43rd EDITION
SA RUGBY ANNUAL

Edited by Duane Heath & Eddie Grieb

Springbok Season Coverage & Comment: Stephen Nell
Statistics: Paul Dobson, Eddie Grieb & Piet Landman
Designer: Ryan Manning
Production Editor: Alison Ward
Text by the Editor, Stephen Nell or as credited
Photographs by Gallo Images or as credited

© 2014 – SARU & MWP MEDIA CC
Printed & bound by Creda Communications,
Eliot Ave, Eppindust II, Cape Town
ISBN 978-0-620-57859-2 SA RUGBY ANNUAL 2014

All rights reserved. No part of this publication may be reproduced, stored in a retrieval system, or transmitted in any form or by any means electronic, mechanical or photocopied, recorded or otherwise without prior consent of the publishers.

Disclaimer: The views expressed in this Annual are those of the editors & contributors and not necessarily those of the South African Rugby Union.

The Editors welcome suggestions and notification of any errors or omissions.
Duane Heath: PO Box 22643 Fish Hoek 7974; 086 684 7068 (fax); duaneh@sarugby.co.za
Eddie Grieb: 702 Mirror Carp Street, Garsfontein 0081; 086 559 0744 (fax); eddieg@sarugby.co.za

South Africa's 14 Rugby Provinces

 Blue Bulls Rugby Union

 Boland Rugby Union

 Border Rugby Union

 Eastern Province Rugby Football Union

 Free State Rugby Union

 Golden Lions Rugby Union

 Griffons Rugby Union

 Griqualand West Rugby Union

 KwaZulu-Natal Rugby Union

 Leopards Rugby Union

 Mpumalanga Rugby Union

 South Western Districts Rugby Football Union

 Valke Rugby Union

 Western Province Rugby Football Union

Foreword

Highs and lows during memorable 2013 season

WITH THE SUN HAVING BARELY set on another memorable year for South African rugby, a new season is once again upon us.

The modern game, both on and off the field, moves at a pace that is sometimes frightening – and whereas in the so-called old days many months of inactivity used to separate one season from the next, in this professional era the lines have blurred sufficiently for there to be very little time to catch one's breath.

You can't blame rugby lovers for becoming engrossed in the latest match, but this doesn't always allow us to see the big picture. And with less than 18 months to go until the 2015 Rugby World Cup, there is no better time than now to take stock of where the Springboks are in their preparations.

No longer is the World Cup years away. But spare a thought for coach Heyneke Meyer and his players, for whom the pressure over the coming season and a half will increase to almost unbearable levels.

Heyneke's first season in charge was, predictably, a season of discovery, but in 2013 he, captain Jean de Villiers and the entire squad gave us glimpses of where this team can end up. No, they are not quite the finished article yet, but therein lies the excitement. These Springboks are no longer a team in transition but rather a side on a steady upward curve.

Ten victories in 12 Tests in 2013 is proof of this. Under Heyneke, and an inspirational skipper in Jean, the Boks are quietly building up to 2015 but at the same time they have not lost sight of the coach's stated goals of trying to win every Test they play along the way.

Record wins over Australia in the Castle Rugby Championship and a first away victory over France in 16 years during a second successive unbeaten European tour have given us a glimpse of just how good the Springboks can become, with the likes of Eben Etzebeth and Willie le Roux adding exuberance to a squad brimming with experience.

Were the World Cup to kick off tomorrow, the Springboks would be second favourites behind the all-conquering All Blacks. But life teaches us that the wheel inevitably turns, and there were enough signs in 2013 to suggest that this squad will be ready to challenge New Zealand's current and unquestioned dominance come 2015.

But, as always, 2013 wasn't only about the men in green and gold, and the season delivered highlights for, amongst others, the Springbok Sevens and the SA President's XV, who won the inaugural IRB Tbilisi Cup. Back home, the Steval Pumas capped off a season to remember by not only winning the Absa Currie Cup First Division but also winning promotion to the Premier Division, where they will come up against the likes of The Cell C Sharks, who beat DHL WP at Newlands to claim the iconic Absa Currie Cup.

At grassroots level, SARU's new Cell C Community Cup breathed life back into club rugby, with GAP Despatch scoring a fairytale victory in the final, 25 years after the legendary Danie Gerber led the unheralded Eastern Cape side to their first national title.

SA rugby was awash with these good news stories in 2013 and such is the passion for the game that these stories will continue to be written and retold to future generations. From the humble club secretary in the platteland town, to the Springbok team manager, there is a collective spirit of purpose in South African rugby which we can be truly proud of.

Finally, I cannot speak about our beloved sport without mentioning our greatest supporter, former president Nelson Mandela, who passed away in December 2013. Madiba will be remembered for so many things, but for us perhaps his most extraordinary act came in 1995 when he used the World Cup to unite all South Africans as never before.

As 2014 unfolds, it is the responsibility of each and every one of us to strive to emulate Madiba's amazing life, to make South African rugby truly inclusive.

Oregan Hoskins
President, South African Rugby Union

CONTENTS
SA RUGBY ANNUAL 2014

Notes & Abbreviations	6
Editor's Notes	7
South African Rugby Union in 2013	9

COMMENT & AWARDS

SARU Award Winners	12
Player of the Year – *Jean de Villiers*	14
Previous Winners	17
Young Player of the Year – *Eben Etzebeth*	18
Previous Winners	21

THE SEASON IN 2013

Team Achievements	24
Match Features	25
Leading Players	26
Career Milestones	27
South Africans playing abroad	28

NATIONAL TEAMS

Review of 2013 International Season	34
Springbok Test Appearances & Points	37
Springbok Squad Members in 2013	38
CASTLE LAGER INCOMING SERIES	
Review	40
South Africa vs Italy	52
South Africa vs Scotland	54
South Africa vs Samoa	56
CASTLE RUGBY CHAMPIONSHIP	
Review	58
South Africa vs Argentina – *Soweto*	70
Argentina vs South Africa – *Mendoza*	72
Australia vs South Africa – *Brisbane*	74
New Zealand vs South Africa – *Auckland*	76
South Africa vs Australia – *Cape Town*	78
South Africa vs New Zealand – *Johannesburg*	80
END-OF-YEAR TOUR	
Review	82
Wales vs South Africa – *Cardiff*	86
Scotland vs South Africa – *Edinburgh*	88
France vs South Africa – *Paris*	90
IRB WORLD CHAMPIONSHIP	
Review	92
IRB WORLD SERIES Review	100
RUGBY WORLD CUP SEVENS	105
SA WOMEN	108
SA SCHOOLS	112
SA PRESIDENT'S XV	115

2013 VODACOM SUPER RUGBY

TOURNAMENT Review	120
Logs & leading scorers	122
Vodacom Bulls	126
Toyota Cheetahs	132
Southern Kings	138
Sharks	144

DHL Stormers	150
PROMOTION-RELEGATION	156
Blues	158
Chiefs	162
Crusaders	166
Highlanders	170
Hurricanes	174
ACT Brumbies	178
Melbourne Rebels	182
New South Wales Waratahs	186
Queensland Reds	190
Western Force	194

2013 DOMESTIC CHAMPIONSHIPS

ABSA CURRIE CUP	200
VODACOM CUP	204
ABSA Under-21 Championships	210
ABSA Under-19 Championships	214

THE PROVINCES

Blue Bulls Rugby Union	220
Boland Rugby Union	228
Border Rugby Union	236
Eastern Province Rugby Union	244
Free State Rugby Union	252
Golden Lions Rugby Union	260
Griffons Rugby Union	268
Griqualand West Rugby Union	276
KwaZulu-Natal Rugby Union	284
Leopards Rugby Union	292
Mpumalanga Rugby Union	300
South Western Districts Rugby Football Union	308
Valke Rugby Union	316
Western Province Rugby Football Union	324

CLUB & AMATEUR RUGBY

YOUTH WEEKS Review & Statistics	334
CELL C COMMUNITY CUP Review & Statistics	346
FNB VARSITY CUP Review & Statistics	349

RECORDS

South African First-Class Records	354
100 Appearances for a Province	356
Vodacom Super Rugby Records	359
Castle Rugby Championship Records	364
Absa Currie Cup Records	368
Vodacom Cup Records	384
SPRINGBOK RECORDS	386
SPRINGBOKS 1891-2013	427
Springbok Sevens Players 1993-2013	448
SA U20 Players	451
South Africans Capped Overseas	453
SA Schools Representatives 1974-2013	455
Referees	462
Obituaries	466
2013 Season First-Class Player List	476

Notes

KEY TO TEAM APPEARANCE LISTS:
R = Replacement. X = Unused replacement.
c = Captain. A dash (–) denotes player not named in match-day squad for that particular match.

1. All records are correct as at 1 January 2014, unless otherwise stated.
2. All teams listed are in the order of fullback (15) to loosehead prop (1).
3. For record purposes, team names at the time of the establishment of the record have been used.
4. Union names and the names of their senior teams in 2013 are as follows:
Blue Bulls Rugby Union (formerly Northern Transvaal) – playing as Vodacom Blue Bulls.
Boland Rugby Union – playing as Regent Boland Cavaliers.
Border Rugby Union – playing as Border Bulldogs.
Eastern Province Rugby Football Union – playing as Eastern Province Kings.
Free State Rugby Union (formerly Orange Free State) – playing as Toyota Free State Cheetahs.
Golden Lions Rugby Union (formerly Transvaal and Gauteng Lions) – playing as MTN Golden Lions.
Griffons Rugby Union (formerly Northern Free State) – playing as Griffons.
Griqualand West Rugby Union – playing as GWK Griquas.
Leopards Rugby Union (formerly Western Transvaal & North West) – playing as Platinum Leopards.
Mpumalanga Rugby Union (formerly South Eastern Transvaal) – playing as the Steval Pumas.
KwaZulu-Natal Rugby Union (formerly Natal) – playing as the Sharks.
South Western Districts Rugby Football Union – playing as SWD Eagles.
Valke Rugby Union (formerly Eastern Transvaal, Gauteng Falcons & Falcons) – playing as the Valke.
Western Province Rugby Football Union – playing as DHL Western Province.
5. Definition of a 'first-class match' and 'first-class appearance':
i) To qualify as a first-class match, it must be played strictly according to the Laws of the game (no more than seven players on the bench).
ii) The following categories of matches qualify for first-class status if point i) is fulfilled:
   a) All matches featuring the South African national team (Springboks);
   b) All matches in senior competitions sanctioned by SARU;
   c) All matches against touring international teams;
   d) All matches between senior provincial teams & touring teams of the same or a higher status;
   e) All matches between senior provincial teams outside of SARU competitions where the strongest possible teams are fielded;
   f) All matches played by senior teams carrying the name of a South African national team;
   g) All matches played by senior composite teams in IRB approved competitions.
iii) Any player appearing in one of the above matches (either in the starting XV or as a replacement – blood replacements and yellow-card replacements included) will be deemed to have made a first-class appearance.

Team Abbreviations

SOUTH AFRICAN TEAMS: *BB* – Blue Bulls, *Bol* – Boland, *Bor* – Border, *EP* – Eastern Province, *ETvl* – Eastern Transvaal, *F* – Falcons (if province), *FS* – Free State, *GF* – Gauteng Falcons, *GL* – Golden Lions, *GW* – Griqualand West, *Mpu* – Mpumalanga, *NEC* – North Eastern Cape, *NED* – North Eastern Districts, *NNtl* – Northern Natal, *NOFS* – Northern Orange Free State, *NTvl* – Northern Transvaal, *OFS* – Orange Free State, *SWD* – South Western Districts, *Tvl* – Transvaal, *WP* – Western Province, *WTvl* – Western Transvaal.

MAJOR INTERNATIONAL TEAMS: *A* – Australia, *Arg* – Argentina, *BI* – British Isles, *E* – England, *F* – France (if opponent), *I* – Ireland, *It* – Italy, *NZ* – New Zealand, *S* – Scotland, *W* – Wales.

OTHER TEAMS: *Bots* – Botswana, *C* – Canada, *Cam* – Cameroon, *Fj* – Fiji, *G* – Georgia, *Gulf* – Gulf States, *IC* – Ivory Coast, *J* – Japan, *Ken* – Kenya, *Mad* – Madagascar, *Mor* – Morocco, *Nam* – Namibia, *Neth* – Netherlands, *Nor* – Norway, *NZC* – New Zealand Cavaliers (1986), *P* – Portugal, *PI* – Pacific Islanders, *R* – Romania, *Russ* – Russia, *Sam* – Samoa, *SAm* – South America, *SETvl* – South Eastern Transvaal, *Sp* – Spain, *SWA* – South West Africa, *Swazi* – Swaziland, *T* – Tonga, *Tan* – Tanzania, *Tun* – Tunisia, *U* – Uruguay, *Ug* – Uganda, *WS* – Western Samoa, *WT* – World XV, *Z* – Zimbabwe, *Zam* – Zambia

Preface

THE 2014 EDITION OF THE *SA RUGBY* *Annual*, like its 42 predecessors, is an attempt to record, in words, pictures, tables and graphs, a season in the life of South Africa's national sport.

It is written, edited, photographed, designed, proofread, printed, bound, ordered, delivered, stocked and – hopefully! – finally sold and read, not only so that future generations may know what unfolded at a particular juncture in the twisting, undulating road that is SA rugby, but also so that they may look back on the year 2013 from a future we may never live to see, and so gain perspective on those on- and off-field events that we might have been blessed enough to witness.

Even a book of record such as the SA Rugby *Annual* is not compiled in a vacuum, its editors and contributors able to freeze the world around them to take a neat historical snapshot. The story of our sport, like that of our lives, is continually unfolding, refusing to be bookended by the beginning and end of a particular calendar year, as the *Annual* is seemingly able to do. Decisions taken in a rugby boardroom might make an impact on the field for years afterwards, their consequences, perhaps good and bad, needing to be recorded; a try-scoring record set the day before this book goes to print may be broken the day after it hits the shelves.

Our task, therefore, is to ensure that the hours we devote to each *Annual* match, or, better still, exceed, those hours put into the preceding edition. By doing so, we ensure there is a continuum from year to year, the pages of one edition flowing seamlessly into the next. If, in the year 2050, a reader is able to piece together from the 2012, 2013 and 2014 *Annuals* the reasons why the Springboks won the 2015 Rugby World Cup, then we would have done our job.

My thanks, as always, go out to everyone involved in the *Annual's* production, so that we are able to act as the eyes and ears for future generations of people for whom South African rugby will be as much a part of the fabric of their lives as it is ours.

History, they say, is written by the winners, and contained in these 512 pages are stories of triumph – from the Springboks' huge victories over Australia in the unforgiving Test arena, to Despatch's rise from the grassroots ashes to once again become the best club in the land, a quarter of a century after Danie Gerber put the unfashionable Eastern Cape town on the map.

But 2013 was also filled with low points, none perhaps as sobering as the Springboks' 50th Test defeat to the All Blacks, at Ellis Park of all places – an eighth loss in nine matches to our greatest rivals and one which sees our historical win ratio against the current world champions slip to just 39 percent.

It was also a year in which rugby lost an irreplaceable group of men and women who blessed our sport with their contributions – from Nelson Mandela, Louis Luyt, Jan Ellis, Morgan Cushe and Fritz Eloff, to those perhaps not as famous, but without whom the fabric of our national game would not be nearly as colourful or meaningful: Koppel Brown, Francis Mellish, Simon Mjo, Pa Pelser, Roderick Rossouw, Sailor van Schalkwyk and Laurie Kay – the pilot of perhaps the most famous Boeing 747 flypast of all time.

Their obituaries, and many others besides, are recorded here so that their contributions may never be forgotten.

For their superhuman efforts once again, I would like to thank my co-editor Eddie Grieb and his team of Piet Landman, Paul Dobson, Heinrich Schulze, Gideon Nieman, Ashley Berry and Frikkie van Rensburg. Thanks as always to Herman le Roux and our overseas stalwarts – John Griffiths (IRB statistician), Geoff Miller (NZRU statistician), Matthew Alvarez (ARU statistician), Stuart Farmer (Stuart Farmer Media Services Ltd, England) and Lee Ashton (New Zealand).

Thank you to Paul Sales and his photographers at Gallo Images for their tireless efforts to visually document our sport, and to the rugby writers whose words make the *Annual* the respected document of record it is. In no particular order they are: John

Preface

Bishop, Simon Borchardt, Paul Dobson, Stephen Nell, Gideon Nieman, Hannes Nienaber and Craig Ray.

JJ Harmse and Zeena Isaacs of SARU also deserve thanks for their contributions, as does Andy Colquhoun, my mentor and colleague at SARU headquarters.

Our friends at the provincial unions must again be thanked for their willingness to help – Saartjie Olivier (Blue Bulls), Willie Small (Boland), Trevor Barnes (KZN), Marius van Rensburg (Mpumalanga), Emil Oelrich & Gesie van der Merwe (Valke), Revenne Maritz (WP), Lewies van Zyl (SWD), Karen Crafford (Leopards), Leah van Wyk (Griffons), Debbie Ellis (EP), Lizette Viviers & Ronel Pienaar (Free State), Akhona Mgijima (Border) and Pieter Bergh (Griquas).

Thanks as always must go to the South African Rugby Union for their unwavering support of a book that we like to think is the best of its kind in world rugby. Without their vision and funding, especially in these tough economic times, the *Annual* would itself become an exhibit at SARU's world-class Springbok Experience museum which opened in 2013 at Cape Town's V&A Waterfront.

I would also like to acknowledge once again the tremendous support given by production editor Alison Ward of MWP, who co-publish the *Annual* together with SARU, as well as Lesley Ackermann and Linda Kay of printers Creda Communications; and everyone at Blue Weaver.

Finally, a special thanks go once again to those colleagues who spent most of the year with their sleeves rolled up as far as they would go: my co-editor and stats guru Eddie Grieb, design wizard Ryan Manning, and rugby writer and author Stephen Nell, whose status as one of the country's most respected authorities on the game made him a natural go-to man to record the Springboks' season in detail.

And, for the fifth year running, on behalf of them I must thank our long-suffering family members whose patience grows with each passing season: Alida Grieb and Lee & Edrich; Vanessa Manning and Hannah & Joshua; and, finally, to my wife Aisling, our son Kian and daughter Emma.

Duane Heath
Kommetjie, Cape Town
December 2013

Looking for back issues of the SA Rugby Annual?

Select Books

Available from Select Books, 232 Long Street, Cape Town, 8001, South Africa

For more information contact David & Karen McLennan
Tel: +27 (0)21 424 6955 • **Fax:** +27 (0)21 424 0866
Email: selectb@mweb.co.za **Website:** www.selectbooks.co.za

Founder member of SABDA (Southern African Book Dealers Association)
VAT Registration number: 4910156449

South African Rugby Union

ADDRESS:
SARU House, Tygerberg Park, 163 Uys Krige Road,
Plattekloof, Cape Town, 7500
TELEPHONE:
+27 21 928 7000
EMAIL:
info@sarugby.co.za

SARU OFFICE-BEARERS

Oregan Hoskins
(President)

Mark Alexander
(Deputy President)

James Stoffberg
(Vice-President)

MEMBERS OF THE EXECUTIVE COUNCIL
Oregan Hoskins
Mark Alexander
James Stoffberg
Mputumi Damane
Boet Fick
Dawie Groenewald
Piet Heymans
Pat Kuhn
Monde Tabata
Tobie Titus
Jurie Roux
Basil Haddad
Dr Ismail Jakoet *(Company Secretary)*

SARU DEPARTMENTS
(AS AT 31 DECEMBER 2013)
Executive Office: Jurie Roux (Chief Executive Officer), Ismail Jakoet (Company Secretary), Ronel Groenewald, Sumantha Gounden.
Commercial and Marketing: Andy Marinos (GM), Corlia Oberholzer, Steven Roos, Coris Zietsman, Zintsika Tashe, Jenny Wentzel, Ziada Martin, Patricia Dlakavu, Mingon van Rooyen, Justine Blacker, Chumani Bembe, Lois Coetzee.
Corporate Affairs: Andy Colquhoun (GM), Rayaan Adriaanse, De Jongh Borchardt, Khaya Mayedwa, JJ Harmse, Dr Hendrik Snyders, Zeena Isaacs, Andrea Pharaoh, Maria Ananias, Eddie Grieb, Romano Lekay, Karen Nell.
Development: Mervin Green (GM), Yusuf Jackson, Herman Masimla, Nico Serfontein, Hilton Adonis, Hazel Solomon, Rudlyn Barnes, Valda Gertse, Louise Barnard, Samantha McDonald, Duane Heath.
High Performance: Rassie Erasmus (GM), Charles Wessels, JJ Fredericks, Clint Readhead, Willie Maree, Sebastian Prim, Mahlubi Puzi, Wayne Viljoen, Ian Schwartz, Zeenat Abdullah, Allie Abrahams, Albie Visser, Debbie Griffiths, Michelle English, Carla van der Merwe.
Human Resources: Ingrid Mangcu (GM), Kolisa Kongo, Lucille MacGibbon, Janet Burgers, Martha Qabo.
Operations and Finance: Basil Haddad (GM), Sesi Sekhosana, Christo Ferreira, Nelda Cozyn, Nomini Malungisa, Marcus Mude, Philicia George, Berenice Knockpaal, Daneille Weston, Unathi Sompondo, Thembisa Magaga, Yandiswa Mbulali, Irven October, Eric Sofisa, Anna Andreas, Arnold Gertse, Malehlonono Selela, Megan Esterhuizen, Max Nodongwe.
Referees: Andre Watson (GM), Eugene de Villiers, Mark Lawrence, Neville Heilbron, Aletta Coetzee.

SECTION 1
COMMENT & AWARDS

SARU Award Winners **12**

PLAYERS OF THE YEAR:
Winner – *Jean de Villiers* **14**
Previous Winners **17**

YOUNG PLAYER OF THE YEAR:
Winner – *Eben Etzebeth* **18**
Previous Winners **21**

Springbok captain Jean de Villiers celebrates victory over Wales. *Scott Heavey/Getty Images*

SARU AWARDS 2013

SA Rugby Player of the Year:
Jean de Villiers
(Other finalists: Bismarck du Plessis, Eben Etzebeth, Willie le Roux, Duane Vermeulen)

Absa Young Player of the Year:
Eben Etzebeth
(Other finalists: Pieter-Steph du Toit, Siya Kolisi, Jan Serfontein, Cheslin Kolbe)

Absa Team of the Year:
Steval Pumas
(Other finalists: Springboks, Sharks Absa Currie Cup)

Jimmy Stonehouse

Absa Coach of the Year:
Jimmy Stonehouse (Steval Pumas, SA President's XV)
(Other finalists: Heyneke Meyer, Brendan Venter)

Springbok Sevens Player of the Year:
Cornal Hendricks
(Other finalists: Frankie Horne, Seabelo Senatla)

SA Under-20 Player of the Year:
Cheslin Kolbe
(Other finalists: Jacques du Plessis, Seabelo Senatla)

Vodacom Super Rugby Player of the Year:
Adriaan Strauss (Toyota Cheetahs)
(Other finalists: Willie le Roux, Duane Vermeulen)

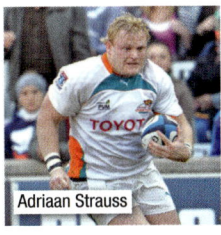
Adriaan Strauss

Scarra Ntubeni

Giovano Fourie

Grant Hermanus

Absa Currie Cup Premier Division Player of the Year:
Scarra Ntubeni (DHL Western Province)
(Other finalists: Cheslin Kolbe, Fred Zeilinga)

Absa Currie Cup First Division Player of the Year:
Rosco Speckman (Steval Pumas)
(Other finalists: Alshaun Bock, Tiger Mangweni)

Vodacom Cup Player of the Year:
Fred Zeilinga (Sharks XV)
(Other finalists: Marnitz Boshoff, Rosco Speckman)

Cell C Community Cup Player of the Tournament:
Giovano Fourie (Gap Management Despatch)

Coca-Cola Craven Week Player of the Tournament:
Grant Hermanus (Western Province)

Marriott Referee Award:
Jonathan Kaplan

Women's Achiever of the Year:
Zenay Jordaan

SARU PLAYER OF THE YEAR
JEAN DE VILLIERS
(DHL Stormers, DHL Western Province, South Africa, Barbarians)

GENTLEMANLY SPRINGBOK CAPTAIN Jean de Villiers was deservedly crowned South Africa's Player of the Year for the second time, following on the achievement of 2008.

De Villiers saw off the challenges of fellow finalists and Springbok team-mates **Bismarck du Plessis** (Sharks, South Africa, Barbarians), **Eben Etzebeth** (DHL Stormers, DHL WP, South Africa), **Willie le Roux** (Toyota Cheetahs, GWK Griquas, South Africa, Barbarians) and **Duane Vermeulen** (DHL Stormers, DHL WP, South Africa, Barbarians).

Like a fine red wine, De Villiers, who turned 32 at the start of the 2013 season, seems to get better with age. The former Paarl Gymnasium schoolboy finished his 13th season of first-class rugby – and his 12th as a Springbok – by leading South Africa on an unbeaten tour of Europe, which included their first win over France in France since 1997, as well as a 28-0 win over Scotland. Twelve Tests the Springboks played in 2013 and 12 times it was De Villiers who led them out in the No 12 jersey – 10 of them victorious, with only the imperious All Blacks preventing a clean sweep of victories.

Since being appointed as captain by coach Heyneke Meyer at the start of the 2012 season – a selection which was described as 'left field' by some – De Villiers has led the Springboks in 24 Tests. Seventeen of those have been won, two have been drawn, and only five have been lost.

His win rate as captain is 71 percent, which places him fourth on the all-time list of Bok skippers who have played 10 or more Tests. Only Morné du Plessis (13/15, 87%), Joost van der Westhuizen (8/10, 80%) and Gary Teichmann (26/36, 72%) have been more successful leaders of the green and gold – and the good news is that De Villiers may yet move up a place or two if he achieves his ultimate personal goal, which is to cap off a remarkable career by lifting the Webb Ellis Cup when the Rugby World Cup final is held at Twickenham on 31 October 2015 – a date just shy of what would be his 35th birthday.

Should this pan out the way he and every rugby lover across the land hopes it will, De Villiers – who has always put team goals ahead of his own, in any case – will also most likely look down from the summit as the most capped Springbok of all time. As it was, he finished the 2013 season on 96 Test caps – 81 of those coming at centre, a South African record which will take some beating. His 25 consecutive appearances in the midfield between 2011 and 2013 is also a Springbok record for a centre.

De Villiers is now fourth on the all-time capped list, not at all far behind former team-mates John Smit (111 Tests), Victor Matfield (110) and Percy Montgomery (102). Fitness permitting, it's most likely he will overtake Montgomery sometime during the 2014 season.

Jean de Villiers, South Africa's 54th Test captain, played a total of 30 first-class matches in 2013 – 12 Tests, 14 Vodacom Super Rugby matches for the DHL Stormers, three Absa Currie Cup games for DHL Western Province, and a season-ending match in London, where he captained the Barbarians to a win over Fiji at Twickenham.

His first-class record now stands at 254 matches, in which he has scored 91 tries – a remarkable strike rate in anyone's language.

Previous Players of the Year

2012: Bryan Habana (Player of the Year, WP), Keegan Daniel (Sharks), Patrick Lambie (Sharks), Eben Etzebeth (Western Province), JP Pietersen (Sharks).

2011: Schalk Burger (Player of the Year, WP), Bismarck du Plessis (Sharks), Patrick Lambie (Sharks), Francois Hogaard (Blue Bulls), Victor Matfield (Blue Bulls).

2010: Gurthrö Steenkamp (Player of the Year, Blue Bulls), Gio Aplon (WP), Schalk Burger (WP), Juan de Jongh (WP), Francois Hougaard (Blue Bulls).

2009: Fourie du Preez (Player of the Year, Blue Bulls), Heinrich Brüssow (Free State), Victor Matfield (Blue Bulls), John Smit (Sharks), Morné Steyn (Blue Bulls).

2008: Jean de Villiers (Player of the Year, Western Province), Tendai Mtawarira, Bismarck du Plessis, Ryan Kankowski, Adrian Jacobs (all KwaZulu Natal).

2007: Bryan Habana (Player of the Year, Blue Bulls), Fourie du Preez (Blue Bulls), Victor Matfield (Blue Bulls), Percy Montgomery (Natal), Juan Smith (Free State).

2006: Fourie du Preez (Player of the Year, Blue Bulls), Os du Randt (Free State), Victor Matfield (Blue Bulls), Pierre Spies (Blue Bulls), Luke Watson (Western Province).

2005: Bryan Habana (Player of the Year, Blue Bulls), Bakkies Botha, Victor Matfield (both Blue Bulls), Jean de Villiers (WP), Ricky Januarie (Lions).

2004: Schalk Burger (Player of the Year, WP), Os du Randt (Free State), De Wet Barry, Marius Joubert (WP), Bakkies Botha (Blue Bulls).

2003: Ashwin Willemse (Player of the Year, Lions), Juan Smith (Free State), Richard Bands, Bakkies Botha (Blue Bulls), Joe van Niekerk (Lions).

2002: Joe van Niekerk (Player of the Year), Jannes Labuschagne, André Pretorius, Lawrence Sephaka (all Lions), Werner Greeff (WP).

2001: André Vos (Player of the Year, Lions), Braam van Straaten (WP), Victor Matfield (Blue Bulls), Lukas van Biljon (Natal), Conrad Jantjes (Lions).

2000: Breyton Paulse (Player of the Year, WP), Thinus Delport, Rassie Erasmus (both Lions), Kennedy Tsimba (Free State), Corné Krige (WP).

1999: André Venter (Player of the Year, Free State), Breyton Paulse, Cobus Visagie (both WP), Joost van der Westhuizen (Blue Bulls), Hennie le Roux (Lions).

1998: Gary Teichmann (Player of the Year, Natal), Joost van der Westhuizen, Krynauw Otto (Blue Bulls), Gaffie du Toit (Griqualand West), Bobby Skinstad (WP).

1997: Os du Randt (Player of the Year, Free State), Pieter Rossouw, Percy Montgomery, Dick Muir (all WP), Johan Roux (Lions).

1996: André Joubert (Player of the Year), Henry Honiball, Gary Teichmann (both Natal), Ruben Kruger, Joost van der Westhuizen (both NTvl).

1995: Ruben Kruger (Player of the Year), Joost van der Westhuizen (both NTvl), Francois Pienaar (Tvl), Joel Stransky (WP), André Joubert (Natal).

1994: Chester Williams (Player of the Year, WP), Mark Andrews, André Joubert (both Natal), Ruben Kruger, Joost van der Westhuizen (both NTvl).

1993: Gavin Johnson (Player of the Year), Francois Pienaar (both Tvl), James Small (Natal), Tiaan Strauss (WP), Joost van der Westhuizen (NTvl).

1992: Tiaan Strauss (Player of the Year), Danie Gerber (both WP), Jacques Olivier, Naas Botha, Adriaan Richter (all NTvl).

1991: Uli Schmidt (Player of the Year), Naas Botha, Gerbrand Grobler (all NTvl), André Joubert (OFS), Wahl Bartmann (Natal).

1990: Uli Schmidt (Player of the Year), Robert du Preez (both NTvl), Wahl Bartmann, Joel Stransky (both Natal), Tiaan Strauss (WP).

1989: Johan Heunis (Player of the Year), Robert du Preez, Burger Geldenhuys (all NTvl), André Joubert (OFS), Carel du Plessis (WP).

1988: Calla Scholtz (Player of the Year), Tiaan Strauss (both WP), Naas Botha, Adolf Malan (both NTvl), Gerhard Mans (SWA).

1987: Naas Botha (Player of the Year), Adri Geldenhuys (both NTvl), Gysie Pienaar (OFS), John Robbie, Jannie Breedt (both Tvl).

1986: Jannie Breedt (Player of the Year), Wahl Bartmann (both Tvl), Carel du Plessis (WP), Uli Schmidt (NTvl), Garth Wright (EP).

1985: Naas Botha (Player of the Year, NTvl), Jannie Breedt (Tvl), Schalk (SWP) Burger (WP), Danie Gerber (EP), Gerrie Sonnekus (OFS).

1984: Danie Gerber (Player of the Year, EP), Rob Louw, Calla Scholtz (both WP), Ray Mordt (NTvl), Errol Tobias (Boland).

1983: Hennie Bekker (Player of the Year), Divan Serfontein, Carel du Plessis (all WP), Liaan Kirkham (Tvl), Ray Mordt (NTvl).

1982: Divan Serfontein (Player of the Year), Colin Beck, Hennie Bekker (all WP), Naas Botha, Johan Heunis (both NTvl).

1981: Naas Botha (Player of the Year), Johan Heunis (both NTvl), Ray Mordt (Tvl), Divan Serfontein, De Villiers Visser (both WP).

1980: Gysie Pienaar (Player of the Year, OFS), Naas Botha, Louis Moolman (both NTvl), Morné du Plessis (WP), Gerrie Germishuys (Tvl).

1979: Naas Botha (Player of the Year), Louis Moolman (both NTvl), Morné du Plessis, Rob Louw, De Villiers Visser (all WP).

1978: Thys Lourens (Player of the Year), Tommy du Plessis, Pierre Edwards (all NTvl), De Wet Ras (OFS), Ian Robertson (Rhodesia).

1977: Moaner van Heerden (Player of the Year), Thys Lourens (both NTvl), Morné du Plessis (WP), Hermanus Potgieter, Theuns Stofberg (both OFS).

*1976: Morné du Plessis (WP), Moaner van Heerden (NTvl), Bryan Williams, Sid Going, Peter Whiting (all NZ).

*1975: Gerald Bosch (Tvl), Gerrie Germishuys (OFS), Pierre Spies, Thys Lourens (both NTvl), Johan Oosthuizen (WP).

*1974: Gareth Edwards, Willie John McBride, JPR Williams (all British Lions), Willem Stapelberg, John Williams (both NTvl).

*1973: Gerald Bosch (Tvl), Dirk de Vos, Moaner van Heerden, Pierre Spies (all NTvl), Johan Oosthuizen (WP).

*1972: Kevin de Klerk (Tvl), Sam Doble (England), Jan Ellis (SWA), Carel Fourie (North East Cape) John Pullin (England).

*1971: Benoit Dauga (France), Frik du Preez (NTvl), Jan Ellis (SWA), Hannes Marais (EP), Hannes Viljoen (Natal).

*1970: Piet Greyling (Tvl), Joggie Jansen (OFS), Ian McCallum (WP), Alan Sutherland, Bryan Williams (both NZ).

* Before 1977, no single player of the year was named.

SARU YOUNG PLAYER OF THE YEAR
EBEN ETZEBETH
(DHL Stormers, DHL Western Province, South Africa)

EBEN ETZEBETH WAS NAMED SOUTH Africa's Young Player of the Year for the second year in a row – a rare achievement which tells you all you need to know about the 22-year-old Springbok lock.

Etzebeth saw off the challenges of fellow finalists and internationals **Pieter-Steph du Toit** (Sharks & South Africa), **Cheslin Kolbe** (DHL WP & Springbok Sevens), **Siya Kolisi** (DHL Stormers, DHL WP & South Africa) and **Jan Serfontein** (Vodacom Bulls, Vodacom Blue Bulls & South Africa).

Etzebeth's meteoric rise was confirmed when he was shortlisted for the title of International Rugby Board Player of the Year – an award that eventually went to the peerless All Black eighthman, Kieran Read.

But for someone who was playing club rugby for UCT in the Varsity Cup rugby as recently as 2011, and who made his first-class debut only in 2012, to think that the 2.03m, 117kg second-rower's status as a worthy replacement for Bakkies Botha has been cemented in such a short space of time is nothing short of remarkable.

As we wrote in these pages only a year ago, there are responsibilities that come attached to wearing the Springboks' No 4 jersey that require a touch of the super-human. Those who have donned it over the years have made it a pointer to the immense physicality embedded in the DNA of South African rugby.

None did it more effectively in the modern era than Botha and it seemed inevitable that his successor would struggle to meet his standards. But in stepped 20-year-old Etzebeth and without even having shed all of his puppy fat he made it look remarkably easy.

His meteoric rise was highlighted by the fact that he played for South Africa even before making his Absa Currie Cup debut for DHL Western Province.

And a year later, having played in all 12 of the Springboks' Tests in 2013 – 11 of them starting – Etzebeth the rookie suddenly has 23 Test caps under his belt and, fitness and form permitting, should have accumulated close to 40 by the time the 2015 Rugby World Cup comes along.

We predicted in the 2013 Annual that greatness beckons for Etzebeth, and, if anything, the 2013 season merely proved that the sky is indeed the limit for the soft-spoken giant.

Springbok coach Heyneke Meyer's masterstroke to recall the veteran Botha for the Boks' end-of-season tour to Wales, Scotland and France also ensured that Etzebeth continued his apprenticeship at a breakneck pace, the wily old Botha imparting all of his immense experience to the newcomer who has so brilliantly filled his massive boots.

Eben Etzebeth played a total of 23 first-class matches in 2013 – 12 Tests, 8 Vodacom Super Rugby matches for the DHL Stormers, and three Absa Currie Cup games for DHL Western Province. His first-class record now stands at 55 matches, in which he has scored three tries.

Previous Young Players of the Year

2012: Eben Etzebeth (Young Player of the Year, WP), Elton Jantjies (Golden Lions), Marcell Coetzee (KZN), Johan Goosen (Free State), Raymond Rhule (Free State).

2011: Patrick Lambie (Young Player of the Year, Sharks), Elton Jantjies (Golden Lions), Johan Goosen (Free State), Jaco Taute (Golden Lions), Francois Hougaard (Blue Bulls).

2010: Elton Jantjies (Young Player of the Year, Golden Lions), Bjorn Basson (Blue Bulls), Juan de Jongh (WP), Francois Hougaard (Blue Bulls), Patrick Lambie (KZN).

2009: Heinrich Brüssow (Young Player of the Year, Free State), Juan de Jongh (WP), Francois Hougaard (Blue Bulls), Lionel Mapoe (Free State), Frans Steyn (Sharks).

2008: Robert Ebersohn (Young Player of the Year, Free State), Heinrich Brüssow (Free State), Nick Koster (WP), Tendai Mtawarira, Bismarck du Plessis (both KZN).

2007: Francois Steyn (Young player of the Year), JP Pietersen, Ryan Kankowski (all KwaZulu-Natal), Heinke van der Merwe (Lions), Richardt Strauss (Free State).

2006: Pierre Spies (Young Player of the Year, Blue Bulls), JP Pietersen, Keegan Daniel (KwaZulu-Natal), Hilton Lobberts (Blue Buls), Gio Aplon (Western Province).

2005: Jongi Nokwe (Young Player of the Year, Boland), Wynand Olivier, Morné Steyn (Blue Bulls), Ruan Pienaar, JP Pietersen (KwaZulu-Natal).

2004: Bryan Habana (Young Player of the Year, Lions), Schalk Burger (WP), Schalk Brits (Lions), Fourie du Preez (Blue Bulls), Luke Watson (Natal).

2003: Ashwin Willemse (Young Player of the Year, Lions), Schalk Burger (WP), John Mametsa (Blue Bulls), Jaque Fourie (Lions), Fourie du Preez (Blue Bulls).

2002: Pedrie Wannenburg (Young Player of the Year, Blue Bulls), Brent Russell (Pumas), Hanyani Shimange (Free State), Jaque Fourie (Lions), Derick Hougaard (Blue Bulls).

2001: Conrad Jantjies (Young Player of the Year), Gcobani Bobo, Joe van Niekerk (all Lions), Adi Jacobs (Falcons), Wylie Human (Free State).

2000: Marius Joubert (Boland), Conrad Jantjes (Lions), De Wet Barry, Adri Badenhorst (both WP), Wylie Human (Free State).

1999: John Smit (Natal), Kaya Malotana (Border), Jannes Labuschagne (Lions), Wayne Julies (Boland), Torros Pretorius (Pumas).

1998: Lourens Venter, Robert Markram (both Griquas), Grant Esterhuizen, Nicky van der Walt (both Blue Bulls), André Vos (Golden Lions).

1997: Thinus Delport (Gauteng Lions), Breyton Paulse, Louis Koen, Bobby Skinstad (all WP), Jan-Harm van Wyk (Free State).

1996: Dawie du Toit, Hannes Venter (both NTvl), Marius Goosen (Boland), MJ Smith (Free State), André Vos (EP).

1995: Stephen Brink, Jorrie Kruger (both OFS), Robbie Kempson (Natal), Danie van Schalkwyk, Joggie Viljoen (both NTvl).

1994: Frikkie Bosman (ETvl), Braam Els (OFS), Harold Karele (EP), André Snyman (NTvl), Justin Swart (WP).

1993: Krynauw Otto, FP Naude (both NTvl), Ryno Oppermann (OFS), Johan Roux (Tvl), Christiaan Scholtz (WP).

1992: Jannie de Beer, Hentie Martens, Brendan Venter, André Venter (all OFS), Joost van der Westhuizen (NTvl).

1991: Pieter Hendriks (Tvl), Hennie le Roux (EP), Pieter Müller (OFS), Johan Nel, Jacques Olivier (both NTvl).

1990: Andrew Aitken (Natal), Jannie Claassens, Theo van Rensburg (both NTvl), Bernard Fourie (WTvl), Ian Macdonald (Tvl).

1989: Stompie Fourie (OFS), Pieter Nel, Verwoerd Roodt (both NTvl), Joel Stransky, Jeremy Thomson (both Natal).

1988: Kobus Burger, Christian Stewart (WP), Jacques du Plessis (EP), André Joubert (OFS), JJ van der Walt (NTvl).

1987: Chris Badenhorst (OFS), Robert du Preez (WTvl), Jan Lock, Charles Rossouw (both NTvl), Andrew Paterson (EP).

1986: Keith Andrews, Tiaan Strauss (both WP), Martin Knoetze (WTvl), Hendrik Kruger (NTvl), Frans Wessels (OFS).

1985: Schalk (SW) Burger, Faffa Knoetze (both WP), Deon Coetzee (Tvl), Christo Ferreira (OFS), Giepie Nel (NTvl).

1984: Paul Botes, Uli Schmidt (both NTvl), Niel Burger (WP), Wessel Lightfoot, Helgard Müller (both OFS).

1983: Wahl Bartmann (Tvl), Jannie Dreyer, Adolf Malan (both NTvl), Calla Scholtz (WP), Gert Smal (WTvl).

1982: Wilfred Cupido (South African Rugby Federation), Michael du Plessis (WP), Liaan Kirkham (Tvl), Piet Kruger (NTvl), Rudie Visagie (OFS).

1981: Harry Viljoen, Jannie Breedt, André Skinner (all NTvl), Jan du Toit, Ernest Viljoen (both OFS).

1980: Colin Beck (WP), Cliffie Brown (Natal), Johan Marais (NTvl), Chris Rogers (Zimbabwe), Japie Wessels (OFS).

1979: Darius Botha (NTvl), Willie du Plessis (WP), Doug Jeffrey (OFS), André Markgraaff (WTvl), Gawie Visagie (Griquas).

1978: Burger Geldenhuys, Okkie Oosthuizen (both NTvl), Eben Jansen (OFS), Ray Mordt, David Smith (both Rhodesia).

1977: Naas Botha, Thys Burger (both NTvl), Agie Koch, Flippie van der Merwe (both WP), Gysie Pienaar (OFS).

1976: Dirk Froneman, Wouter Hugo (both OFS), Divan Serfontein, Nick Mallet (both WP), LM Rossouw (NTvl).

1975: Tommy du Plessis, Christo Wagenaar (both NTvl), Corrie Pypers (Tvl), Hermanus Potgieter, De Wet Ras (both OFS).

1974: Gavin Cowley (EP), Peter Kirsten (WP), John Knox, Louis Moolman (both NTvl), Johan Strauss (Tvl).

1973: Dave Frederickson (Tvl), Wilhelm Landman (WP), Martiens le Roux (OFS), Keith Thoresson (Natal), Barry Wolmarans (Boland).

1972: Paul Bayvel, Gerald Bosch (both Tvl), Pikkie du Toit (OFS), Dugald Macdonald (WP), Jackie Snyman (OFS).

1971: Kevin de Klerk, Gert Schutte (both Tvl), Piet du Plessis (NTvl), Buddy Swartz (Griquas), Johan Wagenaar (OFS).

1970: Francois de Villiers, Johan Walters (both WP), Peter Cronje (Tvl), Jannie van Aswegen (Griquas), John Williams (NTvl).

SECTION 2
THE SEASON IN 2013

Team Achievements **24**

Match Features **25**

Leading Players **26**

Career Milestones **27**

South Africans playing abroad **28**

Please note: 2013 First-Class Player List has moved to Section 8 & begins on pg 476.

Patrick Lambie with the Absa Currie Cup. *Steve Haag/Gallo Images*

SEASON IN 2013

AGGREGATE FIRST-CLASS TEAM RECORDS *Ranked by winning percentage*

TEAM	Competition	Played	Won	Drawn	Lost	Points For	Points Against	Tries For	Tries Against	% Position
SA President's XV	IRB Tbilisi Cup	3	3	0	0	77	33	44	9	100,0%
Pumas	Vodacom Cup/First Division/P&R	28	25	3	0	1283	576	163	64	89,3%
Springboks (Tests)	Incoming/Rugby Champs/EOY Tour	12	10	2	0	404	192	47	19	83,3%
The Sharks	Absa Currie Cup	12	9	3	0	337	264	33	25	75,0%
Sharks XV	Vodacom Cup	8	6	2	0	304	208	33	21	75,0%
Western Province	Vodacom Cup/Absa Currie Cup	21	15	3	3	551	460	56	51	71,4%
Bulls	Vodacom Super Rugby	17	12	5	0	471	356	42	36	70,6%
Golden Lions	Vodacom Cup	10	7	3	0	448	232	59	23	70,0%
Eastern Province Kings	Vodacom Cup/First Division	25	17	7	1	741	603	84	65	68,0%
Cheetahs	Super Rugby	17	10	7	0	395	373	40	33	58,8%
Leopards XV	Vodacom Cup	7	4	3	0	289	158	38	18	57,1%
Stormers	Super Rugby	16	9	7	0	346	292	30	18	56,3%
Leopards	First Division	15	8	7	0	477	430	66	48	53,3%
The Sharks	Super Rugby	16	8	8	0	384	305	40	31	50,0%
Pampas XV	Vodacom Cup	8	4	3	1	275	236	37	30	50,0%
Lions	Super Rugby Promotion & Relegation	2	1	1	0	44	42	4	4	50,0%
Southern Kings	Super Rugby Promotion & Relegation	2	1	1	0	42	44	4	4	50,0%
Free State Cheetahs	Absa Currie Cup	11	5	6	0	284	271	34	29	45,5%
Blue Bulls	Vodacom Cup/Absa Currie Cup	18	8	9	1	691	446	84	52	44,4%
Golden Lions	Absa Currie Cup	11	4	6	1	342	329	41	33	36,4%
SWD Eagles	Vodacom Cup/First Division	22	8	14	0	640	706	79	87	36,4%
Boland Cavaliers	Vodacom Cup/First Division	21	7	12	2	480	649	64	86	33,3%
Griquas	Vodacom Cup/Absa CC/ P&R	20	6	14	0	553	558	65	66	30,0%
Griffons	Vodacom Cup/First Division	21	6	13	2	500	779	67	105	28,6%
Free State XV	Vodacom Cup	7	2	5	0	195	190	25	22	28,6%
Border Bulldogs	Vodacom Cup/First Division	21	6	15	0	420	604	47	80	28,6%
Valke	Vodacom Cup/First Division	21	4	16	1	488	848	63	121	19,0%
Southern Kings	Super Rugby	16	3	12	1	298	564	27	69	18,8%

MATCH FEATURES

Highest score registered by a team
- 161 Golden Lions vs Limpopo Blue Bulls (161-3) Vodacom Cup
- 154 Pumas vs Limpopo Blue Bulls (154-0) Vodacom Cup
- 124 Griquas vs Limpopo Blue Bulls (124-5) Vodacom Cup
- 113 Leopards XV vs Limpopo Blue Bulls (113-3) Vodacom Cup
- 110 Blue Bulls vs vs Limpopo Blue Bulls (110-0) Vodacom Cup
- 89 Blue Bulls vs vs Griffons (89-10) Vodacom Cup

Most tries by a team in a match
- 25 Golden Lions vs Limpopo Blue Bulls (161-3) Vodacom Cup
- 16 Blue Bulls vs vs Limpopo Blue Bulls (110-0) Vodacom Cup
- 13 Blue Bulls vs vs Griffons (89-10) Vodacom Cup
- 12 Blue Bulls vs Valke (74-14) Vodacom Cup
- 10 Sharks XV vs Border (72-06) Vodacom Cup
- 10 Pumas vs Valke (62-0) Vodacom Cup
- 10 Pumas vs Griffons (64-07) Vodacom Cup
- 10 Pumas vs Valke (67-17) First Division

SEASON IN 2013

Biggest winning margin
- 158 Golden Lions vs Limpopo Blue Bulls (161-3) Vodacom Cup
- 154 Pumas vs Limpopo Blue Bulls (154-0) Vodacom Cup
- 119 Griquas vs Limpopo Blue Bulls (124-5) Vodacom Cup
- 110 Leopards XV vs Limpopo Blue Bulls (113-3) Vodacom Cup
- 110 Blue Bulls vs vs Limpopo Blue Bulls (110-0) Vodacom Cup
- 79 Blue Bulls vs vs Griffons (89-10) Vodacom Cup
- 66 Sharks XV vs Border (72-06) Vodacom Cup
- 62 Pumas vs Valke (62-0) Vodacom Cup
- 60 Blue Bulls vs Valke (74-14) Vodacom Cup
- 60 South Africa vs Argentina (73-13) Test
- 57 Pumas vs Griffons (64-07) Vodacom Cup
- 50 Pumas vs Valke (67-17) First Division

Most points by a player in a match
- 47 Anthony Volmink, GL vs Limpopo BB (9t, 1c) Vodacom Cup
- 40 Willie du Plessis, BB vs Limpopo BB (2t, 15c) Vodacom Cup
- 28 Morne Steyn, SA vs Argentina (8c, 4p) Test
- 25 Justin van Staden, SWD vs Leopards (5c, 5p) First Division

Most tries by a player in a match
- 9 Anthony Volmink Golden Lions vs Limpopo Blue Bulls Vodacom Cup
- 5 Marius Schoeman Griquas vs Limpopo Blue Bulls Vodacom Cup
- 5 Rocco Jansen Griquas vs Limpopo Blue Bulls Vodacom Cup
- 4 Sampie Mastriet Blue Bulls vs Valke Vodacom Cup
- 4 Ian Heyns Leopards XV vs Limpopo Blue Bulls Vodacom Cup
- 4 Danwel Demas Pumas vs Limpopo Blue Bulls Vodacom Cup
- 4 JP Mostert Valke vs Limpopo Blue Bulls Vodacom Cup
- 4 Raymond Rhule Free State vs Griquas Currie Cup
- 3 Boom Prinsloo Free State XV vs Pampas XV Vodacom Cup
- 3 Nicky Steyn Griffons vs Limpopo Blue Bulls Vodacom Cup
- 3 Rhyk Welgemoed Leopards XV vs Limpopo Blue Bulls Vodacom Cup
- 3 Jaco Bouwer Pumas vs Limpopo Blue Bulls Vodacom Cup
- 3 Uzair Cassiem Pumas vs Valke Vodacom Cup
- 3 Rosco Speckman Pumas vs Pampas XV Vodacom Cup
- 3 Chris Cloete WP vs EP Kings Vodacom Cup
- 3 JW Bell Pumas vs Griffons First Division
- 3 RW Kember Pumas vs EP Kings First Division
- 3 Ashwin Scott Pumas vs Valke First Division
- 3 Rosco Speckman Pumas vs Valke First Division
- 3 BG Uys Leopards vs Border First Division
- 3 Edmar Marais Leopards vs Valke First Division
- 3 Brendan April Boland vs Griffons First Division
- 3 Alshaun Bock SWD vs Valke First Division
- 3 Alshaun Bock SWD vs EP Kings First Division
- 3 Willie Odendaal Valke vs SWD Eagles First Division

Most conversions by a player in a match
- 15 Willie du Plessis Blue Bulls vs Limpopo Blue Bulls Vodacom Cup
- 14 Andre Pretorius Leopards XV vs Limpopo Blue Bulls Vodacom Cup
- 12 Guy Cronje Golden Lions vs Limpopo Blue Bulls Vodacom Cup
- 12 Francois Brummer Griquas vs Limpopo Blue Bulls Vodacom Cup
- 11 Carl Bezuidenhout Pumas vs Limpopo Blue Bulls Vodacom Cup
- 11 Coenie van Wyk Pumas vs Limpopo Blue Bulls Vodacom Cup
- 9 Scott van Breda EP Kings vs Griffons First Division
- 8 Fred Zeilinga Sharks XV vs Border Vodacom Cup
- 8 Marnitz Boshoff Golden Lions vs Blue Bulls Currie Cup
- 8 Morne Steyn South Africa vs Argentina Test
- 7 Jaun Kotze Valke vs Limpopo Blue Bulls Vodacom Cup
- 7 Carl Bezuidenhout Pumas vs Valke First Division
- 7 Willie du Plessis Blue Bulls vs Valke Vodacom Cup
- 7 Willie du Plessis Blue Bulls vs Griffons Vodacom Cup

Most penalties by a player in a match
- 7 Patrick Lambie Sharks vs Crusaders Super rugby
- 7 Gouws Prinsloo Griquas vs Golden Lions Currie Cup

Most drop goals by a player in a match
- 2 F Zeilinga Sharks vs Golden Lions Currie Cup

Scored in all four ways
- 21 Pts Fred Zeilinga [1T, 2C, 2P, 2DG] Sharks vs Golden Lions Currie Cup

SEASON IN 2013

LEADING PLAYERS IN 2013

MOST POINTS IN 2013 (100 OR MORE)

PLAYER	Team/s	Matches	Tries	Conversions	Penalties	Drop Goals	Points
Morne Steyn	Bulls/SA	29	3	61	86	1	**398**
Carl Bezuidenhout	Pumas	27	6	81	60	2	**378**
Patrick Lambie	Sharks/SA/Barbarians	31	3	35	54	3	**256**
Fred Zeilinga	Sharks XV	19	4	42	44	0	**250**
Demetri Catrakilis	Southern Kings/WP	21	1	19	56	3	**220**
Scott van Breda	EP Kings	20	4	36	42	0	**218**
Marnitz Boshoff	Golden Lions	17	2	38	30	4	**188**
Adriaan Engelbrecht	Leopards/Leop XV/SA Pres XV	25	5	45	19	0	**172**
Joe Pietersen	Stormers	15	0	19	44	0	**170**
Justin van Staden	SWD/SA Univ	12	1	30	26	2	**149**
Kurt Coleman	WP	17	0	21	34	0	**144**
Riaan Smit	FS Cheetahs	18	3	20	26	0	**133**
Jaun Kotze	Valke	21	4	31	11	5	**130**
Rosco Speckman	Pumas/SA Pres XV	28	24	0	0	0	**120**
Handre Pollard	Blue Bulls/SA U/20	26	0	24	20	1	**111**
Elgar Watts	FS Cheetahs/Cheetahs/FS XV	19	4	18	18	0	**110**
Alshaun Bock	SWD Eagles	23	22	0	0	0	**110**
Tony Jantjies	Blue Bulls	9	2	22	18	0	**108**
Elton Jantjies	Golden Lions	24	2	15	20	0	**100**

MOST TRIES (10 OR MORE)

PLAYER	Team/s	Matches	Tries
Rosco Speckman	Pumas/SA Pres XV	28	**24**
Alshaun Bock	SWD Eagles/SA Pres XV	23	**22**
Anthony Volmink	Golden Lions	20	**19**
JW Bell	Pumas	25	**15**
Edmar Marais	Leopards	22	**14**
Marnus Schoeman	Griquas	17	**12**
Raymond Rhule	Cheetahs/FS Cheetahs	27	**12**
Luther Obi	SA U20/Leopards	19	**12**
Jean de Villiers	Stormers/SA/Barbarians	30	**12**
Danie Dames	Leopards	21	**11**
Derrick Minnie	Golden Lions	18	**11**
Coenie van Wyk	Pumas	24	**11**
Sampie Mastriet	Bulls/Blue Bulls	14	**10**
Wiaan Liebenberg	Blue Bulls	16	**10**
Mpho Mbiyozo	Southern Kings/EP	17	**10**

Most Appearances

Player	Team/s	Apps
Wille le Roux	Cheetahs/SA/GW/Barbarians	32
Coenie Oosthuizen	Cheetahs/SA/FS/Barbarians	32
Adriaan Strauss	Cheetahs/SA/FS	31
Patrick Lambie	Sharks/SA/Barbarians	31
Jean de Villiers	Stormers/SA/WP/Barbarians	30

SEASON IN 2013

Players who recorded a 100th appearance for their province in 2013

Player	For & Against	Date
Steph Roberts	Griquas vs Leopards XV	20/04/2013
Werner Griesel	Griffons vs Blue Bulls	27/04/2013
Brok Harris	WP vs Free State	17/08/2013
Clemen Lewis	Boland vs EP Kings	13/09/2013
Keegan Daniel	Sharks vs Golden Lions	27/09/2013
DJ Terblanche	Pumas vs SWD Eagles	04/10/2013
Franco van der Merwe	Golden Lions vs WP	19/10/2013

Players who recorded a 100th appearance for their franchise in 2013

Player	For & Against	Date
Andries Bekker	Stormers vs Cheetahs	06/04/2013
Pierre Spies	Bulls vs Highlanders	18/05/2013

Youngest and oldest first-class players in 2012

Rohan Janse van Rensburg	Blue Bulls vs Pumas, March 16	18 years 186 days
Eddie Fredericks	FS XV vs EP Kings, April 6	35 years 96 days

Tallest, shortest, heaviest and lightest players in 2013

Andries Bekker	Stormers	2.08m
Rory Arnold	Griquas	2.08m
Percy Williams	Golden Lions/SA U/20	1.60m
Dean Hopp	SWD Eagles	142kg
Charlie Ewerts	SWD Eagles	64kg

CAREER LEADERS IN 2013 - *ONLY IN SOUTH AFRICA*

500 CAREER POINTS OR MORE BY A PLAYER ACTIVE IN 2013

PLAYER	Province	Matches	Tries	Conversions	Penalties	Drop Goals	Points
M Steyn	Blue Bulls	279	50	528	521	45	**3004**
AS Pretorius	Leopards	203	28	375	280	42	**1856**
LI Strydom	Griffons	196	16	313	302	11	**1645**
PJ Grant	WP	155	19	180	232	1	**1148**
PJ Lambie	Sharks	118	19	149	198	3	**990**
JC Pietersen	WP	116	32	83	143	5	**770**
ET Jantjies	Golden Lions	94	6	115	166	3	**762**
BG Habana	WP	263	143	0	0	0	**715**
R Pienaar	Sharks	199	27	122	102	3	**694**
EG Watts	FS Cheetahs	117	35	139	72	1	**672**
R Viljoen	Sharks	195	48	80	65	14	**637**
C Bezuidenhout	Pumas	89	16	111	79	2	**545**

Fifty tries

BG Habana	WP	143
J Fourie	WP	95
JL Nokwe	Valke	93
J de Villiers	WP	91
ER Fredericks	FS	89
OM Ndungane	Sharks	86
AZ Ndungane	Blue Bulls	82
NT Nelson	EP	75
AG Bock	SWD	73
J-PR Pietersen	Sharks	68
SJ Pretorius	FS	67
LA Watson	EP	66
MC Joubert	Sharks	61
AG van Rensburg	Golden Lions	61

Two hundred and fifty first-class appearances

LJ Botes	Sharks	280
M Steyn	Blue Bulls	279
JN du Plessis	Sharks	275
JP Botha	Blue Bulls	264
BG Habana	WP	263
F van der Merwe	Golden Lions	260

SOUTH AFRICANS ABROAD

Compiled by Stuart Farmer. South Africans appearing for leading clubs overseas at some point in 2013.
* Springbok   + Overseas international

A

+ NJ (Nick) Abendanon	Bath Rugby	England
HJ (Heini) Adams	Bordeaux-Begles	France
JP (Jacobie) Adriaanse	Scarlets	Wales
CG (Chris) Alcock	Western Force	Australia
RD (Rob) Andrew	Leicester Tigers	England
	London Welsh	England
DZ (Zane) Ansell	Petrarca Padova	Italy

B

C (Conrad) Barnard	Agen	France
	Oyonnax	France
PC (Pat) Barnard	Brive	France
+ BM (Brad) Barritt	Saracens	England
CJ (Coenie) Basson	Lyon O.U.	France
S (Stefan) Basson	Vea-FemiCZ Rovigo	Italy
* A (Andries) Bekker	Kobe Kobelco Steelers	Japan
R (Roland) Bernard	Grenoble	France
JF (Jan-Francois) Bester van den Berg	Macclesfield Blues	England
N (Naude) Beukes	Grenoble	France
JDB (Jannie) Bornman	Castres Olympique	France
PW (Paul) Bosch	Montpellier	France
* HM (Meyer) Bosman	Stade Francais Paris	France
+ WT (Tobias) Botes	Benetton Treviso	Italy
BJ (Berend) Botha	Mont-de-Marsan	France
* BJ (BJ) Botha	Munster	Ireland
* GVG (Gary) Botha	Toulouse	France
* JP (Bakkies) Botha	Toulon	France
+ MJ (Mouritz) Botha	Saracens	England
R (Rudi) Brits	Colomiers	France
* SB (Schalk) Brits	Saracens	England
JL (Lodie) Britz	Mont-de-Marsan	France
* HW (Heinrich) Brussow	NTT Docomo Red Hurricanes	Japan
AM (Albertus) Buckle	Grenoble	France
CB (Craig) Burden	Toulon	France
K (Kevin) Buys	Brive	France

C

D (Dario) Chistolini	Gloucester Rugby	England
	Zebre	Italy
+ AD (Antonie) Claassen	Castres Olympique	France
EF (Errie) Claassens	Worcester Warriors	England
* M (Michael) Claassens	Bath Rugby	England
	Toulon	France
AM (Ashley) Clarke	Massy	France
A (Arno) Coetzee	Aurillac	France
C (Cilliers) Coetzer	Tarbes	France
ML (Michael) Coetzee	Castres Olympique	France
R (Rudi) Coetzee	Grenoble	France

Bakkies Botha representing Toulon and Rory Kockott in Castres Olympique colours.
Getty Images

SOUTH AFRICANS ABROAD

Player	Club	Country
SD (Stuart) Commins	London Wasps	England
SD (Stuart) Commins	Ealing Trailfinders	England
* J (Jacques) Cronje	Racing-Metro 92	France

D

Player	Club	Country
J (Johann) de Bruyn	Rugby Reggio	Italy
SJ (Sebastian) de Chaves	Mont-de-Marsan	France
	Leicester Tigers	England
+ B (Benjamin) de Jager	Cammi Calvisano	Italy
* NA (Neil) de Kock	Saracens	England
+ CA (Carlo Antonio) del Fava		
	Newcastle Falcons	England
M (Marius) Delport	Dax	France
RJE (Robbie) Diack	Ulster	Ireland
WJ (Hanno) Dirksen	Ospreys	Wales
C (Chris) du Plessis	Rugby Viadana	Italy
PJS (JP) du Plessis	Montpellier	France
PVW (Petrus) du Plessis	Saracens	England
CG (Cornell) du Preez	Edinburgh Rugby	Scotland
* PF (Fourie) du Preez	Suntory Sungoliath	Japan
R (Ruaan) du Preez	Oyonnax	France
* WH (Wian) du Preez	Munster	Ireland
	Lyon O.U.	France
JJ (Jaco) du Toit	Pau	France
DO (Dewaldt) Duvenage	Perpignan	France

E

Player	Club	Country
GW (George) Earle	Scarlets	Wales
JM (Sias) Ebersohn	Western Force	Australia
RT (Robert) Ebersohn	Montpellier	France
HO (Henk) Eksteen	Beziers	France
+ J (Jaco) Erasmus	Cammi Calvisano	Italy
	M-Three San Dona	Italy
+ IR (Ian) Evans	Ospreys	Wales
M (Mat) Evans	Ealing Trailfinders	England

F

Player	Club	Country
NS (Nick) Fenton-Wells	Saracens	England
	Bedford Blues	England
SJP (Schalk) Ferreira	Toulouse	France
AR (Adriaan) Fondse	Rugby Viadana	Italy
* J (Jaque) Fourie	Kobe Kobelco Steelers	Japan
BK (Burton) Francis	Agen	France

G

Player	Club	Country
+ Q (Quintin) Geldenhuys	Zebre	Italy
D (Dandre) Gerber	Beziers	France
D (Durandt) Gerber	Mantovani Lazio	Italy
R (Rayno) Gerber	Vea-FemiCZ Rovigo	Italy
SC (Sam) Gerber	Bayonne	France
SE (Stephan) Gerber	Aurillac	France
R (Reggie) Goodes	Wellington Lions	New Zealand
K (Kieran) Goss	Cornish Pirates	England
* PJ (Peter) Grant	Kobe Kobelco Steelers	Japan
JA (Cobus) Grobler	La Rochelle	France
JH (Hans) Grobler	Tarbes	France

H

Player	Club	Country
* BG (Bryan) Habana	Toulon	France
T (Thor) Halvorsen	Marchiol Mogliano	Italy
D (Dean) Hammond	Worcester Warriors	England
H (Drikus) Hancke	Montpellier	France
* AJ (Alistair) Hargreaves	Saracens	England
WJ (Wikus) Harmse	Narbonne	France
	Bourg-en-Bresse	France
PJ (Petrus) Hauman	Brive	France
DS, (Dane) Haylett-Petty	Western Force	Australia
	Toyota Shokki Shuttles	Japan
RW (Rob) Herring	Ulster	Ireland
CO (Cliffie) Hodgson	Coventry	England
T (Tyrone) Holmes	Petrarca Padova	Italy
	Glasgow Warriors	Scotland
JP (Joubert) Horn	Rugby Viadana	Italy
A (Andre) Hough	Pau	France
A (Alten) Hulme	Grenoble	France
WA (Wylie) Human	Pays d'Aix	France
G (Gavin) Hume	Perpignan	France
	Clermont Auvergne	France

J

Player	Club	Country
EA (Rassie) Jansen van Vuuren		
	Montpellier	France
	La Rochelle	France
JC (JC) Janse van Rensburg		
	Bayonne	France
* ER (Ricky) Januarie	Lyon O.U.	France
J (Jody) Jenneker	Oyonnax	France
* AF (Ashley) Johnson	London Wasps	England
G (Gavin) Jones	Blaydon	England
EW (Wessel) Jooste	Castres Olympique	France
	Agen	France
CM (Chris) Jordaan	Petrarca Padova	Italy
E (Ernst) Joubert	Saracens	England

K

Player	Club	Country
* R (Ryan) Kankowski	Toyota Shokki Shuttles	Japan
JB (Kobus) Kemp	Aurillac	France
* Z (Zane) Kirchner	Leinster	Ireland
GP (Graham) Knoop	Ospreys	Wales
RM (Rory) Kockott	Castres Olympique	France
RN (Nick) Koster	Bath Rugby	England
	Bristol Rugby	England
+ DM (Dan) Kotze	Clermont Auvergne	France
AG (Andries) Kruger	Carcassonne	France
* PJJ (Juandre) Kruger	Racing-Metro 92	France

SOUTH AFRICANS ABROAD

L
	Name	Club	Country
	GA (Gideon) la Grange	Benetton Treviso	Italy
+	B (Bernard) le Roux	Racing-Metro 92	France
+	JE (Jacques) le Roux	Coventry	England
	PL (Vickus) Liebenberg	Mont-de-Marsan	France
	RF (Rob) Linde	Bayonne	France
*	H (Hilton) Lobberts	M-Three San Dona	Italy
	W (Werner) Loftus	Tarbes	France
	LFP (Francois) Louw	Bath Rugby	England
	L (Louis) Ludik	Agen	France
	A (Ali) Lyon	Richmond	England

M
	Name	Club	Country
	SJ (Shaun) Malton	Nottingham Rugby	England
	JA (Jandre) Marais	Bordeaux-Begles	France
	GD (Gere) Maree	Coventry	England
	G (George) Marich	Narbonne	France
	RJG (Justin) Melck	Saracens	England
	WG (Jakes) Mjekevu	Perpignan	France
	W (Wouter) Moore	Beziers	France
*	G (Gerhard) Mostert	Stade Francais Paris	France
	GH (Gert) Muller	Agen	France
		Bayonne	France
*	GJ (Johann) Muller	Ulster	Ireland
	J (Jeandre) Mynhardt	Pays d'Aix	France

N
	Name	Club	Country
	J (Jacques) Naude	Dax	France
	WP (WP) Nel	Edinburgh Rugby	Scotland

O
	Name	Club	Country
*	W (Wynand) Olivier	Montpellier	France
	E (Ettienne) Oosthuizen	ACT Brumbies	Australia

P
	Name	Club	Country
	RJ (Richard) Palframan	London Irish	England
	J (Jeff) Perkins	Colomiers	France
	BJM (Ben) Pienaar	Moseley	England
		London Welsh	England
*	R (Ruan) Pienaar	Ulster	Ireland
	JC (Joe) Pietersen	Biarritz Olympique	France
*	JPR (JP) Pietersen	Panasonic Wild Knights	Japan
+	DW (David) Pocock	ACT Brumbies	Australia
	DJ (Danie) Poolman	Connacht	Ireland
*	DJ (Dewald) Potgieter	Yamaha Jubilo	Japan
	JL (Jacques-Louis) Potgieter	Bayonne	France
		Dax	France
+	A (Andries) Pretorius	Cardiff Blues	Wales
*	AS (Andre) Pretorius	Carcassonne	France

R
	Name	Club	Country
*	MC (Chiliboy) Ralepele	Toulouse	France
+	C (Clyde) Rathbone	ACT Brumbies	Australia
	BC (Bryan) Rennie	Bristol Rugby	England
	E (Ethienne) Reynecke	Connacht	Ireland
		Pau	France
	W (Will) Richards	Newport	Wales
	R (Riccardo) Robuschi	M-Three San Dona	Italy
	HL (Hendrik) Roodt	Grenoble	France
*	DJ (Danie) Rossouw	Suntory Sungoliath	Japan
		Toulon	France
	JS (Jacobus) Roux	Benetton Treviso	Italy
	Q (Quinn) Roux	Leinster	Ireland

S
	Name	Club	Country
	DS (Danie) Saayman	Pau	France
	JA (Jarrod) Saffy	Melbourne Rebels	Australia
	D (Donovan) Sanders	Jersey	England
	JJ (Jared) Saunders	Rotherham Titans	England
		Saracens	England
	JH (Johan) Schoonbee	Hawke's Bay Magpies	New Zealand
	DM (Dewald) Senekal	Bayonne	France
	BC (Brett) Sharman	Bath Rugby	England
	RC (Ross) Skeate	Agen	France
	AJ (Bertus) Smit	Pays d'Aix	France
*	JW (John) Smit	Saracens	England
*	JH (Juan) Smith	Toulon	France
	JP (Jean-Pierre) Smith	ACT Brumbies	Australia
	RH (Ruan) Smith	ACT Brumbies	Australia
	J (Joe) Snyman	Scarlets	Wales
	R (Ruan) Snyman	Racing-Metro 92	France
*	RS (Shaun) Sowerby	Grenoble	France
	SL (Scott) Spedding	Bayonne	France
	FA (Frikkie) Spies	Tarbes	France
	CJ (CJ) Stander	Munster A	Ireland
*	GG (Gurthro) Steenkamp	Toulouse	France
+	MJH (Matt) Stevens	Saracens	England
	AJ (Braam) Steyn	Marchiol Mogliano	Italy
		Cammi Calvisano	Italy
*	M (Morne) Steyn	Stade Francais Paris	France
+	CR (Richardt) Strauss	Leinster	Ireland
	JZ (Josh) Strauss	Glasgow Warriors	Scotland
	N (Nic) Strauss	Narbonne	France
	M (Mark) Swanepoel	ACT Brumbies	Australia
		Tasman Makos	New Zealand
	M (Meyer) Swanepoel	Marchiol Mogliano	Italy
	R (Riaan) Swanepoel	Brive	France

T
	Name	Club	Country
	JE (Jarrod) Taylor	Cambridge	England
	PD (PD) Terblanche	Tarbes	France
	MJ (Morgan) Thompson	Ealing Trailfinders	England
	K (Kyle) Tonetti	Connacht	Ireland
+	GA (Greig) Tonks	Edinburgh Rugby	Scotland

SOUTH AFRICANS ABROAD

Francois Louw and Michael Claassens representing Bath. *Getty Images*

U
R (Retief) Uys	Brive	France

V
* PA (Albert) van den Berg	Canon Eagles	Japan
+ DTH (DTH) van der Merwe	Glasgow Warriors	Scotland
FC (Francois) van der Merwe	Racing-Metro 92	France
* HS (Heinke) van der Merwe	Leinster	Ireland
	Stade Francais Paris	France
IP (Izak) van der Westhuizen	Edinburgh Rugby	Scotland
MJ (Martinus) van der Heever	Toulouse	France
MRS (Pellow) van der Westhuizen	Colomiers	France
PW (Wimpie) van der Walt	NTT Docomo	
	Red Hurricanes	Japan
JP (Johan) van Heerden	Bucuresti Wolves	Romania
R (Ruahan) van Jaarsveld	Rugby Viadana	Italy
J (Joe) van Niekerk	Vea-FemiCZ Rovigo	Italy
* JC (Joe) van Niekerk	Toulon	France
AJ (Dries) van Schalkwyk	Zebre	Italy
E (Eugene) van Staden	Biarritz Olympique	France
GJ (GJ) van Velze	Northampton Saints	England
M (Michael) van Vuuren	Zebre	Italy
MT (Michael) van Vuuren	Stade Francais Paris	France
A (Anton) van Zyl	Stade Francais Paris	France
+ CC (Cornelius) van Zyl	Benetton Treviso	Italy
D (Darryl) Veenendaal	Bedford Blues	England
DLR (De la Rey) Veenendaal	Cambridge	England
H (Henno) Venter	Birmingham & Solihull Bees	England
CH (Harry) Vermaas	Beziers	France
* J (Jano) Vermaak	Toulouse	France
FJN (Frans) Viljoen	Lyon O.U.	France
R (Riaan) Viljoen	NTT Docomo	
	Red Hurricanes	Japan
JF (Jan) Volschenk	Oyonnax	France
G (Gerhard) Vosloo	Clermont Auvergne	France

W
B (Brandon) Walker	Hartpury College	England
	Esher	England
* PJ (Pedrie) Wannenburg	Castres Olympique	France
LR (Lorne) Ward	Rosslyn Park	England
C (Tollie) Wegner	Stade Francais Paris	France
* MVZ (Marco) Wentzel	London Wasps	England
PJ (Johan) Wessels	La Rochelle	France
B (Brett) Wilkinson	Connacht	Ireland

Z
C (Cameron) Zeiss	Esher	England

SECTION 3
NATIONAL TEAMS

SPRINGBOKS
Review of the 2013 Season **34**
Springbok Test Appearances
& Points **37**
Springbok Squad Members
in 2013 .... **38**
CASTLE LAGER INCOMING SERIES
Series Review **40**
South Africa vs Italy **52**
South Africa vs Scotland **54**
South Africa vs Samoa **56**
CASTLE RUGBY CHAMPIONSHIP
Tournament Review & statistics .. **58**
Results & Scorers **60**
Squads & Management lists **62**
South Africa vs Argentina –
Soweto **70**
Argentina vs South Africa –
Mendoza **72**
Australia vs South Africa –
Brisbane **74**
New Zealand vs South Africa –
Auckland **76**
South Africa vs Australia –
Cape Town **78**
South Africa vs New Zealand –
Johannesburg **80**

END-OF-YEAR TOUR
Tour Review & statistics **82**
Wales vs South Africa –
Cardiff **86**
Scotland vs South Africa –
Edinburgh **88**
France vs South Africa –
Paris **90**

SA UNDER-20
IRB World Championship
Review & statistics **92**

SEVENS
IRB World Series Review
& statistics **100**
Rugby World Cup Sevens **105**

SA WOMEN
Season Review & statistics **108**

SA SCHOOLS **112**
SA PRESIDENT'S XV **115**

SA Schools scrumhalf Justin Philips sends the ball to the backline against England. *Carl Fourie/Gallo Images*

SPRINGBOKS IN 2013

Bok star shines brightly despite blackout

SPRINGBOK COACH HEYNEKE MEYER'S constitution is such that he will never consider second best as good enough, but he could nevertheless reflect on 2013 as a satisfactory year.

South Africa established a winning culture with 10 victories from 12 Tests, with the two defeats against the All Blacks in Auckland and Johannesburg. The 83% win ratio was 20% higher than the Boks' historic average and the best harvest since 1998, when they won 11 of 12 Tests.

There was progress in just about every area, noticeably in attack where they scored 23 tries in the Castle Rugby Championship. This was helped by sharper play at the breakdowns, where the input of Scottish consultant Richie Gray proved valuable. South Africa also conceded only one try on their end-of-season tour.

While there were weak performances against Scotland in Nelspruit and Argentina in Mendoza, the Boks were generally consistent. Meyer also succeeded in expanding his depth with a view to the 2015 World Cup.

The rise of Willie le Roux at fullback played a big role in transforming South Africa's attacking play. Any doubts Meyer had over him were erased on the end-of-season tour, where Le Roux also displayed tactical nous.

Morné Steyn put an indifferent 2012 behind him by rediscovering his goalkicking touch and consequently also his smile. Patrick Lambie then did a fine stand-in job when Steyn was troubled by a back injury in Cardiff and Edinburgh.

Siya Kolisi proved himself capable of stepping into the Bok loose-trio when injury claimed Willem Alberts, while Frans Malherbe and Coenie Oosthuizen also looked promising at tighthead prop.

The year's biggest disappointment was in Auckland, where Springbok hooker Bismarck du Plessis was unfairly red-carded by French referee Romain Poite. Du Plessis deserved his second yellow card for leading with his elbow, but the first for a legitimate tackle on All Black flyhalf Dan Carter sowed the seeds for the ensuing mess.

A highly-anticipated Test between the two best teams in the world was consequently reduced to a farce early in the second half. It was scant consolation when the International Rugby Board acknowledged the error after New Zealand had won 29-15.

The return match at Ellis Park was an epic as South Africa gave it their all in the quest to achieve the bonus-point victory that could potentially win them the Championship.

They got their four tries, but lost the tournament the moment that the All Blacks' replacement flyhalf, Beauden Barrett, broke and scored his team's fourth try for the single log point the visitors needed. The All Blacks went on to win 38-27.

There were a number of outstanding individual Bok performances. Duane Vermeulen showed that he is second only to the incomparable Kieran Read as a No 8, Bryan Habana remained at the peak of his powers on the wing, skipper Jean de Villiers played some of the best rugby of his career in midfield and Alberts was powerful on defence and attack.

Meyer's biggest positional concern was at scrumhalf, where he recalled veteran Fourie du Preez from Japan to paper over the cracks – when he was available, that is. And while Flip van der Merwe did an impressive holding job, Meyer was also still concerned about his long-term options at No 5 lock, although the rise of Pieter-Steph du Toit should not cause Meyer to lose that much sleep.

Nevertheless, 2013 provided a fine harvest.

Siya Kolisi and Jean de Villiers. *Lee Warren/Gallo Images*

SPRINGBOKS IN 2013

RESULTS

Date	Venue	Opponent	Result	Score	Scorers
June 08	Growthpoint Kings Park, Durban	ITALY	WON	44-10	T: Strauss, Engelbrecht, Habana, De Villiers, Basson. C: Steyn (4), Lambie. P: Steyn (3).
June 15	Mbombela Stadium, Nelspruit	SCOTLAND	WON	30-17	T: Penalty try, Engelbrecht, Serfontein. C: Steyn (2), Lambie. P: Steyn (2), Lambie.
June 22	Loftus Versfeld, Pretoria	SAMOA	WON	56-23	T: Habana (2), Louw (2), Engelbrecht, Basson, Steyn, Nyakane. C: Steyn (3), Lambie (2). P: Steyn (2)
Aug 17	FNB Stadium, Soweto	ARGENTINA	WON	73-13	T: Penalty try, Engelbrecht, Strauss, Alberts, De Villiers, Du Preez, Habana, Vermeulen, B du Plessis. C: Steyn (8). P: Steyn (4).
Aug 24	Estadio Malvinas Argentinas, Mendoza	ARGENTINA	WON	22-17	T: Basson. C: Steyn. P: Steyn (5).
Sept 07	Suncorp Stadium, Brisbane	AUSTRALIA	WON	38-12	T: Oosthuizen, De Villiers, Kirchner, Le Roux. C: Steyn (3). P: Steyn (4).
Sept 14	Eden Park, Auckland	NEW ZEALAND	Lost	15-29	T: B du Plessis, Lambie. C: Steyn. P: Steyn.
Sept 28	DHL Newlands, Cape Town	AUSTRALIA	WON	28-08	T: Strauss, Kirchner, Le Roux. C: Steyn (2). P: Steyn (3).
Oct 05	Ellis Park, Johannesburg	NEW ZEALAND	Lost	27-38	T: Habana (2), Le Roux, De Villiers. C: Steyn (2). P: Steyn .
Nov 09	Millennium Stadium, Cardiff	WALES	WON	24-15	T: De Villiers, B du Plessis, Du Preez. C: Steyn (2), Lambie. P: Steyn
Nov 17	Murrayfield, Edinburgh	SCOTLAND	WON	28-00	T: Alberts, Le Roux, Pietersen, Oosthuizen. C: Lambie (4).
Nov 23	Stade de France, Paris	FRANCE	WON	19-10	T: Pietersen. C: Steyn. P: Steyn(3), Lambie.

SCORERS

PLAYER	Province	Apps	Tries	Conv	Pen	DG	Pts
M Steyn	Blue Bulls	12	1	29	29	0	150
BG Habana	Toulon, France	12	6	0	0	0	30
PJ Lambie	KwaZulu-Natal	12	1	9	2	0	29
J de Villiers	Western Province	12	5	0	0	0	25
WJ le Roux	Griquas	12	4	0	0	0	20
JJ Engelbrecht	Blue Bulls	11	4	0	0	0	20
BA Basson	Blue Bulls	5	3	0	0	0	15
JA Strauss	Free State	12	3	0	0	0	15
BW du Plessis	KwaZulu-Natal	11	3	0	0	0	15
L-FP Louw	Bath, England	11	2	0	0	0	10
CV Oosthuizen	Free State	12	2	0	0	0	10
WS Alberts	KwaZulu-Natal	10	2	0	0	0	10
PF du Preez	Suntory Goliath, Japan	5	2	0	0	0	10
Z Kirchner	Leinster, Ireland	4	2	0	0	0	10
TN Nyakane	Free State	3	1	0	0	0	5
JL Serfontein	Blue Bulls	9	1	0	0	0	5
DJ Vermeulen	Western Province	9	1	0	0	0	5
J-PR Pietersen	Panasonic Wild Knights	3	2	0	0	0	10
Penalty tries	–	0	2	0	0	0	10
		47	38	31	0		404

SPRINGBOKS IN 2013

TEST APPEARANCES & POINTS

SPRINGBOK	Italy	Scotland	Samoa	Argentina 1	Argentina 2	Australia 1	New Zealand 1	Australia 2	New Zealand 2	Wales	Scotland	France	Matches	Tries	Conversions	Penalties	Drop Goals	Points
WJ le Roux	15	15	15	15	15	14	14	14	14	10R	15	15	12	4	–	–	–	20
BG Habana	14	14	14	14	14	11	11	11	11	11	11	11	12	6	–	–	–	30
JJ Engelbrecht	13	13	13	13	13	13	13	13	13	14R	12R	–	11	4	–	–	–	20
J de Villiers	12c	12c	12c	12c	12c	12c	12c	12c	12c	12c	12c	12c	12	5	–	–	–	25
BA Basson	11	11	11	11	11	–	–	–	–	–	–	–	5	3	–	–	–	15
M Steyn	10	10	10	10	10	10	10	10	10	10	6R	10	12	1	29	29	–	150
J Vermaak	9	–	–	–	x	9R	9R	–	–	–	–	x	3	–	–	–	–	0
PJ Spies	8	8	8	–	–	–	–	–	–	–	–	–	3	–	–	–	–	0
AF Botha	7	7	–	–	–	–	–	–	–	–	–	–	2	–	–	–	–	0
L-FP Louw	6	–	6	6	6	6	6	6	6	6	6	6	11	2	–	–	–	10
PJJ Kruger	5	5	5R	5	5	5R	5R	5R	5	–	–	–	9	–	–	–	–	0
E Etzebeth	4	4	4	4	4	4	4	4	4	4	4R	4	12	–	–	–	–	0
JN du Plessis	3	3	3	3	3	3	3	3	3	–	–	–	9	–	–	–	–	0
JA Strauss	2	2	2	2	2	2R	2R	2	2R	2R	2	2R	12	3	–	–	–	15
T Mtawarira	1	1	1	1	1	1	1	1	1	1	1R	1	12	–	–	–	–	0
MC Ralepelle	2R	–	–	–	–	–	–	–	–	–	–	–	1	–	–	–	–	0
TN Nyakane	1R	3R	3R	–	–	–	–	–	–	–	–	–	3	1	–	–	–	5
CV Oosthuizen	3R	1R	1R	3R	3R	3R	3R	3R	3R	3R	3R	3	12	2	–	–	–	10
PR van der Merwe	5R	4R	5	5R	5R	5	5	5	–	5	5	5	11	–	–	–	–	0
MC Coetzee	6R	6	–	–	–	–	–	–	–	–	7R	–	3	–	–	–	–	0
R Pienaar	9R	9	9	9	9	9	x	9R	9R	9R	–	9	11	–	–	–	–	0
PJ Lambie	10R	10R	10R	15R	11R	10R	11R	15R	15R	15	10	10R	12	1	9	2	–	29
JL Serfontein	14R	13R	12R	12R	13R	12R	13R	13R	11R	–	–	–	9	1	–	–	–	5
S Kolisi	–	7R	8R	7R	7R	6R	6R	7R	7R	7R	–	19R	10	–	–	–	–	0
BW du Plessis	–	2R	2R	2R	2R	2	2	2R	2	2	2R	2	11	3	–	–	–	15
PE van Zyl	–	9R	9R	–	–	–	–	–	–	–	–	–	2	–	–	–	–	0
WS Alberts	–	–	7	7	7	7	7	7	7	7	7	7	10	2	–	–	–	10
DJ Vermeulen	–	–	–	8	8	8	8	8	8	8	8	8	9	1	–	–	–	5
GG Steenkamp	–	–	–	1R	1R	1R	1R	1R	1R	1R	1	1R	9	–	–	–	–	0
PF du Preez	–	–	–	9R	–	–	–	9	9	9	9	–	5	2	–	–	–	10
Z Kirchner	–	–	–	–	–	15	15	15	15	–	–	–	4	2	–	–	–	10
F van der Merwe	–	–	–	–	–	–	–	–	5R	–	–	–	1	–	–	–	–	0
JP Pietersen	–	–	–	–	–	–	–	–	–	14	14	14	3	2	–	–	–	10
J Fourie	–	–	–	–	–	–	–	–	–	13	13	13	3	–	–	–	–	0
JF Malherbe	–	–	–	–	–	–	–	–	–	3	3	–	2	–	–	–	–	0
PS du Toit	–	–	–	–	–	–	–	–	–	4R	–	7R	2	–	–	–	–	0
JP Botha	–	–	–	–	–	–	–	–	–	–	4	4R	2	–	–	–	–	0
LC Adriaanse	–	–	–	–	–	–	–	–	–	–	–	3R	1	–	–	–	–	0
Penalty tries	–	–	–	–	–	–	–	–	–	–	–	–	0	2	–	–	–	10
38 Players took the field													**273**	**47**	**38**	**31**	**0**	**404**

c=Captain
Players yellow-carded are indicated by the yellow blocks.

SPRINGBOK SQUAD MEMBERS IN 2013*

	Province	Date of birth	Height	Weight	Career Tests	Tries	Conversions	Penalties	Drop Goals	Career Pts
LC Adriaanse	Griquas	05/02/1988	1,81	115	1	0	0	0	0	0
WS Alberts	KwaZulu-Natal	11/05/1984	1,92	120	30	7	0	0	0	25
GG Aplon **	Western Province	06/10/1982	1,75	80	17	5	0	0	0	25
BA Basson	Blue Bulls	11/02/1987	1,85	84	11	3	0	0	0	15
AF Botha	Blue Bulls	26/10/1991	1,90	102	2	0	0	0	0	0
JP Botha	Toulon, France	22/09/1979	2,02	122	78	7	0	0	0	35
MC Coetzee	KwaZulu-Natal	08/05/1991	1,91	106	15	1	0	0	0	5
JL de Jongh ***	Western Province	15/04/1988	1,77	84	14	3	0	0	0	15
J de Villiers	Western Province	24/02/1981	1,90	100	96	25	0	0	0	125
BW du Plessis	KwaZulu-Natal	22/05/1984	1,89	112	57	9	0	0	0	45
JN du Plessis	KwaZulu-Natal	16/11/1982	1,88	120	51	1	0	0	0	5
PF du Preez	Suntory Goliath, Japan	24/03/1982	1,82	91	67	15	0	0	0	75
PS du Toit	KwaZulu-Natal	20/08/1992	2,00	116	2	0	0	0	0	0
JJ Engelbrecht	Blue Bulls	22/02/1989	1,90	94	12	4	0	0	0	20
E Etzebeth	Western Province	29/10/1991	2,03	117	23	0	0	0	0	0
J Fourie	Kobe Steelers, Japan	04/03/1983	1,90	105	72	32	0	0	0	160
JL Goosen **	Free State	27/07/1992	1,85	85	4	0	1	2	0	8
BG Habana	Toulon, France	12/06/1983	1,80	94	95	53	0	0	0	265
Z Kirchner	Leinster, Ireland	16/06/1984	1,84	92	28	5	0	0	0	25
S Kolisi	Western Province	16/06/1991	1,86	99	10	0	0	0	0	0
PJJ Kruger	Racing Metro, France	06/09/1985	1,99	112	17	0	0	0	0	0
PJ Lambie	KwaZulu-Natal	17/10/1990	1,78	87	32	1	15	11	0	68
WJ Le Roux	Griquas	18/08/1989	1,86	88	12	4	0	0	0	20
L-FP Louw	Bath, England	15/06/1985	1,90	114	28	5	0	0	0	25
JF Malherbe	Western Province	14/03/1991	1,90	120	2	0	0	0	0	0
T Mtawarira	KwaZulu-Natal	01/08/1985	1,83	115	53	2	0	0	0	10
TN Nyakane	Free State	04/05/1989	1,78	109	3	1	0	0	0	5
CV Oosthuizen	Free State	22/03/1989	1,81	127	14	2	0	0	0	10
R Pienaar	Ulster, Ireland	10/03/1984	1,87	92	74	7	22	17	0	130
J-PR Pietersen	Panasonic Wild Knights, Jpn	12/07/1986	1,90	106	51	16	0	0	0	80
MC Ralepelle	Blue Bulls	11/09/1986	1,80	104	22	1	0	0	0	5
JL Serfontein	Blue Bulls	15/04/1993	1,87	97	9	1	0	0	0	5
PJ Spies	Blue Bulls	08/06/1985	1,94	108	53	7	0	0	0	35
GG Steenkamp	Toulouse, France	12/06/1981	1,89	122	49	6	0	0	0	30
M Steyn	Stade Francais, France	11/07/1984	1,84	91	54	8	88	132	8	636
JA Strauss	Free State	18/11/1985	1,84	114	33	5	0	0	0	25
F van der Merwe	Golden Lions	15/03/1983	1,98	116	1	0	0	0	0	0
PR van der Merwe	Blue Bulls	03/06/1985	1,98	120	34	1	0	0	0	5
PE van Zyl	Free State	14/09/1989	1,74	81	2	0	0	0	0	0
J Vermaak	Toulouse, France	01/01/1985	1,70	82	3	0	0	0	0	0
DJ Vermeulen	Western Province	03/07/1986	1,93	108	16	1	0	0	0	5

SPRINGBOK SQUAD MEMBERS IN 2013*

	Province	Date of birth	Height	Weight	Career Tests	Tries	Conversions	Penalties	Drop Goals	Career Pts
FBC Kirsten ****	Blue Bulls	18/08/1988	1,93	120						
S Ntubeni ****	Western Province	18/02/1991	1,77	102						
L Schreuder ****	Western Province	25/04/1990	1,84	82						
44 players					238	126	162	8		1942

(of which 41 are classified as Springboks and have official Springbok numbers - see page 427)
(of which 3 are not classified as Springboks due to a revision of the Springbok capping policy - see footnote below)
(of which 38 made a Test appearance in 2013 - see footnotes below)

Bold letters denote new Springbok - 7 in total in 2013, all of whom took the field in a Test match (Adriaanse, Du Toit, Kolisi, Le Roux, Nyakane, Serfontein, Van Zyl). Additionally, Van der Merwe, Malherbe, Vermaak and AF Botha played their first Tests in 2013 after having won Springbok colours for being part of an official overseas touring squad at some point during 2012.

* *This list of 44 players includes all 38 players who made a Test appearance in 2013, as well as all players - capped or uncapped - who toured overseas with the Springboks, either with the 2013 Castle Rugby Championship squad, or the End-of-Year touring squad to Wales, Scotland and France. Players who were part of Springbok training or Test match squads for 2013 home Tests are not included on this list, as the Springbok capping policy states that a player must take the field in a home Test match to be classified as a Springbok.*

** *Capped Springboks Aplon & Goosen toured Wales, Scotland & France but did not take the field in any Tests.*

*** *Capped Springbok De Jongh toured with the Rugby Championship squad but did not take the field in any Tests.*

**** *A revision of the Springbok capping policy in December 2013, and applied retrospectively to the 2013 end-of-year tour to Wales, Scotland and France, means that Kirsten, Schreuder and Ntubeni are NOT considered Springboks until they take the field in a Test match, whereupon they will be given a Springbok number. Previously, all players who embarked on an overseas tour with the Springboks, up to and including the 2013 Castle Rugby Championship, were awarded Springbok colours and a Springbok number and were considered Springboks, regardless of whether or not they took the field in a Test match. The three players concerned, as well as all uncapped players who in future tour overseas with the Springboks but who do not take the field in a Test match, will be classified as "Springbok tour squad members" until such time as they take the field in a Test match, whereupon they will be considered Springboks and be given a Springbok number.*

CASTLE LAGER INCOMING TOUR

Series provides Bok building blocks

THE QUALITY OF THE PERFORMANCES were a mixed bag, but Springbok coach Heyneke Meyer would have been satisfied with the building blocks that he gained from the groundbreaking Castle Lager Incoming Series against Italy, Scotland and Samoa.

Fullback Willie le Roux, outside centre JJ Engelbrecht, and loose forwards Arno Botha and Siya Kolisi all produced compelling displays to show that they have a lot to offer on the road ahead.

Rising young midfield star Jan Serfontein also provided glimpses of his talent in his cameo performances, which yielded a terrific try at the death in South Africa's 30-17 victory over Scotland in Nelspruit.

Botha sadly suffered a serious, season-ending knee injury early in that match following his busy performance on debut in the 44-10 victory over Italy in Durban.

But the unfortunate development set the stage for Kolisi, who made a big impression with the ball in hand and was crowned man of the match.

There were also Test debuts for scrumhalves Piet van Zyl and Jano Vermaak, as well as loosehead prop Trevor Nyakane. Judgement would be reserved.

South Africa's tendency to do enough to win rather than do it emphatically again reared its unfortunate head. The match against Scotland was actually still in the balance before Serfontein put it beyond doubt with a moment of individual brilliance.

While the scoreboard suggests otherwise, the victory over Italy wasn't particularly impressive as the Springboks faded for 40 minutes before and after half-time.

It followed a similar pattern to the first season under Meyer where they often produced performances that left one with both questions and answers.

But the lasting impression was left by a compelling 56-23 thrashing of Samoa at Loftus Versfeld in Pretoria. The Springboks remained true to their traditional strength of the rolling maul, but this time mixed it up with some cleverly constructed tries.

Le Roux was a key figure in that regard as he joined the line on a number of occasions to create opportunities for his team-mates. It signalled a departure in Meyer's thinking from picking a defensive fullback.

Of course, it added the element of risk considering Le Roux's error rate, but the rewards were substantial.

Wing Bryan Habana also added to the feel-good factor of the victory over Samoa by notching his 50th Test try following a smart blindside play initiated by scrumhalf Ruan Pienaar.

South Africa's discipline was good in the face of extreme provocation by the Samoans, which was a clear sign that the team led by Jean de Villiers was maturing.

The Springboks' scrumming proved a concern when it was put to the test against Italy, who sent revered tighthead prop Martin Castrogiovanni on in the second half of their match.

While the Springboks gave Samoa a mauling in the scrums, it is hardly one of the islanders' traditional strengths and Meyer would have felt the need to expand his front-row depth.

But by and large Springbok fans would have been satisfied with the outcome of the incoming series, which, for the first time in South Africa and possibly the world, saw two Test matches played back to back at the same venue on the same day, three weeks in a row.

The lasting impression was of a team that finished strongly, with a few potential stars being born.

That winning feeling...Skipper Jean de Villiers and his victorious Springboks celebrate at Loftus Versfeld. *Steve Haag/Gallo Images*

2013 INCOMING TOUR

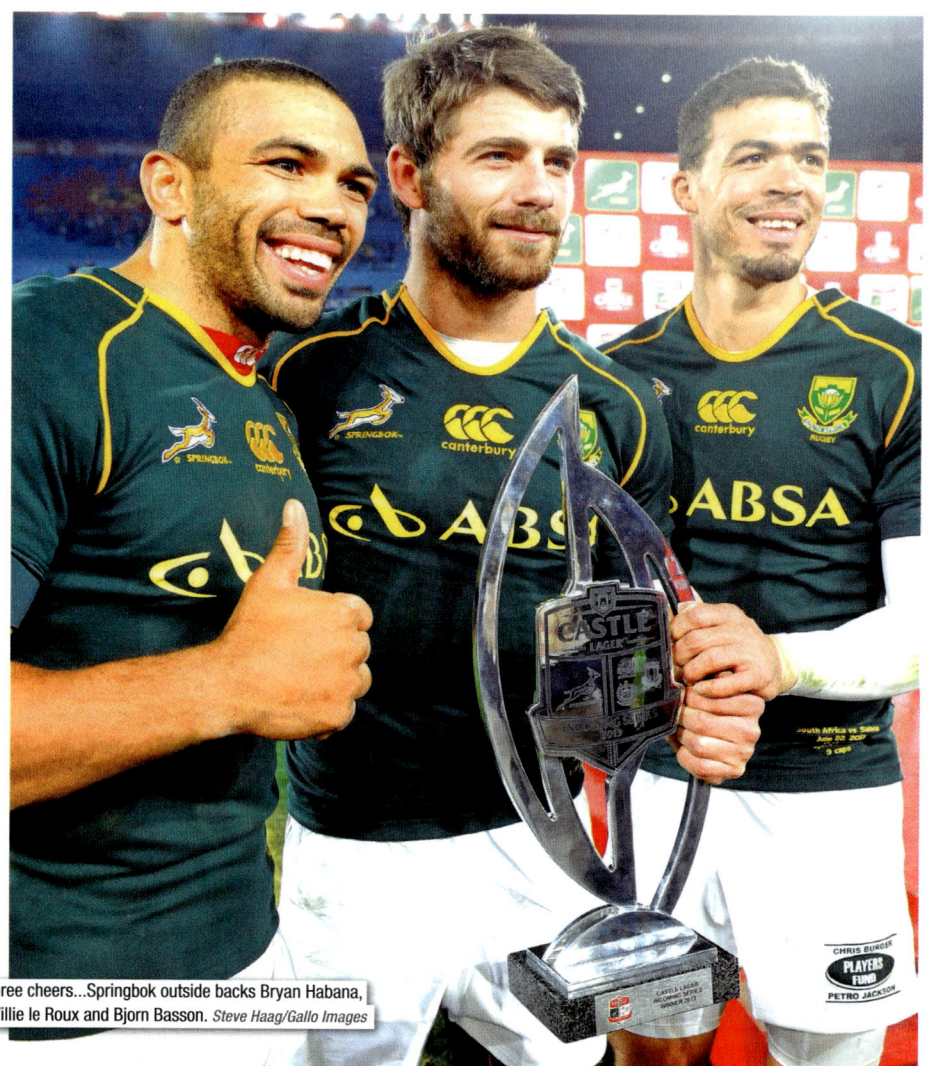

Three cheers...Springbok outside backs Bryan Habana, Willie le Roux and Bjorn Basson. *Steve Haag/Gallo Images*

2013 QUADRANGULAR TOURNAMENT **RESULTS**

Date	Time	Opponents	Venue	Referee
08/06/2013	14:15	Samoa 27, Scotland 17	Growthpoint Kings Park, Durban	John Lacey (Ireland)
08/06/2013	17:15	**South Africa** 44, Italy 10	Growthpoint Kings Park, Durban	Pascal Gauzere (France)
15/06/2013	14:15	Samoa 39, Italy 10	Mbombela Stadium, Nelspruit	Craig Joubert (South Africa)
15/06/2013	17:15	**South Africa** 30, Scotland 17	Mbombela Stadium, Nelspruit	Roman Poite (France)
22/06/2013	14:15	Scotland 30, Italy 29	Loftus Versfeld, Pretoria	Leighton Hodges (Wales)
22/06/2013	17:15	**South Africa** 56, Samoa 23	Loftus Versfeld, Pretoria	Pascal Gauzere (France)

ITALY TOURING SQUAD

	Date of birth	Height	Weight	Club
Andrea Masi	30.03.1981	1,83	99	London Wasps, UK
Giovanbattista Venditti	27.03.1990	1,85	110	Zebre, Italy
Luca Morisi	22.02.1991	1,83	95	Benetton Treviso, Italy
Alberto Sgarbi	26.11.1986	1,90	102	Benetton Treviso, Italy
Luke McLean	29.06.1987	1,90	95	Benetton Treviso, Italy
Alberto di Bernardo	04.11.1980	1,78	87	Benetton Treviso, Italy
Edoardo Gori	05.03.1990	1,80	83	Benetton Treviso, Italy
Sergio Parisse	12.09.1983	1,95	110	Stade Francais, France
Robert Barbieri	05.06.1984	1,85	107	Benetton Treviso, Italy
Alessandro Zanni	31.01.1984	1,93	107	Benetton Treviso, Italy
Marco Bortolami	12.06.1980	1,95	113	Zebre, Italy
Antonio Pavanello	13.10.1982	1,95	112	Benetton Treviso, Italy
Lorenzo Cittadini	17.12.1982	1,90	118	Benetton Treviso, Italy
Leonardo Ghiraldini	26.12.1984	1,83	102	Benetton Treviso, Italy
Alberto de Marchi	13.03.1986	1,83	113	Benetton Treviso, Italy
Davide Giazzon	16.01.1986	1,80	106	Zebre, Italy
Matias Aguero	13.02.1981	1,85	108	Zebre, Italy
Martin Castrogiovanni	21.10.1981	1,88	119	Leicester Tigers, UK
Valerio Bernabo	03.03.1984	1,98	112	Benetton Treviso, Italy
Joshua Furno	21.10.1989	2,01	114	Narbonne, France
Tobias Botes	26.04.1984	1,80	87	Benetton Treviso, Italy
Luciano Orquera	12.10.1981	1,70	79	Zebre, Italy
Tommaso Iannone	16.09.1990	1,83	83	Benetton Treviso, Italy
Mauro Bergamasco	01.05.1979	1,85	98	Zebre, Italy
Gonzalo Canale	11.11.1982	1,83	94	La Rochelle, France
Alberto Chillon	05.12.1990	1,78	77	Zebre, Italy
Gonzalo Garcia	18.02.1984	1,85	96	Zebre, Italy
Andrea Manici	28.04.1990	1,83	101	Zebre, Italy
Francesco Minto	20.05.1987	1,93	104	Benetton Treviso, Italy
Michele Rizzo	16.09.1982	1,88	108	Benetton Treviso, Italy
Leonardo Sarto	15.01.1992	1,93	93	Zebre, Italy
Manoa Vosawai	12.08.1983	1,88	114	Benetton Treviso, Italy
Leandro Cedaro	16.02.1988	196	126	La Rochelle, France

33 Players

COACHES & MANAGEMENT

Jacques Brunel **COACH** Luigi Troiani **TEAM MANAGER** Philipe Berot **ASSISTANT COACH**
David Fonzi **VIDEO ANALYST** Alex Marco **STRENGTH & CONDITIONING** Simone Porcelli **DOCTOR**
Andrea Cimbrico **MEDIA MANAGER** Yarno Celeghin **PHYSIOTHERAPIST** Sante Lugarini **DOCTOR**
Alberto Calabro **BAGGAGE MASTER**

ITALY APPEARANCES & SCORERS

	South Africa	Samoa	Scotland	Matches	Tries	Conversions	Penalties	Drop Goals	Points
Andrea Masi	15	15	15	3	–	–	–	–	0
Giovanbattista Venditti	14	14	14	3	–	–	–	–	0
Luca Morisi	13	–	13	2	–	–	–	–	0
Alberto Sgarbi	12	–	12	2	1	–	–	–	5
Luke McLean	11	11R	11R	3	–	–	–	–	0
Alberto di Bernardo	10	10R	10	3	–	2	1	–	7
Edoardo Gori	9	9	–	2	–	–	–	–	0
Sergio Parisse	8c	8c	8c	3	–	–	–	–	0
Robert Barbieri	7	–	7	2	–	–	–	–	0
Alessandro Zanni	6	6	5R	3	–	–	–	–	0
Marco Bortolami	5	5	5	3	–	–	–	–	0
Antonio Pavanello	4	5R	4R	3	–	–	–	–	0
Lorenzo Cittadini	3	3R	3R	3	–	–	–	–	0
Leonardo Ghiraldini	2	2	2R	3	–	–	–	–	0
Alberto de Marchi	1	1	1R	3	–	–	–	–	0
Davide Giazzon	2R	–	2	2	–	–	–	–	0
Matias Aguero	1R	–	1	2	–	–	–	–	0
Martin Castrogiovanni	3R	3	3	3	–	–	–	–	0
Valerio Bernabo	5R	4	–	2	–	–	–	–	0
Joshua Furno	7R	–	6	2	–	–	–	–	0
Tobias Botes	9R	9R	9	3	–	–	–	–	0
Luciano Orquera	10R	10	–	2	–	–	1	–	3
Tommaso Iannone	13R	11	–	2	–	–	–	–	0
Mauro Bergamasco	–	7	–	1	–	–	–	–	0
Gonzalo Canale	–	13	13R	2	–	–	–	–	0
Alberto Chillon	–	–	9R	1	–	–	–	–	0
Gonzalo Garcia	–	12	–	1	–	–	–	–	0
Andrea Manici	–	2R	–	1	–	–	–	–	0
Francesco Minto	–	–	–		–	–	–	–	0
Michele Rizzo	–	1R	–	1	–	–	–	–	0
Leonardo Sarto	–	–	11	1	–	–	–	–	0
Manoa Vosawai	–	7R	–	1	–	–	–	–	0
Leandro Cedaro	–	–	4	1	–	–	–	–	0
Penalty try	–	–	–	0	1	–	–	–	5
				69	**2**	**2**	**2**	**0**	**20**

R = Substitute; *(c)* = Captain.

ITALY RESULTS & SCORERS

SOUTH AFRICA 44 ITALY 10 (halftime 20-0)
June 8, Growthpoint Kings Park, Durban (23 663). Referee: P Gauzere (France)
SOUTH AFRICA - **TRIES:** Strauss, Engelbrecht, Habana, De Villiers, Basson. **CONVERSIONS:** M Steyn (4), Lambie.
PENALTY GOALS: M Steyn (3).
ITALY - **TRY:** Sgarbi. **CONVERSION:** Di Bernardo. **PENALTY GOAL:** Di Bernardo.
SOUTH AFRICA: WJ le Roux, BG Habana (JL Serfontein, 72)*, JJ Engelbrecht, J de Villiers (C), BA Basson, M Steyn (PJ Lambie, 76) , J Vermaak (R Pienaar, 60),PJ Spies, AF Botha (MC Coetzee 67) , L-FP Louw (MC Coetzee 55-67), PJJ Kruger (PR van der Merwe, 59), E Etzebeth, JN du Plessis (CV Oosthuizen, 67), JA Strauss (MC Ralepelle, 72), T Mtawarira (TN Nyakane, 74). *Serfontein to inside centre, de Villiers to outside centre and Engelbrecht to right wing. TEST DEBUTS: Botha, Vermaak, Le Roux, Nyakane, Serfontein. YELLOW CARD: Basson*
ITALY: A Masi, G Venditti, L Morisi (T Iannone, 68), A Sgarbi, LJ McLean, A di Bernardo (L Orquera, 77), E Gori (WT Botes, 60), SM Parisse (C), RJ Barbieri (RJ Furno, 49), A Zanni, M Bortolami (V Bernabo, 66), A Pavanello, L Cittadini (ML Castrogiovanni, 49), LL Ghiraldini (D Giazzon, 45), A de Marchi (M Aguero, 45).
TEST DEBUT: A di Bernardo. Yellow-card: Bortolami

SAMOA 39 ITALY 10 (halftime 10-3)
June 15, Mbombela Stadium, Nelspruit (30 018). Referee: C Joubert (South Africa)
SAMOA - **TRIES:** Williams, Leiua, Leota, Tuifua, Va'aulu. **CONVERSIONS:** Williams (3), Anufe.
PENALTY GOALS: Williams (2).
ITALY - **TRY:** Penalty try. **CONVERSION:** Di Bernardo. **PENALTY GOAL:** Orquera
SAMOA: BWF Va'aulu, A Leiua, PB Williams (C), JW Leota (SJ Mapusua, 72), AT Tuilagi, T Pisi (K Anufe, 56), JI Sua (AJ Poluleuligaga, 65), T Tuifua, JT Lam (P Faasalele, 56), O Treviranus, DA Leo (K Thompson, 56), TAM Paulo, CIA Johnston (JVI Johnston, HT), W Ole Avei (TT Paulo, 72), S Taulafo (L Mulipola,60). *YELLOW CARD: Leiua*
ITALY: A Masi, G Venditti, GJ Canale, GM Garcia, T Iannone (LJ McLean, 55), L Orquera (A di Bernardo, 44), E Gori (WT Botes, 60), SM Parisse (C), M Bergamasco (M Vosavai, 59), A Zanni, M Bortolami (A Pavanello, 55), V Bernabo, ML Castrogiovanni (L Cittadini, 59), LL Ghiraldini (A Manici, 36), A de Marchi (M Rizzo 55). *TEST DEBUT: A Manici.*

SCOTLAND 30 ITALY 29 (halftime 20-20)
June 22, Loftus Versfeld, Pretoria (35 725). Referee: L Hodges (Wales)
SCOTLAND - **TRIES:** Strokosch, Scott, Lamont. **CONVERSIONS:** Laidlaw (3). **PENALTY GOALS:** Laidlaw (3).
ITALY - **TRIES:** Sarto, Penalty try. **CONVERSIONS:** Di Bernardo (2). **PENALTY GOALS:** DI Bernardo (5).
SCOTLAND: PE Murchie (DM Taylor, 58), TSF Seymour (T Visser, 44), AJ Dunbar, MCM Scott, SF Lamont, TA Heathcote (HB Pyrgos, 49), GD Laidlaw (C), JW Beattie (R Harley, 60), AK Strokosch, DK Senton, AD Kellock, TJM Swinson (GS Gillchrist, 58), EA Murray, S Lawson (FJM Brown, 72), AG Dickinson (M Low, 50/ J Welsh, 72).
TEST DEBUT: Brown
ITALY: A Masi, G Venditti, L Morisi (GJ Canale, 53), A Sgarbi, L Sarto (LJ McLean, 61), A di Bernardo, WT Botes (A Chillon, 69), SM Parisse (C), RJ Barbieri, RJ Furno, M Bortolami (A Zanni, 49), LL Cedaro (A Pavanello, 53), ML Castrogiovanni (L Cittadini, 47), D Giazzon (LL Ghiraldini, 47), M Aguero (A de Marchi,47).
TEST DEBUT: Cedaro, Sarto

2013 INCOMING TOUR

SAMOA TOURING SQUAD

	Date of birth	Height	Weight	Club
James Sooialo	02.04.1989	1,85	83	Wellington Norths, NZ
Alapati Leiua	21.09.1988	1,85	98	Hurricanes, NZ
Paul Williams	22.04.1983	1,87	100	Stade Francais, France
Johnny Leota	21.01.1984	1,83	93	Sale Sharks, UK
Alesana Tuilagi	24.02.1981	1,85	117	NTT Shining Arcs, Japan
Tusiata Pisi	18.06.1982	1,83	93	Hurricanes, NZ
Jeremy Sua	10.11.1988	1,77	92	Crusaders, NZ
Taiasina Tuifua	20.08.1984	1,96	118	Newcastle Falcons, UK
Jack Lam	18.11.1987	1,88	103	Hurricanes, NZ
Ofisa Treviranus	31.03.1984	1,87	108	London Irish, UK
Daniel Leo	02.10.1982	1,98	112	Perpignan, France
Teofilo Paulo	11.06.1987	1,98	122	Cardiff Blues, Wales
Census Johnston	06.05.1981	1,91	138	Toulouse, France
Wayne Ole Avei	13.06.1983	1,78	114	Bordeaux Begles, France
Logovii Mulipola	11.03.1987	1,92	124	Leicester Tigers, UK
Manu Leiataua	26.12.1986	1,80	106	North Harbour, NZ
Sakaria Taulafo	29.01.1983	1,83	120	London Wasps, UK
James Johnston	06.03.1986	1,88	140	Harlequins, UK
Faatiga Lemalu	17.04.1989	2,01	109	Mont-de-Marsan, France
Junior Poluleuligaga	05.02.1981	1,80	98	Exeter Chiefs, UK
Brando Vaaulu	03.05.1987	1,79	94	Tokyo Gas, Japan
Seilala Mapusua	27.02.1980	1,80	120	Kubota Spears, Japan
Alafoti Faosiliva	28.10.1985	1,85	112	Bristol, UK
Kane Thompson	09.01.1982	1,98	112	Canon Eagles, Japan
Ki Anufe	12.04.1987	1,55	85	Marist Auckland, NZ
Piula Faasalele	22.01.1988	1,96	124	Castres Olympique, France
Ti'i Paulo	13.01.1983	1,85	110	Clermont Auvergne, France
Faalemiga Selesele	28.02.1989	1,60	90	Moataa, Samoa
Iosefa Tekori	17.12.1983	1,98	122	Castres Olympique, France
Isaia Tuifua	24.08.1987	1,78	95	Vigo Rugby Club, Spain
Kahn Fotualii	22.05.1982	1,83	96	Ospreys, Wales
Robert Lilomaiava	28.03.1992	1,73	95	Vaiala Rugby Club, Samoa
Sinoti Sinoti	9.09.1985	1,75	92	Zebre, Italy

33 Players

COACHES & MANAGEMENT

Stephen Betham **HEAD COACH**   Namulauulu Sami Leota **TEAM MANAGER**
Darryl Suasua **ASSISTANT COACH - BACKS**   Greg Smith **ASSISTANT COACH - FORWARDS**
Mike Casey **SCRUM COACH**   Junior Narayan **VIDEO ANALYST**   Michael Deasy **STRENGTH & CONDITIONING**
Uitiriai Kapeteni **LOGISTIC OFFICER**   Dr. Navy Collins **TEAM DOCTOR**
Jodie McCarthy **PHYSIOTHERAPIST**   Sue Pescud **PHYSIOTHERAPIST**
Hugh Galvan **SET PIECE SKILLS COACH**   Potumoe Leavasa **DEVELOPMENT COACH**

SAMOA APPEARANCES & SCORERS

	Scotland	Italy	South Africa	Matches	Tries	Conversions	Penalties	Drop Goals	Points
James Sooialo	15	–	15	2	1	3	2	–	17
Alapati Leiua	14	14	14	3	1	–	–	–	5
Paul Williams	13c	13c	13c	3	1	3	2	–	17
Johnny Leota	12	12	12	3	1	–	–	–	5
Alesana Tuilagi	11	11	11	3	2	–	–	–	10
Tusiata Pisi	10	10	10	3	–	–	–	–	0
Jeremy Sua	9	9	9	3	–	–	–	–	0
Taiasina Tuifua	8	8	8	3	1	–	–	–	5
Jack Lam	7	7	7	3	–	–	–	–	0
Ofisa Treviranus	6	6	6	3	–	–	–	–	0
Daniel Leo	5	5	5	3	–	–	–	–	0
Teofilo Paulo	4	4	4	3	–	–	–	–	0
Census Johnston	3	3	1R	3	–	–	–	–	0
Wayne Ole Avei	2	2	2	3	–	–	–	–	0
Logovii Mulipola	1	1R	3	3	–	–	–	–	0
Manu Leiataua	2R	–	–	1	–	–	–	–	0
Sakaria Taulafo	1R	1	1	3	–	–	–	–	0
James Johnston	3R	3R	3R	3	–	–	–	–	0
Faatiga Lemalu	5R	–	–	1	–	–	–	–	0
Junior Poluleuligaga	x	9R	9R	2	–	–	–	–	0
Brando Vaaulu	14R	15	14R	3	1	–	–	–	5
Seilala Mapusua	12R	12R	15R	3	–	–	–	–	0
Alafoti Faosiliva	x	–	6R	1	–	–	–	–	0
Kane Thompson	–	5R	4R	2	–	–	–	–	0
Ki Anufe	–	10R	–	1	–	1	–	–	2
Piula Faasalele	–	7R	–	1	–	–	–	–	0
Ti'i Paulo	–	2R	2R	2	–	–	–	–	0
Faalemiga Selesele	–	–	–	0	–	–	–	–	0
Iosefa Tekori	–	–	–	0	–	–	–	–	0
Isaia Tuifua	–	–	–	0	–	–	–	–	0
Kahn Fotualii	–	–	–	0	–	–	–	–	0
Robert Lilomaiava	–	–	–	0	–	–	–	–	0
Sinoti Sinoti	–	–	–	0	–	–	–	–	0
				67	8	7	4	0	66

R = Substitute; *x* = Unused Substitute; *(c)* = Captain.

SAMOA RESULTS & SCORERS

SCOTLAND 17 SAMOA 27 (halftime 9-14)
June 8, Growthpoint Kings Park, Durban (23 663). Referee: J Lacey (Ireland)
SCOTLAND - TRY: Lamont. **PENALTY GOALS:** Laidlaw (4).
SAMOA - **TRIES:** Tuilagi (2), So'oialo. **CONVERSIONS:** So'oialo (3). **PENALTY GOALS:** So'oialo (2).
SCOTLAND: GA Tonks, SF Lamont, AJ Dunbar, MCM Scott, T Visser (DM Taylor, 70), TA Heathcote (P Horne, 59), GD Laidlaw (HB Pyrgos, 70), JW Beattie, KDR Brown (C - R Wilson, 41), AK Strokosch, AD Kellock (JL Hamilton, 65), GS Gillchrist, EA Murray (GDS Cross, 45), P MacArthur (S Lawrie, 12), AG Dickinson (MJ Low, 65)
TEST DEBUTS: MacArthur, Dunbar, Tonks, Lawrie, Horne, Taylor.
SAMOA: J So'oialo, A Leiua (BWF Va'aulu, 80), PB Williams (C), JW Leota (SJ Mapusua, 74), AT Tuilagi, T Pisi, JI Sua, T Tuifua, JT Lam, O Treviranus, DA Leo (F Lemalu, 55), TAM Paulo, CIA Johnston (JVI Johnston, 55), W Ole Avei (M Leiatua, 55), L Mulipola (S Taulafo, 78). Unused subs: AJ Poluleuligaga, A Fa'osiliva.
TEST DEBUTS: Lam, Leiua, Leiatua, Va'alu.

SAMOA 39 ITALY 10 (halftime 10-3)
June 15, Mbombela Stadium, Nelspruit (30 018). Referee: C Joubert (South Africa)
SAMOA - **TRIES:** Williams, Leiua, Leota, Tuifua, Va'aulu. **CONVERSIONS:** Williams (3), Anufe.
PENALTY GOALS: Williams (2).
ITALY - **TRY:** Penalty try. **CONVERSION:** Di Bernardo. **PENALTY GOAL:** Orquera
SAMOA: BWF Va'aulu, A Leiua, PB Williams (C), JW Leota (SJ Mapusua, 72), AT Tuilagi, T Pisi (K Anufe, 56), JI Sua (AJ Poluleuligaga, 65), T Tuifua, JT Lam (P Faasalele, 56), O Treviranus, DA Leo (K Thompson, 56), TAM Paulo, CIA Johnston (JVI Johnston, HT), W Ole Avei (TT Paulo, 72), S Taulafo (L Mulipola,60).
YELLOW-CARD: Leiua
ITALY: A Masi, G Venditti, GJ Canale, GM Garcia, T Iannone (LJ McLean, 55), L Orquera (A di Bernardo, 44), E Gori (WT Botes, 60), SM Parisse (C), M Bergamasco (M Vosavai, 59), A Zanni, M Bortolami (A Pavanello, 55), V Bernabo, ML Castrogiovanni (L Cittadini, 59), LL Ghiraldini (A Manici, 36), A de Marchi (M Rizzo 55).
TEST DEBUT: A Manici.

SOUTH AFRICA 56 SAMOA 23 (halftime 32-9)
June 22, Loftus Versfeld, Pretoria (35 725). Referee: P Gauzere (France)
SOUTH AFRICA - **TRIES:** Habana (2), Louw (2), Engelbrecht, Basson, Steyn, Nyakane. **CONVERSIONS:** M Steyn (3), Lambie (2). **PENALTY GOALS:** M Steyn (2).
SAMOA - **TRIES:** Paulo, Poluleuligaga. **CONVERSION:** So'oialo, Williams. **PENALTY GOALS:** So'oialo (3).
SOUTH AFRICA: WJ le Roux, BG Habana, JJ Engelbrecht, J de Villiers (C, JL Serfontein, 71), BA Basson, M Steyn (PJ Lambie, 65) , R Pienaar, 60 (PE van Zyl, 67), PJ Spies (S Kolisi, HT/PJJ Kruger, 48-52)*, WS Alberts , L-FP Louw, PR van der Merwe (PJJ Kruger 71), E Etzebeth, JN du Plessis (TN Nyakane, 67)*, JA Strauss (BM du Plessis, 60), T Mtawarira (CV Oosthuizen, 57). * *Kolisi to blindside-flanker, Alberts to No. 8. Nyakane to loose-head prop, Oosthuizen to tight-head prop. YELLOW CARD: Habana*
SAMOA: J So'oialo (SJ Mapusua, 61), A Leiua (BWF Va'aulu, 57), PB Williams (C), JW Leota (SJ Mapusua, 22-27), AT Tuilagi, T Pisi, JI Sua (AJ Poluleuligaga, 65), T Tuifua, JT Lam, O Treviranus (A Fa'osiliva, 67), DA Leo, TAM Paulo (K Thompson, 52), L Mulipola (JVI Johnston, 67), W Ole Avei (TT Paolo, 52), S Taulafo (CIA Johnston, 57).
YELLOW-CARD: Mulipola. RED-CARD: Tuilagi. BROTHERS: Census and James Johnston; Ofisa Treviranus and Alapati Leiua.

SCOTLAND TOURING SQUAD

	Date of birth	Height	Weight	Club
Greig Tonks	20.05.1989	1,85	92	Edinburgh, Scotland
Sean Lamont	15.01.1981	1,88	105	Glasgow Warriors, Scotland
Alex Dunbar	23.04.1990	1,90	100	Glasgow Warriors, Scotland
Matt Scott	30.09.1990	1,88	99	Edinburgh, Scotland
Tim Visser	29.05.1987	1,93	109	Edinburgh, Scotland
Tom Heathcote	11.02.1992	1,78	89	Bath, UK
Greig Laidlaw	12.10.1985	1,75	79	Edinburgh, Scotland
Johnnie Beattie	21.11.1985	1,93	106	Montpellier, France
Kelly Brown	08.06.1982	1,93	108	Saracens, UK
Alasdair Strokosch	21.02.1983	1,90	107	Perpignan, France
Alastair Kellock	14.06.1981	2,03	119	Glasgow Warriors, Scotland
Grant Gilchrist	09.08.1990	2,01	120	Edinburgh, Scotland
Euan Murray	07.08.1980	1,88	115	Worcester Warriors, UK
Pat MacArthur	27.04.1987	1,83	99	Glasgow Warriors, Scotland
Alasdair Dickinson	11.09.1983	1,85	107	Sale Sharks, UK
Steven Lawrie	22.02.1984	1,85	103	Edinburgh, Scotland
Moray Low	28.11.1984	1,88	122	Glasgow Warriors, Scotland
Geoff Cross	11.12.1982	1,83	116	Edinburgh, Scotland
Jim Hamilton	17.11.1982	2,03	124	Glasgow Warriors, Scotland
Ryan Wilson	18.05.1989	1,93	103	Glasgow Warriors, Scotland
Henry Pyrgos	09.07.1989	1,78	80	Glasgow Warriors, Scotland
Peter Horne	05.10.1989	1,83	90	Glasgow Warriors, Scotland
Duncan Taylor	05.09.1989	1,90	92	Saracens, UK
Peter Murchie	07.01.1986	1,90	93	Glasgow Warriors, Scotland
Tommy Seymour	01.07.1988	1,83	94	Glasgow Warriors, Scotland
Ruaridh Jackson	12.02.1988	1,83	86	Glasgow Warriors, Scotland
Tim Swinson	17.02.1987	1,93	111	Glasgow Warriors, Scotland
Scott Lawson	28/09/1981	1,73	96	London Irish, UK
David Denton	05.02.1990	1,95	115	Edinburgh, Scotland
Jon Welsh	13/10/1986	1,85	123	Glasgow Warriors, Scotland
Fraser Brown	20/06.1989	1,80	103	Glasgow Warriors, Scotland
Rob Harley	26/05/1990	1,98	107	Glasgow Warriors, Scotland
John Barclay	24.09.1986	1,90	101	Glasgow Warriors, Scotland
Ryan Grant	08.10.1985	1,85	113	Glasgow Warriors, Scotland
Ross Ford	23.04.1984	1,85	114	Edinburgh, Scotland
Richie Vernon	07.07.1987	1,95	103	Sale Sharks, UK

36 Players

COACHES AND MANAGEMENT

HEAD COACH Scott Johnson **ASSISTANT COACHES** Jonathan Humphreys, Massimo Cuttita & Duncan Hodge
TEAM MANAGER Gavin Scott **STRENGTH & CONDITIONING** Neill Potts & Cedric Unholz
DOCTER Dr Jonathan Hanson **PHYSIO** Paul McGinley **PHYSIO** Stephen Mutch
VODEO ANALYST Robert Holdsworth **BAGGAGE MASTER** John Pennycuick

SCOTLAND APPEARANCES & SCORERS

	Samoa	South Africa	Italy	Matches	Tries	Conversions	Penalties	Drop Goals	Points
Greig Tonks	15	–	–	1	–	–	–	–	0
Sean Lamont	14	11	11	3	2	–	–	–	10
Alex Dunbar	13	13	13	3	1	–	–	–	5
Matt Scott	12	12	12	3	2	–	–	–	10
Tim Visser	11	–	14R	2	–	–	–	–	0
Tom Heathcote	10	–	10	2	–	–	–	–	0
Greig Laidlaw	9	9c	9c	3	–	5	8	–	34
Johnnie Beattie	8	8	8	3	–	–	–	–	0
Kelly Brown	7c	–	–	1	–	–	–	–	0
Alasdair Strokosch	6	6	7	3	1	–	–	–	5
Alastair Kellock	5	5R	5	3	–	–	–	–	0
Grant Gilchrist	4	–	4R	2	–	–	–	–	0
Euan Murray	3	3	3	3	–	–	–	–	0
Pat MacArthur	2	–	–	1	–	–	–	–	0
Alasdair Dickinson	1	1	1	3	–	–	–	–	0
Steven Lawrie	2R	–	–	1	–	–	–	–	0
Moray Low	1R	1R	1R	3	–	–	–	–	0
Geoff Cross	3R	–	–	1	–	–	–	–	0
Jim Hamilton	5R	5	–	2	–	–	–	–	0
Ryan Wilson	7R	7	–	2	–	–	–	–	0
Henry Pyrgos	9R	21R	10R	3	–	–	–	–	0
Peter Horne	10R	10R	–	2	–	–	–	–	0
Duncan Taylor	11R	15R	15R	3	–	–	–	–	0
Peter Murchie	–	15	15	2	–	–	–	–	0
Tommy Seymour	–	14	14	2	–	–	–	–	0
Ruaridh Jackson	–	10	–	1	–	–	–	–	0
Tim Swinson	–	4	4	2	–	–	–	–	0
Scott Lawson	–	2	2	2	–	–	–	–	0
David Denton	–	7R	6	2	–	–	–	–	0
Jon Welsh	–	x	17R	1	–	–	–	–	0
Fraser Brown	–	x	2R	1	–	–	–	–	0
Rob Harley	–	–	8R	1	–	–	–	–	0
John Barclay	–	–	–	0	–	–	–	–	0
Ryan Grant	–	–	–	0	–	–	–	–	0
Ross Ford	–	–	–	0	–	–	–	–	0
Richie Vernon	–	–	–	0	–	–	–	–	0
				67	6	5	8	0	64

R = Substitute; x = Unused Substitute; (c) = Captain.

SCOTLAND RESULTS & SCORERS

SCOTLAND 17 SAMOA 27 (halftime 9-14)
June 8, Growthpoint Kings Park, Durban (23 663). Referee: J Lacey (Ireland)
SCOTLAND - TRY: Lamont. PENALTY GOALS: Laidlaw (4).
SAMOA - TRIES: Tuilagi (2), So'oialo. CONVERSIONS: So'oialo (3). PENALTY GOALS: So'oialo (2).
SCOTLAND: GA Tonks, SF Lamont, AJ Dunbar, MCM Scott, T Visser (DM Taylor, 70), TA Heathcote (P Horne, 59), GD Laidlaw (HB Pyrgos, 70), JW Beattie, KDR Brown (C - R Wilson, 41), AK Strokosch, AD Kellock (JL Hamilton, 65), GS Gillchrist, EA Murray (GDS Cross, 45), P MacArthur (S Lawrie, 12), AG Dickinson (MJ Low, 65)
TEST DEBUTS: MacArthur, Dunbar, Tonks, Lawrie, Horne, Taylor.
SAMOA: J So'oialo, A Leiua (BWF Va'aulu, 80), PB Williams (C), JW Leota (SJ Mapusua, 74), AT Tuilagi, T Pisi, JI Sua, T Tuifua, JT Lam, O Treviranus, DA Leo (F Lemalu, 55), TAM Paulo, CIA Johnston (JVI Johnston, 55), W Ole Avei (M Leiatua, 55), L Mulipola (S Taulafo, 78). Unused subs: AJ Poluleuligaga, A Fa'osiliva.
TEST DEBUTS: Lam, Leiua, Leiatua, Va'alu.

SOUTH AFRICA 30 SCOTLAND 17 (halftime 6-10)
June 15, Mbombela Stadium, Nelspruit (30 018). Referee: R Poite (France)
SOUTH AFRICA - TRIES: Penalty try, Engelbrecht, Serfontein. CONVERSIONS: M Steyn (2), Lambie. PENALTY GOALS: M Steyn (2), Lambie.
SCOTLAND - TRY: Scott, Dunbar. CONVERSION: Laidlaw (2). PENALTY GOAL: Laidlaw.
SOUTH AFRICA: WJ le Roux, BG Habana, JJ Engelbrecht (JL Serfontein, 70)*, J de Villiers (C), BA Basson, M Steyn (PJ Lambie, 70) , R Pienaar, 60 (PE van Zyl, 69), PJ Spies, AF Botha (S Kolisi, 5)*, MC Coetzee, PJJ Kruger, E Etzebeth (PR van der Merwe, 67), JN du Plessis (TN Nyakane, 76)*, JA Strauss (BM du Plessis, 67), T Mtawarira (CV Oosthuizen, 67). * *Serfontein to inside-centre, de Villiers to outside-centre. Kolisi to openside-flanker, Coetzee to -blindside-flanker. Nyakane to loose-head prop, Oosthuizen to tight-head prop. TEST DEBUTS: Kolisi, van Zyl.*
SCOTLAND: PE Murchie (DM Taylor, 75), TSF Seymour, AJ Dunbar, MCM Scott, SF Lamont, RJH Jackson (P Horne, 33/HB Pyrgos, 44), GD Laidlaw (C), JW Beattie, R Wilson (DK Denton, 38), AK Strokosch, JL Hamilton (AD Kellock, 61), TJM Swinson, EA Murray, S Lawson, AG Dickinson (M Low, 64). Unused subs: FJM Brown, J Welsh.
TEST DEBUTS: Murchie, Seymour, Swinson. Yellow-card: Hamilton

SCOTLAND 30 ITALY 29 (halftime 20-20)
June 22, Loftus Versfeld, Pretoria (35 725). Referee: L Hodges (Wales)
SCOTLAND - TRIES: Strokosch, Scott, Lamont. CONVERSIONS: Laidlaw (3). PENALTY GOALS: Laidlaw (3).
ITALY - TRIES: Sarto, Penalty try. CONVERSIONS: Di Bernardo (2). PENALTY GOALS: DI Bernardo (5).
SCOTLAND: PE Murchie (DM Taylor, 58), TSF Seymour (T Visser, 44), AJ Dunbar, MCM Scott, SF Lamont, TA Heathcote (HB Pyrgos, 49), GD Laidlaw (C), JW Beattie (R Harley, 60), AK Strokosch, DK Senton, AD Kellock, TJM Swinson (GS Gillchrist, 58), EA Murray, S Lawson (FJM Brown, 72), AG Dickinson (M Low, 50/ J Welsh, 72).
TEST DEBUT: Brown
ITALY: A Masi, G Venditti, L Morisi (GJ Canale, 53), A Sgarbi, L Sarto (LJ McLean, 61), A di Bernardo, WT Botes (A Chillon, 69), SM Parisse (C), RJ Barbieri, RJ Furno, M Bortolami (A Zanni, 49), LL Cedaro (A Pavanello, 53), ML Castrogiovanni (L Cittadini, 47), D Giazzon (LL Ghiraldini, 47), M Aguero (A de Marchi,47).
TEST DEBUT: Cedaro, Sarto

Habana sets Bok ball rolling

SOUTH AFRICA 44 ITALY 10 (halftime 20-0)

June 8, Growthpoint Kings Park, Durban (23 663). Referee: P Gauzere (France).
SOUTH AFRICA - **TRIES:** Strauss, Engelbrecht, Habana, De Villiers, Basson. **CONVERSIONS:** M Steyn (4), Lambie.
PENALTY GOALS: M Steyn (3).
ITALY - **TRY:** Sgarbi. **CONVERSION:** Di Bernardo. **PENALTY GOAL:** Di Bernardo.

There was much hype about the new blood, but ultimately it was a man four days shy of his 30th birthday that stole the show as the Springboks kicked off their international season with a 44-10 victory over Italy in Durban.

Bryan Habana set off on a magnificent solo run to score the try in the 66th minute that gave the Springboks an unassailable 30-10 lead.

As is so often the case with Habana's tries, nothing appeared to be on. But after receiving a floated pass from hooker Adriaan Strauss, the great wing cut inside, swerved his way past the first line of defence and then made the Italians look pedestrian with a tremendous burst of acceleration.

Earlier, Habana had also played a creative role by setting up a try for outside centre JJ Engelbrecht with a superb counter-attack. It was a try that secured the Springboks a 20-0 lead after just 23 minutes.

Perhaps the plan was coming together too early because the Springboks' performance petered out after that. It also didn't help their cause when left wing Bjorn Basson was yellow-carded for a high tackle early in the second half.

The Springboks also faltered in the set phases, with a key development the decision by Azzurri coach Jacques Brunel to beef up his scrum with the introduction of feared tighthead prop Martin Castrogiovanni off the bench.

By the time Italian flyhalf Albery Di Bernardo was taking aim for the penalty that reduced the deficit to 20-10 in the 58th minute, Italy had dominated territory to the tune of 94% against 6%.

However, the Springboks regained their composure and a breakdown penalty allowed flyhalf Morné Steyn to lift the flags before Habana weaved his magic.

The match was closed out with tries by skipper Jean de De Villiers and Basson. De Villiers scored after a counter-attack from an ill-judged kick by Italy's replacement scrumhalf, the South African-born Tobias Botes. Basson scored his try two minutes before the end after intercepting a pass by Di Bernardo.

Much of the hype in the build-up had centred around the fact that Willie le Roux would be making his Springbok debut. Le Roux had excelled on the wing for the Cheetahs, but was at fullback.

The enterprise he showed was indeed pleasing, while he was also solid under the high ball in fielding a cross kick that otherwise would have led to an Italian try.

Arno Botha also had a satisfactory debut on the flank, while scrumhalf Jano Vermaak was solid in his first Test before limping off with a hamstring injury.

There were two more debutants, with Bulls centre Jan Serfontein sent on as a blood replacement for Habana in the 72nd minute and Cheetahs loosehead prop Trevor Nyakane replacing Tendai Mtawarira six minutes from time.

Notwithstanding some delightful individual moments, this wasn't a good team performance by the Springboks. But, of course, it was the first Test of the year and mission accomplished.

SCORING SEQUENCE

Min	Action	Score
4	Steyn penalty	3-0
10	Steyn penalty	6-0
14	Strauss try, Steyn conversion	13-0
23	Engelbrecht try, Steyn conversion	20-0
47	Sgarbi try, Di Bernardo conversion	20-7
58	Di Bernardo penalty	20-10
64	Steyn penalty	23-10
66	Habana try, Steyn conversion	30-10
75	De Villiers try, Steyn conversion	37-10
78	Basson try, Lambie conversion	44-10

FLYING COLOURS...Bryan Habana goes over for one of his trademark tries for South Africa. *Steve Haag/Gallo Images*

SOUTH AFRICA: WJ le Roux, BG Habana (JL Serfontein, 72)*, JJ Engelbrecht, J de Villiers (C), BA Basson, M Steyn (PJ Lambie, 76) , J Vermaak (R Pienaar, 60), PJ Spies, AF Botha (MC Coetzee 67) , L-FP Louw (MC Coetzee 55-67), PJJ Kruger (PR van der Merwe, 59), E Etzebeth, JN du Plessis (CV Oosthuizen, 67), JA Strauss (MC Ralepelle, 72), T Mtawarira (TN Nyakane, 74). *Serfontein to inside centre, De Villiers to outside centre and Engelbrecht to right wing. TEST DEBUTS: Botha, Vermaak, Le Roux, Nyakane, Serfontein. YELLOW CARD: Basson*

ITALY: A Masi, G Venditti, L Morisi (T Iannone, 68), A Sgarbi, LJ McLean, A di Bernardo (L Orquera, 77), E Gori (WT Botes, 60), SM Parisse (C), RJ Barbieri (RJ Furno, 49), A Zanni, M Bortolami (V Bernabo, 66), A Pavanello, L Cittadini (ML Castrogiovanni, 49), LL Ghiraldini (D Giazzon, 45), A de Marchi (M Aguero, 45). *TEST DEBUT: A di Bernardo. Yellow card: Bortolami*

2013 INCOMING TOUR

Kolisi lights up Mbombela Test

SOUTH AFRICA 30 SCOTLAND 17 (halftime 6-10)

June 15, Mbombela Stadium, Nelspruit (30 018). Referee: R Poite (France)
SOUTH AFRICA - **TRIES:** Penalty try, Engelbrecht, Serfontein. **CONVERSIONS:** M Steyn (2), Lambie.
PENALTY GOALS: M Steyn (2), Lambie.
SCOTLAND - **TRY:** Scott, Dunbar. **CONVERSION:** Laidlaw (2). **PENALTY GOAL:** Laidlaw.

SOUTH AFRICA'S 30-17 VICTORY OVER Scotland in Nelspruit will be remembered for little else than an inspired performance on his Test debut by loose forward Siya Kolisi.

The 22-year-old standout DHL Stormers flank was sent on in the fifth minute after Arno Botha suffered a serious knee injury and produced a busy display in an insipid Springbok effort.

Perhaps the biggest concern was the lack of urgency as Scotland made all the early running and increased a 10-6 half-time lead to 17-6 when outside centre Alex Dunbar finished in the left-hand corner early in the second half.

Dunbar's try followed an incisive run by lock Tim Swinson, though there had been more than a hint of obstruction in the build-up. The controversial try left South Africa with lots to do and the match ultimately turned irreversibly after Swinson's second-row partner, Jim Hamilton, was yellow-carded for shoving Springbok giant Eben Etzebeth in the face in the 52nd minute.

South Africa had been awarded a penalty try four minutes earlier thanks to Scotland transgressing in the face of the good old party trick of the rolling maul.

The Springboks exploited their numerical advantage following Hamilton's sin-binning and took the lead through a try by outside centre JJ Engelbrecht, who ran a good line from which he collected fullback Willie le Roux's delayed pass.

But it was a rare moment of inspired attacking play.

The try that finally put the victory beyond doubt only came in the dying seconds and was thanks to a bit of individual brilliance by the young replacement centre Jan Serfontein, who spun out of two tackles before finishing to give the scoreboard a distinctly flattering look.

So poor were the Springboks in the first half that one genuinely feared for them against markedly inferior opponents. Scotland attacked with gusto and ran clever lines to trouble the South African defence.

One of the most disturbing aspects of South Africa's play was that they didn't know what to do with the ball in hand. Their general attack was poor and flyhalf Morné Steyn twice launched high balls after the Springboks had been awarded free kicks. Why give your opponents an even chance of winning back possession?

Perhaps it was just the fact that they aren't used to winning that prevented Scotland from doing so. They were all over the Springboks and fully deserved to take the lead when inside centre Matt Scott finished under the posts midway through the first half.

His try followed an inspired little chip and gather by left wing Sean Lamont, which was indicative of the dare and freedom with which the Scots played.

But ultimately Hamilton's lack of discipline and South Africa's resolve swung the Test.

The latter is a quality South Africa have always been able to call on, but this was a performance that left their supporters troubled – even more so because they hadn't even played against a full-strength Scottish team.

SCORING SEQUENCE

Min	Action	Score
8	Laidlaw penalty	0-3
14	Steyn penalty	3-3
18	Steyn penalty	6-3
21	Scott try, Laidlaw conversion	6-10
43	Dunbar try, Laidlaw conversion	6-17
47	Steyn missed penalty	6-17
49	Penalty try, Steyn conversion	13-17
56	Engelbrecht try, Steyn conversion	20-17
75	Lambie penalty	23-17
80	Serfontein try, Lambie conversion	30-17

WHITE KNIGHT...Siya Kolisi made his Test debut much earlier than expected after an early injury to Arno Botha.
Steve Haag/Gallo Images

SOUTH AFRICA: WJ le Roux, BG Habana, JJ Engelbrecht (JL Serfontein, 70)*, J de Villiers (C), BA Basson, M Steyn (PJ Lambie, 70) , R Pienaar, 60 (PE van Zyl, 69), PJ Spies, AF Botha (S Kolisi, 5)*, MC Coetzee, PJJ Kruger, E Etzebeth (PR van der Merwe, 67), JN du Plessis (TN Nyakane, 76)*, JA Strauss (BM du Plessis, 67), T Mtawarira (CV Oosthuizen, 67). * *Serfontein to inside centre, De Villiers to outside centre. Kolisi to openside flanker, Coetzee to blindside flanker. Nyakane to loosehead prop, Oosthuizen to tighthead prop.* TEST DEBUTS: Kolisi, Van Zyl.

SCOTLAND: PE Murchie (DM Taylor, 75), TSF Seymour, AJ Dunbar, MCM Scott, SF Lamont, RJH Jackson (P Horne, 33/HB Pyrgos, 44), GD Laidlaw (C), JW Beattie, R Wilson (DK Denton, 38), AK Strokosch, JL Hamilton (AD Kellock, 61), TJM Swinson, EA Murray, S Lawson, AG Dickinson (M Low, 64). UNUSED SUBS: FJM Brown, J Welsh. TEST DEBUTS: Murchie, Seymour, Swinson. YELLOW CARD: Hamilton

Boks keep their eye on the ball

SOUTH AFRICA 56 SAMOA 23 (halftime 32-9)

June 22, Loftus Versfeld, Pretoria (35 725). Referee: P Gauzere (France)
SOUTH AFRICA - **TRIES:** Habana (2), Louw (2), Engelbrecht, Basson, Steyn, Nyakane. **CONVERSIONS:** M Steyn (3), Lambie (2).
PENALTY GOALS: M Steyn (2).
SAMOA - **TRIES:** Paulo, Poluleuligaga. **CONVERSION:** So'oialo, Williams. **PENALTY GOALS:** So'oialo (3).

THIS IS A MATCH THAT, AMONG OTHER things, highlighted that there are different ways of putting a squeeze on your opponent. While Samoa fullback Julian So'oialo's grab of Adriaan Strauss's you-know-what in the 52nd minute left the Springbok hooker shouting his line-out calls in soprano, South Africa went about their business in a far more constructive manner.

So constructive, in fact, that the resounding 56-23 victory inspired confidence for the road ahead.

Fullback Willie le Roux recovered from two early mistakes to play a magnificent playmaking role and had a hand in three of South Africa's eight tries, while JJ Engelbrecht continued to grow in his role as outside centre.

And then, of course, there was the great Bryan Habana. He scored his 50th Test try after scrumhalf Ruan Pienaar feigned to the open side before attacking the blind and passing to Habana on the right to increase the Springboks' lead to a commanding 37-16 in the 59th minute.

Earlier, Habana had scored his 49th try in the first half after an incursion into the line by Le Roux, who beat Samoan left wing Alesana Tuilagi before drawing So'oialo and making the final pass. Beautiful.

It catapulted the Springboks into a 10-6 lead after they had trailed 3-6 and from thereon they produced a performance that challenged the belief that Heyneke Meyer is a conservative coach.

Perhaps the most pleasing aspect was that there was attacking intent and the creativity to match it.

It's not just the backs that played their part. The Springboks dominated the scrums, while flank Francois Louw was a menace at the breakdowns and deservedly anointed man of the match.

Samoa's approach was worthy of contempt. While by far the most obscene, So'oialo's act of foul play was not an isolated incident.

Scrumhalf Jeremy Sua's reckless rucking – he could see full well that Louw's head was in the vicinity – drew blood. Tuilagi was also red-carded in the 58th minute after a late stiff-arm tackle on Springbok captain Jean de Villiers.

Not that the Springbok performance was without blemish. Steyn missed four kicks at goal, while the Springboks were also caught unawares a few times. The Samoans also scored off a line-out move 10 minutes before the end. It was a lapse in concentration that would have been grossly unacceptable to Meyer had the horse not bolted by then.

But the Springboks still cranked up the volume after that and Louw scored his second try before replacement prop Trevor Nyakane had the delight of his first touchdown at the death.

The handsome victory was jut reward for the Springboks keeping their eye on the ball.

The right ball, of course.

SCORING SEQUENCE

Min	Action	Score
3	Steyn penalty	3-0
11	So'oialo penalty	3-3
15	So'oialo penalty	3-6
18	Habana try, Steyn conversion	10-6
25	Louw try, Steyn conversion	17-6
28	Steyn penalty	20-6
31	So'oialo penalty	20-9
34	Engelbrecht try, Steyn missed conversion	25-9
38	Basson try, Steyn conversion	32-9
47	Paulo try, So'oialo conversion	32-16
58	Habana try, Steyn missed conversion	37-16
63	Steyn try, Steyn missed conversion	42-16
70	Poluleuligaga try, Williams conversion	42-23
76	Louw try, Lambie conversion	49-23
80	Nyakane try, Lambie conversion	56-23

CHASING SHADOWS...JJ Engelbrecht evades the tackles of two Samoans during the Loftus Test. *Steve Haag/Gallo Images*

SOUTH AFRICA: WJ le Roux, BG Habana, JJ Engelbrecht, J de Villiers (C, JL Serfontein, 71), BA Basson, M Steyn (PJ Lambie, 65) , R Pienaar, 60 (PE van Zyl, 67), PJ Spies (S Kolisi, HT/PJJ Kruger, 48-52)*, WS Alberts , L-FP Louw, PR van der Merwe (PJJ Kruger 71), E Etzebeth, JN du Plessis (TN Nyakane, 67)*, JA Strauss (BM du Plessis, 60), T Mtawarira (CV Oosthuizen, 57).
* Kolisi to blindside flanker, Alberts to No. 8. Nyakane to loosehead prop, Oosthuizen to tighthead prop. YELLOW CARD: Habana

SAMOA: J So'oialo (SJ Mapusua, 61), A Leiua (BWF Va'aulu, 57), PB Williams (C), JW Leota (SJ Mapusua, 22-27), AT Tuilagi, T Pisi, JI Sua (AJ Poluleuligaga, 65), T Tuifua, JT Lam, O Treviranus (A Fa'osiliva, 67), DA Leo, TAM Paulo (K Thompson, 52), L Mulipola (JVI Johnston, 67), W Ole Avei (TT Paolo, 52), S Taulafo (CIA Johnston, 57).
YELLOW CARD: Mulipola. RED CARD: Tuilagi. BROTHERS: Census and James Johnston; Ofisa Treviranus and Alapati Leiua.

CASTLE LAGER RUGBY CHAMPIONSHIPS

Boks make strides – but All Blacks stay step ahead

THE BIG STRIDES THAT THE SPRINGBOKS took in Heyneke Meyer's second season in charge were reflected in some exceptional performances in the Castle Rugby Championship.

While ultimately heartbreaking due to defeats to the All Blacks – the first in Auckland highly controversial – the Boks' campaign was a successful one. They achieved their biggest ever victory over Argentina (73-13) and put to bed their Brisbane bogey by thrashing Australia 38-12.

The latter set up a mouthwatering away clash against the All Blacks, which was unfortunately ruined by the controversial dismissal of Bok hooker Bismarck du Plessis.

Du Plessis was sin-binned in the first half for a legitimate tackle on Dan Carter, which left the All Black flyhalf nursing a shoulder injury for six weeks.

When the Bok hooker transgressed in the second half by leading with his elbow, he was issued a second yellow card and consequently a red one. The match was effectively ended as a contest then and there as the Springboks were down 17-10 at the time and there was almost a full half left to play.

It was too little and too late when the International Rugby Board issued a statement saying that the match officials had erred, but the entire affair added to the intrigue ahead of South Africa's home leg.

First up were Australia and the Springboks delivered a resounding 28-8 victory at Newlands. However, a great opportunity to achieve a bonus-point victory was spurned.

It meant that the Springboks would have to achieve a four-try win and prevent the All Blacks from getting a bonus point in order to win the tournament.

South Africa appeared to be on course when their inspirational captain, Jean de Villiers, powered his way over the Kiwis' replacement flyhalf, Beauden Barrett, and beat the tackle of centre Ma'a Nonu to score the all-important fourth try.

However, the Boks' chance of winning the Rugby Championship dissipated when Barrett ghosted his way through their defence for the All Blacks' fourth try almost immediately after De Villiers had scored.

It highlighted one of the Boks' biggest weakness of their campaign: defence.

They conceded five tries in the Ellis Park encounter, which was lost 38-27 in spite of the All Blacks twice being reduced to 14 men. But on the whole it was a campaign of positives.

There was a marked improvement in South Africa's proficiency at the breakdowns, while their attacking intent yielded dividends. The Boks fell one try short of the All Blacks' tournament tally of 24, which made a mockery of the charge often levelled at Meyer that he is a conservative coach.

If anything, he was a little too bold as the Springboks played to the All Blacks' strengths with their cavalier approach in Johannesburg. The point is, after all, to score more points, not tries, than your opponent.

Nevertheless, a decent campaign provided confirmation that Meyer was on the right track with the Boks. A number of players also continued to grow in stature, notably No 8 Duane Vermeulen, flank Francois Louw, lock Eben Etzebeth and outside back Willie le Roux.

Then, of course, there were was the impressive old guard. Wing Bryan Habana's brace of tries against the All Blacks at Ellis Park was superb, while the 32-year-old De Villiers was like the finest red wine on the planet.

The Springboks face the Haka. Sandra Mu/Getty Images

2013 CASTLE RUGBY CHAMPIONSHIPS

RESULTS

August 17	ANZ Stadium, Sydney	Australia	29	New Zealand	47
August 17	FNB Stadium, Soweto	SOUTH AFRICA	73	Argentina	13
August 24	Westpac Stadium, Wellington	New Zealand	27	Australia	16
August 24	Malvinas Argentinas Stadium, Mendoza	Argentina	17	SOUTH AFRICA	22
September 7	Waikato Stadium, Hamilton	New Zealand	28	Argentina	13
September 7	Suncorp Stadium, Brisbane	Australia	12	SOUTH AFRICA	38
September 14	Eden Park, Auckland	New Zealand	29	SOUTH AFRICA	15
September 14	Patersons Stadium, Perth	Australia	14	Argentina	13
September 28	Newlands, Cape Town	SOUTH AFRICA	28	Australia	8
September 28	Estadio Ciudad de la Plata, La Plata	Argentina	15	New Zealand	33
October 5	Ellis Park, Johannesburg	SOUTH AFRICA	27	New Zealand	38
October 5	Gigante de Arroyita Ground, Rosario	Argentina	17	Australia	54

LOG

Team	P	W	L	D	PF	PA	Diff	TF	TA	B	Pts
New Zealand	6	6	0	0	202	115	87	24	10	4	28
South Africa	6	4	2	0	203	117	86	23	13	3	19
Australia	6	2	4	0	133	170	-37	12	18	1	9
Argentina	6	0	6	0	88	224	-136	7	25	2	2

Springbok captain Jean de Villiers. *Gallo Images*

SCORERS

PLAYER	Country	Matches	Tries	Conversions	Penalties	Drop Goals	Points
M Steyn	South Africa	6	0	17	18	0	88
CP Lealiifano	Australia	6	0	5	18	0	64
BR Smith	New Zealand	6	8	0	0	0	40
AW Cruden	New Zealand	3	1	7	6	0	37
FN Sanchez	Argentina	6	0	4	9	0	35
BJ Barrett	New Zealand	5	1	6	3	0	26
I Folau	Australia	6	5	0	0	0	25
F Contepomi	Argentina	6	1	3	3	0	20
BG Habana	South Africa	6	3	0	0	0	15
J de Villiers	South Africa	6	3	0	0	0	15
J-M Leguizamon	Argentina	6	3	0	0	0	15
KJ Read	New Zealand	6	3	0	0	0	15
WJ Le Roux	South Africa	6	3	0	0	0	15
TJ Taylor	New Zealand	1	0	1	4	0	14
MT Bosch	Argentina	5	2	0	1	0	13
DW Carter	New Zealand	2	0	3	2	0	12
AL Smith	New Zealand	6	2	0	0	0	10
JA Strauss	South Africa	6	2	0	0	0	10
BW du Plessis	South Africa	6	2	0	0	0	10
SJ Savea	New Zealand	6	2	0	0	0	10
LJ Messam	New Zealand	3	2	0	0	0	10
SJ Cane	New Zealand	5	2	0	0	0	10
Z Kirchner	South Africa	4	2	0	0	0	10
BT Foley	Australia	1	1	2	0	0	9
AP Ashley-Cooper	Australia	6	1	0	0	0	5
BA Robinson	Australia	2	1	0	0	0	5
BA Basson	South Africa	2	1	0	0	0	5
BA Retallick	New Zealand	6	1	0	0	0	5
C Feau-Sautia	Australia	1	1	0	0	0	5
CV Oosthuizen	South Africa	6	1	0	0	0	5
CG Smith	New Zealand	6	1	0	0	0	5
DJ Vermeulen	South Africa	6	1	0	0	0	5
PF du Preez	South Africa	3	1	0	0	0	5
JD O'Connor	Australia	4	1	0	0	0	5
JJ Engelbrecht	South Africa	6	1	0	0	0	5
JM Tomane	Australia	2	1	0	0	0	5
M Landajo	Argentina	6	1	0	0	0	5
PJ Lambie	South Africa	6	1	0	0	0	5
RH McCaw	New Zealand	4	1	0	0	0	5
SW Genia	Australia	5	1	0	0	0	5
WS Alberts	South Africa	6	1	0	0	0	5
QS Cooper	Australia	6	0	1	1	0	5
IJA Dagg	New Zealand	6	0	0	1	0	3
Penalty try	South Africa	0	1	0	0	0	5
			66	49	66	0	626

2013 CASTLE RUGBY CHAMPIONSHIPS

SPRINGBOK SQUAD, APPEARANCES & SCORERS

	Date of birth	Height	Weight	Province	Argentina	Argentina	Australia	New Zealand	Australia	New Zealand	Matches	Tries	Conversions	Penalties	Drop Goals	Points
WJ Le Roux	18/08/1989	1,86	88	Griquas	15	15	14	14	14	14	6	3	-	-	-	15
BG Habana	12/06/1983	1,79	94	Toulon, France	14	14	11	11	11	11	6	3	-	-	-	15
JJ Engelbrecht	22/02/1989	1,90	94	Blue Bulls	13	13	13	13	13	13	6	1	-	-	-	5
J de Villiers (C)	24/02/1981	1,90	100	Western Province	12c	12c	12c	12c	12c	12c	6	3	-	-	-	15
BA Basson	11/02/1987	1,87	84	Blue Bulls	11	11	-	-	-	-	2	1	-	-	-	5
M Steyn	11/07/1984	1,86	91	Stade Francais, France	10	10	10	10	10	10	6	-	17	18	-	88
R Pienaar	10/03/1984	1,86	92	Ulster, N.Ireland	9	9	9	9	x	9R	5	-	-	-	-	0
DJ Vermeulen	03/07/1986	1,92	90	Western Province	8	8	8	8	8	8	6	1	-	-	-	5
WS Alberts	05/11/1984	1,91	119	The Sharks	7	7	7	7	7	7	6	1	-	-	-	5
L-FP Louw	15/06/1985	1,90	114	Bath, England	6	6	6	6	6	6	6	-	-	-	-	0
PJJ Kruger	06/09/1985	1,99	112	Racing Metro, France	5	5	5R	5R	5R	5	6	-	-	-	-	0
E Etzebeth	29/10/1991	2,03	117	Western Province	4	4	4	4	4	4	6	-	-	-	-	0
JN du Plessis	16/11/1982	1,87	119	The Sharks	3	3	3	3	3	3	6	-	-	-	-	0
JA Strauss	18/11/1985	1,84	111	FS Cheetahs	2	2	2R	7R	2	2R	6	2	-	-	-	10
T Mtawarira	01/07/1985	1,83	115	The Sharks	1	1	1	1	1	1	6	-	-	-	-	0
BW du Plessis	22/05/1984	1,89	113	The Sharks	2R	2R	2	2	2R	2	6	2	-	-	-	10
GG Steenkamp	12/06/1981	1,89	124	Toulouse, France	1R	1R	1R	1R	1R	1R	6	-	-	-	-	0
CV Oosthuizen	22/03/1989	1,83	127	FS Cheetahs	3R	3R	3R	3R	3R	3R	6	1	-	-	-	5
PR van der Merwe	03/06/1985	1,99	120	Blue Bulls	5R	5R	5	5	5	-	5	-	-	-	-	0
S Kolisi	16/06/1991	1,86	99	Western Province	7R	7R	6R	6R	7R	7R	6	-	-	-	-	0
PF du Preez	24/03/1982	1,82	91	Suntory Sungoliath, Japan	9R	-	-	-	9	9	3	1	-	-	-	5
PJ Lambie	17/10/1990	1,78	87	The Sharks	15R	11R	10R	10R	15R	15R	6	1	-	-	-	5
JL Serfontein	15/04/1993	1,87	97	Blue Bulls	12R	13R	12R	12R	13R	11R	6	-	-	-	-	0
J Vermaak	01/01/1985	1,75	82	Toulouse, France	-	x	9R	9R	-	-	2	-	-	-	-	0
Z Kirchner	16/06/1984	1,84	92	Leinster, Ireland	-	-	15	15	15	15	4	2	-	-	-	10
F van der Merwe	15/03/1983	1,98	116	Golden Lions	-	-	-	-	-	5R	1	-	-	-	-	0
MC Coetzee	08/05/1991	1,90	106	Kwazulu Natal	-	-	-	-	-	-	0	-	-	-	-	0
PE van Zyl	14/09/1989	1,74	81	FS Cheetahs	-	-	-	-	-	-	0	-	-	-	-	0
LC Adriaanse	05/02/1988	1,8	115	Griquas	-	-	-	-	-	-	0	-	-	-	-	0
JL de Jongh	15/04/1988	1,77	85	Western Province	-	-	-	-	-	-	0	-	-	-	-	0
PS du Toit	20/08/1992	2,00	115	The Sharks	-	-	-	-	-	-	0	-	-	-	-	0
TN Nyakane	04/05/1989	1,78	109	FS Cheetahs	-	-	-	-	-	-	0	-	-	-	-	0
MC Ralepelle	11/09/1986	1,78	104	Toulouse, France	-	-	-	-	-	-	0	-	-	-	-	0
Penalty try	-	-	-	-	-	-	-	-	-	-	0	1	-	-	-	5
33 Players											136	23	17	18	0	203

(c) = Captain

2013 CASTLE RUGBY CHAMPIONSHIPS

NEW ZEALAND SQUAD, APPEARANCES & SCORERS

ALL BLACKS	Date of birth	Height	Weight	Province	Australia	Australia	Argentina	South Africa	Argentina	South Africa	Matches	Tries	Conversions	Penalties	Drop Goals	Points
IJA Dagg	06/06/1988	1,86	94	Hawke's Bay	15	15	15	15	15	15	6	–	-	1	-	3
BR Smith	01/06/1986	1,86	93	Otago	14	14	14	14	14	14	6	8	-	-	-	40
CG Smith	12/10/1981	1,86	95	Wellington	13	13	13	13	13	13	6	1	-	-	-	5
MA Nonu	21/05/1982	1,82	107	Wellington	12	12	-	12	12	12	5	-	-	-	-	0
SJ Savea	07/08/1990	1,92	103	Wellington	11	11	11	11	11	11	6	2	-	-	-	10
AW Cruden	08/01/1989	1,78	83	Manawatu	10	-	-	-	10	10	3	1	7	6	-	37
AL Smith	21/11/1988	1,71	83	Manawatu	9	9	9	9	9	9	6	2	-	-	-	10
KJ Read	26/10/1985	1,93	110	Canterbury	8	8	8	8c	8c	8	6	3	-	-	-	15
RH McCaw (C)	31/12/1980	1,87	107	Canterbury	7c	7c	7c	-	-	7c	4	1	-	-	-	5
DS Luatua	29/04/1991	1,96	110	Auckland	6	6	6	6R	6R	6R	6	-	-	-	-	0
SL Whitelock	12/10/1988	2,02	116	Canterbury	5	5	5	5	5	5	6	-	-	-	-	0
L Romano	16/02/1986	1,99	115	Canterbury	4	-	-	-	-	-	1	-	-	-	-	0
OT Franks	23/12/1987	1,85	118	Canterbury	3	3	-	3	3	-	4	-	-	-	-	0
AK Hore	13/09/1978	1,83	115	Taranaki	2	2	2	-	2	2	5	-	-	-	-	0
TD Woodcock	27/01/1981	1,84	119	North Harbour	1	1	1	1	1	1	6	-	-	-	-	0
KF Mealamu	20/03/1979	1,81	118	Auckland	2R	-	-	2R	2R	-	3	-	-	-	-	0
BJ Franks	27/03/1984	1,03	116	Hawke's Bay	1R	-	3R	-	-	3R	3	-	-	-	-	0
CC Faumuina	24/12/1986	1,84	128	Auckland	3R	3R	3	3R	3R	3	6	-	-	-	-	0
BA Retallick	31/05/1991	2,04	117	Bay of Plenty	4R	4	4	4	4	4	6	1	-	-	-	5
SJ Cane	13/01/1992	1,89	104	Bay of Plenty	7R	x	7R	7	7	4R	5	2	-	-	-	10
TNJ Kerr-Barlow	15/08/1990	1,87	89	Waikato	9R	9R	9R	11R	9R	9R	6	-	-	-	-	0
BJ Barrett	27/05/1991	1,87	90	Taranaki	10R	-	10R	10R	10R	10R	5	1	6	3	-	26
RS Crotty	23/09/1988	1,81	92	Canterbury	12R	-	-	-	-	-	1	-	-	-	-	0
TJ Taylor	11/03/1989	1,83	90	Canterbury	-	10	-	-	-	-	1	-	1	4	-	14
DS Coles	12/10/1986	1,84	103	Wellington	-	2R	2R	2	-	2R	4	-	-	-	-	0
WWV Crockett	24/01/1983	1,93	116	Canterbury	-	1R	1R	1R	1R	1R	5	-	-	-	-	0
JI Thrush	19/04/1985	1,98	109	Wellington	-	x	5R	-	4R	-	2	-	-	-	-	0
CR Slade	10/10/1987	1,83	90	Canterbury	-	12R	-	-	-	-	1	-	-	-	-	0
CT Piutau	31/10/1991	1,83	94	Auckland	-	10R	15R	15R	12R	11R	5	-	-	-	-	0
F Saili	16/02/1991	1,85	99	Auckland	-	-	12	-	-	-	1	-	-	-	-	0
DW Carter	05/03/1982	1,78	94	Canterbury	-	-	10	10	-	-	2	-	3	2	-	12
LJ Messam	25/03/1984	1,90	108	Waikato	-	-	-	6	6	6	3	2	-	-	-	10
MB Todd	24/03/1988	1,85	104	Canterbury	-	-	-	7R	-	-	1	-	-	-	-	0
TTR Perenara	23/01/1993	1,84	94	Wellington	-	-	-	-	-	-	0	-	-	-	-	0
PAT Weepu	07/09/1983	1,78	94	Auckland	-	-	-	-	-	-	0	-	-	-	-	0

35 Players   136   24   17   16   0   202

(c) = Captain

2013 CASTLE RUGBY CHAMPIONSHIPS

AUSTRALIA SQUAD, APPEARANCES & SCORERS

	Date of birth	Height	Weight	Province	New Zealand	New Zealand	South Africa	Argentina	South Africa	Argentina	Matches	Tries	Conversions	Penalties	Drop Goals	Points
JD Mogg	08/06/1989	1,87	90	ACT	15	15	x	–	–	–	2	–	–	–	–	0
I Folau	03/04/1989	1,93	103	NSW	14	14	15	15	15	15	6	5	–	–	–	25
AP Ashley-Cooper	27/03/1984	1,82	98	NSW	13	13	13	13	14	14	6	1	–	–	–	5
CP Lealiifano	24/09/1987	1,79	95	ACT	12	12	12	12	12	12	6	–	5	18	–	64
JD O'Connor	05/07/1990	1,80	88	Melbourne Rebels	11	11	14	14	–	–	4	1	–	–	–	5
MP Toomua	02/01/1990	1,82	89	ACT	10	10	12R	10R	12R	12R	6	–	–	–	–	0
SW Genia	17/01/1988	1,82	85	Queensland	9	9	9c	x	9R	9	5	1	–	–	–	5
BSC Mowen	01/12/1984	1,95	107	ACT	8	8	8	8c	8	8	6	–	–	–	–	0
MK Hooper	29/10/1991	1,82	97	NSW	7	7	7	7	7	7	6	–	–	–	–	0
HJ McMeniman	01/11/1983	2,00	114	Western Force	6	–	–	–	–	–	1	–	–	–	–	0
JE Horwill	29/05/1985	2,00	115	Queensland	5c	5c	–	–	5c	5c	4	–	–	–	–	0
RA Simmons	19/04/1989	2,00	115	Queensland	4	4	4	4	4	4	6	–	–	–	–	0
BE Alexander	13/11/1984	1,89	117	ACT	3	3	3R	3	3	3	6	–	–	–	–	0
ST Moore	20/01/1983	1,86	112	ACT	2	2	2	2	2	2	6	–	–	–	–	0
JA Slipper	06/06/1989	1,85	113	Queensland	1	1	1	1	1	1	6	–	–	–	–	0
SM Fainga'a	02/02/1987	1,87	108	Queensland	2R	2R	2R	2R	2R	2R	6	–	–	–	–	0
ST Sio	16/10/1991	1,87	116	ACT	1R	1R	1R	1R	–	–	4	–	–	–	–	0
SM Kepu	05/02/1986	1,88	125	NSW	3R	3R	3	3R	3R	3R	6	–	–	–	–	0
SM Fardy	05/07/1984	1,98	110	ACT	8R	6	6	6	6	6	6	–	–	–	–	0
LB Gill	08/06/1992	1,84	96	Queensland	6R	8R	7R	–	–	–	3	–	–	–	–	0
NW White	13/06/1990	1,73	82	ACT	9R	9R	9R	9	9	9R	6	–	–	–	–	0
QS Cooper	05/04/1988	1,86	93	Queensland	10R	10R	10	10	10	10	6	–	1	1	–	5
RTRN Kuridrani	31/03/1991	1,96	102	ACT	15R	13R	–	x	13	13	4	–	–	–	–	0
KP Douglas	01/06/1989	2,01	120	NSW	–	4R	5	5	–	–	3	–	–	–	–	0
NM Cummins	05/10/1987	1,89	98	Western Australia	–	–	11	11	–	–	2	–	–	–	–	0
BJ McCalman	09/01/1989	1,80	85	Victoria	–	–	8R	6R	6R	6R	4	–	–	–	–	0
S Timani	19/09/1986	2,02	119	NSW	–	–	–	5R	4R	5R	3	–	–	–	–	0
C Feauai-Sautia	17/11/1993	1,81	88	Queensland	–	–	–	–	11R	–	1	1	–	–	–	5
BA Robinson	19/07/1984	1,83	114	NSW	–	–	–	–	1R	1R	2	1	–	–	–	5
JM Tomane	11/02/1990	1,90	102	ACT	–	–	–	–	11	11	2	1	–	–	–	5
BT Foley	08/09/1989	1,80	85	NSW	–	–	–	–	–	10R	1	1	2	–	–	9
JW Schatz	27/05/1990	1,92	109	Queensland	–	–	–	–	–	–	0	–	–	–	–	0
A Anae	21/06/1989	1,85	114	Queensland	–	–	–	–	–	–	0	–	–	–	–	0

33 Players   135   12   8   19   0   133

(c) = Captain

2013 CASTLE RUGBY CHAMPIONSHIPS

ARGENTINA SQUAD, APPEARANCES & SCORERS

	Date of birth	Height	Weight	Province	South Africa	South Africa	New Zealand	Australia	New Zealand	Australia	Matches	Tries	Conversions	Penalties	Drop Goals	Points
J-M Hernández	07/08/1982	1,87	94	Racing Metro, France	15	–	15	15	15	15	5	–	–	–	–	0
GO Camacho	28/08/1984	1,74	85	Leicester Tigers, UK	14	14	14	–	–	–	3	–	–	–	–	0
MT Bosch	07/01/1984	1,86	92	Saracens, UK	13	13	13	–	13	13	5	2	–	1	–	13
F Contepomi	20/08/1977	1,83	95	Newman	12c	12c	12R	12	12R	12	6	1	3	3	–	20
J-J Imhoff	11/05/1988	1,85	90	Racing Metro, France	11	–	–	11	11	11	4	–	–	–	–	0
FN Sánchez	26/10/1988	1,77	83	Bordeaux Begles, France	10	10	10	10	10	10	6	–	4	9	–	35
M Landajo	14/06/1988	1,71	81	Club Atletico de San Isidro	9	9	9	9R	9	9	6	1	–	–	–	5
LV Senatore	13/05/1984	1,91	106	Worcester, England	8	8	–	–	–	–	2	–	–	–	–	0
J-M Leguizamón	06/06/1983	1,90	104	Lyon, France	7	7	8	8	8	8	6	3	–	–	–	15
P Matera	18/07/1993	1,93	99	Asociacion Alumni	6	6	7	7	7	7	6	–	–	–	–	0
P Albacete	09/02/1981	2,00	122	Toulouse, France	5	–	–	–	5	5	3	–	–	–	–	0
M Carizza	23/08/1984	2,02	118	Unattached	4	–	4	4	4R	4R	5	–	–	–	–	0
MD Diaz Sanchez	16/02/1993	1,85	115	Teque	3	x	–	–	–	3R	2	–	–	–	–	0
E Guiñazú	15/01/1982	1,81	114	Bath, England	2	2	2	2R	2	2	6	–	–	–	–	0
J Figallo	25/03/1988	1,90	115	Montpellier, France	1	3	3	3	3	–	5	–	–	–	–	0
A Creevy	15/03/1985	1,81	110	Worcester, England	2R	2R	2R	2	2R	2R	6	–	–	–	–	0
N Lobo	27/08/1991	1,80	116	Newcastle, England	3R	x	1R	1R	1R	1R	5	–	–	–	–	0
J-P Orlandi	20/06/1983	1,90	119	Bath, England	1R	–	3R	x	3R	3	4	–	–	–	–	0
M Galarza	12/11/1986	2,03	111	Univ de La Plata	4R	5	5R	5R	–	–	4	–	–	–	–	0
JA Farías Cabello	19/09/1978	1,94	110	Tucumán	5R	4	5	5	4	4	6	–	–	–	–	0
TM Cubelli	12/06/1989	1,77	81	Belgrano Athletic	9R	9R	9R	9	x	9R	5	–	–	–	–	0
S Fernández	28/11/1985	1,83	94	Unattached	x	12R	12	13R	12	12R	5	–	–	–	–	0
H Agulla	22/10/1984	1,81	92	Bath, England	15R	11	11	14	14R	14	6	–	–	–	–	0
L González Amorosino	11/02/1985	1,85	93	Unattached	–	15	14R	14R	14	11R	5	–	–	–	–	0
MI Ayerza	12/01/1983	1,86	114	Leicester Tigers, England	–	1	1	1	1	1	5	–	–	–	–	0
T Lavanini	22/01/1993	2,00	118	Hindu	–	5R	–	–	–	–	1	–	–	–	–	0
B Macome	10/01/1986	1,90	106	Tucuman	–	8R	7R	x	8R	8R	4	–	–	–	–	0
J Tuculet	08/08/1989	1,84	86	Unattached	–	x	–	–	–	–	0	–	–	–	–	0
J-M Fernández Lobbe	19/11/1981	1,91	106	Toulon, France	–	–	6c	6c	6c	6c	4	–	–	–	–	0
G Tiesi	24/04/1985	1,84	92	San Isidro Club	–	–	–	13	–	–	1	–	–	–	–	0
M Rodríguez	12/04/1985	1,85	96	Stade Français, France	–	–	–	–	–	–	0	–	–	–	–	0
31 Players											131	7	7	13	0	88

(c) = *Captain*

2013 CASTLE RUGBY CHAMPIONSHIPS

SPRINGBOK COACHES & MANAGEMENT

HEAD COACH: Heyneke Meyer **FORWARDS COACH:** Johan van Graan **BACKS COACH:** Ricardo Loubscher
FITNESS COACH: Basil Carzis **DEFENCE COACH:** John McFarland **TEAM MANAGER:** Ian Schwartz
TEAM DOCTOR: Dr Craig Roberts **PHYSIOTHERAPIST:** Vivian Verwant **MASSEUSE:** Daliah Hurwitz
OPERATIONAL HEAD: Charles Wessels **PR AND ADMIN:** Annelee Murray **LOGISTICS:** JJ Fredericks
TECHNICAL ANALYST: Albé Visser **COMMUNICATIONS MANAGER:** De Jongh Borchardt
CONDITIONING CONSULTANT: Niel du Plessis **KICKING CONSULTANT:** Louis Koen
SCRUM CONSULTANT: Pieter de Villiers **PERFORMANCE ANALYST:** Chean Roux
PHYSIOTHERAPIST: Rene Naylor

NEW ZEALAND COACHES & MANAGEMENT

HEAD COACH: Steve Hansen **MANAGER:** Darren Shand **ASSISTANT MANAGER:** Gilbert Enoka
ASSISTANT COACH: Ian Foster **FORWARDS COACH:** Mike Cron **DEFENCE COACH:** Aussie McLean
KICKING COACH: Mick Byrne **SELECTOR:** Grant Fox **DOCTOR:** Dr Tony Page
PHYSIOTHERAPIST: Peter Gallagher **MANUAL THERAPIST:** George Duncan
STRENGTH & CONDITIONING: Dr Nic Gill **PERFORMANCE ANALYST:** Alistair Rogers
LOGISTICS: Errol Collins **MEDIA MANAGER:** Joe Locke **NUTRITIONIST:** Katrina Darry
EXECUTIVE ASSISTANT: Bianca Thiel

AUSTRALIA COACHES & MANAGEMENT

HEAD COACH: Ewen McKenzie **ATTACK COACH:** Jim McKay **FORWARDS COACH:** Andrew Blades
COACHING ASSISTANT: Nick Scrivener **STRENGTH & CONDITIONING:** Scott Murphy
MANAGER: Bob Egerton **LOGISTICS MANAGER:** Matt Sheppard **DOCTOR:** Dr Richard Brown
HEAD PHYSIOTHERAPIST: Andrew Ryan **SPORTS MEDICINE CO-ORDINATOR:** Ed Fitzgerald
ANALYST: Andrew Sullivan **MEDIA MANAGER:** Brendon Altadonna **PHYSIOTHERAPIST:** Kieran Cleary

ARGENTINA COACHES & MANAGEMENT

TEAM PRESIDENT: Julio Clement **HEAD COACH:** Santiago Phelan
ASSISTANT COACHES: Fabián Turnes, Mauricio Reggiardo, Martín Gaitán & Germán Fernández
TEAM MANAGER: Jimenez Salice **DOCTOR:** Dr Guillermo Botto **MEDIA MANAGER:** Rafael Laría
PHYSIOTHERAPISTS: Maximiliano Marticorena & Lucas Toro **BAGAGE MASTER:** Jorge Ruarte
VIDEO ANALYST: Raúl Pérez **TECHNICAL ADVISER:** Graham Henry **TRAINER:** Gonzalo Santos

2013 CASTLE RUGBY CHAMPIONSHIPS

RESULTS

Australia 29 New Zealand 47 (halftime 19-25)
August 17, ANZ Stadium, Sydney (68 765). Referee: C Joubert (South Africa)
AUSTRALIA - TRY: Genia, O'Connor. CONVERSION: Lealiifano (2). PENALTY GOALS: Lealiifano (5).
NEW ZEALAND - TRIES: B Smith (3), C Smith, Cruden, McCaw. CONVERSION: Cruden (3), Barrett.
PENALTY GOALS: Cruden (3).
AUSTRALIA: JD Mogg (RTRN Kuridrani, 53), I Folau, AP Ashley-Cooper, CP Lealiifano, JD O'Connor, MP Toomua (QS Cooper, 61), SW Genia (NW White, 77), BSC Mowen (SM Fardy, 77), M Hooper (SM Fardy, 61-66), HJ McMeniman (LB Gill, 53), JE Horwill (C), RA Simmons, BE Alexander (SM Kepu, 58), ST Moore (SM Faingaa, 71), JA Slipper (ST Sio, 71). *TEST DEBUT: MP Toomua, RTRN Kuridrani. CHAMPIONSHIP DEBUTS: JD Mogg, I Folau, CP Lealiifano, MP Toomua, BSC Mowen, SM Fardy, ST Sio, NW White, RTRN Kuridrani.*
NEW ZEALAND: IJA Dagg; BR Smith, CG Smith, MA Nonu (RS Crotty, 63), SJ Savea, A Cruden (BJ Barrett, 71), AL Smith (TNJ Kerr-Barlow, 69), KJ Read, RH McCaw (C/SJ Cane, 73), DS Luatua, SL Whitelock, L Romano (BA Rettalick, 17), OT Franks (CC Faumuina, 61), AK Hore (KF Mealamu, 49), TD Woodcock (BJ Franks, 61). *TEST DEBUT: RS Crotty. CHAMPIONSHIP DEBUTS: DS Luatua, RS Crotty, TNJ Kerr-Barlow. YELLOW-CARD: SL Whitelock, 80*

New Zealand 27 Australia 16 (halftime 15-6)
August 24, Westpac Stadium, Wellington (35 583). Referee: J Peyper (South Africa)
NEW ZEALAND - TRIES: B Smith (2). CONVERSION: Taylor. PENALTY GOALS: Taylor (4), Dagg.
AUSTRALIA - TRY: Folau. CONVERSION: Lealiifano. PENALTY GOALS: Lealiifano (3).
NEW ZEALAND: IJA Dagg; BR Smith (CT Piuta, 73-79), CG Smith, MA Nonu (CR Slade, 76), SJ Savea, TJ Taylor (CT Piutau, 79), AL Smith (TNJ Kerr-Barlow, 70), KJ Read, RH McCaw (C), DS Luatua, SL Whitelock, BA Rettalick, OT Franks (CC Faumuina, 66), AK Hore (DS Coles, 48), TD Woodcock (WVV Crockett, 61). *UNUSED SUBSTITUTE: SJ Cane, JI Thrush. TEST DEBUT: TJ Taylor. TEST & CHAMPIONSHIP DEBUTS: TJ Taylor, CT Piutau.*
AUSTRALIA: JD Mogg, I Folau, AP Ashley-Cooper (RTRN Kuridrani, 63), CP Lealiifano, JD O'Connor, MP Toomua (QS Cooper, 58), SW Genia (NW White, 77), BSC Mowen (LB Gill, 65), MK Hooper, SM Fardy, JE Horwill (C), RA Simmons (KP Douglas, 72), BE Alexander (SM Kepu, 54), ST Moore (SM Fainga'a, 77), JA Slipper (ST Sio, 36).

New Zealand 28 Argentina 13 (halftime 15-10)
September 7, Waikato Stadium, Hamilton (22 220) Referee: J Garces (France)
NEW ZEALAND - TRIES: A Smith (2), Savea. CONVERSION: Carter (2). PENALTY GOALS: Carter (2), Barrett.
ARGENTINA - TRY: Leguizamon. CONVERSION: Sanchez. PENALTY: Sanchez (2).
NEW ZEALAND: IJA Dagg (CT Piutau, 71), BR Smith, CG Smith, F Saili, SJ Savea, DW Carter (BJ Barrett, 55 , AL Smith (TNJ Kerr-Barlow, 75), KJ Read, RH McCaw (C, SJ Cane, 60), DS Luatua, SL Whitelock (JI Thrush, 75), BA Rettalick, CC Faumuina (BJ Franks, 71), AK Hore (DS Coles, 46), TD Woodcock (WVV Crockett, 41/CC Faumuina, 78). *TEST DEBUT: F Saili. CHAMPIONSHIP DEBUTS: F Saili, JI Thrush.*
ARGENTINA: J-M Hernandez, GO Camacho (L Gonzales Amorosino, 46) MT Bosch, S Fernandez (F Contepomi, 71), H Agulla, FN Sanchez, M Landajo (TM Cubelli, 66), JM Leguizamon, P Matera (B Macome, 76), J-M Fernandez Lobbe (C), JA Farias Cabello (M Galarza, 55), M Carizza, J Figallo (J-P Orlandi, 63), E Guiñazú (A Creevy, 49) , MI Ayerza (N Lobo, 70). *YELLOW CARD: E Guinazu 23*

The Boks with the Mandela Plate. *Carl Fourie/Gallo Images*

RESULTS

Australia 23 Argentina 19 (halftime 14-3)
September 14, Patersons Stadium, Perth (18 214). Referee: N Owens (Wales)
AUSTRALIA - TRY: Folau. **PENALTY GOALS**: Lealiifano (3).
ARGENTINA - TRY: Leguizamon. **CONVERSION**: Sanchez. **PENALTY GOALS**: Sanchez (2).
AUSTRALIA: I Folau, JD O'Connor, AP Ashley-Cooper, CP Lealiifano, NM Cummins, QS Cooper (MP Toomua, 66), NW White, BSC Mowen (C), MK Hooper, SM Fardy (BJ McCalman, 73), KP Douglas (S Timani, 51), RA Simmons, BE Alexander (SM Kepu, 60), ST Moore (SM Fainga'a, 66), JA Slipper (ST Sio, 46).
UNUSED SUBSTITUTES: SW Genia, RTRN Kuridrani.
ARGENTINA: J-M Hernandez, H Agulla (L Gonzales Amorosino, 52), G Tiesi (S Fernandez, 73, F Contepomi, J-J Imhoff, FN Sanchez, TM Cubelli (M Landajo, 62), JM Leguizamon, P Matera, J-M Fernandez Lobbe (C), JA Farias Cabello (M Galarza, 57), M Carizza, J Figallo, A Creevy (E Guiñazú, 52), Ml Ayerza (N Lobo, 75).
UNUSED SUBSTITUTE: J-P Orlandi, B Macome.

Argentina 15 New Zealand 33 (halftime 9-11)
September 28, Estadio Ciudad, La Plata (40 207). Referee: J Peyper (South Africa)
ARGENTINA - **PENALTY GOALS**: Sanchez (4), Bosch.
NEW ZEALAND - TRIES: B Smith (2), Savea, Cane. **CONVERSIONS**: Cruden, Barrett. **PENALTY GOALS**: Cruden (3).
ARGENTINA: J-M Hernandez, L Gonzales Amorosino (H Agulla, 61), MT Bosch, S Fernandez, (F Contepomi, 61), J-J Imhoff, FN Sanchez, M Landajo, JM Leguizamon (B Macome, 72), P Matera, J-M Fernandez Lobbe (C), P Albacete, JA Farias Cabello (M Carizza, 59), J Figallo (J-P Orlandi, 64), E Guiñazú (A Creevy, 64), Ml Ayerza (N Lobo, 70).
NEW ZEALAND: IJA Dagg, BR Smith, CG Smith, MA Nonu (CT Piutau, 70), SJ Savea, AW Cruden (BJ Barrett, 72), AL Smith (TNJ Kerr-Barlow, 68), KJ Read (C), SJ Cane, LJ Messam (DS Luatua, 61) SL Whitelock, BA Rettalick (JI Thrush, 75), OT Franks (CC Faumuina, 41), AK Hore (KF Mealamu, 53), TD Woodcock (WWV Crockett, 70).

Argentina 17 Australia 54 (halftime 10-25)
October 5, Gigante de Arroyita Ground, Rosario (28 570). Referee: W Barnes (England)
ARGENTINA - TRIES: Bosch, Landajo. **CONVERSION**: Sanchez (2). **PENALTY GOAL**: Sanchez.
AUSTRALIA - TRIES: Folau (3), Ashley-Cooper, Tomane, Robinson, Foley. **CONVERSIONS**: Lealiifano (2), Foley (2), Cooper. **PENALTY GOALS**: Lealiifano (2), Cooper.
ARGENTINA: J-M Hernandez, H Agulla, M Bosch, F Contepomi (S Fernandez, 67), J-J Imhoff (L Gonzales Amorosino, 67), FN Sanchez, M Landajo (TM Cubelli, 73), JM Leguizamon (B Macome, 75), P Matera, J-M Fernandez Lobbe (C), P Albacete, JA Farias Cabello (M Carizza, 50), J-P Orlandi, (MD Diaz, 64), E Guiñazú (A Creevy, 67), Ml Ayerza (N Lobo, 73). *YELLOW CARD: P Matera, 30*
AUSTRALIA: I Folau, AP Ashley-Cooper, RTRN Kuridrani, CP Lealiifano (MP Toomua, 41), JM Tomane, QS Cooper (BT Foley, 66), SW Genia (NW White, 75), BSC Mowen, MK Hooper, SM Fardy (BJ Robinson, 16-25), JE Horwill (C, S Timani, 60), RA Simmons, BE Alexander (SM Kepu, 48), ST Moore (SM Fainga'a, 50), JA Slipper (BA Robinson, 60).
YELLOW CARD: JA Slipper, 15; RA Simmons, 51. TEST AND CHAMPIONSHIP DEBUT: BT Foley.

2013 CASTLE RUGBY CHAMPIONSHIPS

Boks produce Madiba magic

South Africa 73 Argentina 13 (halftime 26-6)

August 17, FNB Stadium, Soweto (52 867). Referee: C Pollock (New Zealand).
SOUTH AFRICA - TRIES: Pen try, Engelbrecht, Strauss, Alberts, De Villiers, Du Preez, Habana, Vermeulen, B du Plessis.
CONVERSIONS: Steyn (8). PENALTY GOALS: Steyn (4).
ARGENTINA - TRY: Contepomi. CONVERSION: Contepomi. PENALTY GOALS: Contepomi (2).

THE DAY WAS DEDICATED TO NELSON Mandela and it was appropriate therefore that the Springboks lifted the nation's mood with a highly impressive victory over Argentina.

South Africa scored nine tries – the big question before kick-off was whether they would get to four for the sake of a bonus point – and Fourie du Preez also made a promising re-entry into Springbok rugby.

The early stages of the game suggested the Springboks might grind their way to victory, but they ended up playing with remarkable freedom in putting the Pumas to the sword.

South Africa's breakthrough came in the 30th minute when they were awarded a penalty try for a deliberate knockdown by Eusebio Guinazu. Referee Chris Pollock also sin-binned the Pumas' former DHL Stormers hooker.

Not long after that a beautiful counter-attack yielded the second try, with outside centre JJ Engelbrecht chasing down a kick by irrepressible fullback Willie le Roux to score.

Flyhalf Morné Steyn then added his fourth penalty to give South Africa a commanding 26-6 lead at half-time.

The Springboks put their driving maul to particularly good use in a second half that yielded seven tries.

Du Preez had made his entry just before De Villiers's try and the 25 minutes the ace scrumhalf spent on the field showed that it had been a masterstroke by coach Heyneke Meyer to call him up from Japan.

Du Preez read the game and distributed masterfully, while he also scored a try in the 62nd minute after a line break by De Villiers. It catapulted the Springboks into a 52-6 lead and by then they were already enjoying themselves.

Wing Bryan Habana was next on the scoresheet after the ball had travelled impressively through Springbok hands before No 8 Duane Vermeulen touched down thanks to a heel against the head.

Vermeulen's try highlighted South Africa's dominance at set-piece, which was particularly significant given suggestions in the build-up that they might struggle against the traditionally powerful Pumas scrum.

The forwards were also impressive in the loose, with lock Eben Etzebeth at his belligerent best.

Flyhalf Steyn also made a big contribution with the boot as he succeeded with 12 out of 13 attempts at goal. And there was another impressive cameo for young centre Jan Serfontein after he had replaced De Villiers in midfield for the last 12 minutes.

As for the Pumas, they only looked dangerous in the final minute when captain and inside centre Felipe Contepomi finished after some impressive handling.

But so big was their hiding that it couldn't even be termed a consolation try.

SCORING SEQUENCE

Min	Action	Score
6	Steyn penalty	3-0
10	Steyn penalty	6-0
17	Contepomi penalty	6-3
19	Steyn penalty	9-3
23	Contepomi penalty	9-6
30	Penalty try, Steyn conversion	16-6
33	Engelbrecht try, Steyn conversion	23-6
38	Steyn penalty	26-6
46	Strauss try, Steyn conversion	33-6
53	Alberts try, Steyn missed conversion	38-6
55	De Villiers try, Steyn conversion	45-6
62	Du Preez try, Steyn conversion	52-6
67	Habana try, Steyn conversion	59-6
70	Vermeulen try, Steyn conversion	66-6
76	B du Plessis try, Steyn conversion	73-6
80	Contepomi try, Contepomi conversion	73-13

Duane Vermeulen celebrates. *Lee Warren/Gallo Images*

SOUTH AFRICA: WJ Le Roux (PJ Lambie, 59), BG Habana, JJ Engelbrecht, J de Villiers (C, JL Serfontein, 68), BA Basson, M Steyn, R Pienaar (PF du Preez, 61), DJ Vermeulen, WS Alberts (S Kolisi, 66), L-F Louw, PJJ Kruger (PR van der Merwe, 57), E Etzebeth, JN du Plessis (CV Oosthuizen, 55), JA Strauss (BW du Plessis, 55), T Mtawarira (GG Steenkamp, 57).
CHAMPIONSHIP DEBUTS: WJ le Roux, JL Serfontein, S Kolisi

ARGENTINA: J-M Hernandez (H Agulla, 31), GO Camacho, MT Bosch, F Contepomi (C), J-J Imhoff (A Creevy 35-41), FN Sanchez, M Landajo (TM Cubelli, 59), L Senatore, JM Leguizamon, P Matera, P Albacete (JA Farias Cabello, 14), M Carizza (M Galarza, 56), M Diaz (N Lobo, 41), E Guiñazú (A Creevy, 57), JG Figallo (J-P Orlandi). *UNUSED SUBSTITUTE: S Fernandez*
CHAMPIONSHIP DEBUTS: F Contepomi, TM Cubelli, P Matera, M Galarza, M Diaz, N Lobi. Yellow-cards: E Guinazu (30), L Senatore (51)

2013 CASTLE RUGBY CHAMPIONSHIPS

Boks survive Mendoza mauling

Argentina 17 South Africa 22 (halftime 17-13)

August 24, Malvinas Argentinas Stadium, Mendoza (23944). Referee: SR Walsh (Australia).
ARGENTINA - **TRIES**: Leguizamon, Bosch. **CONVERSIONS**: Contepomi (2). **PENALTY GOAL**: Contepomi.
SOUTH AFRICA - **TRY**: Basson. **CONVERSION**: M Steyn. **PENALTY GOALS**: M Steyn (5).

PERHAPS IT WAS INEVITABLE THAT the Springboks would struggle against Argentina in Mendoza after hammering them by a 60-point margin just the previous weekend.

But the contrast in performance was so pronounced that it was incredible. Having played extraordinarily well at the FNB Stadium, the Springboks completely lost their focus in Mendoza and had to wait until the last minute to put their narrow victory beyond doubt.

The struggle had its roots in an awful start by the Boks, with Pumas flank Juan-Manuel Leguizamón finishing for the hosts' first try in just the second minute. It was all too easy, with the half-hearted defence by wing Bjorn Basson capturing South Africa's flat-footed opening. Ruan Pienaar had also been caught in possession as Argentina won the turnover that led to the try and it was the start of an unhappy performance by the Springbok scrumhalf.

The match was deadlocked at 10-all after 15 minutes, with Basson finishing for the Springboks' only try after a bizarre sequence of play in which first they and then Argentina had lost possession.

One would have thought that the try would serve as a spur for South Africa to settle into a rhythm. However, their play continued to be plagued by sloppiness in which they struggled at the breakdowns and showed scant regard for possession.

Skipper Jean de Villiers' decision-making also let him down. A good example was the kickable penalty in the 23rd minute from which he opted to set up a lineout for his side to hopefully maul over for the try.

However, the Springboks could not set up the maul and ended up being driven back after having had the opportunity to edge ahead.

Argentina were back in the lead three minutes before half-time, with outside centre Marcelo Bosch exploiting the space between opposite number JJ Engelbrecht and tighthead prop Jannie du Plessis to finish.

Neither Springbok would have felt proud of his effort on defence.

The one Springbok who stood tall was flyhalf Morné Steyn, who struck an important penalty just before half-time to bring the score to 13-17. South Africa then set about grinding their way to victory, but Argentina put up one helluva fight which at times strayed outside the bounds of good sportsmanship.

Steyn reduced the deficit to one point with a penalty early in the half, but the Springboks' performance continued to be error-ridden. They eventually took the lead for the first time eight minutes before the end when Steyn struck his fourth penalty after Argentina had been penalised for collapsing a maul.

De Villiers then surprisingly asked Steyn to kick for the corner after Argentina had been penalised at a ruck in the 78th minute. Fortunately the decision didn't backfire and it ended up being a shrewd move as it helped to wind down the clock.

The only answer the Pumas could muster after the Springboks had set up another maul was to collapse it and Steyn then struck the final blow.

SCORING SEQUENCE

Min	Action	Score
2	Leguizamon try, Contepomi conversion	7-0
9	Steyn penalty	7-3
11	Contepomi penalty	10-3
14	Basson try, Steyn conversion	10-10
34	Contepomi missed penalty	10-10
37	Bosch try, Contepomi conversion	17-10
40	Steyn penalty	17-13
45	Steyn penalty	17-16
62	Bosch missed penalty	17-16
72	Steyn penalty	17-19
81	Steyn penalty	17-22

Bjorn Basson leaps high. *Getty Images*

ARGENTINA: L Gonzales Amorosino, GO Camacho, MT Bosch, F Contepomi (C), S Fernandez, 48), H Agulla, FN Sanchez, M Landajo (TM Cubelli, 57), L Senatore (B Macome, 61), JM Leguizamon, P Matera, M Galarza (T Lavanini, 74), JA Farias Cabello, J Figallo, E Guiñazú (A Creevy, 57), MI Ayerza. *UNUSED SUBSTITUTE: J Tuculet, N Lobo, MD Diaz. Championship debuts: T Lavanini.*

SOUTH AFRICA: WJ Le Roux, BG Habana, JJ Engelbrecht (JL Serfontein, 68) **, J de Villiers (C), BA Basson (PJ Lambie, 62)*, M Steyn, R Pienaar, DJ Vermeulen, WS Alberts (S Kolisi, 68), L-F Louw, PJJ Kruger (PR van der Merwe, 57), E Etzebeth, JN du Plessis (CV Oosthuizen, 68), JA Strauss (BW du Plessis, 53), T Mtawarira (GG Steenkamp, 59). **Lambie to fullback, Habana to left-wing and le Roux to right-wing.** Serfontein to inside-centre and de Villiers to outside-centre.* **UNUSED SUBSTITUTE:** *J Vermaak.* **Other:** *50th Test for BW du Plessis.*

Boks show fine disregard for history

Australia 12 South Africa 38 (halftime 6-16)

September 7, Suncorp Stadium, Brisbane (43 715). Referee: G Clancy (Ireland)
AUSTRALIA - PENALTY GOALS: Lealiifano (4).
SOUTH AFRICA - TRIES: Oosthuizen, De Villiers, Kirchner, Le Roux. CONVERSIONS: Steyn (3). PENALTY GOALS: Steyn (4).

NOT EVEN WHEN THE CASTLE RUGBY Championship was still called the Tri-Nations did the Springboks produce as commanding a performance away from home as this one in Brisbane.

Much was made in the run-up of South Africa's modest record on Australia's Gold Coast, but Jean de Villiers' team showed a fine disregard for history. They pounded Australia up front and struck hard with their backs.

Springbok coach Heyneke Meyer was also vindicated with his selections. He surprised by axing Juandré Kruger to pick Flip van der Merwe as his No 5 lock, while the return of Zane Kirchner at fullback also worked a treat.

Kirchner, of course, is a solid and 'safe' player, which naturally will never quite appeal to your average rugby supporter.

South Africans had so much enjoyed Willie le Roux's pizzazz in the position, but Meyer shrewdly retained his services by moving him to the wing.

The Springboks started particularly well with prop Coenie Oosthuizen – a blood replacement for Jannie du Plessis – barging his way over the tryline in the fifth minute after a lineout in Australia's 22-metre area.

Flyhalf Morné Steyn converted and the hunt for South Africa's first victory in Brisbane since 1971 was off to the perfect start.

However, the Springboks were knocked out of their stride two minutes later when flank Willem Alberts was sin-binned for a deliberate knockdown. Wallaby inside centre Christian Leiliifano raised the flags with a penalty and it was game on.

But even with 14 men the Springboks stood their ground and, by the time Alberts returned, Steyn had restored the seven-point lead.

Leiliifano again reduced the deficit to four points, but it didn't take the Springboks long to find their rhythm and by half-time they were up 16-6 after two more penalties from Steyn.

With the Wallabies having to score at least twice to haul the Boks in, it would make the next score a crucial one. Australia managed it via Leiliifano's boot, but their task of chasing the game was complicated by openside flank Michael Hooper being yellow-carded for dumping Bok wing Bryan Habana on his back.

Australia's demise was inevitable and it came inside an eight-minute Bok blitzkrieg from the 59th to the 68th minute. Springbok captain Jean de Villiers scored the first of the tries after Kruger had plucked Habana's chip kick from the air.

The bonus-point try came after Wallaby flyhalf Quade Cooper coughed up possession. Vermeulen flicked the ball to his right and Le Roux ran through to score, dummying to create a gap through which to ghost. Steyn's conversion made it 38-12 and with that the Springboks had put the finishing touch on their biggest ever win over the Wallabies in Australia.

SCORING SEQUENCE

Min	Action	Score
5	Oosthuizen try, Steyn conversion	**0-7**
9	Lealiifano penalty	**3-7**
13	Steyn penalty	**3-10**
23	Lealiifano penalty	**6-10**
29	Steyn penalty	**6-13**
35	Steyn penalty	**6-16**
40	Steyn missed penalty	**6-16**
44	Lealiifano penalty	**9-16**
50	Steyn penalty	**9-19**
52	Lealiifano penalty	**12-19**
59	De Villiers try, Steyn miossed conversion	**12-24**
66	Kirchner try, Steyn conversion	**12-31**
68	Le Roux try, Steyn conversion	**12-38**

Mercurial Willie le Roux. *Cameron Spencer/Getty Images*

AUSTRALIA: I Folau, JD O'Connor, AP Ashley-Cooper, 63), CP Lealiifano (MP Toomua, 73), NM Cummins, QS Cooper, SW Genia (C, NW White, 69), BSC Mowen (BJ McCalman, 71), MK Hooper (LB Gill, 71), SM Fardy, KP Douglas, RA Simmons (BJ McCalman 30-40), SM Kepu (BE Alexander, 47), ST Moore (SM Fainga'a, 66-69, 75), JA Slipper (ST Sio, 64).*UNUSED SUBSTITUTES:* JD Mogg.
YELLOW CARD: MK Hooper, 49

SOUTH AFRICA: Z Kirchner, WJ Le Roux, JJ Engelbrecht, J de Villiers (C, JL Serfontein, 71), BG Habana, M Steyn (PJ Lambie, 71), R Pienaar (J Vermaak, 77), DJ Vermeulen, WS Alberts, L-F Louw (S Kolisi, 71), PR van der Merwe (PJJ Kruger, 57), E Etzebeth, JN du Plessis (CV Oosthuizen, 4-9, 63), BW du Plessis (JA Strauss, 57), T Mtawarira (GG Steenkamp, 57).
YELLOW CARD: WS Alberts, 8

2013 CASTLE RUGBY CHAMPIONSHIPS

Eden Park retains hoodoo status

New Zealand 29 South Africa 15 (halftime 17-10)

September 14, Eden Park, Auckland (47 362). Referee: R Poite (France)
NEW ZEALAND – TRIES: Read (2), Retallick, Cane. CONVERSION: Carter, Barrett (2). PENALTY GOAL: Barrett.
SOUTH AFRICA – TRY: BW du Plessis, Lambie. CONVERSION: Steyn. PENALTY GOAL: Steyn.

IT WAS SUPPOSED TO BE THE RUGBY event of the year, but the showdown between the All Blacks and Springboks at Eden Park in Auckland degenerated into a refereeing farce of epic proportions.

The incident that sparked the controversy occurred in the 17th minute when referee Romain Poite sent Springbok hooker Bismarck du Plessis to the sin-bin for what was deemed a dangerous tackle on All Black flyhalf Dan Carter.

Du Plessis was neither offside nor could he be accused of not using his arms, but perhaps Poite was sub-consciously guided by one of the greatest flyhalves of the modern era having been injured.

While Du Plessis returned and still scored a try from a rolling maul, he was then red-carded for a second yellow in the 42nd minute after leading with his forearm and striking All Black flank Liam Messam on the throat.

This time the yellow card was justified, but of course, an injustice was done due to Poite's error in the first half.

South Africa were trailing 10-17 at the time of Du Plessis's dismissal and with that their chance of an upset victory evaporated.

A sense of injustice hung in the air and the International Rugby Board took the unusual step of posting a statement on its website that the match officials had admitted to their blunder.

While a commendable step, it didn't change the result and from a South African perspective this was a very unhappy chapter in the history of matches between the game's greatest rivals.

There were more interesting twists late in the match when All Black No 8 Kieran Read was dismissed for lineout interference in the 72nd minute and inside centre Ma'a Nonu for a late charge on Springbok skipper Jean de Villiers two minutes later.

It meant South Africa saw out the match with 14 men against New Zealand's 13, but by then the horse had bolted. The Kiwis were leading 29-10 and there was not nearly enough time for the Springboks to catch up.

South Africa scored a delightful try in the 75th minute when replacement back Pat Lambie finished smartly after a cross-kick by flyhalf Morné Steyn. But it was too little and too late.

The twist of events also paved the way for New Zealand to notch a bonus-point try, with flank Sam Cane finishing in the 69th minute after some relentless attacking play.

South Africa's concentration let them down early in the first half when Read scored from a lineout move, while the defence was awful in the run-up to Kiwi lock Brodie Retallick's try in the 32nd minute.

It appeared as if the Springboks hadn't pitched mentally, while it's important to note that Du Plessis should also have known better than leading with his forearm while taking the ball up.

The red card was scrapped from his record, but not the second yellow. And, of course, nothing will change what it states in black and white in the history books: New Zealand 29 South Africa 15.

SCORING SEQUENCE

Min	Action	Score
4	Read try, Carter conversion	7-0
10	Steyn penalty	7-3
15	Steyn missed penalty	7-3
22	Retallick try, Barrett conversion	14-3
32	B du Plessis try, Steyn conversion	14-10
35	Barrett penalty	17-10
46	Read try, Barrett conversion	24-10
68	Cane try, Barrett missed conversion	29-10
75	Lambie try, Steyn missed conversion	29-15

Duane Vermeulen contests. Sandra Mu/Getty Images

NEW ZEALAND: IJA Dagg (CT Piutau, 41), BR Smith, CG Smith, MA Nonu, SJ Savea (TNJ Kerr-Barlow, 76), DW Carter (BJ Barrett, 16) , AL Smith, KJ Read (C), SJ Cane (MB Todd, 31-40, 71-76), LJ Messam (DS Luatua,62) SL Whitelock, BA Rettalick, OT Franks (CC Faumuina, 65), DS Coles (KF Mealamu, 51), TD Woodcock (WWV Crockett, 70). *CHAMPIONSHIP DEBUT: MB Todd. YELLOW-CARDS: KJ Read, 72; MA Nonu, 74.*

SOUTH AFRICA: Z Kirchner, WJ Le Roux (JL Serfontein, 69-74)*, JJ Engelbrecht (JL Serfontein, 74),** J de Villiers (C), BG Habana (PJ Lambie, 74)***, M Steyn, R Pienaar (J Vermaak, 70), DJ Vermeulen, WS Alberts (JA Strauss, 19-27, 45) , L-F Louw (S Kolisi, 74), PR van der Merwe (PJJ Kruger, 41), E Etzebeth, JN du Plessis (CV Oosthuizen, 55), BW du Plessis, T Mtawarira (GG Steenkamp, 55-71). *YELLOW CARD: BW du Plessis, 42. * Serfontein to inside-centre, De Villiers to outside centre, Engelbrecht to right-wing. ** Serfontein to inside-centre, De Villiers to outside-centre. *** Lambie to fullback, Kirchner to left-wing.*

2013 CASTLE RUGBY CHAMPIONSHIPS

Wallabies fail Newlands examination

South Africa 28 Australia 8 (halftime 23-3)

September 28, Newlands, Cape Town (46 052). Referee: J Garces (France).
SOUTH AFRICA - TRIES: Strauss, Kirchner, Le Roux. CONVERSIONS: Steyn (2). PENALTY GOALS: Steyn (3).
AUSTRALIA - TRY: Feauai-Sautia. PENALTY GOAL: Lealiifano.

IT WAS QUITE AN ANOMALY: A SPRINGBOK team with shoulders drooped after a 20-point pasting of the Wallabies.

But in spite of this being a record victory over Australia at Newlands, it was also an opportunity lost. A bonus point for four tries was within easy reach, but South Africa failed to capitalise.

It may well have something to do with the ease in which they accumulated points early in the first half when a blitzkrieg from the 9th to the 19th minute saw them race into a 20-3 lead.

Hooker Adriaan Strauss and fullback Zane Kirchner scored within two minutes of one another during that period to render the crowd delirious.

The intensity with which South Africa played in that first quarter was remarkable. Lock Eben Etzebeth and No 8 Duane Vermeulen provided a rumbustious edge, while the Springboks also showed a willingness to attack from deep positions.

Skipper Jean de Villiers was also bold in his decision-making and a few times instructed flyhalf Morné Steyn to set up lineouts instead of taking the three-pointer on offer. The second such occasion resulted in Strauss's try. South Africa initially couldn't set up the maul, but Strauss was over two phases after they had been brought to ground.

Vermeulen had taken the ball up aggressively before it was recycled and scrumhalf Fourie du Preez found his marauding hooker with the scoring pass.

South Africa scored their second try straight after the kick-off. After mauling their way up field, the ball travelled down the line and De Villiers found centre partner JJ Engelbrecht with a skip pass out wide.

Engelbrecht raced down the touchline and then passed inside to fullback Kirchner, who beat opposite number Israel Folau to finish.

South Africa could not have created a better platform from which to achieve a bonus-point victory.

The signs looked all the more promising when Wallaby flank Michael Hooper was sin-binned for a dangerous tackle on Etzebeth in the 28th minute. However, the Springboks only managed another penalty by Steyn in his absence and by half-time the scoreboard read 23-3.

It was still a good enough platform, but the Springboks had lost their structure and discipline. Lock Flip van der Merwe was sin-binned in the 40th minute for needlessly elbow-charging Wallaby wing Adam Ashley-Cooper.

The Wallabies didn't have it in them to capitalise on their one-man advantage, but at the same time the Springboks couldn't build a head of steam.

With the sands of time running out, Vermeulen made the Boks' mission an all the more difficult one with a deliberate knockdown of the ball in the 66th minute. Strangely, however, the Boks were the better team in his absence and right wing Willie le Roux scored their third try in the right-hand corner after a blindside pass by Du Preez.

There were eight minutes left – and the task apparently made easier by a yellow card for Wallaby replacement lock Sitaleki Timani – but the Springboks could not make it count.

SCORING SEQUENCE

Min	Action	Score
6	Penalty Lealiifano	0-3
9	Penalty Steyn	3-3
13	Strauss try, Steyn conversion	10-3
15	Kirchner try, Steyn conversion	17-3
19	Penalty Steyn	20-3
32	Penalty Steyn	23-3
72	Le Roux try, Steyn missed conversion	28-3
78	Feauai-Sautia try, Cooper missed conversion	28-8

Adriaan Strauss dives over. *Carl Fourie/Gallo Images*

SOUTH AFRICA: Z Kirchner (PJ Lambie, 75), WJ Le Roux, JJ Engelbrecht (JL Serfontein, 58)*, J de Villiers (C), BG Habana, M Steyn, PF du Preez, DJ Vermeulen, WS Alberts (S Kolisi, 60) , L-F Louw, PR van der Merwe (PJJ Kruger, 60), E Etzebeth, JN du Plessis (CV Oosthuizen, 67), JA Strauss (BW du Plessis, 49), T Mtawarira (GG Steenkamp, 54).
YELLOW CARDS: PR van der Merwe, 40 (he was cited and suspended for one game); DJ Vermeulen, 66. OTHER: 50th Tests for M Steyn & JN du Plessis. * Serfontein to inside-centre. De Villiers to outside-centre. **UNUSED SUBSITUTE:** R Pienaar

AUSTRALIA: I Folau, AP Ashley-Cooper, RTRN Kuridrani, CP Lealiifano (MP Toomua, 73)*, JM Tomane (C Feauai-Sautia, 58), QS Cooper, NW White (SW Genia, 41), BSC Mowen, MK Hooper, SM Fardy (BJ McCalman, 58), JE Horwill (C), RA Simmons (S Timani, 67), BE Alexander (SM Kepu, 55), ST Moore (SM Fainga'a, 67), JA Slipper (BA Robinson, 51). * Toomua to flyhalf. Cooper to inside-centre. TEST AND CHAMPIONSHIP DEBUT: C Feauai-Sautia. YELLOW CARDS: MK Hooper, 28. S Timani, 75

2013 CASTLE RUGBY CHAMPIONSHIPS

All Blacks gain further altitude

South Africa 27 New Zealand 38 (halftime 15-21)

October 5, Ellis Park, Johannesburg (60 634). Referee: N Owens (Wales)
SOUTH AFRICA - TRIES: Habana (2). Le Roux, De Villiers. **CONVERSION**: Steyn (2). **PENALTY GOAL**: Steyn
NEW ZEALAND - TRIES: Messam (2), BR Smith, Barrett, Read. **CONVERSIONS**: Cruden (3), Barrett (2). **PENALTY GOAL**: Barrett.

SELDOM HAS THERE BEEN SUCH A tangible sense of anticipation about an episode in rugby's greatest rivalry as this one.

Apart from the fact that it was the world's two best teams slugging it out, the biggest contributing factor was that the previous meeting in Auckland had been ruined by the poor refereeing that led to Springbok hooker Bismarck du Plessis' red card.

But here we were at last: A chance once more for 15 to play 15. The man with the unenviable task of carrying the whistle was Welshman Nigel Owens, who ultimately contributed to a great spectacle.

South Africa went into the game with only a slim chance of winning the Rugby Championship. They had to win with a bonus point and prevent the Kiwis from getting a single log point.

South Africa got their bonus point for four tries, but perhaps the feverish hunt thereof is what led to them playing a high-tempo game on New Zealand's terms.

The Springboks also contributed to their own demise through poor handling of All Black kick-offs and weak defence.

It was missed tackles that contributed directly to the Kiwis' replacement flyhalf, Beauden Barrett, clinching the Championship with their fourth try in the 61st minute.

Up until then the Springboks had stood toe to toe with the All Blacks, with Jean de Villiers scoring the fourth try in the 58th minute. The Springbok captain ran Jonah Lomu-style over Barrett and then beat the challenges of Ma'a Nonu and Aaron Smith on his way to the tryline.

Earlier, speedster Bryan Habana had left a brief but indelible mark on the match, finishing off two magnificent tries before having to leave field in the 22nd minute with a hamstring injury.

Habana's tries owed much to the deft passing of No 8 Duane Vermeulen and flank Francois Louw.

Vermeulen was in exceptional form, but even he was eclipsed by All Black No 8 Kieran Read, who was at the heart of most of what was good for New Zealand. Read was instrumental in crafting right wing Ben Smith's early try and also won the turnover that led to flank Liam Messam scoring on the stroke of half-time.

He finally also ran in for the try that sealed South Africa's fate after collecting a neat pass from left wing Julian Savea.

That was in spite of New Zealand having been reduced to 14 men – for the second time in the game – with a yellow card to replacement prop Ben Franks in the 63rd minute.

Messam, who notched a brace of tries, had also been sin-binned early in the second half.

Looking back, the Springboks might regret not playing a tighter game with a greater focus on accurate execution.

Dropping kick-offs and shooting out of line on defence were criminal offences.

But ultimately one couldn't begrudge the All Blacks their victory. It proved beyond doubt that they were the foremost team in world rugby.

SCORING SEQUENCE

Min	Action	Score
10	Steyn penalty	**3-0**
12	B Smith try, Cruden conversion	**3-7**
18	Habana try, Steyn conversion	**10-7**
20	Habana try, Steyn missed conversion	**15-7**
26	Messam try, Cruden conversion	**15-14**
40	Messam try, Cruden conversion	**15-21**
46	Le Roux try, Steyn conversion	**22-21**
55	Barrett penalty	**22-24**
58	De Villiers try, Steyn missed conversion	**27-24**
61	Barrett try, Barrett conversion	**27-31**
65	Read try, Barrett conversion	**27-38**

Jean de Villiers and Richie McCaw. *Steve Haag/Gallo Images*

SOUTH AFRICA: Z Kirchner (PJ Lambie, 71), WJ Le Roux, JJ Engelbrecht, J de Villiers (C), BG Habana (JL Serfontein, 22), M Steyn, PF du Preez (R Pienaar, 71), DJ Vermeulen, WS Alberts (S Kolisi, 40) , L-F Louw, PJJ Kruger (F van der Merwe, 62), E Etzebeth, JN du Plessis (CV Oosthuizen, 51), BW du Plessis (JA Strauss, 51), T Mtawarira (GG Steenkamp, 53).
TEST AND CHAMPIONSHIP DEBUT: F van der Merwe. OTHER: 50th Test for T Mtawarira. 50th Test at flyhalf for M Steyn.

NEW ZEALAND: IJA Dagg, BR Smith, CG Smith, MA Nonu, SJ Savea (CT Piutau, 70), AW Cruden (BJ Barrett, 48) , AL Smith (TNJ Kerr-Barlow, 69), KJ Read, RH McCaw (C), LJ Messam (DS Luatua, 64) SL Whitelock, BA Rettalick (SJ Cane, 74), CC Faumuina (BJ Franks, 50), AK Hore (DS Coles, 43), TD Woodcock (WWV Crockett, 53). *YELLOW CARDS:* LJ Messam, 46; BJ Franks 63.

CASTLE LAGER OUTGOING TOUR

Boks give hint of possibilities to come

A SECOND SUCCESSIVE UNBEATEN end-of-season tour was testimony to the excellent progress the Springboks have made under coach Heyneke Meyer.

While there were some nervous moments in the 24-15 victory over Wales in Cardiff, the Boks ultimately left little doubt about their superiority. They were never troubled in their victories over Scotland in Edinburgh (28-0) and France in Paris (19-10).

The uncertainty against Wales stemmed partly from the fact that Meyer had decided to call up centre Jaque Fourie and wing JP Pietersen from their Japan-based clubs.

While it restored a backline combination that had served South Africa very well in the past, there was always the danger that these players would be a little off the pace.

But apart from a nervous first 10 minutes when Welsh midfielder Jonathan Davies cut through the Bok line a few times, there was little doubt by the end of the tour that Fourie and Pietersen could be very useful going forward.

Fourie provided the deft pass from which another Japan-based Bok, scrumhalf Fourie du Preez, killed off the game against the Welsh.

Pietersen's try-scoring prowess also came through as he finished after a sublime kick by fullback Willie le Roux against Scotland and stormed down French scrumhalf Morgan Parra's kick to set the Boks on their way in Paris.

Le Roux's ability to play a tactical game was one of the tour highlights for Meyer, who initially doubted his merits as a Test fullback. However, Meyer saw enough against Wales and Scotland to be convinced that Le Roux could wear the No 15 jersey going forward.

Flank Willem Alberts was immense as he gave Meyer precisely what he wants from a No 7 flank – a momentum-gainer and momentum–stopper, all rolled into one. Alberts was a juggernaut going forward and a bone collector on defence.

Flip van der Merwe also played well as a No 5 lock, while veteran Bakkies Botha, who seemingly retired from Test rugby after the 2011 World Cup, showed that he still has a role to play when Eben Etzebeth was first rested for the game against Scotland and then injured early on against France.

The control with which the Boks played against France and Scotland was particularly impressive. They started the Test at Murrayfield with a magnificent try, taking the ball through phase after phase before rounding off with an unstoppable rolling maul.

South Africa's clinical mauling also allowed them to score a try that put daylight between them and Wales in the first half in Cardiff.

The victory in Paris was the Boks' first in France since 1997. Pietersen's try almost immediately after the kick-off was the perfect start and after that they comfortably subdued the French. Had France not scored a disputed try on the stroke of half-time and had the Boks been more clinical in the second half, the scoreline would have been a lot more emphatic.

But perhaps the fact that the Boks were comfortably the better team in all three Tests yet left room for improvement is precisely what made this a very good tour. It left one pondering the possibilities of what Meyer's team might achieve once he irons out the remaining wrinkles.

Skipper Jean de Villiers on the charge against France. *David Rogers/Getty Images/Gallo Images*

2013 OUTGOING TOUR

The Springboks celebrate Fourie du Preez's match-turning try against Wales. *Gallo Images*

COACHES & MANAGEMENT

HEAD COACH Heyneke Meyer **FORWARDS COACHES** Johann van Graan & Pieter de Villiers
BACKLINE COACH Ricardo Loubscher **DEFENCE COACH** John McFarland
CONDITIONING COACH Basil Carzis **KICKING COACH** Louis Koen **TEAM MANAGER** Ian Schwartz
TEAM DOCTOR Dr Craig Roberts **PHYSIOTHERAPIST** Vivian Verwant
PHYSIOTHERAPIST René Naylor **MASSEUSE** Daliah Hurwitz **OPERATIONAL HEAD** Charles Wessels
PR & ADMIN MANAGER Annelee Murray **LOGISTICS** JJ Fredericks **TECHNICAL ANALYST** Albé Visser
COMMUNICATIONS MANAGER De Jongh Borchardt **PERFORMANCE ANALYST** Chean Roux

2013 OUTGOING TOUR

SPRINGBOK SQUAD TO WALES, SCOTLAND & FRANCE 2013

	Date of birth	Height	Weight	Province	Wales	Scotland	France	Matches	Tries	Conversions	Penalties	Drop Goals	Points
PJ Lambie	17/10/1990	1,77	87	KwaZulu-Natal	15	10	10R	3	0	5	1	0	13
J-PR Pietersen	12/07/1986	1,91	103	Panasonic Wild Knights, Japan	14	14	14	3	2	0	0	0	10
J Fourie	04/03/1983	1,90	105	Kobe Steelers, Japan	13	13	13	3	0	0	0	0	0
J de Villiers	24/02/1981	1,90	100	Western Province	12c	12c	12c	3	1	0	0	0	5
BG Habana	12/06/1983	1,79	94	Toulon, France	11	11	11	3	0	0	0	0	0
M Steyn	11/07/1984	1,86	91	Stade Francais, France	10	6R	10	3	0	3	4	0	18
PF du Preez	24/03/1982	1,82	91	Suntory Goliath, Japan	9	9	–	2	1	0	0	0	5
DJ Vermeulen	03/07/1986	1,92	90	Western Province	8	8	8	3	0	0	0	0	0
WS Alberts	11/05/1984	1,92	120	KwaZulu-Natal	7	7	7	3	1	0	0	0	5
L-FP Louw	15/06/1985	1,90	114	Bath Rugby, England	6	6	6	3	0	0	0	0	0
PR van der Merwe	03/06/1985	1,99	120	Blue Bulls	5	5	5	3	0	0	0	0	0
E Etzebeth	29/10/1991	2,03	117	Western Province	4	4R	4	3	0	0	0	0	0
JF Malherbe	14/03/1991	1,90	120	Western Province	3	3	–	2	0	0	0	0	0
BW du Plessis	22/05/1984	1,89	113	KwaZulu-Natal	2	2R	2	3	1	0	0	0	5
T Mtawarira	01/07/1985	1,88	118	KwaZulu-Natal	1	1R	1	3	0	0	0	0	0
JA Strauss	18/11/1985	1,84	111	Free State	2R	2	2R	3	0	0	0	0	0
GG Steenkamp	12/06/1981	1,89	122	Toulouse, France	1R	1	1R	3	0	0	0	0	0
CV Oosthuizen	22/03/1989	1,81	127	Free State	3R	3R	3	3	1	0	0	0	5
PS du Toit	20/08/1992	2,00	116	KwaZulu-Natal	4R	–	7R	2	0	0	0	0	0
S Kolisi	16/06/1991	1,86	99	Western Province	7R	–	19R	2	0	0	0	0	0
R Pienaar	10/03/1984	1,86	92	Ulster, Ireland	9R	9R	9	3	0	0	0	0	0
JJ Engelbrecht	22/02/1989	1,90	94	Blue Bulls	14R	12R	-	2	0	0	0	0	0
WJ le Roux	18/08/1989	1,86	88	Griquas	10R	15	15	3	1	0	0	0	5
JP Botha	22/09/1979	2,02	122	Toulon, France	-	4	4R	2	0	0	0	0	0
MC Coetzee	08/05/1991	1,90	106	KwaZulu-Natal	-	7R	–	1	0	0	0	0	0
LC Adriaanse	05/02/1988	1,81	115	Griquas	-	-	3R	1	0	0	0	0	0
J Vermaak	01/01/1985	1,75	82	Toulouse, France	-	-	x	0	0	0	0	0	0
GG Aplon	06/10/1982	1,75	80	Western Province	-	-	-	0	0	0	0	0	0
JL Goosen	27/07/1992	1,85	85	Free State	-	-	-	0	0	0	0	0	0
Z Kirchner	16/06/1984	1,84	92	Leinster, Ireland	-	-	-	0	0	0	0	0	0
JL Serfontein	15/04/1993	1,87	97	Blue Bulls	-	-	-	0	0	0	0	0	0
FBC Kirsten**	18/08/1988	1,93	120	Blue Bulls									
S Ntubeni**	18/02/1991	1,77	102	Western Province									
L Schreuder**	25/04/1990	1,84	82	Western Province									
34 Players								68	8	8	5	0	71

*Captain

**A revision of the Springbok capping policy in December 2013, and applied retrospectively to this tour, means that Kirsten, Schreuder and Ntubeni are not considered Springboks until they take the field in a Test match. Previously, all players who embarked on an overseas tour with the Springboks were awarded Springbok colours and a Springbok number, regardless of whether or not they took the field.

2013 OUTGOING TOUR

Boks 'pitch up' in Cardiff

Wales 15 South Africa 24 (halftime 12-17)

November 9, Millennium Stadium, Cardiff (66 490). Referee: ACP Rolland (Ireland)
WALES - PENALTY GOALS: Halfpenny (5).
SOUTH AFRICA - TRIES: De Villiers, B du Plessis, Du Preez. CONVERSIONS: Steyn (2), Lambie. PENALTY GOAL: Steyn

IT WAS HARDLY FLAWLESS, BUT THE Springboks passed a significant character test in beating Wales on an awful pitch at the Millennium Stadium.

South Africa had to overcome two major setbacks before completing their victory. First flyhalf Morné Steyn had to leave the field in the 18th minute due to a back spasm and then, in the 36th minute, flank Francois Louw was sin-binned for shoving Wales hooker Richard Hibbard with his elbow.

Steyn had to leave the field immediately after converting South Africa's second try by hooker Bismarck du Plessis, who was mauled over after skipper Jean de Villiers opted to go for touch rather than ask Steyn to kick for poles.

Just six minutes earlier the Boks had struck their first significant blow when De Villiers touched down. It all started thanks to the genius of left wing Bryan Habana, who dummied and then sped through the Welsh defence from deep. Du Plessis was up in support and smashed his way through the defence before off-loading to De Villiers.

The Boks led 17-6 after Du Plessis's try and were well on top, though Steyn's departure forced them into a reshuffle. Patrick Lambie moved from fullback to flyhalf, with Willie le Roux sent on to man the last outpost.

Wales also suffered a significant early blow when centre Jonathan Davies, one of the stars of the British & Irish Lions' series victory over Australia earlier in the season, had to be substituted in the 12th minute. Davies had started the match superbly, twice cutting through the Boks' midfield in the first eight minutes. South Africa conceded a breakdown penalty in the ensuing play on each occasion, allowing Wales fullback Leigh Halfpenny – the Lions' player of the series against the Wallabies – to edge his side into a 3-0 and then a 6-3 lead.

Perhaps the reintroduction of Japan-based centre Jaque Fourie had created some uncertainty in the Boks' midfield.

Having built a commanding lead, the Springboks lost their way a litte. Wales fought back bravely and edged their way closer with three penalties by Halfpenny reducing the deficit to two points by the 55th minute. But this is where the pedigree of South Africa's experienced players kicked in.

With 15 minutes left, Fourie du Preez kicked the ball down the left touchline and Fourie gathered before passing the ball back between a couple of mesmerised Welsh defenders. Du Preez cantered through to score under the posts and bring up the winning score of 24-15. It was pure genius.

A bizarre turn of events followed three minutes later when referee Alain Rolland sin-binned both Welsh loosehead Gethin Jenkins and the Boks' replacement tighthead, Coenie Oosthuizen, after a scrum had collapsed.

In truth, one could hardly blame the props for a collapsing scrum on a virtually unplayable surface. For tighthead prop Frans Malherbe these were difficult conditions in which to make his debut, but he was outstanding elsewhere in making 15 tackles.

SCORING SEQUENCE

Min	Action	Score
3	Halfpenny penalty	3-0
5	Steyn penalty	3-3
8	Halfpenny penalty	6-3
11	De Villiers try, Steyn conversion	6-10
17	B du Plessis try, Steyn conversion	6-17
25	Halfpenny penalty	9-17
34	Halfpenny penalty	12-17
55	Halfpenny penalty	15-17
62	Lambie missed penalty	15-17
65	Du Preez try, Lambie conversion	15-24

Jean de Villiers receives the winners' trophy from Prince William. *Scott Heavey/Getty Images*

WALES: SL Halfpenny, GP North, JJV Davies (MA Beck, 12)*, MS Williams, LB Williams (JW Hook, 12)*, R Priestland, WM Phillips (LD Williams, 73), TT Faletau, SK Warburton (C), DJ Lydiate (J Tipuric, 64), A-W Jones (LC Charteris, 73), BS Davies, AR Jones (SA Andrews, 31/P James, 41), RM Hibbard (KJ Owens, 64) , GD Jenkins. *Halfpenny to left-wing, Beck to outside-centre, Hook to fullback.* YELLOW CARD: *GD Jenkins, 58*

SOUTH AFRICA: PJ Lambie; J-PR Pietersen (JJ Engelbrecht, 72), J Fourie, J de Villiers (C), BG Habana; M Steyn (WJ le Roux, 18)*, PF du Preez (R Pienaar, 77), DJ Vermeulen, WS Alberts (S Kolisi, 66), L-FP Louw, PR van der Merwe, E Etzebeth (PS du Toit, 69), JF Malherbe (CV Oosthuizen, 55), BW du Plessis (JA Strauss, 66), T Mtawarira (GG Steenkamp, 66).
TEST DEBUTS: JF Malherbe, PS du Toit YELLOW CARDS: L-FP Louw, 36; CV Oosthuizen, 58. * Lambie to flyhalf, Le Roux to fullback.
NOTE: Most experienced backline for SA ever with 447 caps

Bakkies return precipitates whitewash

Scotland 0 South Africa 28 (halftime 0-21)

November 17, Murrayfield, Edinburgh (49 278). Referee: J Garces (France)

SCOTLAND - None

SOUTH AFRICA - TRIES: Alberts, Le Roux, Pietersen, Oosthuizen. **CONVERSIONS**: Lambie (4).

THE THUMBS-UP THAT FLANK FRANCOIS Louw gave from his stretcher as he was carried off as a mere precautionary measure five minutes before the end captured the essence of this Springbok victory perfectly.

In fact, one would venture to say the whitewash of Scotland deserved two thumbs up.

There had been a lingering uncertainty in the build-up brought about by two factors: South Africa had lost at Murrayfield three years previously and coach Heyneke Meyer also took a few calculated selection risks.

Among those was the choice of 34-year-old lock Bakkies Botha, who produced a performance that cemented him in Meyer's long-term plans.

Adriaan Strauss and Gurthrö Steenkamp had also been drafted in at hooker and loosehead prop in place of Bismarck du Plessis and Tendai Mtawarira respectively.

Morné Steyn had recovered from a back spasm on the eve of the kick-off, but Meyer decided to pick Patrick Lambie at flyhalf and Willie le Roux at fullback.

Le Roux's genius was at the heart of the victory, but in truth this was mostly a dominant team effort.

The Boks started superbly, carrying the ball through phase after phase before Scotland eventually couldn't take the body punches anymore. The home side conceded the penalty in their 22-metre area, but the three easy points on offer were not enough for Bok skipper Jean de Villiers.

Instead, Lambie was instructed to kick the ball out in the corner and seconds later flank Willem Alberts finished from the maul.

Alberts, who also shone the previous week against Wales, had a big first half with dominant ball-carries and tackles before being pulled off at half-time to keep him fresh for the following weekend's match against France.

The only anxiety that set in after this was that South Africa struggled for a good while to convert their continued dominance into points.

Scotland's lineout was faltering badly and they lost five of their first six throw-ins inside the first 20 minutes, which kept the ball in Bok hands.

On the one occasion where Scotland threatened to get going, there was a right mess between flyhalf Ruaridh Jackson and fullback Sean Maitland, allowing Le Roux to pounce and score the second try on the half-hour mark.

Le Roux then swung his wand to set up JP Pietersen for a delightful try. The Bok fullback broke through a gap and then kicked the ball masterfully into the right wing's path.

By half-time the score was 21-0 and there was only going to be one winner.

There was nevertheless plenty of Scottish class off the field, with the Murrayfield crowd giving the seriously ill former Bok scrumhalf, Joost van der Westhuizen, a heart-warming round of applause as he was wheeled out at half-time.

It didn't take the Boks long to sew up the match as replacement tighthead prop, Conie Oosthuizen, was driven over from a lineout maul in the 53rd minute. Oosthuizen was an injury substitution for Frans Malherbe and produced a performance that inspired confidence.

SCORING SEQUENCE

Min	Action	Score
5	Alberts try, Lambie conversion	0-7
17	Lambie missed penalty	0-7
30	Le Roux try, Lambie conversion	0-14
32	Pietersen try, Lambie conversion	0-21
53	Oosthuizen try, Lambie conversion	0-28

Duane Vermeulen takes a lineout ball against Scotland.
David Rogers/Getty Images

SCOTLAND: SD Maitland, TF Seymour (MB Evans, 65), NJ De Luca, DM Taylor, SF Lamont, RJH Jackson (D Weir, 55) GD Laidlaw (C, CP Cusiter, 69), DK Denton, JA Barclay (JW Beattie, 65), AK Strokosch, JL Hamilton, RJ Gray (JD Gray, 62), MJ Low, RW Ford (S Lawson, 55) , AG Dickinson (R Grant, 55). *UNUSED SUBSTITUTE: GDS Cross. Test debut: JD Gray. Note: RJ Gray and JD Gray are brothers*

SOUTH AFRICA: WJ Le Roux; J-PR Pietersen, J Fourie, J de Villiers (C, JJ Engelbrecht, 71)*, BG Habana; PJ Lambie, PF du Preez (R Pienaar, 65), DJ Vermeulen, WS Alberts (MC Coetzee, 41), L-FP Louw (M Steyn, 75)** , PR van der Merwe, JP Botha (E Etzebeth, 59), JF Malherbe (CV Oosthuizen, 37), JA Strauss (BW du Plessis,61), GG Steenkamp (T Mtawarira,55). ** Fourie to 12, Engelbrecht to 13. ** Steyn to outside-centre, Engelbrecht to flank. YELLOW CARD: MC Coetzee, 71. NOTE: JP Pietersen played in his 50th Test.*

Boks break their French hoodoo

France 10 South Africa 19 (halftime 7-13)

November 23, Stade de France, Paris (75 600). Referee: W Barnes (England)
FRANCE - TRY: Huget. Conversion: Parra. PENALTY GOAL: Doussain.
SOUTH AFRICA - TRY: Pietersen. CONVERSION: Steyn. PENALTY GOALS: Steyn (3), Lambie.

THE SPRINGBOKS ENDED A 16-YEAR drought in France with a victory that was a lot more convincing than the scoreboard suggested.

Prior to this, South Africa hadn't won there since the spectacular 52-10 annihilation of Les Bleus at the Parc des Princes in 1997. This victory, in the Stade de France, won't go down as a classic, but was significant on various fronts.

Perhaps the most pleasing aspect is that the Boks had moved into a zone where one could expect a consistency of performance. They completed their second successive end-of-season tour unbeaten and delivered an 83% win ratio for 2013.

South Africa could not have hoped for a better start as right wing JP Pietersen scored moments after the kick-off when he stormed down French scrumhalf Morgan Parra's kick. Flyhalf Morné Steyn converted and the nerves were settled.

Thereafter the Boks suffocated and strangled Les Bleus with their imposing defence. Time and again the French ran at them, but on each occasion the South African line held and served as a platform to transfer the pressure.

The accuracy of South Africa's kicking was another pleasing aspect of their play, with France caught in possession in deep areas on a few occasions. And, said French skipper and openside flank Thierry Dusautoir after the game, his side also came off second best at the breakdowns.

Not even the loss of lock enforcer Eben Etzebeth to an ankle injury in the 16th minute took the Boks out of their stride. Bakkies Botha was sent on and normal service resumed.

As time passed, France wilted under the pressure and Steyn's unerring boot took the score up to 13-0 shortly before half-time.

However, the home side got a lucky break in the dying seconds of the first half when the ball popped loose from a ruck. France attacked down the blind side and left wing Yoann Huget finished. Parra converted from the corner and by half-time Les Bleus were back in it at 7-13.

But any local hope that it would turn the tide proved unfounded as the Boks set about purposefully with their work in the second half.

The rewards were initially evasive. Both outside centre Jaque Fourie and openside flank Francois Louw were denied tries by Scottish television match official Iain Ramage. The latter call, it was later revealed, had been a mistake.

But the pressure eventually took its toll, allowing Steyn to strike a crucial penalty from over 40 metres on the hour to give the Boks a nine-point buffer.

One would have expected the yellow-carding of French frontranker Thomas Domingo in the 68th minute to be the catalyst for the Boks to drive home their advantage. However, Louw was himself sin-binned for a bit of foul play and, with seven minutes left, France's replacement scrumhalf, Jean-Marc Doussain, reduced the deficit to six points.

It spurred the Boks into action and Patrick Lambie, on for Steyn, closed out the game with a penalty two minutes from time.

SCORING SEQUENCE

Min	Action	Score
1	Pietersen try, Steyn conversion	0-7
11	Parra missed penalty	0-7
27	Steyn penalty	0-10
39	Steyn penalty	0-13
39	Huget try, Parra conversion	7-13
60	Steyn penalty	7-16
73	Doussain penalty	10-16
78	Lambie penalty	10-19

JP Pietersen celebrates his early try against France.
David Rogers/Getty Images/Gallo Images

FRANCE: B Dulin, S Guitone, F Fritz (M Bastareaud, 60), W Fofana, Y Huget, R Tales (F Michalak, 75), M Parra (J-M Doussain, 67), D Chouly, W Lauret (Y Nyanga, 70), T Dusatoir (C, Y Forestier, 72-79), Y Maestri (S Vahaamahinga, 50), P Pape, N Mas (R Slimani, 57), B Kayser (D Szarzewski, 47), Y Forestier (T Domingo, 41). *YELLOW CARD: T Domingo, 68*

SOUTH AFRICA: WJ Le Roux (PJ Lambie 57-61); J-PR Pietersen, J Fourie, J de Villiers (C), BG Habana; M Steyn (PJ Lambie, 72), R Pienaar, DJ Vermeulen, WS Alberts (PS du Toit, 68), L-FP Louw, PR van der Merwe, E Etzebeth (JP Botha, 16/S Kolisi, 75)*, CV Oosthuizen (LC Adriaanse, 74), BW du Plessis (JA Strauss, 67), T Mtawarira (GG Steenkamp, 57).
*UNUSED SUBSTITUTE: J Vermaak. TEST DEBUT: LC Adriaanse. YELLOW CARD: L-FP Louw, 73. * Du Toit to lock, Kolisi to flank.*

IRB JUNIOR WORLD CHAMPIONSHIP

Junior Boks lose crown but finish on high

SOUTH AFRICA MIGHT HAVE LOST their status as Under-20 world champions by the narrowest of margins but you would be hard-pressed to find too many unkind words spoken about the Junior Springboks after the class of 2013 lifted the collective gloom of South African supporters in the best possible way: with a sensational victory over the old enemy.

Coach Dawie Theron's team surrendered their crown in Vannes, France, after a nail-biting 18-17 semi-final defeat to Wales – a match that turned on the bounce of the ball late in the game, when the South Africans, who had twice come from behind, looked to have done enough to advance to their second final in as many years.

Just a few days later, the defeat – or at least the bitter taste that followed it – had been largely forgotten after the Junior Boks produced a comeback of Lazarus proportions in the third-place play-off against New Zealand, winning 41-34 after trailing 21-0 after half an hour.

Theron rightly praised the fighting spirit displayed by his team against a Junior All Blacks side who, in the process, lost to their great rivals in green and gold for the second year in a row.

South Africa scored three tries in the space of seven minutes late in the first half to throw the game back into the melting pot and sew seeds of doubt in the minds of the four-time champions, who found themselves outplayed in the final quarter of a memorable match.

"The boys displayed that typical South African fighting spirit, even when New Zealand threatened to come back near the end," said Theron afterwards. "For us, this was such a vital match to win because of the manner in which we lost our semi-final. This was a great contest against a very good New Zealand team, and I am so proud of the boys.

"Yes, we did not play in the final, but we did manage to beat England, the current Six Nations champions, France in front of their own supporters and we got the better of New Zealand."

Delighted skipper Ruan Steenkamp said his advice to his retreating team-mates early on was to keep believing in themselves. "We made a terrible start and paid the price for some silly errors," he said. "But we managed to get some pride back. Any win is great against New Zealand."

Nevertheless the South Africans will lament their missed chances in the semi-final against Wales, when twice they reeled in their opponents. Lock forward Irne Herbst collected a short throw at the front of the line-out to crash over for the first try and give South Africa a 7-6 lead on the half hour. Then, replacement flanker Kwagga Smith reclaimed the lead for South Africa with their second try on the hour to make it 14-11.

Handré Pollard converted both tries and added a penalty to give the Junior Boks a 17-11 lead with less than five minutes remaining. However, Wales right wing Ashley Evans dived on flyhalf Sam Davies' chip into the in-goal area and Davies then converted from wide out on the right to give Wales a last-gasp victory.

It was a devastating way to lose the title they had won at Newlands in Cape Town a year earlier, but Theron said afterwards that the foundation for future success at Under-20 level had been laid. "Apart from the loss against Wales, we managed to beat New Zealand and England twice in two years," he said. "I regard these victories as vital stepping stones for the team, because New Zealand were dominating the competition just a short while ago while England are so dominant in the Six Nations."

GAME BREAKER...SA U20 wing Luther Obi was in fine form against the Junior All Blacks.
Roger Sedres/Gallo Images

IRB JUNIOR WORLD CHAMPIONSHIP

FINAL LOG

Pool A	P	W	D	D	PF	PA	TF	TA	B	Pts
SOUTH AFRICA	3	3	0	0	154	43	22	6	1	13
England	3	2	0	1	163	37	23	3	2	10
France	3	1	0	2	70	59	9	6	2	6
USA	3	0	0	3	3	251	0	39	0	0
Pool B	**P**	**W**	**D**	**D**	**PF**	**PA**	**TF**	**TA**	**B**	**Pts**
New Zealand	3	3	0	0	104	42	14	4	2	14
Ireland	3	2	0	1	91	49	10	6	2	10
Australia	3	1	0	2	71	45	10	4	3	7
Fiji	3	0	0	3	21	151	2	22	0	0
Pool C	**P**	**W**	**D**	**D**	**PF**	**PA**	**TF**	**TA**	**B**	**Pts**
Wales	3	3	0	0	93	44	9	4	1	13
Argentina	3	2	0	1	92	54	9	4	2	10
Scotland	3	1	0	2	70	103	9	11	2	6
Samoa	3	0	0	3	52	106	6	14	2	2

FINAL STANDINGS
1. England
2. Wales
3. SA
4. New Zealand
5. France
6. Argentina
7. Australia
8. Ireland
9. Samoa
10. Scotland
11. Fiji
12. USA

MATCH RESULTS & SCORERS

South Africa 97 USA 0 *(halftime 54-0)*
June 5. Stade Henri Desgrange, La Roche-sur-Yon. Referee: Shuhei Kubo (Japan)
SOUTH AFRICA - TRIES: Senatla (4), Kriel (2), Geduld (2), Obi (2), Willemse (2), Beerwinkel, Kolbe, Du Toit, Steenkamp **CONS:** Du Preez (6), Pollard. **PEN:** Pollard.
Kolbe *(Kriel, 41)*, Obi, Geduld *(Swanepoel, 41)*, Pollard, Senatla, Du Preez, Ungerer *(Venter, 69)*, Steenkamp (C), Du Plessis *(Davis, 64)*, Smit, Visser *(Smith, 15)*, Herbst, De Bruin *(Coetzee, 41)*, Du Toit *(Willemse, 41)*, Beerwinkel *(Sithole, 69)*.
USA - None
Conor Kearns, Noah Tarrant, Mike Teo, Eukalafi Okusi, Lemoto Fillkitonga *(Gavin Brown, 55)*, Liam Bourke *(Jared Stewart, 19-27. 41)*, Tom Bliss 9 *(C, Alex Taefu, 76)*, Ross Deacon *(Alex Goff, 45)*, Vili Tolutau, Zachary Bonte *(Brendan Hardiman, 47)*, Christian Ostberg, Teli Veamtahau, Henry Hall *(Solomone Anitema, 61)*, Cameron Falcon *(Casper Huizenga, 61)*, Christopher Banks *(Korbin Lindell, 61)*.

South Africa 31 England 24 *(halftime 21-7)*
June 9. Stade Henri Desgrange, La Roche-sur-Yon. Referee: Mike Fraser (NZ)
SOUTH AFRICA - TRIES: Senatla (2), Du Plessis. **CONS:** Du Preez (2). **PENS:** Du Preez (4).
Kolbe *(Kriel, 66)*, Obi, Geduld *(Swanepoel, 31)*, Pollard, Senatla, Du Preez, Ungerer *(Venter, 59)*, Steenkamp (C), Du Plessis, Smit, Visser, Herbst *(YC, 75)*, De Bruin *(Coetzee, 51)*, Du Toit *(Willemse, 65)*, Beerwinkel *(Sithole, 69)*.
UNUSED SUBS: Davis, Kirsten.
ENGLAND - TRIES: Stooke, Sloan, Purdy. **CONS:** Slade (3). **PEN:** Slade.
Anthony Watson *(Henry Purdy, 41)*, Ben Howard, Harry Sloan, Sam Hill, Jack Nowell, Henry Slade, Alex Day *(Calum Braley, 47)*, Jack Clifford (C), Matt Hankin *(Joel Conlon, 66)*, Ross Moriarty, Dominic Barrow *(Tom Price, 59/ YC, 75)*, Elliott Stooke, Scott Wilson, Luke Cowan-Dickie, Danny Hobbs-Awoyemi *(Alec Hepburn, 59)*.
UNUSED SUBS: Scott Spurling, Tom Smallbone, Ollie Devoto.

IRB JUNIOR WORLD CHAMPIONSHIP

MATCH RESULTS & SCORERS

South Africa 26, France 19 *(halftime 8-7)*
June 13. Stade Henri Desgrange, La Roche-sur-Yon. Referee: Marius Mitreal (Italy)
SOUTH AFRICA - TRIES: Kolbe, Swanepoel, Obi. **CON**: Pollard. **PEN**: Pollard (3).
Kolbe, Obi *(Kriel, 66)*, Swanepoel, Janse van Rensburg, Senatla, Polloard, Venter, Steenkamp *(C, Davis, 11-17)*, Du Plessis, Smit, Visser *(Kirsten, 71)*, Herbst, Coetzee *(Martinus, 57)*, Du Toit *(Willemse, 51)*, Sithole (Beerwinkel, 61). *UNUSED SUBS: Du Preez, Williams.*
FRANCE - TRIES: Serin, Taulegine, Regards. **CONS**: Serin, Selponi.
Teddy Thomas, Gabriel Lacroix, Ettienne Dussartre *(Florian Vialelle, 54)*, Thibault Regard, Stephen Parez, Enzo Selponi *(Francois Bouvier, 75)*, Bastien Duhalde *(Baptiste Serin, 59)*, Marco Taulegne *(Johan Allouat, 52)*, Alban Placine *(Matieu Babilot, 48)*, Yacouba Camara, Jean-Baptiste Singer *(Oleg Ischenko, 75)*, Paul Jedrasiak (C), Khatchik Vartanov *(Alexis Valette, 66)*, Chris Tolofua *(Romain Ruffenach, 66)*, Cyrill Baille.

South Africa 17, Wales 18 *(halftime 7-6) (Semi-Final)*
June 18, Stade de la Rabine, Vannes. Referee: Luke Pearce (England)
SOUTH AFRICA - TRIES: Smith, Herbst. **CONS**: Pollard (2). **PEN**: Pollard.
Kolbe, Obi, Swanepoel *(Geduld, 41)*, Pollard, Senatla, Du Preez, Ungerer *(Williams, 70)*, Steenkamp (C), Du Plessis, Smit *(Smith, 18)*, Visser, Herbst, De Bruin, Du Toit *(Willemse, 63)*, Beerwinkel. *UNUSED SUBS: Sithole, Davis, Kriel, Coetzee.*
WALES - TRIES: Evans, Jenkins. **CON**: Davies. **PENS**: Davies (2).
Jordan Williams, Ashley Jay Evans, Steffan Hughes *(Thomas Pascoe, 76)*, Jack Dixon, Hallam Amos *(Aaron Warren, 70)*, Sam Davies, Rhodri Williams *(Joshua Davies, 75)*, Ieuan Jones *(James Benjamin, 80)*, Ellis Jenkins (C), Sion Bennett *(Daniel Thomas, 70)*, Rhodri Hughes *(Daniel Suter, 80)*, Jack Jones, Nicky Thomas, Ethan Lewis *(Elliott Dee, 41)*, Gareth Thomas *(Thomas Davies, 67)*.

South Africa 41 New Zealand 34 *(halftime 21-26) (Third place Play-off)*
June 23, Stade de la Rabine, Vannes. Referee: Dudley Phillips (Ireland).
SOUTH AFRICA - TRIES: Smith, De Bruin, Obi, Steenkamp, Senatla, Ungerer. **CONS**: Pollard (4). **PEN**: Pollard.
Kolbe, Obi, Kriel, Janse van Rensburg *(Du Preez, 54)*, Senatla, Pollard, Ungerer, Davis *(Smith, 47)*, Du Plessis, Steenkamp (C), Visser, Herbst, De Bruin *(Coetzee, 61)*, Willemse *(Du Toit, 25)*, Sithole. *UNUSED SUBS: Beerwinkel, Stander, Williams, Swanepoel.*
NEW ZEALAND - TRIES: Visinia (2), Webber, Manihera, Edwards. **CON**: Hickey (3). **P**: Hickey.
Joe Webber, Penikolo Latu, Michael Collins, Teihorangi Walden *(Leroy van Dam, 72)*, Lolagi Visinia, Simon Hickey *(Jade Te Rure, 57)*, Sheridan Rangihuna *(Tayler Adams, 41)*, Joseph Edwards, Ardie Savea *(C, Scott Scrafton, 70)*, Jordan Manihera *(YC, 52)*, Patrick Tuipolutou *(Christopher Vui, 68)*, Scott Barrett, Sione Mafileo *(Boyd Wiggins, 76)*, Nick Grogan *(Kalafi Pongi, 61/ YC 61)*, Donald Brighouse *(Daniel Lienert-Brown, 55)*.

IRB JUNIOR WORLD CHAMPIONSHIP

TOURNAMENT RESULTS

JUNE 05					JUNE 18 9th place Semi Final			
SOUTH AFRICA	97	USA	0		Samoa	19	Fiji	18
Ireland	19	Australia	15		Scotland	39	USA	3
Argentina	44	Scotland	13		**5th place Semi Final**			
New Zealand	59	Fiji	6		Argentina	22	Australia	15
Wales	42	Samoa	3		France	9	Ireland	8
France	6	England	30		**Semi Finals**			
JUNE 09					SOUTH AFRICA	17	Wales	18
SOUTH AFRICA	31	England	24		New Zealand	21	England	33
Ireland	46	Fiji	3		**June 23 11th Place Play-Off**			
Wales	26	Scotland	21		Fiji	46	USA	12
New Zealand	14	Australia	10		**9th Place Play-Off**			
France	45	USA	3		Samoa	33	Scotland	24
Argentina	28	Samoa	16		**7th Place Play-Off**			
JUNE 13					Australia	28	Ireland	17
SOUTH AFRICA	26	France	19		**5th Place Play-Off**			
England	109	USA	0		France	37	Argentina	34
Scotland	36	Samoa	33		**3rd Place Play-Off**			
Australia	46	Fiji	12		SOUTH AFRICA	41	New Zealand	34
Wales	25	Argentina	20		**Final**			
New Zealand	31	Ireland	26		England	23	Wales	15

LEADING SCORERS

POINTS

Patricio Fernandez	Argentina	82
Sam Davies	Wales	61
Henry Slade	England	55
Tommy Allan	Scotland	39
Emori Waqa	Fiji	39
Seabelo Senatla	South Africa	35
Handre Pollard	South Africa	34
Simon Hickey	New Zealand	32
Vincent Mallett	France	32
Luke Burton	Australia	31

TRIES

Seabelo Senatla	South Africa	7
Luther Obi	South Africa	4
Rory Scholes	Ireland	4
Lolagi Visinia	New Zealand	4
Emori Waqa	Fiji	4
Mark Bennett	Scotland	3
Alex Day	England	3
Ashley Evans	Wales	3
Epalahame Faiva	New Zealand	3
Patricio Fernandez	Argentina	3
Pablo Matera	Argentina	3
Ross Moriarty	England	3
Melani Nanai	Samoa	3
Alex Northam	Australia	3
Henry Purdy	England	3

JUNIOR SPRINGBOK SQUAD

	Position	Date of birth	Height	Weight	Province
BACKS					
C (Cheslin) Kolbe	Fullback	28/10/1993	1,71	78	Western Province
JA (Jesse) Kriel	Fullback	15/02/1994	1,86	95	Blue Bulls
LBS (Luther) Obi	Wing	29/04/1993	1,75	86	Leopards
SB (Seabelo) Senatla	Wing	10/02/1993	1,86	76	Free State
JG (Justin) Geduld	Centre	01/10/1993	1,75	70	Western Province
H (Handre) Pollard	Centre	11/03/1994	1,88	94	Blue Bulls
AE (Dries) Swanepoel	Centre	19/02/1993	1,84	92	Blue Bulls
R (Rohan) Janse van Rensburg	Centre	11/09/1994	1,86	100	Blue Bulls
RJ (Robert) du Preez	Flyhalf	30/07/1993	1,92	95	Sharks
K (Percy) Williams	Scrumhalf	05/06/1993	1,60	70	Golden Lions
S (Stefan) Ungerer	Scrumhalf	23/11/1993	1,85	88	Sharks
HC (Hanco) Venter	Scrumhalf	07/01/1993	1,76	82	Sharks
FORWARDS					
R (Ruan) Steenkamp (Capt)	No 8	02/02/1993	1,82	92	Blue Bulls
JH (Jannie) Stander	Flanker	21/04/1993	1,96	107	Golden Lions
WHJ (Jacques) du Plessis	Flanker	12/08/1993	2,01	119	Blue Bulls
RA (Roelof) Smit	Flanker	11/01/1993	1,90	90	Blue Bulls
AS (Kwagga) Smith	Flanker	11/06/1993	1,80	80	Golden Lions
JC (Jannes) Kirsten	Flanker	01/12/1993	1,96	107	Blue Bulls
D (Dennis) Visser	Lock	20/01/1993	2,00	120	Blue Bulls
IP (Irne) Herbst	Lock	04/05/1993	1,97	117	Blue Bulls
A (Aidon) Davis	Lock	29/04/1994	1,91	100	EP Kings
DR (Devon) Martinus	Prop	28/01/1993	1,86	120	Golden Lions
L (Luan) de Bruin	Prop	13/02/1993	1,83	124	Free State
A (Andrew) Beerwinkel	Prop	05/03/1993	1,86	115	Blue Bulls
SMS (Sithembiso) Sithole	Prop	31/03/1993	1,79	104	Sharks
M (Marne) Coetzee	Prop	17/09/1993	1,80	114	Blue Bulls
OJJ (Jacques) du Toit	Hooker	19/11/1993	1,86	102	Free State
ME (Michael) Willemse	Hooker	14/02/1993	1,84	103	Western Province

28 Players

COACHES & MANAGEMENT

Dawie Theron **COACH** Brendan Venter **ASSISTANT COACH** Nazeem Adams **ASSISTANT COACH** Jonathan Mokoena **MANAGER** Aneurin Robyn **PHYSIO** Phato Cele **DOCTOR** Norman Laker **VIDEO ANALYST** Yusuf Jackson **SARU REPRESENTATIVE** Warren Adams **CONDITIONING** Rayaan Adriaanse **MEDIA**

APPEARANCES & SCORERS IN 2013

	USA	England	France	Wales (SF)	New Zealand (3rd place)	Matches	Tries	Conversions	Penalties	Drop Goals	Points
Cheslin Kolbe	15	15	15	15	15	5	2	–	–	–	10
Luther Obi	14	14	14	14	14	5	4	–	–	–	20
Justin Geduld	13	13	–	13R	–	3	2	–	–	–	10
Handre Pollard	12	12	10	12	10	5	–	8	6	–	34
Seabelo Senatla	11	11	11	11	11	5	7	–	–	–	35
Robert du Preez	10	10	x	10	12R	4	–	8	4	–	28
Stefan Ungerer	9	9	–	9	9	4	1	–	–	–	5
Ruan Steenkamp	8c	8c	8c	8c	6c	5	2	–	–	–	10
Jacques du Plessis	7	7	7	7	7	5	1	–	–	–	5
Roelof Smit	6	6	6	6	–	4	–	–	–	–	0
Dennis Visser	5	5	5	5	5	5	–	–	–	–	0
Irne Herbst	4	4	4	4	4	5	1	–	–	–	5
Luan de Bruin	3	3	–	3	3	4	1	–	–	–	5
Jacques du Toit	2	2	2	2	2R	5	1	–	–	–	5
Andrew Beerwinkel	1	1	1R	1	x	4	1	–	–	–	5
Michael Willemse	2R	2R	2R	2R	2	5	2	–	–	–	10
Sithembiso Sithole	1R	1R	1	x	1	4	–	–	–	–	0
Aidon Davis	7R	x	8R	x	8	3	–	–	–	–	0
Kwagga Smith	5R	–	–	6R	8R	3	2	–	–	–	10
Hanco Venter	9R	9R	9	–	–	3	–	–	–	–	0
Dries Swanepoel	13R	13R	13	13	x	4	1	–	–	–	5
Jesse Kriel	15R	15R	14R	x	13	4	2	–	–	–	10
Marne Coetzee	3R	3R	3	x	3R	4	–	–	–	–	0
Jannes Kirsten	–	x	5R	–	–	1	–	–	–	–	0
Rohan J van Rensburg	–	–	12	–	12	2	–	–	–	–	0
Percy Williams	–	–	x	9R	x	1	–	–	–	–	0
Devon Martinus	–	–	3R	–	–	1	–	–	–	–	0
Jannie Stander	–	–	–	–	x	0	–	–	–	–	0
28 players						**103**	**30**	**16**	**10**	**0**	**212**

R = Substitute; *x* = Unused Substitute; *(c)* = Captain.

TOURNAMENT WINNERS & SA PERFORMANCES*

2008	New Zealand won in Wales	SA 3rd	Captain: Gerrit-Jan van Velze	Coach: Eric Sauls
2009	New Zealand won in Japan	SA 3rd	Captain: Robert Ebersohn	Coach: Eric Sauls
2010	New Zealand won in Argentina	SA 3rd	Captain: CJ Stander	Coach: Eric Sauls
2011	New Zealand won in Italy	SA 5th	Captain: Arno Botha	Coach: Dawie Theron
2012	South Africa won in SA	SA 1st	Captain: Wiaan Liebenberg	Coach: Dawie Theron
2013	England won in France	SA 3rd	Captain: Ruan Steenkamp	Coach: Dawie Theron

*This competition replaced the Under 19 Rugby World Championship and Under 21 Rugby World Championship.

HAIR WE GO...Seabelo Senatla was a constant thorn in the flesh of opposition teams. Roger Sedres/Gallo Images

SPRINGBOK SEVENS

Inconsistency hampers Sevens Boks

THE 2012/13 HSBC SEVENS WORLD Series promised much, but only in patches did the South African team managed to deliver on those. Instead it became a series where the performance graph showed the highs of being the only team to win three tournaments to the lows of not even making the Cup quarter-finals on two occasions, something that is just not palatable in the South African mental set-up.

It still delivered an overall second place, but so high were the standards demanded that in a season review, SARU and coach Paul Treu reached consensus that the coach's contract would not be renewed when it expired at the end of October 2013.

Former Springbok Sevens captain and 32 HSBC tournament veteran Neil Powell was subsequently appointed as the new Springbok Sevens coach for the 2013/14 season and beyond.

The series started on a positive note for the South Africans. They played with great speed and precision at the Gold Coast 7s, the opening Australian leg of the series.

Very convincing wins on day one over Canada (38-0), USA (33-5) and New Zealand (31-21) confirmed the team as pool A winners and strong favourites for the title. They got past France in the Cup quarter-finals (26-14), but then lost out to bogey team Fiji in the semis, losing 21-10 after two lapses in concentration allowed the Islanders to race away to score.

A great comeback against Kenya (41-7) resulted in a third-place finish as well as the most tries scored. Fiji went on to beat New Zealand 32-14 in the final.

As multiple winners of the Dubai Sevens and with good momentum from the Gold Coast, the team arrived in the United Arab Emirates with high hopes.

What was to follow was hard to predict. They opened their pool C campaign with a win over England, but then slumped to a shock 12-10 defeat to Portugal. A 10-5 loss to Samoa dumped South Africa into the Bowl competition. Even here, it was a battle.

They managed wins against Russia and the USA, but lost to Argentina in a disappointing showing for a lowly bottom-eight finish in the tournament. Kyle Brown also sustained an injury that ruled him out of the remainder of the Series. Samoa won the title by beating New Zealand.

Tournament three – the Nelson Mandela Bay South African Sevens – saw Frankie Horne take over the captaincy and equalling Fabian Juries' record for most tournaments on the circuit. The home crowd's expectations were fuelled on day one, with the South Africans scoring convincing wins over Samoa, France and Australia to top Pool A. They moved into the semi-finals of the Cup by beating USA in the quarter-finals, but in a tight affair, were knocked out by New Zealand 12-5. The Kiwi team went on to beat France in the final, with South Africa outclassing Argentina 35-0 to take third.

Talk before the Wellington event in New Zealand, where South Africa last won a decade ago, was to re-create history, but it turned out to be another disaster for Treu and his troops.

Opening losses to Samoa and Canada almost dumped the team out of contention early and thanks to other pool results and a 21-0 win over Wales, the Springbok Sevens scraped into the Cup competition.

A one-point defeat to fellow Africans Kenya compounded the misery of losing debutant Justin Geduld to a hand injury. A 28-12 loss to Australia in the Plate semi-final again resulted in an early shower at the tournament hotel. England became the fourth team in as many tournaments to come out tops, this time beating a plucky Kenya.

A week in rugby is a long time, but few could pre-

The Springbok Sevens team savour the sweet taste of victory in Glasgow. *Ian MacNicol/Getty Images*

SPRINGBOK SEVENS

dict the South African comeback in Las Vegas. Joined by a fit-again Cecil Afrika and Branco du Preez, the Springbok Sevens team totally dominated the USA Sevens tournament. They opened up strongly against Uruguay (45-0), reversed their loss to Canada a week before (17-5) and beat Kenya 15-5 to top the pool. Another win over Wales (26-0) and suddenly they contesting for a place in the final.

Scores were tied 7-7 at half-time of their semi-final against Samoa, as it was when the final whistle sounded. In extra time, a scorching run by Seabelo Senatla booked their first final spot of the Series.

In the final, they totally dominated New Zealand with a 40-21 win. Senatla, who had debuted in Wellington, had a fantastic tournament and his pace broke his opponents. South Africa's win also resulted in five different winners in the opening five tournaments.

There was real optimism that the Hong Kong bogey could be broken when the Series moved to Asia for the next two tournaments. Alas, massive disappointment was the only dish on the menu as the inconsistency in performance, selection and commitment hampered the squad.

They opened their Pool A campaign with a 21-0 loss to Argentina and dropped day two's opening match to Australia 21-12. A 31-0 win over Wales was scant reward and they missed a second Cup quarter-final spot in three tournaments.

Their Bowl campaign started well with a 28-14 win over Spain in the quarters, but they were dumped out of the tournament in their semi-final, where England scored a 26-14 win. The tournament was won by Fiji, who came from behind to beat Wales.

Japan was not expected to bring any joy to the Springbok Sevens team a week later following their 5-2-3 performance in China, but Afrika, who missed Hong Kong due to a chronic knee ailment, joined the side again and it paid dividends.

They lost to Fiji 29-12 in the opening Pool A match, but a dramatic turnaround was about to happen.

Wins over Portugal (12-0) and Spain (42-7) broke the shackles and they qualified for the Cup stages.

Two close wins over Samoa (19-12) and France (14-12) in the quarters and semis were overshadowed by another stellar showing in the final, again against New Zealand.

The Kiwis jumped into an early 12-0 lead, only to be outplayed in the second half. Treu's troops romped home to a 24-19 win and a second tournament victory.

With the win in Japan, South Africa moved into second spot on the log for the first time, but with two tournaments left, it became clear that the ultra-consistent New Zealand were going to be hard to catch in the title race.

The Springboks found their groove in what was to be a 13-match winning streak and when they left Glasgow with the Cup, they became the only team to win consecutive tournaments as well as three in all.

Scotland probably provided the best effort of the series for Frankie Horne and his men. They beat Kenya (17-14), Canada (17-14) and Samoa (27-0) on day one. In the Cup quarters they overcame USA 22-5, outplayed England 24-17 in the semis and won the title by beating New Zealand (again) 28-21 in the final. The Kiwis did however clinch the overall title by reaching the final.

London was a special tournament for longstanding servant Horne, as he became the first player ever to play in 50 consecutive tournaments. This was however to be the only emotional high for the team. They did open with wins over Australia (5-0) and France 17-14, but after that, the tournament fell flat for South Africa.

They lost to the USA (19-12) in pool play and in the Cup quarters missed the trick against England (19-14). A second loss against the USA (22-5) in the Plate semis was a disappointing way to finish the series.

Seven new players were introduced to the wider WSS audiences. Warren Whiteley, Ruwellyn Isbell (Gold Coast), Kevin Luiters (Dubai), Seabelo Senatla, Justin Geduld (Wellington), WJ Strydom (Edinburgh) and Werner Kok (London) represented their country for the first time in the 2012/13 series.

Cornal Hendricks (38 tries, 130 points) was the leading point-scorer and Chris Dry (17 tries) also weighed in with some telling contributions.

BY JJ HARMSE

IRB SEVENS WORLD SERIES PERFORMANCES & LOG 2012-2013
(Only top 15 countries listed)

Team	Aus	Dub	SA	NZ	USA	HK	JAP	SCO	LON	Points
New Zealand	19	19	22	17	19	17	19	19	22	173
South Africa	17	7	17	10	22	5	22	22	10	132
Fiji	22	10	12	7	15	22	10	10	13	121
Samoa	10	22	7	15	17	13	10	5	5	104
Kenya	15	17	5	19	1	15	5	7	15	99
England	7	3	5	22	5	8	8	17	17	92
Wales	5	13	13	3	10	19	5	15	8	91
Australia	10	1	8	13	3	10	17	8	19	89
France	12	15	19	5	8	3	15	3	7	87
Argentina	13	8	15	10	7	2	7	12	10	84
United States	2	5	10	1	10	5	13	13	12	71
Canada	5	12	1	8	13	12	3	10	5	69
Scotland	3	5	1	12	12	1	12	5	0	51
Portugal	1	10	10	1	1	10	1	1	0	35
Spain	8	2	3	5	5	1	1	1	0	26

2012/13 SERIES TOURNAMENT SUMMARY

TOURNAMENT 1:
Gold Coast, Australia, 13-14 October 2012
With two new caps, Ruwellyn Isbell and Reuben Johannes, the Boks did very well in the pool stage by staying undefeated including beating New Zealand 31-21. The second day was less successful when they beat France in the Cup quarter-final but then lost to Fiji in the semi-final. They bounced back to beat Kenya 41-7 to claim the third place. Cornal Hendriks continued his good form for the Blitzbokke, making use of his pace and strength to score eight tries, which made him the joint top try scorer. Fiji defeated New Zealand 31-14 to win the Cup final.
SA RESULTS: bt Canada 38-0; bt USA 33-5; bt New Zealand 31-21; bt France 26-14 (QF Cup); lost Fiji 10-21 (SF Cup); bt Kenya 41-7 (3rd place)

TOURNAMENT 2:
Dubai, 30 November – 1 December 2012
It turned out to be the worst tournament in more than a decade for the 'Boks. Cecil Afrika was not available due to an due to a niggling knee injury, then Branco du Preez suffered a hamstring injury during training In Dubai and finally captain Kyle Brown suffered a broken ankle in the first half of their pool encounter with England. Losses to Portugal and Samoa meant that they were relegated to the Bowl competition where they lost to Argentina in the semi-final. Samoa won the Cup final by beating New Zealand 26-15.
SA RESULTS: bt England 19-10; lost Portugal 10-12; lost Samoa 5-10; bt Russia 25-12 (QF Bowl); bt USA 22-14 (SF Bowl); lost Argentina 10-14 (Final Bowl)

TOURNAMENT 3:
Nelson Mandela Bay, South Africa
8-9 December 2012
Frankie Horne, the new captain, equaled the record of 44 tournaments held by Fabian Juries as the most capped Springbok Sevens player of all time. The Blitzbokke performed much better in front of their home crowd and went undefeated until the lost their semi-final against New Zealand in the final minute. New Zealand won the Cup final against France 47-12 and SA ended 3rd after defeating Argentina 35-0.
SA RESULTS: bt Samoa 29-7; bt France 12-5; bt Australia 17-7; bt USA 17-7 (QF Cup); lost New Zealand 5-12 (SF Cup); bt Argentina 35-0 (3rd place)

TOURNAMENT 4:
Wellington, New Zealand, 1-2 February 2013

Injuries to several key players opened the door for to two 19-year old debutantes in Justin Geduld and Seabelo Senatlo. They were made to work extremely hard for a quarterfinal spot after losing to Samoa and Canada in the pool games. They were only able to qualify thanks to a better points difference courtesy of a 21-0 win over Wales in their final pool match. England beat Kenya 24-19 to win the Cup final.

SA RESULTS: lost Samoa 10-19; lost Canada 15-26; bt Wales 21-0; lost Kenya 20-21 (QF Cup); lost Australia 12-28 (SF Plate).

TOURNAMENT 5:
United States, February 10-12, 2012

The 'Boks produced a dramatic turnaround to claim their first World Sevens Series title in 21 Months when they Beat New Zealand in the cup final. Earlier the media speculated that Las Vegas could be a moment of Paul Treu's sevens coaching career after some below par performances in this series. The return of Branco Du Preez in the place of injured Justin Geduld, provided the spark the Blitzbokke so desperately needed.

SA RESULTS: bt Uruguay 45-0; bt Canada 17-5; bt Kenya 15-5; bt Wales 26-0 (QF Cup); bt Samoa 12-5 (SF Cup); bt New Zealand 40-21 (Final Cup)

TOURNAMENT 6:
Hong Kong, China 22-24 March 2013

The up-and-down performances of the Blitzbokke continued. Losses to Argentina and Australia had them ending up in the Bowl competition where they were eliminated in the semi-finals. Fiji won the Cup final by defeating Wales 26-19.

SA RESULTS: Lost Argentina 0-21; lost Australia 12-21; bt Wales 31-0; bt Spain 28-14 (QF Bowl); lost England 14-26 (SF Bowl).

TOURNAMENT 7:
Tokyo, Japan, 30-31 March 2013

The inconsistency of the team continued but at least gave a positive result in this tournament. The 'Boks achieved consecutive victories in Cup finals against New Zealand for the first time in 14 years,. They recovered from a loss against Fiji in their opening pool game to reach the final. Seabelo Senatla turned out to be the star for the Boks when he scored two long range tries in critical moments against Samoa and France respectively.

SA RESULTS: lost Fiji 12-29; bt Portugal 12-0; bt Spain 42-7; bt Samoa 19-12 (QF Cup); bt France 14-12 (SF Cup); Bt New Zealand 24-19 (Final Cup).

TOURNAMENT 8:
Glasgow, Scotland 4-5 May 2013

South Africa won their third Cup final in the 2012/13 series beating MNew Zealand 28-21 in the title decider. This makes South Africa the only team in the series to have won three tournaments. The win could not stop New Zealand from winning the overall 2012/12 series. Marius van der Westhuizen became the first referee from a country to handle a final where his compatriots played in.

SA RESULTS: bt Kenya 17-14; bt Canada 17-14; bt Samoa 27-0; bt USA 22-5 (QF Cup); bt England 24-17 (SF Cup); bt New Zealand 28-21 (Final Cup).

TOURNAMENT 9:
London, England 11-12 May 2013

Sevens captain Frankie Horne became the first South African to play 50 tournaments in the HSBC Sevens World Series. The 'Boks only reached the quarter-finals due to their favourable points difference. They lost to England in the cup quarter-final in additional time and then suffered defeat to the USA in the Plate semi-final. New Zealand won the Cup final (and the series) by beating Australia 47-12.

SA RESULTS: bt Australia 5-0; bt France 17-14; lost USA 12-19; lost England 14-19 (QF Cup); lost USA 5-22 (SF Plate).

RUGBY WORLD CUP, Moscow, Russia
28-30 June 2013

Frankie Horne was injured and not available for the tournament but Kyle Brown returned to take over the captaincy. Despite doing well in their pool games they could not get past Fiji in the quarter-

SPRINGBOK SEVENS

finals. A conversion attempt from Cecil Afrika narrowly missed the upright after Sithole scored with less than a minute of play to go. Kyle Brown was suspended for two games (quarter-final & first match of the World Games) after the Scotland pool match for contact with eyes or eye area. New Zealand won the RWC sevens title by beating England 33-0 in the final.

SA RESULTS: bt Russia 31-0; bt Japan 33-0; bt Scotland 41-0; lost Fiji 10-12 (QF)

2013 WORLD GAMES, Cali, Colombia
25 July to 4 August 2013

Only 8 teams competed in this tournament and it kicked of with 4 quarter-finals. The team was coached by former SA sevens stalwarts Vuyo Zangqa (Head coach) and Neil Powell (Assistant coach). The Springbok Sevens won the gold medal match by 33-24 against Argentina. This was the first gold medal for the "Boks after winning bronze and silver at the previous two World Games.

SA RESULTS: bt Uruguay 36-0 (QF); bt France 33-12 (SF); bt Argentina 33-24 (Final)

SA SEVENS PLAYERS 2012-2013

Player	Province	Aus	Dub	SA	NZ	US	HK	Jap	Sco	Lon	RWC	WG
Dry, C (Chris)	SARU contracted	x	x	x	x	x	x	x	x	x	x	–
Isbell, R (Ruwellyn)*	SARU contracted	x	x	x	–	–	–	–	–	–	–	x
Horne, F (Frankie)	SARU contracted	x	x	x(c)	x(c)	x(c)	x(c)	x(c)	x(c)	x(c)	–	–
Johannnes, R (Reuben)*	SARU contracted	x	–	–	–	–	–	–	–	–	–	x
Hendriks, C (Cornal)	SARU contracted	x	x	x	x	x	x	x	x	x	x	x
Brown, K (Kyle)	SARU contracted	x(c)	x(c)	–	–	–	–	–	–	–	x(c)	x(c)
Du Preez, B (Branco)	SARU contracted	x	–	–	–	x	x	x	–	–	x	–
Dippenaar, S (Stephan)	SARU contracted	x	x	x	x	x	x	x	x	x	x	x
Delport, P (Paul)	SARU contracted	x	x	x	x	x	–	–	x	–	–	–
Afrika, C (Cecil)	SARU contracted	x	–	x	–	–	–	x	–	x	x	–
Mbovane, T (Tshotsho)	SARU contracted	x	x	x	x	x	x	–	x	–	–	–
Hunt, S (Steven)	SARU contracted	x	x	–	–	–	x	x	–	–	–	x
Snyman, P (Phillip)	SARU contracted	–	x	x	x	x	x	x	x	x	–	–
Whiteley, W (Warren)*	Golden Lions	–	x	x	x	x	–	–	–	–	–	–
Luiters, K (Kevin)*	FS Cheetahs	–	x	–	–	–	–	–	–	–	–	–
Kolbe, C (Cheslin)	Western Province	–	–	x	x	x	–	–	–	x	–	–
Botha, B (Bernado)	SARU contracted	–	–	x	–	–	–	–	–	x	–	x
Engelbrecht, P (Pieter)*	FS Cheetahs	–	–	–	x	x	–	–	x	x	–	–
Geduld, J (Justin)*	SARU contracted	–	–	–	x	–	x	x	x	–	–	–
Senatla, S (Seabelo)	SARU contracted	–	–	–	x	x	x	x	x	–	x	x
Ulengo, J (Jamba)	SARU contracted*	–	–	–	–	–	x	x	x	x	–	x
Strydom, WJ (Willem-Johannes)*	SARU contracted	–	–	–	–	–	–	–	x	x	–	x
Kok, W (Werner)*	SARU contracted	–	–	–	–	–	–	–	–	x	–	x
Benjamin, R (Ryno)	FS Cheetahs	–	–	–	–	–	–	–	–	–	x	–
Sithole, S (Sibisiso)	Sharks	–	–	–	–	–	–	–	–	–	x	–
Mastriet, S (Sampie)	Blue Bulls	–	–	–	–	–	–	–	–	–	x	–
Richards, M (Mark)*	SARU contracted	–	–	–	–	–	–	–	–	–	–	x

*New caps

RUGBY WORLD CUP SEVENS 2013

Melrose Cup eludes Sevens Boks

THERE WAS MASSIVE DISAPPOINTMENT for South Africa at Moscow's Luzhniki Stadium as both the Springbok Sevens and Springbok Women Sevens team failed to deliver on their potential.

The men lost in the quarter-finals of the Cup and the women, who contested the Bowl competition after winning only one match in pool play, fell apart in their quarter-final clash against Fiji.

The men finished as first seeds after the pool stages, having scored 17 tries and not conceding any. Their 'reward' was a clash with Fiji, who edged them out with a heartbreaking 12-10 defeat.

A conversion attempt from Cecil Afrika narrowly missed the upright after Sibusiso Sithole scored with less than a minute of play to go and from the resulting kick-off Fiji controlled the ball and kicked it into touch for their win.

South Africa were also knocked out at the quarter-final stage of the 2005 Hong Kong and 2009 Dubai World Cup Sevens tournaments.

The Springbok Sevens team started well and were on the scoreboard first after Cheslin Kolbe created some space for Ryno Benjamin and the Free State player dotted down in the corner. Kolbe's conversion was unsuccessful.

Two tries by Fiji in quick succession gave them a 12-5 lead at the break. South Africa came back well in the second half and when Sithole scored, extra time looked a certainty.

But it was not to be, much to the agony of the squad and coach Paul Treu, who lost captain Kyle Brown overnight due to suspension. Brown was found guilty of "recklessly making contact with an opponent's eye" and suspended for two matches.

On day two, the South Africans comfortably beat Japan 33-0 and Scotland 41-0 after their 31-0 romp past hosts Russia on day one to end their Pool B play with a 105 points differential – the best in the competition.

The 17 tries scored by the Springbok Sevens team in their three matches were also more than any other team and they were the only outfit not to concede a try. The Scots hardly had a look-in and the South Africans scored almost at will.

Sampie Mastriet touched down within 18 seconds after a 60-metre sprint and two tries by Afrika before the break laid the foundation for the second-half onslaught.

Kolbe, who started at scrumhalf/sweeper, scored a hat-trick in a matter of minutes and Mastriet finished off a fine performance with his second on the night.

Try-scoring ace Seabelo Senatla did not even needed to move off the bench for this one.

Senatla had been much more active against Japan earlier in the day and scored twice in as many minutes when he was called upon in the second half.

The Asian side gave a determined showing in the first half, but two Philip Snyman tries held them at bay and Japan could not stop all the gaps or handle Senatla's pace in the second half.

The Springbok Women Sevens team also ended their campaign in disappointing fashion when they were beaten 22-5 by Fiji in the Bowl quarter-finals.

The women lost Lorinda Brown in their first match off pool play with a broken leg and the playmaker's absence clearly affected the team, as they lacked composure and direction.

An opening defeat to Ireland, together with Brown's injury, laid a shaky foundation. A win over China lifted the spirits slightly, but Australia totally dominated the final pool match and South Africa, the 2009 semi-finalists in Dubai, were sent packing to contest the Bowl section.

BY JJ HARMSE

Cheslin Kolbe in full flight. *Wessel Oosthuizen/Gallo Images*

SPRINGBOK WOMEN

SA Women qualify for World Cup

THE SA WOMEN'S 2013 SEASON featured a mix of highs and lows, but one of the most memorable moments was undoubtedly the team's record-breaking 63-3 victory against Uganda in their Rugby World Cup qualifier in East London, which earned them a spot in the 2014 IRB Women's Rugby World Cup in France.

The victory marked the team's biggest winning margin since their first Test match in 2004, and granted them entry into their third successive global tournament.

Such was the team's dominance they scored 11 tries to none as they delivered a fine attacking display and backed this up with a solid defensive effort. Uganda's only points were scored compliments of a penalty by Racheal Babirye.

With a 29-0 lead at the break, the Springbok Women dominated proceedings from the outset, but the most encouraging aspect for the coaching staff was that skipper Mandisa Williams and her team continued to apply pressure and reaped the rewards as they stretched their winning margin to 60 points.

Another defining moment of 2013 was the fact that the Springbok Women's 15-a-side team played their first internationals since 2011 when they featured in the Women's Nations Cup in Colorado in August. The tournament included clashes against the USA, Canada and England.

The team's campaign, however, was disappointing as they finished fourth following defeats in all four matches. They started off with a 35-22 defeat against hosts, the USA, but managed to bounce back strongly against England in their second match by building up an encouraging 17-7 lead at the break. Unfortunately they allowed this lead to slip as penalties conceded and a late try by the hosts forced them into an 18-17 lead, which they held onto until the final whistle.

This result was followed by a 53-17 defeat against Canada in their final round-robin match, which booked them a place in the third and fourth-place playoff against the USA. With the home team knocked out of the final and the side determined to salvage some pride at home, they came out firing and registered a convincing 61-5 victory against the Springbok Women.

The SA Under-20 Women's team also featured in the Junior Nations Cup in London in July, and made an early statement by defeating hosts England 24-22 in their opening match. Unfortunately they were unable to build on this victory, as they went down 42-5 to the USA and 37-0 against Canada in their next round-robin matches. These results secured them a place in the third and fourth-place playoff against hosts England.

And similarly to the senior side, they were unable to match the opposition's determination and were forced to settle for a 27-3 defeat and a fourth-place finish in the tournament.

On the Sevens front the SA Women surprised at the first leg of the inaugural IRB Women's Sevens World Series in Dubai, as they beat England, the Netherlands, Brazil and Spain to advance to the Cup final against New Zealand. The Kiwis, however, proved too strong and registered a convincing 41-0 victory in the final. The Springbok Women backed this up with a respectable showing at the Houston leg, by reaching the Cup semi-final against Australia. But they suffered a 17-12 defeat in extra time after finishing the match at 12-12. The team then travelled to the Netherlands, but had a disappointing campaign as they suffered narrow defeats to England and France on day one. They managed to beat China on day two, but were beaten by hosts, the Netherlands, in the Bowl competition.

BY ZEENA ISAACS

SPRINGBOK WOMEN

SA WOMEN RUGBY WORLD CUP QUALIFIER 2013 RESULTS

Date	Venue	Opponent	Result	Score	Referee	Scorers
07 Sept	Buffalo City Stadium, East London	UGANDA	WON	63-3 (29-0)	Jacobus Husselman (Namibia)	T: Nojoko (2), Cronje (2), Hofmeester (2), Simmers, Jordaan, Williams, Ngxatu, Ntoyanto. C: Nojoko (2), Jordaan, Rabie.

2013 RUGBY WORLD CUP QUALIFIER APPEARANCES & SCORERS

	Uganda	Matches	Tries	Conversions	Penalties	Drop Goals	Points
Zandile Nojoko	15	1	2	2	–	–	14
Marlien Cronje	14	1	2	–	–	–	10
Mathrin Simmers	13	1	1	–	–	–	5
Daphne Scheepers	12	1	–	–	–	–	0
Natasha Hofmeester	11	1	2	–	–	–	10
Zenay Jordaan	10	1	1	1	–	–	7
Fudiswa Plaatjie	9	1	–	–	–	–	0
Mandisa Williams	8c	1	1	–	–	–	5
Nwabisa Ngxatu	7	1	1	–	–	–	5
Vuyolwethu Vazi	6	1	–	–	–	–	0
Dolly Mavumengwana	5	1	–	–	–	–	0
Nolusindiso Booi	4	1	–	–	–	–	0
Asathandile Ntoyanto	3	1	1	–	–	–	5
Thandi Xwetu	2	1	–	–	–	–	0
Laurian Johannes	1	1	–	–	–	–	0
Denita Wentzel	2R	1	–	–	–	–	0
Sinazo Tsawu	1R	1	–	–	–	–	0
Amanda Tshidi	4R	1	–	–	–	–	0
Andrea Mentoor	7R	1	–	–	–	–	0
Lamla Momoti	5R	1	–	–	–	–	0
Tayla Kinsey	15R	1	–	–	–	–	0
Veroeshka Grain	11R	1	–	–	–	–	0
Marnezelle Rabie	13R	1	–	1	–	–	2
	23	11	4	0	0	63

R = Substitute; *(c)* = Captain.

SA WOMEN NATIONS CUP 2013 RESULTS

Date	Venue	Opponent	Result	Score	Referee	Scorers
30 July	Univ of Norhern Colorado, Greeley, Col	USA	LOST	22-35(10-20)	Clair Hodnett (Eng)	T: Simmers, Cronje, Jordaan, Williams. C: Nojoko.
3 Aug	Univ of Norhern Colorado, Greeley, Col	ENGLAND	LOST	17-18(17-07)	Sherry Trumbull (Can)	T: Jordaan (2), Booi. C: Rabie.
7 Aug	Univ of Norhern Colorado, Greeley, Col	CANADA	LOST	17-53(10-24)	Leah Berard (USA)	T: Jordaan (2), Cronje. C: Rabie.
10 Aug	Infinity Park, Glendale, Colorado	USA	LOST	05-61(05-39)	Clair Hodnett (Eng)	T: Grain.

NATIONS CUP 2013 APPEARANCES & SCORERS

	USA	England	Canada	USA	Matches	Tries	Conversions	Penalties	Drop Goals	Points
Marnezelle Rabie	15	15	15R	10R	4	–	2	–	–	4
Phumeza Gadu	14	14	11R	14	4	–	–	–	–	0
Mathrin Simmers	13	–	–	x	1	1	–	–	–	5
Vuyolwethu Vazi	12	13	12	12	4	–	–	–	–	0
Marlien Cronje	11	11	14	11	4	2	–	–	–	10
Zenay Jordaan	10	10	10	10	4	5	–	–	–	25
Fudiswa Plaatjie	9	9	9	9	4	–	–	–	–	0
Mandisa Williams	8c	8c	8c	8c	4	1	–	–	–	5
Nwabisa Ngxatu	7	7	5	5	4	–	–	–	–	0
Lamla Momoti	6	6	6	6	4	–	–	–	–	0
Andrea Mentoor	5	6R	4	6R	4	–	–	–	–	0
Nolusindiso Booi	4	4	4R	4	4	1	–	–	–	5
Portia Jonga	3	3	3	–	3	–	–	–	–	0
Celeste Marais	2	–	–	5R	2	–	–	–	–	0
Nedene Botha	1	x	1R	1	3	–	–	–	–	0
Thandi Xwetu	2R	2	2	2R	4	–	–	–	–	0
Laurian Johannes	1R	1	1	1	4	–	–	–	–	0
Annilie Pretorius	4R	x	3R	1R	3	–	–	–	–	0
Vuykazi Mbonda	7R	7R	5R	7R	4	–	–	–	–	0
Nomathamsanqa Faleni	5R	7	7	7	4	–	–	–	–	0
Zandile Nojoko	15R	15R	15	15	4	–	1	–	–	2
Veroeshka Grain	11R	13R	6R	13	4	1	–	–	–	5
Daphne Scheepers	13R	12	13	–	3	–	–	–	–	0
Simone Vosloo	–	2R	2R	2	3	–	–	–	–	0
Lusanda Mtiya	–	x	11	x	1	–	–	–	–	0
25 players					87	11	3	0	0	61

R = Substitute; *(c)* = Captain.

2013 NATIONS CUP LOG

Team	P	W	L	D	PF	PA	B	Pts
England	3	3	0	0	83	29	1	13
Canada	3	2	0	1	97	56	2	10
South Africa	3	1	0	2	51	113	1	5
United States	3	0	0	3	51	75	2	2

TOURNAMENT RESULTS

JULY 30
Canada 29 England 25
USA 35 SOUTH AFRICA 22

AUGUST 4
England 18 SOUTH AFRICA 17
Canada 35 USA 17

AUGUST 7
Canada 53 SOUTH AFRICA 17
USA 21 England 36

AUGUST 10
3rd Place Play-Off
USA 61 SOUTH AFRICA 5
Final
Canada 27 England 13

SA SCHOOLS

Scholars pass acid test

THE SA SCHOOLS TEAM PASSED THEIR mid-year rugby examinations with flying colours with a clean sweep of victories over their counterparts from England, France and Wales.

The four-nation under-18 series, held at three venues in the Western Cape over a period of nine days in mid-August, proved popular once again, with the visitors all indicating their willingness to return in 2014. A fifth team, the Italian Under-18s, also gained valuable experience in curtain-raiser matches against the Western Province, Boland and South Western Districts Craven Week teams.

Head coach Chris October would have been justifiably proud of his charges, who held their collective nerve to eke out three tight wins on the trot against some of the best schoolboy players from Europe.

The SA Schools side opened their account with a 19-14 win over England at City Park in Cape Town, followed by a nailbiting 17-13 victory over France at a cold and wet Outeniqua Park in George. The side then finished on a high when they showed nerves of steel to edge Wales 14-13 in their final match, held at Drostdy Technical High in Worcester, to finish the series unbeaten.

The series began in thrilling fashion at the historic City Park, with England grabbing an early 7-0 lead to signal their intent. But any fears that the SA Schools side would be found wanting were quickly allayed as the hosts fought their way back into the match through a try scored by inspirational captain and No 8, Rikus Bothma, and a penalty from the reliable Grant Hermanus.

A try after the break by wing Duhan van der Merwe was cancelled out by the visitors, who took a one-point lead. But two penalties from Brandon Thomson secured a hard-fought come-from-behind victory.

The electric Van der Merwe was at it again in the second match against France in George, dotting down in the opening minute to give his team the best possible start.

But France, as they so often do, came off the ropes and narrowed the gap to a single point with a drop goal and penalty.

SA stretched their lead in the second half to 17-6 with a penalty, followed by Van der Merwe's second try, but the French countered with a converted try with four minutes remaining to set up a tense finish.

Strong winds in Worcester made for difficult conditions as SA Schools went for the clean sweep.

A penalty from Luke Price gave Wales a 3-0 lead but SA struck back through Jean-Luc du Preez, son of former Springbok scrumhalf Robert, with Thomson converting. The forwards, who came off second best for much of the match against France, were instrumental in the try as they applied pressure upfront and spread the ball wide to Du Preez, who was open on the wing.

But their lead was short-lived as Wales right wing Ashton Hewitt out-sprinted two defenders to dot down. But Leolin Zass crossed just before the break to give SA a 14-8 lead.

Hewitt scored his second try to narrow the gap to one point, but SA, as they had in the previous two matches, showed character on defence to hold out for the victory.

2013 SA SCHOOLS **RESULTS & SCORERS**

Date	Venue	Opponent	Result	Score	Referee	Scorers
Aug 09	Cape Town	ENGLAND	**WON**	17-07	C Evans	T: Bothma, Van der Merwe. P: Thomson (2), Hermanus.
Aug 13	George	FRANCE	**WON**	17-13	Craig Keys	T: Van der Merwe (2). C: Human (2). P: Human.
Aug 18	Worcester	WALES	**WON**	14-13	Craig Keys	T: J-L du Preez, Zas. C: Thomson.

MATCH RESULTS & SCORERS

South Africa 19 England 14
August 9, City Park Stadium, Cape Town.
Referee: C Evans
SOUTH AFRICA - TRIES: Bothma, Van der Merwe.
PENS: Thomson (2), Hermanus.
ENGLAND - TRIES: Chisholm (2). CONS: Olver (2).

South Africa 17 France 13
August 13, Outeniqua Park, George.
Referee: Craig Keys
SOUTH AFRICA - TRIES: Van der Merwe (2). CONS: Human (2). **PEN:** Human.
FRANCE - TRY: Fontaine. CON: Fontaine. PENS: Meret (2).

South Africa 14 Wales 13
August 17, HTS Drostdy, Worcester.
Referee: Craig Keys.
SOUTH AFRICA - TRIES: J-L du Preez, Zas. **CON:** Thomson.
WALES - TRIES: Hewitt (2). **PEN:** Price.

Other matches
August 09 - Wales 47, France 8 (City Park Stadium, Cape Town), August 13 - England 17, Wales 15 (Outeniqua Park, George), August 17 - England 12, France 8 (HTS Drostdy, Worcester)

SA SCHOOLS APPEARANCES & SCORERS

	England	France	Wales	Matches	Tries	Conversions	Penalties	Drop Goals	Points
EW Viljoen	15	15	11R	3	–	–	–	–	0
Grant Hermanus	14	–	15	2	–	–	1	–	3
Warrick Gelant	13	12	13	3	–	–	–	–	0
Daniel du Plessis	12	–	12	2	–	–	–	–	0
Duhan van der Merwe	11	11	11	3	3	–	–	–	15
Brandon Thomson	10	x	10	2	–	1	2	–	8
Justin Phillips	9	x	9R	2	–	–	–	–	0
Rikus Bothma	8c	8c	8c	3	1	–	–	–	5
Jacques Vermeulen	7	6R	6	3	–	–	–	–	0
PJ Toerien	6	–	x	1	–	–	–	–	0
RG Snyman	5	5	5	3	–	–	–	–	0
Daniel du Preez	4	4R	4	3	–	–	–	–	0
Ruan Kramer	3	3R	3	3	–	–	–	–	0
Joseph Dweba	2	2R	2	3	–	–	–	–	0
Ox Nche	1	–	1	2	–	–	–	–	0
Francois Steyn	2R	2	x	2	–	–	–	–	0
Thomas du Toit	1R	1	x	2	–	–	–	–	0
Conraad van Vuuren	3R	3	–	2	–	–	–	–	0
Abongile Nonkontwana	x	4	x	1	–	–	–	–	0
Jean-Luc du Preez	x	7	7	2	1	–	–	–	5
Dewald Human	x	10	x	1	–	2	1	–	7
Marco Jansen van Vuren	x	–	9	1	–	–	–	–	0
Jurie Linde	11R	13	–	2	–	–	–	–	0
Leolin Zas	–	14	14	2	1	–	–	–	5
Remu Malan	–	9	–	1	–	–	–	–	0
Refuoe Rampeta	–	6	–	1	–	–	–	–	0
Malcolm Jaer	–	11R	–	1	–	–	–	–	0
Thabani Mtsi	–	x	1R	1	–	–	–	–	0
28 players				**57**	**6**	**3**	**4**	**0**	**48**

R = Substitute; *(c)* = Captain.

COACHES & MANAGEMENT

Chris October **COACH** David Coert **MANAGER** Roean Bezuidenhout **ASST COACH**
Gerhard Coetzer **DOCTOR** Bash Mohamed **PHYSIO** Warren Adams **CONDITIONING**
Jacques Nienaber **DEFENCE COACH** Dawie Theron **ADDITIONAL COACH**

SA PRESIDENT'S XV

President's XV win inaugural Tbilisi Cup

SOUTH AFRICA'S TREMENDOUS strength in depth was once again evident in Georgia from 7-16 June when the SA President's XV claimed the International Rugby Board's inaugural Tbilisi Cup with a 21-16 victory over the tournament hosts.

The Tbilisi Cup is part of the IRB's ongoing strategy of increasing the competition schedule for Tier Two nations and in its maiden run gave ever-improving World Cup finalists Georgia a chance to test themselves against fellow RWC 2015 hopefuls Uruguay, Emerging Ireland, and a team made up of the best players from the Absa Currie Cup First Division provinces.

The President's XV, coached by Pumas mentor Jimmy Stonehouse, finished the Tbilisi Cup unbeaten. They overcame an injury-hit Uruguay 37-9 in their opening match and carried that form into the match against Emerging Ireland, which the South Africans won 19-8.

With the tournament winner decided by log points over the three matches, the South Africans had to beat Georgia in their final match to lift the trophy, and they duly accomplished this at the Avchala Stadium thanks to a brave forward effort, tries from wing Rosco Speckman and lock Eduan van der Walt, and accurate goal-kicking from flyhalf Carl Bezuidenhout.

"We are delighted to get the victory and win the tournament overall. It was a physical battle and I was quite impressed with the performance," said coach Stonehouse. "The tournament has been an excellent developmental tool for our players and will be fantastic for their progression as players."

The final match was the most physical of the tournament, with the South Africans outmuscled by the abrasive Georgians, whose indiscretions however allowed Bezuidenhout to put the visitors 6-0 up.

The next 20 minutes belonged to the home side. Beka Tsiklauri kicked a difficult long-range penalty to cut the deficit to three points before the Georgian pack stamped their authority on the match.

A surge by the forwards from 15 metres out resulted in a try for Levan Chilachava, which was greeted by rapturous applause from the partisan home crowd. Tsiklauri converted to give the Lelos the lead. Bezuidenhout and Tsiklauri traded penalties before Specman came off his wing and glided through the hosts' defence to put his side back in front. Bezuidenhout kicked the resulting conversion to make it 16-13 to South Africa at half-time.

With the wind at their backs in the second half the Lelos quickly levelled the scores after a third penalty for winger, Tsiklauri, but it was Van der Walt who sealed the result when he bundled his way over the line for what proved to be the match-winning try.

SA PRESIDENT'S XV

IRB TBILISI CUP RESULTS & SCORERS

Date	Venue	Opponent	Result	Score	Scorers
June 07	Avchala Stadium, Tbilisi	Uruguay	WON	37-19	T: Cassiem (2), Bothma, Engelbrecht, Louw, Mkhafu. C: Croy (2). P: Croy.
June 11	Avchala Stadium, Tbilisi	Emerging Ireland	WON	19-08	T: Bock. C: Bezuidenhout. P: Bezuidenhout (4).
June 16	Avchala Stadium, Tbilisi	Georgia	WON	21-16	T: Van der Walt, Speckman. C: Bezuidenhout. P: Bezuidenhout (3).

MATCH RESULTS & SCORERS

JUNE 07
South Africa President's XV 37 Uruguay 9 (Avchala Stadium, Tbilisi)
SA PRES XV – TRIES: Cassiem (2), Engelbrecht, Mkhafu, Bothma, Louw. CONS: Croy (2). PEN: Croy.
URUGUAY – PENS: Etcheverry (2). DG: Etcheverry.

Georgia 15 Emerging Ireland 20 (Avchala Stadium, Tbilisi)
GEORGIA - TRIES: Chkhaidze, Mchedlidze. CON: Tsiklauri. PEN: Tsiklauri
EMERGING IRELAND – TRY: Kearney. PENS: Keatley (5).

JUNE 11
South Africa President's XV 19 Emerging Ireland 8 (Avchala Stadium, Tbilisi)
SA PRES XV - TRY: Bock. CON: Bezuidenhout. PENS: Bezuidenhout (4).
EMERGING IRELAND - TRY: Allen. PEN: Keatley.

Georgia 27 Uruguay 3 (Avchala Stadium, Tbilisi)
GEORGIA – TRIES: Todua, Zibzibadze, Nemsadze. CON: Tsiklauri (3). PENS: Tsiklauri (2).
URUGUAY – PEN: Albanell.

JUNE 16
South Africa President's XV 21 Georgia 16 (Avchala Stadium, Tbilisi)
SA PRES XV - TRIES: Van der Walt, Speckman. CON: Bezuidenhout. PENS: Bezuidenhout (3)
GEORGIA – TRY: Chilachava. CON: Tsiklauri. PENS: Tsiklauri (3).

URUGUAY 33 Emerging Ireland 42 (Avchala Stadium, Tbilisi)
URUGUAY – TRIES: Gaminara, Tassistro, Albanell, Roman, Lamanna. CON: Prada (3), Etcheverry.
EMERGING IRELAND – TRIES: Keatley (2), Morris (2), O'Halloran, Annett. CONS: Keatley (6).

Warm-up game
MAY 24
South Africa President's XV 26 Welwitchias 23 (Hage Geingob Stadium, Windhoek)
SA PRES XV - TRIES: Maritz, Bock, Croy, Jordaan. CONS: Croy (3)
WELWITCHIAS - TRIES: Dames, Swanepoel. CONS: Kotze (2). PENS: Kotze (2)
SA Pres XV: Hoffman Maritz (Carl Bezuidenhout), Joe Seerane (Jaquin Jansen), Jerome Pretorius, Adriaan Engelbrecht, Alshaun Bock, Ricardo Croy, Inus Kritzinger (Ntando Kebe), Zandre Jordaan, Brian Shabangu, Vincent Gwavu (Uzair Cassiem), Lubabalo Mtyanda, Brendon Snyman (C), Jaco Bouwer, Ruan Dreyer (Ivann Espag), Ashton Constant (Frank Herne), Kwezi Mkhafu

SA PRESIDENT'S XV

IRB TBILISI CUP LOG

Team	P	W	L	D	PF	PA	Diff	TF	TA	B	Pts
SA President's XV	3	3	0	0	77	33	44	9	2	1	13
Emerging Ireland	3	2	0	1	70	67	3	8	8	1	9
Georgia	3	1	0	2	58	44	14	6	3	2	6
Uruguay	3	0	0	3	45	106	-61	5	15	1	1

IRB TBILISI CUP APPEARANCES & SCORERS

	Uruguay	Emerging Ireland	Georgia	Matches	Tries	Conversions	Penalties	Drop Goals	Points
Jansen, J (Jaquin)	15	–	–	1	–	–	–	–	0
Pretorius, J (Jerome)	14	14R	x	2	–	–	–	–	0
Watermeyer, S (Stefan)	13	12R	15R	3	–	–	–	–	0
Engelbrecht, AE (Adriaan)	12	12	12	3	1	–	–	–	5
Louw, WD (Wilmaure)	11	13	13	3	1	–	–	–	5
Croy, R (Ricardo)	10	–	–	1	–	2	1	–	7
Nyoka, S (Sinovuyo)	9	9R	9	3	–	–	–	–	0
Bothma, R (Renaldo)	8	–	8	2	1	–	–	–	5
Cassiem, U (Uzair)	7	7	7	3	2	–	–	–	10
Bouwer, WJ (Jaco)	6	8R	6	3	–	–	–	–	0
Mtyanda, L (Lubabalo)	5	4R	4R	3	–	–	–	–	0
Snyman, BM (Brendon) - capt.	4c	4c	4c	3	–	–	–	–	0
Dreyer, MC (Martin)	3	3R	3R	3	–	–	–	–	0
Constant, A (Ashton)	2	–	2R	2	–	–	–	–	0
Mkhafu, K (Kwezi)	1	x	–	1	1	–	–	–	5
Herne, F (Frank)	2R	2	2	3	–	–	–	–	0
Espag, I (Ivann)	3R	3	3	3	–	–	–	–	0
Van der Walt, ER (Eduan)	4R	5	5	3	1	–	–	–	5
Shabangu, SB (Brian)	8R	6	x	2	–	–	–	–	0
Kebe, NL (Ntando)	9R	9	9R	3	–	–	–	–	0
Speckman, RS (Rosco)	13R	11	11	3	1	–	–	–	5
Van Wyk, CG (Coenie)	15R	15	15	3	–	–	–	–	0
Bock, AG (Alshaun)	–	14	14	2	1	–	–	–	5
Bezuidenhout, C (Carl)	–	10	10	2	–	2	7	–	25
Jordaan, Z (Zandre)	–	8	–	1	–	–	–	–	0
Koch, VP (Vincent)	–	1	1	2	–	–	–	–	0
26 players				63	9	4	8	0	77

R = Substitute; *(c)* = Captain.

SECTION 4
VODACOM SUPER RUGBY

Tournament Review **120**
Logs & leading scorers **122**

SOUTH AFRICA
Vodacom Bulls **126**
Toyota Cheetahs **132**
Southern Kings **138**
Sharks **144**
DHL Stormers **150**
Promotion-relegation **156**

NEW ZEALAND
Blues **158**
Chiefs **162**
Crusaders **166**
Highlanders **170**
Hurricanes **174**

AUSTRALIA
ACT Brumbies **178**
Melbourne Rebels **182**
New South Wales Waratahs **186**
Queensland Reds **190**
Western Force **194**

Cornell du Preez goes high for Southern Kings in their match against the Highlanders. *Richard Huggard/Gallo Images*

VODACOM SUPER RUGBY

Cheetah clawback leaves lasting impression

THE VODACOM BULLS WERE THE PICK of the bunch, but it was the Toyota Cheetahs that warmed the hearts of South Africans in the 2013 Super Rugby campaign.

Tipped to finish in the bottom half of the table, Naka Drotské's underdogs produced some inspirational performances to provide cheer for their long-suffering fans as well as win over the neutrals.

Their roll of honour included a hat-trick of tour victories against the Highlanders, Waratahs and Force before they also accounted for among others the DHL Stormers, Reds and Blues in Bloemfontein.

But the Cheetahs' inspirational tale came to an unfortunate end in Canberra, where they were beaten 15-13 by the Brumbies. Jake White's side also accounted for the Bulls in the semi-final at Loftus.

While the Bulls finished second on the overall log behind the Chiefs, they never quite created the impression that they were championship material. If anything, they were perhaps a team where the sum was greater than its parts thanks to a winning culture that had been established over several years.

However, there was no one in their ranks that one might have classified as a player that only comes once in a generation, as was the case in the recent past when they had the likes of Victor Matfield and Fourie du Preez.

Of course, it also didn't help that key lock Juandré Kruger's contract with French club Racing Metro kicked in before the Bulls' season had even been completed. He missed their last three games.

One of the big positives of the Bulls' campaign is that it provided a springboard for flyhalf Morné Steyn to play himself back into form. The Springboks ended up being major beneficiaries in the June incoming Tests and later in the Castle Rugby Championship.

Perhaps the biggest disappointment of South Africa's Super Rugby story was the Stormers' inconsistent form. They had spent big in a bid to take the next step, bringing in several MTN Lions players in flyhalf Elton Jantjies, fullback Jaco Taute, utility prop Pat Cilliers and flank Michael Rhodes.

But Jantjies hardly proved the catalyst to unlock their star-studded backline, while Taute's form was poor before he suffered a major knee injury early in the campaign.

Rhodes also struggled with injuries, while Cilliers didn't give the Stormers' scrum the muscle they had hoped for.

Injuries played a massive part in the Stormers' demise, while they also suffered from a few refereeing shockers. They recovered to win their last five games, but by then the horse had bolted.

The Sharks, who also promised a lot before the season started, failed to deliver amid reports of massive in-fighting and back-stabbing at the union. It clearly spilled over into the team environment and led to coach John Plumtree's demise.

In Port Elizabeth the Southern Kings almost delivered a fairytale. Going by attendance figures, they were the third-best supported team in the tournament. Sadly it ended in tears when they were edged on points difference in the promotion-relegation play-offs against the Lions.

The Kings felt much of that stemmed from referee Jaco Peyper's failure to consult the television match official in the build-up to Lions centre Stokkies Hanekom's try in the second half.

That in itself demonstrated problems on a much larger scale: too much time was spent talking about referees as opposed to the quality of the rugby throughout the tournament, while the promotion-relegation system did South African rugby no good.

The Cheetahs surprised friend and foe alike in 2013 with their spirited displays.
Cameron Spencer/Getty Images

VODACOM SUPER RUGBY

FINAL LOG

Team	P	W	L	D	PF	PA	Diff	TF	TA	B7	B4	B	Pts*
Chiefs	16	12	4	0	458	364	94	50	38	2	8	10	66
Bulls	16	12	4	0	448	330	118	41	34	2	5	7	63
Brumbies	16	10	4	2	430	295	135	43	31	3	5	8	60
Crusaders	16	11	5	0	446	307	139	44	31	3	5	8	60
Reds	16	10	4	2	321	296	25	31	23	2	4	6	58
Cheetahs	16	10	6	0	382	358	24	38	32	4	2	6	54
Stormers	16	9	7	0	346	292	54	30	18	5	1	6	50
Sharks	16	8	8	0	384	305	79	40	31	5	3	8	48
Waratahs	16	8	8	0	411	371	40	45	34	4	1	5	45
Blues	16	6	10	0	347	364	-17	40	36	6	6	12	44
Hurricanes	16	6	10	0	386	457	-71	41	49	5	4	9	41
Rebels	16	5	11	0	382	515	-133	44	65	5	4	9	37
Force	16	4	11	1	267	366	-99	26	34	5	0	5	31
Highlanders	16	3	13	0	374	496	-122	40	55	5	4	9	29
Southern Kings	16	3	12	1	298	564	-266	27	69	0	2	2	24
	240	117	117	6	5680	5680	0	580	580	56	54	110	710

Include eight points per team for two byes.

PLAY-OFF RESULTS

PLAY-OFF: Crusaders 38 Reds 9 (halftime 21-6)
AMI Stadium, Addington, Christchurch, Saturday July 20
Referee: Jaco Peyper (SA)
Crusaders - TRIES: Crotty (2), Carter, Marshall. CONVERSIONS: Carter (3). PENALTIES: Carter (3), Taylor.
Reds - PENALTIES: Cooper (3).

PLAY-OFF: Brumbies 15 Cheetahs 13 (halftime 6-5)
Canberra Stadium, Canberra, Sunday, July 21
Referee: Glen Jackson (NZ)
Brumbies - PENALTIES: Lealiifano (4), White.
Cheetahs - TRIES: Sadie, Benjamin. PENALTY: Smit.

SEMI-FINAL: Chiefs 20 Crusaders 19 (halftime 3-9)
Waikato Stadium, Hamilton, Saturday July 27
Referee: Steve R Walsh (Aus)
Chiefs - TRIES: Cruden, Masaga. CONVERSIONS: Cruden (2). PENALTY: Cruden (2).
Crusaders - TRY: Dagg. CONVERSION: Carter. PENALTIES: Carter (4).

SEMI-FINAL: Bulls 23 Brumbies 26 (halftime 11-16)
Loftus Versfeld, Pretoria, Saturday, July 27.
Referee: Craig Joubert (SA)
Bulls - TRY: Engelbrecht. PENALTIES: Steyn (6).
Brumbies - Tries: Mogg, Kuridrani. Conversions: Lealiifano (2). Penalties: Lealiifano (2).

FINAL: Chiefs 27 Brumbies 22 (halftime 9-16)
Waikato Stadium, Hamilton, Saturday August 3
Referee: Craig Joubert (SA)
Chiefs - TRIES: Messam, Robinson. CONVERSION: Cruden. PENALTIES: Cruden (5).
Gareth Anscombe *(Robbie Robinson, 59)*, Lelia Masaga, Charlie Ngatai, Andrew Horrell *(Bundi Aki, 46)*, Asaeli Tikoirutuma *(Michael FitGerald, 78)*, Aaron Cruden, Tawera Kerr-Barlow *(Augustine Pulu, 65)*, Matt Vant-Leven *(Sam Cane, 49)*, Tanerau Latimer, Liam Messam, Brodie Retallick, Craig Clarke (c), Ben Tameifuna *(Ben Afeaki, 46)*, Hika Elliott *(Rhys Marshall, 78)*, Toby Smith.
Brumbies - TRY: Lealiifano. CONVERSION: Lealiifano. PENALTIES: Lealiifano (5).
Jesse Mogg, Henry Speight, Tevita Kuridrani *(Andrew Smith, 72)*, Christian Lealiifano, Clyde Rathbone *(Joe Tomane, 59)*, Matt Toomua, Nic White *(Ian Prior, 78)*, Ben Mowen (c), George Smith, Peter Kimlin, Sam Carter *(Fotu Auelua, 65)*, Scott Fardy, Ben Alexander *(Ruan Smith, 78)*, Stephen Moore, Scott Sio
Unused subs: Siliva Siliva, Colby Faingaa.

2013 VODACOM SUPER RUGBY *LEADING SCORERS*

50 POINTS OR MORE

PLAYER	Team	Tries	Conversions	Penalties	Drop Goals	Points
Morné Steyn	Bulls	2	32	57	1	248
Christian Lealiifano	Brumbies	3	22	58	0	233
Beauden Barrett	Hurricanes	2	28	40	0	186
Quade Cooper	Reds	3	20	38	1	172
Patrick Lambie	Sharks	1	17	43	1	171
Dan Carter	Crusaders	3	31	31	0	170
Joe Pietersen	Stormers	0	19	44	0	170
Gareth Anscombe	Chiefs	5	30	27	0	166
Demetri Catrakilis	Southern Kings	0	14	37	1	142
Brendan McKibbin	Waratahs	0	20	33	0	139
Colin Slade	Highlanders	2	20	27	0	131
James O'Connor	Rebels	1	21	23	0	116
Aaron Cruden	Chiefs	2	10	24	0	102
Chris Noakes	Blues	1	14	15	0	78
Jayden Hayward	Force	0	9	17	0	69
Jason Woodward	Rebels	3	12	9	0	66
Tyler Bleyendaal	Crusaders	2	4	15	0	63
Sias Ebersohn	Force	1	5	14	2	63
Burton Francis	Cheetahs	0	7	15	1	62
Tom Taylor	Crusaders	1	4	14	0	55
Riaan Smit	Cheetahs	1	5	13	0	54
Baden Kerr	Blues	0	11	10	0	52
Frank Halai	Blues	10	0	0	0	50

FIVE TRIES

Player	Team	Tries	Player	Team	Tries
Frank Halai	Blues	10	Gareth Anscombe	Chiefs	5
Cam Crawford	Waratahs	8	Bernard Foley	Waratahs	5
Henry Speight	Brumbies	8	Alifeleti (Alfi) Mafi	Force	5
Hosea Gear	Highlanders	8	Charles Piutau	Blues	5
Israel Folau	Waratahs	8	George Whitelock	Crusaders	5
Julian Savea	Hurricanes	7	Hugh Pyle	Rebels	5
TJ Perenara	Hurricanes	7	Jano Vermaak	Bulls	5
Jesse Mogg	Brumbies	6	Jean de Villiers	Stormers	5
Ben R Smith	Highlanders	6	Johann Sadie	Cheetahs	5
Ben Tameifuna	Chiefs	6	Kade Poki	Highlanders	5
Bundee Aki	Chiefs	6	Lelia Masaga	Chiefs	5
Rene Ranger	Blues	6	Peter Betham	Waratahs	5
Scott Higginbotham	Rebels	6	Raymond Rhule	Cheetahs	5
Tim Nanai-Williams	Chiefs	6	Rod Davies	Reds	5
Willie Le Roux	Cheetahs	6	Ryan Crotty	Crusaders	5
Wimpie van der Walt	Southern Kings	6	Tom English	Rebels	5

VODACOM SUPER RUGBY 1996-2013

TEAM	1996	1997	1998	1999	2000	2001	2002	2003	2004	2005
Crusaders	12th	6th	**2nd**	**4th**	**2nd**	10th	**1st**	2nd	2nd	**1st**
ACT Brumbies	5th	2nd	10th	5th	1st	**1st**	3rd	4th	**1st**	5th
Blues	2nd	**1st**	1st	9th	6th	11th	6th	**1st**	5th	7th
NSW Waratahs	7th	9th	6th	8th	9th	8th	2nd	5th	8th	2nd
Sharks/Natal	4th	4th	3rd	7th	12th	2nd	10th	11th	7th	12th
Stormers/WP	11th	-	9th	2nd	5th	7th	7th	9th	3rd	9th
Bulls/NTransvaal	3rd	8th	11th	12th	11th	12th	12th	6th	6th	3rd
Hurricanes	9th	3rd	8th	10th	8th	9th	9th	3rd	11th	4th
Chiefs	6th	11th	7th	6th	10th	6th	8th	10th	4th	6th
Queensland Reds	1st	10th	5th	1st	7th	4th	5th	8th	10th	10th
Highlanders	8th	12th	4th	3rd	3rd	5th	4th	7th	9th	8th
Free State/Cheetahs	-	7th	-	-	-	-	-	-	-	-
Western Force	-	-	-	-	-	-	-	-	-	-
Lions/Cats	10th	5th	12th	11th	4th	3rd	11th	12th	12th	11th
Melbourne Rebels	-	-	-	-	-	-	-	-	-	-
Southern Kings	-	-	-	-	-	-	-	-	-	-

Bold type indicates champion

WINNING PERCENTAGE LOG

TEAM	Played	Won	Lost	Drawn	Pts For	Pts Against	Difference	Tries For	Tries Against	Bonus Tries	Bonus >7	Points	% Win
Crusaders	250	168	76	6	7405	6456	949	814	579	28	88	700	67,20%
ACT Brumbies	237	138	94	5	6393	5246	1147	751	541	38	87	620	58,23%
Blues	234	132	98	4	6433	5607	826	771	603	43	90	629	56,41%
NSW Waratahs	231	120	107	4	5814	5170	644	654	547	48	71	582	51,95%
Stormers	218	113	100	5	5013	5010	3	512	523	41	45	523	51,83%
Chiefs	230	117	108	5	5915	5855	60	659	650	46	67	547	50,87%
Sharks	236	119	110	7	5868	5647	221	653	609	47	66	567	50,42%
Hurricanes	229	115	109	5	5874	5847	27	670	641	31	73	568	50,22%
Queensland Reds	230	115	110	5	5254	5595	-341	568	618	43	54	531	50,00%
Bulls	234	116	111	7	6132	6296	-164	651	718	32	62	522	49,57%
Highlanders	228	101	125	2	5412	5826	-414	579	664	46	46	511	44,30%
Cheetahs	125	42	81	2	2843	3466	-623	302	391	29	20	209	33,60%
Western Force	113	36	70	7	2238	2804	-566	227	314	29	16	201	31,86%
Melbourne Rebels	48	12	36	0	1025	1605	-580	111	198	12	9	64	25,00%
Lions	209	52	152	5	4575	6555	-1980	480	765	47	42	327	24,88%
Southern Kings	16	3	12	1	298	564	-266	27	69	0	2	2	18,75%
	3068	1499	1499	70	76492	77549	-1057	8429	8430	560	838	7103	

VODACOM SUPER RUGBY

LOG BY AVERAGE POSITION

2006	2007	2008	2009	2010	2011	2012	2013	Play-offs	Semi-finals	Finals	Total	Champions	Ave Position
1st	3rd	1st	4th	4th	3rd	4th	4th	3	15	10	28	7	3,66
6th	5th	9th	7th	6th	13th	7th	3rd	1	7	5	13	2	5,16
8th	4th	6th	9th	7th	4th	12th	10th	1	6	4	11	3	6,05
3rd	13th	2nd	5th	3rd	5th	11th	9th	1	5	2	8	-	6,44
5th	1st	3rd	6th	9th	6th	6th	8th	2	7	4	11	-	6,44
11th	10th	5th	10th	2nd	2nd	1st	7th	-	5	1	6	-	6,50
4th	2nd	10th	1st	1st	7th	5th	2nd	2	7	3	12	3	6,22
2nd	8th	4th	3rd	8th	9th	8th	11th	-	6	1	7	-	7,00
7th	6th	7th	2nd	11th	10th	2nd	1st	-	4	3	7	2	6,66
12th	14th	12th	13th	5th	1st	3rd	5th	2	4	1	7	1	6,94
9th	9th	11th	11th	12th	8th	9th	14th	-	4	1	6	-	8,11
10th	11th	13th	14th	10th	11th	10th	6th	1	-	-	1	-	10,22
14th	7th	8th	8th	13th	12th	14th	13th	-	-	-	0	-	11,13
13th	12th	14th	12th	14th	14th	15th	-	-	2	-	2	-	10,88
-	-	-	-	15th	13th	12th	-	-	-	-	0	-	14,00
-	-	-	-	-	-	-	15th	-	-	-	0	-	15,00

The Southern Kings' star shone brightly, albeit briefly.
Richard Huggard/Gallo Images

VODACOM BULLS

Bulls falter in final straight

GROUND
Loftus Versfeld
CAPACITY
50 000
ADDRESS
Kirkness St, Sunnyside, Pretoria, 0132
TELEPHONE NUMBER
012-420 0700
WEBSITE
www.vodacombulls.co.za
COLOURS
Navy fading from chest to hem. Herringbone design under arms and sides. Navy collar with faded sleeves. Navy shorts with herringbone insert.
COACH
Frans Ludeke
CAPTAIN
Pierre Spies
CEO
Barend van Graan
CHAIRMAN
Louis Nel

BY CRAIG RAY,
THE TIMES

AFTER SIX GAMES OF WHAT WAS SHAPING UP TO BE A superb season, the Vodacom Bulls' 2013 Vodacom Super Rugby play-off aspirations appeared to be all but over after three straight losses.

But Frans Ludeke's men, in only their second season of rebuilding following the retirement and departure of half a dozen key players in late 2011, summoned the spirit of their best years and reeled off nine consecutive victories.

It was an amazing run spearheaded by flyhalf Morné Steyn, who returned to his best form after a forgettable 2012 season.

Steyn contributed 248 points – his second-highest single season contribution after the 263 he amassed in 2010 – to take the Bulls to the top of the SA conference and second on the overall standings.

The Bulls had the chance to secure top spot going in to the final round, but lost 30-13 to the DHL Stormers at Newlands to allow the defending champion Chiefs to smooth the path to retaining their title by taking the No 1 position on the standings.

However, the daunting task of travelling to Hamilton to meet the Chiefs in the final never materialised as the Bulls inexplicably lost the plot during their Loftus semi-final against Jake White's Brumbies.

In a tight tussle the Bulls finally hit the front at 20-19 on the hour when Steyn landed his fifth penalty. The momentum had swung the way of the Bulls and from that position, at Loftus, they should have driven home the advantage.

Over the next 12 minutes the Bulls earned four successive penalties that were all well within Steyn's range. Captain Dewald Potgieter instructed Steyn to kick the first three for the corner instead of at the posts.

Ludeke was fuming in the coaches' box and after three failed lineout drives Potgieter relented to let Steyn kick the fourth. He duly landed the penalty and it opened the gap to 23-19, but crucially still left the Brumbies within striking distance.

The visitors' centre Tevita Kuridrani broke Bulls hearts when he skipped through for a last-minute try to seal a famous win – the Bulls' first-ever post-season loss at Loftus in their sixth play-off game in Pretoria.

Potgieter claimed afterwards he wanted to keep the Brumbies pinned back, but his logic didn't wash with the Bulls' tried and tested method of taking points when on offer. It was probably good timing for the unfortunate Potgieter that it also happened to be his last game before taking up a contract in Japan.

While there was a sense of what might have been after the semi, from a playing perspective the emergence of centres Jan Serfontein and JJ Engelbrecht, as well as flank Arno Botha, was a boost for 2014.

The Bulls celebrate winning the South African conference.
Ashley Vlotman/Gallo Images

VODACOM SUPER RUGBY

COACHES & MANAGEMENT

HEAD COACH: Frans Ludeke **BACKLINE COACH:** Pieter Rossouw
FORWARDS/ATTACK COACH: Victor Matfield **DEFENCE COACH:** Pine Pienaar **MANAGER:** Wynie Strydom **KICKING COACH:** Vlok Cilliers **STRENGTH AND CONDITIONING:** André Volsteedt
CONDITIONING AND REHABILITATION: Stephen Plummer **TEAM DOCTOR:** Dr Org Strauss
PHYSIOTHERAPISTS: Roneé Eksteen & Karabo Morokane **BAGGAGE MASTER:** Andries Kabinde
MASSEUSE: Elzanne van Coller **MARKETING & COMMUNICATIONS MANAGER:** Richard Papo

APPEARANCES & POINTS IN SUPER RUGBY

BULLS	BULLS CAREER							SUPER RUGBY CAREER					
	Province	Debut	Matches	Tries	Conversions	Penalties	Drop Goals	Points	Debut	Matches	Tries	Conversions	Penalties	Drop Goals	Points
BA (Bjorn) Basson	BB	2011	46	20	–	–	–	100	2009	55	26	–	–	–	130
U (Ulrich) Beyers	BB	2013	2	–	–	–	–	0	2013	2	–	–	–	–	0
AF (Arno) Botha	BB	2012	22	1	–	–	–	5	2012	22	1	–	–	–	5
JG (Jean) Cook	BB	2013	1	–	–	–	–	0	2013	1	–	–	–	–	0
WHJ (Jacques) du Plessis	BB	2013	1	–	–	–	–	0	2013	1	–	–	–	–	0
JJ (JJ) Engelbrecht	BB	2012	33	7	–	–	–	35	2012	33	7	–	–	–	35
LD van Z (Louis) Fouche	BB	2012	21	2	5	5	–	35	2012	21	2	5	5	–	35
MD (Dean) Greyling	BB	2008	38	4	–	–	–	20	2008	38	4	–	–	–	20
GN (Grant) Hattingh	BB	2013	12	–	–	–	–	0	2012	21	1	–	–	–	5
F (Francois) Hougaard	BB	2008	56	18	–	–	–	90	2008	56	18	–	–	–	90
Z (Zane) Kirchner	BB	2008	82	21	–	–	–	105	2008	82	21	–	–	–	105
FBC (Frik) Kirsten	BB	2009	31	–	–	–	–	0	2009	31	–	–	–	–	0
PJJ (Juandre) Kruger	BB	2012	31	1	–	–	–	5	2012	31	1	–	–	–	5
W (Werner) Kruger	BB	2008	92	8	–	–	–	40	2008	92	8	–	–	–	40
GLS (Lionel) Mapoe	Lions	2013	12	2	–	–	–	10	2010	40	5	–	–	–	25
S (Sampie) Mastriet	BB	2013	1	1	–	–	–	5	2013	1	1	–	–	–	5
MM (Morne) Mellett	BB	2013	12	–	–	–	–	0	2013	12	–	–	–	–	0
AZ (Akona) Ndungane	BB	2005	96	32	–	–	–	160	2005	96	32	–	–	–	160
W (Wynand) Olivier	BB	2005	110	29	–	–	–	145	2005	110	29	–	–	–	145
R (Rudy) Paige	BB	2013	4	–	–	–	–	0	2013	4	–	–	–	–	0
DJ (Dewald) Potgieter	BB	2008	67	4	–	–	–	20	2008	67	4	–	–	–	20
UJ (Jacques) Potgieter	BB	2012	23	4	–	–	–	20	2012	23	4	–	–	–	20
MC (Chiliboy) Ralepelle	BB	2006	69	4	–	–	–	20	2006	69	4	–	–	–	20
JM (Jono) Ross	BB	2013	4	–	–	–	–	0	2013	4	–	–	–	–	0
JL (Jan) Serfontein	BB	2013	12	2	–	–	–	10	2013	12	2	–	–	–	10
R (Ruan) Snyman	BB	2010	1	1	–	–	–	5	2010	1	1	–	–	–	5
PJ (Pierre) Spies	BB	2005	102	25	–	–	–	125	2005	102	25	–	–	–	125
JWA (Wilhelm) Steenkamp	BB	2008	36	–	–	–	–	0	2008	54	1	–	–	–	5
GJ (Deon) Stegmann	BB	2008	75	5	–	–	–	25	2008	75	5	–	–	–	25
M (Morne) Steyn	BB	2005	123	13	242	275	25	1449	2005	123	13	242	275	25	1449
PR (Flip) van der Merwe	BB	2010	57	2	–	–	–	10	2007	63	3	–	–	–	15
HJ (Hencus) van Wyk	BB	2013	1	–	–	–	–	0	2013	1	–	–	–	–	0
JF (Francois) Venter	BB	2012	11	–	–	–	–	0	2012	11	–	–	–	–	0
J (Jano) Vermaak	BB	2012	31	6	–	–	–	30	2006	104	17	3	4	–	103
C-T (Callie) Visagie	Lions	2013	7	1	–	–	–	5	2012	23	1	–	–	–	5
PJ (Jurgen) Visser	BB	2013	11	1	–	–	–	5	2013	11	1	–	–	–	5
FW (Willie) Wepener	BB	2012	23	1	–	–	–	5	2006	63	2	–	–	–	10
P (Paul) Willemse	BB	2013	5	–	–	–	–	0	2013	6	–	–	–	–	0
Totals			1361	215	247	280	25	2484		1561	239	250	284	25	2602

NOTE: **BB** = *Blue Bulls*

VODACOM SUPER RUGBY

FINAL LOG POSITIONS

2013	2nd	2009	1st	2005	3rd	2001	12th	1997* 8th
2012	5th	2008	10th	2004	6th	2000	11th	1996* 3rd
2011	7th	2007	2nd	2003	6th	1999	12th	* As Northern
2010	1st	2006	4th	2002	12th	1998	11th	Transvaal

APPEARANCES & POINTS IN 2013

	Stormers	W Force	Blues	Crusaders	Reds	Brumbies	Cheetahs	Kings	Waratahs	Hurricanes	Highlanders	Sharks	Cheetahs	Kings	Sharks	Stormers	Brumbies	Matches	Tries	Conversions	Penalties	Drop Goals	Points
Kirchner	15	15	15	15	15	15	–	–	–	–	–	14R	15	15	15	15	–	11	1	–	–	–	5
Mapoe	14	13	11	–	14	14	11	11	14R	13R	11	14R	14	–	–	–	–	12	2	–	–	–	10
Engelbrecht	13	–	13	13	13	13	13	13	13	13	13	13	13R	13	13	13	–	16	4	–	–	–	20
Olivier	12	12	12	12	–	–	–	–	12	–	12	–	13	–	–	–	–	7	–	–	–	–	0
Basson	11	11	–	–	11	–	–	13R	11	11	14R	11	11	11	11	11	11	13	1	–	–	–	5
Steyn, M	10	10	10	10	10R	10	10	10	10	10	10	10	10	10R	10	10	10	17	2	32	57	1	248
Hougaard	9	9	14R	x	–	–	–	9R	9R	9	9	9	9	9	9	–	9	11	2	–	–	–	10
Spies	8c	8c	8c	8c	8c	8c	8c	8c	8c	8c	8c	8c	8c	–	–	–	–	13	1	–	–	–	5
Potgieter, D	7	–	–	–	7	7	7	–	6	7	7	7	6R	8c	8c	8c	8c	13	–	–	–	–	0
Stegmann	6	–	6	6	6	6	6	–	6	6	6	6	6	6	6	6	6	15	4	–	–	–	20
Kruger, J	5	5	5	5	4R	5	5	5	5	5	5	5	5	4R	–	–	–	14	–	–	–	–	0
Van der Merwe	4	4	4	4	–	4	4	4	4	4	4	4	4	4	4	4	4	15	–	–	–	–	0
Kruger, W	3	3	3R	3R	3	3	3R	3R	3	3	3R	3R	3	3	3	3	3	17	2	–	–	–	10
Ralepelle	2	2	2R	2R	2	2	2	2	2	2	2	2	2	2	2	2	2	17	2	–	–	–	10
Mellett	1	1	1	1	1	1	1	1	–	–	1	–	–	–	1R	1R	1R	12	–	–	–	–	0
Wepener	2R	2R	2	2	2R	2R	–	–	2R	2R	–	2R	–	2R	–	–	–	10	–	–	–	–	0
Kirsten	3R	1R	3	3	3R	3R	3	3	–	1R	3	3	1R	1R	3R	3R	3R	16	–	–	–	–	0
Hattingh	6R	4R	5R	4R	5	–	–	–	–	5R	4R	x	5R	5	5	5	5	12	–	–	–	–	0
Botha	7R	6	7	7	–	6R	7R	7	7	8R	7R	7R	7	–	–	–	–	12	1	–	–	–	5
Vermaak	9R	9R	9	9	9	9	9	9	9	9R	9R	9R	–	9R	9	14R	–	16	5	–	–	–	25
Fouche	10R	11R	x	12R	10	x	10R	10R	15R	12R	12R	–	13R	10	–	–	–	11	2	4	5	–	33
Venter	13R	–	–	–	12	x	–	–	–	–	–	–	–	–	–	–	–	3	–	–	–	–	0
Potgieter, J	–	7	6R	7R	6R	–	–	6R	6R	–	–	–	–	7	7	7	7	10	2	–	–	–	10
Cook	–	7R	–	–	–	–	–	–	–	–	–	–	–	–	–	–	–	1	1	–	–	–	5
Serfontein	–	13R	–	14R	11R	12	12	12	12	–	12	x	12	12	12	–	12	12	2	–	–	–	10
Mastriet	–	14	–	–	–	–	–	–	–	–	–	–	–	–	–	–	–	1	1	–	–	–	5
Ndungane	–	–	14	14	–	–	14	14	14	14	14	–	14	14	14	14	–	12	4	–	–	–	20
Visser	–	–	11R	11	–	11	15	15	–	15	15	15	15	–	12R	10R	x	11	1	–	–	–	5
Willemse	–	–	–	–	4	4	4R	4R	–	–	–	–	–	–	–	–	5R	5	–	–	–	–	0
Snyman	–	–	–	–	x	x	–	–	–	–	–	–	–	–	–	–	–	0	–	–	–	–	0
Steenkamp	–	–	–	–	x	–	–	4R	–	–	–	–	–	5R	–	–	–	2	–	–	–	–	0
Visagie	–	–	–	–	–	2R	18R	–	–	2R	–	2R	–	2R	2R	2R	–	7	1	–	–	–	5
Beyers	–	–	–	–	–	15R	–	15	–	–	–	–	–	–	–	–	–	2	–	–	–	–	0
Paige	–	–	–	–	–	9R	9R	–	–	–	–	–	14R	–	9R	–	–	4	–	–	–	–	0
Greyling	–	–	–	–	–	–	1	1	–	1	1	1	1	1	1	–	1	8	1	–	–	–	5
Van Wyk	–	–	–	–	–	–	1R	–	–	–	–	–	–	–	–	–	–	1	–	–	–	–	0
Ross	–	–	–	–	–	–	–	–	–	–	–	7R	7R	7R	7R	–	–	4	–	–	–	–	0
Du Plessis	–	–	–	–	–	–	–	–	–	–	–	–	–	–	4R	–	–	1	–	–	–	–	0
38 players																			364	42	36	62	1	471

▓ *Yellow Card* ■ *Red Card*

VODACOM SUPER RUGBY

Pass master...Morné Steyn was back to his best in 2013 after a forgettable 2012 season. *Duif du Toit/Gallo Images*

2013 **RESULTS & SCORERS**

Date	Venue	Opponent	Result	Score	Referee	Scorers
Febr 22	Pretoria	STORMERS	WON	25-17	J Peyper	T: Ralepelle. C: Steyn. P: Steyn (6).
Mrch 02	Pretoria	W FORCE	WON	36-26	J Jaftha	T: W Kruger, Mastriet, Steyn. C: Steyn (2). P: Steyn (4).
Mrch 10	Auckland	BLUES	WON	28-21	G Williamson	T: Ndungane, Botha, Mapoe. C: Steyn (2). P: Steyn (3).
Mrch 16	Christchurch	CRUSADERS	LOST	19-41	C Pollock	T: Stegmann. C: Steyn. P: Steyn (4).
Mrch 23	Brisbane	REDS	LOST	18-23	J Leckie	P: Fouche (5), Steyn.
Mrch 30	Canberra	BRUMBIES	LOST	20-23	J White	T: Engelbrecht, Visser. C: Steyn (2). P: Steyn (2).
April 13	Pretoria	CHEETAHS	WON	26-20	J Jaftha	T: Vermaak, Visagie. C: Steyn (2). P: Steyn (4).
April 20	Port Elizabeth	KINGS	WON	34-0	F Pastrana	T: Ndungane, J Potgieter, Serfontein, Vermaak. C: Steyn (2), Fouche (2). P: Steyn. DG: Steyn.
April 27	Pretoria	WARATAHS	WON	30-19	F Pastrana	T: Steyn, Hougaard. C: Steyn. P: Steyn (6).
May 04	Pretoria	HURRICANES	WON	48-14	L vd Merwe	T: Ndungane, Greyling, Stegmann, Engelbrecht, Mapoe, Fouche. C: Steyn (5), Fouche. P: Steyn (2).
May 18	Pretoria	HIGHLANDERS	WON	35-18	J Peyper	T: Ndungane, Vermaak, Engelbrecht, Spies. C: Steyn (3). P: Steyn (3).
May 25	Durban	SHARKS	WON	18-16	J Kaplan	P: Steyn (6).
Jun 01	Bloemfontein	CHEETAHS	WON	30-25	J Jaftha	T: Stegmann, W Kruger, Vermaak. C: Steyn (3). P: Steyn (3).
Jun 29	Pretoria	KINGS	WON	48-18	L vd Merwe	T: Ralepelle, Stegmann, Hougaard, J Potgieter, Serfontein, Fouche. C: Steyn (5), Fouche. P: Steyn (2).
July 06	Pretoria	SHARKS	WON	20-19	J Jaftha	T: Basson, Vermaak. C: Steyn (2). P: Steyn (2).
July 13	Cape Town	STORMERS	LOST	13-30	C Joubert	T: Kirchner. C: Steyn (2). P: Steyn (2).
Semi-final						
July 27	Pretoria	BRUMBIES	LOST	23-26	C Joubert	T: Engelbrecht. P: Steyn (6).

Played	Won	Lost	Drawn	Points for	Points against	Tries for	Tries against
17	**12**	**5**	**0**	**471**	**356**	**42**	**36**

VODACOM BULLS RECORDS

MATCH RECORDS

Biggest win	89	v Queensland Reds (92-3)	Pretoria	2007
Heaviest defeat	64	v ACT Brumbies (9-73)	Canberra	1999
Highest score	92	v Queensland Reds (92-3)	Pretoria	2007
Most points conceded	75	v Crusaders (25-75)	Christchurch	2000
Most tries	13	v Queensland Reds (92-3)	Pretoria	2007
Most tries conceded	11	v Crusaders (25-75)	Christchurch	2000
Most points by a player	39	JH Kruger (1t 5c 8p) v Highlanders	Pretoria	1996
Most tries by a player	3	AJ Richter v Blues	Pretoria	1997
	3	PF du Preez v Cats	Pretoria	2004
	3	W Olivier vs Rebels	Pretoria	2011
Most conversions by a player	11	DJ Hougaard v Queensland Reds	Pretoria	2007
Most penalties by a player	8	JH Kruger v Highlanders	Pretoria	1996
	8	DJ Hougaard v Crusaders	Pretoria	2007
Most drop goals by a player	4	M Steyn vs Crusaders	Pretoria	2009

SEASON RECORDS

Most team points	500	from 15 matches	2010
Most points by a player	263	M Steyn	2010
Most team tries	52	from 17 matches	2012
Most tries by a player	10	BA Basson	2011-2012
Most conversions by a player	38	M Steyn	2010
	38	M Steyn	2012
Most penalties by a player	57	M Steyn	2013
Most drop goals by a player	11	M Steyn	2009

CAREER RECORDS

Most appearances	123	M Steyn	2005-2013
Most points	1449	M Steyn	2005-2013
Most tries	37	BG Habana	2005-2009
Most conversions	242	M Steyn	2005-2013
Most penalties	275	M Steyn	2005-2013
Most drop goals	25	M Steyn	2005-2013

TOYOTA CHEETAHS

Cheetahs release their handbrake

THE TOYOTA CHEETAHS ENJOYED THEIR MOST SUCCESSFUL season in Vodacom Super Rugby, making the play-offs for the first time in their history while unearthing superb new talent along the way.

Although they fell to eventual finalists the Brumbies in Canberra in a wild card play-off game after finishing sixth on the overall standings, 10 wins from 16 league games signalled massive progress for the Bloemfontein-based side.

Their success came down largely to their improved fitness and defensive structure, which ensured they were competitive in almost every match.

The assistance of Springbok defence coach John McFarland, who spent some time with the team in pre-season, played a big role in the Cheetahs' defensive improvement while a more 'position- and match-specific approach' to fitness training ensured that they had few injuries.

Five of the pack – props Lourens Adriaanse and Coenie Oosthuizen, hooker Adriaan Strauss, lock Lood de Jager and No 8 Phillip van der Walt – featured in all 17 matches. Prop Trevor Nyakane and flank Lappies Labuschagne played in 16 while Heinrich Brüssow featured in 15 matches. There was remarkable consistency in selection and fitness.

Behind the scrum the situation was similar with wings Raymond Rhule and Willie le Roux, centres Robert Ebersohn and Johann Sadie and scrumhalf Piet van Zyl involved in every match. Fullback Hennie Daniller missed only one game and reserve scrumhalf Sarel Pretorius featured in 15 matches.

The Cheetahs' only serious issue was at flyhalf where they lost Springbok Johan Goosen for the season in a freak training-ground accident on tour in Sydney.

But in Goosen's absence, stand-in Burton Francis made the position his own for the bulk of the season after landing an injury-time penalty to beat the DHL Stormers in a crunch game. He finished as the franchise's leading scorer with 62 points.

Wing Le Roux, enjoying his second season at this level, was the playmaker around which the Cheetahs' attacking gameplan centred and, despite an initial reticence by Springbok coach Heyneke Meyer to select him, Le Roux was almost a permanent fixture in the Springbok No 14 jersey just a few months later.

Le Roux's ability to take the ball as first receiver, pop up at centre, or hit the line from fullback, created havoc in opposing defences.

The Cheetahs' season started inauspiciously with a home loss to the Sharks, while a 45-3 thrashing at the hands of the defending champion Chiefs in Hamilton during their tour-opener the following week suggested another long season was in store.

But the Cheetahs rallied with tour wins over the Highlanders, Waratahs and Force, followed by home wins over the Rebels and Stormers. Their five-match winning streak was a franchise record.

BY CRAIG RAY,
THE TIMES

GROUND
Free State Stadium
CAPACITY
46 000
ADDRESS
Att Horak Ave, Bloemfontein
TELEPHONE
051-407 1700
COLOURS
White jersey with an orange collar and russet orange and Biscay bay detail. White shorts, russet orange socks
WEBSITE
www.fscheetahs.co.za
COACH
Naka Drotske
CAPTAIN
Adriaan Strauss
MANAGER
Eugene van Wyk
MANAGING DIRECTOR
Harold Verster
CHAIRMAN
Randal September

Dynamo...wing Willie le Roux. *Johan Pretorius/Gallo Images*

COACHES & MANAGEMENT

HEAD COACH: Naka Drotské **ASSISTANT COACHES:** Hawies Fourie & Oersond Gorgonzola
FORWARDS & SCRUM COACH: Os du Randt **STRENGTH & CONDITIONING:** Niel du Plessis
VIDEO ANALYST: Charl Strydom **MANAGER:** Eugene van Wyk **DOCTOR:** Dr Ferdie Wesso
PHYSIOTHERAPIST: JP du Toit **LOGISTICS:** Sakkie Wessels **MEDIA OFFICER:** Ronel Pienaar
DEFENCE COACH: Michael Horak

APPEARANCES & POINTS IN SUPER RUGBY

			CHEETAHS CAREER						SUPER RUGBY CAREER					
	Province	Debut	Matches	Tries	Conversions	Penalties	Drop Goals	Points	Debut	Matches	Tries	Conversions	Penalties	Drop Goals	Points
LC (Lourens) Adriaanse	GW	2011	30	–	–	–	–	0	2011	30	–	–	–	–	0
RJ (Ryno) Barnes	GW	2010	30	–	–	–	–	0	2010	30	–	–	–	–	0
RS (Rayno) Benjamin	FS	2011	28	7	–	–	–	35	2006	51	9	–	–	–	45
F (Francois) Brummer	GW	2013	1	–	–	1	–	3	2010	2	–	1	1	–	5
HW (Heinrich) Brüssow	FS	2007	70	6	–	–	–	30	2007	70	6	–	–	–	30
HJ (Hennie) Daniller	FS	2008	76	7	–	–	–	35	2004	83	7	–	–	–	35
MJ (Tewis) de Bruyn	FS	2008	57	3	2	2	–	25	2008	57	3	2	2	–	25
L (Lodewyk) de Jager	FS	2013	17	–	–	–	–	0	2013	17	–	–	–	–	0
RT (Robert) Ebersohn	FS	2010	59	11	–	–	–	55	2010	59	11	–	–	–	55
BK (Burton) Francis	FS	2013	6	–	7	15	1	62	2008	33	1	20	27	2	132
AD (Barry) Geel	FS	2010	8	–	–	–	–	0	2010	8	–	–	–	–	0
JL (Johan) Goosen	FS	2012	13	3	25	40	1	188	2012	13	3	25	40	1	188
PHC (Pieter) Labuschagne	FS	2012	19	2	–	–	–	10	2012	19	2	–	–	–	10
RJ (Rynard) Landman	GW	2013	14	–	–	–	–	–	2013	14	–	–	–	–	0
WJ (Willie) le Roux	GW	2012	33	13	–	–	–	65	2012	33	13	–	–	–	65
XH (Howard) Mnisi	GW	2013	1	–	–	–	–	0	2013	1	–	–	–	–	0
TN (Trevor) Nyakane	FS	2012	27	2	–	–	–	10	2012	27	2	–	–	–	10
CR (Caylib) Oosthuizen	FS	–	0	–	–	–	–	0	2012	6	1	–	–	–	5
CV (Coenie) Oosthuizen	FS	2010	57	8	–	–	–	40	2010	57	8	–	–	–	40
SJ (Sarel) Pretorius	FS	2009	53	19	–	–	–	95	2009	67	21	–	–	–	105
JG (Boom) Prinsloo	FS	2012	13	1	–	–	–	5	2012	13	1	–	–	–	5
RK (Raymond) Rhule	FS	2013	17	5	–	–	–	25	2013	17	5	–	–	–	25
J (Johann) Sadie	FS	2013	17	5	–	–	–	25	2011	34	7	–	–	–	35
AJ (Riaan) Smit	FS	2011	24	3	11	23	–	106	2011	24	3	11	23	–	106
JA (Adriaan) Strauss	FS	2007	81	8	–	–	–	40	2006	89	8	–	–	–	40
FJ (Francois) Uys	FS	2009	33	–	–	–	–	0	2009	33	–	–	–	–	0
CP (Philip) van der Walt	FS	2010	41	3	–	–	–	15	2010	41	3	–	–	–	15
PE (Piet) van Zyl	FS	2012	32	5	–	–	–	25	2012	32	5	–	–	–	25
FJN (Frans) Viljoen	FS	2006	34	1	–	–	–	5	2006	34	1	–	–	–	5
PV (Waltie) Vermeulen	FS	2010	23	1	–	–	–	5	2010	23	1	–	–	–	5
EG (Elgar) Watts	FS	2013	6	–	7	8	–	38	2013	6	–	7	8	–	38
Totals			**891**	**106**	**45**	**81**	**2**	**942**		**958**	**121**	**59**	**93**	**3**	**1011**

NOTE: *FS* = *Free State*, *GW* = *Griqualand West*

FINAL LOG POSITIONS

2013	6th	2011	11th	2009	14th	2007	11th
2012	10th	2010	10th	2008	13th	2006	10th

1997 7th

APPEARANCES & POINTS IN 2013

CHEETAHS

	Sharks	Chiefs	Highlanders	Waratahs	Force	Rebels	Stormers	Bulls	Sharks	Kings	Hurricanes	Reds	Kings	Bulls	Stormers	Blues	Brumbies	Matches	Tries	Conversions	Penalties	Drop Goals	Points
Daniller	15	15	15	15	15	15	15	15	15	15	15	15	15	15	–	15	15	16	1	–	–	–	5
Le Roux	14	14	14	14	14	14	14	14	14	14	14	14	11	14	15	14	14	17	6	–	–	–	30
Sadie	13	13	13	13	13	13	13	13	13	13	13	13	13	13	13	13	13	17	5	–	–	–	25
Ebersohn	12	12	12	12	12	12	12	12	12	12	12	12	12	12	12	12	12	17	4	–	–	–	20
Rhule	11	11	11	11	11	11	11	11	11	11	11	11	14R	11	11	11	11	17	5	–	–	–	25
Goosen	10	10	10	10	–	–	–	–	–	–	–	–	–	–	–	–	–	4	–	8	9	–	43
Van Zyl	9	9R	9R	9R	9R	9R	9	9	9	9	9	9	9	9	9	9	9	17	3	–	–	–	15
Van der Walt	8	8	8	8	8	8	8	8	8	8	8	8	8	8	8	8	8	17	2	–	–	–	10
Labuschagne	7	7	7	7	7	7	7	7	7	7	–	7	7	7	7	7	7	16	2	–	–	–	10
Viljoen	6	6	6	6	–	–	6R	7R	7R	7	–	–	–	–	–	–	–	8	–	–	–	–	0
Uys	5	5	5	5	5	5	5	5	5	5	5	5	5	–	–	–	–	14	–	–	–	–	0
De Jager	4	4	4	4	4	4	4	4	4	4	4	4	4	4	4	4	4	17	–	–	–	–	0
Adriaanse	3	3	3	3	3	3	3	3	3	3	3	3	3	3	3	3	3	17	–	–	–	–	0
Strauss	2c	2c	2c	2c	2c	2c	2c	2c	2c	2c	2c	2c	2c	2c	2c	2c	2c	17	–	–	–	–	0
Nyakane	1	1	1	1	1	1	1	1	–	3R	3R	3R	3R	3R	3R	3R	3R	16	2	–	–	–	10
Barnes	18R	2R	2R	x	x	2R	x	x	x	x	x	2R	2R	x	2R	2R	x	8	–	–	–	–	0
Oosthuizen, Coenie	3R	3R	3R	1R	3R	3R	3R	3R	1	1	1	1	1	1	1	1	1	17	2	–	–	–	10
Vermeulen	4R	–	–	–	–	–	–	–	–	–	–	–	–	5R	5R	4R	–	4	–	–	–	–	0
Prinsloo	8R	6R	–	–	8R	8R	6R	–	–	–	7R	6R	6R	8R	6R	7R	7R	12	1	–	–	–	5
Pretorius	9R	9	9	9	9	9	9R	–	–	9R	9R	9R	9R	9R	14	9R	9R	15	4	–	–	–	20
Watts	x	–	–	–	–	–	–	10R	10R	10	10	x	9R	10R	x	–	–	6	–	7	8	–	38
Benjamin	12R	13R	12R	x	13R	13R	20R	15R	13R	14R	11R	13R	14	12R	–	14R	11R	15	2	–	–	–	10
Landman	–	4R	4R	4R	4R	4R	4R	4R	x	4R	x	4R	4R	5R	5	5	5	14	–	–	–	–	0
Smit	–	10R	x	x	10	–	–	–	–	–	10R	11R	10	10	10	10	–	8	1	5	13	–	54
Brussow	–	–	6R	6R	6	6	6	6	6	6	6	6	6	6	6	6	6	15	–	–	–	–	0
Francis	–	–	–	–	x	10	10	10	10	10	10	–	–	–	–	–	–	6	–	7	15	1	62
Geel	–	–	–	–	12R	–	–	–	–	–	–	–	–	–	–	–	–	1	–	–	–	–	0
Brummer	–	–	–	–	–	x	10R	x	–	–	–	–	–	–	–	–	–	1	–	–	1	–	3
De Bruyn	–	–	–	–	–	–	9R	x	–	–	–	–	–	–	–	–	–	1	–	–	–	–	0
Oosthuizen, Caylib	–	–	–	–	–	–	–	x	–	–	–	–	–	–	–	–	–	0	–	–	–	–	0
Mnisi	–	–	–	–	–	–	–	–	–	–	–	–	–	13R	–	–	–	1	–	–	–	–	0
De Bruyn	–	–	–	–	–	–	–	–	–	–	–	–	–	x	–	–	–	0	–	–	–	–	0
32 players																		351	40	27	46	1	395

▓ *Yellow Card* ■ *Red Card*

VODACOM SUPER RUGBY

No way through...the Cheetahs were a completely different defensive team in 2013.
Loren Battersby / Gallo Images

2013 TOYOTA CHEETAHS SUPERRUGBY RESULTS & SCORERS

Date	Venue	Opponent	Result	Score	Referee	Scorers
Febr 23	Bloemfontein	SHARKS	LOST	22-29	J Kaplan	T: Van der Walt, Sadie, Labuschagne. C: Goosen (2). P: Goosen.
Mrch 02	Hamilton	CHIEFS	LOST	3-45	M Fraser	P: Goosen.
Mrch 09	Invercargill	HIGHLANDERS	WON	36-19	N Briant	T: Pretorius (2), Ebersohn. C: Goosen (3). P: Goosen (5).
Mrch 15	Sydney	WARATAHS	WON	27-26	G Williamson	T: Rhule (2), Ebersohn. C: Goosen (3). P: Goosen (2).
Mrch 23	Perth	FORCE	WON	19-10	G Williamson	T: Le Roux. C: Smit. P: Smit (4).
Mrch 30	Bloemfontein	REBELS	WON	34-16	G Jackson	T: Daniller, Rhule, Sadie, Le Roux, Benjamin. C: Francis (3). P: Francis.
April 06	Bloemfontein	STORMERS	WON	26-24	S Berry	T: Ebersohn, Pretorius. C: Francis (2). P: Francis (3). DG: Francis.
April 13	Pretoria	BULLS	LOST	20-26	J Jaftha	T: Nyakane. P: Francis (4), Brummer.
April 20	Durban	SHARKS	WON	12-6	J White	T: Rhule, Le Roux. C: Francis.
April 27	Bloemfontein	KINGS	WON	26-12	J White	T: Rhule, Labuschagne, Le Roux. C: Francis. P: Francis (3).
May 10	Bloemfontein	HURRICANES	LOST	34-39	S Berry	T: Oosthuizen (2), Ebersohn. C: Watts (2). P: Francis (4), Watts (2).
May 17	Bloemfontein	REDS	WON	27-13	C Joubert	T: Van Zyl (2). C: Watts. P: Watts (5).
May 25	Port Elizabeth	KINGS	WON	34-22	S Berry	T: Sadie (2), Van Zyl, Le Roux. C: Watts (4). P: Watts (2).
Jun 01	Bloemfontein	BULLS	LOST	25-30	J Jaftha	T: Le Roux, Nyakane, Smit. C: Smit (2). P: Smit (2).
Jun 29	Cape Town	STORMERS	LOST	03-28	S Berry	P: Smit.
July 06	Bloemfontein	BLUES	WON	34-13	J Peyper	T: Van der Walt, Pretorius, Prinsloo. C: Smit (2). P: Smit (5).
Play-off						
July 21	Canberra	BRUMBIES	LOST	13-15	G Jackson	T: Sadie, Benjamin. P: Smit.

Played	Won	Lost	Drawn	Points for	Points against	Tries for	Tries against
17	**10**	**7**	**0**	**395**	**373**	**40**	**33**

TOYOTA CHEETAHS RECORDS

MATCH RECORDS

Biggest win	49	vs. Lions (59-10)	Welkom	2010
Heaviest defeat	46	vs. Brumbies (15-61)	Canberra	2010
Highest score	59	vs. Lions (59-10)	Welkom	2010
Most points conceded	61	vs. Brumbies (15-61)	Canberra	2010
Most tries	9	vs. Lions (59-10)	Welkom	2010
Most tries conceded	9	vs. Brumbies (15-61)	Canberra	2010
Most points by a player	26	HM Bosman vs. Stormers	Cape Town	2006
Most tries by a player	3	SJ Pretorius vs Hurricanes	Bloemfontein	2011
	3	R Viljoen vs Lions	Johannesburg	2011
	3	RS Benjamin vs Stormers	Bloemfontein	2011
Most conversions by a player	7	JH de Beer vs. Highlanders	Invercargill	1997
Most penalties by a player	8	HM Bosman vs. Stormers	Cape Town	2006
Most drop goals by a player	2	JM Ebersohn vs Hurricanes	Bloemfontein	2011
	2	R Viljoen vs Brumbies	Bloemfontein	2011

SEASON RECORDS

Most team points	435	in 16 games	2011
Most points by a player	179	JM Ebersohn	2011
Most team tries	44	in 16 games	2011
Most tries by a player	9	SJ Pretorius	2011
Most conversions by a player	32	JM Ebersohn	2011
Most penalties by a player	33	JM Ebersohn	2011
Most drop goals by a player	2	IP Olivier	2010
	2	JM Ebersohn	2011
	2	R Viljoen	2011

CAREER RECORDS

Most appearances	81	JA Strauss	2007-2013
Most points	220	JM Ebersohn	2010-2012
Most tries	19	SJ Pretorius	2009-2013
Most conversions	36	JM Ebersohn	2010-2012
Most penalties	44	JM Ebersohn	2010-2012
Most drop goals	2	IP Olivier	2009-2010
	2	JM Ebersohn	2010-2011
	2	R Viljoen	2010-2011

SOUTHERN KINGS

Kings-for-a-season lose their crown

CONSIDERING THE BASE THE KINGS STARTED FROM, WITH confirmation of their inclusion in Vodacom Super Rugby only coming in August 2012, their debut season was hugely positive even if their final position on the standings didn't reflect that fact.

Three wins and a draw in 16 matches does not sound like a season worthy of anything other than strong criticism. But for a team that only existed on paper five months before the 2013 Super Rugby campaign started, it was a remarkable effort.

Ultimately the Kings would finish last with 24 points, but their three wins matched those of the Highlanders who finished one place above them.

The Kings built their game on a solid set piece, superb fitness, committed and organised defence and the steady boot of Western Province's Currie Cup-winning flyhalf Demetri Catrakilis, who contributed 142 points. They had very little time to do more than that.

The impressive Nelson Mandela Bay Stadium in Port Elizabeth was also a colourful new addition to the tournament and an average home crowd of nearly 31,000 made the Kings the second-most watched team in the tournament behind the DHL Stormers.

Alan Solomons, despite having the title 'director of rugby', was quite clearly the man behind building a squad with few stars, several journeymen and a handful of up-and-coming young talents. Solomons moulded a competitive unit quickly even though captain Luke Watson sustained a throat injury in their opening game against the Force that would keep him out for five weeks.

After gloomy predictions that the newcomers would be cannon fodder the Kings silenced their detractors with a 22-10 win over the Force in game one. Several unknown players such as flank Wimpie van der Walt and the 18-year-old wing Sergeal Pietersen caught the eye as the Kings won new friends.

Two home losses followed, to the 2012 finalists the Sharks and Chiefs, where the Kings competed admirably before their maiden Australasian tour.

Not surprisingly the Kings fell to the All Black-laden Crusaders (55-20) and Hurricanes (46-30) before securing arguably the surprise result of the tournament when they held the Brumbies, eventual runners-up, to a 28-28 draw in Canberra. A 30-27 victory over the Rebels concluded a successful tour.

The Kings secured their third victory with a 34-27 win over the Highlanders in PE in week 13 but finished with five consecutive losses that ultimately left them stranded at the bottom of the standings.

After propping up the SA conference the Kings played a promotion-relegation series against the MTN Lions. Each team won their away leg, but the Kings lost out by two points on aggregate and won't participate in the 2014.

GROUND
Nelson Mandela Bay Stadium, Port Elizabeth
CAPACITY
46 000
ADDRESS
70 Prince Alfred Road, Sydenham, PE
TELEPHONE NUMBER
+ 27 41 408 8902
COLOURS
Black jersey with Team Charcoal/Ebony inserts and white piping. Black shorts and socks
WEBSITE
www.skings.co.za
COACH
Matt Sexton
CAPTAIN
Luke Watson
CHARMAIN
Cheeky Watson
CEO
Charl Crous

BY CRAIG RAY,
THE TIMES

Charging King...Jacques Engelbrecht. *Johan Pretorius/Gallo Images*

COACHES & MANAGEMENT

DIRECTOR OF RUGBY: Alan Solomons **HEAD COACH:** Matt Sexton
DEFENCE & BREAKDOWN: Omar Mouneimne **BACKS AND ATTACK COACH:** Bradley Mooar
PERFORMANCE ANALYST: Southy Steenkamp **STRENGTH & CONDITIONING:** Johan Pretorius
PHYSIOTHERAPIST: James Fleming **DOCTOR:** Dr Conrad van Hagen **MASSEUR:** Lelani van der merwe
ASST PHYSIOTHERAPIST: Kim Naidoo **MANAGER:** Willem Oliphant **LOGISTICS MANAGER:** Sydney Goba

APPEARANCES & POINTS IN SUPER RUGBY

			KINGS CAREER						SUPER RUGBY CAREER					
	Province	Debut	Matches	Tries	Conversions	Penalties	Drop Goals	Points	Debut	Matches	Tries	Conversions	Penalties	Drop Goals	Points
DO (Daniel) Adongo	EP	2013	5	–	–	–	–	0	2013	5	–	–	–	–	0
RM (Rynier) Bernardo	EP	2013	10	–	–	–	–	–	2013	10	–	–	–	–	–
DJ (David) Bulbring	EP	2013	18	–	–	–	–	–	2010	21	–	–	–	–	0
K (Kevin) Buys	EP	2013	17	–	–	–	–	–	2010	30	–	–	–	–	0
D (Demetri) Catrakilis	EP	2013	15	–	14	40	1	151	2013	–	–	14	40	1	151
RJ (Ronnie) Cooke	EP	2013	17	2	–	–	–	10	2006	41	7	–	–	–	35
A (Aidon) Davis	EP	2013	1	–	–	–	–	–	2013	1	–	–	–	–	0
CF (Charl) du Plessis	EP	2013	3	–	–	–	–	–	2013	3	–	–	–	–	0
CG (Cornell) du Preez	EP	2013	16	3	–	–	–	15	2013	16	3	–	–	–	15
WR (Wesley) Dunlop	EP	–	0	–	–	–	–	–	–	0	–	–	–	–	0
JJ (Jacques) Engelbrecht	EP	2013	17	1	–	–	–	5	2013	17	1	–	–	–	5
J (Jaco) Engels	EP	2013	4	–	–	–	–	–	2006	44	2	–	–	–	10
SJP (Schalk) Ferreira	EP	2013	17	2	–	–	–	10	2007	33	2	–	–	–	10
J (Hannes) Franklin	EP	2013	10	1	–	–	–	5	2010	22	3	–	–	–	15
SE (Shane) Gates	EP	2013	7	–	–	–	–	–	2013	7	–	–	–	–	0
S (Siyanda) Grey	EP	2013	4	–	–	–	–	–	2013	4	–	–	–	–	0
JD (Johan) Herbst	SWD	2013	1	–	–	–	–	–	2013	1	–	–	–	–	0
GD (Grant) Kemp	SWD	2013	13	–	–	–	–	–	2013	13	–	–	–	–	0
M (Micheal) Killian	EP	2013	4	–	–	–	–	–	2009	41	10	–	–	–	50
V (Virgille) Lacombe	EP	2013	4	–	–	–	–	–	2013	4	–	–	–	–	0
T (Tomas) Leonardi	EP	2013	1	–	–	–	–	–	2013	1	–	–	–	–	0
BG (Bandise) Maku	EP	2013	18	–	–	–	–	–	2008	51	–	–	–	–	0
T (Thabo) Mamojele	EP	2013	1	–	–	–	–	–	2013	1	–	–	–	–	0
SP (SP) Marais	EP	2013	10	–	–	–	–	–	2013	10	–	–	–	–	0
E (Edgar) Marutlulle	Leo	2013	4	–	–	–	–	–	2011	12	–	–	–	–	0
MM (Mpho) Mbiyozo	EP	2013	1	1	–	–	–	5	2013	1	1	–	–	–	5
WM (Waylon) Murray	EP	2013	8	–	–	–	–	–	2006	63	8	–	–	–	40
DP (Darron) Nell	EP	2013	7	–	–	–	–	–	2007	17	2	–	–	–	10
DA (Devin) Oosthuizen	EP	2013	11	–	–	–	–	–	2013	11	–	–	–	–	0
H (Hadleigh) Parkes	EP	2013	7	–	–	–	–	–	2012	20	2	–	–	–	10
S (Sergeal) Petersen	EP	2013	8	4	–	–	–	20	2013	8	4	–	–	–	20
MED (Marcello) Sampson	EP	2013	14	1	–	–	–	5	2013	14	1	–	–	–	5
SS (Siviwe) Soyizwapi	EP	2013	6	–	–	–	–	–	2013	6	–	–	–	–	0
AJ (Andries) Strauss	EP	2013	14	–	–	–	–	–	2006	54	4	–	–	–	20
SR (Steven) Sykes	EP	2013	15	2	–	–	–	10	2007	84	11	–	–	–	55
S (Scott) van Breda	EP	2013	2	12	3	–	–	18	2013	2	1	2	3	–	18
PW (Wimpie) van der Walt	EP	2013	17	6	–	–	–	30	2013	17	6	–	–	–	30
E (Elric) van Vuuren	SWD	2013	2	–	–	–	–	–	2013	2	–	–	–	–	0
SH (Shaun) Venter	Pumas	2013	18	2	–	–	–	10	2013	18	2	–	–	–	10
N (Nicolas) Vergallo	EP	2013	14	1	–	–	–	5	2013	14	1	–	–	–	5
LA (Luke) Watson	EP	2013	6	2	–	–	–	10	2003	88	13	–	–	–	65
GA (George) Whitehead	EP	2013	17	2	6	3	–	31	2013	17	2	6	3	–	31
			384	42	23	43	1	340							

NOTE: EP = Eastern Province Kings, **SWD** = South Western Districts, **LEO** = Leopards

VODACOM SUPER RUGBY

FINAL LOG POSITIONS

2013 15th

APPEARANCES & POINTS IN 2013

KINGS

Player	Force	Sharks	Chiefs	Crusaders	Hurricanes	Brumbies	Rebels	Bulls	Cheetahs	Waratahs	Highlanders	Cheetahs	Stormers	Bulls	Stormers	Sharks	Lions	Lions	Matches	Tries	Conversions	Penalties	Drop Goals	Points
Marais	15	15	15	–	–	–	–	–	–	11R	15	15	15	15	–	15	15	10	–	–	–	–	–	0
Petersen	14	14	14	14	14	14	14	–	–	14	–	–	–	–	–	–	–	–	8	4	–	–	–	20
Cooke	13	13	13	13	13	11	11	14	13	13	13	13	13	13	–	13	13	17	2	–	–	–	–	10
Strauss	12	12	12R	–	12c	12c	12c	12	12c	12c	12	12	12	12c	12c	–	–	14	–	–	–	–	–	0
Sampson	11	11	11	11	–	11R	14R	11	–	–	11	11	11	11	11	11	–	14	1	–	–	–	–	5
Catrakilis	10	10	10	10	10	15R	10	10	10	10	10	–	10	10	–	10	–	15	–	14	40	1	–	151
Venter	9	9	9	9	9	9R	9	9	9	9	9	9	9R	9	9	9R	9	9	18	2	–	–	–	10
Du Preez	8	6	6	6	–	8	8	6	6	6	8	8	6	6	–	6	6	16	3	–	–	–	–	15
Watson	7c	–	–	–	–	–	8c	8R	7R	7c	7c	–	–	–	–	–	–	6	2	–	–	–	–	10
Van der Walt	6	7	7	7	7	7	7	7	7	7	6	6	7	7	7	7	7	17	6	–	–	–	–	30
Sykes	5	4	4c	–	4	4	4	4	4	4	4	–	–	4R	4c	4R	4R	15	2	–	–	–	–	10
Bulbring	4	5R	5	5	5	5R	5R	5	5R	5R	5	5	5	5	5	5	5	18	–	–	–	–	–	0
Buys	3	3	3	3	3	3R	3R	3	3	3	3	3	3	–	3	3	3	17	–	–	–	–	–	0
Maku	2	2	2	2	2	2R	2R	2	2	2	2	2	2	2	2R	2	2	18	–	–	–	–	–	0
Ferreira	1	1	1	1c	1	1	1	1	1	1	1	1	1	1	–	1	1	17	2	–	–	–	–	10
Marutlulle	2R	2R	2R	2R	–	–	–	–	–	–	–	–	–	–	–	–	–	4	–	–	–	–	–	0
Engels	3R	1R	3R	3R	–	–	–	–	–	–	–	–	–	–	–	–	–	4	–	–	–	–	–	0
Adongo	x	8R	5R	4	6R	–	–	–	–	4R	–	x	–	–	–	–	–	5	–	–	–	–	–	0
Engelbrecht	8R	8	8	8	8	6R	6R	8R	8	8	–	6R	8	8	8	8	8	17	1	–	–	–	–	5
Herbst	9R	–	–	–	–	–	–	–	–	–	–	–	–	–	–	–	–	1	–	–	–	–	–	0
Whitehead	x	14R	15R	15	15	10	15	15	15	15	15	10R	10	10R	15R	10	10R	10	17	2	6	3	–	31
Parkes	x	12R	12	12	11	–	–	–	–	–	–	–	–	–	14	14	11	7	–	–	–	–	–	0
Nell	–	5c	–	–	–	–	–	–	–	–	4	4	4	5R	4c	4c	–	7	–	–	–	–	–	0
Vergallo	–	9R	9R	9R	9R	9	x	9R	9R	8R	9R	9	9R	9R	9	x	x	14	1	–	–	–	–	5
Leonardi	–	–	4R	–	–	–	–	–	–	–	–	–	–	–	–	–	–	1	–	–	–	–	–	0
Bernardo	–	–	–	4R	5R	5	5	4R	5	5	–	5R	4R	4R	–	–	–	10	–	–	–	–	–	0
Murray	–	–	–	12R	11R	13	13	13	x	12R	–	–	–	–	13	x	12	8	–	–	–	–	–	0
Van Vuuren	–	–	–	10R	10R	–	–	–	–	–	–	–	–	–	–	–	–	2	–	–	–	–	–	0
Oosthuizen	–	–	–	7R	6	6	–	–	–	6R	–	8R	8R	8R	7	8R	7R	11	–	–	–	–	–	0
Kemp	–	–	–	–	3R	3	3	3R	3R	3R	3R	3R	3R	3R	3	3R	3R	13	–	–	–	–	–	0
Franklin	–	–	–	–	2R	2	2	2R	–	–	–	2R	2R	2R	2	2R	2R	10	1	–	–	–	–	5
Soyizwapi	–	–	–	–	–	15	13R	10R	x	14R	–	–	14	–	–	15	–	6	–	–	–	–	–	0
Van Breda	–	–	–	–	–	–	13R	–	–	–	–	–	–	–	–	–	14	2	1	2	3	–	18
Grey	–	–	–	–	–	–	–	14	11	14	14	–	–	–	–	–	–	4	–	–	–	–	–	0
Killian	–	–	–	–	–	–	–	11	–	–	–	–	14	14	11R	–	–	4	–	–	–	–	–	0
Lacombe	–	–	–	–	–	–	–	2R	2R	2R	2R	–	–	–	–	–	–	4	–	–	–	–	–	0
Gates	–	–	–	–	–	–	–	–	–	12R	14R	x	12R	13R	12	12	12R	7	–	–	–	–	–	0
Du Plessis	–	–	–	–	–	–	–	–	–	–	–	–	3R	1	–	3R	3	–	–	–	–	–	0
Mbiyozo	–	–	–	–	–	–	–	–	–	–	–	–	–	6	–	–	–	1	1	–	–	–	–	5
Davis	–	–	–	–	–	–	–	–	–	–	–	–	–	6R	–	–	–	1	–	–	–	–	–	0
Mamojele	–	–	–	–	–	–	–	–	–	–	–	–	–	4R	–	–	–	1	–	–	–	–	–	0
Dunlop	–	–	–	–	–	–	–	–	–	–	–	–	–	–	–	–	x	–	–	–	–	–	–	0
42 players																		**384**	**31**	**22**	**46**	**1**	**340**

▓ *Yellow Card* ■ *Red Card* ▓ *Promotion/Relagation Match*

VODACOM SUPER RUGBY

Together as one...the Kings were a tight unit in 2013.
Loren Battersby / Gallo Images

2013 **RESULTS & SCORERS**

Date	Venue	Opponent	Result	Score	Referee	Scorers
Febr 23	Port Elizabeth	FORCE	**WON**	22-10	L vd Merwe	T: Petersen (2). P: Catrakilis (4).
Mrch 09	Port Elizabeth	SHARKS	LOST	12-21	J Jaftha	P: Catrakilis (4).
Mrch 15	Port Elizabeth	CHIEFS	LOST	24-35	S Berry	T: Engelbrecht, Petersen. C: Catrakilis. P: Catrakilis (4).
Mrch 23	Chrischurch	CRUSADERS	LOST	20-55	R Hoffman	T: Van der Walt, Whitehead. C: Catrakilis, Whitehead. P: Catrakilis (2).
Mrch 30	Wellington	HURRICANES	LOST	30-46	N Briant	T: Sykes, Cooke, Franklin. C: Catrakilis (2), Whitehead
April 05	Canberra	BRUMBIES	DREW	28-28	J Peyper	T: Du Preez (2), Ferreira, Van der Walt. C: Whitehead (3), Catrakilis.
April 13	Melbourne	REBELS	**WON**	30-27	A Lees	T: Cooke, Venter, Van der Walt. C: Catrakilis (3). P: Catrakilis (2). DG: Catrakilis.
April 20	Port Elizabeth	BULLS	LOST	0-34	F Pastrana	
April 27	Bloemfontein	CHEETAHS	LOST	12-26	J White	P: Catrakilis (4).
May 04	Port Elizabeth	WARATAHS	LOST	10-72	J Kaplan	T: Petersen. C: Catrakilis. P: Catrakilis.
May 11	Port Elizabeth	HIGHLANDERS	**WON**	34-27	J Jaftha	T: Watson (2), Du Preez, Venter. C: Catrakilis (4). P: Catrakilis (2).
May 25	Port Elizabeth	CHEETAHS	LOST	22-34	S Berry	T: Vergallo. C: Whitehead. P: Catrakilis (5).
Jun 01	Cape Town	STORMERS	LOST	11-19	C Joubert	T: Van der Walt. P: Whitehead (2).
Jun 29	Pretoria	BULLS	LOST	18-48	L vd Merwe	T: Van der Walt (2). C: Catrakilis. P: Catrakilis (2).
July 06	Port Elizabeth	STORMERS	LOST	12-24	L vd Merwe	P: Catrakilis (4).
July 13	Durban	SHARKS	LOST	13-58	S Berry	T: Mbiyozo, Whitehead. P: Whitehead.
Promotion & relegation						
July 26	Port Elizabeth	LIONS	LOST	19-26	J Peyper	T: Sykes, Sampson. P: Catrakilis (3)
Aug 03	Johannesburg	LIONS	WON	23-18	S Berry	T: Ferreira, Van Breda. C: Van Breda (2). P: Van Breda (3).

Played	Won	Lost	Drawn	Points for	Points against	Tries for	Tries against
18	**4**	**13**	**1**	**340**	**608**	**31**	**73**

SOUTHERN KINGS RECORDS

MATCH RECORDS

Biggest win	12	vs. Western Force (22-10)	Port Elizabeth	2013
Heaviest defeat	62	vs. Waratahs (10-72)	Port Elizabeth	2013
Highest score	34	vs. Highlanders (34-27)	Port Elizabeth	2013
Most points conceded	72	vs. Waratahs (10-72)	Port Elizabeth	2013
Most tries	4	vs. Brumbies (28-28)	Canberra	2013
	4	vs. Highlanders (34-27)	Port Elizabeth	2013
Most tries conceded	11	vs. Waratahs (10-72)	Port Elizabeth	2013
Most points by a player	18	S van Breda vs. Lions (1t, 2c, 3p)	Johannesburg	2013
Most tries by a player	2	S Petersen vs. Force	Port Elizabeth	2013
	2	CG du Preez vs. Brumbies	Canberra	2013
	2	LA Watson vs. Highlanders	Port Elizabeth	2013
	2	PW van der Walt vs. Bulls	Pretoria	2013
Most conversions by a player	4	D Catrakilis vs. Highlanders	Port Elizabeth	2013
Most penalties by a player	5	D Catrakilis vs. Cheetahs	Port Elizabeth	2013
Most drop goals by a player	1	D Catrakilis vs. Rebels	Melbourne	2013

SEASON RECORDS

Most team points	340	from 18 matches	2013
Most points by a player	151	D Catrakilis	2013
Most team tries	31	from 18 matches	2013
Most tries by a player	6	PW van der Walt	2013
Most conversions by a player	14	D Catrakilis	2013
Most penalties by a player	46	D Catrakilis	2013
Most drop goals by a player	1	D Catrakilis	2013

CAREER RECORDS

Most appearances	18	SH Venter	2013
	18	DJ Bulbring	2013
	18	BG Maku	2013
Most points	151	D Catrakilis	2013
Most tries	6	PW van der Walt	2013
Most conversions	14	D Catrakilis	2013
Most penalties	46	D Catrakilis	2013
Most drop goals	1	D Catrakilis	2013

SHARKS

Stuttering season for disrupted Sharks

GROUND
Mr Price KINGS PARK

CAPACITY
52 000

ADDRESS
Isaiah Ntshangane Road, Durban

TELEPHONE NUMBER
031-308 8400

COLOURS
Grey jersey with black and white trim, blacks shorts and socks

WEBSITE
www.sharksrugby.co.za

COACH
John Plumtree (resigned before the end of the season)

CAPTAIN
Keegan Daniel

CEO
Brian van Zyl

CHAIRMAN
Stephen Saad

THE best-laid sporting plans can come horribly unstuck, as head coach John Plumtree and the Sharks found during a disrupted 2013 Vodacom Super Rugby campaign.

The Sharks, with good reason, were touted as one of the tournament favourites, yet the season will be remembered for all the wrong reasons – the horrific injury toll, the patchy form of high-profile players, the undignified, late-tournament ditching of their head coach, and a disappointing mid-table finish.

Plumtree had a formidable squad in harness with quality cover in every area, settled combinations and strong leadership fore and aft. Their advance to two 2012 finals (Absa Currie Cup & Super Rugby) was an endorsement of the players, their coaching staff and their style of rugby.

But there were disruptions from the start and the Sharks had between 10 and 15 players sidelined, most with serious injury, for most of the competition and they were never able to reproduce the panache of the 2012 season.

They still made the start they wanted with five wins in their first six games. The most significant were against the Toyota Cheetahs (29-22) in Bloemfontein, and the DHL Stormers (12-6) and Crusaders (21-17) in Durban.

But the team then lost their way and six defeats in their next seven outings, including three on their Antipodean tour, left them playing for pride instead of a place in the play-offs.

The narrow losses in matches they should have won – against the Cheetahs (12-6) and Vodacom Bulls (18-16) at home, and the lowly Highlanders (25-22) in Dunedin – effectively killed off their challenge.

Plumtree, who had planned to use the depth in the squad to rotate and freshen up players during the marathon season, was forced to select on fitness rather than form as he tried to plug holes. Players were fielded out of position and four were borrowed from other franchises.

But, in spite of all the many setbacks, the Sharks should have performed better. Plumtree, in praising the example set by such youngsters as Pieter-Steph du Toit, Kyle Cooper and Wiehahn Herbst, at times questioned the attitude and intensity of some of his senior players. The Sharks only found form and momentum when their big forwards (Bismarck du Plessis, Beast Mtawarira, Willem Alberts and Jean Deysel) finally returned but by then it was too late.

Plumtree was the fall guy and he departed with three rounds remaining after a career which saw the Sharks reach five finals and win two Currie Cup titles in six years.

Who would have thought that, just a few months later, the Sharks would turn the tide and win the Absa Currie Cup?

BY JOHN BISHOP

Black attack...skipper Keegan Daniel on the charge for the Sharks. *Steve Haag/Gallo Images*

COACHES & MANAGEMENT

COACH: John Plumtree **ASSISTANT COACHES:** Grant Bashford & Hugh Reece-Edwards
TECHNICAL ANALYST: Clinton Isaacs **MANAGER:** Trevor Barnes **DOCTOR:** Alan Kourie
PHYSIOTHERAPIST: Deane Macquet **CONDITIONING TRAINER:** Mark Steele
ADMIN MANAGER: Piet Strydom **MASSEUR:** Robert Russell **MEDIA OFFICER:** Piet Strydom
NOTE: Plumtree resigned before the end of the season. Bashford and Reece-Edwards took over.

APPEARANCES & POINTS IN SUPER RUGBY

THE SHARKS	Province	SHARKS CAREER							SUPER RUGBY CAREER						
		Debut	Matches	Tries	Conversions	Penalties	Drop Goals	Points	Debut	Matches	Tries	Conversions	Penalties	Drop Goals	Points
WS (Willem) Alberts	Sharks	2010	48	5	–	–	–	25	2007	85	9	–	–	–	45
HM (Meyer) Bosman	Sharks	2011	47	7	11	–	–	57	2006	108	11	38	38	–	245
CB (Craig) Burden	Sharks	2006	47	4	–	–	–	20	2006	47	4	–	–	–	20
LJ (Jacques) Botes	Sharks	2005	114	27	–	–	–	135	2005	114	27	–	–	–	135
A (Anton) Bresler	Sharks	2011	34	1	–	–	–	0	2011	34	1	–	–	–	5
A (Andries) Coetzee	Lions	2013	1	–	–	–	–	0	2012	13	–	–	–	1	3
M (Marcell) Coetzee	Sharks	2011	39	5	–	–	–	25	2011	39	5	–	–	–	25
KL (Kyle) Cooper	Sharks	2012	17	1	–	–	–	5	2012	17	1	–	–	–	5
KR (Keegan) Daniel	Sharks	2006	96	15	–	–	–	75	2006	96	15	–	–	–	75
JR (Jean) Deysel	Sharks	2008	54	–	–	–	–	0	2008	54	–	–	–	–	0
BW (Bismarck) du Plessis	Sharks	2005	103	14	–	–	–	70	2005	103	14	–	–	–	70
JN (Jannie) du Plessis	Sharks	2008	88	–	–	–	–	0	2006	114	–	–	–	–	0
PS (Pieter-Steph) du Toit	Sharks	2012	19	–	–	–	–	0	2012	19	–	–	–	–	0
MS (Monde) Hadebe	Sharks	–	0	–	–	–	–	0	–	0	–	–	–	–	0
WJ (Wiehahn) Herbst	Sharks	2010	39	–	–	–	–	0	2010	39	–	–	–	–	0
EW (Edwin) Hewitt	Sharks	2013	3	–	–	–	–	0	2013	3	–	–	–	–	0
AD (Butch) James	Sharks	2001	59	6	63	74	4	390	2001	75	7	71	84	4	441
JC (JC) Janse van Rensburg	Lions	2013	3	–	–	–	–	–	2008	53	1	–	–	–	5
PA (Paul) Jordaan	Sharks	2012	18	2	–	–	–	10	2012	18	2	–	–	–	10
R (Ryan) Kankowski	Sharks	2007	82	18	–	–	–	90	2007	82	18	–	–	–	90
P (Patrick) Lambie	Sharks	2010	50	8	65	114	1	515	2010	50	8	65	114	1	515
PJ (Piet) Lindeque	Sharks	2013	5	1	–	–	–	5	2013	5	1	–	–	–	5
L (Louis) Ludik	Sharks	2011	40	7	–	–	–	35	2007	76	11	–	–	–	55
JA (Jandre) Marais	Sharks	2012	12	1	–	–	–	5	2012	12	1	–	–	–	5
C (Charl) McLeod	Sharks	2008	55	5	–	–	–	25	2008	55	5	–	–	–	25
TC (Tian) Meyer	Sharks	–	0	–	–	–	–	0	2012	11	2	–	–	–	10
DJ (Danie) Mienie	Sharks	2013	1	–	–	–	–	–	2013	1	–	–	–	–	–
DJ (Derick) Minnie	Lions	2013	3	3	–	–	–	15	2010	45	9	–	–	–	45
T (Tendai) Mtawarira	Sharks	2007	88	2	–	–	–	10	2007	88	2	–	–	–	10
LS (Lubabalo) Mtembu	Sharks	2012	7	1	–	–	–	5	2012	7	1	–	–	–	5
LN (Lwazi) Mvovo	Sharks	2010	52	17	–	–	–	85	2010	52	17	–	–	–	85
OM (Odwa) Ndungane	Sharks	2005	95	24	–	–	–	120	2004	105	27	–	–	–	135
J-P R (JP) Pietersen	Sharks	2006	98	33	–	–	–	165	2006	98	33	–	–	–	165
JM (Cobus) Reinach	Sharks	2012	13	1	–	–	–	5	2012	13	1	–	–	–	5
SJ (Sean) Robinson	Sharks	2013	3	–	–	–	–	0	2013	3	–	–	–	–	0
SCT (S'bura) Sithole	Sharks	2013	2	–	–	–	–	0	2013	2	–	–	–	–	0
FPL (Francois) Steyn	Sharks	2007	50	4	7	10	7	85	2007	50	4	7	10	7	85
F (Franco) van der Merwe	Lions	2013	16	–	–	–	–	–	2007	91	7	–	–	–	35
J (Jaco) van Tonder	Sharks	2013	1	–	–	–	–	–	2013	1	–	–	–	–	0
R (Riaan) Viljoen	Sharks	2012	23	8	–	–	–	40	2010	49	13	1	4	2	85
FJ (Fred) Zeilinga	Sharks	2013	1	1	–	–	–	5	2013	1	1	–	–	–	5
Totals			**1526**	**221**	**146**	**198**	**12**	**2022**		**1928**	**258**	**182**	**250**	**15**	**2449**

VODACOM SUPER RUGBY

FINAL LOG POSITIONS

2013	8th	2009	6th	2005	12th	2001	2nd	1997	4th
2012	6th	2008	3rd	2004	7th	2000	12th	1996	4th
2011	6th	2007	1st	2003	11th	1999	7th		
2010	9th	2006	5th	2002	10th	1998	3rd		

APPEARANCES & POINTS IN 2013

THE SHARKS

	Cheetahs	Stormers	Kings	Brumbies	Rebels	Crusaders	Stormers	Cheetahs	Chiefs	Highlanders	Reds	Force	Bulls	Blues	Bulls	Kings	Matches	Tries	Conversions	Penalties	Drop Goals	Points
Ludik	15	15	15	15	15	–	–	–	–	–	–	–	13	13	13	8	3	–	–	–	15
Pietersen	14	14	14	11	14	11	14	–	–	14	13	13	–	–	–	14	11	–	–	–	–	0
Jordaan	13	13	13	13	13	13	13	13	–	–	–	–	–	–	–	–	8	–	–	–	–	0
Steyn	12c	12c	12c	12	14R	15	15	12R	13	13	–	–	–	–	–	–	10	–	–	–	–	0
Mvovo	11	11	11	14R	11	–	–	–	–	11	11	11	11	11	11	11	12	2	–	–	–	10
Lambie	10	10	10	10	10	10	10	10	10	10	10	10	10	10	12	–	15	1	17	43	1	171
Reinach	9	9	9	9R	9	9	9	9	9R	–	–	–	–	9R	9R	9R	12	1	–	–	–	5
Kankowski	8	8	8	8	7R	6R	7	–	–	–	–	–	–	–	–	–	7	2	–	–	–	10
Coetzee, M	7	6	6	6	7	7	6	6	7R	7	6	6	6	6	6	6	16	4	–	–	–	20
Botes	6	7R	7R	8R	6	6	–	–	–	–	–	–	–	8R	7R	6R	9	1	–	–	–	5
Van der Merwe	5	5	5	5	5	5	5	5R	5	5	5	5	5	5	5	5	16	–	–	–	–	0
Bresler	4	4	4	4	–	5R	5R	4	4	x	4R	4	–	–	–	–	10	–	–	–	–	0
Du Plessis, J	3	3	3	3	1R	3	3	3R	3	3	3R	3	3	3	3	3	16	–	–	–	–	0
Burden	2	2	2	2	15R	2R	2R	2R	2	x	–	–	–	–	–	–	9	–	–	–	–	0
Mtawarira	1	1	1	1	1	1	1	1	–	–	–	–	1	1	1	1	12	2	–	–	–	10
Cooper	2R	2R	2R	2R	2	2	2	2	2R	2	2	2	2	2R	2R	–	16	1	–	–	–	5
Herbst	3R	3R	3R	3R	3	3R	3R	3	1	1	3	3R	3R	3R	3R	3R	16	–	–	–	–	0
Du Toit	4R	4R	4R	4R	4	4	4	7	5	4	4	4R	4	–	–	–	13	–	–	–	–	0
Deysel	8R	7	7	–	–	–	–	4R	7c	20R	7	x	7R	7R	7	7	11	–	–	–	–	0
McLeod	x	x	9R	9	9R	9R	9R	x	9	9	9	9	9	9	9	9	13	2	–	–	–	10
Bosman	15R	x	12R	15R	12	12	12	12	12	12	12	12	–	–	–	12	13	3	9	–	–	33
Ndungane	11R	x	11R	14	–	14	14R	14	14	–	14R	14	14	14	14	15	13	2	–	–	–	10
Daniel	–	–	–	7c	8c	8c	8c	8c	6R	6c	8c	8c	8c	8c	8R	8c	13	4	–	–	–	20
Viljoen	–	–	–	–	10R	x	15R	15	15	15	15	15	15	15	15	10	11	4	–	–	–	20
Marais	–	–	–	4R	–	–	–	–	–	–	–	–	x	4R	4R	4R	4	–	–	–	–	0
Sithole	–	–	–	–	14R	–	–	20R	–	–	–	–	–	–	–	–	2	–	–	–	–	0
Robinson	–	–	–	–	–	–	11	11R	–	–	–	12R	–	–	–	–	3	–	–	–	–	0
Mthembu	–	–	–	–	–	–	7R	6R	8	8	–	7R	6R	–	–	–	6	1	–	–	–	5
Coetzee, A	–	–	–	–	–	–	–	11	–	–	–	–	–	–	–	–	1	–	–	–	–	0
Lindeque	–	–	–	–	–	–	–	–	11	13R	14	13R	13	–	–	–	5	1	–	–	–	5
Minnie	–	–	–	–	–	–	–	–	6	8R	6R	–	–	–	–	–	3	3	–	–	–	15
Mienie	–	–	–	–	–	–	–	–	1R	–	–	–	–	–	–	–	1	–	–	–	–	0
Janse van Rensburg	–	–	–	–	–	–	–	–	–	3R	1	1	–	–	–	–	3	–	–	–	–	0
Meyer	–	–	–	–	–	–	–	–	–	–	x	x	x	–	–	–	0	–	–	–	–	0
Hadebe	–	–	–	–	–	–	–	–	–	–	x	x	x	–	–	–	0	–	–	–	–	0
Alberts	–	–	–	–	–	–	–	–	–	7R	7	7	7	8	7R	–	6	–	–	–	–	0
Du Plessis, B	–	–	–	–	–	–	–	–	–	–	–	–	2R	2	2	–	3	1	–	–	–	5
James	–	–	–	–	–	–	–	–	–	–	–	–	12	10c	–	–	2	–	–	–	–	0
Hewitt	–	–	–	–	–	–	–	–	–	–	–	–	4	4	4	–	3	–	–	–	–	0
Van Tonder	–	–	–	–	–	–	–	–	–	–	–	–	x	12R	–	–	1	–	–	–	–	0
Zeilinga	–	–	–	–	–	–	–	–	–	–	–	–	–	–	–	14R	1	1	–	–	–	5
Penalty try	–	–	–	–	–	–	–	–	–	–	–	–	–	–	–	–	0	1	–	–	–	5

41 players   334   40   26   43   1   384

Yellow Card ■ *Red Card*

VODACOM SUPER RUGBY

Gotcha...the Rebels were beaten 64-7. Steve Haag/Gallo Images

2013 RESULTS & SCORERS

Date	Venue	Opponent	Result	Score	Referee	Scorers
Febr 23	Bloemfontein	CHEETAHS	WON	29-22	J Kaplan	T: Botes. C: Mvovo, Coetzee. C: Lambie (2). P: Lambie (5).
Mrch 02	Durban	STORMERS	WON	12-06	J Kaplan	P: Lambie (4).
Mrch 09	Port Elizabeth	KINGS	WON	21-12	J Jaftha	P: Lambie (6). DG: Lambie.
Mrch 16	Durban	BRUMBIES	LOST	10-29	J Kaplan	T: Kankowski. C: Lambie. P: Lambie.
Mrch 23	Durban	REBELS	WON	64-07	L vd Merwe	T: Ludik (2), Reinach, Botes, Daniel, Cooper, Coetzee, Viljoen, Kankowski, Mtawarira. C: Bosman (5), Lambie (2)
April 05	Durban	CRUSADERS	WON	21-17	L vd Merwe	P: Lambie (7).
April 13	Cape Town	STORMERS	LOST	15-22	C Joubert	P: Lambie (5).
April 20	Durban	CHEETAHS	LOST	06-12	J White	P: Lambie (2).
April 27	Hamilton	CHIEFS	LOST	29-37	C Pollock	T: Minnie (2), Daniel, Mtembu. C: Lambie (3). P: Lambie.
May 04	Dunedin	HIGHLANDERS	LOST	22-25	SR Walsh	T: Bosman (2), Mvovo. C: Lambie (2). P: Lambie.
May 10	Brisbane	REDS	LOST	17-32	G Jackson	T: Minnie, Lindeque. C: Lambie (2). P: Lambie.
May 17	Perth	FORCE	WON	23-13	J Leckie	T: Daniel, Viljoen. C: Lambie (2). P: Lambie (3).
May 25	Durban	BULLS	LOST	16-18	J Kaplan	T: McLeod. C: Lambie. P: Lambie (3).
Jun 29	Durban	BLUES	WON	22-20	J Peyper	T: McLeod, Coetzee, Viljoen. C: Lambie (2). P: Lambie.
July 06	Pretoria	BULLS	LOST	19-20	J Jaftha	T: Lambie, Ndungane. P: Lambie (3).
July 13	Durban	KINGS	WON	58-13	S Berry	T: Mtawarira, Viljoen, Ndungane, Bosman, Coetzee, Ludik, Daniel, Zeilinga, B du Plessis, pen try. C: Bosmman (4).

Played	Won	Lost	Drawn	Points for	Points against	Tries for	Tries against
16	8	8	0	384	305	40	31

SHARKS RECORDS

MATCH RECORDS

Biggest win	57	v Rebels (64-7)	Durban	2013
Heaviest defeat	43	v Crusaders (34-77)	Christchurch	2005
Highest score	75	v Highlanders (75-43)	Durban	1997
Most points conceded	77	v Crusaders (34-77)	Christchurch	2005
Most tries	10	v Rebels (64-7)	Durban	2013
Most tries conceded	11	v Crusaders (34-77)	Christchurch	2005
Most points by a player (Natal)	50	GE Lawless (4t, 9c, 4p) v Highlanders	Durban	1997
Most points by a player (Sharks)	28	P Lambie (1t, 1c, 7p) v Highlanders	Durban	2012
Most tries by a player (Natal)	4	GE Lawless v Highlanders	Durban	1997
Most tries by a player (Sharks)	4	CS Terblanche v Chiefs	Port Elizabeth	1998
Most conversions by a player	9	GE Lawless v Highlanders	Durban	1997
Most penalties by a player	7	GE Lawless v NSW Waratahs	Durban	1997
	7	PJ Lambie v Highlanders	Durban	2012
	7	PJ Lambie v Crusaders	Durban	2013
Most drop goals by a player	2	FPL Steyn v Blues	Albany	2007
	2	F Michalak vs Stormers	Cape Town	2012

SEASON RECORDS

Most team points	453	in 13 matches	1996
Most points by a player	193	P Lambie	2011
Most team tries	56	in 13 matches	1996
Most tries by a player (Natal)	13	JT Small	1996
Most tries by a player (Sharks)	12	J-PR Pietersen	2007
Most conversions by a player	28	P Lambie	2011
Most penalties by a player	43	PJ Lambie	2013
Most drop goals by a player	4	FPL Steyn	2007

CAREER RECORDS

Most appearances	125	JW Smit	1999-2010
Most points	515	PJ Lambie	2010-2013
Most tries	35	CS Terblanche	1998-2011
Most conversions	65	PJ Lambie	2010-2013
Most penalties	114	PJ Lambie	2010-2013
Most drop goals	7	FPL Steyn	2007-2012

DHL STORMERS

Stormers fall short playing catch-up

THE DHL STORMERS ENDURED THEIR WORST VODACOM Super Rugby campaign since 2009, failing to make the semi-finals for the first time in four seasons after an horrific injury run and a tough fixture list conspired against them.

Despite all this, in the end the Cape side finished seventh on the overall standings, agonisingly and frustratingly missing out on a play-off place by a single position.

But they were always playing catch-up after a miserable first half of the tournament and ran out of time to recover lost ground despite finishing the season with five consecutive wins.

The fact that they ended the group phase as the form team in the SA Conference was scant consolation for a campaign that promised much but delivered little.

The Stormers' inability to score tries, which had been evident in previous seasons, ultimately cost them a play-off berth. They only managed 30 tries in 16 games. Only the 13th-placed Force and 15th-placed Kings scored fewer touchdowns.

The Stormers struggled to grow their attack with constant injuries, which saw 16 players sitting out at various times throughout the campaign.

Five of the matches they lost were by seven points or less, underlining how their lack of tries cost them victory on several occasions. Just one more try here and there could have made a massive difference to the season.

The Stormers started their campaign with away matches against the Sharks and Bulls followed by home games against the defending champion Chiefs, eventual finalists the Brumbies and perennial favourites the Crusaders.

After losing the first two the Cape side bounced back with wins over the Chiefs and Brumbies but a loss to the Crusaders, and then the following week to a last-minute penalty at the Cheetahs, left the season at a crossroads.

The Stormers dug in to secure a win over the Sharks in the return fixture at Newlands before embarking on what looked like, on paper anyway, a comfortable tour – if there is ever such a thing.

The trip started well with a tough two-point win over the Hurricanes but the wheels were about to come off. Stormers substitutes were accused of harassing a match official during that fixture and after three weeks of SANZAR investigations the Stormers eventually accepted a R240,000 fine. They also had to apologise to the official.

The fallout from that episode dogged the rest of the tour and in retrospect it was the beginning of the end of their play-off aspirations as they lost three matches on tour and fell out of play-off contention.

GROUND
Newlands
CAPACITY
49 000
ADDRESS
11 Boundary Road,
Newlands, Cape Town
TELEPHONE NUMBER
021-659 4500
COLOURS
Navy blue jersey with blue hoops, navy shorts and socks
WEBSITE
www.iamastormer.com
COACH
Allister Coetzee
CAPTAIN
Jean de Villiers
CEO
Rob Wagner
CHAIRMAN
Sam Dube

BY CRAIG RAY,
THE TIMES

High flyer...Bryan Habana does what he knows best.
Carl Fourie/Gallo Images

VODACOM SUPER RUGBY

COACHES & MANAGEMENT

COACH: Allister Coetzee **ASSISTANT COACHES:** Robbie Fleck & Matthew Proudfoot
DEFENCE COACH: Jacques Nienaber **DOCTOR:** Dr Arthur Williams
STRENGHT & CONDITIONING: Stephan du Toit **KICKING COACH:** Greg Hechter
PHYSIOTHERAPIST: Wayne Hector **MASSEUR:** Greg Daniels **MEDIA OFFICER:** Howard Kahn
MANAGER: Chippie Solomon **VIDEO ANALYST:** Human Kriek

APPEARANCES & POINTS IN SUPER RUGBY

	STORMERS CAREER								SUPER RUGBY CAREER						
	Province	Debut	Matches	Tries	Conversions	Penalties	Drop Goals	Points	Debut	Matches	Tries	Conversions	Penalties	Drop Goals	Points
GG (Gio) Aplon	DHL WP	2007	76	16	–	1	86	66	2007	76	16	–	1	1	86
D (Don) Armand	DHL WP	2012	15	–	–	–	–	0	2012	15	–	–	–	–	0
A (Andries) Bekker	DHL WP	2005	105	15	–	–	–	75	2005	105	15	–	–	–	75
MJ (Martin) Bezuidenhout	Lions	2013	8	–	–	–	–	–	2011	32	3	–	–	–	15
N (Nizaam) Carr	DHL WP	2012	21	–	–	–	–	0	2012	21	–	–	–	–	0
PM (Pat) Cilliers	DHL WP	2013	13	–	–	–	–	–	2007	44	1	–	–	–	5
M (Marius) Coetzer	Pumas	2013	1	–	–	–	–	–	2012	6	–	–	–	–	0
KK (Kurt) Coleman	DHL WP	2011	6	1	4	6	0	31	2011	6	1	4	6	0	31
D (Damian) de Allende	DHL WP	2013	14	–	–	–	–	0	2013	14	–	–	–	–	0
JL (Juan) de Jongh	DHL WP	2010	57	9	–	–	–	45	2010	57	9	–	–	–	45
J (Jean) de Villiers	DHL WP	2005	96	27	–	–	–	135	2005	96	27	–	–	–	135
DO (Dewaldt) Duvenage	DHL WP	2009	67	2	4	4	–	30	2009	67	2	4	4	–	30
R (Rynhardt) Elstadt	DHL WP	2011	37	–	–	–	–	0	2011	37	–	–	–	–	0
E (Eben) Etzebeth	DHL WP	2012	21	2	–	–	–	10	2012	21	2	–	–	–	10
DA (Deon) Fourie	DHL WP	2008	70	10	–	–	–	50	2008	70	10	–	–	–	50
R (Ross) Geldenhuys	EP Kings		0	–	–	–	–	–	2008	19	–	–	–	–	0
NJ (Nick) Groom	DHL WP	2011	11	1	–	–	–	5	2011	11	1	–	–	–	5
PJ (Peter) Grant	DHL WP	2006	90	10	116	179	0	819	2006	90	10	116	179	0	819
DG (Gerbrandt) Grobler	DHL WP	2013	5	–	–	–	–	–	2013	5	–	–	–	–	0
BG (Bryan) Habana	DHL WP	2010	57	19	–	–	–	95	2005	118	56	–	–	–	280
J (Brok) Harris	DHL WP	2007	84	2	–	–	–	10	2007	84	2	–	–	–	10
C (Chris) Heiberg	DHL WP	–	0	–	–	–	–	0	–	0	–	–	–	–	0
ET (Elton) Jantjies	Lions	2013	13	–	1	3	–	11	2011	40	–	34	56	1	239
R (Rohan) Kitshoff	DHL WP	2013	1	–	–	–	–	–	2013	1	–	–	–	–	0
S (Steven) Kitshoff	DHL WP	2011	35	–	–	–	–	0	2011	35	–	–	–	–	0
C (Cheslin) Kolbe	DHL WP	–	0	–	–	–	–	–	–	0	–	–	–	–	0
S (Siya) Kolisi	DHL WP	2012	29	3	–	–	–	15	2012	29	3	–	–	–	15
CR (Tiaan) Liebenberg	DHL WP	2007	67	5	–	–	–	25	2006	80	6	–	–	–	30
JF (Frans) Malherbe	DHL WP	2011	32	–	–	–	–	0	2011	32	–	–	–	–	0
S (Siya) Ntubeni	DHL WP	2011	11	–	–	–	–	0	2011	11	–	–	–	–	0
JC (Joe) Pietersen	DHL WP	2006	50	2	6	25	–	97	2006	50	9	35	86	0	373
MK (Michael) Rhodes	DHL WP	2013	3	1	–	–	–	5	2011	14	3	–	–	–	15
L (Louis) Schreuder	DHL WP	2011	27	1	–	–	–	5	2011	27	1	–	–	–	5
M De K (De Kock) Steenkamp	DHL WP	2010	47	–	–	–	–	0	2010	47	–	–	–	–	0
JJ (Jaco) Taute	Lions	2013	4	–	–	–	–	0	2010	35	9	–	2	–	51
GJ (Gary) van Aswegen	DHL WP	2011	15	–	3	7	1	30	2011	15	–	3	7	1	30
GJ (Gerhard) van den Heever	DHL WP	2012	26	2	–	–	–	10	2009	57	14	–	–	–	70
DJ (Duane) Vermeulen	DHL WP	2009	62	2	–	–	–	10	2007	82	5	–	–	–	25
Totals			1276	130	134	225	87	1579		1549	205	196	341	3	2449

NOTE: DHL WP = *Western Province*, **EP Kings** = *Eastern Province*

VODACOM SUPER RUGBY

FINAL LOG POSITIONS

2013	7th	2009	10th	2005	9th	2001	7th	1996*	11th
2012	1st	2008	5th	2004	3rd	2000	5th		
2011	2nd	2007	10th	2003	9th	1999	2nd	*As Western	
2010	2nd	2006	11th	2002	7th	1998	9th	Province	

APPEARANCES & POINTS IN 2013

	Bulls	Sharks	Chiefs	Brumbies	Crusaders	Cheetahs	Sharks	Hurricanes	Blues	Waratahs	Rebels	Reds	Kings	Cheetahs	Kings	Bulls	Matches	Tries	Conversions	Penalties	Drop Goals	Points
Taute	15	–	–	11R	11R	15	–	–	–	–	–	–	–	–	–	–	4	–	–	–	–	0
Aplon	14	14	14	11	11	11	11	14	14	14	14	14	14	14	14	15	16	4	–	–	–	20
De Villiers	13c	13c	13c	12c	12c	12c	12c	12c	12c	12c	12c	13c	13c	–	–	12c	14	5	–	–	–	25
De Allende	12	12	12	12R	13R	15R	14	11R	13R	–	–	12	12	12	12	14R	14	–	–	–	–	0
Habana	11	11	11	–	–	–	–	11	11	11	11	11	11	11	11	11	12	3	–	–	–	15
Jantjies	10	10	10	10	10	10	–	–	10R	x	10	10	10	10	10	10R	13	–	1	3	–	11
Groom	9	9	9	9R	10R	9	–	x	–	–	9R	–	–	–	9R	9R	9	1	–	–	–	5
Vermeulen	8	8	8	8	8	8	8	8	8	8	–	–	–	–	–	–	10	–	–	–	–	0
Elstadt	7	7	7	7	7	–	–	6	7	7	–	–	–	–	7R	7	10	–	–	–	–	0
Kolisi	6	6	6	6	6	6	6	–	6	6	7	6	6	6	–	–	13	2	–	–	–	10
Bekker	5	5	5	5	5	5	5	5	5	5	5	–	–	–	–	–	11	4	–	–	–	20
Steenkamp	4	4	4	4	4	4	4	4	–	–	–	5	5	5	5	–	13	–	–	–	–	0
Cilliers	3	3R	3R	3R	1	3R	3R	3	3R	3R	3	–	–	–	3R	1R	13	–	–	–	–	0
Fourie	2	2	2	2R	2	2	2	2	2	2	6	–	7	7c	6c	6	15	4	–	–	–	20
Kitshoff, S	1	1	1	1	–	1	1	1	1	1	1	1	1	1	1	1	15	–	–	–	–	0
Bezuidenhout	3R	2R	–	–	14R	x	2R	–	–	–	2	x	x	2R	2R	2R	8	–	–	–	–	0
Malherbe	3R	3	3	3	3	3	3	3R	3	3	3R	–	–	–	–	–	11	–	–	–	–	0
Armand	x	5R	x	5R	7R	–	–	–	7R	6R	7	7R	7R	7	7R	–	10	–	–	–	–	0
Carr	7R	6R	6R	6R	6R	6R	x	7R	7R	7R	8	8	8	8	8	8	15	–	–	–	–	0
Duvenage	9R	–	9R	9	9	–	9	9	9	9	–	9R	9R	9R	–	–	11	–	–	–	–	0
Van den Heever	11R	14R	11R	14	14	–	–	–	–	–	x	14R	14R	14R	15R	14	11	1	–	–	–	5
Pietersen	14R	15	15	15	15	14	15	15	15	15	15	15	15	15	15	–	15	–	19	44	–	170
Grant	–	10R	10R	–	–	–	–	–	–	–	–	–	–	–	–	–	2	–	–	–	–	0
Schreuder	–	9R	–	–	–	9R	9R	x	9R	x	9	9	9	9	9	9	10	1	–	–	–	5
Liebenberg	–	–	7R	2	–	–	–	–	–	–	–	2	2	–	–	–	4	–	–	–	–	0
De Jongh	–	–	–	13	13	13	13	13	13	13	–	–	13	13	13	–	11	3	–	–	–	15
Harris	–	–	–	–	1R	–	–	1R	–	–	x	3	3	3	3	3	7	–	–	–	–	0
Rhodes	–	–	–	–	–	7	7	7	–	–	–	–	–	–	–	–	3	1	–	–	–	5
Van Aswegen	–	–	–	–	–	10R	10	10	10	10	10R	x	13R	10R	x	10	9	–	3	3	–	15
Grobler	–	–	–	–	–	x	5R	–	–	–	x	4	x	4R	5R	4R	5	–	–	–	–	0
Coleman	–	–	–	–	–	–	10R	–	–	–	–	–	–	–	–	–	1	–	–	–	–	0
Kolbe	–	–	–	–	–	–	x	–	–	–	–	–	–	–	–	–	0	–	–	–	–	0
Ntubeni	–	–	–	–	–	–	–	6R	6R	2R	–	–	–	2	2	2	6	–	–	–	–	0
Etzebeth	–	–	–	–	–	–	–	4R	4	4	5	4	4	4	4	4	8	1	–	–	–	5
Coetzer	–	–	–	–	–	–	–	–	–	–	4R	–	–	–	–	–	1	–	–	–	–	0
Kitshoff, R	–	–	–	–	–	–	–	–	–	–	7R	–	–	–	–	–	1	–	–	–	–	0
Heiberg	–	–	–	–	–	–	–	–	–	–	x	x	–	–	–	–	0	–	–	–	–	0
Geldenhuys	–	–	–	–	–	–	–	–	–	–	–	–	x	–	–	–	0	–	–	–	–	0
Penalty try	–	–	–	–	–	–	–	–	–	–	–	–	–	–	–	–	0	–	–	–	–	0
38 players																	**331**	**30**	**23**	**50**	**0**	**346**

▓ *Yellow Card* ■ *Red Card*

VODACOM SUPER RUGBY

Tall story...Andries Bekker leaps high.
Carl Fourie / Gallo Images

2013 RESULTS & SCORERS

Date	Venue	Opponent	Result	Score	Referee	Scorers
Febr 22	Pretoria	BULLS	LOST	17-25	J Peyper	T: De Villiers, Bekker. C: Pietersen (2). P: Pietersen.
Mrch 02	Durban	SHARKS	LOST	6-12	J Kaplan	P: Pietersen (2)
Mrch 09	Cape Town	CHIEFS	WON	36-34	J Peyper	T: Aplon (2), Groom. C: Pietersen (3). P: Pietersen (5).
Mrch 23	Cape Town	BRUMBIES	WON	35-22	G Jackson	T: Bekker (2), Aplon, Van den Heever. C: Pietersen (3). P: Pietersen (3)
Mrch 30	Cape Town	CRUSADERS	LOST	14-19	C Joubert	T: Kolisi. P: Pietersen (3).
April 06	Bloemfontein	CHEETAHS	LOST	24-26	S Berry	T: De Jongh (2). C : Pietersen. P: Pietersen (4).
April 13	Cape Town	SHARKS	WON	22-15	C Joubert	T: De Jongh. C : Pietersen. P: Pietersen (5).
April 26	Palmerston North	HURRICANES	WON	18-16	SR Walsh	T: Aplon, Rhodes. C: Pietersen. P: Pietersen (2).
May 03	Albany	BLUES	LOST	17-18	G Jackson	T: De Villiers (2). C: Pietersen (2). P: Pietersen.
May 11	Sydney	WARATAHS	LOST	15-21	C Pollock	P: Pietersen (5).
May 17	Melbourne	REBELS	LOST	21-30	M Fraser	T: Bekker, Habana, Schreuder. C: Pietersen (3)
May 25	Cape Town	REDS	WON	20-15	J Peyper	T: De Villiers. P: Pietersen (5).
Jun 01	Cape Town	KINGS	WON	19-11	C Joubert	T: Fourie. C: Pietersen. P: Pietersen (4).
Jun 29	Cape Town	CHEETAHS	WON	28-03	S Berry	T: Habana, Fourie, Kolisi. C: Pietersen (2). P: Pietersen (3).
July 06	Port Elizabeth	KINGS	WON	24-12	L vd Merwe	T: Fourie (2). C: Jantjies. P: Jantjies (3), Pietersen.
July 13	Cape Town	BULLS	WON	30-13	C Joubert	T: Habana, Etzebeth, De Villiers. C: Van Aswegen (3). P: Van Aswegen (3).

Played	Won	Lost	Drawn	Points for	Points against	Tries for	Tries against
16	9	7	0	346	292	30	18

DHL STORMERS RECORDS

MATCH RECORDS

Biggest win	38	vs. Lions (56-18)	Cape Town	2009
Heaviest defeat	61	vs. Bulls (14-75)	Pretoria	2005
Highest score	56	vs. Lions (56-18)	Cape Town	2009
Most points conceded	75	vs. Bulls (14-75)	Pretoria	2005
Most tries	8	vs. Blues (51-23)	Auckland	2004
	8	vs. Lions (56-18)	Cape Town	2009
Most tries conceded	11	vs. Blues (28-74)	Auckland	1998
Most points by a player	28	AJJ van Straaten (1t 4c 5p) vs. Hurricanes	Cape Town	2000
Most tries by a player	3	BJ Paulse vs. Bulls	Pretoria	2001
	3	PWG Rossouw vs. Chiefs	Hamilton	2002
Most conversions by a player	6	PJ Grant vs W Force	Cape Town	2011
Most penalties by a player	7	JT Stransky vs. Transvaal	Johannesburg	1996
	7	AJJ van Straaten vs. Bulls	Pretoria	1999
	7	PJ Grant vs. Crusaders	Cape Town	2010
	7	PJ Grant vs Cheetahs	Cape Town	2011
Most drop goals by a player	2	PC Montgomery vs. Cats	Johannesburg	2000

SEASON RECORDS

Most team points	410	in 17 matches	2011
Most points by a player	170	JC Pietersen	2013
Most team tries	39	in 15 matches	2010
Most tries by a player	11	PWG Rossouw	2002
Most conversions by a player	23	AJJ van Straaten	2000
Most penalties by a player	44	JC Pietersen	2013
Most drop goals by a player	2	PC Montgomery	2000

CAREER RECORDS

Most appearances	105	A Bekker	2005-2013
Most points	819	PJ Grant	2006-2013
Most tries	35	BJ Paulse	1998-2007
Most conversions	116	PJ Grant	2006-2013
Most penalties	179	PJ Grant	2006-2013
Most drop goals	2	PC Montgomery	1996-2002

SUPER RUGBY PROMOTION/RELEGATION

Holding on...The Kings on the defence against a Lions rolling maul. Duif du Toit/Gallo Images

APPEARANCES & POINTS IN 2013 PROMOTION/RELEGATION SERIES

KINGS	Lions	Lions	Matches	Tries	Conversions	Penalties	Drop Goals	Points	LIONS	Kings	Kings	Matches	Tries	Conversions	Penalties	Drop Goals	Points
SP Marais	15	15	2	–	–	–	–	0	Ruan Combrinck	15	15	2	–	–	–	–	0
Hadleigh Parkes	14	11	2	–	–	–	–	0	Deon van Rensburg	14	–	1	–	–	–	–	0
Ronnie Cooke	13	13	2	–	–	–	–	0	Stokkies Hanekom	13	13	2	2	–	–	–	10
Shane Gates	12	12R	2	–	–	–	–	0	Dylan des Fountain	12	12	2	–	–	–	–	0
Marcello Sampson	11	–	1	1	–	–	–	5	Anthony Volmink	11	11	2	–	–	–	–	0
Demetri Catrakilis	10	–	1	–	–	3	–	9	Elton Jantjies	10	10	2	–	3	6	–	24
Shaun Venter	9	9	2	–	–	–	–	0	Vian van der Watt	9	–	1	–	–	–	–	0
Jacques Engelbrecht	8	8	2	–	–	–	–	0	Warren Whiteley	8	8	2	–	–	–	–	0
Wimpie van der Walt	7	7	2	–	–	–	–	0	Derrick Minnie	7	7	2	1	–	–	–	5
Cornell du Preez	6	6	2	–	–	–	–	0	Jaco Kriel	6	6	2	1	–	–	–	5
David Bulbring	5	5	2	–	–	–	–	0	Franco van der Merwe	5	5	2	–	–	–	–	0
Darron Nell	4c	4c	2	–	–	–	–	0	Hendrik Roodt	4	4	2	–	–	–	–	0
Kevin Buys	3	3	2	–	–	–	–	0	Julian Redelinghuys	3	3	2	–	–	–	–	0
Bandise Maku	2	2	2	–	–	–	–	0	Martin Bezuidenhout	2	2	2	–	–	–	–	0
Schalk Ferreira	1	1	2	1	–	–	–	5	JC Janse van Rensburg	1c	1c	2	–	–	–	–	0
Hannes Franklin	2R	2R	2	–	–	–	–	0	Robbie Coetzee	2R	2R	2	–	–	–	–	0
Grant Kemp	3R	–	1	–	–	–	–	0	Ruan Dreyer	3R	3R	2	–	–	–	–	0
Steven Sykes	4R	4R	2	1	–	–	–	5	Willie Britz	8R	8R	2	–	–	–	–	0
Devin Oosthuizen	8R	7R	2	–	–	–	–	0	Warwick Tecklenburg	6R	6R	2	–	–	–	–	0
Nicolas Vergallo	x	x	0	–	–	–	–	0	Guy Cronje	9R	9R	2	–	–	–	–	0
Waylon Murray	x	12	1	–	–	–	–	0	Marnitz Boshoff	10R	x	1	–	–	–	–	0
George Whitehead	10R	10	2	–	–	–	–	0	Chrysander Botha	14R	14R	2	–	–	–	–	0
Scott van Breda	–	14	1	1	2	3	–	18	Deon Helberg	–	14	1	–	–	–	–	0
Charl du Plessis	–	3R	1	–	–	–	–	0	Ross Cronje	–	9	1	–	–	–	–	0
Wesley Dunlop	–	x	0	–	–	–	–	0	24 players			43	4	3	6	0	44
25 players			40	4	2	6	0	42									

SOUTHERN KINGS RESULTS & SCORERS

Date	Venue	Opponent	Result	Score	Referee	Scorers
July 26	Port Elizabeth	LIONS	LOST	19-26	J Peyper	T: Sykes, Sampson. P: Catrakilis (3)
Aug 03	Johannesburg	LIONS	WON	23-18	S Berry	T: Ferreira, Van Breda. C: Van Breda (2). P: Van Breda (3).

Played	Won	Lost	Drawn	Points for	Points against	Tries for	Tries against
2	1	1	0	42	44	4	4

MTN LIONS RESULTS & SCORERS

Date	Venue	Opponent	Result	Score	Referee	Scorers
July 26	Port Elizabeth	KINGS	WON	26-19	J Peyper	T: Hanekom (2). C: Jantjies (2). P: Jantjies (4).
Aug 03	Johannesburg	KINGS	LOST	18-23	S Berry	T: Kriel, Minnie. C: Jantjies. P: Jantjies (2).

Played	Won	Lost	Drawn	Points for	Points against	Tries for	Tries against
2	1	1	0	44	42	4	4

BLUES

RECORDS

MATCH RECORDS

Biggest win	53	vs. Hurricanes (60-7)	Wellington 2002
Heaviest defeat	47	vs. Crusaders (12-59)	Christchurch 2012
Highest score	74	vs. Stormers (74-28)	Auckland 1998
Most points conceded	63	vs. Chiefs (34-63)	Hamilton 2009
Most tries	11	vs. Stormers (74-28)	Auckland 1998
Most tries conceded	9	vs. Chiefs (34-63)	Hamilton 2009
Most points by a player	29	GW Anscombe (2t, 2c, 5p) vs. Bulls	Pretoria 2012
Most tries by a player	4	J Vidiri vs. Bulls	Auckland 2000
	4	DC Howlett vs. Hurricanes	Wellington 2002
	4	JM Muliaina vs. Bulls	Auckland 2002
Most conversions by a player	7	AR Cashmore vs. Stormers	Auckland 1998
	7	AR Cashmore vs. Bulls	Auckland 2000
	7	CJ Spencer vs. Bulls	Auckland 2002
Most penalties by a player	6	AR Cashmore vs. Chiefs	Auckland 1998
	6	AR Cashmore vs. Hurricanes	Auckland 1999
	6	JA Arlidge vs. Bulls	Auckland 2001
	6	SA Brett vs. Bulls	Auckland 2010
	6	C Noakes vs. Stormers	Albany 2013
Most drop goals by a player	1	on eleven occasions	

SEASON RECORDS

Most team points	513	in 13 matches	1997
Most points by a player	180	AR Cashmore	1998
Most team tries	70	in 13 matches	1996
Most tries by a player	12	DC Howlett	2003
Most conversions by a player	34	AR Cashmore	1998
Most penalties by a player	34	AR Cashmore	1999
Most drop goals by a player	2	O Ai'i	2000
	2	SA Brett	2010

CAREER RECORDS

Most appearances	152	KF Mealamu	2000-2013
Most points	619	AR Cashmore	1996-2000
Most tries	55	DC Howlett	1999-2007
Most conversions	120	CJ Spencer	1996-2005
Most penalties	114	AR Cashmore	1996-2000
Most drop goals	3	CJ Spencer	1996-2005

HONOURS
CHAMPIONS
1996
1997
2003

GROUNDS
Eden Park

CAPACITY
42 500

ADDRESS
Walters Road, Mount Eden, Auckland

TELEPHONE NUMBER
+64 9 815 4850

COLOURS
Blue with navy sleeves and white piping, blue shorts and socks

WEBSITE
www.theblues.co.nz

CAPTAIN
Ali Williams

CEO
Andy Dalton

CHAIRMAN
Gary Whetton

COACH
Sir John Kirwan

Centre of attention: the gifted Rene Ranger played most of the season in the No 13 jersey, scoring six tries. Phil Walter/Getty Images

2013 RESULTS & SCORERS

Date	Venue	Opponent	Result	Score	Referee	Scorers
Febr 23	Wellington	HURRICANES	WON	34-20	G Jackson	T: Halai (2), Piutau, Ranger. C: Weepu. P: Weepu (4).
Mrch 01	Auckland	CRUSADERS	WON	34-15	C Pollock	T: Halai (2), Moala, Braid, Luatua. C: Weepu, Noakes, Kerr. P: Weepu.
Mrch 10	Auckland	BULLS	LOST	21-28	G Williamson	T: Piutau, Ranger. C: Kerr. P: Kerr (3).
Mrch 24	Sydney	WARATAHS	LOST	27-30	F Pastrana	T: Parsons, Noakes, Puitau. C: Noakes (3). P: Noakes (2).
Mrch 30	Mt Manganui	CHIEFS	LOST	16-23	J Kaplan	T: Moala. C: Kerr. P: Noakes (3).
April 05	Auckland	HIGHLANDERS	WON	29-18	SR Walsh	T: Weepu (2), Ta'avao, Luatua. C: Noakes (2), Kerr. P: Noakes.
April 13	Auckland	HURRICANES	WON	28-6	J Peyper	T: Piutau, Halai, Parsons, McCartney. C: Noakes (4).
April 26	Brisbane	REDS	LOST	11-12	C Joubert	T: Willison. P: Noakes, Nikoro.
May 03	Stormers	STORMERS	WON	18-17	G Jackson	P: Noakes (6).
May 11	Auckland	REBELS	WON	36-32	G Williamson	T: Halai (3), F Saiili (2), Ranger. C: Noakes (2), Kerr.
May 18	Christchurch	CRUSADERS	LOST	3-23	G Jackson	P: Noakes.
May 25	Auckland	BRUMBIES	LOST	13-20	L vd Merwe	T: Ranger. C: Noakes. P: Noakes, Kerr.
June 01	Dunedin	HIGHLANDERS	LOST	28-38	J White	T: Braid, Ranger, Luatua, Nahole. C: Kerr (4).
June 29	Durban	SHARKS	LOST	20-22	J Peyper	T: Halai (2), Ranger. C: Noakes. P: Kerr.
July 06	Bloemfontein	CHEETAHS	LOST	13-34	J Peyper	T: Gibson-Park. C: Kerr. P: Kerr (2).
July 13	Auckland	CHIEFS	LOST	16-26	C Pollock	T: Piutau. C: Kerr. P: Kerr (3).

Played	Won	Drawn	Lost	Points for	Points against	Tries for	Tries against
16	6	10	0	347	364	40	36

COACHES & MANAGEMENT

HEAD COACH: Sir John Kirwan **ASSISTANT COACH:** Grant Doorey **FORWARDS COACH:** Mick Byrne
SCRUM COACH: Mike Casey **STRENGTH & CONDITIONING:** Wally Rifle **DOCTOR:** Dr Stephen Kara
PHYSIOTHERAPIST: Mark Plummer **ANALYST:** Troy Webber **MANAGER:** Bryce Anderson
MEDIA OFFICER: Jo Coleman **SKILLS COACH:** Jeff Wilson **TECHNICAL ADVISOR:** Sir Graham Henry

APPEARANCES & POINTS IN SUPER RUGBY

BLUES

	Date of Birth	Height	Weight	Matches	Tries	Conversions	Penalties	Drop Goals	Points
KS (Kane) Barrett	16/04/1990	1,94	111	3	–	–	–	–	0
AF (Anthony) Boric	27/12/1983	2,00	113	72	3	–	–	–	15
LG (Luke) Braid	05/101988	1,85	101	57	6	–	–	–	30
CC (Charlie) Faumuina	24/12/1986	1,86	128	45	2	–	–	–	10
M (Malakai) Fekitoa	10/05/1992	1,89	99	0	–	–	–	–	0
J (Jamison) Gibson-Park	23/02/1992	1,76	80	11	1	–	–	–	5
F (Frank) Halai	06/03/1988	1,95	105	16	10	–	–	–	50
BD (Bryn) Hall	03/02/1993	1,83	89	1	–	–	–	–	0
BH (Baden) Kerr	09/06/1989	1,90	90	12	–	11	10	–	52
DS (Steven) Luatua	29/04/1991	1,96	115	20	4	–	–	–	20
TS (Tevita) Mailau	25/04/1985	1,85	115	38	2	–	–	–	10
TR (Tom) McCartney	06/09/1985	1,85	109	58	2	–	–	–	10
QJRWJ (Quentin) MacDonald	25/09/1988	1,81	102	30	1	–	–	–	5
MR (Marty) McKenzie	14/08/1992	1,81	108	3	–	–	–	–	0
KF (Keven) Mealamu	20/03/1979	1,81	108	152	10	–	–	–	50
G (George) Moala	05/11/1990	1,83	104	14	2	–	–	–	10
L (Liaki) Moli	04/01/1990	1,98	114	16	1	–	–	–	5
WR (Waisake) Naholo	08/05/1991	1,75	90	1	1	–	–	–	5
W (Wayne) Ngaluafe	13/10/1988	1,75	90	1	–	–	–	–	0
AN (Albert) Nikoro	07/08/1992	1,84	99	4	–	–	1	–	3
CM (Chris) Noakes	21/07/1985	1,81	88	25	2	28	30	–	164
BR (Brendon) O'Connor	11/09/1989	1,86	100	17	–	–	–	–	0
JW (James) Parsons	27/11/1986	1,85	105	20	2	–	–	–	10
TG (Tim) Perry	01/08/1988	1,88	116	7	–	–	–	–	0
CT (Charles) Piutau	31/10/1991	1,86	95	18	6	–	–	–	30
SMJ (Sam) Prattley	16/01/1990	1,96	115	4	–	–	–	–	0
R (Ronald) Raaymakers	07/04/1990	1,93	108	2	–	–	–	–	0
RMN (Rene) Ranger	30/09/1986	1,82	101	65	25	–	–	–	125
CJ (Culum) Retallick	08/05/1984	1,98	113	41	–	–	–	–	0
F (Francis) Saili	16/02/1991	1,78	99	21	3	–	–	–	15
P (Peter) Saili	04/01/1988	1,88	111	60	4	–	–	–	20
A (Angus) Ta'avo	22/03/1990	1,94	125	22	1	–	–	–	5
AOHM (Oofa) Tu'ungafasi	17/01/1993	1,95	129	5	–	–	–	–	0
L (Lolagi) Visinia	17/01/1993	1,94	99	1	–	–	–	–	0
PAT (Piri) Weepu	07/09/1983	1,78	96	114	6	51	57	–	303
AJ (Ali) Williams	30/04/1981	2,02	118	117	6	–	–	–	30
JDK (Jackson) Willison	05/09/1988	1,83	94	52	7	–	–	–	35
Totals				**1145**	**107**	**90**	**98**	**0**	**1017**

VODACOM SUPER RUGBY

FINAL LOG POSITIONS

2013	10th	2009	9th	2005	7th	2001	11th	**1997** 1st
2012	12th	2008	6th	2004	5th	2000	6th	**1996** 2nd
2011	4th	2007	4th	**2003**	**1st**	1999	9th	
2010	7th	2006	8th	2002	6th	1998	1st	

APPEARANCES & POINTS IN 2013

BLUES

	Hurricanes	Crusaders	Bulls	Waratahs	Chiefs	Highlanders	Hurricanes	Reds	Stormers	Rebels	Crusaders	Brumbies	Highlanders	Sharks	Cheetahs	Chiefs	Matches	Tries	Conversions	Penalties	Drop Goals	Points
Piutau	15	15	15	15	15	15	15	15	15	15	15	15	15	15	15	15	16	5	–	–	–	25
Halai	14	14	14	14	14	14	14	14	14	14	14	14	14	14	14	14	16	10	–	–	–	50
Ranger	13	13	13	13	13	13	11	13	11	13	13	13	13	11R	11	13	16	6	–	–	–	30
Saili, F	12	12	12	12	12	11R	13	11R	13	12	12R	12	12	12	12	12	16	2	–	–	–	10
Moala	11	11	–	11	11	11	–	–	–	11	11	11	–	11	13R	–	10	2	–	–	–	10
Noakes	10	10	–	10	10	10	10	10	10	10	10	–	10	–	–	–	12	1	14	15	–	78
Weepu	9	9	9	9	9	9	9	9	9	9	9	9	9	–	9		15	2	2	5	–	29
Saili, P	8	8	–	8	8	8	8	8	8	8	8	8	8	8	8		15	–	–	–	–	0
Braid, L	7	7	7	7	7	7	7	7	7	8R	7	7	7	7	7	7	16	2	–	–	–	10
Luatua	6	6	8	6	6	6	6	6	6	6	–	6	6	6			14	3	–	–	–	15
Williams	5c	5c	5c	5c	5c	5c	5c	5c	5c	5c	5c	5c	5c	5c	5c	5c	16	–	–	–	–	0
Retallick	4	4	–	4	4	4	4	4	4	–	4	4	x	–	4R	–	11	–	–	–	–	0
Faumuina	3	3	3	–	–	–	–	–	–	–	–	–	–	–	–	–	4	–	–	–	–	0
Parsons	2	2	2R	2	2	2	2	2	–	–	–	2R	2	2	2	2R	13	2	–	–	–	10
McCartney	1	1	–	1	1	–	1	1	1	–	–	–	–	–	–	–	7	1	–	–	–	5
MacDonald	x	2R	2	x	2R	–	–	–	2R	2	2R	–	–	x	–	–	6	–	–	–	–	0
Ta'avao	3R	3R	3R	3R	3	3	3	3	3	3	3	3	3	3	3	3	16	1	–	–	–	5
Moli	4R	4R	4	–	–	–	–	–	–	–	–	–	–	–	–	4R	4	–	–	–	–	0
O'Connor	8R	8R	6R	8R	8R	6R	7R	8R	x	7	6R	6	8R	6R	6R	8R	15	–	–	–	–	0
Hall	x	9R	–	–	–	–	–	–	–	–	–	–	–	–	–	–	1	–	–	–	–	0
Kerr	x	10R	10	x	10R	10R	10R	10R	x	10R	x	10R	10	10R	10	10	12	–	11	10	–	52
Willison	x	14R	–	13R	12R	12	12	12	12	–	12	11R	11R	13	13	14R	13	1	–	–	–	5
Naholo	–	–	11	–	–	–	–	–	–	–	–	11	–	–	–	–	2	1	–	–	–	5
Barrett	–	–	6	–	–	–	–	–	–	–	x	–	8R	–	6		3	–	–	–	–	0
Perry	–	–	1	–	–	1	–	–	1	1	1	1	1	–	–	–	7	–	–	–	–	0
Raaymakers	–	–	4R	–	–	–	–	4R	–	x	–	–	–	–	–	–	2	–	–	–	–	0
Gibson-Park	–	–	9R	9R	9R	9R	9R	9R	x	9R	x	x	9R	9R	9	9R	11	1	–	–	–	5
McKenzie	–	–	10R	–	–	–	–	–	–	–	–	–	x	–	10R	10R	3	–	–	–	–	0
Nikoro	–	–	11R	–	–	–	13R	11	–	–	–	–	–	–	–	–	3	–	–	1	–	3
Boric	–	–	–	5R	5R	4R	4R	–	x	4	x	4R	4	4	4	4	10	–	–	–	–	0
Tu'ungafasi	–	–	–	–	x	x	1R	x	x	3R	–	–	–	1R	1R	3R	5	–	–	–	–	0
Mealamu	–	–	–	–	2R	2R	2R	2	–	2	2	2R	–	2R	2		9	–	–	–	–	0
Visinia	–	–	–	–	–	–	–	x	–	–	–	–	–	–	–	11	1	–	–	–	–	0
Sua	–	–	–	–	–	–	–	–	x	–	–	–	–	–	–	–	0	–	–	–	–	0
Prattley	–	–	–	–	–	–	–	–	–	1R	x	1R	–	–	1	1	4	–	–	–	–	0
Ngaluafe	–	–	–	–	–	–	–	–	–	–	–	–	–	9R	–	–	1	–	–	–	–	0

36 players — 325 40 27 31 0 347

 Yellow Card ■ Red Card

www.theblues.co.nz

CHIEFS

HONOURS
CHAMPIONS
2012
2013

GROUND
Waikato Stadium
CAPACITY
25 000
ADDRESS
Seddon Road, Hamilton
TELEPHONE NUMBER
+64 7 839 5675
COLOURS
Black jersey with red and yellow panels.
Black shorts and socks
WEBSITE
www.chiefs.co.nz
COACH
Dave Rennie
CAPTAIN
Craig Clarke
CEO
Gary Dawson
CHAIRMAN
Dallas Fisher

RECORDS

MATCH RECORDS

Biggest win	38	vs. Transvaal (47-9)	Hamilton	1997
Heaviest defeat	50	vs. Cats (3-53)	Bloemfontein	2000
Highest score	72	vs. Lions (72-65)	Johannesburg	2010
Most points conceded	65	vs. Lions (72-65)	Johannesburg	2010
Most tries	9	vs. Western Force (64-36)	Hamilton	2007
	9	vs. Blues (63-34)	Hamilton	2009
	9	vs. Lions (72-65)	Johannesburg	2010
Most tries conceded	9	vs. Lions (72-65)	Johannesburg	2010
Most points by a player	32	SR Donald (1t, 9c, 3p) vs. Lions Johannesburg		2010
Most tries by a player	4	SW Sivivatu vs. Blues	Hamilton	2009
	4	AT Tikoirotuma vs Blues	Albany	2012
Most conversions by a player	9	SR Donald vs. Lions	Johannesburg	2010
Most penalties by a player	6	GW Jackson vs. Queensland Reds Rotorua		2001
	6	SR Donald vs. Crusaders	Christchurch	2007
Most drop goals by a player	1	on eight occasions		

SEASON RECORDS

Most team points	369	in 15 matches	2009
Most points by a player	251	AW Cruden	2012
Most team tries	53	in 18 matches	2012
Most tries by a player	12	RQ Randle	2002
Most conversions by a player	43	AW Cruden	2012
Most penalties by a player	50	AW Cruden	2012
Most drop goals by a player	2	ID Foster	1996

CAREER RECORDS

Most appearances	113	LJ Messam	2006-2013
Most points	857	SR Donald	2005-2011
Most tries	42	SW Sivivatu	2003-2011
Most conversions	150	SR Donald	2005-2011
Most penalties	153	SR Donald	2005-2011
Most drop goals	2	ID Foster	1996-1998
	2	GW Jackson	1999-2004

No Messam around...All Black flanker Liam Messam and skipper Craig Clarke celebrate.
Hannah Johnston/Getty Images

2013 RESULTS & SCORERS

Date	Venue	Opponent	Result	Score	Referee	Scorers
Febr 22	Dunedin	HIGHLANDERS	WON	41-27	SR Walsh	T: Nanai-Williams (2), Osborne, Tikorotuma. C: Anscombe (3). P: Anscombe (5).
Mrch 02	Hamilton	CHEETAHS	WON	45-3	M Fraser	T: Tikorotuma, Afeaki, Tameifuna, Anscombe, Messam, Marshall. C: Anscombe (6). P: Anscombe.
Mrch 09	Cape Town	STORMERS	LOST	34-36	J Peyper	T: Ngatai (2), Horrell, Nanai-Williams. C: Anscombe (4). P: Anscombe (2).
Mrch 15	Port Elizabeth	KINGS	WON	35-24	S Berry	T: Masaga (3), Cane. C: Anscombe (3). P: Anscombe (3).
Mrch 22	Hamilton	HIGHLANDERS	WON	19-7	J White	T: Nanai-Williams. C: Anscombe. P: Anscombe (4).
Mrch 30	Mt Manganui	BLUES	WON	23-16	J Kaplan	T: Kahui, Tameifuna. C: Anscombe (2). P: Anscombe (3).
April 13	Hamilton	REDS	LOST	23-31	SR Walsh	T: Aki, Osborne. C: Anscombe (2). P: Anscombe (3).
April 19	Sydney	WARATAHS	LOST	20-25	C Joubert	T: Anscombe, Tameifuna. C: Anscombe (2). P: Anscombe (2).
April 27	Hamilton	SHARKS	WON	37-29	C Pollock	T: Nanai-Williams (2), Tikoirotuma, Aki. C: Anscombe (4). P: Anscombe (2), Cruden.
May 03	Rebels	MELBOURNE	WON	39-33	G Williamson	T: Anscombe (3), Retallick, Aki, Cane. C: Anscombe (3). P: Anscombe.
May 10	Pukekohe	FORCE	WON	22-21	M Fraser	T: Masaga. C: Cruden. P: Cruden (5).
May 17	Wellington	BLUES	WON	17-12	L vd Merwe	T: Latimer. P: Cruden (4).
May 24	Hamilton	CRUSADERS	WON	28-19	SR Walsh	T: Cruden, Aki, Clarke. C: Cruden (2). P: Cruden (3).
June 28	Hamilton	HURRICANES	WON	34-22	G Williamson	T: Tameifuna, Aki, Vant-Leven, Kerr-Barlow. C: Cruden (4). P: Cruden (2).
July 05	Christchurch	CRUSADERS	LOST	15-43	J White	T: Tikorotuma, Ngatai. C: Horrell. P: Cruden.
July 13	Auckland	BLUES	WON	26-16	C Pollock	T: Tameifuna (2), Aki, Elliott. P: Cruden, Anscombe.
Semi-final						
July 27	Hamilton	CRUSADERS	WON	20-19	SR Walsh	T: Cruden, Masaga. C: Cruden (2). P: Cruden (2).
Final						
Aug 03	Hamilton	BRUMBIES	WON	27-22	C Joubert	T: Robinson, Messam. C: Cruden. P: Cruden (5).

Played	Won	Lost	Drawn	Points for	Points against	Tries for	Tries against
18	14	4	0	505	405	54	40

www.chiefs.co.nz

COACHES & MANAGEMENT

HEAD COACH: Dave Rennie **ASSISTANT COACHES:** Wayne Smith, Tom Coventry & Andrew Strawbridge
STRENGHT & CONDITIONING COACH: Phil Healey **VIDEO ANALYST:** Regan Hall
DOCTOR: Dr James McGarvey **PHYSIOTHERAPIST:** Paul Cameron **MANAGER:** Stewart Williams
MEDIA OFFICER: Kylie Sousa

APPEARANCES & POINTS IN SUPER RUGBY

	Date of Birth	Height	Weight	Matches	Tries	Conversions	Penalties	Drop Goals	Points
BTP (Ben) Afeaki	12/01/1988	1,93	127	35	1	–	–	–	5
B (Bundee) Aki	07/04/1990	1,82	92	14	6	–	–	–	30
GW (Gareth) Anscombe	10/05/1991	1,84	90	23	7	43	48	1	268
SJ (Sam) Cane	13/01/1992	1,84	104	40	3	–	–	–	15
CBJ (Craig) Clarke	01/08/1983	2,00	114	88	2	–	–	–	10
NJ (Nick) Crosswell	03/04/1986	1,95	110	38	–	–	–	–	0
AW (Aaron) Cruden	08/01/1989	1,78	85	61	9	71	104	–	499
HTP (Hika) Elliott	22/01/1986	1,86	112	85	7	–	–	–	35
RA (Ross) Filipo	14/04/1979	1,98	114	47	8	–	–	–	40
MJ (Michael) FitzGerald	03/02/1987	1,97	114	27	–	–	–	–	0
RJ (Romana) Graham	29/05/1986	2,02	116	19	–	–	–	–	0
AA (Andrew) Horrell	18/07/1988	1,82	93	25	2	1	–	–	12
RD (Richard) Kahui	09/06/1985	1,90	104	68	18	–	–	–	90
MZH (Michael) Kaianga	28/01/1991	1,85	120	3	–	–	–	–	0
TNJ (Tawera) Kerr-Barlow	15/08/1990	1,87	90	41	4	–	–	–	20
TD (Tanerau) Latimer	06/05/1986	1,85	97	98	8	–	–	–	40
AF (Fritz) Lee	29/08/1989	1,90	108	21	2	–	–	–	10
BG (Brendon) Leonard	16/04/1985	1,82	92	73	18	–	–	–	90
P (Pauliasi) Manu	23/12/1987	1,84	115	17	–	–	–	–	0
R (Rhys) Marshall	12/10/1992	1,84	104	9	1	–	–	–	5
LCT (Lelia) Masaga	30/08/1986	1,80	95	91	37	–	–	–	185
LJ (Liam) Messam	25/03/1984	1,90	108	113	24	–	–	–	120
TT (Tim) Nanai-Williams	12/06/1989	1,82	87	51	16	1	2	–	88
CJ (Charlie) Ngatai	17/08/1990	1,86	97	26	4	–	–	–	20
PJJ (Patrick) Osborne	14/06/1987	1,89	105	9	2	–	–	–	10
AW (Augustin) Pulu	04/01/1990	1,80	93	24	1	–	–	–	5
BA (Brodie) Retallick	31/05/1991	2,04	117	35	2	–	–	–	10
RB (Robbie) Robinson	22/08/1989	1,81	89	45	4	7	9	1	64
S (Solomoana) Sakalia	02/02/1991	1,90	118	0	–	–	–	–	0
MM (Mahonri) Schwalger	15/09/1979	1,80	107	55	–	–	–	–	0
TJ (Toby) Smith	10/10/1988	1,90	115	37	3	–	–	–	15
BVC (Ben) Tameifuna	30/08/1991	1,82	137	33	7	–	–	–	35
AT (Asaeli) Tikoirutuma	24/06/1986	1,87	92	33	11	–	–	–	55
S (Save) Tokula	15/06/1985	1,92	97	7	1	–	–	–	5
MJ (Matt) Vant-Leven	23/10/1987	1,91	106	12	1	–	–	–	5
DJ (Dan) Waenga	06/11/1985	1,78	91	1	–	–	–	–	0
Totals				**1404**	**209**	**123**	**163**	**2**	**1786**

FINAL LOG POSITIONS

2013	1st	**2009**	2nd	**2005**	6th	**2001**	6th	**1997**	11th
2012	2nd	**2008**	7th	**2004**	4th	**2000**	10th	**1996**	6th
2011	10th	**2007**	6th	**2003**	10th	**1999**	6th		
2010	11th	**2006**	7th	**2002**	8th	**1998**	7th		

APPEARANCES & POINTS IN 2013

	Highlanders	Cheetahs	Stormers	Kings	Highlanders	Blues	Reds	Waratahs	Sharks	Rebels	Force	Blues	Crusaders	Hurricanes	Crusaders	Blues	Crusaders	Brumbies	Matches	Tries	Conversions	Penalties	Drop Goals	Points
Anscombe	15	15	15	15	15	15	15	15R	15	15	–	–	–	–	–	13R	15	15	13	5	30	27	–	166
Osborne	14	10R	14R	14R	–	x	14R	–	–	11R	11	–	14	–	14	–	–	–	9	2	–	–	–	10
Nanai-Williams	13	13	13	13	13	–	14	12R	13	13	–	–	–	13	12R	13	–	–	12	6	–	–	–	30
Aki	12	12	–	–	–	12	12	–	12	12	12	12	12	12	12	12	12R	12R	14	6	–	–	–	30
Tikoiorutuma	11	11	11	11	11	11	11	11	11	11R	11	11	11	11	11R	11	11	11	18	4	–	–	–	20
Cruden	10	10	10	10	10	10	10	10	10	10	10	10	10	10	10	10	10	10	18	2	10	24	–	102
Kerr-Barlow	9	9R	9	9	9	–	–	–	–	–	9	9	9	9	9	9	9	9	13	1	–	–	–	5
Lee	8	8	–	–	–	8	6R	8	–	–	–	–	–	–	–	–	–	–	5	–	–	–	–	0
Cane	7	7	7	8R	7	8R	7	7	8R	7	7	–	8R	7R	7	8R	8R	8R	17	2	–	–	–	10
Messam	6	6c	8	6	6c	6c	8c	6c	6	6	6	6	6	–	6	6	6	–	17	2	–	–	–	10
Retallick	5	5	5	4R	5	5	5	5	5	5	5	5	5	5	5	5	5	–	18	1	–	–	–	5
Clarke	4c	4R	4c	4c	–	–	–	–	4c	4c	4c	4c	4c	4c	4c	4c	4c	4c	14	1	–	–	–	5
Afeaki	3	3	3	3	3R	3	–	–	–	–	3	3	–	3	3R	–	3R	3R	12	1	–	–	–	5
Marshall	2	2R	–	x	2R	2R	2R	2R	2R	–	–	–	–	–	–	–	2R	2R	9	1	–	–	–	5
Manu	1	1	1	1R	1	–	–	1	–	1	–	1	1	1	1	3R	–	–	12	–	–	–	–	0
Smith	1R	–	–	1	–	1	1	–	1	1R	1	–	3R	–	–	1	1	1	11	–	–	–	–	0
Tameifuna	3R	1R	1R	–	3	3R	3	3	3R	3	3R	3R	3	3R	3	3	3	3	17	6	–	–	–	30
FitzGerald	4R	4	4R	5	4	4	4	4	4R	4R	x	4R	x	5R	7R	5R	x	11R	15	–	–	–	–	0
Latimer	8R	8R	6	7	8R	7	6	8R	7	8R	8R	7	7	6R	7	7	7	7	18	1	–	–	–	5
Pulu	9R	9	9R	9R	13R	9	9	9R	9	9R	x	x	9R	9R	9R	7R	9R	9R	16	–	–	–	–	0
Ngatai	13R	12R	12	13R	12R	–	–	13	12R	–	12R	13	13	13R	13	–	13	13	14	3	–	–	–	15
Masaga	14R	14	14	14	14	14	–	14	14	14	14	14R	14	–	14	14	14	14	16	5	–	–	–	25
Elliott	–	2	2R	2	2	2	2	2	–	2R	2	2	2	2	2	2	2	2	16	1	–	–	–	5
Schwalger	–	–	2	–	–	–	–	2	2	2R	2R	2R	2R	2R	2R	–	–	–	9	–	–	–	–	0
Horrell	–	–	12R	12	12	13R	22R	15	–	–	–	–	15R	10R	15	12	12	–	11	1	1	–	–	7
Croswell	–	–	6R	–	8	4R	4R	4R	8	–	–	8R	–	–	–	–	–	–	7	–	–	–	–	0
Filipo	–	–	–	8	–	–	–	–	–	–	–	–	–	6	–	–	–	–	2	–	–	–	–	0
Kahui	–	–	–	–	14R	13	13	12	–	–	–	–	–	–	–	–	–	–	4	1	–	–	–	5
Graham	–	–	–	–	4R	–	–	–	–	–	–	–	–	–	–	–	–	–	1	–	–	–	–	0
Leonard	–	–	–	–	–	9R	9R	9	9R	9	–	–	–	–	–	–	–	–	5	–	–	–	–	0
Kainga	–	–	–	–	–	3R	3R	3	–	–	–	–	–	–	–	–	–	–	3	–	–	–	–	0
Robinson	–	–	–	–	–	–	15R	13R	15	15	15	15	15	15	11	14R	15R	–	10	1	–	–	–	5
Vant-Leven	–	–	–	–	–	–	–	8	8	8	8	8	8	8	8	8	–	–	9	1	–	–	–	5
Tokula	–	–	–	–	–	–	–	–	13	13R	–	–	–	–	–	–	–	–	2	–	–	–	–	0
Waenga	–	–	–	–	–	–	–	–	–	x	12R	–	–	–	–	–	–	–	1	–	–	–	–	0
36 players																			**388**	**54**	**41**	**51**	**0**	**505**

Yellow Card ■ Red Card

CRUSADERS

HONOURS
CHAMPIONS
1998
1999
2000
2002
2005
2006
2008

GROUND
AMI Stadium
CAPACITY
39 000
ADDRESS
30 Stevens Street,
Christchurch
TELEPHONE
+ 64 3 379 8300
COLOURS
Red jersey with black side panels. Black shorts and black socks
WEBSITE
www.crusaders.co.nz
COACH
Todd Blackadder
CAPTAIN
Richie McCaw
CEO
Hamish Riach
CHAIRMAN
Murray Ellis

RECORDS

MATCH RECORDS

Biggest win	77	vs. NSW Waratahs (96-19)	Christchurch	2002
Heaviest defeat	36	vs. Queensland Reds (16-52)	Brisbane	1996
Highest score	96	vs. NSW Waratahs (96-19)	Christchurch	2002
Most points conceded	58	vs. Natal (26-58)	Durban	1996
Most tries	14	vs. NSW Waratahs (96-19)	Christchurch	2002
Most tries conceded	8	vs. Natal (26-58)	Durban	1996
Most points by a player	31	TJ Taylor (1t, 1c, 8p) vs. Stormers	Christchurch	2012
Most tries by a player	4	CS Ralph vs. NSW Waratahs	Christchurch	2002
	4	SD Maitland vs. Brumbies	Nelson	2011
Most conversions by a player	13	AP Mehrtens vs. NSW Waratahs	Christchurch	2002
Most penalties by a player	8	TJ Taylor vs. Stormers	Christchurch	2012
Most drop goals by a player	3	AP Mehrtens vs. Highlanders	Christchurch	1998

SEASON RECORDS

Most team points	541	from 13 matches	2005
Most points by a player	221	DW Carter	2006
Most team tries	71	from 13 matches	2005
Most tries by a player	15	RL Gear	2005
Most conversions by a player	37	DW Carter	2005
Most penalties by a player	43	AP Mehrtens	1999
Most drop goals by a player	4	AP Mehrtens	1998, 1999, 2002

CAREER RECORDS

Most appearances	134	CR Flynn	2002-2013
Most points	1547	DW Carter	2003-2013
Most tries	52	CS Ralph	1999-2008
Most conversions	259	DW Carter	2003-2013
Most penalties	277	DW Carter	2003-2013
Most drop goals	17	AP Mehrtens	1996-2005

Handful...The Crusaders played with their usual verve but fell at the penultimate hurdle.
Steve Haag/Gallo Images

2013 **RESULTS & SCORERS**

Date	Venue	Opponent	Result	Score	Referee	Scorers
Mrch 01	Auckland	BLUES	LOST	15-34	C Pollock	P: Carter (5).
Mrch 08	Wellington	HURRICANES	LOST	28-29	A Lees	T: Flynn, Carter, Dagg, Crotty. C: Carter (4).
Mrch 16	Christchurch	BULLS	WON	41-19	C Pollock	T: McNicholl, Read, Fruean, Marshall, Heinz, Crockett. C: Carter (4). P: Carter.
Mrch 23	Christchurch	KINGS	WON	55-20	R Hoffman	T: G Whitelock (3), L Whitelock, Todd, Heinz, Crockett. C: Carter (5), Bleyendaal (2). P: Carter (2).
Mrch 30	Cape Town	STORMERS	WON	19-14	C Joubert	T: Todd. C: Bleyendaal. P: Bleyendaal (4).
April 05	Durban	SHARKS	LOST	17-21	L vd Merwe	T: Ellis. P: Bleyendaal (4).
April 13	Perth	FORCE	LOST	14-16	J Kaplan	T: Romano. P: Bleyendaal (3).
April 20	Christchurch	HIGHLANDERS	WON	24-8	G Williamson	T: Fruean, T Taylor. C: Bleyendaal. P: Bleyendaal (4).
April 28	Christchurch	REBELS	WON	30-26	N Briant	T: Bleyendaal, Guildford. C: Taylor. P: Taylor (6).
May 05	Canberra	BRUMBIES	WON	30-23	C Joubert	T: Ellis, Dagg, Guildford. C: Carter (3). P: Carter (3)
May 18	Christchurch	BLUES	WON	23-3	G Jackson	T: G Whitelock, Crotty. C: Taylor (2). P: Taylor (3).
May 25	Hamilton	CHIEFS	LOST	19-28	SR Walsh	T: Todd. C: Taylor. P: Taylor (4).
May 31	Christchurch	WARATAHS	WON	23-22	G Jackson	T: Flynn, Todd. C: Carter (2). P: Carter (3).
June 29	Dunedin	HIGHLANDERS	WON	40-12	SR Walsh	T: Ellis, Carter, G Whitelock, Veainu. C: Carter (4). P: Carter (4).
July 05	Christchurch	CHIEFS	WON	43-15	J White	T: Read (2), Dagg, Crotty, Bleyendaal. C: Carter (3). P: Carter (4).
July 13	Christchurch	Hurricanes	WON	25-17	G Jackson	T: Ellis, Marshall, Guildford. C: Carter (2). P: Carter (2).
Play-off						
July 20	Christchurch	Reds	WON	38-9	J Peyper	T: Crotty (2), Carter, Marshall. C: Carter (3). P: Carter (3), Taylor.
Semi-final						
July 27	Hamilton	Chiefs	LOST	19-20	SR Walsh	T: Dagg. C: Carter. P: Carter (4).

Played	Won	Lost	Drawn	Points for	Points against	Tries for	Tries against
18	12	6	0	503	336	49	33

COACHES & MANAGEMENT

HEAD COACH: Todd Blackadder **ASSISTANT COACHES:** Dave Hewett, Aaron Mauger & Tabai Matson
HIGH PERFORMANCE LEADER: Steve Lancaster **ANALYST:** Jamie Hamilton **TRAINER:** Mark Drury
PERFORMANCE CO-ORDINATOR: Carl Jennings **LOGISTICS:** John Miles **DOCTOR:** Deb Robinson
PHYSIOTHERAPIST: John Roche **MANAGER:** Angus Gardiner **MEDIA OFFICER:** Anne Newman

APPEARANCES & POINTS IN SUPER RUGBY

CRUSADERS

	Date of Birth	Height	Weight	Matches	Tries	Conversions	Penalties	Drop Goals	Points
DJ (Dominic) Bird	09/04/1991	2,06	112	10	–	–	–	–	0
T (Tyler) Bleyendaal	31/05/1990	1,85	96	16	2	8	27	–	107
DW (Dan) Carter	05/03/1982	1,78	94	123	33	259	277	11	1547
S (Shane) Christie	23/09/1985	1,84	107	1	–	–	–	–	0
WWW (Wyatt) Crockett	24/01/1983	1,93	116	122	8	–	–	–	40
RS (Ryan) Crotty	23/09/1988	1,81	91	63	10	–	–	–	50
IJA (Israel) Dagg	06/06/1988	1,86	96	68	24	18	20	–	213
TJS (Tom) Donnelly	01/10/1981	2,00	113	84	–	–	–	–	0
AM (Andy) Ellis	21/02/1984	1,82	89	107	20	–	–	3	109
CR (Corey) Flynn	05/01/1981	1,84	108	134	18	–	–	–	90
OT (Owen) Franks	23/12/1987	1,85	118	75	2	–	–	–	10
R (Robbie) Fruean	13/07/1988	1,90	104	62	15	–	–	–	75
BCJ Ben) Funnell	06/06/1990	1,80	105	16	–	–	–	–	0
ZR (Zac) Guildford	08/02/1989	1,82	94	79	30	–	–	–	150
WA (Willi) Heinz	24/11/1986	1,79	93	41	3	–	–	–	15
NE (Nepo) Laulala	06/11/1989	1,84	116	3	–	–	–	–	0
TG (Tom) Marshall	07/05/1990	1,83	91	42	6	–	–	–	30
RH (Richie) McCaw	31/12/1980	1,87	108	122	26	–	–	–	130
JZ (Johnny) McNicholl	24/09/1990	1,85	96	4	1	–	–	–	5
J (Joe) Moody	18/09/1988	1,88	112	16	–	–	–	–	0
KJ (Kieran) Read	26/10/1985	1,93	110	96	16	–	–	–	80
L (Luke) Romano	13/05/1987	1,98	110	46	5	–	–	–	25
J (Jordan) Taufua	29/01/1992	1,82	100	5	–	–	–	–	0
C (Codie) Taylor	31/03/1991	1,83	106	3	–	–	–	–	0
TJ (Tom) Taylor	11/03/1989	1,83	90	25	2	19	51	–	201
MB (Matt) Todd	24/03/1988	1,85	104	51	8	–	–	–	40
J (Jimmy) Tupou	08/08/1992	1,96	109	2	–	–	–	–	0
TK (Telusa) Veainu	26/12/1990	1,80	85	9	1	–	–	–	5
AJ (Adam) Whitelock	17/04/1987	1,85	95	53	7	–	–	–	35
GB (George) Whitelock	30/03/1986	1,90	106	78	8	–	–	–	40
LC (Luke) Whitelock	29/01/1991	1,90	104	28	1	–	–	–	5
SL (Sam) Whitelock	12/10/1988	2,02	116	59	2	–	–	–	10
Totals				**1643**	**248**	**304**	**375**	**14**	**3012**

VODACOM SUPER RUGBY

FINAL LOG POSITIONS

2013	4th	2009	4th	2005	1st	2001	10th
2012	4th	**2008**	**1st**	2004	2nd	**2000**	**2nd**
2011	3rd	2007	3rd	2003	2nd	**1999**	**4th**
2010	4th	**2006**	**1st**	**2002**	**1st**	1998	2nd
						1997	6th
						1996	12th

APPEARANCES & POINTS IN 2013

CRUSADERS	Blues	Hurricanes	Bulls*	Kings	Stormers	Sharks**	Force	Highlanders	Rebels	Brumbies	Blues	Chiefs	Waratahs	Highlanders	Chiefs	Hurricanes	Reds	Chiefs	Matches	Tries	Conversions	Penalties	Drop Goals	Points
Taylor, T	15	13R	–	–	–	–	–	12R	12	15	15	12	12	12	12	12	12	12	13	1	4	14	–	55
Whitelock, A	14	21R	12R	13R	11R	11	11	x	x	13R	11R	x	–	–	–	15R	12R	11	11	–	–	–	–	0
Fruean	13	13	13	13	13	13	13	13	–	13	13	13R	12R	–	–	–	–	–	12	2	–	–	–	10
Crotty	12	12	12	12	12	12	12	12	13	12	12	13	13	13	13	13	13	13	18	5	–	–	–	25
Dagg	11	15	15	–	–	14R	15	15	15	12R	13R	15	15	15	15	15	15	15	16	4	–	–	–	20
Carter	10	10	10	10	–	–	–	10R	10	10	10	10	10	10	10	10	10	10	14	3	31	31	–	170
Ellis	9	9	9	15R	9R	9	9	9	9R	9	9	9	9	9R	9	9	9	9	18	4	–	–	–	20
Read	8c	8c	8c	8c	–	–	–	–	–	8c	8c	8c	7R	8c	8c	8c	8c	–	12	3	–	–	–	15
Todd	7	7	7	7	7	7	–	7	7	7	7	7	7	7	7	7	7	7	17	4	–	–	–	20
Whitelock, G	6	6	6	6	6c	6c	6c	6c	6c	6c	6	6	6	6c	6	6	6	6	18	5	–	–	–	25
Whitelock, S	5	4	4	5	5	5R	5	5	5	5	5	–	5	5	5	5	5	–	17	–	–	–	–	0
Romano	4	–	–	4	4	4	4	4	4	4	4	4R	4	–	4	4	–	–	15	1	–	–	–	5
Franks	3	3	3	3	3	3	3	3	3	3	–	–	–	3	3	3	3	–	14	–	–	–	–	0
Flynn	2	2	2	2	2	–	2	2	2	2	–	2	2R	2	2	2	2	2	15	2	–	–	–	10
Crockett	1	1	1	1	1	1	1	1	1R	1	1	1	1R	1	1	1	1	1	18	2	–	–	–	10
Funnell	2R	2R	2R	–	x	2	x	2R	2R	2R	2	2R	2	2R	2R	2R	2R	–	15	–	–	–	–	0
Moody	1R	1R	3R	3R	3R	1R	x	8R	1	x	1R	1R	1	1R	1R	1R	1R	1R	16	–	–	–	–	0
Bird	4R	5	5	5R	x	5R	–	x	5R	19R	4R	5R	5	–	–	–	–	–	10	–	–	–	–	0
Whitelock, L	6R	6R	8R	7R	8	8	8	8	8	8	6R	6R	8R	8	6R	6R	4R	4R	18	1	–	–	–	5
Heinz	9R	9R	9R	9	9	9R	9R	9R	9	9R	9R	9R	9	9R	9R	9R	9R	9R	18	2	–	–	–	10
Blyendaal	x	–	13R	10R	10	10	10	10	10	–	–	–	–	13R	13R	12R	10R	x	11	2	4	15	–	63
Marshall	13R	14	14	15	15	15	14	14	14	14	14	14	14	14	14	14	14	14	18	3	–	–	–	15
McNicholl	–	11	11	14	11	–	–	–	–	–	–	–	–	–	–	–	–	–	4	1	–	–	–	5
Donnelly	–	x	5R	–	–	–	5	–	–	–	–	4	4R	4	–	–	–	–	5	–	–	–	–	0
Guildford	–	–	–	11	14	14	11R	11	11	11	11	11	11	11	11	11	11	11	15	3	–	–	–	15
Taylor, C	–	–	–	2R	–	x	–	–	–	2R	2	–	–	–	–	–	–	–	3	–	–	–	–	0
Taufua	–	–	–	–	8R	8R	7R	x	8R	6R	–	–	–	–	–	–	–	–	5	–	–	–	–	0
Christie	–	–	–	–	x	–	7	–	–	–	–	–	–	–	–	–	–	–	1	–	–	–	–	0
Veainu	–	–	–	–	x	15R	–	–	–	–	x	–	11R	14R	14R	–	–	–	4	1	–	–	–	5
Laulala	–	–	–	–	–	–	–	–	–	3	3	3	3	–	–	–	–	–	4	–	–	–	–	0
Tupou	–	–	–	–	–	–	–	–	–	–	5R	–	–	4R	–	–	–	–	2	–	–	–	–	0
McCaw	–	–	–	–	–	–	–	–	–	–	–	–	–	–	7R	7R	–	–	2	–	–	–	–	0
33 players																				**379**	**49**	**39**	**60**	**0**	**503**

▨ *Yellow Card* ■ *Red Card*

* *all four Whitelocks on the field from the 66th min onwards.*
** *all four Whitelocks in the starting line-up. A first in SR history.*

HIGHLANDERS

GROUND
Forsyth Barr Stadium
CAPACITY
30 748
ADDRESS
Anzac Avenue, Long Park
TELEPHONE NUMBER
+64 3 446 4010
COLOURS
Blue jersey with gold stripes. Blue shorts and socks
WEBSITE
www.highlanders rugby.co.nz
CAPTAIN
Andrew Hore
GENERAL MANAGER
Roger Clark
CHAIRMAN
Ross Laidlaw

RECORDS

MATCH RECORDS

Biggest win	42	vs. Bulls (65-23)	Invercargill	1999
Heaviest defeat	44	vs. ACT Brumbies (26-70)	Canberra	1996
Highest score	65	vs. Bulls (65-23)	Invercargill	1999
Most points conceded	75	vs. Sharks (43-75)	Durban	1997
Most tries	9	vs. Bulls (65-23)	Invercargill	1999
Most tries conceded	9	vs. ACT Brumbies (26-70)	Canberra	1996
Most points by a player	28	BA Blair vs. Sharks	Durban	2005
Most tries by a player	3	TM Vaega vs. Western Province	Cape Town	1996
	3	DC Howlett vs. Chiefs	Hamilton	1997
	3	JW Wilson vs. Stormers	Cape Town	1998
	3	JC Stanley vs. Stormers	Cape Town	1998
	3	TR Nicholas vs. Bulls	Pretoria	2002
	3	BA Blair vs. Sharks	Durban	2005
	3	IJA Dagg vs. Bulls	Pretoria	2010
	3	AJ Thomson vs. Rebels	Invercargill	2012
	3	KI Poki vs. Cheetahs	Invercargill	2013
Most conversions by a player	7	TE Brown vs. Bulls	Invercargill	1999
Most penalties by a player	8	WC Walker vs. Chiefs	Hamilton	2003
Most drop goals by a player	1	on 18 occasions		

SEASON RECORDS

Most team points	374	from 12 matches	1998
	374	from 16 matches	2013
Most points by a player	150	TE Brown	2000
Most team tries	40	from 12 matches	1998
	40	from 16 matches	2013
Most tries by a player	10	JW Wilson	1998
Most conversions by a player	21	TE Brown	1999
Most penalties by a player	34	TE Brown	2000
Most drop goals by a player	2	SD Culhane	1996
	2	BJ Laney	1999
	2	NJ Evans	2005

CAREER RECORDS

Most appearances	127	AD Oliver	1996-2007
Most points	857	TE Brown	1996-2011
Most tries	35	JW Wilson	1996-2002
Most conversions	137	TE Brown	1996-2011
Most penalties	180	TE Brown	1996-2011

Old hand...Andrew Hore brought his vast experience to the Highlanders' front row.
Hannah Johnston/Getty Images

2013 RESULTS & SCORERS

Date	Venue	Opponent	Result	Score	Referee	Scorers
Febr 22	Dunedin	CHIEFS	LOST	27-41	SR Walsh	T: B Smith, Gear, Poki. C: Sopoaga (3). P: Sopoaga (2).
Mrch 09	Invercargill	CHEETAHS	LOST	19-36	N Briant	T: Poki (3). C: Slade, Sopoaga.
Mrch 15	Dunedin	HURRICANES	LOST	19-23	F Pastrana	T: Gear. C: Slade. P: Slade (4)
Mrch 22	Hamiltom	CHIEFS	LOST	7-19	J White	T: A Smith. C: Slade.
Mrch 29	Dunedin	REDS	LOST	33-34	J Peyper	T: Dixon, Gear, Nonu. C: Sopoaga (2), Slade. P: Slade (3), Sopoaga.
April 05	Auckland	BLUES	LOST	28-29	SR Walsh	T: B Smith, Burleigh. C: Slade. P: Slade (2).
April 12	Dunedin	BRUMBIES	LOST	19-30	C Pollock	T: A Smith. C: Parker. P: Parker (4).
April 20	Christchurch	CRUSADERS	LOST	8-24	G Williamson	T: Emery. P: Slade.
May 04	Dunedin	SHARKS	WON	25-22	SR Walsh	T: A Smith, Slade, Treeby. C: Slade (2). P: Slade (2).
May 11	Port Elizabeth	KINGS	LOST	27-34	J Jaftha	T: Thorn, Slade, Gear, Treeby. C: Slade (2). P: Slade.
May 18	Pretoria	BULLS	LOST	18-35	J Peyper	T: Ellison, Tanaka. C: Parker. P: Slade (2).
May 25	Perth	FORCE	LOST	18-19	A Lees	P: Slade (4), Parker (2).
June 01	Dunedin	BLUES	WON	38-28	J White	T: B Smith (2), Gear, Ellison. C: Slade (3). P: Slade (3), Parker.
June 29	Dunedin	CRUSADERS	LOST	12-40	SR Walsh	T: B Smith, Gear. C: Slade.
July 06	Wellington	HURRICANES	WON	49-44	M Fraser	T: A Smith, Dixon, Gear, Poki, Tuiali'i. Elisson. C: Slade (3), Parker (2). P: Slade (3).
July 12	Melbourne	REBELS	LOST	37-38	A Lees	T: B Smith, Gear, Elisson, Woodcock. C: Slade (4). P: Slade (2), Parker.

Played	Won	Drawn	Lost	Points for	Points against	Tries for	Tries against
16	3	13	0	374	496	40	55

COACHES & MANAGEMENT

HEAD COACH: Jamie Joseph **ASSISTANT COACH:** Scott McLeod and Jon Preston
ADMINISTRATOR: Diane Ede **CONDITIONING COACH:** Andrew Beardmore **DOCTOR:** Dr Greg MacLeod
PHYSIOTHERAPIST: Adam Letts **VIDEO ANALYST:** Chris Lapage **MANAGER:** Graham Purvis
MEDIA OFFICER: Doug McSweeney **COMMERCIAL MANAGER:** Mike Kerr **SCRUM COACH:** Kees Meeuws

APPEARANCES & POINTS IN SUPER RUGBY

	Date of Birth	Height	Weight	Matches	Tries	Conversions	Penalties	Drop Goals	Points
JJG (Josh) Bekhuis	26/04/1986	2,00	111	71	2	–	–	–	10
TP (Tim) Boys	19/02/1984	1,89	98	45	1	–	–	–	5
PD (Phil) Burleigh	22/10/1986	1,81	92	23	3	–	–	–	15
LJ (Liam) Coltman	25/01/1990	1,85	109	13	–	–	–	–	0
EC (Elliot) Dixon	04/09/1989	1,95	110	15	2	–	–	–	10
TE (Tamati) Ellison	01/04/1983	1,85	99	77	13	–	–	–	65
JWC (Jason) Emery	21/09/1993	1,73	88	11	1	–	–	–	5
AC (Tony) Ensor	11/05/1991	1,87	87	1	–	–	–	–	0
SLM (Ma'afu) Fia	22/01/1989	1,80	114	24	–	–	–	–	0
HE (Hosea) Gear	16/03/1984	1,88	103	102	39	–	–	–	195
JI (John) Hardie	27/07/1988	1,83	103	38	1	–	–	–	5
JMRA (Jarrad) Hoeata	12/12/1983	1,95	115	45	1	–	–	–	5
AK (Andrew) Hore	13/09/1978	1,83	110	141	21	–	–	–	105
TJ (TJ) Ioane	09/05/1989	1,82	104	13	–	–	–	–	0
CC (Chris) King	30/04/1981	1,86	118	107	7	–	–	–	35
JL (Jamie) Mackintosh	20/02/1985	1,92	130	67	2	–	–	–	10
LT (Nasi) Manu	15/08/1988	1,89	112	49	2	–	–	–	10
BT (Brayden) Mitchell	24/01/1989	1,83	104	8	–	–	–	–	0
BI (Bronson) Murray	06/11/1982	1,84	118	46	1	–	–	–	5
TWM (Tino) Nemani	24/05/1991	1,85	100	7	–	–	–	–	0
MA (Ma'a) Nonu	21/05/1982	1,82	107	133	1	–	–	–	5
JW (Jake) Paringatai	13/04/1980	1,85	106	10	–	–	–	–	0
HJ (Hayden) Parker	19/11/1990	1,75	80	10	–	4	8	–	32
KI (Kade) Poki	17/01/1988	1,76	92	42	12	–	–	–	60
B (Buxton) Popoali'i	04/12/1989	1,73	87	14	–	–	–	–	0
TWK (Trent) Renata	13/05/1988	1,80	90	3	–	–	–	–	0
JK (Jason) Rutledge	15/12/1977	1,75	100	60	8	–	–	–	40
CR (Colin) Slade	10/10/1987	1,83	90	47	4	40	43	1	232
AL (Aaron) Smith	21/11/1988	1,71	83	44	7	–	–	–	35
BR (Ben) Smith	01/06/1986	1,90	92	72	16	–	–	–	80
LZ (Lima) Sopoaga	03/02/1991	1,75	91	16	1	11	19	–	84
F (Fumiaki) Tanaka	03/01/1985	1,63	75	14	1	–	–	–	5
BC (Brad) Thorn	03/02/1975	1,95	112	107	12	–	–	–	60
MM (Mose) Tuiali'i	25/03/1981	1,94	112	77	1	–	–	–	5
S (Shaun) Treeby	26/01/1989	1,75	85	26	4	–	–	–	20
JT (Joe) Wheeler	20/10/1987	2,00	111	14	–	–	–	–	0
FS (Frae) Wilson	09/02/1989	1,77	92	3	–	–	–	–	0
TD (Tony) Woodcock	27/01/1981	1,84	119	125	9	–	–	–	45
Totals				1720	172	55	70	1	1183

FINAL LOG POSITIONS

2013	14th	2009	11th	2005	8th	2001	5th	1997	12th
2012	9th	2008	11th	2004	9th	2000	3rd	1996	8th
2011	8th	2007	9th	2003	7th	1999	3rd		
2010	12th	2006	9th	2002	4th	1998	4th		

APPEARANCES & POINTS IN 2013

	Chiefs	Cheetahs	Hurricanes	Chiefs	Reds	Blues	Brumbies	Crusaders	Sharks	Kings	Bulls	Force	Blues	Crusaders	Hurricanes	Rebels	Matches	Tries	Conversions	Penalties	Drop Goals	Points
Smith, B	15	15	15	15	15	15	15	15	15	15	15	15	15	15	15	15	16	6	–	–	–	30
Poki	14	14	14	14	–	–	14	–	–	–	–	–	–	14	14	14	8	5	–	–	–	25
Burleigh	13	13	12	13R	13R	13R	13	–	14	–	–	–	–	–	–	–	8	1	–	–	–	5
Nonu	12	–	–	12	12	12	12	12	–	–	–	12	12R	12R	–	–	9	1	–	–	–	5
Gear	11c	11	11	11	11	11	11	11	11	11	11	11	11	11	11	11	16	8	–	–	–	40
Sopoaga	10	10	16R	10R	10R	14R	–	–	–	–	–	–	10R	–	–	–	7	–	6	3	–	21
Smith, A	9	9	9	9	9	9	9R	9	9	9	9	9	9R	9R	9	9	16	4	–	–	–	20
Manu	8	–	–	–	–	–	–	–	–	–	–	–	–	–	–	–	1	–	–	–	–	0
Hardie	7	7	7	7	7	7	7	7	7	7	7	7	7	–	–	–	13	–	–	–	–	0
Wheeler	6	6	6	8R	–	–	–	–	6R	6R	6	5R	–	–	5R	6R	10	–	–	–	–	0
Bekhuis	5	5	–	5	5	5	5R	5	5	5	–	5	5	5	5	5	14	–	–	–	–	0
Hoeata	4	5R	5	6	6	6	5	6	6	6	5	–	6	6	–	–	13	–	–	–	–	0
Fia	3	3	3R	1	3R	3R	3	3R	1R	3R	–	3	3	3	3	3	15	–	–	–	–	0
Mitchell	2	2R	2R	–	–	–	–	–	–	–	–	–	–	–	–	–	3	–	–	–	–	0
Woodcock	1	1	1	–	1	–	–	1	1	1	1R	1	–	1	1	1	12	1	–	–	–	5
Coltman	2R	–	–	2	2R	2R	x	2R	2R	2R	2R	2	2R	2R	2	2R	13	–	–	–	–	0
Murray	3R	–	–	1R	–	–	–	–	–	–	3R	3R	3R	3R	3R	–	7	–	–	–	–	0
Dixon	8R	–	8	8	8	21R	8R	6R	8R	–	8R	7R	8R	7	7	x	13	2	–	–	–	10
Boys	4R	6R	–	7R	7R	–	–	–	–	–	–	–	–	–	–	–	4	–	–	–	–	0
Tanaka	9R	9R	9R	–	x	9R	9	9R	9R	9R	9R	9R	9	9	9R	9R	14	1	–	–	–	5
Parker	10R	–	–	–	–	–	10	10	13R	10R	10R	10	10R	–	10R	10R	10	–	4	8	–	32
Popoalii	14R	13R	13R	–	14	14	–	–	–	–	–	–	–	14R	–	–	6	–	–	–	–	0
Treeby	–	12	–	–	–	–	–	12	12	12	–	12	12	12	13R	–	8	2	–	–	–	10
Paringatai	–	8	8R	–	–	–	–	8R	–	–	–	–	5R	8R	6	–	6	–	–	–	–	0
Thorn	–	4	4	4c	4	4	4	4	4	4	4c	4	4	4c	4	–	15	1	–	–	–	5
Hore	–	2c	2c	–	2c	2c	2c	2c	2c	2c	2c	2R	2c	2c	2R	2c	14	–	–	–	–	0
Slade	–	10R	10	10	10	10	x	10R	10	10	10	10R	10	10	10	10	14	2	20	27	–	131
King	–	3R	3	3	3	3	3R	3	3	3	3	–	–	–	–	–	10	–	–	–	–	0
Emery	–	–	–	13	13	13	14R	13	14R	14R	12R	14	–	–	–	13	11	1	–	–	–	5
Ioane	–	–	5R	–	8R	8R	6	8	8	8	5R	6	6R	6R	6	8	13	–	–	–	–	0
Rutledge	–	–	–	2R	–	–	–	–	–	–	–	–	–	–	–	–	1	–	–	–	–	0
Wilson	–	–	–	9R	–	–	–	–	–	–	–	–	–	–	–	–	1	–	–	–	–	0
Tuiali'i	–	–	–	–	–	8	8	–	–	8R	8	8	8	8	8	7	9	1	–	–	–	5
MacKintosh	–	–	–	–	1	1	1R	–	–	1	–	1	–	–	–	–	5	–	–	–	–	0
Ensor	–	–	–	–	–	–	14	–	–	–	–	–	–	–	–	–	1	–	–	–	–	0
Ellison	–	–	–	–	–	–	–	13	13	13	13	13	13	13	13	12	8	4	–	–	–	20
Nemani	–	–	–	–	–	–	–	–	14	14	9R	–	–	–	–	–	3	–	–	–	–	0
Renata	–	–	–	–	–	–	–	–	–	–	14	–	–	–	–	–	1	–	–	–	–	0
38 players																	348	40	30	38	0	374

Yellow Card ■ *Red Card*

HURRICANES

GROUND
Westpac Stadium
CAPACITY
34 500
ADDRESS
Waterloo Quay,
Wellington
TELEPHONE NUMBER
+ 64 4 389 0020
COLOURS
Yellow jersey with black piping, black shorts and socks
WEBSITE
www.hurricanes.co.nz
COACH
Mark Hammett
CAPTAIN
Conrad Smith
CEO
James te Puni
CHAIRMAN
Brian Roche

RECORDS

MATCH RECORDS

Biggest win	49	vs. ACT Brumbies (56-7)	Wellington	2009
Heaviest defeat	53	vs. Blues (7-60)	Wellington	2002
Highest score	64	vs. Northern Transvaal (64-32)	New Plymouth	1997
	66	vs Melbourne Rebels (66-24)	Wellington	2012
Most points conceded	60	vs. Blues (7-60)	Wellington	2002
Most tries	9	vs. Highlanders (60-34)	Wellington	1997
	9	vs Melbourne Rebels (66-24)	Wellington	2012
Most tries conceded	8	vs. Blues (7-60)	Wellington	2002
Most points by a player	30	DE Holwell (1t, 2c, 7p) vs. Highlanders	Napier	2001
Most tries by a player	3	JF Umaga vs. Northern Transvaal	New Plymouth	1997
	3	JF Umaga vs. Highlanders	Wellington	1997
	3	CM Cullen vs. Free State	Wellington	1997
	3	JD O'Halloran vs. Blues	Wellington	1998
	3	JF Umaga vs. Queensland Reds	New Plymouth	2000
	3	MA Nonu vs. ACT Brumbies	Wellington	2005
	3	HE Gear vs. Reds	Wellington	2010
	3	AK Hore vs. Chiefs	Wellington	2006
	3	TJ Perenara vs Force	Perth	2012
	3	SJ Savea vs Melbourne Rebels	Wellington	2012
Most conversions by a player	9	BJ Barrett vs Melbourne Rebels	Wellington	2012
Most penalties by a player	7	JB Cameron vs. Blues	Palmerston North	1996
	7	DE Holwell vs. Highlanders	Napier	2001
Most drop goals by a player	1	By three players		

SEASON RECORDS

Most team points	489	from 16 matches	2012
Most points by a player	197	BJ Barrett	2012
Most team tries	58	from 16 matches	2012
Most tries by a player	12	JF Umaga	1997
Most conversions by a player	35	BJ Barrett	2012
Most penalties by a player	40	BJ Barrett	2013
Most drop goals by a player	1	By three players	

CAREER RECORDS

Most appearances	122	JF Umaga	1996-2007
Most points	676	DE Holwell	1998-2006
Most tries	56	CM Cullen	1996-2003
Most conversions	118	DE Holwell	1998-2006
Most penalties	135	DE Holwell	1998-2006
Most drop goals	1	By three players	

Gold Smith...Hurricanes skipper Conrad Smith led from the front. Hagan Hopkins/Getty Images

2013 RESULTS & SCORERS

Date	Venue	Opponent	Result	Score	Referee	Scorers
Febr 23	Wellington	Blues	LOST	20-34	G Jackson	T: J Savea, Penalty try. C: Barrett (2). P: Barrett (2).
Mrch 01	Brisbane	Reds	LOST	12-18	SR Walsh	P: Barrett (4).
Mrch 08	Wellington	Crusaders	WON	29-28	A Lees	T: Leiua, J Savea. C: Barrett (2). P: Barrett (5).
Mrch 15	Dunedin	Highlanders	WON	23-19	F Pastrana	T: Smith, Perenara, Franks. C: Barrett. P: Barrett (2).
Mrch 30	Wellington	Kings	WON	46-30	N Briant	T: Leiua, May, Shields, Smith, Thrush, Perenara. C: Barrett (5). P: Barrett (2).
April 06	Wellington	Waratahs	WON	41-29	J Kaplan	T: J Savea (2), Matu'u, Goodes. C: Barrett (3). P: Barrett (5)
April 13	Auckland	Blues	LOST	6-28	J Peyper	P: Barrett. DG: Pisi.
April 19	Wellington	Force	WON	22-16	N Briant	T: Toomaga-Allen, Shields, Pisi. C: Barrett (2). P: Barrett.
April 26	Palmerston North	Stormers	LOST	16-18	SR Walsh	T: Taylor, Proctor. P: Barrett (2).
May 04	Pretoria	Bulls	LOST	14-48	L vd Merwe	T: Perenara (2). C: Barrett (2).
May 10	Bloemfontein	Cheetahs	WON	39-34	S Berry	T: Barrett, J Savea, Perenara, Vito. C: Barrett (2). P: Barrett (5).
May 17	Wellington	Chiefs	LOST	12-17	L vd Merwe	P: Barrett (4).
May 31	Canberra	Brumbies	LOST	23-30	J Peyper	T: Lee-Lo, Perenara. C: Barrett (2). P: Barrett (3).
June 28	Wellington	Chiefs	LOST	22-34	G Williamson	T: Leiua, Barrett, Perenara. C: Barrett (2). P: Barrett.
July 06	Wellington	Highlanders	LOST	44-49	M Fraser	T: Dixon, Franks, Smylie, Broadhurst, J Savea. C: Barrett (5) P: Barrett (3).
July 13	Christchurch	Crusaders	LOST	17-25	G Jackson	T: Shields, J Savea, Vito. C: Taylor.

Played	Won	Lost	Drawn	Points for	Points against	Tries for	Tries against
16	6	10	0	386	457	41	49

COACHES & MANAGEMENT

HEAD COACH: Mark Hammett **ASSISTANT COACH:** Alama Ieremia **SCRUM COACH:** Dan Cron
CONDITIONING COACHES: David Gray & Paul Downes **DOCTOR:** Dr Theo Dorfling **MANAGER:** Tony Ward
TECHNICAL ADVISOR: Richard Watt **PHYSIOTHERAPISTS:** Cam Shaw & Lee Van Santos
MEDIA OFFICER: Bronwyn Williams **SKILLS COACH:** Clark Laidlaw **MASSEUR:** Paul Minehan

APPEARANCES & POINTS IN SUPER RUGBY

	Date of Birth	Height	Weight	Matches	Tries	Conversions	Penalties	Drop Goals	Points
BJ (Beauden) Barrett	27/05/1991	1,87	92	36	4	64	79	–	385
TES (Tim) Bateman	03/06/1987	1,83	91	62	6	–	–	–	30
JP (James) Broadhurst	01/12/1987	2,03	122	41	2	–	–	–	10
DS (Dane) Coles	12/10/1986	1,84	103	53	5	–	–	–	25
AL (Ash) Dixon	01/09/1988	1,82	102	1	–	–	–	–	5
JJ (Jason) Eaton	21/08/1982	2,02	105	95	10	–	–	–	50
BJ (Ben) Franks	27/03/1984	1,84	118	98	4	–	–	–	20
R (Reg) Goodes	04/04/1992	1,84	112	20	1	–	–	–	5
J (Jack) Lam	18/11/1987	1,88	103	37	2	–	–	–	10
R (Reynold) Lee-Lo	20/02/1986	1,81	96	12	1	–	–	–	5
A (Alapati) Leiua	21/09/1988	1,85	96	35	6	–	–	–	30
FJ (Faifile) Levave	15/01/1986	1,92	110	66	6	–	–	–	30
KW (Karl) Lowe	17/09/1984	1,81	104	41	3	–	–	–	15
JR (James) Marshall	07/12/1988	1,83	90	8	–	–	–	–	0
M (Motu) Matu'u	30/04/1987	1,84	108	22	2	–	–	–	10
B (Ben) May	13/10/1982	1,93	124	64	1	–	–	–	5
O (Opetera) Peleseuma	11/02/1992	1,75	87	1	–	–	–	–	0
TJ (TJ) Perenara	23/01/1993	1,84	94	29	14	–	–	–	70
T (Tusi) Pisi	18/06/1982	1,83	91	18	1	–	–	1	8
M (Matt) Proctor	26/10/1992	1,80	90	4	1	–	–	–	5
MJ (Mark) Reddish	03/03/1985	1,96	112	24	–	–	–	–	0
A (Ardie) Savea	14/10/1993	1,92	103	40	–	–	–	–	0
SJ (Julian) Savea	07/08/1990	1,92	103	40	16	–	–	–	80
JE (John) Schwalger	28/09/1983	1,87	122	78	3	–	–	–	15
BDF (Brad) Shields	02/04/1991	1,93	111	29	3	–	–	–	15
CG (Conrad) Smith	12/10/1981	1,86	95	96	18	–	–	–	90
CB (Chris) Smylie	22/03/1982	1,80	91	58	3	–	–	–	15
AS (Andre) Taylor	11/01/1988	1,78	93	45	13	2	1	–	72
BN (Blade) Thomson	04/12/1990	1,98	106	1	–	–	–	–	0
JI (Jeremy) Thrush	19/04/1985	1,98	115	80	8	–	–	–	40
J (Jeffrey) Toomaga-Allen	19/11/1990	1,92	125	25	2	–	–	–	10
VVJ (Victor) Vito	27/03/1987	1,93	109	60	8	–	–	–	40
Totals				1319	143	66	80	1	1095

FINAL LOG POSITIONS

2013	11th	2009	3rd	2005	4th	2001	9th	1997	3rd
2012	8th	2008	4th	2004	11th	2000	8th	1996	9th
2011	9th	2007	8th	2003	3rd	1999	10th		
2010	8th	2006	2nd	2002	9th	1998	8th		

APPEARANCES & POINTS IN 2013

	Blues	Reds	Crusaders	Highlanders	Kings	Waratahs	Blues	Force	Stormers	Bulls	Cheetahs	Chiefs	Brumbies	Chiefs	Highlanders	Crusaders	Matches	Tries	Conversions	Penalties	Drop Goals	Points
Taylor	15	15	15	15R	15	15	10R	10R	15	15	15	15	15	–	–	10R	14	1	1	–	–	7
Leiua	14	14	14	14	14	14	14	14	14	14	14	14	14	14R	14	–	15	3	–	–	–	15
Smith	13c	13c	13c	13c	13c	13c	13c	13c	13c	13c	–	–	13c	13c	13c	13c	14	2	–	–	–	10
Bateman	12	12	12	12	12	12	12	12	12	13R	12	12	–	–	–	–	12	–	–	–	–	0
Savea, J	11	11	11	11	11	11	11	11	–	11	11	11	11	11	11	11	15	7	–	–	–	35
Barrett	10	10	10	10	10	10	15	15	10	10	10	10	10	10	10	10	16	2	28	40	–	186
Perenara	9	9	9	9	9	9	9	9R	9	9	9	9	9	9	9	9	16	7	–	–	–	35
Shields	8	8	6	6	6	6	6	6	6	6	6R	6R	6	6	6R	6	16	3	–	–	–	15
Lowe	7	7	7	7	7	–	–	7R	7	7	–	–	–	7	7	7	11	–	–	–	–	0
Vito	6	6	8	8	8	–	–	–	8	8	8c	8c	8	8	8	8	13	2	–	–	–	10
Eaton	5	5	5	5	5	5	–	5	5	5	5	–	–	–	–	–	11	–	–	–	–	0
Thrush	4	4	4	4	4	–	–	4	4	4	4	4	4	4	4	4	14	1	–	–	–	5
May	3	–	3R	3	3	3	3	–	1R	3R	3	3	3	3	3	3	14	1	–	–	–	5
Coles	2	2	2	–	2	2R	–	–	–	–	–	2	–	–	–	–	6	–	–	–	–	0
Franks	1	1	1	1	1	–	1	1	1	1	1	1	1	1	1	1	15	2	–	–	–	10
Dixon	x	–	–	2R	–	2R	–	x	2R	2	2	2	x	2	2R	2	9	1	–	–	–	5
Goodes	3R	1R	–	3R	3R	1	–	1R	–	1R	2R	3R	x	3R	1R	17R	12	1	–	–	–	5
Reddish	5R	–	–	–	5R	4	4	5	4R	4R	–	–	5R	4R	20R	–	10	–	–	–	–	0
Levave	8R	8R	6R	7R	8R	8	8	8	6R	8R	6	6	6R	6R	6	7R	16	1	–	–	–	5
Smylie	9R	9R	9R	x	9R	9R	9R	9	9R	9R	x	9R	x	9R	9R	9R	13	1	–	–	–	5
Marshall	x	x	15R	15	–	–	–	–	–	–	15R	15R	15R	15	15	15	8	–	–	–	–	0
Lee-Lo	13R	x	16R	–	12R	12R	12R	12R	–	–	13	13	12	12	12	12	12	1	–	–	–	5
Toomaga-Allen	–	3	3	–	–	3R	3R	3	3	3	3R	3R	–	–	–	–	9	1	–	–	–	5
Broadhurst	–	5R	5R	5R	–	5R	4R	5R	–	–	5R	5R	5	5	5	5	12	1	–	–	–	5
Matu'u	–	2R	2R	2	2R	2	2	2	2	–	–	–	–	–	–	–	8	1	–	–	–	5
Pisi	–	–	–	14R	15R	15R	10	10	12R	12	12R	12R	12R	x	–	–	10	1	–	–	1	8
Savea, A	–	–	–	–	–	7	7	–	7R	–	–	–	–	–	–	–	3	–	–	–	–	0
Lam	–	–	–	–	–	6R	7R	7	–	7R	7	7	7	–	7R	–	8	–	–	–	–	0
Proctor	–	–	–	–	–	–	–	11	–	–	–	–	–	14	14R	14	4	1	–	–	–	5
Schwalger	–	–	–	–	–	–	–	–	–	–	–	–	–	x	3R	3R	2	–	–	–	–	0
Thomson	–	–	–	–	–	–	–	–	–	–	–	–	–	–	–	5R	1	–	–	–	–	0
Peleseuma	–	–	–	–	–	–	–	–	–	–	–	–	–	–	–	12R	1	–	–	–	–	0
Penalty try	–	–	–	–	–	–	–	–	–	–	–	–	–	–	–	–	0	1	–	–	–	5
32 players																	340	41	29	40	1	386

▩ *Yellow Card* ■ *Red Card*

ACT BRUMBIES

HONOURS
CHAMPIONS
2001
2004

GROUND
Canberra Stadium
CAPACITY
27 000
ADDRESS
Battye St, Bruce ACT
TELEPHONE NUMBER
+61 2 6260 8588
COLOURS
Navy blue jersey with gold trim and white sides, navy shorts and socks
WEBSITE
www.brumbies.com.au
COACH
Jake White
CAPTAIN
Ben Mowen
CEO
Andrew Fagan
CHARMAIN
Sean Hammond
PRESIDENT
Geoff Larkham

RECORDS

MATCH RECORDS

Biggest win	64	vs. Bulls (73-9)	Canberra	1999
	64	vs. Cats (64-0)	Canberra	2000
Heaviest defeat	49	vs. Hurricanes (07-56)	Wellington	2009
Highest score	73	vs. Bulls (73-9)	Canberra	1999
Most points conceded	56	vs. Hurricanes (07-56)	Wellington	2009
Most tries	10	vs. Bulls (73-9)	Canberra	1999
	10	vs. Cats (64-16)	Canberra	2002
	10	vs. Cats (68-28)	Canberra	2004
Most tries conceded	8	vs. Hurricanes (07-56)	Wellington	2009
Most points by a player	25	SA Mortlock (1t 4c 4p) vs. Stormers Canberra		2001
	25	JWC Roff (1t 7c 2p) vs. Chiefs Canberra		2003
Most tries by a player	4	JWC Roff vs. Sharks	Manuka	1996
Most conversions by a player	9	JWC Roff vs. Cats	Canberra	2004
Most penalties by a player	6	J Huxley vs. Highlanders	Canberra	2002
Most drop goals by a player	1	on 21 occasions		

SEASON RECORDS

Most team points	487	in 13 matches	2004
Most points by a player	233	CP Lealiifano	2013
Most team tries	67	in 13 matches	2004
Most tries by a player	15	JWC Roff	1997
Most conversions by a player	51	JWC Roff	2004
Most penalties by a player	57	CP Lealiifano	2013
Most drop goals by a player	2	GM Gregan	2001
	2	SJ Larkham	2001 & 2002
	2	CP Lealiifano	2009

CAREER RECORDS

Most appearances	142	GB Smith	2000-2013
Most points	1019	SA Mortlock	1998-2010
Most tries	57	JWC Roff	1996-2004
Most conversions	161	SA Mortlock	1998-2010
Most penalties	144	SA Mortlock	1998-2010
Most drop goals	5	SJ Larkham	

Jake White was instrumental in the Brumbies' turnaround. Duif du Toit/Gallo Images

2013 **RESULTS & SCORERS**

Date	Venue	Opponent	Result	Score	Referee	Scorers
Febr 16	Canberra	REDS	WON	24-06	A Lees	T: Mogg (2). C: Prior. P: Mogg (2), White (2).
Febr 22	Melbourne	REBELS	WON	30-13	J Leckie	T: Mogg, Mowen, Rathbone, Coleman. C: Lealiifano (2). P: Lealiifano (2)
Mrch 09	Canberra	WARATAHS	WON	35-06	J White	T: Mowen, Lealiifano, Speight, Coleman. C: Lealiifano (2), Prior. P: Lealiifano (3).
Mrch 16	Durban	SHARKS	WON	29-10	J Kaplan	T: Speight, Mogg, Tomane, Toomua. C: Lealiifano (3). P: Lealiifano.
Mrch 23	Cape Town	STORMERS	LOST	22-35	G Jackson	T: Speight. C: Lealiifano. P: Lealiifano (5).
Mrch 30	Canberra	BULLS	WON	23-20	J White	T: Coleman. P: Lealiifano (6).
April 05	Canberra	KINGS	DREW	28-28	J Peyper	T: Speight, Tomane. P:Lealiifano (5), White.
April 12	Dunedin	HIGHLANDERS	WON	30-19	C Pollock	T: Speight, G Smith, Tomane. C: Lealiifano (3). P: Lealiifano (2), White.
April 20	Brisbane	REDS	DREW	19-19	G Jackson	T: Lealiifano. C: Lealiifano. P: Lealiifano (4).
April 27	Canberra	FORCE	WON	41-07	A Gardner	T: Speight (2), Mogg, Tomane, Siliva, Kuridrani. C: Lealiifano (4). P: Lealiifano.
May 05	Canberra	CRUSADERS	LOST	23-30	C Joubert	T: Mowen, Toomua. C: Lealiifano, Toomua. P: Lealiifano (3).
May 18	Sydney	WARATAHS	LOST	22-28	SR Walsh	T: Mowen, Kuridrani. P: Mogg (3), Lealiifano.
May 25	Auckland	BLUES	WON	20-13	L vd Merwe	T: White. P: Lealiifano (5).
May 31	Canberra	HURRICANES	WON	30-23	J Peyper	T: White, Kimlin. C: Lealiifano. P: Laeliifano (6).
Jun 07	Canberra	REBELS	WON	39-17	R Hoffman	T: Rathbone (2),
July 13	Perth	FORCE	LOST	15-21	R Hoffman	T: Fardy, Kuridrani. C: Lealiifano. P: Lealiifano.
Play-off						
July 21	Canberra	CHEETAHS	WON	15-13	G Jackson	P: Lealiifano (4), White.
Semi-final						
July 27	Pretoria	BULLS	WON	26-23	C Joubert	T: Mogg, Kuridrani. C: Lealiifano (2), P: Lealiifano (4).
Final						
Aug 03	Hamilton	CHIEFS	LOST	22-27	C Joubert	T: Lealiifano. C: Lealiifano. P: Lealiifano (5).

Played	Won	Lost	Drawn	Points for	Points against	Tries for	Tries against
19	**12**	**5**	**2**	**493**	**358**	**46**	**36**

COACHES & MANAGEMENT

COACH: Jake White **BACKS COACH:** Stephen Larkham **FORWARDS COACH:** Laurie Fisher
GENERAL MANAGER: George De Crespigny **PERFORMANCE ANALYST:** Warrick Harrington
DOCTOR: Dr Angus Bathgate **PHYSIOTHERAPIST:** Byron Field & Hamish Macauley
ASSISTANT MANAGER: Garry Quinlivan **CAREER AND EDUCATION ADVISER:** Sue Crawford
ADMINISTRATIVE DIRECTOR: Nick Leah **MEDIA OFFICER:** Elliott Woods
ATHLETIC PERFORMANCE DIRECTOR: Dean Benton
ATHLETIC PERFORMANCE COACH: Aled Walters

APPEARANCES & POINTS IN SUPER RUGBY

	Date of Birth	Height	Weight	Matches	Tries	Conversions	Penalties	Drop Goals	Points
BE (Ben) Alexander	14/11/1988	1,88	116	81	16	–	–	–	80
FM (Fotu) Auelua	29/01/1984	1,89	115	25	1	–	–	–	5
S (Sam) Carter	10/09/1989	2,00	110	34	2	–	–	–	10
RJ (Robbie) Coleman	03/08/1990	1,79	83	37	7	–	–	–	35
CG (Colby) Faingaa	31/03/1991	1,82	95	35	1	–	–	–	5
SM (Scott) Fardy	05/07/1984	1,98	113	30	3	–	–	–	15
ZA (Zack) Holmes	30/05/1990	1,75	87	10	3	8	16	–	79
PJ (Peter) Kimlin	11/07/1985	1,98	114	79	6	–	–	–	30
RTRN (Tevita) Kuridrani	31/03/1991	1,96	102	26	4	–	–	–	20
CP (Christian) Lealiifano	25/09/1991	1,80	89	70	12	39	83	2	396
JW (John) Mann-Rea	19/02/1981	1,81	105	2	–	–	–	–	0
P (Pat) McCabe	21/03/1988	1,85	90	49	6	–	–	–	30
JD (Jesse) Mogg	08/06/1989	1,87	90	32	10	1	11	–	85
ST (Stephen) Moore	20/01/1983	1,90	112	118	8	–	–	–	40
BSC (Ben) Mowen	12/01/1984	1,95	106	75	8	–	–	–	40
RA (Ruaidhri) Murphy	05/07/1987	1,87	119	19	1	–	–	–	5
DP (Dan) Palmer	13/09/1988	1,80	115	45	–	–	–	–	0
DW (David) Pocock	23/04/1988	1,83	101	72	7	–	–	–	35
LW (Leon) Power	27/02/1986	2,00	116	10	–	–	–	–	0
IG (Ian) Prior	21/08/1990	1,79	83	31	1	5	–	–	15
E (Etienne) Oosthuizen	22/12/1992	1,98	120	6	–	–	–	–	0
C (Clyde) Rathbone	23/07/1981	1,80	97	63	18	–	–	–	90
S (Siliva) Siliva	11/12/1991	1,78	113	11	1	–	–	–	5
ST (Scott) Sio	16/10/1991	1,87	116	22	1	–	–	–	5
J (Jordan) Smiler	19/06/1985	1,91	102	4	–	–	–	–	0
A (Andrew) Smith	10/01/1985	1,93	105	38	6	–	–	–	30
GB (George) Smith	15/07/1984	1,80	101	142	18	–	–	–	90
R-H (Ruan) Smith	24/01/1990	1,87	125	9	–	–	–	–	0
HV (Henry) Speight	24/03/1988	1,86	97	46	19	–	–	–	95
M (Mark) Swanepoel	26/10/1990	1,81	92	6	–	–	–	–	0
JM (Joe) Tomane	02/02/1990	1,90	102	31	8	–	–	–	40
MP (Matt) Toomua	03/01/1994	1,83	88	47	5	2	–	1	32
NW (Nic) White	13/06/1990	1,76	84	34	3	–	8	–	39
Totals				**1339**	**172**	**55**	**110**	**3**	**1351**

VODACOM SUPER RUGBY

FINAL LOG POSITIONS

2013	3rd	2009	7th	2005	5th	2001	1st	1997	2nd
2012	7th	2008	9th	2004	1st	2000	1st	1996	5th
2011	13th	2007	5th	2003	4th	1999	5th		
2010	6th	2006	6th	2002	3rd	1998	10th		

APPEARANCES & POINTS IN 2013

BRUMBIES

	Reds	Rebels	Waratahs	Sharks	Stormers	Bulls	Kings	Highlanders	Reds	Force	Crusaders	Waratahs	Blues	Hurricanes	Rebels	Force	Cheetahs	Bulls	Chiefs	Matches	Tries	Conversions	Penalties	Drop Goals	Points
Mogg	15	15	15	15	–	–	–	15	15	15	15	15	15	15	15	15	15	15	15	16	6	–	6	–	48
Speight	14	–	14	14	14	14	14	14	14	14	14	14	14	14	14	14	14	14	14	18	8	–	–	–	40
Smith, A	13	13	13	–	–	x	12R	13	–	–	–	–	–	–	12R	x	x	13R		7	–	–	–	–	0
Lealiifano	12	12	12	12	12	12	10	12	12	12	12	12	12	12	–	12	12	12	12	18	3	22	57	–	233
Rathbone	11	11	11	14R	11R	x	–	–	11R	–	–	–	14R	x	11	–	11	11	11	11	3	–	–	–	15
Toomua	10	10	10	10	10	10	–	10	10	10	10	10	10	10	10	10	10	10	10	18	2	1	–	–	12
White	9	9	9	9	–	9	9	9	9	9	9	9	9	9	9c	–	9	9	9	17	2	–	5	–	25
Mowen	8c	8c	8c	6c	6c	8c	6c	8c	8c	8c	8c	8c	8c	8c	–	8c	8c	8c	8c	18	4	–	–	–	20
Pocock	7	7	7	–	–	–	–	–	–	–	–	–	–	–	–	–	–	–	–	3	–	–	–	–	0
Kimlin	6	6	6	4	4	6	4	4	4	4	4	6	6	6	8	6	6	6	6	19	1	–	–	–	5
Carter	5	5	5	5	5	–	5R	5	5	5	5	5	5	5	5	5	5	5	5	18	–	–	–	–	0
Fardy	4	4	4	8R	5R	4	–	–	–	–	4	4	4	4	6	4	4	4	4	14	1	–	–	–	5
Palmer	3	3	3	–	3	3	3	3	3	–	3	–	–	–	3	–	–	–	–	10	–	–	–	–	0
Moore	2	2	2	2	2	2	2R	2	2	2	2	2	2	2	–	2	2	2	2	18	–	–	–	–	0
Alexander	1	1	1	3	3R	3R	1	1	1	3	1	3	3	3	–	3	3	3	3	18	–	–	–	–	0
Siliva	2R	2R	2R	2R	2R	x	2	x	x	2R	2R	2R	x	x	2	2R	x	x	x	11	1	–	–	–	5
Murphy	3R	–	–	1R	–	–	–	–	1R	–	–	–	–	–	–	–	–	–	–	3	–	–	–	–	0
Auelua	5R	5R	5R	8	8	5R	8	6R	6	6	6	4R	5R	5R	–	6R	5R	5R	5R	18	–	–	–	–	0
Faingaa	7R	7R	–	4R	8R	4R	8R	7R	6R	7R	6R	7R	7	7	7	7R	x	x		16	1	–	–	–	5
Prior	9R	9R	9R	9R	9	x	x	9R	9R	9R	9R	9R	x	x	9R	9	x	x	9R	13	–	5	–	–	10
Coleman	11R	11R	11R	15R	15	15	15	–	–	15R	15R	22R	x	x	11R	14R	–	–	–	12	3	–	–	–	15
Tomane	14R	14	13R	11	11	11	11	11	11	11	11	11	11	11	–	11	11R	11R	11R	18	4	–	–	–	20
Sio	–	3R	3R	1	1	1	3R	3R	3R	1	3R	1	1	1	1	1	1	1	1	18	1	–	–	–	5
Kuridrani	–	14R	–	13	13	13	13R	13	13	13	13	13	13	13	13	13	13	13	13	17	4	–	–	–	20
Smith, G	–	–	7R	7	7	7	7	7	7	7	7	–	–	7R	7	7	7			14	1	–	–	–	5
Holmes	–	–	–	15R	–	x	–	–	–	–	–	10R	–	–	–	–	–	–	–	2	1	–	–	–	5
Swanepoel	–	–	–	–	9R	–	–	–	–	–	–	–	–	–	9R	–	–	–	–	2	–	–	–	–	0
Oosthuizen	–	–	–	–	–	5	5	–	–	–	–	–	5R	–	–	–	–	–	–	3	–	–	–	–	0
McCabe	–	–	–	–	–	–	12	15R	10R	13R	13R	12R	–	–	12	–	–	–	–	7	–	–	–	–	0
Smiler	–	–	–	–	–	–	–	6	7R	–	–	–	–	x	18R	4R	–	–	–	4	–	–	–	–	0
Power	–	–	–	–	–	–	–	–	6R	5R	–	–	–	–	4	–	–	–	–	3	–	–	–	–	0
Smith, R	–	–	–	–	–	–	–	–	–	–	–	3R	1R	1R	3R	3R	3R	3R	3R	8	–	–	–	–	0
Mann-Rea	–	–	–	–	–	–	–	–	–	–	–	–	–	–	2R	–	–	–	–	1	–	–	–	–	0

33 players 393 46 28 68 0 493

▨ *Yellow Card* ■ *Red Card*

MELBOURNE REBELS

GROUND
AAMI Park, Melbourne
CAPACITY
30 000
ADDRESS
Visy Park Gate, Level 2, Royal Parade, Carlton North
TELEPHONE NUMBER
+ 61 3 9221 0700
COLOURS
Dark blue jersey with white and red trim. Dark blue shorts with white trim. Dark blue socks with white band.
WEBSITE
www.melbournerebels.com.au
COACH
Damien Hill
CAPTAIN
Gareth Delve
CEO
Steven Boland
CHARMAIN
Harold Mitchell AC
PRESIDENT
Gary Grey

RECORDS

MATCH RECORDS

Biggest win	17	vs Hurricanes (42-25)	Melbourne 2011
Heaviest defeat	57	vs Sharks (7-64)	Durban 2013
Highest score	42	vs Hurricanes (42-25)	Melbourne 2011
Most points conceded	66	vs Hurricanes (24-66)	Wellington 2012
Most tries	6	vs Hurricanes (42-25)	Melbourne 2011
Most tries conceded	10	vs Sharks (7-64)	Durban 2013
Most points by a player	24	JD O'Connor vs Blues	Melbourne 2012
Most tries by a player	2	AM Campbell vs Hurricanes	Melbourne 2011
		KC Vuna vs Bulls	Melbourne 2012
		NJ Phipps vs Crusaders	Melbourne 2012
		C Neville vs Western Force	Perth 2012
		KC Vuna vs Hurricanes	Wellington 2012
		HW Pyle vs Lions	Johannesburg 2012
		J Woodward vs Force	Perth 2013
		HW Pyle vs Chiefs	Melbourne 2013
		M Inman vs Blues	Auckland 2013
		T English vs Waratahs	Melbourne 2013
		B Hegarty vs Highlanders	Melbourne 2013
		KC Vuna vs Highlanders	Melbourne 2013
		T English vs Highlanders	Melbourne 2013
Most conversions by a player	5	KJ Beale vs Bulls	Melbourne 2012
Most penalties by a player	6	DJ Cipriani vs Brumbies	Melbourne 2011
Most drop goals by a player	0		

SEASON RECORDS

Most team points	382	from 16 matches	2013
Most points by a player	116	JD O'Connor	2013
Most team tries	44	from 16 matches	2013
Most tries by a player	7	KC Vuna	2012
Most conversions by a player	21	JD O'Connor	2013
Most penalties by a player	25	DJ Cipriani	2011
Most drop goals by a player	0		

CAREER RECORDS

Most appearances	47	NJ Phipps	2011-2013
Most points	201	JD O'Connor	2012-2013
Most tries	13	KC Vuna	2011-2013
Most conversions	27	JD O'Connor	2012-2013
Most penalties	44	JD O'Connor	2012-2013

Threat...the multi-talented James O'Connor scored 116 points during the season.
Bradley Kanaris/Getty Images

2013 RESULTS & SCORERS

Date	Venue	Opponent	Result	Score	Referee	Scorers
Febr 15	Melbourne	FORCE	WON	30-23	A Gardner	T: Robinson, Pyle, Kingi. C: O"Connor (3). P: O'Connor (3).
Febr 22	Melbourne	BRUMBIES	LOST	13-30	J Leckie	T: Higginbotham. C: O'Connor. P: O'Connor (2).
Mrch 01	Sydney	WARATAHS	LOST	26-31	R Hoffman	T: Robinson, Beale. C: O'Connor (2). P: O'Connor (4).
Mrch 08	Melbourne	REDS	LOST	13-23	F Pastrana	T: Mitchell. C: O'Connor. P: O'Connor (2).
Mrch 23	Durban	SHARKS	LOST	07-64	L vd Merwe	T: Higginbotham. C: O'Connor.
Mrch 30	Bloemfontein	CHEETAHS	LOST	16-34	G Jackson	T: Neville. C: O'Connor. P: O'Connor (3).
April 06	Perth	FORCE	WON	30-23	M Fraser	T: Woodward (2), Kingi, Pyle. C: O'Connor (2). P: O'Connor (2).
April 13	Melbourne	KINGS	LOST	27-30	A Lees	T: Roberts, Robinson, Inman. C: O'Connor (3). P: O'Connor (2).
April 28	Christchurch	CRUSADERS	LOST	26-30	N Briant	T: Robinson, O'Connor, Higginbotham. C: O'Connor. P: O'Connor (3).
May 03	Melbourne	CHIEFS	LOST	33-39	G Williamson	T: Pyle (2), Beale, Phipps, Higginbotham. C: O'Connor (4).
May 11	Auckland	BLUES	LOST	32-36	G Williamson	T: Inman (2), Woodward, Mitchell, Higginbotham. C: Woodward (2). P: Woodward.
May 17	Melbourne	STORMERS	WON	30-21	M Fraser	T: Pyle, Higginbotham, Penalty try. C: Woodward (3). P: Woodward (2).
May 25	Melbourne	WARATAHS	WON	24-22	G Williamson	T: English (2). C: Woodward. P: Woodward (4).
Jun 01	Brisbane	REDS	LOST	20-33	J Leckie	T: Sidey, Fuglistaller. C: O'Connor (2). P: O'Connor (2).
Jun 07	Canberra	BRUMBIES	LOST	17-39	R Hoffman	T: Alo-Emile, English. C: Woodward (2). P: Woodward.
July 12	Melbourne	HIGHLANDERS	WON	38-37	A Lees	T: Hegarty (2), Vuna (2), English (2). C: Woodward (4).

Played	Won	Lost	Drawn	Points for	Points against	Tries for	Tries against
16	5	11	0	382	515	44	65

VODACOM SUPER RUGBY

COACHES & MANAGEMENT

HEAD COACH: Damien Hill **ASSISTANT COACHES:** John Muggletone, Nathan Grey & Matt Cockbain
HEAD CONDITIONING COACH: Zane Leonard **CONDITIONING COACH:** Mark Andrews
VIDEO ANALYST: Damon Edmonds **DOCTOR:** Dr Tracy Peters **PHYSIO:** David Rundle
ASST PHYSIO: Paul Percy **MEDIA OFFICER:** Adam Freier **MANAGER:** Scott Harrison
SCRUM COACH: Matt Tink **ASST TEAM MANAGER:** Hannah Catchpole

APPEARANCES & POINTS IN SUPER RUGBY

	Date of Birth	Height	Weight	Matches	Tries	Conversions	Penalties	Drop Goals	Points
P (Paul) Alo-Emile	22/12/1991	1,80	120	18	1	–	–	–	5
KJ (Kurtley) Beale	06/01/1989	1,85	88	82	16	74	60	–	417
L (Luke) Burgess	20/08/1983	1,80	83	59	4	–	–	–	20
TF (Tim) Davidson	03/11/1982	1,94	105	40	1	–	–	–	5
GL (Gareth) Delve	30/12/1982	1,91	115	43	4	–	–	–	20
T (Tom) English	08/03/1991	1,88	96	10	5	–	–	–	25
S (Scott) Fuglistaller	16/04/1987	1,83	88	16	1	–	–	–	5
B (Bryce) Hegarty	28/08/1992	1,85	90	5	2	–	–	–	10
NJ (Nic) Henderson	01/05/1981	1,85	117	119	–	–	–	–	0
S (Scott) Higginbotham	05/09/1986	1,95	102	79	23	–	–	–	115
JK (James) Hilgendorf	29/03/1982	1,82	93	32	4	–	–	–	20
S (Shota) Horie	21/01/1986	1,80	104	6	–	–	–	–	0
M (Mitch) Inman	24/10/1988	1,91	102	46	3	–	–	–	15
LM (Luke) Jones	02/04/1991	2,01	108	31	–	–	–	–	0
J (James) King	16/03/1987	2,01	111	1	–	–	–	–	0
RTI (Richard) Kingi	17/03/1989	1,76	80	36	3	4	–	–	23
P (Pat) Leafa	16/03/1989	1,80	108	1	–	–	–	–	0
LV (Lachlan) Mitchell	30/09/1977	1,82	94	45	6	–	–	–	30
C (Cadeyrn) Neville	09/11/1988	2,02	120	24	3	–	–	–	15
JD (James) O'Connor	05/07/1990	1,80	79	59	13	50	114	–	507
NJ (Nick) Phipps	09/01/1989	1,80	87	47	6	–	–	–	30
HW (Hugh) Pyle	21/09/1988	2,01	118	43	9	–	–	–	45
J (Jordy) Reid	03/10/1991	1,85	107	9	–	–	–	–	0
A (Angus) Roberts	17/12/1990	1,85	92	7	1	–	–	–	5
GP (Ged) Robinson	02/06/1983	1,80	104	51	7	–	–	–	35
A (Alex) Rokobaro	06/10/1989	1,75	81	2	–	–	–	–	0
JA (Jarrod) Saffy	24/10/1984	1,91	106	35	2	–	–	–	10
RJ (Rory) Sidey	04/07/1986	1,88	100	46	6	–	–	–	30
K (Kimani) Sitauti	12/04/1991	1,83	95	4	–	–	–	–	0
N (Nick) Stirzaker	08/03/1991	1,79	80	15	–	–	–	–	0
KC (Cooper) Vuna	05/07/1987	1,82	101	36	13	–	–	–	65
LS (Laurie) Weeks	05/04/1986	1,81	114	61	1	–	–	–	5
J (Jason) Woodward	17/05/1990	1,88	82	12	3	12	9	–	66
Totals				1120	137	128	174	0	1523

VODACOM SUPER RUGBY

FINAL LOG POSITIONS

2013 12th   **2012** 13th   **2011** 15th

APPEARANCES & POINTS IN 2013

	Force	Brumbies	Waratahs	Reds	Sharks	Cheetahs	Force	Kings	Crusaders	Chiefs	Blues	Stormers	Waratahs	Reds	Brumbies	Highlanders	Matches	Tries	Conversions	Penalties	Drop Goals	Points
O'Connor	15	15	15	10c	15	15	15	10	10	10	10	–	–	10	–	15R	13	1	21	23	–	116
Kingi	14	14	14	14	13R	14	14	15	–	–	–	–	–	–	–	–	8	2	–	–	–	10
Inman	13	13	13	13	12	13	13	13	13	13	13	13	13	13	–	–	15	3	–	–	–	15
Sidey	12	12	12	11R	11R	12R	12	12	12	12	–	12	12	12	12	12	15	1	–	–	–	5
Mitchell	11	11	11	12	14	12	–	13	14R	10R	12	11	11	11	11	–	14	2	–	–	–	10
Beale	10	10	10	–	–	–	–	–	15R	–	–	–	–	–	–	–	4	2	–	–	–	10
Phipps	9	9	9	9	9	9	9	9	9	9	9	9R	9	9	–	9	15	1	–	–	–	5
Delve	8c	8c	–	–	6c	6c	–	–	6R	7R	6R	6R	6R	8R	8c	8c	12	–	–	–	–	0
Fuglistaller	7	7	7	7	7	7R	7	7	7	7	7	7	7	7	7	7	16	1	–	–	–	5
Higginbotham	6	6	8	8	8	8	8c	8c	8c	8c	8c	8c	8c	–	–	–	14	6	–	–	–	30
Jones	5	5	6	6	5	5	6	5R	5R	5R	5R	5	5	5	6R	–	16	–	–	–	–	0
Pyle	4	4	4	4	4	4	4	4	4	4	4	4	–	4	–	–	15	5	–	–	–	25
Weeks	3	3	3	3	3	3R	3R	3R	3	3	3	3	3	3	–	–	16	–	–	–	–	0
Robinson	2	2	2	2	2	2	2	2	2	2R	2	2	2	2	–	–	16	4	–	–	–	20
Henderson	1	1	1	1	1	1	1	1	1	1	1	1	1	1	–	–	16	–	–	–	–	0
Horie	x	2R	2R	x	6R	2R	x	x	x	x	2	x	x	2R	–	x	6	–	–	–	–	0
Alo-Emile	1R	3R	7R	3R	3R	3	3	3	3R	3R	3R	3R	3R	3R	–	3R	16	1	–	–	–	5
Neville	4R	8R	5	5	4R	6R	5	5	5	5	5	5R	4R	4	–	5	16	1	–	–	–	5
Saffy	7R	7R	7R	7R	–	x	7R	5R	6	6	6	6	6	–	–	6	13	–	–	–	–	0
Stirzaker	x	9R	x	9R	9R	9R	9R	9R	9R	x	9R	9	9R	x	–	9	11	–	–	–	–	0
Rokobaro	x	15R	–	11	–	–	–	–	–	–	–	–	–	–	–	–	2	–	–	–	–	0
English	x	10R	x	21R	–	–	x	–	14	14	14	14	14	14	–	13	10	5	–	–	–	25
Reid	–	–	5R	5R	7R	7	5R	7R	–	–	–	7R	–	–	6	7R	9	–	–	–	–	0
Roberts	–	–	x	15	10	10	10	15R	x	–	10R	–	–	–	x	15	7	1	–	–	–	5
Woodward	–	–	–	–	13	11	11	14	14	15	15	15	15	15	–	14	12	3	12	9	–	66
Vuna	–	–	–	–	11	–	10R	11	11	11	11	–	–	–	–	11	7	2	–	–	–	10
Hegarty	–	–	–	–	–	–	–	–	–	21R	10	10	15R	–	–	10	5	2	–	–	–	10
Sitauti	–	–	–	–	–	–	–	–	–	–	–	13R	11R	11R	11R	x	4	–	–	–	–	0
Hilgendorf	–	–	–	–	–	–	–	–	–	–	–	–	x	–	10	–	1	–	–	–	–	0
Davidson	–	–	–	–	–	–	–	–	–	–	–	–	–	–	8R	–	1	–	–	–	–	0
Leafa	–	–	–	–	–	–	–	–	–	–	–	–	–	–	2R	–	1	–	–	–	–	0
Burgess	–	–	–	–	–	–	–	–	–	–	–	–	–	–	9R	–	1	–	–	–	–	0
King	–	–	–	–	–	–	–	–	–	–	–	–	–	–	5R	–	1	–	–	–	–	0
Penalty try	–	–	–	–	–	–	–	–	–	–	–	–	–	–	–	–	–	1	–	–	–	5

33 players 328 44 33 32 0 382

▨ *Yellow Card*   ■ *Red Card*

NSW WARATAHS

GROUND
Sydney Football Stadium

CAPACITY
44 000

ADDRESS
Driver Avenue, Moore Park

TELEPHONE NUMBER
+ 61 2 8354 3300

COLOURS
Sky blue jersey with navy collar, navy shorts and sky blue socks

WEBSITE
www.waratahs.com.au

COACH
Michael Cheika

CAPTAIN
Dave Dennis

CEO
Jason Allen

CHARMAIN
Roger Davis

RECORDS

MATCH RECORDS

Biggest win	62	vs. Kings (72-10)	Port Elizabeth	2013
	61	vs. Lions (73-12)	Sydney	2010
Heaviest defeat	77	vs. Crusaders (19-96)	Christchurch	2002
Highest score	53	vs. Bulls (53-7)	Sydney	2001
	73	vs. Lions (73-12)	Sydney	2010
Most points conceded	96	vs. Crusaders (19-96)	Christchurch	2002
Most tries	11	vs. Lions (73-12)	Sydney	2010
	11	vs. Kings (72-10)	Port Elizabeth	2013
Most tries conceded	14	vs. Crusaders (19-96)	Christchurch	2002
Most points by a player	34	PG Hewat (3t 2c 5p) vs. Bulls Sydney		2005
	4	DA Mitchell vs. Lions	Sydney	2010
Most tries by a player	3	A Murdoch vs. Hurricanes	Sydney	1996
	3	MC Burke vs. Northern Transvaal Sydney		1997
	3	S Taupeaafe vs. Sharks	Sydney	1998
	3	SNG Staniforth vs. Chiefs	Rotorua	2002
	3	PG Hewat vs. Bulls	Sydney	2005
	3	JC Crawford vs. Kings	Port Elizabeth	2013
Most conversions by a player	9	BS Barnes	Sydney	2010
Most penalties by a player	7	MC Burke vs. Blues	Sydney	2001
Most drop goals by a player	1	on eleven occasions		

SEASON RECORDS

Most team points	411	from 17 matches	2011
Most points by a player	191	PG Hewat	2006
Most team tries	50	from 17 matches	2011
Most tries by a player	10	PG Hewat	2005
Most conversions by a player	31	MC Burke	2002
Most penalties by a player	36	PG Hewat	2000
Most drop goals by a player	3	BS Barnes	2010

CAREER RECORDS

Most appearances	132	PR Waugh	2000-2011
Most points	959	MC Burke	1996-2004
Most tries	29	LD Tuqiri	2003-2009
Most conversions	160	MC Burke	1996-2004
Most penalties	173	MC Burke	1996-2004
Most drop goals	3	KJ Beale	2007-2010

Israel Folau in full flight. His form was rewarded with selection to the Wallabies. Richard Huggard/Gallo Images

2013 RESULTS & SCORERS

Date	Venue	Opponent	Result	Score	Referee	Scorers
Febr 23	Brisbane	REDS	LOST	17-25	C Pollock	T: Folau, Volovola. C: Foley (2). P: McKibbin.
Mrch 01	Sydney	REBELS	WON	31-26	R Hoffman	T: Foley, Hooper, Ryan. C: McKibbin (2). P: McKibbin (4).
Mrch 09	Canberra	BRUMBIES	LOST	06-35	J White	P: Mckibbin (2).
Mrch 15	Sydney	CHEETAHS	LOST	26-27	G Williamson	T: Ashley-Cooper, Betham. C: McKibbin (2). P: McKibbin (4).
Mrch 24	Sydney	BLUES	WON	30-27	F Pastrana	T: Mitchell, Folau, Foley. C: Foley (2), McKibbin. P: Foley (2), McKibbin.
Mrch 31	Sydney	FORCE	WON	23-19	SR Walsh	T: Ashley-Cooper. P: McKibbin (6).
April 06	Wellington	HURRICANES	LOST	29-41	J Kaplan	T: Ashley-Cooper, Foley, Folau. C: McKibbin. P: McKibbin (4).
April 19	Sydney	CHIEFS	WON	25-20	C Joubert	T: Crawford, Folau, Ulugia. C: McKibbin (2). P: McKibbin (2)
April 27	Pretoria	BULLS	LOST	19-30	F Pastrana	T: Foley, Folau, Ryan. C: McKibbin (2).
May 04	Port Elizabeth	KINGS	WON	72-10	J Kaplan	T: Crawford (3), Betham (2), Dennis, Folau, Douglas, Hooper, Kingston, Volavola. C: McKibbin (5), Lucas (2). P: McKibbin.
May 11	Sydney	STORMERS	WON	21-15	C Pollock	T: Crawford, Folau. C: Barnes. P: McKibbin (2), Barnes.
May 18	Sydney	BRUMBIES	WON	28-22	SR Walsh	T: Barnes, Hooper, Betham. C: Barnes (2). P: McKibbin (2), Barnes.
May 25	Melbourne	REBELS	LOST	22-24	G Williamson	T: Folau. C: Barnes. P: Barnes (4), McKibbin.
May 31	Christchurch	CRUSADERS	LOST	22-23	G Jackson	T: Foley, Crawford, Betham. C: McKibbin (2). P: McKibbin.
Jun 09	Perth	FORCE	WON	28-13	A Gardner	T: Crawford, Atkins, Kingston. C: McKibbin (2). P: McKibbin (2), Foley.
Jul 13	Sydney	Reds	LOST	12-14	SR Walsh	T: Crawford, Barnes. C: McKibbin.

Played	Won	Lost	Drawn	Points for	Points against	Tries for	Tries against
16	8	8	0	411	371	45	34

www.waratahs.com.au

COACHES & MANAGEMENT

HEAD COACH: Michael Cheika **ASSISTANT COACHES:** Allan Gaffney & Daryl Gibson
COACHING CO-ORDINATOR: Greg Mumm **SPEED COACH:** Matt Shirvington **KICKING COACH:** Matt Burke
HIGH PERFORMANCE ANALYST: Anthony Wakeling **DOCTOR:** Dr Sharron Flahive
MATCH DAY DOCTOR: Dr Luke Inman **PHYSIOTHERAPISTS:** Kieran Cleary & Alex Hill
STRENGTH & CONDITIONING: Tom Tombleson **MANAGER:** Chris Webb

APPEARANCES & POINTS IN SUPER RUGBY

WARATAHS

	Date of Birth	Height	Weight	Matches	Tries	Conversions	Penalties	Drop Goals	Points
HRHL (Richard) Aho	24/04/1987	1,91	120	1	–	–	–	–	0
AP (Adam) Ashley-Cooper	28/03/1984	1,83	96	108	18	–	–	1	93
OH (Ollie) Atkins	12/8/1988	2,01	117	2	1	–	–	–	5
BS (Berrick) Barnes	28/05/1986	1,83	87	88	10	48	42	9	299
PJJ (Peter) Betham	06/01/1989	1,91	98	22	6	–	–	–	30
TJO (Tom) Carter	25/02/1983	1,88	101	76	15	–	–	–	75
MJ (Mitchell) Chapman	15/03/1983	1,97	110	82	4	–	–	–	20
AP (Adam) Coleman	07/10/1991	2,04	122	1	–	–	–	–	0
JC (Cam) Crawford	14/11/1988	1,93	98	7	8	–	–	–	40
DA (Dave) Dennis	01/10/1986	1,92	104	62	7	–	–	–	35
KP (Kane) Douglas	01/06/1989	2,01	115	58	1	–	–	–	5
I (Israel) Folau	03/04/1989	1,93	103	14	8	–	–	–	40
BT (Bernard) Foley	08/09/1989	1,80	85	30	8	4	4	–	60
AJ (AJ) Gilbert	19/06/1987	1,83	105	3	–	–	–	–	0
TR (Terrence) Hepetema	03/01/1992	1,83	96	1	–	–	–	–	0
JG (Jed) Holloway	02/11/1992	1,96	108	4	–	–	–	–	0
LR (Luke) Holmes	14/04/1983	1,84	108	34	1	–	–	–	5
MK (Michael) Hooper	29/10/1991	1,82	97	46	8	–	–	–	40
RG (Rob) Horne	15/08/1989	1,85	83	59	11	–	–	–	55
SM (Sekope) Kepu	05/02/1986	1,88	115	61	1	–	–	–	5
TJ (Tom) Kingston	19/09/1991	1,91	90	29	7	–	–	–	35
MJ (Mat) Lucas	29/01/1992	1,75	78	12	–	2	–	–	4
PJ (Pat) McCutcheon	24/06/1987	1,87	100	24	1	–	–	–	5
B (Brendan) McKibbin	19/09/1985	1,75	86	46	1	41	52	–	243
DA (Drew) Mitchell	26/03/1984	1,83	90	112	35	–	–	–	175
WL (Wycliff) Palu	27/07/1982	1,93	118	90	12	–	–	–	60
GH (Greg) Peterson	26/03/1991	2,03	123	1	–	–	–	–	0
SUT (Tatafu) Polota-Nau	26/07/1985	1,80	110	102	12	–	–	–	60
BA (Benn) Robinson	19/07/1984	1,83	109	109	6	–	–	–	30
PJ (Paddy) Ryan	09/08/1986	1,91	120	28	2	–	–	–	10
WRJ (Will) Skelton	05/03/1992	2,03	135	6	–	–	–	–	0
JD (Jeremy) Tilse	06/02/1986	1,94	117	21	–	–	–	–	0
L (Lopeti) Timani	28/09/1990	1,93	117	19	–	–	–	–	0
S (Sitaleki) Timane	19/09/1986	2,02	119	53	5	–	–	–	25
LD (Lachlan) Turner	11/05/1987	1,88	88	71	25	–	–	–	125
JJ (John) Ulugia	17/01/1986	1,78	119	52	2	–	–	–	10
BTT (Ben) Volavola	13/01/1991	1,88	88	8	2	–	–	–	10
LJ (Liam) Winton	06/03/1986	1,95	111	1	–	–	–	–	0
Totals				**1543**	**217**	**95**	**98**	**10**	**1599**

VODACOM SUPER RUGBY

FINAL LOG POSITIONS

2013	9th	2009	5th	2005	2nd	2001	8th	1997	9th
2012	11th	2008	2nd	2004	8th	2000	9th	1996	7th
2011	5th	2007	13th	2003	5th	1999	8th		
2010	3rd	2006	3rd	2002	2nd	1998	6th		

APPEARANCES & POINTS IN 2013

WARATAHS

	Reds	Rebels	Brumbies	Cheetahs	Blues	Force	Hurricanes	Chiefs	Bulls	Kings	Stormers	Brumbies	Rebels	Crusaders	Force	Reds	Matches	Tries	Conversions	Penalties	Drop Goals	Points
Folau	15	15	14	15	15	15	15	15	15	15	15	15	15	15	–	–	14	8	–	–	–	40
Kingston	14	14	–	–	14R	14R	14R	–	11	13R	–	x	11R	–	13	13	10	2	–	–	–	10
Ashley-Cooper	13	13	13	13	13	13	13	13	13	13	13	13	13	13	–	–	14	3	–	–	–	15
Carter	12	12	12	–	–	–	–	–	–	–	–	–	–	–	12c	–	4	–	–	–	–	0
Mitchell	11	11	11	–	11	11	11	11	–	11R	11	11	14R	15	–	–	12	1	–	–	–	5
Foley	10	10	10	10	10	10	10	10	10	10	10	10	10	10	10	10	16	5	4	3	–	42
Mckibbin	9	9	9	9	9	9	9	9	9	9	9	9	9R	9	9	9	16	–	20	33	–	139
Palu	8	8	–	–	–	–	8R	8	8	8	8	8	–	–	–	–	9	–	–	–	–	0
Hooper	7	7	7	7	7	7	7	7	7	7	7	7	7	–	–	7	15	3	–	–	–	15
Dennis	6c	6c	8c	6c	6c	6c	6c	6c	6c	6c	6c	6c	8c	–	8c	–	15	1	–	–	–	5
Douglas	5	5	5	5	5	5	5	5	5	5	5	5	5	–	5	–	15	1	–	–	–	5
Timani, S	4	–	4	4	4	4	4	4	4	4	4	4	4	–	–	4	14	–	–	–	–	0
Kepu	3	3	3	–	3R	3R	3	3	3	3	3R	3	3	–	–	3	14	–	–	–	–	0
Polota-Nau	2	2	2	–	–	2R	–	2	2	2	2	2	–	–	–	–	9	–	–	–	–	0
Tilse	1	1R	–	1R	–	–	–	–	–	–	–	–	–	1	3R	–	5	–	–	–	–	0
Ulugia	2R	2R	–	2	2	2	2	2R	2R	2R	x	2R	2	2	2	2	14	1	–	–	–	5
Robinson	1R	1	1	1	1	1	1	1	1	1	1	1	1	–	1	–	15	–	–	–	–	0
Ryan	3R	3R	3R	3	3	3	1R	3R	3R	3R	3R	3	3R	3R	3	–	15	2	–	–	–	10
Chapman	4R	4	6	4R	5R	4R	4R	4R	4R	8R	8R	5R	8R	–	–	5R	14	–	–	–	–	0
Timani, L	8R	8R	6R	8R	–	–	–	–	–	–	–	–	–	6	–	–	5	–	–	–	–	0
Lucas	14R	9R	9R	x	9R	x	9R	x	9R	9R	9R	9	9R	9R	x	–	12	–	2	–	–	4
Volavola	13R	14R	15	14R	x	x	x	x	10R	12R	–	–	–	–	14R	11R	8	2	–	–	–	10
Peterson	–	7R	x	–	–	–	–	–	–	–	–	–	–	–	–	–	1	–	–	–	–	0
Holmes	–	–	2R	x	2R	–	x	–	–	–	–	2R	2R	2R	2R	–	6	–	–	–	–	0
Turner	–	–	12R	14	–	–	–	–	–	–	–	–	–	–	–	–	2	–	–	–	–	0
McCutcheon	–	–	4R	8	8	8	8	8R	8R	5R	–	–	–	6	–	6R	10	–	–	–	–	0
Barnes	–	–	–	12	–	–	–	–	10R	12R	12	12R	–	12	–	12	6	2	4	6	–	36
Betham	–	–	–	11	14	14	14	11R	11R	11	11	14	11	11	11	11	13	5	–	–	–	25
Horne	–	–	–	12R	12	12	12	12	12	12	12	12	12R	12	–	13	12	–	–	–	–	0
Holloway	–	–	–	–	x	8R	–	–	–	–	–	–	8R	8	6	–	4	–	–	–	–	0
Crawford	–	–	–	–	–	–	14	14	14	14	–	–	14	14	15	–	7	8	–	–	–	40
Skelton	–	–	–	–	–	–	–	–	–	4R	4R	4R	4R	–	4	4R	6	–	–	–	–	0
Gilbert	–	–	–	–	–	–	–	–	–	–	–	–	–	7	–	–	1	–	–	–	–	0
Atkins	–	–	–	–	–	–	–	–	–	–	–	–	–	5	–	–	1	1	–	–	–	5
Aho	–	–	–	–	–	–	–	–	–	–	–	–	–	3R	–	–	1	–	–	–	–	0
Coleman	–	–	–	–	–	–	–	–	–	–	–	–	–	1	–	–	1	–	–	–	–	0
Winton	–	–	–	–	–	–	–	–	–	–	–	–	–	6R	–	–	1	–	–	–	–	0
Hepetema	–	–	–	–	–	–	–	–	–	–	–	–	–	13R	–	–	1	–	–	–	–	0
38 players																	**338**	**45**	**30**	**42**	**0**	**411**

▨ *Yellow Card* ■ *Red Card*

QUEENSLAND REDS

HONOURS
CHAMPIONS
2011

GROUND
Suncorp Stadium
ADDRESS
Castlemaine Street, Milton
TELEPHONE
+ 61 7 3354 9333
CAPACITY
52 000
COLOURS
Cardinal red jersey, socks and shorts
WEBSITE
www.redsrugby.com.au
COACH
Ewen McKenzie
CAPTAIN
James Horwill
CEO
Jim Carmichael
CHAIRMAN
Rod McCall
PRESIDENT
Tony Shaw

RECORDS

MATCH RECORDS

Biggest win	50	vs. Rebels (53-3)	Brisbane	2011
Heaviest defeat	89	vs. Bulls (3-92)	Pretoria	2007
Highest score	53	vs. Rebels (53-3)	Brisbane	2011
Most points conceded	92	vs. Bulls (3-92)	Pretoria	2007
Most tries	7	vs. Blues (51-13)	Brisbane	1996
	7	vs. Bulls (48-12)	Brisbane	2002
	7	vs. Force (50-10)	Brisbane	2010
	7	vs. Rebels (53-3)	Brisbane	2011
Most tries conceded	13	vs. Bulls (3-92)	Pretoria	2007
Most points by a player	31	QS Cooper (2t, 3c, 5p) vs Crusaders Brisbane		2010
Most tries by a player	3	RW Davies vs Blues	Brisbane	2011
Most conversions by a player	5	JA Eales on four occasions		
	5	EJ Flatley vs. Stormers	Brisbane	2002
	5	QS Cooper vs. Force	Brisbane	2010
	5	QS Cooper vs. Rebels	Brisbane	2011
Most penalties by a player	7	QS Cooper vs. Brumbies	Canberra	2011
	7	MJ Harris vs Force	Brisbane	2012
Most drop goals by a player	2	BS Barnes vs. Brumbies	Canberra	2008

SEASON RECORDS

Most team points	477	from 18 matches	2011
Most points by a player	228	QS Cooper	2011
Most team tries	51	from 18 matches	2011
Most tries by a player	10	CE Latham	2002
Most conversions by a player	31	QS Cooper	2010
	31	QS Cooper	2011
Most penalties by a player	43	QS Cooper	2011
Most drop goals by a player	4	BS Barnes	2008
	4	QS Cooper	2011

CAREER RECORDS

Most appearances	123	SP Hardman	2000-2010
Most points	629	EJ Flatley	1996-2006
Most tries	41	CE Latham	1997-2008
Most conversions	92	EJ Flatley	1996-2006
Most penalties	130	EJ Flatley	1996-2006
Most drop goals	6	BS Barnes	2006-2009

Genial genius...Will Genia was a world-class presence for the Reds. Bradley Kanaris/Getty Images

2013 RESULTS & SCORERS

Date	Venue	Opponent	Result	Score	Referee	Scorers
Febr 16	Canberra	Brumbies	LOST	6-24	A Lees	P: Harris (2).
Febr 23	Brisbane	Waratahs	WON	25-17	C Pollock	T: Tapuai (2), Shipperley. C: Harris (2). P: Harris (2).
Mrch 01	Brisbane	Hurricanes	WON	18-12	SR Walsh	T: Ioane, Simmons. C: Cooper. P: Cooper (2).
Mrch 08	Melbourne	Rebels	WON	23-13	F Pastrana	T: Tapuai, Frisby. C: Cooper (2). P: Cooper (3).
Mrch 16	Brisbane	Force	LOST	12-19	A Gardner	P: Cooper (4).
Mrch 23	Brisbane	Bulls	WON	23-18	J Leckie	T: Lance, Cooper. C: Cooper (2). P: Cooper (3).
Mrch 29	Dunedin	Highlanders	WON	34-33	J Peyper	T: Schatz, Hanson, Gill, Genia. C: Cooper (4). P: Cooper (2).
April 13	Hamilton	Chiefs	WON	31-23	SR Walsh	T: Davies (2), Schatz, Cooper. C: Cooper (4). P: Cooper.
April 20	Brisbane	Brumbies	DREW	19-19	G Jackson	T: Schatz, Gill, Davies. C: Cooper (2).
April 26	Brisbane	Blues	WON	12-11	C Joubert	P: Cooper (4).
May 04	Perth	Force	DREW	11-11	R Hoffman	T: Feauai-Sautia. P: Cooper (2)
May 10	Brisbane	Sharks	WON	32-17	G Jackson	T: Davies (2), S Faingaa, A Faingaa. C: Cooper (3). P: Cooper (2).
May 18	Bloemfontein	Cheetahs	LOST	13-27	C Joubert	T: Lucas. C: Cooper. P: Cooper (2).
May 25	Cape Town	Stormers	LOST	15-20	J Peyper	P: Cooper (5).
Jun 01	Brisbane	Rebels	WON	33-20	J Leckie	T: Lucas, Schatz, Morahan, Cooper. C: Harris, Cooper. P: Cooper (2). DG: Cooper.
July 13	Sydney	Waratahs	WON	14-12	SR Walsh	T: Lucas. P: Cooper (3).
Play-off						
July 20	Christchurch	Crusaders	LOST	9-38	J Peyper	P: Cooper (3).

Played	Won	Lost	Lost	Points for	Points against	Tries for	Tries against
17	**10**	**5**	**2**	**330**	**334**	**31**	**27**

COACHES & MANAGEMENT

DIRECTOR OF COACHING: Ewen McKenzie **HEAD COACH:** Richard Graham
ASSISTANT COACHES: Jim McKay & Matt Taylor **DOCTOR:** Dr Abhi Varshney
PHYSIOTHERAPIST: Nathan Carlos, Sep Rafiee, Andrew Plastow **PERFORMANCE COACH:** Damian Marsh
ASST PERFORMANCE COACH: Matthew Lieschke **MANAGER:** Shane Sullivan
MEDIA OFFICER: Brendan Altadonna **STRATEGY COACH:** Philip Fowler **SCRUM COACH:** Alec Evans
VIDEO ANALYST: Ben McGahan **PERFORMANCE ANALYST:** Peter Wilkins **DIETITIAN:** Gary Slater
CONDITIONING COACH: Oliver Richardson **LOGISTICS MANAGER:** Michael Atkinson

APPEARANCES & POINTS IN SUPER RUGBY

REDS	Date of Birth	Height	Weight	Matches	Tries	Conversions	Penalties	Drop Goals	Points
A (Albert) Anae	21/06/1989	1,85	114	17	–	–	–	–	0
C (Curtis) Browning	30/10/1993	1,88	106	1	–	–	–	–	0
JM (Jarrad) Butler	20/07/1991	1,85	102	12	–	–	–	–	0
QS (Quade) Cooper	05/04/1988	1,85	83	88	19	84	109	6	608
BP (Ben) Daley	27/06/1988	1,83	106	57	1	–	–	–	5
RW (Rod) Davies	18/05/1989	1,80	88	44	15	–	–	–	75
AS (Anthony) Fainga'a	02/02/1987	1,78	88	62	5	–	–	–	25
SM (Saia) Fainga'a	02/02/1987	1,87	100	95	8	–	–	–	40
C (Chris) Feauai-Sautia	17/11/1993	1,81	88	16	3	–	–	–	15
NH (Nick) Frisby	29/10/1992	1,85	80	18	3	–	–	–	15
SW (Will) Genia	17/01/1988	1,75	82	86	16	1	1	–	85
LB (Liam) Gill	08/06/1992	1,83	96	41	5	–	–	–	25
JE (James) Hanson	15/09/1988	1,80	100	50	5	–	–	–	25
MJ (Mike) Harris	08/07/1988	1,86	96	31	3	30	41	1	201
GS (Greg) Holmes	11/06/1983	1,83	110	104	6	–	–	–	30
JE (James) Horwill	29/05/1985	2,01	113	87	6	–	–	–	30
DAN (Digby) Ioane	14/07/1985	1,78	92	86	22	–	–	–	110
JB (Jono) Lance	07/02/1990	1,83	90	20	2	–	1	–	13
BJ (Ben) Lucas	30/12/1987	1,80	79	62	5	5	7	–	56
LJ (Luke) Morahan	13/04/1990	1,87	93	46	11	–	–	–	55
ECT (Ed) O'Donoghue	26/06/1982	1,98	112	37	–	–	–	–	0
J (Jono) Owen	01/11/1986	1,88	120	18	–	–	–	–	0
EC (Ed) Quirk	28/08/1991	1,91	106	29	–	–	–	–	0
BS (Beau) Robinson	15/08/1986	1,81	97	58	1	–	–	–	5
UR (Radike) Samo	09/07/1976	1,97	116	69	9	–	–	–	45
JW (Jake) Schatz	25/07/1990	1,90	104	49	4	–	–	–	20
DP (Dom) Shipperley	04/01/1991	1,86	94	35	11	–	–	–	55
JA (James) Slipper	06/06/1989	1,85	113	51	3	–	–	–	15
RA (Rob) Simmons	19/04/1989	2,00	118	65	1	–	–	–	5
BNL (Ben) Tapuai	19/01/1989	1,78	95	39	7	–	–	–	35
AM (Aidan) Toua	19/01/1990	1,81	89	5	–	–	–	–	0
AR (Adam) Wallace-Harrison	24/09/1979	2,00	114	67	5	–	–	–	25
Totals				1545	176	120	159	7	1618

VODACOM SUPER RUGBY

FINAL LOG POSITIONS

2013	5th	**2009**	13th	**2005**	10th	**2001**	4th	**1997** 10th
2012	3rd	**2008**	12th	**2004**	10th	**2000**	7th	**1996** 1st
2011	1st	**2007**	14th	**2003**	8th	**1999**	1st	
2010	5th	**2006**	12th	**2002**	5th	**1998**	5th	

APPEARANCES & POINTS IN 2013

REDS

	Brumbies	Waratahs	Hurricanes	Rebels	Bulls	Highlanders	Chiefs	Brumbies	Blues	Force	Sharks	Cheetahs	Stormers	Rebels	Waratahs	Crusaders	Matches	Tries	Conversions	Penalties	Drop Goals	Points
Harris	15	15	15R	12R	13	13R	–	–	–	–	–	–	–	12R	12	–	8	–	3	4	–	18
Shipperley	14	14	14	14	x	–	14	14	14R	14R	14	–	–	–	14R	14	11	1	–	–	–	5
Toua	13	–	15	–	x	–	x	x	–	–	–	–	–	–	–	–	2	–	–	–	–	0
Tapuai	12	12	12	12	12	12	12	12	12	12	12	x	15R	x	13	13	15	3	–	–	–	15
Ioane	11	11	11	11	–	11	–	–	11	11	11	11	–	–	–	–	10	1	–	–	–	5
Cooper	10	10	10	10	10	10	10	10	10	10	10	10	10	10	10	10	17	3	20	38	1	172
Lucas	9	9	9	x	–	–	x	x	15R	15R	15R	11R	x	15	15	15	10	2	–	–	–	10
Schatz	8	8	8	8	8	8	8	8	8	8	8	8	6	8	8	8	17	4	–	–	–	20
Gill	7	7	7	7	7	–	7	7	7	7	7	7	7	7R	7	7	16	2	–	–	–	10
Quirk	6	6	6	6	6	6	6	6	6	6	6	6	8R	6	6	6	17	–	–	–	–	0
Simmons	5	5	5	5	5	5R	4	4	4	4	4	4	4	4	5	4	17	1	–	–	–	5
Wallace-Harrison	4	4R	x	4R	5R	–	–	–	–	–	5R	–	–	–	–	–	5	–	–	–	–	0
Slipper	3c	3c	3c	3c	3	3	3	3	3	1R	3	3	3	3	3c	3	17	–	–	–	–	0
Faingaa, S	2	2	2	2	2	x	–	–	2R	2	2	2	2	2R	2	2	14	1	–	–	–	5
Holmes	1	1	1	1	1	1	1	1	1R	3	1	1	1	1	1	1	17	–	–	–	–	0
Hanson	2R	2R	2R	2R	2R	2	2	2	2	2R	2R	2R	2R	2	–	–	15	1	–	–	–	5
Anae	1R	3R	1R	3R	1R	3R	x	3R	–	–	1	3R	–	–	1R	2R	11	–	–	–	–	0
O'Donoghue	4R	4	4	4	4	4	5R	4R	4R	4R	5R	5	4R	4R	x	4	16	–	–	–	–	0
Butler	8R	8R	–	–	8R	7	7R	6R	x	6R	8R	6R	6R	–	x	–	10	–	–	–	–	0
Frisby	9R	9R	9R	9	9R	9R	–	–	–	–	–	–	–	11R	9	14R	9	1	–	–	–	5
Lance	12R	x	–	15	15	15	15	15	15	15	15	–	15	–	12R	12	13	2	–	–	–	10
Feauai-Sautia	13R	13	13	14R	11	14	–	14R	x	12R	14R	13	13	–	–	11	13	1	–	–	–	5
Morahan	–	13R	11R	–	14	–	11	–	–	–	–	15	11	11	11	12R	9	1	–	–	–	5
Samo	–	–	6R	8R	–	–	–	–	–	–	–	8	6R	4R	6R	–	6	–	–	–	–	0
Faingaa, A	–	–	–	13	–	13	13	13	13	13	13	12	12	12	12	–	11	1	–	–	–	5
Genia	–	–	–	–	9c	9	9	9	9	9	9c	9	9	–	–	9	12	1	–	–	–	5
Horwill	–	–	–	–	–	5c	5c	5c	5c	5c	5c	–	5c	5c	5c	–	10	–	–	–	–	0
Browning	–	–	–	–	–	7R	–	–	–	–	–	–	–	–	–	–	1	–	–	–	–	0
Ah Wong	–	–	–	–	–	x	–	–	–	–	–	–	–	–	–	–	0	–	–	–	–	0
Daley	–	–	–	–	–	–	1R	1R	1R	1	–	–	1R	1R	1R	–	7	–	–	–	–	0
Davies	–	–	–	–	–	–	14R	11	14	14	–	14	14	14	14	–	9	5	–	–	–	25
Robinson	–	–	–	–	–	–	–	–	–	6R	7R	6R	7R	7	6R	8R	7	–	–	–	–	0
Owen	–	–	–	–	–	–	–	–	–	–	–	–	–	x	–	1R	1	–	–	–	–	0
33 players																	353	31	23	42	1	330

Yellow Card ■ Red Card

WESTERN FORCE

GROUND
nib Stadium
CAPACITY
20526
ADDRESS
310 Pier Street, Perth, WA 6000
TELEPHONE NUMBER
+ 61 8 9387 0700
COLOURS
Ocean blue jersey with black shorts and socks
WEBSITE
www.rugbywa.com.au
COACH
Michael Foley
CAPTAIN
Matt Hodgson
CEO
Mark Sinderberry
CHARMAIN
Dr Russel Perry
PRESIDENT
David Redpath

RECORDS

MATCH RECORDS

Biggest win	41	vs. Lions (55-14)	Perth	2009
Heaviest defeat	53	vs. Crusaders (0-53)	Christchurch	2007
Highest score	55	vs. Lions (55-14)	Perth	2009
Most points conceded	53	vs. Crusaders (0-53)	Christchurch	2007
Most tries	8	vs. Lions (55-14)	Perth	2009
Most tries conceded	8	vs. Crusaders (0-53)	Christchurch	2007
Most points by a player	25	CB Shepherd vs. Bulls (2t, 3c, 3p)	Pretoria	2007
Most tries by a player	3	SNG Staniforth vs. Cats	Johannesburg	2006
	3	CB Shepherd vs. Brumbies	Canberra	2009
Most conversions by a player	6	MJ Giteau vs. Lions	Perth	2009
Most penalties by a player	6	JD O'Connor vs. Bulls	Perth	2011
Most drop goals by a player	2	JM Ebersohn vs. Bulls	Pretoria	2013

SEASON RECORDS

Most team points	333	from 16 matches	2011
Most points by a player	170	JD O'Connor	2011
Most team tries	42	from 13 matches	2009
Most tries by a player	9	SNG Staniforth	2006
Most conversions by a player	28	MJ Giteau	2009
Most penalties by a player	47	JD O'Connor	2011
Most drop goals by a player	2	JM Ebersohn	2013

CAREER RECORDS

Most appearances	97	MJ Hodgson	2006-2013
Most points	372	CB Shepherd	2006-2012
Most tries	30	CB Shepherd	2006-2012
Most conversions	55	MJ Giteau	2007-2009
Most penalties	70	JD O'Connor	2009-2011
Most drop goals	2	JM Ebersohn	2013

No way through...the Force could only score 26 tries in 16 matches. Paul Kane/Getty Images

2013 **RESULTS & SCORERS**

Date	Venue	Opponent	Result	Score	Referee	Scorers
Febr 15	Melbourne	REBELS	LOST	23-30	A Gardner	T: Mafi (2), Brown. C: Godwin. P: Godwin (2).
Febr 23	Port Elizabeth	KINGS	LOST	10-22	L vd Merwe	T: Mafi, Cowan.
Mrch 02	Pretoria	BULLS	LOST	26-36	J Jaftha	T: Cottrell, Lynn. C: Ebersohn (2), P: Ebersohn. DG: Ebersohn (2).
Mrch 16	Brisbane	REDS	WON	19-12	A Gardner	T: Mafi. C: Ebersohn. P: Ebersohn (4).
Mrch 23	Perth	CHEETAHS	LOST	10-19	G Williamson	T: Stanley. C: Ebersohn. P: Hayward.
Mrch 31	Sydney	WARATAHS	LOST	19-23	SR Walsh	T: Mafi. C: Ebersohn. P: Ebersohn (4).
April 06	Perth	REBELS	LOST	23-30	M Fraser	T: Dellitt, Tupou, Stanley. C: Godwin. P: Ebersohn (2).
April 13	Perth	CRUSADERS	WON	16-14	J Kaplan	T: Norton-Knight. C: Hayward. P: Hayward (3).
April 19	Wellington	HURRICANES	LOST	16-22	N Briant	T: Mathewson. C: Hayward. P: Hayward (3)
April 27	Canberra	BRUMBIES	LOST	7-41	A Gardner	T: Hodgson. C: Hayward.
May 04	Perth	REDS	DREW	11-11	R Hoffman	T: McCalman. P: Ebersohn (2).
May 10	Pukekohe	CHIEFS	LOST	21-22	M Fraser	T: Dellitt (2). C: Hayward. P: Hayward (3).
May 17	Perth	SHARKS	LOST	13-23	J Leckie	T: Godwin. C: Hayward. P: Hayward (2).
May 25	Perth	HIGHLANDERS	WON	19-18	A Lees	T: Ebersohn. C: Hayward. P: Hayward (4).
June 09	Perth	WARATAHS	LOST	13-28	A Gardner	T: Godwin, Cowan. P: Hayward.
July 13	Perth	BRUMBIES	WON	21-15	R Hoffman	T: McCalman, Rasolea, Hodgson. C: Hayward (3).

Played	Won	Lost	Drawn	Points for	Points against	Tries for	Tries against
16	4	11	1	267	366	26	34

www.rugbywa.co.au

COACHES & MANAGEMENT

HEAD COACH: Michael Foley **BACKS COACH:** Steve Meehan **FORWARDS COACH:** Nick Stiles
DEFENCE & SKILLS COACH: Phil Blake **CONDITIONING COACH:** Charlie Higgins
ASST CONDIOTIONING COACH: Brendyn Appleby **ACADEMY CONDITIONING COACH:** Louis Dallimore
VIDEO ANALYST: Scott Anderson **THERAPIST:** Rob Naish **DOCTOR:** Dr Mike Cadogan
MEDIA OFFICER: Nick Smith **MANAGER:** Mitch Hardy **RUGBY STRATEGIST:** Philip Fowler
ATHLETIC PERFORMANCE: David Joyce **PHYSIOTHERAPISTS:** Emidio Pacceca & Ben Mather

APPEARANCES & POINTS IN SUPER RUGBY

FORCE	Date of Birth	Height	Weight	Matches	Tries	Conversions	Penalties	Drop Goals	Points
CB (Chris) Alcock	24/06/1988	1,82	103	41	1	–	–	–	5
PD (Phoenix) Battye	28/09/1990	2,04	115	11	–	–	–	–	0
RN (Richard) Brown	28/08/1989	1,88	104	89	5	–	–	–	25
NL (Nathan) Charles	09/01/1989	1,83	103	44	1	–	–	–	5
S (Sam) Christie	26/09/1986	1,81	91	4	–	–	–	–	0
AJ (Angus) Cottrell	20/11/1989	1,91	105	16	1	–	–	–	5
PJM (Pekahou) Cowan	02/06/1986	1,83	109	75	3	–	–	–	15
NM (Nick) Cummins	05/10/1987	1,88	94	59	9	–	–	–	45
P (Patrick) Dellitt	21/08/1986	1,91	92	31	3	–	–	–	15
JM (Sias) Ebersohn	23/02/1989	1,75	81	54	3	41	58	4	283
T (Tetera) Faulkner	26/07/1988	1,80	114	14	–	–	–	–	0
KW (Kyle) Godwin	30/07/1992	1,87	87	17	3	3	2	–	27
J (Jayden) Hayward	11/08/1987	1,85	95	10	–	9	17	–	69
J (James) Hilterbrand	21/05/1989	1,85	108	2	–	–	–	–	0
MJ (Matt) Hodgson	25/06/1981	1,85	101	97	7	–	–	–	35
BA (Ben) Jacobs	17/05/1982	1,83	92	41	6	–	–	–	30
KA (Kieran) Longbottom	20/12/1985	1,80	107	41	–	–	–	–	0
TR (Toby) Lynn	06/10/1984	1,97	113	62	2	–	–	–	10
SL (Salesi) Ma'afu	22/03/1983	1,84	125	74	4	–	–	–	20
A (Alfi) Mafi	08/06/1988	1,86	89	54	11	–	–	–	55
S (Salesi) Manu	26/09/1990	1,85	122	9	–	–	–	–	0
AS (Alby) Mathewson	13/12/1985	1,73	86	99	18	–	–	–	90
B (Ben) McCalman	18/03/1988	1,92	106	51	4	–	–	–	20
HJ (Hugh) McMeniman	01/11/1983	2,01	112	37	1	–	–	–	5
SH (Sam) Norton-Knight	02/12/1983	1,88	88	64	11	–	–	–	55
J (Junior) Rasolea	29/04/1991	1,96	100	12	1	–	–	–	5
BR (Brett) Sheehan	16/09/1979	1,79	90	93	2	2	4	–	26
M (Mick) Snowden	18/12/1987	1,85	91	5	–	–	–	–	0
WTN (Winston) Stanley	11.02.1989	1,84	95	25	4	–	–	–	20
E (Ed) Stubbs	02/02/1989	1,83	102	3	–	–	–	–	0
HR (Heath) Tessman	03/03/1984	1,82	105	23	–	–	–	–	0
W (Will) Tupou	20/07/1990	1,89	101	13	1	–	–	–	5
R (Rory) Walton	11/04/1989	1,96	111	8	–	–	–	–	0
B (Ben) Whittaker	10/10/1989	1,89	111	32	1	–	–	–	5
SL (Sam) Wykes	25/04/1988	1,95	106	59	2	–	–	–	10
Totals				**1369**	**104**	**55**	**81**	**4**	**885**

VODACOM SUPER RUGBY

FINAL LOG POSITIONS

2013	13th	2011	12th	2009	8th	2007	7th
2012	14th	2010	13th	2008	8th	2006	14th

APPEARANCES & POINTS IN 2013

	Rebels	Kings	Bulls	Reds	Cheetahs	Waratahs	Rebels	Crusaders	Hurricanes	Brumbies	Reds	Chiefs	Sharks	Highlanders	Waratahs	Brumbies	Matches	Tries	Conversions	Penalties	Drop Goals	Points
Tupou	15	15	15	15	15	–	15	–	–	–	–	–	–	–	–	–	6	1	–	–	–	5
Dellit	14	–	–	14	14	14	14	11R	14	14	14	14	14	14	14	14	14	3	–	–	–	15
Stanley	13	13	13	13	13	13	13	–	13	13R	–	–	–	–	–	–	9	2	–	–	–	10
Godwin	12	12	12	12	12	12	12	12	–	12	12	12	12	12	12	12	14	2	2	2	–	20
Mafi	11	11	14	11	11	15	11	14	11R	–	–	–	–	–	–	–	9	5	–	–	–	25
Christie	10	10	–	–	–	9R	10R	–	–	–	–	–	–	–	–	x	4	–	–	–	–	0
Mathewson	9	9	9	9	9	9	9	9	9	9	9	9R	9	9	9	9	16	1	–	–	–	5
McCalman	8	8	8R	8R	6R	6	8	6	–	6	8	8	8	8	–	8	14	2	–	–	–	10
Alcock	7	6R	7R	7	7	8R	3R	6R	7R	8R	7	7	7	7	7	7	16	–	–	–	–	0
Cottrell	6	6	6	6	6	–	6	–	6	–	–	–	–	8R	8	–	9	1	–	–	–	5
Lynn	5	4R	4	4	4	4	4	4	4	4	4	4	4	x	4R	–	15	1	–	–	–	5
Wykes	4	4	5R	–	4R	4R	5R	5	5	5	5	5	5	5	5	4	15	–	–	–	–	0
Faulkner	3	3	3R	3R	3R	–	1R	3R	3	–	x	1R	3R	3R	–	–	11	–	–	–	–	0
Charles	2	2	2	2	2	–	–	–	–	–	–	–	–	–	–	–	5	–	–	–	–	0
Cowan	1c	1	1	1c	1c	1	–	1	1	1	1	1	1	1	1c	1	15	2	–	–	–	10
Tessman	2R	2R	x	x	2R	2	2	2	2	2	2	2	2	2	2	–	13	–	–	–	–	0
Longbottom	3R	3R	–	–	–	3R	1	–	3R	3R	3	3	3	3	3	–	11	–	–	–	–	0
Battye	4R	–	–	4R	–	–	–	–	–	–	–	–	–	–	–	–	2	–	–	–	–	0
Brown	8R	8R	8	8	8	8	–	8	8	8	8R	8R	7R	7R	–	5R	14	1	–	–	–	5
Snowden	x	13R	10R	x	x	–	9R	9R	x	9R	–	–	–	–	–	–	5	–	–	–	–	0
Ebersohn	10R	–	10	10	10	10	10	13R	x	22R	10	10	10	10	10	10	14	1	5	14	2	63
Rasolea	13R	12R	–	11R	–	11	–	13	12	13	x	13R	14R	11	11	12	12	1	–	–	–	5
Cummins	–	14	11	–	–	–	–	–	–	11	11	11	–	–	–	11	6	–	–	–	–	0
Hodgson	–	7c	7c	–	7R	7c	7c	7c	7c	7c	6c	6c	6c	6c	4R	6c	14	2	–	–	–	10
McMeniman	–	5	5	5	5	5	5	–	–	–	–	–	–	–	6	5	8	–	–	–	–	0
Ma'afu	–	–	3	3	3	3	3	–	3	–	–	–	–	–	3R	3	9	–	–	–	–	0
Hayward	–	–	13R	x	10R	–	–	15	15	15	x	15	15	15	15	15	10	–	9	17	–	69
Whittaker	–	–	–	–	–	x	2R	2R	–	–	–	–	–	–	–	x	2	–	–	–	–	0
Norton-Knight	–	–	–	–	15R	11R	10	10	10	15	x	10R	10R	x	x	–	8	1	–	–	–	5
Eaton	–	–	–	–	x	–	–	–	–	–	–	–	–	–	–	–	0	–	–	–	–	0
Stubbs	–	–	–	–	–	–	11	11	11	–	–	–	–	–	x	–	3	–	–	–	–	0
Walton	–	–	–	–	–	5R	5R	4R	5R	5R	5R	4R	4	–	–	–	8	–	–	–	–	0
Hilterbrand	–	–	–	–	–	–	x	2R	x	x	x	x	2	–	–	–	2	–	–	–	–	0
Jacobs	–	–	–	–	–	–	–	–	13	13	13	13	13	–	–	–	6	–	–	–	–	0
Sheehan	–	–	–	–	–	–	–	–	–	9R	9	9R	9R	9R	x	–	5	–	–	–	–	0
Manu	–	–	–	–	–	–	–	–	–	–	–	–	–	–	–	3R	1	–	–	–	–	0
36 players																	**325**	**26**	**16**	**33**	**2**	**267**

■ Yellow Card   ■ Red Card

SECTION 5
DOMESTIC CHAMPIONSHIPS

ABSA CURRIE CUP 2013
Tournament Review & statistics **200**

VODACOM CUP 2013
Tournament Review & statistics **204**
Pampas XV team details **208**

ABSA UNDER-21 CHAMPIONSHIP 2013
Tournament Review **210**
Logs & statistics **211**

ABSA UNDER-19 CHAMPIONSHIP 2013
Tournament Review **213**
Logs & statistics **214**

MISCELLANEOUS PROVINCIAL CHAMPIONSHIPS
Amateur Provincial Competitions **216**
Sub-Union Tournaments **216**
Interprovincial Sevens **217**
Women's Interprovincial Tournament **217**

Sharks coach Brendan Venter gives Frans Steyn some instructions before they took on DHL Western Province in the 2013 Absa Currie Cup final at Newlands. *Steve Haag/Gallo Images*

ABSA CURRIE CUP

Sharks rediscover their bite

THE SHARKS WON THEIR SEVENTH Absa Currie Cup title, and their third in six years, when they beat DHL Western Province 33-19 in front of a capacity crowd at Newlands.

WP, who had gone through the league stage of the Premier Division unbeaten – winning eight matches and drawing two – went into the final as favourites having already defeated the Sharks twice, in Cape Town earlier in the season and in Durban when both sides had their Springboks back. Apart from their losses to WP, the Sharks also suffered a shock opening-round defeat to GWK Griquas at Kings Park.

But when all was said and done, they won the match that really mattered, on 26 October, with scrumhalf Charl McLeod scoring their two tries and flyhalf Pat Lambie contributing the rest of the points – 23 in all – with the boot. It was a fantastic result not just for captain Keegan Daniel and his players, but for the new Sharks coaching team of Brendan Venter, Brad Macleod-Henderson and Sean Everitt, as well as new CEO John Smit, who had made those appointments.

The other two Premier Division semi-finalists, the Toyota Free State Cheetahs and MTN Golden Lions, both lost five matches during the league stage of the tournament, and were no match for the Sharks and WP respectively in the semi-finals. Having lost eight Springboks to overseas-based clubs after Vodacom Super Rugby, a young and inexperienced Vodacom Blue Bulls team failed to make the play-offs after winning just three of their 10 matches.

Griquas, who had started the competition so well against the Sharks, went on to lose the rest of their matches, although six of those defeats were by seven points or less. They finished bottom of the Premier Division and had to play two promotion-relegation matches against the Steval Pumas, who had won the First Absa Division with considerable ease. Griquas scored a late converted try to win the first match 21-19 in Kimberley, but the Pumas scored three unanswered tries in the return leg in Nelspruit to win 33-15 and earn promotion to the Premier Division for 2014. Griquas, though, were given a lifeline when SARU's general council voted to expand the Currie Cup Premier Division from six to eight teams, with the EP Kings also joining the top flight.

The Pumas enjoyed an outstanding First Division campaign, winning all 14 of their league matches and scoring an average of 43 points and 5.4 tries per game. They were as impressive in the play-offs, putting 52 points and six tries past the SWD Eagles in their semi-final and 53 points and six tries past the EP Kings in the final.

In the domestic U21 final, Western Province claimed a 30-23 win against a Blue Bulls team that included Springbok centre Jan Serfontein and several other players with senior Currie Cup experience. WP won 11 of their 12 league matches and edged the Golden Lions 44-41 in extra time of their semi-final.

In the U19 decider, the Blue Bulls claimed their 14th successive win of the season when they beat the Golden Lions 35-23. It was the perfect send-off for coach Paul Anthony, who was set to join the Sharks' senior coaching team for the 2014 season.

BY SIMON BORCHARDT,
SA RUGBY MAGAZINE

The Sharks celebrate their 2013 Currie Cup final victory. Luke Walker/Gallo Images

ABSA CURRIE CUP PREMIER DIVISION LOG

Team	P	W	L	D	PF	PA	Diff	TF	TA	B	Pts
DHL Western Province	10	8	0	2	245	201	44	23	21	1	37
Sharks	10	7	3	0	271	223	48	28	21	5	33
Toyota Free State Cheetahs	10	5	5	0	262	238	24	31	26	6	26
MTN Golden Lions	10	4	5	1	326	296	30	40	31	8	26
Vodacom Blue Bulls	10	3	6	1	225	253	-28	24	28	3	17
GWK Griquas	10	1	9	0	208	326	-118	17	36	7	11

2013 ABSA CURRIE CUP PLAY-OFF RESULTS

PLAY-OFF RESULTS
SEMI-FINALS: Sharks bt FS **Cheetahs 33-22** (Durban). **Western Province** bt **Golden Lions 33-16** (Cape Town)

2013 ABSA CURRIE CUP FINAL
DHL Newlands, Cape Town, Saturday 26 October 2013
Referee: Jonathan Kaplan. Crowd: 49 000
WP 19 (13) **(TRY:** De Allende. **CONVERSION:** Catrakilis. **PENALTIES:** Catrakilis 3, Coleman)
Sharks 33 (19) **(TRIES:** McLeod 2. **CONVERSION:** Lambie. **PENALTIES:** Lambie 5. **DG:** Lambie 2)
WP: Gio Aplon, Gerhard van den Heever (Juan de Jongh, 52), Jean de Villiers, Damian de Allende, Cheslin Kolbe, Demetri Catrakilis (Kurt Coleman, 48), Louis Schreuder (Nick Groom, 52). Duane Vermeulen, Siya Kolisi (Schalk Burger, 6-17, 59), Deon Fourie (c), De Kock Steenkamp (Michael Rhodes, 55), Eben Etzebeth, Pat Cilliers (Frans Malherbe, 55), Scarra Ntubeni (Brok Harris, 74), S Kitshoff.
Sharks: SP Marais, Odwa Ndungane, Louis Ludik, Francois Steyn (Heimar Williams, 72), Lwazi Mvovo, Patrick Lambie, Charl McLeod (Cobus Reinach, 65), Keegan Daniel (c), Willem Alberts (Jacques Botes, 75, Marcell Coetzee, Pieter-Steph du Toit, Peet Marais (Stephan Lewies, 59) Jannie du Plessis (Wiehahn Herbst, 45), Bismarck du Plessis (Kyle Cooper, 80), Tendai Mtawarira. *UNUSED SUB:* Fred Zeilinga.

2013 ABSA CURRIE CUP LEADING SCORERS

50 POINTS OR MORE

PLAYER	Team	Tries	Conversions	Penalties	Drop Goals	Points
Marnitz Boshoff	Golden Lions	2	20	14	0	92
Fred Zeilinga	Sharks	1	13	17	3	91
Kurt Coleman	WP	0	9	21	0	81
Riaan Smit	Free State	2	12	12	0	70
Demetri Catrakilis	WP	1	5	16	2	69
Elton Jantjies	Golden Lions	2	11	11	0	65
Elgar Watts	Free State	4	8	9	0	63
Handre Pollard	Blue Bulls	0	10	13	1	62
Nico Scheepers	Griquas	1	5	12	0	51

FIVE TRIES

Raymond Rhule	Free State	7	Derrick Minnie	Golden Lions	6
Anthony Volmink	Golden Lions	6	Jaco Kriel	Golden Lions	5

PROMOTION & RELEGATION PLAY-OFF RESULTS

Griquas beat **Pumas 21-19**, GWK Park, Kimberley, Friday 18 October, 2013
Pumas beat **Griquas 33-15**, Mbombela Stadium, Friday 25 October, 2013

ABSA CURRIE CUP PROMOTION & RELEGATION LOG

Team	P	W	L	D	PF	PA	Diff	TF	TA	B	Pts
Pumas	2	1	1	0	52	36	16	4	3	1	5
Griquas	2	1	1	0	36	52	-16	3	4	0	4

ABSA CURRIE CUP REVIEW

FIRST DIVISION LOG

Team	P	W	L	D	PF	PA	Diff	TF	TA	B	Pts
Pumas	14	14	0	0	601	254	347	76	31	10	66
EP Kings	14	10	4	0	441	297	144	52	34	11	51
Leopards	14	8	6	0	448	398	50	64	46	12	44
SWD Eagles	14	7	7	0	460	452	8	58	59	13	41
Boland Cavaliers	14	6	7	1	329	393	-64	45	54	6	32
Griffons	14	3	9	2	367	534	-167	49	72	11	27
Border	14	4	10	0	277	365	-88	32	46	9	25
Valke	14	2	11	1	349	579	-230	45	79	8	18

FIRST DIVISION PLAY-OFF RESULTS

PLAY-OFF RESULTS
SEMI-FINALS: EP Kings bt **Leopards** 32-29 (Port Elizabeth). **Pumas** bt **SWD Eagles** 52-33 (Nelspruit).

2013 ABSA CUP FINAL
Mbombela Stadium, Nelspruit, Friday, 11 October 2013. Referee: Craig Joubert. Crowd: 3000
Pumas 53 (TRIES: Van Wyk 3, Bell, Kember, Bothma. CONVERSION: Bezuidenhout 2, Roos 2. PENALTIES: Bezuidenhout 5).
EP Kings 30 (TRIES Dukisa, Van Zyl, Penalty try. CONVERSIONS: Van Breda 3, PENALTIES: Van Breda 3).
Pumas: Coenie van Wyk, JW Bell, Wilmaure Louw (Dewald Pretorius, 72), Stefan Watermeyer, Rosco Speckman, Carl Bezuidenhout (JC Roos, 68), Faf de Klerk (Reynier van Rooyen, 71), RW Kember (Christo Le Roux, 68), Renaldo Bothma (Christo le Roux, 2-7), Corne Steenkamp (C), Eduan van der Walt, Rudi Mathee (Giant Mtyanda), DJ Terblanche (Vincent Koch, 55), Frank Herne (Francois du Toit, 71), Corne Fourie.
EP Kings: SP Marais, PL Perez, IW Stevens, S Mangweni, MED Sampson, GA Whitehead (WR Dunlop, 65), NH Oelschig (S Mathie, 68), CG du Preez, PW van der Walt, DA Oosthuizen (MM Mbiyozo, 77), DJ Bulbring, DP Nell (c, W van Heerden, 72), CJ Newland, J Franklin, SJP Ferreira (A Schlechter, 23). Unused subs: F Herne, M Kilian.

FIRST DIVISION LEADING SCORERS
50 POINTS OR MORE

PLAYER	Team	Tries	Conversions	Penalties	Drop Goals	Points
Carl Bezuidenhout	Pumas	3	47	35	1	217
Adriaan Engelbrecht	Leopards	2	43	19	0	153
Scott van Breda	EP Kings	1	27	29	0	146
Justin van Staden	SWD	1	25	26	2	139
Jaun Kotze	Valke	3	21	7	4	90
Alshaun Bock	SWD	17	0	0	0	85
Louis Strydom	Griffons	0	15	14	1	75
Dale Sabbagh	Border	0	11	17	0	73
Eric Zana	Boland	1	18	8	0	65
JC Roos	Valke/Pumas	0	16	10	0	62
Edmar Marais	Leopards	11	0	0	0	55
Rosco Speckman	Pumas	11	0	0	0	55
JW Bell	Pumas	10	0	0	0	50

TEN TRIES

Alshaun Bock	SWD	17	Rosco Speckman	Pumas	11
Edmar Marais	Leopards	11	JW Bell	Pumas	10

VODACOM CUP

Lions roar for record fifth time

THE MTN GOLDEN LIONS, playing as the Young Lions, won the Vodacom Cup for a record fifth time when they beat the Steval Pumas 42-28 in the final played at Mbombela Stadium in Nelspruit.

It was the second year in a row that the visiting team managed to lift the trophy, following on the heels of DHL WP's triumph over GWK Griquas in Kimberley in 2012. The men from the Cape put up a spirited defence of their title under coach John Dobson, finishing second in the South section, but WP were well beaten by the Lions (44-25) in the semi-final played at Johannesburg's Ellis Park.

Victory in the final also meant that the Lions could finally lay claim to be the most successful team in the 16-year history of the competition, although it took them nine years to earn bragging rights, their last win coming in 2004, which, incidentally, was also the last time the men from Gauteng reached the final.

At one stage during the season it looked as if the Lions, still smarting from their exclusion from Vodacom Super Rugby in favour of the Southern Kings, would not make it to Mbombela: they lost three of their first four pool matches before turning their season around with six straight wins.

The Pumas, who topped the North Section, were playing in their first final at this level but they could not clear the final hurdle. The team from Mpumalanga did however have the consolation of having 11 of their players included in the SA President's XV squad for the inaugural IRB Tbilisi Cup, while their coach, Jimmy Stonehouse, was appointed to take charge of the team bound for Georgia [see Section 3: National Teams].

In a final in which the two sides scored three tries apiece, it was the boot of Lions flyhalf Marnitz Boshoff that made all the difference, the pivot slotting all 10 of his kicks at goal for a personal contribution of 27 points. The home side started well and went 10-0 ahead early in the match, with centre Stefan Watermeyer going over in the corner for his team's opening try. He was followed onto the scoresheet by fullback Coenie van Wyk, who dotted down from a deft grubber by flyhalf Carl Bezuidenhout later in the half.

Johan Ackermann & Kevin de Klerk.
Duif du Toit/Gallo Images

The visitors however went into the break 23-20 ahead, thanks to tries by wing Anthony Volmink and eighthman and captain, Warren Whiteley.

The second half was a more tense affair, with flanker Warwick Tecklenburg's try nine minutes from time finally putting the result beyond doubt for the Lions. Fittingly, it was Boshoff who had the final say, slotting a neat drop goal in the 79th minute.

Volmink finished the season as the competition's top try-scorer with 13 touchdowns, followed by Pumas speedster Rosco Speckman on 11. The Sharks XV's Fred Zeilinga finished as top point-scorer with 154, with Bezuidenhout second with 128. Boshoff's final haul saw him move into third place with 96.

The sweet taste of victory!
Duif du Toit/Gallo Images

VODACOM CUP REVIEW

VODACOM CUP NORTH SECTION LOG

Team	P	W	L	D	PF	PA	Diff	TF	TA	LB	TB	Pts
Pumas	7	6	1	0	414	131	283	60	15	0	5	29
Blue Bulls	7	5	2	0	435	159	276	60	20	2	6	28
Griquas	7	4	3	0	296	161	135	44	24	0	6	22
Young Lions	7	4	3	0	320	154	166	47	17	1	4	21
Leopards XV	7	4	3	0	289	158	131	38	18	2	3	21
Valke	7	3	4	0	133	245	-112	18	33	0	1	13
Griffons	7	2	5	0	139	269	-130	18	42	0	1	9
Limpopo	7	0	7	0	32	781	-749	3	119	0	0	0

VODACOM CUP SOUTH SECTION LOG

Team	P	W	L	D	PF	PA	Diff	TF	TA	LB	TB	Pts
Sharks XV	7	6	1	0	279	166	113	32	18	1	4	32
WP	7	5	1	1	208	153	55	26	20	1	4	26
EP Kings	7	5	1	1	191	154	37	22	16	0	3	24
Pampas XV	7	4	2	1	238	192	46	32	25	0	4	21
Free State XV	7	2	5	0	195	190	5	25	22	5	4	21
SWD	7	1	6	0	147	202	-55	18	22	4	2	14
Border	7	2	5	0	143	239	-96	15	34	1	0	7
Boland	7	1	5	1	151	256	-105	19	32	2	1	6

Note: LB = Lost Bonus, TB = Try Bonus

VODACOM CUP PLAY-OFF RESULTS

PLAY-OFF RESULTS
QUARTER FINALS: Blue Bulls lost to **EP Kings 31-34** (Pretoria), **Pumas** beat **Pampas XV 44-37** (Nelspruit)
Sharks XV lost to **Golden Lions 25-42** (Durban), **WP** beat **Griquas 21-13** (Cape Town)
SEMI-FINALS: Golden Lions beat **WP 44-25** (Johannesburg), **Pumas** beat **EP Kings 39-13** (Nelspruit)

FINAL: Mbombela Stadium, Nelspruit, Friday, May 17. Referee: Marius van der Westhuizen. 19:10
Pumas 28 (TRIES: Watermeyer, Van Wyk, J Pretorius. CONVERSIONS: Bezuidenhout 2. PENALTIES: Bezuidenhout 3)
Golden Lions 42 (TRIES: Volmink, Whiteley, Tecklenburg. CONVERSIONS: Boshoff 3. PENALTIES: Boshoff 6. DROP GOAL: Boshoff)
Pumas: Coenie van Wyk, JW Bell, Wilmaure Louw (Dewald Pretorius, 72), Stefan Watermeyer (Jerome Pretorius, 60), Rosco Specman, Carl Bezuidenhout, Faf de Klerk, Renaldo Bothma (Jacques Momberg, 74), Jaco Bouwer (Marius Coetzer, 66), Corne Steenkamp (c, RW Kember, 53), Eduan van der Walt, Uzair Cassiem, Ivann Espag (DJ Terblanche, 41), Frank Herne, Vincent Koch (Corne Fourie, 53).
Golden Lions: Chrysander Botha, Deon Helberg (Lionel Cronje, 74), Deon van Rensburg, Alwyn Hollenbach (Dylan des Fountain, 22-24, 73), Anthony Volmink, Marnitz Boshoff, Michael Bondesio (Ross Cronje, 67), Warren Whiteley (cv), Warwick Tecklenburg, Jaco Kriel (Willie Britz, 74), Hugo Kloppers (JJ Breet, 77), Hendrik Roodt, Ruan Dreyer, Robbie Coetzee (Francois du Toit, 74), Jacques van Rooyen (Van Zyl Botha, 77).

2013 VODACOM CUP LEADING SCORERS

50 POINTS OR MORE

PLAYER	Team	Tries	Conversions	Penalties	Drop Goals	Points
Fred Zeilinga	Sharks XV	3	29	27	0	154
Carl Bezuidenhout	Pumas	3	31	16	1	128
Marnitz Boshoff	Young Lions	0	18	16	4	96
Andre Pretorius	Leopards XV	2	28	9	0	93
Tony Jantjies	Blue Bulls	2	18	11	0	79
Willie du Plessis	Blue Bulls	2	30	0	0	70
Anthony Volmink	Young Lions	13	1	0	0	67
Santiago Gonzalez Iglesias	Pampas XV	2	18	7	0	67
Karlo Aspeling	Border	0	6	18	0	66
Kurt Coleman	WP	0	12	13	0	63
Rosco Speckman	Pumas	11	0	0	0	55
Scott van Breda	EP Kings	2	7	10	0	54
Tewis de Bruyn	Free State XV	2	5	10	0	50
Jeff Taljard	SWD	1	9	9	0	50

TEN TRIES

Anthony Volmink	Young Lions	13	Boom Prinsloo	Free State XV	5
Rosco Specman	Pumas	11	Chris Cloete	WP	5
Marnus Schoeman	Griquas	9	Courtnal Skosan	Blue Bulls	5
Sampie Mastriet	Blue Bulls	9	Danie Dames	Leopards XV	5
Wiaan Liebenberg	Blue Bulls	8	Frank Herne	Pumas	5
Manuel Montero	Pampas XV	7	Jaco Bouwer	Pumas	5
Dries Swanepoel	Blue Bulls	6	JW Bell	Pumas	5
Leon Karemaker	Griquas	6	Rocco Jansen	Griquas	5
Travis Ismaiel	Blue Bulls	6	Sizo Maseko	Sharks XV	5
Chrysander Botha	Young Lions	5	Vincent Koch	Pumas	5

PAMPAS XV

COLOURS Navy blue jersey with white stripes, navy blue shorts, navy blue socks
FOUNDED 2010 (afffiliated to the Argentina Rugby Union) **HEAD COACH** Daniel Hourcade
ASSISTANT COACHES Emiliano Bergamaschi, Raul Perez, Mauricio Reggiardo
DOCTOR Pablo Carias. Pedro Gauna **PHYSIO** Claudio Fernandez **PF** Guillermo Fantoni
KITMAN Federico Garcia **CAPTAIN** Mariano Galarza

2013 RESULTS AND SCORERS

VODACOM CUP Played **8** Won **4** Drawn **1** Lost **3** Points for **275** Points against **236** Tries for **37** Tries against **30**

Date	Venue	Opponent	Result	Score	Referee	Scorers
Mrch 09	Port Elizabeth	EP Kings	DREW	20-20	F Pretorius	T: Montero. P: Madero (5).
Mrch 15	George	Eagles	WON	22-17	M vd Westhuizen	T: Montero, Cubelli, Penalty try. C: Iglesias (2). P: Iglesias.
Mrch 23	Stellenbosch	Bulldogs	WON	45-26	M Jonker	T: De la Fuente (2), Masera, Cordero, Macome, Frutero, Penalty try. C: Madero (4), Iglesias.
April 06	Wellington	Cavaliers	WON	65-23	M Kemp	T: Montero (2), Iglesias (2), Landajo (2), De la Vega, Bruno. C: Iglesias (6), Madero (2). P: Iglesias (3).
April 13	Cape Town	WP	LOST	17-28	PJ van Vuuren	T: Masera, Montero, Senatore. C: Madero.
April 20	Stellenbosch	Free State XV	WON	38-32	F Pretorius	T: Barrea (2), Montero, Cubelli, Bruno. C: Iglesias (5). P: Iglesias.
April 26	Durban	Sharks XV	LOST	31-46	R Rasivhenge	T: Estelles (2), Moyano, Senatore, Galarza. C: Madero (3).
QUARTER-FINAL						
May 03	Nelspruit	Pumas	LOST	37-44	J van Heerden	T: Moyano, Montero, Cubelli, Baez, Veiga. C: Iglesias (3). P: Iglesias (2).

APPEARANCES & POINTS IN VODACOM CUP 2013

	EP Kings	Eagles	Bulldogs	Cavaliers	WP	Free State XV	Sharks XV	Pumas	Matches	Tries	Conversions	Penalties	Drop Goals	Points
Ramiro Moyano	15	11R	15	–	–	15	15	15	6	2	–	–	–	10
Santiago Cordero	14	15	11	–	–	–	–	–	3	1	–	–	–	5
Jeronimo de la Fuente	13	–	13	15R	13	–	–	12R	5	2	–	–	–	10
Javier Rojas	12	–	12	12	–	12	12	12	6	–	–	–	–	0
Manuel Montero	11	11	–	11	11	11	–	11	6	7	–	–	–	35
Benjamin Madero	10	13R	10	10R	10	–	10	13R	7	–	10	5	–	35
Martin Landajo	9	9R	9	9R	9	9R	9	9R	8	2	–	–	–	10
Lisandro Ahuali de Chazal	8	–	8	–	–	8	7R	–	4	–	–	–	–	0
Benjamin Macome	7	5R	7	7	–	7	7	7	7	1	–	–	–	5
Rodrigo Baez	6	–	6	7R	6	6	–	6	6	1	–	–	–	5
Mariano Galarza	5c	–	5c	5c	–	5c	5c	5c	6	1	–	–	–	5
Tomas Vallejos	4	4	–	4	4	–	4	–	5	–	–	–	–	0
Juan Gomez	3	–	3	–	3R	3	3R	3	6	–	–	–	–	0
Martin Garcia Veiga	2	2R	2	2R	2	–	2	2	7	1	–	–	–	5
Bruno Postiglioni	1	–	1	–	1	2R	1	1R	6	–	–	–	–	0
Emilano Coria	2R	2	2R	2	–	2	–	–	5	–	–	–	–	0
Ramiro Herrera	3R	3	–	3R	3	3R	–	3R	6	–	–	–	–	0
Rodrigo Bruno	4R	8	–	4R	5	4	–	4	6	2	–	–	–	10
Javier Ortega Desio	6R	6	7R	–	8R	6R	4R	–	6	–	–	–	–	0
Tomas Cubelli	9R	9c	9R	9	9R	9	9R	9	8	3	–	–	–	15
Santiago Gonzales Iglesias	10R	10	10R	10	10R	10	10R	10	8	2	17	7	–	65
Matias Orlando	13R	12	–	13	14	13	11R	13	7	–	–	–	–	0
Facundo Barrea	–	14	15R	–	–	14	14	14	5	2	–	–	–	10
Juan Pablo Estelles	–	13	–	14	12	–	13	–	4	2	–	–	–	10
Pablo Matera	–	7	–	–	–	–	–	–	1	–	–	–	–	0
Matias Allemanno	–	5	5R	–	4R	5R	–	8R	5	–	–	–	–	0
Francisco Piccinini	–	1	–	1	1R	1	1R	1	6	–	–	–	–	0
Ariel Castelina	–	1R	3R	3	–	–	3	–	4	–	–	–	–	0
Cesar Frutero	–	7R	4	–	–	–	–	–	2	1	–	–	–	5
Penalty try	–	–	–	–	–	–	–	–	–	2	–	–	–	10
Matias Masera	–	–	14	15	15	–	11	–	4	2	–	–	–	10
Leonardo Senatore	–	–	8	8c	7R	8	8	–	5	2	–	–	–	10
Tomas de la Vega	–	–	–	7	7	–	6	7R	4	1	–	–	–	5
Juan Ignacio Brex	–	–	–	–	12R	13R	–	–	2	–	–	–	–	0
33 Players									**176**	**37**	**27**	**12**	**0**	**275**

ABSA UNDER-21 CHAMPIONSHIP

Sweet revenge for WP

WP were deserved U21 champions.
Ashley Vlotman/Gallo Images

WESTERN PROVINCE WON THE Absa Under-21 Championship final in front of their home fans when a brace of tries from their captain, Josh Katzen, helped them to beat the Blue Bulls 30-23 in a curtain-raiser to the Absa Currie Cup final at Newlands.

It was just reward for WP and their head coach John Dobson, as the Cape side lost just once in 2013 despite losing a number of star players to injury. It was WP's first title since 2010.

WP finished their regular season with a staggering 54 log points from 12 matches – scoring 478 points and conceding just 193. In the process, they also scored the most tries – 97 – and conceded the fewest – 26 – of all the teams in the competition.

Flyhalf Tim Swiel, who scored 15 points in the final, ended as the competition's top point-scorer with 180, whilst outside backs Craig Barry (nine) and Devon Williams (eight) finished amongst the top try-scorers.

"It was a pleasing win for us against a star-studded Bulls team," said coach John Dobson, referring to the Bulls' selection of Springbok Jan Serfontein.

"We had some big injury disruptions heading into the play-offs, losing key men like Ollie Kebble, Gerbrandt Grobler and Jurie van Vuuren, but the guys stuck to their guns and showed great commitment. I am a proud coach, but (also) thankful to my fellow coaches and players."

The Blue Bulls led 13-9 just before the break but WP showed grit and an option to kick for the corner from a kickable penalty was rewarded when Katzen drove over behind his pack to give his side a 16-13 half-time lead.

The second half started with WP extending their lead with another Katzen try following a rolling maul; again a decision for the attacking line-out was rewarded. The visitors' Handre Pollard kicked a penalty but Pat Howard scored a converted try that forced the Bulls to play catch-up rugby.

Having to score twice forced the Blue Bulls into a more attacking pattern and the introduction of some fresh legs off the bench gave them impetus.

A converted try by replacement wing Dries Swanepoel gave the Blue Bulls a sniff, but WP held on for a deserved win.

ABSA UNDER-21 CUP PLAY-OFF RESULTS

FINALS RESULTS
FINALS - SECTION A
DHL Newlands Rugby Stadium, Cape Town. Saturday, 26 October. Referee: Rasta Rasivhenge
WP 30 (TRIES: Katzen (2), Howard. CONS: Swiel (3). PENS: Swiel (3).
Blue Bulls 23 (TRIES: Small-Smith, Swanepoel. CON: Pollard, Jantjies. PENS: Pollard (3).
WP: D Leyds, P Howard (C Barry, 71), J Kotzé, JP van Wyk, D Williams, TG Swiel, GHD Masimla (FJ Nel, 72), R Smid (E Bredenkamp, 70), S Notshe, JM Katzen (c), R Botha, J Kleyn, JCE Swanepoel (D Chowles, 52), SH Coetzee (M Willemse, 41), J Ackerman. Unused subs: C du Preez, JP Lewis.
Blue Bulls: JN Rossouw (D Swanepoel, 71), KS Mahlo, WT Small-Smith, JL Serfontein, T Ismaiel, H Pollard (A Jantjies, 70), R van Rooyen (C Engelbrecht, 52), C Davids (R Steenkamp, 70), J du Plessis (N van der Walt, 61), W Liebenberg (c), IP Herbst (yc, 50) (D Visser, 61), P Willemse, H van Wyk, GJ Visagie, J Forwood (A Beerwinkel, 67).

FINALS - SECTION B
Mbombela Stadium, Nelspruit. Friday, 11 October. Referee: Francois de Bruin.
EP Kings 59 (TRIES: Olivier, Tshidibi, Van der Westhuyzen, Barnard, Ludick, Punguzwa, Soyiwapi, Kuhle. CONS: Allerston (3), Hauptfleisch, Van Niekerk. PENS: Allerston (3).
Boland 19 (TRY: Pretorius. CON: Esau. PENS: Esau (4).
EP Kings: SS Soyizwapi, EP Barnard, M van Niekerk, S Gates (G Hauptfleisch, 67), SNP Msutwana (A Jho, 58-64), R Allerston, I Ludick (SQ Majola, 67), A Davis (SQ Punguzwa, 64), C Tshidibi, WL Smith, K Kaba (S Zaayman, 55), S Kuhle, MG Sofisa, DR van der Westhuyzen (c) (FP Roberts, 67), BH Olivier (P Stemmet, 25-33, 41).
Boland: JD Joseph, A Fortuin, R Swarts (SC Dyson, 60), G Moses, K Horsemend, A Esau, J de Koker (TJ Ramat, 61), C Pretorius (yc, 24-34), C Willemse (c), FD Basson, WW Schoor (E Claassen, 52, yc, 58-68), JSA Lambrechts (T Marsh, 60, yc, 69), CK Swarts (A Moerat, 52), KW Fikster (B Hunter, 52), SP Wessels (FH Langenhoven, 51). UNUSED SUB: J Slabber.

Team	P	W	L	D	PF	PA	Diff	TF	TA	BP<7	BP	Pts
Western Province	12	11	1	0	478	193	285	67	26	1	9	54
Blue Bulls	12	8	4	0	449	282	167	60	34	2	7	41
Sharks	12	8	4	0	423	301	122	56	39	1	7	40
Golden Lions	12	7	5	0	392	336	56	53	41	2	6	36
Free State	12	6	6	0	332	360	-28	44	48	1	6	31
Leopards	12	2	10	0	321	500	-179	42	69	1	6	15
Border	12	0	12	0	228	651	-423	33	98	0	3	3

Team	P	W	L	D	PF	PA	Diff	TF	TA	BP<7	BP	Pts
EP Kings	7	7	0	0	388	110	278	55	15	0	7	35
Boland	7	6	1	0	334	139	195	52	18	0	6	30
Limpopo Blue Bulls	7	5	2	0	284	136	148	44	16	2	6	28
Griquas	7	3	4	0	159	244	-85	22	38	2	3	17
Griffons	7	3	4	0	156	263	-107	21	43	0	3	15
Valke	7	2	5	0	156	316	-160	24	47	1	4	13
Pumas	7	2	5	0	156	224	-68	22	35	1	2	11
SWD	7	0	7	0	125	326	-201	18	46	1	2	3

ABSA CURRIE CUP REVIEW

ABSA UNDER-21 CUP *LEADING SCORERS*

50 POINTS OR MORE

PLAYER	Team	Tries	Conversions	Penalties	Drop Goals	Points
TG Swiel	WP	5	46	20	1	180
M Schmidt	Golden Lions	5	37	19	0	156
R Du Preez	Sharks	4	23	14	0	108
A Esau	Boland	3	31	7	0	98
R Allerston	EP Kings	0	33	10	0	96
MES Scholtz	Limpopo Blue Bulls	3	27	2	2	81
K Marais	Blue Bulls	1	23	8	1	78
W Gilbert	Leopards	1	19	9	1	73
T Jantjies	Blue Bulls	2	19	7	0	69

Tim Swiel. *Ashley Vlotman/Gallo Images*

SEVEN TRIES

S Soyizwapi	EP Kings	10	SQ Punguzwa	EP Kings	8
C Barry	Western Province	9	D Williams	Western Province	8
A Esterhuizen	Sharks	9	J Buys	Leopards	7
K Horsemend	Boland	9	JD Joseph	Boland	7
S de Wit	Golden Lions	8	WG Engelbrecht	Limpopo Blue Bulls	7
F Olivier	Valke	8	W Smith	EP Kings	7

ABSA UNDER-19 CHAMPIONSHIP

Perfect Blue Bulls take title

The future looks bright at the Blue Bulls.
Peter Heeger/Gallo Images

THE BLUE BULLS CROWNED A PERFECT season by beating the Golden Lions 35-23 in the Absa Under-19 Provincial Championship final, held at Newlands in Cape Town.

This was the team's 14th win of the season and they remained undefeated in the competition.

The Blue Bulls scored four tries to two and never surrendered their strong 21-9 lead at the break. The win was a perfect send-off for coach Paul Anthony, having lost the last three finals the team contested. Anthony will be off to Durban in 2014 to take up a position with the Sharks.

The Blue Bulls were on the scoreboard first when flyhalf Kobus Marais kicked an early penalty, cancelled out shortly afterwards by Golden Lions pivot Jako van der Walt.

Marais, who only kicked six from eleven, pulled his second penalty attempt, but slotted a longer range effort shortly after to punt his side back into a 6-3 lead, which increased to 9-3.

A good Golden Lions maul resulted in a penalty and replacement flyhalf Brendan Hewitt kicked his first penalty to close the gap.

A counter-attack from deep by winger Duncan Matthews resulted in Blue Bulls prop Pierre Schoeman crashing over for first try of match. Marais converted for a 16-6 lead.

Hewitt kicked a snap drop goal after good driving play by his forwards, but the Blue Bulls finished the half strongly when Keagon Gordon was worked over in the corner with second left to play in the half, giving the Blue Bulls a 21-9 lead.

A Duncan Matthews try, converted by Marais, made it 28-9 but the Golden Lions' scrumhalf Jan Meyer scored after a great dummy close to the line. The Lions scored another soon after through hooker Malcolm Marx and when Hewitt converted, the Lions were suddenly in touching distance again (28-23).

Marais pushed another penalty attempt to the right and the Blue Bulls again reverted to their running game to clinch matters. Another turn-over, followed by a strong run from Jesse Kriel saw Gordon over for his second try to seal the win.

ABSA UNDER-19 CUP PLAY-OFF RESULTS

FINALS RESULTS
FINALS - SECTION A
DHL Newlands Rugby Stadium, Cape Town, Saturday, 26 October. Referee: Rodney Bonaparte.
Golden Lions 23 (TRIES: Meyer, Marx. CONS: Hewit (2). PENS: Hewit, Van der Walt. DG: Hewit).
Blue Bulls 35 (TRIES: Gordon (2), Matthews, Schoeman. CONS: Marais (3). PENS: Marais (3).
Golden Lions: BD Herbst, C McKay, KP Marx (K van Dalen, 53), DJ Arries, C Nel (G van der Walt, 35), J van der Walt (B Hewit, 21), CJP Meyer (A Sihunu, 69), J Venter (rc, 54), CJ Brink, ST Mabuza, J-P du Preez (RD Snyman, 66), VK Sekekete (E Enslin, 58), PE Scholtz (Q Terblanche, 55), M Marx, D Smith (c) (FP van Heerden, 55).
Blue Bulls: J Kriel (c), DV Matthews, DD Kriel, R Janse van Resburg (L-RM van Wyk, 70), K Gordon (G May, 70), K Marais, J-P Smith (C Anthony, 69), CH Massyn (rc, 54), J Droste, HW Viljoen (N Ralepelle, 56), NJ Janse van Rensburg, J Basson (CH Cooper, 66), DL van der Westhuizen (W Louw, 56), CW Els (A van Wyk, 66), P Schoeman (P Strauss, 69).

FINALS - SECTION B
Mbombela Stadium, Nelspruit, Friday, 11 October. Referee: Christie du Preez.
Valke 40 (TRIES: Schutte, FJ Ueckermann, Van Zyl, MP Ueckermann. CONS: Venter (4). PENS: Venter (2). DG: Venter (2).
EP Kings 56 (TRIES: Malotana (3), Davids (3), Moore, Petersen. CONS: Davids (5). PENS: Davids (2)).
Valke: D Cloete (R Faber, 70), WR Thompson, EN Schoeman, MN Ueckermann, JF Malan (A Kotzé, 37), MC Venter (c), FJ Ueckermann (R Slippers, 62), J-C van Zyl (J Linde, 63), J-R Swanepoel, C Anderson, WJ Botes (P Terblanche, 38), D Steyl, GS van Niekerk (DJ Binneman, 62), J Roux, AS Schutte. Unused subs: E Ernst/E Snyman.
EP Kings: K Malotana, S Petersen, S Davids, L Nieuwoudt, SM Slater, AB Banfield, JDA Baggott (JF Nel, 62), E Slabbert, TW Paul, JH Schmidt, G Huisamen, S Ebersohn, ML Moore (c), J-P Jamieson (J Ford, 53), DG Murray. Unused replacements: S Qinela, BC Cafu, D Meyer, ED Fortuin, WB Swarts, MN Khumalo.

ABSA UNDER-19 LOG – SECTION A

Team	P	W	L	D	PF	PA	Diff	TF	TA	BP<7	BP	Pts
Blue Bulls	12	12	0	0	502	149	353	70	17	0	8	56
Golden Lions	12	8	4	0	294	239	55	37	31	2	5	39
Sharks	12	8	4	0	333	226	107	43	29	1	5	38
Leopards	12	5	7	0	297	367	-70	45	46	4	8	32
Western Province	12	4	7	1	301	289	12	41	39	3	4	25
Free State	12	4	7	1	260	376	-116	35	54	1	5	24
Border	12	0	12	0	130	471	-341	15	70	1	0	1

ABSA UNDER-19 LOG – SECTION B

Team	P	W	L	D	PF	PA	Diff	TF	TA	BP<7	BP	Pts
Valke	7	7	0	0	267	151	116	37	20	0	6	34
Boland	7	5	2	0	180	169	11	27	23	0	5	25
EP Kings	7	4	3	0	213	164	49	33	22	2	5	23
SWD	7	4	3	0	199	167	32	24	25	1	3	20
Griffons	7	3	4	0	187	229	-42	23	32	2	3	17
Limpopo Blue Bulls	7	2	5	0	209	190	19	32	23	3	3	14
Griquas	7	3	4	0	171	188	-17	22	26	2	3	8
Pumas	7	0	7	0	108	276	-168	14	41	1	0	1

ABSA UNDER-19 CUP LEADING SCORERS

50 POINTS OR MORE

PLAYER	Team	Tries	Conversions	Penalties	Drop Goals	Points
MC Venter	Valke	2	34	14	2	126
K Marais	Blue Bulls	3	35	13	0	124
B Hewit	Golden Lions	0	25	23	1	122
J-L Du Plessis	Sharks	5	17	18	1	116
C Smith	Western Province	1	25	13	1	97
D Taljaard	Griffons	3	14	13	0	82
L Eksteen	SWD	6	14	6	0	76
S Davids	EP Kings	4	15	4	0	62
W Boonzaaier	Boland	2	13	5	0	51

Keagon Gordon. Peter Heeger/Gallo Images

SEVEN TRIES

FJ Ueckermann	Valke	9	B Makhavhu	Leopards	7
M Cloete	Sharks	8	K Malotana	EP Kings	7
K Gordon	Blue Bulls	8	C Nel	Golden Lions	7
P Schoeman	Blue Bulls	8	J Rudolph	Leopards	7
D Stokes	Leopards	8			

AMATEUR TOURNAMENTS

Blue Bulls show who's boss

THE BLUE BULLS WERE CROWNED THE 2013 Amateur Provincial Champions in a thrilling year for amateur rugby as they ground out a 31-30 victory against Emerging Western Province at DHL Newlands in the grand finale to the season.

The teams met in the final round-robin match between the winners of the Southern (Emerging WP), Northern (Blue Bulls) and Central (KZN Duikers) Amateur Provincial tournaments, and with the Duikers suffering defeats in both their matches, the last game effectively doubled as an unofficial final.

The Blue Bulls had an edge in the first half and built up a 17-13 lead at the break. But Western Province fought back with intent and worked their way into a 30-26 lead late in the second half. This lead, however, was cancelled out as the Blue Bulls scored a valuable try to sneak into a 31-30 lead.

In a dramatic end to the match, WP were awarded a penalty with 30 seconds to go, which could have secured them a last-gasp victory, but the goal attempt was unsuccessful.

In the Sub-Union competitions, hosts the KwaZulu-Natal Wildebeest and Valke were crowned the Southern and Northern Sub-Union champions respectively.

The KwaZulu-Natal Wildebeest took top honours in Margate as they produced a scintillating performance in the final for an emphatic 41-12 victory against Eastern Province.

The KZN side entered the final high on confidence following their impressive 63-0 victory against Griquas, and they managed to transfer that onto the field in the final by producing a balanced effort on attack and defence. Boland also finished the tournament on a high as they powered their way to a convincing 82-16 victory to win the plate final.

In the Northern Sub-Union tournament in Kempton Park the Valke registered a hard-fought 24-18 victory against the Golden Lions to claim the title in front of their home crowd.

Both teams entered the final unbeaten and were closely matched on form, which was illustrated by each side managing to score only two tries. But the Valke were handed an edge as the Lions received a yellow card for a high tackle. They were again reduced to 14 men in the dying minutes after receiving an automatic red card following a second yellow-card offence.

The victory for the Valke marked their third win in the competition and earned them the bragging rights as the only unbeaten team.

The Blue Bulls, meanwhile, won the plate final thanks to their 40-23 victory against the Pumas in which they outscored the opposition five tries to four.

In the final amateur tournament, Sea Harvest emerged as winners of the annual South African Fish Industries tournament in Velddrif on the West Coast after grinding out a 16-12 victory in the final against Club Mykonos in front of close to 4000 spectators.

Sea Harvest booked their place in the final after pipping West Point 11-10 in the semi-final, while Club Mykonos defeated Pioneer Fishing 15-10.

Sea Harvest got off to a strong start and built up an encouraging 13-3 lead at the break. This served as a wake-up call for Club Mykonos, who staged a dramatic second-half comeback. But unfortunately for the team the 11 points scored by Sea Harvests' goal-kicker Ambrose Barends and a try by Donovan Williams was sufficient to cancel out the two tries and one conversion scored by Club Mykonos.

Elandsbaai won the plate final 15-3 against Coastal Link, while Cerebos-B emerged victorious in the shield final by defeating Oceana Brands 16-9 and I&J defeated the Walvis Bay Kudos 15-10 in the bowl.

BY ZEENA ISAACS

INTERPROVINCIAL SEVENS

Leopards, EP take titles

THE LEOPARDS MEN'S TEAM AND Eastern Province Women's team took top honours at the annual SARU Interprovincial Sevens at GWK Park in Kimberley.

The Leopards men defeated the Pumas 34-21 in the Cup final and the Blue Bulls beat Free State 31-14 to take the Plate final, while the Eastern Province Women's team beat Border 24-15 to win the trophy and the Free State Women won the Plate final after defeating the Pumas 17-12.

In the men's competition, the Leopards beat Western Province 26-14, Free State 24-7, Lowveld 31-7 and the Valke 17-12 to advance to the Cup semi-final against Eastern Province.

They continued their solid form in the semifinal and outplayed the Port Elizabeth team 19-5 to book their place in the final against the Pumas.

The Pumas had an equally impressive tournament featuring round-robin victories against Eastern Province, SWD, the Blue Bulls and Griquas, while they beat Western Province 28-7 to book their place in the final.

The Leopards scored six tries to four for a 34-21 victory and the title of SARU Interprovincial Sevens champions.

WOMEN'S INTERPROVINCIAL

Border make women's history

BORDER MADE HISTORY BY LIFTING the Women's Interprovincial trophy for the first time since the competition's inception in 2003.

The team registered an emphatic 41-8 victory against defending champions Western Province at the Buffalo City Municipal Stadium in East London to win the title, while Griquas defeated the Limpopo Blue Bulls 39-20 to win the B Division final.

Border entered their clash as narrow favourites with home-ground advantage and their strong defence counting in their favour. Western Province, meanwhile, had to undertake the journey by road to East London, which may have contributed to their disappointing display.

So dominant were the East London team that they racked up an impressive seven tries, while allowing WP to cross their tryline only once. As if that were not enough, all the Cape side's points were scored in the first half, with the home team controlling proceedings in the second half.

SECTION 6
THE PROVINCES

Blue Bulls Rugby Union **220**

Boland Rugby Union **228**

Border Rugby Union **236**

Eastern Province Rugby Union **244**

Free State Rugby Union **252**

Golden Lions Rugby Union **260**

Griffons Rugby Union **268**

Griqualand West Rugby Union **276**

KwaZulu-Natal Rugby Union **284**

Leopards Rugby Union **292**

Mpumalanga Rugby Union **300**

South Western Districts Rugby Football Union **308**

Valke Rugby Union **316**

Western Province Rugby Football Union **324**

Warren Whiteley of the Golden Lions drives into the tackle during their Vodacom Cup final clash against the Pumas. *Duif du Toit/Gallo Images*

BLUE BULLS RUGBY UNION

FOUNDED 1938
(as Northern Transvaal)
GROUND Loftus Versfeld, Pretoria
CAPACITY
50 000
ADDRESS
Kirkness Street, Sunnyside, Pretoria, 0002
POSTAL ADDRESS
PO Box 27856, Sunnyside, Pretoria, 0132
TELEPHONE NUMBER
012-420 0700
WEBSITE
www.thebulls.co.za
COLOURS
Sky blue jersey and socks, navy shorts
HEAD COACH
Frans Ludeke
CURRIE CUP COACH Pine Pienaar
VODACOM CUP COACH
Denzil Frans
CAPTAIN
Jono Ross
PRESIDENT
Louis Nel
COMPANY CEO
Barend van Graan
UNION CEO
Dr Eugene Hare

Stuttering season for 'green' Blue Bulls

THE VODACOM BLUE BULLS FAILED TO REACH THE ABSA Currie Cup Premier Division semi-finals for the first time in 12 years as an inexperienced group of players produced a predictably inconsistent season, although there were positive signals that the future is bright.

Coach Pine Pienaar and his charges were probably not expected to win the Currie Cup, given the exodus of big-name players over the preceding weeks and months, but few would've thought they'd be flirting so dangerously with the relegation zone during a season that never quite got going.

In the final analysis the men from Pretoria finished safely in fifth place in the six-team Premier Division, their three wins, a draw and six losses ensuring a six-point cushion between them and GWK Griquas, who not only grabbed the wooden spoon but were also relegated to the First Division.

The threat of relegation was certainly more front of mind than any thoughts of reaching the semi-finals: the Blue Bulls finished nine points adrift of the fourth-placed MTN Golden Lions.

Things started off well enough when the Blue Bulls visited Newlands in round one and came away with a 24-all draw against DHL WP, the reigning Currie Cup champions.

But their remaining nine games produced a neat sequence of nagging inconsistency: a win, followed by two losses – a 'one step forward, two steps back' cycle that would be repeated three times.

The Blue Bulls edged Griquas 15-9 in Pretoria in round two, only to suffer an ignominious 62-23 defeat to the Golden Lions at Loftus Versfeld the following week. A trip to Durban to face the Sharks only made matters worse when the Blue Bulls went down 34-18.

Back in Pretoria, the side bounced back against the Toyota Cheetahs but then lost at home to WP and to the Lions away.

A 52-10 win over Griquas in Kimberley in round eight ensured the Bulls would remain in the Premier Division, before their season ended with consecutive losses to the Sharks and Cheetahs.

Flyhalf Handré Pollard finished the season as the team's top point-scorer with 62, while centre Francois Venter was the Blue Bulls' top try-scorer with four touchdowns.

The fact that the Bulls could score only 24 tries in 10 matches tells its own story, although, in their defence, the team's negative points differential of just -28 suggests a team who never quite gave up, even if they were never going to win the title.

VODACOM CUP LOG POSITIONS

2013	3rd	2010	1st	2007	3rd	2004	3rd	2001	1st	1998	9th
2012	4th	2009	2nd	2006	3rd	2003	1st	2000	4th		
2011	2nd	2008	1st	2005	1st	2002	3rd	1999	7th		

ABSA CURRIE CUP LOG POSITIONS

2013	5th	2010	4th	2007	4th	2004	1st	2001	7th	1998	2nd
2012	4th	2009	3rd	2006	2nd	2003	1st	2000	10th	1997	5th
2011	5th	2008	2nd	2005	1st	2002	4th	1999	5th	1996	2nd

2013 RESULTS & SCORERS

VODACOM CUP Played **8** Won **5** Drawn **0** Lost **3** Points for **466** Points against **193** Tries for **64** Tries against **24** Winning Percentage **63%**

Date	Venue	Opponent	Result	Score	Referee	Scorers
Mrch 09	Kimberley	Griquas	WON	40-32	R Rasivhenge	T: Snyman (2), Mastriet, Swanepoel, Venter, Liebenberg. C: Jantjies (3), Pollard (2).
Mrch 16	Pretoria	Pumas	LOST	42-44	S Mayende	T: Swanepoel (2), Ismaiel, Mastriet, Smit. C: Jantjies (4). P: Jantjies (3).
Mrch 23	Johannesburg	Golden Lions	WON	54-26	S Mayende	T: Liebenberg, Janse van Rensburg, Ismaiel, Jantjies, Penalty try. C: Jantjies (5), Beyers. P: Jantjies (4).
April 06	Pretoria	Leopards	LOST	26-33	J Jaftha	T: Cook, Smit. C: Jantjies (2). P: Jantjies (4).
April 13	Springs	Valke	WON	74-14	L van der Merwe	T: Mastriet (4), Ismaiel (2), Liebenberg (2), Skosan (2), Blommetjies, Lindeque. C:Du Plessis (7).
April 20	Lephalale	Limpopo	WON	110-0	R Rasivhenge	T: Ismaiel (2), W du Plessis (2), Snyman (2), Greyling (2), Skosan (2), Blommetjies, Janse van Rensburg, Van Wyk, Liebenberg, Mastriet, Van der Walt. C: W du Plessis (15).
April 27	Pretoria	Griffons	WON	10-89	S Mayende	T: Swanepoel (2), Janse van Rensburg (2), Van der Walt (2), Blommetjies, Skosan, Mastriet, J du Plessis, Liebenberg, Jantjies, Willis. C: W du Plessis (8), Jantjies (4).
QUARTER-FINAL						
May 04	Pretoria	EP Kings	LOST	31-34	T Jonker	T: Swanepoel, Mastriet, Liebenberg, Short. C: Pollard (4). P: Pollard.

ABSA CURRIE CUP Played **10** Won **3** Lost **6** Drawn **1** Points for **225** Points against **253** Tries for **24** Tries against **28**

Date	Venue	Opponent	Result	Score	Referee	Scorers
Aug 10	Cape Town	WP	DREW	24-24	R Rasivhenge	T: Venter, Cook. C: Jantjies. P: Jantjies (4).
Aug 16	Pretoria	Griquas	WON	15-09	M vd Westhuizen	P: Visser (3), Jantjies (2).
Aug 24	Pretoria	Golden Lions	LOST	23-62	J Kaplan	T: Venter, Visser, Ismaiel. C: Visser. P: Visser, Jantjies.
Aug 31	Durban	Sharks	LOST	18-34	J Kaplan	T: Ndungane (2). C: Pollard. P: Pollard (2).
Sep 07	Pretoria	Cheetahs	WON	26-10	S Berry	T: Liebenberg, Willemse. C: Pollard (2). P: Pollard (4).
Sep 14	Pretoria	WP	LOST	18-29	M Jonker	T: Ross, Bullbring. C: Pollard. P: Pollard. D: Pollard.
Sep 21	Johannesburg	Golden Lions	LOST	26-35	S Berry	T: Basson (2), Venter, Paige. C: Jantjies (3).
Sep 28	Kimberley	Griquas	WON	52-10	Q Immelman	T: Small-Smith (2), Willemse (2), Visser, Du Plessis, Liebenberg. C: Pollard (4). P: Pollard (3).
Oct 04	Pretoria	Sharks	LOST	16-18	M vd Westhuizen	T: Venter. C: Pollard. P: Pollard (3).
Oct 12	Bloemfontein	Cheetahs	LOST	07-22	M Jonker	T: Van der Merwe. C: Pollard.

BLUE BULLS SQUAD IN 2013 / BLUE BULLS CAREER

PLAYER	Appearances	Tries	Conversions	Penalties	Drop Goals	Points	Career Matches	Career Tries	Conversions	Penalties	Drop Goals	Points
S (Shaun) Adendorff	3	–	–	–	–	0	3	–	–	–	–	0
LE (Louis) Albertse	6	–	–	–	–	0	6	–	–	–	–	0
BA (Bjorn) Basson	3	2	–	–	–	10	15	13	–	–	–	65
U (Ulrich) Beyers	13	0	1	0	0	2	27	3	1	0	1	20
CA (Clayton) Blommetjies	13	3	–	–	–	15	32	8	–	–	–	40
C (Christopher) Bosch	1	–	–	–	–	0	1	–	–	–	–	0
DJ (David) Bullbring	6	1	–	–	–	5	6	1	–	–	–	5
JG (Jean) Cook	9	2	–	–	–	10	17	3	–	–	–	15

BLUE BULLS RUGBY UNION

BLUE BULLS SQUAD IN 2013 | BLUE BULLS CAREER

PLAYER	Appearances	Tries	Conversions	Penalties	Drop Goals	Points	Career Matches	Career Tries	Conversions	Penalties	Drop Goals	Points
WHJ (Jacques) du Plessis	12	2	–	–	–	10	12	2	–	–	–	10
WNF (Willie) du Plessis	4	2	30	0	0	70	7	4	33	0	0	86
JJ (JJ) Engelbrecht	1	–	–	–	–	0	9	–	–	–	–	0
JJ (Jacques) Engelbrecht	8	–	–	–	–	0	8	–	–	–	–	0
MD (Dean) Greyling	6	2	–	–	–	10	69	7	–	–	–	35
GN (Grant) Hattingh	10	–	–	–	–	0	18	–	–	–	–	0
KS (Kurt) Haupt	2	–	–	–	–	0	2	–	–	–	–	0
CN (Cornell) Hess	4	–	–	–	–	0	39	–	–	–	–	0
TK (Travis) Ismaiel	10	7	–	–	–	35	10	7	–	–	–	35
WJ (Lohan) Jacobs	9	–	–	–	–	0	15	–	–	–	–	0
R (Rohan) Janse van Rensburg	6	4	–	–	–	20	6	4	–	–	–	20
A (Tony) Jantjies	9	2	22	18	0	108	14	3	32	24	0	151
FBC (Frik) Kirsten	7	–	–	–	–	0	47	–	–	–	–	0
JC (Jannes) Kirsten	1	–	–	–	–	0	1	–	–	–	–	0
W (Werner) Kruger	7	–	–	–	–	0	112	7	–	–	–	35
WA (Wiaan) Liebenberg	16	10	–	–	–	50	18	10	–	–	–	50
PJ (Piet) Lindeque	1	1	–	–	–	5	1	1	–	–	–	5
BG (Bandise) Maku	8	–	–	–	–	0	69	3	–	–	–	15
JJ (Kobus) Marais	2	–	–	–	–	0	2	–	–	–	–	0
S (Sampie) Mastriet	13	9	–	–	–	45	34	20	–	–	–	100
MT (Bongi) Mbonambi	13	–	–	–	–	0	19	–	–	–	–	0
MM (Morne) Mellet	5	–	–	–	–	0	23	2	–	–	–	10
WM (Waylon) Murray	6	–	–	–	–	0	6	–	–	–	–	0
AZ (Akona) Ndungane	7	2	–	–	–	10	62	27	–	–	–	135
MB (Burger) Odendaal	1	–	–	–	–	0	1	–	–	–	–	0
R (Rudi) Paige	14	1	–	–	–	5	18	2	–	–	–	10
H (Handre) Pollard	8	0	16	14	1	77	8	0	16	14	1	77
UJ (Jacques) Potgieter	1	–	–	–	–	0	9	2	–	–	–	10
SJP (Stephan) Pretorius	4	–	–	–	–	0	10	–	–	–	–	0
JM (Jono) Ross	10	1	–	–	–	5	22	2	–	–	–	10
JL (Jan) Serfontein	1	–	–	–	–	0	11	4	–	–	–	20
BG (Basil) Short	2	1	–	–	–	5	9	2	–	–	–	10
CD (Courtnal) Skosan	4	5	–	–	–	25	12	7	–	–	–	35
WT (William) Small-Smith	4	2	–	–	–	10	6	3	–	–	–	15
RA (Roelof) Smit	3	2	–	–	–	10	3	2	–	–	–	10
R (Ruan) Snyman	11	4	–	–	–	20	69	12	–	–	–	60
WJ (Wilhelm) Steenkamp	11	–	–	–	–	0	87	5	–	–	–	25
HD (Heinrich) Steyl	2	–	–	–	–	0	2	–	–	–	–	0
D (Dawie) Steyn	6	–	–	–	–	0	15	–	–	–	–	0
JK (Jade) Stiglingh	1	–	–	–	–	0	1	–	–	–	–	0
AE (Dries) Swanepoel	6	6	–	–	–	30	6	6	–	–	–	30
ENG (Emile) Temperman	1	–	–	–	–	0	1	–	–	–	–	0
JN (Jason) Thomas	1	–	–	–	–	0	1	–	–	–	–	0
SM (Sidney) Tobias	1	–	–	–	–	0	1	–	–	–	–	0
FJ (Francois) Tredoux	1	–	–	–	–	0	1	–	–	–	–	0
M (Marcel) van der Merwe	8	1	–	–	–	5	8	1	–	–	–	5
HB (Nardus) van der Walt	8	3	–	–	–	15	8	3	–	–	–	15
PS (Schalk) van Heerden	3	–	–	–	–	0	4	–	–	–	–	0
D (Damian) van Wyk	3	–	–	–	–	–	3	–	–	–	–	0
HJ (Hencus) van Wyk	4	1	–	–	–	5	5	1	–	–	–	5
JF (Francois) Venter	10	5	–	–	–	25	43	12	–	–	–	60
TJ (Jacques) Verwey	1	–	–	–	–	0	2	–	–	–	–	0
C-T (Callie) Visagie	4	–	–	–	–	0	4	–	–	–	–	0
GJ (Jaco) Visagie	4	–	–	–	–	0	4	–	–	–	–	0
PJ (Jurgen) Visser	10	2	1	4	0	24	37	7	2	5	0	54
FW (Willie) Wepener	3	–	–	–	–	0	25	1	–	–	–	5
MP (Mike) Williams	3	–	–	–	–	0	3	–	–	–	–	0
P (Paul) Willemse	12	3	–	–	–	15	12	3	–	–	–	15
VS (Vainon) Willis	1	1	–	–	–	5	12	3	–	–	–	15
NS (Ngubeko) Zulu	4	–	–	–	–	0	4	–	–	–	–	0
68 Players												

BLUE BULLS RUGBY UNION

APPEARANCES & POINTS IN VODACOM CUP 2013

	Griquas	Pumas	Golden Lions	Leopards	Valke	Limpopo	Griffons	EP Kings QF	Matches	Tries	Conversions	Penalties	Drop Goals	Points
Ulrich Beyers	15	13	15	15	–	13	–	–	5	–	1	–	–	2
Travis Ismaiel	14	14	14	14	14	14	–	14R	7	6	–	–	–	30
Dries Swanepoel	13	12	13	13	–	–	13	13	6	6	–	–	–	30
Francois Venter	12	–	–	–	–	–	–	–	1	1	–	–	–	5
Sampie Mastriet	11	11	–	–	11	11	11	11	6	9	–	–	–	45
Tony Jantjies	10	10	10	10	–	–	10R	–	5	2	18	11	–	79
Ruan Snyman	9	9	–	9	9	9	–	9R	6	4	–	–	–	20
Jean Cook	8	8	8	8	8	–	–	8	6	1	–	–	–	5
Nardus van der Walt	7	7	7	7	8R	8	8	7	8	3	–	–	–	15
Wiaan Liebenberg	6	6	6	–	6	6	6c	6	7	8	–	–	–	40
Wilhelm Steenkamp	5c	5c	5c	5c	5c	5c	–	5c	7	–	–	–	–	0
Paul Willemse	4	4	–	–	–	–	–	–	2	–	–	–	–	0
Stephan Pretorius	3	3	3	3R	–	–	–	–	4	–	–	–	–	0
Kurt Haupt	2	–	2R	–	–	–	–	–	2	–	–	–	–	0
Dawie Steyn	1	1	1	1R	–	–	1	1	6	–	–	–	–	0
Bongi Mbonambi	2R	–	–	–	2R	2R	2	2	5	–	–	–	–	0
Louis Albertse	3R	3R	3R	–	1R	3R	3	–	6	–	–	–	–	0
Cornell Hess	4R	4R	4	4	–	–	–	–	4	–	–	–	–	0
Jacques Verwey	6R	–	–	–	–	–	–	–	1	–	–	–	–	0
Rudy Paige	x	–	9	9R	–	–	9	9	4	–	–	–	–	0
Handre Pollard	10R	–	–	–	–	–	–	10	2	–	6	1	–	15
Damian van Wyk	11R	15	–	11R	–	–	–	–	3	–	–	–	–	0
Jason Thomas	–	2	–	–	–	–	–	–	1	–	–	–	–	0
Jaco Visagie	–	2R	–	–	–	–	2R	6R	3	–	–	–	–	0
Roelof Smit	–	7R	7R	6	–	–	–	–	3	2	–	–	–	10
Lohan Jacobs	–	9R	–	–	9R	9R	9R	–	4	–	–	–	–	0
Francois Tredoux	–	x	10R	–	–	–	–	–	1	–	–	–	–	0
Rohan Janse van Rensburg	–	15R	12	12	–	12	12	12	6	4	–	–	–	20
Heinrich Steyl	–	–	11	11	–	–	–	–	2	–	–	–	–	0
Callie Visagie	–	–	2	2	–	–	–	–	2	–	–	–	–	0
Ngubeko Zulu	–	–	4R	–	4R	5R	5R	–	4	–	–	–	–	0
Emile Temperman	–	–	9R	–	–	–	–	–	1	–	–	–	–	0
Jade Stiglingh	–	–	11R	–	–	–	–	–	1	–	–	–	–	0
Hencus van Wyk	–	–	–	3	3	3	–	3	4	1	–	–	–	5
Dean Greyling	–	–	–	1	1	1	–	–	3	2	–	–	–	10
Sidney Tobias	–	–	–	8R	–	–	–	–	1	–	–	–	–	0
Jannes Kirsten	–	–	–	4R	–	–	–	–	1	–	–	–	–	0
Kobus Marais	–	–	–	10R	10R	–	–	–	2	–	–	–	–	0
Clayton Blommetjies	–	–	–	–	15	15	15	15	4	3	–	–	–	15
Piet Lindeque	–	–	–	–	13	–	–	–	1	1	–	–	–	5
Burger Odendaal	–	–	–	–	12	–	–	–	1	–	–	–	–	0
Willie du Plessis	–	–	–	–	10	10	10	15R	4	2	30	–	–	70
Jacques Potgieter	–	–	–	–	7	–	–	–	1	–	–	–	–	0
Mike Williams	–	–	–	–	4	–	4	4	3	–	–	–	–	0
Willie Wepener	–	–	–	–	2	2	–	–	2	–	–	–	–	0
Courtnall Skosan	–	–	–	–	12R	13R	14	14	4	5	–	–	–	25
Jacques du Plessis	–	–	–	–	–	7	7	–	2	1	–	–	–	5
Schalk van Heerden	–	–	–	–	–	4	5	4R	3	–	–	–	–	0
Shaun Adendorff	–	–	–	–	–	7R	7R	7R	3	–	–	–	–	0
Christopher Bosch	–	–	–	–	–	14R	–	–	1	–	–	–	–	0
Basil Short	–	–	–	–	–	–	3R	1R	2	1	–	–	–	5
Vainon Willis	–	–	–	–	–	–	14R	–	1	1	–	–	–	5
Penalty try										1	–	–	–	5
52 Players									174	64	55	12	0	466

APPEARANCES & POINTS IN ABSA CURRIE CUP 2013

	WP	Griquas	Golden Lions	Sharks	Cheetahs	WP	Golden Lions	Griquas	Sharks	Cheetahs	Matches	Tries	Conversions	Penalties	Drop Goals	Points
Jurgen Visser	15	15	15	15	15	15	15R	15	15	15	10	2	1	4	–	24
Sampie Mastriet	14	14	14	14	14	14	–	14	x	–	7	–	–	–	–	0
Ulrich Beyers	13	13	13	12	13R	–	13	12R	12R	–	8	–	–	–	–	0
Francois Venter	12	12	12	–	12	12	12	12	12	12R	9	4	–	–	–	20
Travis Ismaiel	11	11	11	–	–	–	–	–	–	–	3	1	–	–	–	5
Tony Jantjies	10	10	10	–	–	–	10	–	–	–	4	0	4	7	0	29
Rudi Paige	9	9	9R	9R	9R	9	9	9	9	9	10	1	–	–	–	5
Jono Ross	8c	8c	8c	8c	8c	8c	8c	8c	8c	6c	10	1	–	–	–	5
Jacques du Plessis	7	7	7	7	7R	7	7	7	7	7	10	1	–	–	–	5
Wiaan Liebenberg	6	6	6	6	6	6	6	6	6	–	9	2	–	–	–	10
Grant Hattingh	5	5	5	5	5	5	5R	5R	5R	5R	10	–	–	–	–	0
Paul Willemse	4	4	4	4	4	4	4	4	4	4	10	3	–	–	–	15
Frik Kirsten	3	–	–	3	3	3	1R	–	3	3	7	–	–	–	–	0
Willie Wepener	2	–	–	–	–	–	–	–	–	–	1	–	–	–	–	0
Morne Mellett	1	1	1	1	–	–	1	–	–	–	5	–	–	–	–	0
Callie Visagie	2R	2	–	–	–	–	–	–	–	–	2	–	–	–	–	0
Marcel van der Merwe	1R	3R	1R	–	1	1	–	1	1	1	8	1	–	–	–	5
Wilhelm Steenkamp	5R	5R	5R	–	–	–	5	–	–	–	4	–	–	–	–	0
Jean Cook	7R	7R	–	–	–	–	–	–	–	8R	3	1	–	–	–	5
Ruan Snyman	9R	9R	9	9	9	–	–	–	–	–	5	–	–	–	–	0
Waylon Murray	13R	12R	11R	13	13	13	–	–	–	–	6	–	–	–	–	0
Clayton Blommetjies	11R	10R	10R	15R	11R	15R	15	11R	–	14R	9	–	–	–	–	0
Werner Kruger	–	3	3	1R	1R	–	3	3	–	1R	7	–	–	–	–	0
Bongi Mbonambi	–	2R	2	2	2	2	–	2R	2	2	8	–	–	–	–	0
Bandise Maku	–	–	2R	2R	2R	2R	2	2	2R	2R	8	–	–	–	–	0
Jacques Engelbrecht	–	–	7R	8R	7	7R	4R	6R	6R	8	8	–	–	–	–	0
Akhona Ndungane	–	–	–	11	11	11	14	11	14	14	7	2	–	–	–	10
Handre Pollard	–	–	–	10	10	10	–	10	10	10	6	0	10	13	1	62
David Bullbring	–	–	–	5R	5R	5R	–	5	5	5	6	1	–	–	–	5
Tian Schoeman	–	–	–	x	–	–	–	–	–	–	0	0	–	–	–	0
Dean Greyling	–	–	–	–	–	–	1R	–	3R	1R	3	–	–	–	–	0
Lohan Jacobs	–	–	–	–	–	–	9R	9R	9R	9R	5	–	–	–	–	0
William Small-Smith	–	–	–	–	–	–	13R	13R	13	13	4	2	–	–	–	10
Bjorn Basson	–	–	–	–	–	–	11	–	11	11	3	2	–	–	–	10
Jaco Visagie	–	–	–	–	–	–	2R	–	–	–	1	–	–	–	–	0
JJ Engelbrecht	–	–	–	–	–	–	–	–	–	13	1	–	–	–	–	0
Jan Serfontein	–	–	–	–	–	–	–	–	–	12	1	–	–	–	–	0
37 Players											218	24	15	24	1	225

LIMPOPO BLUE BULLS APPEARANCES & POINTS IN VODACOM CUP 2013

	Griffons	Leopards XV	Griquas	Valke	Pumas	Blue Bulls	Golden Lions	Matches	Tries	Conversions	Penalties	Drop Goals	Points
Robin Goliath	15	11	–	–	10R	10R	15	5	–	–	–	–	0
Ruan Muller	14	13	13	10	13	13	–	6	1	–	–	–	5
Werner van Heese	13	–	–	13	–	–	–	2	–	–	–	–	0
Ludwig Gossmann	12	10	10	13R	10	10	10	7	–	–	–	–	0
Damian Flink	11	14	11	11	–	11R	11	6	–	–	–	–	0
Bronwyn Craill	10	15	15	15	–	15	13	6	–	1	5	–	17
Theyman Jongbloed	9	9	–	–	–	–	–	2	–	–	–	–	0
Jaco Swart	8c	8c	8c	8c	8c	–	8R	6	–	–	–	–	0
Arrie van der Berg	7	7	7	7	7	7	8	7	–	–	–	–	0
Jaco Louw	6	6	–	6	–	6R	7c	5	–	–	–	–	0
Wiehann Uys	5	5	5	5	–	–	–	4	–	–	–	–	0
JJ de Lange	4	4	4	4	6	–	6	6	–	–	–	–	0
Bernardt Groenewald	3	3	3R	2	2	2R	–	6	1	–	–	–	5
Chris Crous	2	2	–	–	–	–	–	2	–	–	–	–	0
Johan Coetzer	1	1	1	1	1	1	1	7	–	–	–	–	0
Dickson Ndiweni	2R	–	2R	–	8R	8c	2	5	–	–	–	–	0
Thulani Mathonsi	16R	3R	3	3	3	3	3	7	–	–	–	–	0
Marius Swanepoel	x	–	–	–	–	–	–	0	–	–	–	–	0
Willem Snyman	6R	–	–	–	–	–	–	1	–	–	–	–	0
Andries Botha	9R	9R	–	–	–	–	–	2	–	–	–	–	0
Wickus Davel	12R	12	12	12	12	–	14R	6	–	–	–	–	0
Justin Pelser	11R	14R	14	12R	12R	12	12	7	–	–	–	–	0
JP Ferreira	–	2R	2	–	2R	2	–	4	–	–	–	–	0
Roedolf Grobler	–	4R	–	5R	4	4	4	5	1	–	–	–	5
Photole Mokoto	–	20R	–	–	5R	12R	18R	4	–	–	–	–	0
Stefan van Wyk	–	12R	9	11R	11R	9R	9R	6	–	–	–	–	0
Sinthamdile Memese	–	–	6	–	–	–	–	1	–	–	–	–	0
Shane Mienie	–	–	1R	1R	4R	–	–	3	–	–	–	–	0
Phanuel Nkuna	–	–	x	8R	5	5	5	4	–	–	–	–	0
Nollie Davel	–	–	9R	9	9	9	9	5	–	–	–	–	0
Pieter Booyse	–	–	12R	–	11	11	–	3	–	–	–	–	0
Deano Kruger	–	–	x	–	–	–	–	0	–	–	–	–	0
Rory Cresswell	–	–	–	4R	–	–	–	1	–	–	–	–	0
Mynhardt Smith	–	–	–	14	14	14	–	3	–	–	–	–	0
Zander Byleveldt	–	–	–	–	15	–	–	1	–	–	–	–	0
Cornelius van Greyen	–	–	–	–	–	6	–	1	–	–	–	–	0
Walter Pretorius	–	–	–	–	–	4R	4R	2	–	–	–	–	0
Jean Pieters	–	–	–	–	–	–	14	1	–	–	–	–	0
Albertus Seegers	–	–	–	–	–	–	2R	1	–	–	–	–	0
Willie Louw	–	–	–	–	–	–	22R	1	–	–	–	–	0
40 Players								**151**	**3**	**1**	**5**	**0**	**32**

LIMPOPO BLUE BULLS RESULTS & SCORERS IN 2013

VODACOM CUP Played **7** Won **0** Drawn **0** Lost **7** Points For **32** Points Against **781** Tries For **3** Tries Against **19**

Date	Venue	Opponent	Result	Score	Referee	Scorers
Mrch 9	Polokwane	Griffons	LOST	14-50	N Rocono	T: Groenewald. P: Craill (3).
Mrch 15	Potchefstroom	Leopards XV	LOST	3-113	R Rasivhenge	P: Craill.
Mrch 23	Groblersdal	Griquas	LOST	5-124	L Jam	T: Muller.
April 6	Tzaneen	Valke	LOST	07-69	S Geldenhuys	T: Grobler. C: Craill.
April 13	Nelspruit	Pumas	LOST	0-154	T Jonker	
April 20	Lephalale	Blue Bulls	LOST	0-110	R Rasivhenge	
April 27	Alberton	Golden Lions	LOST	3-161	L Pretorius	P: Craill.

BLUE BULLS RUGBY UNION

ABSA UNDER-21 CHAMPIONSHIP (Runner-up, 2nd, Section A)

Played	Won	Drawn	Lost	Points for	Points against	Tries for	Tries against	Winning %
14	9	0	5	508	325	66	38	64,00%

RESULTS: Bt Leopards (a) 59-17. Lost WP (a) 6-14. Bt Border (a) 66-14. Bt Lions (h) 26-20. Bt Free State (h) 40-27. Lost Sharks (a) 15-19. Bt Leopards (h) 48-33. Lost WP (h) 21-32. Bt Border (h) 70-19. Bt Lions (a) 40-25. Lost Sharks (a) 29-35. Bt Free State (a) 29-27. SEMI FINAL Bt Sharks (h) 36-13. FINAL Lost WP (a) 23-30.

SCORERS: 78 Kobus Marais (1t,23c,8p,1d); 65 Tony Jantjies (3t,16c,6p); 52 Handre Pollard (1t,7c,11p); 25 Roelof Smit, Travis Ismaiel, Hencus van Wyk, Jacques Rossouw, Dries Swanepoel (5t each); 24 Rudi van Rooyen (4t,2c]; 15 Nardus van der Walt, Carlo Engelbrecht (3t each); 10 Jade Stiglingh, Jermaine Kleinsmith, Damian van Wyk, Christopher Bosch, Jaco Visagie, Shaun Adendorff, Burger Odendaal (2t each); 5 Christoph Gouws, Kefentse Mahlo, Rohan Janse van Rensburg, Paul Willemse, Lwandile Sompontsha, Ruan Steenkamp, Irne Herbst, Dennis Visser, Justin Forwood, Jan Serfontein, Wiaan Liebenberg, William Small-Smith (1t each); 4 Malcolm Theo (2c).

ABSA U19 CHAMPIONSHIP (Champions, 1st, Section A)

Played	Won	Drawn	Lost	Points for	Points against	Tries for	Tries against	Winning %
14	14	0	0	574	193	79	22	100,00%

RESULTS: Bt Leopards (a) 61-14. Bt WP (a) 34-10. Bt Border (a) 56-7. Bt Lions (h) 15-12. Bt Free State (h) 56-21. Bt Sharks (a) 28-19. Bt Leopards (h) 48-12. Bt WP (h) 46-16. Bt Border (h) 59-3. Bt Lions (a) 24-8. Bt Sharks (h) 23-13. Bt Free State (a) 52-14. SEMI FINAL Bt Leopards (h) 37-21. FINAL Bt Lions (a) 35-23.

SCORERS: 126 Kobus Marais (3t,36c,13p); 45 Keagon Gordon (9t); 42 Jesse Kriel (5t,7c,1p); 40 Pierre Schoeman (8t); 31 Juan-Phillip Smith (1t,10c,2p); 30 Rohan Janse van Rensburg,Daniel Kriel (6t each); 25 Ganfried May, Hendrik Viljoen (5t each); 23 Leight-on-Ras van Wyk (3t,4c); 20 Duncan Matthews (4t); 20 Jacobus Wolmarans (1t,6c,1p); 15 Cornelius Els (3t); 10 Arno van Wyk, Jean Droste, Arend Bannink, Christiaan van Dijk, Dayan van der Westhuizen, Wilco Louw, Christiaan Massyn (2t each); 5 Nicolaas Janse van Rensburg, Nqoba Mxoli, Riekert Hattingh, Ngwako Ralepelle, Marcus Kleinbooi, Petrus Strauss (1t each); 2 Joshua Stander (1c).

ABSA UNDER-21 CHAMPIONSHIP (3rd, Section B)
Limpopo Blue Bulls

Played	Won	Drawn	Lost	Points for	Points against	Tries for	Tries against	Winning %
8	5	0	3	306	161	48	20	63,00%

RESULTS: Bt SWD (a) 60-0. Bt Pumas (h) 53-19. Lost Boland (h) 25-31. Bt Griffons (a) 41-20. Bt Valke (h) 48-10. Bt Griquas (a) 24-19. Lost EP (h) 33-37. SEMI FINAL Lost Boland (a) 22-25.

SCORERS: 81 Marcel Scholtz (3t,27c,2p,2d); 35 Willem Engelbrecht (7t); 25 Werner van Heese (5t); 15 Bernard Nortje, Donovan O'Grady, Oskar Calitz, Pieter Kruger, James Wepener (3t each); 10 Corne Ras, Trent Williams, Jonty Shelton, Robey Leibrandt (2t each); 5 Wolta Mtsweni, Anrich du Plessis, Divan Nel, Graham Logan, Jan-Boland Deysel, Primo Ncube, Barend Wessels, Daniel Hart, Bernhardt Gemholtz, Jerome Bastick (1t each).

ABSA UNDER-19 CHAMPIONSHIP (7th, Section B)
Limpopo Blue Bulls

Played	Won	Drawn	Lost	Points for	Points against	Tries for	Tries against	Winning %
7	2	0	5	209	190	32	23	29,00%

RESULTS: Bt SWD (a) 18-16. Bt Pumas (h) 62-14. Lost Boland (h) 18-22. Lost Griffons (a) 38-40. Lost Valke (h) 18-32. Lost Griquas (a) 38-40. Lost EP (h) 17-26.

SCORERS: 25 Zander Richter (5t); 24 William Parker (1t,8c,1p); 20 Alistair van Schoor (4t); 19 Ruan Booyse (1t,4c,2p); 18 Wade Worthington (3t,1p); 15 Stephan Smith, Willie Lloyd (3t each); 11 Casper du Plessis (4c,1p); 10 Visscher Strydom, Kallie Jantjies (2t each); 5 Chris du Plooy, Dean van Heerden, Ettienne du Plessis, Shaun Potgieter, Michael van Damme, Ruan Brink, Johannes Smit, Sipho Siboza (1t each); 2 Marinus Gubitz (1c).

AMATEUR CHAMPIONSHIP
Assupol Blue Bulls (Winners, North Section, Pretoria)

Played	Won	Drawn	Lost	Points for	Points against	Winning %
3	3	0	0	101	53	100%

RESULTS: Bt Pumas 49-10. Bt Leopards 28-20. Bt Lions 24-23. Playoffs: Bt KZN 56-18. FINAL: Bt WP 31-30.

Assupol Blue Bulls XV (Winners Plate, North Section, Pretoria)

Played	Won	Drawn	Lost	Points for	Points against	Winning %
3	2	0	1	108	66	66%

RESULTS: Lost Lions 27-29. Bt Limpopo 41-17. Bt Pumas 40-20.

Blue Bulls Limpopo (North Section, Pretoria)

Played	Won	Drawn	Lost	Points for	Points against	Winning %
3	1	0	2	62	96	33%

RESULTS: Lost Valke 18-31. Lost Blue Bulls XV 17-41. Bt Lowveld 27-24.

BLUE BULLS RUGBY UNION

SUB-UNION CHAMPIONSHIP
Assupol Blue Bulls (North Section, Kempton Park)

Played	Won	Drawn	Lost	Points for	Points against	Winning %
3	2	0	1	111	85	66%

RESULTS: Lost Leopard 23-33. Bt Blue Bulls Limpopo 48-29. Bt Pumas 40-23.

Blue Bulls Limpopo (North Section, Kempton Park)

Played	Won	Drawn	Lost	Points for	Points against	Winning %
3	1	0	2	172	99	33%

RESULTS: Lost Valke 40-44. Lost Blue Bulls 29-48. Bt Lowveld 103-7.

BLUE BULLS RECORDS

MATCH RECORDS

Biggest win	147-8	vs. South Western Districts (CC) *(Currie Cup Record)* Polokwane	1996
Heaviest defeat	13-57	vs. Transvaal (CC) Johannesburg	1994
Highest score	147	vs. South Western Districts (147-8, CC) Polokwane	1996
Most points conceded	64	vs. Wellington Hurricanes (32-64) New Plymouth	1997
Most tries	23	vs. South Western Districts (147-8, CC) *(Currie Cup Record)* Polokwane	1996
Most points by a player	40	CP Steyn vs. SWD Eagles (CC) Pretoria	2000
Most tries by a player	7	J Olivier vs. SWD (CC) *(Currie Cup Record)* Polokwane	1996
Most conversions by a player	14	LR Sherrell vs. SWD (CC) *(Currie Cup Record)* Polokwane	1996
	15	W du Plessis vs Limpopo (VC) Lephalele	2013
Most penalties by a player	9	JH Kruger vs. Western Province (CC) *(SA Record)* Pretoria	1996
	9	DJ Hougaard vs. Western Province (CC) *(SA Record)* Pretoria	2002
Most drop goals by a player	5	HE Botha vs. Natal *(CC Record)* Pretoria	1992

SEASON RECORDS

Most team points	1193	28 matches	1996
Most team points in Currie Cup	783	13 matches	1997
Most points by a player	361	CP Steyn	1999
Most Currie Cup points	268	JW Heunis (Currie Cup Record)	1989
Most team tries	142	28 matches	2004
Most tries by a player	25	PJ Spies	1975
Most Currie Cup tries by a player	18	E Botha	2004

CAREER RECORDS

Most appearances	184	SB Geldenhuys	1977-1989
Most points	2511	HE Botha (179 matches)	1977-1992
Most tries	85	DE Oosthuysen (140 matches)	1986-1994

HONOURS

ABSA Currie Cup	1946, 1956, 1968, 1969, 1971 (shared), 1973, 1974, 1975, 1977, 1978, 1979 (shared), 1980, 1981, 1987, 1988, 1989 (shared), 1991, 1998, 2002, 2003, 2004, 2006 (shared), 2009.
Lion Cup	1985, 1990, 1991
Bankfin Cup	2000
Vodacom Cup	2001, 2008, 2009

BOLAND RUGBY UNION

FOUNDED
1939
GROUND
Boland Stadium
CAPACITY
11 000
ADDRESS
50 Fontein Street,
Wellington
POSTAL ADDRESS
PO Box 127, Wellington,
7654
**TELEPHONE
NUMBER**
021-873 2317
WEBSITE
www.bolandrugby.com
COLOURS
Pink, black and white
jersey, black shorts
**CURRIE CUP
COACH**
Eugene Eloff
**VODACOM CUP
COACH**
Abe Davids
CAPTAIN
Franzel September
PRESIDENT
Francois Davids
CEO
Willie Small

Cavaliers get back on the horse

THE BOLAND CAVALIERS BOUNCED BACK FROM A NIGHTMARE 2012 season to finish one position shy of the Absa Currie Cup First Division semi-finals in 2013.

Six wins and a draw, and fifth position on the log, was a satisfactory and encouraging turnaround for coach Loffie Eloff and his charges, given the highs and lows – in that order – of the previous two seasons.

They say a year is a long time in South African rugby and for Boland supporters double that time must have seemed like an eternity, for the Cavaliers romped to the First Division title as recently as 2011 when they beat their man rivals, the EP Kings, by an astonishing 31 points in the final.

But the success didn't last, and the Cavaliers meekly surrendered their title when they won just three matches en route to a sixth-placed finish in 2012.

Against this backdrop, nothing less than a noticeable improvement in 2013 would do, and the Cavaliers, while never exactly setting the world alight, duly delivered.

Things started disastrously when they lost 45-17 to the Leopards in round one – in Wellington. But the Cavaliers pulled themselves together and won their next four matches on the trot – including a 30-23 win over the EP Kings in Port Elizabeth – to lower their supporters' blood pressure.

But any hopes of a second title in three years were quickly shown to be optimistic, as the Cavaliers' inconsistency resulted in a sequence of mid-season wins and losses.

A 35-30 win over the SWD Eagles in round nine looked to have laid the platform for a run into the semi-finals, but the Cavaliers then conspired to lose four and draw one of their last five matches to see them finish nine points behind the fourth-placed Eagles.

The hammer blow came in round 11, when they lost 28-21 to the Valke, who would eventually finish with the wooden spoon.

Despite the disappointment of missing out on the play-offs, a number of players had seasons to remember.

Fullback Jaquin Jansen was his consistent self at fullback and scored four tries in 11 matches, while wing Brendon April was the side's top try-scorer with seven touchdowns. Eric Zana was equally impressive at flyhalf and fullback and also kicked 60 points.

Up front, utility forward PJ van Zyl – who played in every match and alternated between eighthman, blindside flank and lock for good measure – scored four tries as did flanker and inspirational skipper Franzel September.

Clemen Lewis throws in for the Boland Cavaliers.
Carl Fourie/Gallo Images

BOLAND RUGBY UNION

VODACOM CUP LOG POSITIONS

2013	15th	2010	3rd	2007	6th	2004	8th	2001	2nd	1998	6th
2012	9th	2009	11th	2006	6th	2003	7th	2000	8th		
2011	11th	2008	5th	2005	2nd	2002	2nd	1999	3rd		

ABSA CURRIE CUP LOG POSITIONS

2013	11th	2010	11th	2007	7th	2004	9th	2001	9th	1998	10th
2012	12th	2009	8th	2006	10th	2003	10th	2000	5th	1997	7th
2011	9th	2008	7th	2005	6th	2002	13th	1999	12th	1996	8th

2013 RESULTS & SCORERS

VODACOM CUP Played **7** Won **1** Drawn **1** Lost **5** Points for **151** Points against **256** Tries for **19** Tries against **32** Winning% **14%**

Date	Venue	Opponent	Result	Score	Referee	Scorers
Mrch 09	Ceres	WP	DREW	17-17	J Sylvestre	T: Constant, Buckle. C: Croy, Jansen. P: Jansen.
Mrch 16	Bloemfontein [1]	Free State XV	WON	27-23	A Sehlako	T: Halvorsen (2), Adams. C: Croy (2), G April. P: Croy (2).
Mrch 23	Robertson	SWD Eagles	LOST	12-44	J Sylvestre	T: Trytsman, Van Zyl. C: G April
April 06	Wellington	Pampas XV	LOST	23-65	M Kemp	T: B April, Roberts, Adams, Pretorius. P: Croy.
April 12	Durban [2]	Sharks XV	LOST	24-54	Q Immelman	T: Jansen, Pretorius, Penalty try. C: Croy (3). P: Croy
April 19	East London	Border	LOST	25-26	L vd Merwe	T: Pretorius (2), Gerber. C: Croy (2). P: Croy (2).
April 27	Malmesbury	EP Kings	LOST	23-27	G de Bruin	T: Constant, Van der Merwe. C: Jansen (2). P: Jansen (3).

[1] CUT Field, [2] Kings Park 1.

ABSA CURRIE CUP Played **14** Won **6** Lost **7** Drawn **1** Points for **329** Points against **393** Tries for **45** Tries against **54** Winning% **43%**

Date	Venue	Opponent	Result	Score	Referee	Scorers
Jun 29	Wellington	Leopards	LOST	17-45	B Crouse	T: Gerber, Jansen. C: Zana (2). P: Zana.
Jul 06	George	SWD	WON	22-17	M vd Westhuizen	T: Gerber, Astle, Jordaan. C: Olivier (2). P: Olivier.
Jul 12	Wellington	Border	WON	22-20	Q Immelman	T: Jansen (2), September. C: Olivier (2). P: Olivier.
Jul 19	Wellington	Valke	WON	20-07	M vd Westhuizen	T: Van der Merwe (2), September. C: Olivier. P: Olivier.
Jul 26	Port Elizabeth	EP Kings	WON	30-23	J Jaftha	T: Jansen, Van Zyl, Jordaan. C: Olivier (3). P: Olivier (3).
Aug 02	Wellington	Pumas	LOST	05-35	L vd Merwe	T: Jordaan.
Aug 10	Welkom	Griffons	WON	55-35	L Legoete	T: April (2), Williams, Lewis, Zana, Van Zyl, Pretorius, Pienaar. C: Zana (6). P: Zana.
Aug 17	Potchefstroom	Leopards	LOST	17-22	S Berry	T: April, Williams, Francke. C: Zana.
Aug 24	Wellington	SWD	WON	35-30	Q Immelman	T: Gerber, Williams, September, Francke. C: Zana (3). P: Zana (3).
Aug 30	East London	Border	LOST	19-21	L vd Merwe	T: September, Van Zyl. P: Zana (3).
Sep 07	Kempton Park	Valke	LOST	21-28	Q Immelman	T: Bester, April, Van Zyl. C: Jansen (3).
Sep 13	Wellington	EP Kings	LOST	19-40	J Kaplan	T: Kriel (2), Pretorius. C: Zana (2)
Sep 21	Nelspruit	Pumas	LOST	21-44	M vd Westhuizen	T: Gerber, Francke, Kebe. C: Olivier (2), Zana.
Sep 27	Wellington	Griffons	DREW	26-26	T Jonker	T: April (3), Kruger. C: Zana (3).

BOLAND RUGBY UNION

BOLAND SQUAD IN 2013 — BOLAND CAREER

PLAYER	Appearances	Tries	Conversions	Penalties	Drop Goals	Points	Career Matches	Career Tries	Conversions	Penalties	Drop Goals	Points
KM (Keenan) Abrahams	1	–	–	–	–	0	1	–	–	–	–	0
TF (Tythan) Adams	8	2	–	–	–	10	8	2	–	–	–	10
BT (Brendon) April	18	8	–	–	–	40	66	34	–	–	–	170
GG (Garth) April	4	–	2	–	–	4	4	–	2	–	–	4
J-C (JC) Astle	13	1	–	–	–	5	13	1	–	–	–	5
A (Alwyn) Bester	10	1	–	–	–	5	64	10	–	–	–	59
CJ (Chris) Buckle	3	1	–	–	–	5	12	2	–	–	–	10
N (Nolan) Clark	9	–	–	–	–	0	28	3	–	–	–	15
A (Ashton) Constant	6	2	–	–	–	10	48	6	–	–	–	30
R (Ricardo) Croy	13	–	8	6	–	34	25	–	14	15	–	73
DL (Dual) Erasmus	2	–	–	–	–	0	2	–	–	–	–	0
R (Reinhardt) Erwee	3	–	–	–	–	0	3	–	–	–	–	0
AA (Ashley) Esau	1	–	–	–	–	0	1	–	–	–	–	0
BA (Bradley) Fortuin	20	–	–	–	–	0	20	–	–	–	–	0
A (Armon) Fourie	1	–	–	–	–	0	1	–	–	–	–	0
JC (Jonathan) Francke	20	3	–	–	–	15	55	16	–	–	–	80
JA (Braam) Gerber	19	5	–	–	–	25	46	7	–	–	–	35
G (Gerhardus) Goosen	1	–	–	–	–	0	1	–	–	–	–	0
T (Thor) Halvorsen	10	2	–	–	–	10	39	3	–	–	–	15
PF (Francois) Hanekom	18	–	–	–	–	0	32	–	–	–	–	0
AJ (Adri) Jacobs	2	–	–	–	–	0	2	–	–	–	–	0
ML (Marko) Janse van Rensburg	4	–	–	–	–	0	4	–	–	–	–	0
J (Jacquin) Jansen	17	5	6	4	–	49	66	21	60	39	–	342
Z (Zandré) Jordaan	10	3	–	–	–	15	66	21	–	–	–	105
NL (Ntando) Kebe	21	1	–	–	–	5	21	1	–	–	–	5
JJ (Hanno) Kitshoff	8	–	–	–	–	0	15	–	–	–	–	0
JF (Johannes) Kleinhans	1	–	–	–	–	0	1	–	–	–	–	0
AJ (Jacques) Kotze	13	–	–	–	–	0	13	–	–	–	–	0
J (Jason) Kriel	1	2	–	–	–	10	1	2	–	–	–	10
R (Rossouw) Kruger	11	1	–	–	–	5	41	3	–	–	–	15
C (Clemen) Lewis	17	1	–	–	–	5	102	7	–	–	–	35
S (Sabelo) Nhlapo	8	–	–	–	–	0	8	–	–	–	–	0
L (Len) Olivier	6	–	10	6	–	38	6	–	10	6	–	38
WC (Wynand) Pienaar	6	1	–	–	–	5	6	1	–	–	–	5
UD (Ulrich) Pretorius	16	6	–	–	–	30	16	6	–	–	–	30
CD (Cheslyn) Roberts	11	1	–	–	–	5	11	1	–	–	–	5
RD (Ricky) Schroeder	10	–	–	–	–	0	10	–	–	–	–	0
FJ (Franzel) September	18	4	–	–	–	20	65	24	–	–	–	120
CG (Callie) Steenkamp	1	–	–	–	–	0	1	–	–	–	–	0
JA (Andries) Truter	2	–	–	–	–	0	2	–	–	–	–	0
AM (Albert) Trytsman	3	1	–	–	–	5	3	1	–	–	–	5
JL (Lodewyk) Uys	7	–	–	–	–	0	7	–	–	–	–	0
SDC (Senan) van der Merwe	11	3	–	–	–	15	26	6	–	–	–	30
PJ (PJ) van Zyl	21	5	–	–	–	25	58	10	–	–	–	50
BCG (Ben) Venter	18	–	–	–	–	0	18	–	–	–	–	0
AF (Alistair) Vermaak	3	–	–	–	–	0	3	–	–	–	–	0
C (Cheswin) Williams	12	3	–	–	–	15	22	4	1	4	–	34
ES (Eric) Zana	13	1	18	8	–	65	25	5	19	8	–	87
Penalty try	0	1	–	–	–	5	–	1	–	–	–	5
48 players	**451**	**64**	**44**	**24**	**0**	**480**	**1077**	**204**	**133**	**62**	**3**	**1506**

www.bolandrugby.com

APPEARANCES & POINTS IN VODACOM CUP 2013

	WP	Free State XV	SWD	Pampas XV	Sharks XV	Border	EP Kings	Matches	Tries	Conversions	Penalties	Drop Goals	Points
Jaquin Jansen	15	10	–	15	15	15	15	6	1	3	4	–	23
Cheslyn Roberts	14	14	14	14	14	–	–	5	1	–	–	–	5
Jonathan Francke	13	13	13	–	13	13	13R	6	–	–	–	–	0
Albert Trytsman	12	12	12	–	–	–	–	3	1	–	–	–	5
Brendon April	11	11	11R	11	11	11	12R	7	1	–	–	–	5
Ricardo Croy	10	10R	–	10	10	10	10	6	–	8	6	–	34
Ntando Kebe	9	9	9	9	9R	9	9R	7	–	–	–	–	0
Zandré Jordaan	8	–	8	–	–	8	8	4	–	–	–	–	0
PJ van Zyl	7	6R	4	7R	4R	7	6R	7	1	–	–	–	5
Franzel September	6	6	6	6	6	6	–	6	–	–	–	–	0
Nolan Clark	5	5R	5	5	5	5	5	7	–	–	–	–	0
Ben Venter	4	4	–	4	4	4	4	6	–	–	–	–	0
Francois Hanekom	3	3	1	3	3	–	3	6	–	–	–	–	0
Chris Buckle	2	2R	–	–	–	–	–	2	1	–	–	–	5
Ashton Constant	1c	1c	2c	–	1c	1c	1c	6	2	–	–	–	10
Marko Janse van Rensburg	20R	2	3R	2	–	–	–	4	–	–	–	–	0
Rossouw Kruger	x	3R	3	–	–	3	3R	4	–	–	–	–	0
Hanno Kitshoff	4R	5	–	–	–	–	–	2	–	–	–	–	0
Alwyn Bester	7R	8	7R	8c	8	–	–	5	–	–	–	–	0
Bradley Fortuin	6R	8R	4R	8R	7R	6R	7	7	–	–	–	–	0
Garth April	10R	15	15	13	–	–	–	4	–	2	–	–	4
Tythan Adams	11R	14R	11	11R	14R	14	11	7	2	–	–	–	10
Thor Halvorsen	–	7	7	7	7	–	–	4	2	–	–	–	10
Ashley Esau	–	–	10	–	–	x	–	1	–	–	–	–	0
Armon Fourie	–	–	2R	–	–	x	–	1	–	–	–	–	0
Dual Erasmus	–	–	9R	–	–	–	9	2	–	–	–	–	0
Braam Gerber	–	–	10R	12	12	12	12	5	1	–	–	–	5
Johannes Kleinhans	–	–	–	1	–	–	–	1	–	–	–	–	0
Cheswin Williams	–	–	–	13R	–	x	13	2	–	–	–	–	0
Ulrich Pretorius	–	–	–	2R	2	4R	6	4	4	–	–	–	20
Andries Truter	–	–	–	9R	9	–	–	2	–	–	–	–	0
Callie Steenkamp	–	–	–	3R	–	–	–	1	–	–	–	–	0
Senan van der Merwe	–	–	–	–	11R	11R	14	3	1	–	–	–	5
Alistair Vermaak	–	–	–	–	3R	3R	8R	3	–	–	–	–	0
Clemen Lewis	–	–	–	–	2R	2	2	3	–	–	–	–	0
Gerhardus Goosen	–	–	–	–	–	–	4R	1	–	–	–	–	0
Penalty try	–	–	–	–	–	–	–	0	1	–	–	–	5
36 players									150	19	13	10	0	151

BOLAND RUGBY UNION

APPEARANCES & POINTS IN ABSA CURRIE CUP 2013

	Leopards	SWD	Border	Valke	EP Kings	Pumas	Griffons	Leopards	SWD	Border	Valke	EP Kings	Pumas	Griffons	Matches	Tries	Conversions	Penalties	Drop Goals	Points
Jaquin Jansen	15	15	15	15	15	15	15	15	15	–	15	10R	–	–	11	4	3	–	–	26
Brendon April	14	–	–	11	11	11	11	11	11	11	11	–	13R	11	11	7	–	–	–	35
Reinhardt Erwee	13	11	11	–	–	–	–	–	–	–	–	–	–	–	3	–	–	–	–	0
Braam Gerber	12	12	12	12	12	12	12	12	12R	12	12	12	12	12	14	4	–	–	–	20
Senan van der Merwe	11	11R	14R	14	14	14	–	–	x	14	14	–	–	–	8	2	–	–	–	10
Eric Zana	10	15R	11R	15R	10R	–	10	10	10	10	10	15	15	15	13	1	18	8	–	65
Ricky Schroeder	9	–	–	9R	9R	9R	9	9R	9R	9	9R	9R	–	–	10	–	–	–	–	0
PJ van Zyl	8	7	4	4	4	4	7	7	8	8	8	5	8	8	14	4	–	–	–	20
Ben Venter	7	–	7R	4R	4R	7R	4	4	4	4	–	4	4R	4	12	–	–	–	–	0
Franzel September	6c	6c	6c	6c	6c	6c	6c	–	6c	6c	6c	6c	–	6c	12	4	–	–	–	20
Nolan Clark	5	5	–	–	–	–	–	–	–	–	–	–	–	–	2	–	–	–	–	0
JC Astle	4	4	5	5	5	5	5	5	5	5	–	5	5	5	13	1	–	–	–	5
Rossouw Kruger	3	–	–	1R	–	–	1R	–	–	x	3	3R	1R	3	7	1	–	–	–	5
Clemen Lewis	2	2	2	2	2	2	2	2	2	2	2R	2	2c	2	14	1	–	–	–	5
Francois Hanekom	1	3	3	–	3R	3R	1	3	1R	3	–	3	1	1	12	–	–	–	–	0
Ulrich Pretorius	2R	2R	2R	x	2R	2R	2R	4R	7R	x	2	8R	6	2R	12	2	–	–	–	10
Sabelo Nhlapo	3R	1	1	1	1	1	–	1	1	–	–	–	–	–	8	–	–	–	–	0
Thor Halvorsen	8R	5R	7	7	7	–	4R	–	–	–	–	–	–	–	6	–	–	–	–	0
Bradley Fortuin	5R	8R	4R	7R	7R	7	8R	6R	7	x	4R	7	7	7	13	–	–	–	–	0
Ntando Kebe	9R	9	9	9	9	9	9R	9	9	9R	9	9	9	9	14	1	–	–	–	5
Wynand Pienaar	10R	–	–	–	–	12R	12R	12R	12	–	–	–	–	14R	6	1	–	–	–	5
Jonathan Francke	14R	13	13	13	13	13	13	13	13	14R	13	11R	13	–	14	3	–	–	–	15
Cheslyn Roberts	–	14	14	–	–	–	15R	14R	–	–	–	–	14	14	6	–	–	–	–	0
Leonard Olivier	–	10	10	10	10	–	–	–	–	–	–	–	10	10	6	–	10	6	–	38
Zandre Jordaan	–	8	8	8	8	8	–	8c	–	–	–	–	–	–	6	3	–	–	–	15
Jacques Kotze	–	1R	1R	3	3	3	3	1R	3	1	1	1	3	1R	13	–	–	–	–	0
Ricardo Croy	–	10R	12R	–	–	10	–	–	–	x	14R	10	10R	10R	7	–	–	–	–	0
Cheswin Williams	–	–	–	10R	12R	10R	14	14	14	15	13	11	–	9R	10	3	–	–	–	15
Alwyn Bester	–	–	–	–	–	8R	8	6	–	–	7R	8	–	–	5	1	–	–	–	5
Lodewyk Uys	–	–	–	–	–	–	–	7R	7R	7	7	4R	4	7R	7	–	–	–	–	0
Hanno Kitshoff	–	–	–	–	–	–	–	4R	4R	4	6R	7R	4R	–	6	–	–	–	–	0
Tythan Adams	–	–	–	–	–	–	–	–	–	x	–	–	11	–	1	–	–	–	–	0
Keenan Abrahams	–	–	–	–	–	–	–	–	–	1R	–	–	–	–	1	–	–	–	–	0
Adri Jacobs	–	–	–	–	–	–	–	–	–	–	–	14	13	–	2	–	–	–	–	0
Jason Kriel	–	–	–	–	–	–	–	–	–	–	–	14R	–	–	1	2	–	–	–	10
Chris Buckle	–	–	–	–	–	–	–	–	–	–	–	6R	–	–	1	–	–	–	–	0
36 players															301	45	31	14	0	329

ABSA UNDER-21 CHAMPIONSHIP (Runners-up, 2nd, Section B)

Played	Won	Drawn	Lost	Points for	Points against	Tries for	Tries against	Winning %
9	7	0	2	378	220	57	30	78,00%

RESULTS Bt Griquas (a) 78-28. Bt SWD (h) 56-24. Bt Limpopo Blue Bulls (a) 31-25. Bt Valke (a) 69-08. Lost EP (h) 17-31. Bt Mpumalanga (a) 31-10. Bt Griffons (h) 13-52. SEMI-FINAL Bt Limpopp Blue Bulls (h) 25-22. FINAL Lost EP (a) 19-59.

SCORERS 98 Ashley Esau (3t, 31c, 7p). 45 Kirwan Horsemend (9t). 35 Juandré Joseph (7t). 35 Conway Pretorius (5t). 20 Arno Fortuin, Jovelian de Koker (4t each). 15 Johann Lambrechts (3t). 10 Branden Hunter, Chaney Willemse, Francois Basson, Gerswin Moses, Siphokuhle Mbobosi, Stephan Wessels, Wade Schoor (2t each), Sherwin Dyson (5c). 5 Ernst Claassen, Glendon du Plessis, Kelvin Fikster, Kyle Mettler, Lee-Heino Appollis, Roland Swarts, Tiaan Ramat (1t each).

ABSA UNDER-19 CHAMPIONSHIP (2nd, Section B)

Played	Won	Drawn	Lost	Points for	Points against	Tries for	Tries against	Winning %
8	5	0	3	210	214	31	29	63,00%

RESULTS Bt Griquas (a) 23-22. Bt SWD (h) 24-14. Bt Limpopo Blue Bulls (a) 22-18. Lost Valke (a) 24-41. Bt EP (h) 26-24. Bt Mpumalanga (a) 39-20. Lost Griffons (h) 22-30. SEMI-FINAL Lost EP (h) 30-45.

SCORERS 51 Willbur Boonzaaier (2t, 13c, 5p). 27 Phil-Lee George (5t, 1c). 25 Valentino Wellman (5t). 20 Anzo Stubbs, Louis Carstens (4t each). 15 Francois Pienaar (3t). 12 Gilbert Abrahams (3c, 2p). 10 Brandon Meyer, Deno-Chaunzey van Turha (2t each). 5 Chad Kleinsmidt, Edward Lange, Kennedy Rorwana, Marshall Africa (1t each).

The Cavaliers gave the ball plenty of air as always.
Carl Fourie/Gallo Images

BOLAND RECORDS

MATCH RECORDS

Biggest win	96-5	vs Zimbabwe	1996
Biggest win (Currie Cup)	65-5	vs. Mpumalanga	2007
Heaviest defeat	8-96	vs Western Province	1993
	3-91	vs Free State Cheetahs (Currie Cup)	2007
Highest score	96	vs Zimbabwe (96-5)	1996
Highest score (Currie Cup)	79	vs Valke (79-26)	2012
Moist points conceded	96	vs Western Province (8-96)	1993
Moist points conceded (Currie Cup)	91	vs Free State Cheetahs	2007
Most tries	15	vs Zimbabwe	1996
Most tries (Currie Cup)	12	vs Valke	2012
Most points by a player	34	F Horn vs South Western Districts	1996
Most points by a player (Currie Cup)	25	P O'Neill vs Northern Free State	1997
Most tries by a player (Currie Cup)	6	FP Marais vs North Eastern Districts	1952

SEASON RECORDS

Most team points	956	24 matches	2001
Most team points (Currie Cup)	566	12 matches	2011
Most points by a player	355	F Horn	1996
Most points by a player (Currie Cup)	197	EG Watts	2011
Most team tries	137	24 matches	2001
Most team tries (Currie Cup)	75	12 matches	2011
Most tries by a player	20	CS Terblanche	1997
Most tries by a player (Currie Cup)	16	RS Benjamin	2006

CAREER RECORDS

Most appearances	154	N Papier	2001-2012
Most points	524	P O'Neill	1996-2002
Most tries	82	JI Daniels	1998-2008

HONOURS

Currie Cup First Division	2001, 2003, 2004, 2006, 2011
Vodacom Shield	2004

BORDER RUGBY FOOTBALL UNION

Bulldogs rediscover some bite

FOUNDED
1891
GROUND
BCM Stadium (formerly the Basil Kenyon Stadium)
CAPACITY
15 000
ADDRESS
Recreation Road, East London, 5201
POSTAL ADDRESS
PO Box 75, East London, 5200
TELEPHONE NUMBER
043-743 5998
WEBSITE
www.borderbulldogs.co.za
COLOURS
Brown jersey with white, red and green stripes and white shorts with green stripes. Brown socks with two white stripes.
HEAD COACH
Paul Flanagan
CAPTAIN
Gareth Krause
PRESIDENT
Phumlani Mkolo
UNION GENERAL MANAGER
Lefty Ngece

THE BORDER BULLDOGS PULLED THEMSELVES TOGETHER after a miserable 2012 season, during which the East London-based side lost every one of their 14 Absa Currie Cup First Division matches, to stage a creditable recovery in 2013.

They might have handed over the wooden spoon to the Valke, but captain Gareth Krause and his side will know that their results, while a dramatic improvement on the year before, don't guarantee anything.

That said, the Bulldogs picked up four wins en route to a seventh-place finish, with their 26-22 victory in Potchefstroom over the Leopards, who would finish third on the final standings, the most impressive.

Their other three wins – against the Griffons, Boland Cavaliers and Valke – all came at home.

Even in defeat, there was enough on display in some matches to suggest that the men from East London need no longer be the pushovers they've become in recent years.

They were somewhat unlucky to lose 23-16 to the Steval Pumas in Nelspruit in round two – a remarkable effort considering the way in which the Pumas swept all before them in 2013, culminating in a First Division title, a promotion-relegation series win over GWK Griquas, and the Team of the Year award at the SA Rugby Awards.

A number of narrow defeats could also so easily have turned the season into an even better success, notably their 22-20 defeat to the Cavaliers in Wellington, a 34-29 loss to the Valke in Kempton Park and a nailbiting 9-6 defeat to the EP Kings in Port Elizabeth.

As always, a number of players in coach Paul Flanagan's squad stuck up their hands. Fullback Dale Sabbagh missed the first six matches but kicked 73 points in the last eight.

Utility back Quinton Crocker played fullback, inside centre and outside centre and scored two tries, while the halfback combination of flyhalf Karlo Aspeling and scrumhalf Shannon Rick gave the team much needed direction. The main beneficiary of this was wing Andrew van Wyk, whose five tries were the most by any player.

Up front, Krause was his usual tireless self in the number seven jersey while prop Khwezi Mkhafu had the honour of being the forwards' top try-scorer, with three touchdowns. Krause's flanker partner, Brian Shabangu, also enjoyed a solid season, and was rewarded with two tries.

Border Bulldogs wing Andrew van Wyk charges at the Valke defence.
Duif du Toit/Gallo Images

BORDER RUGBY FOOTBALL UNION

VODACOM CUP LOG POSITIONS

2013	13th	2010	9th	2007	13st	2004	6th	2001	11th	1998	12th
2012	10th	2009	10th	2006	13th	2003	8th	2000	9th		
2011	15th	2008	13th	2005	13th	2002	3rd	1999	11th		

ABSA CURRIE CUP LOG POSITIONS

2013	13th	2010	13th	2007	14th	2004	10th	2001	12th	1998	12th
2012	13th	2009	13th	2006	13th	2003	13th	2000	13th	1997	11th
2011	14th	2008	14th	2005	14th	2002	10th	1999	8th	1996	10th

2013 RESULTS AND SCORERS

VODACOM CUP Played **7** Won **2** Drawn **0** Lost **5** Points for **143** Points against **239** Tries for **15** Tries against **34**

Date	Venue	Opponent	Result	Score	Referee	Scorers
Mrch 08	Durban	Sharks XV	LOST	06-72	M Jonker	P: Aspeling (2).
Mrch 16	Mthatha	EP Kings	LOST	22-30	B Crouse	T: Seerane (2), Nyoka. C: Aspeling (2). P: Aspeling.
Mrch 23	Stellenbosch	Pampas XV	LOST	26-45	M Jonker	T: Seerane, Qrocker, Pretorius. C: Aspeling. P: Aspeling (3).
April 06	Paarl	WP	LOST	13-22	J Sylvestre	T: Adams, Bester. P: Aspeling.
April 14	Alice	Free State XV	LOST	25-26	F Groenewald	T: N Jacobs, Mkhafu, Van Wyk. C: Aspeling (2). P: Aspeling (2).
April 19	East London	Cavaliers	**WON**	26-25	L vd Merwe	T: Seerane, Muir, Mkhafu. C: Sabbagh. P: Aspeling (3).
April 26	George	Eagles	**WON**	25-19	A Sehlako	T: Van Schalkwyk. C: Aspeling. P: Aspeling (6).

ABSA CURRIE CUP Played **14** Won **4** Lost **10** Drawn **0** Points for **277** Points against **365** Tries for **32** Tries against **46**

Date	Venue	Opponent	Result	Score	Referee	Scorers
Jun 28	East London	Eagles	LOST	12-36	L Legoete	T: Van Schalkwyk, Mkhafu. C: Aspeling.
July 05	Nelspruit	Pumas	LOST	16-23	R Raslvhenge	T: Muir. C: Aspeling. P: Aspeling (3).
July 12	Wellington	Cavaliers	LOST	20-22	Q Immelman	T: Crocker, Taljaard. C: Dumond (2). P: Dumond, Aspeling.
July 20	East London	Griffons	**WON**	22-20	M Jonker	T: Aspeling, A van Wyk, Crocker. C: Aspeling (2). P: Aspeling.
July 26	Kempton Park	Valke	LOST	29-34	M Jonker	T: A van Wyk, Mhlongo, Mkhafu, Shabangu. C: Crocker (2), N Jacobs. P: N Jacobs.
Aug 03	East London	Leopards	LOST	10-26	M vd Westhuizen	T: Spring, A van Wyk.
Aug 09	Port Elizabeth	EP Kings	LOST	06-09	J Kaplan	P: Sabbagh (2).
Aug 16	George	Eagles	LOST	31-36	R Rasivhenge	T: R van Wyk (2), Booi, Gerber. C: Aspeling. P: Sabbagh (2). D: Aspeling.
Aug 23	East London	Pumas	LOST	10-42	J Kotze	T: Kyd. C: Sabbagh. P: Sabbagh.
Aug 30	East London	Cavaliers	**WON**	21-19	L van der Merwe	T: Krause, Pretorius. C: Sabbagh. P: Sabbagh (3).
Sep 07	Welkom	Griffons	LOST	19-24	J Kaplan	T: A van Wyk (2), Booi. C: Sabbagh (2).
Sep 13	East London	Valke	**WON**	35-14	J van Heerden	T: Rick (2), Jenner, Muir. C: Sabbagh (3). P: Sabbagh (3).
Sep 20	Potchefstroom	Leopards	**WON**	26-22	J van Heerden	T: Mkhafu, Shabangu. C: Sabbagh (2). P: Sabbagh (4).
Sep 27	East London	EP Kings	LOST	20-38	B Crouse	T: Jenner, Spring. C: Sabbagh (2). P: Sabbagh (2).

BORDER RUGBY FOOTBALL UNION

BORDER SQUAD IN 2013 — BORDER CAREER

PLAYER	Appearances	Tries	Conversions	Penalties	Drop Goals	Points	Career Matches	Career Tries	Conversions	Penalties	Drop Goals	Points
DHN (Duane) Adams	4	1	–	–	–	5	4	1	–	–	–	5
L (Lukhanyo) Am	2	–	–	–	–	0	2	–	–	–	–	0
KG (Karlo) Aspeling	20	1	11	23	1	99	20	1	11	23	1	99
J (Juan) Bester	2	1	–	–	–	5	3	1	–	–	–	5
CN (Chumani) Booi	4	2	–	–	–	10	105	28	14	7	–	189
WW (Wesley) Cloete	21	–	–	–	–	0	34	–	–	–	–	0
Q (Quinton) Crocker	21	3	2	0	0	19	32	4	5	2	–	36
C (Cecil) Dumond	7	0	2	1	0	7	7	0	2	1	0	7
G (George) Fritz	1	–	–	–	–	0	2	–	–	–	–	0
SE (Stephan) Gerber	12	1	–	–	–	5	12	1	–	–	–	5
AJ (Anthonie) Gronum	3	–	–	–	–	0	34	–	–	–	–	0
N (Niell) Jacobs	21	1	1	1	0	10	31	3	1	1	–	20
R (Ruan) Jacobs	17	–	–	–	–	0	23	4	–	–	–	20
D (Dwayne) Jenner	8	2	–	–	–	10	26	3	–	–	–	15
AE (Alister) Keet	7	–	–	–	–	0	7	–	–	–	–	0
GE (Gareth) Krause	19	1	–	–	–	5	78	13	–	–	–	65
PG (Pieter) Kruger	1	–	–	–	–	0	1	–	–	–	–	0
BJ (Blake) Kyd	14	1	–	–	–	5	33	2	–	–	–	10
E (Ernst) Ladendorf	3	–	–	–	–	0	3	–	–	–	–	0
W (Wayne) Lemley	7	–	–	–	–	0	7	–	–	–	–	0
S (Siya) Mdaka	17	1	–	–	–	5	20	1	–	–	–	5
SS (Sthembiso) Mhlongo	9	1	–	–	–	5	9	1	–	–	–	5
K (Kwezi) Mkhafu	21	5	–	–	–	25	70	6	–	–	–	30
D (Dean) Muir	18	3	–	–	–	15	31	4	–	–	–	20
SD (Shaun) Nieuwenhuyzen	2	–	–	–	–	0	2	–	–	–	–	0
S (Sinovuyo) Nyoka	16	1	–	–	–	5	49	2	–	–	–	10
JH (Juan) Pretorius	20	2	–	–	–	10	20	2	–	–	–	10
SMK (Shannon) Rick	18	2	–	–	–	10	18	2	–	–	–	10
DG (Dale) Sabbagh	11	0	12	17	0	75	22	0	23	26	1	127
R (Walla) Schoeman	16	–	–	–	–	0	40	–	–	–	–	0
J (Johannes) Seerane	7	4	–	–	–	20	10	6	–	–	–	30
SB (Brian) Shabangu	12	2	–	–	–	10	26	4	–	–	–	20
D (Dillon) Smit	5	–	–	–	–	0	5	–	–	–	–	0
SM (Shane) Spring	11	1	–	–	–	5	42	7	–	–	–	35
M (Matthew) Taljaard	5	1	–	–	–	5	67	8	–	–	–	40
N (Nomani) Tonga	11	–	–	–	–	0	67	5	–	–	–	25
CJ (Chrislyn) van Schalkwyk	15	2	–	–	–	10	25	6	–	–	–	30
AJD (Andrew) van Wyk	12	5	–	–	–	25	12	5	–	–	–	25
RI (Rynardt) van Wyk	21	3	–	–	–	15	27	4	–	–	–	20
LY (Lolo) Waka	6	–	–	–	–	0	6	–	–	–	–	0

40 players

APPEARANCES & POINTS IN VODACOM CUP 2013

Player	Sharks XV	EP Kings	Pampas XV	WP	Free State XV	Cavaliers	Eagles	Matches	Tries	Conversions	Penalties	Drop Goals	Points
Shaun Nieuwenhuyzen	15	15	–	–	–	–	–	2	–	–	–	–	0
Chrislyn van Schalkwyk	14	11	11	14	–	–	14	5	1	–	–	–	5
Ruan Jacobs	13	13	13	–	–	14	13	5	–	–	–	–	0
Quinton Crocker	12	12	12c	13	13	13	15	7	1	–	–	–	5
Joe Seerane	11	14	14	11	14	11	11	7	4	–	–	–	20
Karlo Aspeling	10	10	10	10	10	15	10	7	–	6	18	–	66
Shannon Rick	9	9	9	–	–	9R	x	4	–	–	–	–	0
Juan Pretorius	8	8	8	8	8	–	8	6	1	–	–	–	5
Gareth Krause	7c	4c	–	4c	4c	4c	4c	6	–	–	–	–	0
Shane Spring	6	6R	6R	7R	–	8	–	5	–	–	–	–	0
Antonie Gronum	5	–	–	–	–	–	–	1	–	–	–	–	0
Nomani Tonga	4	5	4R	5R	–	5	5	6	–	–	–	–	0
Wesley Cloete	3	3	3R	3R	3R	3	3R	7	–	–	–	–	0
Kwezi Mkhafu	2	2	2	2	2	1	1	7	2	–	–	–	10
Blake Kyd	1	1	1	1	1	3R	1R	7	–	–	–	–	0
PG Kruger	3R	–	–	–	–	–	–	1	–	–	–	–	0
Renier Schoeman	8R	x	3	3	3	–	3	5	–	–	–	–	0
Allister Keet	5R	4R	5	5	5	–	–	5	–	–	–	–	0
Rynardt van Wyk	4R	7	7	8R	6R	7	7	7	1	–	–	–	5
Dillon Smit	9R	–	11R	9R	x	–	–	3	–	–	–	–	0
Niell Jacobs	15R	13R	13R	12	12	12	12	7	1	–	–	–	5
Lolo Waka	14R	–	–	–	11	11R	x	3	–	–	–	–	0
Siya Mdaka	–	6	6	7	7	8R	7R	6	–	–	–	–	0
Wayne Lemley	–	7R	4	–	–	–	–	2	–	–	–	–	0
Sinovuyo Nyoka	–	9R	9R	9	9	9	9	6	1	–	–	–	5
Dale Sabbagh	–	15R	15	–	x	10	–	3	–	1	–	–	2
George Fritz	–	–	2R	–	–	x	–	1	–	–	–	–	0
Duane Adams	–	–	–	15	15	10R	11R	4	1	–	–	–	5
Juan Bester	–	–	–	6	6	–	–	2	1	–	–	–	5
Dean Muir	–	–	–	2R	1R	2	2	4	1	–	–	–	5
Lukhanyo Am	–	–	–	14R	12R	–	–	2	–	–	–	–	0
Ernst Ladendorf	–	–	–	–	8R	5R	5R	3	–	–	–	–	0
Brian Shabangu	–	–	–	–	–	6	6	2	–	–	–	–	0
33 Players								148	15	7	18	0	143

BORDER RUGBY FOOTBALL UNION

APPEARANCES & POINTS IN ABSA CURRIE CUP 2013

Player	Eagles	Pumas	Cavaliers	Griffons	Valke	Leopards	EP Kings	Eagles	Pumas	Cavaliers	Griffons	Valke	Leopards	EP Kings	Matches	Tries	Conversions	Penalties	Drop Goals	Points
Quinton Crocker	15	12	12	12	12	12	13	13	13	13	13	13	13	13	14	2	2	0	0	14
Chrislyn van Schalkwyk	14	11	11	11	11	10R	11	11	–	11	–	–	14R	–	10	1	–	–	–	5
Ruan Jacobs	13	13	13	13	13	13	–	11R	14	x	15R	13R	8R	12R	12	–	–	–	–	0
Niell Jacobs	12	11R	15R	10	10	10	12R	12R	12R	12R	12R	12R	10R	10R	14	0	1	1	0	5
Lolo Waka	11	–	–	–	–	–	–	14R	–	14R	–	–	–	–	3	–	–	–	–	0
Karlo Aspeling	10	15	15	15	10R	–	10	10	10	10	10	10	10	10	13	1	5	5	1	33
Shannon Rick	9	9R	9R	9	9	9	9R	9R	9R	9R	9	9	9	9	14	2	–	–	–	10
Juan Pretorius	8	8	8	8	8	8	4R	4R	5R	4R	6R	6R	8	8R	14	1	–	–	–	5
Gareth Krause	7c	7c	7c	7c	7c	7c	7c	7c	7c	7c	7c	7c	–	–	13	1	–	–	–	5
Shane Spring	6	–	–	8R	x	11	–	–	–	–	–	11	11	11	6	1	–	–	–	5
Stephan Gerber	5	5	5	5	–	5	5	5	–	5	5	5	5	5	12	1	–	–	–	5
Sthembiso Mhlongo	4	–	4	4	4	–	–	4	4	4	4	4	–	–	9	1	–	–	–	5
Renier Schoeman	3	3	3	3	3	3R	3R	x	3R	3R	3R	3R	–	–	11	–	–	–	–	0
Dean Muir	2	2	2	2	2	2	2	2	2	2	2	2	2	2	14	2	–	–	–	10
Khwezi Mkhafu	1	1	1	1	1	1	1R	1R	1R	1	1	1	1	1	14	3	–	–	–	15
Matthew Taljaard	x	2R	2R	2R	–	–	–	8R	–	2R	–	–	–	–	5	1	–	–	–	5
Wesley Cloete	3R	3R	3R	3R	3R	3	3	3	3	3	3	3	3	3	14	–	–	–	–	0
Nomani Tonga	x	4	4R	–	5	–	6R	–	–	–	–	5R	–	4R	6	–	–	–	–	0
Siyabulela Mdaka	8R	4R	8R	x	x	19R	6	6	6	6	6	6	–	7	11	1	–	–	–	5
Rynardt van Wyk	6R	8R	6R	6	6	6	8	8	8	8	8	6	6	8	14	2	–	–	–	10
Sinovuyo Nyoka	9R	9	9	9R	9R	11R	9	9	9	9	–	–	–	–	10	–	–	–	–	0
Cecil Dummond	11R	10	10	10R	15	15	–	–	–	–	–	14R	–	–	7	0	2	1	0	7
Andrew van Wyk	–	14	14	14	14	14	14R	–	11	14	11	14	14	14	12	5	–	–	–	25
Brian Shabangu	–	6	6	4R	4R	6R	–	–	6R	8R	4R	–	7R	6c	10	2	–	–	–	10
Dale Sabbagh	–	x	–	–	–	–	15	15	15	15	15	15	15	15	8	0	11	17	0	73
Wayne Lemley	–	–	–	–	5R	4R	–	–	5	–	–	–	4R	7R	5	–	–	–	–	0
Antonie Gronum	–	–	–	–	–	–	4	4	–	–	–	–	–	–	2	–	–	–	–	0
Chumani Booi	–	–	–	–	–	9R	14	14	–	–	14	–	–	–	4	2	–	–	–	10
Dwayne Jenner	–	–	–	–	–	–	12	12	12	12	12	12	12	12	8	2	–	–	–	10
Blake Kyd	–	–	–	–	–	–	1	1	1	–	1R	1R	3R	3R	7	1	–	–	–	5
Alistar Keet	–	–	–	–	–	–	–	–	–	–	–	–	4	4	2	–	–	–	–	0
Dillon Smit	–	–	–	–	–	–	–	–	–	–	–	–	12R	9R	2	–	–	–	–	0
32 Players															**300**	**32**	**21**	**24**	**1**	**277**

ABSA UNDER-21 CHAMPIONSHIP (7th, Section A)

Played	Won	Drawn	Lost	Points for	Points against	Tries for
12	0	0	12	228	653	33

RESULTS: Lost Sharks (h) 31-53. Lost Free State (h) 15-32. Lost Leopards (a) 17-26. Lost Blue Bulls (h) 14-66. Lost WP (a) 20-38. Lost Golden Lions (h) 16-45. Lost Sharks (a) 20-71. Lost Free State (a) 29-45. Lost Leopards (h) 28-57. Lost Blue Bulls (a) 19-70. Lost WP (h) 12-74. Lost Golden Lions (a) 7-76.

SCORERS: 29 Angus Cleophas (4t,3c,1p); 29 Shaun Nieuwenhuyzen (3t,7c); 20 Janco Lehmann (4c,4p); 15 Juan Bester,Ernst Ladendord (3t each); 12 Dillon Smit (2t,1c); 11 Hendri Rust (1t,3c); 10 Johan Wagenaar, Leroy Afrika, Mario Noordman, Jan-Hendrik Botha (2t each); 9 Wayne Gardner (3c,1p); 8 Fanelesibonge Zwane (1t,1p); 5 James Flynn, Duane Adams, Etienne Taljaard, Stephan Deyzel, Siphesihle Ngubane, Nicol du Plessis, Marlyn Williams, Penalty try (1t each).

ABSA U19 CHAMPIONSHIP (7th, Section A)

Played	Won	Drawn	Lost	Points for	Points against	Tries for
12	0	0	12	130	464	16

RESULTS: Lost Sharks (h) 24-32. Lost Free State (h) 13-29. Lost Leopards (a) 15-36. Lost Blue Bulls (h) 7-56. Lost WP (a) 0-62. Lost Golden Lions (h) 3-19. Lost Sharks (a) 5-41. Lost Free State (a) 20-28. Lost Leopards (h) 16-19. Lost Blue Bulls (a) 3-59. Lost WP (h) 7-36. Lost Golden Lions (a) 17-47.

SCORERS: 46 Werner Barnard (1t,7c,9p); 20 Conor-Terrah Brockschmidt (4t); 7 Michael Haley (1t,1c); Dylan Rust (2c,1p); 5 Funani Mabala, Johan Gericke, Oliver Cracknell, Soso Xakalashe, Luzuko Mafu, Russel Weavill, Athenkosi Mabinda, Johannes Jonker, Charl Carelse, Devon van Eeden (1t each).

AMATEUR CHAMPIONSHIP

BORDER (South Section, Saldanha)

Played	Won	Drawn	Lost	Points for	Points against	Winning %
3	2	0	1	97	80	66%

RESULTS: Bt Boland 32-20. Lost SWD 25-27. Bt EP 40-33.

BORDER RURAL (South Section, Saldanha)

Played	Won	Drawn	Lost	Points for	Points against	Winning %
3	1	0	2	96	71	33%

RESULTS: Lost SWD 25-36. Lost Boland 22-28. Bt EP Rural 49-7.

SOUTHERN SUB-UNION CHAMPIONSHIP (Margate)

Played	Won	Drawn	Lost	Points for	Points against	Winning %
3	0	0	3	52	99	0%

RESULTS: Lost KZN Wildebeest 6-28. Lost Free State 18-30. Lost SWD 28-41.

BORDER RECORDS

MATCH RECORDS

Biggest win	85-3	vs. Zimbabwe	1996
Biggest Currie Cup win	56-23	vs. Northern Free State	1997
Heaviest defeat	14-87	vs. Griqualand West (Currie Cup)	1998
	9-84	vs. Griqualand West (Vodacom Cup)	2011
Highest score	85	vs. Zimbabwe (85-3)	1996
Most points conceded	87	vs. Griqualand West (14-87)	1998
Most tries	15	vs. Zimbabwe (85-3)	1996
Most Currie Cup tries	8	vs. Northern Free State (56-23)	1997
Most points by a player	31	L Basson vs. Valke	2010
Most Currie Cup points by player	31	L Basson vs. Valke	2010
Most tries by a player	4	A Stephenson vs. Far North	1976
	4	RG Bennett vs. Zimbabwe	1996

SEASON RECORDS

Most team points	778	27 matches	1996
Most Currie Cup points by team	332	12 matches	2004
Most points by a player	299	M Flutey	1995
Most Currie Cup points by player	125	R Gerber	2004
Most team tries	101	27 matches	1996
Most Currie Cup tries by team	42	14 matches	2012
Most tries by a player	20	RG Bennett	1996
Most Currie Cup tries by a player	10	AZ Ndungane	2004

CAREER RECORDS

Most appearances	183	W Weyer	1988-2000
Most points	672	GK Miller	1996-2001
Most tries	44	A Alexander	

HONOURS

ABSA Currie Cup	1932 (shared), 1934 (shared)
Vodacom Shield	2003

EASTERN PROVINCE RUGBY UNION

FOUNDED
1888
GROUND
Nelson Mandela Bay
CAPACITY 45000
ADDRESS
70 Prince Alfred Road,
North End, Port Elizabeth,
6001
POSTAL ADDRESS
PO Box 13111, Humewood, 6013
TELEPHONE NUMBER
041-408 8902
EMAIL
info@eprugby.co.za
COLOURS
Red and black hooped jersey, black shorts, red and black socks
CURRIE CUP COACH
David Maidza
VODACOM CUP COACH
David Maidza
CAPTAIN
Darron Nell
PRESIDENT
Cheeky Watson
COMPANY CEO (ACTING)
Charl Crous

Frustrated Kings play second fiddle

WHATEVER YOUR THOUGHTS ON THE RUGBY IN THE Eastern Cape, it goes without saying that the Eastern Province Kings had a season that won't be forgotten in a hurry.

The Southern Kings, of which the EPRU is the main franchise partner, enjoyed a cameo performance in the Vodacom Super Rugby competition before losing their status to the Lions in a promotion-relegation series by the narrowest of margins.

Against this backdrop, there were ongoing deliberations during 2013 about how to accommodate the Kings in the Absa Currie Cup Premier Division from 2014, in order to prepare them for a possible permanent entry into Super Rugby from 2016 when that tournament looks set to expand.

Various models were proposed and discussed, including expanding the Premier Division to eight team to accommodate both the Kings and the Steval Pumas, who would later beat the EP Kings 53-30 to win the Absa Currie Cup 2013 First Division final.

However, at the time of writing, it seemed a foregone conclusion that the status quo would remain for 2014, with the Kings remaining in the First Division wilderness, where they would be joined by GWK Griquas, who were no match for the Pumas' power in their promotion-relegation series.

While the loss in the final was disappointing, it was their second place on the final log, behind the men from Nelspruit, which really hurt the Kings.

By not finishing top of the log, the Kings missed out on the opportunity to challenge the bottom-placed Premier Division team (in this case, Griquas) for a place in the top flight on merit.

It was clear from the opening weekend that the Kings would be up against it, when they were well beaten, 29-13, by the Pumas in Port Elizabeth. A heartbreaking 33-32 defeat in the return match in Nelspruit put paid to any hopes of topping the log, despite a six-match winning streak that followed the Mbombela loss, which included a 63-7 win over the Griffons – EP's biggest-ever Currie Cup victory.

The departure of star players after their Super Rugby exit meant the Kings used over 50 players during the Currie Cup campaign, with fullback Scott van Breda scoring 146 points and evergreen flanker Mpho Mbiyozo finishing as the top try-scorer, with six touchdowns.

The Kings now go into 2014 uncertain of what their future holds, which is a remarkable state of mind to be in considering where they were just a year ago, when big-time rugby was about to return to Port Elizabeth and there was a tangible buzz of excitement in the air.

Veteran Mpho Mbiyozo was one of the Kings' stalwarts in 2013.
Duif du Toit/Gallo Images

VODACOM CUP LOG POSITIONS

2013	5th	2010	14th	2007	8th	2004	13th	2001	10th	1998	8th			
2012	5th	2009	14th	2006	12th	2003	11th	2000	7th					
2011	10th	2008	12th	2005	12th	2002	11th	1999	9th					

ABSA CURRIE CUP LOG POSITIONS

2013	8th	2010	10th	2007	10th	2004	13th	2001	11th	1998	9th
2012	7th	2009	12th	2006	12th	2003	11th	2000	11th	1997	14th
2011	10th	2008	14th	2005	12th	2002	11th	1999	7th	1996	9th

2013 RESULTS AND SCORERS

VODACOM CUP Played **9** Won **6** Drawn **1** Lost **2** Points for **238** Points against **224** Tries for **27** Tries against **23** Winning% **70%**

Date	Venue	Opponent	Result	Score	Referee	Scorers
Mrch 09	Port Elizabeth	Pampas XV	DREW	20-20	F Pretorius	T: Van Breda. P: Dunlop (4), Van Breda.
Mrch 16	Mthatha	Bulldogs	WON	30-22	B Crouse	T: Soyizwapi, Schoeman, Oosthuizen, Lacombe. C: Dunlop (2). P: Dunlop, Van Breda.
Mrch 22	Port Elizabeth	WP	LOST	18-43	L Legoete	T: Mbiyozo, Britz. C: Dunlop. P: Dunlop (2).
April 06	Bloenfontein	Free State XV	WON	17-13	S Mayende	T: Stevens. P: Van Breda (4).
April 12	Uitenhage	Eagles	WON	52-10	M vd Westhuizen	T: Grey (2), Ngam (2), Van Breda, Mangweni, Watson. C: Van Breda (7). P: Van Breda.
April 20	Port Elizabeth	Sharks XV	WON	27-23	B Crouse	T: Dukisa, Grey, Willemse. C: Van Zyl (2), Dukisa. P: Van Zyl, Dukisa.
April 27	Malmesbury	Cavaliers	WON	27-23	G de Bruin	T: Van Zyl, Schoeman, Oosthuizen, Willemse. C: Van Zyl (2). P: Van Breda.
QUARTER-FINAL						
May 04	Pretoria	Blue Bulls	WON	34-31	T Jonker	T: Willemse, Gqoboka, Davis, Mbiyozo. C: Dunlop (3), Van Zyl. P: Van Breda (2).
SEMI-FINAL						
May 10	Nelspruit	Pumas	LOST	12-39	T Jonker	T: Mbiyozo. C: Dunlop. P: Dunlop (2).

ABSA CURRIE CUP Played **16** Won **11** Drawn **0** Lost **5** Points for **503** Points against **379** Tries for **57** Tries against **42** Winning% **69%**

Date	Venue	Opponent	Result	Score	Referee	Scorers
Jun 28	Port Elizabeth	Pumas	LOST	13-29	M Jonker	T: Dunlop. C: Dunlop. P: Dunlop (2).
July 06	Welkom	Griffons	WON	37-21	J Kotze	T: Soyizwapi, Parkes, A Davis, D Davis, Geldenhuys. C: Dunlop (3). P: Dunlop (2).
July 12	Port Elizabeth	Leopards	LOST	18-22	S Mayende	P: Van Breda (4), Dunlop (2).
July 19	George	Eagles	WON	35-34	L Legoete	T: Mbiyozo (2), Soyizwapi, Van Niekerk, A Davis. C: Van Niekerk, Van Zyl. P: Dukisa (2).
July 26	Port Elizabeth	Cavaliers	LOST	23-30	J Jaftha	T: Soyizwapi, Stevens, Mbiyozo. C: Van Breda. P: Van Breda, Dunlop.
Aug 02	Brakpan	Valke	WON	44-18	J Peyper	T: Mbiyozo (3), Grey, Dukisa. C: Dukisa (5). P: Dukisa (3).
Aug 09	Port Elizabeth	Bulldogs	WON	09-06	J Kaplan	P: Dukisa (2). D: Dukisa.
Aug 16	Nelspruit	Pumas	LOST	32-33	M Jonker	T: Van Breda, Killian, Mangweni, Vergallo, Sykes. C: Whitehead (2). P: Van Breda.
Aug 23	Port Elizabeth	Griffons	WON	63-07	M Jonker	T: Stevens (2), Fihlani (2), Killian, Agaba, Oosthuizen, Franklin, Mamojele. C: Van Breda (9).
Aug 30	Potchefstroom	Leopards	WON	44-26	T Jonker	T: Willemse (2), Killian, Mangweni, Du Preez, Fihlani. C: Van Breda (4). P: Van Breda (2)
Sep 06	Port Elizabeth	Eagles	WON	15-09	L vd Merwe	P: Van Breda (5).
Sep 13	Wellington	Cavaliers	WON	40-19	J Kaplan	T: Killian, Skosana, Du Preez, Willemse, Sykes, Penalty try. C: Whitehead (3), Van Breda (2).
Sep 20	Port Elizabeth	Valke	WON	30-23	J Jaftha	T: Willemse (2), Mangweni. C: Van Breda (3). P: Van Breda (3).
Sep 27	East London	Bulldogs	WON	38-20	B Crouse	T: Whitehead (2), Sykes, Nell. C: Van Breda (3). P: Van Breda (4).
SEMI FINAL						
Oct 04	Port Elizabeth	Leopards	WON	32-29	B Crouse	T: Agaba, Van Zyl. C: Van Breda (2). P: Van Breda (6).
FINAL						
Oct 11	Nelspruit	Pumas	LOST	30-53	C Joubert	T: Van Zyl, Dukisa, Penalty try. C: Van Breda (3). P: Van Breda (3).

EASTERN PROVINCE KINGS SQUAD IN 2013 / EP KINGS CAREER

PLAYER	Appearances	Tries	Conversions	Penalties	Drop Goals	Points	Career Matches	Career Tries	Conversions	Penalties	Drop Goals	Points
YW (Boela) Abrahams	7	–	–	–	–	0	20	–	–	–	–	0
DO (Daniel) Adongo	4	–	–	–	–	0	4	–	–	–	–	0
TEVK (Tim) Agaba	12	2	–	–	–	10	12	2	–	–	–	10
EP (Eben) Barnard	4	–	–	–	–	0	4	–	–	–	–	0
R (Rynier) Bernardo	5	–	–	–	–	0	17	–	–	–	–	0
T (Thembelani) Bholi	4	–	–	–	–	0	4	–	–	–	–	0
CJ (Coenraad) Britz	13	1	–	–	–	5	31	4	–	–	–	20
RJ (Ronnie) Cooke	4	–	–	–	–	0	4	–	–	–	–	0
A (Aidon) Davis	7	2	–	–	–	10	7	2	–	–	–	10
D (Dalton) Davis	10	2	–	–	–	10	10	2	–	–	–	10
AJ (Albie) de Swardt	11	–	–	–	–	0	11	–	–	–	–	0
CF (Charl) du Plessis	16	–	–	–	–	0	27	–	–	–	–	0
CG (Cornell) du Preez	4	2	–	–	–	10	23	11	–	–	–	55
N (Ntabeni) Dukisa	18	3	6	8	1	54	18	3	6	8	1	54
WR (Wesley) Dunlop	10	1	11	16	0	75	28	5	38	29	0	194
RJ (Robert) Dyer	2	–	–	–	–	0	37	5	–	–	–	25
J (Jaco) Engels	5	–	–	–	–	0	34	4	–	–	–	20
RD (Renier) Erasmus	1	–	–	–	–	0	1	–	–	–	–	0
LS (Samora) Fihlani	17	3	–	–	–	15	17	3	–	–	–	15
J (Hannes) Franklin	8	1	–	–	–	5	53	3	–	–	–	15
S (Shane) Gates	4	–	–	–	–	0	10	2	–	–	–	10
R (Ross) Geldenhuys	14	1	–	–	–	5	14	1	–	–	–	5
LP (Lizo) Gqoboka	21	1	–	–	–	5	30	2	–	–	–	10
S (Siyanda) Grey	9	4	–	–	–	20	30	14	–	–	–	70
A (Andile) Jho	6	–	–	–	–	0	6	–	–	–	–	0
D (Dwayne) Kelly	12	–	–	–	–	0	12	–	–	–	–	0
M (Michael) Killian	15	4	–	–	–	20	83	27	–	–	–	135
V (Virgile) Lacombe	3	1	–	–	–	5	3	1	–	–	–	5
T (Tomas) Leonardi	4	–	–	–	–	0	4	–	–	–	–	0
M (Marzuq) Maarman	1	–	–	–	–	0	1	–	–	–	–	0
T (Thabo) Mamojele	11	1	–	–	–	5	16	2	–	–	–	10
S (Tiger) Mangweni	23	4	–	–	–	20	64	11	–	–	–	55
S (Scott) Mathie	13	–	–	–	–	0	23	–	–	–	–	0
MM (Mpho) Mbiyozo	16	9	–	–	–	45	54	10	–	–	–	50
AE (Enoch) Mnyaka	1	–	–	–	–	0	1	–	–	–	–	0
K (Kuselo) Moyake	8	–	–	–	–	0	8	–	–	–	–	0
WM (Waylon) Murray	1	–	–	–	–	0	1	–	–	–	–	0
DP (Darron) Nell	8	1	–	–	–	5	50	9	–	–	–	45
NT (Norman) Nelson	1	–	–	–	–	0	92	56	–	–	–	280
Y (Yamkela) Ngam	3	2	–	–	–	10	3	2	–	–	–	10
LN (Lonwabo) Ntleki	2	–	–	–	–	0	4	–	–	–	–	0
SW (Schalk) Oelofse	1	–	–	–	–	0	1	–	–	–	–	0
BH (Brenden) Olivier	15	–	–	–	–	0	17	–	–	–	–	0
DA (Devin) Oosthuizen	14	3	–	–	–	15	52	10	–	–	–	50
H (Hadleigh) Parkes	2	1	–	–	–	5	2	1	–	–	–	5
S (Sergeal) Petersen	3	–	–	–	–	0	3	–	–	–	–	0
MED (Marcello) Sampson	5	–	–	–	–	0	37	19	–	–	–	95
P (Paul) Schoeman	8	2	–	–	–	10	8	2	–	–	–	10
MBJ (Brian) Skosana	12	1	–	–	–	5	12	1	–	–	–	5
SS (Siviwe) Soyizwapi	8	4	–	–	–	20	9	4	–	–	–	20
PF (Pieter) Stemmet	1	–	–	–	–	0	1	–	–	–	–	0
IW (Wayne) Stevens	21	4	–	–	–	20	56	13	–	–	–	65
SR (Steven) Sykes	6	3	–	–	–	15	6	3	–	–	–	15
S (Scott) van Breda	19	3	34	39	0	200	39	8	34	45	0	243
DR (Dane) van der Westhuyzen	10	–	–	–	–	0	10	–	–	–	–	0
W (Wayne) van Heerden	13	–	–	–	–	0	121	22	–	–	–	110
M du P (Marlou) van Niekerk	6	1	1	0	0	7	6	1	1	0	0	7

info@eprugby.co.za

EASTERN PROVINCE SQUAD IN 2013 | EP KINGS CAREER

PLAYER	Appearances	Tries	Conversions	Penalties	Drop Goals	Points	Career Matches	Career Tries	Conversions	Penalties	Drop Goals	Points
KD (Kayle) van Zyl	15	3	6	1	0	30	15	3	6	1	0	30
N (Nicolas) Vergallo	5	1	–	–	–	5	5	1	–	–	–	5
LA (Luke) Watson	1	1	–	–	–	5	27	24	–	–	–	120
GA (George) Whitehead	9	2	5	0	0	20	39	8	59	27	–	239
S (Stefan) Willemse	16	8	–	–	–	40	16	8	–	–	–	40
S (Stefan) Zaayman	2	–	–	–	–	0	2	–	–	–	–	0
MR (Mzwanele) Zito	1	–	–	–	–	0	1	–	–	–	–	0
64 Players	**531**	**82**	**63**	**64**	**1**	**731**	**1356**	**309**	**144**	**110**	**1**	**2172**

ABSA U21 CHAMPIONSHIP (Champions, 1st, Section B)

Played	Won	Drawn	Lost	Points for	Points against	Tries for	Tries against
9	9	0	0	491	155	72	20

RESULTS: Bt Pumas (a) 46-20. Bt Griffons (h) 58-7. Bt Griquas (a) 53-0. Bt SWD (h) 76-16. Bt Boland (a) 31-17. Bt Valke (h) 87-17. Bt Limpopo (a) 37-33. SEMI FINAL Bt Griquas (h) 44-26. FINAL Bt Boland (a) 59-19.

SCORERS: 96 Ruan Allerston (33c,10p); 50 Siviwe Soyizwapi (10t); 40 Siphesihle Pungwuza (8t); 37 Marlou van Niekerk (5t,6c); 35 Wayven Smith (7t); 27 Sonwabo Majola (5t,1c); 25 Eben Barnard, Aidon Davis (5t each); 16 Shane Gates (2t,3c); 15 Lonwabo Ntleki, Ayabulela Dlepu, Sonkosi Kuhle (3t each); 10 Mzuvukile Sofisa, Claude Tshidibi, Siphumelele Msutwana (2t each), Gavin Hauptfleisch (5c); 7 Juan Smit (1t,1c); 5 Kevin Kaba, Sergeal Petersen, Frederik Roberts, Brandon Hector, Yakha Quinela, Sinethemba Nditi, Brenden Olivier, Ivan Ludick, Dane van der Westhuizen (1t each); 3 Andile Jho (1p).

ABSA U19 CHAMPIONSHIP (Champions, 3rd, Section B)

Played	Won	Drawn	Lost	Points for	Points against	Tries for	Tries against
9	6	0	3	314	234	45	30

RESULTS: Bt Pumas (a) 46-18. Bt Griffons (h) 42-20. Bt Griquas (a) 26-7. Lost SWD (h) 10-35. Lost Boland (a) 24-26. Lost Valke (h) 39-41. Bt Limpopo (a) 26-17. SEMI FINAL Bt Boland (a) 45-30. FINAL Bt Valke (a) 56-40.

SCORERS: 62 Selwyn Davids (4t,15c,4p); 35 Khaya Malotana (7t); 31 Warren Swarts (2t,9c,1p); 22 Juandre Fourie (4t,1c); 17 Matthew Moore (3t,1c), Alex Banfield (2t,2c,1p); 15 Johannes Nel, Kevin Kaba, Sergeal Petersen (3t each); 11 Jason Baggot (1c,3p); 10 John Schmidt, Khanya Mzilikazi, Stephan Ebersohn (2t each); 5 Gerrit Huisamen, Sherwin Slater, Jean-Pierre Jamieson, Lyle Lombard, Francois van der Walt, Dewald Meyer, Kuhle Mbiko, Whayburn Howley (1 t each); 4 Mitchel Turner (2c).

AMATEUR CHAMPIONSHIP
Eastern Province (South Section, Saldanha)

Played	Won	Drawn	Lost	Points for	Points against	Winning %
3	1	0	2	79	91	33%

RESULTS: Bt EP Rural 16-12. Lost WP 30-39. Lost Border 33-40.

EP Rural (South Section, Saldanha)

Played	Won	Drawn	Lost	Points for	Points against	Winning %
3	0	0	3	37	87	0%

RESULTS: Lost EP 12-16. Lost Boland XV 18-22. Lost Border Rural 7-49.

SOUTHERN SUB-UNION CHAMPIONSHIP (Runner-up, Margate)

Played	Won	Drawn	Lost	Points for	Points against	Winning %
3	2	0	1	62	85	66%

RESULTS: Bt Boland 23-20. Bt WP 27-24. Lost KZN Wildebeest 12-41.

EASTERN PROVINCE RUGBY UNION

APPEARANCES & POINTS IN VODACOM CUP 2013

	Pampas XV	Border	WP	Free State XV	Eagles	Sharks XV	Cavaliers	Blue Bulls	Pumas	Matches	Tries	Conversions	Penalties	Drop Goals	Points
Siwiwe Soyizwapi	15	15	15	–	–	–	–	–	–	3	1	–	–	–	5
Siyanda Grey	14	14	14	14	14	14	–	–	–	6	3	–	–	–	15
Scott van Breda	13	11	–	15	15	–	13	13	15	6	2	7	10	–	54
Wayne Stevens	12	13	13	13c	13	–	–	13	13	7	1	–	–	–	5
Norman Nelson	11	–	–	–	–	–	–	–	–	1	–	–	–	–	0
Wesley Dunlop	10	10	10	–	–	–	11R	12R	10	6	–	7	9	–	41
Scott Mathie	9	9	9	9	9	9	9	9	9	9	–	–	–	–	0
Devin Oosthuizen	8	6	–	–	–	6	6	6	–	5	2	–	–	–	10
Mpho Mbiyozo	7c	7c	7c	–	7c	7c	–	8R	7c	7	3	–	–	–	15
Tomas Leonardi	6	–	–	–	–	–	7	7	6	4	–	–	–	–	0
Samora Fihlani	5	5	5	5	5	4	–	5R	5R	8	–	–	–	–	0
Rynier Bernardo	4	4	–	–	–	–	–	–	–	2	–	–	–	–	0
Ross Geldenhuys	3	3	3	3	3	–	–	1R	1R	7	–	–	–	–	0
Virgile Lacombe	2	2	–	–	2R	–	–	–	–	3	1	–	–	–	5
Brenden Olivier	1	–	1R	3R	3R	–	–	–	–	4	–	–	–	–	0
Dane vd Westhuyzen	2R	2R	7R	7R	2R	–	–	–	2R	6	–	–	–	–	0
Charl du Plessis	1R	1	1	1	–	3R	3	3	3	8	–	–	–	–	0
Aidon Davis	5R	4R	6	–	–	–	–	–	–	3	–	–	–	–	0
Kuselo Moyake	6R	7R	–	–	–	–	–	–	–	2	–	–	–	–	0
Boela Abrahams	9R	9R	9R	–	–	–	–	–	–	3	–	–	–	–	0
Ntabeni Dukisa	x	10R	10R	10	10R	15	–	–	–	5	1	1	1	–	10
Andile Jho	x	–	–	18R	13R	13	13R	–	–	4	–	–	–	–	0
Tiger Mangweni	–	12	12	12	12	12	12c	12c	12	8	1	–	–	–	5
Paul Schoeman	–	8	8	8	6	8	8	8	8	8	2	–	–	–	10
Lizo Gqoboka	–	1R	–	–	1	1	1	1	1	6	1	–	–	–	5
Waylon Murray	–	12R	–	–	–	–	–	–	–	1	–	–	–	–	0
Yamkela Ngam	–	–	11	11	11	–	–	–	–	3	2	–	–	–	10
Thabo Mamojele	–	–	4	6R	–	–	–	–	–	2	–	–	–	–	0
Coenraad Britz	–	–	2	2	2	2	2R	2R	2	7	1	–	–	–	5
Wayne van Heerden	–	–	4R	–	–	–	–	–	–	1	–	–	–	–	0
Dalton Davis	–	–	8R	7	6R	–	–	7R	8R	5	1	–	–	–	5
Lonwabo Ntleki	–	–	11R	–	–	–	–	–	21R	2	–	–	–	–	0
Tim Agaba	–	–	–	6	–	x	7R	–	–	2	–	–	–	–	0
Mzwanele Zito	–	–	–	4	–	–	–	–	–	1	–	–	–	–	0
Schalk Oelofse	–	–	–	4R	–	–	–	–	–	1	–	–	–	–	0
Kayle van Zyl	–	–	–	9R	9R	15R	15	15R	15	6	1	5	1	–	18
Marlou van Niekerk	–	–	–	10R	–	x	–	–	15R	2	–	–	–	–	0
Shane Gates	–	–	–	–	10	10	10	10	–	4	–	–	–	–	0
Luke Watson	–	–	–	–	8	–	–	–	–	1	1	–	–	–	5
Darron Nell	–	–	–	–	4	–	4	–	5	3	–	–	–	–	0
Stefan Willemse	–	–	–	–	4R	4R	4R	4	4	5	3	–	–	–	15
Michael Killian	–	–	–	–	–	11	–	14	11	3	–	–	–	–	0
Daniel Adongo	–	–	–	–	–	5	5	5	–	3	–	–	–	–	0
Jaco Engels	–	–	–	–	–	3	3R	–	–	2	–	–	–	–	0
Brian Skosana	–	–	–	–	–	x	14	–	14	2	–	–	–	–	0
Eben Barnard	–	–	–	–	–	–	11	–	–	1	–	–	–	–	0
Hannes Franklin	–	–	–	–	–	–	2	2	–	2	–	–	–	–	0
Dwayne Kelly	–	–	–	–	–	–	9R	–	9R	2	–	–	–	–	0
Marcello Sampson	–	–	–	–	–	–	–	11	–	1	–	–	–	–	0
49 Players										193	27	20	21	0	238

EASTERN PROVINCE RUGBY UNION

APPEARANCES & POINTS IN ABSA CURRIE CUP 2013

	Pumas	Griffons	Leopards	Eagles	Cavaliers	Valke	Bulldogs	Pumas	Griffons	Leopards	Eagles	Cavaliers	Valke	Bulldogs	Leopards	Pumas	Matches	Tries	Conversions	Penalties	Drop Goals	Points
S van Breda	15	15	15	–	14	–	–	15	15	15	15	15	15	15	15	15	13	1	27	29	–	146
S Soyizwapi	14	14	–	15	15	15	–	–	–	–	–	–	–	–	–	–	5	3	–	–	–	15
W Stevens	13	13	13	13	13	–	12R	13R	13	13	13	13	13	13R	x	12R	14	3	–	–	–	15
T Mangweni	12c	12c	12c	12c	12c	–	12c	12	12c	12	12c	12c	12c	12	12	12	15	3	–	–	–	15
H Parkes	11	11	–	–	–	–	–	–	–	–	–	–	–	–	–	–	2	1	–	–	–	5
W Dunlop	10	10	10	–	10	–	–	–	–	–	–	–	–	–	–	–	4	1	4	7	–	34
D Kelly	9	9R	9R	9	–	–	–	–	9R	9R	–	–	9R	9	9	9	10	–	–	–	–	0
T Agaba	8	–	–	–	–	–	–	7	8	7	7	8R	8	8	8	8	10	2	–	–	–	10
K Moyake	7	6R	7	–	–	–	7R	–	8R	–	–	–	6R	–	–	–	6	–	–	–	–	0
D Davis	6	6	8	8	6	–	–	–	–	–	–	–	–	–	–	–	5	1	–	–	–	5
D Adongo	5	–	–	–	–	–	–	–	–	–	–	–	–	–	–	–	1	–	–	–	–	0
S Willemse	4	–	–	6	5	6	–	x	6	8R	7R	7	6	–	7R	7R	11	5	–	–	–	25
C du Plessis	3	–	–	–	–	–	–	–	3	3	3	3	–	3	3	3	8	–	–	–	–	0
C Britz	2	–	–	2	2	–	2R	–	–	x	2R	2R	–	x	–	–	6	–	–	–	–	0
L Gqoboka	1	–	3R	3R	3R	3	3	3	3R	3R	1R	1	3R	1	1	1	15	–	–	–	–	0
D vd Westhuyzen	2R	2	2	–	–	2R	–	–	–	–	–	–	–	–	–	–	4	–	–	–	–	0
B Olivier	1R	1	1	1	1	–	1	1	1	1	–	1	–	–	–	–	11	–	–	–	–	0
A Davis	5R	8	–	5	8	–	–	–	–	–	–	–	–	–	–	–	4	2	–	–	–	10
M Mbiyozo	7R	7	–	7	7	7c	7	–	–	–	–	–	7	7	7	7	9	6	–	–	–	30
S Mathie	9R	9	9	–	9	–	–	–	–	–	–	–	–	–	–	–	4	–	–	–	–	–
N Dukisa	14R	10R	14	10	12R	10	15	10R	10R	14R	x	10R	x	10R	x	10R	13	2	5	7	1	44
M van Niekerk	6R	–	10R	14	–	–	10	–	–	–	–	–	–	–	–	–	4	1	1	–	–	7
T Mamojele	–	5	–	5R	–	5R	5R	–	5R	4R	5	4R	x	7R	–	–	9	1	–	–	–	5
S Fihlani	–	4	4	4	4	4	–	4	4	4	–	–	–	–	–	–	9	3	–	–	–	15
R Geldenhuys	–	3	3	–	–	–	–	–	–	–	3R	3	3R	3R	3R	3R	7	1	–	–	–	5
A de Swardt	–	2R	2R	2R	2R	2	2	x	2R	–	–	2	2	2	2	–	11	–	–	–	–	0
P Stemmet	–	3R	–	–	–	–	–	–	–	–	–	–	–	–	–	–	1	–	–	–	–	0
W van Heerden	–	5R	19R	6R	6R	5	5	–	–	–	4R	5	5	5R	5R	4R	12	–	–	–	–	0
S Petersen	–	13R	–	–	–	11R	14	–	–	–	–	–	–	–	–	–	3	–	–	–	–	0
E Barnard	–	–	11	11	–	11	–	–	–	–	–	–	–	–	–	–	3	–	–	–	–	0
T Bholi	–	–	6	–	8R	6R	6	–	–	–	–	–	–	–	–	–	4	–	–	–	–	0
R Bernardo	–	–	5	–	–	–	–	5R	5	–	–	–	–	–	–	–	3	–	–	–	–	0
R Erasmus	–	–	7R	–	–	–	–	–	–	–	–	–	–	–	–	–	1	–	–	–	–	0
A Jho	–	–	14R	x	–	12	–	–	–	–	–	–	–	–	–	–	2	–	–	–	–	0
J Engels	–	–	–	3	3	3R	–	–	–	–	–	–	–	–	–	–	3	–	–	–	–	0
B Abrahams	–	–	–	9R	9R	9	9	x	–	–	–	–	–	–	–	–	4	–	–	–	–	0
K van Zyl	–	–	–	10R	10R	9R	9R	–	–	x	9R	9	9R	9R	9R	9R	9	2	1	–	–	12
M Killian	–	–	–	–	11	14	11	11	14	14	14	14	14	14	14	11	12	4	–	–	–	20
S Grey	–	–	–	–	–	13	13	14	–	–	–	–	–	–	–	–	3	1	–	–	–	5
S Zaayman	–	–	–	–	–	8	8	–	–	–	–	–	–	–	–	–	2	–	–	–	–	0
B Skosana	–	–	–	–	–	13R	10R	–	14R	11R	11R	11	11	11	11	14	10	1	–	–	–	5
M Maarman	–	–	–	–	–	–	1	–	–	–	–	–	–	–	–	–	1	–	–	–	–	0
E Mnyaka	–	–	–	–	–	–	3R	x	–	–	–	–	–	–	–	–	1	–	–	–	–	0
R Cooke	–	–	–	–	–	–	–	13	–	–	–	–	–	13	13	13	4	–	–	–	–	0
G Whitehead	–	–	–	–	–	–	–	10	10	10	10	10	10	10	10	10	9	2	5	0	–	20
N Vergallo	–	–	–	–	–	–	–	9	9	9	9	9	–	–	–	–	5	1	–	–	–	5
C du Preez	–	–	–	–	–	–	–	8	–	8	8	8	–	–	–	–	4	2	–	–	–	10
D Oosthuizen	–	–	–	–	–	–	–	6	7	6	6	6	7	6	6	6	9	1	–	–	–	5
S Sykes	–	–	–	–	–	–	–	5	–	–	–	4	4	4	4	4	6	3	–	–	–	15
D Nell	–	–	–	–	–	–	–	4c	–	5c	–	–	5c	5c	5c	–	5	1	–	–	–	5

APPEARANCES & POINTS IN ABSA CURRIE CUP 2013

	Pumas	Griffons	Leopards	Eagles	Cavaliers	Valke	Bulldogs	Pumas	Griffons	Leopards	Eagles	Cavaliers	Valke	Bulldogs	Leopards	Pumas	Matches	Tries	Conversions	Penalties	Drop Goals	Points
H Franklin	–	–	–	–	–	–	–	2	2	2	2	–	2R	–	–	2	6	1	–	–	–	5
M Sampson	–	–	–	–	–	–	–	11	11	11	13R	–	–	–	–	–	4	–	–	–	–	0
Y Ngam	–	–	–	–	–	–	–	–	–	–	–	–	x	–	–	–	0	–	–	–	–	0
B Dyer	–	–	–	–	–	–	–	–	–	–	–	–	–	–	2R	2R	2	–	–	–	–	0
Penalty try	–	–	–	–	–	–	–	–	–	–	–	–	–	–	–	–	0	2	–	–	–	10
54 Players																	**338**	**57**	**43**	**43**	**1**	**503**

EP KINGS RECORDS

MATCH RECORDS
Biggest win	110-17	vs. Welwitschias (Namibia)	2001
Biggest Currie Cup win	63-7	vs. Griffons	2013
Heaviest defeat	12-80	vs. Griqualand West	1998
Heaviest Currie Cup defeat	3-65	vs. Northern Transvaal	1984
Highest score	110	vs. Welwitschias (Namibia) (110-17)	2001
Most points conceded	80	vs. Griqualand West (12-80)	1998
Most tries	16	vs. Welwitschias (Namibia) (110-17)	2001
Most Currie Cup tries	11	vs. Griffons (67-26)	2011
Most points by a player	38	HP le Roux vs. Eastern Transvaal	1991
Most Currie Cup points by a player	29	AP Kruger vs. North West	1996
Most tries by a player	5	FW Knoetze vs. Stellaland	1991
	5	FG Crous vs. Western Transvaal	1994
	5	N Nelson vs. Valke (Currie Cup, First Div.)	2010

SEASON RECORDS
Most team points	875	27 matches	2012
Most Currie Cup points by team	611	18 matches	2012
Most points by a player	282	AP Kruger	1996
Most Currie Cup points by a player	153	B Hennessey	2002
Most team tries	103	24 matches	2003
	103	27 matches	2012
Most Currie Cup tries by team	76	18 matches	2012
Most tries by a player	14	M Van Vuuren	1994
	14	H Pedro	1998
	14	FM Juries	2003
Most Currie Cup tries by a player	13	H Pedro	1998
	13	LA Watson	2012

CAREER RECORDS
Most appearances	173	BC Pinnock	1993-2002
Most points	1126	GC van Zyl	1981-1988
Most Currie Cup points	755	GC van Zyl	1981-1988
Most tries	56	NT Nelson	2006-2013

HONOURS
Vodacom Shield   2002
First Division   2010, 2012

FREE STATE RUGBY UNION

FOUNDED 1895
(as Orange Free State)
GROUND
Free State Stadium
CAPACITY
46 000
ADDRESS
Att Horak St,
Bloemfontein, 9300
POSTAL ADDRESS
P.O. Box 15,
Bloemfontein, 9300
TELEPHONE
051-407 1700
WEBSITE
www.fscheetahs.co.za
COLOURS
White jersey with orange stripes, black shorts
CURRIE CUP COACH
Naka Drotské
VODACOM CUP COACH
Joe Beukes
CAPTAIN
Adriaan Strauss
PRESIDENT
Lindsay Mould
COMPANY CEO
Harold Verster
UNION CEO
Gerda von Solms
(passed away during the season)

Cheetahs back up to speed

THE TOYOTA FREE STATE CHEETAHS PUT A FORGETTABLE 2012 Absa Currie Cup season behind them to once again be title contenders in 2013.

But their nagging inconsistency in recent times, which saw them finish last on the log in 2012 with just three wins, continued to be a factor in 2013, coach Naka Drotské and his charges winning five and losing five in the round-robin stages.

Other results meant that this was still good enough to finish third on the six-team log behind the unbeaten DHL Western Province and the Sharks, and ahead of the fourth-placed MTN Golden Lions. But the Cheetahs' inability to win more than two matches in a row came back to bite them when it counted most, as the Sharks ran out 33-22 winners in Durban to advance to the final.

A look at the season's results show that the Cheetahs, for all their effort, just couldn't string together a consistent set of results. The men from Bloemfontein started off well enough when they beat the Lions 30-29 in Johannesburg on the opening weekend. But they followed up this invaluable win on the road with two losses – the second of which came at home against the Sharks.

GWK Griquas and the Lions were dispatched at the Free State Stadium but a 26-10 loss to the struggling Vodacom Blue Bulls at Loftus Versfeld, and a 29-27 defeat to WP back in Bloem, left the Cheetahs with too much work to do in their final two games to challenge for a home semi-final.

Against the Sharks in the Durban semi, the Cheetahs ran into an in-form Patrick Lambie, who scored 22 points, but they also made far too many basic errors – something which had dogged them all season. Despite the loss, Drotské will have taken heart from the fact that his side had bounced back from their horror 2012 season, while a number of players put their hands up for 2014 Vodacom Super Rugby consideration.

The Cheetahs' backline selections were remarkably consistent, with scrumhalf Sarel Pretorius missing only the semi-final, flyhalf Elgar Watts, centres Robert Ebersohn and Johann Sadie, and fullback Hennie Daniller playing in every match, while wings Raymond Rhule and Riaan Smit missed just three matches between them.

Rhule continued to grow as a player, scoring seven tries in 10 matches, while Watts matured as a playmaker, scoring four tries of his own and kicking 43 points. Springbok pivot Johan Goosen also made a long-awaited return, coming on as a replacement in the last two games of the season, which will give Drotské plenty of options as he looks to 2014.

The back row combination of No. 8 Philip van der Walt, blindsider Lappies Labuschagne and skipper Boom Prinsloo were very effective, while Lodewyk de Jager showed promise at lock alongside the industrious Oupa Mohoje.

Boom Prinsloo leaps high for the Cheetahs.
Steve Haag/Gallo Images

VODACOM CUP LOG POSITIONS

2013	10th	2010	2nd	2007	4th	2004	2nd	2001	4th	1998	11th
2012	11th	2009	6th	2006	8th	2003	2nd	**2000**	**3rd**		
2011	7th	2008	2nd	2005	5th	2002	5th	1999	12th		

ABSA CURRIE CUP LOG POSITIONS

2013	3rd	2010	3rd	**2007**	**1st**	2004	3rd	2001	4th	1998	5th
2012	6th	2009	4th	**2006**	**1st**	2003	5th	2000	4th	1997	3rd
2011	3rd	2008	3rd	**2005**	**4th**	2002	2nd	1999	3rd	1996	3rd

2013 RESULTS & SCORERS

VODACOM CUP (as Free State XV) Played **7** Won **2** Drawn **0** Lost **5** Points for **195** Points against **190** Tries for **25** Tries against **22** Winning Percentage **29%**

Date	Venue	Opponent	Result	Score	Referee	Scorers
Mrch 08	George	SWD	WON	31-08	S Berry	T: Fredericks, Erasmus, Claassen. C: De Bruyn (2). P: De Bruyn (4)
Mrch 16	Bloemfontein [1]	Boland	LOST	23-27	A Sehlako	T: Erasmus, De Bruyn, Engelbrecht. C: De Bruyn. P: De Bruyn (2).
Mrch 23	Durban	Sharks XV	LOST	33-34	C Joubert	T: Huggett, Engelbrecht, De Klerk, Ngoza. C: De Bruyn (2). P: De Bruyn (3).
April 06	Bloemfontein	EP Kings	LOST	13-17	S Mayende	T: Mohoje, Erasmus. P: De Bruyn.
April 13	Alice	Border	WON	26-25	F Groenewald	T: Daniller (2), Engelbrecht, Marx. C: Scheepers (2), Watts.
April 20	Stellenbosch [2]	Pampas XV	LOST	32-38	F Pretorius	T: Prinsloo (3). Engelbrecht, Tom. C: Watts (2). P: Watts
April 27	Bloemfontein	WP	LOST	37-41	M Jonker	T: Prinsloo (2), Mohoje, de Bruyn. C: Smit (3), Scheepers. P: Scheepers (2), Smit.

[1] CUT Field, [2] AF Markotter Stadium.

ABSA Currie Cup Played **11** Won **5** Lost **6** Drawn **0** Points for **284** Points against **271** Tries for **34** Tries against **29** Winning Percentage **45%**

Date	Venue	Opponent	Result	Score	Referee	Scorers
Aug 10	Johannesburg	Golden Lions	WON	30-29	M vd Westhuizen	T: Prinsloo, Sadie, Ebersohn, Pretorius. C: Smit, Watts. P: Smit, Watts.
Aug 17	Cape Town	WP	LOST	14-15	J Kaplan	T: Watts, Smit. C: Watts, Smit.
Aug 23	Bloemfontein	Sharks	LOST	15-18	J Jaftha	T: Labuschagne, Rhule. C: Smit. P: Smit.
Aug 31	Bloemfontein	Griquas	WON	40-20	C Joubert	T: Prinsloo (2), Watts, Luiters, Rhule. C: Smit (2), Watts. P: Watts (2), Smit.
Sep 07	Pretoria	Blue Bulls	LOST	10-26	S Berry	T: Smit, Watts.
Sep 13	Bloemfontein	Golden Lions	WON	26-23	M vd Westhuizen	T: Sadie, Pretorius. C: Smit (2). P: Smit (4).
Sep 21	Durban	Sharks	LOST	26-50	M Jonker	T: Rhule, Le Roux. C: Smit (2). P: Smit (4).
Sep 27	Bloemfontein	WP	LOST	27-29	M Jonker	T: Daniller (2), Pretorius. C: Smit (2), Watts. P: Smit, Watts.
Oct 05	Kimberley	Griquas	WON	52-21	J Kaplan	T: Rhule (4), Van Zyl, Van der Merwe. C: Du Plessis (3), Watts (2). P: Watts (4)
Oct 12	Bloemfontein	Blue Bulls	WON	22-07	M Jonker	T: Strauss, Watts, Ebersohn. C: Watts (2). P: Watts.
Oct 19 Semi-final	Durban	Sharks	LOST	22-33	M vd Westhuizen	T: Sadie, Labuschagne, Van der Merwe, C: Smit, Goosen. P: Goosen.

FREE STATE RUGBY UNION

FREE STATE CHEETAHS SQUAD IN 2013

PLAYER	Appearances	Tries	Conversions	Penalties	Drop Goals	Points	Career Matches	Career Tries	Conversions	Penalties	Drop Goals	Points
RS (Ryno) Benjamin	4	–	–	–	–	0	19	2	–	–	–	10
HJ (Hennie) Daniller	11	2	–	–	–	10	71	11	–	–	–	55
T (Tertius) Daniller	0	–	–	–	–	0	0	–	–	–	–	0
L (Lodewyk) de Jager	10	–	–	–	–	0	10	–	–	–	–	0
PR (Rossouw) de Klerk	7	–	–	–	–	0	7	–	–	–	–	0
WNF (Willie) du Plessis	9	–	3	–	–	6	9	–	3	–	–	6
WH (Wian) du Preez	5	–	–	–	–	0	110	7	–	–	–	35
RT (Robert) Ebersohn	11	2	–	–	–	10	72	11	–	–	–	55
GJ (Joubert) Engelbrecht	1	–	–	–	–	0	1	–	–	–	–	0
JL (Johan) Goosen	2	–	1	1	–	5	17	2	23	26	3	143
JR (John-Roy) Jenkinson	2	–	–	–	–	0	2	–	–	–	–	0
PHC (Pieter) Labuschagne	11	2	–	–	–	10	39	10	–	–	–	50
AJ (AJ) le Roux	4	1	–	–	–	5	7	1	–	–	–	5
HJ (Hercu) Liebenberg	9	–	–	–	–	0	57	–	–	–	–	0
PJ (Piet) Lindeque	6	–	–	–	–	0	6	–	–	–	–	0
K (Kevin) Luiters	4	1	–	–	–	5	4	1	–	–	–	5
TS (Oupa) Mohoje	11	–	–	–	–	0	11	–	–	–	–	0
TFN (Freddy) Ngoza	4	–	–	–	–	0	4	–	–	–	–	0
TN (Trevor) Nyakane	9	–	–	–	–	0	37	2	–	–	–	10
CR (Caylib) Oosthuizen	3	–	–	–	–	0	3	–	–	–	–	0
CV (Coenie) Oosthuizen	2	–	–	–	–	0	53	11	–	–	–	55
SJ (Sarel) Pretorius	10	3	–	–	–	15	22	7	–	–	–	35
JG (Boom) Prinsloo	11	3	–	–	–	15	31	9	–	–	–	45
D (Davon) Raubenheimer	6	–	–	–	–	0	16	–	–	–	–	0
E (Ethienne) Reynecke	4	–	–	–	–	0	4	–	–	–	–	0
RK (Raymond) Rhule	10	7	–	–	–	35	22	15	–	–	–	75
J (Johann) Sadie	11	3	–	–	–	15	11	3	–	–	–	15
AJ (Riaan) Smit	9	2	12	12	–	70	35	10	20	19	–	147
JA (Adriaan) Strauss	2	1	–	–	–	5	56	9	–	–	–	45
FJ (Francois) Uys	4	–	–	–	–	0	58	7	–	–	–	35
SW (Schalk) van der Merwe	5	2	–	–	–	10	15	2	–	–	–	10
CP (Philip) van der Walt	8	–	–	–	–	0	31	4	–	–	–	20
PE (Piet) van Zyl	7	1	–	–	–	5	31	6	–	–	–	30
PV (Waltie) Vermeulen	5	–	–	–	–	0	44	–	–	–	–	0
EG (Elgar) Watts	11	4	8	9	–	63	11	4	8	9	–	63
35 players	228	34	24	22	0	284	926	134	54	54	3	949

APPEARANCES & POINTS IN ABSA CURRIE CUP 2013

FREE STATE RUGBY UNION

Player	Golden Lions	WP	Sharks	Griquas	Blue Bulls	Golden Lions	Sharks	WP	Griquas	Blue Bulls	Sharks SF	Matches	Tries	Conversions	Penalties	Drop Goals	Points
Hennie Daniller	15	15	15	15	15	15	15	15	15	15	15	11	2	–	–	–	10
Riaan Smit	14	14	14	14	14	14	14	14	–	–	14	9	2	12	12	–	70
Johann Sadie	13	13	13	13	13	13	13	13	13	13	13	11	3	–	–	–	15
Robert Ebersohn	12	12	12	12	12	12	12	12	12	12	12	11	2	–	–	–	10
Raymond Rhule	11	11	11	11	11	11	11	–	11	11	11	10	7	–	–	–	35
Elgar Watts	10	10	10	10	10	10	10	10	10	10	10	11	4	8	9	–	63
Sarel Pretorius	9	9	9	9	9	9	9	9	9	9	–	10	3	–	–	–	15
Philip van der Walt	8	8	8	8	8	–	–	–	6R	8	8	8	–	–	–	–	0
Pieter Labuschagne	7	7	7	7	7	7	7	7	7	7	7	11	2	–	–	–	10
Boom Prinsloo	6c	6c	6c	6c	6c	8c	8c	8c	8c	6	6	11	3	–	–	–	15
Waltie Vermeulen	5	5	–	5R	x	5	5	–	–	–	–	5	–	–	–	–	0
Lodewyk de Jager	4	4	5	5	5	–	4	5	5	5	5	10	–	–	–	–	0
John-Roy Jenkinson	3	3	–	–	–	–	–	–	–	–	–	2	–	–	–	–	0
Hercu Liebenberg	2	2	2	2	2	2	2	2	2	–	x	9	–	–	–	–	0
Caylib Oosthuizen	1	1	1	–	–	–	–	–	–	–	–	3	–	–	–	–	0
Ethienne Reynecke	2R	6R	x	2R	2R	x	–	–	–	–	–	4	–	–	–	–	0
Wian du Preez	1R	1R	–	3R	3R	3R	–	–	–	–	–	5	–	–	–	–	0
Oupa Mohoje	5R	4R	4	4	4	4	5R	6	6	4R	4R	11	–	–	–	–	0
Davon Raubenheimer	x	7R	7R	7R	8R	6	6	x	–	–	–	6	–	–	–	–	0
Piet van Zyl	9R	9R	–	–	–	–	12R	9R	9R	14R	9	7	1	–	–	–	5
Joubert Engelbrecht	x	x	–	–	–	–	–	–	12R	–	–	1	–	–	–	–	0
Piet Lindeque	14R	–	x	14R	14R	12R	–	11	14	–	–	6	–	–	–	–	0
Willie du Plessis	–	x	10R	15R	10R	15R	10R	10R	10R	15R	15R	9	–	3	–	–	6
Trevor Nyakane	–	–	3	1	1	1	1	3	3R	3	3	9	–	–	–	–	0
Rossouw de Klerk	–	–	1R	3	3	3	3	1R	3	–	–	7	–	–	–	–	0
Kevin Luiters	–	–	9R	9R	9R	9R	–	–	–	–	–	4	1	–	–	–	5
Freddy Ngoza	–	–	x	–	–	x	7R	4	5R	x	6	4	–	–	–	–	0
Tertius Daniller	–	–	–	–	x	–	–	–	–	–	–	0	–	–	–	–	0
Ryno Benjamin	–	–	–	–	–	11R	14R	–	14	14R	–	4	–	–	–	–	0
Schalk van der Merwe	–	–	–	–	–	3R	1	1	1R	1R	–	5	2	–	–	–	10
AJ le Roux	–	–	–	–	–	2R	2R	2R	2R	–	–	4	1	–	–	–	5
Francois Uys	–	–	–	–	–	–	4R	4	4	4	–	4	–	–	–	–	0
Adriaan Strauss	–	–	–	–	–	–	–	–	2c	2c	–	2	1	–	–	–	5
Coenie Oosthuizen	–	–	–	–	–	–	–	–	1	1	–	2	–	–	–	–	0
Johan Goosen	–	–	–	–	–	–	–	–	–	10R	10R	2	–	1	1	–	5
35 players													228	34	24	22	0	284

FREE STATE XV SQUAD (Vodacom Cup squad)

PLAYER	Appearances	Tries	Conversions	Penalties	Drop Goals	Points	Career Matches	Career Tries	Conversions	Penalties	Drop Goals	Points
LH (Leroy) Bitterhout	2	–	–	–	–	0	4	2	–	–	–	10
JG (Gys) Briedenhann	1	–	–	–	–	0	1	–	–	–	–	0
M (Marnus) Briedenhann	6	–	–	–	–	0	6	–	–	–	–	0
N (Neil) Claassen	7	1	–	–	–	5	2	–	–	–	–	0
FH (Erick) Colyn	1	–	–	–	–	0	1	–	–	–	–	0
T (Tertius) Daniller	7	2	–	–	–	10	7	2	–	–	–	10
MJ (Tewis) de Bruyn	5	2	5	10	–	50	5	2	5	10	–	59
PR (Rossouw) de Klerk	7	1	–	–	–	5	7	1	–	–	–	5
MS (Maputhla) Dolo	5	–	–	–	–	0	5	–	–	–	–	0
JJ (Jay) du Toit	0	–	–	–	–	0	0	–	–	–	–	0
GJ (Joubert) Engelbrecht	7	4	–	–	–	20	7	4	–	–	–	20
EL (Ludwig) Erasmus	7	3	–	–	–	15	7	3	–	–	–	15
AS (Andries) Ferreira	3	–	–	–	–	0	3	–	–	–	–	0
ER (Eddie) Fredericks	4	1	–	–	–	5	4	1	–	–	–	5
AD (Barry) Geel	1	–	–	–	–	0	6	3	–	–	–	15
E (Elandre) Huggett	5	1	–	–	–	5	12	2	–	–	–	10
HJ (Hercu) Liebenberg	7	–	–	–	–	0	7	–	–	–	–	0
DN (Niell) Jordaan	4	–	–	–	–	0	4	–	–	–	–	0
K (Kevin) Luiters	4	–	–	–	–	0	6	–	–	–	–	0
CM (Charles) Marais	4	–	–	–	–	0	8	–	–	–	–	0
DR (Niel) Marais	6	–	–	–	–	0	6	–	–	–	–	0
NPJ (Noel) Marx	3	1	–	–	–	5	3	1	–	–	–	5
P (Pieter) Matthee	3	–	–	–	–	0	3	–	–	–	–	0
TS (Oupa) Mohoje	5	2	–	–	–	10	5	2	–	–	–	10
IJ (Ignis) Nagel	3	–	–	–	–	0	3	–	–	–	–	0
TFN (Freddy) Ngoza	2	1	–	–	–	5	2	1	–	–	–	5
Q (Quinton) Norris	1	–	–	–	–	0	1	–	–	–	–	0
CR (Caylib) Oosthuizen	3	–	–	–	–	0	3	–	–	–	–	0
JG (Boom) Prinsloo	3	5	–	–	–	25	3	5	–	–	–	25
DS (Davon) Raubenheimer	3	–	–	–	–	0	6	–	–	–	–	0
JN (Nico) Scheepers	4	–	3	2	–	12	8	3	12	5	–	54
AJ (Riaan) Smit	1	–	3	1	–	9	6	1	11	3	1	39
S (Siphosethu) Tom	5	1	–	–	–	5	6	2	–	–	–	10
FJ (Franco) van der Merwe	2	–	–	–	–	0	2	–	–	–	–	0
AJ (Andre) van der Walt	6	–	–	–	–	0	13	–	–	–	–	0
TG (Torsten) van Jaarsveld	2	–	–	–	–	0	2	–	–	–	–	0
R (Robbie) van Schalkwyk	1	–	–	–	–	0	3	1	–	–	–	5
OP (Ockie) van Zyl	2	–	–	–	–	0	9	2	–	–	–	10
PV (Waltie) Vermeulen	1	–	–	–	–	0	4	–	–	–	–	0
EG (Elgar) Watts	2	–	3	1	–	9	2	–	3	1	–	9
AW (Arthur) Williams	1	–	–	–	–	0	1	–	–	–	–	0
41 Players	146	25	14	14	0	195	193	38	31	19	1	321

FREE STATE RUGBY UNION

APPEARANCES & POINTS IN VODACOM CUP 2013 (Free State XV)

Player	SWD Eagles	Boland	Sharks XV	EP Kings	Border	Pampas XV	WP	Matches	Tries	Conversions	Penalties	Drop Goals	Points
Leroy Bitterhout	15	15	–	–	–	–	–	2	–	–	–	–	0
Eddie Fredericks	14	14	14	14	–	–	–	4	1	–	–	–	5
Joubert Engelbrecht	13	13	12	12	13	13	12	7	4	–	–	–	20
Niel Marais	12	12	–	12R	12	12	12R	6	–	–	–	–	0
Ludwig Erasmus	11	11	15	15	15	15	13	7	3	–	–	–	15
Tewis de Bruyn	10	10	10	10	–	–	9	5	2	5	10	–	50
Andre van der Walt	9	9	9	9	9R	x	6R	6	–	–	–	–	0
Tertius Daniller	8c	8c	8c	8c	8c	8c	7R	7	2	–	–	–	10
Davon Raubenheimer	7	7	–	7	–	–	–	3	–	–	–	–	0
Torsten van Jaarsveld	6	6	–	–	–	–	–	2	–	–	–	–	0
Neil Claassen	5	5	5	5	5	5	5R	7	1	–	–	–	5
Marnus Briedenhann	4	4	–	4R	4R	4R	4	6	–	–	–	–	0
Rossouw de Klerk	3	3	3	3	3	3	3	7	1	–	–	–	5
Hercu Liebenberg	2	2	2	2	2	2	2c	7	–	–	–	–	0
Franco van der Merwe	1	1	–	–	–	–	–	2	–	–	–	–	0
Ignis Nagel	1R	1R	x	1R	–	x	–	3	–	–	–	–	0
Gys Briedenhann	4R	–	–	–	–	–	–	1	–	–	–	–	0
Ockie van Zyl	x	4R	5R	–	–	–	–	2	–	–	–	–	0
Pieter Matthee	8R	6R	7	–	–	–	–	3	–	–	–	–	0
Erick Colyn	x	9R	–	–	–	–	–	1	–	–	–	–	0
Arthur Williams	x	12R	–	–	–	–	–	1	–	–	–	–	0
Quinton Norris	14R	x	–	–	–	–	–	1	–	–	–	–	0
JJ du Toit	–	x	–	–	–	–	–	0	–	–	–	–	0
Robbie van Schalkwyk	–	–	13	–	–	–	–	1	–	–	–	–	0
Maputhla Dolo	–	–	11	11	15R	14	14	5	–	–	–	–	0
Elandre Huggett	–	–	6	5R	2R	6R	8R	5	1	–	–	–	5
Oupa Mohoje	–	–	4	6	7	7	7	5	2	–	–	–	10
Charles Marais	–	–	1	–	1R	1	1R	4	–	–	–	–	0
Nico Scheepers	–	–	15R	–	14	11R	15	4	–	3	2	–	12
Freddy Ngoza	–	–	7R	7R	–	–	–	2	1	–	–	–	5
Kevin Luiters	–	–	9R	9R	9	9	–	4	–	–	–	–	0
Niell Jordaan	–	–	6R	–	6R	8R	8	4	–	–	–	–	0
Siphosethu Tom	–	–	13R	14R	11	11	11	5	1	–	–	–	5
Barry Geel	–	–	–	13	–	–	–	1	–	–	–	–	0
Andries Ferreira	–	–	–	4	4	4	–	3	–	–	–	–	0
Caylib Oosthuizen	–	–	–	1	1	–	1	3	–	–	–	–	0
Elgar Watts	–	–	–	–	10	10	–	2	–	3	1	–	9
Boom Prinsloo	–	–	–	–	6	6	6	3	5	–	–	–	25
Noel Marx	–	–	–	–	10R	12R	10R	3	1	–	–	–	5
Riaan Smit	–	–	–	–	–	–	10	1	–	3	1	–	9
Waltie Vermeulen	–	–	–	–	–	–	5	1	–	–	–	–	0
41 players								**146**	**25**	**14**	**14**	**0**	**195**

ABSA UNDER-21 CHAMPIONSHIP (5th, Section A)
Played 12 Won 6 Drawn 0 Lost 6 Points for 332 Points against 360 Tries for 44 Tries against 48
RESULTS Bt WP (h) 18-16. Bt Border (a) 32-15. Bt Golden Lions (a) 25-23. Lost KZN (h) 25-36. Lost Blue Bulls (a) 27-40. Bt Leopards (h) 29-40. Lost WP (a) 13-32. Bt Border (h) 43-29. Lost Golden Lions (h) 28-43. Lost KZN (a) 16-39. Bt Leopards (a) 38-29. Lost Blue Bulls (h) 27-29.
SCORERS 56 Marco Mason (3t, 7c, 9p). 46 Niel Marais (11c, 8p). 30 Neil Claassen (6t). 25 Stephan Griesel, Tienie Burger (5t each). 20 Maputha Dolo (4t). 15 Jan de Klerk, Philip Botha, Sethu Tom, Raymond Rhule (3t each), Noël Marx (1t, 2c, 2dg), Jan Strumpher (5p). 10 Henco Greyling, Henco Venter, Tertius Kruger (2t each). 5 Gerhard Olivier, Kevin Luiters, Luan de Bruin, Niell Jordaan, Ockert du Toit (1t each).

FREE STATE CHEETAHS RECORDS

MATCH RECORDS
Biggest win	132-3	vs. Eastern Orange Free State	1977
Biggest Currie Cup win	106-0	vs. Northern Free State	1997
Heaviest defeat	0-50	vs. Eastern Province *(Currie Cup)*	1993
Highest score	132	vs. Eastern Orange Free State (132-3)	1977
Highest Currie Cup score	113	vs. South Western Districts (113-11)	1996
Most points conceded	64	vs. Griqualand West (17-64)	1998
Most tries	23	vs. Eastern Orange Free State (132-3)	1977
Most Currie Cup tries	17	vs. South Western Districts (113-11)	1996
Most points by a player	48	WJdeW Ras vs. Eastern Orange Free State	1977
Most Currie Cup points by player	46	JH de Beer vs. Northern Free State	1977
Most tries by a player	6	HL Potgieter vs. Eastern Orange Free State	1977
Most Currie Cup tries by a player	4	On seven occasions	
Most conversions by a player	20	WJdeW Ras vs. Eastern Orange Free State *(SA Record)*	1977
Most Currie Cup conversions	14	JH de Beer vs. Northern Free State	1977
Most penalties by a player	8	AF Fourie vs. Griqualand West *(Currie Cup)*	1997

SEASON RECORDS
Most team points	1434	31 matches *(SA Record)*	1996
Most Currie Cup points by team	703	15 matches	1997
Most points by a player	460	MJ Smith	1996
Most Currie Cup points by player	230	K Tsimba	2003
Most team tries	191	31 matches *(SA Record)*	1996
Most Currie Cup tries by team	91	15 matches	1997
Most tries by a player	24	J-H van Wyk	1996
Most Currie Cup tries by a player	16	J-H van Wyk	1997

CAREER RECORDS
Most appearances	245	HL Müller *(SA Record)*	1983-1998
Most Currie Cup appearances	142	HL Müller	1983-1998
Most points	1707	WJdeW Ras	1974-1986
Most Currie Cup points	1101	WJdeW Ras	1974-1986
Most tries	136	C Badenhorst	1986-1999
Most Currie Cup tries	65	C Badenhorst	1986-1999

HONOURS
ABSA Currie Cup	1976, 2005, 2006 (shared), 2007
Lion Cup	1983
Bankfin Nite Series	1996
Vodacom Cup	2000

ABSA UNDER-19 CHAMPIONSHIP (6th Section A)
Played 12 Won 4 Drawn 1 Lost 7 Points for 260 Points against 376 Tries for 35 Tries against 54
RESULTS Drew WP (h) 18-18. Bt Border (a) 29-13. Lost Golden Lions (a) 14-26. Lost KZN (h) 31-55. Lost Blue Bulls (a) 21-56. Lost Leopards (h) 16-34. Lost WP (a) 05-22. Bt Border (h) 28-20. Bt Golden Lions (h) 35-34. Lost KZN (a) 22-26. Bt Leopards (a) 27-20. Lost Blue Bulls (h) 14-52.
SCORERS 40 Pieter Jordaan (2t, 9c, 4p). 37 Warren Potgieter (11c, 4p, 1dg). 23 Nicolaas Lee (4t, 1p). 22 Len le Roux (4t, 1c). 15 Barend Bornman, Donovan Gissing, Jan Venter, Louis Venter (3t each). 11 Stephen Rautenbach (1c, 3p). 10 Jean-Luke van Zyl, SWD Oosthuizen, Vuyani Maqina (2t each) 5 Brandon Krause, Cameron van Heerden, Gilbert Chalmers, Henco van der Westhuizen, Mthokozisi Mkhabela, Naldo Meyer, Stephan van Rensburg (1t each). 2 Michael Marx (1c).

GOLDEN LIONS RUGBY UNION

Lightning strikes twice for Lions

FOUNDED 1889
GROUND
Coca-Cola Park
(previously Ellis Park)
CAPACITY
60 000
ADDRESS
South Office Block,
Johannesburg Stadium,
124 Van Beek Street,
Doornfontein 2094
POSTAL ADDRESS
PO Box 15724, Doornfontein, 2028
TELEPHONE NUMBER
011-402 2960
WEBSITE
www.lionsrugby.co.za
COLOURS
White and red trim
jersey, black shorts
and black socks
CURRIE CUP COACH
Johan Ackermann
VODACOM CUP COACH
Timmy Goodwin
CAPTAIN
Derrick Minnie
PRESIDENT
Kevin de Klerk
COMPANY CEO
Ruben Moggee

THE MTN GOLDEN LIONS, THE 2011 ABSA CURRIE CUP champions, had their quest for another title dashed for the second year in a row by DHL Western Province.

In both instances the Lions' season ended abruptly in the semi-finals, but whereas the 2012 play-off saw WP break the Lion's hearts with a last-gasp 21-16 win at Ellis Park, the result was slightly more emphatic in 2013 at Newlands.

On another day the Lions might well have come out on top, but WP had the mercurial Gio Aplon to thank for the victory. With WP leading 10-9 with half-time fast approaching, it was the hosts who struck the vital psychological blow as Aplon went on a trademark 50-metre try-scoring run that brought the crowd to its feet and knocked some of the stuffing out of what had been, up to that point, a brave Lions effort.

Flyhalf Demetri Catrakilis then kicked a penalty and suddenly WP were nine points to the good at the break – a lead that the visitors never quite looked like reeling in.

But despite this, Lions coach Johan Ackermann could look back on a successful season in charge, with the early highlights being the team's Vodacom Cup title and their re-entry into Vodacom Super Rugby, thanks to victory over the Southern Kings in a tightly-contested promotion-relegation series.

These successes gave the Lions momentum going into the Currie Cup, and although they lost their opening two games, against the Cheetahs and Sharks, the men from Johannesburg lost only once in their next five encounters to set themselves up for the semis.

Another highlight for all concerned – perhaps the highlight of the year for many supporters, was the Lions' magnificent, and quite unexpected, 62-23 victory over the Vodacom Blue Bulls at Loftus Versfeld in round three.

That they followed this up with a 35-26 win at Ellis Park in the return leg was merely icing on the cake.

But it was WP that had the Lions' number in 2013, the teams drawing 31-all at Ellis Park before the streeptruie ran out 36-23 winners at Newlands in the penultimate round. The semi-final two weeks later then followed a similar script.

Ackermann however will go into 2014 with confidence that his team can take the step up to Super Rugby. Marnitz Boshoff showed consistency at flyhalf and fullback, while left wing Anthony Volmink, with six tries, gave the side teeth on attack.

Up front, nobody gave more to the cause than skipper and flanker Derrick Minnie, and he was duly rewarded with six touchdowns to cap off a year to remember for all the right reasons.

VODACOM CUP LOG POSITIONS

2013	1st 🏆	**2010**	5th	**2007**	11th	**2004**	1st 🏆	**2001**	8th	**1998**	2nd
2012	5th	**2009**	8th	**2006**	4th	**2003**	3rd	**2000**	5th		
2011	2nd	**2008**	7th	**2005**	10th	**2002**	1st 🏆	**1999**	1st 🏆		

ABSA CURRIE CUP LOG POSITIONS

2013	4th	**2010**	3rd	**2007**	3rd	**2004**	4th	**2001**	3rd	**1998**	8th
2012	3rd	**2009**	6th	**2006**	5th	**2003**	4th	**2000**	3rd	**1997**	4th
2011	1st 🏆	**2008**	4th	**2005**	2nd	**2002**	3rd	**1999**	1st 🏆	**1996**	4th

2013 RESULTS & SCORERS

VODACOM CUP (Young Lions XV) P **10** W **7** D **0** L **3** Points For **448** Points Against **232** Tries For **59** Tries Against **23** Winning Percentage **70%**

Date	Venue	Opponent	Result	Score	Referee	Scorers
Mrch 09	Johannesburg	Leopards	WON	45-15	M vd Westhuizen	T: A Coetzee, Van Rensburg, Volmink, L Cronje, Whiteley, Breet, R Coetzee C: Boshoff (3), L Cronje (2).
Mrch 15	Kempton Park	Valke	LOST	22-27	N Rocono	T: Davids, Newman, Botha, H Boshoff. C: Deale.
Mrch 23	Johannesburg	Blue Bulls	LOST	26-54	S Mayende	T: Davids (2), R Nel, Vorster. C: Davids (3).
April 05	Welkom	Griffons	LOST	19-30	J Kotze	T: Lerm, Van der Walt. P: Schmidt (3).
April 12	Johannesburg	Griquas	WON	24-11	D van Heerden	T: Van Rensburg, Bondesio, Whiteley. C: Boshoff (3). P: Boshoff.
April 19	Nelspruit	Pumas	WON	23-14	L Jam	T: Minnie, Kriel. C: Boshoff (2). P: Boshoff (2). D: Boshoff.
April 27	Alberton	Limpopo	WON	161-3	L Pretorius	T: Volmink (9), Botha (2), Kriel (2), L Cronje (2), G Cronje (2), Helberg, Du Plessis, Whiteley, Redelinghuys, Du Toit, Breet, Van der Walt, Des Fountain. C: G Cronje (12), R Cronje (3), Botha, De Kock, Volmink.
QUARTER-FINAL						
May 03	Durban	Sharks XV	WON	42-25	B Crouse	T: Botha, Volmink, Van Rensburg. C: Boshoff (3). P: Boshoff (6). D: Boshoff.
SEMI-FINAL						
May 11	Johannesburg	WP	WON	44-25	M Jonker	T: C Botha (2), Helberg, Van Rensburg, Volmink, Britz. C: Boshoff (4). P: Boshoff. D: Boshoff.
FINAL						
May 17	Nelspruit	Pumas	WON	42-28	M vd Westhuizen	T: Volmink, Whiteley, Tecklenburg. C: Boshoff (3). P: Boshoff (6). D: Boshoff.

ABSA CURRIE CUP Played **11** Won **4** Lost **6** Drawn **1** Points For **343** Points Against **329** Tries For **41** Tries Against **33** Winning Percentage **36%**

Date	Venue	Opponent	Result	Score	Referee	Scorers
Aug 10	Johannesburg	Cheetahs	LOST	29-30	M vd Westhuizen	T: Hanekom, Britz, Dreyer. C: Boshoff. P: Boshoff (4).
Aug 16	Durban	Sharks	LOST	25-33	B Crouse	T: Volmink (2), Kriel. C: Jantjies (2). P: Jantjies (2).
Aug 24	Pretoria	Blue Bulls	WON	62-23	J Kaplan	T: Minnie (2), Helberg, Volmink, Britz, Kriel, Tecklenburg, Jantjies. C: Boshoff (8). P: Boshoff (2).
Aug 30	Johannesburg	WP	DREW	31-31	J Peyper	T: Helberg, Jantjies, Minnie, Penalty try. C: Boshoff (4). P: Boshoff.
Sep 07	Kimberley	Griquas	WON	38-32	J Jaftha	T: Boshoff, A Coetzee, Volmink, Kriel, Van der Merwe, R Coetzee. C: Jantjies (3), Boshoff.
Sep 13	Bloemfontein	Cheetahs	LOST	23-26	M vd Westhuizen	T: Volmink, Nel. C: Jantjies (2). P: Jantjies (3).
Sep 21	Johannesburg	Blue Bulls	WON	35-26	S Berry	T: Boshoff, A Coetzee, Kriel, Dreyer, Van Rooyen. C: Jantjies (2). P: Jantjies, Boshoff.
Sep 27	Johannesburg	Sharks	LOST	25-31	J Jaftha	T: Whiteley, Minnie, Kriel. C: Jantjies (2). P: Jantjies (2)
Oct 05	Cape Town	WP	LOST	23-36	S Berry	T: Minnie. C: Boshoff (2). P: Boshoff (3).
Oct 12	Johannesburg	Griquas	WON	35-28	J Peyper	T: Volmink, Wepener, Van Rooyen, Britz. C: Boshoff (3). P: Boshoff (3).
SEMI-FINAL						
Oct 19	Cape Town	WP	LOST	16-33	M Jonker	T: Whiteley. C: Boshoff. P: Jantjies (3).

GOLDEN LIONS RUGBY UNION

GOLDEN LIONS CURRIE CUP SQUAD IN 2013 | CAREER

PLAYER	Appearances	Tries	Conversions	Penalties	Drop Goals	Points	Career Matches	Career Tries	Conversions	Penalties	Drop Goals	Points
MJ (Martin) Bezuidenhout	2	–	–	–	–	0	33	1	–	–	–	5
M (Michael) Bondesio	2	–	–	–	–	0	25	–	–	–	–	0
ML (Marnitz) Boshoff	11	2	20	14	0	92	11	2	20	14	0	92
CA (Chrysander) Botha	6	–	–	–	–	0	6	–	–	–	–	0
J-J (JJ) Breet	2	–	–	–	–	0	2	–	–	–	–	0
WS (Willie) Britz	10	3	–	–	–	15	20	3	–	–	–	15
A (Andries) Coetzee	8	2	–	–	–	10	18	3	1	–	–	17
RL (Robbie) Coetzee	10	1	–	–	–	5	10	1	–	–	–	5
G (Guy) Cronje	6	–	–	–	–	0	8	–	1	–	–	2
L (Lionel) Cronje	5	–	–	–	–	0	5	–	–	–	–	0
R (Ross) Cronje	7	–	–	–	–	0	16	1	–	–	–	5
RJ (Robert) de Bruyn	7	–	–	–	–	0	7	–	–	–	–	0
JJ (Kobus) de Kock	2	–	–	–	–	0	2	–	–	–	–	0
D (Dylan) des Fountain	8	–	–	–	–	0	17	1	–	–	–	5
RM (Ruan) Dreyer	9	2	–	–	–	10	13	2	–	–	–	10
F (Francois) du Toit	1	–	–	–	–	0	3	–	–	–	–	0
S (Stephan) Greeff	2	–	–	–	–	0	2	–	–	–	–	0
LS (Lambert) Groenewald	6	–	–	–	–	0	6	–	–	–	–	0
NJ (Nico) Hanekom	1	1	–	–	–	5	1	1	–	–	–	5
GG (Deon) Helberg	10	2	–	–	–	10	18	5	–	–	–	25
GD (Grant) Janke	1	–	–	–	–	0	1	–	–	–	–	0
ET (Elton) Jantjies	9	2	11	11	0	65	42	4	75	101	2	479
PH (Hugo) Kloppers	4	–	–	–	–	0	4	–	–	–	–	0
JA (Jaco) Kriel	10	5	–	–	–	25	23	7	–	–	–	35
LG (Lionel) Mapoe	3	–	–	–	–	0	20	5	–	–	–	25
TC (Tian) Meyer	6	–	–	–	–	0	6	–	–	–	–	0
DJ (Derick) Minnie	11	6	–	–	–	30	60	19	–	–	–	95
AR (Ruhan) Nel	3	1	–	–	–	5	3	1	–	–	–	5
J (Julian) Redelinghuys	3	–	–	–	–	0	3	–	–	–	–	0
JS (Bees) Roux	2	–	–	–	–	0	2	–	–	–	–	0
WJ (Warwick) Tecklenburg	11	1	–	–	–	5	11	1	–	–	–	5
CJ (CJ) van der Linde	9	–	–	–	–	0	18	–	–	–	–	0
F (Franco) van der Merwe	8	1	–	–	–	5	100	10	–	–	–	50
J (Jacques) van Rooyen	11	2	–	–	–	10	11	2	–	–	–	10
CM (Chris) van Zyl	7	–	–	–	–	0	7	–	–	–	–	0
RC (Ruan) Venter	2	–	–	–	–	0	2	–	–	–	–	0
AA (Anthony) Volmink	11	6	–	–	–	30	16	9	–	–	–	45
FW (Willie) Wepener	9	1	–	–	–	5	40	7	–	–	–	35
WR (Warren) Whiteley	4	2	–	–	–	10	41	5	–	–	–	25
39 Players	**239**	**40**	**31**	**25**	**0**	**337**	**633**	**90**	**97**	**115**	**2**	**995**

GOLDEN LIONS RUGBY UNION

APPEARANCES & POINTS IN ABSA CURRIE CUP 2013

Player	Cheetahs	Sharks	Blue Bulls	WP	Griquas	Cheetahs	Blue Bulls	Sharks	WP	Griquas	WP SF	Matches	Tries	Conversions	Penalties	Drop Goals	Points
Chrysander Botha	15	14R	15	–	–	–	–	14	15	14		6	–	–	–	–	0
Deon Helberg	14	14	14	14	13R	13R	13	13	13R	14	–	10	2	–	–	–	10
Nico Hanekom	13	–	–	–	–	–	–	–	–	–	–	1	1	–	–	–	5
Dylan des Fountain	12	12	12	12	12	12	12	12	–	–	–	8	–	–	–	–	0
Anthony Volmink	11	11	11	11	11	11	11	11	11	11	11	11	6	–	–	–	30
Marnitz Boshoff	10	15	10	15	15	15	15	15	10	10	15	11	2	20	14	0	92
Guy Cronje	9	9	9	9	–	–	9R	10R	–	–	–	6	–	–	–	–	0
Willie Britz	8	8	8	4	8	8	–	4R	4	5R	4R	10	3	–	–	–	15
Warwick Tecklenburg	7	6R	4R	6	7R	6	7	6R	6R	6	6R	11	1	–	–	–	5
Derrick Minnie	6c	7c	7c	7c	7c	7c	8c	7c	7c	7c	7c	11	6	–	–	–	30
Hugo Kloppers	5	5	–	x	–	4R	–	–	4R	–	–	4	–	–	–	–	0
Stephan Greeff	4	–	–	–	–	–	4	–	–	–	–	2	–	–	–	–	0
Ruan Dreyer	3	3	3	3	3	–	3	3	3	–	3	9	2	–	–	–	10
Martin Bezuidenhout	2	2	–	–	–	–	–	–	–	–	–	2	–	–	–	–	0
Jacques van Rooyen	1	1	1	1R	1	1R	1R	1R	1R	1	1R	11	2	–	–	–	10
Francois du Toit	2R	–	–	–	–	–	–	–	–	–	–	1	–	–	–	–	0
CJ van der Linde	1R	1R	1R	1	3R	1	1	1	–	–	1	9	–	–	–	–	0
Lambert Groenewald	6R	4R	6R	8	–	–	6R	–	–	6R	–	6	–	–	–	–	0
Jaco Kriel	4R	6	6	4R	6	8R	6	6	6	–	6	10	5	–	–	–	25
Tian Meyer	9R	9R	9R	9R	9	9	–	–	–	–	x	6	–	–	–	–	0
Elton Jantjies	10R	10	15R	10	10	10	10	10	–	–	10	9	2	11	11	–	65
Robert de Bruyn	13R	13	13	13	13	13	–	–	–	–	10R	7	–	–	–	–	0
Chris van Zyl	–	4	4	–	–	–	4R	4	5	4	4	7	–	–	–	–	0
Robbie Coetzee	–	2R	2R	2R	2	2R	2	2	2	2R	2R	10	1	–	–	–	5
Lionel Cronje	–	15R	13R	–	–	–	11R	–	12	10R	–	5	–	–	–	–	0
Franco van der Merwe	–	–	5	5	5	5	5	5	–	5	5	8	1	–	–	–	5
Willie Wepener	–	–	2	2	2R	2	2R	2R	2R	2	2	9	1	–	–	–	5
JJ Breet	–	–	–	8R	4R	–	–	–	–	–	–	2	–	–	–	–	0
Andries Coetzee	–	–	–	14R	14	14	14	14	15	12	12	8	2	–	–	–	10
Ruan Venter	–	–	–	–	4	4	–	–	–	–	–	2	–	–	–	–	0
Ross Cronje	–	–	–	–	9R	9R	9	9	9R	9R	9	7	–	–	–	–	0
Ruhan Nel	–	–	–	–	x	15R	14R	14R	–	–	–	3	1	–	–	–	5
Bees Roux	–	–	–	–	–	3	–	–	3R	–	–	2	–	–	–	–	0
Warren Whiteley	–	–	–	–	–	–	–	8	8	8	8	4	2	–	–	–	10
Grant Janke	–	–	–	–	–	–	–	12R	–	–	–	1	–	–	–	–	0
Lionel Mapoe	–	–	–	–	–	–	–	–	13	13	13	3	–	–	–	–	0
Michael Bondesio	–	–	–	–	–	–	–	–	9	9	–	2	–	–	–	–	0
Julian Redelinghuys	–	–	–	–	–	–	–	–	1	3	3R	3	–	–	–	–	0
Kobus de Kock	–	–	–	–	–	–	–	–	12R	14R	–	2	–	–	–	–	0
Penalty try	–	–	–	–	–	–	–	–	–	–	–		1	–	–	–	5
39 Players													**239**	**41**	**31**	**25**	**0**	**342**

GOLDEN LIONS RUGBY UNION

YOUNG LIONS SQUAD (Vodacom Cup squad) — CAREER

PLAYER	Appearances	Tries	Conversions	Penalties	Drop Goals	Points	Career Matches	Career Tries	Conversions	Penalties	Drop Goals	Points
LD (Leroy) Afrika	1	–	–	–	–	0	1	–	–	–	–	0
GB (Gavin) Annandale	2	–	–	–	–	0	2	–	–	–	–	0
M (Michael) Bondesio	6	1	–	–	–	5	14	4	–	–	–	20
FCF (Fabian) Booysen	1	–	–	–	–	0	3	–	–	–	–	0
SJ (Fanie) Booysen	1	–	–	–	–	0	1	–	–	–	–	0
HB (Henri) Boshoff	2	1	–	–	–	5	2	1	–	–	–	5
ML (Marnitz) Boshoff	6	–	18	16	4	96	6	0	18	16	4	96
CA (Chrysander) Botha	5	5	1	–	–	27	5	5	1	0	0	27
V (Van Zyl) Botha	4	1	–	–	–	5	7	1	–	–	–	5
JJ (JJ) Breet	5	2	–	–	–	10	5	2	–	–	–	10
WS (Willie) Britz	7	1	–	–	–	5	7	1	–	–	–	5
A (Andries) Coetzee	1	1	–	–	–	5	2	2	5	–	–	20
RL (Robbie) Coetzee	6	1	–	–	–	5	6	1	–	–	–	5
G (Guy) Cronje	2	2	12	–	–	34	6	2	24	9	0	85
L (Lionel) Cronje	5	3	2	–	–	19	5	3	2	0	0	19
R (Ross) Cronje	5	–	3	–	–	6	7	0	3	0	0	6
A (Ashlon) Davids	2	3	3	–	–	21	2	3	3	0	0	21
JJ (Hanco) Deale	2	–	1	–	–	2	2	0	1	0	0	2
JJ (Kobus) de Kock	3	–	1	–	–	2	3	0	1	0	0	2
D (Dylan) des Fountain	6	1	–	–	–	5	8	2	–	–	–	10
RM (Ruan) Dreyer	7	–	–	–	–	0	17	1	–	–	–	5
JP (Jean-Pierre) du Plessis	2	1	–	–	–	5	3	1	–	–	–	5
F (Francois) du Toit	7	1	–	–	–	5	14	3	–	–	–	15
DC (Damien) Engledoe	1	–	–	–	–	0	1	–	–	–	–	0
J-RA (JR) Esterhuizen	1	–	–	–	–	0	4	3	–	–	–	15
S (Stephan) Greeff	1	–	–	–	–	0	2	–	–	–	–	0
NJ (Stokkies) Hanekom	1	–	–	–	–	0	1	–	–	–	–	0
GG (Deon) Helberg	7	2	–	–	–	10	7	2	–	–	–	10
AWCJ (Alwyn) Hollenbach	5	–	–	–	–	0	13	2	–	–	–	10
GD (Grant) Janke	1	–	–	–	–	0	1	–	–	–	–	0
JC (JC) Janse van Rensburg	2	–	–	–	–	0	10	1	–	–	–	5
FW (Wiseman) Kamanga	1	–	–	–	–	0	4	–	–	–	–	0
PH (Hugo) Kloppers	4	–	–	–	–	0	4	–	–	–	–	0
AJ (Jacques) Kotze	1	–	–	–	–	0	1	–	–	–	–	0
JA (Jaco) Kriel	6	3	–	–	–	15	26	7	–	–	–	35
E (Eugene) le Maitre	1	–	–	–	–	0	1	–	–	–	–	0
R (Ruan) Lerm	1	1	–	–	–	5	8	1	–	–	–	5
DR (Devon) Martinus	3	–	–	–	–	0	3	–	–	–	–	0
DJ (Derrick) Minnie	2	1	–	–	–	5	22	5	–	–	–	25
BJ (Bradley) Moolman	1	–	–	–	–	0	8	4	–	–	–	20
W (Whestley) Moolman	1	–	–	–	–	0	1	–	–	–	–	0
FJ (Franco) Mostert	3	–	–	–	–	0	3	–	–	–	–	0
KM (Keith) Murray	1	–	–	–	–	0	1	–	–	–	–	0
AR (Ruhan) Nel	3	1	–	–	–	5	4	1	–	–	–	5
JJ (Jacques) Nel	3	–	–	–	–	0	3	–	–	–	–	0
CW (Willie) Newman	3	1	–	–	–	5	3	1	–	–	–	5
D (Dylan) Peterson	3	–	–	–	–	0	3	–	–	–	–	0

YOUNG LIONS SQUAD (2013 Vodacom Cup)

PLAYER	Appearances	Tries	Conversions	Penalties	Drop Goals	Points	Career Matches	Career Tries	Conversions	Penalties	Drop Goals	Points
M (Mark) Pretorius	1	–	–	–	–	0	1	–	–	–	–	0
J (Julian) Redelinghuys	4	1	–	–	–	5	4	1	–	–	–	5
HL (Hendrik) Roodt	6	–	–	–	–	0	12	1	–	–	–	5
D (Marais) Schmidt	1	–	–	3	–	9	6	1	10	7	0	46
JH (Janneman) Stander	1	–	–	–	–	0	1	–	–	–	–	0
JH (Jannie) Stander	3	–	–	–	–	0	3	–	–	–	–	0
WJ (Warwick) Tecklenburg	7	1	–	–	–	5	7	1	–	–	–	5
CK (Claude) Tshibidi	2	–	–	–	–	0	2	–	–	–	–	0
V (Vian) van der Walt	2	2	–	–	–	10	3	2	–	–	–	10
X (Xander) vd Westhuizen	1	–	–	–	–	0	1	–	–	–	–	0
R (Rikus) van Niekerk	3	–	–	–	–	0	3	–	–	–	–	0
AG (Deon) van Rensburg	6	4	–	–	–	20	6	4	–	–	–	20
J (Jacques) van Rooyen	6	–	–	–	–	0	6	–	–	–	–	0
CM (Chris) van Zyl	3	–	–	–	–	0	3	–	–	–	–	0
WJ (Wynand) Venter	1	–	–	–	–	0	1	–	–	–	–	0
C-T (Callie) Visagie	1	–	–	–	–	0	1	–	–	–	–	0
A (Anthony) Volmink	7	13	1	–	–	67	14	19	1	0	0	97
HW (Harold) Vorster	3	1	–	–	–	5	6	1	–	–	–	5
PJ (PJ) Walters	2	–	–	–	–	0	2	–	–	–	–	0
WR (Warren) Whiteley	7	4	–	–	–	20	11	4	–	–	–	20
K (Percy) Williams	3	–	–	–	–	0	3	–	–	–	–	0
68 players	**214**	**59**	**42**	**19**	**4**	**448**	**355**	**93**	**69**	**32**	**4**	**711**

ABSA UNDER-21 CHAMPIONSHIP (4th, Section A)
Played 13 Won 7 Lost 6 Drawn 0 Points for 433 Points against 380 Tries for 58 Tries against 47 Winning percentage 54%
RESULTS: Bt Sharks (a) 24-17. Lost Free State (h) 23-25. Bt Leopards (a) 24-23. Lost Blue Bulls (a) 20-26. Bt Border (a) 45-16. Lost WP (h) 26-53. Bt Sharks (h) 39-31. Bt Free State (a) 43-28. Bt Leopards (h) 42-31. Lost Blue Bulls (h) 25-40. Lost WP (a) 5-39. Bt Border (h) 76-7. SEMI FINAL Lost WP (a) 41-44.
SCORERS: 156 Marais Schmidt (5t,37c,19p); 40 Stephan de Wit (8t); 30 Jacques Nel, Damian Engledoe (6t each); 25 Ruan Lerm, Peter-John Walters (5t each); 20 Albert Smith (4t); 17 Jaco van der Walt (1t, 6c); 15 Harold Vorster (3t); 10 Lourens Erasmus, Mark Pretorius (2t each); 5 Henri Boshoff, Gideon Meiring, Percy Williams, Ashlon Davids, Ruhan Janse van Rensburg, Ruan Venter, Devon Martinus, Nico du Plessis, Jannie Stander, Fabian Booysen, Matt Torrance (1t each).

ABSA UNDER-19 CHAMPIONSHIP (Runner-up, 2nd, Section A)
Played 14 Won 9 Lost 5 Drawn 0 Points for 344 Points against 299 Tries for 41 Tries against 38 Winning percentage 64%
RESULTS: Bt Sharks (a) 21-13. Bt Free State (h) 26-14. Bt Leopards (a) 34-27. Lost Blue Bulls (a) 12-15. Bt Border (a) 19-3. Bt WP (h) 31-26. Lost Sharks (h) 9-25. Lost Free State (a) 34-35. Bt Leopards (h) 32-27. Lost Blue Bulls (h) 8-24. Bt WP (a) 21-13. Bt Border (h) 47-17. SEMI FINAL Bt Sharks (h) 27-25. FINAL Lost Blue Bulls (a) 23-35.
SCORERS: 122 Brandan Hewit (25c,23p,1d); 35 Carlisle Nel (7t); 30 Jano Venter (6t); 25 Koch Marx (5t); 20 Malcolm Marx (4t); 15 Barend Herbst, Victor Sekekete, Sikhumbuzo Mabuza (3t each); 14 Gabriel du Toit (4c,2p); 10 Jaun Vorster, Sampie Hearn (2t each); 5 Calvin Smith, Kyle van Dalen, Cyle Brink, Chad McKay, Francois van Heerden, Christiaan Meyer (1t each); 3 Jaco van der Walt (1p).

PROVINCIAL AMATEUR CHAMPIONSHIP (Runner-up, Northern Section, Pretoria)
Played 3 Won 2 Lost 1 Drawn 0 Points for 87 Points against 57 Winning percentage 66%
RESULTS: Bt Lowveld 81-3. Bt Griffons 28-27. Lost Valke 18-24.

SUB-UNION CHAMPIONSHIP (Runner-up, Northern Sub-Unions, Kempton Park)
Played 3 Won 2 Lost 1 Drawn 0 Points for 127 Points against 54 Winning percentage 67%
RESULTS: Bt Lowveld 81-3. Bt Griffons 28-27. Lost Valke 18-24.

YOUNG LIONS XV - APPEARANCES & POINTS IN VODACOM CUP 2013

Player	Leopards	Valke	Blue Bulls	Griffons	Griquas	Pumas	Limpopo	Sharks XV OF	WP SF	Pumas F	Matches	Tries	Conversions	Penalties	Drop Goals	Points
Andries Coetzee	15	–	–	–	–	–	–	–	–	–	1	1	–	–	–	5
Deon van Rensburg	14	–	–	–	13	13	–	13	13	13	6	4	–	–	–	20
Dylan des Fountain	13	–	13R	–	–	–	12R	13R	11R	12R	6	1	–	–	–	5
JP du Plessis	12	–	–	–	–	–	12	–	–	–	2	1	–	–	–	5
Anthony Volmink	11	–	–	–	11	11	11	11	11	11	7	13	1	0	0	67
Lionel Cronje	10	–	–	–	12R	10R	15	x	x	14R	5	3	2	0	0	19
Whestley Moolman	9	–	–	–	–	–	–	–	–	–	1	–	–	–	–	0
Warren Whiteley	8	–	–	–	8	8	8c	8c	8c	8c	7	4	–	–	–	20
JJ Breet	7	–	–	–	–	–	5R	17R	5R	5R	5	2	–	–	–	10
Jaco Kriel	6	–	–	–	4R	6	6	6	–	6	6	3	–	–	–	15
Franco Mostert	5	–	–	–	5	5	–	–	–	–	3	–	–	–	–	0
Hendrik Roodt	4	–	–	–	4	4	–	4	4	4	6	–	–	–	–	0
Ruhan Dreyer	3	–	–	–	1	3	3R	1	3	3	7	–	–	–	–	0
Robbie Coetzee	2	–	–	–	2	2	–	2	2	2	6	1	–	–	–	5
JC Janse van Rensburg	1c	–	–	–	1c	–	–	–	–	–	2	–	–	–	–	0
Callie Visagie	2R	–	–	–	–	–	–	–	–	–	1	–	–	–	–	0
Jacques van Rooyen	1R	1	–	–	–	1	3R	1	1	6	–	–	–	–	0
Gavin Annandale	4R	–	–	–	–	4	–	x	–	–	2	–	–	–	–	0
Warwick Tecklenburg	6R	–	–	–	6	6R	6R	7	6	7	7	1	–	–	–	5
Michael Bondesio	9R	–	–	–	9c	–	–	9	9	9	6	1	–	–	–	5
Marnitz Boshoff	10R	–	–	–	10	10	–	10	10	10	6	0	18	16	4	96
Ruan Nel	13R	–	15	–	15	–	–	–	–	–	3	1	–	–	–	5
Hanco Deale	–	15	–	15	–	–	–	–	–	–	2	0	1	0	0	2
Jacques Nel	–	14	14	14	–	–	–	–	–	–	3	–	–	–	–	0
Xander vd Westhuizen	–	13	–	–	–	–	–	–	–	–	1	–	–	–	–	0
Harold Vorster	–	12	12	12	–	–	–	–	–	–	3	1	–	–	–	5
Leroy Afrika	–	11	–	–	–	–	–	–	–	–	1	–	–	–	–	0
Ashlon Davids	–	10	10	–	–	–	–	–	–	–	2	3	3	0	0	21
Percy Williams	–	9	9	9	–	–	–	–	–	–	3	–	–	–	–	0
Chris van Zyl	–	8c	5c	5c	–	–	–	–	–	–	3	–	–	–	–	0
Dylan Peterson	–	7	7	4	–	–	–	–	–	–	3	–	–	–	–	0
Willie Newman	–	6	6	7R	–	–	–	–	–	–	3	1	–	–	–	5
Stephan Greeff	–	5	–	–	–	–	–	–	–	–	1	–	–	–	–	0
Jannie Stander	–	4	4	4R	–	–	–	–	–	–	3	–	–	–	–	0
Van Zyl Botha	–	3	3R	–	–	–	–	1R	1R	–	4	1	–	–	–	5
Rikus van Niekerk	–	2	2R	2	–	–	–	–	–	–	3	–	–	–	–	0
Henri Boshoff	–	1	–	1	–	–	–	–	–	–	2	1	–	–	–	5
Keith Murray	–	2R	–	–	–	–	–	–	–	–	1	–	–	–	–	0
Devon Martinus	–	3R	3	3R	–	–	–	–	–	–	3	–	–	–	–	0
Tiaan Benade	–	x	x	–	–	–	–	–	–	–	0	–	–	–	–	0
Claude Tshibidi	–	7R	8R	–	–	–	–	–	–	–	2	–	–	–	–	0
Wynand Venter	–	x	9R	–	–	–	–	–	–	–	1	–	–	–	–	0
Damien Engledoe	–	11R	–	–	–	–	–	–	–	–	1	–	–	–	–	0
Fanie Booysen	–	10R	–	–	–	–	–	–	–	–	1	–	–	–	–	0
Nico Hanekom	–	–	13	–	–	–	–	–	–	–	1	–	–	–	–	0
Deon Helberg	–	–	11	–	14R	12R	13	14	14	14	7	2	–	–	–	10
Willie Britz	–	–	8	–	7R	7R	7	6R	7	6R	7	1	–	–	–	5
Francois du Toit	–	–	2	–	2R	2R	2	2R	2R	2R	7	1	–	–	–	5
PJ Walters	–	–	11R	11	–	–	–	–	–	–	2	–	–	–	–	0
Bradley Moolman	–	–	–	13	–	–	–	–	–	–	1	–	–	–	–	0
Marais Schmidt	–	–	–	10	–	–	–	–	–	–	1	0	0	3	0	9
Ruan Lerm	–	–	–	8	–	–	–	–	–	–	1	1	–	–	–	5
Fabian Booysen	–	–	–	7	–	–	–	–	–	–	1	–	–	–	–	0
Janneman Stander	–	–	–	6	–	–	–	–	–	–	1	–	–	–	–	0
Jacques Kotze	–	–	–	3	–	–	–	–	–	–	1	–	–	–	–	0
Eugene le Maitre	–	–	–	2R	–	–	–	–	–	–	1	–	–	–	–	0
Vian van der Walt	–	–	–	9R	–	–	9R	–	–	–	2	2	–	–	–	10
Kobus de Kock	–	–	–	10R	–	15	15R	–	–	–	3	0	1	0	0	2
Grant Janke	–	–	–	14R	–	–	–	–	–	–	1	–	–	–	–	0

YOUNG LIONS XV - APPEARANCES & POINTS IN VODACOM CUP 2013

	Leopards	Valke	Blue Bulls	Griffons	Griquas	Pumas	Limpopo	Sharks XV QF	WP SF	Pumas F	Matches	Tries	Conversions	Penalties	Drop Goals	Points
JR Esterhuizen	–	–	–	–	14	–	–	–	–	–	1	–	–	–	–	0
Alwyn Hollenbach	–	–	–	–	12	12	–	12	12	12	5	–	–	–	–	0
Derrick Minnie	–	–	–	–	7	7	–	–	–	–	2	1	–	–	–	5
Julian Redelinghuys	–	–	–	–	3	1R	3	3	–	–	4	1	–	–	–	5
Wiseman Kamanga	–	–	–	–	6R	–	–	–	–	–	1	–	–	–	–	0
Guy Cronje	–	–	–	–	9R	–	9	–	–	–	2	2	12	0	0	34
Chrysander Botha	–	–	–	–	–	14	14	15	15	15	5	5	1	0	0	27
Ross Cronje	–	–	–	–	–	9R	10	9R	9R	9R	5	0	3	0	0	6
Hugo Kloppers	–	–	–	–	–	–	5	5	5	5	4	–	–	–	–	0
Mark Pretorius	–	–	–	–	–	–	2R	–	–	–	1	–	–	–	–	0
69 Players											214	59	42	19	4	448

GOLDEN LIONS RECORDS

MATCH RECORDS

Biggest win	116-10	vs. South Eastern Transvaal	1993
Biggest Currie Cup win	99-9	vs. Far North	1973
	104-14	vs. Vodacom Eagles	2003
Heaviest defeat	10-74	vs. British Lions	2009
Heaviest Currie Cup defeat	5-59	vs. Free State	2006
Highest score	116	vs. South Eastern Transvaal (116-10)	1993
Most points conceded	74	vs. British Lions (10-74)	2009
Most tries	18	vs. Madrid XV (96-6)	1979
Most Currie Cup tries	16	vs. Far North (99-9)	1973
Most points by a player	40	L Barnard vs. North East Cape	1979
Most Currie Cup points by a player	36	GR Bosch vs. Far North	1973
Most tries by a player	6	SA Smit vs. Orange Free State	1941
Most Currie Cup tries by a player	4	On seven occasions (most recently by GM Delport vs. Griffons 1997)	
Most conversions by a player	16	L Barnard vs. North East Cape	1979
Most Currie Cup conversions	13	GR Bosch vs. Far North	1973
Most penalties by a player	7	On five occasions in Currie Cup	
Most drop goals by a player	3	GR Bosch vs. Eastern Transvaal (CC, 1972) & vs. WP (CC, 1974)	
	3	JC Robbie vs. Eastern Province (1987)	1987
	3	AS Pretorius vs. Griquas (CC)	2005

SEASON RECORDS

Most team points	1390	33 matches	1999
Most team points in Currie Cup	580	14 matches	1997
Most points by a player	414	J Engelbrecht	1999
Most Currie Cup points by a player	263	GE Lawless	1996
Most team tries	181	33 matches	1999
Most team tries in Currie Cup	74	14 matches	1997
Most tries by a player	23	P Hendriks	1994
Most Currie Cup tries by a player	14	JA van der Walt	1996

CAREER RECORDS

Most appearances	153	HP le Roux	1992-2000
Most Currie Cup appearances	108	PJJ Grobbelaar	2003-2012
Most points	896	GR Bosch	1972-1978
Most Currie Cup points	521	GR Bosch	1972-1978
Most tries	89	P Hendriks	1990-1997
Most Currie Cup tries	38	P Hendriks	1990-1997

HONOURS

ABSA Currie Cup 1922, 1939, 1950, 1952, 1971 (shared), 1972, 1993, 1994, 1999, 2011
Lion Cup 1986, 1987, 1992, 1993, 1994
Super 10 1993
Vodacom Cup 1999, 2002, 2003, 2004, 2013

GRIFFONS RUGBY UNION

FOUNDED
1968 (as Northern Free State)
GROUND
North West Stadium, Welkom
CAPACITY
8 500
ADDRESS
Rugby Street, Welkom
POSTAL ADDRESS
PO Box 631, Welkom 9460
TELEPHONE NUMBER
057 352 6482
EMAIL
rugbybond@icon.co.za
COLOURS
Purple and yellow jersey, white shorts
CURRIE CUP COACH
Oersond Gorgonzola
VODACOM CUP COACH
Oersond Gorgonzola
CAPTAIN
Werner Griesel
PRESIDENT
Randal September
COMPANY CEO
Eugene van Wyk

Griffons select reverse gear

IT WAS A CASE OF ONE STEP FORWARD, TWO STEPS BACK FOR the Griffons in 2013.

A three-year slide had been halted in 2012 when the men from the northern Free State finished a creditable third on the new-look eight-team Absa Currie Cup First Division log, following a decision to reinstate a top-six Premier Division and a so-called 'bottom eight'.

The Griffons eventually lost 37-30 in the 2012 semi-finals, to the tough Pumas at their Nelspruit fortress, and there was every indication that, having effectively finished ninth out of 14 provinces after finishing 11th, 12th and 12th in 2009, 2010 and 2011 respectively, the class of 2013 could perhaps replicate the heroics of 2008.

But five years after beating the Leopards in Potchefstroom to win the First Division title, the Griffons were left contemplating yet another slide after managing just three wins in 14 matches to finish well off the pace in sixth place.

The team certainly had no problem scoring tries – their tally of 49 touchdowns came at an average of 3.5 per match – but like so many First Division also-rans their leaky defence was an Achilles heel. The side conceded 72 tries during the campaign – more than five per match on average – with only wooden-spoonists the Valke (79 conceded) spending more time behind their tryline.

Having ended their Vodacom Cup campaign on the receiving end of an 89-10 thumping at the hands of the Blue Bulls in Pretoria, the Griffons kicked off their First Division campaign well enough when they drew 30-all on the road against the Valke.

But thereafter followed five demoralising defeats in their next six games, including a 46-point loss to the Pumas in Nelspruit, a two-point defeat in East London against the Bulldogs, and a five-point reversal in George against the Eagles.

Mid-table First Division teams cannot afford to constantly be on the wrong end of tight results, and the Griffons paid the price in the final analysis.

Despite their poor results, a number of players can look back on a difficult season with heads held high. Tertius Maarman, who played in every match in either the fullback or flyhalf position, was consistent and scored four tries, as did regular skipper, centre Werner Griesel.

Griesel's centre partner, Japie Nel, missed his team's opening match, but made up for it with eight tries in 12 appearances to tie the Griffons record for tries scored in a season.

Up front, eighthman Nicky Steyn was his tireless self, even though he managed only eight appearances, and his presence on a more regular basis might have made all the difference to a team who were always punching above their weight.

The Griffons won plenty of ball in 2013 but their defence was a weakness.
Duif du Toit/Gallo Images

GRIFFONS RUGBY UNION

VODACOM CUP LOG POSITIONS

2013	11th	**2010**	12th	**2007**	14th	**2004**	14th	**2001**	9th	**1998** 13th
2012	12th	**2009**	12th	**2006**	11th	**2003**	14th	**2000**	13th	
2011	10th	**2008**	13th	**2005**	14th	**2002**	13th	**1999**	13th	

ABSA CURRIE CUP LOG POSITIONS

2013	12th	**2010**	12th	**2007**	11th	**2004**	14th	**2001**	13th	**1998** 14th
2012	9th	**2009**	11th	**2006**	14th	**2003**	14th	**2000**	14th	**1997** 12th
2011	12th	**2008**	9th	**2005**	11th	**2002**	14th	**1999**	13th	**1996** 12th

2013 RESULTS AND SCORERS

VODACOM CUP Played **7** Won **3** Drawn **0** Lost **4** Points for **133** Points against **245** Tries for **18** Tries against **33** Winning % **43%**

Date	Venue	Opponent	Result	Score	Referee	Scorers
Mrch 09	Polokwane	Limpopo BB	WON	50-14	N Rocono	T: Steyn (3), Hancke (2), Sithole, Nortjie, McDonald. C: Strydom (5).
Mrch 16	Welkom	Griquas	LOST	12-26	J van Heerden	T: Herbert, Nagel. C: Graaff.
Mrch 23	Nelspruit [1]	Pumas	LOST	07-64	T Jonker	T: Mahoney. C: Graaff.
April 05	Welkom	Golden Lions	WON	30-19	J Kotze	T: Griesel, Hancke, Mbotho. C: Graaff (3). P: Graaff (2). DG: Graaff.
April 12	Potchefstroom	Leopards XV	LOST	07-27	C Jadezweni	T: McDonald. C: Herbert.
April 19	Welkom	Valke	WON	17-06	E Nel	T: Nortjie, Mbotho. C: Graaff (2). P: Graaff.
April 27	Pretoria	Blue Bulls	LOST	10-89	S Mayende	T: McDonald. C: Graaff. P: Graaff.

[1] Nelspruit RC

ABSA CURRIE CUP Played **14** Won **3** Lost **9** Drawn **2** Points for **367** Points against **534** Tries for **49** Tries against **72** Winning % **21%**

Date	Venue	Opponent	Result	Score	Referee	Scorers
Jun 28	Kempton Park	Valke	DREW	30-30	S Mayende	T: Steyn, Maarman, Griesel. C: Strydom (3), P: Strydom (3).
July 06	Welkom	EP Kings	LOST	21-37	J Kotze	T: Ehlers, Huggett, Koekemoer. C: Strydom (3).
July 12	Nelspruit	Pumas	LOST	10-56	J van Heerden	T: Nel. C: Engelbrecht. P: Engelbrecht.
July 20	East London	Border	LOST	20-22	M Jonker	T: Steyn, Maarman. C: Strydom (2). P: Strydom (2).
July 27	Welkom	Leopards	WON	34-28	L vd Merwe	T: Nortjie (2), le Roux, Griesel. C: Strydom (4). P: Strydom. DG: Strydom.
Aug 02	George	SWD	LOST	25-30	J Kaplan	T: Jordaan. C: Strydom. P: Strydom (6).
Aug 10	Welkom	Boland	LOST	35-55	P Legoete	T: Demas, Kritzinger, Nel, Daniller, Griesel. C: Strydom (2). P: Strydom (2).
Aug 17	Welkom	Valke	WON	50-35	J Jaftha	T: Groenewald (2), Van Heerden, Kritzinger, Nel, Jordaan, Briedenhann, Griesel. C: Kritzinger (4), Maarman
Aug 23	Port Elizabeth	EP Kings	LOST	07-63	M Jonker	T: Nel. C: Kritzinger.
Aug 30	Welkom	Pumas	LOST	24-42	J Jaftha	T: Maarman (2), Sithole, Ngoza. C: Engelbrecht (2).
Sep 07	Welkom	Border	WON	24-19	J Kaplan	T: Kritzinger, Nel, Nelson, Daniller. C: Engelbrecht (2).
Sep 13	Potchefstroom	Leopards	LOST	33-40	C Joubert	T: Le Roux (2), Kritzinger, Nelson, S van der Merwe. C: Du Toit (4).
Sep 21	Welkom	SWD	LOST	28-51	C Joubert	T: Nel (2), Sithole (2). C: Du Toit (3), Maarman.
Sep 27	Wellington	Boland	DREW	26-26	T Jonker	T: Nel, Sithole, Engelbrecht, Nelson. C: Du Toit (3).

GRIFFONS RUGBY UNION

GRIFFONS SQUAD IN 2013 / GRIFFONS CAREER

PLAYER	Appearances	Tries	Conversions	Penalties	Drop Goals	Points	Career Matches	Career Tries	Conversions	Penalties	Drop Goals	Points
DE (Enrico) Acker	1	–	–	–	–	0	1	–	–	–	–	0
M (Mlungisi) Bali	13	–	–	–	–	0	13	–	–	–	–	0
AH (Alfredo) Barends	2	–	–	–	–	0	2	–	–	–	–	0
BC (Bernado) Botha	5	–	–	–	–	0	5	–	–	–	–	0
M (Marnus) Briedenhann	5	1	–	–	–	5	40	3	–	–	–	15
RM (Rudi) Britz	15	–	–	–	–	0	30	2	–	–	–	10
T (Tertius) Danniller	11	2	–	–	–	10	11	2	–	–	–	10
MJ (Tewis) de Bruyn	1	–	–	–	–	0	1	–	–	–	–	0
PR (Rossouw) de Klerk	1	–	–	–	–	0	1	–	–	–	–	0
D (Danwel) Demas	2	1	–	–	–	5	2	1	–	–	–	5
FC (Franna) du Toit	4	–	10	–	–	20	4	–	10	–	–	20
C-E (Chris) Ehlers	14	1	–	–	–	5	32	3	–	–	–	15
GJ (Joubert) Engelbrecht	9	1	5	1	–	18	9	1	5	1	–	18
R (Reinhardt) Erwee	2	–	–	–	–	0	24	4	20	12	–	96
AS (Andries) Ferreira	1	–	–	–	–	0	1	–	–	–	–	0
GP (Deon) Gouws	1	–	–	–	–	0	1	–	–	–	–	0
JPJ (Hansie) Graaff	9	–	8	4	1	31	27	7	46	15	2	178
W (Werner) Griesel	19	5	–	–	–	25	114	26	–	–	–	130
H (Dirk) Grobbelaar	2	–	–	–	–	0	2	–	–	–	–	0
WR (Wilmar) Groenewald	8	2	–	–	–	10	15	2	–	–	–	10
S (Shane) Hancke	13	3	–	–	–	15	79	23	–	–	–	115
C (Colin) Herbert	7	1	1	–	–	7	9	1	1	–	–	7
E (Elandre) Huggett	3	1	–	–	–	5	3	1	–	–	–	5
J (Jeremy) Jordaan	14	2	–	–	–	10	14	2	–	–	–	10
HL (Lehan) Koekemoer	14	1	–	–	–	5	14	1	–	–	–	5
A (Armandt) Koster	5	–	–	–	–	0	11	–	–	–	–	0
IM (Inus) Kritzinger	10	4	5	–	–	30	19	6	5	–	–	40
AJ (AJ) le Roux	5	2	–	–	–	10	5	2	–	–	–	10
HF (Erik) le Roux	10	1	–	–	–	5	29	2	–	–	–	10
SJ (Sarel) Louw	7	–	–	–	–	0	140	13	–	–	–	65
T (Tertius) Maarman	14	4	2	–	–	24	70	20	4	–	–	108
AS (Andries) Mahoney	9	1	–	–	–	5	7	3	–	–	–	15
BB (Brenvin) Marais	1	–	–	–	–	0	1	–	–	–	–	0
CM (Charles) Marais	1	–	–	–	–	0	6	1	–	–	–	5
F da S (Franco) Mateus	3	–	–	–	–	0	3	–	–	–	–	0
V (Vuyo) Mbotho	16	2	–	–	–	10	16	2	–	–	–	10
AN (Aubrey) McDonald	15	3	–	–	–	15	15	3	–	–	–	15
TS (Teboho) Mohoje	5	–	–	–	–	0	6	–	–	–	–	0
J (Japie) Nel	18	9	–	–	–	45	79	30	–	–	–	150
NT (Norman) Nelson	5	3	–	–	–	15	5	3	–	–	–	15
TFN (Freddy) Ngoza	5	1	–	–	–	5	5	1	–	–	–	5
O (Oshwill) Nortjie	19	4	–	–	–	20	26	6	–	–	–	30
S (Shaun) Prins	5	–	–	–	–	0	5	–	–	–	–	0
DS (Davon) Raubenheimer	5	–	–	–	–	0	5	–	–	–	–	0
EO (Egbert) Ras	4	–	–	–	–	0	4	–	–	–	–	0
HR (Heinrich) Roelfse	8	–	–	–	–	0	14	–	–	–	–	0
DA (Dean) Rossouw	0	–	–	–	–	0	0	–	–	–	–	0
AH (Ashwin) Scott	2	–	–	–	–	0	2	–	–	–	–	0
FL (Frans) Sisita	1	–	–	–	–	0	1	–	–	–	–	0
SM (Martin) Sithole	16	5	–	–	–	25	38	14	–	–	–	70
KB (Kevin) Stevens	15	–	–	–	–	0	72	3	–	–	–	15
NPJ (Nicky) Steyn	13	5	–	–	–	25	88	38	–	–	–	190
LI (Louis) Strydom	7	–	20	14	1	85	33	5	45	59	1	295
MJ (Martin) van der Heever	1	–	–	–	–	0	1	–	–	–	–	0
DJ (Danie) van der Merwe	15	–	–	–	–	0	18	2	–	–	–	10
SW (Schalk) van der Merwe	5	1	–	–	–	5	5	1	–	–	–	5
D (Derrick) van Heerden	17	1	–	–	–	5	61	4	–	–	–	20
JC (JC) van Wyk	9	–	–	–	–	0	14	–	–	–	–	0
58 players	**447**	**67**	**51**	**19**	**2**	**500**	**1258**	**238**	**136**	**87**	**3**	**1732**

APPEARANCES & POINTS IN VODACOM CUP 2013

Player	Limpopo BB	Griquas	Pumas	Golden Lions	Leopards XV	Valke	Blue Bulls	Matches	Tries	Conversions	Penalties	Drop Goals	Points
Hansie Graaff	15	10	10	10	10	10	10	7	–	8	4	1	31
Aubrey McDonald	14	15	15	15	15	15	15	7	3	–	–	–	15
Vuyo Mbotho	13	14	14	14	14	14	14	7	2	–	–	–	10
Colin Herbert	12	13	13	7R	10R	14R	–	6	1	1	–	–	7
Shane Hancke	11	11	11	11	11	11	11	7	3	–	–	–	15
Louis Strydom	10	–	–	–	–	–	–	1	–	5	–	–	10
Andries Mahoney	9	9	9	9R	–	–	12R	5	1	–	–	–	5
Nicky Steyn	8c	8c	8c	8c	8c	–	–	5	3	–	–	–	15
Mlungisi Bali	7	4	5	4R	4R	5R	4R	7	–	–	–	–	0
Martin Sithole	6	7	6	6	6	6	6	7	1	–	–	–	5
Lehan Koekemoer	5	5	4	5	5	5	5	7	–	–	–	–	0
Jeremy Jordaan	4	–	4R	4	4	4	4	6	–	–	–	–	0
Rudi Britz	3	3	3	3	1	1	3R	7	–	–	–	–	0
Derick van Heerden	2	2	–	5R	2R	2	2	6	–	–	–	–	0
Kevin Stevens	1	1	1	1	1R	1R	1R	7	–	–	–	–	0
Martin van der Heever	2R	x	–	–	–	–	–	1	–	–	–	–	0
Heinrich Roelfse	3R	1R	1R	x	–	–	–	3	–	–	–	–	0
Franco Mateus	7R	5R	2R	–	–	–	–	3	–	–	–	–	0
Dirk Grobbelaar	4R	6	–	–	–	–	–	2	–	–	–	–	0
Oshwill Nortje	9R	9R	9R	9	14R	9R	9	7	2	–	–	–	10
Brenvin Marais	12R	x	–	–	–	–	–	1	–	–	–	–	0
Alfredo Barends	10R	11R	–	–	–	–	–	2	–	–	–	–	0
Japie Nel	–	12	12	12	12	12	12	6	1	–	–	–	5
Egbert Ras	–	6R	8R	6R	7R	–	–	4	–	–	–	–	0
Armandt Koster	–	–	7	7	7	7	7	5	–	–	–	–	0
JC van Wyk	–	–	2	2	2	2R	2R	5	–	–	–	–	0
Werner Griesel	–	–	13R	13	13	13c	13c	5	1	–	–	–	5
Erik le Roux	–	–	6R	–	8R	8	8	4	–	–	–	–	0
Sarel Louw	–	–	–	1R	–	–	1	2	–	–	–	–	0
Inus Kritzinger	–	–	–	–	9	9	–	2	–	–	–	–	0
Danie van der Merwe	–	–	–	–	3	3	3	3	–	–	–	–	0
Wilmar Groenewald	–	–	–	–	–	6R	6R	2	–	–	–	–	0
Reinhardt Erwee	–	–	–	–	–	11R	14R	2	–	–	–	–	0
33 players								**151**	**18**	**14**	**4**	**1**	**133**

GRIFFONS RUGBY UNION

APPEARANCES & POINTS IN ABSA CURRIE CUP 2013

Player	Valke	EP Kings	Pumas	Border	Leopards	SWD	Boland	Valke	EP Kings	Pumas	Border	Leopards	SWD	Boland	Matches	Tries	Conversions	Penalties	Drop Goals	Points
Tertius Maarman	15	15	10	15	15	11	15R	10	10	10	10	15R	10R	10R	14	4	2	–	–	24
Aubrey McDonald	14	14	15	x	15R	15	15	15	15	–	x	x	–	–	8	–	–	–	–	0
Hansie Graaff	13	13	–	–	–	–	–	–	–	–	–	–	–	–	2	–	–	–	–	0
Werner Griesel	12	13R	14c	14	14	13c	13c	13c	13c	14c	14c	12c	14c	14c	14	4	–	–	–	20
Shane Hancke	11	11	11	–	–	11R	–	–	11	11	–	–	–	–	6	–	–	–	–	0
Louis Strydom	10	10	–	10	10	10	10	–	–	–	–	–	–	–	6	–	15	14	1	75
Tewis de Bruyn	9	–	–	–	–	–	–	–	–	–	–	–	–	–	1	–	–	–	–	0
Nicky Steyn	8c	–	–	8c	8c	–	–	–	6R	6R	8	8	8	8	8	2	–	–	–	10
Erik le Roux	7	6	6	6	6	8	–	–	–	–	–	–	–	–	6	1	–	–	–	5
Wilmar Groenewald	6	–	–	–	–	6R	6	6	–	–	–	4R	8R	–	6	2	–	–	–	10
Lehan Koekemoer	5	5c	5	5R	4R	5	5	–	–	–	–	–	–	–	7	1	–	–	–	5
Andries Ferreira	4	–	–	–	–	–	–	–	–	–	–	–	–	–	1	–	–	–	–	0
Daniel van der Merwe	3	3	3	3	3	3	3	–	–	3R	3R	3	3	1	12	–	–	–	–	0
Elandre Huggett	2	2	–	2	–	–	–	–	–	–	–	–	–	–	3	1	–	–	–	5
Kevin Stevens	1	1	1	1	1	1	1	–	5R	–	–	–	–	–	8	–	–	–	–	0
Derrick van Heerden	x	2R	2	2R	2	2R	x	2	2	2	2R	x	2	2	11	1	–	–	–	5
Rudi Britz	3R	1R	–	1R	1R	1R	–	–	–	–	–	3R	1	3R	8	–	–	–	–	0
Chris Ehlers	4R	4	4	4	4	4	4	5	5	5	5	5	5	5	14	1	–	–	–	5
Davon Raubenheimer	7R	7	8	7	7	–	–	–	–	–	–	–	–	–	5	–	–	–	–	0
Tertius Daniller	6R	8	4R	8R	8R	–	8	–	8	8	8	–	7	7	11	2	–	–	–	10
Ossie Nortjie	11R	9	9	9	9	9	9	9	10R	9R	9R	x	9R	x	12	2	–	–	–	10
Shaun Prins	14R	–	–	–	–	11R	11	13R	15R	–	–	–	–	–	5	–	–	–	–	0
Japie Nel	–	12	12	12	12	12	12	12	12	12	12	–	12	12	12	8	–	–	–	40
Joubert Engelbrecht	–	14R	13	13	13	–	–	–	–	13	13	13	13	13	9	1	5	1	–	18
Enrico Acker	–	9R	–	–	–	–	–	–	–	–	–	–	–	–	1	–	–	–	–	0
Teboho Mohoje	–	4R	7	5	5	7	–	–	–	–	–	–	–	–	5	–	–	–	–	0
Martin Sithole	–	6R	–	–	–	6	6	–	6R	6	6	6	6	6	9	4	–	–	–	20
Charles Marais	–	–	1R	–	–	–	–	–	–	–	–	–	–	–	1	–	–	–	–	0
JC van Wyk	–	–	2R	–	2R	2	2	–	–	–	–	–	–	–	4	–	–	–	–	0
Andries Mahoney	–	–	9R	9R	9R	9R	–	–	–	–	–	–	–	–	4	–	–	–	–	0
Sarel Louw	–	–	3R	–	–	–	–	1	3	3	3	–	–	–	5	–	–	–	–	0
Colin Herbert	–	–	5R	–	–	–	–	–	–	–	–	–	–	–	1	–	–	–	–	0
Vuyo Mboto	–	–	x	11	11	14	–	15R	14	15	–	14	15R	14R	9	–	–	–	–	0
Freddy Ngoza	–	–	–	6R	5R	–	–	8	–	7	7	–	–	–	5	1	–	–	–	5
Jeremy Jordaan	–	–	–	–	–	5R	4R	4	4	–	4R	4	4	4	8	2	–	–	–	10
Mlungisi Bali	–	–	–	–	–	x	7	4R	7R	5R	–	7	4R	–	6	–	–	–	–	0
Danwel Demas	–	–	–	–	–	–	14	14	–	–	–	–	–	–	2	1	–	–	–	5
Ashwin Scott	–	–	–	–	–	–	11R	11	–	–	–	–	–	–	2	–	–	–	–	0
Inus Kritzinger	–	–	–	–	–	–	9R	9R	9	9	9	9	9	9	8	4	5	–	–	30
Heinrich Roelfse	–	–	–	–	–	–	1R	3	3R	–	–	–	1R	3	5	–	–	–	–	0
Marnus Briedenhann	–	–	–	–	–	–	–	7	7	4	4	–	–	8R	5	1	–	–	–	5
Schalk van der Merwe	–	–	–	–	–	–	–	1R	1	1	1	1	–	–	5	1	–	–	–	5
AJ le Roux	–	–	–	–	–	–	–	2R	2R	2R	2	2	–	–	5	2	–	–	–	10
Rossouw de Klerk	–	–	–	–	–	–	–	3R	–	–	–	–	–	–	1	–	–	–	–	0
Bernado Botha	–	–	–	–	–	–	–	–	15R	15	15	15	15	–	5	–	–	–	–	0
Norman Nelson	–	–	–	–	–	–	–	–	11R	11	11	11	11	–	5	3	–	–	–	15
Franna du Toit	–	–	–	–	–	–	–	–	–	10R	10	10	10	10	4	–	10	–	–	20
Frans Sisita	–	–	–	–	–	–	–	–	–	–	8R	–	–	–	1	–	–	–	–	0
Deon Gouws	–	–	–	–	–	–	–	–	–	–	–	–	2R	x	1	–	–	–	–	0
Dean Rossouw	–	–	–	–	–	–	–	–	–	–	–	–	–	x		–	–	–	–	0
50 players															296	49	37	15	1	367

ABSA UNDER-21 CHAMPIONSHIP (4th, Section B)

Played	Won	Drawn	Lost	Points for	Points against	Tries for	Tries against	Winning %
8	3	0	5	185	288	26	43	38,00%

RESULTS Lost Boland (h) 28-78. Bt Valke (a) 39-28. Lost EP (h) 00-53. Bt Mpumalanga (a) 24-20. Lost Griffons (h) 24-31. Lost Limpopo Blue Bulls (h) 19-24. Bt SWD (a) 25-10. SEMI-FINAL Lost EP (a) 26-44.

SCORERS 52 Jonty Gray (2t, 9c, 8p). 23 Marthinus van der Merwe (4t, 1p). 17 Leroy Bitterhout (3t, 1c). 11 Hendri Rust (1t, 3c). 10 George du Raan, Johann Strauss, Nicolaas Steyn, Renier Botha, (2t each). 8 Juan Vos (4c). 5 Arrie van der Berg, Elgernon Diamonds, Hendrik Pretorius, Jacob de Jager, Lyvette Shikwambana, Reynardt Muller, Rossouw Pienaar, Ruan Roets, Stephan Steyn (1t each).

ABSA U19 CHAMPIONSHIP (7th, Section B)

Played	Won	Drawn	Lost	Points for	Points against	Tries for	Tries against	Winning %
7	3	0	4	171	188	22	26	43,00%

RESULTS Lost Boland (h) 22-23. Lost Valke (a) 20-31. Lost EP (h) 07-26. Bt Mpumalanga (a) 31-20. Bt Griffons (h) 25-21. Bt Limpopo Blue Bulls (h) 40-38. Lost SWD (a) 26-26.

SCORERS 36 Deon van Zyl (6c, 7p, 1dg). 28 Christo Coetzee (1t, 7c, 3p) 25 Johan Nel (5t). 15 Marthinus Kemp, Ryno Smith (3t each). 10 Bjorn van Wyk, Luxolo Koza, McPherson Maketlo (2t each). 5 Hillford Clarke, Hugo Strydom, Juan le Roux, Willem van Aswegen (1t each). 2 Stefan Schutte (1c).

Oshwill Nortje gets the ball away against the Vodacom Blue Bulls in the Vodacom Cup.
Duif du Toit/Gallo Images

GRIFFONS RECORDS

MATCH RECORDS

Biggest win	72-12	vs Stellaland	1992
Biggest win (Currie Cup)	74-06	vs Eastern Orange Free State	1988
Heaviest defeat	8-91	vs Free State	1995
Heaviest defeat (Currie Cup)	0-106	vs Free State Cheetahs	1997
Highest score	72	vs Stellaland (72-12)	1992
Highest score (Currie Cup)	74	vs Eastern Orange Free State (74-6)	1988
Moist points conceded	91	vs Free State (8-91)	1995
Moist points conceded (Currie Cup)	106	vs Free State Cheetahs (0-106)	1997
Most tries	11	vs Stellaland (72-12)	1992
Most tries (Currie Cup)	12	vs Eastern Orange Free State (74-6)	1988
Most points by a player	36	E Herbert vs Stellaland	1992
Most points by a player (Currie Cup)	36	E Herbert vs Falcons	1997
Most tries by a player (Currie Cup)	5	P Maritz vs SE Tvl	1982
Most conversions by a player	11	E Herbert vs Stellaland	1992
Most conversions by a player (Currie Cup)	10	E Herbert vs EOFS	1988
Most penalties by a player	9	E Herbert vs Pumas	2001
Most penalties by a player (Currie Cup)	9	E Herbert vs Falcons	1997
Most drop goals by a player (Currie Cup)	3	E Herbert vs FS Cheetahs	2000

SEASON RECORDS

Most team points	657	24 matches	2001
Most team points (Currie Cup)	506	15 matches	2012
Most points by a player	263	E Herbert	2001
Most points by a player (Currie Cup)	195	E Herbert	1988
Most team tries	86	21 matches	2012
Most team tries (Currie Cup)	68	15 matches	2012
Most tries by a player	14	O Damons	2004
Most tries by a player (Currie Cup)	8	GA Passens	1999
	8	MP Goosen	2005
	8	CS Afrika	2008
	8	J Nel	2013
Most conversions by a player	43	E Herbert	2001
Most penalties by a player	56	E Herbert	2001
Most drop goals by a player	10	E Herbert	1988

CAREER RECORDS

Most appearances	205	E Herbert	1986-2001
Most consecutive games	102	A Gerber	1979-1985
Most matches as captain	95	JJ Jerling	1989-1997
Most points	2608	E Herbert	1986-2001
Most tries	38	NPJ Steyn	2008-2013
Most conversions by a player	331	E Herbert	1986-2001
Most penalties by a player	544	E Herbert	1986-2001
Most drop goals by a player	66	E Herbert	1986-2001

HONOURS

Paul Roos Trophy	1970
Vodacom Shield	2001
Bankfin Cup	2008

GRIQUALAND WEST RUGBY UNION

FOUNDED
1886
GROUND
GWK Park, Kimberley
CAPACITY
11 000
ADDRESS
Jacobus Smit Avenue, New Park, Kimberley
POSTAL ADDRESS
PO Box 110825, Hadison Park, Kimberley 8306
TELEPHONE NUMBER
053-832 8773
WEBSITE
www.griquasrugby.co.za
COLOURS
Peacock blue and white hooped jersey, black shorts
CURRIE CUP COACH
Pote Human
VODACOM CUP COACH
Pote Human
CAPTAIN
Ryno Barnes
PRESIDENT
Hennie van der Merwe
COMPANY CEO
Arni van Rooyen

Lower league beckons for Griquas

THE 2014 SEASON WILL BE THE DAWNING OF A NEW ERA FOR the Griqualand West Rugby Union as Hawies Fourie will take over the reins as head coach from Pote Human. Fourie has been backline coach of the Toyota Free State Cheetahs Cheetahs since 2008 after joining them from Boland. Human will coach the University of Pretoria in the Varsity Cup, while the 2014 season also sees backline coach Abré Minnie leaving Kimberley to pursue business opportunities in George.

Minnie joined Griquas in 2003 and his visionary backline coaching played a major part in the Peacock Blues drinking out of the Vodacom Cup three times during his tenure. Fourie moves to Kimberley as the city prepares to open a much-needed university, which could help the team to hang onto their prospective talents as well as lure players to the union.

Whatever happens, what cannot be disputed is that 2013 was forgettable. Griquas finished last in the Absa Currie Cup Premier Division and then lost their promotion/relegation series against the Steval Pumas. Griquas managed to squeak a 21-19 victory at their fortress of GWK Park, but were outplayed 33-15 in the Mbombela Stadium in Nelspruit.

They start their campaign on a high, beating eventual champions the Sharks in the first match of the competition, 32-30 in Durban, but thereafter there were only losses to account for.

But it wasn't all doom and gloom for Griquas. They gave eventual finalists DHL Western Province a fright before going down 19-13 at a wet Newlands, while they lost 20-19 to WP at home.

The Sharks had to work hard for an equally close 25-24 win in Kimberley. Rarely has two points been so important in the greater scheme of things.

The highlight of the season without a doubt was the fact that Griquas managed to produce yet another two Springboks. Fullback Willie le Roux and prop Lourens Adriaanse became the union's 62nd and 63rd international players after excellent performances during Vodacom Super Rugby for the Cheetahs. However, both players are lost to the union for 2014, with Le Roux joining the Cheetahs and Adriaanse deciding to further his career at the Sharks.

In the Vodacom Cup, WP halted Griquas' progress in the quarter-finals with a 21-13 victory in Cape Town.

BY HANNES NIENABER

Hilton Lobberts in action for Griquas against the Sharks.
Steve Haag/Gallo Images

GRIQUALAND WEST RUGBY UNION

VODACOM CUP LOG POSITIONS

2013	6th	2010	6th	2007	2nd	2004	12th	2001	3rd	**1998** **1st**
2012	2nd	**2009**	**1st**	2006	9th	2003	9th	2000	1st	
2011	4th	2008	4th	2005	3rd	2002	10th	1999	2nd	

ABSA CURRIE CUP LOG POSITIONS

2013	6th	2010	6th	2007	6th	2004	6th	2001	8th	**1998** **1st**
2012	5th	2009	5th	2006	6th	2003	7th	2000	8th	1997 6th
2011	6th	2008	6th	2005	7th	2002	7th	1999	6th	1996 6th

2013 RESULTS & SCORERS

VODACOM CUP PLAYED **8** WON **4** DRAWN **0** LOST **4** POINTS FOR **309** POINTS AGAINST **180** TRIES FOR **45** TRIES AGAINST **26** WINNING PERCENTAGE **50%**

Date	Venue	Opponent	Result	Score	Referee	Scorers
Mrch 09	Kimberley	Blue Bulls	LOST	32-40	R Rasivhenge	T: Hewitt, Schoeman, Vermeulen, Westraadt, Penalty try. C: Brummer, Vermeulen. P: Brummer.
Mrch 16	Welkom	Griffons	WON	26-12	J van Heerden	T: Boshoff, Downey, Karemaker, Schoeman. C: Brummer (3).
Mrch 23	Groblersdal	Limpopo BB	WON	124-5	L Jam	T: Schoeman (5), Jansen (5), Vulindlu (2), Carney, Acker, Brummer, Coetzee, Downey, Karemaker, Lawson, Pen try. C: Brummer (12).
April 05	Kimberley	Pumas	LOST	31-47	B Crouse	T: Carney, Adendorf, Karemaker, Lawson. C: De Wet (4). P: De Wet.
April 12	Johannesburg¹	Golden Lions	LOST	11-24	J van Heerden	T: Coetzee. P: De Wet (2).
April 20	Kimberley	Leopards XV	WON	32-26	L Legoete	T: Coetzee, Stemmet, Karemaker, Schoeman. C: De Wet (3). P: De Wet. DG: De Wet.
April 27	Kempton Park	Valke	WON	40-07	J van Heerden	T: Karemaker (2), Van Niekerk (2), Badenhorst, Acker. C: De Wet (5).
Quarter-final						
May 04	Cape Town	WP	LOST	13-21	S Mayende	T: Schoeman. C: De Wet. P: De Wet (2).

ABSA CURRIE CUP PLAYED **12** WON **2** LOST **0** DRAWN **10** POINTS FOR **244** POINTS AGAINST **378** TRIES FOR **20** TRIES AGAINST **40** WINNING PERCENTAGE **17%**

Date	Venue	Opponent	Result	Score	Referee	Scorers
Aug 09	Durban	Sharks	WON	32-30	J Jaftha	T: Greeff, M Schoeman. C: Scheepers (2). P: Scheepers (6).
Aug 16	Pretoria	Blue Bulls	LOST	09-15	M vd Westhuizen	P: Brummer (3).
Aug 24	Kimberley	WP	LOST	19-20	S Mayende	T: Vermeulen. C: Gerber. P: Scheepers (4).
Aug 31	Bloemfontein	Free State	LOST	20-40	C Joubert	T: Jansen, Arnold. C: Scheepers (2). P: Scheepers (2).
Sep 07	Kimberley	Golden Lions	LOST	32-38	J Jaftha	T: Greeff, Mnisi, Stemmett, Vermeulen. C: Brummer (3). P: Brummer (2).
Sep 14	Kimberley	Sharks	LOST	24-25	J Peyper	T: M Schoeman, B Schoeman. C: Brummer. P: Brummer (4).
Sep 20	Cape Town	WP	LOST	13-19	L vd Merwe	T: Scheepers. C: Scheepers. P: Brummer, Prinsloo.
Sep 28	Kimberley	Blue Bulls	LOST	10-52	Q Immelman	T: Penalty try. C: Prinsloo. P: Prinsloo.
Oct 05	Kimberley	Free State	LOST	21-52	J Kaplan	T: Davis, Nepgen, Arnold. C: Prinsloo (3).
Oct 12	Johannesburg	Golden Lions	LOST	28-35	J Peyper	T: Jansen. C: Prinsloo. P: Prinsloo (7).
PROMOTION & RELEGATION						
Oct 18	Kimberley	Pumas	WON	21-19	J Kaplan	T: Greeff, Stemmet, M Schoeman. C: Prinsloo (3).
Oct 25	Nelspruit	Pumas	LOST	15-33	C Joubert	P: Gouws (5).

GRIQUAS SQUAD IN 2013 — GRIQUAS CAREER

PLAYER	Appearances	Tries	Conversions	Penalties	Drop Goals	Points	Career Matches	Career Tries	Conversions	Penalties	Drop Goals	Points
DE (Enrico) Acker	6	2	–	–	–	10	16	3	–	–	–	15
JW (Jonathan) Adendorf	9	1	–	–	–	5	19	2	–	–	–	10
LC (Lourens) Adriaanse	5	–	–	–	–	0	37	3	–	–	–	15
RW (Rory) Arnold	6	2	–	–	–	10	6	2	–	–	–	10
WHB (Brummer) Badenhorst	13	1	–	–	–	5	13	1	–	–	–	5
RJ (Ryno) Barnes	11	–	–	–	–	0	82	9	–	–	–	45
LA (Logan) Basson	1	–	–	–	–	0	12	2	8	1	0	29
JH (Jannie) Boshoff	4	1	–	–	–	5	13	7	–	–	–	35
F (Francois) Brummer	16	1	20	11	–	78	33	3	38	33	2	196
EF (Eugene) Butterworth	2	–	–	–	–	0	6	–	–	–	–	0
D (Deon) Carney	8	2	–	–	–	10	8	2	–	–	–	10
J (Jacques) Coetzee	20	3	–	–	–	15	39	6	–	–	–	30
D (Dalton) Davis	3	1	–	–	–	5	3	1	–	–	–	5
JJS (JJ) de Klerk	1	–	–	–	–	0	1	–	–	–	–	0
P-S (Pieter-Steyn) de Wet	5	–	13	6	1	47	5	–	13	6	1	47
MG (Matthew) Dobson	18	–	–	–	–	0	41	2	–	–	–	10
J (Justin) Downey	8	2	–	–	–	10	48	4	–	–	–	20
PJJ (Pieter) Engelbrecht	1	–	–	–	–	0	1	–	–	–	–	0
JC (Jonathan) Francke	1	–	–	–	–	0	1	–	–	–	–	0
D (Du Randt) Gerber	6	–	1	–	–	2	6	–	1	–	–	2
CFK (Carel) Greeff	8	3	–	–	–	15	8	3	–	–	–	15
EW (Edwin) Hewitt	8	1	–	–	–	5	32	1	–	–	–	5
JP (Joubert) Horn	5	–	–	–	–	0	5	–	–	–	–	0
APM (Marnus) Hugo	17	–	–	–	–	0	47	1	–	–	–	5
PG (Gerhard) Human	1	–	–	–	–	0	9	–	–	–	–	0
RR (Rocco) Jansen	18	7	–	–	–	35	65	28	–	–	–	140
L (Leon) Karemaker	15	6	–	–	–	30	59	23	–	–	–	115
VE (Victor) Kruger	2	–	–	–	–	0	2	–	–	–	–	0
RJ (Rynard) Landman	4	–	–	–	–	0	23	7	–	–	–	35
RJ (Richard) Lawson	10	2	–	–	–	10	47	14	–	–	–	70
WJ (Willie) le Roux	2	–	–	–	–	0	11	1	–	–	–	5
RJ (RJ) Liebenberg	9	–	–	–	–	0	9	–	–	–	–	0
H (Hilton) Lobberts	4	–	–	–	–	0	4	–	–	–	–	0
XH (Howard) Mnisi	11	1	–	–	–	5	11	1	–	–	–	5
JP (JP) Nel	9	–	–	–	–	0	12	–	–	–	–	0
J (Jaco) Nepgen	12	1	–	–	–	5	48	4	–	–	–	20
PL (Pat) O'Brien	9	–	–	–	–	0	9	–	–	–	–	0
B (Brendan) Pitzer	1	–	–	–	–	0	1	–	–	–	–	0
N (Nico) Pretorius	1	–	–	–	–	0	1	–	–	–	–	0
JG (Gouws) Prinsloo	9	–	8	14	–	58	9	–	8	14	–	58
WAS (Steph) Roberts	17	–	–	–	–	0	111	4	–	–	–	20
JN (Nico) Scheepers	7	1	5	12	–	51	7	1	5	12	–	51
DB (Burger) Schoeman	10	1	–	–	–	5	37	5	–	–	–	25
M (Marnus) Schoeman	17	12	–	–	–	60	41	25	–	–	–	125
NP (Nick) Schonert	14	–	–	–	–	0	14	–	–	–	–	0
JH (Jean) Stemmet	15	3	–	–	–	15	45	15	–	–	–	75
SG (Stephan) van der Merwe	3	–	–	–	–	0	3	–	–	–	–	0
E (Ewald) van der Westhuizen	1	–	–	–	–	0	1	–	–	–	–	0
JL (Janro) van Niekerk	10	2	–	–	–	10	22	4	–	–	–	20
PJ (PJ) Vermeulen	13	3	1	–	–	17	21	5	1	–	–	27
W (Walter) Venter	4	–	–	–	–	0	14	1	–	–	–	5
L (Luzuko) Vulindlu	8	2	–	–	–	10	11	2	–	–	–	10
S (Simon) Westraadt	7	1	–	–	–	5	54	9	–	–	–	45
Penalty try	0	3	–	–	–	15	0	1	–	–	–	5
53 players	**425**	**65**	**48**	**43**	**1**	**553**	**1183**	**202**	**74**	**66**	**3**	**1365**

GRIQUALAND WEST RUGBY UNION

APPEARANCES & POINTS IN VODACOM CUP 2013

	Blue Bulls	Griffons	Limpopo XV	Pumas	Golden Lions	Leopards XV	Valke	WP	Matches	Tries	Conversions	Penalties	Drop Goals	Points
Rocco Jansen	15	11	11	11	15	11	–	–	6	5	–	–	–	25
Jannie Boshoff	14	14	–	14	14	–	–	–	4	1	–	–	–	5
Jean Stemmet	13	13	13	15R	13	13	13	13	8	1	–	–	–	5
PJ Vermeulen	12c	12c	12c	13c	–	15c	11c	11c	7	1	1	–	–	7
Richard Lawson	11	15	15	15	–	–	–	–	4	2	–	–	–	10
Francois Brummer	10	10	10	–	–	–	15	15	5	1	16	1	–	40
Marnus Hugo	9	–	9R	9	9R	–	9R	14R	6	–	–	–	–	0
Leon Karemaker	8	8	8	8	8c	8	8	8	8	6	–	–	–	30
Justin Downey	7	7	8R	7	7	7	7	7	8	2	–	–	–	10
Marnus Schoeman	6	6	6	6	6	6	2R	6	8	9	–	–	–	45
Jaco Nepgen	5	5	–	–	–	–	5R	5	4	–	–	–	–	0
Edwin Hewitt	4	4	4	4	4	4	4R	4	8	1	–	–	–	5
Eugene Butterworth	3	3	–	–	–	–	–	–	2	–	–	–	–	0
Matthew Dobson	2	2R	2R	2	2	2R	2	2	8	–	–	–	–	0
Steph Roberts	1	1	1	1	1	1	–	–	6	–	–	–	–	0
Simon Westraadt	2R	2	2	2R	2R	2	–	–	6	1	–	–	–	5
Janro van Niekerk	1R	1R	–	1R	1R	1R	1	1	7	2	–	–	–	10
Joubert Horn	4R	5R	x	–	–	4R	4	5R	5	–	–	–	–	0
Deon Carney	6R	8R	7	6R	4R	6R	6	8R	8	2	–	–	–	10
Enrico Acker	9R	9R	9	–	–	22R	9	x	5	2	–	–	–	10
Jacques Coetzee	10R	9	14	9R	9	–	9	14R	8	3	–	–	–	15
Luzuko Vulindlu	11R	–	14R	13R	11	14	14	14	7	2	–	–	–	10
Brummer Badenhorst	–	3R	3	3R	3R	3R	3	3R	7	1	–	–	–	5
Walter Venter	–	15R	13R	12	x	12R	–	–	4	–	–	–	–	0
Jonathan Adendorf	–	–	5	5	5	5	5	4R	6	1	–	–	–	5
Nick Schonert	–	–	3R	3	3	3	3R	3	6	–	–	–	–	0
Pieter-Steyn de Wet	–	–	–	10	10	10	10	10	5	–	13	6	1	47
Pieter Engelbrecht	–	–	–	–	12	–	–	–	1	–	–	–	–	0
Stephan van der Merwe	–	–	–	–	x	12	12	2	3	–	–	–	–	0
Gerhard Human	–	–	–	–	–	7R	–	–	1	–	–	–	–	0
JJ de Klerk	–	–	–	–	–	–	–	12R	1	–	–	–	–	0
Penalty try	–	–	–	–	–	–	–	–	0	2	–	–	–	10
31 players									172	45	30	7	1	309

APPEARANCES & POINTS IN ABSA CURRIE CUP 2013

	Sharks	Blue Bulls	WP	Free State	Golden Lions	Sharks	WP	Blue Bulls	Free State	Golden Lions	Pumas	Pumas	Matches	Tries	Conversions	Penalties	Drop Goals	Points
Gouws Prinsloo	15	15	–	–	–	15R	15	15	15	15	15	15	9	–	8	14	–	58
Nico Scheepers	14	14	14	14	13R	14	14	–	–	–	x	x	7	1	5	12	–	51
JP Nel	13	13	13	13	–	13	–	13	13	12R	x	12R	9	–	–	–	–	0
Howard Mnisi	12	12	12	12	12	12	12	12	12	–	12	12	11	1	–	–	–	5
PJ Vermeulen	11	11	15	15	15	15	–	–	–	–	–	–	6	2	–	–	–	10
Francois Brummer	10	10	10	10	10	10	10	10	10	–	10	10	11	–	4	10	–	38
Jacques Coetzee	9	9	9R	9R	9R	9R	9	9R	9R	9	9R	9	12	–	–	–	–	0
Burger Schoeman	8	8	8R	7	7	7	7	7	–	–	8	7	10	1	–	–	–	5
Jaco Nepgen	7	5	4	–	–	–	5	5	5	7	5	–	8	1	–	–	–	5
Marnus Schoeman	6	–	–	6R	6	6	6	6	6	–	6	6R	9	3	–	–	–	15
Rynard Landman	5	–	–	–	–	–	–	–	–	4	4	4	4	–	–	–	–	0
Hilton Lobberts	4	4	7	4	–	–	–	–	–	–	–	–	4	–	–	–	–	0
Lourens Adriaanse	3	3	–	–	–	–	–	–	–	3c	3	3	5	–	–	–	–	0
Ryno Barnes	2c	2c	2c	2c	2c	2c	2c	2c	2c	–	2c	2c	11	–	–	–	–	0
Steph Roberts	1	1	1	1	1	1	1	1	1	–	1	1	11	–	–	–	–	0
Matthew Dobson	x	2R	x	3R	3R	3R	3R	17R	3R	2	3R	2	10	–	–	–	–	0
Nick Schonert	3R	3R	3	3	3	3	3	–	–	–	–	3R	8	–	–	–	–	0
Jonathan Adendorff	4R	7	5	–	–	–	–	–	–	–	–	–	3	–	–	–	–	0
Carel Greeff	6R	6	6	6	8	8	–	–	–	–	7R	8	8	3	–	–	–	15
Marnus Hugo	9R	9R	9	9	9	9	9R	9	9	–	9	9R	11	–	–	–	–	0
Du Randt Gerber	x	x	10R	x	10R	x	10R	10R	10R	10	–	–	6	–	1	–	–	2
Rocco Jansen	13R	15R	11	11	11	11	11	11	11	11	11	11	12	2	–	–	–	10
Leon Karemaker	–	8R	8	8	–	–	8	8	8	8	–	–	7	–	–	–	–	0
RJ Liebenberg	–	6R	7R	–	7R	7R	x	7R	7	6	7	6	9	–	–	–	–	0
Brummer Badenhorst	–	–	1R	1R	1R	6R	x	–	1R	1R	–	–	6	–	–	–	–	0
Richard Lawson	–	–	14R	13R	14	–	11R	14	14	–	–	–	6	–	–	–	–	0
Rory Arnold	–	–	–	5	–	4	4	4	4R	5	–	–	6	2	–	–	–	10
Pat O'Brien	–	–	–	4R	4	5R	4R	4R	7R	5R	5R	5	9	–	–	–	–	0
Jean Stemmet	–	–	–	–	13	–	13	13R	13R	13	13	13	7	2	–	–	–	10
Victor Kruger	–	–	–	5	5	–	–	–	–	–	–	–	2	–	–	–	–	0
Dalton Davis	–	–	–	4R	–	–	–	4	5R	–	–	–	3	1	–	–	–	5
Ewald vd Westhuizen	–	–	–	–	–	–	3	–	–	–	–	–	1	–	–	–	–	0
Brendan Pitzer	–	–	–	–	–	–	3R	–	–	–	–	–	1	–	–	–	–	0
Nico Pretorius	–	–	–	–	–	–	–	3	–	–	–	–	1	–	–	–	–	0
Luzuko Vulindlu	–	–	–	–	–	–	–	–	–	14	–	–	1	–	–	–	–	0
Jonathan Francke	–	–	–	–	–	–	–	–	–	12	–	–	1	–	–	–	–	0
Janro van Niekerk	–	–	–	–	–	–	–	–	–	1	1R	1R	3	–	–	–	–	0
Enrico Acker	–	–	–	–	–	–	–	–	–	9R	–	–	1	–	–	–	–	0
Simon Westraadt	–	–	–	–	–	–	–	–	–	8R	–	–	1	–	–	–	–	0
Logan Basson	–	–	–	–	–	–	–	–	–	14R	–	–	1	–	–	–	–	0
Willie le Roux	–	–	–	–	–	–	–	–	–	–	14	14	2	–	–	–	–	0
Penalty try	–	–	–	–	–	–	–	–	–	–	–	–	0	1	–	–	–	5
40 players													253	20	18	36	0	244

GRIQUALAND WEST RUGBY UNION

ABSA UNDER-21 CHAMPIONSHIP (4th, Section B)

Played	Won	Drawn	Lost	Points for	Points against	Tries for	Tries against	Winning %
8	3	0	5	185	288	26	43	38,00%

RESULTS Lost Boland (h) 28-78. Bt Valke (a) 39-28. Lost EP (h) 00-53. Bt Mpumalanga (a) 24-20. Lost Griffons (h) 24-31. Lost Limpopo Blue Bulls (h) 19-24. Bt SWD (a) 25-10. SEMI-FINAL Lost EP (a) 26-44.

SCORERS 52 Jonty Gray (2t, 9c, 8p). 23 Marthinus van der Merwe (4t, 1p). 17 Leroy Bitterhout (3t, 1c). 11 Hendri Rust (1t, 3c). 10 George du Raan, Johann Strauss, Nicolaas Steyn, Renier Botha, (2t each). 8 Juan Vos (4c). 5 Arrie van der Berg, Elgernon Diamonds, Hendrik Pretorius, Jacob de Jager, Lyvette Shikwambana, Reynardt Muller, Rossouw Pienaar, Ruan Roets, Stephan Steyn (1t each).

ABSA U19 CHAMPIONSHIP (7th, Section B)

Played	Won	Drawn	Lost	Points for	Points against	Tries for	Tries against	Winning %
7	3	0	4	171	188	22	26	43,00%

RESULTS Lost Boland (h) 22-23. Lost Valke (a) 20-31. Lost EP (h) 07-26. Bt Mpumalanga (a) 31-20. Bt Griffons (h) 25-21. Bt Limpopo Blue Bulls (h) 40-38. Lost SWD (a) 26-26.

SCORERS 36 Deon van Zyl (6c, 7p, 1dg). 28 Christo Coetzee (1t, 7c, 3p) 25 Johan Nel (5t). 15 Marthinus Kemp, Ryno Smith (3t each). 10 Bjorn van Wyk, Luxolo Koza, McPherson Maketlo (2t each). 5 Hillford Clarke, Hugo Strydom, Juan le Roux, Willem van Aswegen (1t each). 2 Stefan Schutte (1c).

Willie le Roux became Griquas' 62nd Springbok.
Manus van Dyk/Gallo Images

GRIQUAS RECORDS

MATCH RECORDS

Biggest win	94-0	vs. South Western Districts Federation	1978
Biggest win (Currie Cup)	87-14	vs. Border	1998
	80-07	vs Cavaliers	2009
Heaviest defeat	3-75	vs. Western Province	1985
Heaviest defeat (Currie Cup)	7-78	vs. Natal Sharks	2002
Highest score	94	vs. South Western Districts Federation (94-0)	1978
Highest score (Currie Cup)	87	vs. Border (87-14)	1998
Moist points conceded	75	vs. Western Province	1985
Moist points conceded (Currie Cup)	78	vs. Natal Sharks (7-78)	2002
	78	vs. Western Province (31-78)	2004
Most tries	18	vs. South Western Districts Federation	1978
Most tries (Currie Cup)	14	vs. Griffons (84-12)	2002
Most points by a player	42	IP Olivier vs. Griffons	2009
Most points by a player (Currie Cup)	33	PJ Visagie vs. Rhodesia	1968
Most tries by a player	7	J Jonker vs. Namibia	1996
Most tries by a player (Currie Cup)	4	D Prins vs. Eastern Province	1978
	4	J Nicholas vs. North West	1998
	4	BA Basson vs. Sharks	2010
Most conversions by a player (Currie Cup)	11	JC Wessels vs. Border	1998

SEASON RECORDS

Most team points	1428	32 matches	1998
Most team points (Currie Cup)	489	14 matches	1998
Most points by a player	361	GS du Toit	1998
Most points by a player (Currie Cup)	173	IP Olivier	2010
Most team tries	210	32 matches	1998
Most team tries (Currie Cup)	86	21 matches	2003
Most tries by a player	29	BA Basson	2010
Most tries by a player (Currie Cup)	21	BA Basson	2010
Most conversions by a player	98	GS du Toit	1998
Most drop goals by a player	7	GS du Toit	1998

CAREER RECORDS

Most appearances	161	AWA van Wyk	1984-1995
Most appearances (Currie Cup)	69	D Prins	1979-1987
Most consecutive games	97	P Smith	1963-1973
Most matches as captain	66	AWA van Wyk	1989-1994
Most points	719	JMF Lubbe	1995-2001
Most points (Currie Cup)	440	CS Erasmus	1977-1985
Most tries	61	J Nicholas	1998-2002
Most tries (Currie Cup)	37	D Prins	1979-1987
Most conversions by a player	133	JMF Lubbe	1995-2001
Most penalties by a player	91	JMF Lubbe	1995-2001
Most drop goals by a player	15	PJ Visagie	1964-1974
Most drop goals by a player (Currie Cup)	8	PJ Visagie	1964-1974

HONOURS

Bankfin Currie Cup	1899, 1911, 1970
Vodacom Cup	1998, 2005, 2007, 2009

KWAZULU-NATAL RUGBY UNION

FOUNDED 1890
(as Natal Rugby Union)
GROUND
Growthpoint Kings Park
CAPACITY 53 000
ADDRESS
Jacko Jackson Drive,
Stamford Hill, Durban
POSTAL ADDRESS
PO Box 307, Durban, 4000
TELEPHONE NUMBER
031-308 8400
WEBSITE
www.sharksrugby.co.za
COLOURS
Black and white jersey
and socks, white shorts
CURRIE CUP COACH
Brad MacLeod-Henderson
VODACOM CUP COACH
Swys de Bruin
CAPTAIN
Keegan Daniel
PRESIDENT
Graham MacKenzie
COMPANY CEO
John Smit
UNION CEO
Pete Smith

BY JOHN BISHOP

New-look Sharks surge to title

IT WAS A CAMPAIGN WHICH STARTED IN DISARRAY BUT ENDED in heady triumph as the Sharks, cleverly and ruthlessly, went from the ridiculous to the sublime in beating DHL Western Province at Newlands to regain the Absa Currie Cup title they had last won in 2010.

It was the fourth successive final for the Sharks and, as underdogs, they duly followed the modern trend by toppling the favourites.

Few would have expected the Sharks to scale such heights following the dramatic and acrimonious mid-year changes at King's Park. But, under new CEO John Smit and coaches Brendan Venter, Brad Macleod-Henderson and Sean Everitt, they snuck up and mugged Province in their own backyard to take South African rugby's richest prize. Jake White now takes over from the Flying Doctor Venter at the Sharks and he has the most difficult act to follow.

The road to the final was not the smoothest and the Sharks were forced to grind out narrow wins, often in the closing moments of tense contests.

The season started with a 32-30 home loss to GWK Griquas which immediately placed the Sharks, and their management, under pressure. Victories over MTN Golden Lions (33-25) and the Toyota Cheetahs (18-15) in Bloemfontein brought relief but they lost to Western Province both away (25-19) and at home (17-13). These defeats ultimately cost them a home final.

A late try by prop Wiehahn Herbst edged them home 25-24 against struggling Griquas in Kimberley, young flyhalf Fred Zeilinga had a field day in their 31-25 win over the Lions at Ellis Park and veteran Butch James calmly kicked two late penalties for an 18-16 win at Loftus to secure a home semi-final.

Their most balanced display came in the home game against Free State when they romped home 50-26 and they again beat the Cheetahs in the semi-final (33-22) when Pat Lambie flourished.

Flank Jean Deysel had enjoyed an excellent season until he went down with an injury in the semi-final while veteran Jacques Botes, in becoming the most capped player in Currie Cup history, Kyle Cooper, Keegan Daniel, Charl McLeod and Odwa Ndungane provided the experience as the Sharks advanced.

Young talent also emerged. Fullback SP Marais, signed from the EP Kings, centre Heimar Williams and Zeilinga are clearly players for the future.

But it was the late return of their Springboks which transformed the willing young squad into champions, adding muscle, skill and rugby nous at the critical moment. Pieter-Steph du Toit solved the lineout problem, the Test front-row propped up the scrum, Willem Alberts, Marcell Coetzee, Bismarck du Plessis and Frans Steyn added the physical edge and McLeod and Lambie scored the points. And it all came together with the Currie Cup final.

The Sharks celebrate their Currie Cup triumph. *Steve Haag/Gallo Images*

KWAZULU-NATAL RUGBY UNION

VODACOM CUP LOG POSITIONS

2013	2nd	**2010**	4th	**2007**	9th	**2004**	4th	**2001**	5th	**1998**	4th
2012	5th	**2009**	3rd	**2006**	1st	**2003**	4th	**2000**	12th		
2011	5th	**2008**	9th	**2005**	12th	**2002**	9th	**1999**	4th		

ABSA CURRIE CUP LOG POSITIONS

2013	2nd	**2010**	1st 🏆	**2007**	2nd	**2004**	5th	**2001**	2nd	**1998**	3rd
2012	1st	**2009**	1st 🏆	**2006**	4th	**2003**	2nd	**2000**	1st	**1997**	2nd
2011	2nd	**2008**	1st 🏆	**2005**	5th	**2002**	1st	**1999**	2nd	**1996**	1st 🏆

2013 RESULTS & SCORERS

VODACOM CUP (as Sharks XV) Played **8** Won **6** Drawn **0** Lost **2** Points for **304** Points against **208** Tries for **33** Tries against **21** Winning Percentage **75%**

Date	Venue	Opponent	Result	Score	Referee	Scorers
Mrch 08	Durban	Border Bulldogs	WON	72-06	M Jonker	T: Fisher (2), Maseko (2), Zeilinga (2), Sithole, Williams, Venter, Prinsloo. C: Zeilinga (8). P: Zeilinga (2).
Mrch 16	Cape Town	WP	WON	24-23	M Kemp	T: Viljoen, Sithole, Maseko. C: Zeilinga (3). P: Zeilinga.
Mrch 23	Durban	Free State XV	WON	34-33	C Joubert	T: Sithole, Maseko, F Marais. C: Zeilinga (4). P: Zeilinga (2).
April 05	George	Eagles	WON	26-22	Q Immelman	T: Kleinhans, Robinson. C: Zeilinga (2). P: Zeilinga (4).
April 12	Durban	Cavaliers	WON	54-24	Q Immelman	T: Stander (2), Sithole, Williams, Bondesio, Van Tonder. C: Zeilinga (6). P: Zeilinga (4).
April 20	Port Elizabeth	EP Kings	LOST	23-27	B Crouse	T: Alexander. P: Zeilinga (6).
April 26	Durban	Pampas XV	WON	46-31	R Rasivhenge	T: Alberts (2), Van Tonder, Matsushima, Joubert, Harris. C: Zeilinga (5). P: Zeilinga (2).
QUARTER-FINAL:						
May 03	Durban	Golden Lions	LOST	25-42	B Crouse	T: Maseko. C: Zeilinga. P: Zeilinga (6).

ABSA CURRIE CUP Played **12** Won **9** Lost **3** Drawn **0** Points for **337** Points against **264** Tries for **33** Tries against **25** Winning Percentage **75%**

Date	Venue	Opponent	Result	Score	Referee	Scorers
Aug 09	Durban	Griquas	LOST	30-32	J Jaftha	T: Botes (2), Mvovo. C: James (3). P: James (3).
Aug 16	Durban	Golden Lions	WON	33-25	B Crouse	T: SP Marais, Williams, Stander. C: James (2), Zeilinga. P: James (3), Zeilinga.
Aug 23	Bloemfontein	Cheetahs	WON	18-15	J Jaftha	T: Ludik, Deysel. C: Zeilinga. P: Zeilinga. D: Zeilinga.
Aug 31	Durban	Blue Bulls	WON	34-18	J Kaplan	T: SP Marais, Williams, Wentzel, McLeod. C: Zeilinga (4). P: Zeilinga (2).
Sep 07	Cape Town	WP	LOST	19-25	C Joubert	T: Mvovo, Botes, Cooper. C: Zeilinga (2).
Sep 14	Kimberley	Griquas	WON	25-24	J Peyper	T: Maseko, Herbst. P: James (3), Zeilinga (2).
Sep 21	Durban	Cheetahs	WON	50-26	M Jonker	T: Mvovo (2), SP Marais, Whitehead, Williams, Daniel, Reinach. C: Zeilinga (3). P: Zeilinga (3).
Sep 27	Johannesburg	Golden Lions	WON	31-25	J Jaftha	T: SP Marais, Zeilinga, Reinach. C: Zeilinga (2). P: Zeilinga (2). D: Zeilinga (2).
Oct 04	Pretoria	Blue Bulls	WON	18-16	M vd Westhuizen	P: Zeilinga (4), James (2).
Oct 12	Durban	WP	LOST	13-17	J Kaplan	T: Daniel. C: Lambie. P: Zeilinga (2).
SEMI-FINAL:						
Oct 19	Durban	Cheetahs	WON	33-22	M vd Westhuizen	T: Lambie, Botes, Williams. C: Lambie (3). P: Lambie (4).
FINAL:						
Oct 26	Cape Town	WP	WON	33-19	J Kaplan	T: McLeod (2). C: Lambie. P: Lambie (5). D: Lambie (2).

KWAZULU-NATAL RUGBY UNION

SHARKS CURRIE CUP SQUAD IN 2013

PLAYER	Appearances	Tries	Conversions	Penalties	Drop Goals	Points	Career Matches	Career Tries	Conversions	Penalties	Drop Goals	Points
WS (Willem) Alberts	1	–	–	–	–	0	19	4	–	–	–	20
LJ (Jacques) Botes	10	4	–	–	–	20	120	32	–	–	–	210
CB (Craig) Burden	5	–	–	–	–	0	71	23	–	–	–	115
DM (Dale) Chadwick	9	–	–	–	–	0	34	2	–	–	–	10
MC (Marcell) Coetzee	5	–	–	–	–	0	24	1	–	–	–	5
KL (Kyle) Cooper	12	1	–	–	–	5	38	2	–	–	–	10
KR (Keegan) Daniel	10	2	–	–	–	10	104	33	–	–	–	165
JR (Jean) Deysel	9	1	–	–	–	5	61	7	–	–	–	35
J (Justin) Downey	4	–	–	–	–	0	7	–	–	–	–	0
BW (Bismarck) du Plessis	3	–	–	–	–	0	39	10	–	–	–	50
JN (Jannie) du Plessis	2	–	–	–	–	0	35	3	–	–	–	15
P-S (Pieter-Steph) du Toit	5	–	–	–	–	0	5	–	–	–	–	0
R (Rayno) Gerber	5	–	–	–	–	0	5	–	–	–	–	0
MS (Monde) Hadebe	4	–	–	–	–	0	13	–	–	–	–	0
WJ (Wiehahn) Herbst	12	1	–	–	–	5	52	1	–	–	–	5
EW (Edwin) Hewitt	9	–	–	–	–	0	9	–	–	–	–	0
AD (Butch) James	8	0	5	11	0	43	73	11	96	81	1	493
P (Patrick) Lambie	3	1	5	9	2	48	28	6	47	63	2	319
SJ (Stephan) Lewies	5	–	–	–	–	0	5	–	–	–	–	0
L (Louis) Ludik	9	1	–	–	–	5	44	7	–	–	–	35
PC (Peet) Marais	12	–	–	–	–	0	18	–	–	–	–	0
SP (SP) Marais	11	4	–	–	–	20	11	4	–	–	–	20
SS (Sizo) Maseko	4	1	–	–	–	5	4	1	–	–	–	5
C (Charl) McLeod	12	3	–	–	–	15	59	12	–	–	–	60
DJ (Danie) Mienie	6	–	–	–	–	0	6	–	–	–	–	0
T (Beast) Mtawarira	2	–	–	–	–	0	37	3	–	–	–	15
LS (Tera) Mtembu	5	–	–	–	–	0	11	1	–	–	–	5
LN (Lwazi) Mvovo	12	4	–	–	–	20	57	25	–	–	–	125
OM (Odwa) Ndungane	9	–	–	–	–	0	78	29	1	–	–	147
JM (Cobus) Reinach	12	2	–	–	–	10	26	4	–	–	–	20
B (Brynard) Stander	4	1	–	–	–	5	8	1	–	–	–	5
FPL (Frans) Steyn	2	–	–	–	–	0	20	4	12	6	1	65
J (Jaco) van Tonder	6	–	–	–	–	0	6	–	–	–	–	0
M van Z (Marco) Wentzel	5	1	–	–	–	5	5	1	–	–	–	5
TJ (Tim) Whitehead	7	1	–	–	–	5	14	1	–	–	–	5
H (Heimar) Williams	9	4	–	–	–	20	9	4	–	–	–	20
FJ (Fred) Zeilinga	10	1	13	17	3	91	10	1	13	17	3	91
37 Players	258	33	23	37	5	337	1165	233	169	167	7	2075

KWAZULU-NATAL RUGBY UNION

APPEARANCES & POINTS IN ABSA CURRIE CUP 2013

Player	Griquas	Golden Lions	Cheetahs	Blue Bulls	WP	Griquas	Cheetahs	Golden Lions	Blue Bulls	Cheetahs SF	WP F	Matches	Tries	Conversions	Penalties	Drop Goals	Points
Odwa Ndungane	15	15	–	14	–	–	14	14	14	14	14	9	–	–	–	–	0
Sizo Maseko	14	–	14	–	14	14	–	–	–	–	–	4	1	–	–	–	5
Louis Ludik	13	13	13	13	13	13	–	x	13R	13	13	9	1	–	–	–	5
Tim Whitehead	12	–	–	12	12	13	13	13	13	–	–	7	1	–	–	–	5
Lwazi Mvovo	11	11	11	11	11	11	11	11	11	11	11	12	4	–	–	–	20
Butch James	10	10	10R	10R	10	10	10R	x	10R	–	–	8	0	5	11	0	43
Charl McLeod	9	9	9	9R	9R	9	9	9	9R	9	9	12	3	–	–	–	15
Jacques Botes	8c	8c	8c	8c	8c	8c	–	–	6	8c	7R	10	4	–	–	–	20
Jean Deysel	7	7	7	7	7	7	–	–	7	7	7	9	1	–	–	–	5
Brynard Stander	6	6	–	–	–	–	8R	6R	–	–	–	4	1	–	–	–	5
Marco Wentzel	5	5	5	5	5	–	–	–	–	–	–	5	1	–	–	–	5
Edwin Hewitt	4	4	4	4R	5R	4	4R	5R	5R	–	–	9	–	–	–	–	0
Wiehahn Herbst	3	3	3	3	3R	3	3	3	3	3R	3	3R	12	1	–	–	–	5
Kyle Cooper	2	2	2	2R	2R	2	2	2	2	2R	2R	2R	12	1	–	–	–	5
Dale Chadwick	1	1	1	1	–	3R	1	1	1	–	1	–	9	–	–	–	–	0
Craig Burden	2R	2R	2R	2	2	–	–	–	–	–	–	5	–	–	–	–	0
Rayno Gerber	3R	3R	3R	3R	3	–	–	–	–	–	–	5	–	–	–	–	0
Peet Marais	4R	4R	4R	4	4	4R	4	4	4	4	4	12	–	–	–	–	0
Tera Mtembu	6R	6R	7R	–	–	–	7	7	–	–	–	5	–	–	–	–	0
Cobus Reinach	9R	9R	9R	9	9	9R	9R	9	9R	9R	9R	12	2	–	–	–	10
Fred Zeilinga	12R	10R	10	10	10R	10R	10	10	10	x	x	10	1	13	17	3	91
Jaco van Tonder	14R	15R	15R	14R	x	x	15R	14R	–	–	–	6	–	–	–	–	0
SP Marais	–	14	15	15	15	15	15	15	15	15	15	11	4	–	–	–	20
Heimar Williams	–	12	12	12	–	–	12	12	12	12R	12R	9	4	–	–	–	20
Keegan Daniel	–	–	6	6	6	6	8c	8c	8c	8R	8c	8c	10	2	–	–	–	10
Justin Downey	–	–	–	7R	7R	7R	–	6	–	–	–	4	–	–	–	–	0
Danie Mienie	–	–	–	–	1	1	3R	3R	3R	–	3R	–	6	–	–	–	–	0
Pieter-Steph du Toit	–	–	–	–	–	5	5	–	–	5	5	5	5	–	–	–	–	0
Monde Hadebe	–	–	–	–	–	2R	2R	2R	2R	–	–	4	–	–	–	–	0
Marcelle Coetzee	–	–	–	–	–	–	6	–	6R	6	6	6	5	–	–	–	–	0
Stephan Lewies	–	–	–	–	–	–	–	5	5	4R	4R	4R	5	–	–	–	–	0
Jannie du Plessis	–	–	–	–	–	–	–	–	3	–	3	2	–	–	–	–	0
Bismarck du Plessis	–	–	–	–	–	–	–	–	2	2	2	3	–	–	–	–	0
Beast Mtawarira	–	–	–	–	–	–	–	–	1	–	1	2	–	–	–	–	0
Patrick Lambie	–	–	–	–	–	–	–	–	10R	10	10	3	1	5	9	2	48
Francois Steyn	–	–	–	–	–	–	–	–	–	12	12	2	–	–	–	–	0
Willem Alberts	–	–	–	–	–	–	–	–	–	–	7	1	–	–	–	–	0
37 Players												**258**	**33**	**23**	**37**	**5**	**337**

SHARKS XV SQUAD IN 2013 (Vodacom Cup) — CAREER

PLAYER	Appearances	Tries	Conversions	Penalties	Drop Goals	Points	Career Matches	Career Tries	Conversions	Penalties	Drop Goals	Points
WS (Willem) Alberts	2	2	–	–	–	10	2	2	–	–	–	10
GWC (Guy) Alexander	2	1	–	–	–	5	2	1	–	–	–	5
M (Murray) Bondesio	2	1	–	–	–	5	2	1	–	–	–	5
AM (Allan) Dell	6	–	–	–	–	0	10	–	–	–	–	0
AP (Andre) Esterhuizen	3	–	–	–	–	0	3	–	–	–	–	0
TL (Tyler) Fisher	5	2	–	–	–	10	5	2	–	–	–	10
MS (Monde) Hadebe	8	–	–	–	–	0	19	–	–	–	–	0
RL (Robbie) Harris	2	1	–	–	–	5	20	2	–	–	–	10
W (Wiehan) Hay	1	–	–	–	–	0	1	–	–	–	–	0
MC (Marius) Joubert	7	1	–	–	–	5	11	1	–	–	–	5
R (Ryan) Kankowski	1	–	–	–	–	0	3	–	–	–	–	0
S (Simon) Kerrod	2	–	–	–	–	0	2	–	–	–	–	0
F (Francois) Kleinhans	7	1	–	–	–	5	20	3	–	–	–	15
G (Gideon) Koegelenberg	1	–	–	–	–	0	1	–	–	–	–	0
JST (Stephan) Lewies	1	–	–	–	–	0	2	–	–	–	–	0
K (Khaya) Majola	7	–	–	–	–	0	8	–	–	–	–	0
FS (Franco) Marais	8	1	–	–	–	5	8	1	–	–	–	5
JA (Jandre) Marais	7	–	–	–	–	0	36	2	–	–	–	10
PC (Peet) Marais	8	–	–	–	–	0	23	–	–	–	–	0
SS (Sizo) Maseko	8	5	–	–	–	25	8	5	–	–	–	25
K (Kotaro) Matsushima	2	1	–	–	–	5	2	1	–	–	–	5
JG (Johan) Meyer	5	–	–	–	–	0	5	–	–	–	–	0
TC (Tian) Meyer	4	–	–	–	–	0	4	–	–	–	–	0
DJ (Daniel) Mienie	6	–	–	–	–	0	13	–	–	–	–	0
LS (Lubabalo) Mtembu	4	–	–	–	–	0	16	4	–	–	–	20
JG (Gouws) Prinsloo	8	1	–	–	–	5	21	7	28	30	–	181
SJ (Sean) Robinson	1	1	–	–	–	5	1	1	–	–	–	5
SCT (Sibusiso) Sithole	5	4	–	–	–	20	20	12	–	–	–	60
B (Brynard) Stander	8	2	–	–	–	10	16	5	–	–	–	25
S (Stefan) Ungerer	4	–	–	–	–	0	4	–	–	–	–	0
NJJ (Nico) van Dyk	8	–	–	–	–	0	10	–	–	–	–	0
J (Jaco) van Tonder	6	2	–	–	–	10	8	2	–	–	–	10
HC (Hanco) Venter	6	1	–	–	–	5	7	1	–	–	–	5
R (Riaan) Viljoen	2	1	–	–	–	5	2	1	–	–	–	5
H (Heimar) Williams	8	2	–	–	–	10	23	2	–	–	–	10
FJ (Fred) Zeilinga	8	3	29	27	–	154	19	3	30	27	–	156
36 players	173	33	29	27	0	304	357	59	58	57	0	582

KWAZULU-NATAL RUGBY UNION

SHARKS XV - APPEARANCES & POINTS IN VODACOM CUP 2013

Player	Border	WP	Free State XV	Eagles	Cavaliers	EP Kings	Pampas XV	Golden Lions QF	Matches	Tries	Conversions	Penalties	Drop Goals	Points
Riaan Viljoen	15	15	–	–	–	–	–	–	2	1	–	–	–	5
S'bura Sithole	14	14	14	–	14	14	–	–	5	4	–	–	–	20
Tyler Fisher	13	11R	12R	x	–	–	13R	13R	5	2	–	–	–	10
Heimar Williams	12	12	12	12	12	12	12	12	8	2	–	–	–	10
Sizo Maseko	11	11	11	11	11	11	11	11	8	5	–	–	–	25
Fred Zeilinga	10	10	10	10	10	10	10	10	8	3	29	27	–	154
Stefan Ungerer	9	9	9R	–	–	–	–	9R	4	–	–	–	–	0
Lubabalo Mtembu	8	8	8	8	–	–	–	–	4	–	–	–	–	0
Brynard Stander	7	7	7	7	7	7	7	6	8	2	–	–	–	10
Francois Kleinhans	6	6	–	6	6	6	6	7R	7	1	–	–	–	5
Peet Marais	5	5	5	5	5	5	5	5	8	–	–	–	–	0
Jandre Marais	4c	4c	–	4	4	4	4	4	7	–	–	–	–	0
Allan Dell	3	1	1	3	1	1R	–	–	6	–	–	–	–	0
Monde Hadebe	2	2	2	2	2	2	2	2	8	–	–	–	–	0
Danie Mienie	1	3R	1R	1	3R	1	–	–	6	–	–	–	–	0
Franco Marais	2R	2R	2R	2R	2R	2R	2R	3R	8	1	–	–	–	5
Nico van Dyk	1R	3	3	1R	3	3	3	3	8	–	–	–	–	0
Johan Meyer	8R	5R	7R	7R	–	–	8R	–	5	–	–	–	–	0
Khaya Majola	6R	6R	6	x	7R	6R	7R	6R	7	–	–	–	–	0
Hanco Venter	11R	9R	9	9	–	–	9R	9	6	1	–	–	–	5
Andre Esterhuizen	14R	–	–	–	12R	12R	–	–	3	–	–	–	–	0
Gouws Prinsloo	15R	14R	15	15	15	15	15R	11R	8	1	–	–	–	5
Marius Joubert	–	13	13c	13c	13c	13c	13c	13c	7	1	–	–	–	5
Wiehan Hay	–	–	4	–	–	–	–	–	1	–	–	–	–	0
Stephan Lewies	–	–	4R	–	–	–	–	–	1	–	–	–	–	0
Jaco van Tonder	–	–	15R	14	15R	15R	15	15	6	2	–	–	–	10
Tian Meyer	–	–	–	9R	9	9	9	–	4	–	–	–	–	0
Sean Robinson	–	–	–	11R	–	–	–	–	1	1	–	–	–	5
Guy Alexander	–	–	–	–	8	8	–	–	2	1	–	–	–	5
Gideon Koegelenberg	–	–	–	–	4R	x	–	–	1	–	–	–	–	0
Murray Bondesio	–	–	–	–	6R	8R	–	–	2	–	–	–	–	0
Kotaro Matsushima	–	–	–	–	–	–	14	14	2	1	–	–	–	5
Willem Alberts	–	–	–	–	–	–	8	7	2	2	–	–	–	10
Robbie Harris	–	–	–	–	–	–	1	1	2	1	–	–	–	5
Simon Kerrod	–	–	–	–	–	–	3R	1R	2	–	–	–	–	0
Ryan Kankowski	–	–	–	–	–	–	–	8	1	–	–	–	–	0
36 Players									173	33	29	27	0	304

ABSA UNDER-21 CHAMPIONSHIP (4th, Section A) Played 13 Won 8 Drawn 0 Lost 5 Points for 436 Points against 337 Tries for 57 Tries against 41
RESULTS: Bt Border (a) 53-31. Lost Golden Lions (h) 17-24. Bt Free State (a) 36-25. Bt Leopards (a) 62-18. Lost WP (a) 3-20. Bt Blue Bulls (h) 19-15. Bt Border (h) 71-20. Lost Golden Lions (a) 31-39. Bt Free State (a) 39-16. Bt Leopards (h) 33-13. Bt Blue Bulls (a) 35-29. Lost WP (h) 24-51. SEMI FINAL Lost Blue Bulls (a) 13-36.
SCORERS: 113 Robert du Preez (5t,23c,14p); 45 Andre Esterhuizen (9t); 40 Duncan Campbell (11c,6p); 30 Brendon Cope (2t,7c,2p); 28 Stefan Ungerer (5t,1d); 20 Allan Dell, Sean Robinson, Johan Meyer, Garath Meikle (4t each); 15 Tyler Fisher, Alcino Izaacs, Guy Alexander, Kotaro Matsushima (3t each); 10 Hanco Venter, Dylan Nel (2t each); 5 Jacques Taylor, Khaya Majola, Wade Elliot, Wiehan Hay (1t each).

ABSA U19 CHAMPIONSHIP (3rd, Section A)
Played 13 Won 8 Drawn 0 Lost 5 Points for 358 Points against 253 Tries for 46 Tries against 31
RESULTS: Bt Border (h) 32-24. Lost Golden Lions (h) 13-21. Bt Free State (a) 55-31. Bt Leopards (a) 24-17. Bt WP (a) 25-19. Lost Blue Bulls (h) 19-28. Bt Border (h) 41-5. Bt Golden Lions (a) 25-9. Bt Free State (h) 26-22. Lost Leopards (h) 22-

KZN SHARKS RECORDS

MATCH RECORDS
Biggest win	90-9	vs. South Eastern Transvaal (Currie Cup)	1996
Heaviest defeat	6-62	vs. Northern Transvaal	1991
Heaviest Currie Cup defeat	0-52	vs. Western Province	1932
Highest score	90	vs. South Eastern Transvaal (Currie Cup) (90-9)	1996
Most points conceded	62	vs. Northern Transvaal (6-62)	1991
Most tries	15	vs. Northern Natal (78-0)	1990
Most Currie Cup tries	13	vs. South Eastern Transvaal (90-9)	1996
Most points by a player	50	GK Lawless vs. Otago Highlanders	1997
Most Currie Cup points by a player	38	HW Honiball vs. Boland	1996
Most tries by a player	4	By 11 players - most recently by JP Pietersen vs. Leopards	2005
Most conversions by a player	11	HW Honiball vs. South Eastern Transvaal (Currie Cup)	1996
Most penalties by a player	8	GS du Toit vs. Western Province (Currie Cup)	2001
Most drop goals by a player	4	WJdeW Ras vs. Western Province (Currie Cup)	1979

SEASON RECORDS
Most team points	1348	30 matches	1996
Most Currie Cup points by team	792	15 matches	1996
Most points by a player	304	JT Stransky	1990
Most Currie Cup points by a player	205	P Lambie	2010
Most team tries	184	30 matches	1996
Most Currie Cup tries by team	112	15 matches	1996
Most tries by a player	28	JF van der Westhuizen	1993
Most Currie Cup tries by a player	13	JF van der Westhuizen	1996
	13	J Joubert	1996
	13	H Mentz	2005

CAREER RECORDS
Most appearances	165	HM Reece-Edwards	1982-1995
	165	S Atherton	1988-2000
Most points	1114	HM Reece-Edwards	1982-1995
Most tries	90	JF van der Westhuizen	1992-1998

HONOURS
ABSA Currie Cup   1990, 1992, 1995, 1996, 2008, 2010, 2013

27. Lost Blue Bulls (a) 13-23. Bt WP (h) 38-0. SEMI FINAL Lost Golden Lions (a) 25-27.
SCORERS: 116 Jean-Luc du Plessis (5t,17c,18p,1d); 40 Michael Cloete (8t); 32 Colin Willemse (10c,4p); 28 Sandile Kubeka (5t,1d); 20 Barend Potgieter, Themba Williams (4t each); 15 Neil Maritz, Alrin Eksteen, Christopher de Beer (3t each); 10 Joseph Jones, Cameron Wright, Wion Robbertse, Bartho le Roux (2t each); 5 Hendrik Botha, Nkululeko Marwana, Stefan van Schalkwyk (1t each); 2 Gabriel le Roux (1c).

AMATEUR CHAMPIONSHIP
KZN DUIKERS (Champion, Central Section, Kimberley)
Played 3 Won 3 Drawn 0 Lost 0 Points for 112 Points against 55 Winning% 100%
RESULTS: Bt Free State Rural 44-12. Bt Free State 39-17.

Bt Griquas 29-26. Playoffs: Lost WP 21-25. Lost Blue Bulls 18-56.

KZN WILDEBEEST RURAL (Central Section)
Played 3 Won 1 Drawn 0 Lost 2 Points for 77 Points against 80 Winning% 33%
RESULTS: Lost Free State 11-31. Bt Free State Rural 49-10. Lost Griffons Rural 17-39.

SUB-UNION CHAMPIONSHIP
KZN WILDEBEEST (Champions, Southern Section, Margate)
Played 3 Won 3 Drawn 0 Lost 0 Points for 132 Points against 18 Winning % 100%
RESULTS: Bt Border 28-6. Bt Griquas 63-0. Bt EP 41-12.

LEOPARDS RUGBY UNION

FOUNDED 1920
(as Western Transvaal)
GROUND
Profert Olen Park
CAPACITY
22 000
ADDRESS
Cnr of James Moroka
and Piet Bosman Streets
POSTAL ADDRESS
PO Box 422, Potchefstroom 2520
TELEPHONE NUMBER
018-297 5304/5
EMAIL karen@leopardsrugby.co.za
COLOURS
Green & red jersey, white shorts
CURRIE CUP COACH
Jorrie Muller
VODACOM CUP COACH
Jorrie Muller
CAPTAIN
Brendon Snyman
PRESIDENT
Adv. André May
COMPANY CEO
Louis du Plessis

Kings spoil Leopards' party again

HISTORY HAS A NASTY WAY OF REPEATING ITSELF, AND SO IT proved for the Leopards in 2013 when they fell to the same opponents at the same hurdle in the most important match of their season once again.

The men from Potchefstroom finished fourth on the 2012 Absa Currie Cup First Division log, earning them a ticket to Port Elizabeth to face the all-conquering EP Kings in the semi-finals. It proved a bridge too far for the Leopards, the Kings winning easily, 50-27.

One year later and it must have felt like a scene from the Hollywood movie Groundhog Day. The Leopards had managed to improve their log position, up to third after eight wins in their 14 matches, but the imperious rise of eventual champions the Steval Pumas meant that the Kings finished second and, for the second time in a row, would host the North West side in a semi-final.

This time around it was a lot closer, the Kings running out 32-29 winners, but this would have been scant consolation for the Leopards and their management, who had managed to see off the Kings 22-18 at the Nelson Mandela Bay Stadium in the round-robin stages.

The semi-final loss would also cost coach Jorrie Muller his job, and he will be replaced by former Springbok scrumhalf Robert du Preez in 2014. For Du Preez, who coached Jonsson College Rovers to the final of the inaugural Cell C Community Cup in April 2013, it will be an emotional homecoming after years spent in Durban. He will take charge of the Pukke in the Varsity Cup before turning his attentions to the Leopards.

The team were well served by a number of players, flyhalf Adriaan Engelbrecht playing in all 15 of their Currie Cup matches – the last five at centre – and scoring 153 points in the process.

Wing Edmar Marais too did not miss a game, and scored 11 tries in the process, while his wing partner Luther Obi bagged eight touchdowns while missing only one match.

Up front, the side was well led by lock Brendon Snyman, with hooker Edgar Marutlulle deputising with aplomb for five matches when Snyman was injured. Marutlulle also did the hard yards and was rewarded with six tries – an excellent return for a tight forward in just 13 matches.

Their semi-final loss apart, the Leopards were impressive in a number of outings, with their win in PE in round three and an opening-round drubbing (45-17) of the Boland Cavaliers in Wellington the highlights.

Edgar Marutlulle had a season to remember for the Leopards.
Duif du Toit/Gallo Images

LEOPARDS RUGBY UNION

VODACOM CUP LOG POSITIONS

2013	9th	**2010**	8th	**2007**	7th	**2004**	7th	**2001**	12th	**1998** 14th
2012	10th	**2009**	4th	**2006**	12th	**2003**	4th	**2000**	9th	
2011	13th	**2008**	6th	**2005**	4th	**2002**	6th	**1999**	14th	

ABSA CURRIE CUP LOG POSITIONS

2013	9th	**2010**	8th	**2007**	13th	**2004**	11th	**2001**	10th	**1998**	13th
2012	12th	**2009**	7th	**2006**	9th	**2003**	9th	**2000**	12th	**1997**	13th
2011	8th	**2008**	10th	**2005**	8th	**2002**	12th	**1999**	12th	**1996**	13th

2013 RESULTS & SCORERS

VODACOM CUP (Leopards XV) PLAYED **7** WON **4** DRAWN **0** LOST **3** POINTS FOR **289** POINTS AGAINST **158** TRIES FOR **38** TRIES AGAINST **18** WINNING% **57%**

Date	Venue	Opponent	Result	Score	Referee	Scorers
Mrch 09	Johannesburg [1]	Golden Lions	LOST	15-45	M vd Westhuizen	T: Van der Merwe, Dames. C: Pretorius. P: Gilbert.
Mrch 15	Umzimuhle	Limpopo Blue Bulls	WON	113-3	R Rasivhenge	T: Heyns (4), Welgemoed (3), Vermaak (2), Engelbrecht (2), Marais (2), Pretorius, Dames, Smith, Swart. C: Pretorius (14).
Mrch 22	Potchefstroom	Valke	WON	47-16	J van Heerden	T: Hanekom (2), van der Merwe, Uys, Marais, Olivier, Dames. C: Pretorius (6).
April 06	Pretoria [2]	Blue Bulls	WON	33-26	J Jaftha	T: Hanekom, Welgemoed. C: Pretorius. P: Pretoriuis (7).
April 12	Potchefstroom	Griffons	WON	27-07	C Jadezweni	T: Dames (2), Hanekom. C: Pretorius (3). P: Pretorius (2).
April 20	Kimberley	Griquas	LOST	26-32	L Legoete	T: Pretorius, Skorbinski, Okafor, Kruger. C: Pretorius (3).
April 27	Potchefstroom	Pumas	LOST	28-29	J Kaplan	T: Kruger, H Swart, Maritz. C: Engelbrecht (2). P: Gilbert (3).

[1] Pirates RC, [2] Loftus B.

ABSA CURRIE CUP PLAYED **15** WON **8** LOST **7** DRAWN **0** POINTS FOR **477** POINTS AGAINST **430** TRIES FOR **66** TRIES AGAINST **48** WINNING % **53%**

Date	Venue	Opponent	Result	Score	Referee	Scorers
July 05	Potchefstroom	Valke	WON	50-25	L Legoete	T: Marais (3), Engelbrecht, Marutlulle, Skorbinski, Mahuza. C: Engelbrecht (6). P: Engelbrecht.
July 12	Port Elizabeth	EP Kings	WON	22-18	S Mayende	T: Marais, Laker, Hanekom. C: Engelbrecht (2). P: Engelbrecht.
July 19	Potchefstroom	Pumas	LOST	27-35	L vd Merwe	T: Dames, Marais, Laker. C: Engelbrecht (3). P: Engelbrecht (2).
July 27	Welkom	Griffons	LOST	28-34	L vd Merwe	T: Marais (2), Obi, Marutlulle. C: Engelbrecht (4).
Aug 03	East London	Border	WON	26-10	M vd Westhuizen	T: Snyman, Swart, Obi. C: Engelbrecht. P: Engelbrecht (3).
Aug 09	Potchefstroom	SWD	LOST	47-50	S Mayende	T: Hanekom (2), Marutlulle, Buys, Laker, Dreyer. C: Engelbrecht (4). P: Engelbrecht (3).
Aug 17	Potchefstroom	Boland	WON	22-17	S Berry	T: Obi (2), Dames. C: Engelbrecht (2). P: Engelbrecht.
Aug 24	Kempton Park	Valke	WON	38-27	R Rasivhenge	T: Obi (2), Dames, Tossel, Kruger, Bezuidenhout. C: Engelbrecht (4).
Aug 30	Potchefstroom	EP Kings	LOST	26-44	T Jonker	T: Maruitlulle, Tossel, Obi, Lusaseni. C: Engelbrecht (3).
Sep 06	Nelspruit	Pumas	LOST	20-38	J Peyper	T: Buys, Obi. C: Engelbrecht (2). P: Engelbrecht (2).
Sep 13	Potchefstroom	Griffons	WON	40-33	C Joubert	T: Marais (2), Snyman, Dames, Marutlulle, Buys. C: Engelbrecht (4), Buys.
Sep 20	Potchefstroom	Border	LOST	22-26	J van Heerden	T: Uys (3), Dames. C: Gilbert.
Sep 27	George	SWD	WON	35-24	L vd Merwe	T: De Wet (2), Engelbrecht, Snyman, Dames, Laker, Niemand.
Semi-final						
Oct 04	Port Elizabeth	EP Kings	LOST	29-32	B Crouse	T: Marais, Dorfling. C: Engelbrecht (2). P: Engelbrecht (5).

karen@leopardsrugby.co.za

LEOPARDS ABSA CURRIE CUP SQUAD IN 2013 | LEOPARDS CAREER

PLAYER	Appearances	Tries	Conversions	Penalties	Drop Goals	Points	Career Matches	Career Tries	Conversions	Penalties	Drop Goals	Points
GB (Gavin) Annandale	1	–	–	–	–	0	1	–	–	–	–	0
SM (Stephan) Bezuidenhout	6	1	–	–	–	5	38	1	–	–	–	5
JA (Jarryd) Buys	8	4	1	–	–	22	8	4	1	–	–	22
HDP (Danie) Dames	14	6	–	–	–	30	58	22	–	–	–	110
PA (Philip) de Wet	8	2	–	–	–	10	29	13	–	–	–	65
TA (Tiaan) Dorfling	9	1	–	–	–	5	12	1	–	–	–	5
MC (Martin) Dreyer	11	1	–	–	–	5	11	1	–	–	–	5
AE (Adriaan) Engelbrecht	15	2	43	19	–	153	36	9	48	23	–	210
WJ (Warren) Gilbert	6	–	1	–	–	2	6	–	1	–	–	2
S (Stephan) Greeff	2	–	–	–	–	0	2	–	–	–	–	0
FJ (Jaco) Grobler	4	–	–	–	–	0	18	2	–	–	–	10
M (Morne) Hanekom	11	3	–	–	–	15	29	5	–	–	–	25
JR (John-Roy) Jenkinson	6	–	–	–	–	0	16	–	–	–	–	0
DB (Danie) Jordaan	1	–	–	–	–	0	2	–	–	–	–	0
RA (Robert) Kruger	10	1	–	–	–	5	33	2	–	–	–	10
VE (Victor) Kruger	2	–	–	–	–	0	14	1	–	–	–	5
JJB (Johann) Laker	14	4	–	–	–	20	40	8	–	–	–	40
L (Luvuyiso) Lusaseni	14	1	–	–	–	5	43	2	–	–	–	10
S (Sylvian) Mahuza	3	1	–	–	–	5	3	1	–	–	–	5
E (Edmar) Marais	15	11	–	–	–	55	15	11	–	–	–	55
E (Edgar) Marutlulle	13	6	–	–	–	30	26	10	–	–	–	50
D (Dumisani) Matyeshana	2	–	–	–	–	0	36	15	–	–	–	75
SJ (SJ) Niemand	6	1	–	–	–	5	7	2	–	–	–	10
GJ (Gerhard) Nortier	1	–	–	–	–	0	15	2	2	1	–	17
JC (JC) Oberholzer	3	–	–	–	–	0	8	–	–	–	–	0
LBS (Luther) Obi	14	8	–	–	–	40	14	8	–	–	–	40
SW (SW) Oosthuizen	2	–	–	–	–	0	2	–	–	–	–	0
AH (Henry) Skorbinski	8	2	–	–	–	10	18	3	–	–	–	15
J (Joe) Smith	8	–	–	–	–	0	9	–	–	–	–	0
BM (Brendon) Snyman	12	3	–	–	–	15	46	5	–	–	–	25
HP (HP) Swart	9	1	–	–	–	5	13	2	–	–	–	10
BM (Marnus) Tack	1	–	–	–	–	0	1	–	–	–	–	0
GD (George) Tossel	14	4	–	–	–	20	31	9	2	2	–	55
BG (BG) Uys	14	3	–	–	–	15	61	8	–	–	–	40
AHP (Akker) van der Merwe	9	–	–	–	–	0	9	–	–	–	–	0
AP (Peet) van der Walt	12	–	–	–	–	0	12	–	–	–	–	0
BD (Bernie) van Rooyen	13	–	–	–	–	0	19	–	–	–	–	0
ED (Elardus) Venter	10	–	–	–	–	0	10	–	–	–	–	0
JC (Jacques) Vermaak	6	–	–	–	–	0	6	–	–	–	–	0
R (Rhyk) Welgemoed	2	–	–	–	–	0	2	–	–	–	–	0
CFM (Charl) Weideman	5	–	–	–	–	0	16	–	–	–	–	0
41 players	324	66	45	19	0	477	775	147	54	26	0	921

LEOPARDS RUGBY UNION

LEOPARDS XV - APPEARANCES & POINTS IN VODACOM CUP 2013

	Golden Lions	Limpopo BB	Valke	Blue Bulls	Griffons	Griquas	Pumas	Matches	Tries	Conversions	Penalties	Drop Goals	Points
Danie Dames	15	15	15	15	14	14	14	7	5	–	–	–	25
Andrew van Wyk	14	–	14	14	14R	–	x	4	–	–	–	–	0
Charl Weideman	13	13	13	–	–	–	–	3	–	–	–	–	0
Adriaan Engelbrecht	12	12	12	12	12	12	12	7	2	2	–	–	14
Edmar Marais	11	11	11	11	11	11	11	7	3	–	–	–	15
Warren Gilbert	10	–	10R	x	10R	–	10	4	–	–	4	–	12
Jacques Olivier	9	9	9	9	9R	–	–	5	1	–	–	–	5
Rhyk Welgemoed	8	6	6	6	6	6R	8R	7	4	–	–	–	20
Robert Kruger	7	7	7	7	7	7	6	7	2	–	–	–	10
Marcel Groenewald	6	–	–	–	–	–	–	1	–	–	–	–	0
Brendon Snyman	5c	5c	5c	5c	5c	5c	5c	7	–	–	–	–	0
Peet van der Walt	4	4	4	–	–	4	4R	5	–	–	–	–	0
Stephan Bezuidenhout	3	3	–	–	–	–	–	2	–	–	–	–	0
Jacques Vermaak	2	2	2	2	2R	–	–	5	2	–	–	–	10
BG Uys	1	1	1	–	1	–	1	5	1	–	–	–	5
Akker van der Merwe	2R	–	2R	2R	2	2R	2	6	2	–	–	–	10
Buhle Mxunyelwa	3R	3R	3R	–	–	–	–	3	–	–	–	–	0
Kenny Okafor	8R	4R	4R	4	4R	4R	–	6	1	–	–	–	5
Morne Hanekom	6R	8	8	8	8	8	8	7	4	–	–	–	20
Malherbe Swart	9R	9R	9R					3	1	–	–	–	5
Andre Pretorius	10R	10	10	10	10	10	–	6	2	28	9	–	93
George Tossel	13R	14R	13R	13	13	13	13	7	–	–	–	–	0
Ian Heyns	–	14	–	–	–	–	–	1	4	–	–	–	20
Arno Nel	–	7R	–	–	–	–	–	1	–	–	–	–	0
Johan Smith	–	1R	–	1R	–	3R	–	3	1	–	–	–	5
Johnny Welthagen	–	13R	–	–	–	–	–	1	–	–	–	–	0
Elardus Venter	–	–	3	3	3	3	3	5	–	–	–	–	0
Bernie van Rooyen	–	–	6R	–	–	–	–	1	–	–	–	–	0
Martin Dreyer	–	–	–	1	3R	1	3R	4	–	–	–	–	0
HP Swart	–	–	–	7R	6R	8R	7	4	1	–	–	–	5
Tiaan Dorfling	–	–	–	9R	9	9R	9	4	–	–	–	–	0
Hoffman Maritz	–	–	–	14R	15	15	15	4	1	–	–	–	5
Luvuyiso Lusaseni	–	–	–	4R	4	6	4	4	–	–	–	–	0
Jaco Grobler	–	–	–	–	–	9	10R	2	–	–	–	–	0
JC Oberholzer	–	–	–	–	–	2	–	1	–	–	–	–	0
Hennie Skorbinski	–	–	–	–	–	13R	13R	2	1	–	–	–	5
Edgar Marutlulle	–	–	–	–	–	–	2R	1	–	–	–	–	0
37 players								152	38	30	13	0	289

LEOPARDS APPEARANCES & POINTS IN ABSA CURRIE CUP 2013

Player	Boland	Valke	EP Kings	Pumas	Griffons	Border	SWD	Boland	Valke	EP Kings	Pumas	Griffons	Border	SWD	EP Kings	Matches	Tries	Conversions	Penalties	Drop Goals	Points
Jarryd Buys	15	–	–	–	15	14R	15	x	15R	13R	15R	10	–	–	–	8	4	1	–	–	22
Danie Dames	14	15	15	15	–	15	14	15	15	15	15	15	15	15	15	14	6	–	–	–	30
Hennie Skorbinski	13	13	13	13	13	13	13	–	–	13	–	–	–	–	–	8	2	–	–	–	10
George Tossel	12	12	12	12	12	12	12	12	12	12	13	12	12	–	13R	14	4	–	–	–	20
Edmar Marais	11	14	11	11	11	11	11R	11	11	11	11	11	11	11	11	15	11	–	–	–	55
Adriaan Engelbrecht	10	10	10	10	10	10	10	10	10	12	13	13	12	12	–	15	2	43	19	–	153
Johann Laker	9	9	9	9	9	9	9	9	–	9	9	9	9	9	9	14	4	–	–	–	20
Morne Hanekom	8	8	8	8	–	8	8	8	–	–	–	6R	7	7	7	11	3	–	–	–	15
Robert Kruger	7	7	7	7	7	–	7	–	7	7	7	7	–	–	–	10	1	–	–	–	5
Bernie van Rooyen	6	6	6	6R	6	4R	8R	6	6R	6R	6R	–	6R	4R	–	13	–	–	–	–	0
Brendon Snyman	5c	5c	5c	5c	5c	5c	5c	5c	–	–	–	4R	5	5c	5c	12	3	–	–	–	15
Luvuyiso Lusaseni	4	4	4R	4R	4	4	4	4	4	5	5	4	–	7R	4R	14	1	–	–	–	5
John Roy Jenkinson	3	–	3	3	3	–	–	–	–	3R	3R	–	–	–	–	6	–	–	–	–	0
Edgar Marutlulle	2	2	2	2	2	2	2	–	2c	2c	2c	2c	2c	–	2R	13	6	–	–	–	30
BG Uys	1	1	1	1	1	1	1	1	1	1	–	1	1	1	1	14	3	–	–	–	15
JC Oberholzer	2R	2R	2R	–	–	–	–	–	–	–	–	–	–	–	–	3	–	–	–	–	0
Joe Smith	1R	3R	1R	–	–	–	–	–	–	1R	1R	1R	1R	1R	–	8	–	–	–	–	0
Martin Dreyer	3R	3	3R	3R	3R	3	3R	8R	1R	1R	1	–	–	–	–	11	1	–	–	–	5
Peet van der Walt	8R	4R	4	4	–	7	4R	5R	5	4	–	–	4	4	4	12	–	–	–	–	0
HP Swart	x	8R	6R	6	8	6	6	7	8	–	–	–	–	–	7R	9	1	–	–	–	5
Jaco Grobler	11R	9R	9R	9R	–	–	–	–	–	–	–	–	–	–	–	4	–	–	–	–	0
Warren Gilbert	9R	12R	–	x	12R	–	–	–	–	–	–	–	10	10	10	6	–	1	–	–	2
Luther Obi	–	11	14	14	14	14	11	14	14	14	14	14	14	14	14	14	8	–	–	–	40
Sylvian Mahuza	–	15R	11R	14R	–	–	–	–	–	–	–	–	–	–	–	3	1	–	–	–	5
Akker van der Merwe	–	–	–	2R	2R	2R	2R	2	2R	2R	2R	–	–	2R	–	9	–	–	–	–	0
Rhyk Welgemoed	–	–	–	–	8R	6R	–	–	–	–	–	–	–	–	–	2	–	–	–	–	0
Jacques Vermaak	–	–	–	–	4R	–	–	2R	–	–	–	2R	2R	2	2	6	–	–	–	–	0
Charl Weideman	–	–	–	–	13R	13R	13R	13	13	–	–	–	–	–	–	5	–	–	–	–	0
Tiaan Dorfling	–	–	–	–	9R	9R	9R	x	9	x	10R	9R	9R	9R	9R	9	1	–	–	–	5
Elardus Venter	–	–	–	–	–	3R	3	3	3	3	3	3	3R	3	3	10	–	–	–	–	0
Philip de Wet	–	–	–	–	–	–	6R	6	6	6	6	6	6	6	6	8	2	–	–	–	10
Stephan Bezuidenhout	–	–	–	–	–	–	3R	3R	–	–	3R	3	3R	3R	–	6	1	–	–	–	5
Victor Kruger	–	–	–	–	–	–	4R	4R	–	–	–	–	–	–	–	2	–	–	–	–	0
Marnus Tack	–	–	–	–	–	–	12R	–	–	–	–	–	–	–	–	1	–	–	–	–	0
SJ Niemand	–	–	–	–	–	–	–	8	8	8	8	8	8	–	–	6	1	–	–	–	5
Gerhard Nortier	–	–	–	–	–	–	–	–	–	10	–	–	–	–	–	1	–	–	–	–	0
Stephan Greeff	–	–	–	–	–	–	–	–	–	4	5	–	–	–	–	2	–	–	–	–	0
Danie Jordaan	–	–	–	–	–	–	–	–	–	4R	–	–	–	–	–	1	–	–	–	–	0
SW Oosthuizen	–	–	–	–	–	–	–	–	–	x	12R	13R	–	–	–	2	–	–	–	–	0
Gavin Annandale	–	–	–	–	–	–	–	–	–	–	4R	–	–	–	–	1	–	–	–	–	0
Dumisani Matyeshane	–	–	–	–	–	–	–	–	–	–	–	–	–	13	13	2	–	–	–	–	0
41 players																324	66	45	19	0	477

LEOPARDS RUGBY UNION

ABSA UNDER-21 CHAMPIONSHIP (6th, Section A)

Played	Won	Drawn	Lost	Points for	Points against	Tries for	Tries against	Winning %
12	2	0	10	321	500	42	69	17,00%

RESULTS Lost Blue Bulls (h) 17-59. Lost WP (a) 10-55. Bt Border (h) 26-17. Lost Golden Lions (h) 23-24. Lost KZN (h) 18-62. Lost Free State (a) 29-40. Lost Blue Bulls (a) 33-48. Lost WP (h) 35-54. Bt Border (a) 57-28. Lost Golden Lions (a) 31-42. Lost KZN (a) 13-33. Lost Free State (h) 29-38.

SCORERS 73 Warren Gilbert (1t, 19c, 9p, 1dg). 35 Jaco Buys (7t). 33 Ryno Smith (2t, 7c, 3p). 30 Adriaan Oosthuizen (6t) 20 Tiaan Loots (4t). 15 Jaco Jordaan (3t), Jaco du Plessis (6c, 1p). 10 Erno Nagy, Eugene Pettit, Jaco Grobler, Marnus Tack, Sylvian Mahuza (2t each). 5 Armandt Stoman, Arno Ebersohn, Corné Duvenhage, Louis Vorster, Louwrens Strydom, Marnus Redelinghuys, Rowayne Beukman, Ryno Pienaar, Sarel Smith, Thomas Meyer (1t each).

ABSA U19 CHAMPIONSHIP (4th, Section A)

Played	Won	Drawn	Lost	Points for	Points against	Tries for	Tries against	Winning %
13	5	0	8	318	404	48	50	39,00%

RESULTS Lost Blue Bulls (h) 14-61. Bt WP (a) 28-27. Bt Border (h) 36-15. Lost Golden Lions (h) 27-34. Lost KZN (h) 17-24. Bt Free State (a) 16-34. Lost Blue Bulls (a) 12-48. Lost WP (h) 36-45. Bt Border (a) 19-16. Lost Golden Lions (a) 27-32. Bt KZN (a) 27-22. Lost Free State (h) 20-27. SEMI-FINAL Lost Blue Bulls (a) 21-37.

SCORERS 48 Lourens Boddington (4t, 11c, 2p). 40 Deon Stokes (8t). 35 Blessing Makhavu, Jeandré Rudolph, (7t each). 27 Lloyd Greeff (5t, 1c). 21 Cornelius Swart (9c, 1p). 20 Chriswill September (4t). 15 Andries du Plooy (3t). 13 Schalk Hugo (1t, 4c) 10 Esthehan Visagie, Roche Steenkamp, Sias Koen (2t each). 7 Gysbert van Wyk (1t, 1c), Janko Barnard (2c, 1dg). 5 Courtney Cupido, Johan Breiers, Kwena Moremi, Marchell Hattingh (1t each).

Morne Hanekom attempts to score a try during the First Division semi-final against EP Kings *Michael Sheehan/Gallo Images*

LEOPARDS RECORDS

MATCH RECORDS
Biggest win	80-3	vs Niteroi, Brazilia	1993
Biggest win (Currie Cup)	103-9	vs Eastern Orange Free State	1988
Heaviest defeat	12-98	vs Transvaal	1996
Heaviest defeat (Currie Cup)	21-92	vs Blue Bulls	2011
Highest score	83	vs Uruguay (83-10)	1994
Highest score (Currie Cup)	103	vs Eastern Orange Free State (103-9)	1988
Most points conceded	98	vs Transvaal (12-98)	1996
Most points conceded (Currie Cup)	92	vs Blue Bulls (21-92)	2011
Most tries (Currie Cup)	18	vs Eastern Orange Free State	1988
Most points by a player	41	D Basson vs Namibia	1994
Most points by a player (Currie Cup)	31	T Marais vs Eastern Orange Free State	1988
	31	IP Olivier vs Pumas	2005
Most tries by a player	5	T Van Niekerk vs Eastern Transvaal	1965
Most tries by a player (Currie Cup)	5	A Kettledas vs SWD Eagles	2012

SEASON RECORDS
Most points by a player	368	D Basson	1994
Most points by a player (Currie Cup)	204	C Durand	2008
Most tries by a player	25	CR Lloyd	2006
Most tries by a player (Currie Cup)	19	CR Lloyd	2006

CAREER RECORDS
Most appearances	191	WH (Werner) Lessing	1998-2007
Most matches as captain	129	E Hare	1989-1996
Most points	1183	D Basson	1991-1998
Most points (Currie Cup)	703	T Marais	1980-1988
Most tries	48	CR (Colin) Lloyd	2004-2011

MPUMALANGA RUGBY UNION

FOUNDED
1969 (as South Eastern Transvaal)
GROUND
Mbombela Stadium
CAPACITY
43 500
ADDRESS
1 Bafana Bafana Str, Nelspruit
POSTAL ADDRESS
Box 1574, Witbank 1035
TELEPHONE NUMBER
013-7574600
EMAIL
arrie@pumas.co.za
COLOURS
Dove grey, black and pink jersey, shorts and socks
CURRIE CUP COACH
Jimmy Stonehouse
VODACOM CUP COACH
Jimmy Stonehouse
CAPTAIN
Corne Steenkamp
PRESIDENT
Hein Mentz
COMPANY CEO
Koos Kruger

Pumas leap back into top flight

THE STEVAL PUMAS CAPPED OFF A TRULY MEMORABLE SEASON in which they were, by some distance, the most successful first-class provincial team in South African rugby, by winning promotion back to the Absa Currie Cup Premier Division for 2014.

Not enough can be said about coach Jimmy Stonehouse and his men from the Lowveld – a team revitalised and transformed following a change in management and their relocation from Witbank to Nelspruit.

Where to begin? Perhaps right at the tail-end of the fairytale is most appropriate. On October 25, playing in front of their adoring home fans, the Pumas overwhelmed GWK Griquas 33-15 in the second leg of their promotion-relegation tussle to ensure that they will play in the top flight in 2014.

The Pumas' victory was one-sided and thoroughly deserved, and revealed the steely character that Stonehouse has instilled in the side, for they lost they had lost the week before in the first leg in Kimberley, to a late try, and a lesser team, even one playing at home, might have doubted deep down their ability to cross the substantial mental barrier that exists between the Premier and First Divisions.

In so doing, the Pumas finished off the season with 25 victories from their 28 Vodacom Cup and Currie Cup matches (including the play-offs and promotion-relegation series) – their 89 percent win ratio making them the second most successful of the 28 teams that played first-class rugby in 2013. And considering that the SA President's Team – coached by Stonehouse! – who won the IRB Tbilisi Cup, topped that list with a 100 percent score but played only three matches, there is little doubt as to who could claim the statistical title of 'best team in SA'.

The Pumas lost just twice in the Vodacom Cup, the killer blow coming in the final, in Nelspruit, against the Golden Lions, when they went down 42-28.

But thereafter began a dream unbeaten run of 16 successive victories in the Absa Currie Cup First Division – 14 in the round-robin stages, followed by massive wins in the semi-final (52-33 over SWD) and final (53-30 over the EP Kings).

Their 154-0 win over the Limpopo Blue Bulls in the Vodacom Cup is a first-class record, as is the tally of 22 tries scored in that match. Most team points in a season (1283 in 28 matches), most Currie Cup points (758 in 18), most points by a player (353 – Carl Bezuidenhout), most Currie Cup points (225 – Bezuidenhout), Most team tries (163) and most Currie Cup tries (92) are the statistical markers of what will be remembered as a near-perfect year.

Bezuidenhout was the perfect general at flyhalf, setting up his backs while scoring 225 points himself. His halfback partner, Francois de Klerk, was consistently good, while left wing Rosco Speckman, with 12 Currie Cup tries, provided the Pumas with the teeth that they had been lacking in previous seasons.

The Pumas swept all before them in 2013.
Duif du Toit/Gallo Images

VODACOM CUP LOG POSITIONS

2013	2nd	2010	9th	2007	5th	2004	10th	2001	14th	1998	5th
2012	3rd	2009	9th	2006	5th	2003	12th	2000	10th		
2011	6th	2008	11th	2005	7th	2002	8th	1999	5th		

ABSA CURRIE CUP LOG POSITIONS

2013	7th	2010	7th	2007	12th	2004	10th	2001	6th	1998	11th
2012	8th	2009	9th	2006	8th	2003	7th	2000	7th	1997	9th
2011	7th	2008	12th	2005	10th	2002	6th	1999	9th	1996	7th

PUMAS SQUAD IN 2013 / PUMAS CAREER

PLAYER	Appearances	Tries	Conversions	Penalties	Drop Goals	Points	Career Matches	Career Tries	Conversions	Penalties	Drop Goals	Points
JW (JW) Bell	25	15	–	–	–	75	25	15	–	–	–	75
C (Carl) Bezuidenhout	25	6	79	53	2	353	67	12	101	65	2	463
R (Renaldo) Bothma	18	8	–	–	–	40	37	15	–	–	–	75
WJ (Jaco) Bouwer	21	8	–	–	–	40	97	44	–	–	–	220
U (Uzair) Cassiem	23	7	–	–	–	35	33	11	–	–	–	55
M (Marius) Coetzer	13	1	–	–	–	5	67	1	–	–	–	5
F (Francois) de Klerk	28	1	–	–	–	5	46	3	–	–	–	15
D (Danwel) Demas	2	6	–	–	–	30	19	8	–	–	–	40
F (Francois) du Toit	10	1	–	–	–	5	10	1	–	–	–	5
I (Ivann) Espag	10	1	–	–	–	5	10	1	–	–	–	5
C (Corne) Fourie	28	3	–	–	–	15	52	6	–	–	–	30
F (Frank) Herne	21	8	–	–	–	40	21	8	–	–	–	40
RW (RW) Kember	24	9	–	–	–	45	58	16	–	–	–	80
VP (Vincent) Koch	26	6	–	–	–	30	30	6	–	–	–	30
SC (Stephan) Kotze	5	–	–	–	–	0	5	–	–	–	–	0
C (Christo) le Roux	17	4	–	–	–	20	97	14	–	–	–	70
WH (Wilhelm) Loock	11	4	–	–	–	20	33	13	–	–	–	65
WD (Wilmaure) Louw	24	1	–	–	–	5	24	1	–	–	–	5
T (Tiaan) Marx	14	2	17	2	–	50	82	15	31	17	1	191
R (Rudi) Mathee	10	1	–	–	–	5	50	4	–	–	–	20
CJ (Jacques) Momberg	17	2	–	–	–	10	17	2	–	–	–	10
L (Lubabalo) Mtyanda	18	2	–	–	–	10	18	2	–	–	–	10
DP (Dewald) Pretorius	16	1	–	–	–	5	37	7	–	–	–	35
J (Jerome) Pretorius	17	5	–	–	–	25	25	7	–	–	–	35
J-C (JC) Roos	7	–	18	14	1	81	30	2	78	63	1	358
D (Deon) Scholtz	1	–	–	–	–	0	34	9	–	–	–	45
AR (Ashwin) Scott	3	4	–	–	–	20	50	11	–	–	–	55
WJ (Willem) Serfontein	10	–	–	–	–	0	62	1	–	–	–	5
RS (Rosco) Speckman	25	23	–	–	–	115	25	23	–	–	–	115
CJ (Corne) Steenkamp	22	5	–	–	–	25	141	28	–	–	–	140
DJ (De-Jay) Terblanche	27	3	–	–	–	15	103	6	–	–	–	30
D (Drew) van Coller	10	1	–	–	–	5	22	2	–	–	–	10
ER (Eduan) van der Walt	22	3	–	–	–	15	94	10	–	–	–	50
R (Reynier) van Rooyen	13	1	–	–	–	5	13	1	–	–	–	5
CG (Coenie) van Wyk	24	11	12	–	–	79	64	32	35	20	–	290
SH (Shaun) Venter	3	–	–	–	–	0	105	28	–	–	–	140
S (Stefan) Watermeyer	24	9	–	–	–	45	24	9	–	–	–	45
Penalty tries	0	1	–	–	–	5	0	1	–	–	–	5
37 players	614	163	126	69	3	1283	1727	375	245	165	4	2872

MPUMALANGA RUGBY UNION

2013 RESULTS & SCORERS

VODACOM CUP Played **10** Won **8** Drawn **0** Lost **2** Points for **525** Points against **223** Tries for **71** Tries against **24** Winning% **80%**

Date	Venue	Opponent	Result	Score	Referee	Scorers
Mrch 09	Nelspruit	Valke	WON	62-00	G de Bruin	T: Cassiem (3), Koch (2), Bouwer (2), Loock, Marx, Terblanche. C: Marx (6)
Mrch 16	Pretoria [1]	Blue Bulls	WON	44-42	S Mayende	T: Espag, Coetzer, Bothma, Specman, Watermeyer, Koch. C: Marx (4). P: Marx, Bezuidenhout.
Mrch 23	Nelspruit [2]	Griffons	WON	64-07	T Jonker	T: Herne (2), Specman (2), Bezuidenhout, Steenkamp, De Klerk, Bell, Watermeyer, Loock. C: Marx (4), Bezuidenhout (3)
April 05	Kimberley	Griquas	WON	47-31	B Crouse	T: Specman (2), Bezuidenhout, Bell, Bothma, Watermeyer, Loock. C: Bezuidenhout (5), Marx.
April 13	Nelspruit	Limpopo Blue Bulls	WON	154-0	T Jonker	T: Demas (4), Bouwer (3), Bell (2), Bothma (2), Herne (2), Scott, Le Roux, Fourie, Terblanche, Van Coller, Van der Walt, J Pretorius, Kember, D Pretorius. C: Bezuidenhout (11), Van Wyk (11).
April 19	Nelspruit	Golden Lions	LOST	14-23	L Jam	T: Specman, Herne. C: Bezuidenhout, Van Wyk.
April 26	Potchefstroom	Leopards XV	WON	29-28	J Kaplan	T: Specman, Cassiem, Koch. C: Bezuidenhout. P: Bezuidenhout (4).
Quarter-final						
May 03	Nelspruit	Pampas XV	WON	44-37	J van Heerden	T: Specman (3), Koch, Bezuidenhout. C: Bezuidenhout (5). P: Bezuidenhout (3).
Semi-final						
May 10	Nelspruit	EP Kings	WON	39-13	T Jonker	T: Specman, Bell, Van Wyk. C: Bezuidenhout (3). P: Bezuidenhout (5). DG: Bezuidenhout.
Final						
May 17	Nelspruit	Golden Lions	LOST	28-42	M vd Westhuizen	T: Van Wyk, J Pretorius, Watermeyer. C: Bezuidenhout (2). P: Bezuidenhout (3).

[1] Loftus B. [2] Nelspruit RC

ABSA CURRIE CUP Played **18** Won **17** Drawn **0** Lost **1** Points for **758** Points against **353** Tries for **92** Tries against **40** Winning% **94%**

Date	Venue	Opponent	Result	Score	Referee	Scorers
Jun 28	Port Elizabeth	EP Kings	WON	29-13	M Jonker	T: J Pretorius (2). C: Bezuidenhout (2). P: Bezuidenhout (4). DG: Bezuidenhout.
July 05	Nelspruit	Border	WON	23-16	R Rasivhenge	T: Steenkamp, Bouwer. C: Bezuidenhout (2). P: Bezuidenhout (3)
July 12	Nelspruit	Griffons	WON	56-10	J van Heerden	T: Bell (3), Bezuidenhout, Steenkamp, Specman, Kember. C: Bezuidenhout (4), Marx (2).
July 19	Potchefstroom	Leopards	WON	35-27	L vd Merwe	T: Van Wyk, Speckman. C: Bezuidenhout (2). P: Bezuidenhout (7).
July 27	Nelspruit	SWD	WON	60-20	B Crouse	T: Herne (2), Bell (2), Bezuidenhout, Van der Walt, Mtyanda, Kember, Koch. C: Bezuidenhout (6). P: Bezuidenhout.
Aug 02	Wellington	Boland	WON	35-05	L vd Merwe	T: Cassiem (2), Van Wyk, Herne, Speckman. C: Bezuidenhout (2). P: Bezuidenhout, Marx.
Aug 10	Nelspruit	Valke	WON	69-12	T Jonker	T: Watermeyer (2), Fourie, Terblanche, Bouwer, Momberg, Bell, Speckman, Kember. C: Bezuidenhout (9). P: Bezuidenhout (2).
Aug 16	Nelspruit	EP Kings	WON	33-32	M Jonker	T: Kember (3), Momberg. C: Bezuidenhout (2). P: Bezuidenhout (3).
Aug 23	East London	Border	WON	42-10	J Kotze	T: Van der Walt, Bouwer, Bell, Mtyanda, Speckman, Marx. C: Roos (6).
Aug 31	Welkom	Griffons	WON	42-24	J Jaftha	T: Le Roux, Van Wyk, Fourie, Du Toit, Bothma. C: Roos (3), Bezuidenhout. P: Roos (3).
Sep 06	Nelspruit	Leopards	WON	38-20	J Peyper	T: Van Wyk, Steenkamp, J Pretorius, Bothma, Speckman. C: Roos (2). P: Roos (3).
Sep 13	George	SWD	WON	28-27	Q Immelman	T: Speckman (2), Van Wyk. C: Roos (2). P: Roos (3).
Sep 21	Nelspruit	Boland	WON	44-21	M vd Westhuizen	T: Demas (2), Bezuidenhout, Van Rooyen, Mathee, Cassiem, Loock. C: Bezuidenhout (3). P: Bezuidenhout.
Sep 27	Kempton Park	Valke	WON	67-17	L Jam	T: Scott (3), Specman (3), Bell (2), Le Roux, Watermeyer. C: Bezuidenhout (7). P: Bezuidenhout.
Semi-final						
Oct 04	Nelspruit	SWD	WON	52-33	R Rasivhenge	T: Le Roux, Van Wyk, Steenkamp, Bothma, Kember, Watermeyer. C: Bezuidenhout (5). P: Bezuidenhout (4).
Final						
Oct 11	Nelspruit	EP Kings	WON	53-30	C Joubert	T: Van Wyk (3), Bell, Bothma, Kember. C: Bezuidenhout (2), Roos (2). P: Bezuidenhout (5).
PROMOTION & RELEGATION						
Oct 18	Kimberley	Griquas	LOST	19-21	J Kaplan	T: Louw. C: Bezuidenhout. P: Bezuidenhout (2), Roos (2).
Oct 25	Nelspruit	Griquas	WON	33-15	C Joubert	T: Specman, Watermeyer, Penalty try. C: Roos (3). P: Roos (3). DG: Roos.

arrie@pumas.co.za

APPEARANCES & POINTS IN VODACOM CUP 2013

	Valke	Blue Bulls	Griffons	Griquas	Limpopo BB	Golden Lions	Leopards XV	Pampas XV	EP Kings	Golden Lions	Matches	Tries	Conversions	Penalties	Drop Goals	Points
Coenie van Wyk	15	15	–	–	10R	10R	14R	15	15	15	8	2	12	–	–	34
Wilhelm Loock	14	14	14	14	–	14	14	–	–	–	6	3	–	–	–	15
Wilmaure Louw	13	13	13	13	12R	13	13	13	13	13	10	–	–	–	–	0
Stefan Watermeyer	12	12	12	12	–	12	12	12	12	12	9	4	–	–	–	20
Rosco Speckman	11	11	11	11	–	11	11	11	11	11	9	11	–	–	–	55
Tiaan Marx	10	10	10	10	–	–	–	–	–	–	4	1	15	1	–	38
Reynier van Rooyen	9	9	9R	9	9R	9	–	–	–	–	6	–	–	–	–	0
Christo le Roux	8	8	–	6R	8	8R	–	–	–	–	5	1	–	–	–	5
Uzair Cassiem	7	7	7	7	5R	7	4	4	4	4	10	4	–	–	–	20
Corne Steenkamp	6c	6c	6c	6c	–	6c	6c	6c	6c	6c	9	1	–	–	–	5
Eduan van der Walt	5	–	–	–	4	5	5	5	5	5	7	1	–	–	–	5
Willem Serfontein	4	4	4	4	–	4	5R	5R	–	–	7	–	–	–	–	0
Ivann Espag	3	3	–	3	–	3	3	3	3	3	7	1	–	–	–	5
Jacques Momberg	2	2	2	2	–	2	2R	2R	8R	8R	9	–	–	–	–	0
Vincent Koch	1	1	1	1	1R	1R	1	1	1	1	10	5	–	–	–	25
Drew van Coller	2R	6R	–	–	3	–	–	–	–	–	3	1	–	–	–	5
Corne Fourie	1R	1R	3R	1R	1	1	1R	1R	1R	1R	10	1	–	–	–	5
DJ Terblanche	3R	3R	3	3R	3R	3	3R	3R	3R	3R	10	2	–	–	–	10
RW Kember	8R	–	8	–	7	–	6R	8R	7R	6R	7	1	–	–	–	5
Jaco Bouwer	5R	5R	7R	5R	6	4R	7	7	7	7	10	5	–	–	–	25
Francois de Klerk	9R	9R	9	9R	9	9R	9	9	9	9	10	1	–	–	–	5
Carl Bezuidenhout	10R	10R	15	15	10	10	10	10	10	10	10	3	31	16	1	128
Marius Coetzer	–	5	5	5	5	–	–	–	5R	7R	6	1	–	–	–	5
Renaldo Bothma	–	8R	8R	8	7R	8	8	8	8	8	9	4	–	–	–	20
Frank Herne	–	–	2R	2R	2	2R	2	2	2	2	8	5	–	–	–	25
Jerome Pretorius	–	–	12R	–	13	13R	13R	12R	12R	12R	7	2	–	–	–	10
JW Bell	–	–	10R	10R	15	15	15	14	14	14	8	5	–	–	–	25
Danwel Demas	–	–	–	–	14	–	–	–	–	–	1	4	–	–	–	20
Dewald Pretorius	–	–	–	–	12	–	–	x	2R	13R	3	1	–	–	–	5
Ashwin Scott	–	–	–	–	11	–	–	–	–	–	1	1	–	–	–	5
30 Players											219	71	58	17	1	525

MPUMALANGA RUGBY UNION

APPEARANCES & POINTS IN ABSA CURRIE CUP 2013

	EP Kings	Border	Griffons	Leopards	SWD	Boland	Valke	EP Kings	Border	Griffons	Leopards	SWD	Boland	Valke	SWD	EP Kings	Griquas	Griquas	Matches	Tries	Conversions	Penalties	Drop Goals	Points
C van Wyk	15	15	15	15	15	15	15	15	–	15	15	15	15	–	15	15	15	15	16	9	–	–	–	45
Jerome Pretorius	14	12	13	–	–	–	11R	15R	14	13	13	14	–	–	–	–	–	14R	10	3	–	–	–	15
Wilmaure Louw	13	–	–	13	13	13	13	13	13	–	–	13	13	13	13	13	13	13	14	1	–	–	–	5
Stefan Watermeyer	12	–	12	12	–	12	12	12	12	12	12	12	–	12	12	12	12	12	15	5	–	–	–	25
Rosco Speckman	11	–	11	11	11	11	11	11	11	11	11	11	–	11	11	11	11	11	16	12	–	–	–	60
Carl Bezuidenhout	10	10	10	10	10	10	10	10	–	10R	10R	–	10	10	10	10	10	–	15	3	48	37	1	225
Francois de Klerk	9	9R	9	9	9	9	9	9	9R	9	9	9	9R	9	9	9	9	9	18	–	–	–	–	0
RW Kember	8	8c	8	8	8c	8	8c	8	8	8R	8	8	–	8c	8	8	8	8	17	8	–	–	–	40
Uzair Cassiem	7	–	7	7	7	7	7	7	7R	–	–	–	7	7R	5R	–	8R	5R	13	3	–	–	–	15
Corne Steenkamp	6c	6R	6c	6c	–	–	–	–	6R	6c	6c	6c	6R	6c	6c	6c	6c	6c	13	4	–	–	–	20
Eduan van der Walt	5	–	5	5	5	5c	–	5c	5c	5c	5	5	–	5	5	5	5	4R	15	2	–	–	–	10
Lubabalo Mtyanda	4	4	4	4	4	4	4	4	4	4	4R	5	4R	4R	4R	5R	5	–	18	2	–	–	–	10
Ivann Espag	3	–	–	–	–	–	–	–	3	–	–	–	–	–	–	3	–	–	3	–	–	–	–	0
Jacques Momberg	2	2R	2R	2R	2	2	2	2	–	–	–	–	–	–	–	–	–	–	8	2	–	–	–	10
Vincent Koch	1	–	1	1	1R	1	3R	1R	1	1	3R	1	1	–	1	3R	1R	1	16	1	–	–	–	5
Drew van Coller	2R	2	3R	–	–	–	1R	–	2	2	–	–	–	–	–	–	3R	–	7	–	–	–	–	0
Corne Fourie	1R	1	1R	1R	1	1R	1	1	2R	2R	1	3	3	1	3	1	1	1R	18	2	–	–	–	10
DJ Terblanche	3R	3	3	3	3	3	3	3	3	–	3	1R	1R	3	1R	3	3R	3	17	1	–	–	–	5
Marius Coetzer	4R	5	–	18R	4R	–	5	4R	–	4R	–	–	–	–	–	–	–	–	7	–	–	–	–	0
Jaco Bouwer	6R	6	–	–	–	4R	6	2R	6	6	6R	8R	6R	6	–	–	–	–	11	3	–	–	–	15
JW Bell	14R	11R	14	14	14	14	14	14	15	14	14	13R	–	15	14	14	14	14	17	10	–	–	–	50
Tiaan Marx	12R	13R	10R	12R	12	12R	13R	–	12R	11R	–	–	15R	–	–	–	–	–	10	1	2	1	–	12
Wilhelm Loock	–	14	–	–	11R	–	–	–	11R	–	–	11	–	11R	–	–	–	–	5	1	–	–	–	5
Dewald Pretorius	–	13	9R	13R	12R	22R	–	–	–	11R	12R	12	11R	12R	13R	14R	13R	–	13	–	–	–	–	0
Deon Scholtz	–	11	–	–	–	–	–	–	–	–	–	–	–	–	–	–	–	–	1	–	–	–	–	0
Reynier van Rooyen	–	9	–	9R	9R	9R	–	–	–	–	–	x	9	9R	–	9R	–	–	7	1	–	–	–	5
Christo Le Roux	–	7	–	–	7R	2R	7R	7R	7	7	8R	–	7R	7	8R	8R	–	–	12	3	–	–	–	15
Stephan Kotze	–	1R	–	–	3R	3R	–	3R	–	–	–	–	–	1R	–	–	–	–	5	–	–	–	–	0
Willem Serfontein	–	5R	4R	–	–	–	4R	–	–	–	–	–	–	–	–	–	–	–	3	–	–	–	–	0
Frank Herne	–	–	2	2	6	6	–	6	–	–	2R	2R	2	2	2	2	2	2R	13	3	–	–	–	15
Rudi Mathee	–	–	6R	4R	–	–	–	–	–	5R	4	4	4	4	4	4	4	4	10	1	–	–	–	5
Shaun Venter	–	–	–	–	–	–	9R	9R	9	–	–	–	–	–	–	–	–	–	3	–	–	–	–	0
JC Roos	–	–	–	–	–	–	–	10	10	10	10	–	–	–	10R	10R	10	7	–	18	14	1	81
Francois du Toit	–	–	–	–	–	–	–	2R	3R	2	2	2R	2R	2R	2R	2R	2	–	10	1	–	–	–	5
Renaldo Bothma	–	–	–	–	–	–	–	8R	8	7	7	8	–	7	7	7	7	7	9	4	–	–	–	20
Danwel Demas	–	–	–	–	–	–	–	–	–	–	–	–	14	–	–	–	–	–	1	2	–	–	–	10
Ashwin Scott	–	–	–	–	–	–	–	–	–	–	–	12R	14	–	–	–	–	–	2	3	–	–	–	15
Penalty try	–	–	–	–	–	–	–	–	–	–	–	–	–	–	–	–	–	–	0	1	–	–	–	5
37 Players																				395	92	68	52	2	758

arrie@pumas.co.za

MPUMALANGA RUGBY UNION

ABSA UNDER-21 CHAMPIONSHIP (7th Section B)

Played	Won	Drawn	Lost	Points for	Points against	Tries for	Tries against	Winning %
7	2	0	5	156	224	22	35	29,00%

RESULTS Lost EP (h) 20-46. Lost Limpopo Blue Bulls (a) 19-53. Bt Griffons (a) 36-12. Lost Griquas (h) 20-24. Bt SWD (a) 32-31. Lost Boland (h) 10-31. Lost Valke (a) 19-27.

SCORERS 31 Juan van der Merwe (8c, 5p). 25 Pule Sibiya (5t). 19 Christo Nelson (2t, 3c, 1p). 12 Johan Pretorius, Kyran Odendaal (2t, 1c each). 10 Cornelius Rautenbach, Dirk Louwies, Edwin Olivier, Pieter Killian (2t each). 5 Jan Els, Nkululeko Ngozo, Thembinkosi Thabang (1t each). 2 Morné van den Berg (1c).

ABSA U19 CHAMPIONSHIP (8th, Section B)

Played	Won	Drawn	Lost	Points for	Points against	Tries for	Tries against	Winning %
7	0	0	7	108	276	14	41	0,00%

RESULTS Lost EP (h) 18-46. Lost Limpopo Blue Bulls (a) 14-62. Lost Griffons (a) 21-22. Lost Griquas (h) 20-31. Lost SWD (a) 12-55. Lost Boland (h) 20-39. Lost Valke (a) 03-21.

SCORERS 23 Marthinus Snyman (3t, 1c, 1p, 1dg), Jaun-dré (7c, 3p). 22 Juandré van Wyk (3t, 2c, 1p). 10 Deon Joubert, Wian van Schalkwyk (2t each). 5 David Pieterse, Michael Chimbila, Shane Pretorius, Winson Theron (1t each).

Jimmy Stonehouse, Corne Steenkamp and MJ Mentz hold the ABSA First Division trophy.
Duif du Toit/Gallo Images

PUMAS RECORDS

MATCH RECORDS
Biggest win	154-00	vs. Limpopo Blue Bulls	2013
Biggest Currie Cup win	111-14	vs. Vodacom Eagles	2001
Heaviest defeat	10-116	vs. Transvaal	1993
Heaviest Currie Cup defeat	9-90	vs. Natal	1996
Highest score	154	vs. Limpopo Blue Bulls (154-0)	2013
Most points conceded	116	vs. Transvaal (10-116)	1993
Most tries	22	vs. Limpopo Blue Bulls	2013
Most Currie Cup tries	16	vs. Vodacom Eagles (111-14)	2001
Most points by a player	37	J Benade vs. Lowveld	1995
	37	CP Steyn vs. Vodacom Cheetahs (Currie Cup)	2003
Most tries by a player	5	D Pretorius vs. South Western Districts Federation	1978
Most Currie Cup tries by a player	4	A Fourie vs. North West	1998

SEASON RECORDS
Most team points	1283	28 matches	2013
Most Currie Cup points by team	758	18 matches	2013
Most points by a player	353	C Bezuidenhout	2013
Most Currie Cup points by a player	225	C Bezuidenhout	2013
Most team tries	163	28 matches	2013
Most Currie Cup tries by team	92	18 matches	2013
Most tries by a player	24	A Kettledas	2009
Most Currie Cup tries by a player	18	A Kettledas	2009

CAREER RECORDS
Most appearances	183	FJ Rossouw	1991-2000
Most points	869	JH Muller	1973-1985
Most tries	57	K Grobler	1979-1990

HONOURS
ABSA Currie Cup (First Division) 2005, 2009, 2013

SOUTH WESTERN DISTRICTS RUGBY FOOTBALL UNION

FOUNDED
1899
GROUND
Outeniqua Park
CAPACITY
7500
ADDRESS
CJ Langenhoven Road, George
POSTAL ADDRESS
PO Box 10471, George 6530
TELEPHONE NUMBER
044-873 0137
EMAIL
rugby@swdeagles.co.za
COLOURS
White & green jersey, white shorts and green socks
CURRIE CUP COACH
Bevin Fortuin
VODACOM CUP COACH
Eddie Myners
CAPTAIN
Kabamba Floors
PRESIDENT
Hennie Bartmann
UNION CEO
Johan Prinsloo

Eagles fall at penultimate hurdle

THE SWD EAGLES ERASED THE PAIN OF 2012, WHEN THEY missed out on the Absa Currie Cup First Division semi-finals by a single log point, by reaching the semi-finals under their new coach, former Springbok fullback Bevin Fortuin.

This was a genuine team effort from a side assembled on a shoestring budget, but if one has to single out individuals then the Eagles' hero was undoubtedly veteran left wing Alshaun Bock.

Bock's achievements in 2013 were remarkable by any measure: he played in all 14 of the Eagles' First Division matches and scored 17 tries – a Union record. His three touchdowns in six appearances in the Vodacom Cup brought his season tally to 20 in 20 games – also an SWD record.

Bock's contribution to the Eagles' First Division cause cannot be underestimated: he began with a brace in the side's 36-12 round-one victory over the Border Bulldogs in East London, and then proceeded to score at least once in each of the next nine matches, including hat-tricks against the Valke in round three and EP a week later.

Bock then went scoreless in the final four rounds before scoring in their semi-final against the eventual champions, the Steval Pumas, in Nelspruit, a match the Eagles lost 52-33.

The Eagles won seven and lost seven to reach that stage, finishing fourth on the table behind the Pumas, EP Kings and Leopards.

Under Fortuin, who, until the previous year, had still been an active player-coach at local club Blanco, whom he led to the 2012 National Club Championships, the team played an attractive brand of rugby and won over many supporters. Their semi-final appearance was just reward for the hard work put in by management and the players, and there is confidence going into 2014.

The Eagles used a total of 37 players in the First Division campaign, and, apart from Bock, boasted a number of star performers. At the back, Bock's wing partner Clint Wagman scored four tries in 13 appearances, while centres Gerrit Smith and Jeff Taljard took care of some of the goalkicking, scoring 74 points in total between them. Flyhalf-cum-fullback Justin van Staden was the team's top point-scorer with 139.

Up front, the team was superbly led by Fortuin's former Bok team-mate, eighthman/flanker Kabamba Floors, while livewire flanker Shaun Raubenheimer and loosehead prop Roy Godfrey – who also played in every match – each scored five tries to sum up just the type of enterprising game the Eagles dished up in 2013.

Loose forward Christo du Plessis was the first graduate of the Cell C Community Cup to play provincial rugby, and the former Blanco and Evergreens player took his opportunity well.
Petri Oeschger/Gallo Images

SWD RUGBY FOOTBALL UNION

VODACOM CUP LOG POSITIONS

Year	Pos	Year	Pos	Year	Pos	Year	Pos	Year	Pos	Year	Pos
2013	12th	2010	13th	2007	12th	2004	9th	2001	7th	1998	3rd
2012	15th	2009	5th	2006	14th	2003	13th	2000	14th		
2011	11th	2008	10th	2005	8th	2002	12th	1999	8th		

ABSA CURRIE CUP LOG POSITIONS

Year	Pos	Year	Pos	Year	Pos	Year	Pos	Year	Pos	Year	Pos
2013	10th	2010	9th	2007	9th	2004	8th	2001	14th	1998	7th
2012	11th	2009	10th	2006	11th	2003	8th	2000	6th	1997	8th
2011	9th	2008	11th	2005	13th	2002	9th	1999	4th	1996	14th

2013 RESULTS & SCORERS

VODACOM CUP Played **7** Won **1** Drawn **0** Lost **6** Points for **147** Points against **202** Tries for **18** Tries against **22** Winning% **14%**

Date	Venue	Opponent	Result	Score	Referee	Scorers
Mrch 08	George	Free State XV	LOST	08-31	S Berry	T: Kemp. P: Van Vuuren.
Mrch 15	George	Pampas	LOST	17-22	M vd Westhuizen	T: Bock, Hartnick. C: Van Vuuren (2). P: Van Vuuren.
Mrch 23	Robertson	Boland	WON	44-12	J Sylvestre	T: Rhoode, Herbst, Floors, Hartnick, Penalty try. C: Taljard (5). P: Taljard (3).
April 05	George	Sharks XV	LOST	22-26	Q Immelman	T: Dyanti. C: Taljard. P: Taljard (5).
April 12	Port Elizabeth¹	EP Kings	LOST	10-52	M vd Westhuizen	T: Floors, Taljard.
April 20	Strand	WP	LOST	27-34	J Jaftha	T: Bock, Du Plessis, Wagman, Luckan. C: Taljard (2). P: Taljard
April 26	George	Border	LOST	19-25	A Sehlako	T: Bock, Wagman, Du Toit. C: Taljard, Van Vuuren.

¹ NMMU Stadium

ABSA CURRIE CUP Played **15** Won **7** Drawn **0** Lost **8** Points for **493** Points against **504** Tries for **61** Tries against **65** Winning% **47%**

Date	Venue	Opponent	Result	Score	Referee	Scorers
Jun 28	East London	Border	WON	36-12	L Legoete	T: Bock (2), Du Plessis, Wagman, Ferreira. C: Smith (2), Taljard (2). P: Taljard.
July 05	George	Boland	LOST	17-22	M vd Westhuizen	T: Bock, Du Plessis. C: Taljard (2). P: Taljard.
July 12	Kempton Park	Valke	WON	38-37	R Rasivhenge	T: Bock (3), Du Plessis, Van Staden, Du Toit. C: Taljard (3), Van Staden.
July 19	George	EP Kings	LOST	34-35	L Legoete	T: Bock (3), Taljard, Raubenheimer. C: Taljard (3). P: Van Staden.
July 27	Nelspruit	Pumas	LOST	20-60	B Crouse	T: Bock, Godfrey. C: Van Staden (2). P: Van Staden (2).
Aug 02	George	Griffons	WON	30-25	J Kaplan	T: Bock, Kemp, Floors. C: Van Staden (3). P: Van Staden (3).
Aug 09	Potchefstroom	Leopards	WON	50-47	S Mayende	T: Bock, Meslane, Smith, Du Toit, Raubenheimer. C: Van Staden (5). P: Van Staden (5)
Aug 16	George	Border	WON	36-31	R Rasivhenge	T: Bock, Wagman, Parks, Zito, Godfrey. C: Van Staden (4). P: Van Staden.
Aug 24	Wellington	Boland	LOST	30-35	Q Immelman	T: Bock, Wagman, Le Roux, Ferreira. C: Smith, Van Staden. P: Van Staden (2).
Aug 30	George	Valke	WON	58-42	M Jonker	T: Bock (2), Godfrey (2), Delo, Pedro, Du Toit, Zito. C: Van Staden (5), Smith. P: Van Staden (2).
Sep 06	Port Elizabeth	EP Kings	LOST	09-15	L vd Merwe	P: Van Staden (2). DG: Van Staden.
Sep 13	George	Pumas	LOST	27-28	Q Immelman	T: Smith, Oelofse. C: Van Staden. P: Van Staden (4). DG: Van Staden.
Sep 21	Welkom	Griffons	WON	51-28	C Joubert	T: Hartnick (2), Raubenheimer (2), Smith, Blom, Dyantyi, Ferreira. C: Smith (4). P: Smith.
Sep 27	George	Leopards	LOST	24-35	L vd Merwe	T: Boesak, Godfrey, Raubenheimer. C: Smith (3). P: Smith.
Semi-final						
Oct 04	Nelspruit	Pumas	LOST	33-52	R Rasivhenge	T: Bock, Venter, Wagman. C: Van Staden (3). P: Van Staden (4).

SWD RUGBY FOOTBALL UNION

SWD EAGLES SQUAD IN 2013 | SWD CAREER

PLAYER	Appearances	Tries	Conversions	Penalties	Drop Goals	Points	Career Matches	Career Tries	Conversions	Penalties	Drop Goals	Points
KR (Kerwin) Apollis	1	1	–	–	–	5	1	1	–	–	–	5
J (Jandre) Blom	12	1	–	–	–	5	45	5	26	23	–	146
AG (Alshaun) Bock	20	20	–	–	–	100	35	29	–	–	–	145
M (Marshell) Boesak	2	1	–	–	–	5	2	1	–	–	–	5
AD (Armand) Coetzee	1	–	–	–	–	0	1	–	–	–	–	0
LC (Lionel) Cornelius	2	–	–	–	–	0	2	–	–	–	–	0
LA (Layle) Delo	14	1	–	–	–	5	27	2	–	–	–	10
CJ (Christo) du Plessis	18	4	–	–	–	20	33	5	–	–	–	25
LM (Lourens) du Toit	4	–	–	–	–	0	4	–	–	–	–	0
OM (Martin) du Toit	18	4	–	–	–	20	22	4	–	–	–	20
M (Mzo) Dyantyi	14	2	–	–	–	10	55	7	–	–	–	35
CD (Charlton) Ewerts	2	–	–	–	–	0	6	1	–	–	–	5
M (Martin) Ferreira	12	3	–	–	–	15	12	3	–	–	–	15
L (Kabamba) Floors	17	3	–	–	–	15	50	21	–	–	–	105
MZ (Merlin) Geswindt	1	–	–	–	–	0	1	–	–	–	–	0
RAM (Roy) Godfrey	14	5	–	–	–	25	14	5	–	–	–	25
LL (Lyndon) Hartnick	14	4	–	–	–	20	56	9	–	–	–	45
JD (Johan) Herbst	3	1	–	–	–	5	23	10	–	–	–	50
KR (Kirsten) Heyns	2	–	–	–	–	0	2	–	–	–	–	0
DLJ (Dean) Hopp	9	–	–	–	–	0	41	4	–	–	–	20
EG (Eldred) James	1	–	–	–	–	0	1	–	–	–	–	0
C (Creswin) Josephs	3	–	–	–	–	0	3	–	–	–	–	0
GD (Grant) Kemp	10	2	–	–	–	10	24	4	–	–	–	20
W (Wayne) Khan	5	–	–	–	–	0	7	–	–	–	–	10
RJ (Raoul) Larson	12	–	–	–	–	0	14	–	–	–	–	0
G (Grant) le Roux	14	1	–	–	–	5	32	3	–	–	–	15
L (Wikus) Louwrens	2	–	–	–	–	0	2	–	–	–	–	0
G (Ghafoer) Luckan	10	1	–	–	–	5	15	7	–	–	–	35
DK (Dumisane) Meslane	10	1	–	–	–	5	26	8	–	–	–	40
L (Lubabalo) Mtyanda	7	–	–	–	–	0	70	8	–	–	–	40
SW (Schalk) Oelofse	11	1	–	–	–	5	11	1	–	–	–	5
MX (Mbembe) Payi	5	–	–	–	–	0	5	–	–	–	–	0
BJ (Buran) Parks	16	1	–	–	–	5	25	1	–	–	–	5
HN (Hentzwill) Pedro	3	1	–	–	–	5	3	1	–	–	–	5
AQ (Quinten) Petzer	0	–	–	–	–	0	8	–	–	–	–	0
S (Shaun) Raubenheimer	12	5	–	–	–	25	59	20	–	–	–	100
DE (Deroy) Rhoode	14	1	–	–	–	5	53	4	12	3	–	53
DC (Daniel) Roberts	10	–	–	–	–	0	10	–	–	–	–	0
JJ (Jean) Rossouw	7	–	–	–	–	0	21	1	–	–	–	5
XG (Xavier) Scholtz	1	–	–	–	–	0	15	–	–	–	–	0
WS (Wentsley) Scott	7	–	–	–	–	0	33	5	–	–	–	25
GPJ (Gerrit) Smith	12	3	11	2	–	43	12	3	11	2	–	43
JJ (Jeff) Taljard	18	2	19	11	–	81	51	10	19	11	–	121
HJ (Hans) van Dyk	12	–	–	–	–	0	22	–	–	–	–	0
J-L (James) van Rooyen	6	–	–	–	–	0	6	–	–	–	–	0
J (Justin) van Staden	12	1	25	26	2	139	12	1	25	26	2	139
E (Elric) van Vuuren	3	–	3	2	–	12	31	14	66	37	–	313
A (Anver) Venter	1	1	–	–	–	5	1	1	–	–	–	5
M (Michael) Vermaak	8	–	–	–	–	0	26	2	–	–	–	10
L (Luzuko) Vulindlu	3	–	–	–	–	0	3	–	–	–	–	0
CA (Clinton) Wagman	17	6	–	–	–	30	43	12	–	–	–	60
MR (Mzwanele) Zito	12	2	–	–	–	10	12	2	–	–	–	10
52 players	**444**	**79**	**58**	**41**	**2**	**640**	**1088**	**215**	**159**	**102**	**2**	**1715**

rugby@swdeagles.co.za

SWD RUGBY FOOTBALL UNION

APPEARANCES & POINTS IN VODACOM CUP 2013

Player	Free State XV	Pampas XV	Boland	Sharks XV	EP Kings	WP	Border	Matches	Tries	Conversions	Penalties	Drop Goals	Points
Elric van Vuuren	15	15	–	–	–	–	11R	3	–	3	2	–	12
Charlie Ewerts	14	–	–	–	11R	–	–	2	–	–	–	–	0
Wentsley Scott	13	11R	13	13	13	13	13	7	–	–	–	–	0
Jeff Taljard	12	12	12	12	12	12	12	7	1	9	9	–	50
Alshaun Bock	11	13	14	11	–	15	15	6	3	–	–	–	15
Martin du Toit	10	10	10	10	10	10	10	7	1	–	–	–	5
Johan Herbst	9	11	11	–	–	–	–	3	1	–	–	–	5
Michael Vermaak	8	x	5R	8R	8	5	5	6	–	–	–	–	0
Lyndon Hartnick	7c	8	8	8	17R	8	8c	7	2	–	–	–	10
Dumisane Meslane	6	–	–	–	–	7	7	3	–	–	–	–	0
Grant le Roux	5	5	5	5	5	–	–	5	–	–	–	–	0
Lubabalo Mtyanda	4	4	4	4	4	4	4	7	–	–	–	–	0
Grant Kemp	3	–	–	–	–	–	–	1	1	–	–	–	5
Hansie van Dyk	2	–	2	2	2	2	2	6	–	–	–	–	0
Jean Rossouw	1	3R	1R	1R	1R	–	–	5	–	–	–	–	0
Wayne Khan	2R	2	–	–	–	–	–	2	–	–	–	–	0
Raoul Larson	x	3	3	3	3	3	3	6	–	–	–	–	0
Armand Coetzee	4R	–	–	–	–	–	–	1	–	–	–	–	0
Buran Parks	6R	7	6R	x	5R	–	–	4	–	–	–	–	0
Mzo Dyantyi	14R	9	9	9	9	9R	9	7	1	–	–	–	5
Lionel Cornelius	x	9R	10R	–	–	–	–	2	–	–	–	–	0
Merlin Geswindt	13R	–	–	–	–	–	–	1	–	–	–	–	0
Ghafoer Luckan	–	14	–	–	11	11	11	4	1	–	–	–	5
Kabamba Floors	–	6c	6c	6c	6c	6c	–	5	2	–	–	–	10
Layle Delo	–	1	1	1	1	–	1	5	–	–	–	–	0
James van Rooyen	–	2R	3R	3R	3R	3R	3R	6	–	–	–	–	0
Deroy Rhoode	–	13R	15	15	15	9	10R	6	1	–	–	–	5
Christo du Plessis	–	7R	7	7	7	8R	6	6	1	–	–	–	5
Creswin Josephs	–	–	13R	x	–	10R	12R	3	–	–	–	–	0
Kirsten Heyns	–	–	11R	x	12R	–	–	2	–	–	–	–	0
Clinton Wagman	–	–	–	14	14	14	14	4	2	–	–	–	10
Kerwin Appollis	–	–	–	9R	–	–	–	1	1	–	–	–	5
Daniel Roberts	–	–	–	–	15R	14R	–	2	–	–	–	–	0
Wikus Louwrens	–	–	–	–	–	1	1R	2	–	–	–	–	0
Shaun Raubenheimer	–	–	–	–	–	6R	7R	2	–	–	–	–	0
Xavier Scholtz	–	–	–	–	17R	–	–	1	–	–	–	–	0
Quinten Petzer	–	–	–	–	–	–	x	0	–	–	–	–	0
37 players								**147**	**18**	**12**	**11**	**0**	**147**

SWD RUGBY FOOTBALL UNION

APPEARANCES & POINTS IN ABSA CURRIE CUP 2013

Player	Border	Boland	Valke	EP Kings	Pumas	Griffons	Leopards	Border	Boland	Valke	EP Kings	Pumas	Griffons	Pumas	Matches	Tries	Conversions	Penalties	Drop Goals	Points
Daniel Roberts	15	15	15R	15R	14	15	x	x	15R	15R	–	–	–	–	8	–	–	–	–	0
Clinton Wagman	14	14	14	11R	–	14	14	14	14	14	14	14	14	14	13	4	–	–	–	20
Gerrit Smith	13	–	–	13	12	12	13	13	13	13	13	15	12	12	12	3	11	2	–	43
Jeff Taljard	12	12	12	12	–	13R	12	12	12	12	12	12	–	–	11	1	10	2	–	31
Alshaun Bock	11	11	11	11	11	11	11	11	11	11	11	11	11	11	14	17	–	–	–	85
Martin du Toit	10	10	10	10	10	–	10	10	10	10	10	–	–	10	11	3	–	–	–	15
Mzo Dyantyi	9	–	–	–	13R	9R	9R	x	9R	–	–	–	9	10R	7	1	–	–	–	5
Kabamba Floors	8c	8c	8c	8c	–	6c	8c	8c	6c	6c	6c	8c	–	8c	12	1	–	–	–	5
Christo du Plessis	7	7	7	7	8	8	–	6R	8	8	8	7R	8	–	12	3	–	–	–	15
Shaun Raubenheimer	6	6	6R	6	7	6	7	–	–	–	–	6	6	6	10	5	–	–	–	25
Grant le Roux	5	5	–	–	–	–	4	4R	4R	4R	4R	4	4R	–	9	1	–	–	–	5
Michael Vermaak	4	5R	–	–	–	–	–	–	–	–	–	–	–	–	2	–	–	–	–	0
Dean Hopp	3	4R	3R	3R	3	–	–	3R	–	3R	–	3R	–	3R	9	–	–	–	–	0
Martin Ferreira	2	2	2R	2R	2R	2	2	2	2	–	–	2	2	2	12	3	–	–	–	15
Roy Godfrey	1	1	1	1	1c	1	1	1	1	1	1	1	1c	1	14	5	–	–	–	25
Wayne Khan	2R	–	x	–	–	x	–	–	–	–	2	2R	–	–	3	–	–	–	–	0
Layle Delo	1R	3R	–	x	3R	3R	2R	x	–	2R	2R	–	1R	2R	9	1	–	–	–	5
Buran Parks	7R	–	4R	6R	6R	8R	6	7	7	7R	7	7	–	7	12	1	–	–	–	5
Dumisane Meslane	6R	–	6	–	6	–	7R	6	6R	–	–	–	8R	–	7	1	–	–	–	5
Deroy Rhoode	9R	9R	9R	–	9	–	–	–	–	9R	x	9	15	9	8	–	–	–	–	0
Mbembe Payi	15R	15R	–	–	14R	15R	10R	x	–	–	–	–	–	–	5	–	–	–	–	0
Ghafoer Luckan	14R	13	13	14	13	13	–	–	–	–	–	–	–	–	6	–	–	–	–	0
Jandre Blom	–	9	9	9	9R	9	9	9	9	9	9	13R	10	–	12	1	–	–	–	5
Schalk Oelofse	–	4	–	4	4	4	4	–	4	4	4	4	4R	4	11	1	–	–	–	5
Raoul Larson	–	3	3	3	–	–	3R	–	3R	–	3R	–	–	–	6	–	–	–	–	0
Hansie van Dyk	–	2R	2	2	2	–	–	–	2R	2	–	–	–	–	6	–	–	–	–	0
Justin van Staden	–	10R	15	15	15	10	15	15	15	15	15	10	–	15	12	1	25	26	2	139
Mzwanele Zito	–	–	5	5	5	5	5	5	5	5	5	5	5	5	12	2	–	–	–	10
Lourens du Toit	–	–	4	x	4R	5R	4R	–	–	–	–	–	–	–	4	–	–	–	–	0
Grant Kemp	–	–	–	–	–	3	3	3	3	3	3	3	3	3	9	1	–	–	–	5
Lyndon Hartnick	–	–	–	–	–	–	4R	7R	7	8R	6R	7	7R	–	7	2	–	–	–	10
Hentzwill Pedro	–	–	–	–	–	–	–	14R	–	x	13R	11R	–	–	3	1	–	–	–	5
Luzuko Vulindlu	–	–	–	–	–	–	–	–	14R	13	13	–	–	–	3	–	–	–	–	0
Jean Rossouw	–	–	–	–	–	–	–	–	–	1R	–	3R	–	–	2	–	–	–	–	0
Eldred James	–	–	–	–	–	–	–	–	–	–	–	15R	–	–	1	–	–	–	–	0
Marshell Boesak	–	–	–	–	–	–	–	–	–	–	–	–	12R	14R	2	1	–	–	–	5
Anver Venter	–	–	–	–	–	–	–	–	–	–	–	–	–	13	1	1	–	–	–	5
37 players															297	61	46	30	2	493

rugby@swdeagles.co.za

SWD RUGBY FOOTBALL UNION

ABSA UNDER-21 CHAMPIONSHIP (8th, Section B)

Played	Won	Drawn	Lost	Points for	Points against	Tries for	Tries against	Winning %
7	0	0	7	125	326	18	46	0,00%

RESULTS Lost Limpopo Blue Bulls (h) 00-60. Lost Boland (a) 24-56. Lost Valke (h) 22-36. Lost EP (a) 16-76. Lost Mpumalanga (h) 31-32. Lost Griffons (a) 22-41. Lost Griquas (h) 10-25.

SCORERS 45 Chris Willemse (3t, 9c, 4p). 30 Jerome Fillies (6t). 15 Dillin Snel (3t). 10 Linden Rhode (2t). 5 Jade Roelfse, Kirsten Heyns, Marcelino Marais, Nathan Luiters, C-Than Moos (1t each).

ABSA U19 CHAMPIONSHIP (7th, Section A)

Played	Won	Drawn	Lost	Points for	Points against	Tries for	Tries against	Winning %
8	4	0	4	223	196	26	27	50,00%

RESULTS Lost Limpopo Blue Bulls (h) 16-18. Lost Boland (a) 14-24. Lost Valke (h) 20-50. Bt EP (a) 35-10. Bt Mpumalanga (h) 55-12. Bt Griffons (a) 30-27. Bt Griquas (h) 29-26. SEMI-FINAL Lost Valke (h) 24-29.

SCORERS 76 Leighton Eksteen (6t, 14c, 6p). 28 Elfrido Ayford (1t, 4c, 5t). 23 Macdelin Saayman (4t, 1dg). 20 Elroy Havenga (4t). 15 Curtley Kiewiet (3t) 13 Johan Steyn (2c, 3p). 8 Lee-Roy Pojie (1t, 1p). 5 Brandon Haas, Dean January, Hardus Coetzee, Hendrik Oosthuizen, Jason Mesuur, Lenesteyo Nomdo, Lodewikus Oosthuizen, Simon Snyman (1t each).

Alshaun Bock made try-scoring history in 2013.
Ashley Vlotman/Gallo Images

SWD RECORDS

MATCH RECORDS

Biggest win	102-0	vs. Transkei	1995
Biggest win (Currie Cup)	102-0	vs. Griffons	1999
Heaviest defeat	0-97	vs. British Lions	1974
Heaviest defeat (Currie Cup)	8-147	vs. Northern Transvaal	1996
Highest score	105	vs. Transkei (105-8)	1994
Highest score (Currie Cup)	102	vs. Griffons (102-0)	1999
Most points conceded	97	vs. British Lions (0-97)	1974
Most points conceded (Currie Cup)	147	vs. Northern Transvaal (8-147)	1996
Most tries	16	vs. Transkei (102-0)	1995
Most tries (Currie Cup)	16	vs. Griffons (102-0)	1999
Most points by a player	28	AJJ Van Straaten	1997
Most points by a player (Currie Cup)	29	CR Van As vs. Leopards	2002
Most tries by a player	4	G Cilliers vs. North Eastern Districts	1965
	4	F Amsterdam vs. Northern Natal	1992
Most tries by a player (Currie Cup)	4	MG Joubert vs. Valke	2009

SEASON RECORDS

Most team points	943	29 matches	1998
Most team points (Currie Cup)	493	15 matches	2013
Most points by a player	252	AJJ Van Straaten	1997
Most points by a player (Currie Cup)	173	CR Van As	2002
Most team tries	132	29 matches	1998
Most team tries (Currie Cup)	79	21 matches	2003
Most tries by a player	20	AG Bock	2013
Most tries by a player (Currie Cup)	17	AG Bock	2013

CAREER RECORDS

Most appearances	191	C Botha	1993-2011
Most points	638	CR Van As	2000-2004
Most points (Currie Cup)	480	CR Van As	2000-2004
Most tries	53	DB Coeries	1998-2005
Most conversions by a player	134	CR Van As	2000-2004
Most penalties by a player	105	CR Van As	2000-2004

HONOURS

Bankfin Cup	2002
ABSA Cup (First Division)	2007

VALKE RUGBY UNION

FOUNDED
1947
(as Eastern Transvaal)
GROUND
Barnard Stadium,
Kempton Park
CAPACITY
7 000
ADDRESS
CR Swart Avenue,
Kempton Park
POSTAL ADDRESS
PO Box 12703, Edleen
1625
TELEPHONE NUMBER
011-975 2822/2487
EMAIL
valke@global.co.za
COLOURS
Red jersey, shorts and socks
CURRIE CUP COACH
John Williams
VODACOM CUP COACH
John Williams
CAPTAIN
JP Mostert
PRESIDENT
Vivian Lottering
CEO
Jurie Coetzee

Valke take wooden spoon

THE VALKE ENDURED YET ANOTHER TORRID YEAR IN THE wilderness of the Absa Currie Cup First Division, their heroics of seasons past – most notably a convincing and well deserved Vodacom Cup title as recently as 2006 – fading faster with each passing year.

In 2012, the East Rand union began the Currie Cup with high hopes but finished the competition with just three wins from their 14 round-robin matches. In their desperate search for positives, supporters were able to point out that the dreaded wooden spoon had at least eluded their side, albeit by a single rung on the ladder.

The winless Border Bulldogs might have occupied the basement position in the provincial pecking order in 2012 but a year later the roles were reversed, with the team once feared as the Red Devils slipping to eighth, their two wins and a draw seeing them finish seven points adrift of the seventh-placed Bulldogs, whose forgettable campaign did have the consolation of twice the number of victories.

Perhaps a more noteworthy and telling stat is that the Valke scored 13 more tries than the Bulldogs (45 to 32) but crucially the Eastern Cape outfit conceded an incredible 33 fewer touchdowns.

And therein lies the story of the Valke: plenty of heart, decent options on attack – but without ball in hand the most porous provincial team in the country.

Their season began on a neutral note when they drew 30-30 against the Griffons at their home base of Barnard Stadium, Kempton Park, but thereafter followed three straight defeats to the Leopards (50-25), SWD Eagles (38-37) and Boland Cavaliers (20-7) that forced plenty of introspection.

The Valke looked to have turned their season around when they rallied to beat the Bulldogs 34-29 at home in round five, but it proved a false dawn as they proceeded to lose the next five games by conceding a truckload of points on each occasion – 44, 69, 50, 38, 58.

The Cavaliers were beaten 28-21 in round 11, but once again the Valke could not take advantage, and their season slipped away with a hat-trick of meek defeats during which they shipped a combined 132 points, including a 50-point hiding in front of what was left of their home fans, at the hands of the all-conquering Pumas.

The Valke used a total of 39 players through their miserable campaign, but credit must be given to those players who never gave up. Fullback Kyle Hendricks played in all 14 Currie Cup matches and caught the eye on occasion, while utility back Juan Kotze scored 90 points in his 14 appearances.

Scrumhalf Anrich Richter and centre Willie Odendaal, who also played in every match, each scored six tries while upfront skipper and eighthman JP Mostert bravely led his team week in and week out and was rewarded with four tries – all of them coming against Limpopo, to put him in the records books.

Sandile Ngcobo played in 12 Currie Cup First Division matches in 2013.
Duif du Toit/Gallo Images

VALKE RUGBY UNION

VODACOM CUP LOG POSITIONS

Year	Pos	Year	Pos	Year	Pos	Year	Pos	Year	Pos	Year	Pos
2013	14th	2010	12th	2007	9th	2004	4th	2001	13th	1998	7th
2012	12th	2009	13th	2006	2nd	2003	6th	2000	2nd		
2011	11th	2008	9th	2005	9th	2002	4th	1999	6th		

ABSA CURRIE CUP LOG POSITIONS

Year	Pos	Year	Pos	Year	Pos	Year	Pos	Year	Pos	Year	Pos
2013	14th	2010	12th	2007	8th	2004	12th	2001	5th	1998	6th
2012	12th	2009	14th	2006	7th	2003	12th	2000	11th	1997	10th
2011	11th	2008	8th	2005	9th	2002	8th	1999	10th	1996	11th

2013 RESULTS & SCORERS

VODACOM CUP Played **7** Won **2** Drawn **0** Lost **5** Points for **139** Points against **269** Tries for **18** Tries against **42** Winning% **29%**

Date	Venue	Opponent	Result	Score	Referee	Scorers
Mrch 09	Nelspruit	Pumas	LOST	00-62	G de Bruin	
Mrch 15	Kempton Park	Golden Lions	WON	27-22	N Rocono	T: Engelbrecht (2), Hendricks. C: Roberts (3). P: J Kotze (2).
Mrch 22	Potchefstroom	Leopards	LOST	16-47	D van Heerden	T: Olivier. C: Roberts. P: Roberts (2). D: J Kotze.
April 06	Tzaneen	Limpopo	WON	69-07	S Geldenhuys	T: Mostert (4), Nokwe (2), Van Wyk, Cronje, Poley, Van Eeden, Powell. C: J Kotze (7).
April 13	Springs	Blue Bulls	LOST	14-74	L van der Merwe	T: J Kotze, Richter. C: J Kotze (2).
April 19	Welkom	Griffons	LOST	06-17	E Nel	P: J Kotze (2).
April 27	Kempton Park	Griquas	LOST	07-40	D van Heerden	T: Ngcobo. C: J Kotze.

ABSA CURRIE CUP Played **14** Won **2** Drawn **1** Lost **11** Points for **349** Points against **579** Tries for **45** Tries against **79** Winning% **14%**

Date	Venue	Opponent	Result	Score	Referee	Scorers
June 29	Kempton Park	Griffons	DREW	30-30	S Mayende	T: Odendaal, Nokwe, Richter. C: Roberts (3). P: Roberts (3).
July 05	Potchefstroom	Leopards	LOST	25-50	L Legoete	T: Odendaal, Richter, Kotze. C: Roberts {2}. P: Roberts (2).
July 12	Kempton Park	Eagles	LOST	37-38	R Rasivheng	T: Odendaal (3), Cronje, Kirkwood. C: Kotze (3). P: Kotze. D: Kotze.
July 19	Wellington	Cavaliers	LOST	07-20	M vd Westhuizen	T: Richter. C: Kotze.
July 26	Kempton Park	Bulldogs	WON	34-29	M Jonker	T: Cronje, Mostert, Bothma, De Bruin. C: Kotze (4). P: Kotze (2).
Aug 02	Brakpan	EP Kings	LOST	18-44	J Peyper	T: Roberts, Richter. C: Kotze. P: Kotze. D: Kotze.
Aug 10	Nelspruit	Pumas	LOST	12-69	T Jonker	T: Kotze, Gwavu. C: Kotze.
Aug 17	Welkom	Griffons	LOST	35-50	J Jaftha	T: Nokwe (2), Cronje, Odendaal. C: Kotze (2), Roos. P: Roos. D: Kotze (2).
Aug 24	Kempton Park	Leopards	LOST	27-38	R Rasivheng	T: Hendricks (2), Nokwe, Maritz. C: Hendricks, Roberts. P: Kotze.
Aug 30	George	Eagles	LOST	42-58	M Jonker	T: Hendricks, Cronje, Mostert, Muller, Du Rand, Penalty try. C: Kotze (6).
Sep 07	Kempton Park	Cavaliers	WON	28-21	Q Immelman	T: Muller (2), Odendaal, Kotze. C: Kotze. P: Kotze (2).
Sep 13	East London	Bulldogs	LOST	14-35	J van Heerden	T: Richter (2). C: Kotze (2).
Sep 20	Port Elizabeth	EP Kings	LOST	23-30	J Jaftha	T: Ngcobo, Oosthuizen. C: Hendricks (2). P: Hendricks (3).
Sep 27	Kempton Park	Pumas	LOST	17-67	L Jam	T: Mostert (2), Powell. C: Hendricks.

VALKE RUGBY UNION

VALKE SQUAD IN 2013 — VALKE CAREER

PLAYER	Appearances	Tries	Conversions	Penalties	Drop Goals	Points	Career Matches	Career Tries	Conversions	Penalties	Drop Goals	Points
GDJ (Jacques) Alberts	17	–	–	–	–	0	32	1	–	–	–	5
F (Franco) Booysen	1	–	–	–	–	0	39	6	–	–	–	30
RL (Rinus) Bothma	9	1	–	–	–	5	9	1	–	–	–	5
JG (JP) Brummer	3	–	–	–	–	0	4	–	–	–	–	0
CF (Coert) Cronje	20	6	–	–	–	30	57	26	–	–	–	130
JM (Johan) de Bruin	5	1	–	–	–	5	63	7	–	–	–	35
V (Vernon) du Preez	3	–	–	–	–	0	15	1	–	–	–	5
CW (Wessel) du Rand	12	1	–	–	–	5	12	1	–	–	–	5
NJE (Nico) Engelbrecht	11	2	–	–	–	10	46	6	–	–	–	30
FP (Francois) Fourie	13	–	–	–	–	0	13	–	–	–	–	0
W (Willem) Greyvenstein	1	–	–	–	–	0	1	–	–	–	–	0
LV (Vincent) Gwavu	14	1	–	–	–	5	14	1	–	–	–	5
WR (Wayne) Havenga	1	–	–	–	–	0	4	–	–	–	–	0
K (Kyle) Hendricks	20	4	4	3	0	37	61	28	16	10	0	202
D (Devlin) Hope	1	–	–	–	–	0	1	–	–	–	–	0
G (Gido) Horn	1	–	–	–	–	0	18	2	11	5	0	47
C (Christo) Joubert	3	–	–	–	–	0	3	–	–	–	–	0
SM (Shane) Kirkwood	9	1	–	–	–	5	9	1	–	–	–	5
FA (Arafaat) Kock	7	–	–	–	–	0	8	–	–	–	–	0
J (Jaun) Kotze	21	4	31	11	5	130	42	8	66	27	6	271
SJP (Paul) Kruger	5	–	–	–	–	0	5	–	–	–	–	0
JB (Johann) Louw	2	–	–	–	–	0	2	–	–	–	–	0
GCF (Franco) Maritz	4	1	–	–	–	5	4	1	–	–	–	5
SS (Shaun) McGeer	9	–	–	–	–	0	9	–	–	–	–	0
J-PF (JP) Mostert	18	8	–	–	–	40	20	8	–	–	–	40
B (Bruce) Muller	12	3	–	–	–	15	18	4	–	–	–	20
R-H (Reg) Muller	1	–	–	–	–	0	72	26	–	–	–	130
SC (Stix) Ngcobo	17	2	–	–	–	10	30	6	–	–	–	30
JL (Jongi) Nokwe	14	6	–	–	–	30	14	6	–	–	–	30
WA (Willie) Odendaal	18	6	–	–	–	30	63	14	–	–	–	70
F (Friedle) Olivier	9	1	–	–	–	5	9	1	–	–	–	5
J (Jaco) Oosthuizen	5	1	–	–	–	5	16	4	–	–	–	20
AP (Arno) Poley	12	1	–	–	–	5	43	3	1	–	1	20
AH (Birtie) Powell	17	2	–	–	–	10	22	2	–	–	–	10
N (Nico) Pretorius	17	–	–	–	–	0	53	1	–	–	–	5
A (Anrich) Richter	21	7	–	–	–	35	43	15	–	–	–	75
WA (Wesley) Roberts	15	1	10	7	0	46	15	1	10	7	0	46
JC (JC) Roos	1	0	1	1	0	5	1	0	1	1	0	5
S (Stefan) Schoeman	7	–	–	–	–	0	7	–	–	–	–	0
JP (Jaco) Snyman	6	–	–	–	–	0	46	8	–	–	–	40
DPJ (Dauw) Steyn	3	–	–	–	–	0	3	–	–	–	–	0
BTR (Brendan) Tshoshane	5	–	–	–	–	0	5	–	–	–	–	0
D (Dandre) vd Westhuizen	10	–	–	–	–	0	14	–	–	–	–	0
MP (Marco) van Eeden	17	1	–	–	–	5	17	1	–	–	–	5
JCB (Baksteen) van Heerden	5	–	–	–	–	0	9	1	–	–	–	5
RS (Russell) van Wyk	11	1	–	–	–	5	11	1	–	–	–	5
TJ (Jacques) Verwey	12	–	–	–	–	0	12	–	–	–	–	0
47 players	445	62	46	22	5	483	1014	192	105	50	7	1341

valke@global.co.za

APPEARANCES & POINTS IN VODACOM CUP 2013

	Pumas	Golden Lions	Leopards	Limpopo	Blue Bulls	Griffons	Griquas	Matches	Tries	Conversions	Penalties	Drop Goals	Points
Kyle Hendricks	15	15	15	–	15	11	11	6	1	–	–	–	5
Arno Poley	14	14	14	11	11	11R	15R	7	1	–	–	–	5
Coert Cronje	13	13	–	13	13	13	13	6	1	–	–	–	5
Willie Odendaal	12c	12c	12c	12c	12c	12c	12c	7	–	–	–	–	0
Jongi Nokwe	11	11	11	14	14	–	–	5	2	–	–	–	10
Wesley Roberts	10	10	10	–	–	10R	10R	5	–	4	2	–	14
Anrich Richter	9	9	9	14R	9	9	9	7	1	–	–	–	5
MP van Eeden	8	6	6	6	6	6	6	7	1	–	–	–	5
Friedle Olivier	7	7	8	4R	6R	4R	8R	7	1	–	–	–	5
Vincent Gwavu	6	–	–	–	7	7	7	4	–	–	–	–	0
Jacques Alberts	5	5	5	5	5	5	5	7	–	–	–	–	0
Shaun McGeer	4	5R	8R	4	5R	5R	1R	7	–	–	–	–	0
Nico Pretorius	3	3	3R	3	3	3	–	6	–	–	–	–	0
Baksteen van Heerden	2	2	2	2R	1R	–	–	5	–	–	–	–	0
Nico Engelbrecht	1	1	3	–	–	3R	3	5	2	–	–	–	10
JP Brummer	2R	2R	1R	–	–	–	–	3	–	–	–	–	0
Stefan Schoeman	1R	3R	1	1	1	1	1	7	–	–	–	–	0
Paul Kruger	4R	4R	4	5R	4R	–	–	5	–	–	–	–	0
Francois Fourie	7R	4	7	7	4	4	4	7	–	–	–	–	0
Johann Louw	9R	–	–	9R	–	–	–	2	–	–	–	–	0
Jaun Kotze	10R	10R	10R	10	10	10	10	7	1	10	4	1	40
Russell van Wyk	15R	11R	11R	15	11R	15	15	7	1	–	–	–	5
Fredericque Kock	–	15R	–	9	–	15R	9R	4	–	–	–	–	0
Reg Muller	–	8	–	–	–	–	–	1	–	–	–	–	0
Franco Booysen	–	–	13	–	–	–	–	1	–	–	–	–	0
Wayne Havenga	–	–	6R	–	–	–	–	1	–	–	–	–	0
Sandile Ngcobo	–	–	14R	11R	14R	14	14	5	1	–	–	–	5
JP Mostert	–	–	–	8	8	8	8	4	4	–	–	–	20
Birtie Powell	–	–	–	2	2	2	2	4	1	–	–	–	5
Vernon du Preez	–	–	–	6R	2R	x	2R	3	–	–	–	–	0
Willem Greyvenstein	–	–	–	–	–	–	3R	1	–	–	–	–	0
31 Players								**153**	**18**	**14**	**6**	**1**	**139**

VALKE RUGBY UNION

APPEARANCES & POINTS IN ABSA CURRIE CUP 2013

Player	Griffons	Leopards	Eagles	Cavaliers	Bulldogs	EP Kings	Pumas	Griffons	Leopards	Eagles	Cavaliers	Bulldogs	EP Kings	Pumas	Matches	Tries	Conversions	Penalties	Drop Goals	Points
Kyle Hendricks	15	15	15	15	14	14	14R	15	15	15	15	15	15	14	14	3	4	3	0	32
Arno Poley	14	14	–	–	–	–	14	–	–	–	11	11	–	–	5	–	–	–	–	0
Coert Cronje	13	13	13	13	13	13	13	13	13	13	13	13	13	13	14	5	–	–	–	25
Willie Odendaal	12	12	12	12	12	–	–	12R	12	12	12	–	12	12	11	6	–	–	–	30
Jongi Nokwe	11	11	–	–	–	11R	11	11	11	11	–	14R	11	–	9	4	–	–	–	20
Wesley Roberts	10	10	10R	15R	15	15	15	–	10R	11R	10R	–	–	–	10	1	6	5	0	32
Anrich Richter	9	9	9	9	9	9	11R	9	9	9R	9R	9	9R	11	14	6	–	–	–	30
JP Mostert	8c	8c	8c	8c	8c	8c	5c	8c	8c	5c	5c	5c	8c	7c	14	4	–	–	–	20
Jacques Verwey	7	7	6	6	7	–	8	7	–	7	7	7	7	6	12	–	–	–	–	0
Vince Gwavu	6	6	–	–	–	–	8R	6	6	6	6	6	6	8R	10	1	–	–	–	5
Rinus Bothma	5	5	5	5	5	5	–	–	–	–	–	8R	5	5	9	1	–	–	–	5
Shane Kirkwood	4	4	4	4	–	–	–	–	4	4	4	4	4	4	9	1	–	–	–	5
Dandre vd Westhuizen	3	1	1	3	x	3R	3	3	x	3R	3	3R	–	–	10	–	–	–	–	0
Birtie Powell	2	2	2	2	2R	2	2	2	2	2	2	2	–	2	13	1	–	–	–	5
Wessel du Rand	1	–	–	1	1	1R	1	1	3	6R	3R	3	3R	1	12	1	–	–	–	5
Bruce Muller	7R	2R	2R	x	2	6	6	–	1R	1	1	1	2	3R	12	3	–	–	–	15
Nico Pretorius	1R	3	3	3R	3	3	1R	1R	–	3	–	–	3	3	11	–	–	–	–	0
Nico Engelbrecht	3R	3R	3R	–	3R	1	3R	–	–	–	–	–	–	–	6	–	–	–	–	0
Jacques Alberts	5R	–	7R	x	7R	5R	4	5	5	4R	–	x	7R	4R	10	–	–	–	–	0
Arafaat Kock	x	–	9R	x	x	9R	9	–	–	–	–	–	–	–	3	–	–	–	–	0
Jaun Kotze	14R	10R	10	10	10	10	10	10	10	10	10	10	14R	15	14	3	21	7	4	90
Russell van Wyk	x	14R	14	14	–	–	–	–	–	–	–	–	–	9R	4	–	–	–	–	0
Bovril de Bruin	–	6R	7	7	4	4	–	–	–	–	–	–	–	–	5	1	–	–	–	5
Marco van Eeden	–	7R	5R	4R	6	–	–	7	8	8	8	5R	8	–	10	–	–	–	–	0
Sandile Ngcobo	–	22R	11	11	11	11	–	14	14	14	14	14	14	15R	12	1	–	–	–	5
Dauw Steyn	–	–	11R	–	–	–	–	–	–	–	–	–	15R	12R	3	–	–	–	–	0
Johan van Heerden	–	–	–	x	–	–	–	–	–	–	–	–	–	–	0	–	–	–	–	0
Francois Fourie	–	–	–	–	6R	7	7	4	4	8R	x	–	–	–	6	–	–	–	–	0
Gido Horn	–	–	–	–	12R	–	–	–	–	–	–	–	–	–	1	–	–	–	–	0
Christo Joubert	–	–	–	–	–	12	12	15R	–	–	–	–	–	–	3	–	–	–	–	0
Shaun McGeer	–	–	–	–	–	7R	–	4R	x	–	x	–	–	–	2	–	–	–	–	0
Jaco Oosthuizen	–	–	–	–	–	12R	–	–	–	–	11R	12	10	10	5	1	–	–	–	5
Friedle Olivier	–	–	–	–	–	7R	5R	x	–	–	–	–	–	–	2	–	–	–	–	0
Franco Maritz	–	–	–	–	–	12R	12	13R	x	–	12R	–	–	–	4	1	–	–	–	5
Brendan Tshoshane	–	–	–	–	–	–	3R	1	–	8R	2R	1	–	–	5	–	–	–	–	0
JC Roos	–	–	–	–	–	–	11R	–	–	–	–	–	–	–	1	–	1	1	–	5
Jaco Snyman	–	–	–	–	–	–	–	9R	9	9	9R	9	9	–	6	–	–	–	–	0
Ian Oosthuizen	–	–	–	–	–	–	–	–	–	–	–	x	–	–	0	–	–	–	–	0
Devlin Hope	–	–	–	–	–	–	–	–	–	–	–	–	16R	–	1	–	–	–	–	0
Penalty try	–	–	–	–	–	–	–	–	–	–	–	–	–	–	–	1	–	–	–	5
39 Players															**292**	**45**	**32**	**16**	**4**	**349**

valke@global.co.za

VALKE RUGBY UNION

ABSA UNDER-21 CHAMPIONSHIP (6th, Section B)

Played	Won	Drawn	Lost	Points for	Points against	Tries for	Tries against	Winning %
7	2	0	5	156	316	24	47	29%

RESULTS: Lost Griffons (a) 30-32. Lost Griquas (h) 28-39. Bt SWD (a) 36-22. Lost Boland (h) 8-69. Lost Limpopo (a) 10-48. Lost EP (a) 17-87. Bt Pumas (h) 27-19.

SCORERS: 40 Friedle Olivier (8t); 24 Deon Hendrikz (1t,2c,4p,1d); 12 Ruben Smith (2t,1c); 11 Kazlo Holtzhausen (4c,1p); 10 Ernst Behr, Maxwell Sehoole, Adriaan van den Berg (2t each); 5 Gary Woolls, John Spence, JP Brummer, Juan van der Merwe, Mandla Mdaka, Daymin Jansen van Vuuren, Fanie Raseroka (1t each); 4 Paul Walters (2c).

ABSA U19 CHAMPIONSHIP (Runner-up, 1st, Section B)

Played	Won	Drawn	Lost	Points for	Points against	Tries for	Tries against	Winning %
9	8	0	1	336	231	44	28	89%

RESULTS: Bt Griffons (a) 51-27. Bt Griquas (h) 31-20. Bt SWD (a) 50-20. Bt Boland (h) 41-24. Bt Limpopo (a) 32-18. Bt EP (a) 41-39. Bt Pumas (h) 21-3. SEMI FINAL Bt SWD (h) 29-24. FINAL Lost EP (a) 40-56.

SCORERS: 126 Matthys Venter (2t,34c,14p,2d); 45 Francwa Ueckermann (9t); 35 Elden Schoeman (7t); 25 Charlton Anderson (5t); 20 Jaques Malan (4t); 15 Dominic Cloete, Willem Smith, Andries Schutte (3t each); 10 Divan Binneman, Jean-Claude van Zyl (2t each); 5 Ruben Faber, Wietsse Botes, Ruan Ernst, Marthinus Ueckermann, Penalty try (1t each).

AMATEUR CHAMPIONSHIP

Valke (North Section, Pretoria)

Played	Won	Drawn	Lost	Points for	Points against	Winning %
3	1	0	2	52	105	33%

RESULTS: Bt Limpopo 31-18. Lost Lions 6-35. Lost Leopards 15-52.

SUB-UNION CHAMPIONSHIP (Winner, Northern Unions, Kempton Park)

Played	Won	Drawn	Lost	Points for	Points against	Winning %
3	3	0	0	90	66	100%

RESULTS: Bt Limpopo Blue Bulls 44-40. Bt Leopards 22-8. Bt Golden Lions 24-18.

VALKE RECORDS

MATCH RECORDS

Biggest win	109-0	vs. Vagabonds	1998
Biggest Currie Cup win	65-15	vs. North West	1999
Heaviest defeat	3-151	vs. Western Province	1995
Heaviest Currie Cup defeat	14-95	vs. Pumas	2009
Highest score	109	vs. Vagabonds (109-0)	1998
Most points conceded	151	vs. Western Province (3-151)	1995
Most points conceded (CC)	95	vs. Pumas (14-95)	2009
Most tries	17	vs. Vagabonds	1998
Most Currie Cup tries	11	vs. Griquas	2001
	11	vs. Griffons	2003
Most points by a player	33	A de Kock vs. Eastern Orange Free State	1994
	33	A de Kock vs. Namibia	1995
Most Currie Cup points by a player	27	G Peens vs. Border	1997
Most tries by a player	4	C van Zyl vs. North West Cape	1980
	4	P Hiten vs. Curda	1986
	4	D Nortje vs. Eastern Orange Free State	1989
	4	W Geyer vs. Northern Free State	1998
	4	W Geyer vs. Blue Bulls	1998
	4	J Houtsamer vs. Mighty Elephants	2001
	4	LD Lubbe vs. Griffons	2003
	4	G Mbangeni vs. Leopards	2004
	4	JP Mostert vs Limpopo	2013

SEASON RECORDS

Most team points	884	35 matches	1998
Most Currie Cup points by team	393	14 matches	2012
Most points by a player	277	J Viljoen	1996
Most Currie Cup points by a player	158	Louis Strydom	2005
Most team tries	118	35 matches	1998
Most Currie Cup tries by team	56	14 matches	2012
Most tries by a player	22	W Geyer	1998
Most Currie Cup tries by a player	10	LD Lubbe	1989
	10	E Botha	2001

CAREER RECORDS

Most appearances	158	E Rossouw	1997-2004
Most points	732	H Labuschagne	
Most tries	55	L Lubbe	

HONOURS

Vodacom Cup	2006

WESTERN PROVINCE RFU

W.P. RUGBY

FOUNDED
1883
GROUND
Newlands
CAPACITY
49 000
ADDRESS
11 Boundary Road, Newlands
POSTAL ADDRESS
PO Box 66, Newlands 7725
TELEPHONE NUMBER
021-659 4500
WEBSITE
www.wprugby.com
COLOURS
Royal blue & white hoops, black shorts & socks
CURRIE CUP COACH
Allister Coetzee
VODACOM CUP COACH
John Dobson
CAPTAIN
Deon Fourie
PRESIDENT
Thelo Wakefield
COMPANY MD
Rob Wagner
UNION CEO
Theuns Roodman

Cup loss takes gloss off season

D**HL WESTERN PROVINCE WENT THROUGH THE LEAGUE** stage of the Absa Currie Cup undefeated, winning eight matches and drawing two, before beating the MTN Golden Lions 33-16 in their semi-final. But that counted for little when they lost 33-19 in the final at Newlands, to a Sharks team they had beaten 17-13 in Durban a fortnight earlier to top the log.

Coach Allister Coetzee said afterwards that Province had not expected the Sharks to play direct rugby with a big focus on tactical kicking, which was an indictment on him and his coaching team.

The Sharks had made good use of the boot all season, and their chip kicks in behind WP's midfield ruck and high balls on WP's smaller backs, Cheslin Kolbe and Gio Aplon, were poorly dealt with. The hosts also struggled at the lineouts and their failure to control the restarts cost them momentum and points.

There was a lot of talk going into the final about how Province would cope with the pressure of playing in front of an expectant home crowd. The DHL Stormers had lost their last two play-off matches at Newlands, in 2011 and 2012, and WP, in 2013, had a chance to prove they could handle the favourites' tag. It was one they didn't take, as they once again lost the mental battle.

While WP did not retain their title, a number of their players used the Currie Cup to enhance their reputations. Damian de Allende kept Springbok centre Juan de Jongh out of the starting XV, Kolbe was a constant threat on the wing with ball in hand, and Aplon's good form saw him force his way back into the Springbok squad for their end-of-year tour, where he was joined by uncapped hooker Scarra Ntubeni. Captain and flank Deon Fourie had another excellent season and was named WP's Player of the Year, while Bok flank Schalk Burger returned after an 18-month injury and illness-enforced absence, coming off the bench in WP's last five matches of the tournament.

Flyhalf Demetri Catrakilis, back in the Cape after a Super Rugby stint with the Kings, played an important part in WP's wins against the Sharks in Durban and in the semi-final against the Lions, while Kurt Coleman did well for the senior side when given the opportunity.

Coleman wore the No 10 jersey for WP during their Vodacom Cup campaign earlier in the year, which ended with the defending champions losing 44-25 to the Golden Lions in the semi-finals.

Unfortunately for Province, there was more play-off pain to come.

BY SIMON BORCHARDT,
SA RUGBY MAGAZINE

Cheslin Kolbe was a revelation for WP during the Currie Cup. *Carl Fourie/Gallo Images*

WESTERN PROVINCE RFU

VODACOM CUP LOG POSITIONS

2013	4th	2010	7th	2007	1st	2004	11th	2001	6th	1998	10th
2012	1st	2009	7th	2006	7th	2003	10th	2000	6th		
2011	3rd	2008	3rd	2005	5th	2002	14th	1999	10th		

ABSA CURRIE CUP LOG POSITIONS

2013	1st	2010	2nd	2007	5th	2004	2nd	2001	4th	1998	4th
2012	3rd	2009	2nd	2006	3rd	2003	3rd	2000	2nd	1997	1st
2011	4th	2008	5th	2005	3rd	2002	5th	1999	11th	1996	5th

2013 RESULTS & SCORERS

VODACOM CUP Played **9** Won **6** Drawn **1** Lost **2** Points for **254** Points against **210** Tries for **30** Tries against **27** Winning Percentage **67%**

Date	Venue	Opponent	Result	Score	Referee	Scorers
Mrch 09	Ceres	Boland	DREW	17-17	J Sylvestre	T: Cloete, Williams, Reyneke. C: Van Aswegen.
Mrch 16	Cape Town [1]	Sharks XV	LOST	23-24	M Kemp	T: Van der Spuy, Smid. C: Van Aswegen (2). P: Van Aswegen (2). DG: Van Aswegen
Mrch 22	Port Elizabeth	EP Kings	WON	43-18	P Legoete	T: Cloete (3), Kolbe, Botha. C: Swiel (3). P: Van Aswegen (3). DG: Van Aswegen.
April 06	Paarl	Border	WON	22-13	J Sylvestre	T: Cloete, Williams, Reyneke. C: Coleman (2). P: Coleman.
April 13	Cape Town	Pampas XV	WON	28-17	P J van Vuuren	T: Howard (2), Notshe, Swiel. C: Leyds. P: Leyds. DG: Swiel
April 20	Strand	SWD	WON	34-27	J Jaftha	T: Notshe, Smid, Van der Spuy, Van Wyk. C: Coleman (4). P: Coleman (2).
April 27	Bloemfontein	Free State XV	WON	41-37	M Jonker	T: Klaasen (2), Kolbe, Van Wyk, Van der Spuy. C: Coleman (5). P: Coleman (2).
Quarter-final						
May 04	Cape Town	Griquas	WON	21-13	S Mayende	T: Kolbe (2). C: Coleman. P: Coleman (3).
Semi-final						
May 11	Johannesburg	Golden Lions	LOST	25-44	M Jonker	T: Swiel, Van Wyk. P: Coleman (5).

[1] City Park, Crawford.

ABSA CURRIE CUP Played **12** Won **9** Lost **1** Drawn **2** Points for **297** Points against **250** Tries for **26** Tries against **24** Winning Percentage **75%**

Date	Venue	Opponent	Result	Score	Referee	Scorers
Aug 10	Cape Town	Blue Bulls	DREW	24-24	R Rasivhenge	T: Aplon, Carr, Howard. C: Van Aswegen (3). P: Van Aswegen.
Aug 17	Cape Town	Free State	WON	15-14	J Kaplan	T: Fourie, Rhodes. C: Van Aswegen. P: Van Aswegen.
Aug 24	Kimberley	Griquas	WON	20-19	S Mayende	T: Fourie, de Jongh. C: Coleman (2). P: Coleman (2).
Aug 30	Johannesburg	Golden Lions	DREW	31-31	J Peyper	T: Kolbe, de Allende, Liebenberg. C: Coleman (2). P: Coleman (4).
Sep 07	Cape Town	Sharks	WON	25-19	C Joubert	T: Kolbe, Aplon, De Jongh. C: Van Aswegen, Coleman. P: Coleman (2).
Sep 14	Pretoria	Blue Bulls	WON	29-18	M Jonker	T: De Allende, Aplon. C: Coleman (2). P: Coleman (3), Van Aswegen (2).
Sep 20	Cape Town	Griquas	WON	19-13	L vd Merwe	T: Groom. C: Coleman. P: Coleman (3), Catrakilis.
Sep 27	Bloemfontein	Free State	WON	29-27	M Jonker	T: Kolbe, Rhodes. C: Coleman, Catrakilis. P: Coleman (3), Catrakilis. DG: Catrakilis.
Oct 05	Cape Town	Golden Lions	WON	36-23	S Berry	T: De Allende, Fourie, Van den Heever, Rhodes. C: Catrakilis (2). P: Catrakilis (3), Coleman.
Oct 12	Durban	Sharks	WON	17-13	J Kaplan	T: Fourie. P: Catrakilis (3). DG: Catrakilis.
Semi-final						
Oct 19	Cape Town	Golden Lions	WON	33-16	M Jonker	T: Catrakilis, Aplon. C: Catrakilis. P: Catrakilis (5), Coleman (2).
Final						
Oct 26	Cape Town	Sharks	LOST	19-33	J Kaplan	T: De Allende. C: Catrakilis. P: Catrakilis (3), Coleman.

WESTERN PROVINCE RFU

WESTERN PROVINCE SQUAD IN 2013 | WP CAREER

PLAYER	Appearances	Tries	Conversions	Penalties	Drop Goals	Points	Career Matches	Career Tries	Conversions	Penalties	Drop Goals	Points
GG (Gio) Aplon	12	4	–	–	–	20	95	32	2	–	–	164
E (Ederies) Arendse	1	–	–	–	–	0	15	5	–	–	–	25
DW (Don) Armand	1	–	–	–	–	0	19	1	–	–	–	5
R (Ruan) Botha	1	1	–	–	–	5	1	1	–	–	–	5
MG (Marcel) Brache	5	–	–	–	–	0	44	6	–	–	–	30
SWP (Schalk) Burger	5	–	–	–	–	0	37	7	–	–	–	35
N (Nizaam) Carr	9	1	–	–	–	5	17	1	–	–	–	5
D (Demetri) Catrakilis	6	1	5	16	2	69	40	1	66	111	8	494
PM (Pat) Cilliers	12	–	–	–	–	0	12	–	–	–	–	0
CA (Chris) Cloete	4	5	–	–	–	25	4	5	–	–	–	25
SH (Stephan) Coetzee	8	–	–	–	–	0	8	–	–	–	–	0
KC (Kurt) Coleman	17	–	21	34	–	144	39	6	31	39	–	209
JHJ (Bolla) Conradie	7	–	–	–	–	0	7	–	–	–	–	0
D (Damian) de Allende	12	4	–	–	–	20	24	6	–	–	–	30
JL (Juan) de Jongh	7	2	–	–	–	10	29	14	–	–	–	70
J (Jean) de Villiers	3	–	–	–	–	0	50	30	–	–	–	150
HC (Carel) du Preez	3	–	–	–	–	0	3	–	–	–	–	0
R (Rynhardt) Elstad	7	–	–	–	–	0	24	–	–	–	–	0
E (Eben) Etzebeth	3	–	–	–	–	0	6	–	–	–	–	0
HMS (Hendrik) Ferreira	6	–	–	–	–	0	6	–	–	–	–	0
DA (Deon) Fourie	10	4	–	–	–	20	90	22	–	–	–	110
MG (Mthetheleli) Fuzani	9	–	–	–	–	0	9	–	–	–	–	0
DG (Gerbrandt) Grobler	14	–	–	–	–	0	15	–	–	–	–	0
NJ (Nic) Groom	12	1	–	–	–	5	49	7	–	–	–	35
J (Brok) Harris	14	–	–	–	–	0	109	14	–	–	–	70
C (Chris) Heiberg	7	–	–	–	–	0	7	–	–	–	–	0
PB (Patrick) Howard	11	3	–	–	–	15	14	3	–	–	–	15
VT (Vincent) Jobo	1	–	–	–	–	0	1	–	–	–	–	0
JM (Josh) Katzen	2	–	–	–	–	0	2	–	–	–	–	0
R (Rohan) Kitshoff	7	–	–	–	–	0	22	7	–	–	–	35
S (Steven) Kitshoff	12	–	–	–	–	0	32	1	–	–	–	5
JAG (James) Kilroe	1	–	–	–	–	0	1	–	–	–	–	0
BW (Berton) Klaasen	10	2	–	–	–	10	24	–	–	–	–	0
GP (Graham) Knoop	3	–	–	–	–	0	3	–	–	–	–	0
C (Cheslin) Kolbe	19	7	–	–	–	35	19	7	–	–	–	35
S (Siya) Kolisi	3	–	–	–	–	0	23	5	–	–	–	25
HW (Helmut) Lehman	1	–	–	–	–	0	8	–	–	–	–	0
DY (Dillyn) Leyds	2	–	1	1	–	5	2	–	1	1	–	5
CR (Tiaan) Liebenberg	3	1	–	–	–	5	61	6	–	–	–	30
JF (Frans) Malherbe	4	–	–	–	–	0	33	–	–	–	–	0
GHD (Godlen) Masimla	9	–	–	–	–	0	9	–	–	–	–	0
JA (Cobus) Nel	4	–	–	–	–	0	4	–	–	–	–	0
RD (Ryan) Nell	2	–	–	–	–	0	2	–	–	–	–	0
S (Sikumbuzo) Notshe	9	2	–	–	–	10	9	2	–	–	–	10
S (Scarra) Ntubeni	12	–	–	–	–	0	32	1	–	–	–	5
R (Ryan) Olivier	2	–	–	–	–	0	2	–	–	–	–	0
M (Micheal) Poppmeier	2	–	–	–	–	0	2	–	–	–	–	0
JT (Jody) Reynecke	6	2	–	–	–	10	6	2	–	–	–	10
MK (Michael) Rhodes	11	3	–	–	–	15	11	3	–	–	–	15
D (Dylan) Rogers	3	–	–	–	–	0	3	–	–	–	–	0
L (Louis) Schreuder	12	–	–	–	–	0	44	3	–	–	–	15
RD (Ricky) Schroeder	1	–	–	–	–	0	7	–	–	–	–	0
R (Rayn) Smid	10	2	–	–	–	10	10	2	–	–	–	10
M de K (De Kock) Steenkamp	12	–	–	–	–	0	62	1	–	–	–	5
TG (Tim) Swiel	9	2	3	–	1	19	9	2	3	–	1	19
GJ (Gary) van Aswegen	7	–	8	9	2	49	13	–	16	16	2	86
GJ (Gerhard) van den Heever	12	1	–	–	–	5	24	3	–	–	–	15

WESTERN PROVINCE RFU

WESTERN PROVINCE SQUAD IN 2013 — WP CAREER

PLAYER	Appearances	Tries	Conversions	Penalties	Drop Goals	Points	Career Matches	Career Tries	Conversions	Penalties	Drop Goals	Points
W (Wilhelm) van der Sluys	5	—	—	—	—	0	19	—	—	—	—	0
MG (Michael) van der Spuy	13	3	—	—	—	15	24	5	—	—	—	25
FD (Francois) van Wyk	2	—	—	—	—	0	2	—	—	—	—	0
JP (Kobus) van Wyk	5	3	—	—	—	15	5	3	—	—	—	15
DJ (Duane) Vermeulen	3	—	—	—	—	0	38	7	—	—	—	35
AD (Ashley) Wells	8	—	—	—	—	0	8	—	—	—	—	0
ME (Michael) Willemse	6	—	—	—	—	0	6	—	—	—	—	0
DF (Devon) Williams	8	2	—	—	—	10	8	2	—	—	—	10
65 players	447	56	38	60	5	551	1363	223	119	167	11	1887

APPEARANCES & POINTS IN VODACOM CUP 2013

Player	Boland	Sharks XV	EP Kings	Border	Pampas XV	SWD Eagles	Free State XV	Griquas QF	Golden Lions SF	Matches	Tries	Conversions	Penalties	Drop Goals	Points
Cheslin Kolbe	15	15	11	15	—	15	15	15	—	7	4	—	—	—	20
Patrick Howard	14	14	14	14	14	14	14	14	—	9	2	—	—	—	10
Berton Klaasen	13	13	13	13	12R	12	13	13	13	9	2	—	—	—	10
Michael van der Spuy	12	12R	13R	13R	13	13	12	—	12	8	3	—	—	—	15
Devon Williams	11	11	—	11	15	11	11	11	11	8	2	—	—	—	10
Kurt Coleman	10	—	10	10	—	10	10	10	10	7	—	12	13	—	63
Bolla Conradie	9c	9	9R	9R	9	—	9	—	9c	7	—	—	—	—	0
Rayn Smid	8	8	8	8	8	8	8	8	8	9	2	—	—	—	10
Sikumbuzo Notshe	7	5R	7	6R	6	6	6	8R	7R	9	2	—	—	—	10
Chris Cloete	6	6	6	6	—	—	—	—	—	4	5	—	—	—	25
Gerbrandt Grobler	5	5	5	—	—	5c	5	7	4	7	—	—	—	—	0
Ryan Olivier	4	4	—	—	—	—	—	—	—	2	—	—	—	—	0
Ashley Wells	3	1	1	—	1	1	1	1R	1	8	—	—	—	—	0
Stephan Coetzee	2	2	2	2	6R	—	2	2R	2	8	—	—	—	—	0
Dylan Rogers	1	3R	—	—	3R	—	—	—	—	3	—	—	—	—	0
Jody Reyneke	7R	2R	2R	2R	—	6R	—	—	2R	6	2	—	—	—	10
Hendrik Ferreira	3R	19R	—	—	—	5R	1R	1	3R	6	—	—	—	—	0
Vincent Jobo	6R	—	—	—	—	—	—	—	—	1	—	—	—	—	0
Carel du Preez	8R	—	—	—	7	—	7R	—	—	3	—	—	—	—	0
Godlen Masimla	9R	9R	9	9	13R	9	9R	9	9R	9	—	—	—	—	0
Gary van Aswegen	10R	10	10R	—	—	—	—	—	—	3	—	3	5	2	27
Tim Swiel	11R	11R	15	—	10	11R	15R	11R	15	8	2	3	—	1	19
Marcel Brache	—	12c	12c	12c	12c	—	—	12c	—	5	—	—	—	—	0
Don Armand	—	7	—	—	—	—	—	—	—	1	—	—	—	—	0
Chris Heiberg	—	3	—	1R	1R	3	3	3	3	7	—	—	—	—	0
Ruan Botha	—	—	4	—	—	—	—	—	—	1	1	—	—	—	5
Brok Harris	—	—	3	3	3	—	—	—	—	3	—	—	—	—	0
Michael Rhodes	—	—	7R	—	—	—	—	—	—	1	—	—	—	—	0
Francois van Wyk	—	—	1R	1	—	—	—	—	—	2	—	—	—	—	0
Cobus Nel	—	—	7R	7	7R	—	7	—	—	4	—	—	—	—	0
Michael Poppmeier	—	—	—	5	4R	—	—	—	—	2	—	—	—	—	0
Mthetheleli Fuzani	—	—	—	4	4	4	5R	4	4R	6	—	—	—	—	0
James Kilroe	—	—	—	5R	—	—	—	—	—	1	—	—	—	—	0
Kobus van Wyk	—	—	—	11R	—	12R	12R	12R	13R	5	3	—	—	—	15
Ederies Arendse	—	—	—	—	11	—	—	—	—	1	—	—	—	—	0
Wilhelm van der Sluys	—	—	—	—	5	4R	4	5	5	5	—	—	—	—	0
Michael Willemse	—	—	—	—	2	2	2R	2	—	4	—	—	—	—	0
Dillyn Leyds	—	—	—	—	11R	—	—	—	14R	2	—	1	1	—	5
Graham Knoop	—	—	—	—	—	7	—	4R	7	3	—	—	—	—	0
Ricky Schroeder	—	—	—	—	—	9R	—	x	—	1	—	—	—	—	0
Rohan Kitshoff	—	—	—	—	—	—	—	6	—	1	—	—	—	—	0
Helmut Lehmann	—	—	—	—	—	—	—	—	6	1	—	—	—	—	0
40 players										197	30	19	19	3	254

WESTERN PROVINCE RFU

APPEARANCES & POINTS IN ABSA CURRIE CUP 2013

	Blue Bulls	Free State	Griquas	Golden Lions	Sharks	Blue Bulls	Griquas	Free State	Golden Lions	Sharks	Golden Lions SF	Sharks F	Matches	Tries	Conversions	Penalties	Drop Goals	Points
Gio Aplon	15	15	15	15	15	15	15	15	15	15	15	15	12	4	–	–	–	20
Gerhard van den Heever	14	14	14	14	14	14	14	14	14	14	14	14	12	1	–	–	–	5
Patrick Howard	13	13	–	–	–	–	–	–	–	–	–	–	2	1	–	–	–	5
Damian de Allende	12	12	12	12	12	12	12	12	12	12	12	12	12	4	–	–	–	20
Cheslin Kolbe	11	11	11	11	11	11	11	11	11	11	11	11	12	3	–	–	–	15
Gary van Aswegen	10	10	–	–	10R	10R	–	–	–	–	–	–	4	–	5	4	–	22
Louis Schreuder	9	9	9	9R	9	9	9R	9R	9	9	9	9	12	–	–	–	–	0
Nizaam Carr	8	8	8	8	8	8	8	8	8	–	–	–	9	1	–	–	–	5
Rynhardt Elstadt	7	7	7	7	7	6	–	–	7	–	–	–	7	–	–	–	–	0
Deon Fourie	6c	6c	6c	6c	6c	–	–	6c	6c	6c	6c	6c	10	4	–	–	–	20
De Kock Steenkamp	5	5	5	5	5	5c	5c	5	5	5	5	5	12	–	–	–	–	0
Gerbrandt Grobler	4	4R	4R	4R	4R	8R	4R	x	–	–	–	–	7	–	–	–	–	0
Brok Harris	3	3	3R	1R	3R	3R	3R	x	3R	1R	6R	2R	11	–	–	–	–	0
Scarra Ntubeni	2	2	2	2R	2	2	2	2	2	2	2	2	12	–	–	–	–	0
Steven Kitshoff	1	1	1	1	1	1	1	1	1	1	1	1	12	–	–	–	–	0
Ross Geldenhuys	x	–	–	–	–	–	–	–	–	–	–	–	0	–	–	–	–	0
Pat Cilliers	3R	3R	3	3	3	3	3	3	3	3	3	3	12	–	–	–	–	0
Michael Rhodes	4R	4	4	4	4	7	–	7	4	x	5R	5R	10	3	–	–	–	15
Rohan Kitshoff	8R	x	8R	8R	6R	4R	6	–	–	–	–	–	6	–	–	–	–	0
Nick Groom	9R	9R	9R	9	9R	9R	9	9	9R	9R	9R	9R	12	1	–	–	–	5
Kurt Coleman	x	10R	10	10	10	10	10	10	10R	x	10R	10R	10	–	9	21	–	81
Berton Klaasen	11R	–	–	–	–	–	–	–	–	–	–	–	1	–	–	–	–	0
Ryan Nell	–	13R	x	–	–	–	–	–	14R	–	–	–	2	–	–	–	–	0
Tiaan Liebenberg	–	2R	2R	2	–	–	–	–	–	–	–	–	3	1	–	–	–	5
Juan de Jongh	–	–	13	13	13	13	13	–	–	–	14R	14R	7	2	–	–	–	10
Tim Swiel	–	–	x	15R	–	–	–	–	–	–	–	–	1	–	–	–	–	0
Michael van der Spuy	–	–	–	x	12R	12R	x	13	13	13	–	–	5	–	–	–	–	0
Michael Willemse	–	–	–	–	2R	2R	x	x	–	–	–	–	2	–	–	–	–	0
Mtheleli Fuzani	–	–	–	–	–	4	4	4	–	–	–	–	3	–	–	–	–	0
Rayn Smid	–	–	–	–	–	–	7	–	–	–	–	–	1	–	–	–	–	0
Demetri Catrakilis	–	–	–	–	–	–	10R	10R	10	10	10	10	6	1	5	16	2	69
Josh Katzen	–	–	–	–	–	–	6R	8R	x	–	–	–	2	–	–	–	–	0
Schalk Burger	–	–	–	–	–	–	–	4R	7R	7R	7R	7R	5	–	–	–	–	0
Frans Malherbe	–	–	–	–	–	–	–	–	1R	3R	3R	3R	4	–	–	–	–	0
Duane Vermeulen	–	–	–	–	–	–	–	–	8	8	8	8	3	–	–	–	–	0
Siya Kolisi	–	–	–	–	–	–	–	–	7	7	7	7	3	–	–	–	–	0
Eben Etzebeth	–	–	–	–	–	–	–	–	4	4	4	4	3	–	–	–	–	0
Jean de Villiers	–	–	–	–	–	–	–	–	13R	13	13	13	3	–	–	–	–	0
38 players													250	26	19	41	2	297

WESTERN PROVINCE RFU

ABSA UNDER-21 CHAMPIONSHIP (CHAMPIONS, 1st, Section A)

Played	Won	Drawn	Lost	Points for	Points against	Tries for	Tries against	Winning %
14	13	0	1	552	257	77	33	93,00%

RESULTS Lost Free State (a) 16-18. Bt Leopards (h) 55-10. Bt Blue Bulls (h) 14-06. Bt Border (h) 38-20. Bt KZN (h) 20-03. Bt Golden Lions (a) 53-26. Bt Free State (h) 32-13. Bt Leopards (a) 54-35. Bt Blue Bulls (a) 32-21. Bt Border (a) 74-12. Bt Golden Lions (h) 39-05. Bt KZN (a) 51-24. SEMI-FINAL Bt Golden Lions (h) 44-41. FINAL Bt Blue Bulls (h) 30-23.

SCORERS 180 Tim Swiel (5t, 46c, 20p, 1dg). 45 Graig Barry (9t). 42 Dillyn Leyds (4t, 8c, 2p). 40 Devon Williams (8t). 30 Pat Howard (6t). 25 Eital Bredenkamp, Justin Benn, Joshua Katzen (5t each). 20 Kobus van Wyk (4t). 15 Godlen Masimla, JP Lewis (3t each). 10 Carel du Preez, Frederik Nel, Johnny Kotze, Kyle Lombard, Rayn Smid, Stephan Coetzee (2t each). Justin Ackermann, Michael Willemse, Oliver Kebble, Sikumbuzo Notshe, Sithembiso Sithole, penalty try (1t each).

ABSA U19 CHAMPIONSHIP (5th, Section A)

Played	Won	Drawn	Lost	Points for	Points against	Tries for	Tries against	Winning %
12	4	1	7	301	289	41	39	33,00%

RESULTS Drew Free State (a) 18-18. Lost Leopards (h) 27-28. Lost Blue Bulls (h) 10-34. Bt Border (h) 69-00. Lost KZN (h) 19-25. Lost Golden Lions (a) 26-31. Bt Free State (h) 22-05. Bt Leopards (a) 45-36. Lost Blue Bulls (a) 16-46. Bt Border (a) 36-07. Lost Golden Lions (h) 13-21. Lost KZN (a) 00-38.

SCORERS 97 Chris Smith (1t, 25c, 13p, 1dg). 30 Pieter Schoonraad (6t). 24 Jason Worrall (4t, 2c). 20 Ramone Samuels (4t). 15 Steven Meiring (3t). 10 Chad Solomon, Chris Mouton, Luke van der Smit, Ruan Rossouw (2t each). 5 Attie van Rensburg, Devon Nash, Dewald Naudé, Gareth de Bruin, Jason Morris, Johan de Villiers, Jonathan Bredell, Joshua Moon, Liam Hendricks, Lindokuhle Mvelase-Julyan, Michael Hazner, Sebastian Negri, Sebastian Ferreira, Solomon Ferreira, Wesley Adonis (1t each).

WESTERN PROVINCE RECORDS

MATCH RECORDS

Biggest win	151-3	vs. Eastern Transvaal	1995
Biggest win (Currie Cup)	107-23	vs. South Western Districts	1996
Heaviest defeat	18-58	vs. Pumas	2002
Heaviest defeat (Currie Cup)	13-50	vs. Lions	2002
Highest score	151	vs. Eastern Transvaal (151-3)	1995
Highest score (Currie Cup)	107	vs. South Western Districts (107-23)	1996
Moist points conceded	62	vs. Griqualand West (26-62)	1998
Moist points conceded (Currie Cup)	66	vs. Transvaal	1992
Most tries	23	vs. Easten Transvaal (151-3)	1995
Most tries (Currie Cup)	17	vs. South Western Districts (107-23)	1996
Most points by a player	46	JT Stransky vs. Eastern Transvaal	1995
Most points by a player (Currie Cup)	33	C Rossouw vs. Blue Bulls	2003
Most tries by a player	6	S Berridge vs. Eastern Transvaal	1995
Most tries by a player (Currie Cup)	5	J Swart vs. Northern Free State	1996
	5	BJ Paulse vs. Falcons	1997
	5	ER Seconds vs. Griquas	2004
	5	A Bekker vs. Valke	2008
Most conversions by a player	18	JT Stransky vs. Eastern Transvaal	1995
Most conversions by a player (Currie Cup)	11	LJ Koen vs. South Western Districts	1996
Most penalties by a player (Currie Cup)	7	LR Sherrell vs. Northern Transvaal	1991
	7	NV Cilliers vs. Transvaal	1993
	7	C Rossouw vs. Falcons	2001
	7	AJJ van Straaten vs. Cheetahs	2001
Most drop goals by a player (Currie Cup)	4	L Rodriguez vs. Griqualand West	1950

SEASON RECORDS

Most team points	1357		31 matches	1997
Most team points (Currie Cup)	619		15 matches	1997
Most points by a player	391	NB Scholtz		1988
Most points by a player (Currie Cup)	227	NB Scholtz		1988
Most team tries	182		31 matches	1997
Most team tries (Currie Cup)	84		15 matches	1997
Most tries by a player	25	CJ du Plessis		1989
	25	J Swart		1997
Most tries by a player (Currie Cup)	19	CJ du Plessis		1989
Most conversions by a player	80	NB Scholtz		1989
Most penalties by a player	73	LR Sherrell		1991
Most drop goals by a player	5	NV Cilliers		1997

CAREER RECORDS

Most appearances	156	CP Strauss	1986-1995
Most points	1570	NB Scholtz (116 matches)	1982-1989
Most points (Currie Cup)	992	NB Scholtz	1982-1989
Most tries	95	NJ Burger	1982-1991
Most tries (Currie Cup)	70	BJ Paulse	1996-2007
Most conversions by a player	293	NB Scholtz	1982-1989
Most penalties by a player	256	NB Scholtz	1982-1989
Most drop goals by a player	12	NB Scholtz	1982-1989

HONOURS

Bankfin Currie Cup	1889, 1892, 1894, 1895, 1897, 1898, 1904, 1906, 1908, 1914, 1920, 1925, 1927, 1929, 1932 (shared), 1934 (shared), 1936, 1947, 1954, 1959, 1964, 1966, 1979 (shared), 1982, 1983, 1984, 1985, 1986, 1989 (shared), 1997, 2000, 2001, 2012
Vodacom Cup	2012
Lion Cup	1984, 1988, 1989
Bankfin Nite Series	1997

SECTION 7
CLUB & AMATEUR RUGBY

YOUTH WEEKS Review & Statistics **334**

CELL C COMMUNITY CUP Review & Statistics **346**

FNB VARSITY CUP Review & Statistics **349**

Note: Referees & Obituaries have moved to Section 8 & begin on pg 462 & 466 respectively.

Former Springbok teammates Adri Geldenhuys (head coach) and Danie Gerber celebrate GAP Despatch's inaugural Cell C Community Cup triumph at Outeniqua Park in George. Both men played for the club during their glory years. *Roger Sedris/ImageSA*

COCA-COLA CRAVEN WEEK

WP graduate top of the class

WESTERN PROVINCE PROVED TO be in a class of their own at the 2013 Youth Weeks as they won the unofficial finals at the Under-13 and Under-18 Coca-Cola Craven Weeks, the Coca-Cola Under-16 Grant Khomo Week as well as the LSEN Week.

WP's form at the flagship U18 tournament in Polokwane was particularly impressive as they advanced through the competition unbeaten with a series of emphatic victories.

The team began their campaign with an encouraging 40-24 victory against the Pumas, but the true sign of their class was their convincing 30-6 victory against the Blue Bulls in their second match – a game many thought had the potential to be a final.

This win booked WP's spot in the final match of the tournament against the Golden Lions. WP emulated this dominant showing in their final match against the Golden Lions despite the Johannesburg team showing their fighting spirit in the second half.

The Cape side opened up the scoring with two early penalties by in-form wing Grant Hermanus for a 6-0 lead. They continued to reap the rewards as they dominated territory and possession, which earned them two tries in quick succession by Thomas du Toit and Herschel Jantjies, and another penalty for a 23-0 lead. The pressure got to the Lions, with the team opting for a penalty goal minutes before half-time, which proved unsuccessful.

The Lions, however, clawed their way back into the game early in the second half with a well-worked try by Erwin Harris who took advantage of an overlap on attack. WP, however, inflated their lead to 30-7 with yet another try created by Hermanus, who danced his way through the defence to put his team on the front foot. But the Lions refused to lie down and ran in two late tries. WP's Daniel du Plessis, however, sealed the win with three minutes to spare as he scored his team's fifth try.

WP were equally impressive at the Coca-Cola Under-16 Grant Khomo Week and delivered a fantastic 50-12 victory against the Leopards in the opening match to kick off their successful campaign. They built on this form against EP for a 34-22 win, before beating the Blue Bulls 22-15 in the final match.

The team stamped their authority early on against the Blue Bulls and created two try-scoring chances in the opening minutes, but the Bulls' tenacious defence shut them out. The tables soon turned to attack as the Bulls scored two tries in quick succession to take a 12-0 lead. This, however, was short lived as Western Province right wing Moegamat Cassiem-February sprinted to the tryline in the 21st minute, which was supported by a second try minutes later by centre Taigh Schoor, to level the scores at 12-12 at the break.

A penalty by Blue Bulls flyhalf Eduard Fouche two minutes into the second half broke the deadlock and pushed the team into a 15-12 lead. But the arm-wrestle continued as WP scrumhalf Jondre Williams slotted over a tough penalty to leave the scores locked at 15-15 with 10 minutes to go.

The Cape team backed this up with a stunning try by Juandre Grobler whose dummy pass earned him a clear path to the tryline and a seven-point victory.

The same two provinces also battled it out in the grand finale of the Under-13 Craven Week, but a penalty four minutes from time secured Western Province's 11-10 victory. In the LSEN Week, Western Province defeated Eastern Cape 26-12 in the unofficial final.

SWD, meanwhile, took the honours at the Coca-Cola Under-18 Academy Week following victories against the Golden Lions, WP and Eastern Province.

COCA-COLA CRAVEN WEEK *RESULTS*

DAY ONE: JULY 08

Griquas (03) **17** – T: Dimitrio Tieties, Gideon Bruwer. C: Tieties (2). P: Tieties. **Zimbabwe** (13) **35** – T: Jabulani Mutukwa (2), Brendon Mandivenga, Munyaradzi Mashaya. C: Mandivenga (3). P: Mandivenga (3).
Border (17) **38** – T: Jedwyn Harty, Justin Hollis, Lungelo Gosa, Robert Lyons, Somila Jho. C: Simon Bolze (5). P: Bolze. **Namibia** (07) **20** – T: Justin Newman (2). C: Chris Arries (2). P: Arries (2).
WP (19) **40** – T: Daniel du Plessis (4), Dewald Naudé, Heinrich Buhr. C: Grant Hermanus (5). **Pumas** (17) **24** – T: Thulane Mkhonto, Odwa Nkunjana, Mauro Bucuchane, Jaco van Vuuren. C: Rowan Gouws (2).
Blue Bulls (17) **46** - T: Johan Linde (2), Jade Solomons, Ivan van Zyl, Hyron Andrews, Franco Naudé, penalty try. C: Van Zyl (4). P: Van Zyl. **KZN** (17) **22** - T: Ayron Schramm (2), Muziwandile Mazibuko. C: Tristan Tedder (2). P: Tedder.
Limpopo BB (14) **26** – T: J-P van Wyk (2), Mlungisi Ntimane, Andries Bruwer. C: Van Wyk (3). **Boland** (17) **31** – T: Hanro Liebenberg (2), Johan du Toit, Leolin Zas, Raylinn Philander. C: Ewan Adams (2), Zas.

DAY TWO: JULY 09

EP CD (21) **35** – T: Gordon-Wayne Plaatjes, Qhama Masiza, Robert Ball, Sintu Manjezi. C: Jason Vers (3). P: Vers (3). **Leopards** (05) **10** – T: Enrico Smith, Paul Hurn.
Griquas CD (36) **51** – T: Jonathan Steenkamp (4), Chris Oppermann (2), Abraham Burger, Hendrik Nel, Jasper Wiese. C: Pieter Toua (2), Lukas van Niekerk. **Border CD** (00) **00**
Valke (10) **37** – T: Marco Holmes (2), Cameron Rooi, Ruan Potgieter, Sampie Hearn. C: Potgieter (3). P: Potgieter. DG: Potgieter. **Griffons** (23) **37** – T: Gregan Hull (2), Mlumzana Nkala, Shaun Reynolds. C: Reynolds (4). P: Reynolds (3).
Golden Lions (20) **34** – T: Devon Henson, Gerdus van der Walt, Gunther Janse van Vuuren, Ralton October. C: Erwin Harris (4). P: Harris (2). **SWD** (15) **27** – T: Gene Wiilemse (2), Dewald Human, Geor Malan, Jayden Onkers. C: Malan.
EP (18) **21** – T: Luan Nieuwoudt, Malcolm Jaer. C: Theo Stapelberg. P: Stapelberg (3). **Free State** (15) **32** – T: Ox Nche, Paul Wipplinger, Stephan Rautenbach, Thamaha Maruping. C: Rautenbach (3). P: Rautenbach (2).

DAY THREE: JULY 10

Namibia (06) **27** – T: Johan Retief, Milaan van Wyk. C: Chris Arries. P: Arries (5). **Griquas** (05) **10** – T: Gerhard Holtzhausen, Luke Mason.
Limpopo BB (00) **05** – T: Saudevandre Rolls. **Zimbabwe** (15) **43** – T: Barend Moolman, Brendon Boshi, Brendon Mandivenga, Edo Chikwezvero, Jabulani Mutukwa, Tawanda Ngosi. C: Mandivenga (5). P: Mandivenga.
Boland (05) **19** – T: Ewan Adams, Mishaun Arendse, Tiaan Lambrechts. C: Leolin Zas (2). **Border** (22) **37** – T: Jedwyn Harty (3), Somila Jho (2), Nanelamandlane Tyali. C: Lungelo Gosa (2). P: Gosa.
KZN (06) 18 – T: Kelvin Elder, Kurt Webster. C: Webster. P: Webster (2). Pumas (13) 40 – T: Mauro Bucuchane (2), Mzwakhe Fransman, Willandré Kotenberg. C: Brandon Thomson (4). P: Thomson (4).
Blue Bulls (03) 06 – P: Jemeel Warnick (2). WP (13) 30 – T: Heinrich Buhr, Herschel Jantjies, Petrus Bothma. C: Grant Hermanus (3). P: Hermanus (3).

DAY FOUR: JULY 11

Leopards (40) **64** – T: Gopolang Molefe (2), Mick Carroll (2), Tiaan Bezuidenhout (2), Markus Coetzer, Paul Hurn, Thabo Chirwa. C: Coetzer (8). P: Coetzer. **CD** (00) **00**.
Valke (18) **44** – T: Darren de Bruin, Eldron van Rooyen, Marco Holmes, Marco van Vuuren, Pieter Jansen, Ruan Potgieter. C: Potgieter (4). P: Potgieter (2). **Griquas CD** (05) **24** – T: Abraham Burger (4). C: Pieter Toua (2).
Griffons (17) **26** – T: André van Vuuren, Roelof Scheepers. C: Shaun Reynolds (2). P: Reynolds (4). **EP CD** (07) **20** – T: Thomas Filmer, Robert Ball. C: Jason Vers (2). P: Vers (2).
EP (00) **14** – T: Erich de Jager, Johann van Niekerk. C: Theo Stapelberg (2). **SWD** (14) **40** – T: Duhan van der Merwe (2), Benjamin Jansen van Vuuren, Brandon Haas, Donovan van der Berg, J-P Coetzee. C: Dewald Human (5).
Free State (09) **19** – T: Andrew du Plessis. C: Stephan Rautenbach. P: Rautenbach (4). **Golden Lions** (11) **20** – T: Fernando Kermis. P: Erwin Harris (4), Gerdus van der Walt.

DAY FIVE: JULY 13

Limpopo BB (12) **36** – T: Adrian Maebane (3), Christopher Durow, Matjikinyane Molapo, Mlungisi Ntimane. C: Arno Maree (3). **EP CD** (34) **39** – T: Thomas Filmer (2), Jason Baggott, Sintu Manjezi, Tsepho Mabitsela. C: Jason Vers (4). P: Vers (2).
Boder CD (00) **05** – T: Thabang Rixi. **Griquas** (54) **94** – T: Johan Nel (3), Leon Becker (3), Gerhard Holtzhausen (2), Dimitrio Tieties (2), Doctor Booysen, Gideon Bruwer, Jacques van Zyl, Ryan de Wee. C: Tieties (10), Holtzhausen, Katlego Mabeleng.
Zimbabwe (10) **10** – T: Brendon Mandivenga. C: Mandivenga. P: Mandivenga. **Namibia** (19) **33** – T: Justin Newman (2), Chris Arries. C: Arries (3). P: Arries (4).
Border (07) **14** – T: Keegan Gray, Kewan Gibb. C: Gibb (2). **KZN** (42) **77** – T: Akhona Nela (2), Jean-Luc du Preez (2), Marcel Coetzee (2), Ayron Schramm, Daniel du Preez, Jaco Coetzee, Morné Joubert, Reece McHardy. C: Tristan Tedder (7), Kurt Webster (4).
Griquas CD (17) **17** – T: Jasper Wiese, Chris Oppermann. C: Pieter Toua (2). P: Toua. **Leopards** (19) **34** – T: Beyers van Sittert, Frederick Pretorius, Gideon van der Merwe, Gopolang Molefe, Paul Hurn. C: Markus Coetzer (3). P: Coetzer.
Griffons (20) **34** – T: André Jansen van Vuuren, Gregan Hull, Shane Grobler, Shaun Reynolds. C: Reynolds (3). P: Reynolds (2). **Boland** (22) **27** – T: Rohaan Adams (2), Martin van Wyk, Warren Williams. C: Leon Zas (2). P: Zas.
EP (18) **29** – T: Arno Lötter, Johann van Niekerk, Keanu Vers. C: Theo Stapelberg. P: Stapelberg (4). **Valke** (03) **18** – T: Ruan Potgieter, Sampie Hearn. C: Potgieter. P: Potgieter (2).
Blue Bulls (24) **29** – T: Eduan Keyter, Hyron Andrews, Ivan van Zyl, Jade Solomons, Justin Phillips. C: Van Zyl (2). **SWD** (20) **37** – T: Dewald Human, Duhan van der Merwe, Geor Malan, Nemo Roelofse. C: Human (4). P: Human (3).
Free State (19) **22** – T: EW Viljoen (2), Marius Louw. C: Stephan Rautenbach (2). P: Rautenbach. **Pumas** (16) **25** - T: Johan du Plooy. C: Brandon Thomson. P: Thomson (6).
WP (23) **45** – T: Daniël du Plessis, Dewald Naudé, Herschel Jantjies, Johan Vermeulen, Thomas du Toit. C: Grant Hermanus (4). P: Hermanus (4). **Golden Lions** (00) **29** – T: Erwin Harris, Johan Esterhuizen, S'busiso Nkosi, Sibongumusa Radebe. C: Harris (2), Radebe. P: Harris.

COCA-COLA-CRAVEN WEEK

ENRISTA BLUE BULLS U/18

No.	Name & Surname	School	Town	ID	Weight	Height
1	Xander van Wyk	Waterkloof	Pretoria	9504125123085	115	183
2	Francois Steyn	Affies	Pretoria	9506195027088	98	176
3	Johan van Wyk	Waterkloof	Pretoria	9501125013084	112	185
4	Hyron Andrews	Garsfontein	Pretoria	9507065124088	102	203
5	RG Snyman	Affies	Pretoria	9501295013088	113	205
6	Calvonn Allisson	Affies	Pretoria	9503235168089	110	194
7	PJ Toerien	Garsfontein	Pretoria	9602175053085	95	183
8	Salmon van Huyssteen	Affies	Pretoria	9603035013087	86	188
9	Justin Phillips	Waterkloof	Pretoria	9502035034087	76	181
10	Jemeel Warnick	Garsfontein	Pretoria	950518518087	78	173
11	Jade Solomons	Garsfontein	Pretoria	9512175134084	84	178
12	Franco Naude	Garsfontein	Pretoria	9603285193084	91	185
13	Jurie Linde	Affies	Pretoria	9503135048084	86	185
14	Ethan Sias	Garsfontein	Pretoria	9502135210082	78	179
15	Eduan Keyter	Affies	Pretoria	9606135048085	86	183
16	Wildon March	Garsfontein	Pretoria	9601185155088	84	175
17	WP Eloff	Affies	Pretoria	9501185107081	116	195
18	Veaan Roodt	Centurion	Centurion	9508195271088	106	183
19	Abongile Nonkwatane	St Albans	Pretoria	9504105329082	108	195
20	Ivan van Zyl	Affies	Pretoria	9506305030089	80	180
21	Jose Shaw	St Albans	Pretoria	9506295074089	80	173
22	George-Lee Erasmus	Garsfontein	Pretoria	9503035232085	73	175
23	Derik Bezuidenhout	Affies	Pretoria	9505315211085	94	185
24	Reinach Venter	Waterkloof	Pretoria	9501035009081	100	175

TEAM MANAGER Koos de Jager **MEDICAL** Wikus Naude **COACHES** Gert vd Westhuizen, Cobus van Dyk
PERMANENT REPRESENTATIVE DOLF JONKER **BIOKINETICIST** Fanus Venter

BOLAND U/18

No.	Name & Surname	School	Town	ID	Weight	Height
1	Wiaan Lombaard	Augsberg	Clanwilliam	9507265242086	106	190
2	Martin van Wyk	Hermanus	Hermanus	9503035025083	100	184
3	Ferrel Kelly	Drostdy	Worcester	9503125128086	117	180
4	Herman Le Roux	Montague	Montague	9505245301089	105	196
5	Johan Du Toit	Swartland	Malmesbury	9509085114081	96	192
6	Brand Taljaard	Robertson	Robertson	9501215022086	95	186
7	Cheslin Korasie	Schoonspruit	Malmesbury	9503095367086	75	178
8	Hanro Liebenberg	Drostdy	Worcester	9510105044084	102	195
9	Killian von Mollendorff	Labori	Paarl	9511245093080	80	179
10	Evan Adams	Hermanus	Hermanus	9507215185088	70	165
11	Rohaan Adams	Drostdy	Worcester	9509075128083	71	173
12	Chemandre van Schalkwyk	Swartland	Malmesbury	9502275171086	76	180
13	Leolin Zass	Hermanus	Hermanus	9510205196081	82	180
14	Mishaun Arendse	Schoonspruit	Malmesbury	9510315189083	75	173
15	Raylinn Philander	Hugenote	Wellington	9601265244083	75	175
16	Tiaan Lambrechts	Bredasdorp	Bredasdorp	9508185151084	98	173
17	Tobie Wiese	Augsberg	Clanwilliam	9501245249089	98	175
18	Carl Heydenrich	Worcester Gim	Worcester	9510275110087	130	192
19	Jurie Fick	Drostdy	Worcester	9610055171083	103	185
20	Georon Claasen	Vredendal	Vredendal	9505045268082	63	173
21	Warren Williams	New Orleans	Paarl	9508225134082	67	182
22	Fabio Africa	Weston	Vredenburg	9605025121085	69	170

TEAM MANAGER Mervin Petersen **COACHES** Wylie Seroot, JP Van Rhyn
PERMANENT REPRESENTATIVE David Coert

COCA-COLA-CRAVEN WEEK

BORDER COUNTRY DISTRICTS U/18

No.	Name & Surname	School	Town	ID	Weight	Height
1	Patric Kayanja	Elliot high	Elliot	9507285629080	87	157
2	Rixi Thabang	Dalibaso	Mqanduli	9511055895087	75	166
3	Bulela Kawe	Indwe high	Indwe	9512075909080		
4	Thembani Gobodo	Indwe High	Indwe	9610075781085	96	167
5	Buhle Nojekwa	Indwe High	Indwe	9510245184089	103	193
6	Siphamandla Dubase	Jamangile	Maclear	9606096092080	56	151
7	Amahle Bhungeni	Dalibaso	Mqanduli	9607075707086	89	190
8	Phiwe Makalala	Mthatha high	Mthatha	9501035764081	78	179
9	Okuhle Fumba	Ugie high	Ugie	9601265507083		
10	Simphiwe Ncwina	KSD FET	Mthatha	9602215671086	70	165
11	Cameron Groom	Ugie high	Ugie	9512115351087	72	186
12	Azola Mabhulu	Dalibaso	Mqanduli	9606126379085	70	166
13	Chuma Wana	Ugie high	Ugie	9601195603085	67	176
14	Siphosethu Tyali	Dalibaso	Mqanduli	9510106352080	73	190
15	Liza Ntlahla	Jonguhlang	Mthatha	9503185638081	85	159
16	Xhanti Malindi	UCMSC	Mthatha	9511295810086	82	183
17	Abongile Keti	KSD FET	Mthatha	9505195533087	80	168
18	Tevan Lehman	KEH		9502175056080	92	188
19	Sihle Vunguvungu	Sibabale	Ugie	9510135596087	81	183
20	Ntshengulana Vuyisanani	Maclear high	Maclear	9610096037087	70	188
21	Wandile Mgqukuza	CHB	Libode			
22	Ayanda Mvimbi	Thomas Ntaba	Maclear			

TEAM MANAGERS B. Ndinisa **COACHES** Sizwe Sodinga, V Mdluli.

BORDER CITY U/18

No.	Name & Surname	School	Town	Id	Weight	Height
1	Thabani Mtsi	Selborne	East London	950111 5411 082	98	180
2	Jayson Reinecke	Cambridge	East London	951208 5086 085	94	182
3	Matthew Nelson	Selborne	East London	950424 6120 085	122	181
4	Jason Steyn	Selborne	East London	960220 5204 088	101	186
5	Robert Lyons	Selborne	East London	960626 5140 082	103	187
6	Damian Wolvaard	Selborne	East London	951006 5148 081	84	191
7	Jedwyn Harty	Selborne	East London	951119 5208 084	97	185
8	Justin Hollis	Queens	Queenstown	951017 5187 086	92	186
9	Kewan Gibb	Queens	Queenstown	951231 5010 087	80	180
10	Lungelo Gosa	Selborne	East London	950131 5142 081	80	178
11	Jerry Danquah	Queens	King William's Town	960119 6252 080	86	176
12	Simon Bolze	Queens	Queenstown	950730 5206 083	84	181
13	Somila Jho	Dale	King William's Town	950825 5350 087	78	180
14	Lilitha Jonas	Queens	Queenstown	950326 5124 085	72	176
15	Ayavuya Mavuso	Dale	King William's Town	950507 5387 083	73	186
16	Sinako George	Dale	King William's Town	951112 5395 084	92	171
17	Sibusiso Lali	Stirling	East London	950303 5209 083	96	180
18	Lona Ntsila	Queens	Queenstown	950628 5451 081	81	188
19	Mihlali Nchukana	Dale	King William's Town	950226 5403 085	81	190
20	Keegan Gray	Selborne	East London	950711 5060 064	71	171
21	Kyle Brown	Queens	Queenstown	950117 5170 081	84	180
22	Nanele Tyali	Selborne	East London	950611 5116 086	82	178

TEAM MANAGER Mtobeli Kweliti, Sivuyile Vakele **COACHES** Lefty Dakuse, Clinton Loest
PERMANENT REPRESENTATIVE Mongezi Mncono

E.P. COUNTRY DICTRICTS U/18

No.	Name & Surname	School	Town	ID	Weight	Height
1	Nicolaas Oosthuizen	Marlow	Cradock	9611195088038		
2	Thomas Filmer	St Andrews	Grahamstown	9595195156087		178
3	Ronald Beyl	Marlow	Cradock	9508055140084	123	176
4	Tyler Paul	St Andrews	Grahamstown	9501205049081	106	193
5	Sintu Manjezi	St Andrews	Grahamstown	9504075681082	95	195
6	Cornelius van Heerden	Marlow	Cradock	9511035293080	83	177
7	Stuart Stopforth	St Andrews	Grahamstown	9503265141089	95	192
8	Luigy van Jaarsveld	Marlow	Gradock	9608215132086	96	191
9	Jason Baggott	St Andrews	Grahamstown	9507125107081	88	186
10	Jason Vers	Union	G/Reinett	9504195146081		
11	Xhantilomzi Sandi	Greame	Grahamstown	9505305366089	84	179
12	Peet Schoeman	Marlow	Gradock	9504285240083	92	190
13	Robert Ball	St Andrews	Grahamstown	9603145205086	82	185
14	Aphiwe Dinga	Aliwal North	Aliwal North	9509125669086	73	173
15	Tsepho Mabitsela	Volkskool	Graaff Reinet	9501066350081	70	170
16	Jacobus Blom	Marlow	Cradock	9508075128085	91	181
17	David Murray	St Andrews	Grahamstown	9503075226088	105	180
18	Johannes Viljoen	Marlow	Gradock	9608305184088	86	191
19	Ockert du Preez	Marlow	Gradock	9507205236081	87	188
20	Qhama Masiza	Gymnasium	Adelaide	9608235313088	70	
21	Siphosethu Pinini	Graeme	Grahamstown	9503045264086	76	169
22	Gordon-Lynne Plaatjies	Graeme	Grahamstown	9502075144085	90	186

TEAM MANAGERS George Malan **COACHES** Allan Miles, Derik Olivier

EASTERN PROVINCE U/18

No.	Name & Surname	School	Town	ID	Weight	Height
1	Kaden Prince	Brandwag	Uitenhage	9610075069085	115	179
2	Justin Antonie	Pearson	Port Elizabeth	9501245354087	100	176
3	Erich de Jager	Brandwag	Uitenhage	9602295075083	117	183
4	Elandre Van Der Merwe	Brandwag	Uitenhage	9505055090087	97	189
5	Stephan Ebersohn	Grey	Port Elizabeth	9502085017081	116	194
6	Cyril-John Velleman (C)	Grey	Port Elizabeth	95022452201088	89	180
7	Morney Moos	Brandwag	Uitenhage	9605105118084	89	186
8	Martin Groenewald	Grey	Port Elizabeth	9506025200087	107	190
9	Luciano Daniels	Otto Du Plessis	Port Elizabeth	9505265370089	63	161
10	Ernst Stapelberg	Framesby	Port Elizabeth	9502065218089	90	187
11	Keanu Vers	Grey	Port Elizabeth	9602045832080	73	173
12	Luan Nieuwoudt	Nico Malan	Humansdorp	9504175173089	88	184
13	Siyambuka Lawu	Pearson	Port Elizabeth	9505215372086	85	179
14	Dylan Vermaak	Grey	Port Elizabeth	9612095195080	80	185
15	Malcom Jaer	Brandwag	Uitenhage	9506295128083	70	174
16	Arno Lotter	Daniel Pienaar	Uitenhage	9503085088080	104	189
17	Jody Bambie	HTS Newton	Port Elizabeth	9503085277089	108	186
18	Anru Botha	Framesby	Port Elizabeth	9509155240089	94	186
19	Bathandwa Cafu	Grey	Port Elizabeth	9506285364086	97	181
20	Matthew Alborough	Grey	Port Elizabeth	9502085040083	82	175
21	Jeremy Ward	Grey	Port Elizabeth	9601105037085	85	180
22	Reynold King	Pearson	Port Elizabeth	9505155168080	77	175
23	Johann van Niekerk	Grey	Port Elizabeth	9601305141083	90	190

TEAM MANAGER Sebenzile Hoko **COACHES** Gordon Nolan, Pedro Somerset

COCA-COLA-CRAVEN WEEK

FREE STATE U/18

No.	Name & Surname	School	Town	ID	Weight	Height
1	Retshegofaditswe Nche	HTS Louis Botha	Bloemfontein	9507235415085	105	177
2	Andrew du Plessis	Grey College	Bloemfontein	9501145197081	100	177
3	Ruan Kramer	Grey College	Bloemfontein	9508035227084	117	187
4	De Wet Bezuidenhout	Grey College	Bloemfontein	9609105385081	90	184
5	Casper Fourie	Grey College	Bloemfontein	9502096068081	97	188
6	Refuoe Rampeta	HTS Louis Botha	Bloemfontein	9503235268087	87	174
7	Marius Louw (c)	Grey College	Bloemfontein	9510245355085	91	183
8	Andries Kriek	Grey College	Bloemfontein	9501185207089	97	185
9	Heinrich Sander	Grey College	Bloemfontein	9506225268082	73	170
10	Julian Delicado	Grey College	Bloemfontein	9502165274081	76	174
11	Sheldon Fortuin	HTS Louis Botha	Bloemfontein	9503305259081	75	170
12	Aliqhayiya Mgijima	HTS Louis Botha	Bloemfontein	9502115194082	90	186
13	Stephan Rautenbach	Grey College	Bloemfontein	9511035075081	92	189
14	Henry Immelman	Grey College	Bloemfontein	9505265179084	88	189
15	EW Viljoen	Grey College	Bloemfontein	9505095231089	92	192
16	Martin Wippliger	Grey College	Bloemfontein	9501175217080	105	185
17	Ruben Terblanche	Grey College	Bloemfontein	9602215255088	97	177
18	Victor Maruping	HTS Louis Botha	Bloemfontein	9608245686085	89	186
19	Wahseem Gallant	HTS Louis Botha	Bloemfontein	9503286036086	91	185
20	Shirwin Cupido	HTS Louis Botha	Bloemfontein	9610155285080	62	165
21	Masego Toolo	HTS Louis Botha	Bloemfontein	9506265403086	65	177
22	Dale Koopman	HTS Louis Botha	Bloemfontein	9604105093082	86	178

TEAM MANAGER Jimmy Jimlongwe **COACHES** Dirkie Groenewald, Roelf Meyer
PERMANENT REPRESENTATIVE Michael Barker

GOLDEN LIONS U/18

No.	Name & Surname	School	Town	ID	Weight	Height
1	Andrew Acton	Jeppe	Johannesburg	9503275165086	108	186
2	Joseph Dweba	Hoërskool Florida	Florida	9510255434085	105	174
3	Roan Grobbelaar	Helpmekaar Kollege	Johannesburg	9503065040085	113	183
4	Rhyno Herbst	Monument	Krugersdorp	9607055022084	106	197
5	Devon Henson	St. John's College	Johannesburg	9603185151083	106	193
6	Dwayne Pienaar	Monument	Krugersdorp	9501175055084	90	181
7	Dylan Vlok	Monument	Krugersdorp	9506095184088	88	183
8	Wiehan Jacobs	Monument	Krugersdorp	9504185103084	96	190
9	Johan Esterhuizen (C)	Monument	Krugersdorp	9503305913083	70	172
10	Innocent Radebe	St. Stithians	Johannesburg	9501035231081	81	175
11	Ralton October	Hoërskool Florida	Florida	9606205264083	70	171
12	Gerdus van der Walt	Monument	Krugersdorp	9504205246087	85	183
13	Godfrey Ramaboea	King Edward Vii	Johannesburg	9506185166086	79	178
14	S' Busiso Nkosi	Jeppe High School	Johannesburg	9601215259082	96	183
15	Erwin Harris	Hoërskool Florida	Florida	9501145139083	88	178
16	Emmanuel Morowane	Jeppe	Johannesburg	9503205198082	102	170
17	Cornelius Greeff	Monument	Krugersdorp	9507035201081	115	192
18	Gunther Janse van Vuuren	Monument	Krugersdorp	9508245028082	108	186
19	Nyasha Tarusenga	St. Benedict's	Johannesburg	75-2021644E-07	80	185
20	Brandan Rieck	Hoërskool Florida	Florida	9505135014081	75	169
21	Erick Fourie	Monument	Krugersdorp	9505095052089	86	184
22	Fernando Kermis	Hoërskool Florida	Johannesburg	9509045205086	85	174
23	Vincent Dlamini	Jeppe	Johannesburg	9504105529087	76	170

TEAM MANAGER Richard Van Rensburg **COACHES** Golie Gouws, Werner J Van Rensburg, Stephan Louwrens

COCA-COLA-CRAVEN WEEK

GRIFFONS U/18

No.	Name & Surname	School	Town	ID	Weight	Height
1	Ernest Sumner	Voortrekker	Bethlehem	9503065013082	111	185
2	Cheslin Van Rayner	Hentie Cilliers	Virginia	9501225088085	94	185
3	Shane Grobler	HTS	Welkom	9501165040088	108	178
4	Arno de Blom	HTS	Welkom	9506145288087	95	187
5	FP Pelser	Witteberg	Bethlehem	9503305126082	105	200
6	André J. Van Vuuren	Voortrekker	Bethlehem	9507135112089	93	174
7	Gerrit Otto	AHS	Kroonstad	9506125119088	92	184
8	Gregan Hull	Hentie Cilliers	Virginia	9508315148083	90	185
9	Roelof Scheepers	Voortrekker	Bethlehem	9502105171082	77	178
10	Shaun Reynolds	Goudveld	Welkom	9506155285080	91	187
11	Jonathan April	Hentie Cilliers	Virginia	9603255143085	70	170
12	Wian Van der Watt	Voortrekker	Bethlehem	9502035146089	87	181
13	Wessel Hefer	Bothaville H/S	Bothaville	9512065050085	92	193
14	Jamie Joseph	Hentie Cilliers	Virginia	PO 334962	84	182
15	Sechaba Matsoele	Voortrekker	Bethlehem	9501275892085	88	183
16	Albert Brummer	Gimnasium	Welkom	9502045158082	85	180
17	Kyle Ess	Hentie Cilliers	Virginia	9510155149080	107	182
18	Mpho Ramokhoase	Gimnasium	Welkom	9507205162089	103	174
19	Francois Stemmet	AHS	Kroonstad	9606115014081	93	185
20	Damian May	Hentie Cilliers	Virginia	9504055175089	94	186
21	Rian Pretorius	Hentie Cilliers	Virginia	9502155164086	82	181
22	Nazo Nkala	Hentie Cilliers	Virginia	9603015339080	85	183
23	Nick Fortein	Gimnasium	Welkom	96011165312089	87	177

TEAM MANAGER Wilfred Berling **BIOCENETICUS** Dawie De Jager
COACHES Kassie Kasselman, Roean Bezuidenhoudt **TECH. ADVISOR** Andries Kruger

GRIQUAS COUNTRY DISTRICT U/18

No.	Name & Surname	School	Town	ID	Weight	Height
1	Jan-Hendrik van Wyk	HS Duineveld	Upington	9507035158083	112	191
2	Hanro Visagie	HS Duineveld	Upington	9504195102084	100	179
3	Scott Fritz	HS Calvinia	Calvinia	9502125107082	110	175
4	Rayno Nel	HS Duineveld	Upington	9505095100086	92	187
5	Dylan du Plessis	HS Kalahari	Kuruman	9509145298080	80	189
6	Theunis Visser	HS Duineveld	Upington	9512045290082	86	176
7	Junior Burger	HS Duineveld	Upington	9510305071085	100	191
8	Jasper Wiese	HS Upington	Upington	9510215094086	96	188
9	AJ Le Roux	HS Kalahari	Kuruman	9511215207082	65	164
10	Cobus van Niekerk	HS Duineveld	Upington	9507135085087	84	177
11	Josh van Heerden	HS Namakwa	Springbok	9511275331087	71	175
12	Ruan Venter	HS Kalahari	Kuruman	9508075657083	92	170
13	Clinton Toua	HS Kalahari	Kuruman	9502105106088	84	183
14	Gavian Cloete	HS Concordia	Concordia	9506205198085	77	178
15	Darryl de Wee	HS Upington	Upington	9506265196086	70	175
16	Morgan Engelbrecht	HS Namakwa	Springbok	9505185229084	87	175
17	Henri Nel	HS Duineveld	Upington	9511285072085	90	176
18	Ryno Karstens	HS Duineveld	Upington	9608285015088	104	193
19	Sergio Boer	HS Upington	Upington	9608255138084	90	180
20	Bokang Tsabang	HS Kalahari	Kuruman	9602025667084	84	188
21	Jonathan Steenkamp	HS Upington	Upington	9507215026084	74	174
22	Romario van Rooyen	HS Danielskuil	Danielskuil	9512185124083	65	168

TEAM MANAGER Sebenzile Hoko **COACHES** Gordon Nolan, Pedro Somerset

COCA-COLA-CRAVEN WEEK

GRIQUAS U/18

No.	Name & Surname	School	Town	ID	Weight	Height
1	Obakeng Pholoholo	HS Hartswater	Hartswater	9502075685087	101	181
2	Danie van Zyl	HS Diamantveld	Kimberley	9503125031082	79	180
3	Doctor Booysen	HS Noordkaap	Kimberley	9501155118089	102	174
4	Thulani Njenje	HS Noordkaap	Kimberley	9605188503080	90	198
5	Bradley Leijdekkers	HS Noordkaap	Kimberley	9503165062088	95	191
6	BJ Miller	HS Hartswater	Hartswater	9503125013080	80	179
7	Nardus Bosman	HS Diamantveld	Kimberley	9604255039083	87	191
8	Jacques van Zyl	HS Diamantveld	Kimberley	9506075283082	95	185
9	GM Bruwer	HS Noordkaap	Kimberley	9503215019088	74	172
10	Wentzel Mathys	HS Prieska	Prieska	9502115111086	80	179
11	Katlego Mabaleng	HS Landboudal	Jacobsdal	9509115424088	70	177
12	Luke Mason	HS Noordkaap	Kimberley	9505235155081	85	176
13	Dimitrio Tieties	HS Noordkaap	Kimberley	9503095137083	81	176
14	Leon Becker	HS Noordkaap	Kimberley	9601015209089	83	184
15	Ryan de Wee	HS Noordkaap	Kimberley	9508295254083	69	174
16	Willie van Aswegen	HS Noordkaap	Kimberley	9508075011083	88	176
17	Francois Jacobs	HS Landboudal	Jacobsdal	9502035237086	108	190
18	Kosie Human	HS De Aar	De Aar	9505035136083	98	186
19	Gerhard Holtzhausen	HS Noordkaap	Kimberley	9611145178088	81	185
20	Saint- Art Pergoa	HS De Aar	De Aar	9506045196083	60	173
21	Aldro Heyns	HS Noordkaap	Kimberley	9505285155080	81	176
22	Jacques Nel	HS Hartswater	Harstswater	9505045064085	95	186

TEAM MANAGERS Adam Botha **COACHES** Ezzard Alexander, Cassie Carstens
TECHNICAL ADVISOR Bok Makram

KWAZULU NATAL U/18

No.	Name & Surname	School	Town	ID	Weight	Height
1	Mzamo Majola	Westville	Durban	9502205292085	103	182
2	Kerron van Vuuren	Glenwood	Durban	9505235067088	98	184
3	Jacobus Tredoux	Glenwood	Durban	9602235174087	110	181
4	Ntokozo Vidima	Glenwood	Durban	9505135187085	96	189
5	Daniel Du Preez	Kearsney	Durban	9508055129087	110	196
6	Muziwandile Mazibuko	Glenwood	Durban	9503065058087	89	187
7	Jean-Luc du Preez	Kearsney	Durban	9508055130085	112	196
8	Ayron Schramm	Kearsney	Durban	9504185141084	101	192
9	Reece McHardy	Westville	Durban	9507175217087	82	173
10	Tristan Tedder	Kearsney	Durban	9604175067081	72	179
11	Sphamandla Ngcobo	Glenwood	Durban	9507286194084	70	158
12	Akhona Nela	Glenwood	Durban	9504035349085	88	178
13	Marcel Coetzee	Maritzburg College	Durban	9512146047084	86	180
14	Banele Ngwenya	Maritzburg College	Durban	9508025205082	71	169
15	Cornelis Vermaak	Glenwood	Durban	9502185166085	89	183
16	Njabulo Gumede	Maritzburg College	Durban	9501035596087	103	183
17	Jordan Meaker	Kearsney	Durban	9508185195081	82	170
18	Thabiso Zuma	Maritzburg College	Durban	9504255518088	105	175
19	Jakobus Coetzee	Glenwood	Durban	9606105058080	93	187
20	Kurt Webster	DHS	Durban	9601125131082	81	174
21	Kelvin Elder	Maritzburg College	Durban	9501205311085	84	184
22	Morne Joubert	Glenwood	Durban	9601195049081	76	179
23	Tijde Visser	Kearsney	Durban	9609215045088	97	174
24	Chris Lines`	Kearsney	Durban	9602165063088	83	184

TEAM MANAGER Dean Moodley **PHYSIOTHERAPIST** Brent Brimsley
COACHES Barend Steyn, Sean Erasmus

COCA-COLA-CRAVEN WEEK

LEOPARDS U/18

No.	Name & Surname	School	Town	ID	Weight	Height
1	Fanie Rankane	Brits HS	Brits	9501065147082	90	177
2	Eric Smith	Klerksdorp HS	Kerksdorp	9506145206089	94	178
3	Feedie Pieterse	Rustenburg HS	Rustenburg	9611075145081	123	184
4	Ferdie Pretorius	Klerksdorp HS	Klerksdorp	9508165103089	105	198
5	Gopolang Molefe	Bafokeng HS	Bafokeng	9510186196084	97	198
6	Isaih Billa	Orkney HS	Orkney	9509145317088	85	170
7	Gideon vd Merwe	Gimnasium	Potchefstroom	9501275203089	87	178
8	Tiaan Bezuidenhout	Rustenburg HS	Rustenburg	9504285036085	89	189
9	Garann Kriek	Gimnasium	Potchefstroom	9601155140086	74	176
10	CR Botha	Lichtenburg HS	Lichtenburg	9503015142080	80	178
11	Mick Carrol	Lichtenburg HS	Lichtenburg	9501205019084	86	180
12	Michael Hurn	Volkskool	Potchefstroom	950716516 3085	84	178
13	Markus Coetzer	Bergsig Akademie	Rustenburg	9605145417082	90	188
14	Paul Moluleke	Klerksdorp HS	Klerksdorp	9604055554083	84	188
15	Brent September	Brits HS	Brits	9505085073087	90	177
16	Onthatile Ramarola	Boys High	Potchefstroom	9505145453089	96	170
17	Beyers van Sittert	Klerksdorp HS	Klerksdorp	9502065153088	101	180
18	Thabo Chirwa	Orkney HS	Orkney	9512225513089	92	184
19	Jaco Swanepoel	Schweizer Reneke	Schweizer Reneke	9602235141086	92	200
20	Jaco Smith	Schweizer Reneke	Schweizer Reneke	9607235023085	83	179
21	Solomon Mmutle	Boys High	Potchefstroom	9503225470081	71	183
22	Thabang Tsheko	Boys High	Potchefstroom	9509285498086	82	178

TEAM MANAGER Johnnie Robbetze **COACHES** Johan Herbst, Koot Booysen

LIMPOPO BLUE BULLS U/18

No.	Name & Surname	School	Town	ID	Weight	Height
1	Madot Mabokela	Ben Vorster	Tzaneen	9607155640082	103	181
2	Mitch Mametsa	Ben Vorster	Tzaneen	9604295791081	96	181
3	Mogau Mabokela	Ben Vorster	Tzaneen	9502025114089	120	182
4	Nico Bezuidenhout	Ben Vorster	Tzaneen	9501165020080	95	190
5	Armand Naude	Nylstroom	Modimolle	9506095037088	88	194
6	Erick van Niekerk	Ben Vorster	Tzaneen	9504265193088	100	197
7	Christopher Durow	Ben Vorster	Tzaneen	9506045134084	87	190
8	Mlungisi Ntimane	Ben Vorster	Tzaneen	9505045483087	80	182
9	Theo Maree	Ben Vorster	Tzaneen	9503025059084	80	181
10	Andries Bruwer	Ben Vorster	Tzaneen	9504195007085	80	175
11	Arno van Staden	Pietersburg	Polokwane	9501055212086	85	185
12	Jean-Pierre van Wyk	Louis Trichardt	Louis Trichardt	9506185319081	93	176
13	Adrian Maebane	Ben Vorster	Tzaneen	9508085904087	85	175
14	Matjikinyane Molapo	Ben Vorster	Tzaneen	9501025067081	101	183
15	Arno Maree	Pietersburg	Polokwane	9501055212986	85	185
16	Raymond Pieterse	Louis Trichardt	Louis Trichardt	9503055014082	95	180
17	Henton Minnaar	Nylstroom	Modimolle	9501115012088	108	175
18	Richard Coetzee	Hans Strijdom	Mookgopong	9504275074088	84	184
19	Mosesile Mahlo	Ben Vorster	Tzaneen	9605095492085	87	184
20	Wiaan Cornelesin	Nylstroom	Modimolle	9505315012087	68	175
21	Saudevandre Rolls	Warmbad	Bela Bela	9612035288086	87	185
22	Ngaka Mathabela	Ben Vorster	Tzaneen	9601175345082	70	175

TEAM MANAGERS Dirk Oosthuizen, David Mathabatha **COACHES** Andre May, Eben Lingenfelder, Hein Wagner
PERMANENT REPRESENTATIVE Johan Calitz

COCA-COLA-CRAVEN WEEK

NAMIBIA U/18

No.	Name & Surname	School	Town	Id/DOB	Weight	Height
1	Hans Breedt	Tsumeb Gim	Tsumeb	04/07/96	110	180
2	Desmond Stramis	W/Hoek Gim	Windhoek	08/11/95	101	181
3	Torsten Stahn	W/Hoek Gim	Windhoek	21/07/95	98	185
4	Muharua Katjiteko	WHS	Windhoek	23/04/95	103	200
5	Andre Augustyn	WHS	Windhoek	13/04/95	85	190
6	Karl Grundling	WAP	Windhoek	20/06/95	85	180
7	Adriaan Booysen	Elnatan	Stampriet	17/05/96	90	189
8	Johan Retief (C)	W/Hoek Gim	Windhoek	10/10/95	100	193
9	Stefan Potgieter	Tsumeb Gim	Tsumeb	30/04/96	70	168
10	Chris Arries(V/C)	WHS	Windhoek	11/10/95	73	173
11	Sharaeve Titus	Ojtiwarongo	Otjiwaro	23/03/95	65	165
12	Justin Newman	W/Hoek Gim	Windhoek	17/02/95	86	171
13	Brendon Du Plessis	Elnatan	Stampriet	06/09/95	83	185
14	Wilrico Theron	Edugate	Otjiwarongo	21/12/95	77	166
15	Pj Singarem	W/Hoek Gim	Windhoek	12/03/96	82	186
16	Jandre Van Wyk	Elnatan	Stampriet	25/01/96	90	170
17	Jason Benade	Dr Lemmer	Rehoboth	16/04/95	100	185
18	Conraad Willemse	Tsumeb / Gim	Windhoek	24/05/96	87	190
19	Freddy Puriza	WHS	Windhoek	02/01/95	86	180
20	Dian Von Solms	W/Hoek Gim	Windhoek	02/08/95	74	175
21	Eugene Joubert	Elnatan	Windhoek	14/03/95	75	172
22	Milan Van Wyk	W/Hoek Gim	Windhoek	30/04/96	80	168

TEAM MANAGERS Thys Reynecke **COACHES** Henry Kemp, Christo Alexander
PERMANENT REPRESENTATIVE Fanie Van Zyl

FORD PUMAS U/18

No.	Name & Surname	School	Town	ID	Weight	Height
1	JP Herbst	HTS Middelburg	Middelburg	9502155150085	100	185
2	Tristan Jooste	HTS Witbank	Witbank	9510305018086	89	178
3	Conrad van Vuuren	Hoërskool Nelspruit	Nelspruit	9509045161081	107	180
4	Thulane Mkhonto	Hoërskool Middelburg	Middelburg	9503076356082	81	189
5	Michael Basson	HTS Middelburg	Middelburg	9501305110080	105	195
6	Willandrè Kotzenberg	HTS Middelburg	Middelburg	9502095437080	84	176
7	Daniël Maartins	Hoërskool Nelspruit	Nelspruit	9505045222089	85	182
8	Menzi Nhlabathi	Hoërskool Nelspruit	Nelspruit	9503205248085	91	187
9	Rowan Gouws	HTS Middelburg	Middelburg	9508065007083	72	175
10	Brandon Thomson	Hoërskool Ermelo	Ermelo	9503075035083	88	184
11	Bennie Mashbane	Hoërskool Middelburg	Middelburg	9506255567080	95	176
12	Helgaard Viljoen	Hoërskool Nelspruit	Nelspruit	9509155040083	86	177
13	Mauro Bucuchane	Hoërskool Nelspruit	Nelspruit	100701778085C	86	175
14	Odwa Nkunjane	HTS Witbank	Witbank	9602135334088	66	175
15	Lindelwe Zungu	Hoërskool Piet Retief	Piet Retief	9505165510081	73	172
16	Jaco Vosloo	Hoërskool Nelspruit	Nelspruit	9503135017089	85	180
17	Bheki Shongwe	Hoërskool Barberton	Barberton	9609205033086	110	177
18	Cauwen Mashaba	Generaal Hertzog	Witbank	9602035287089	91	168
19	Christopher van Leeuwen	Hoërskool Middelburg	Middelburg	9504265019085	101	194
20	Christiaan Erasmus	Hoërskool Nelspruit	Nelspruit	9507155211084	82	175
21	Ruan du Plooy	HTS Middelburg	Middelburg	9511015453084	85	183
22	Mzwakhe Fransman	HTS Witbank	Witbank	9508045013086	79	180

TEAM MANAGER Koos de Jager **MEDICAL** Wikus Naude **COACHES** Gert vd Westhuizen, Cobus van Dyk
PERMANENT REPRESENTATIVE Dolf Jonker **BIOKINETICIST** Fanus Venter

COCA-COLA-CRAVEN WEEK

SWD U/18

No.	Name & Surname	School	Town	ID	Weight	Height
1	Juandre Dique	Oakdale HLS	Riversdale	9505095116082	104	185
2	Marne Botha	Outeniqua HS	George	950105 5239 089	90	180
3	Stefan Grundlingh	Outeniqua HS	George	9508295105087	130	183
4	Donovan Van Der Berg	Oakdale HLS	Riversdale	9506135143086	97	190
5	Eduard Zandberg	Outeniqua HS	George	9602145143081	115	201
6	Geor Malan (C)	Outeniqua HS	George	9505085413085	87	180
7	Daniel Maree	Oakdale HLS	Riversdale	9601265134086	100	190
8	Dian Koen	Outeniqua HS	George	9511065039080	107	189
9	Remu Malan	Outeniqua HS	George	9505085414083	78	178
10	Dewald Human	Outeniqua HS	George	9505195192082	65	167
11	Duhan Van Der Merwe	Outeniqua HS	George	950604506080	96	194
12	Gene Willemse	Oakdale HLS	Riversdale	9504135226084	88	182
13	Douw Schoeman	Outeniqua HS	George	9502185158082	90	179
14	Lorenzo Gordon	Oakdale HLS	Riversdale	9505195174080	81	183
15	Hennie Barnard	Outeniqua HS	George	9503205151081	84	180
16	Brendon Haas	Langhoven Gimnasium	Oudtshoorn	9504065053086	100	180
17	Nemo Roelofse	Oakdale HLS	Riversdale	9506065078088	103	180
18	Anton Smit	Outeniqua HS	George	9608055193081	91	194
19	Benjamin JV Vuuren	Oakdale HLS	Riversdale	9509195107082	87	180
20	Maurice White	Oakdale HLS	Riversdale	9603185082080	86	178
21	Jayden Onkers	Oudtshoorn	Oudtshoorn	9503235149089	80	178
22	JP Coetzee	Oakdale HLS	Riversdale	9503245269083	90	190

TEAM MANAGER Chris Hendricks **HEADCOACH** Kobus Fielies
ASS COACHES Jacques Wolfaart, Pine Marais

VALKE U/18

No.	Name & Surname	School	Town	ID	Weight	Height
1	Thabo Pitsi	Rhodes	Kempton Park	950812 5031 081	105	170
2	Pieter Jansen	Eg.Jansen	Boksburg	9503215035084	103	183
3	Donovan Venter	Gimnasium	Vereeniging	960708 5258 088	102	181
4	Rholane Ncubuka	Ahs Sasol	Sasolburg	950609 5202 088	96	191
5	Estian Enslin	Eg.Jansen	Boksburg	950309 5171 082	107	197
6	Joswin De Wee	Gimnasium.	Vereeniging	950726 5086 087	90	170
7	Marco Holmes	Eg.Jansen	Boksburg	950209 5095 085	95	185
8	Morne Swart	Eg.Jansen	Boksburg	950302 5080 080	90	187
9	Marco Van Vuren	Transvalia	Vd Bijl Park	950121 5216 084	83	175
10	Ruan Potgieter	Eg.Jansen	Boksburg	9509285093085	85	180
11	Eldron Van Rooyen	Gimnasium	Vereeniging	950415 5219 084	70	163
12	Zander Cronje	Eg.Jansen	Boksburg	950809 5119 080	92	187
13	Sampie Hearn	Eg.Jansen	Boksburg	950628 5064 082	104	188
14	Jacqone De Villiers	Gimnasium	Vereeniging	950402 5050 081	77	177
14	Darren De Bruyn	Jeugland	Kempton Park	960611 5196 086	73	176
15	Kobus Engelbrecht	Eg.Jansen	Boksburg	950220 5281 088	78	179
16	Marius Greyvensteyn	Eg.Jansen	Boksburg	950516 5072 082	108	175
17	Arnout Malherbe	Transvalia	Vd Bijl Park	950828 5381 086	108	182
18	Ben Wepener	Kempton	Kempton Park	950420 5143 086	100	180
19	Edward Mlotsha	Kempton	Kempton Park	950314 5028 084	91	183
20	Ryan Solomons	C. De Wet	Sasolburg	950917 5019 083	74	177
21	Cameron Rooi	Anker	Brakpan	950608 5919 089	75	176
22	Darren De Bruyn	Jeugland	Kempton Park	960611 5196 086	73	176

TEAM MANAGERS Allan Arnold **COACHES** Philip Lemmer, Kwagga Loubsher

COCA-COLA-CRAVEN WEEK

DHL WESTERN PROVINCE U/18

No.	Name & Surname	School	Town	ID	Weight	Height
1	Thomas du Toit	Hoër Jongenskool	Paarl	950505 5162 084	120	187
2	Daniel du Plessis	Hoër Jongenskool	Paarl	950224 5016 080	107	178
3	Francois van der Merwe	Hoër Jongenskool	Paarl	950603 5094 082	117	187
4	Burger van Niekerk	Hoër Jongenskool	Paarl	950101 5589 086	104	198
5	Johan Momsen	Hoërskool Gimnasium	Paarl	950821 5073 084	94	192
6	Charlton Jonas	Hoër Jongenskool	Paarl	950212 5171 088	92	179
7	Jacques Vermeulen	Hoërskool Gimnasium	Paarl	950208 5086 086	103	197
8	Rikus Bothma (Capt)	Hoërskool Gimnasium	Paarl	951017 5166 080	102	186
9	Herschel Jantjies	Paul Roos Gimnasium	Stellenbosch	960422 5232081	70	167
10	Dennis Cox	Excelsior Sekondêr	Bellville	950201 5020 080	72	172
11	Dewald Naude	Hoër Jongenskool	Paarl	950824 5115 087	80	175
12	Daniel du Plessis	Paul Roos Gimnasium	Stellenbosch	950317 5369 085	93	187
13	Jarryd Sage	Wynberg Boys High School	Cape Town	950818 5124 081	93	196
14	Grant Hermanus	Hoërskool Gimnasium	Paarl	951111 5040 088	76	179
15	Khanyo Ngcukana	Rondebosch Boys High	Cape Town	950510 5223 084	82	180
16	Ruan Brits	Hoër Jongenskool	Paarl	960113 5028 088	102	184
17	Gavin van den Berg	Hoërskool Gimnasium	Paarl	960110 5140 087	115	185
18	Brett Paulse	Rondebosch Boys High	Cape Town	950911 5060 080	118	186
19	Saud Abrahams	Diocesan College	Cape Town	960104 5227 085	96	181
20	Damian Stevens	Hoër Jongenskool	Paarl	950602 6116 084	65	163
21	Siya Alam	Wynberg Boys High School	Cape Town	950719 5401 083	79	173
22	Heinrich Buhr	Hoër Landbouskool Boland	Paarl	950602 5087 088	84	173
23	Dante van der Merwe	Hoër Jongenskool	Paarl	951102 5332 088	71	181

TEAM MANAGER Petrie Stofberg **COACHES** Hein Kriek, Peter Links
PERMANENT REPRESENTATIVE Kervin Grove **BIOKINETICIST** Lukas Holtzhauzen

---

ZIMBABWE U/18

No.	Name & Surname	School	Town	ID	Weight	Height
1	Thabani Mujeni	St Georges	Harare	BN635191	102	176
2	Alexander Zwart	St Johns	Harare	BN953962	92	180
3	Tapiwa Muringani	Peterhouse	Marondera	BN406770	103	180
4	Tafadzwa Kufazvinei	St Georges	Harare	BN669145	89	188
5	Nicholas Burnett	St Johns	Harare	BN733947	92	192
6	Ivan Bawden	St Georges	Harare	BN726275	92	186
7	Daniel Moolman	Peterhouse	Marondera	BN850060	89	184
8	Tinashe Gonese	Hillcrest	Mutare	BN676360	85	186
9	Tinashe Gwisai	M.C.C	Gweru	CN602799	62	165
10	Rukudzo Gona	St Johns	Harare	CN141874	75	176
11	Jabulani Mutukwa	St Georges	Harare	BN929415	83	179
12	Munyaradzi Mashaya	St Georges	Harare	BN819598	84	179
13	Thomas Chadwick	St Johns	Harare	A02197053	83	183
14	Brandon Boshi	St Georges	Harare	CN071796	86.5	186
15	Brendon Mandivenga	Peterhouse	Marondera	BN541153	83	178
16	Stephen Bhasera	Falcon	Esigodini	CN871114	110	181
17	Glynne Rorke	St Johns	Harare	BN708278	95	182
18	Tanaka Chikwezvero	Prince Edward	Harare	BN820667	102	180
19	Philangezwi Mudambanuki	Peterhouse	Marondera	BN700524	96	181
20	Andrew Dollar	Peterhouse	Marondera	BN519290	68	165
21	Justin Zietsman	Falcon	Esigodini	CN386018	85	184
22	Tawanda Ngosi	M.C.C	Gweru	BN974427	78	183

TEAM MANAGERS Tungamirai Mashungu **COACHES** Godwin Murambiwa, Brendon Brider

CELL C COMMUNITY CUP

Despatch write new club chapter

DESPATCH ROSE FROM THE ASHES TO claim their first national club rugby title in 25 years when they beat favourites Jonsson College Rovers in the inaugural Cell C Community Cup final at Outeniqua Park in George on Easter Monday.

In a fairytale finish, Despatch fullback Monty Dumond slotted a long-range penalty after the hooter to ensure his team would be the first in many years to drink out of the Gold Cup – an iconic trophy brought out of mothballs and painstakingly restored for the tournament.

It was a triumph not only for the Eastern Cape side but for club rugby as a whole, with SARU making the bold move to replace the ailing National Club Championships, which had been going since 1975, with a new televised tournament that promised to breathe life back into the club game.

Circumstances dictated that the first Community Cup kicked off less than five months after the final Club Champs was successfully staged in Rustenburg, as the traditional week-long season-ending event for 16 teams was replaced by a World Cup-style tournament played in the pre-season.

The enlarged field of 20 teams were divided into four pools of five, with a total of 40 pool matches being played across the length and breadth of the country before the top eight progressed to a knock-out event over the Easter weekend – a throwback to the old Toyota Club Championships which had been so successful in Durban for many years.

But perhaps the major shift was a decision to restrict the Community Cup to non-university or so-called 'open' clubs only – with the general feeling being that the university teams, who had dominated the Club Champs throughout its 38-year history, were adequately catered for by the Varsity Cup and Shield.

The cross-over to a national club tournament featuring only open clubs actually took place at the 2012 Club Champs, which was expertly hosted by the Rustenberg Impala Rugby Club. College Rovers, who came from behind to beat Despatch in the match of the week in the quarter-finals, went on to claim their second Club Champs title in three years and so earned the right to host the opening match of the Community Cup.

With Rovers and Despatch drawn in the same Pool, the decision to build on their new-found rivalry was an easy one and so it was that the two sides opened the Community Cup era with a surprisingly one-sided encounter in Durban which Rovers won comfortably.

Who would have thought that, seven weeks and 51 matches later, the same two sides would be at it again in the final, this time decided in the very last seconds?

Veteran Dumond had a 47-metre effort a minute earlier falling a couple of metres short, but when afforded another kick 45 metres out after Rovers had hands in the ruck, he slotted it as the hooter sounded and was promptly mobbed by team-mates.

Rovers had retaken the lead three minutes earlier with a Greg Goosen penalty, but a last desperate surge by Despatch resulted in them giving Dumond his glory moment. And fittingly, Springbok legend Danie Gerber, who had led Despatch to famous Club Champs triumphs in 1985 and 1988 and who was never far from the team throughout their 2013 campaign, was on hand to drink out of the Cup together with head coach Adri Geldenhuys, who played for South Africa alongside Gerber against the All Blacks in 1992.

The moment was not as triumphant for a third member of the Bok class of '92, former scrumhalf and Rovers coach Robert du Preez, who, in one of those rare twists, had played for Tukkies 25 years earlier when Gerber's Despatch claimed their second title.

Their third might have taken a quarter of a century, but the feeling in George was that, in the context of the where club rugby was headed, it was perhaps their greatest.

"We want to put Despatch back on the map and this is only the beginning," said their captain, Elroy Ligman.

"We want to thank everyone for their effort and also Cell C and SARU for making this happen."

COMMUNITY CUP LOG 2013

POOL A	P	W	L	D	PF	PA	Diff	TF	TA	LB	TB	Pts
Jonsson College Rovers (KZN)	4	4	0	0	165	76	89	23	9	0	4	20
GAP Despatch (EP)	4	3	1	0	151	113	38	21	13	0	3	15
SK Walmers (WP)	4	2	2	0	138	125	13	17	15	1	3	12
United Bulk Villagers Worcester (Boland)	4	1	3	0	90	179	-89	9	25	0	0	4
Aveng Moolmans Sishen (Griquas)	4	0	4	0	96	147	-51	13	21	2	1	3

POOL B	P	W	L	D	PF	PA	Diff	TF	TA	LB	TB	Pts
Pretoria Police (Blue Bulls)	4	4	0	0	219	96	123	31	13	0	4	20
Durbanville-Bellville (WP)	4	3	1	0	262	81	181	40	11	0	4	16
African Bombers (EP)	4	2	2	0	128	143	-15	17	22	0	3	11
Welkom Rovers (Griffons)	4	1	3	0	89	202	-113	9	27	0	2	6
Bloemfontein Police (Free State)	4	0	4	0	76	252	-176	12	36	0	0	0

POOL C	P	W	L	D	PF	PA	Diff	TF	TA	LB	TB	Pts
Rustenburg Impala (Leopards)	4	3	0	1	192	77	115	26	9	0	2	16
Roodepoort (Lions)	4	3	1	0	158	91	67	21	11	0	2	14
Raiders (Lions)	4	2	1	1	132	75	57	17	7	1	3	14
Bloemfontein Crusaders (Free State)	4	1	3	0	77	153	-76	10	23	0	1	5
BB Truck Noordelikes (Limpopo)	4	0	4	0	74	237	-163	11	35	0	1	1

POOL D	P	W	L	D	PF	PA	Diff	TF	TA	LB	TB	Pts
East Rand Cranes Brakpan (Valke)	4	3	1	0	260	65	195	39	9	1	3	16
Evergreens (SWD)	4	3	1	0	117	76	41	17	10	1	2	15
Broubart Old Selbornians (Border)	4	3	1	0	117	77	40	16	11	1	1	14
Roses United (Boland)	4	1	3	0	132	177	-45	18	26	1	2	7
White River (Mpumalanga)	4	0	4	0	80	311	-231	13	47	0	2	2

Note: *LB=Losing Bonus TB=Tries Bonus*

CELL C COMMUNITY CUP EASTER TOURNAMENT - GEORGE

THURSDAY, 28 MARCH
Brakpan beat Roodepoort 39-13
Despatch beat Pretoria Police 33-25
College Rovers beat Durbanville-Bellville 27-17
Rustenburg Impala beat Evergreens 50-10

SATURDAY, 30 MARCH
Durbanville-Belville beat Roodepoort 23-10
College Rovers beat Brakpan 29-25
Pretoria Police beat Evergreens 41-12
Despatch beat Rustenburg Impala 21-20

MONDAY, 1 APRIL
Roodepoort beat Evergreens 47-24
Durbanville-Bellville beat Pretoria Police 30-3
Brakpan beat Rustenburg Impala 58-8
Despatch beat College Rovers 26-24 (FINAL)
Despatch 26 (TRIES: Swanepoel, Lewis, Van Tonder. CONVERSION: Dumond. PENALTIES: Dumond 3)
College Rovers 24 (TRIES: Jordaan, Torrens. CONVERSION: Goosen. PENALTIES: Goosen 3, Micklewood)
Despatch: Monty Dumond, Elcardo Mintoor, Rosseau Prinsloo, Basil de Doncker, Baldwin McBean, Ryan Brown, Marlon Lewis (Bronwin Gysman, 65), Jaco Swanepoel, Elroy Ligman (c), Bobby Dyer (Morne Strydom, 61), Trichardt van Tonder, Ashley Viviers, Ayanda Nogampula (Dyllan Lamprecht, 52), Giovano Fourie, Dewald Barnard (Jean Meyer, 68). *UNUSED SUBS: Elandre Smit, Darren van winkel, Derrick Memanie, Deon Booysen.*
College Rovers: Christopher Micklewood (c), Jors Dannhauser, Sergio Torrens, Jean Botha (Andrew Borgen, 25-30, 69), Chris Jordaan (Kyle Wilkinson, 49), Greg Goosen, Tian Meyer, Juan Language, Conrad Stoltz (Wade Elliott, 3-5, 54), Murray Bondesio, Nikolai Blignaut, Francois Robertse (Simba Bwanyana, 78), Simon Kerrod, Mark Goosen (Chris Kemp, 61), Sangoni Mxoli. *UNUSED SUBS: Thulani Ngidi, Ivan Ludick, Gideon Bruwer.*

2013 CELL C COMMUNITY CUP LEADING SCORERS

50 POINTS OR MORE

PLAYER	Tries	Conversions	Penalties	Drop Goals	Points
Charl Nieuwenhuis (Brakpan)	3	43	8	0	125
Naas Olivier (Rustenburg Impala)	0	23	4	0	88
Adnaan Osman (SK Walmers)	4	13	9	0	73
Steven Griffiths (Roodepoort)	0	15	11	1	66
Ryan Brown (Despatch)	1	13	9	0	58
Dillon Laubscher (Pretoria Police)	0	17	8	0	58
Hagen Mumba (Roses United)	3	10	6	0	53
Jors Dannhauser (College Rovers)	3	8	7	0	52
Raynor Becker (Durbanville-Bellville)	5	10	2	0	51

FIVE TRIES

Ruan van Loo (Pretoria Police)	8	Raynor Becker (Durbanville-Bellville)	5
Gerrit Theron (Durbanville-Bellville)	8	Baldwin McBean (Despatch)	5
Leon du Plessis (Rustenburg Impala)	7	Danwill Erasmus (SK Walmers)	5
Michael Nienaber (Pretoria Police)	7	Duran Alberts (Old Selbornians)	5
Sergio Torrens (College Rovers)	7	Elcardo Mintoor (Despatch)	5
Wikus van der Berg (Brakpan)	7	Morne Meningke (Durbanville-Bellville)	5
Franco Booysen (Brakpan)	6	Wandile Mjekevu (College Rovers)	5
Jaco Lotter (Brakpan)	6		

FNB VARSITY CUP

Tuks top of the class again

FNB UP-TUKS RETAINED THEIR FNB Varsity Cup title by storming to a comprehensive 44-5 victory over hosts Maties at the Danie Craven Stadium in Stellenbosch.

The powerful Pretoria unit, who made their intentions known with a 61-24 drubbing of UJ in the semi-finals, made a mockery of pre-match predictions of a more even final, scoring five tries to hand the home side their first defeat of the season, and just their third loss at home in the tournament's six years.

Things never went right for Maties from the get-go, as they lost two early line-outs which gave Tuks all the attacking platform they needed to take the early lead through two quick tries to open up a 16-0 advantage.

Scrumhalf Danie Faasen was first to score when he burst over following some sustained pressure from his powerful forward pack on the Maties' tryline. Faasen's halfback partner Willie du Plessis followed that up soon afterwards when he finished off a flowing movement to give Tuks the upper hand at the first strategy break.

Another lost Maties line-out saw Tuks wing Vainon Willis come within inches of scoring the visitors' third try, but he was forced into touch as he went to ground the ball in the corner, much to the relief of the Stellenbosch crowd.

But this was a night on which the dam wall would eventually burst, and Tuks were rewarded once more when skipper Jono Ross bounced out of a tackle to get over next to the poles just before halftime, giving his side a commanding 24-0 lead at the break.

There was not let-off from Tuks after the break, and it was not long before wing Courtnall Skosan forced his way over for their fourth try after another period of sustained pressure.

Despite their hopeless situation, Maties, the three-time champions who had snuck into the final on the back of a 16-15 semi-final win over NMMU, did not give in and eventually got on the scoreboard when the ball was worked out to wing Clearance Khumalo, who dived over in the corner for a try which reduced the gap to 32-5.

The defending champions, as champions do, responded by applying further pressure, which resulted in a penalty to SA Under-20 star Handre Pollard before fullback Clayton Blommetjies made the most of a dropped pass by popping over a drop-goal to put Tuks out of sight at 36-5.

The final blow was struck just minutes before the final whistle when Willis, somewhat appropriately, snatched an intercept to race away for the try which secured not only more silverware for Tuks but also the record for the biggest victory margin in a Varsity Cup final.

It was not quite what the organisers would have wanted, but even the most diehard Maties fan could not quibble at the result, or the professional manner in which it was achieved.

In the Varsity Shield final, the Central University of Technology Ixias beat the University of the Western Cape, coached by former Springbok coach Peter de Villiers, 29-19, in Bloemfontein to claim their second Shield title.

BACK OF THE TOURNAMENT Howard Mnisi (NMMU)
FORWARD OF THE TOURNAMENT Reniel Hugo (Maties)
OVERALL PLAYER OF THE TOURNAMENT Oupa Mohoje (Shimlas)

Varsity Cup Log 2013

Team	P	W	L	D	PF	PA	Diff	TF	TA	LB	TB	Pts
Maties	7	7	0	0	205	117	88	28	16	0	5	33
UP-Tuks 1	7	4	3	0	179	114	65	25	13	3	3	22
UJ	7	3	3	1	218	179	39	31	23	2	5	21
NMMU	7	4	2	1	120	103	17	14	15	2	1	21
NWU-Pukke	7	4	3	0	237	222	15	33	30	1	4	21
Shimlas	7	2	3	2	183	132	51	24	19	1	2	15
UCT	7	1	4	2	159	198	-39	22	27	1	2	11
Wits	7	0	7	0	133	369	-236	17	51	0	1	1

Note: LB=Losing Bonus TB=Tries Bonus

FNB VARSITY CUP PLAY-OFF RESULTS

SEMI-FINALS: Maties beat **NMMU** 16-15 (Stellenbosch); **Tuks** beat **UJ** 61-24 (Pretoria)

FINAL RESULTS
Danie Craven Stadium, Stellenbosch, Monday 8 April. Referee: Marius van der Westhuizen
MATIES: 5 (0) (**TRY**: Khumalo)
TUKS 44 (24) (**TRIES**: Skosan, Faasen, Ross, Willis, Du Plessis. **CONVERSIONS**: Pollard 5. **PENALTY**: Pollard. **DROP GOAL**: Blommetjies)
MATIES: Craig Barry (JP Lewis, 52), Clearance Khumalo, Mark Hodgskiss, Ryan Nell, Dean Hammond, JH Potgieter (Dean Grant, 59), James Alexander (Jean Nel, 59), Reniel Hugo, Lungelo Chonco (Beyers de Villiers, 48), Helmut Lehman (c,), Wilhelm van der Sluys, Jan de Klerk (Reuben Johannes, 68), Stephan Hamman (Brendan Pitzer, 59), Charl de Villiers (Johan Kirsten, 48), Alistair Vermaak (Niel Oelofse, 59).
TUKS: Clayton Blommetjies, Vainon Willis, Piet Lindeque (Christoper Bosch, 58), Handre Pollard, Courtnall Skosan, Willie du Plessis (Riaan Britz, 68), Danie Faasen (Emile Tempermann, 63), Jono Ross (c), Jacques Verwey (Wiaan Liebenberg, 59), Shaun Adendorff, Marvin Orie (Schalk van Heerden, 23), Mike Williams, Basil Short (Christoph Gouws, 63), Mbongeni Mbonambi (Jaco Visagie, 72), Juan Schoeman (Sabelo Nhlapo, 35-41, 72).

FNB VARSITY CUP LEADING SCORERS

50 POINTS OR MORE

PLAYER	TEAM	Tries	Conversions	Penalties	Drop Goals	Points
Kobus de Kock	UJ	5	22	0	0	91
Handre Pollard	Tuks	1	19	3	0	68
Gerhard Nortier	Pukke	1	15	2	0	54
Justin van staden	NMMU	0	10	10	0	50

FIVE TRIES

Hoffman Maritz	Pukke	7	Cortnall Skosan	Tuks	5
Kobus de Kock	UJ	5	Shaun Adendorff	Tuks	5
Carel Greeff	Wits	5	Liam Bax	UCT	5

FNB VARSITY SHIELD

BACK OF THE TOURNAMENT Freddie Muller (UWC)
FORWARD OF THE TOURNAMENT Billy Dutton (UFH)
OVERALL PLAYER OF THE TOURNAMENT Inus Kritzinger (CUT)

Varsity Shield Log 2013

Team	P	W	L	D	PF	PA	Diff	TF	TA	LB	TB	Pts
CUT	8	8	0	0	296	159	137	41	19	0	5	37
UWC	8	4	4	0	225	160	65	28	19	1	4	21
UKZN	8	4	4	0	143	215	-72	17	29	0	0	16
UFH	8	3	5	0	159	194	-35	20	24	1	2	15
TUT	8	1	7	0	122	217	-95	12	27	3	1	8

Note: LB=Losing Bonus TB=Tries Bonus

FNB VARSITY SHIELD PLAY-OFF RESULTS

FINAL RESULT
CUT Rugby Stadium, Bloemfontein. Monday 1 April.
Referee: Stephan Geldenhuys
CUT 29 (TRIES: Pretorius 2, Kritzinger, Mhlanga.
CONVERSION: Marx. PENALTIES: Marx 3)
UWC 19 (TRIES: Marcus, Julies. CONVERSION: Muller.
PENALTIES: Muller 2)
CUT: Kholo Ramashala, Charles Hitccock (Alex Mhlanga, 36), Johan van Schalkwyk, Leon Pretorius, Meyer van Tonder, Noel Marx, Inus Kritzinger (c, Christoff Swanepoel, 80), Juan Hugo, Frans Sisita (Dean Kouprihanoff, 45), Moekoa Bolofo, Andrew Bester, Johan Klopper (Lyvette Shikwambana, 72), Danie van der Merwe (Petri Coetzee, 52), Deon Gouws (Anrich Bitzi, 51), Carl Gersbach (Rudi Fuls, 51).
UWC: Warrick Rhoda, Donovan Williams (Charl van Vollenhoven, 76), Kenwinn Wiener, Justin McKay, Minenhle Mthuthwa (Quaid Langeveldt, 76), Freddie Muller (Yondels Stampu, 62), Denzel Willemse, Heinrich Marcus, Samuel Borsaah (Njabulo Ndlovu, 41), Jose Julies, Mtheteleli Fuzani, Pallo Manual, Kelvin de Bruyn, Charlton van Jaarsveld (c), Michael September.
UNUSED SUBS: Ludwe Ntlokondala, Siphiwo Bakeni, Jaycee Jooste, Seth Maphumulo.

FNB VARSITY SHIELD LEADING SCORERS

50 POINTS OR MORE

PLAYER	TEAM	Tries	Conversions	Penalties	Drop Goals	Points
Freddie Muller	UWC	3	15	5	1	73
Morne Hugo	TUT	1	10	15	1	68
Noel Marx	CUT	1	17	6	0	68
Meyer van Tonder	CUT	6	11	1	0	65
Lukhanyiso Komani	UFH	2	9	8	0	53

FIVE TRIES

Inus Kritzinger	CUT	8	Heinrich Marcus	UWC		5
Meyer van Tonder	CUT	6	Kenvin Wiener	UWC		5
Alex Mhlanga	CUT	5	Lundi Ralarala	UFH		5
Deon Gouws	CUT	5				

SECTION 8
RECORDS

FIRST-CLASS RECORDS
South African First-Class Records **354**
100 Appearances for a Province **356**

INTERNATIONAL RECORDS
SANZAR – Vodacom Super Rugby Records **359**
SANZAR – Castle Rugby Championship Records **364**

DOMESTIC RECORDS
Absa Currie Cup Records **368**
Currie Cup Final Players & Captains **373**

Vodacom Cup Records **384**

SPRINGBOK RECORDS & PLAYER LISTS **386**

SPRINGBOKS A-Z (1891 to 2013) **427**

OTHER PLAYER LISTS
Springbok Sevens Internationals 1993-2013 .... **448**
SA U20 Players **451**
South Africans Capped Overseas **453**
SA Schools Representatives 1974-2013 .... **455**
Referees **462**

Obituaries **466**
2013 Season First-Class Player List **476**

Joost van der Westhuizen holds the record for the most tries in a Springbok jersey. *Carl Fourie/Gallo Images*

SOUTH AFRICAN FIRST-CLASS RECORDS

MATCH RECORDS

Scores of 150 points
163	Lowveld vs Transkei	1994
161	Golden Lions vs Limpopo BB	2013
154	Pumas vs Limpopo BB	2013
151	Western Province vs Eastern Transvaal	1995

Wins by 130 points
158	GL vs Limpopo BB (161-3)	2013
154	Pumas vs Limpopo BB (154-0)	2013
153	Lowveld vs Transkei (163-10)	1994
148	WP vs Eastern Transvaal (151-3)	1995
139	Northern Transvaal vs SWD (147-8)	1996

Twenty-five tries
26	Lowveld vs Transkei	1994

Forty-eight points by a player
50	GE Lawless, Sharks vs Highlanders	1997
48	WJ de W Ras, OFS vs EOFS	1977
48	JH de Beer, SA Students vs Taiwan	1992
48	J Nel, Lowveld vs Transkei	1994

Seven tries by a player
9	AA Volmink, GL vs Limpopo BB	2013
8	M Watson, Lowveld vs Transkei	1994
7	C Fourie, Gazelles vs Neuquen (Arg.)	1972
7	J Olivier, N.Transvaal vs SWD	1996
7	J Jonker, Griquas vs Namibia	1996

Twenty conversions by a player
20	WJ de W Ras, OFS vs EOFS	1977

Nine penalty goals by a player
9	JH Kruger, N.Transvaal vs WP	1996
9	E Herbert, NFS vs Falcons	1997
9	E Herbert, Griffons vs Pumas	2001
9	DJ Hougaard, Blue Bulls vs WP	2002
9	PC Montgomery, SA XV vs World XV	2006

Five drop goals by a player
5	HE Botha, N.Transvaal vs Natal	1992
5	JH de Beer, SA vs England	1999

SEASON RECORDS

Most points by a team
1434	Free State	1996
1390	Lions	1999
1348	Natal Sharks	1996
1284	Pumas	2013

Most tries by a team
191	Free State	1996
184	Natal Sharks	1996
181	Lions	1999
163	Pumas	2013

400 points by a player
528	NB Scholtz, Western Province	1988
471	M Steyn, Bulls, Blue Bulls, SA	2010
460	MJ Smith, Free State	1996
456	J Engelbrecht, Lions	1999
444	DJB Basson, Western Transvaal	1994
443	E Herbert, NFS & Free State	1994
434	M Steyn, Bulls, Blue Bulls, SA	2009
427	JT Stransky, Western Province	1994
424	CP Steyn, Blue Bulls	1999
406	K Tsimba, Vodacom Cheetahs	2002
401	HE Botha, Northern Transvaal	1987

30 tries by a player
35	P Hendriks, Transvaal	1992
34	BA Basson, Cheetahs, GW, SA	2010
34	C Fourie, North East Cape & Gazelles	1972
32	BJ Paulse, Western Province	2000
30	AJ Joubert, Natal	1996

CAREER RECORDS

1 500 points
3781	HE Botha (NTvl & SA)	1977-95
3525	E Herbert (NFS & OFS)	1986-2001
3004	M Steyn (Blue Bulls, Bulls, SA)	2002-13
2358	WJ de W Ras (OFS, Natal & SA)	1974-86
2303	AJ Joubert (OFS, Natal & SA)	1986-99
2140	JT Stransky (NTvl, Natal, WP & SA)	1987-96
1914	AJJ van Straaten	1994-2005

SOUTH AFRICAN FIRST-CLASS RECORDS

		(NTvl, SWD, Falcons, WP, Griquas, Stormers, SA)	
1880	PC Montgomery	(WP, Stormers, Sharks, SA)	1994-2009
1862	NB Scholtz (Boland, WP, Gazelles)		1980-88
1856	AS Pretorius (Golden Lions, Leopards, SA)		2002-13
1853	W de Waal (Leop, FS, WP)		2002-10
1789	LJ Koen (WP, Stormers, Lions, Cats, Bulls, SA)		1996-2003
1766	JF van Wyk (EOFS)		1985-95
1753	JH de Beer (Tvl, FS, Bulls, Cats, SA)		1990-2000
1671	CP Steyn (Far North, Blue Bulls, Pumas)		1993-2006
1658	LR Sherrell (Natal, WP, Tvl, NTvl & SA)		1986-98
1569	R Blair (WP, Tvl & SA)		1974-84
1515	KC Tsimba (FS, BB, Pumas, NFS)		2000-09

100 tries

173	C Badenhorst (OFS, SA)	1986-99
159	BJ Paulse (WP, Stormers, SA)	1997-2007
158	DM Gerber (EP, OFS, WP, SA)	1978-95
157	JT Small (Tvl, Natal, WP, SA)	1988-99
156	JS Germishuys (OFS, Tvl, SA)	1971-85
156	JI Daniels (Boland, Lions, Cats, Bulls)	1998-2008
155	CS Terblanche (Boland, Natal, Sharks, SA)	1994-2011
143	BG Habana (Lions, BB, WP, SA)	2004-13
139	JH van der Westhuizen (Blue Bulls, SA)	1992-2003
135	AJ Joubert (OFS, Natal & SA)	1986-99
128	PWG Rossouw (WP, Stormers, SA)	1991-2004
119	P Hendriks (Tvl, SA)	1989-97
116	RH Mordt (Zimbabwe, NTvl, Tvl, SA)	1977-85
113	CJ du Plessis (WP, Tvl, SA)	1980-89
113	D Oosthuysen (WTvl, NTvl, SA)	1986-94
109	JF van der Westhuizen (Natal, WP, Tvl, SA)	1989-97
106	NJ Burger (WP)	1982-91
105	S Brink (FS, Natal, Sharks)	1993-2004

450 conversions

669	HE Botha (NTvl, SA)	1977-95
528	M Steyn (Blue Bulls, Bulls, SA)	2002-13
484	WJ de W Ras (OFS, Natal, SA)	1974-86
478	E Herbert (NFS & OFS)	1986-2001
346	W de Waal (Leopards, FS, WP)	2002-10
316	LJ Koen (WP, Lions, Boland)	1996-10

300 penalty goals

710	E Herbert (NFS, OFS)	1986-2001
545	HE Botha (NTvl, SA)	1977-95
521	M Steyn (Blue Bulls, Bulls, SA)	2002-13

75 drop goals

210	HE Botha (NTvl, SA)	1977-95
90	WJ de W Ras (OFS, Natal, SA)	1974-86
83	E Herbert (NFS, OFS)	1986-2001

Most appearances in a single position for a province

159	Fullback	HM Reece-Edwards
221	Wing	C Badenhorst
225	Centre	HL Müller
205	Flyhalf	E Herbert
162	Scrumhalf	E Hare
154	No. 8	AWA van Wyk
183	Flank	SB Geldenhuys
191	Lock	WH Lessing
177	Prop	CJ Botha
157	Hooker	T van der Walt

100 matches as a provincial captain

129	E Hare (WTvl)	1989-96
128	HE Botha (NTvl)	1980-92
103	M du Plessis (WP)	1972-80
102	JC Breedt (Tvl)	1986-92
101	M Reitz (Boland)	1989-94
100	JR van Rensburg (Vaal Triangle)	1983-89

Fastest to 100 games

CJ Kapp (SWD) 3 years 240 days 1997-2000

Youngest player to 100 games

P Hendriks (Tvl) 24 years 339 days on 18/03/1995

Played for seven provinces

J-P Joubert NFS, SWD, Bol, GW, BB, FS, GL
R Geldenhuys* Bor, Pum, GL, Bol, Griff, FS, EP
*He sat on the bench for WP in 2006 and in 2013 without going on

Played for six provinces

St E Wilken	EP, FS, Tvl, NTvl, Griquas, Natal
J Nel	WTvl, EP, WP, Boland, Tvl, FS
H Rheeders	Blue Bulls, EP, FS, Pumas, Griffons, SWD
JN Van der Walt	Blue Bulls, Valke, Sharks, Griquas, Griffons, SWD Eagles
TC Kokoali	GL, FS, NFS, KZN, BB, Valke
PH Myburgh	KZN, Valke, BB, Bol, FS, NFS
LI Strydom	Griff, BB, Valke, Lions, Cheetahs, EP
AJ van Schalkwyk	FS, Valke, Boland, BB, GL, Leopards

More than 300 first-class matches*

345	V Matfield (BB, GW, Cats, Bulls, SA)
344	CS Terblanche (Bol, KZN, Sharks, SA)
343	A-H le Roux (FS, KZN, Cheetahs, SA)
338	PA van den Berg (Vaal Triangle, GW, KZN, SA)
328	JW Smit (KZN, Sharks, SA)

*only in SA

100 APPEARANCES FOR A PROVINCE

A
Alcock, C.D (Chad) Eastern Province 113. **Allan, J** (John) Natal 126. **Andrews, K.S** (Keith) Western Province 147. **Andrews, M.G** (Mark) Natal 122. **Appelgryn, J** (Kobie) NFS 103. **Atherton, S** (Steve) Natal 165.

B
Badenhorst, C (Chris) Free State 221. **Badenhorst, M.J.L** (Thys) NFS 103. **Bedford, T.P** (Tommy) Natal 119. **Bekker, H.J** (Hennie) Western Province 108. **Bekker, I.A** (Sakkie) EOFS 100. **Berry, D.P** (Don) Western Transvaal 104. **Bester, H** (Hennie) NFS 100. **Beukes, J** (Joe) OFS 121. **Beukes, J.A** (Boela) Vaal Triangle 115. **Blakeway, A.D** (Andrew) Natal 111. **Blom, L.F** (Louis) Western Province 125. **Booi CN** (Chumani) Border 105. **Booysen, J** (Jaco) Eastern Transvaal 134. **Bosman, M** (Marius) South Eastern Transvaal 107. **Botes, LJ** (Jacques) Natal Sharks 120. **Botha, A** (Anton) Border 119. **Botha, A.A** (André) Natal 137. **Botha, C.J** (Connie) SWD 191. **Botha, H.E** (Naas) Northern Transvaal 179. **Botha, J.N** (Taai) Eastern Transvaal 122. **Brandt, F** (Fabian) Boland Cavaliers 132. **Breedt, J.C** (Jannie) Transvaal 118. **Breedt, J.P.F** (Jan) NFS 148. **Bucholz, A.P** (Pierre) Vaal Triangle 152. **Burger, N.J** (Niel) Western Province 126. **Burke, JC** (Conrad) Boland Cavaliers 113.

C
Campher, L (Lourens) Northern Transvaal 106. **Claasen, A.D** (André) Border 141. **Claassen, J.T** (Johan) Western Transvaal 105. **Claassens, J.P** (Jannie) Northern Transvaal 102. **Cloete, A.** (André) OFS 152. **Cockrell, R.J** (Robert) Western Province 102. **Coeries, D.B** (Darryll) SWD Eagles 118. **Coetzee, H** (Harry) SWD 108. **Coetzee, J** (Jaco) OFS 141. **Coetzee, J** (Jannie) Boland 140. **Coetzee, J** (Japie) Namibia 119. **Coetzee, J.H.H** (Boland) Western Province 127. **Cooke, R.E** (Richard) South Eastern Transvaal 112.

D
Daniel, KR (Keegan) Natal Sharks 104. **De Jager, J.J** (Jakkie) Northern Natal 122. **De Klerk, K.B.H** (Kevin) Transvaal 107. **De Lange, P** (Draadkar) South Eastern Transvaal 114. **De Villiers, T.T.C.R** (Tielman) Griqualand West 101. **De Villiers, A** (André) EOFS 106. **De Villiers, F** (Frikkie) Griqualand West 112. **De Wet, F.P** (Eric) NWC 124. **Dixon, T** (Tommy) Boland Cavaliers 103. **Domoney, W** (Wayne) Border 111. **Douw, T.J** (Turtius) Falcons 108. **Drotské, A.E** (Naka) FS Cheetahs 127. **Du Plessis, C.J** (Carel) Western Province 108. **Du Plessis, H** (Henley) Boland Cavaliers 133. **Du Plessis, M** (Morné) Western Province 112. **Du Plessis, T.D** (Tommy) Northern Transvaal 126. **Du Plooy, A.J.J** (Amos) Eastern Province 102. **Du Preez, GJD** (Delarey) Border Bulldogs 103. **Du Preez, F.C.H** (Frik) Northern Transvaal 109. **Du Preez, J** (Kosie) Vaal Triangle 100. **Du Preez, WH** (Wian) FS Cheetahs 110. **Du Randt, J.P** (Os) FS Cheetahs 105. **Du Toit, H.B** (Manie) SWD Eagles 109. **Du Toit, H.J** (Hein) Boland 104. **Du Toit, P.A** (Fonnie) Northern Transvaal 102. **Durrheim, E.A** (Ertjies) Eastern Transvaal 152.

E
Edwards, W (Bull) Border 103. **Els, J.C.W** (Jannie) Eastern Transvaal 117. **Els, W.W** (Braam) OFS 155. **Engelbrecht, H** (Herklaas) NWC 126. **Erasmus, F.S** (Frans) Eastern Province 119. **Erasmus, J** (Johan/Rassie) FS Cheetahs 117.

F
Ferreira, C.F (Freddie) Western Province 100. **Fihlani, I.Z** (Ian) Border Bulldogs 129. **Fortuin, BA** (Bevin) SWD Eagles 122. **Fourie, M.J** (Pote) Northern Transvaal 105. **Fourie, P.D** (Kleinboet) Eastern Transvaal 109. **Fredericks, E.R** (Eddie) Free State 114. **Froneman, P** (Philip) Border 117.

G
Garvey, A.C (Adrian) Natal 109. **Geldenhuys, A** (Adri) Eastern Province 110. **Geldenhuys, S.B** (Burger) Northern Transvaal 184. **Gelderbloom, G** (Glen) Border 115. **Gerber, A** (André) NFS 111. **Gerber, D.M** (Danie) Eastern Province 116. **Geyser, F.M** (Frikkie) NFS 118. **Greeff, J** (Jacques) Eastern Province 101. **Greyling, M** (Tienie) EOFS 171. **Griesel, W** (Werner) Griffons 114. **Grimes, H** (Henry) SWD Eagles 103. **Grobbelaar, PJJ** (Cobus) Golden Lions 113. **Grobler, G** (Gerbrand) Northern Transvaal 108.

H
Hankinson, R.G (Rob) Natal 110. **Hare, E** (Eugene) Western Transvaal 176. **Harris, J** (Brok) Western Province 109. **Harrison, J** (Julian) NFS 102. **Hendriks, P** (Pieter) Transvaal 138. **Herbert, E** (Eric) NFS 205.

100 APPEARANCES FOR A PROVINCE

Heunis, D.F (Danie) Eastern Transvaal 124. Heunis, J.W (Johan) Northern Transvaal 109. Heymans, J.H (Dougie) OFS 154. Honiball, H.W (Henry) Natal 111. Hugo, D.P (Niel) Western Province 146. Human, J (Hannes) Leopards 125. Human, P.G (Pote) Eastern Province 116.

J
Jacobs, B.J (Bennie) Border 179. Jamieson, C.M (Craig) Natal 123. Jansen, E (Eben) OFS 125. Jerling, J.J (Jurie) NFS 174. Johnson, A.M (Andrew) Eastern Province 123. Jonck, C (Chris) Mighty Elephants 121. Joubert, B (Bobby) Border 101. Joubert, P.C (Piet) South Eastern Transvaal 112. Julies, R (Randile) Boland Cavaliers 104.

K
Kahts, W.J.H (Willie) Northern Transvaal 110. Kapp, C.J (Johan) SWD 124. Karg, D.H (Deon) Namibia 102. Knoetze, F (Faffa) Western Province 110. Koch, A.C (Chris) Boland 112. Koch, W (Willem) Boland 101. Kruger, CR (Chris) FS Cheetahs 100. Kruger, W (Werner) Blue Bulls 112. Kuun, GWF (Derick) Blue Bulls 100.

L
Labuschagne, H.J (Hendrik) Eastern Transvaal 107. Labuschagne, J.J (Jannes) Lions 103. Lamprecht, J.C (Johann) Northern Transvaal 101. Le Roux, A-H (Ollie) Natal Sharks/Wildebeest 101*. Le Roux, H.P (Hennie) Transvaal 153. Le Roux, J.H.S (Johan) Transvaal 100. Le Roux, M (Martiens) OFS 162. Lessing, W.H (Werner) Leopards 191. Lewis, C (Clemen) Boland Cavaliers 102. Ligman, EJ (Elroy) Eastern Province 101. Linee, M (Tinus) Western Province 112. Lock, J.L (Jan) Northern Transvaal 106. Lombard, JR (Nardi) Mighty Elephants 104. Loots, P (Pietie) Border Bulldogs 121. Losper, S.J (Sarel) Namibia 116. Lötter, J.G (Deon) Griqualand West 104. Lotz, J.W (Jan) Transvaal 114. Lourens, M.J (Thys) Northern Transvaal 168. Louw, SJ (Sarel) Griffons 140. Lubbe, J.M.F (Edrich) Griqualand West 114. Lubbe, L (Leon) Eastern Transvaal 119. Luus, NJ (Nico) Valke 134.

M
Macdonald, I (Ian) Transvaal 145. Malan, A.W (Adolf) Northern Transvaal 159. Mametsa, SJ (John) Blue Bulls 136. Marais, F.S (Frans) Boland 101. Maritz, A (Dries) Transvaal 141. Maritz, W (Willem) Namibia 103. Matthys, P (Piet) Eastern Transvaal 110. Mbulali, V (Vusumzi) Border 100. Meintjes, J (Kobus) Boland 102. Meiring, F.A (FA) Northern Transvaal 105. Meyer, E (Eugene) Eastern Transvaal 110. Meyer, N.J (Nico) Eastern Province 107. Meyer, W (Willie) Eastern Province 105. Moolman, J.H (Jannie) NEC 100. Moolman, L.C (Louis) Northern Transvaal 171. Mortassagne, A.M (Mort) Natal 100. Mtimka, LJJ (Black) Border Bulldogs 109. Muir, D.J (Dick) Natal 148. Mulder, J.C (Japie) Transvaal 113. Müller, H.L (Helgard) OFS 245. Muller, J.H (Harry) South Eastern Transvaal 126. Myburgh, J.L (Mof) Northern Transvaal 109.

N
Nel, D (Donie) Far North 140. Nicholas, J (Jearus) Griqualand West 116. Nieuwenhuis, J (Jacques) Valke 100. Nieuwenhuyzen, S.L (Stephen) NFS 151.

O
Olivier, J (Jacques) Northern Transvaal 137. Oosthuysen, D.E (Deon) Northern Transvaal 140. Opperman, R.J (Ryno) OFS 137. Oxlee, K (Keith) Natal 102.

P
Papier, N (Neil) Boland Cavaliers 154. Patterson, A.C (Andrew) Western Province 131. Pienaar, J.F (Francois) Transvaal 100. Pienaar, Z.M.J (Gysie) OFS 165. Pinnock, B.C (Barry) Eastern Province 173. Potgieter, CJ (Chris) Boland Cavaliers 115. Potgieter, R (Riaan) Eastern Province 108. Potgieter, R (Riaan) South Eastern Transvaal 109. Povey, S.A (Shaun) Western Province 103. Pretorius, A.J (Attie) Stellaland 124. Pretorius, D.B (Dawie) EOFS 117. Prins, D.R (Dave) Griqualand West 107. Putt, K.B (Kevin) Natal 118.

R
Rademeyer, H.N (Hempas) Transvaal 105. Ras, W.J.de W (De Wet) OFS 141. Reece-Edwards, H.M (Hugh) Natal 165. Reitz, M (Takkies) Boland 101. Richter, A.J (Adriaan) Northern Transvaal 137. Roberts, WAS (Steph) Griqualand West 111. Rodgers, P.H (Heinrich) Northern Transvaal 115. Roets, J (Johan) Blue Bulls 105. Rossouw, E (Naas) Falcons 158. Rossouw, F.J (Francois) South Eastern Transvaal 183. Rossouw, P.W.G (Pieter) Western Province 126. Roux, J.P (Johan) Transvaal 111. Roux, WG (Wessel) Blue Bulls 114. Ryan, M.W (Mike) NFS 115.

S
Santon, D (Dale) Boland Cavaliers 120. Schmidt, U.L (Uli) Northern Transvaal 136. Schoeman, M (Matthys) Stella-

100 APPEARANCES FOR A PROVINCE

land 112. **Scholtz, H** (Hendro) FS Cheetahs 147. **Scholtz, N.B** (Calla) Western Province 116. **Senekal, C** (Chris) Namibia 101. **Serfontein, D.J** (Divan) Western Province 100. **Serfontein, J.L** (Jan) Eastern Province 117. **Slade, J** (John) Natal 101. **Smit, F.C** (FC) Western Province 104. **Smit, J** (Koos) Vaal Triangle 101. **Smith, J.D** (Tos) Griqualand West 137. **Smith, M.J** (MJ) OFS 117. **Sonnekus, G.H.H** (Gerrie) OFS 160. **Steenkamp, CJ** (Corne) Pumas 141. **Stewart, J.C** (Christian) Western Province 136. **Stoop, L** (Leon) Namibia 105. **Strauss, C.P** (Tiaan) Western Province 156. **Strauss, J.H.P** (Johan) Transvaal 105. **Strydom, J.J** (Hannes) Transvaal 115. **Swart, D.P** (DP) Western Transvaal 117. **Swart, EJ** (Eddie) Border 111. **Swart, G.J** (Hakkies) South Eastern Transvaal 158. **Swart, I.S. De V** (Balie) Transvaal 108. **Swart, M** (Marius) Border 131.

T
Teichmann, G.H (Gary) Natal 144. **Terblanche, CS** (Stefan) Natal Sharks 104. **Terblanche, DJ** (DJ) Pumas 103. **Theron, D.F** (Dawie) Griqualand West 108. **Thomson, J.R.D** (Jeremy) Natal 152. **Treu, P.M** (Paul) SWD 105.

V
Van der Linde, A (Toks) Western Province 133. **Van der Merwe, C.A** (Chris) Boland 137. **Van der Merwe, D** (Danie) Namibia 106. **Van der Merwe, F** (Franco) Golden Lions 100. **Van der Merwe, L** (Leonard) Griffons 111. **Van der Merwe, W.J** (Wessel) Western Transvaal 122. **Van Niekerk, JJ** (Janru) Boland Cavaliers 106. **Van der Walt, J.A** (Jannie) Transvaal 116. **Van der Walt, T** (Tjaart) Eastern Transvaal 157. **Van der Westhuizen, J.F** (Cabous) Natal 128. **Van der Westhuizen, J.H** (Joost) Northern Transvaal 144. **Van Greunen, M** (Markus) Leopards 111. **Van Heerden, W** (Wayne) Eastern Province 121. **Van Rensburg, J.R** (James) Vaal Triangle 101. **Van Rooyen, J.C.O** (Kobus) Eastern Transvaal 134. **Van Schouwenburg, FJ** (Francois) Blue Bulls 112. **Van Tonder, H.V** (Hendry) South Eastern Transvaal 103. **Van Wyk, A.W.A** (André) Griqualand West 161. **Van Wyk, J.F** (Japie) EOFS 150. **Van Zyl, C.A.A** (Carlo) Border 115. **Van Zyl, C.G.P** (Sakkie) OFS 121. **Van Zyl, G.C** (Giepie) Eastern Province 109. **Van Zyl, WP** (Piet) Boland Cavaliers 144. **Venter, A.G** (André) OFS 115. **Venter, B** (Brendan) OFS 122. **Venter, De W** (De Waal) Griqualand West 106. **Venter, J.A** (Barabas) Transvaal 106. **Venter, S** (Shaun) Pumas 105. **Verhoeven, A** (Antonius) Boland Cavaliers 124. **Vermeulen, A** (André) Griqualand West 121. **Vermeulen, R** (Ruan) Blue Bulls 115. **Visagie, R** (Richard) Boland 105. **Visagie, R.G** (Rudi) OFS 109. **Visagie, R.G** (Rudi) Natal 109. **Visser, J. de V** (Div) Western Province 106. **Vos, J** (Johnny) Border 104.

W
Wagener, O (Otto) NFS 128. **Watson, A.C** (Tony) Natal 144. **Webb, T.C** (Tommie) SWD Eagles 119. **Wessels, H** (Hedley) Griqualand West 131. **Wessels, H.J** (Japie) OFS 145. **Wessels, J.C** (Boeta) Griqualand West 111. **Weyer, W.A** (Wayne) Border 183. **Wiese, J.J** (Kobus) Transvaal 128. **Willemse, C** (Chaka) South Eastern Transvaal 101. **Williamson, G** (Gunder) Falcons 139. **Wolfaardt, E.P** (Elmo) Boland 117. **Wolfaardt, J** (Jacques) SWD 121. **Wolmarans, B.J** (Barry) OFS 116.

Ollie le Roux played 100 games for the KZN Sharks and one for the KZN Wildebeest

100 APPEARANCES FOR A FRANCHISE

Bekker, A (Andries)	Stormers	105	Rossouw, DJ (Danie)	Bulls	116
Botes, LJ (Jacques)	Sharks	114	Smit, JW (John)	Sharks	125
Botha, JP (Bakkies)	Bulls	100	Spies, PJ (Pierre)	Bulls	102
Du Plessis, BW (Bismarck)	Sharks	103	Steyn, M (Morne)	Bulls	123
Du Preez, PF (Fourie)	Bulls	112	Terblanche, CS (Stefan)	Sharks	122
Matfield, V (Victor)	Bulls	116	Wannenburg, PJ (Pedrie)	Bulls	113
Olivier, W (Wynand)	Bulls	110			

VODACOM SUPER RUGBY RECORDS

CHAMPIONS

1996	Blues	2000	Crusaders	2005	Crusaders	2010	Vodacom Bulls
1997	Blues	2001	ACT Brumbies	2006	Crusaders	2011	Reds
1998	Crusaders	2002	Crusaders	2007	Vodacom Bulls	2012	Chiefs
1999	Crusaders	2003	Blues	2008	Crusaders	2013	Chiefs
		2004	ACT Brumbies	2009	Vodacom Bulls		

RESULTS OF FINALS

Year	Winner	Score	Loser	Score	Venue
1996	**Blues**	45	Sharks	21	Auckland
1997	**Blues**	23	ACT Brumbies	7	Auckland
1998	**Blues**	13	Crusaders	20	Auckland
1999	Highlanders	19	**Crusaders**	24	Dunedin
2000	ACT Brumbies	19	**Crusaders**	20	Canberra
2001	**ACT Brumbies**	36	Sharks	6	Canberra
2002	**Crusaders**	31	ACT Brumbies	13	Christchurch
2003	**Blues**	21	Crusaders	17	Auckland
2004	**ACT Brumbies**	47	Crusaders	38	Canberra
2005	**Crusaders**	35	NSW Waratahs	25	Christchurch
2006	**Crusaders**	19	Hurricanes	12	Christchurch
2007	Sharks	19	**Vodacom Bulls**	20	Durban
2008	**Crusaders**	20	Waratahs	12	Christchurch
2009	**Vodacom Bulls**	61	Chiefs	17	Pretoria
2010	**Vodacom Bulls**	25	Vodacom Stormers	17	Soweto
2011	**Reds**	18	Crusaders	13	Brisbane
2012	**Chiefs**	37	Sharks	6	Hamilton
2013	**Chiefs**	27	ACT Brumbies	22	Hamilton

MATCH RECORDS

75 points
96-19 Crusaders vs. NSW Waratahs Christchurch 2002
92-03 Vodacom Bulls vs. Queensland Reds Pretoria 2007
77-34 Crusaders vs. Sharks Christchurch 2005
75-43 Natal vs. Highlanders Durban 1997
75-27 Crusaders vs. Bulls Christchurch 2000
75-14 Bulls vs. Stormers Pretoria 2005

Wins by 50 points
89 Vodacom Bulls vs. Queensland Reds (92-3) Pretoria 2007
77 Crusaders vs. Waratahs (96-19) Christchurch 2002
64 ACT Brumbies vs. Bulls (73-9) Canberra 1999
64 ACT Brumbies vs. Cats (64-0) Canberra 2000
61 Bulls vs. Stormers (75-14) Pretoria 2005
53 Blues vs. Hurricanes (60-7) Wellington 2002
53 Crusaders vs. Western Force (53-0) Christchurch 2007
50 Cats vs. Chiefs (53-3) Bloemfontein 2000
50 Reds vs. Melbourne Rebels (53-3) Brisbane 2011

Eleven tries
14 Crusaders vs. Waratahs (96-19) Christchurch 2002
13 Vodacom Bulls vs. Queensland Reds (92-3) Pretoria 2007
11 Blues vs. Stormers (74-28) Auckland 1998
11 Crusaders vs. Bulls (75-27) Christchurch 2000
11 Crusaders vs. Sharks (77-34) Christchurch 2005

Thirty-five points by a player
50 GE Lawless (4t, 9c, 4p) Natal vs. Highlanders 1997
39 JH Kruger (1t, 5c, 8p) NTvl vs. Highlanders 1996
35 M Steyn (1t, 9c, 4p) Bulls vs. Stormers 2005
35 M Steyn (2t, 5c, 5p) Bulls vs. Brumbies 2010

VODACOM SUPER RUGBY RECORDS

Four tries by a player

4	JWC Roff, ACT Brumbies vs. Natal	1996
4	GE Lawless, Natal vs. Highlanders	1997
4	CS Terblanche, Sharks vs. Chiefs	1998
4	J Vidiri, Blues vs. Bulls	2000
4	DC Howlett, Blues vs. Hurricanes	2002
4	M Muliaina, Blues vs. Bulls	2002
4	CS Ralph, Crusaders vs. NSW Waratahs	2002
4	SW Sivivatu, Chiefs vs. Blues	2009
4	DA Mitchell, Waratahs vs Lions	2010
4	SD Maitland, Crusaders vs Brumbies	2011
4	AT Tikoroituma, Chiefs vs Blues	2012

Ten conversions by a player

13	AP Mehrtens, Crusaders vs. Waratahs	2002
11	DJ Hougaard, Vodacom Bulls vs. Queensland Reds	2007

Eight penalty goals by a player

9	ET Jantjies, Lions vs Cheetahs	2012
8	JH Kruger, N.Transvaal vs. Highlanders	1996
8	WC Walker, Highlanders vs. Chiefs	2003
8	HM Bosman, Cheetahs vs. Stormers	2006
8	DJ Hougaard, Vodacom Bulls vs. Crusaders	2007
8	TJ Taylor, Crusaders vs. Stormers	2012

Three drop goals by a player

4	M Steyn, Bulls vs. Crusaders	2009
3	AP Mehrtens, Crusaders vs. Highlanders	1998
3	LJ Koen, Bulls vs. Cats	2003

SEASON RECORDS

200 POINTS OR MORE

	PLAYER	Province	Season	Tries	Conversions	Penalties	Drop Goals
263	M Steyn	Bulls	2010	5	38	51	3
251	AW Cruden	Chiefs	2012	3	43	50	0
240	M Steyn	Bulls	2013	2	32	57	1
228	QS Cooper	Reds	2011	5	31	43	4
221	DW Carter	Crusaders	2006	5	38	37	3
216	M Steyn	Bulls	2011	–	33	46	4
206	AP Mehrtens	Crusaders	1998	5	23	41	4
201	DW Carter	Crusaders	2004	6	27	39	0

12 tries

15	JWC Roff	ACT Brumbies	1997
15	RL Gear	Crusaders	2005
13	JT Small	Natal	1996
13	AM Walker	ACT Brumbies	2000
12	AJ Joubert	Natal	1996
12	JF Umaga	Hurricanes	1997
12	RQ Randle	Chiefs	2002
12	DC Howlett	Blues	2003
12	JP Pietersen	Sharks	2007

35 or more conversions

51	JWC Roff	ACT Brumbies	2004
43	AW Cruden	Chiefs	2012
39	SA Mortlock	ACT Brumbies	2000
38	DW Carter	Crusaders	2006
38	M Steyn	Bulls	2010
37	DW Carter	Crusaders	2005
36	SR Donald	Crusaders	2009
35	JWC Roff	ACT Brumbies	2003

40 or more penalty goals

58	CP Lealiifano	Brumbies	2013
57	M Steyn	Bulls	2013
51	M Steyn	Bulls	2010
50	AW Cruden	Chiefs	2012
47	JD O'Connor	Western Force	2011
46	M Steyn	Bulls	2011
44	JC Pietersen	Stormers	2013
43	AP Mehrtens	Crusaders	1999
43	QS Cooper	Reds	2011
43	PJ Lambie	Sharks	2013

VODACOM SUPER RUGBY RECORDS

42	DW Carter	Crusaders	2011	**Five or more drop goals**			
41	AP Mehrtens	Crusaders	1998	11	M Steyn	Bulls	2009
40	NR Spooner	Queensland Reds	1999	7	LJ Koen	Bulls	2003
40	BJ Barrett	Hurricanes	2013	6	AS Pretorius	Lions	2009

TEAM RECORDS

Most points in a log season
469   Crusaders   2002

Most points in all matches
541   Crusaders (13 matches)   2005

Most points conceded
585   Lions   2010

Most log points
66   Reds   2011
66   Stormers   2012
66   Chiefs   2013

Fewest log points
4   Bulls   2002

Fewest log points to reach semi-finals
30   Sharks   1997

Most tries in a log season
61   Crusaders   2005

Most tries in all matches
71   Crusaders   2005

Fewest tries scored
13   Lions   2007
15   Blues   1999
15   Queensland Reds   2007

Most tries conceded
74   Melbourne Rebels   2011
72   Lions   2010
69   Southern Kings   2013
67   Bulls   2002

Most wins in a log season
14   Stormers   2012
13   Reds   2011

Fewest wins in a season
0   Lions   2010
0   Bulls   2002

CAREER RECORDS

40 tries
59	DC Howlett	Hurricanes/Highlanders/Blues	104 matches
58	CS Ralph	Chiefs/Crusaders	135 matches
57	JWC Roff	ACT Brumbies	83 matches
56	CM Cullen	Hurricanes	85 matches
56	BG Habana	Bulls/Stormers	118 matches
55	SA Mortlock	ACT Brumbies	138 matches
48	JF Umaga	Hurricanes/Chiefs	129 matches
46	MA Nonu	Hurricanes/Blues/High	133 matches
43	J Vidiri	Blues	61 matches
42	LR MacDonald	Crusaders	127 matches
42	SW Sivivatu	Chiefs	89 matches
41	CE Latham	Reds	109 matches
41	SNG Staniforth	Waratahs/Western Force	106 matches
40	RL Gear	Crusaders	79 matches
40	JT Rokocoko	Blues	96 matches
37	J Fourie	Cats/Lions/Stormers	98 matches
36	CB Shepherd	Waratahs/Western Force	78 matches
35	JW Wilson	Highlanders	72 matches
35	M Vunibaka	Crusaders	50 matches
35	BJ Paulse	Stormers	79 matches
35	CS Terblanche	Sharks	122 matches
33	SJ Larkham	ACT Brumbies	116 matches
33	MJ Giteau	Brumbies/Force	104 matches
33	DA Mitchell	Reds/Force/ Waratahs	96 matches
32	RQ Randle	Chiefs	64 matches
32	AM Walker	ACT Brumbies/Reds	56 matches
31	PWG Rossouw	Stormers	75 matches
31	BN Tune	Queensland Reds	98 matches

Bryan Habana extended his SA try-scoring record to 56. *Peter Heeger/Gallo Images*

VODACOM SUPER RUGBY RECORDS

100 conversions

259	DW Carter	Crusaders	123 matches
242	M Steyn	Bulls	123 matches
162	SA Mortlock	ACT Brumbies/Rebels	138 matches
160	MC Burke	NSW Waratahs	79 matches
150	SR Donald	Chiefs	85 matches
147	TE Brown	Highl./Sharks/Stormers	107 matches
134	AP Mehrtens	Crusaders	87 matches
123	DE Holwell	Hurricanes/Blues	82 matches
121	CS Spencer	Blues/Lions	108 matches
113	MJ Giteau	Brumbies/Force	104 matches
106	AR Cashmore	Blues	57 matches
102	AS Pretorius	Cats/Lions	72 matches

500 POINTS OR MORE

	PLAYER	Province	Season	Tries	Conversions	Penalties	Drop Goals
1547	DW Carter	Crusaders	123	33	259	271	11
1431	M Steyn	Bulls	123	13	242	275	25
1036	SA Mortlock	ACT Brumbies	142	55	162	146	0
990	AP Mehrtens	Crusaders	87	13	134	202	17
959	MC Burke	NSW Waratahs	79	24	160	173	0
942	TE Brown	Highl/Sharks/Stormers	107	5	148	199	8
857	SR Donald	Chiefs	85	19	150	153	1
819	PJ Grant	Stormers	90	10	116	179	0
751	MJ Giteau	Brumbies/Force	104	33	113	117	3
700	DE Holwell	Hurricanes/Blues	82	8	123	138	0
661	AS Pretorius	Cats/Lions	72	11	102	121	13
629	EJ Flatley	Queensland Reds	87	11	92	130	0
625	CJ Spencer	Blues/Lions	108	28	121	78	3
619	AR Cashmore	Blues	47	13	106	113	1
607	QS Cooper	Reds	88	19	84	109	6
588	JWC Roff	ACT Brumbies	83	57	99	34	1
555	LJ Koen	Stormers/Bulls/Cats	51	5	79	113	11
520	PG Hewat	NSW Waratahs	40	17	66	101	0
515	PJ Lambie	Sharks	50	8	65	114	1

100 penalty goals

277	DW Carter	Crusaders	123 matches
275	M Steyn	Bulls	123 matches
202	AP Mehrtens	Crusaders	87 matches
199	TE Brown	Highl./Sharks/Stormers	107 matches
179	PJ Grant	Stormers	90 matches
173	MC Burke	NSW Waratahs	71 matches
172	M Steyn	Bulls	89 matches
153	SR Donald	Chiefs	85 matches
144	SA Mortlock	ACT Brumbies	123 matches
138	DE Holwell	Hurricanes/Blues	82 matches
130	EJ Flatley	Reds	87 matches
121	AS Pretorius	Cats/Lions	72 matches
117	MJ Giteau	Brumbies/Force	104 matches
113	AR Cashmore	Blues	57 matches
113	LJ Koen	Stormers/Bulls/Cats	51 matches
108	AJJ van Straaten	Bulls/Stormers	45 matches
101	P Hewat	NSW Waratahs	40 matches

Five drop goals

21	M Steyn	Bulls	123 matches
17	AP Mehrtens	Crusaders	87 matches
13	AS Pretorius	Cats/Lions	72 matches
11	LJ Koen	Bulls	51 matches
11	DW Carter	Crusaders	123 matches
10	DJ Hougaard	Bulls	51 matches
9	BS Barnes	Reds/Waratahs	59 matches
8	TE Brown	Highlanders/Sharks	107 matches
6	AJD Mauger	Crusaders	89 matches

VODACOM SUPER RUGBY RECORDS

5	SJ Larkham	ACT Brumbies	116 matches	109	B Robinson	Waratahs
5	GS du Toit	Sharks, Stormers & Cheetahs		108	A Ashley-Cooper	Waratahs/Brumbies
			67 matches	108	HM Bosman	Cheetahs/Sharks
				108	QJ Cowan	Highlanders

100 appearances

162	NC Sharpe	Reds/Force		108	A-H Le Roux	Sharks/Cheetahs
152	KF Mealamu	Blues/Chiefs		108	CJ Spencer	Blues/Lions
146	SA Mortlock	ACT Brumbies/Rebels		107	CJ Whitaker	NSW Waratahs
142	GB Smith	ACT Brumbies		107	TE Brown	Highl./Stormers/Sharks
141	AK Hore	Highl/Hurr/Crus		107	AM Ellis	Crusaders
136	CS Ralph	Chiefs/Crusaders/Reds		107	MA Gerrard	Rebels/Brum/NSW
136	GM Gregan	ACT Brumbies		106	CC King	Highlanders/Crusaders
134	CR Flynn	Crusaders		106	OM Ndungane	Bulls/Sharks
134	MA Nonu	Highl/Hurr/Blues		106	BJ Cannon	Waratahs/Force
132	PR Waugh	NSW Waratahs		106	AKE Baxter	NSW Waratahs
131	GM Somerville	Crusaders/Rebels		106	SNG Staniforth	Waratahs/Force
129	RD Thorne	Crusaders		105	JW Marshall	Crusaders
128	JF Umaga	Hurricanes/Chiefs		104	DC Howlett	Highlanders/Blues
127	AD Oliver	Highlanders		104	MJ Giteau	Brumbies/Force
127	LR MacDonald	Crusaders/Chiefs		104	JM Muliaina	Chiefs/Blues
125	TD Woodcock	Blues/Highlanders		104	A Bekker	Stormers
125	AJ Venter	Cats/Sharks/Stormers		104	AL Freier	Rebels/Brum/NSW
125	JW Smit	Sharks		104	J Vermaak	Bulls/Lions/Cats
124	V Matfield	Cats/Bulls		103	BW du Plessis	Sharks
123	SP Hardman	Reds		103	JA Collins	Blues/Chiefs
123	M Steyn	Bulls		103	MD Chisholm	ACT Brumbies
122	WVV Crockett	Crusaders		102	PA van den Berg	Cats/Sharks
122	RH McCaw	Crusaders		102	HE Gear	Highlanders/Hurricanes
122	CS Terblanche	Sharks		102	PJ Spies	Bulls
121	AKE Baxter	NSW Waratahs		101	R So'oialo	Hurricanes
121	DW Carter	Crusaders		101	IF Afoa	Blues
118	BG Habana	Bulls/Stormers		101	NS Tialata	Hurricanes
118	NJ Henderson	Rebels/Force/ACT		101	SUT Polota-Nau	Waratahs
118	ST Moore	Brumbies/Reds		100	DJ Lyons	Waratahs
117	AJ Williams	Blues/Crusaders		100	WK Young	ACT Brumbies
116	SJ Larkham	ACT Brumbies		100	JP Botha	Bulls
116	DJ Rossouw	Bulls				

Tallest

114	LJ Botes	Sharks		2.08m	Andries Bekker	Stormers
114	JN du Plessis	Sharks/Cheetahs		2.06m	Dominic Bird	Crusaders
114	P Weepu	Blues/Hurricanes				
113	JA Paul	ACT Brumbies				
113	LJ Messam	Chiefs				
113	PJ Wannenburg	Bulls				
113	AA Jacobs	Cats/Bulls/Sharks				
112	PF du Preez	Bulls				
111	MJ Dunning	NSW Waratahs/Force				
111	A Mitchell	Reds/Force/NSW				
110	CR Jack	Crusaders				
110	W Olivier	Bulls				
109	CE Latham	Waratahs/Reds				

RUGBY CHAMPIONSHIP RECORDS

CHAMPIONS

1996	New Zealand	2000	Australia	2005	New Zealand	2010	New Zealand
1997	New Zealand	2001	Australia	2006	New Zealand	2011	Australia
1998	South Africa	2002	New Zealand	2007	New Zealand	2012	New Zealand
1999	New Zealand	2003	New Zealand	2008	New Zealand	2013	New Zealand
		2004	South Africa	2009	South Africa		

MATCH RECORDS

Fifty points
- 73-13 South Africa vs. Argentina 17/08/2013 Soweto
- 61-22 South Africa vs. Australia 23/08/1997 Pretoria
- 55-35 New Zealand vs. South Africa 09/08/1997 Auckland
- 54-15 New Zealand vs. Argentina 29/09/2012 La Plata
- 54-17 Australia vs. Argentina 06/10/2013 Rosario
- 53-08 South Africa vs. Australia 30/08/2008 Johannesburg
- 52-16 New Zealand vs. South Africa 19/07/2003 Pretoria
- 50-21 New Zealand vs. Australia 26/07/2003 Sydney

Wins by 35 points
- 60 South Africa vs. Argentina 17/08/2013 Soweto
- 49 Australia vs. South Africa (49-0) 15/07/2006 Brisbane
- 45 South Africa vs. Australia (53-8) 30/08/2008 Johannesburg
- 39 South Africa vs. Australia (61-22) 23/08/1997 Pretoria
- 39 New Zealand vs. Argentina (54-15) 29/09/2012 La Plata
- 37 New Zealand vs. Australia (43-6) 06/07/1996 Wellington
- 37 Australia vs. Argentina (54-17) 06/10/2013 Rosario
- 36 New Zealand vs. South Africa (52-16) 19/07/2003 Pretoria

Fifty points away from home
- 54 New Zealand vs. Argentina 29/09/2012 La Plata
- 54 Australia vs. Argentina, Rosario 06/10/2013 Rosario
- 52 New Zealand vs. South Africa 19/07/2003 Pretoria
- 50 New Zealand vs. Australia 26/07/2003 Sydney

Most by SA is 38 vs. Australia, Brisbane, 2013.

Six tries
- 9 South Africa vs. Argentina 17/08/2013 Soweto
- 8 South Africa vs. Australia 23/08/1997 Pretoria
- 8 South Africa vs. Australia 30/08/2008 Johannesburg
- 7 New Zealand vs. South Africa 09/08/1997 Auckland
- 7 New Zealand vs. South Africa 19/07/2003 Pretoria
- 7 New Zealand vs. Australia 26/07/2003 Sydney
- 7 New Zealand vs. Australia 31/07/2010 Melbourne
- 7 New Zealand vs. Argentina 29/09/2012 La Plata
- 7 Australia vs. Argentina 06/10/2013 Rosario
- 6 New Zealand vs. Australia 06/07/1996 Wellington
- 6 South Africa vs. New Zealand 19/08/2000 Johannesburg
- 6 Australia vs. South Africa 15/07/2006 Brisbane
- 6 New Zealand vs. South Africa 30/07/2011 Wellington
- 6 New Zealand vs. Australia 17/08/2013 Sydney

No points conceded in a test match
- 28-0 New Zealand vs South Africa 10/07/1999 Dunedin
- 49-0 Australia vs South Africa 15/07/2006 Brisbane
- 19-0 New Zealand vs South Africa 16/08/2008 Cape Town
- 22-0 New Zealand vs Australia 25/08/2012 Auckland

Twenty-five points by a player
- 31 M Steyn (1t, 1c, 8p), SA vs. NZ 01/08/2009 Durban
- 29 AP Mehrtens (1c, 9p), NZ vs. Australia 24/07/1999 Auckland
- 28 M Steyn (8c, 4p), SA vs. Argentina 17/08/2013 Soweto
- 26 JH de Beer (1t, 6c, 3p), SA vs. Australia 23/08/1997 Pretoria
- 25 CJ Spencer (1t, 4c, 4p), NZ vs. SA 09/08/1997 Auckland

CASTLE RUGBY CHAMPIONSHIP RECORDS

25 JT Stransky (1t, 1c, 6p), SA vs. Aus.
  03/08/1996 Bloemfontein
25 DW Carter (2c, 7p), NZ vs. SA 22/07/2006 Wellington
Most by an Australian: 24 by MC Burke (2t, 1c, 4p) vs. NZ in Melbourne, 11/07/1998

Three tries by a player
4 JL Nokwe, SA vs. Australia 30/08/2008 Johannesburg
3 JT Rokocoko, NZ vs. Australia 26/07/2003 Sydney
3 MC Joubert, SA vs. NZ 14/08/2004 Johannesburg
3 DC Howlett, NZ vs. Australia 03/09/2005 Auckland
3 BG Habana, SA vs. Australia 29/09/2012 Pretoria
3 CS Jane, NZ vs. Argentina 29/09/2012 La Plata
3 BR Smith, NZ vs. Australia 17/08/2013 Sydney
3 I Folau, Australia vs. Argentina 06/10/2013 Rosario

Five conversions by a player
8 M Steyn, SA vs. Argentina 17/08/2013 Soweto
6 JH de Beer, SA vs. Australia 23/08/1997 Pretoria
5 AJJ van Straaten, SA vs. NZ 19/08/2000 Johannesburg
5 SA Mortlock, Australia vs. SA 15/07/2006 Brisbane

Seven penalty goals by a player
9 AP Mehrtens, NZ vs. Australia 24/07/1999 Auckland
8 M Steyn, SA vs NZ 01/08/2009 Durban
7 MC Burke, Australia vs. NZ 28/08/1999 Sydney
7 AP Mehrtens, NZ vs. SA 07/08/1999 Pretoria
7 DW Carter, NZ vs. SA 22/07/2006 Wellington
7 DW Carter, NZ vs. Australia 21/07/2007 Auckland
7 M Steyn, SA vs Australia 08/08/2009 Cape Town

Two drop goals by a player
2 JH de Beer, SA vs. NZ 19/07/1997 Johannesburg
2 FPL Steyn, SA vs. Australia 16/06/2007 Cape Town

SEASON RECORDS BY TEAM

One hundred and sixty points
203	South Africa	2013
202	New Zealand	2013
184	New Zealand	2010
179	New Zealand	2006
177	New Zealand	2012
162	Australia	2010

One hundred and seventy points conceded
224	Argentina	2013
194	South Africa	2010
188	Australia	2010
185	South Africa	2006
170	Australia	2013

Most by New Zealand - 131 in 2009

Sixty or fewer points conceded
54	South Africa	1998
57	Australia	1999
59	New Zealand	2007

Fifteen tries
24	New Zealand	2013
23	South Africa	2013
22	New Zealand	2010
18	South Africa	1997
18	New Zealand	2012
17	New Zealand	1997
17	New Zealand	2003
17	New Zealand	2006
17	Australia	2010
16	New Zealand	2008

Fifteen tries conceded
22	South Africa	2010
21	Australia	2008
21	Australia	2010
18	South Africa	1997
18	South Africa	2006
17	Australia	1997
16	Argentina	2012

Most conceded by New Zealand - 13 in 1997 & 2000

Three tries or fewer conceded
| 3 | Australia | 1999 |
| 3 | South Africa | 2001 |

Fewest tries conceded by New Zealand - 4 in 2001

Nineteen or more log points
28	New Zealand	2013
27	New Zealand	2010
26	New Zealand	2012
23	New Zealand	2006
21	South Africa	2009
19	New Zealand	2008
19	South Africa	2013

Most by Australia is 14 (2000 & 2008)

CASTLE RUGBY CHAMPIONSHIP RECORDS

SEASON RECORDS BY A PLAYER

Seventy points
99	DW Carter	New Zealand	2006
95	M Steyn	South Africa	2009
88	M Steyn	South Africa	2013
84	CJ Spencer	New Zealand	1997
82	DW Carter	New Zealand	2008
77	M Steyn	South Africa	2010
72	MJ Giteau	Australia	2009
71	SA Mortlock	Australia	2000

Four tries
8	BR Smith	New Zealand	2013
7	CM Cullen	New Zealand	2000
7	BG Habana	South Africa	2012
6	JT Rokocoko	New Zealand	2003
5	DC Howlett	New Zealand	2003
5	CS Jane	New Zealand	2012
5	I Folau	Australia	2013
4	CM Cullen	New Zealand	1997
4	SA Mortlock	Australia	2000
4	JL Nokwe	South Africa	2008
4	JD O'Connor	Australia	2010
4	JM Muliaina	New Zealand	2010

Ten conversions
17	M Steyn	South Africa	2013
14	DW Carter	New Zealand	2006
13	CJ Spencer	New Zealand	1997
12	JH de Beer	South Africa	1997
12	SA Mortlock	Australia	2006
12	DW Carter	New Zealand	2008
11	MJ Giteau	Australia	2008
11	MJ Giteau	Australia	2010
11	DW Carter	New Zealand	2010
10	M Steyn	South Africa	2010

Fifteen penalty goals
23	M Steyn	South Africa	2009
21	DW Carter	New Zealand	2006
19	AP Mehrtens	New Zealand	1996
19	AP Mehrtens	New Zealand	1999
19	M Steyn	South Africa	2010
18	M Steyn	South Africa	2013
18	CP Lealiifano	Australia	2013
16	CJ Spencer	New Zealand	1997
15	DW Carter	New Zealand	2007
15	DW Carter	New Zealand	2008

Two drop goals
3	M Steyn	South Africa	2009
2	JH de Beer	South Africa	1997
2	AP Mehrtens	New Zealand	2000
2	PC Montgomery	South Africa	2005
2	AS Pretorius	South Africa	2005
2	FPL Steyn	South Africa	2007
2	BS Barnes	Australia	2009

Jean de Villiers equalled Victor Matfields appearances in the Rugby Championship with 43. Duif du Toit/Gallo Images

CAREER RECORDS

80 POINTS OR MORE

PLAYER	Country	Appearances	Tries	Conversions	Penalties	Drop Goals	Points
DW Carter	New Zealand	39	6	72	115	4	531
AP Mehrtens	New Zealand	26	1	34	82	3	328
M Steyn	Souh Africa	25	1	39	75	4	320
MC Burke	Australia	28	7	19	65	1	271
MJ Giteau	Australia	37	7	36	46	3	254
PC Montgomery	South Africa	34	4	26	43	3	210
SA Mortlock	Australia	31	9	21	37	0	198
CJ Spencer	New Zealand	13	3	21	32	0	153
AJJ van Straaten	South Africa	9	0	5	28	0	94
CM Cullen	New Zealand	24	16	0	0	0	80

Nine tries

17	BG Habana	South Africa
16	CM Cullen	New Zealand
15	JT Rokocoko	New Zealand
13	DC Howlett	New Zealand
12	RH McCaw	New Zealand
10	MA Nonu	New Zealand
9	JW Marshall	New Zealand
9	SA Mortlock	Australia
9	LD Tuqiri	Australia
9	J Fourie	South Africa
9	CS Jane	New Zealand

Eighteen conversions

72	DW Carter	New Zealand
39	M Steyn	South Africa
36	MJ Giteau	Australia
34	AP Mehrtens	New Zealand
26	PC Montgomery	South Africa
21	CJ Spencer	New Zealand
21	SA Mortlock	Australia

Forty penalty goals

115	DW Carter	New Zealand
82	AP Mehrtens	New Zealand
75	M Steyn	South Africa
65	MC Burke	Australia
46	MJ Giteau	Australia
43	PC Montgomery	South Africa

Three drop goals

4	AS Pretorius	South Africa
4	M Steyn	South Africa
4	DW Carter	New Zealand
3	AP Mehrtens	New Zealand
3	PC Montgomery	South Africa
3	MJ Giteau	Australia
3	B Barnes	Australia

Thirty appearances

49	RH McCaw	New Zealand
48	GM Gregan	Australia
47	NC Sharpe	Australia
47	KF Mealamu	New Zealand
44	TD Woodcock	New Zealand
43	JM Muliaina	New Zealand
43	V Matfield	South Africa
43	J de Villiers	South Africa
41	GB Smith	Australia
39	DW Carter	New Zealand
39	JW Smit	South Africa
38	SJ Larkham	Australia
38	BG Habana	South Africa
37	AP Ashley-Cooper	Australia
37	MJ Giteau	Australia
35	JW Marshall	New Zealand
34	PC Montgomery	South Africa
33	PAT Weepu	New Zealand
32	RD Elsom	Australia
31	SA Mortlock	Australia
30	PR Waugh	Australia
30	GM Somerville	New Zealand

ABSA CURRIE CUP RECORDS

CHAMPIONS

Year	Champion	Year	Champion	Year	Champion
1892[1]	Western Province	1956	Northern Transvaal	1989	Northern Transvaal
1894	Western Province	1957-59[3]	Western Province		& Western Province
1895	Western Province	1964	Western Province	1990	Natal
1897	Western Province	1966	Western Province	1991	Northern Transvaal
1898	Western Province	1968	Northern Transvaal	1992	Natal
1899[2]	Griqualand West	1969	Northern Transvaal	1993	Transvaal
1904	Western Province	1970	Griqualand West	1994	Transvaal
1906	Western Province	1971	Northern Transvaal	1995	Natal
1908	Western Province		& Transvaal	1996	Natal
1911	Griqualand West	1972	Transvaal	1997	Western Province
1914	Western Province	1973	Northern Transvaal	1998	Blue Bulls
1920	Western Province	1974	Northern Transvaal	1999	The Lions
1922	Transvaal	1975	Northern Transvaal	2000	Western Province
1925	Western Province	1976	Orange Free State	2001	Western Province
1927	Western Province	1977	Northern Transvaal	2002	Blue Bulls
1929	Western Province	1978	Northern Transvaal	2003	Blue Bulls
1932	Western Province	1979	Northern Transvaal	2004	Blue Bulls
	& Border		& Western Province	2005	Free State
1934	Western Province	1980	Northern Transvaal	2006	Free State &
	& Border	1981	Northern Transvaal		Blue Bulls
1936	Western Province	1982	Western Province	2007	Free State
1939	Transvaal	1983	Western Province	2008	Natal Sharks
1946	Northern Transvaal	1984	Western Province	2009	Blue Bulls
1947	Western Province	1985	Western Province	2010	Natal Sharks
1950	Transvaal	1986	Western Province	2011	Golden Lions
1952	Transvaal	1987	Northern Transvaal	2012	Western Province
1954	Western Province	1988	Northern Transvaal	2013	Natal Sharks

[1] The Currie Cup was first presented to the South African inter-provincial champions in 1892. It had been given by Sir Donald Currie (owner of the Castle Shipping Line) to WE Maclagan, captain of the first British Isles team on their departure for South Africa, with instructions that it should be awarded to the first side to beat the tourists and thereafter become a floating trophy for the South African inter-provincial champions. In the event they won all 19 of their games and the cup was presented to Griqualand West who lost only 3-0. Griquas in turn handed over the trophy to the South African Rugby Board as per Currie's instructions.
[2] Western Province and Transvaal did not compete due to the impending Anglo-Boer war.
[3] Contested over two seasons (suspended in 1958 due to tour by France).

Note: Western Province won the SA Rugby Board Trophy at the tournament in Kimberley in 1889.

RESULTS OF FINALS

Year	Team	Score	Team	Score	Venue
1939[1]	Western Province	6	Transvaal	17	Cape Town
1946	Northern Transvaal	11	Western Province	9	Pretoria
1947	Western Province	16	Transvaal	12	Cape Town
1950	Transvaal	22	Western Province	11	Johannesburg
1952	Boland	9	Transvaal	11	Wellington
1954	Western Province	11	Northern Transvaal	8	Cape Town
1956	Natal	8	Northern Transvaal	9	Durban
1968	Northern Transvaal	16	Transvaal	3	Pretoria
1969	Northern Transvaal	28	Western Province	13	Pretoria

ABSA CURRIE CUP RECORDS

Year	Winner	Score	Loser	Score	Venue
1970	Griqualand West	11	Northern Transvaal	9	Kimberley
1971	Transvaal	14	Northern Transvaal	14	Johannesburg
1972	Eastern Transvaal	19	Transvaal	25	Springs
1973	Northern Transvaal	30	Orange Free State	22	Pretoria
1974	Northern Transvaal	17	Transvaal	15	Pretoria
1975	Orange Free State	6	Northern Transvaal	12	Bloemfontein
1976	Orange Free State	33	Western Province	16	Bloemfontein
1977	Northern Transvaal	27	Orange Free State	12	Pretoria
1978	Orange Free State	9	Northern Transvaal	13	Bloemfontein
1979	Western Province	15	Northern Transvaal	15	Cape Town
1980	Northern Transvaal	39	Western Province	9	Pretoria
1981	Northern Transvaal	23	Orange Free State	6	Pretoria
1982	Western Province	24	Northern Transvaal	7	Cape Town
1983	Northern Transvaal	3	Western Province	9	Pretoria
1984	Western Province	19	Natal	9	Cape Town
1985	Western Province	22	Northern Transvaal	15	Cape Town
1986	Western Province	22	Transvaal	9	Cape Town
1987	Transvaal	18	Northern Transvaal	24	Johannesburg
1988	Northern Transvaal	19	Western Province	18	Pretoria
1989	Western Province	16	Northern Transvaal	16	Cape Town
1990	Northern Transvaal	12	Natal	18	Pretoria
1991	Northern Transvaal	27	Transvaal	15	Pretoria
1992	Transvaal	13	Natal	14	Johannesburg
1993	Natal	15	Transvaal	21	Durban
1994	Orange Free State	33	Transvaal	56	Bloemfontein
1995	Natal	25	Western Province	17	Durban
1996	Transvaal	15	Natal	33	Johannesburg
1997	Western Province	14	Free State	12	Cape Town
1998	Blue Bulls	24	Western Province	20	Pretoria
1999	Natal	9	Lions	32	Durban
2000	Natal	15	Western Province	25	Durban
2001	Western Province	29	Natal	24	Cape Town
2002	Lions	7	Blue Bulls	31	Johannesburg
2003	Blue Bulls	40	Natal Sharks	19	Pretoria
2004	Blue Bulls	42	Free State Cheetahs	33	Pretoria
2005	Blue Bulls	25	Free State Cheetahs	29	Pretoria
2006	Free State	28	Blue Bulls	28	Bloemfontein
2007	Free State	20	Lions	18	Bloemfontein
2008	Natal	14	Blue Bulls	9	Durban
2009	Blue Bulls	36	Free State Cheetahs	24	Pretoria
2010	Natal Sharks	30	Vodacom Western Province	10	Durban
2011	Golden Lions	42	Natal Sharks	16	Johannesburg
2012	Natal Sharks	18	DHL Western Province	25	Durban
2013	DHL Western Province	19	Natal Sharks	33	Cape Town

[1] A final has decided the winner in every competition since 1939 except 1957-59, 1964 & 1966.

MOST TITLES

32	Western Province (four times shared)	last	2001	
23	Blue Bulls (four times shared)	last	2009	
10	Lions (once shared)	last	2011	
7	Natal	last	2013	
4	Free State (once shared)	last	2007	
3	Griqualand West	last	1970	
2	Border (twice shared)	last	1934	

FINAL RECORDS

Most points
- 56 Transvaal vs Free State, 1994 final score 56-33*
- 42 Blue Bulls vs FS Cheetahs, 2004 final score 42-33
- 42 Golden Lions vs Sharks, 2011, final score 42-16
- 40 Blue Bulls vs Sharks , 2003 final score 40-19
- 39 Northern Transvaal vs WP, 1980 final score 39-9
- 36 Blue Bulls vs FS Cheetahs, 2009 final score 36-24
- 33 Free State vs WP, 1976 final score 33-16
- 33 Free State vs Lions, 1994 final score 33-56
- 33 Natal vs Lions, 1996 final score 33-15
- 33 FS Cheetahs vs Blue Bulls, 2004 final score 33-42
- 33 Sharks vs WP, 2013 final score 33-19

The match aggregate of 89 points is also a finals record

Five tries
- 7 Lions vs Free State on 1 October 1994
- 6 Blue Bulls vs Cheetahs on 23 October 2004
- 5 Blue Bulls vs WP on 4 October 1980
- 5 Lions vs Sharks on 11 September 1999
- 5 Blue Bulls vs Sharks on 1 November 2003

Twenty points by a player
- 26 Derick Hougaard Blue Bulls vs Lions, 2002
  (1try, 5 penalties, 2 drop goals)
- 25 Patrick Lambie Sharks vs Western Province, 2010
  (2 tries, 3 conversions, 3 penalties)
- 24 Naas Botha Blue Bulls vs Lions, 1987
  (4 penalties, 4 drop goals)
  Braam van Straaten vs Sharks, 2001
  (1try, 2 conversions, 5 penalties)
  Elton Jantjies vs Sharks, 2011
  (3 conversions, 5 penalties, 1 drop goal)
- 23 Patrick Lambie Sharks vs Western Province, 2013
  (1 conversion, 5 penalties, 1 drop goal)
- 21 Gavin Johnson Lions vs Free State ,1994
  (6 conversions,3 penalties)
  Morné Steyn Blue Bulls vs FS Cheetahs, 2009
  (3 conversions, 4 penalties, 1 drop goal)
- 20 Thierry Lacroix Natal vs WP, 1995
  (6 penalties, 1 conversion)

Six conversions by a player
- 6 Gavin Johnson Lions vs Cheetahs, 1994

Six penalty goals by a player
- 6 Thierry Lacroix Natal vs WP, 1995
- 6 Patrick Lambie Sharks vs WP, 2012

Four drop goals by a player
- 4 Naas Botha Northern Transvaal vs Transvaal, 1987

Most appearances in finals
- 11 Burger Geldenhuys Blue Bulls
  Northern Transvaal   1977-1989
  Naas Botha Blue Bulls
  Northern Transvaal   1977-1991
- 9 Louis Moolman Blue Bulls
  Northern Transvaal   1975-1986

Forty points in finals
- 138 Naas Botha   1t, 10c, 20p, 18dg   1977-1991
- 62   Willem de Waal   7c, 16p   2004-2010
- 54   Morné Steyn   6c, 12p, 2dg   2005-2009
- 45   Calla Scholtz   1t, 4c, 9p, 2dg   1983-1988
- 44   Derick Hougaard   1t, 3c, 8p, 3dg   2002-2006
- 41   Joel Stransky   1c, 13p   1990-1995

Three tries in finals
- 4 Ettienne Botha   Blue Bulls   2003-2004
- 3 Neil Burger   WP   1982-1985
- 3 Edrich Krantz   FS & N Tvl   1976-1980

Oldest and youngest winning captains
35 years 138 days   Thys Lourens   Northern Transvaal 1978
22 years 217 days   Naas Botha   Northern Transvaal 1980

Most wins as Coach
11* Brigadier Buurman van Zyl   Northern Transvaal 1968-1981

including two draws

Most finals as a referee
- 7 Andre Watson (Valke/SARU)
- 6 Steve Strydom (Free State)
- 5 Freek Burger (WP)
- 5 Jonathan Kaplan (SARU)

Youngest winning coach
32 years 351 days Johan Erasmus (FS Cheetahs in 2005)
33 years 89 days Dawie Snyman (WP in 1982)

ABSA CURRIE CUP RECORDS

MATCH RECORDS

One hundred and ten points
147	Blue Bulls vs SWD (147-8)	Pietersburg	1996
113	Cheetahs vs SWD (113-11)	Bloemfontein	1996
111	Pumas vs SWD (111-14)	Witbank	2001

Wins by 100 points
139	Blue Bulls vsSWD (147-8)	Pietersburg	1996
106	Cheetahs vs NFS (106-0)	Bloemfontein	1997
102	Cheetahs vs SWD (113-11)	Bloemfontein	1996
102	SWD Eagles vs NFS (102-0)	George	1999

Sixteen tries
23	Blue Bulls vs SWD (147-8)	1996
18	Western Transvaal vs EOFS (103-9)	1988
16	Transvaal vs Far North (99-9)	1973
16	SWD Eagles vs NFS (102-0)	1999
16	Pumas vs SWD Eagles (111-14)	2001

Thirty-five points by a player
46	Jannie de Beer (3t, 14c, 1p)	FS vs NFS	1997
40	Casper Steyn (2t, 3c, 8p)	BB vs SWD	2000
38	Henry Honiball (4t, 6c, 2p)	Natal vs Bol	1996
38	Lance Sherrell (2t, 14c)	BB vs SWD	1996
37	Casper Steyn (2t, 3c, 7p)	Pumas vs FS	2003
36	Gerald Bosch (1t, 13c, 2dg)	Tvl vs FN	1973
36	Eric Herbert (3c, 9p, 1dg)	NFS vs Valke	1997
36	Casper Steyn (1t, 7c, 7p)	BB vs Pumas	2000
35	Jacques Olivier (7t)	BB vs SWD	1996
	Kennedy Tsimba (1t, 9c, 4p)	FS vs GW	2003
	Braam Pretorius (2t, 11c, 1p)	Pumas vs Valke	2009

Six tries by a player
7	Jacques Olivier	Blue Bulls vs SWD (147-8)	1996
6	Buks Marais	Boland vs NED (33-3)	1952

Fourteen conversions by a player
14	Tjaart Marais	W-Tvl vs Eastern Free State	1988
14	MJ Smith	Free State vs SWD	1996
14	Lance Sherrell	Blue Bulls vs SWD	1996
14	Jannie de Beer	FS vs NFS	1997
14	Nel Fourie	Pumas vs SWD Eagles	2001

Nine penalty goals by a player
9	Eric Herbert	NFS vs Valke	1997
9	Derick Hougaard	BB vs WP	2002

Five drop goals by a player
5	Naas Botha	N Transvaal vs Natal	1992

SEASON RECORDS

Seven hundred and fifty points
792	Natal	15 matches	1996
783	Northern Transvaal	13 matches	1996

One hundred tries by a team
112	Natal	15 matches	1996
102	Northern Transvaal	13 matches	1996

Two hundred and fifty points by a player
268	Johan Heunis	N Transvaal	1989
263	Gavin Lawless	Transvaal	1996
252	Casper Steyn	Blue Bulls	1999

Fifteen tries
21	Bjorn Basson	Griquas	2010
19	Carel du Plessis	WP	1989
19	Colin Lloyd	Leopards	2006
18	Ettienne Botha	Blue Bulls	2004
18	Allister Kettledas	Pumas	2009
17	Alshaun Bock	SWD	2013
16	Jan-Harm van Wyk	FS	1997
16	Rayno Benjamin	Boland	2006
15	Philip Burger	FS	2006
15	Danwel Demas	Boland	2011

Fifty conversions
62	Louis Koen	WP	1997
55	Jannie de Beer	FS	1997
54	Braam Pretorius	Pumas	2009

Forty penalties
50	Willem de Waal	WP	2010
48	Gavin Lawless	Transvaal	1996
47	Willem de Waal	FS	2005
45	Lance Sherrell	WP	1991
	Johan Heunis	N Transvaal	1987
	Cameron Oliver	Transvaal	1989
42	Cameron Oliver	Transvaal	1990
	Andre Joubert	FS	1989

Twenty drop goals
20	Naas Botha	N Transvaal	1985

CAREER RECORDS

One hundred matches

145	Jacques Botes	Pumas & Sharks	2002-2013
142	Helgard Muller	FS	1983-1998
141	Rudi Visagie	FS, Ntl & SE-TVL	1980-1996
136	Chris Badenhorst	FS, Ntl & SE-TVL	1986-1999
132	Louis Strydom	Griff,BB,Valke,Lions,FS, EP	2001-2013
129	Franco van der Merwe	Leopards & Golden Lions	2004-2013
128	Burger Geldenhuys	N Tvl	1977-1989
	Ollie le Roux	FS & Natal	1993-2007
	Stefan Terblanche	Boland & Sharks	1994-2011
126	Andre Joubert	FS & Natal	1986-1999
125	Eric Herbert	NFS & FS	1986-2001
123	Naas Botha	N Tvl	1977-1992
122	Kabamba Floors	SWD & Free State	2003-2013
119	Eddie Fredericks	Leop, FS, NFS	1998-2011
118	Willie Meyer	EP, FS & Lions	1989-2002
118	Tewis de Bruyn	Leop, SWD, Bol,FS, Griff	2002-2013
116	Hannes Franklin	Pumas, Valke, SWD, EP	2003-2012
115	AJ Venter	FS, Lions & Sharks	1997-2008
114	Piet Krause	Lions, GW, BB, Valke	1996-2007
114	Bevin Fortuin	SWD/FS	2000-2010
113	Jaco Engels	Leop, Bol, BB, EP	2003-2012
113	Skipper Badenhorst	Valke,Pumas,Sharks,FS	2000-2010
112	Louis Moolman	N Tvl	1974-1986
111	Willem de Waal	Leop, FS, WP	2002-2010
110	Justin Peach	EP & Boland	2001-2010
110	Barry Geel	Leopards, GW, FS	2002-2012
108	Willem Stoltz	Lions, Leop, EP	1998-2010
108	Adrian Jacobs	Valke/Sharks	2000-2011
108	Cobus Grobbelaar	Golden Lions	2003-2012
108	Hendro Scholtz	FS	1999-2012
107	Odwa Ndungane	Border, BB, Sharks	2000-2013
106	Martiens le Roux	FS	1973-1986
106	De Wet Ras	FS & Natal	1974-1986
106	Gavin Passens	Griff, Pumas, BB, FS, GW	1999-2010
106	Jaco Engels	Leop, Bol, BB, EP	2003-2011
106	Tiaan Liebenberg	Griquas, WP	2003-2013
104	Gerrie Sonnekus	FS	1974-1985
103	Uli Schmidt	N Tvl & Tvl	1983-1994
103	Albert van den Berg	GW & Natal	1996-2009
103	Tiaan Liebenberg	Griquas, WP	2003-2011
103	Keegan Daniel	Sharks	2006-2013
102	Adolf Malan	N Tvl	1983-1992
102	John Daniels	Boland & Lions	1998-2008
102	Wikus van Heerden	Lions, Blue Bulls	2001-2011
102	Conrad Jantjies	Lions, WP	2000-2011
101	Gysie Pienaar	FS	1974-1987
101	Brok Harris	Western Province	2006-2013
100	Chumani Booi	Border, Pum, GW, WP	2001-2013

One thousand points

1699	Naas Botha	N Transvaal	1977-1992
1433	Willem de Waal	FS & WP	2002-2010
1402	Eric Herbert	NFS & FS	1986-2001
1210	De Wet Ras	FS & Natal	1974-1986
1165	Andre Joubert	FS & Natal	1986-1999
1022	Louis Strydom	Griff, BB, Valke, GL, FS, EP	2001-2013
1017	Calla Scholtz	Boland & WP	1980-1989

Fifty tries

77	John Daniels	Boland & Lions	1998-2008
70	Breyton Paulse	WP	1996-2007
65	Chris Badenhorst	FS	1986-1999
60	Stefan Terblanche	Boland & Natal	1996-2011
58	Andre Joubert	FS & Natal	1986-1999
54	Eddie Fredericks	WP, NFS, Leop, FS	1998-2011
52	Egon Seconds	WP & Griquas	2001-2009
51	Gerrie Germishuys	FS & Transvaal	1971-1985
	Carel du Plessis	WP & Transvaal	1980-1989
	Neil Burger	WP	1982-1991
	Jan-Harm van Wyk	FS & Pumas	1996-2001
50	Fabian Juries	EP, FS & NFS	2001-2009

Fifty drop goals

135	Naas Botha	Northern Transvaal	1977-1992
69	De Wet Ras	Free State & Natal	1974-1986

ABSA CURRIE CUP FINAL PLAYERS 1939 - 2013

COMPILED BY ASHLEY BERRY

A complete list of all players who have played in a Currie Cup final since the first one was contested in 1939.

Key to Abbreviations: WP > Western Province; BB > Blue Bulls; N Tvl > Northern Transvaal; OFS > Orange Free State; TVL > Transvaal; GL > Golden Lions; E Tvl > Eastern Transvaal; GW > Griqualand West; Ntl > Natal.

Name	Province	First & last final	Matches	Won	Lost	Drawn	Winning%
A							
Ackermann D.S.P.(Dawie)	WP	1954	1	1	0	0	100%
Adams H.J.(Heini)	BB	2006	1	0	0	1	0%
Aitken A.D.(Andrew)	Ntl/WP	1990, 97	2	2	0	0	100%
Alberts F.N.F.(Frannie)	N Tvl	1969-70	2	1	1	0	50%
Alberts W.S.(Willem)	Ntl	2010-13	4	2	2	0	50%
Allan J.(John)	Ntl	'92-93, 95	3	2	1	0	67%
Anderson W.	WP	1939	1	0	1	0	0%
Andrews K.S.(Keith)	WP	'86, 88, 97	3	2	1	0	67%
Andrews M.G.(Mark)	Ntl	1993, 95-96, 00	4	2	2	0	50%
Aplon G.G.(Gio)	WP	2010, 12-13	3	1	2	0	33%
Armand D.(Don)	WP	2012	1	1	0	0	100%
Arnold P.(Peet)	WP	1997	1	1	0	0	100%
Atherton S.(Steve)	Ntl	1990, 92-93, 96, 99	5	3	2	0	60%
Aucamp C.(Cobus)	Ntl	1984	1	0	1	0	0%
Aucamp J.J.(Floors)	N Tvl	1973	1	1	0	0	100%
B							
Badenhorst A.J.(Adri)	WP	2000	1	1	0	0	100%
Badenhorst C.(Chris)	OFS	1994, 97	2	0	2	0	0%
Badenhorst C.J.	Tvl	1939	1	1	0	0	100%
Badenhorst D.S.(Daan)	Tvl	1986-87	2	0	2	0	0%
Bands R.E.(Richard)	BB	2002, 04	2	2	0	0	100%
Barnard J.H.(Jannie)	Tvl/WP/Tvl	1968-69, 71	3	0	2	1	0%
Barnard R.W.(Robbie)	Tvl	1968, 71	2	0	1	1	0%
Barrit B.M.(Bradley)	Ntl	2008	1	1	0	0	100%
Barry D.(De Wet)	WP	2000-01	2	2	0	0	100%
Bartmann W.J.(Wahl)	Tvl/Ntl	1986-87, 90, 92-93	5	2	3	0	40%
Basson S.(Stefan)	BB	2006	1	0	0	1	0%
Basson W.W.(Wium)	BB	1998	1	1	0	0	100%
Bates A.J.(Albie)	N Tvl	1973-74	2	2	0	0	100%
Bayvel P.C.R.(Paul)	Tvl	1972, 74	2	1	1	0	50%
Beck J.J.(Colin)	WP	1980, 82	2	1	1	0	50%
Bekker H.(Manie)	WP	1947	1	1	0	0	100%
Bekker H.J.(Hennie)	OFS/WP	1977-80, 82-85	8	4	3	1	50%
Bekker H.P.J.(Jaap)	N Tvl	1954	1	0	1	0	0%
Bekker M.J.(Martiens)	N Tvl	1954, 56	2	1	1	0	50%
Bekker R.P.(Dolph)	N Tvl	1956	1	1	0	0	100%
Bekker S.(Schutte)	BB	1998	1	1	0	0	100%
Benade J.J.	Tvl	1939	1	1	0	0	100%
Beneke J.I.(Izak)	N Tvl	1983	1	0	1	0	0%
Benjamin R.S.(Ryno)	GL	2007	1	0	1	0	0%
Bennet R.G.(Russell)	Ntl	1999	1	0	1	0	0%
Bestbier A.(André)	OFS	1973	1	0	1	0	0%
Bester F.	Bol	1952	1	0	1	0	0%
Bester J.	WP	1939	1	0	1	0	0%
Beukes J.H.T.(Joe)	OFS	1994	1	0	1	0	0%
Beyers N.(Nellis)	WP	1946	1	0	1	0	0%
Bezuidenhoudt N.S.E.(Nic)	N Tvl	1975, 77	2	2	0	0	100%
Bezuidenhout M.J.(Martin)	Tvl	2011	1	1	0	0	100%
Bierman P.(Peet)	E Tvl	1972	1	0	1	0	0%
Blair R.(Robbie)	WP	1979-80	2	0	1	1	0%
Blakeway A.D.(Andrew)	Ntl	1992-93	2	1	1	0	50%
Blom L.F.(Louis)	WP	1995, 97	2	1	1	0	50%
Boer P.(Piet)	BB	1998	1	1	0	0	100%
Bolton W.J.C.(Willie)	OFS	1981	1	0	1	0	0%
Bolus R.(Rob)	WP	1980	1	0	1	0	0%
Bondesio M.(Michael)	Tvl	2011	1	1	0	0	100%
Boome C.S.(Selborne)	WP	1998	1	0	1	0	0%
Booyens V.(Vic)	N Tvl	1973	1	1	0	0	100%
Booysen J.(Jaco)	GL	2002	1	0	1	0	0%
Bosch G.R.(Gerald)	Tvl	1972, 74	2	1	1	0	50%
Bosch P.W.(Paul)	WP	2010	1	0	1	0	0%
Bosch R.G.	Tvl	1947	1	0	1	0	0%
Boshoff J.H.(Jannie)	GL	2007	1	0	1	0	0%
Boshoff L.(Leon)	GL	1999	1	1	0	0	100%
Bosman H.M.(Meyer)	FS/Ntl	2005-07, 09, 12	5	2	2	1	40%
Bosman P.(Piet)	Tvl	1968, 72	2	1	1	0	50%
Botes L.J.(Jacques)	Ntl	2008, 10, 13	3	3	0	0	100%
Botes P.J.(Paul)	N Tvl	1985	1	0	1	0	0%
Botha A.(Attie)	N Tvl	1946	1	1	0	0	100%
Botha A.A.(André)	Ntl	1984, 90	2	1	1	0	50%
Botha B.J.	Ntl	2003	1	0	1	0	0%
Botha D.S.(Darius)	N Tvl	1978-82	5	3	1	1	60%
Botha E.(Ettienne)	BB	2003-04	2	2	0	0	100%
Botha G.v G.(Gary)	BB	2002-06	5	3	1	1	60%
Botha H.E.(Naas)	N Tvl	1977-81, 85, 87-91	11	7	2	2	64%
Botha J.F.(Jan)	N Tvl	1946	1	1	0	0	100%
Botha J.F.(Johan)	OFS	1973	1	0	1	0	0%
Botha J.J.(Koos)	Tvl	1952	1	1	0	0	100%
Botha J.P.(Bakkies)	BB	2002, 04-05, 09	4	3	1	0	75%

ABSA CURRIE CUP FINAL PLAYERS 1939 - 2013

Name	Province	First & last final	Matches	Won	Lost	Drawn	Winning%
Bothma A.(Arnold)	Tvl	1974	1	0	1	0	0%
Boyes R.E.	WP	1950	1	0	1	0	0%
Brand C.P.(Piet)	N Tvl	1969-70	2	1	1	0	50%
Breedt J.C.(Jannie)	N Tvl/Tvl	1981-83, 86-87, 91-92	7	1	6	0	14%
Breedt N.(Nico)	FS	2009	1	0	1	0	0%
Bresler A.(Anton)	Ntl	2010, 12	2	1	1	0	50%
Brewis J.D.(Hansie)	N Tvl	1946, 54	2	1	1	0	50%
Breytenbach C.L.(Conrad)	BB	1998	1	1	0	0	100%
Brink R.A.(Rob)	WP	1995, 00	2	1	1	0	50%
Brink S.(Stephen)	Ntl	2000	1	0	1	0	0%
Brits J.(Johan)	E Tvl	1972	1	0	1	0	0%
Britz G.J.J.(Gerrie)	FS	2004	1	0	1	0	0%
Britz S.(Stefan)	BB	1998	1	1	0	0	100%
Britz W.K.(Warren)	Ntl	1999, 01	2	0	2	0	0%
Broderick F.(Frans)	Tvl	1952	1	1	0	0	100%
Brooks J.Z.(Jannie)	BB	1998	1	1	0	0	100%
Brosnihan W.G.(Warren)	Ntl/BB	2000-01, 04	3	1	2	0	33%
Brown C.G.(Cliffie)	N Tvl	1982	1	0	1	0	0%
Brunow H.L.(Harry)	WP	1939	1	0	1	0	0%
Brüssow H.W.(Heinrich)	FS	2006-07, 09	3	1	1	1	33%
Buchler J.U.(Johnny)	Tvl	1950	1	1	0	0	100%
Burden C.B.(Craig)	Ntl	2010-12	3	1	2	0	33%
Burger J.(Hannes)	N Tvl	1956	1	1	0	0	100%
Burger J.(Jan)	Bol	1952	1	0	1	0	0%
Burger J.M.(Kobus)	WP	1985, 88-89	3	1	1	1	33%
Burger M.B.(Thys)	N Tvl	1978-81	4	3	0	1	75%
Burger N.J.(Niel)	WP	1982, 84-85	3	3	0	0	100%
Burger P.B.(Philip)	FS	2005-06	2	1	0	1	50%
Burger S.W.(Schalk)	WP	1985, 88	2	1	1	0	50%
Burger S.W.P.(Schalk) jnr.	WP	2010, 13	2	0	2	0	0%
Burger S.W.P.(Schalk) snr.	WP	1984-86	3	3	0	0	100%
Butler B.L.(Basil)	WP	1946	1	0	1	0	0%
C							
Cabannes L.(Laurent)	WP	1995	1	0	1	0	0%
Calldo J.G.(Cobus)	FS	2007	1	1	0	0	100%
Carey F.(Fraser)	Tvl	1947	1	0	1	0	0%
Carstens P-D.(Deon)	Ntl/WP	2001, 03, 08, 12	4	2	2	0	50%
Carstens W.(Cassie)	WP	1998	1	0	1	0	0%
Catrakilis D.(Demetri)	WP	2012-13	2	1	1	0	50%
Cilliers P.M.(Pat)	GL/WP	2011, 13	2	1	1	0	50%
Claassen K.(Koos)	Tvl	1968	1	0	1	0	0%
Claassen W.(Wynand)	N Tvl/Ntl	1975, 77, 79, 84	4	2	1	1	50%
Claassens J.H.(Jacques)	FS	2004	1	0	1	0	0%
Claassens J.P.(Jannie)	N Tvl	1990-91	2	1	1	0	50%
Claassens M.(Michael)	FS	2004-06	3	1	1	1	33%
Clarke T.A.(Bossie)	WP	1976, 79-80	3	0	2	1	0%
Cloete A.(Abe)	N Tvl	1954	1	0	1	0	0%
Cockrell C.H.(Charlie)	WP	1969	1	0	1	0	0%
Cockrell R.J.(Robert)	WP	1976, 80	2	0	2	0	0%
Cockrell W.J.(William)	WP	1986	1	1	0	0	100%
Coetzee D.(Danie)	BB	2002, 04-05	3	2	1	0	67%
Coetzee D.A.(Deon)	N Tvl	1982	1	0	1	0	0%
Coetzee E.L.(Eduard)	Ntl	2003	1	0	1	0	0%
Coetzee J.(Johan)	E Tvl	1972	1	0	1	0	0%
Coetzee J.H.(Johan)	OFS	1981	1	0	1	0	0%
Coetzee J.H.H.(Jan-Boland)	WP	1969, 76, 79	3	0	2	1	0%
Coetzee J.J.(Jaco)	OFS	1994	1	0	1	0	0%
Coetzee J.L.(Koot)	N Tvl	1978	1	1	0	0	100%
Coetzee M.C.(Marcell)	Ntl	2011-13	3	1	2	0	33%
Coetzer J.H.(Joe)	Tvl	1974	1	0	1	0	0%
Coleman K.K.(Kurt)	WP	2013	1	0	1	0	0%
Combrinck G.J.(Gerhard)	Tvl	1994	1	1	0	0	100%
Combrinck J.(James)	GW	1970	1	1	0	0	100%
Conradie J.H.J.(Bolla)	WP	2001	1	1	0	0	100%
Cooper K.L.(Kyle)	Ntl	2012-13	2	1	1	0	50%
Craig B.K.(Pat)	Tvl	1947	1	0	1	0	0%
Cronjé G.(Geo)	BB	2002-03	2	2	0	0	100%
Cronjé J.(Jacques)	BB/GL	2003-05, 07	4	2	2	0	50%
Cronjé L.(Lionel)	WP	2010	1	0	1	0	0%
Cronje P.A.(Peter)	Tvl	1971-72	2	1	0	1	50%
Cronjé R.(Ross)	Ntl	2011	1	0	1	0	0%
Cupido W.(Wilfred)	WP	1983	1	1	0	0	100%
D							
Dalton J.(James)	Tvl	1996	1	0	1	0	0%
Daniel K.R.(Keegan)	Ntl	2008, 10-13	5	3	2	0	60%
Daniels J.I.(John)	GL	2002	1	0	1	0	0%
Daniller H.J.(Hennie)	FS	2009	1	0	1	0	0%
Dannhauser G.(Gert)	Tvl	1947, 50	2	1	1	0	50%
Dannhauser T.(Toy)	Tvl	1968	1	0	1	0	0%
Davids Q.(Quinton)	WP	2000-01	2	2	0	0	100%
Davidson C.D.(Craig)	Ntl	1999-03	4	0	4	0	0%
Dawson M.(Murray)	Ntl	1984	1	0	1	0	0%
De Allende D.(Damian)	WP	2012-13	2	1	1	0	50%
De Beer J.H.(Jannie)	FS	1997	1	0	1	0	0%
De Beer M.C.	N Tvl	1954	1	0	1	0	0%
De Beer R.C.(Ski-Hi)	N Tvl	1954, 56	2	1	1	0	50%
De Bruyn M.J.(Tewis)	FS	2007, 09	2	1	1	0	50%
De Jager S.H.F.(Frans)	N Tvl	1956	1	1	0	0	100%
De Jongh J.L.(Juan)	WP	2010, 12-13	3	1	2	0	33%
De Klerk I.J.(Sakkie)	Tvl	1968	1	0	1	0	0%
De Klerk K.B.H.(Kevin)	Tvl	1971-72, 74	3	1	1	1	33%
De Klerk P.R.(Rossouw)	BB	2009	1	1	0	0	100%
De Klerk W.P.(Moffie)	N Tvl	1973	1	1	0	0	100%
De Kock C.(Con)	WP	1946	1	0	1	0	0%
De Kock D.(Deon)	GL	2002	1	0	1	0	0%
De Kock N.A.(Neil)	WP	2001	1	1	0	0	100%
De Meyer O.A.(Oeloff)	N Tvl	1969, 75	2	2	0	0	100%
De Villers A.P.(Apie)	WP	1939	1	0	1	0	0%
De Villers D.J.(David)	FS	2009	1	0	1	0	0%
De Villiers H.(Dirkie)	WP	1947	1	1	0	0	100%
De Villiers H.O.	WP	1969	1	0	1	0	0%

ABSA CURRIE CUP FINAL PLAYERS 1939 - 2013

Name	Province	First & last final	Matches	Won	Lost	Drawn	Winning%
De Villiers J.(Hannes)	N Tvl	1946	1	1	0	0	100%
De Villiers J.(Jean)	WP	2010, 13	2	0	2	0	0%
De Vos D.J.J.(Dirk)	Tvl/N Tvl	1968, 73-74	3	2	1	0	67%
De Waal W.(Willem)	FS/WP	2004-07, 10	5	2	2	1	40%
De Wet A.(Bertie)	WP	1983-84	2	2	0	0	100%
De Wet D.J.(Daan)	OFS	1973	1	0	1	0	0%
De Wet P.	WP	1939	1	0	1	0	0%
De Wet P.J.(Piet)	WP	1939	1	0	1	0	0%
Delaporte C.(Dollie)	Tvl	1939	1	1	0	0	100%
Delport G.M.(Thinus)	GL	1999	1	1	0	0	100%
Delport M.(Marius)	BB	2006, 08	2	0	1	1	0%
Demas D.(Danwel)	FS	2009	1	0	1	0	0%
Dercksen B.(Bennie)	E Tvl	1972	1	0	1	0	0%
Des Dountain D.(Dylan)	Tvl	2011	1	1	0	0	100%
Deuchar B.(Butch)	WP	1976	1	0	1	0	0%
Deysel J.R.(Jean)	Ntl	2008, 11-12	3	1	2	0	33%
Dirks C.A.(Chris)	Tvl	1993	1	1	0	0	100%
Dixon P.J.(Peter)	WP	2000-01	2	2	0	0	100%
Dorrington I.(Ivor)	WP	1954	1	1	0	0	100%
Downes G.(Graham)	Ntl	1984	1	0	1	0	0%
Dreyer J.N.(Jannie)	N Tvl	1983	1	0	1	0	0%
Dreyer K.L.(Kon)	Tvl	1972	1	1	0	0	100%
Drotské A.E.(Naka)	OFS	1994-97, 04-05	4	1	3	0	25%
Dryburgh R.G.(Roy)	WP/Ntl	1950, 54, 56	3	1	2	0	33%
Du Plessis A.J.(Tiny)	OFS	1976	1	1	0	0	100%
Du Plessis B.W.(Bismarck)	Ntl	2008, 10-11, 13	4	3	1	0	75%
Du Plessis C.J.(Carel)	WP/Tvl/WP	1982-84, 86-89	7	4	2	1	57%
Du Plessis D.C.(Daan)	N Tvl	1973-75, 77-77	6	5	0	1	83%
Du Plessis D.F.(Francois)	N Tvl	1991	1	1	0	0	100%
Du Plessis F.(Felix)	Tvl	1947	1	0	1	0	0%
Du Plessis F.(Francois)	N Tvl	1982-83	2	0	2	0	0%
Du Plessis J.N.(Jannie)	FS/Ntl	2005-08, 10-13	8	5	2	1	63%
Du Plessis M.(Morné)	WP	1976, 79	2	0	1	1	0%
Du Plessis M.(Thys)	WP	1950	1	0	1	0	0%
Du Plessis M.J.(Michael)	WP/Tvl/WP	1982, 84-85, 87-89	6	3	2	1	50%
Du Plessis P.G.(Piet)	N Tvl	1971	1	0	0	1	0%
Du Plessis T.D.(Tommy)	N Tvl	1975, 77-82, 85	8	5	2	1	63%
Du Plessis W.(Willie)	WP	1979-80, 82	3	1	1	1	33%
Du Plooy T.J.(Boela)	FS	2004	1	0	1	0	0%
Du Preez F.C.H.(Frik)	N Tvl	1968-71	4	2	1	1	50%
Du Preez G.J.D.(Delarey)	GL	2002	1	0	1	0	0%
Du Preez P.F.(Fourie) jnr.	BB	2003-05, 08-09	5	3	2	0	60%
Du Preez P.F.(Fourie) snr.	N Tvl	1968-70	3	2	1	0	67%
Du Preez R.J.(Robert)	N Tvl/Ntl	1988-92	5	3	1	1	60%
Du Preez W.H.(Wian)	FS	2005-07, 09	4	2	1	1	50%
Du Rand D.(Salty)	Tvl	1974	1	0	1	0	0%
Du Rand H.G.J.(Hennie)	N Tvl	1968, 75	2	2	0	0	100%
Du Rand J.A.(Salty)	WP/N Tvl	1947, 54	2	1	1	0	50%
Du Randt J.P.(Os)	OFS	1994, 97, 04-05	4	1	3	0	25%
Du Toit F.P.(Pikkie)	OFS	1973, 75	2	0	2	0	0%
Du Toit G.S.(Gaffie)	Ntl/FS	2000-01, 06	3	0	2	1	0%
Du Toit J.(John)	WP	1954	1	1	0	0	100%
Du Toit J.C.(Jan)	OFS	1981	1	0	1	0	0%
Du Toit P.A.(Fonnie)	N Tvl	1946, 54	2	1	1	0	50%
Du Toit P.G.(Hempies)	WP	1979-80, 83, 85	4	2	1	1	50%
Du Toit P.S.(Pieter-Steph)	Ntl	2013	1	1	0	0	100%
Du Toit T.(Tobias)	Tvl	1968, 71	2	0	1	1	0%
Duffett D.	WP	1950	1	0	1	0	0%
Duffy G.(Gavin)	Ntl	1956	1	0	1	0	0%
Dukas D.	WP	1950	1	0	1	0	0%
Duncan R.(Rory)	FS	2006-07	2	1	0	1	50%
Durr J.(Johan)	WP	1983	1	1	0	0	100%
Duvenhage D.O.(Dewaldt)	WP	2010	1	0	1	0	0%
Duvenhage F.P.(Floris)	Tvl	1939	1	1	0	0	100%

E

Name	Province	First & last final	Matches	Won	Lost	Drawn	Winning%
East M.(Mike)	WP	1954	1	1	0	0	100%
Edmunds P.(Peter)	Ntl	1984	1	0	1	0	0%
Edwards P.(Pierre)	N Tvl	1977-83	7	4	2	1	57%
Ellis C.E.(Clark)	WP	1986	1	1	0	0	100%
Eloff M.C.(Giel)	N Tvl	1973	1	1	0	0	100%
Els W.W.(Braam)	OFS	1994, 97	2	0	2	0	0%
Engelbrecht G.(Giel)	Bol	1952	1	0	1	0	0%
Engelbrecht K.(Kobus)	GL	1999	1	1	0	0	100%
Engels J.(Jaco)	BB	2006	1	0	0	1	0%
Erasmus J.(Johan)	FS	1997, 04	2	0	2	0	0%
Esterhuizen G.(Grant)	GL	2002	1	0	1	0	0%
Esterhuizen J.(Johan)	Tvl	1972	1	1	0	0	100%
Esterhuizen W.C.(Willa)	N Tvl	1956	1	1	0	0	100%
Etzebeth E.(Eben)	WP	2012-13	2	1	1	0	50%

F

Name	Province	First & last final	Matches	Won	Lost	Drawn	Winning%
Faure C.L.(Chris)	Ntl	1984	1	0	1	0	0%
Ferreira A.P.(Fief)	N Tvl	1971	1	0	0	1	0%
Ferreira F.C.(Freddie)	WP	1985-86, 88-89	4	2	1	1	50%
Ferreira P.S.(Kulu)	WP	1984	1	1	0	0	100%
Fitchet C.(Christo)	OFS	1981	1	0	1	0	0%
Fleck R.F.(Robbie)	WP	1998, 00	2	1	1	0	50%
Flemix J.F.(Jan)	N Tvl	1968	1	1	0	0	100%
Floors L.(Kabamba)	FS	2005-07, 09	4	2	1	1	50%
Fondse A.R.(Adriaan)	WP	2010	1	0	1	0	0%
Fortuin B.A.(Bevin)	FS	2005-06	2	1	0	1	50%
Fourie A.(Braam)	GW	1970	1	1	0	0	100%
Fourie A.J.(Stompie)	Tvl	1991	1	0	1	0	0%
Fourie B.G.(Bernard)	Tvl	1993-94	2	2	0	0	100%

ABSA CURRIE CUP FINAL PLAYERS 1939 - 2013

Name	Province	First & last final	Matches	Won	Lost	Drawn	Winning%	Name	Province	First & last final	Matches	Won	Lost	Drawn	Winning%
Fourie D.A.(Deon)	WP	2010, 12-13	3	1	2	0	33%	Hamilton G.(Greg)	Ntl	1984	1	0	1	0	0%
Fourie J.(Jaque)	GL	2002	1	0	1	0	0%	Hankinson R.G.(Rob)	Ntl	1984	1	0	1	0	0%
Fourie M.J.(Pote)	N Tvl	1987-91	5	3	1	1	60%	Harding G.(Gerard)	Ntl	1990, 92	2	2	0	0	100%
Fourie S.A.(Andries)	Tvl	1986	1	0	1	0	0%	Hargreaves A.J.(Alistair)	Ntl	2010-11	2	1	1	0	50%
Fourie T.T.(Polla)	N Tvl	1968, 70	2	1	1	0	50%	Harris J.(Brok)	WP	2010, 12-13	3	1	2	0	33%
Fredericks E.R.(Eddie)	FS	2004-05, 07	3	2	1	0	67%	Harris T.A.(Tony)	Tvl	1939	1	1	0	0	100%
Fredericks K.P.(Keegan)	BB	2004	1	1	0	0	100%	Hattingh S.J.(Ian)	Tvl	1994, 96	2	1	1	0	50%
Frederickson C.A.(Dave)	Tvl	1974	1	0	1	0	0%	Henderson S.(Skip)	E Tvl	1972	1	0	1	0	0%
Froneman D.C.(Dirk)	OFS	1976, 78	2	1	1	0	50%	Hendriks P.(Pieter)	Tvl	1991-94	4	2	2	0	50%
Fry D.J.(Dennis)	WP	1946-47, 50	3	1	2	0	33%	Herbert E.(Eric)	OFS	1994	1	0	1	0	0%
Fry S.P.(Stephen)	WP	1946-47, 50	3	1	2	0	33%	Herbst C.(Freddie)	Tvl	1952	1	1	0	0	100%
Fuls H.T.(Heinrich)	Tvl	1992	1	0	1	0	0%	Herbst W.J.(Wiehann)	Ntl	2012-13	2	1	1	0	50%
Fynn E.E.(Etienne)	Ntl	1999-01	3	0	3	0	0%	Heunis J.W.(Johan)	N Tvl	1981, 83, 87, 89	4	2	1	1	50%
Fyvie W.S.(Wayne)	Ntl	1995-96, 99	3	2	1	0	67%	Heymans J.H.(Dougie)	OFS	1994	1	0	1	0	0%
G								Heynecke J.(Johnny)	N Tvl	1954	1	0	1	0	0%
Garvey A.C.(Adrian)	Ntl	1995-96	2	0	2	0	0%	Hinrichsen W.	WP	1939	1	1	0	0	100%
Geel P.J.(Flip)	N Tvl	1946	1	1	0	0	100%	Hirst H.(Dummy)	Tvl	1939	1	1	0	0	100%
Geffin A.O.(Okey)	Tvl	1947, 50	2	1	1	0	50%	Hoffman D.(Dirk)	N Tvl	1981-82	2	1	1	0	50%
Geldenhuys A.(Adri)	N Tvl	1987, 89	2	1	0	1	50%	Hoffman R.S.(Steve)	Bol	1952	1	0	1	0	0%
Geldenhuys J.(Jan)	WP	1980	1	0	1	0	0%	Hoffman T.(Teddy)	WP	1969	1	0	1	0	0%
Geldenhuys S.B.(Burger)	N Tvl	1977-83, 85, 87-89	11	6	3	2	55%	Hoffmann C.F.(Carel)	Ntl	2011	1	0	1	0	0%
Gerber H.J.(Hendrik)	WP	2000-01	2	2	0	0	100%	Hollenbach A.W.C.J.(Alwyn)	FS/GL	2005, 07, 11	3	3	0	0	100%
Gerber L.J.(Len)	N Tvl	1974-75	2	2	0	0	100%	Holtzhausen C.(Christo)	E Tvl	1972	1	0	1	0	0%
Gerber R.(Rayno)	FS/BB	2004, 06, 08	3	0	2	1	0%	Honiball H.W.(Henry)	Ntl	1992, 95-96	3	3	0	0	100%
Germishuys J.S.(Gerrie)	OFS	1973, 75-77	4	1	3	0	25%	Horn H.(Hendrik)	E Tvl	1972	1	0	1	0	0%
Geyer C.(Chris)	N Tvl	1954	1	0	1	0	0%	Hougaard D.J.(Derick)	BB	2002, 04-06	4	2	1	1	50%
Gibson B.	Bol	1952	1	0	1	0	0%	Hougaard F.(Francois)	BB	2009	1	1	0	0	100%
Gie W.	WP	1939	1	0	1	0	0%	Hugo D.P.(Niel)	WP	1986, 88-89	3	1	1	1	33%
Gillingham J.W.(Joe)	Tvl/Ntl	1996, 99	2	0	2	0	0%	Hugo W.J.(Wouter)	OFS	1975-78	4	1	3	0	25%
Gioia L.(Lieb)	N Tvl	1956	1	1	0	0	100%	Human A.W.J.(Andries)	BB	2003, 05	2	1	1	0	50%
Goodes B.(Barry)	FS	2005	1	1	0	0	100%	Human P.R.(Flip)	Tvl	1950, 52	2	2	0	0	100%
Gous R.(Riaan)	WP	1989	1	0	0	1	0%	Human W.A.(Wylie)	BB/GL	2002, 07	2	1	1	0	50%
Gouws J.J.(Koos)	N Tvl	1989	1	0	0	1	0%	Hurter M.H.(Marius)	WP	1998	1	0	1	0	0%
Grace R.(Bobby)	Tvl	1968	1	0	1	0	0%	**I**							
Gradwell D.V.(Dudley)	N Tvl	1971	1	0	0	1	0%	Immelman K.(Kobus)	WP	1976	1	0	1	0	0%
Greeff W.W.(Werner)	WP	2001	1	1	0	0	100%	Irvine B.(Brian)	Ntl	1956	1	0	1	0	0%
Greyling P.J.F.(Piet)	Tvl	1971-72	2	1	0	1	50%	**J**							
Griffiths W.(Billy)	WP	1946	1	1	0	0	100%	Jacklin B.(Brian)	Ntl	1956	1	0	1	0	0%
Grobbelaar D.J.E.(Derrick)	BB	1998	1	1	0	0	100%	Jacobs A.A.(Adrian)	Ntl	2008, 11	2	1	1	0	50%
Grobbelaar P.J.J.(Cobus)	GL	2007, 11	2	1	1	0	50%	James A.D.(Butch)	Ntl/GL	2000, 03, 11	3	1	2	0	33%
Grobler C.J.(Kleintjie)	OFS	1973, 75	2	0	2	0	0%	Jamieson C.M.(Craig)	Ntl	1984, 90	2	1	1	0	50%
Grobler G.(Gerbrand)	N Tvl/Tvl	1987-91, 94	6	4	1	1	67%	Jansen E.(Eben)	OFS	1976-77	2	1	1	0	50%
Grobler R.N.(Renier)	N Tvl	1969	1	1	0	0	100%	Jansen J.S.(Joggie)	OFS	1976, 78	2	1	1	0	50%
Groom N.J.(Nick)	WP	2012-13	2	1	1	0	50%	Jantjes C.A.(Conrad)	WP	2010	1	0	1	0	0%
Grundlingh H.E.W.(Henk)	N Tvl	1971	1	0	0	1	0%	Jantjies E.T.(Elton)	Tvl	2011	1	1	0	0	100%
H								Januarie E.R.(Enrico)	WP	2010	1	0	1	0	0%
Haarhoff R.A.(Ronnie)	Ntl	1984	1	0	1	0	0%	Johnson A.F.(Ashley)	FS	2009	1	0	1	0	0%
Habana B.G.(Bryan)	BB/WP	2005, 08-10, 12	5	2	3	0	40%	Johnson G.K.(Gavin)	Tvl	1993-94, 96	3	2	1	0	67%
								Johnstone B.(Brett)	GL	1999	1	1	0	0	100%
Hall D.B.(Dean)	GL	1999	1	1	0	0	100%	Jonker J.W.	FS	2006	1	0	0	1	0%
Halstead T.M.(Trevor)	Ntl	1999-01	3	0	3	0	0%	Jordaan G.J.(Gert)	OFS	1981	1	0	1	0	0%

ABSA CURRIE CUP FINAL PLAYERS 1939 - 2013

Name	Province	First & last final	Matches	Won	Lost	Drawn	Winning%
Jordaan N.(Norman)	BB	2002-03	2	2	0	0	100%
Jordaan P.A.(Paul)	Ntl	2012	1	0	1	0	0%
Jordaan R.P.(Jorrie)	N Tvl	1946	1	1	0	0	100%
Joubert A.J.(André)	Ntl	1993, 95-96, 99	4	2	2	0	50%
Joubert C.H.B.(Tiaan)	BB	2002	1	1	0	0	100%
Joubert E.(Ernst)	GL	2007	1	0	1	0	0%
Joubert J.(Joos)	Ntl	1995-96	2	2	0	0	100%
Joubert J-P.(J.P.)	FS	2009	1	0	1	0	0%
Joubert M.C.(Marius)	FS/Ntl	2007, 11	2	1	1	0	50%
Juries F.M.(Fabian)	FS	2009	1	0	1	0	0%
K							
Kahts W.J.H.(Willie)	N Tvl	1974-75, 77-80, 82	7	5	1	1	71%
Kamana J.(James)	Tvl	2011	1	1	0	0	100%
Kankowski R.(Ryan)	Ntl	2008, 10-11	3	2	1	0	67%
Kayser D.J.(Deon)	Ntl	2000-01, 03	3	0	3	0	0%
Kebble G.R.(Guy)	WP/Ntl	1988-90, 93	4	1	2	1	25%
Kempson R.B.(Rob)	Ntl/WP	1995-96, 00-01	4	4	0	0	100%
Killian M.(Michael)	Tvl	2011	1	1	0	0	100%
Kirchner Z.(Zane)	BB	2008-09	2	1	1	0	50%
Kirkham T.A.(Tobie)	OFS	1994	1	0	1	0	0%
Kirkham W.H.(Liaan)	Tvl	1986-87	2	0	2	0	0%
Kirsten J.J.N.(Kobus)	WP	1989	1	0	0	1	0%
Kirsten J.M.(Michael)	WP	1995	1	0	1	0	0%
Kitshoff S.(Steven)	WP	2012-13	2	1	1	0	50%
Klopper C.(Chris)	Ntl	1956	1	0	1	0	0%
Klopper J.	Tvl	1939	1	1	0	0	100%
Knoetze F.(Faffa)	WP	1985-86, 88-89	4	2	1	1	50%
Knoetze M.J.(Martin)	Tvl	1991	1	0	1	0	0%
Knoetze N.J.(Kallie)	N Tvl	1974	1	1	0	0	100%
Knox J.(John)	N Tvl	1973-74, 77-79	5	4	0	1	80%
Koch A.C.(Chris)	Bol	1952	1	0	1	0	0%
Koch B.(Agie)	WP	1980	1	0	1	0	0%
Koch H.V.(Bubbles)	WP/Bol	1946-52	2	0	2	0	0%
Koch W.(Willem)	Bol	1952	1	0	1	0	0%
Koch W.J.(Wilhelm)	GL	2007	1	0	1	0	0%
Kockott R.M.(Rory)	Ntl	2008, 10	2	2	0	0	100%
Koen L.J.(Louis)	WP	1997	1	1	0	0	100%
Kokoali T.C.(Tsepo)	FS	2004	1	0	1	0	0%
Kolbe C.(Cheslin)	WP	2013	1	0	1	0	0%
Kolisi S.(Siya)	WP	2013	1	0	1	0	0%
Kotze G.J.M.(Gert)	WP	1969	1	0	1	0	0%
Kotze J.J.(Jimmy)	Tvl	1947, 50	2	1	1	0	50%
Krantz E.F.W.(Edrich)	OFS/N Tvl	1976-78, 80	4	2	2	0	50%
Krause J.(Jackie)	Tvl	1991	1	0	1	0	0%
Krause P.(Piet)	BB	2003	1	1	0	0	100%
Kriel P.B.(Piet)	Bol	1952	1	0	1	0	0%
Kriel P.C.(Piet)	WP	1939, 46, 50	3	0	3	0	0%
Krige C.P.J.(Corné)	WP	1997-98, 00-01	4	3	1	0	75%
Kritzinger J.C.	WP	2010	1	0	1	0	0%
Kritzinger J.L.(Klippies)	Tvl/OFS	1974-76	3	1	2	0	33%
Kruger C.R.(Chris)	FS	2004-05	2	1	1	0	50%
Kruger G.H.J.(Gert)	Tvl	1950, 52	2	2	0	0	100%
Kruger H.C.(Herkie)	Ntl	2001	1	0	1	0	0%
Kruger H.E.(Hendrik)	N Tvl	1985, 87, 90	3	1	2	0	33%
Kruger P.E.(Piet)	N Tvl/Tvl	1982-83, 86-87	4	0	4	0	0%
Kruger T.(Tjaart)	E Tvl	1972	1	0	1	0	0%
Kruger W.(Werner)	BB	2008-09	2	1	1	0	50%
Kuün G.W.F.(Derick)	BB	2006, 08-09	3	1	1	1	33%
L							
La Grange G.(Doppies)	Tvl	2011	1	1	0	0	100%
La Marque D.(Derek)	Ntl	1984	1	0	1	0	0%
Labuschagne C.(Cas)	Ntl	1956	1	0	1	0	0%
Labuschagne J.J.(Jannes)	GL	1999, 02	2	1	1	0	50%
Labuschagne L.(Lappies)	Ntl	1956	1	0	1	0	0%
Labuschagne W.A.(Lappies)	Tvl	1986, 91-92	3	0	3	0	0%
Lacroix T.(Thierry)	Ntl	1995	1	1	0	0	100%
Laing B.(Balfour)	Ntl	1956	1	0	1	0	0%
Lambie P.(Patrick)	Ntl	2010-13	4	2	2	0	50%
Lamprecht J.C.(Johann)	N Tvl	1985, 87-90	5	2	2	1	40%
Lategan M.T.(Tjol)	WP	1947	1	1	0	0	100%
Laubscher T.G.(Tommie)	WP	1995, 97	2	1	1	0	50%
Lawless G.E.(Gavin)	Tvl	1996	1	0	1	0	0%
Lawless M.J.(Mike)	WP	1969	1	0	1	0	0%
Lawton T.A.(Tom)	Ntl	1990	1	1	0	0	100%
Le Roux A-H.(Ollie)	OFS/Ntl/FS	1994-95, 00-01, 03, 05-06	7	2	4	1	29%
Le Roux H.P.(Hennie)	Tvl	1992-94, 96, 99	5	3	2	0	60%
Le Roux J.H.S.(Johan)	Tvl	1991	1	0	1	0	0%
Le Roux M.(Martiens)	OFS	1973, 75-78, 81	6	1	5	0	17%
Lensing G.(Kees)	BB	2004-05	2	1	1	0	50%
Leonard A.(Anton)	BB	2002-05	4	3	1	0	75%
Lewies J.S.T.(Stephan)	Ntl	2013	1	1	0	0	100%
Lightfoot W.(Wessel)	WP	1988	1	0	1	0	0%
Linee M.(Tinus)	WP	1995	1	0	1	0	0%
Lobberts H.(Hilton)	BB	2006	1	0	0	1	0%
Lochner G.P.(Flappie)	WP	1939	1	0	1	0	0%
Lock J.L.(Jan)	N Tvl	1985, 87-88, 90	4	2	2	0	50%
Lockyear R.J.(Dick)	WP	1954	1	1	0	0	100%
Lombaard P.(Piet)	WP	1950	1	0	1	0	0%
Lötter D.(Deon)	WP/Tvl	1986, 91, 93	3	2	1	0	67%
Lotz J.W.(Jan)	Tvl	1939, 47	2	1	1	0	50%
Loubscher H.(Hennie)	WP	1954	1	1	0	0	100%
Loubser J.(Kootjie)	Bol	1952	1	0	1	0	0%

ABSA CURRIE CUP FINAL PLAYERS 1939 - 2013

Name	Province	First & last final	Matches	Won	Lost	Drawn	Winning%
Lourens J.P.(Johnnie)	N Tvl	1946	1	1	0	0	100%
Lourens M.J.(Thys)	N Tvl	1968-69, 71, 73-75, 77-78	8	7	0	1	88%
Louw F.H.(Hottie)	WP/BB	1998, 00-01, 06	4	2	1	1	50%
Louw L-F.P.(Francois)	WP	2010	1	0	1	0	0%
Louw M.J.(Martiens)	Tvl	1971	1	0	0	1	0%
Louw P.(Pierre)	WP	1939	1	0	1	0	0%
Louw R.J.(Rob)	WP	1979-80, 82-85	6	4	1	1	67%
Louw S.C.(Fanie)	Tvl	1939	1	1	0	0	100%
Luck A.(Aubrey)	WP	1969	1	0	1	0	0%
Ludik L.(Louis)	GL/Ntl	2007, 10, 12-13	4	2	2	0	50%
Lurie M.(Max)	Tvl	1947	1	0	1	0	0%
Luther C.F.(Chris)	N Tvl	1970-71, 74	3	1	1	1	33%
M							
Maartens C.(Chris)	Tvl	1968	1	0	1	0	0%
Macdonald I.(Ian)	Tvl	1991-93, 96	4	1	3	0	25%
Maku B.G.(Bandise)	BB/GL	2009, 11	2	2	0	0	100%
Malan A.W.(Adolf)	N Tvl	1983, 85, 87-91	7	3	3	1	43%
Malan P.(Piet)	Tvl	1947, 50	2	1	1	0	50%
Malherbe J.F.(Frans)	WP	2012-13	2	1	1	0	50%
Mallet N.V.H.(Nick)	WP	1982-84	3	3	0	0	100%
Mametsa S.J.(John)	BB	2003, 08	2	1	1	0	50%
Mapoe L.G.(Lionel)	FS	2009	1	0	1	0	0%
Marais C.(Charlie)	WP	1980, 89	2	0	1	1	0%
Marais C.F.(Charl)	WP	1998, 00-01	3	2	1	0	67%
Marais D.D.(Dawie)	N Tvl	1983	1	0	1	0	0%
Marais F.P.(Buks)	Bol	1952	1	0	1	0	0%
Marais J.A.(Jandré)	Ntl	2012	1	0	1	0	0%
Marais J.H.(Johan)	N Tvl	1981-82, 85	3	1	2	0	33%
Marais L.(Toetie)	OFS	1981	1	0	1	0	0%
Marais P.C.(Peet)	Ntl	2013	1	1	0	0	100%
Marais S.P.	Ntl	2013	1	1	0	0	100%
Marchant A.R.(Reg)	N Tvl	1983	1	0	1	0	0%
Marinos A.W.N.(Andy)	WP	1998	1	0	1	0	0%
Maritz A.(Dries)	Tvl	1986	1	0	1	0	0%
Markgraaff A.T.(André)	WP	1983	1	1	0	0	100%
Marshall F.(Frank)	Ntl	1956	1	0	1	0	0%
Martens H.J.(Hentie)	OFS/Ntl	1994-99	2	0	2	0	0%
Masina M.(Mac)	GL	1999	1	1	0	0	100%
Matfield V.(Victor)	BB	2002, 04-05, 08-09	5	3	2	0	60%
Mather D.(Doug)	WP	1976	1	0	1	0	0%
McCallum R.J.(Roy)	WP	1979	1	0	0	1	0%
McKechnie R.(Richard)	E Tvl	1972	1	0	1	0	0%
McLean D.A.(Des)	Ntl	1984	1	0	1	0	0%
McLeod C.(Charl)	Ntl	2010, 12-13	3	2	1	0	67%
McLeod-Henderson B.M.(Brad)	Ntl	2003	1	0	1	0	0%
Meiring F.A.	N Tvl	1991	1	1	0	0	100%
Meiring J.(Koos)	N Tvl	1968	1	1	0	0	100%
Mellish F.C.B.(Francis)	WP	1946-47	2	1	1	0	50%
Mellish H.T.	WP	1939	1	0	1	0	0%
Mendez F.E.A.(Fredrico)	Ntl	1996	1	1	0	0	100%
Menter M.A.(Alan)	N Tvl	1968	1	1	0	0	100%
Mentz H.(Henno)	Ntl	2003	1	0	1	0	0%
Meyer H.P.(Hendrik)	FS	2006-07	2	1	0	1	50%
Meyer W.(Willie)	FS/GL	1997, 99, 02	3	1	2	0	33%
Meyer W.(Wim)	BB	1998	1	1	0	0	100%
Michalak F.(Frederic)	Ntl	2008, 11	2	1	1	0	50%
Mills P.M.G.(Pat)	N Tvl	1956	1	1	0	0	100%
Minnaar W.(Walter)	GL	1999	1	1	0	0	100%
Minnie D.J.(Derrick)	Tvl	2011	1	1	0	0	100%
Möller J.D.	WP	2010	1	0	1	0	0%
Monkley D.(Duane)	WP	1998	1	0	1	0	0%
Montgomery P.C.(Percy)	WP	1997-98, 00-01	4	3	1	0	75%
Moolman L.C.(Louis)	N Tvl	1975, 77-83, 85	9	5	3	1	56%
Moore N.(Nick)	GL	1999	1	1	0	0	100%
Mordt R.H.(Ray)	N Tvl	1983, 85	2	0	2	0	0%
Morkel C.T.(Charlie)	WP	1954	1	1	0	0	100%
Morkel J.(Hannes)	WP	1939, 46-47, 50	4	1	3	0	25%
Mostert M.(Marius)	GL	1999	1	1	0	0	100%
Moyle B.S.(Brent)	Ntl	1999-00	2	0	2	0	0%
Mtawarira T.(Tendai)	Ntl	2008, 10-13	5	3	2	0	60%
Muir D.J.(Dick)	Ntl/WP	1990-97	5	4	1	0	80%
Mulder J.C.(Japie)	Tvl	1991, 93-94, 96	4	2	2	0	50%
Mulder K.(Koos)	E Tvl	1972	1	0	1	0	0%
Müller G.H.(Gert)	WP/Tvl	1969, 72, 74	3	1	2	0	33%
Muller G.J.(George)	Tvl	1950	1	1	0	0	100%
Muller G.J.(Johann)	Ntl	2008	1	1	0	0	100%
Müller G.P.(Jorrie)	GL	2002	1	0	1	0	0%
Müller H.L.(Helgard)	OFS	1994, 97	2	0	2	0	0%
Muller H.S.V.(Hennie)	Tvl	1947, 50	2	1	1	0	50%
Müller L.F.(Louis)	N Tvl	1969-70, 75	3	2	1	0	67%
Müller L.J.J.(Lood)	Ntl	1992-93	1	1	0	0	100%
Müller P.G.(Pieter)	Ntl	1992-93	2	1	1	0	50%
Murray W.M.(Waylon)	Ntl	2008	1	1	0	0	100%
Mvovo L.N.(Lwazi)	Ntl	2010-13	4	2	2	0	50%
Myburgh J.L.(Mof)	N Tvl	1968-71	4	2	1	1	50%
Myburgh K.(Kat)	GW	1970	1	1	0	0	100%
N							
Naudé F.S.(Frikkie)	OFS/WP	1973, 79	2	0	1	1	0%
Naude J.(Johan)	Bol	1952	1	0	1	0	0%
Naudé S.W.(Schalk)	Tvl	1986-87	2	0	2	0	0%
Ndungane A.Z.(Akona)	BB	2005-06	2	0	1	1	0%
Ndungane O.M.(Odwa)	Ntl	2008, 10-13	5	3	2	0	60%
Neethling J.B.(Tiny)	WP	1969	1	0	1	0	0%

ABSA CURRIE CUP FINAL PLAYERS 1939 - 2013

Name	Province	First & last final	Matches	Won	Lost	Drawn	Winning%
Nel C.(Christo)	WP	1976	1	0	1	0	0%
Nel G.P.(Giepie)	N Tvl	1982, 85, 87, 89	4	1	2	1	25%
Nel H.J.(Hennie)	N Tvl	1956	1	1	0	0	100%
Nel J.(Johan)	N Tvl	1991	1	1	0	0	100%
Nel J.P.	BB	2002-06	5	3	1	1	60%
Nel J.T.	WP	1939	1	0	1	0	0%
Nel P.J.L.(Pieter)	N Tvl	1987-88	2	2	0	0	100%
Nel S.(Soon)	GW	1970	1	1	0	0	100%
Nel W.P.	FS	2009	1	0	1	0	0%
Nell D.P.(Darron)	FS	2006-07	2	1	0	1	50%
Nell H.(Hekkie)	Tvl	1968	1	0	1	0	0%
Neuhoff C.M.(Mauritz)	N Tvl	1968	1	1	0	0	100%
Newham C.(Charlie)	Tvl	1947	1	0	1	0	0%
Nieuwoudt G.(Bill)	WP	1984, 86	2	2	0	0	100%
Noble C.D.(Christie)	Ntl	1990	1	1	0	0	100%
Nomis S.H.(Syd)	Tvl	1968	1	0	1	0	0%
Nortjé B.D.(Bennie)	GL	2002	1	0	1	0	0%
Norwood S.T.(Simon)	Tvl	1971-72	2	1	0	1	50%
Ntubeni S.(Siyabonga)	WP	2012-13	2	1	1	0	50%
O							
Oberholzer A.F.(Anton)	Tvl	1971-72, 74	3	1	1	1	33%
Oberholzer J.H.(Jan)	N Tvl	1978-82	5	3	1	1	60%
Ochse J.K.(Chum)	WP	1950, 54	2	1	1	0	50%
Oelofse J.S.A.(Hansie)	Tvl	1952	1	1	0	0	100%
Oelschig N.H.(Noël)	FS	2004-07	4	2	1	1	50%
Olivier E.(Eben)	WP	1969	1	0	1	0	0%
Olivier J.(Jacques)	N Tvl	1991, 98	2	2	0	0	100%
Olivier W.(Wynand)	BB	2005, 08-09	3	1	2	0	33%
Oosthuizen C.V.(Coenie)	FS	2009	1	0	1	0	0%
Oosthuizen J.J.(Johan)	WP	1976	1	0	1	0	0%
Oosthuizen J.P. de V.(Jan)	N Tvl	1971	1	0	0	1	0%
Oosthuizen O.W.(Okkie)	N Tvl	1980-81	2	2	0	0	100%
Oosthuizen P.(Pierre)	WP	1979	1	0	0	1	0%
Oosthuizen S.(Schalk)	OFS	1981	1	0	1	0	0%
Oosthuysen D.E.(Deon)	N Tvl	1988-91	4	2	1	1	50%
Opperman R.J.(Ryno)	OFS	1994, 97	2	0	2	0	0%
Otto K.(Krynauw)	BB	1998	1	1	0	0	100%
Oxlee K.(Keith)	Ntl	1956	1	0	1	0	0%
P							
Passens G.A.(Gavin)	BB/FS	2002-04, 06-07	5	4	0	1	80%
Patterson A.C.(Andrew)	WP	1989	1	0	1	0	0%
Paulse B.J.(Breyton)	WP	1998, 00-01	3	2	1	0	67%
Pawson A.L.(André)	OFS	1994	1	0	1	0	0%
Payne S.(Shaun)	Ntl	1999	1	0	1	0	0%
Peens P.W.S.(Pierre)	N Tvl	1980	1	1	0	0	100%
Pelser E.(Eugene)	N Tvl	1983	1	0	1	0	0%
Pelser P.A.(Piet)	Tvl	1952	1	1	0	0	100%
Perry M.(Floris)	N Tvl	1946	1	1	0	0	100%
Piater H.W.(Hein)	N Tvl	1977	1	1	0	0	100%
Pickard J.A.J.(Jan)	WP	1954	1	1	0	0	100%
Pienaar J.A.(Japie)	OFS	1973	1	0	1	0	0%
Pienaar J.F.(Francois)	Tvl	1991-94, 96	5	2	3	0	40%
Pienaar R.(Ruan)	Ntl	2008	1	1	0	0	100%
Pienaar Z.M.J.(Gysie)	OFS	1976-78	3	1	2	0	33%
Pieterse B.H.(Barend)	FS	2004-07	4	2	1	1	50%
Pieterse C.(Charles)	Tvl	1987	1	0	1	0	0%
Pietersen J.(Joe)	WP	2012	1	1	0	0	100%
Pietersen J-P.R.(J.P.)	Ntl	2008, 11-12	3	1	2	0	33%
Pitout C.A.(Anton)	FS	2004	1	0	1	0	0%
Pitzer G.(Gys)	N Tvl	1968-70	3	2	1	0	67%
Platford S.(Shaun)	Ntl	1992	1	1	0	0	100%
Plumtree J.(John)	Ntl	1990, 96	2	2	0	0	100%
Pope C.F.(Chris)	WP	1976	1	0	1	0	0%
Potgieter D.J.(Dewald)	BB	2008-09	2	1	1	0	50%
Potgieter H.L.(Hermanus)	OFS	1975, 77-78	3	0	3	0	0%
Potgieter J-L.(Jacques-Louis)	FS	2009	1	0	1	0	0%
Potgieter R.(Ronnie)	N Tvl	1968-71	4	2	1	1	50%
Potgieter W.C.(Wilhelm)	OFS	1975	1	0	1	0	0%
Povey S.A.(Shaun)	WP	1979, 82-86	6	5	0	1	83%
Powell J.D.(Neil)	BB	2006	1	0	0	1	0%
Pretorius A.S.(André)	GL/Ntl	2002, 10	2	1	1	0	50%
Pretorius J.C.(Jaco)	GL/N Tvl	2002, 07, 09	3	1	2	0	33%
Pretorius J.J.D.(Jannie)	Tvl	1987	1	0	1	0	0%
Pretorius P.I.L.(Piet)	N Tvl	1991	1	1	0	0	100%
Pretorius W.J.J.(Fatty)	Tvl	1939	1	1	0	0	100%
Putt K.B.(Kevin)	Ntl	1993, 95-96	3	2	1	0	67%
Pypers C.G.(Corrie)	Tvl	1974	1	0	1	0	0%
R							
Rademeyer H.N.(Hempas)	Tvl	1986-87	2	0	2	0	0%
Rahn J.A.(Jackie)	Tvl	1952	1	1	0	0	100%
Ralepelle M.C.(Chiliboy)	BB	2008	1	0	1	0	0%
Ras A.(Abel)	N Tvl	1954	1	0	1	0	0%
Ras W.J. de W.(De Wet)	OFS	1975-78, 81	5	1	4	0	20%
Rautenbach S.J.(Faan)	WP	2000	1	1	0	0	100%
Reece-Edwards H.M.(Hugh)	Ntl	1984, 90, 92	3	2	1	0	67%
Reinach J.M.(Cobus)	Ntl	2012-13	2	1	1	0	50%
Rens I.J.(Natie)	Tvl	1952	1	1	0	0	100%
Retief D.F.(Daan)	N Tvl	1946, 54	2	1	1	0	50%
Reynecke E.(Ethienne)	GL	2007	1	0	1	0	0%
Rheeder G.(Gert)	WP	1954	1	1	0	0	100%
Rhodes M.K.(Michael)	GL/WP	2011,13	2	1	1	0	50%
Ribbens P.J.(Pierre)	BB	1998	1	1	0	0	100%
Richter A.H.(Adriaan)	N Tvl	1991	1	1	0	0	100%
Robbie J.C.(John)	Tvl	1986-87	2	0	2	0	0%
Roberts H.(Harry)	Tvl	1991-92	2	0	2	0	0%
Robertson P.(Preston)	WP	1969	1	0	1	0	0%
Robinson J.(Johnny)	Tvl	1950	1	1	0	0	100%
Rodgers P.H.(Heinrich)	N Tvl/Tvl	1985, 87-90, 92-93	7	3	3	1	43%
Rodriguez L.(Len)	WP	1954	1	1	0	0	100%
Roets J.(Johan)	BB	2003-06	4	2	1	1	50%
Rogers C.D.(Chris)	Tvl	1986-87	2	0	2	0	0%

ABSA CURRIE CUP FINAL PLAYERS 1939 - 2013

Name	Province	First & last final	Matches	Won	Lost	Drawn	Winning%
Roos G.J.	Tvl	1939	1	1	0	0	100%
Rose E.E.(Earl)	GL	2007	1	0	1	0	0%
Rossouw C. le C.(Chris)	Tvl/Ntl	1996, 00	2	0	2	0	0%
Rossouw C.(Charles)	Tvl	1994	1	1	0	0	100%
Rossouw C.(Chris)	WP	2000-01	2	2	0	0	100%
Rossouw D.J.(Danie)	BB	2004-06, 08-09	5	2	2	1	40%
Rossouw P.W.G.(Pieter)	WP	1995, 97-98, 00-01	5	3	2	0	60%
Roumat O.(Olivier)	Ntl	1995	1	1	0	0	100%
Roux C.(Chean)	WP	1998	1	0	1	0	0%
Roux F. du T.(Mannetjies)	GW	1970	1	1	0	0	100%
Roux F.(Francois)	N Tvl	1954	1	0	1	0	0%
Roux J.P.(Johan)	N Tvl/Tvl	1991, 93-94, 96	4	3	1	0	75%
Roux O.A.(Tonie)	N Tvl	1970-71	2	0	1	1	0%
Roux W.G.(Wessel)	BB	2002-05	4	3	1	0	75%
Russell R.B.(Brent)	Ntl	2003	1	0	1	0	0%
S							
Sauerman A.(Archie)	Bol	1952	1	0	1	0	0%
Sauermann J.T.(Theo)	Tvl	1971-72, 74	3	1	1	1	33%
Scheepers G.(Gert)	GW	1970	1	1	0	0	100%
Schlebusch J.J.J.(Jan)	OFS	1973, 75, 77	3	0	3	0	0%
Schmidt B.O.(Barry)	Tvl	1950, 52	2	2	0	0	100%
Schmidt U.L.(Uli)	N Tvl/Tvl	1985, 87-91, 93-94	8	5	2	1	63%
Schoeman B.J.(Barry)	OFS	1981	1	0	1	0	0%
Scholtz A.W.(Dries)	BB	2002, 06	2	1	0	1	50%
Scholtz C.P.(Christiaan)	Tvl	1994	1	1	0	0	100%
Scholtz H.(Hendro)	FS	2004-05, 07	3	2	1	0	67%
Scholtz N.B.(Calla)	WP	1983-86, 88	5	4	1	0	80%
Schreuder L.(Louis)	WP	2012-13	2	1	1	0	50%
Schutte G.A.(Gert)	Tvl	1971	1	0	0	1	0%
Schutte P.J.W.(Phillip)	N Tvl/Tvl	1990-91, 94	3	2	1	0	67%
Scriba H.M.(Hans)	WP	1985, 89	2	1	0	1	50%
Scrooby C.W.(Chris)	Tvl	1939	1	1	0	0	100%
Sephaka L.D.(Lawrence)	GL	2002, 07	2	0	2	0	0%
Serfontein D.J.(Divan)	WP	1976, 79-80, 82-84	6	3	2	1	50%
Sherrell R.(Reg)	Ntl	1956	1	0	1	0	0%
Simpson B.(Barry)	Ntl	1956	1	0	1	0	0%
Sinclair D.J.(Des)	Tvl	1950	1	1	0	0	100%
Sinclair J.(Jebb)	WP	2012	1	1	0	0	100%
Skeate R.C.(Ross)	Ntl	2011	1	0	1	0	0%
Skene A.L.(Alan)	WP	1954	1	1	0	0	100%
Skinner A.(André)	N Tvl/Tvl/N Tvl	1981-82, 87, 88, 90	5	2	3	0	40%
Skinstad R.B.(Bob)	WP	1997-98, 01	3	2	1	0	67%
Slade J.(John)	Ntl	1999	1	0	1	0	0%
Smal G.P.(Gert)	WP	1985-86, 88-89	4	2	1	1	50%
Small J.T.(James)	Tvl/Ntl/WP	1991-93, 95-97	6	3	3	0	50%
Smit B.C.(Chris)	WP	1986	1	1	0	0	100%
Smit F.C.	WP	1995	1	0	1	0	0%
Smit G.A.(Gert)	N Tvl	1956	1	1	0	0	100%
Smit J.W.(John)	Ntl	1999-01, 08	4	1	3	0	25%
Smit P.L.(Phillip)	Ntl	2001, 03	2	0	2	0	0%
Smit W.J.	Tvl	1939	1	1	0	0	100%
Smith J.	E Tvl	1972	1	0	1	0	0%
Smith J.H.(Juan)	FS	2004-05	2	1	1	0	50%
Smith K.(Kat)	WP	1969	1	0	1	0	0%
Smith M.J.	FS	1997	1	0	1	0	0%
Smith P.(Peet)	GW	1970	1	1	0	0	100%
Smith P.F.(Franco)	OFS/BB	1994, 98	2	1	1	0	50%
Smith R.F.(Rodger)	Ntl	2000-01	2	0	2	0	0%
Smith T.(Tos)	GW	1970	1	1	0	0	100%
Snyman A.H.(André)	BB/Ntl	1998, 01, 03	3	1	2	0	33%
Snyman D.S.L.(Dawie)	WP	1976	1	0	1	0	0%
Snyman J.C.P.(Jackie)	OFS	1973	1	0	1	0	0%
Sonnekus G.H.H.(Gerrie)	OFS	1975-78, 81	5	1	4	0	20%
Sonnekus P.J.(Pieter)	N Tvl	1983	1	0	1	0	0%
Sowerby R.S.(Shaun)	Ntl	2000-01, 03	3	0	3	0	0%
Spangenberg J.C.(Christo)	N Tvl	1987-89	3	2	0	1	67%
Spies J.J.(Johan)	N Tvl	1968-71	4	2	1	1	50%
Spies P.J.(Pierre) jnr.	BB	2006, 08-09	3	1	1	1	33%
Spies P.J.(Pierre) snr.	N Tvl	1975, 77	2	2	0	0	100%
Stander B.(Ben)	E Tvl	1972	1	0	1	0	0%
Stander J.C.J.(Rampie)	OFS	1973, 76, 78	3	1	2	0	33%
Stapelberg W.P.(Willem)	N Tvl	1968, 73-74	3	3	0	0	100%
Steenkamp G.G.(Gurthrö)	FS/BB	2004, 08-09	3	1	2	0	33%
Steenkamp M.D.(De Kock)	WP	2010, 12-13	3	1	2	0	33%
Stegmann G.J.(Deon)	BB	2008-09	2	1	1	0	50%
Steinhobel J.(Tiny)	Tvl	1947	1	0	1	0	0%
Stewart J.C.(Christian)	WP	1988, 95, 98	3	0	3	0	0%
Steyn F.P.L.(Francois)	Ntl	2008, 13	2	2	0	0	100%
Steyn M.(Morné)	BB	2005-06, 08-09	4	1	2	1	25%
Stofberg M.T.S.(Theuns)	OFS/N Tvl/WP	1976-80, 82-83	7	4	2	1	57%
Stoltz W.(Willem)	GL	2002	1	0	1	0	0%
Stolz T.(Thys)	WP	2000-01	2	2	0	0	100%
Straeuli R.A.W.(Rudolf)	N Tvl/Tvl	1990, 93, 96	3	1	2	0	33%
Stransky J.T.(Joel)	Ntl/WP	1990, 95	3	1	2	0	33%
Strauss A.J.(Andries)	Ntl	2010	1	1	0	0	100%
Strauss C.P.(Tiaan)	WP	1986, 88-89, 95	4	1	2	1	25%
Strauss C.R.(Richardt)	FS	2006-07, 09	3	1	1	1	33%
Strauss J.A.(Adriaan)	BB/FS	2006, 09	2	0	1	1	0%
Strauss J.A.(Attie)	WP	1984	1	1	0	0	100%
Strauss J.C.	N Tvl	1981, 83	2	1	1	0	50%
Strauss J.H.P.(Johan)	Tvl	1974	1	0	1	0	0%
Strauss J.Z.(Joshua)	Tvl	2011	1	1	0	0	100%
Strydom A.(Andries)	E Tvl	1972	1	0	1	0	0%

ABSA CURRIE CUP FINAL PLAYERS 1939 - 2013

Name	Province	First & last final	Matches	Won	Lost	Drawn	Winning%
Strydom A.(Basie)	Tvl	1968	1	0	1	0	0%
Strydom G.J.(Gert)	Tvl	1972, 74	2	1	1	0	50%
Strydom J.J.(Hannes)	Tvl	1993, 96, 99	3	2	1	0	67%
Strydom L.I.(Louis)	BB	2003, 07	2	1	1	0	50%
Strydom L.J.(Louis)	N Tvl	1946	1	1	0	0	100%
Strydom P.A.(Piet)	OFS	1975	1	0	1	0	0%
Strydom W.T.(Willie)	OFS	1973	1	0	1	0	0%
Swanepoel R.(Riaan)	Ntl	2010	1	1	0	0	100%
Swanepoel W.(Werner)	FS	1997	1	0	1	0	0%
Swart F.J.(Francois)	BB	2003	1	1	0	0	100%
Swart I.S. de V.(Balie)	WP/Tvl	1989, 92-94	4	2	1	1	50%
Swart J.C.(Jakes)	OFS	1973	1	0	1	0	0%
Swart J.S.(Justin)	WP/Ntl	1995, 97, 99, 01, 03	5	1	4	0	20%
Swartz B.(Buddy)	GW	1970	1	1	0	0	100%
Swartz E.(Enrico)	Ntl	2003	1	0	1	0	0%
Sykes S.R.(Steven)	Ntl	2008, 10, 12	3	2	1	0	67%
Symington A.(George)	N Tvl	1946	1	1	0	0	100%
Symons T.A.W.(Tommy)	Tvl	1971-72, 74	3	1	1	1	33%
T							
Taute J.J.(Jaco)	Tvl	2011	1	1	0	0	100%
Taylor P.(Peter)	Ntl	1956	1	0	1	0	0%
Taylor T.(Tich)	Ntl	1956	1	0	1	0	0%
Teichmann G.H.(Gary)	Ntl	1992-93, 95-96, 99	5	3	2	0	60%
Terblanche C.S.(Stefan)	Ntl	2000-01, 08, 10-11	5	2	3	0	40%
Thiart D.(Danie)	BB	2006	1	0	0	1	0%
Thomson J.R.D.(Jeremy)	Ntl/Tvl/Ntl	1990, 92, 95-96	4	3	1	0	75%
Thoresson K.R.(Keith)	N Tvl	1975	1	1	0	0	100%
Thorne B.(Bruce)	GL	1999	1	1	0	0	100%
Thorne G.S.(Grahame)	N Tvl	1971	1	0	0	1	0%
Tiedt J.A.(Jannie)	Tvl	1986	1	0	1	0	0%
Townsend A.(Ashton)	Tvl/Ntl	1952, 56	2	1	1	0	50%
Tromp J.A.(Kleinjan)	GL	2002	1	0	1	0	0%
Truscott J.A.(Andries)	BB	1998	1	1	0	0	100%
Truter H.J.(Hendrik)	Tvl/OFS	1991, 94	2	0	2	0	0%
Trytsman J.W.(Johnny)	WP	1998	1	0	1	0	0%
Turner F.G.(Freddie)	WP	1939	1	0	1	0	0%
Tyibilika S.(Solly)	Ntl	2003	1	0	1	0	0%
U							
Uys C.J.(Corné)	FS	2009	1	0	1	0	0%
Uys P. de W.(Piet)	N Tvl	1968-70	3	2	1	0	67%
V							
Van As H.P.(Hugo)	Tvl	1986-87	2	0	2	0	0%
Van Aswegen H.J.(Henning)	OFS/WP	1977, 79-80, 82-83, 85	6	3	2	1	50%
Van Aswegen J.(Jannie)	GW/Tvl	1970-71	2	1	0	1	50%
Van Biljon L.(Lukas)	Ntl	2001, 03	2	0	2	0	0%
Van Blerk J.A.R.	WP	1947	1	1	0	0	100%
Van Blommenstein J.(Johan)	N Tvl	1969-70	2	1	1	0	50%
Van den Berg D.S.(Derek)	WP	1969, 76	2	0	2	0	0%
Van den Berg P.A.(Albert)	Ntl	2000-01, 08	3	2	1	0	67%
Van den Heever D.J.(Daantjie)	N Tvl	1956	1	1	0	0	100%
Van den Heever G.J.(Gerhard)	BB/WP	2009, 12-13	3	2	1	0	67%
Van der Berg C.R.(Riaan)	BB	2005	1	0	1	0	0%
Van der Linde A.(Toks)	WP	1995, 97-98, 00-01	5	3	2	0	60%
Van der Linde C.J.	FS/GL	2004-05, 11	3	2	1	0	67%
Van der Merwe A.J.(Bertus)	Bol	1952	1	0	1	0	0%
Van der Merwe B.S.(Fiks)	N Tvl	1946	1	1	0	0	100%
Van der Merwe C.E.(Erik)	GL	1999	1	1	0	0	100%
Van der Merwe F.(Franco)	GL	2007, 11	2	1	1	0	50%
Van der Merwe G.(Tjokkie)	N Tvl	1978-80	3	2	0	1	67%
Van der Merwe H.S.(Heinke)	GL	2007	1	0	1	0	0%
Van der Merwe P.(Piet)	WP	1954	1	1	0	0	100%
Van der Merwe R.C.(Ryno)	FS	2005-06	2	1	0	1	50%
Van der Ryst F.E.(Franz)	Tvl	1950, 52	2	2	0	0	100%
Van der Schyff P.J.(Johan)	Tvl	1968	1	0	1	0	0%
Van der Spuy S.J.(Fanie)	Tvl	1939	1	1	0	0	100%
Van der Walt J.A.(Jannie)	Tvl	1996, 99	2	1	1	0	50%
Van der Walt J.J.	N Tvl	1988-89	2	1	0	1	50%
Van der Walt J.N.(Nicky)	BB	1998	1	1	0	0	100%
Van der Walt K.(Kobus)	BB	2003	1	1	0	0	100%
Van der Walt L.(Louis)	N Tvl	1974	1	1	0	0	100%
Van der Watt A.E.(Andy)	WP	1969	1	0	1	0	0%
Van der Westhuizen J.F.(Cabous)	Ntl	1992-93, 95	3	2	1	0	67%
Van der Westhuizen J.H.(Joost) (C)	BB	1998, 02	2	2	0	0	100%
Van der Westhuyzen J.N.B.(Jaco)	BB	2002	1	1	0	0	100%
Van Deventer J.(Jannie)	Tvl	1968, 71-72	3	1	1	1	33%
Van Deventer J.D.(Doerie)	N Tvl	1946	1	1	0	0	100%
Van Deventer P.I.(Piet)	GW	1970	1	1	0	0	100%
Van Dyk S.(Stompie)	WP	1946	1	0	1	0	0%
Van Dyk S.W.A.(Schalk)	N Tvl	1956	1	1	0	0	100%
Van Greuning K.(Kapstok)	Tvl	1996	1	0	1	0	0%
Van Heerden F.J.(Fritz)	WP	1995-97	2	1	1	0	50%
Van Heerden H.J.N.(Herman)	OFS	1981	1	0	1	0	0%
Van Heerden J.J.(Goggie)	WP	1984, 86	2	2	0	0	100%
Van Heerden J.L.(Moaner)	N Tvl	1973-74, 77, 80, 82	5	4	1	0	80%
Van Heerden J.L.(Wikus)	GL/BB/GL	2002, 08, 11	3	1	2	0	33%
Van Heerden N.(Nols)	WP	1947	1	1	0	0	100%
Van Heerden P.J.L.(Wickus)	Ntl	1995-96	2	2	0	0	100%
Van Jaarsveld C.J.(Hoppy)	Tvl	1947, 52	2	1	1	0	50%
Van Niekerk J.C.(Joe)	GL	2002	1	0	1	0	0%
Van Niekerk O.(Otto)	Tvl/WP	1939, 46-47	3	2	1	0	67%
Van Niekerk P.(Pietman)	GL	2002	1	0	1	0	0%
Van Niekerk W.(Willouw)	WP	1982	1	1	0	0	100%
Van Reenen A.	Bol	1952	1	0	1	0	0%
Van Reenen J.N.R.(Ross)	OFS	1975-78	4	1	3	0	25%
Van Renen G.L.(George)	WP	1946-47	2	1	1	0	50%
Van Rensburg A.G.(Deon)	Tvl	2011	1	1	0	0	100%

ABSA CURRIE CUP FINAL PLAYERS 1939 - 2013

Name	Province	First & last final	Matches	Won	Lost	Drawn	Winning%
Van Rensburg C.(Clinton)	Ntl	1999	1	0	1	0	0%
Van Rensburg C.Q.(Charl)	Ntl	1999-01, 03	4	0	4	0	0%
Van Rensburg D.(Deon)	E Tvl	1972	1	0	1	0	0%
Van Rensburg J.C.J.(J.C.)	GL	2007, 11	2	1	1	0	50%
Van Rensburg J.T.J.(Theo)	N Tvl/Tvl	1990, 92	2	0	2	0	0%
Van Rensburg P.J.(Vuile)	N Tvl	1946	1	1	0	0	100%
Van Schalkwyk D.(Danie)	BB	1998	1	1	0	0	100%
Van Schalkwyk H.J.(Jaco)	FS	2004	1	0	1	0	0%
Van Schouwenburg F.J.(Francois)	BB	2006	1	0	0	1	0%
Van Staden E.(Eugene)	Ntl	2010-11	2	1	1	0	50%
Van Staden F.(Fred)	N Tvl	1971	1	0	0	1	0%
Van Staden H.J.(Fancy)	Tvl	1950	1	1	0	0	100%
Van Staden J.A.(André)	N Tvl	1969-71, 73-74	5	3	1	1	60%
Van Straaten A.J.J.(Braam)	WP	2000-01	2	2	0	0	100%
Van Vollenhoven K.T.(Tom)	N Tvl	1954	1	0	1	0	0%
Van Vuuren B.J.J.(Koos)	N Tvl	1956	1	1	0	0	100%
Van Wyk C.J.(Basie)	Tvl	1950, 52	2	2	0	0	100%
Van Wyk J.(Johan)	WP	1997-98	2	1	1	0	50%
Van Wyk J-H.(Jan-Harm)	FS	1997	1	0	1	0	0%
Van Wyngaardt J.J.M.(Johan)	Tvl	1971, 74	2	0	1	1	0%
Van Zyl A.(Anton)	GL/WP	2007, 10	2	0	2	0	0%
Van Zyl C.C.(Corniel)	FS	2005, 07	2	2	0	0	100%
Van Zyl D.J.(Dan)	WP	1998, 00	2	1	1	0	50%
Van Zyl J.F.F.(Freddie)	GL	2007	1	0	1	0	0%
Van Zyl M.C.(Thys)	N Tvl	1956	1	1	0	0	100%
Van Zyl P.(Pierre)	N Tvl	1973, 79	2	1	0	1	50%
Van Zyl P.A.(Piet)	OFS	1973	1	0	1	0	0%
Venter A.G.(André)	OFS	1994, 97	2	0	2	0	0%
Venter A.J.	FS/GL/Ntl	1997, 99-01, 03	5	1	4	0	20%
Venter B.(Brendan)	OFS	1994, 97	2	0	2	0	0%
Venter J.(Hannes)	BB	1998	1	1	0	0	100%
Venter J.A.(Barabas)	Tvl	1986-87, 91	3	0	3	0	0%
Venter W.(Walter)	GL	2007	1	0	1	0	0%
Venter W.(Wickus)	GL	1999	1	1	0	0	100%
Vermaak B.S.(Bian)	FS	2006	1	0	0	1	0%
Vermaak J.(Jano)	GL	2007	1	0	1	0	0%
Vermeulen D.J.(Duane)	FS/WP	2007, 10, 12-13	4	2	2	0	50%
Vermeulen R.(Ruan)	BB	2002-03	2	2	0	0	100%
Verster J.J.P.(Basie)	OFS	1975	1	0	1	0	0%
Victor D.P.(Dennis)	N Tvl	1956	1	1	0	0	100%
Vijoen E.J.(Ernest)	OFS	1981	1	0	1	0	0%
Viljoen F.J.N.(Frans)	FS	2009	1	0	1	0	0%
Viljoen J.F.(Joggie)	GW	1970	1	1	0	0	100%
Viljoen L.(Lucas)	N Tvl	1973	1	1	0	0	100%
Viljoen R.(Joggie)	WP	1997	1	1	0	0	100%
Villet J.V.(John)	WP	1982-83	2	2	0	0	100%
Vintcent A.N.(Nellis)	WP	1947	1	1	0	0	100%
Visagie G.P.(Gawie)	Ntl	1984	1	0	1	0	0%
Visagie I.J.(Cobus)	WP	1998, 01	2	1	1	0	50%
Visagie J.C.	Tvl	1952	1	1	0	0	100%
Visagie P.J.(Piet)	GW	1970	1	1	0	0	100%
Visagie R.G.(Vleis)	OFS/Ntl	1981, 90	2	1	1	0	50%
Visser B.(Broekies)	WP	1954	1	1	0	0	100%
Visser J. de V.(De Villiers)	WP	1979-80, 82, 88-89	5	1	2	2	20%
Visser J.(Jan)	WP	1950	1	0	1	0	0%
Visser J.G.	WP	1950	1	0	1	0	0%
Visser M.(Mornay)	WP/Ntl	1995, 99	2	0	2	0	0%
Von Hoeslin D.J.B.(Dave)	Ntl	2001, 03	2	0	2	0	0%
Von Wezel S.A.(Syd)	Tvl	1947	1	0	1	0	0%
Vorster D.(Denys)	GW	1970	1	1	0	0	100%
Vos A.N.(André)	GL	2002	1	0	1	0	0%
Vos J.J.(Jack)	WP	1946-47	2	1	1	0	50%

W

Name	Province	First & last final	Matches	Won	Lost	Drawn	Winning%
Wagenaar C.(Christo)	N Tvl	1975, 77-79, 81	5	4	0	1	80%
Wagner I.J.(Sias)	BB	2002-03	2	2	0	0	100%
Wahl J.J.(Ballie)	WP	1946-47, 50	3	1	2	0	33%
Waldeck J.(Koos)	GW	1970	1	1	0	0	100%
Wannenburg P.J.(Pedrie)	BB	2002-06, 09	6	4	1	1	67%
Wasserman J.G.(Johan)	BB	2002-03, 05	3	2	1	0	67%
Watson A.C.(Tony)	Ntl	1990, 92	2	2	0	0	100%
Watson K.(Ken)	WP	1950	1	0	1	0	0%
Watson L.A.(Luke)	Ntl	2003	1	0	1	0	0%
Weber J.J.(Hans)	N Tvl	1974	1	1	0	0	100%
Wegner C.A.(Callie)	OFS	1981	1	0	1	0	0%
Wegner G.N.(Nico)	Ntl	1999	1	0	1	0	0%
Welsh B.F.(Frikkie)	BB	2003-04	2	2	0	0	100%
Wepener F.W.(Willie)	GL	2007	1	0	1	0	0%
Wessels F.H.(Frans)	N Tvl	1985	1	0	1	0	0%
Wessels H.J.(Japie)	OFS	1978	1	0	1	0	0%
Whipp P.J.M.(Peter)	WP	1976, 79	2	0	1	1	0%
Whitehead T.(Tim)	Ntl	2012	1	0	1	0	0%
Whiteley W.R.(Warren)	Tvl	2011	1	1	0	0	100%
Wiese J.J.(Kobus)	Tvl	1991-94, 96	5	2	3	0	40%
Wilkens V.(Vic)	N Tvl	1954	1	0	1	0	0%
Wilkenson B.(Boesman)	E Tvl	1972	1	0	1	0	0%
Williams C.M.(Chester)	WP/GL	1995, 98, 99	3	1	2	0	33%
Williams H.(Heimar)	Ntl	2013	1	1	0	0	100%
Williams J.G.(John)	N Tvl	1973-75	3	3	0	0	100%
Williamson A.(Andrew)	N Tvl	1987	1	1	0	0	100%
Winter R.G.(Russell)	GL	1999, 02	2	1	1	0	50%
Wolmarans B.J.(Barry)	OFS	1975-78	4	1	3	0	25%
Wright G.D.(Garth)	Tvl	1992	1	0	1	0	0%

Z

Name	Province	First & last final	Matches	Won	Lost	Drawn	Winning%
Zeeman W.(Willie)	WP	1976	1	0	1	0	0%
Zietsman D.W.(Dave)	WP	1976	1	0	1	0	0%

ABSA CURRIE CUP FINAL CAPTAINS 1939 - 2013

Name	Province	First & last final	Matches	Won	Lost	Drawn	Winning%
Andrews M.G.(Mark)	Natal	2000	1	0	1	0	0%
Bartmann W.J.(Wahl)	Natal	1992-93	2	1	1	0	50%
Bates A.J.(Albie)	NT	1973	1	1	0	0	100%
Bekker H.J.(Hennie)	WP	1980	1	0	1	0	0%
Botha G. v G.(Gary)	BB	2006	1	0	0	1	0%
Botha H.E.(Naas)	NT	1980-91	7	5	2	0	71%
Breedt J.C.(Jannie)	TVL	1986-92	4	0	4	0	0%
Brewis J.D.(Hansie)	NT	1954	1	0	1	0	0%
Burger J.(Jan)	Boland	1952	1	0	1	0	0%
Burger S.W.P.(Schalk)	WP	2010	1	0	1	0	0%
Claassen W.(Wynand)	Natal	1984	1	0	1	0	0%
Daniel, KR (Keegan)	Natal	2011-13	2	1	1	0	50%
Dannhauser T.(Toy)	TVL	1968	1	0	1	0	0%
De Wet D.J.(Daan)	OFS	1973	1	0	1	0	0%
Drotské A.E.(Naka)	OFS	2005	1	1	0	0	100%
Du Plessis C.J.(Carel)	WP	1986-89	3	1	1	1	33%
Du Plessis D.C.(Daan)	NT	1979	1	0	0	1	0%
Du Plessis M.(Morné)	WP	1976-79	2	0	1	1	0%
Du Preez F.C.H.(Frik)	NT	1971	1	0	0	1	0%
Duncan R.(Rory)	FS	2007	1	1	0	0	100%
Erasmus J.(Johan)	FS	2004	1	0	1	0	0%
Fourie, D.A (Deon)	WP	2012-13	2	1	1	0	50%
Geel P.J.(Flip)	NT	1946	1	1	0	0	100%
Geldenhuys S.B.(Burger)	NT	1983-89	2	0	1	1	0%
Greyling P.J.F.(Piet)	TVL	1971-72	2	1	0	1	50%
Henderson S.(Skip)	ET	1972	1	0	1	0	0%
Hugo W.J.(Wouter)	OFS	1976-78	3	1	2	0	33%
Jamieson C.M.(Craig)	Natal	1990	1	1	0	0	100%
Joubert E.(Ernst)	GL	2007	1	0	1	0	0%
Kriel P.C.(Piet)	WP	1946	1	0	1	0	0%
Krige C.P.J.(Corné)	WP	2000-01	2	2	0	0	100%
Kritzinger J.L.(Klippies)	OFS	1975	1	0	1	0	0%
Le Roux A-H.(Ollie)	OFS	2006	1	0	0	1	0%
Le Roux M.(Martiens)	OFS	1981	1	0	1	0	0%
Leonard A.(Anton)	BB	2003-05	3	2	1	0	67%
Lotz J.W.(Jan)	TVL	1947	1	0	1	0	0%
Lourens M.J.(Thys)	NT	1974-78	4	4	0	0	100%
Louw S.C.(Fanie)	TVL	1939	1	1	0	0	100%
Matfield V.(Victor)	BB	Sep-08	2	1	1	0	50%
Morkel J.(Hannes)	WP	1950	1	0	1	0	0%
Muir R.J.(Dick)	WP	1997	1	1	0	0	100%
Muller G.J.(Johann)	Natal	2008	1	1	0	0	100%
Müller H.L.(Helgard)	OFS	1994-97	2	0	2	0	0%
Muller H.S.V.(Hennie)	TVL	1950	1	1	0	0	100%
Neethling J.B.(Tiny)	WP	1969	1	0	1	0	0%
Nel H.J.(Hennie)	NT	1956	1	1	0	0	100%
Oberholzer A.F.(Anton)	TVL	1974	1	0	1	0	0%
Oberholzer J.H.(Jan)	NT	1982	1	0	1	0	0%
Pickard J.A.J.(Jan)	WP	1954	1	1	0	0	100%
Pienaar J.F.(Francois)	TVL	1993-96	3	2	1	0	67%
Roux F. du T.(Mannetjies)	GW	1970	1	1	0	0	100%
Serfontein D.J.(Divan)	WP	1982-84	3	3	0	0	100%
Skinstad R.B.(Bob)	WP	1998	1	0	1	0	0%
Smit J.W.(John)	Natal	2001	1	0	1	0	0%
Sowerby R.S.(Shaun)	Natal	2003	1	0	1	0	0%
Strauss C.P.(Tiaan)	WP	1995	1	0	1	0	0%
Strauss J.A.(Adriaan)	FS	2009	1	0	1	0	0%
Strauss, JZ (Josh)	GL	2011	1	1	0	0	100%
Strydom J.J.(Hannes)	TVL	1999	1	1	0	0	100%
Taylor P.(Peter)	Natal	1956	1	0	1	0	0%
Teichmann G.H.(Gary)	Natal	1995-99	3	2	1	0	67%
Terblanche C.S.(Stefan)	Natal	2010	1	1	0	0	100%
Turner F.G.(Freddie)	WP	1939	1	0	1	0	0%
Uys P. de W.(Piet)	NT	1968-70	3	2	1	0	67%
Van Aswegen H.J.(Henning)	WP	1985	1	1	0	0	100%
Van der Westhuizen J.H.(Joost)	B.B.	1998-02	2	2	0	0	100%
Van Renen G.L.(George)	WP	1947	1	1	0	0	100%
Van Wyk C.J.(Basie)	TVL	1952	1	1	0	0	100%
Vos A.N.(André)	GL	2002	1	0	1	0	0%

Keegan Daniel and John Smit hold the Absa Currie Cup trophy.
Steve Haag/Gallo Images

VODACOM CUP RECORDS

CHAMPIONS
1998	Griquas	2003	Lions	2009	Griquas
1999	Lions	2004	Lions	2010	Blue Bulls
2000	Cheetahs	2005	Griquas	2011	Pampas XV
2001	Blue Bulls	2006	Falcons	2012	Western Province
2002	Lions	2007	Griquas	2013	Golden Lions
		2008	Blue Bulls		

RESULTS OF FINALS
Year	Winner	Score	Loser	Score	Venue
1998	Griquas	57	Lions	0	Kimberley
1999	Lions	73	Griquas	7	Johannesburg
2000	Cheetahs	44	Griquas	24	Bloemfontein
2001	Blue Bulls	42	Boland Cavaliers	24	Pretoria
2002	Lions	54	Blue Bulls	38	Johannesburg
2003	Blue Bulls	17	Lions	26	Pretoria
2004	Lions	35	Blue Bulls	16	Johannesburg
2005	Wildeklawer Griquas	27	Leopards	25	Kimberley
2006	Falcons	25	Natal	17	Brakpan
2007	Griquas	33	Blue Bulls	29	Kimberley
2008	Blue Bulls	25	Free State	21	Pretoria
2009	Blue Bulls	19	Griquas	28	Pretoria
2010	Blue Bulls	31	Free State	29	Pretoria
2011	Pampas XV	14	Blue Bulls	9	Potchefstroom
2012	Griquas	18	Western Province	20	Kimberley
2013	Pumas	28	Golden Lions	42	Nelspruit

MATCH RECORDS

90 or more points
Score	Match	Venue/Year
161-03	Golden Lions vs Limpopo BB	Alberton 2013
154-00	Pumas vs Limpopo BB	Nelspruit 2013
124-05	Griquas vs Limpopo BB	Groblersdal 2013
113-03	Leopards XV Limpopo BB	Umzimuhle 2013
110-00	Blue Bulls vs Limpopo BB	Lephalale 2013
110-17	EP vs Welwits.	Port Elizabeth 2001
101-20	Lions vs Welwits.	Johannesburg 2001
92-08	Natal vs North West	Durban 1998
92-25	Blue Bulls vs Welwits.	Pretoria 2000

Won by 80 or more
Score	Match	Venue/Year
158	GL vs L BB (161-03)	Alberton 2013
154	Pumas vs Limpopo BB	Nelspruit 2013
119	Griquas vs Limpopo BB	Groblersdal 2013
110	Leopards XV vs Limpopo BB	Umzimuhle 2013
110	Blue Bulls vs Limpopo BB	Lephalale 2013
93	EP vs Welwits. (110-17)	Port Elizabeth 2001
84	Natal vs North West (92-8)	Durban 1998
81	Lions vs Welwits. (101-20)	Johannesburg 2001
80	Griquas vs Valke (83-3)	Kimberley 2012

15 or more tries
Tries	Match	Venue	Year
16	EP vs Welwits. (110-17)	Port Elizabeth	2001
15	Lions vs Welwits. (101-20)	Johannesburg	2001

35 or more points by a player
Pts	Player/Match	Year
47	AA Volmink (9t, 1c), GL vs LBB	2013
42	IP Olivier (4t, 11c) Griquas vs Griffons	2009
40	WNF du Plessis (2t, 15c) BB vs LBB	2013
38	RG Jordaan (2t, 11c, 2p) Elephants vs Welwits.	2001
36	C Barnard (2t, 10c, 2p) Cheetahs vs Falcons	2004
36	J Peach (2t, 7c, 4p) Boland vs Eagles	2006
35	GS du Toit (3t, 10c) Griquas vs EP	1998

4 or more tries by a player
Tries	Player/Match	Year
9	AA Volmink, Lions vs Limpopo BB	2013
5	S Brink, Natal vs Griffons	1998
5	M Schoeman, Griquas vs Limpopo BB	2013
5	RR Jansen, griquas vs Limpopo BB	2013
5	JA van der Walt, Lions vs Welwits.	2001
4	C Manuel, Natal vs North West	1998
4	W Geyer, Falcons vs Welwits	1998
4	H Swart, Pumas vs Leopards	1999
4	S Marot, Griffons vs SWD	2002
4	G Mbangeni, Falcons vs Leopards	2004
4	E Seconds, WP vs SWD	2006
4	IP Olivier, Griquas vs Griffons	2009
4	J Tuculet, Pampas XV vs Valke	2011
4	JJ Engelbrecht, WP vs Griffons	2011
4	I Heyns, Leopards XV vs Limpopo BB	2013
4	JP Mostert, Valke vs Limpopo BB	2013
4	D Demas, Pumas vs Limpopo BB	2013

VODACOM CUP RECORDS

Ten or more conversions by a player
15	WNF du Plessis, Blue Bulls vs Limpopo BB		2013
14	AS Pretorius, Leopards XV vs Limpopo BB		2013
12	F Brummer, Griquas vs Limpopo BB		2013
12	G Cronje, Golden Lions vs Limpopo BB		2013
11	C Bezuidenhout, Pumas vs Limpopo BB		2013
11	CG van wyk, Pumas vs Limpopo BB		2013
11	RG Jordaan, Elephants vs Welwits.		2001
11	IP Olivier, Griquas vs Griffons		2009
10	GS du Toit, Griquas vs EP		1998
10	C Barnard, Cheetahs vs Falcons		2004

Nine penalty goals by a player
9	E Herbert, Griffons vs Pumas		2001

Two drop goals by a player
2	GS du Toit, Griquas vs Cheetahs		1998
2	J Benade, Pumas vs Falcons		1999
2	A Hough, Griffons vs Border		2006
2	F Brummer, Blue Bulls vs Leopards		2009
2	F Brummer, Blue Bulls vs FS Cheetahs		2010

SEASON RECORDS

700 or more points
731	Griquas		1998
698	Golden Lions		1999

150 or more points by a player
236	GS du Toit	Griquas	1998
193	E Herbert	Griffons	2001
186	J Engelbrecht	Lions	1999
166	KC Tsimba	Cheetahs	2000
163	KC Tsimba	Cheetahs	2002
163	A Hough	Griffons	2006
158	F Brummer	Blue Bulls	2009
154	FJ Zeilinga	Sharks XV	2013
150	JD du Toit	Falcons	1999

100 or more team tries
109	Griquas		1998

50 or more conversions
72	GS du Toit	Griquas	1998

40 or more penalties
44	E Herbert	Griffons	2001

12 or more tries by a player
15	J Daniels	Boland Cavaliers	1998
14	JNB van der Westhuyzen	Natal	1998
	RR Jansen	Blue Bulls	2008
13	AA Volmink	Lions	2013
12	PA van den Berg	Griquas	1998
12	DB Hall	Lions	1999
12	RF Smith	Griquas	1999
12	J Daniels	Lions	2006

Four or more drop goals
6	BK Francis	Blue Bulls	2008
6	F Brummer	Blue Bulls	2010
4	GS du Toit	Griquas	1998
4	J Kotze	Welwitchias	2001

CAREER RECORDS

400 or more points
682	J Peach	EP, Boland
476	C Barnard	Cheetahs, KZN, Griquas
449	K Tsimba	Cheetahs, Pumas
440	Ll Strydom	Griff, Blue Bulls, Valke, FS
425	QJ van Tonder	Griquas, Lions

20 or more tries
63	J Daniels	Boland, Lions
34	J Booysen	Lions
32	J Nicholas	Griquas
24	JA Juries	SWD, Pumas
23	AC Rafferty	Cheetahs
22	JNB van der Westhuyzen	KZN, Pumas, Blue Bulls
22	RF Smith	Griquas, WP, KZN, Cheetahs
21	J Peach	EP/Boland
20	T Douw	Falcons

80 or more conversions
110	J Peach	EP/Boland
99	K Tsimba	Cheetahs, Pumas
83	J Engelbrecht	Lions
80	C April	WP, Blue Bulls, Boland, SWD

60 or more penalty goals
119	J Peach	EP
90	Ll Strydom	Griffons, Blue Bulls, Valke, FS
69	E Herbert	Griffons
67	G Goosen	Border, Boland, Leopards, WP
64	R de Marigny	KZN, Leopards, Blue Bulls

Five or more drop goals
12	J Schutte	KZN, Pumas, Blue Bulls
12	F Brummer	Blue Bulls
7	QJ van Tonder	Griquas, Lions

SPRINGBOK RECORDS

SOUTH AFRICA'S TEST RESULTS SUMMARY 1891-2013

OPPONENTS	Played	Won	Lost	Drawn	% Won	Points For	Points Against	SOUTH AFRICA				OPPONENTS			
								Tries	Conversions	Penalties	Drop goals	Tries	Conversions	Penalties	Drop goals
Argentina	17	16	0	1	94%	682	324	84	65	43	1	30	24	41	1
Australia	78	44	33	1	56%	1501	1357	179	105	166	18	139	87	169	12
British Isles	46	23	17	6	50%	600	516	95	48	52	7	68	30	59	14
Canada	2	2	0	0	100%	71	18	10	6	3	0	2	1	2	0
England	36	22	12	2	61%	749	564	69	47	97	13	39	25	103	7
Fiji	3	3	0	0	100%	129	41	16	11	9	0	4	3	5	0
France	39	22	11	6	56%	783	578	89	60	93	7	51	28	81	19
Georgia	1	1	0	0	100%	46	19	7	4	1	0	1	1	4	0
Ireland	21	16	4	1	76%	417	248	60	32	33	5	24	14	36	3
Italy	11	11	0	0	100%	577	139	79	64	18	0	12	8	20	1
Namibia	2	2	0	0	100%	192	13	27	24	3	0	1	1	2	0
New Zealand	87	34	50	3	39%	1355	1679	133	86	173	28	177	106	203	20
NZ Cavaliers	4	3	1	0	75%	96	62	7	7	15	3	5	3	11	1
Pacific Islands	1	1	0	0	100%	38	24	4	3	4	0	4	2	0	0
Romania	1	1	0	0	100%	21	8	2	1	3	0	1	0	1	0
Scotland	24	19	5	0	79%	597	264	75	52	49	5	27	20	32	3
South America	6	5	1	0	83%	156	86	22	16	6	6	7	5	13	3
S America & Spain	2	2	0	0	100%	54	28	9	3	4	0	3	2	4	0
Spain	1	1	0	0	100%	47	3	7	6	0	0	0	0	1	0
Tonga	2	2	0	0	100%	104	35	16	9	2	0	4	3	3	0
USA	3	3	0	0	100%	145	42	23	16	2	0	4	1	6	1
Uruguay	3	3	0	0	100%	245	12	38	23	3	0	0	0	4	0
Wales	27	25	1	1	93%	739	382	92	61	57	2	32	18	62	2
W Samoa/Samoa	8	8	0	0	100%	385	93	53	36	15	1	12	6	7	0
World Teams	3	3	0	0	100%	87	59	11	5	10	1	9	7	3	0
	428	272	135	21	63,55%	9816	6594	1207	790	861	97	656	395	872	87

SOUTH AFRICA'S WIN PERCENTAGE COMPARED TO THAT OF THEIR MAJOR RIVALS*

TEAM	Played	Won	% Won
New Zealand	512	390	76,2%
South Africa	428	272	63,6%
France	698	383	54,9%
Argentina	375	205	54,7%
England	668	358	53,6%
Wales	656	338	51,5%
Australia	562	286	50,9%
Scotland	628	265	42,2%
Ireland	631	264	41,8%

* as at 24/11/2013

SPRINGBOK RECORDS

TEST MATCHES BY DECADE

DECADE	Played	Won	Lost	Drawn	Win %	Prog. win %
1891-1900	7	1	6	0	14.3%	14.3%
1901-1910	10	5	2	3	50.0%	35.3%
1911-1920	5	5	0	0	100.0%	50.0%
1921-1930	11	6	3	2	54.5%	51.5%
1931-1940	17	13	4	0	76.5%	60.0%
1941-1950	4	4	0	0	100.0%	63.0%
1951-1960	28	18	8	2	64.3%	63.4%
1961-1970	46	26	14	6	56.5%	60.9%
1971-1980	28	20	6	2	71.4%	62.8%
1981-1990	18	14	4	0	77.8%	64.4%
1991-2000	94	60	32	2	63.8%	64.2%
2001-2010	127	78	47	2	61.4%	63.3%
2011-2020	33	22	9	2	66,7%	63,6%
	428	**272**	**135**	**21**		

SOUTH AFRICA'S TEST RECORD BY SEASON

YEAR	Played	Won	Drawn	Lost	Points For	Points Against	% Won Season	% Won Overall	Total Wins	Total Tests
1891	3	0	0	3	0	11	0.00	0.00	0	3
1896	4	1	0	3	16	34	25.00	14.29	1	7
1903	3	1	2	0	18	10	33.33	20.00	2	10
1906	4	2	1	1	29	21	50.00	28.57	4	14
1910	3	2	0	1	38	23	66.67	35.29	6	17
1912-13	5	5	0	0	104	8	100.00	50.00	11	22
1921	3	1	1	1	14	18	33.33	48.00	12	25
1924	4	3	1	0	43	15	75.00	51.72	15	29
1928	4	2	0	2	39	26	50.00	51.52	17	33
1931-32	4	4	0	0	29	9	100.00	56.76	21	37
1933	5	3	0	2	50	42	60.00	57.14	24	42
1937	5	4	0	1	72	47	80.00	59.57	28	47
1938	3	2	0	1	61	36	66.67	60.00	30	50
1949	4	4	0	0	47	28	100.00	62.96	34	54
1951-52	5	5	0	0	100	14	100.00	66.10	39	59
1953	4	3	0	1	79	38	75.00	66.67	42	63
1955	4	2	0	2	75	49	50.00	65.67	44	67
1956	6	3	0	3	47	41	50.00	64.38	47	73
1958	2	0	1	1	8	12	0.00	62.67	47	75
1960-61	10	7	2	1	81	43	70.00	63.53	54	85
1961	3	3	0	0	75	22	100.00	64.77	57	88
1962	4	3	1	0	48	20	75.00	65.22	60	92
1963	4	2	0	2	50	29	50.00	64.58	62	96
1964	2	1	0	1	30	11	50.00	64.29	63	98
1965	8	1	0	7	55	102	12.50	60.38	64	106
1967	4	2	1	1	62	31	50.00	60.00	66	110

SPRINGBOK RECORDS

SOUTH AFRICA'S TEST RECORD BY SEASON - *Continued*

YEAR	Played	Won	Drawn	Lost	Points For	Points Against	% Won Season	% Won Overall	Total Wins	Total Tests
1968	6	5	1	0	89	58	83.33	61.21	71	116
1969-70	8	4	2	2	101	62	50.00	60.48	75	124
1970	4	3	0	1	59	35	75.00	60.94	78	128
1971	5	4	1	0	81	40	80.00	61.65	82	133
1972	1	0	0	1	9	18	0.00	61.19	82	134
1974	6	2	1	3	57	91	33.33	60.00	84	140
1975	2	2	0	0	71	43	100.00	60.56	86	142
1976	4	3	0	1	55	46	75.00	60.96	89	146
1977	1	1	0	0	45	24	100.00	61.22	90	147
1980	9	8	0	1	208	130	88.89	62.82	98	156
1981	6	4	0	2	128	83	66.67	62.96	102	162
1982	2	1	0	1	62	39	50.00	62.80	103	164
1984	4	4	0	0	122	52	100.00	63.69	107	168
1986	4	3	0	1	96	62	75.00	63.95	110	172
1989	2	2	0	0	42	35	100.00	64.37	112	174
1992	5	1	0	4	79	130	20.00	63.13	113	179
1993	7	3	1	3	169	146	42.86	62.37	116	186
1994	9	5	1	3	225	164	55.56	62.05	121	195
1995	10	10	0	0	308	121	100.00	63.90	131	205
1996	13	8	0	5	352	260	61.54	63.76	139	218
1997	13	8	0	5	535	307	61.54	63.64	147	231
1998	12	11	0	1	361	136	91.67	65.02	158	243
1999	13	8	0	5	447	236	61.54	64.84	166	256
2000	12	6	0	6	301	301	50.00	64.18	172	268
2001	11	5	1	5	271	223	45.45	63.44	177	279
2002	11	5	0	6	284	318	45.45	62.76	182	290
2003	12	7	0	5	338	280	58.33	62.58	189	302
2004	13	9	0	4	408	276	69.23	62.86	198	315
2005	12	8	1	3	416	243	66.67	63.00	206	327
2006	12	5	0	7	258	321	41.67	62.24	211	339
2007	17	14	0	3	658	257	82.35	63.20	225	356
2008	13	9	0	4	360	195	69.23	63.41	234	369
2009	12	8	0	4	276	249	66.67	63.51	242	381
2010	14	8	0	6	397	344	57.14	63.29	250	395
2011	9	5	0	4	229	133	55.56	63.12	255	404
2012	12	7	2	3	245	204	58.33	62.98	262	416
2013	12	10	0	2	404	192	83.00	63.60	272	428
Totals	**428**	**272**	**21**	**135**	**9816**	**6594**				

SPRINGBOK RECORDS

OFFICIAL LIST OF ALL 767 TEST & TOUR MATCHES PLAYED BY SOUTH AFRICA 1891-2013

TEST NO.	TOUR MATCH	Date	Venue	Opponent	Captain	Result	Points For	Points against
1		30/07/1891	Port Elizabeth	BRITISH ISLES	HH Castens	Lost	0	4
2		29/08/1891	Kimberley	BRITISH ISLES	RCD Snedden	Lost	0	3
3		05/09/1891	Cape Town	BRITISH ISLES	AR Richards	Lost	0	4
4		30/07/1896	Port Elizabeth	BRITISH ISLES	FTD Aston	Lost	0	8
5		22/08/1896	Johannesburg	BRITISH ISLES	FTD Aston	Lost	8	17
6		29/08/1896	Kimberley	BRITISH ISLES	FTD Aston	Lost	3	9
7		05/09/1896	Cape Town	BRITISH ISLES	BH Heatlie	Won	5	0
8		26/08/1903	Johannesburg	BRITISH ISLES	A Frew	Drew	10	10
9		05/09/1903	Kimberley	BRITISH ISLES	JM Powell	Drew	0	0
10		12/09/1903	Cape Town	BRITISH ISLES	BH Heatlie	Won	8	0
	1	27/09/1906	Northampton	East Midlands	PJ Roos	Won	37	0
	2	29/09/1906	Leicester	Midland Counties	PJ Roos	Won	29	0
	3	03/10/1906	Blackheath	Kent	PJ Roos	Won	21	0
	4	06/10/1906	West Hartlepool	Durham	PJ Roos	Won	22	4
	5	10/10/1906	Newcastle	Northumberland	PJ Roos	Won	44	0
	6	13/10/1906	Leeds	Yorkshire	PJ Roos	Won	34	0
	7	17/10/1906	Plymouth	Devon	PJ Roos	Won	22	6
	8	20/10/1906	Taunton	Somerset	WAG Burger	Won	14	0
	9	24/10/1906	Richmond	Middlesex	PJ Roos	Won	9	0
	10	27/10/1906	Newport	Newport	PJ Roos	Won	8	0
	11	31/10/1906	Cardiff	Glamorgan	PJ Roos	Won	6	3
	12	03/11/1906	Gloucester	Gloucestershire	HW Carolin	Won	23	0
	13	07/11/1906	Oxford	Oxford University	PJ Roos	Won	24	3
	14	10/11/1906	Cambridge	Cambridge University	FJ Dobbin	Won	29	0
	15	13/11/1906	Hawick	South of Scotland	HW Carolin	Won	32	5
11		17/11/1906	Glasgow	SCOTLAND	HW Carolin	Lost	0	6
	16	20/11/1906	Aberdeen	North of Scotland	FJ Dobbin	Won	35	3
12		24/11/1906	Belfast	IRELAND	PJ Roos	Won	15	12
	17	27/11/1906	Dublin	Dublin University	HW Carolin	Won	28	3
13		01/12/1906	Swansea	WALES	PJ Roos	Won	11	0
14		08/12/1906	London	ENGLAND	PJ Roos	Drew	3	3
	18	12/12/1906	Manchester	Lancashire	PJ Roos	Won	11	8
	19	15/12/1906	Carlisle	Cumberland	PJ Roos	Won	21	0
	20	19/12/1906	Richmond	Surrey	PJ Roos	Won	33	0
	21	22/12/1906	Redruth	Cornwall	PJ Roos	Won	9	3
	22	26/12/1906	Newport	Monmouthshire	PJ Roos	Won	17	0
	23	29/12/1906	Llanelli	Llanelli	PJ Roos	Won	16	3
	24	01/01/1907	Cardiff	Cardiff	PJ Roos	Lost	0	17
15		06/08/1910	Johannesburg	BRITISH ISLES	DFT Morkel	Won	14	10
16		27/08/1910	Port Elizabeth	BRITISH ISLES	WA Millar	Lost	3	8
17		03/09/1910	Cape Town	BRITISH ISLES	WA Millar	Won	21	5
	25	03/10/1912	Bath	Somerset	WA Millar	Won	24	3
	26	05/10/1912	Exeter	Devon	WA Millar	Won	8	0
	27	10/10/1912	Redruth	Cornwall	DFT Morkel	Won	15	6
	28	12/10/1912	Newport	Monmouthshire	WA Millar	Won	16	0
	29	17/10/1912	Cardiff	Glamorgan	WA Millar	Won	35	3
	30	19/10/1912	Llanelli	Llanelli	FJ Dobbin	Won	8	7
	31	24/10/1912	Newport	Newport	WA Millar	Lost	3	9
	32	26/10/1912	Blackheath	London	WA Millar	Won	12	8
	33	30/10/1912	Portsmouth	United Services	WA Millar	Won	18	16
	34	02/11/1912	Northampton	East Midlands	WA Millar	Won	14	5
	35	06/11/1912	Oxford	Oxford University	WA Millar	Won	6	0
	36	09/11/1912	Leicester	Midland Counties	WA Millar	Won	25	3

SPRINGBOK RECORDS

OFFICIAL LIST OF ALL 767 TEST & TOUR MATCHES PLAYED BY SOUTH AFRICA 1891-2013

TEST NO.	TOUR MATCH	Date	Venue	Opponent	Captain	Result	Points For	Points against
	37	14/11/1912	Cambridge	Cambridge University	DFT Morkel	Won	24	0
	38	16/11/1912	Twickenham	London	WA Millar	Lost	8	10
	39	20/11/1912	Newcastle	North of England	DFT Morkel	Won	17	0
18		23/11/1912	Edinburgh	SCOTLAND	FJ Dobbin	Won	16	0
	40	27/11/1912	Glasgow	West of Scotland	WA Millar	Won	38	3
19		30/11/1912	Dublin	IRELAND	WA Millar	Won	38	0
	41	04/12/1912	Belfast	Ulster	WA Millar	Won	19	0
	42	07/12/1912	Birkenhead	North of England	DFT Morkel	Won	21	8
20		14/12/1912	Cardiff	WALES	WA Millar	Won	3	0
	43	19/12/1912	Neath	Neath	WA Millar	Won	8	3
	44	21/12/1912	Cardiff	Cardiff	WA Millar	Won	7	6
	45	26/12/1912	Swansea	Swansea	WA Millar	Lost	0	3
	46	28/12/1912	Bristol	Gloucestershire	DFT Morkel	Won	11	0
21		04/01/1913	Twickenham	ENGLAND	DFT Morkel	Won	9	3
22		11/01/1913	Bordeaux	FRANCE	WA Millar	Won	38	5
	47	25/06/1921	Sydney	New South Wales	TB Pienaar	Won	25	10
	48	27/06/1921	Sydney	New South Wales	TB Pienaar	Won	16	11
	49	02/07/1921	Sydney	New South Wales	WH Morkel	Won	28	9
	50	06/07/1921	Sydney	Metropolitan	WH Morkel	Won	14	8
	51	13/07/1921	Wanganui	Wanganui	TB Pienaar	Won	11	6
	52	16/07/1921	New Plymouth	Taranaki	WH Morkel	Drew	0	0
	53	20/07/1921	Masterton	Wairarapa-Bush	TB Pienaar	Won	18	3
	54	23/07/1921	Wellington	Wellington	TB Pienaar	Won	8	3
	55	27/07/1921	Greymouth	West Coast - Buller	HJL Morkel	Won	33	3
	56	30/07/1921	Christchurch	Canterbury	TB Pienaar	Lost	4	6
	57	03/08/1921	Timaru	South Canterbury	WH Morkel	Won	34	3
	58	06/08/1921	Invercargill	Southland	TB Pienaar	Won	12	0
	59	10/08/1921	Dunedin	Otago	WH Morkel	Won	11	3
23		13/08/1921	Dunedin	NEW ZEALAND	WH Morkel	Lost	5	13
	60	17/08/1921	Palmerston N.	Manawatu-Horowhenua	TB Pienaar	Won	3	0
	61	20/08/1921	Auckland	Auckland - North Auckland	TL Krüger	Won	24	8
	62	24/08/1921	Rotorua	Bay of Plenty	TL Krüger	Won	17	9
24		27/08/1921	Auckland	NEW ZEALAND	WH Morkel	Won	9	5
	63	31/08/1921	Hamilton	Waikato	TB Pienaar	Won	6	0
	64	03/09/1921	Napier	Hawkes Bay - Poverty Bay	TB Pienaar	Won	14	8
	65	07/09/1921	Napier	New Zealand Maoris	WH Morkel	Won	9	8
	66	10/09/1921	Nelson	Nelson, Marlborough & Golden Bay - Motueka	JP Michau	Won	26	3
25		17/09/1921	Wellington	NEW ZEALAND	WH Morkel	Drew	0	0
26		16/08/1924	Durban	BRITISH ISLES	PK Albertyn	Won	7	3
27		23/08/1924	Johannesburg	BRITISH ISLES	PK Albertyn	Won	17	0
28		13/09/1924	Port Elizabeth	BRITISH ISLES	PK Albertyn	Drew	3	3
29		20/09/1924	Cape Town	BRITISH ISLES	PK Albertyn	Won	16	9
30		30/06/1928	Durban	NEW ZEALAND	PJ Mostert	Won	17	0
31		21/07/1928	Johannesburg	NEW ZEALAND	PJ Mostert	Lost	6	7
32		18/08/1928	Port Elizabeth	NEW ZEALAND	PJ Mostert	Won	11	6
33		01/09/1928	Cape Town	NEW ZEALAND	PJ Mostert	Lost	5	13
	67	03/10/1931	Bristol	Gloucestershire & Somerset	BL Osler	Won	14	3
	68	08/10/1931	Newport	Newport	BL Osler	Won	15	3
	69	10/10/1931	Swansea	Swansea	JC van der Westhuizen	Won	10	3
	70	14/10/1931	Abertillery	Abertillery & Cross Keys	BL Osler	Won	10	9
	71	17/10/1931	Twickenham	London	BL Osler	Won	30	3

SPRINGBOK RECORDS

OFFICIAL LIST OF ALL 767 TEST & TOUR MATCHES PLAYED BY SOUTH AFRICA 1891-2013

TEST NO.	TOUR MATCH	Date	Venue	Opponent	Captain	Result	Points For	Points against
	72	21/10/1931	Birmingham	Midland Counties	PJ Mostert	Won	13	3
	73	24/10/1931	Sunderland	Durham & Northumberland	JC van der Westhuizen	Won	41	0
	74	28/10/1931	Glasgow	Glasgow	JC van der Westhuizen	Won	21	13
	75	31/10/1931	Melrose	South of Scotland	MM Louw	Drew	0	0
	76	04/11/1931	Cambridge	Cambridge University	BL Osler	Won	21	9
	77	07/11/1931	Twickenham	Combined Services	BL Osler	Won	23	0
	78	12/11/1931	Oxford	Oxford University	BL Osler	Won	24	3
	79	14/11/1931	Leicester	Midland Counties	JC van der Westhuizen	Lost	21	30
	80	18/11/1931	Devonport	Devon & Cornwall	BL Osler	Drew	3	3
	81	21/11/1931	Cardiff	Cardiff	BL Osler	Won	13	5
	82	24/11/1931	Llanelli	Llanelli	MM Louw	Won	9	0
	83	28/11/1931	Neath	Neath & Aberavon	BL Osler	Won	8	3
34		05/12/1931	Swansea	WALES	BL Osler	Won	8	3
	84	09/12/1931	Liverpool	Lancashire & Cheshire	BL Osler	Won	20	9
	85	12/12/1931	Belfast	Ulster	MM Louw	Won	30	3
35		19/12/1931	Dublin	IRELAND	BL Osler	Won	8	3
	86	26/12/1931	Twickenham	London	BL Osler	Won	16	8
36		02/01/1932	Twickenham	ENGLAND	BL Osler	Won	7	0
	87	06/01/1932	Workington	Yorkshire & Cumberland	BL Osler	Won	27	5
	88	09/01/1932	Aberdeen	North of Scotland	JC van der Westhuizen	Won	9	0
37		16/01/1932	Edinburgh	SCOTLAND	BL Osler	Won	6	3
38		08/07/1933	Cape Town	AUSTRALIA	PJ Nel	Won	17	3
39		22/07/1933	Durban	AUSTRALIA	BL Osler	Lost	6	21
40		12/08/1933	Johannesburg	AUSTRALIA	PJ Nel	Won	12	3
41		26/08/1933	Port Elizabeth	AUSTRALIA	PJ Nel	Won	11	0
42		02/09/1933	Bloemfontein	AUSTRALIA	PJ Nel	Lost	4	15
	89	12/06/1937	Melbourne	Victoria	PJ Nel	Won	45	11
	90	16/06/1937	Orange	Combined Western Districts	GH Brand	Won	63	0
	91	19/06/1937	Sydney	New South Wales	PJ Nel	Lost	6	17
43		26/06/1937	Sydney	AUSTRALIA	PJ Nel	Won	9	5
	92	30/06/1937	Newcastle	Newcastle	PJ Nel	Won	58	8
	93	03/07/1937	Brisbane	Australian XV	PJ Nel	Won	36	3
	94	07/07/1937	Toowoomba	Toowoomba	PJ Nel	Won	60	0
	95	10/07/1937	Brisbane	Queensland	PJ Nel	Won	39	4
44		17/07/1937	Sydney	AUSTRALIA	PJ Nel	Won	26	17
	96	24/07/1937	Auckland	Auckland	PJ Nel	Won	19	5
	97	28/07/1937	Hamilton	Waikato-King Country-Thames Valley	PJ Nel	Won	6	3
	98	31/07/1937	New Plymouth	Taranaki	PJ Nel	Won	17	3
	99	04/08/1937	Palmerston N.	Manawatu	PJ Nel	Won	39	3
	100	07/08/1937	Wellington	Wellington	GH Brand	Won	29	0
45		14/08/1937	Wellington	NEW ZEALAND	DH Craven	Lost	7	13
	101	18/08/1937	Blenheim	Nelson-Golden Bay-Motueka-Marlborough	PJ Nel	Won	22	0
	102	21/08/1937	Christchurch	Canterbury	PJ Nel	Won	23	8
	103	25/08/1937	Greymouth	West Coast-Buller	PJ Nel	Won	31	6
	104	28/08/1937	Timaru	South Canterbury	PJ Nel	Won	43	6
46		04/09/1937	Christchurch	NEW ZEALAND	PJ Nel	Won	13	6
	105	08/09/1937	Invercargill	Southland	PJ Nel	Won	30	17
	106	11/09/1937	Dunedin	Otago	DH Craven	Won	47	7
	107	15/09/1937	Napier	Hawke's Bay	PJ Nel	Won	21	12

SPRINGBOK RECORDS

OFFICIAL LIST OF ALL 767 TEST & TOUR MATCHES PLAYED BY SOUTH AFRICA 1891-2013

TEST NO.	TOUR MATCH	Date	Venue	Opponent	Captain	Result	Points For	Points against
	108	18/09/1937	Gisborne	Poverty Bay-Bay of Plenty-East Coast	PJ Nel	Won	33	3
47		25/09/1937	Auckland	NEW ZEALAND	PJ Nel	Won	17	6
	109	29/09/1937	Whangarei	North Auckland	PJ Nel	Won	14	6
48		06/08/1938	Johannesburg	BRITISH ISLES	DH Craven	Won	26	12
49		03/09/1938	Port Elizabeth	BRITISH ISLES	DH Craven	Won	19	3
50		10/09/1938	Cape Town	BRITISH ISLES	DH Craven	Lost	16	21
51		16/07/1949	Cape Town	NEW ZEALAND	F du Plessis	Won	15	11
52		13/08/1949	Johannesburg	NEW ZEALAND	F du Plessis	Won	12	6
53		03/09/1949	Durban	NEW ZEALAND	F du Plessis	Won	9	3
54		17/09/1949	Port Elizabeth	NEW ZEALAND	BJ Kenyon	Won	11	8
	110	10/10/1951	Bournemouth	South Eastern Counties	BJ Kenyon	Won	31	6
	111	13/10/1951	Plymouth	South Western Counties	HSV Muller	Won	17	8
	112	18/10/1951	Pontypool	Pontypool & Newbridge	BJ Kenyon	Won	15	6
	113	20/10/1951	Cardiff	Cardiff	HSV Muller	Won	11	9
	114	23/10/1951	Llanelli	Llanelli	BJ Kenyon	Won	20	11
	115	27/10/1951	Liverpool	North Western Counties	BJ Kenyon	Won	16	9
	116	31/10/1951	Glasgow	Glasgow & Edinburgh	HSV Muller	Won	43	11
	117	03/11/1951	Newcastle	North Eastern Counties	BJ Kenyon	Won	19	8
	118	08/11/1951	Cambridge	Cambridge University	HSV Muller	Won	30	0
	119	10/11/1951	Twickenham	London Counties	HSV Muller	Lost	9	11
	120	15/11/1951	Oxford	Oxford University	HSV Muller	Won	24	3
	121	17/11/1951	Port Talbot	Neath & Aberavon	HSV Muller	Won	22	0
55		24/11/1951	Edinburgh	SCOTLAND	HSV Muller	Won	44	0
	122	28/11/1951	Aberdeen	North of Scotland	JA du Rand	Won	14	3
	123	01/12/1951	Belfast	Ulster	HSV Muller	Won	27	5
56		08/12/1951	Dublin	IRELAND	HSV Muller	Won	17	5
	124	11/12/1951	Limerick	Munster	PA du Toit	Won	11	6
	125	15/12/1951	Swansea	Swansea	HSV Muller	Won	11	3
57		22/12/1951	Cardiff	WALES	HSV Muller	Won	6	3
	126	26/12/1951	Twickenham	Combined Services	SP Fry	Won	24	8
	127	29/12/1951	Leicester	Midland Counties	B Myburgh	Won	3	0
58		05/01/1952	Twickenham	ENGLAND	HSV Muller	Won	8	3
	128	10/01/1952	Newport	Newport	HSV Muller	Won	12	6
	129	12/01/1952	Bristol	Western Counties	PA du Toit	Won	16	5
	130	16/01/1952	Coventry	Midland Counties	PA du Toit	Won	19	8
	131	19/01/1952	Hawick	South of Scotland	HSV Muller	Won	13	3
	132	26/01/1952	Cardiff	Barbarians	HSV Muller	Won	17	3
	133	02/02/1952	Lyon	South Eastern France	HSV Muller	Won	9	3
	134	07/02/1952	Bordeaux	South Western France	SP Fry	Won	20	12
	135	09/02/1952	Toulouse	France 'B'	HSV Muller	Won	9	6
59		16/02/1952	Paris	FRANCE	HSV Muller	Won	25	3
60		22/08/1953	Johannesburg	AUSTRALIA	HSV Muller	Won	25	3
61		05/09/1953	Cape Town	AUSTRALIA	HSV Muller	Lost	14	18
62		19/09/1953	Durban	AUSTRALIA	HSV Muller	Won	18	8
63		26/09/1953	Port Elizabeth	AUSTRALIA	HSV Muller	Won	22	9
64		06/08/1955	Johannesburg	BRITISH ISLES	SP Fry	Lost	22	23
65		20/08/1955	Cape Town	BRITISH ISLES	SP Fry	Won	25	9
66		03/09/1955	Pretoria	BRITISH ISLES	SP Fry	Lost	6	9
67		24/09/1955	Port Elizabeth	BRITISH ISLES	SP Fry	Won	22	8
	136	15/05/1956	Canberra	Australian Capital Territories	SS Vivier	Won	41	6
	137	19/05/1956	Sydney	New South Wales	SS Vivier	Won	29	9

SPRINGBOK RECORDS

OFFICIAL LIST OF ALL 767 TEST & TOUR MATCHES PLAYED BY SOUTH AFRICA 1891-2013

TEST NO.	TOUR MATCH	Date	Venue	Opponent	Captain	Result	Points For	Points against
	138	22/05/1956	Tamworth	New South Wales Country	JAJ Pickard	Won	15	8
68		26/05/1956	Sydney	AUSTRALIA	SS Vivier	Won	9	0
	139	29/05/1956	Brisbane	Queensland	SS Vivier	Won	47	3
69		02/06/1956	Brisbane	AUSTRALIA	SS Vivier	Won	9	0
	140	09/06/1956	Hamilton	Waikato	JAJ Pickard	Lost	10	14
	141	13/06/1956	Whangarei	North Auckland	SS Vivier	Won	3	0
	142	16/06/1956	Auckland	Auckland	SS Vivier	Won	6	3
	143	20/06/1956	Palmerston N.	Manawatu-Horowhenua	AC Koch	Won	14	3
	144	23/06/1956	Wellington	Wellington	JA du Rand	Won	8	6
	145	27/06/1956	Gisborne	Poverty Bay-East Coast	JA du Rand	Won	22	0
	146	30/06/1956	Napier	Hawke's Bay	JA du Rand	Won	20	8
	147	04/07/1956	Nelson	Nelson, Marlborough & Golden Bay - Motueka	JA du Rand	Won	41	3
	148	07/07/1956	Dunedin	Otago	JA du Rand	Won	14	9
70		14/07/1956	Dunedin	NEW ZEALAND	JA du Rand	Lost	6	10
	149	18/07/1956	Timaru	S Canterbury, Mid Canterbury & North Otago	JAJ Pickard	Won	20	8
	150	21/07/1956	Christchurch	Canterbury	JA du Rand	Lost	6	9
	151	25/07/1956	Westport	West Coast-Buller	SS Vivier	Won	27	6
	152	28/07/1956	Invercargill	Southland	JA du Rand	Won	23	12
	153	31/07/1956	Masterton	Wairarapa-Bush	SS Vivier	Won	19	8
71		04/08/1956	Wellington	NEW ZEALAND	SS Vivier	Won	8	3
	154	08/08/1956	Wanganui	Wanganui-King Country	SS Vivier	Won	36	16
	155	11/08/1956	New Plymouth	Taranaki	SS Vivier	Drew	3	3
72		18/08/1956	Christchurch	NEW ZEALAND	SS Vivier	Lost	10	17
	156	22/08/1956	Wellington	New Zealand Universities	SS Vivier	Lost	15	22
	157	25/08/1956	Auckland	New Zealand Maoris	SS Vivier	Won	37	0
	158	28/08/1956	Rotorua	Bay of Plenty-Thames Valley-Counties	SS Vivier	Won	17	6
73		01/09/1956	Auckland	NEW ZEALAND	SS Vivier	Lost	5	11
74		26/07/1958	Cape Town	FRANCE	JT Claasen	Drew	3	3
75		16/08/1958	Johannesburg	FRANCE	JT Claasen	Lost	5	9
76		30/04/1960	Port Elizabeth	SCOTLAND	DC van Jaarsveld	Won	18	10
77		25/06/1960	Johannesburg	NEW ZEALAND	RG Dryburgh	Won	13	0
78		23/07/1960	Cape Town	NEW ZEALAND	RG Dryburgh	Lost	3	11
79		13/08/1960	Bloemfontein	NEW ZEALAND	AS Malan	Drew	11	11
80		27/08/1960	Port Elizabeth	NEW ZEALAND	AS Malan	Won	8	3
	159	22/10/1960	Hove	Southern Counties	AS Malan	Won	29	9
	160	26/10/1960	Oxford	Oxford University	RJ Lockyear	Won	24	5
	161	29/10/1960	Cardiff	Cardiff	AS Malan	Won	13	0
	162	02/11/1960	Pontypool	Pontypool & Cross Keys	JT Claasen	Won	30	3
	163	05/11/1960	Leicester	Midland Counties	RJ Lockyear	Drew	3	3
	164	09/11/1960	Cambridge	Cambridge University	AS Malan	Won	12	0
	165	12/11/1960	Twickenham	London Counties	AS Malan	Won	20	3
	166	16/11/1960	Glasgow	Glasgow & Edinburgh	JT Claasen	Won	16	11
	167	19/11/1960	Hawick	South of Scotland	AS Malan	Won	19	3
	168	23/11/1960	Manchester	North Western Counties	JT Claasen	Won	11	0
	169	26/11/1960	Swansea	Swansea	RJ Lockyear	Won	19	3
	170	29/11/1960	Ebbw Vale	Ebbw Vale & Abertillery	AS Malan	Won	3	0
81		03/12/1960	Cardiff	WALES	AS Malan	Won	3	0
	171	07/12/1960	Camborne	South Western Counties	AS Malan	Won	21	9
	172	10/12/1960	Gloucester	Western Counties	AS Malan	Won	42	0

SPRINGBOK RECORDS

OFFICIAL LIST OF ALL 767 TEST & TOUR MATCHES PLAYED BY SOUTH AFRICA 1891-2013

TEST NO.	TOUR MATCH	Date	Venue	Opponent	Captain	Result	Points For	Points against
	173	13/12/1960	Llanelli	Llanelli	AS Malan	Won	21	0
82		17/12/1960	Dublin	IRELAND	AS Malan	Won	8	3
	174	21/12/1960	Cork	Munster	JT Claasen	Won	9	3
	175	26/12/1960	Twickenham	Combined Services	AS Malan	Won	14	5
	176	28/12/1960	Birmingham	Midland Couties	AS Malan	Won	16	5
	177	31/12/1960	Gosforth	North Eastern Counties	JT Claasen	Won	21	9
	178	03/01/1961	Bournemouth	South Eastern Counties	AS Malan	Won	24	0
83		07/01/1961	Twickenham	ENGLAND	AS Malan	Won	5	0
	179	11/01/1961	Newport	Newport	AS Malan	Won	3	0
	180	14/01/1961	Neath	Neath & Aberavon	AS Malan	Won	25	5
84		21/01/1961	Edinburgh	SCOTLAND	AS Malan	Won	12	5
	181	25/01/1961	Aberdeen	North of Scotland	AS Malan	Won	22	9
	182	28/01/1961	Belfast	Ulster	JT Claasen	Won	19	6
	183	01/02/1961	Dublin	Leinster	AS Malan	Won	12	5
	184	04/02/1961	Cardiff	Barbarians	AS Malan	Lost	0	6
	185	08/02/1961	Bordeaux	South Western France	RJ Lockyear	Won	29	3
	186	11/02/1961	Toulouse	France 'B'	RJ Lockyear	Won	26	10
	187	14/02/1961	Bayonne	Coast of Basque	AS Malan	Won	36	9
85		18/02/1961	Paris	FRANCE	AS Malan	Drew	0	0
86		13/05/1961	Cape Town	IRELAND	JT Claasen	Won	24	8
87		05/08/1961	Johannesburg	AUSTRALIA	JT Claasen	Won	28	3
88		12/08/1961	Port Elizabeth	AUSTRALIA	JT Claasen	Won	23	11
89		23/06/1962	Johannesburg	BRITISH ISLES	JT Claasen	Drew	3	3
90		21/07/1962	Durban	BRITISH ISLES	JT Claasen	Won	3	0
91		04/08/1962	Cape Town	BRITISH ISLES	JT Claasen	Won	8	3
92		25/08/1962	Bloemfontein	BRITISH ISLES	JT Claasen	Won	34	14
93		13/07/1963	Pretoria	AUSTRALIA	GF Malan	Won	14	3
94		10/08/1963	Cape Town	AUSTRALIA	GF Malan	Lost	5	9
95		24/08/1963	Johannesburg	AUSTRALIA	AS Malan	Lost	9	11
96		07/09/1963	Port Elizabeth	AUSTRALIA	GF Malan	Won	22	6
97		23/05/1964	Durban	WALES	GF Malan	Won	24	3
98		25/07/1964	Springs	FRANCE	CM Smith	Lost	6	8
	188	03/04/1965	Belfast	Combined Provinces (Ireland)	AS Malan	Drew	8	8
	189	06/04/1965	Limerick	Combined Universities, Past & Present	AS Malan	Lost	10	12
99		10/04/1965	Dublin	IRELAND	AS Malan	Lost	6	9
	190	13/04/1965	Hawick	Scottish Districts XV	DJ de Villiers	Lost	8	16
100		17/04/1965	Edinburgh	SCOTLAND	AS Malan	Lost	5	8
	191	10/06/1965	Perth	Western Australia	DJ de Villiers	Won	60	0
	192	12/06/1965	Melbourne	Victoria	CM Smith	Won	52	6
	193	14/06/1965	Sydney	New South Wales	DJ de Villiers	Lost	3	12
101		19/06/1965	Sydney	AUSTRALIA	CM Smith	Lost	11	18
	194	22/06/1965	Brisbane	Queensland	CM Smith	Won	50	5
102		26/06/1965	Brisbane	AUSTRALIA	CM Smith	Lost	8	12
	195	30/06/1965	Gisborne	Poverty Bay - East Coast	CM Smith	Won	32	3
	196	03/07/1965	Wellington	Wellington	CM Smith	Lost	6	23
	197	07/07/1965	Palmerston N.	Manawatu-Horowhenua	DJ de Villiers	Won	30	8
	198	10/07/1965	Dunedin	Otago	DJ de Villiers	Won	8	6
	199	14/07/1965	Christchurch	New Zealand Juniors	CM Smith	Won	23	3
	200	17/07/1965	New Plymouth	Taranaki	DJ de Villiers	Won	11	3
	201	21/07/1965	Invercargill	Southland	CM Smith	Won	19	6
	202	24/07/1965	Christchurch	Canterbury	DJ de Villiers	Won	6	5

SPRINGBOK RECORDS

OFFICIAL LIST OF ALL 767 TEST & TOUR MATCHES PLAYED BY SOUTH AFRICA 1891-2013

TEST NO.	TOUR MATCH	Date	Venue	Opponent	Captain	Result	Points For	Points against
	203	27/07/1965	Greymouth	West Coast-Buller	CM Smith	Won	11	0
103		31/07/1965	Wellington	NEW ZEALAND	DJ de Villiers	Lost	3	6
	204	04/08/1965	Wanganui	Wanganui-King Country	DJ de Villiers	Won	24	19
	205	07/08/1965	Hamilton	Waikato	CM Smith	Won	26	13
	206	11/08/1965	Whangarei	North Auckland	CM Smith	Won	14	11
	207	14/08/1965	Auckland	Auckland	DJ de Villiers	Lost	14	15
	208	17/08/1965	Blenheim	Marlborough, Nelson & Golden Bay- Motueka	CM Smith	Won	45	6
104		21/08/1965	Dunedin	NEW ZEALAND	CM Smith	Lost	0	13
	209	25/08/1965	Timaru	S Canterbury, Mid Canterbury & North Otago	DJ de Villiers	Won	28	13
	210	28/08/1965	Wellington	New Zealand Maoris	DJ de Villiers	Won	9	3
	211	31/08/1965	Masterton	Wairarapa-Bush	CM Smith	Won	36	0
105		04/09/1965	Christchurch	NEW ZEALAND	DJ de Villiers	Won	19	16
	212	08/09/1965	Auckland	New Zealand Universities	CM Smith	Won	55	11
	213	11/09/1965	Napier	Hawke's Bay	DJ de Villiers	Won	30	12
	214	14/09/1965	Rotorua	Bay of Plenty-Counties-Thames Valley	DJ de Villiers	Won	33	17
106		18/09/1965	Auckland	NEW ZEALAND	DJ de Villiers	Lost	3	20
107		15/07/1967	Durban	FRANCE	DJ de Villiers	Won	26	3
108		22/07/1967	Bloemfontein	FRANCE	DJ de Villiers	Won	16	3
109		29/07/1967	Johannesburg	FRANCE	DJ de Villiers	Lost	14	19
110		12/08/1967	Cape Town	FRANCE	DJ de Villiers	Drew	6	6
111		08/06/1968	Pretoria	BRITISH ISLES	DJ de Villiers	Won	25	20
112		22/06/1968	Port Elizabeth	BRITISH ISLES	DJ de Villiers	Drew	6	6
113		13/07/1968	Cape Town	BRITISH ISLES	DJ de Villiers	Won	11	6
114		27/07/1968	Johannesburg	BRITISH ISLES	DJ de Villiers	Won	19	6
	215	29/10/1968	Toulon	Littoral-Provence	DJ de Villiers	Won	24	3
	216	02/11/1968	Lyon	South Eastern France	TP Bedford	Won	3	0
	217	05/11/1968	Clermont-Ferrand	Auvergne-Limousin	DJ de Villiers	Won	26	9
115		09/11/1968	Bordeaux	FRANCE	DJ de Villiers	Won	12	9
	218	11/11/1968	Toulouse	South Western France	TP Bedford	Lost	3	11
116		16/11/1968	Paris	FRANCE	DJ de Villiers	Won	16	11
117		02/08/1969	Johannesburg	AUSTRALIA	DJ de Villiers	Won	30	11
118		16/08/1969	Durban	AUSTRALIA	TP Bedford	Won	16	9
119		06/09/1969	Cape Town	AUSTRALIA	TP Bedford	Won	11	3
120		20/09/1969	Bloemfontein	AUSTRALIA	DJ de Villiers	Won	19	8
	219	05/11/1969	Twickenham	Oxford University	DJ de Villiers	Lost	3	6
	220	08/11/1969	Leicester	Midland Counties (E)	TP Bedford	Won	11	9
	221	12/11/1969	Newport	Newport	DJ de Villiers	Lost	6	11
	222	15/11/1969	Swansea	Swansea	DJ de Villiers	Won	12	0
	223	19/11/1969	Ebbw Vale	Gwent	JFK Marais	Lost	8	14
	224	22/11/1969	Twickenham	London Counties	DJ de Villiers	Won	22	6
	225	26/11/1969	Manchester	North Western Counties	DJ de Villiers	Won	12	9
	226	02/12/1969	Aberdeen	North & Midlands of Scotland	DJ de Villiers	Won	37	3
121		06/12/1969	Edinburgh	SCOTLAND	TP Bedford	Lost	3	6
	227	10/12/1969	Aberavon	Aberavon & Neath	TP Bedford	Won	27	0
	228	13/12/1969	Cardiff	Cardiff	DJ de Villiers	Won	17	3
	229	16/12/1969	Aldershot	Combined Services	JFK Marais	Won	14	6
122		20/12/1969	Twickenham	ENGLAND	DJ de Villiers	Lost	8	11
	230	27/12/1969	Exeter	South Western Counties	DJ de Villiers	Won	9	6

SPRINGBOK RECORDS

OFFICIAL LIST OF ALL 767 TEST & TOUR MATCHES PLAYED BY SOUTH AFRICA 1891-2013

TEST NO.	TOUR MATCH	Date	Venue	Opponent	Captain	Result	Points For	Points against
	231	31/12/1969	Bristol	Western Counties	TP Bedford	Drew	3	3
	232	03/01/1970	Gosforth	North Eastern Counties	DJ de Villiers	Won	24	11
	233	06/01/1970	Coventry	Midland Counties (W)	TP Bedford	Won	21	6
123		10/01/1970	Dublin	IRELAND	DJ de Villiers	Drew	8	8
	234	14/01/1970	Limerick	Munster	DJ de Villiers	Won	25	9
	235	17/01/1970	Galashiels	South of Scotland	TP Bedford	Drew	3	3
	236	20/01/1970	Llanelli	Llanelli	DJ de Villiers	Won	10	9
124		24/01/1970	Cardiff	WALES	DJ de Villiers	Drew	6	6
	237	28/01/1970	Gloucester	Southern Counties	TP Bedford	Won	13	0
	238	31/01/1970	Twickenham	Barbarians	DJ de Villiers	Won	21	12
125		25/07/1970	Pretoria	NEW ZEALAND	DJ de Villiers	Won	17	6
126		08/08/1970	Cape Town	NEW ZEALAND	DJ de Villiers	Lost	8	9
127		29/08/1970	Port Elizabeth	NEW ZEALAND	DJ de Villiers	Won	14	3
128		12/09/1970	Johannesburg	NEW ZEALAND	DJ de Villiers	Won	20	17
129		12/06/1971	Bloemfontein	FRANCE	JFK Marais	Won	22	9
130		19/06/1971	Durban	FRANCE	JFK Marais	Drew	8	8
	239	26/06/1971	Perth	Western Australia	JFK Marais	Won	44	18
	240	30/06/1971	Adelaide	South Australia	TP Bedford	Won	43	0
	241	03/07/1971	Melbourne	Victoria	JFK Marais	Won	50	0
	242	06/07/1971	Sydney	Sydney	JFK Marais	Won	21	12
	243	10/07/1971	Sydney	New South Wales	JFK Marais	Won	25	3
	244	13/07/1971	Orange	New South Wales Country	PJF Greyling	Won	19	3
131		17/07/1971	Sydney	AUSTRALIA	JFK Marais	Won	19	11
	245	21/07/1971	Canberra	Australian Capital Territories	JFK Marais	Won	34	3
	246	24/07/1971	Brisbane	Queensland	JFK Marais	Won	33	14
	247	27/07/1971	Brisbane	Junior Wallabies	JFK Marais	Won	31	12
132		31/07/1971	Brisbane	AUSTRALIA	JFK Marais	Won	14	6
	248	03/08/1971	Toowoomba	Queensland Country	PJF Greyling	Won	45	14
133		07/08/1971	Sydney	AUSTRALIA	JFK Marais	Won	18	6
134		03/06/1972	Johannesburg	ENGLAND	PJF Greyling	Lost	9	18
135		08/06/1974	Cape Town	BRITISH ISLES	JFK Marais	Lost	3	12
136		22/06/1974	Pretoria	BRITISH ISLES	JFK Marais	Lost	9	28
137		13/07/1974	Port Elizabeth	BRITISH ISLES	JFK Marais	Lost	9	26
138		27/07/1974	Johannesburg	BRITISH ISLES	JFK Marais	Drew	13	13
	249	06/11/1974	Nice	South Eastern France	JFK Marais	Won	10	7
	250	09/11/1974	Lyon	North Eastern France	DSL Snyman	Won	25	12
	251	13/11/1974	Agen	South Western France	JFK Marais	Won	16	3
	252	16/11/1974	Tarbes	Second Division Clubs	JFK Marais	Won	36	4
	253	20/11/1974	Clermont-Ferrand	Central France	DSL Snyman	Won	29	10
139		23/11/1974	Toulouse	FRANCE	JFK Marais	Won	13	4
	254	27/11/1974	Angoulême	Western France	JCP Snyman	Lost	4	7
140		30/11/1974	Paris	FRANCE	JFK Marais	Won	10	8
	255	04/12/1974	Reims	Northern France	JFK Marais	Won	27	19
141		21/06/1975	Bloemfontein	FRANCE	M du Plessis	Won	38	25
142		28/06/1975	Pretoria	FRANCE	M du Plessis	Won	33	18
143		24/07/1976	Durban	NEW ZEALAND	M du Plessis	Won	16	7
144		14/08/1976	Bloemfontein	NEW ZEALAND	M du Plessis	Lost	9	15
145		04/09/1976	Cape Town	NEW ZEALAND	M du Plessis	Won	15	10
146		18/09/1976	Johannesburg	NEW ZEALAND	M du Plessis	Won	15	14
147		27/08/1977	Pretoria	WORLD TEAM	M du Plessis	Won	45	24
148		26/04/1980	Johannesburg	SOUTH AMERICA	M du Plessis	Won	24	9
149		03/05/1980	Durban	SOUTH AMERICA	M du Plessis	Won	18	9

SPRINGBOK RECORDS

OFFICIAL LIST OF ALL 767 TEST & TOUR MATCHES PLAYED BY SOUTH AFRICA 1891-2013

TEST NO.	TOUR MATCH	Date	Venue	Opponent	Captain	Result	Points For	Points against
150		31/05/1980	Cape Town	BRITISH ISLES	M du Plessis	Won	26	22
151		14/06/1980	Bloemfontein	BRITISH ISLES	M du Plessis	Won	26	19
152		28/06/1980	Port Elizabeth	BRITISH ISLES	M du Plessis	Won	12	10
153		12/07/1980	Pretoria	BRITISH ISLES	M du Plessis	Lost	13	17
	256	09/10/1980	Asunción	Paraguay Invitation XV	RB Prentiss	Won	84	6
	257	11/10/1980	Asunción	South America Invitation XV	MTS Stofberg	Won	79	18
	258	14/10/1980	Montevideo	British Schools Old Boys	MTS Stofberg	Won	83	13
154		18/10/1980	Montevideo	SOUTH AMERICA	MTS Stofberg	Won	22	13
	259	21/10/1980	Santiago	Chile Invitation XV	M du Plessis	Won	78	12
155		25/10/1980	Santiago	SOUTH AMERICA	M du Plessis	Won	30	16
156		08/11/1980	Pretoria	FRANCE	M du Plessis	Won	37	15
157		30/05/1981	Cape Town	IRELAND	W Claasen	Won	23	15
158		06/06/1981	Durban	IRELAND	W Claasen	Won	12	10
	260	22/07/1981	Gisborne	Poverty Bay	E Jansen	Won	24	6
	261	29/07/1981	New Plymouth	Taranaki	W Claasen	Won	34	9
	262	01/08/1981	Palmerston N.	Manawatu	MTS Stofberg	Won	31	19
	263	05/08/1981	Wanganui	Wanganui	W Claasen	Won	45	9
	264	08/08/1981	Invercargill	Southland	MTS Stofberg	Won	22	6
	265	11/08/1981	Dunedin	Otago	W Claasen	Won	17	13
159		15/08/1981	Christchurch	NEW ZEALAND	MTS Stofberg	Lost	9	14
	266	22/08/1981	Nelson	Nelson Bays	W Claasen	Won	83	0
	267	25/08/1981	Napier	New Zealand Maoris	DJ Serfontein	Drew	12	12
160		29/08/1981	Wellington	NEW ZEALAND	W Claasen	Won	24	12
	268	02/09/1981	Rotorua	Bay of Plenty	MTS Stofberg	Won	29	24
	269	05/09/1981	Auckland	Auckland	W Claasen	Won	39	12
	270	08/09/1981	Whangarei	North Auckland	E Jansen	Won	19	10
161		12/09/1981	Auckland	NEW ZEALAND	W Claasen	Lost	22	25
	271	19/09/1981	Wisconsin	Midwest	MTS Stofberg	Won	46	12
	272	22/09/1981	New York	Eastern	W Claasen	Won	41	0
162		25/09/1981	New York	USA	W Claasen	Won	38	7
163		27/03/1982	Pretoria	SOUTH AMERICA	W Claasen	Won	50	18
164		03/04/1982	Bloemfontein	SOUTH AMERICA	W Claasen	Lost	12	21
165		02/06/1984	Port Elizabeth	ENGLAND	MTS Stofberg	Won	33	15
166		09/06/1984	Johannesburg	ENGLAND	MTS Stofberg	Won	35	9
167		20/10/1984	Pretoria	S AMERICA & SPAIN	DJ Serfontein	Won	32	15
168		27/10/1984	Cape Town	S AMERICA & SPAIN	DJ Serfontein	Won	22	13
169		10/05/1986	Cape Town	NZ CAVALIERS	HE Botha	Won	21	15
170		17/05/1986	Durban	NZ CAVALIERS	HE Botha	Lost	18	19
171		24/05/1986	Pretoria	NZ CAVALIERS	HE Botha	Won	33	18
172		31/05/1986	Johannesburg	NZ CAVALIERS	HE Botha	Won	24	10
173		26/08/1989	Cape Town	WORLD TEAM	JC Breedt	Won	20	19
174		02/09/1989	Johannesburg	WORLD TEAM	JC Breedt	Won	22	16
175		15/08/1992	Johannesburg	NEW ZEALAND	HE Botha	Lost	24	27
176		22/08/1992	Cape Town	AUSTRALIA	HE Botha	Lost	3	26
	273	03/10/1992	Bordeaux	French Selection	HE Botha	Lost	17	24
	274	07/10/1992	Pau	Aquitaine XV	WJ Bartmann	Won	29	22
	275	10/10/1992	Toulouse	Midi-Pyrenées XV	HE Botha	Won	18	15
	276	13/10/1992	Marseilles	Provence-Côte D'Azur XV	RJ du Preez	Won	41	12
177		17/10/1992	Lyon	FRANCE	HE Botha	Won	20	15
	277	20/10/1992	Béziers	Languedoc XV	RJ du Preez	Won	36	15
178		24/10/1992	Paris	FRANCE	HE Botha	Lost	16	29
	278	28/10/1992	Tours	French Universities	RJ du Preez	Lost	13	18
	279	31/10/1992	Lille	French Barbarians	HE Botha	Lost	20	25

SPRINGBOK RECORDS

OFFICIAL LIST OF ALL 767 TEST & TOUR MATCHES PLAYED BY SOUTH AFRICA 1891-2013

TEST NO.	TOUR MATCH	Date	Venue	Opponent	Captain	Result	Points For	Points against
	280	04/11/1992	Leicester	Midland Division	HE Botha	Won	32	9
	281	07/11/1992	Bristol	England 'B'	HE Botha	Won	20	16
	282	10/11/1992	Leeds	Northern Division	RJ du Preez	Won	19	3
179		14/11/1992	**Twickenham**	**ENGLAND**	**HE Botha**	**Lost**	**16**	**33**
180		26/06/1993	**Durban**	**FRANCE**	**JF Pienaar**	**Drew**	**20**	**20**
181		03/07/1993	**Johannesburg**	**FRANCE**	**JF Pienaar**	**Lost**	**17**	**18**
	283	14/07/1993	Perth	Western Australia	JF Pienaar	Won	71	8
	284	17/07/1993	Adelaide	South Australian Invitation XV	CP Strauss	Won	90	3
	285	21/07/1993	Melbourne	Victoria	AH Richter	Won	78	3
	286	24/07/1993	Sydney	New South Wales	JF Pienaar	Lost	28	29
	287	27/07/1993	Orange	New South Wales Country	AH Richter	Won	41	7
182		31/07/1993	**Sydney**	**AUSTRALIA**	**JF Pienaar**	**Won**	**19**	**12**
	288	04/08/1993	Canberra	Australian Capital Territories	AH Richter	Won	57	10
	289	08/08/1993	Brisbane	Queensland	JF Pienaar	Won	17	3
	290	11/08/1993	Mackay	Queensland Country	AH Richter	Won	63	5
183		14/08/1993	**Brisbane**	**AUSTRALIA**	**JF Pienaar**	**Lost**	**20**	**28**
	291	18/08/1993	Sydney	Sydney	AH Richter	Won	31	20
184		21/08/1993	**Sydney**	**AUSTRALIA**	**JF Pienaar**	**Lost**	**12**	**19**
	292	27/10/1993	Cordoba	Provincial XV	CP Strauss	Won	55	37
	293	30/10/1993	Buenos Aires	Buenos Aires XV	WJ Bartmann	Lost	27	28
	294	03/11/1993	Tucumán	Tucumán	CP Strauss	Won	40	12
185		06/11/1993	**Buenos Aires**	**ARGENTINA**	**JF Pienaar**	**Won**	**29**	**26**
	295	09/11/1993	Rosario	Provincial XV	WJ Bartmann	Won	40	26
186		13/11/1993	**Buenos Aires**	**ARGENTINA**	**JF Pienaar**	**Won**	**52**	**23**
187		04/06/1994	**Pretoria**	**ENGLAND**	**JF Pienaar**	**Lost**	**15**	**32**
188		11/06/1994	**Cape Town**	**ENGLAND**	**JF Pienaar**	**Won**	**27**	**9**
	296	23/06/1994	Taupo	King Country	JF Pienaar	Won	46	10
	297	25/06/1994	Pukekohe	Counties	WJ Bartmann	Won	37	26
	298	28/06/1994	Wellington	Wellington	JF Pienaar	Won	36	26
	299	02/07/1994	Invercargill	Southland	AH Richter	Won	51	15
	300	05/07/1994	Timaru	Hanan Shield Districts	CP Strauss	Won	67	19
189		09/07/1994	**Dunedin**	**NEW ZEALAND**	**CP Strauss**	**Lost**	**14**	**22**
	301	13/07/1994	New Plymouth	Taranaki	RAW Straeuli	Won	16	12
	302	16/07/1994	Hamilton	Waikato	CP Strauss	Won	38	17
	303	19/07/1994	Palmerston N.	Manawatu	JF Pienaar	Won	47	21
190		23/07/1994	**Wellington**	**NEW ZEALAND**	**JF Pienaar**	**Lost**	**9**	**13**
	304	27/07/1994	Dunedin	Otago	CP Strauss	Lost	12	19
	305	30/07/1994	Christchurch	Canterbury	JF Pienaar	Won	21	11
	306	02/08/1994	Rotorua	Bay of Plenty	CP Strauss	Won	33	12
191		06/08/1994	**Auckland**	**NEW ZEALAND**	**JF Pienaar**	**Drew**	**18**	**18**
192		08/10/1994	**Port Elizabeth**	**ARGENTINA**	**JF Pienaar**	**Won**	**42**	**22**
193		15/10/1994	**Johannesburg**	**ARGENTINA**	**JF Pienaar**	**Won**	**46**	**26**
	307	22/10/1994	Cardiff	Cardiff	RAW Straeuli	Won	11	6
	308	26/10/1994	Newport	Wales 'A'	RAW Straeuli	Won	25	13
	309	29/10/1994	Llanelli	Llanelli	JF Pienaar	Won	30	12
	310	02/11/1994	Neath	Neath	CP Strauss	Won	16	13
	311	05/11/1994	Swansea	Swansea	JF Pienaar	Won	78	7
	312	09/11/1994	Melrose	Scotland 'A'	CP Strauss	Lost	15	17
	313	12/11/1994	Glasgow	Scottish Combined Districts	JF Pienaar	Won	33	6
	314	15/11/1994	Aberdeen	Scottish Select	CP Strauss	Won	35	10
194		19/11/1994	**Edinburgh**	**SCOTLAND**	**JF Pienaar**	**Won**	**34**	**10**
	315	22/11/1994	Pontypridd	Pontypridd	CP Strauss	Won	9	3

SPRINGBOK RECORDS

OFFICIAL LIST OF ALL 767 TEST & TOUR MATCHES PLAYED BY SOUTH AFRICA 1891-2013

TEST NO.	TOUR MATCH	Date	Venue	Opponent	Captain	Result	Points For	Points against
195		26/11/1994	Cardiff	WALES	JF Pienaar	Won	20	12
	316	29/11/1994	Belfast	Combined Provinces	RAW Straeuli	Won	54	19
	317	03/12/1994	Dublin	Barbarians	JF Pienaar	Lost	15	23
196		13/04/1995	Johannesburg	WESTERN SAMOA	JF Pienaar	Won	60	8
197		25/05/1995	Cape Town	AUSTRALIA	JF Pienaar	Won	27	18
198		30/05/1995	Cape Town	ROMANIA	AJ Richter	Won	21	8
199		03/06/1995	Port Elizabeth	CANADA	JF Pienaar	Won	20	0
200		10/06/1995	Johannesburg	WESTERN SAMOA	JF Pienaar	Won	42	14
201		17/06/1995	Durban	FRANCE	JF Pienaar	Won	19	15
202		24/06/1995	Johannesburg	NEW ZEALAND	JF Pienaar	Won	15	12
203		02/09/1995	Johannesburg	WALES	JF Pienaar	Won	40	11
204		12/11/1995	Rome	ITALY	JF Pienaar	Won	40	21
205		18/11/1995	Twickenham	ENGLAND	JF Pienaar	Won	24	14
206		02/07/1996	Pretoria	FIJI	JF Pienaar	Won	43	18
207		13/07/1996	Sydney	AUSTRALIA	JF Pienaar	Lost	16	21
208		20/07/1996	Christchurch	NEW ZEALAND	JF Pienaar	Lost	11	15
209		03/08/1996	Bloemfontein	AUSTRALIA	JF Pienaar	Won	25	19
210		10/08/1996	Cape Town	NEW ZEALAND	JF Pienaar	Lost	18	29
211		17/08/1996	Durban	NEW ZEALAND	GH Teichmann	Lost	19	23
212		24/08/1996	Pretoria	NEW ZEALAND	GH Teichmann	Lost	26	33
213		31/08/1996	Johannesburg	NEW ZEALAND	GH Teichmann	Won	32	22
	318	05/11/1996	Rosario	Rosario	WS Fyvie	Won	45	36
214		09/11/1996	Buenos Aires	ARGENTINA	GH Teichmann	Won	46	15
	319	12/11/1996	Mendoza	Mendoza	WS Fyvie	Won	89	19
215		16/11/1996	Buenos Aires	ARGENTINA	GH Teichmann	Won	44	21
	320	23/11/1996	Brive	French Barbarians	WS Fyvie	Lost	22	30
	321	26/11/1996	Lyon	South East Selection	WS Fyvie	Won	36	20
216		30/11/1996	Bordeaux	FRANCE	GH Teichmann	Won	22	12
	322	03/12/1996	Lille	French Universities	WS Fyvie	Lost	13	20
217		07/12/1996	Paris	FRANCE	GH Teichmann	Won	13	12
218		15/12/1996	Cardiff	WALES	GH Teichmann	Won	37	20
219		10/06/1997	Cape Town	TONGA	GH Teichmann	Won	74	10
220		21/06/1997	Cape Town	BRITISH ISLES	GH Teichmann	Lost	16	25
221		28/06/1997	Durban	BRITISH ISLES	GH Teichmann	Lost	15	18
222		05/07/1997	Johannesburg	BRITISH ISLES	GH Teichmann	Won	35	16
223		19/07/1997	Johannesburg	NEW ZEALAND	GH Teichmann	Lost	32	35
224		02/08/1997	Brisbane	AUSTRALIA	GH Teichmann	Lost	20	32
225		09/08/1997	Auckland	NEW ZEALAND	GH Teichmann	Lost	35	55
226		23/08/1997	Pretoria	AUSTRALIA	GH Teichmann	Won	61	22
227		08/11/1997	Bologna	ITALY	GH Teichmann	Won	62	31
	323	11/11/1997	Biarritz	French Barbarians	AD Aitken	Lost	22	40
228		15/11/1997	Lyon	FRANCE	GH Teichmann	Won	36	32
	324	18/11/1997	Toulon	France 'A'	AD Aitken	Lost	7	21
229		22/11/1997	Paris	FRANCE	GH Teichmann	Won	52	10
230		29/11/1997	Twickenham	ENGLAND	GH Teichmann	Won	29	11
231		06/12/1997	Edinburgh	SCOTLAND	GH Teichmann	Won	68	10
232		13/06/1998	Bloemfontein	IRELAND	GH Teichmann	Won	37	13
233		20/06/1998	Pretoria	IRELAND	GH Teichmann	Won	33	0
234		27/06/1998	Pretoria	WALES	GH Teichmann	Won	96	13
235		04/07/1998	Cape Town	ENGLAND	GH Teichmann	Won	18	0
236		18/07/1998	Perth	AUSTRALIA	GH Teichmann	Won	14	13
237		25/07/1998	Wellington	NEW ZEALAND	GH Teichmann	Won	13	3
238		15/08/1998	Durban	NEW ZEALAND	GH Teichmann	Won	24	23

SPRINGBOK RECORDS

OFFICIAL LIST OF ALL 767 TEST & TOUR MATCHES PLAYED BY SOUTH AFRICA 1891-2013

TEST NO.	TOUR MATCH	Date	Venue	Opponent	Captain	Result	Points For	Points against
239		22/08/1998	Johannesburg	AUSTRALIA	GH Teichmann	Won	29	15
	325	10/11/1998	Firhill	Glasgow Caledonians	RB Skinstad	Won	62	9
240		14/11/1998	London	WALES	GH Teichmann	Won	28	20
	326	17/11/1998	Edinburgh	Edinburgh Reivers	RB Skinstad	Won	49	3
241		21/11/1998	Edinburgh	SCOTLAND	GH Teichmann	Won	35	10
	327	24/11/1998	Cork	Combined Provinces	AN Vos	Won	32	5
242		28/11/1998	Dublin	IRELAND	GH Teichmann	Won	27	13
	328	01/12/1998	Belfast	Ireland 'A'	AN Vos	Won	50	19
243		05/12/1998	Twickenham	ENGLAND	GH Teichmann	Lost	7	13
244		12/06/1999	Port Elizabeth	ITALY	GH Teichmann	Won	74	3
245		19/06/1999	Durban	ITALY	CPJ Krige	Won	101	0
246		26/06/1999	Cardiff	WALES	GH Teichmann	Lost	19	29
247		10/07/1999	Dunedin	NEW ZEALAND	GH Teichmann	Lost	0	28
248		17/07/1999	Brisbane	AUSTRALIA	J Erasmus	Lost	6	32
249		07/08/1999	Pretoria	NEW ZEALAND	JH van der Westhuizen	Lost	18	34
250		14/08/1999	Cape Town	AUSTRALIA	JH van der Westhuizen	Won	10	9
251		03/10/1999	Edinburgh	SCOTLAND	JH van der Westhuizen	Won	46	29
252		10/10/1999	Edinburgh	SPAIN	AN Vos	Won	47	3
253		15/10/1999	Glasgow	URUGUAY	JH van der Westhuizen	Won	39	3
254		24/10/1999	Paris	ENGLAND	JH van der Westhuizen	Won	44	21
255		30/10/1999	London	AUSTRALIA	JH van der Westhuizen	Lost	21	27
256		04/11/1999	Cardiff	NEW ZEALAND	JH van der Westhuizen	Won	22	18
257		10/06/2000	East London	CANADA	AN Vos	Won	51	18
258		17/06/2000	Pretoria	ENGLAND	AN Vos	Won	18	13
259		24/06/2000	Bloemfontein	ENGLAND	AN Vos	Lost	22	27
260		08/07/2000	Melbourne	AUSTRALIA	AN Vos	Lost	23	44
261		22/07/2000	Christchurch	NEW ZEALAND	AN Vos	Lost	12	25
262		29/07/2000	Sydney	AUSTRALIA	AN Vos	Lost	6	26
263		19/08/2000	Johannesburg	NEW ZEALAND	AN Vos	Won	46	40
264		26/08/2000	Durban	AUSTRALIA	AN Vos	Lost	18	19
	329	08/11/2000	Tucuman	Argentina 'A'	DJ van Zyl	Won	32	21
265		12/11/2000	Buenos Aires	ARGENTINA	AN Vos	Won	37	33
	330	15/11/2000	Limerick	Ireland 'A'	A-H le Roux	Lost	11	28
266		19/11/2000	Dublin	IRELAND	AN Vos	Won	28	18
	331	22/11/2000	Cardiff	Wales 'A'	DJ van Zyl	Won	34	15
267		26/11/2000	Cardiff	WALES	AN Vos	Won	23	13
	332	28/11/2000	Worcester	England National Divisions XV	V Matfield	Lost	30	35
268		02/12/2000	Twickenham	ENGLAND	AN Vos	Lost	17	25
	333	09/12/2000	Cardiff	Barbarians	AN Vos	Won	41	31
269		16/06/2001	Johannesburg	FRANCE	AN Vos	Lost	23	32
270		23/06/2001	Durban	FRANCE	AN Vos	Won	20	15
271		30/06/2001	Port Elizabeth	ITALY	RB Skinstad	Won	60	14
272		21/07/2001	Cape Town	NEW ZEALAND	RB Skinstad	Lost	3	12
273		28/07/2001	Pretoria	AUSTRALIA	RB Skinstad	Won	20	15
274		18/08/2001	Perth	AUSTRALIA	RB Skinstad	Drew	14	14
275		25/08/2001	Auckland	NEW ZEALAND	RB Skinstad	Lost	15	26
276		10/11/2001	Paris	FRANCE	RB Skinstad	Lost	10	20
277		17/11/2001	Genoa	ITALY	RB Skinstad	Won	54	26
278		24/11/2001	London	ENGLAND	RB Skinstad	Lost	9	29
279		01/12/2001	Houston	USA	AN Vos	Won	43	20
280		08/06/2002	Bloemfontein	WALES	RB Skinstad	Won	34	19
281		15/06/2002	Cape Town	WALES	RB Skinstad	Won	19	8
282		29/06/2002	Springs	ARGENTINA	CPJ Krige	Won	49	29

SPRINGBOK RECORDS

OFFICIAL LIST OF ALL 767 TEST & TOUR MATCHES PLAYED BY SOUTH AFRICA 1891-2013

TEST NO.	TOUR MATCH	Date	Venue	Opponent	Captain	Result	Points For	Points against
283		06/07/2002	Pretoria	SAMOA	CPJ Krige	Won	60	18
284		20/07/2002	Wellington	NEW ZEALAND	CPJ Krige	Lost	20	41
285		27/07/2002	Brisbane	AUSTRALIA	CPJ Krige	Lost	27	38
286		10/08/2002	Durban	NEW ZEALAND	CPJ Krige	Lost	23	30
287		17/08/2002	Johannesburg	AUSTRALIA	CPJ Krige	Won	33	31
288		09/11/2002	Marseilles	FRANCE	CPJ Krige	Lost	10	30
289		16/11/2002	Edinburgh	SCOTLAND	CPJ Krige	Lost	6	21
290		23/11/2002	London	ENGLAND	CPJ Krige	Lost	3	53
291		07/06/2003	Durban	SCOTLAND	JH van der Westhuizen	Won	29	25
292		14/06/2003	Johannesburg	SCOTLAND	JH van der Westhuizen	Won	28	19
293		28/06/2003	Port Elizabeth	ARGENTINA	CPJ Krige	Won	26	25
294		12/07/2003	Cape Town	AUSTRALIA	CPJ Krige	Won	26	22
295		19/07/2003	Pretoria	NEW ZEALAND	CPJ Krige	Lost	16	52
296		02/08/2003	Brisbane	AUSTRALIA	CPJ Krige	Lost	9	29
297		09/08/2003	Dunedin	NEW ZEALAND	CPJ Krige	Lost	11	19
298		11/10/2003	Perth	URUGUAY	JH van der Westhuizen	Won	72	6
299		18/10/2003	Perth	ENGLAND	CPJ Krige	Lost	6	25
300		24/10/2003	Sydney	GEORGIA	JW Smit	Won	46	19
301		01/11/2003	Brisbane	SAMOA	CPJ Krige	Won	60	10
302		08/11/2003	Melbourne	NEW ZEALAND	CPJ Krige	Lost	9	29
303		12/06/2004	Bloemfontein	IRELAND	JW Smit	Won	31	17
304		19/06/2004	Cape Town	IRELAND	JW Smit	Won	26	17
305		26/06/2004	Pretoria	WALES	JW Smit	Won	53	18
306		17/07/2004	Gosford	PACIFIC ISLANDS	JW Smit	Won	38	24
307		24/07/2004	Christchurch	NEW ZEALAND	JW Smit	Lost	21	23
308		31/07/2004	Perth	AUSTRALIA	JW Smit	Lost	26	30
309		14/08/2004	Johannesburg	NEW ZEALAND	JW Smit	Won	40	26
310		21/08/2004	Durban	AUSTRALIA	JW Smit	Won	23	19
311		06/11/2004	Cardiff	WALES	JW Smit	Won	38	36
312		13/11/2004	Dublin	IRELAND	JW Smit	Lost	12	17
313		20/11/2004	London	ENGLAND	JW Smit	Lost	16	32
314		27/11/2004	Edinburgh	SCOTLAND	JW Smit	Won	45	10
315		04/12/2004	Buenos Aires	ARGENTINA	JW Smit	Won	39	7
316		11/06/2005	East London	URUGUAY	JW Smit	Won	134	3
317		18/06/2005	Durban	FRANCE	JW Smit	Drew	30	30
318		25/06/2005	Port Elizabeth	FRANCE	JW Smit	Won	27	13
319		09/07/2005	Sydney	AUSTRALIA	JW Smit	Lost	12	30
320		23/07/2005	Johannesburg	AUSTRALIA	JW Smit	Won	33	20
321		30/07/2005	Pretoria	AUSTRALIA	JW Smit	Won	22	16
322		06/08/2005	Cape Town	NEW ZEALAND	JW Smit	Won	22	16
323		20/08/2005	Perth	AUSTRALIA	JW Smit	Won	22	19
324		27/08/2005	Dunedin	NEW ZEALAND	JW Smit	Lost	27	31
325		05/11/2005	Buenos Aires	ARGENTINA	JW Smit	Won	34	23
326		19/11/2005	Cardiff	WALES	JW Smit	Won	33	16
327		26/11/2005	Paris	FRANCE	JW Smit	Lost	20	26
328		10/06/2006	Durban	SCOTLAND	JW Smit	Won	36	16
329		17/06/2006	Port Elizabeth	SCOTLAND	JW Smit	Won	29	15
330		24/06/2006	Cape Town	FRANCE	JW Smit	Lost	26	36
331		15/07/2006	Brisbane	AUSTRALIA	JW Smit	Lost	0	49
332		22/07/2006	Wellington	NEW ZEALAND	JW Smit	Lost	17	35
333		05/08/2006	Sydney	AUSTRALIA	JW Smit	Lost	18	20
334		26/08/2006	Pretoria	NEW ZEALAND	JW Smit	Lost	26	45
335		02/09/2006	Rustenburg	NEW ZEALAND	JW Smit	Won	21	20

SPRINGBOK RECORDS

OFFICIAL LIST OF ALL 767 TEST & TOUR MATCHES PLAYED BY SOUTH AFRICA 1891-2013

TEST NO.	TOUR MATCH	Date	Venue	Opponent	Captain	Result	Points For	Points against
336		09/09/2006	Johannesburg	AUSTRALIA	JW Smit	Won	24	16
337		11/11/2006	Dublin	IRELAND	JW Smit	Lost	15	32
338		18/11/2006	London	ENGLAND	JW Smit	Lost	21	23
339		25/11/2006	London	ENGLAND	JW Smit	Won	25	14
	334	03/12/2006	Leicester	World XV	GvG Botha	Won	32	7
340		26/05/2007	Bloemfontein	ENGLAND	JW Smit	Won	58	10
341		02/06/2007	Pretoria	ENGLAND	JW Smit	Won	55	22
342		09/06/2007	Johannesburg	SAMOA	JW Smit	Won	35	8
343		16/06/2007	Cape Town	AUSTRALIA	JW Smit	Won	22	19
344		23/06/2007	Durban	NEW ZEALAND	V Matfield	Lost	21	26
345		07/07/2007	Sydney	AUSTRALIA	RB Skinstad	Lost	17	25
346		14/07/2007	Christchurch	NEW ZEALAND	GJ Muller	Lost	6	33
347		15/08/2007	Cape Town	NAMIBIA	V Matfield	Won	105	13
	335	21/08/2007	Galway	Connacht	RB Skinstad	Won	18	3
348		25/08/2007	Edinburgh	SCOTLAND	V Matfield	Won	27	3
349		09/09/2007	Paris	SAMOA	JW Smit	Won	59	7
350		14/09/2007	St Denis	ENGLAND	JW Smit	Won	36	0
351		22/09/2007	Lens	TONGA	RB Skinstad	Won	30	25
352		30/09/2007	Montpellier	USA	JW Smit	Won	64	15
353		07/10/2007	Marseilles	FIJI	JW Smit	Won	37	20
354		14/10/2007	St Denis	ARGENTINA	JW Smit	Won	37	13
355		20/10/2007	St Denis	ENGLAND	JW Smit	Won	15	6
356		24/11/2007	Cardiff	WALES	JW Smit	Won	34	12
	336	01/12/2007	London	Barbarians	GJ Muller	Lost	5	22
357		07/06/2008	Bloemfontein	WALES	JW Smit	Won	43	17
358		14/06/2008	Pretoria	WALES	JW Smit	Won	37	21
359		21/06/2008	Cape Town	ITALY	V Matfield	Won	26	0
360		05/07/2008	Wellington	NEW ZEALAND	JW Smit	Lost	8	19
361		12/07/2008	Dunedin	NEW ZEALAND	V Matfield	Won	30	28
362		19/07/2008	Perth	AUSTRALIA	V Matfield	Lost	9	16
363		09/08/2008	Johannesburg	ARGENTINA	V Matfield	Won	63	9
364		16/08/2008	Cape Town	NEW ZEALAND	V Matfield	Lost	0	19
365		23/08/2008	Durban	AUSTRALIA	V Matfield	Lost	15	27
366		30/08/2008	Johannesburg	AUSTRALIA	V Matfield	Won	53	8
367		08/11/2008	Cardiff	WALES	JW Smit	Won	20	15
368		15/11/2008	Edinburgh	SCOTLAND	JW Smit	Won	14	10
369		22/11/2008	London	ENGLAND	JW Smit	Won	42	6
370		20/06/2009	Durban	BRITISH ISLES	JW Smit	Won	26	21
371		27/06/2009	Pretoria	BRITISH ISLES	JW Smit	Won	28	25
372		04/07/2009	Johannesburg	BRITISH ISLES	JW Smit	Lost	9	28
373		25/07/2009	Bloemfontein	NEW ZEALAND	JW Smit	Won	28	19
374		01/08/2009	Durban	NEW ZEALAND	JW Smit	Won	31	19
375		08/08/2009	Cape Town	AUSTRALIA	JW Smit	Won	29	17
376		29/08/2009	Perth	AUSTRALIA	JW Smit	Won	32	25
377		05/09/2009	Brisbane	AUSTRALIA	JW Smit	Lost	6	21
378		12/09/2009	Hamilton	NEW ZEALAND	JW Smit	Won	32	29
	337	06/11/2009	Leicester	Leicester Tigers	MC Ralepelle	Lost	17	22
379		13/11/2009	Toulouse	FRANCE	JW Smit	Lost	13	20
	338	17/11/2009	London	Saracens	DJ Potgieter	Lost	23	24
380		21/11/2009	Florence	ITALY	JW Smit	Won	32	10
381		28/11/2009	Dublin	IRELAND	JW Smit	Lost	10	15
382		05/06/2010	Cardiff	WALES	JW Smit	Won	34	31
383		12/06/2010	Cape Town	FRANCE	JW Smit	Won	42	17

SPRINGBOK RECORDS

OFFICIAL LIST OF ALL 767 TEST & TOUR MATCHES PLAYED BY SOUTH AFRICA 1891-2013

TEST NO.	TOUR MATCH	Date	Venue	Opponent	Captain	Result	Points For	Points against
384		19/06/2010	Witbank	ITALY	V Matfield	Won	29	13
385		26/06/2010	East London	ITALY	JW Smit	Won	55	11
386		10/07/2010	Auckland	NEW ZEALAND	JW Smit	Lost	12	32
387		17/07/2010	Wellington	NEW ZEALAND	JW Smit	Lost	17	31
388		24/07/2010	Brisbane	AUSTRALIA	JW Smit	Lost	13	30
389		21/08/2010	Soweto	NEW ZEALAND	JW Smit	Lost	22	29
390		28/08/2010	Pretoria	AUSTRALIA	JW Smit	Won	44	31
391		04/09/2010	Bloemfontein	AUSTRALIA	JW Smit	Lost	39	41
392		06/11/2010	Dublin	IRELAND	V Matfield	Won	23	21
393		13/11/2010	Cardiff	WALES	V Matfield	Won	29	25
394		20/11/2010	Edinburgh	SCOTLAND	V Matfield	Lost	17	21
395		27/11/2010	London	ENGLAND	V Matfield	Won	21	11
	339	04/12/2010	London	Barbarians	JH Smith	Lost	20	26
396		23/07/2011	Sydney	AUSTRALIA	JW Smit	Lost	20	39
397		30/07/2011	Wellington	NEW ZEALAND	JW Smit	Lost	7	40
398		13/08/2011	Durban	AUSTRALIA	JW Smit	Lost	9	14
399		20/08/2011	Port Elizabeth	NEW ZEALAND	V Matfield	Won	18	5
400		11/09/2011	Wellington	WALES	JW Smit	Won	17	16
401		17/09/2011	Wellington	FIJI	JW Smit	Won	49	3
402		22/09/2011	Albany	NAMIBIA	JW Smit	Won	87	0
403		30/09/2011	Albany	SAMOA	V Matfield	Won	13	5
404		09/10/2011	Wellington	AUSTRALIA	JW Smit	Lost	9	11
405		09/06/2012	Durban	ENGLAND	J de Villiers	Won	22	17
406		16/06/2012	Johannesburg	ENGLAND	J de Villiers	Won	36	27
407		23/06/2012	Port Elizabeth	ENGLAND	J de Villiers	Drawn	14	14
408		18/08/2012	Cape Town	ARGENTINA	J de Villiers	Won	27	6
409		25/08/2012	Mendoza	ARGENTINA	J de Villiers	Drawn	16	16
410		08/09/2012	Perth	AUSTRALIA	J de Villiers	Lost	19	26
411		15/09/2012	Dunedin	NEW ZEALAND	J de Villiers	Lost	11	21
412		29/09/2012	Pretoria	AUSTRALIA	J de Villiers	Won	31	8
413		06/10/2012	Soweto	NEW ZEALAND	J de Villiers	Lost	16	32
414		10/11/2012	Dublin	IRELAND	J de Villiers	Won	16	12
415		17/11/2012	Edinburgh	SCOTLAND	J de Villiers	Won	21	10
416		24/11/2012	London	ENGLAND	J de Villiers	Won	16	15
417		08/06/2013	Durban	ITALY	J de Villiers	Won	44	10
418		15/06/2013	Nelspruit	SCOTLAND	J de Villiers	Won	30	17
419		22/06/2013	Pretoria	SAMOA	J de Villiers	Won	56	23
420		17/08/2013	Soweto	ARGENTINA	J de Villiers	Won	73	13
421		24/08/2013	Mendoza	ARGENTINA	J de Villiers	Won	22	17
422		07/09/2013	Brisbane	AUSTRALIA	J de Villiers	Won	38	12
423		14/09/2013	Auckland	NEW ZEALAND	J de Villiers	Lost	15	29
424		28/09/2013	Cape Town	AUSTRALIA	J de Villiers	Won	28	8
425		05/10/2013	Johannesburg	NEW ZEALAND	J de Villiers	Lost	27	38
426		09/11/2013	Cardiff	WALES	J de Villiers	Won	24	15
427		17/11/2013	Edinburgh	SCOTLAND	J de Villiers	Won	28	0
428		23/11/2013	Paris	FRANCE	J de Villiers	Won	19	10
						TEST	9816	6594
						TOUR	8268	2758

SPRINGBOK RECORDS

SOUTH AFRICA'S TEST RESULTS BY OPPONENT

ARGENTINA
Played 17 - Won 16 - Lost 0 - Drawn 1 - PF 682 - PA 324

Year	Winner	Score	Venue
1993	South Africa	29-26	Buenos Aires
1993	South Africa	52-23	Buenos Aires
1994	South Africa	42-22	Port Elizabeth
1994	South Africa	46-26	Johannesburg
1996	South Africa	46-15	Buenos Aires
1996	South Africa	44-21	Buenos Aires
2000	South Africa	37-33	Buenos Aires
2002	South Africa	49-29	Springs
2003	South Africa	26-25	Port Elizabeth
2004	South Africa	39-7	Buenos Aires
2005	South Africa	34-23	Buenos Aires
2007	South Africa	37-13	Paris
2008	South Africa	63-9	Johannesburg
2012	South Africa	27-6	Cape Town
2012	Drawn	16-16	Mendoza
2013	South Africa	73-13	Soweto
2013	South Africa	22-17	Mendoza

AUSTRALIA
Played 78 - Won 44 - Lost 33 - Draw 1 - PF 1501 - PA 1357

Year	Winner	Score	Venue
1933	South Africa	17-3	Cape Town
1933	Australia	6-21	Durban
1933	South Africa	12-3	Johannesburg
1933	South Africa	11-0	Port Elizabeth
1933	Australia	4-15	Bloemfontein
1937	South Africa	9-5	Sydney
1937	South Africa	26-17	Sydney
1953	South Africa	25-3	Johannesburg
1953	Australia	14-18	Cape Town
1953	South Africa	18-8	Durban
1953	South Africa	22-9	Port Elizabeth
1956	South Africa	9-0	Sydney
1956	South Africa	9-0	Brisbane
1961	South Africa	28-3	Johannesburg
1961	South Africa	23-11	Port Elizabeth
1963	South Africa	14-3	Pretoria
1963	Australia	5-9	Cape Town
1963	Australia	9-11	Johannesburg
1963	South Africa	22-6	Port Elizabeth
1965	Australia	11-18	Sydney
1965	Australia	8-12	Brisbane
1969	South Africa	30-11	Johannesburg
1969	South Africa	16-9	Durban
1969	South Africa	11-3	Cape Town
1969	South Africa	19-8	Bloemfontein
1971	South Africa	19-11	Sydney
1971	South Africa	14-6	Brisbane
1971	South Africa	18-6	Sydney
1992	Australia	3-26	Cape Town
1993	South Africa	19-12	Sydney
1993	Australia	20-28	Brisbane
1993	Australia	12-19	Sydney
1995	South Africa	27-18	Cape Town
1996	Australia	16-21	Sydney
1996	South Africa	25-19	Bloemfontein
1997	Australia	20-32	Brisbane
1997	South Africa	61-22	Pretoria
1998	South Africa	14-13	Perth
1998	South Africa	29-15	Johannesburg
1999	Australia	6-32	Brisbane
1999	South Africa	10-9	Cape Town
1999	Australia	21-27	London
2000	Australia	23-44	Melbourne
2000	Australia	6-26	Sydney
2000	Australia	18-19	Durban
2001	South Africa	20-15	Pretoria
2001	Drawn	14-14	Perth
2002	Australia	27-38	Brisbane
2002	South Africa	33-31	Johannesburg
2003	South Africa	26-22	Cape Town
2003	Australia	9-29	Brisbane
2004	Australia	26-30	Perth
2004	South Africa	23-19	Durban
2005	Australia	12-30	Sydney
2005	South Africa	33-20	Johannesburg
2005	South Africa	22-16	Pretoria
2005	South Africa	22-19	Perth
2006	Australia	0-49	Brisbane
2006	Australia	18-20	Sydney
2006	South Africa	24-16	Johannesburg
2007	South Africa	22-19	Cape Town
2007	Australia	17-25	Sydney
2008	Australia	9-16	Perth
2008	Australia	15-27	Durban
2008	South Africa	53-8	Johannesburg
2009	South Africa	29-17	Cape Town
2009	South Africa	32-25	Perth
2009	Australia	6-21	Brisbane
2010	Australia	13-30	Brisbane
2010	South Africa	44-31	Pretoria
2010	Australia	39-41	Bloemfontein
2011	Australia	20-39	Sydney
2011	Australia	9-14	Durban
2011	Australia	9-11	Wellington
2012	Australia	19-26	Perth
2012	South Africa	31-8	Pretoria
2013	South Africa	38-12	Brisbane
2013	South Africa	28-8	Cape Town

BRITISH ISLES/BRITISH & IRISH LIONS
Played 46 - Won 23 - Lost 17 - Drawn 6 - PF 600 - PA 516

Year	Winner	Score	Venue
1891	British Isles	0-4	Port Elizabeth
1891	British Isles	0-3	Kimberley
1891	British Isles	0-4	Cape Town
1896	British Isles	0-8	Port Elizabeth
1896	British Isles	8-17	Johannesburg
1896	British Isles	3-9	Kimberley
1896	South Africa	5-0	Cape Town
1903	Drawn	10-10	Johannesburg

SPRINGBOK RECORDS

SOUTH AFRICA'S TEST RESULTS BY OPPONENT

Year	Winner	Score	Venue
1903	Drawn	0-0	Kimberley
1903	South Africa	8-0	Cape Town
1910	South Africa	14-10	Johannesburg
1910	British Isles	3-8	Port Elizabeth
1910	South Africa	21-5	Cape Town
1924	South Africa	7-3	Durban
1924	South Africa	17-0	Johannesburg
1924	Drawn	3-3	Port Elizabeth
1924	South Africa	16-9	Cape Town
1938	South Africa	26-12	Johannesburg
1938	South Africa	19-3	Port Elizabeth
1938	British Isles	16-21	Cape Town
1955	British Isles	22-23	Johannesburg
1955	South Africa	25-9	Cape Town
1955	British Isles	6-9	Pretoria
1955	South Africa	22-8	Port Elizabeth
1962	Drawn	3-3	Johannesburg
1962	South Africa	3-0	Durban
1962	South Africa	8-3	Cape Town
1962	South Africa	34-14	Bloemfontein
1968	South Africa	25-20	Pretoria
1968	Drawn	6-6	Port Elizabeth
1968	South Africa	11-6	Cape Town
1968	South Africa	19-6	Johannesburg
1974	British Isles	3-12	Cape Town
1974	British Isles	9-28	Pretoria
1974	British Isles	9-26	Port Elizabeth
1974	Drawn	13-13	Johannesburg
1980	South Africa	26-22	Cape Town
1980	South Africa	26-19	Bloemfontein
1980	South Africa	12-10	Port Elizabeth
1980	British Isles	13-17	Pretoria
1997	British Isles	16-25	Cape Town
1997	British Isles	15-18	Durban
1997	South Africa	35-16	Johannesburg
2009	South Africa	26-21	Durban
2009	South Africa	28-25	Pretoria
2009	British Isles	9-28	Johannesburg

CANADA
Played 2 - Won 2 - Lost 0 - Drawn 0 - PF 71 - PA 18

Year	Winner	Score	Venue
1995	South Africa	20-0	Port Elizabeth
2000	South Africa	51-18	East London

ENGLAND
Played 36 - Won 22 - Lost 12 - Drawn 2 - PF 749 - PA 564

Year	Winner	Score	Venue
1906	Drawn	3-3	Crystal Palace
1913	South Africa	9-3	Twickenham
1932	South Africa	7-0	Twickenham
1952	South Africa	8-3	Twickenham
1961	South Africa	5-0	Twickenham
1969	England	8-11	Twickenham
1972	England	9-18	Johannesburg
1984	South Africa	33-15	Port Elizabeth
1984	South Africa	35-9	Johannesburg
1992	England	16-33	Twickenham
1994	England	15-32	Pretoria
1994	South Africa	27-9	Cape Town
1995	South Africa	24-14	Twickenham
1997	South Africa	29-11	Twickenham
1998	South Africa	18-0	Cape Town
1998	England	7-13	Twickenham
1999	South Africa	44-21	Paris
2000	South Africa	18-13	Pretoria
2000	England	22-27	Bloemfontein
2000	England	17-25	Twickenham
2001	England	9-29	Twickenham
2002	England	3-53	Twickenham
2003	England	6-25	Perth
2004	England	16-32	Twickenham
2006	England	21-23	Twickenham
2006	South Africa	25-14	Twickenham
2007	South Africa	58-10	Bloemfontein
2007	South Africa	55-22	Pretoria
2007	South Africa	36-0	Paris
2007	South Africa	15-6	Paris
2008	South Africa	42-6	Twickenham
2010	South Africa	21-11	Twickenham
2012	South Africa	22-17	Durban
2012	South Africa	36-27	Johannesburg
2012	Drawn	14-14	Port Elizabeth
2012	South Africa	16-15	Twickenham

FIJI
Played 3 - Won 3 - Lost 0 - Drawn 0 - PF 129 - PA 41

Year	Winner	Score	Venue
1996	South Africa	43-18	Pretoria
2007	South Africa	37-20	Marseille
2011	South Africa	49-3	Wellington

FRANCE
Played 39 - Won 22 - Lost 11 - Drawn 6 - PF 783 - PA 578

Year	Winner	Score	Venue
1913	South Africa	38-5	Bordeaux
1952	South Africa	25-3	Paris
1958	Drawn	3-3	Cape Town
1958	France	5-9	Johannesburg
1961	Drawn	0-0	Paris
1964	France	6-8	Springs
1967	South Africa	26-3	Durban
1967	South Africa	16-3	Bloemfontein
1967	France	14-19	Johannesburg
1967	Drawn	6-6	Cape Town
1968	South Africa	12-9	Bordeaux
1968	South Africa	16-11	Paris
1971	South Africa	22-9	Bloemfontein
1971	Drawn	8-8	Durban
1974	South Africa	13-4	Toulouse
1974	South Africa	10-8	Paris
1975	South Africa	38-25	Bloemfontein
1975	South Africa	33-18	Pretoria
1980	South Africa	37-15	Pretoria

SPRINGBOK RECORDS

SOUTH AFRICA'S TEST RESULTS BY OPPONENT

Year	Winner	Score	Venue
1992	South Africa	20-15	Lyon
1992	France	16-29	Paris
1993	Drawn	20-20	Durban
1993	France	17-18	Johannesburg
1995	South Africa	19-15	Durban
1996	South Africa	22-12	Bordeaux
1996	South Africa	13-12	Paris
1997	South Africa	36-32	Lyon
1997	South Africa	52-10	Paris
2001	France	23-32	Johannesburg
2001	South Africa	20-15	Durban
2001	France	10-20	Paris
2002	France	10-30	Marseilles
2005	Drawn	30-30	Durban
2005	South Africa	27-13	Port Elizabeth
2005	France	20-26	Paris
2006	France	26-36	Cape Town
2009	France	13-20	Toulouse
2010	South Africa	42-17	Cape Town
2013	South Africa	19-10	Paris

GEORGIA
Played 1 - Won 1 - Lost 0 - Drawn 0 - PF 46 - PA 19

Year	Winner	Score	Venue
2003	South Africa	46-19	Sydney

IRELAND
Played 21 - Won 16 - Lost 4 - Drawn 1 - PF 417 - PA 248

Year	Winner	Score	Venue
1906	South Africa	15-12	Belfast
1912	South Africa	38-0	Dublin
1931	South Africa	8-3	Dublin
1951	South Africa	17-5	Dublin
1960	South Africa	8-3	Dublin
1961	South Africa	24-8	Cape Town
1965	Ireland	6-9	Dublin
1970	Drawn	8-8	Dublin
1981	South Africa	23-15	Cape Town
1981	South Africa	12-10	Durban
1998	South Africa	37-13	Bloemfontein
1998	South Africa	33-0	Pretoria
1998	South Africa	27-13	Dublin
2000	South Africa	28-18	Dublin
2004	South Africa	31-17	Bloemfontein
2004	South Africa	26-17	Cape Town
2004	Ireland	12-17	Dublin
2006	Ireland	15-32	Dublin
2009	Ireland	10-15	Dublin
2010	South Africa	23-21	Dublin
2012	South Africa	16-12	Dublin

ITALY
Played 11 - Won 11 - Lost 0 - Drawn 0 - PF 577 - PA 139

Year	Winner	Score	Venue
1995	South Africa	40-21	Rome
1997	South Africa	62-31	Bologna
1999	South Africa	74-3	Port Elizabeth
1999	South Africa	101-0	Durban
2001	South Africa	60-14	Port Elizabeth
2001	South Africa	54-26	Genoa
2008	South Africa	26-0	Cape Town
2009	South Africa	32-10	Udine
2010	South Africa	29-13	Witbank
2010	South Africa	55-11	East London
2013	South Africa	44-10	Durban

NAMIBIA
Played 2 - Won 2 - Lost 0 - Drawn 0 - PF 192 - PA 13

Year	Winner	Score	Venue
2007	South Africa	105-13	Cape Town
2011	South Africa	87-0	Albany

NEW ZEALAND
Played 87 - Won 34 - Lost 50 - Draw 3 - PF 1355 - PA 1679

Year	Winner	Score	Venue
1921	New Zealand	5-13	Dunedin
1921	South Africa	9-5	Auckland
1921	Drawn	0-0	Wellington
1928	South Africa	17-0	Durban
1928	New Zealand	6-7	Johannesburg
1928	South Africa	11-6	Port Elizabeth
1928	New Zealand	5-13	Cape Town
1937	New Zealand	7-13	Wellington
1937	South Africa	13-6	Christchurch
1937	South Africa	17-6	Auckland
1949	South Africa	15-11	Cape Town
1949	South Africa	12-6	Johannesburg
1949	South Africa	9-3	Durban
1949	South Africa	11-8	Port Elizabeth
1956	New Zealand	6-10	Dunedin
1956	South Africa	8-3	Wellington
1956	New Zealand	10-17	Christchurch
1956	New Zealand	5-11	Auckland
1960	South Africa	13-0	Johannesburg
1960	New Zealand	3-11	Cape Town
1960	Drawn	11-11	Bloemfontein
1960	South Africa	8-3	Port Elizabeth
1965	New Zealand	3-6	Wellington
1965	New Zealand	0-13	Dunedin
1965	South Africa	19-16	Christchurch
1965	New Zealand	3-20	Auckland
1970	South Africa	17-6	Pretoria
1970	New Zealand	8-9	Cape Town
1970	South Africa	14-3	Port Elizabeth
1970	South Africa	20-17	Johannesburg
1976	South Africa	16-7	Durban
1976	New Zealand	9-15	Bloemfontein
1976	South Africa	15-10	Cape Town
1976	South Africa	15-14	Johannesburg
1981	New Zealand	9-14	Christchurch
1981	South Africa	24-12	Wellington
1981	New Zealand	22-25	Auckland
1992	New Zealand	24-27	Johannesburg

SOUTH AFRICA'S TEST RESULTS BY OPPONENT

Year	Winner	Score	Venue
1994	New Zealand	14-22	Dunedin
1994	New Zealand	9-13	Wellington
1994	Drawn	18-18	Auckland
1995	South Africa	15-12	Johannesburg
1996	New Zealand	11-15	Christchurch
1996	New Zealand	18-29	Cape Town
1996	New Zealand	19-23	Durban
1996	New Zealand	26-33	Pretoria
1996	South Africa	32-22	Johannesburg
1997	New Zealand	32-35	Johannesburg
1997	New Zealand	35-55	Auckland
1998	South Africa	13-3	Wellington
1998	South Africa	24-23	Durban
1999	New Zealand	0-28	Dunedin
1999	New Zealand	18-34	Pretoria
1999	South Africa	22-18	Cardiff
2000	New Zealand	12-25	Christchurch
2000	South Africa	46-40	Johannesburg
2001	New Zealand	3-12	Cape Town
2001	New Zealand	15-26	Auckland
2002	New Zealand	20-41	Wellington
2002	New Zealand	23-30	Durban
2003	New Zealand	16-52	Pretoria
2003	New Zealand	11-19	Dunedin
2003	New Zealand	9-29	Melbourne
2004	New Zealand	21-23	Christchurch
2004	South Africa	40-26	Johannesburg
2005	South Africa	22-16	Cape Town
2005	New Zealand	27-31	Dunedin
2006	New Zealand	17-35	Wellington
2006	New Zealand	26-45	Pretoria
2006	South Africa	21-20	Rustenburg
2007	New Zealand	21-26	Durban
2007	New Zealand	6-33	Christchurch
2008	New Zealand	8-19	Wellington
2008	South Africa	30-28	Dunedin
2008	New Zealand	0-19	Cape Town
2009	South Africa	28-19	Bloemfontein
2009	South Africa	31-19	Durban
2009	South Africa	32-29	Hamilton
2010	New Zealand	12-32	Auckland
2010	New Zealand	17-31	Wellington
2010	New Zealand	22-29	Soweto
2011	New Zealand	7-40	Wellington
2011	South Africa	18-5	Port Elizabeth
2012	New Zealand	11-21	Dunedin
2012	New Zealand	16-32	Soweto
2013	New Zealand	15-29	Auckland
2013	New Zealand	27-38	Johannesburg

NEW ZEALAND CAVALIERS
Played 4 - Won 3 - Lost 1 - Drawn 0 - PF 96 - PA 62

Year	Winner	Score	Venue
1986	South Africa	21-15	Cape Town
1986	NZ Cavaliers	18-19	Durban
1986	South Africa	33-18	Pretoria
1986	South Africa	24-10	Johannesburg

PACIFIC ISLANDS
Played 1 - Won 1 - Lost 0 - Drawn 0 - PF 38 - PA 24

Year	Winner	Score	Venue
2004	South Africa	38-24	Gosford

ROMANIA
Played 1 - Won 1 - Lost 0 - Drawn 0 - PF 21 - PA 8

Year	Winner	Score	Venue
1995	South Africa	21-8	Cape Town

SAMOA
Played 8 - Won 8 - Lost 0 - Drawn 0 - PF 385 - PA 93

Year	Winner	Score	Venue
1995	South Africa	60-8	Johannesburg
1995	South Africa	42-14	Johannesburg
2002	South Africa	60-18	Pretoria
2003	South Africa	60-10	Brisbane
2007	South Africa	35-8	Johannesburg
2007	South Africa	59-7	Paris
2011	South Africa	13-5	Albany
2013	South Africa	56-23	Pretoria

SCOTLAND
Played 24 - Won 19 - Lost 5 - Drawn 0 - PF 597 - PA 264

Year	Winner	Score	Venue
1906	Scotland	0-6	Glasgow
1912	South Africa	16-0	Edinburgh
1932	South Africa	6-3	Edinburgh
1951	South Africa	44-0	Edinburgh
1960	South Africa	18-10	Port Elizabeth
1961	South Africa	12-5	Edinburgh
1965	Scotland	5-8	Edinburgh
1969	Scotland	3-6	Edinburgh
1994	South Africa	34-10	Edinburgh
1997	South Africa	68-10	Edinburgh
1998	South Africa	35-10	Edinburgh
1999	South Africa	46-29	Edinburgh
2002	Scotland	6-21	Edinburgh
2003	South Africa	29-25	Durban
2003	South Africa	28-19	Johannesburg
2004	South Africa	45-10	Edinburgh
2006	South Africa	36-16	Durban
2006	South Africa	29-15	Port Elizabeth
2007	South Africa	27-3	Edinburgh
2008	South Africa	14-10	Edinburgh
2010	Scotland	17-21	Edinburgh
2012	South Africa	21-10	Edinburgh
2013	South Africa	30-17	Nelspruit
2013	South Africa	28-0	Edinburgh

SOUTH AMERICA (*indicates includes Spain)
Played 8 - Won 7 - Lost 1 - Drawn 0 - PF 210 - PA 114

Year	Winner	Score	Venue
1980	South Africa	24-9	Johannesburg
1980	South Africa	18-9	Durban
1980	South Africa	22-13	Montevideo
1980	South Africa	30-16	Santiago

SPRINGBOK RECORDS

SOUTH AFRICA'S TEST RESULTS BY OPPONENT

Year	Winner	Score	Venue
1982	South Africa	50-18	Pretoria
1982	South America	12-21	Bloemfontein
1984*	South Africa	32-15	Pretoria
1984*	South Africa	22-13	Cape Town

SPAIN
Played 1 - Won 1 - Lost 0 - Drawn 0 - PF 47 - PA 3

Year	Winner	Score	Venue
1999	South Africa	47-3	Edinburgh

TONGA
Played 2 - Won 2 - Lost 0 - Drawn 0 - PF 104 - PA 35

Year	Winner	Score	Venue
1997	South Africa	74-10	Cape Town
2007	South Africa	30-25	Lens

UNITED STATES OF AMERICA
Played 3 - Won 3 - Lost 0 - Drawn 0 - PF 145 - PA 42

Year	Winner	Score	Venue
1981	South Africa	38-7	Glenville
2001	South Africa	43-20	Houston
2007	South Africa	64-15	Montpellier

URUGUAY
Played 3 - Won 3 - Lost 0 - Drawn 0 - PF 245 - PA 12

Year	Winner	Score	Venue
1999	South Africa	39-3	Glasgow
2003	South Africa	72-6	Perth
2005	South Africa	134-3	East London

WALES
Played 27 - Won 25 - Lost 1 - Drawn 1 - PF 739 - PA 382

Year	Winner	Score	Venue
1906	South Africa	11-0	Swansea
1912	South Africa	3-0	Cardiff
1931	South Africa	8-3	Swansea
1951	South Africa	6-3	Cardiff
1960	South Africa	3-0	Cardiff
1964	South Africa	24-3	Durban
1970	Drawn	6-6	Cardiff
1994	South Africa	20-12	Cardiff
1995	South Africa	40-11	Johannesburg
1996	South Africa	37-20	Cardiff
1998	South Africa	96-13	Pretoria
1998	South Africa	28-20	Wembley
1999	Wales	19-29	Cardiff
2000	South Africa	23-13	Cardiff
2002	South Africa	34-19	Bloemfontein
2002	South Africa	19-8	Cape Town
2004	South Africa	53-18	Pretoria
2004	South Africa	38-36	Cardiff
2005	South Africa	33-16	Cardiff
2007	South Africa	34-12	Cardiff
2008	South Africa	43-17	Bloemfontein
2008	South Africa	37-21	Pretoria
2008	South Africa	20-15	Cardiff
2010	South Africa	34-31	Cardiff
2010	South Africa	29-25	Cardiff
2011	South Africa	17-16	Wellington, NZ
2013	South Africa	24-15	Cardiff

WORLD TEAMS
Played 3 - Won 3 - Lost 0 - Drawn 0 - PF 87 - PA 59

Year	Winner	Score	Venue
1977	South Africa	45-24	Pretoria
1989	South Africa	20-19	Cape Town
1989	South Africa	22-16	Johannesburg

George North is hit by some aggressive Springbok defence during their 2013 clash at the Millennium Stadium. *Scott Heavey/Getty Images*

SPRINGBOK RECORDS

SPRINGBOK TOURS 1906-2013 (Excludes tours where only Test matches were played)

Year	Tour	Captain	Tour Matches	Tests	Tot Matches	Won	Lost	Drawn	Points for	Pts against	Tries for	Tries against
1906/07	British Isles, Ireland & France	PJ Roos	24	4	28	25	2	1	553	79	130	19
1912/13	British Isles, Ireland & France	WA Millar	22	5	27	24	3	0	441	101	103	22
1921	Australia & New Zealand	TB Pienaar	20	3	23	19	2	2	327	119	74	21
1931/32	British Isles & Ireland	BL Osler	22	4	26	23	1	2	407	124	86	23
1937	Australia & New Zealand	PJ Nel	21	5	26	24	2	0	753	169	161	29
1951/52	British Isles, Ireland & France	BJ Kenyon	26	5	31	30	1	0	562	167	120	26
1956	Australia & New Zealand	SS Vivier	23	6	29	22	6	1	520	203	108	31
1960/61	British Isles, Ireland & France	AS Malan	29	5	34	31	1	2	567	132	132	25
1965	Ireland & Scotland	AS Malan	3	2	5	0	4	1	37	53	7	8
1965	Australia & New Zealand	DJ de Villiers	24	6	30	22	8	0	669	285	144	42
1968	France	DJ de Villiers	4	2	6	5	1	0	84	43	12	5
1969/70	British Isles & Ireland	DJ de Villiers	20	4	24	15	5	4	323	157	59	23
1971	Australia	JFK Marais	10	3	13	13	0	0	396	102	76	11
1974	France	JFK Marais	7	2	9	8	1	0	170	74	23	10
1980	South America	M du Plessis	4	2	6	6	0	0	376	78	66	8
1981	New Zealand & USA	W Claassen	13	4	17	14	2	1	535	190	81	16
1992	France & England	HE Botha	10	3	13	8	5	0	297	236	30	16
1993	Australia	JF Pienaar	9	3	12	9	3	0	527	147	75	15
1993	Argentina	JF Pienaar	4	2	6	5	1	0	243	152	32	11
1994	New Zealand	JF Pienaar	11	3	14	10	3	1	445	241	58	22
1994	Wales, Scotland & Ireland	JF Pienaar	11	2	13	11	2	0	375	151	50	12
1996	Argentina, France & Wales	GH Teichmann	5	5	10	8	2	0	367	205	53	19
1997	Italy, France, England & Scotland	GH Teichmann	2	5	7	5	2	0	276	155	40	16
1998	British Isles & Ireland	GH Teichmann	4	4	8	7	1	0	290	92	42	6
2000	Argentina, Ireland, Wales & England	AN Vos	5	4	9	6	3	0	253	219	30	20
2006	Ireland & England	JW Smit	1	3	4	2	2	0	93	76	9	8
2007	Ireland & Scotland	JW Smit	1	1	2	2	0	0	18	3	2	0
2007	Wales & England	JW Smit	1	1	2	1	1	0	39	34	6	5
2009	France, Italy, Ireland & England	JW Smit	2	3	5	1	4	0	95	91	10	5
2010	British Isles & Ireland	V Matfield	1	4	5	3	2	0	110	104	10	10
			339	105	444	359	70	15	10148	3982	1829	484

INTERNATIONAL TOURS TO SOUTH AFRICA 1891-2013
(Excludes tours where only Test matches were played)

Year	Tour	Captain	Tour Matches	Tests	Total Matches	Won	Lost	Drawn	Points for	Points against	Tries for	Tries against
1891	British Isles	WE Maclagan (Scotland)	16	3	19	19	0	0	224	1	89	1
1896	British Isles	JF Hammond (Cambridge University)	17	4	21	19	1	1	310	45	64	10
1903	British Isles	MC Morrison (Scotland)	19	3	22	11	8	3	231	138	49	29
1910	British Isles	T Smyth (Ireland)	21	3	24	13	8	3	290	236	68	54
1924	British Isles	R Cove-Smith (England)	17	4	21	9	9	3	175	155	45	26
1928	New Zealand	MJ Brownlie (Hawke's Bay)	18	4	22	16	5	1	339	144	70	23
1933	Australia	AW Ross (New South Wales)	18	5	23	12	10	1	299	195	67	29
1938	British Isles	S Walker (Ireland)	20	3	23	17	6	0	407	272	79	43
1949	New Zealand	FR Allen (Auckland)	20	4	24	14	7	3	230	146	43	8
1953	Australia	HJ Solomon (New South Wales)	23	4	27	16	10	1	450	413	92	68
1955	British Isles	RH Thompson (Ireland)	20	4	24	18	5	1	418	271	94	39
1958	France	M Celaya (Biarritz)	8	2	10	5	3	2	137	124	26	17

INTERNATIONAL TOURS TO SOUTH AFRICA 1891-2013 (Continued)

Year	Tour	Captain	Tour Matches	Tests	Tot Matches	Won	Lost	Drawn	Points for	Pts against	Tries for	Tries against
1960	Scotland	GH Waddell (Cambridge University)	2	1	3	2	1	0	61	45	13	9
1960	New Zealand	WJ Whineray (Auckland)	22	4	26	20	4	2	441	164	75	23
1961	Ireland	AR Dawson (Wanderers)	3	1	4	3	1	0	59	36	8	6
1961	Australia	KW Catchpole (New South Wales)	4	2	6	3	2	1	90	80	15	16
1962	British Isles	AR Smith (Scotland)	20	4	24	15	5	4	351	208	62	37
1963	Australia	JE Thornett (New South Wales)	20	4	24	15	8	1	303	233	46	28
1964	Wales	DCT Rowlands (Pontypool)	3	1	4	2	2	0	43	58	5	6
1964	France	M Crauste (Lourdes)	5	1	6	5	1	0	117	55	18	4
1967	France	C Darrouy (Mont-de-Marsan)	9	4	13	8	4	1	209	161	30	23
1968	British Isles	TJ Kiernan (Ireland)	16	4	20	15	4	1	377	181	55	21
1969	Australia	GV Davis (New South Wales)	22	4	26	15	11	0	465	353	78	54
1970	New Zealand	BJ Lochore (Wairarapa)	20	4	24	21	3	0	687	228	135	23
1971	France	C Carrère (Toulon)	7	2	9	7	1	1	228	92	42	9
1972	England	JV Pullin (Bristol)	6	1	7	6	0	1	166	58	23	4
1974	British Isles	WJ McBride (Ireland)	18	4	22	21	0	1	729	207	107	16
1975	France	J Fouroux (La Voulte) & R Astre (Béziers)	9	2	11	6	4	1	282	190	41	20
1976	New Zealand	AR Leslie (Wellington)	20	4	24	18	6	0	610	291	89	27
1977	World Team	WJ McBride (Ireland)	2	1	3	0	3	0	76	142	13	23
1980	South America	H Porta (Argentina)	5	2	7	4	3	0	174	134	23	16
1980	British Isles	WB Beaumont (England)	14	4	18	15	3	0	401	244	47	27
1980	France	J-P Rives (Toulouse)	3	1	4	3	1	0	90	95	13	12
1981	Ireland	JF Slattery (Blackrock College)	5	2	7	3	4	0	207	90	30	10
1982	South America	H Porta (Argentina)	12	2	14	12	1	1	448	179	62	25
1984	England	JP Scott (Cardiff)	5	2	7	4	2	1	156	145	19	18
1984	South America & Spain	H Porta (Argentina)	5	2	7	4	3	0	146	140	17	20
1986	New Zealand Cavaliers	AG Dalton (Counties)	8	4	12	8	4	0	275	229	33	16
1989	World Team	P Berbizier (France)	3	2	5	1	4	0	100	130	14	20
1992	New Zealand	SBT Fitzpatrick (Auckland)	4	1	5	5	0	0	167	79	20	6
1992	Australia	NC Farr-Jones (New South Wales)	3	1	4	4	0	0	130	41	15	4
1993	France	J-F Tordo (Nice)	6	2	8	4	2	2	169	159	14	12
1994	England	WDC Carling (Harlequins)	6	2	8	3	5	0	152	165	11	13
1994	Argentina	MH Lofreda (Buenos Aires)	4	2	6	3	3	0	216	216	27	28
1995	Western Samoa	P Fatialofa (Auckland, New Zealand)	2	1	3	0	3	0	38	104	4	12
1995	Wales	JM Humphreys (Cardiff)	1	1	2	0	2	0	17	87	1	10
1996	Fiji	J Veitayaki (King Country, New Zealand)	1	1	2	1	1	0	62	80	7	9
1996	New Zealand	SBT Fitzpatrick (Auckland)	4	3	7	5	1	1	190	139	24	14
1997	British Isles	MO Johnson (England)	10	3	13	11	2	0	480	278	56	32
1997	Tonga	L Katoa (Siutaka)	3	1	4	2	2	0	77	149	9	23
1998	Ireland	PS Johns (Saracens, England)	5	2	7	2	5	0	126	214	11	26
1998	Wales	R Howley (Cardiff)	4	1	5	0	5	0	94	224	9	32
1999	Italy	M Giovanelli (Narbonne, France)	2	2	4	0	4	0	30	267	3	40
2000	England	MO Johnson (Leicester)	3	2	5	4	1	0	183	105	20	6
2001	Italy	A Moscardi (Benetton Treviso)	1	1	2	0	2	0	25	102	2	14
2002	Argentina	A Pichot (Bristol, England)	1	1	2	0	2	0	65	91	7	11
2002	Samoa	S Sititi (Borders, Scotland)	2	1	3	1	2	0	75	117	9	15
2003	Argentina	G Longo (Narbonne, France)	1	1	2	0	1	1	55	56	6	5
2009	British Isles	PJ O'Connell (Ireland)	7	3	10	7	2	1	309	169	34	15
2012	England	CDC Robshaw (Harlequins)	2	3	5	2	2	1	169	129	21	15
			557	147	704	459	204	41	13630	9279	2209	1202

TEST MATCH RECORDS

Highest scores

Score	Opponent	Venue	Year
134-3	vs. Uruguay	East London	2005
105-13	vs. Namibia	Cape Town	2007
101-0	vs. Italy	Durban	1999
96-13	vs. Wales	Pretoria	1998
87-0	vs. Namibia	Albany	2011
74-10	vs. Tonga	Cape Town	1997
74-3	vs. Italy	Port Elizabeth	1999
73-13	vs. Argentina	Soweto	2013
72-6	vs. Uruguay	Perth	2003
68-10	vs. Scotland	Edinburgh	1997
64-15	vs. USA	Montpellier	2007
63-9	vs. Argentina	Johannesburg	2008
62-31	vs. Italy	Bologna	1997
61-22	vs. Australia	Pretoria	1997
60-8	vs. Western Samoa	Johannesburg	1995
60-14	vs. Italy	Port Elizabeth	2001
60-18	vs. Samoa	Pretoria	2002
60-10	vs. Samoa	Brisbane	2003

Biggest margins of victory

Margin	Match	Venue	Year
131	vs. Uruguay (134-3)	East London	2005
101	vs. Italy (101-0)	Durban	1999
92	vs. Namibia (105-13)	Cape Town	2007
87	vs. Namibia (87-0)	Albany	2011
83	vs. Wales (96-13)	Pretoria	1998
71	vs. Italy (74-3)	Port Elizabeth	1999
66	vs. Uruguay (72-6)	Perth	2003
64	vs. Tonga (74-10)	Cape Town	1997
60	vs. Argentina (73-13)	Soweto	2013
58	vs. Scotland (68-10)	Edinburgh	1997
54	vs. Argentina (63-9)	Johannesburg	2008
52	vs. Western Samoa (60-8)	Johannesburg	1995
52	vs. Samoa (59-7)	Paris	2007
50	vs. Samoa (60-10)	Brisbane	2003

Most tries

Tries	Opponent	Venue	Year
21	vs. Uruguay	East London	2005
15	vs. Italy	Durban	1999
15	vs. Wales	Pretoria	1998
15	vs. Namibia	Cape Town	2007
12	vs. Uruguay	Perth	2003
12	vs. Tonga	Cape Town	1997
12	vs. Namibia	Albany	2011
11	vs. Italy	Port Elizabeth	1999
10	vs. Scotland	Edinburgh	1997
10	vs. Ireland	Dublin	1912

Most points conceded

Score	Opponent	Venue	Year
55-35	vs. New Zealand	Auckland	1997
53-3	vs. England	Twickenham	2002
52-16	vs. New Zealand	Pretoria	2003
49-0	vs. Australia	Brisbane	2006
45-26	vs. New Zealand	Pretoria	2006
44-23	vs. Australia	Melbourne	2000
41-20	vs. New Zealand	Wellington	2002
41-39	vs. Australia	Bloemfontein	2010
40-46	vs. New Zealand	Johannesburg	2000
40-7	vs. New Zealand	Wellington	2011
39-20	vs. Australia	Sydney	2011
38-27	vs. Australia	Brisbane	2002
38-27	vs. New Zealand	Johannesburg	2013
36-38	vs. Wales	Cardiff	2004
36-26	vs. France	Cape Town	2006
35-32	vs. New Zealand	Johannesburg	1997
35-17	vs. New Zealand	Wellington	2006

Biggest margins of defeat

Margin	Match	Venue	Year
50	England (3-53)	Twickenham	2002
49	Australia (0-49)	Brisbane	2006
36	New Zealand (16-52)	Pretoria	2003
33	New Zealand (7-40)	Wellington	2011
28	New Zealand (0-28)	Dunedin	1999
27	New Zealand (6-33)	Christchurch	2007
26	Australia (6-32)	Brisbane	1999
23	Australia (3-26)	Cape Town	1992
21	Australia (23-44)	Melbourne	2000
21	New Zealand (20-41)	Wellington	2002
20	New Zealand (35-55)	Auckland	1997
20	Australia (6-26)	Sydney	2000
20	England (9-29)	Twickenham	2001
20	France (10-30)	Marseilles	2002
20	Australia (9-29)	Brisbane	2003
20	New Zealand (9-29)	Melbourne	2003
20	New Zealand (12-32)	Auckland	2010

Most points by a player

Pts	Player vs. Opponent (breakdown)	Venue	Year
35	PC Montgomery vs. Namibia (1t, 12c, 2p)	Cape Town	2007
34	JH de Beer vs. England (2c, 5p, 5dg)	Paris	1999
31	PC Montgomery vs. Wales (2t, 9c, 1p)	Pretoria	1998
31	M Steyn vs. New Zealand (1t, 1c, 8p)	Durban	2009
30	T Chavhanga vs. Uruguay (6t)	East London	2005
29	GS du Toit vs. Italy (2t, 8c, 1p)	Port Elizabeth	1999
29	PC Montgomery vs. Samoa (2t, 5c, 3p)	Paris	2007
28	M Steyn vs. Argentina (8c, 4p)	Soweto	2013

SPRINGBOK RECORDS

28	GK Johnson vs. W Samoa (3t, 5c, 1p)	Johannesburg 1995
26	JH de Beer vs. Australia (1t, 6c, 3p)	Pretoria 1997
26	PC Montgomery vs. Scotland (2t, 8c)	Edinburgh 1997
26	M Steyn vs. Italy (2t, 5c, 2p)	East London 2010
25	JT Stransky vs. Australia (1t, 1c, 6p)	Bloemfontein 1996
25	CS Terblanche vs. Italy (5t)	Durban 1999

Most tries by a player

6	T Chavhanga vs. Uruguay	East London 2005
5	CS Terblanche vs. Italy	Durban 1999
4	CM Williams vs. W Samoa	Johannesburg 1995
4	PWG Rossouw vs. France	Paris 1997
4	CS Terblanche vs. Ireland	Bloemfontein 1998
4	BG Habana vs. Samoa	Paris 2007
4	JL Nokwe vs. Australia	Johannesburg 2008
3	EE McHardy vs. Ireland	Dublin 1912
3	JA Stegmann vs. Ireland	Dublin 1912
3	KT van Vollenhoven vs. B. Isles	Cape Town 1955
3	HJ van Zyl vs. Australia	Johannesburg 1961
3	RH Mordt vs. New Zealand	Auckland 1981
3	RH Mordt vs. USA	New York 1981
3	DM Gerber vs. South America	Pretoria 1982
3	DM Gerber vs. England	Johannesburg 1984
3	GK Johnson vs. W Samoa	Johannesburg 1995
3	JH van der Westhuizen vs. Wales	Cardiff 1996
3	AH Snyman vs. Tonga	Cape Town 1997
3	PWG Rossouw vs. Wales	Pretoria 1998
3	BJ Paulse vs. Italy	Port Elizabeth 1999
3	DJ Kayser vs. Italy	Durban 1999
3	JH van der Westhuizen vs. Uruguay	Perth 2003
3	MC Joubert vs. New Zealand	Johannesburg 2004
3	JH Smith vs. Namibia	Cape Town 2007
3	SWP Burger vs. Namibia	Cape Town 2007
3	BG Habana vs. Australia	Pretoria 2012

Most conversions by a player

12	PC Montgomery vs. Namibia	Cape Town 2007
9	PC Montgomery vs. Wales	Pretoria 1998
9	AD James vs. Argentina	Johannesburg 2008
8	PC Montgomery vs. Scotland	Edinburgh 1997
8	GS du Toit vs. Italy	Port Elizabeth 1999
8	GS du Toit vs. Italy	Durban 1999
8	M Steyn vs. Argentina	Soweto 2013

Most penalty goals by a player

8	M Steyn vs. New Zealand	Durban 2009
7	PC Montgomery vs. Scotland	Port Elizabeth 2006
7	PC Montgomery vs. France	Cape Town 2006
7	M Steyn vs. Australia	Cape Town 2009
6	GR Bosch vs. France	Pretoria 1975
6	JT Stransky vs. Australia	Bloemfontein 1996
6	JH de Beer vs. Australia	Twickenham 1999
6	AJJ van Straaten vs. England	Pretoria 2000
6	AJJ van Straaten vs. Australia	Durban 2000
6	PC Montgomery vs. France	Johannesburg 2001
6	LJ Koen vs. Scotland	Johannesburg 2003
6	M Steyn vs. Australia	Bloemfontein 2010

Most drop goals by a player

5	JH de Beer vs. England	Paris 1999
4	AS Pretorius vs. England	Twickenham 2006
3	HE Botha vs. South America	Durban 1980
3	HE Botha vs. Ireland	Durban 1981
3	JNB van der Westhuyzen vs. Scotland	Edinburgh 2004

Scored all points in a Test (>18)

31*	M Steyn vs. New Zealand	Durban 2009
25	JT Stransky vs. Australia	Bloemfontein 1996
21	JH de Beer vs. Australia	Twickenham 1999
18	AJJ van Straaten vs. England	Pretoria 2000
18	AJJ van Straaten vs. Australia	Durban 2000
18	M Steyn vs. New Zealand	Port Elizabeth 2011

World record

Scored in all four ways in a Test

22	JT Stransky (22 pts - 1t, 1c, 4p, 1dg) vs. Australia	1995
18	AS Pretorius (18 pts - 1t, 2c, 2p, 1dg) vs. New Zealand	2002
21	DJ Hougaard (21 pts - 1t, 5c, 1p, 1dg) vs. Samoa	2003

Most points by a player against SA

29	SA Mortlock, Australia (2t, 2c, 5p)	Melbourne 2000
27	CR Andrew, England (1t, 2c, 5p, 1d)	Pretoria 1994
27	JP Wilkinson, England (8p, 1d)	Bloemfontein 2000
27	G Merceron, France (1t, 2c, 6p)	Johannesburg 2001
27	CC Hodgson, England (1t, 2c, 5p, 1d)	Twickenham 2004
25	CJ Spencer, New Zealand (1t, 4c, 4p)	Auckland 1997
25	DW Carter, New Zealand (2c, 7p)	Wellington 2006
24	MC Burke, Australia (8p)	Twickenham 1999
23	DW Carter, New Zealand (1t, 3c, 4p)	Christchurch 2007
23	DW Carter, New Zealand (1c, 6p, 1d)	Dunedin 2008
22	CJ Spencer, New Zealand (1t, 4c, 3p)	Pretoria 2003
21	H Porta, S America (1t, 1c, 4p, 1d)	Bloemfontein 1982
21	SE Meson, Argentina (1t, 2c, 4p)	Buenos Aires 1993
21	J-L Cilley, Argentina (1t, 2c, 4p)	Johannesburg 1994
21	D Dominguez, Italy (1t, 2c, 4p)	Bologna 1997

SPRINGBOK RECORDS

21	AP Mehrtens, New Zealand (7p)		Pretoria 1999	2	GL Henson (Wales)		Cardiff 2004
21	SA Mortlock, Australia (1t, 2c, 4p)		Sydney 2000	2	MJ Giteau (Australia)		Sydney 2005
21	JP Wilkinson, England (7p)		Twickenham 2001	2	JT Rokocoko (New Zealand)		Dunedin 2005
21	SM Jones, Wales (3c, 5p)		Cardiff 2004	2	V Clerc (France)		Cape Town 2006
21	DA Parks, Scotland (6p, 1d)		Edinburgh 2010	2	MJ Giteau (Australia)		Brisbane 2006
20	CJ Spencer, New Zealand (1t, 3c, 3p)		Johannesburg 1997	2	T Croft (British Isles)		Durban 2009
20	AP Mehrtens, New Zealand (4c, 3p, 1d)		Johannesburg 2000	2	SM Williams (British Isles)		Johannesburg 2009
20	JP Wilkinson, England (1c, 6p)		Twickenham 2000	2	MJ Giteau (Australia)		Perth 2009
20	JP Wilkinson, England (1c, 4p, 2d)		Perth 2003	2	JD O'Connor (Australia)		Pretoria 2010
20	DW Carter, New Zealand (4c, 3p)		Pretoria 2006	2	G North (Wales)		Cardiff 2010
20	SM Jones, British Isles (1c, 5p, 1d)		Pretoria 2009	2	ZR Guildford (New Zealand)		Wellington 2011
20	MJ Giteau, Australia (2t, 2c, 2p)		Perth 2009	2	CS Jane (New Zealand)		Wellington 2011
				2	BR Youngs (England)		Johannesburg 2012
				2	KJ Read (New Zealand)		Auckland 2013
				2	LJ Messam (New Zealand)		Johannesburg 2013

Most tries by a player against SA

2	HS Sugars (Ireland)		Belfast 1906
2	JL Sullivan (New Zealand)		Christchurch 1937
2	IST Smith (New Zealand)		Auckland 1965
2	B Dauga (France)		Bordeaux 1968
2	JJ Williams (British Isles)		Pretoria 1974
2	JJ Williams (British Isles)		Port Elizabeth 1974
2	J-L Averous (France)		Pretoria 1977
2	PV Carozza (Australia)		Cape Town 1992
2	A Penaud (France)		Lyon 1992
2	JS Little (Australia)		Brisbane 1993
2	JW Wilson (New Zealand)		Pretoria 1996
2	FE Bunce (New Zealand)		Johannesburg 1997
2	BN Tune (Australia)		Brisbane 1997
2	CM Cullen (New Zealand)		Auckland 1997
2	JW Roff (Australia)		Brisbane 1999
2	CM Cullen (New Zealand)		Pretoria 1999
2	SA Mortlock (Australia)		Melbourne 2000
2	CM Cullen (New Zealand)		Christchurch 2000
2	CM Cullen (New Zealand)		Johannesburg 2000
2	JF Umaga (New Zealand)		Johannesburg 2000
2	CE Latham (Australia)		Brisbane 2000
2	WJH Greenwood (England)		Twickenham 2000
2	JT Rokocoko (New Zealand)		Pretoria 2003
2	DC Howlett (New Zealand)		Pretoria 2003
2	S Sivivatu (Pacific Islands)		Gosford 2004

Most conversions by a player against SA

5	SA Mortlock (Australia)		Brisbane 2006
4	A Cameron (British Isles)		Johannesburg 1955
4	PE McLean (World Team)		Pretoria 1977
4	CJ Spencer (New Zealand)		Auckland 1997
4	AP Mehrtens (New Zealand)		Johannesburg 2000
4	CJ Spencer (New Zealand)		Pretoria 2003
4	DW Carter (New Zealand)		Pretoria 2006
4	MJ Giteau (Australia)		Pretoria 2010
4	MJ Giteau (Australia)		Bloemfontein 2010
4	JD O'Connor		Sydney 2011

Most penalty goals by a player against SA

8	MC Burke (Australia)		Twickenham 1999
8	JP Wilkinson (England)		Bloemfontein 2000
7	AP Mehrtens (New Zealand)		Pretoria 1999
6	JP Wilkinson (England)		Twickenham 2000
6	G Merceron (France)		Johannesburg 2001
6	DW Carter (New Zealand)		Dunedin 2008
6	DA Parks (Scotland)		Edinburgh 2010

Most drop goals by a player against SA

2	G Camberabero (France)		Johannesburg 1967
2	P Bennett (British Isles)		Port Elizabeth 1974
2	JP Wilkinson (England)		Perth 2003

TEAM SEASON RECORDS
Most points scored

					397	14 tests	28.4 per game	2010
658	17 tests	38.7 per game	2007		361	12 tests	30.1 per game	1998
535	13 tests	41.2 per game	1997		360	13 tests	27.7 per game	2008
447	13 tests	34.4 per game	1999		352	13 tests	27.1 per game	1996
416	12 tests	34.7 per game	2005		338	12 tests	28.2 per game	2003
408	13 tests	31.4 per game	2004		308	10 tests	30.8 per game	1995
404	12 tests	33.7 per game	2013		301	12 tests	25.1 per game	2000

SPRINGBOK RECORDS

Most tries scored
81	17 tests	4.8 per game	2007
74	13 tests	5.7 per game	1997
52	13 tests	4.0 per game	1999

Most conversions
62	17 tests	3.7 per game	2007
54	13 tests	4.2 per game	1997

Most penalty goals
46	14 tests	3.3 per game	2010
42	12 tests	3.5 per game	2009
41	17 tests	2.4 per game	2007
40	13 tests	3.1 per game	1996

Most drop goals
8	13 tests	1999

Most consecutive Test wins
17	23 August 1997 to 28 November 1998

Most consecutive Test defeats
7	25 July 1964 to 21 August 1965

Most consecutive Tests without conceding a try
5	1999

Most consecutive Tests without scoring a try
4	1891 to 1896 & 1972 to 1974

PLAYER SEASON RECORDS

Most points
219	PC Montgomery in 14 tests (5t, 52c, 30p)	2007
185	M Steyn in 13 tests (3t, 25c, 40p)	2010
158	PC Montgomery in 12 tests (1t, 24c, 32p, 3d)	2005
154	PC Montgomery in 11 tests (1t, 28c, 31p)	2004
150	M Steyn in 12 tests (1t, 29c, 29p)	2013
137	M Steyn in 12 tests (1t, 12c, 31p, 5d)	2009
136	AJJ van Straaten in 11 tests (2t, 12c, 34p)	2000
120	LJ Koen in 11 tests (15c, 28p, 2d)	2003
112	JT Stransky in 9 tests (2t, 12c, 23p, 3d)	1995
111	PC Montgomery in 12 tests (2t, 25c, 17p)	1998
102	JH de Beer in 6 tests (18c, 16p, 6d)	1999
102	AS Pretorius in 10 tests (2t, 22c, 15p, 1d)	2002

Most tries
13	BG Habana in 11 tests	2007
12	BG Habana in 12 tests	2005
10	PWG Rossouw in 11 tests	1997
9	CS Terblanche in 12 tests	1998
9	J Fourie in 12 tests	2007
8	JT Small in 7 tests	1993
8	CM Williams in 6 tests	1995
8	PC Montgomery in 10 tests	1997
8	JH van der Westhuizen in 12 tests	1998
8	JH Smith in 13 tests	2007

Most conversions
52	PC Montgomery in 14 tests	2007
29	M Steyn in 12 tests	2013
28	PC Montgomery in 11 tests	2004
25	PC Montgomery in 12 tests	1998
25	M Steyn in 13 tests	2010
24	PC Montgomery in 12 tests	2005
23	HW Honiball in 12 tests	1997
22	AS Pretorius in 10 tests	2002

Most penalty goals
40	M Steyn in 13 tests	2010
34	AJJ van Straaten in 11 tests	2000
32	PC Montgomery in 12 tests	2005
31	PC Montgomery in 11 tests	2004
31	M Steyn in 12 tests	2009
30	PC Montgomery in 14 tests	2007

Most drop goals
6	HE Botha in 9 tests	1980
6	JH de Beer in 6 tests	1999
5	HE Botha in 6 tests	1981
5	AS Pretorius in 6 tests	2006
5	M Steyn in 12 tests	2009

André Pretorius in 2006.
Duif du Toit/Gallo Images

CAREER RECORDS

Most Test match appearances

111	JW Smit	2000-2011
110	V Matfield	2001-2011
102	PC Montgomery	1997-2008
96	J de Villiers	2002-2013
95	BG Habana	2004-2013
89	JH van der Westhuizen	1993-2003
80	JP du Randt	1994-2007
78	JP Botha	2002-2013
77	MG Andrews	1994-2001
75	CJ van der Linde	2002-2011
74	R Pienaar	2006-2013
72	J Fourie	2003-2013
69	JH Smith	2003-2010
68	SWP Burger	2003-2011
67	PF du Preez	2004-2013
66	AG Venter	1996-2001
64	BJ Paulse	1999-2007
63	DJ Rossouw	2003-2011
57	BW du Plessis	2007-2013
54	A-H le Roux	1994-2002
54	M Steyn	2009-2013
53	FPL Steyn	2006-2012
53	PJ Spies	2006-2013
53	T Mtawarira	2008-2013
52	JC van Niekerk	2001-2010
51	PA van den Berg	1999-2007
51	JN du Plessis	2007-2013
51	J-PR Pietersen	2006-2013

Most appearances in all Springbok matches

114	V Matfield	2001-2011
112	JW Smit	2000-2011
111	JH van der Westhuizen	1993-2003
104	PC Montgomery	1997-2008
97	BG Habana	2004-2013
96	J de Villiers	2002-2013
87	FCH du Preez	1961-1971
85	JP du Randt	1994-2007
79	CJ van der Linde	2002-2011
79	R Pienaar	2006-2013
78	JP Botha	2002-2013
75	JFK Marais	1963-1974
74	JH Ellis	1965-1976
74	BJ Paulse	1999-2007
71	JL Gainsford	1960-1967
71	JH Smith	2003-2010
71	J Fourie	2003-2011
70	AG Venter	1996-2001

Most points in Test matches

893	PC Montgomery (102 tests)	1997-2008
636	M Steyn (54 tests)	2009-2013
312	HE Botha (28 tests)	1980-1992
265	BG Habana (95 tests)	2004-2013
240	JT Stransky (22 tests)	1993-1996
221	AJJ van Straaten (21 tests)	1999-2001
190	JH van der Westhuizen (89 tests)	1993-2003
181	JH de Beer (13 tests)	1997-1999
171	AS Pretorius (31 tests)	2002-2007
160	J Fourie (69 tests)	2003-2011
156	HW Honiball (35 tests)	1993-1999
154	AD James (42 tests)	2001-2011

Most points in all Springbok matches

906	PC Montgomery (104 matches)	1997-2008
636	M Steyn (54 matches)	2009-2013
485	HE Botha (40 matches)	1980-1992
329	JT Stransky (36 matches)	1993-1996
294	AJJ van Straaten (27 matches)	1999-2001
293	GH Brand (46 matches)	1928-1938
280	JH van der Westhuizen (111 matches)	1993-2003
265	BG Habana (97 matches)	2004-2013
258	AJ Joubert (49 matches)	1989-1997
240	PJ Visagie (44 matches)	1967-1971
201	K Oxlee (48 matches)	1960-1965

Most tries in Test matches

53	BG Habana (95 tests)	2004-2013
38	JH van der Westhuizen (89 tests)	1993-2003
32	J Fourie (72 tests)	2003-2013
26	BJ Paulse (64 tests)	1999-2007
25	PC Montgomery (102 tests)	1997-2008
25	J de Villiers (96 tests)	2002-2013
21	PWG Rossouw (43 tests)	1997-2003
20	JT Small (47 tests)	1992-1997
19	DM Gerber (24 tests)	1980-1992
19	CS Terblanche (37 tests)	1998-2003

Most tries in all Springbok matches

56	JH van der Westhuizen (111 matches)	1993-2003
53	BG Habana (97 matches)	2004-2013
44	JP Engelbrecht (67 matches)	1960-1969
39	BJ Paulse (74 matches)	1999-2007
32	JH Ellis (74 matches)	1965-1976
32	J Fourie (74 matches)	2003-2013
31	JL Gainsford (71 matches)	1960-1967

SPRINGBOK RECORDS

Most conversions in Test matches
153	PC Montgomery (102 tests)	1997-2008
88	M Steyn (54 matches)	2009-2013
50	HE Botha (28 tests)	1980-1992
38	HW Honiball (35 tests)	1993-1999
33	JH de Beer (13 tests)	1997-1999
31	AS Pretorius (31 tests)	2002-2007
30	JT Stransky (22 tests)	1993-1996

Most conversions in all Springbok matches
157	PC Montgomery (104 matches)	1997-2008
100	GH Brand (46 matches)	1928-1938
91	HE Botha (40 matches)	1980-1992
88	M Steyn (54 matches)	2009-2013
55	JT Stransky (36 matches)	1993-1996

Most penalty goals in Test matches
148	PC Montgomery (102 tests)	1997-2008
132	M Steyn (54 tests)	2009-2013
55	AJJ van Straaten (21 tests)	1999-2001
50	HE Botha (28 tests)	1980-1992
47	JT Stransky (22 tests)	1993-1996
31	LJ Koen (15 tests)	2000-2003
28	AD James (42 tests)	2001-2011
27	JH de Beer (13 tests)	1997-1999
25	HW Honiball (35 tests)	1993-1999
25	AS Pretorius (31 tests)	2002-2007

Most penalty goals in all Springbok matches
148	PC Montgomery (104 matches)	1997-2008
88	M Steyn (54 matches)	2009-2013
66	HE Botha (40 matches)	1980-1992
59	AJJ van Straaten (27 matches)	1999-2001
55	JT Stransky (36 matches)	1993-1996

Most drop goals in Test matches
18	HE Botha (28 tests)	1980-1992
8	JH de Beer (13 tests)	1997-1999
8	AS Pretorius (31 tests)	2002-2007
8	M Steyn (54 tests)	2009-2013
6	PC Montgomery (102 tests)	1997-2008
5	JD Brewis (10 tests)	1949-1953
5	PJ Visagie (25 tests)	1967-1971

Most drop goals in all Springbok matches
27	HE Botha (40 matches)	1980-1992
8	BL Osler (30 matches)	1924-1933
8	PJ Visagie (44 matches)	1967-1971
8	JH de Beer (14 matches)	1997-1999
8	AS Pretorius (33 matches)	2002-2007
8	M Steyn (54 tests)	2009-2013

Most Test match appearances against SA
30	GM Gregan (Australia)	1994-2007
25	NC Sharpe (Australia)	2002-2012
23	SJ Larkham (Australia)	1996-2007
22	JW Marshall (New Zealand)	1995-2005
22	GB Smith (Australia)	2000-2009
22	JM Muliaina (New Zealand)	2003-2011
22	RH McCaw (New Zealand)	2002-2013
22	KF Mealamu (New Zealand)	2003-2013
21	MJ Giteau (Australia)	2002-2010
20	RD Elsom (Australia)	2005-2011

Most points in Tests against SA
245	DW Carter (New Zealand) (18 tests)	2003-2013
209	AP Mehrtens (New Zealand) (16 tests)	1995-2004
159	MJ Giteau (Australia) (21 tests)	2002-2010
150	SA Mortlock (Australia) (18 tests)	2000-2009
140	MC Burke (Australia) (16 tests)	1993-2004
127	JP Wilkinson (England) (9 tests)	1998-2007
113	NR Jenkins (Wales & BI) (11 tests)	1994-2002

Most tries in Tests against SA
10	CM Cullen (New Zealand) (15 tests)	1996-2002
9	JT Rokocoko (New Zealand) (15 tests)	2003-2010
9	MJ Giteau (Australia) (21 Tests)	2002-2010
7	SA Mortlock (Australia) (18 tests)	2000-2009
6	SJ Larkham (Australia) (23 tests)	1996-2007
5	JW Wilson (New Zealand) (15 tests)	1993-2001
5	JW Roff (Australia) (15 tests)	1995-2004
5	JW Marshall (New Zealand) (22 tests)	1995-2005
5	BN Tune (Australia) (13 tests)	1996-2002
5	CE Latham (Australia) (15 tests)	1998-2007
5	DC Howlett (New Zealand) (11 tests)	2000-2007
5	JD O'Connor (Australia) (10 tests)	2008-2013

Most conversions in Tests against SA
31	DW Carter (New Zealand) (17 tests)	2003-2013
21	MJ Giteau (Australia) (21 tests)	2002-2010
19	AP Mehrtens (New Zealand) (16 tests)	1995-2004
17	SA Mortlock (Australia) (18 tests)	2000-2009
16	SM Jones (Wales & BI) (13 tests)	1998-2010
12	MC Burke (Australia) (16 tests)	1993-2004
12	CJ Spencer (New Zealand) (7 tests)	1997-2004

SPRINGBOK RECORDS

Most penalty goals in Tests against SA
54	DW Carter (New Zealand) (18 tests)		2003-2013
53	AP Mehrtens (New Zealand) (16 tests)		1995-2004
36	MC Burke (Australia) (16 tests)		1993-2004
36	JP Wilkinson (England) (9 tests)		1998-2007
35	NR Jenkins (Wales & BI) (11 tests)		1994-2002
28	SM Jones (Wales & BI) (13 tests)		1998-2010
27	SA Mortlock (Australia) (18 tests)		2000-2009

Most drop goals in Tests against SA
4	AP Mehrtens (New Zealand) (16 tests)	1995-2004
3	JP Wilkinson (England) (9 tests)	1998-2007
3	RJR O'Gara (Ireland) (7 tests)	2000-2012

MISCELLANEOUS RECORDS

Most Test match appearances in each position
Position	Player	Appearances
Fullback	PC Montgomery [1]	87
Wing	BG Habana [2]	94
Centre	J de Villiers [3]	81
Flyhalf	M Steyn [4]	52
Scrumhalf	JH van der Westhuizen [5]	87
Prop	JP du Randt	80
Hooker	JW Smit [6]	96
Lock	V Matfield	110
Flank	SWP Burger [7]	66
Eighthman	PJ Spies [8]	48
Captain	JW Smit	83

[1] Also made nine appearances at centre, five at flyhalf and one at wing. [2] Also made one appearance at centre. [3] Also made 15 appearances at wing. [4] Also made one appearance as a fullback and one as a centre. [5] Also made two appearances as replacement wing. [6] Also made two appearances as replacement prop and thirteen at prop in the starting 15. [7] Also made two appearances at No 8. [8] Also made four appearances as a flank and one as replacement wing.

Most consecutive Test match appearances
46	JW Smit (hooker)	2003-2007
39	GH Teichmann (eighthman)	1996-1999
30	M Steyn (Flyhalf/fullback)	2010-2012
28	V Matfield (lock)	2008-2010
26	AH Snyman (centre/wing)	1996-1998
26	AN Vos (eighthman/flank)	1999-2001
25	J de Villiers (centre)	2011-2013

Most Test match tries in each position
Position	Tries	Player	Tests
Fullback	18	PC Montgomery	*87 tests
Wing	53	BG Habana	*94 tests
Centre	28	J Fourie	*61 tests
Flyhalf	8	M Steyn	*52 tests
Scrumhalf	38	JH van der Westhuizen	*87 tests
Prop	6	GG Steenkamp	49 tests
Hooker	8	BW du Plessis	57 tests
Lock	12	MG Andrews	*75 tests
Flank	11	SWP Burger	*66 tests
	11	JH Smith	*59 tests
Eighthman	7	PJ Spies	*48 tests

*Excludes Tests played in other positions

Most consecutive Test match appearances by position
Position	Player	Appearances
Fullback	PC Montgomery (1997-1999)	24
Wing	PWG Rossouw (1997-1999)	24
Centre	J de Villiers (2011-2013)	25
Flyhalf	BL Osler (1924-1933)	17
	HE Botha (1980-1982)	17
	JNB van der Westhuyzen (2004-2005)	17
Scrumhalf	PF du Preez (2004-2006)	21
Prop	A-H le Roux (1998-1999)	25
Hooker	JW Smit (2003-2007)	46
Lock	V Matfield (2008-2010)	28
Flank	RJ Kruger (1995-1997)	22
Eighthman	GH Teichmann (1996-1999)	39
Captain	JW Smit (2004-2007)	43

Longest international career
14 seasons	JP du Randt (1994-2007)	13 years, 12 days
13 seasons	HE Botha (1980-1992)	12 years, 202 days
13 seasons	DM Gerber (1980-1992)	12 years, 27 days
13 seasons	BH Heatlie (1891-1903)	12 years, 14 days
13 seasons	JM Powell (1891-1903)	12 years, 7 days

Most Test matches as a replacement
Replacements	Player	Total Tests
43	A-H le Roux	54
35	R Pienaar	63
35	CJ van der Linde	75
28	PA van den Berg	51
23	PR van der Merwe	34
20	DJ Rossouw	63
19	MC Ralepelle	21

SPRINGBOK RECORDS

Most Test matches as an unused substitute

		Test caps
22	W Swanepoel	20
20	AE Drotské	26
16	JB Neethling	8
15	JH van der Westhuizen	89
14	DJJ de Vos	3
14	J Dalton	43
14	OA Roux	7
12	HM Shimange	9
12	JP Roux	12

Oldest living Springboks*

P Malan	b 13/02/1919	94 years, 321 days
C Moss	b 12/02/1925	88 years, 322 days
MT Lategan	b 29/09/1925	88 years, 93 days

**Age as at 31/12/2013*

Most appearances as a Test match combination

Fullback/wings	PC Montgomery, CS Terblanche & PWG Rossouw (1998-1999)	13
Centres	J de Villiers & J Fourie (2005-2013)	29
Halfbacks	JH van der Westhuizen & HW Honiball (1993-1999)	24
Locks	V Matfield & JP Botha (2003-2010)	62*
Front row	T Mtawarira, BW du Plessis, JN du Plessis (2008-2013)	15
Loose forwards	AG Venter, RJ Kruger & GH Teichmann (1996-1997)	14
	AG Venter, J Erasmus & GH Teichmann (1997-1999)	14

World record

Springboks sent off in Tests (7)

Player	Opponent	Referee	Venue	Date
JT Small	vs. Australia	EF Morrison (England)	Brisbane	1993
J Dalton	vs. Canada	DTM McHugh (Ireland)	Port Elizabeth	1995
AG Venter	vs. New Zealand	WD Bevan (Wales)	Auckland	1997
B Venter	vs. Uruguay	PL Marshall (Australia)	Glasgow	1999
MC Joubert	vs. Australia	PD O'Brien (New Zealand)	Johannesburg	2002
JJ Labuschagne	vs. England	PD O'Brien (New Zealand)	Twickenham	2002
PC Montgomery*	vs Wales	SJ Dickinson (Australia)	Cardiff	2005
BW du Plessis **	vs. New Zealand	R Poite (France)	Auckland	2013

Montgomery's first yellow card was subsequently dismissed by a disciplinary commission and his red card rescinded.
** Du Plessis' first yellow card was subsequently dismissed by a disciplinary commission and his red card recinded.

Springboks yellow-carded in Tests (76)

Player	Opponent	Referee	Venue	Date
RF Fleck	vs. Canada	A Lewis (Ireland)	East London	2000
W Meyer	vs. England	CJ Hawke (New Zealand)	Pretoria	2000
JH van der Westhuizen	vs. England	SJ Dickinson (Australia)	Bloemfontein	2000
CPJ Krige	vs. New Zealand	C White (England)	Christchurch	2000
RB Kempson	vs. Ireland	SJD Lander (England)	Dublin	2000
GM Delport	vs. Ireland	SJD Lander (England)	Dublin	2000
RF Fleck	vs. Wales	SR Walsh (New Zealand)	Cardiff	2000
MG Andrews	vs. France	C White (England)	Durban	2001
D Barry	vs. France	C White (England)	Durban	2001
AD James	vs. Australia	SR Walsh (New Zealand)	Perth	2001
RB Skinstad	vs. Australia	SR Walsh (New Zealand)	Perth	2001
AJJ van Straaten	vs. Italy	WD Erickson (Australia)	Genoa	2001
IJ Visagie	vs. USA	D Méné (France)	Houston	2001
W Meyer	vs. Wales	AJ Spreadbury (England)	Cape Town	2002
MC Joubert	vs. New Zealand	SJ Dickinson (Australia)	Wellington	2002
WW Greeff	vs. Australia	SJD Lander (England)	Brisbane	2002
SJ Rautenbach	vs. Australia	Retrospectively	Brisbane	2002

SPRINGBOK RECORDS

Player	Opponent	Referee	Venue	Year
D Barry	vs. Australia	PD O'Brien (New Zealand)	Johannesburg	2002
JP Botha	vs. France	ACP Rolland (Ireland)	Marseilles	2002
V Matfield	vs. Scotland	J Jutge (France)	Durban	2003
JH van der Westhuizen	vs. Scotland	J Jutge (France)	Durban	2003
RB Kempson	vs. Scotland	S Young (Australia)	Johannesburg	2003
D Barry	vs. Australia	SR Walsh (New Zealand)	Cape Town	2003
D Coetzee	vs. Australia	PD O'Brien (New Zealand)	Brisbane	2003
RB Kempson	vs. Australia	PD O'Brien (New Zealand)	Brisbane	2003
H Scholtz	vs. Georgia	SJ Dickinson (Australia)	Sydney	2003
SWP Burger	vs. Ireland	AJ Spreadbury (England)	Bloemfontein	2004
W Julies	vs. Ireland	J Jutge (France)	Cape Town	2004
PC Montgomery	vs. Australia	PD O'Brien (New Zealand)	Durban	2004
BJ Paulse	vs. Australia	PD O'Brien (New Zealand)	Durban	2004
SWP Burger	vs. Wales	PD O'Brien (New Zealand)	Cardiff	2004
SWP Burger	vs. Ireland	PG Honiss (New Zealand)	Dublin	2004
V Matfield	vs. Scotland	N Williams (Wales)	Edinburgh	2004
JP Botha	vs. Scotland	N Williams (Wales)	Edinburgh	2004
SWP Burger	vs. France	D Courtney (Ireland)	Port Elizabeth	2005
BJ Paulse	vs. Australia	SR Walsh (New Zealand)	Johannesburg	2005
SWP Burger	vs. Australia	SR Walsh (New Zealand)	Johannesburg	2005
BJ Paulse	vs. Australia	ACP Rolland (Ireland)	Perth	2005
J de Villiers	vs. Argentina	AJ Spreadbury (England)	Buenos Aires	2005
PC Montgomery	vs. Wales	SJ Dickinson (Australia)	Cardiff	2005
V Matfield	vs. Australia	PG Honiss (New Zealand)	Brisbane	2006
J de Villiers	vs. England	SR Walsh (New Zealand)	Twickenham	2006
BG Habana	vs. England	J Jutge (France)	Pretoria	2007
RB Skinstad	vs. Samoa	M Changleng (Scotland)	Johannesburg	2007
PJ Spies	vs. Australia	W Barnes (England)	Cape Town	2007
PJ Wannenburg	vs. New Zealand	ACP Rolland (Ireland)	Durban	2007
GvG Botha	vs. Australia	PG Honiss (New Zealand)	Sydney	2007
GJ Muller	vs. Australia	PG Honiss (New Zealand)	Sydney	2007
PJ Wannenburg	vs. New Zealand	SJ Dickinson (Australia)	Christchurch	2007
FPL Steyn	vs. Tonga	W Barnes (England)	Lens	2007
BG Habana	vs. Tonga	W Barnes (England)	Lens	2007
JH Smith	vs. Argentina	SR Walsh (New Zealand)	Paris	2007
PA van den Berg	vs. Wales	CR White (England)	Cardiff	2007
BW du Plessis	vs. Wales	CR White (England)	Cardiff	2007
CJ van der Linde	vs. Wales	D Pearson (England)	Bloemfontein	2008
V Matfield	vs. New Zealand	M Goddard (Australia)	Dunedin	2008
J Fourie	vs. Wales	ACP Rolland (Ireland)	Cardiff	2008
T Mtawarira	vs. England	N Owens (Wales)	Twickenham	2008
CA Jantjes	vs. England	N Owens (Wales)	Twickenham	2008
SWP Burger	vs. British Isles	C Berdos (France)	Pretoria	2009
J-PR Pietersen	vs. New Zealand	N Owens (Wales)	Durban	2009
JP Botha	vs. New Zealand	N Owens (Wales)	Durban	2009
M Steyn	vs. France	W Barnes (England)	Toulouse	2009
R Kankowski	vs. France	W Barnes (England)	Toulouse	2009
PR van der Merwe	vs France	BJ Lawrence (New Zealand)	Cape Town	2010
JP Botha	vs New Zealand	DA Lewis (Ireland)	Auckland	2010
DJ Rossouw	vs New Zealand	ACP Rolland (Ireland)	Wellington	2010

SPRINGBOK RECORDS

J Fourie	vs Australia	G Clancy (Ireland)	Brisbane	2010
BJ Botha	vs Australia	G Clancy (Ireland)	Brisbane	2010
BG Habana	vs Ireland	N Owens (Wales)	Dublin	2010
JW Smit	vs Samoa	N Owens (Wales)	Albany	2011
T Mtawarira	vs. Australia	N Owens (Wales)	Perth	2012
MD Greyling	vs. New Zealand	GJ Clancy (Ireland)	Dunedin	2012
J-PR Pietersen	vs. Ireland	W Barnes (England)	Dublin	2012
PR van der Merwe	vs. Scotland	GJ Clancy (Ireland)	Edinburgh	2012
BA Basson	vs. Italy	P Gauzere (France)	Durban	2013
BG Habana	vs. Samoa	P Gauzere (France)	Pretoria	2013
WS Alberts	vs. Australia	GJ Clancy (Ireland)	Brisbane	2013
BW du Plessis	vs. New Zealand	R Poite (France)	Auckland	2013
PR van der Merwe	vs. Australia	J Garces (France)	Cape Town	2013
DJ Vermeulen	vs. Australia	J Garces (France)	Cape Town	2013

Players sent off in Tests against South Africa (4)

Player	Team	Referee	Venue	Date
R Snow	Canada	DTM McHugh (Ireland)	Port Elizabeth	1995
GL Rees	Canada	DTM McHugh (Ireland)	Port Elizabeth	1995
GR Jenkins	Wales	J Dumé (France)	Johannesburg	1995
PW Williams	Samoa	N Owens (France)	Albany	2011
AT Tuilagi	Samoa	P Gauzere (France)	Pretoria	2013

Players yellow-carded in Tests against South Africa (37)

Player	Team	Referee	Venue	Date
PBT Greening	England	CJ Hawke (New Zealand)	Pretoria	2000
J Leonard	England	SJ Dickinson (Australia)	Bloemfontein	2000
LBN Dallaglio	England	SJ Dickinson (Australia)	Bloemfontein	2000
MJ Cockbain	Australia	PG Honiss (New Zealand)	Durban	2000
PM Clohessy	Ireland	SJD Lander (England)	Dublin	2000
O Magne	France	C White (England)	Durban	2001
A Lo Cicero	Italy	WD Erickson (Australia)	Genoa	2001
E Reed	USA	D Méné (France)	Houston	2001
T Leota	Samoa	AJ Cole (Australia)	Pretoria	2002
JBG Harrison	Australia	SJD Lander (England)	Brisbane	2002
JA Paul	Australia	SJD Lander (England)	Brisbane	2002
R Alvarez	Argentina	N Williams (Wales)	Port Elizabeth	2003
LD Tuqiri	Australia	Retrospectively	Cape Town	2003
KJ Meeuws	New Zealand	ACP Rolland (Ireland)	Pretoria	2003
M Kvirikashvili	Georgia	SJ Dickinson (Australia)	Sydney	2003
R Corrigan	Ireland	J Jutge (France)	Cape Town	2004
CL Horsman	Wales	SJ Dickinson (Australia)	Cardiff	2005
S So'oalo	Samoa	M Changleng (Scotland)	Johannesburg	2007
JH Va'a	Samoa	M Changleng (Scotland)	Johannesburg	2007
J Vaka	Tonga	W Barnes (England)	Lens	2007
S Rabeni	Fiji	PG Honiss (New Zealand)	Marseille	2007
F Contepomi	Argentina	SR Walsh (New Zealand)	Paris	2007
R Hibbard	Wales	D Pearson (England)	Bloemfontein	2008
C-A Del Fava	Italy	G Clancey (Ireland)	Cape Town	2008
SD Shaw	British Isles	SJ Dickinson (Australia)	Johannesburg	2009

SPRINGBOK RECORDS

IB Ross	New Zealand	N Owens (Wales)	Durban	2009
MJ Giteau	Australia	ACP Rolland (Ireland)	Cape Town	2009
RN Brown	Australia	ACP Rolland (Ireland)	Cape Town	2009
GB Smith	Australia	ACP Rolland (Ireland)	Cape Town	2009
S Favaro	Italy	ACP Rolland (Ireland)	Udine	2009
D Yachvili	France	BJ Lawrence (New Zealand)	Cape Town	2010
QS Cooper	Australia	G Clancy (Ireland)	Brisbane	2010
SM Fainga'a	Australia	W Barnes (England)	Bloemfontein	2010
DM Hartley	England	SR Walsh (Australia)	Port Elizabeth	2012
JA Slipper	Australia	ACP Rolland (Ireland)	Pretoria	2012
IJA Dagg	New Zealand	ACP Rolland (Ireland)	Soweto	2012
JPR Heaslip	Ireland	W Barnes (England)	Dublin	2012
M Bortolami	Italy	P Gauzere (France)	Durban	2013
JL Hamilton	Scotland	R Poite (France)	Nelspruit	2013
L Mulipola	Samoa	P Gauzere (France)	Pretoria	2013
E Guinazu	Argentina	C Pollock (NZ)	Soweto	2013
L Senatore	Argentina	C Pollock (NZ)	Soweto	2013
MK Hooper	Australia	G Clancy (Ireland)	Brisbane	2013
KJ Read	New Zealand	R Poite (France)	Auckland	2013
MA Nonu	New Zealand	R Poite (France)	Auckland	2013
MK Hooper	Australia	J Garces (France)	Cape Town	2013
S Rtimani	Australia	J Garces (France)	Cape Town	2013
LJ Messam	New Zealand	N Owens (Wales)	Johannesburg	2013
BJ Franks	New Zealand	N Owens (Wales)	Johannesburg	2013
GD Jenkins	Wales	ACP Rolland (Ireland)	Cardiff	2013
T Domingo	France	W Barnes (England)	Paris	2013

International referees in Tests involving South Africa

Tests	Referee	Country	SA Won	SA Lost	Drawn	% Wins
17	ACP Rolland	Ireland	10	7	-	63%
14	SR Walsh	NZ/Australia	10	1	3	77%
12	PD O'Brien	New Zealand	7	5	-	58%
11	SJ Dickinson	Australia	3	8	-	27%
10	CJ Hawke	New Zealand	7	3	-	70%
9	WD Bevan	Wales	7	2	-	78%
9	EF Morrison	England	3	6	-	33%
9	N Owens	Wales	6	3	-	67%
9	W Barnes	England	6	3	-	67%
8	PG Honiss	New Zealand	3	5	-	38%
8	PL Marshall	Australia	3	5	-	38%
8	CR White	England	6	2	-	75%
8	DA Lewis	Ireland	4	3	1	50%

Highest winning percentage as a Springbok (20 or more Tests)

	Played	Won	Lost	Drawn	% Wins
AC Garvey	28	24	4	0	86%
M du Plessis	22	18	4	0	82%
J Dalton	43	35	8	0	81%
MTS Stofberg	21	17	4	0	81%
JS Germishuys	20	16	4	0	80%

SPRINGBOK RECORDS

Lowest winning percentage as a Springbok (20 or more Tests)

	Played	Won	Lost	Drawn	% Wins
AJJ van Straaten	21	9	11	1	43%
D Barry	39	18	20	1	46%
CPJ Krige	39	18	21	0	46%
W Olivier	34	16	18	0	47%
EP Andrews	23	11	11	1	48%
IJ Visagie	29	14	14	1	48%

SPRINGBOK CAPTAINS & COACHES

TEST CAPTAINS 1891-2013

	CAPTAIN	TESTS AS CAPTAIN (TOTAL TESTS)	DEBUT AS CAPTAIN	DEBUT MATCH
1	HH Castens - Prop, Western Province	1 (1)	1891	British Isles 1st test
2	RCD Snedden - Prop, Griqualand West	1 (1)	1891	British Isles 2nd test
3	AR Richards - Flyhalf, Western Province	1 (3)	1891	British Isles 3rd test
4	FTD Aston - Centre & wing, Transvaal	3 (4)	1896	British Isles 1st test
5	BH Heatlie - Prop & lock, Western Province	2 (6)	1896	British Isles 4th test
6	A Frew - Prop, Transvaal	1 (1)	1903	British Isles 1st test
7	JM Powell - Flyhalf, Griqualand West	1 (4)	1903	British Isles 2nd test
8	HW Carolin - Flyhalf, Western Province	1 (3)	1906	Scotland
9	PJ Roos - Prop, Western Province	3 (4)	1906	Ireland
10	DFT Morkel - Prop, Transvaal	2 (9)	1910	British Isles 1st test
11	WA Millar - No. 8 & flank, Western Province	5 (6)	1910	British Isles 2nd test
12	FJ Dobbin - Scrumhalf, Griqualand West	1 (9)	1912	Scotland
13	TB Pienaar - Prop, Western Province	0 (0)	1921	Did not play in tests
14	WH Morkel - No. 8, Transvaal	3 (9)	1921	New Zealand 1st test
15	PK Albertyn - Centre, South Western Districts	4 (4)	1924	British Isles 1st test
16	PJ Mostert - Prop & hooker, Western Province	4 (14)	1928	New Zealand 1st test
17	BL Osler - Flyhalf, Western Province	5 (17)	1931	Wales
18	PJ Nel - Lock & prop, Natal	8 (16)	1933	Australia 1st test
19	DH Craven - Flyhalf & scrumhalf, Eastern Province	4 (16)	1937	New Zealand 1st test
20	F du Plessis - Lock, Transvaal	3 (3)	1949	New Zealand 1st test
21	BJ Kenyon - Flank, Border	1 (1)	1949	New Zealand 4th test
22	HSV Muller - No. 8, Transvaal	9 (13)	1951	Scotland
23	SP Fry - Flank, Western Province	4 (13)	1955	British Isles 1st test
24	SS Viviers - Fullback & flyhalf	5 (5)	1956	Australia 1st test
25	JA du Rand - Lock, Northern Transvaal	1 (21)	1956	New Zealand 1st test
26	JT Claassen - Lock, Western Transvaal	9 (28)	1958	France 1st test
27	DC van Jaarsveldt - Flank, Rhodesia	1 (1)	1960	Scotland
28	RG Dryburgh - Fullback, Natal	2 (8)	1960	New Zealand 1st test
29	AS Malan - Lock, Transvaal	10 (16)	1960	New Zealand 3rd test
30	GF Malan - Hooker, Transvaal	4 (18)	1963	Australia 1st test
31	CM Smith - Scrumhalf, Orange Free State	4 (7)	1964	France
32	DJ de Villiers - Scrumhalf, Western Province	22 (25)	1965	New Zealand 1st test
33	TP Bedford - No. 8, Natal	3 (25)	1969	Australia 2nd test
34	JFK Marais - Prop, Eastern Province	11 (35)	1971	France 1st test
35	PJF Greyling - Flank, Transvaal	1 (25)	1972	England

SPRINGBOK RECORDS

TEST CAPTAINS 1891-2013

	CAPTAIN	TESTS AS CAPTAIN (TOTAL TESTS)	DEBUT AS CAPTAIN	DEBUT MATCH
36	M du Plessis - No. 8, Western Province	15 (22)	1975	France 1st test
37	MTS Stofberg - Flank, Northern Transvaal	4 (21)	1980	South America 1st test
38	W Claassen - No. 8, Natal	7 (7)	1981	Ireland 1st test
39	DJ Serfontein - Scrumhalf, Western Province	2 (19)	1984	South America & Sp. 1st test
40	HE Botha - Flyhalf, Northern Transvaal	9 (28)	1986	NZ Cavaliers 1st test
41	JC Breedt - No. 8, Transvaal	2 (8)	1989	World Team 1st test
42	JF Pienaar - Flank & No. 8, Transvaal	29 (29)	1993	France 1st test
43	CP Strauss - Flank, Western Province	1 (15)	1994	New Zealand 1st test
44	AJ Richter - No. 8, Northern Transvaal	1 (10)	1995	Romania
45	GH Teichmann - No. 8, Natal	36 (42)	1996	New Zealand 1st test
46	CPJ Krige - Flank, Western Province	18 (39)	1999	Italy 2nd test
47	J Erasmus - Flank, Golden Lions	1 (36)	1999	Australia 1st test
48	JH van der Westhuizen - Scrumhalf, Blue Bulls	10 (89)	1999	New Zealand 2nd test
49	AN Vos - No. 8, Golden Lions	16 (33)	1999	Spain
50	RB Skinstad - No. 8, Western Province	12 (42)	2001	Italy
51	JW Smit - Hooker, Natal	83 (111)	2003	Georgia
52	V Matfield - Lock, Blue Bulls	17 (110)	2007	New Zealand 1st test
53	GJ Muller - Lock, Natal	1 (24)	2007	New Zealand 2nd test
54	J de Villiers - Centre, Western Province	24 (96)	2012	England 1st test

WINNING PERCENTAGES OF SPRINGBOK CAPTAINS (10 OR MORE TESTS)

	PLAYER	Matches	Won	Drawn	Lost	Points For	Points Against
86,67%	M du Plessis	15	13	0	2	357	230
80,00%	JH van der Westhuizen	10	8	0	2	329	191
72,22%	GH Teichmann	36	26	0	10	1228	661
70,83%	J de Villiers	24	17	2	5	649	396
70,59%	V Matfield	17	12	0	5	499	250
65,52%	JF Pienaar	29	19	2	8	780	503
65,06%	JW Smit	83	54	1	28	2436	1668
56,25%	AN Vos	16	9	0	7	434	371
54,55%	JFK Marais	11	6	2	3	138	131
50,00%	AS Malan	10	5	2	3	67	50
50,00%	RB Skinstad	12	6	1	5	285	233
38,89%	CPJ Krige	18	7	0	11	495	502

Percentage of total Springbok points scored by a player during a Test career

	Player	Player points	Springbok points
50.73%	HE Botha	312	615
44,16%	M Steyn	636	1440
42.02%	AJJ van Straaten	221	526
39.47%	JT Stransky	240	608
38.68%	LJ Koen	135	349
35.46%	JH de Beer	181	510
34.39%	PJ Visagie	130	378
27.00%	PC Montgomery	893	3307

Percentage of total Springbok tries scored by a player during a Test career

	Player	Tries	Springbok tries
26.76%	DM Gerber	19	71
18,46%	BG Habana	53	287
13.97%	CS Terblanche	19	136
13.83%	BJ Paulse	26	188
13.11%	J Fourie	32	244
12.80%	PWG Rossouw	21	164
12.75%	JH van der Westhuizen	38	298
12.42%	JT Small	20	161

SPRINGBOK RECORDS

BIOGRAPHICAL FEATURES

Springbok relationships
Father & son	Ten sets	Last PR van der Merwe (1981-89) & PR van der Merwe (2010-2013)
Three brothers	Three sets	Last W (1980-82), CJ (1981-89) & MJ (1984-89) du Plessis
Two brothers	Thirty two sets	Last AK & OM Ndungane 2008

Brothers in Tests *(since World War II)*
Twice	HPJ & RP Bekker	1953
Once	ID & RJ McCallum	1974
Once	DSL & JCP Snyman	1974
Once	HE & DS Botha	1981
Twice	CJ & W du Plessis	1982
Eight times	CJ & MJ du Plessis	1984-1989
Twice	G & J Cronjé	2004
Thirty one times	JN & BW du Plessis	2007-2013

Tallest, shortest, heaviest, lightest
Tallest	A Bekker	2.08m (6ft 10in)
Shortest	TA Gentles	1.60m (5ft 3in)
Heaviest	RG Visagie	138kgs (21st 8lbs)
Lightest	WD Sendin	60kgs (9st 6lbs)

Youngest Springboks on Test debut
18 Years, 18 days	AJ Hartley	British Isles (3rd test)1891
19 Years, 8 days	DG Cope	British Isles (2nd test)1896
19 Years, 37 days	JA Loubser	British Isles (3rd test)1903
19 Years, 51 days	RCB van Ryneveld	British Isles (2nd test)1910
19 Years, 72 days	WJ Mills	British Isles (2nd test)1910
19 Years, 112 days	FG Turner	Australia (1st test)1933
19 Years, 126 days	BH Heatlie	British Isles (2nd test)1891
19 Years, 158 days	SC de Melker	British Isles (2nd test)1903

Oldest Springboks (in their final Test)
37 Years, 34 days	JN Ackermann	Australia (2nd test)2007
36 Years, 258 days	WH Morkel	New Zealand (3rd test)1921
35 Years, 277 days	D Lötter	Australia (2nd test)1993
35 Years, 252 days	FCH du Preez	Australia (3rd test)1971
35 Years, 208 days	PJ Geel	New Zealand (3rd test)1949
35 Years, 130 days	LC Moolman	NZ Cavaliers (4th test)1986

Least and most experienced Springbok starting XV since 1992

115 Caps - vs. Italy, Durban, 1999:
PC Montgomery (23); BJ Paulse (1), RF Fleck (1), JC Mulder (26), CS Terblanche (13); GS du Toit (2), DNB von Hoesslin (1); AN Vos (1), J Erasmus (18), CPJ Krige (0), CS Boome (1), PA van den Berg (1), W Meyer (1), AE Drotské (14), RB Kempson (12).

836 Caps - vs. Australia, Wellington, 2011:
P Lambie (10); J-PR Pietersen (41), J Fourie (68), J de Villiers (71), BG Habana (73); M Steyn (33), PF du Preez (61); PJ Spies (46), SWP Burger (67), HW Brüssow (19), V Matfield (109), DJ Rossouw (62), JN du Plessis (29), JW Smit (110), GG Steenkamp (37).
(This is the most experienced Springbok side of all time)

SPRINGBOK COACHES SINCE 1992

	First & Last Test	P	W	L	D	PF	PA	Diff	TF	TA	Win%
JG Williams	Aug 92 - Nov 92	5	1	4	0	79	130	-51	7	14	20.00%
GHH Sonnekus	Did not take up appointment										
IB McIntosh	June 93 - Aug 94	12	4	6	2	252	240	12	25	14	33.33%
GM Christie	Oct 94 - Nov 95	14	14	0	0	450	191	259	54	16	100.00%
AT Markgraaff	July 96 - Dec 96	13	8	5	0	352	260	92	38	21	61.54%
CJ du Plessis	June 97 - Aug 97	8	3	5	0	288	213	75	39	22	37.50%
NVH Mallett	Nov 97 - Aug 00	38	27	11	0	1251	678	573	152	49	71.05%
HJ Viljoen	Nov 00 - Dec 01	15	8	6	1	376	312	64	38	18	53.33%
RAW Straeuli	Jun 02 - Nov 03	23	12	11	0	622	598	24	71	61	52.17%
JA White	Jun 04 -Dec 07	54	36	17	1	1740	1097	643	194	110	66.67%
P de Villiers	Jun 08 - Oct 11	48	30	18	0	1262	921	341	126	87	62,50%
H Meyer	Jun 12 -	24	17	5	2	649	396	253	70	35	70,08%
South Africa's record since 1992		**254**	**160**	**88**	**6**	**7321**	**5036**	**2285**	**814**	**447**	**62,99%**

SPRINGBOK RECORDS

VENUES

LIST OF ALL 21 VENUES THAT HAVE HOSTED SPRINGBOK TESTS IN SOUTH AFRICA

		P	W	L	D	PF	PA	TF	TA	Ave.score	%Win
Rustenburg	Royal Bafokeng Sports Palace	1	1	0	0	21	20	2	2	21-20	100%
East London	Border Rugby Stadium	3	3	0	0	240	32	36	3	80-11	100%
Johannesburg	Wanderers (New)	1	1	0	0	24	9	3	1	24-9	100%
Witbank	Puma Stadium	1	1	0	0	29	13	4	1	29-13	100%
Nelspruit	Mbombela Stadium	1	1	0	0	30	17	3	2	30-17	100%
Port Elizabeth	EPRU Stadium	16	14	1	1	423	182	49	17	26-11	88%
Durban	Kingsmead	5	4	1	0	57	35	7	7	11-7	80%
Pretoria	Loftus Versfeld	32	24	8	0	1072	650	130	65	34-20	75%
Bloemfontein	Free State Stadium	18	13	4	1	504	307	57	28	28-17	72%
Johannesburg	Ellis Park	45	31	12	2	1184	719	148	66	26-15	69%
Cape Town	Newlands	50	34	14	2	966	601	125	64	19-12	68%
Durban	Kings Park	29	18	8	3	686	455	69	40	24-16	62%
Port Elizabeth	Crusader Ground	10	6	3	1	102	57	18	15	10-06	60%
Port Elizabeth	Nelson Mandela Bay Stadium	2	1	0	1	32	19	1	2	16-10	50%
Johannesburg	Wanderers (Old)	4	2	1	1	49	37	12	7	12-9	50%
Springs	PAM Brink Stadium	2	1	1	0	55	37	7	3	28-19	50%
Soweto	FNB Stadium	3	1	2	0	111	74	11	8	37-25	33%
Bloemfontein	Springbok Park	1	0	1	0	4	15	0	3	4-15	0%
Kimberley	Eclectic Ground	1	0	1	0	0	3	0	0	0-3	0%
Kimberley	KAC Ground	2	0	1	1	3	9	1	1	2-5	0%
Port Elizabeth	Cricket Club Ground	1	0	1	0	0	4	0	2	0-4	0%
		227	156	58	13	5592	3291	683	335	25-14	69%

LIST OF ALL 52 VENUES THAT HAVE HOSTED SPRINGBOK TESTS OUTSIDE SOUTH AFRICA

		P	W	L	D	PF	PA	TF	TA	Ave.score	%Win
Gosford, Australia	Advocate Express	1	1	0	0	38	24	4	4	38-24	100%
Belfast	Balmoral Ground	1	1	0	0	15	12	4	3	15-12	100%
Bologna	Stadio Dall 'Ara	1	1	0	0	62	31	9	3	62-31	100%
Bordeaux	Route de Médoc, Le Bouscat	1	1	0	0	38	5	9	1	38-5	100%
Bordeaux	Municipal Stadium	1	1	0	0	12	9	0	3	12-9	100%
Bordeaux	Parc Lescure	1	1	0	0	22	12	2	0	22-12	100%
Brisbane	Exhibition Ground	2	2	0	0	23	6	5	0	12-3	100%
Buenos Aires	Ferro Carril Oeste Stadium	4	4	0	0	171	85	24	8	43-22	100%
Buenos Aires	River Plate Stadium	1	1	0	0	37	33	5	3	37-33	100%
Buenos Aires	Velez Sarsfield Stadium	2	2	0	0	73	30	8	4	37-15	100%
Edinburgh	Inverleith	1	1	0	0	16	0	4	0	16-0	100%
Genoa	Luigi Ferraris Stadium	1	1	0	0	54	26	8	2	54-26	100%
Glenville, New York	Owl Creek Polo Field	1	1	0	0	38	7	8	1	38-7	100%
Houston, Texas	Robertson Stadium	1	1	0	0	43	20	6	1	43-20	100%
Lens	Stade Felix Bollaert	1	1	0	0	30	25	4	3	30-25	100%
London	Wembley Stadium	1	1	0	0	28	20	3	1	28-20	100%
Lyon	Stade Gerland	2	2	0	0	56	47	7	5	28-24	100%
Montevideo	Wanderers Club	1	1	0	0	22	13	3	2	22-13	100%
Montpellier	Stade de la Mosson	1	1	0	0	64	15	9	2	64-15	100%
Rome	Olympic Stadium	1	1	0	0	40	21	4	2	40-21	100%

SPRINGBOK RECORDS

LIST OF ALL 52 VENUES THAT HAVE HOSTED SPRINGBOK TESTS OUTSIDE SOUTH AFRICA

		P	W	L	D	PF	PA	TF	TA	Ave.score	%Win
Santiago	Prince of Wales Country Club	1	1	0	0	30	16	6	2	30-16	100%
Swansea	St Helen's	2	2	0	0	19	3	5	1	10-2	100%
Hamilton	Waikato Stadium	1	1	0	0	32	29	2	2	32-29	100%
Udine	Stadio Friuli	1	1	0	0	32	10	4	1	32-10	100%
Albany	North Harbour Stadium	2	2	0	0	100	5	13	1	50-3	100%
Cardiff [1]	Millennium Stadium	16	14	1	1	351	251	38	18	22-16	88%
Sydney	Sydney Cricket Ground	6	5	1	0	92	57	18	8	15-10	83%
Paris	Parc des Princes	5	4	1	0	150	66	18	6	30-13	80%
Edinburgh	Murrayfield	17	13	4	0	458	159	63	14	27-09	76%
Paris	Stade de France	7	5	2	0	181	96	13	6	26-14	71%
Paris	Colombes Stadium	3	2	0	1	41	14	9	1	41-14	67%
Dublin	Lansdowne Road/Aviva Stadium	12	8	3	1	206	141	31	13	17-12	67%
London	Twickenham	19	10	9	0	304	323	27	26	16-17	53%
Toulouse	Municipal Stadium	2	1	1	0	26	24	2	2	13-12	50%
Sydney	Aussie Stadium	4	2	2	0	93	71	13	4	23-18	50%
Marseille	Stade Velodrome	2	1	1	0	47	50	6	4	24-25	50%
Glasgow	Hampden Park	2	1	1	0	39	9	5	2	20-5	50%
Mendoza	Malvinas Argentinas Stadium	2	1	0	1	38	33	2	3	19-17	50%
Perth	Subiaco Oval	9	4	4	1	214	174	24	16	24-19	44%
Wellington	Athletic Park	7	3	3	1	64	50	5	6	9-7	43%
Wellington	Wellington Regional Stadium	8	2	6	0	144	196	16	20	18-25	25%
Christchurch	Jade Stadium	8	2	6	0	101	149	13	17	13-19	25%
Brisbane [2]	Suncorp Stadium	9	2	7	0	160	227	19	21	18-25	22%
Auckland	Eden Park	10	2	7	1	151	227	19	26	15-23	20%
Dunedin	Carisbrook	8	1	7	0	93	164	9	18	12-21	13%
Brisbane	Ballymore	1	0	1	0	20	28	2	3	20-28	0%
Brisbane	The Gabba	1	0	1	0	27	38	4	4	27-38	0%
Melbourne	Telstra Dome	2	0	2	0	32	73	3	8	16-37	0%
Sydney	Telstra Stadium	5	0	5	0	73	140	6	17	15-28	0%
London	Crystal Palace	1	0	0	1	3	3	1	1	3-3	0%
Dublin	Croke Park	1	0	1	0	10	15	1	0	10-15	0%
Dunedin	Forsyth Barr Stadium	1	0	1	0	11	21	1	2	11-21	0%
AWAY RECORD		**201**	**116**	**77**	**8**	**4224**	**3303**	**524**	**321**	**21-16**	**58%**

[1] Includes records of the original Cardiff Arms Park on the Millennium Stadium site.
[2] Includes one match at Lang Park on which site the Suncorp Stadium was developed.

SPRINGBOKS 1891-2013 (854 players)

A

Springbok No 324 Ackermann, DSP (Dawie) b 03/06/1930 d 01/01/1970 - WP - 8 Tests (3 - 1T) 19 matches (27 - 9T) 1955: BI2,3,4. 1956: A1,2, NZ1,3. 1958: F2.

632 Ackermann, JN (Johan) b 03/06/1970 - NTvl - 13 Tests (-) 15 matches (-) 1996: Fj, A1, NZ1, A2. 2001: F2(R), It1, NZ1(R), A1. 2006: I, E1,2. 2007: Sm1, A2.

805 Adams, HJ (Heinie) b 29/05/1980 - BB - No Tests - 2 matches (-) Toured F, It, I & E 2009.

853 Adriaanse, LC (Lourens) b 05/02/1988 - GW - 1 Test (-) 1 match (-) 2013: Rugby Championship squad - no tests, F(R).

658 Aitken, AD (Andrew) b 10/06/1968 - WP - 7 Tests (-) 9 matches (-) 1997: F2(R), E. 1998: I2(R), W1(R), NZ1,2(R), A2(R).

822 Alberts, WS (Willem) b 05/11/1984 - KZN - 30 Tests (35 - 7T) 31 matches (35 - 7T) 2010: W2(R), S(t+R), E(R). 2011: NZ2, [W(R), Fj(R), Nam, Sm(t+R), A3(t+R).]. 2012: E1, 2, Arg1, 2, A1, NZ1, A2, NZ2, A1, S, F.4. 2013: Sam, Arg1, Arg2, A1, NZ1, A2, NZ2, W, S, F.

179 Albertyn, PK (Pierre) b 27/05/1897 d 07/03/1973 - SWD - 4 Tests (3 - 1T) 4 matches (3 - 1T) 1924: BI1*, 2*, 3*, 4*.

673 Alcock, CD (Chad) b 09/01/1973 - EP - No Tests - 4 matches (5 - 1T) Toured BI & I. 1998.

13 Alexander, FA (Fred) b 30/12/1870 d 20/04/1937 - GW - 2 Tests (-) 2 matches (-) 1891: BI1, 2.

594 Allan, J (John) b 25/11/1963 - Natal - 13 Tests (-) 25 matches (30 - 6T) 1993: A1(R), Arg1, 2(R). 1994: E1, 2, NZ1, 2, 3. 1996: Fj, A1, NZ1, A2, NZ2.

355 Allen, PB (Peter) b 10/04/1930 d 22/01/1998 - EP - 1 Test (-) 1 match (-) 1960: S.

121 Allport, PH (Percy) b 24/03/1885 d 01/01/1959 - WP - 2 Tests (3 - 1T) 2 matches (3 - 1T) 1910: BI2, 3.

31 Anderson, JH (Biddy) b 26/04/1874 d 11/03/1926 - WP - 3 Tests (-) 3 matches (-) 1896: BI1, 3, 4.

89 Anderson, JW (Joe) b 31/12/1881 d 02/11/1953 - WP - 1 Test (-) 1 match (-) 1903: BI3.

47 Andrew, JB (Ben) b 15/05/1870 d 09/04/1911 - Tvl - 1 Test (-) 1 match (-) 1896: BI2.

759 Andrews, EP (Eddie) b 18/03/1977 - WP - 23 Tests (-) 23 matches (-) 2004: I1, 2, W1(t+R), PI, NZ1, A1, NZ2, A2, W2, I3, E. 2005: F1, A2, NZ2(t), Arg(R), F3(R). 2006: S1, 2, F, A1(R), NZ1(t). 2007: A2(R), NZ2(R).

574 Andrews, KS (Keith) b 03/05/1962 - WP - 9 Tests (-) 31 matches (-) 1992: E. 1993: F1,2,A1(R),2,3,Arg1(R),2.1994: NZ3.

602 Andrews, MG (Mark) b 21/02/1972 - Natal - 77 Tests (60 - 12T) 90 matches (60 - 12T) 1994: E2, NZ1, 2, 3, Arg1, 2, S, W. 1995: WS1, [A, WS2, F, NZ], W, It, E. 1996: Fj, A1, NZ1, A2, NZ2, 3, 4, 5, Arg1, 2, F1, 2, W. 1997: T(R), BI1, 2, NZ1, A1, NZ2, A2, It, F1, 2, E, S. 1998: I1, 2, W1, E1, A1, NZ1, 2, A2, W2, S, I3, E2. 1999: NZ1, 2(R), A2(R), [S, U, E, A3, NZ3]. 2000: A2, NZ2, A3, Arg, I, W, E3. 2001: F1, 2, It1, NZ1, A1, 2, NZ2, F3, E.

358 Antelme, JGM (Mike) b 23/04/1934 - Tvl - 5 Tests (-) 25 matches (45 - 15T) 1960: NZ1, 2, 3, 4. 1961: F.

816 Aplon, GG (Gio) b 06/10/1982 - WP - 17 Tests (25 - 5T) 18 matches (25 - 5T) 2010: W1, F, It1, 2, NZ1(R), 2(R), A1, NZ3, A3(R), I, W2, S, E. 2011: A1, 2. [Nam.]. 2012: E3. 2013: Tour of W, S & F - no Tests.

243 Apsey, JT (John) b 16/04/1911 d 12/11/1987 - WP - 3 Tests (-) 3 matches (-) 1933: A4, 5. 1938: BI2.

76 Ashley, S (Syd) b 23/02/1880 d 20/01/1959 - WP - 1 Test (-) 1 match (-) 1903: BI2.

32 Aston, FTD (Ferdy) b 18/09/1871 d 15/10/1926 - Tvl - 4 Tests (-) 4 matches (-) 1896: BI1*, 2*, 3*, 4.

576 Atherton, S (Steve) b 17/03/1965 - Natal - 8 Tests (-) 23 matches (5 - 1T) 1993: Arg1, 2. 1994: E1, 2, NZ1, 2, 3. 1996: NZ2.

178 Aucamp, J (Hans) b 27/10/1898 d 14/03/1970 - WTvl - 2 Tests (3 - 1T) 2 matches (3 - 1T) 1924: BI1, 2.

B

376 Baard, AP (Attie) b 17/05/1933 d 01/05/2009 - WP - 1 Test (-) 13 matches (9 - 3T) 1960: I.

246 Babrow, L (Louis) b 24/04/1915 d 26/01/2004 - WP - 5 Tests (9 - 3T) 16 matches (42 - 14T) 1937: A1, 2, NZ1, 2, 3.

712 Badenhorst, AJ (Adri) b 18/07/1978 - WP - No Tests - 1 match (-) Toured E. 2000.

610 Badenhorst, C (Chris) b 12/12/1965 - OFS - 2 Tests (10 - 2T) 12 matches (45 - 9T) 1994: Arg2. 1995: WS1(R).

745 Bands, RE (Richard) b 25/03/1974 - BB - 11 Tests (10 - 2T) 11 matches (10 - 2T) 2003: S1, 2, Arg(R), A1, NZ1, A2, NZ2, [U, E, Sm(R), NZ3(R)].

538 Barnard, AS (Anton) b 07/04/1958 - EP - 4 Tests (-) 4 matches (-) 1984: S. Am&Sp1, 2. 1986: NZC1, 2.

399 Barnard, JH (Jannie) b 29/01/1945 d 21/02/1985 Tvl - 5 Tests (-) 18 matches (21 - 7T) 1965: S, A1, 2, NZ3, 4.

442 Barnard, RW (Robbie) b 26/11/1941 d 20/10/2013 - Tvl - 1 Test (-) 10 matches (9 - 3T) 1969-70: tour of UK - no tests. 1970: NZ2(R). 1971: tour of A - no tests.

285 Barnard, WHM (Willem) b 07/08/1923 d 13/06/2012 - NTvl - 2 Tests (-) 14 matches (3 - 1T) 1949: NZ4. 1951: W.

690 Barry, D (De Wet) b 24/06/1978 - WP - 39 Tests (15 - 3T) 41 matches (20 - 4T) 2000: C, E1, 2, A1(R), NZ1, A2. 2001: F1, 2, US(R). 2002: W2, Arg, Sm, NZ1, A1, NZ2, A2. 2003: A1, NZ1, A2, [U, E, Sm, NZ3]. 2004: PI, NZ1, A1, NZ2, A2, W2, I3, E, Arg(t). 2005: F1, 2, A1, NZ(R), F3(R).

Notes: Number preceding name is player's Springbok number. A change in capping policy in Dec 2013, retrospectively applied to 2013 End-of-Year tour, means only players who henceforth have appeared in a Test will be considered Springboks. S Ntubeni, FBC Kirsten & L Schreuder are included in this list to reflect only that they were part of a Springbok touring squad, but they are not Springboks and do not have a Springbok number. For detailed explanation, please see p39. Figures in brackets following the number of Tests or matches are pts scored, followed by breakdown of method of scoring. Figure following Test appearance indicates which match of a sequence against any one opponent it may have been in that year and does not always refer to a Test in a rubber (i.e. Springboks played 5 Tests vs New Zealand in 1996 but only 3 were officially part of the series). A player's province is the one for which he was appearing on his Springbok debut. **Key:** *b > born; d > died; * captain; (R) replacement appearance; (t) temporary replacement; [Square brackets] enclose Rugby World Cup matches; ?? indicates date unknown. Dm > Drop goal from a mark.*

SPRINGBOKS 1891-2013

2006: F.
63 Barry, J (Joe) b 16/03/1876 d 29/03/1961 - WP - 3 Tests (3 - 1T) 3 matches (3 - 1T) 1903: BI1,2,3.
545 Bartmann, WJ (Wahl) b 13/06/1963 - Tvl - 8 Tests (-) 15 matches (5 - 1T) 1986: NZC1, 2, 3, 4. 1992: NZ, A, F1,2.
817 Basson, BA (Bjorn) b 11/02/1987 - GW - 11 Tests (15 - 3T) 11 matches (15 - 3T) 2010: W1(R), It1(R), I, W2. 2011: A1, NZ1. 2013: It, S, Sam, Arg1, Arg2.
661 Basson, WW (Wium) b 23/10/1975 d 22/04/2001 - BB - No Tests - 2 matches (-) Toured It, F,E & S. 1997.
252 Bastard, WE (Ebbo) b 10/12/1912 d 14/02/1949 - Natal - 6 Tests (6 - 2T) 18 matches (15 - 5T) 1937: A1, NZ1, 2, 3. 1938: BI1,3.
438 Bates, AJ (Albie) b 18/04/1941 - WTvl - 4 Tests (-) 18 matches (3 - 1T) 1969: E. 1970: NZ1,2. 1972: E.
468 Bayvel, PCR (Paul) b 28/03/1949 - Tvl - 10 Tests (-) 13 matches (-) 1974: BI2,4,F1,2. 1975: F1,2. 1976: NZ1,2,3,4.
524 Beck, JJ (Colin) b 27/03/1959 - WP - 3 Tests (4 - 1T) 12 matches (35 - 5T, 3C,2P,1D) 1981: NZ2(R), 3(R), US.
387 Bedford, TP (Tommy) b 08/02/1942 - Natal - 25 Tests (3 - 1T) 48 matches (12 - 4T) 1963: A1,2,3,4. 1964: W, F 1965: I, A1,2. 1968: BI1,2,3,4,F1,2. 1969: A1,2*,3*,4,S*,E. 1970: I,W. 1971: F1,2.
795 Bekker, A (Andries) b 05/12/1983 - WP - 29 Tests (5 - 1T) 31 matches (5 - 1T) 2008: W1,2(R), It(R), NZ1(R), 2(t+R), A1(t+R), Arg(R), NZ3, A2, 3, W3(R), S(R), E(R). 2009: BI1(R), 2(R), NZ2(R), A1(R), 2(R), F(t+R), It, I. 2010: It2, NZ1(R), 2(R). 2012: Arg1, 2, NZ1(t+R), A2, NZ2.
527 Bekker, HJ (Hennie) b 12/09/1952 - WP - 2 Tests (4 - 1T) 10 matches (16 - 4T) 1981: NZ1,3.
298 Bekker, HPJ (Jaap) b 11/02/1925 d 06/08/1999 - NTvl - 15 Tests (3 - 1T) 39 matches (12 - 4T) 1952: E, F. 1953: A1, 2, 3,4. 1955: BI2,3,4. 1956: A1,2, NZ1,2,3,4.
353 Bekker, MJ (Martiens) b 03/05/1930 d 10/11/1971 - NTvl - 1 Test (-) 1 match (-) 1960: S.
308 Bekker, RP (Dolph) b 15/12/1926 d 17/06/2012 - NTvl - 2 Tests (3 - 1T) 2 matches (3 - 1T) 1953: A3,4.
639 Bekker, S (Schutte) b 21/10/1971 - NTvl - 1 Test (-) 3 matches (3 - 3T) 1997: A2(t).

640 Bennett, RG (Russell) b 27/11/1971 - Border - 6 Tests (10 - 2T) 10 matches (25 - 5T) 1997: T(R), BI1(R), 3, NZ1, A1, NZ2.
228 Bergh, WF v R v O (Ferdie) b 02/11/1906 d 28/05/1973 - SWD - 17 Tests (21 - 7T) 41 matches (42 - 14T) 1931: W, I. 1932: E, S. 1933: A1, 2, 3, 4, 5. 1937: A1,2, NZ1,2,3. 1938: BI1,2,3.
485 Bestbier, A (André) b 31/03/1946 - OFS - 1 Test (-) 5 matches (-) 1974: F2(R).
186 Bester, JJN (Jack) b 02/03/1898 d 27/10/1943 - WP - 2 Tests (3 - 1T) 2 matches (3 - 1T) 1924: BI2,4.
247 Bester, JLA (Johnny) b 25/12/1917 d 14/05/1977 - WP - 2 Tests (6 - 2T) 14 matches (30 - 10T) 1938: BI2,3.
49 Beswick, AM (Allan) b 30/06/1870 d 06/09/1908 - Border - 3 Tests (-) 3 matches (-) 1896: BI2,3,4.
383 Bezuidenhout, CE (Chris) b 13/10/1937 d ??/??/2002 - NTvl - 3 Tests (-) 3 matches (-) 1962: BI2,3,4.
751 Bezuidenhout, CJ (Christo) b 14/05/1970 - Mpu - 4 Tests (-) 4 matches (-) 2003: NZ2(R), [E, Sm, NZ3].
457 Bezuidenhout, NSE (Niek) b 04/08/1950 - NTvl - 9 Tests (-) 13 matches (-) 1972: E. 1974: BI2,3,4,F1,2. 1975: F1,2. 1977: WT.
225 Bierman, JN (Nic) b 13/02/1910 d 08/06/1977 - Tvl - 1 Test (-) 14 matches (18 - 6T) 1931: I.
8 Bisset, WM (William) b 11/09/1867 d 23/02/1958 - WP - 2 Tests (-) 2 matches (-) 1891: BI1,3.
494 Blair, R (Robbie) b 03/06/1953 - WP - 1 Test (21 - 3C,5P) 1 match (21 - 3C, 5P) 1977: WT.
747 Bobo, G (Gcobani) b 12/09/1979 - GL - 6 Tests (-) 6 matches (-) 2003: S2(R), Arg, A1(R), NZ2. 2004: S(R). 2008: It.
670 Boome, CS (Selborne) b 16/05/1975 - WP - 20 Tests (10 - 2T) 25 matches (15 - 3T) 1999: It1,2,W, NZ1(R), A1, NZ2, A2. 2000: C, E1, 2. 2003: S1(R), 2(R), Arg(R), A1(R), NZ1(R), A2, NZ2(R), [U(R), G, NZ3(R)].
467 Bosch, GR (Gerald) b 12/05/1949 - Tvl - 9 Tests (89 - 7C,23P,2D) 14 matches (132 - 15C, 31P,3D) 1974: BI2, F1, 2. 1975: F1, 2. 1976: NZ1, 2, 3, 4.
771 Bosman, HM (Meyer) b 19/04/1985 - FS - 3 Tests (7 - 2C, 1P) 6

matches (7 - 2C, 1P) 2005: W, F3. 2006: A1(R).
185 Bosman, NJS (Nico) b 06/10/1902 d ??/??/1990 - Tvl - 3 Tests (-) 3 matches (-) 1924: BI2,3,4.
843 Botha, AF (Arno) b 26/10/1991 - BB - No Tests - No matches Toured I, S & E. 2012.
778 Botha, BJ (BJ) b 04/01/1980 - KZN - 25 Tests (5 - 1T) 26 matches (5 - 1T) 2006: NZ2(R), 3, A3, I(R), E1, 2. 2007: E1, Sm1, A1, NZ1, N(R), S(t+R), [Sm(R), E3, T(R), US.]. 2008: W2. 2009: It(R), I. 2010: W1, F, It2(R), NZ1(R), 2(R), A1.
522 Botha, DS (Darius) b 26/06/1955 - NTvl - 1 Test (-) 8 matches (12 - 3T) 1981: NZ1.
770 Botha, GvG (Gary) b 12/10/1981 - BB - 12 Tests (-) 14 matches (-) 2005: A3(R), F3(R). 2007: E1(R), 2(R), Sm1(R), A1(R), NZ1, A2, NZ2(R), N, S, [T.].
502 Botha, HE (Naas) b 27/02/1958 - NTvl - 28 Tests (312 - 2T,50C,50P,18D) 40 matches (485 - 6T,91C, 66P,27D) 1980: S. Am1, 2, BI1, 2, 3, 4, S. Am3, 4, F. 1981: I1, 2, NZ1,2,3,US. 1982: S. Am1,2. 1986: NZC1*, 2*, 3*, 4*. 1989: WT1, 2. 1992: NZ*, A*, F1*,2*,E*.
90 Botha, JA (John) b 19/11/1879 d 08/12/1920 - Tvl - 1 Test (-) 1 match (-) 1903: BI3.
733 Botha, JP (Bakkies) b 22/09/1979 - BB - 78 Tests (35 - 7T) 79 matches (40 - 8T) 2002: F.2003: S1,2,A1,NZ1,A2(R), [U, E, G, Sm, NZ3]. 2004: I1, PI, NZ1, A1, NZ2, A2, W2, I3, E, S, Arg. 2005: A1, 2, 3, NZ1, A4, NZ2, Arg, W, F3. 2007: E1, 2, A1, NZ1, N, S, [Sm, E3, T, US(R), Fiji, Arg, E4.], W. 2008: W1, 2, It, NZ1, 2, A1, Arg, W3, S, E. 2009: BI1, 2, NZ1, 2, A1, 2, 3, NZ3, F, It. 2010: It1, 2, NZ1, I, W2, S, E. 2011: A2, NZ2, [Fj, N.]. 2013: S2, F(R).
374 Botha, JPF (Hannes) b 11/05/1937 d 30/08/2011 - NTvl - 3 Tests (-) 10 matches (9 - 3T) 1962: BI2,3,4.
412 Botha, PH (Piet) b 13/11/1935 - Tvl - 2 Tests (-) 11 matches (3 - 1T) 1965: A1,2.
4 Boyes, HC (Harry) b 12/03/1868 d 26/10/1892 - GW - 2 Tests (-) 2 matches (-) 1891: BI1,2.
149 Braine, JS (Jack) b 01/05/1891 d 25/10/1940 - GW - No Tests - 11 matches (-) Toured BI, I & F. 1912/13.
204 Brand, GH (Gerry) b 08/10/1906 d 04/02/1996 - WP - 16 Tests (55 - 13 C, 7P,

SPRINGBOKS 1891-2013

2D) 46 matches (293 - 2T, 100C, 25P, 3D) 1928: NZ2, 3. 1931: W, I. 1932: E, S. 1933: A1, 2, 3, 4, 5. 1937: A1, 2, NZ2, 3. 1938: BI1.
39 Bredenkamp, MJ (Mike) b 02/05/1873 d 22/12/1940 - GW - 2 Tests (-) 2 matches (-) 1896: BI1, 3.
547 Breedt, JC (Jannie) b 04/06/1959 - Tvl - 8 Tests (-) 8 matches (-) 1986: NZC1, 2, 3, 4. 1989: WT1*, 2*. 1992: NZ, A.
268 Brewis, JD (Hannes) b 15/06/1920 d 09/09/2007 - NTvl - 10 Tests (18 - 1T, 5D) 19 matches (36 - 6T, 6D) 1949: NZ1, 2, 3, 4. 1951: S, I, W. 1952: E, F. 1953: A1.
313 Briers, TPD (Theuns) b 11/07/1929 - WP - 7 Tests (15 - 5T) 12 matches (27 - 9T) 1955: BI1, 2, 3, 4. 1956: NZ2, 3, 4.
104 Brink, DJ (Koei) b 07/11/1882 d 29/10/1970 - WP - 3 Tests (-) 18 matches (9 - 3T) 1906: S, W, E.
626 Brink, RA (Robby) b 21/07/1971 - WP - 2 Tests (-) 2 matches (-) 1995: [R, C].
799 Brits, SB (Schalk) b 16/05/1981 - WP - 5 Tests (-) 5 matches (-) 2008: It(R), NZ2(R), A1. 2012: S(R), E4(R).
760 Britz, GJJ (Gerrie) b 14/04/1978 - FS - 13 Tests (-) 14 matches (-) 2004: I1(R), 2(R), W1(R), PI, A1, NZ2, A2(R), I3(t), S(t+R), Arg(R). 2005: U. 2006: E2(R). 2007: NZ2(R).
725 Britz, WK (Warren) b 07/11/1973 - Natal - 1 Test (-) 1 match (-) 2002: W1.
244 Broodryk, JA (Tallie) b 11/04/1910 d 22/10/1993 - Tvl - No Tests - 6 matches (22 - 6T, 1D) Toured A & NZ. 1937.
100 Brooks, D (Cocky) b 22/09/1881 d 14/11/1962 - Border - 1 Test (-) 11 matches (3 - 1T) 1906: S.
655 Brosnihan, WG (Warren) b 28/12/1971 - GL - 6 Tests (5 - 1T) 10 matches (10 - 2T) 1997: A2. 2000: NZ1(t+R), A2(t+R), NZ2(R), A3(R), E3(R).
74 Brown, CB (Charlie) b 29/01/1878 d 18/06/1944 - WP - 3 Tests (-) 3 matches (-) 1903: BI1, 2, 3.
801 Brüssow, HW (Heinrich) b 21/07/1986 - FS - 20 Tests (5 - 1T) 20 matches (5 - 1T) 2008: E(R). 2009: BI1, 2(R), 3, NZ1, 2, A1, 2, 3, NZ3, F, It, I. 2011: A2, NZ2, [W, Fj, N(R), Sm, A3.].
407 Brynard, GS (Gertjie) b 21/10/1938 - WP - 7 Tests (6 - 2T) 21 matches (42 - 14T) 1965: A1, NZ1, 2, 3, 4. 1968: BI3, 4.

287 Buchler, JU (Johnny) b 07/04/1930 - Tvl - 10 Tests (8 - 1C, 1P, 1D) 26 matches (26 - 4C, 5P, 1D) 1951: S, I, W. 1952: E, F. 1953: A1, 2, 3, 4. 1956: A2.
837 Burden, CB (Craig) b 13/05/1985 - KZN - No Tests - No matches Castle Rugby Championship Squad 2012
108 Burdett, AF (Adam) b 20/08/1882 d 04/11/1918 - WP - 2 Tests (-) 11 matches (6 - 2T) 1906: S, I.
552 Burger, JM (Kobus) b 31/03/1964 - WP - 2 Tests (-) 2 matches (-) 1989: WT1, 2.
511 Burger, MB (Thys) b 10/11/1954 - NTvl - 3 Tests (8 - 2T) 13 matches (52 - 13 T) 1980: BI2(R), S.Am3. 1981: US(R).
535 Burger, SWP (Schalk) b 06/10/1955 - WP - 6 Tests (-) 6 matches (-) 1984: E1, 2. 1986: NZC1, 2, 3, 4.
754 Burger, SWP (Schalk) b 13/04/1983 - WP - 68 Tests (65 - 13T) 68 matches (65 - 13T) 2003: [G(R), Sm(R), NZ3(R)]. 2004: I1, 2, W1, PI, NZ1, A1, NZ2, A2, W2, I3, E. 2005: F1, 2, A1, 2(R), 3(R), NZ1, A4, NZ2, Arg(R), W, F3. 2006: S1, 2. 2007: E1, 2, A1, NZ1, N, S, [Sm, US, Fiji, Arg, E4.]. W. 2008: It(R), NZ1, 2, A1, NZ3, A2, 3, W3, S, E. 2009: BI2, A2(R), NZ3, F, I. 2010: F, It2, NZ1, 2, A1, NZ3, A2, 3. 2011: [W, Fj, N, Sm, A3.].
99 Burger, WAG (Bingo) b 12/08/1883 d 08/08/1963 - Border - 4 Tests (-) 23 matches (3 - 1T) 1906: S, I, W. 1910: BI2.
91 Burmeister, ARD (Arthur) b 01/05/1885 d 25/05/1952 - WP - No Tests - 10 matches (-) Toured BI & F. 1906/07.

C

395 Carelse, G (Gawie) b 21/07/1941 d 03/08/2002 - EP - 14 Tests (-) 30 matches (5 - 1T, 1C) 1964: W, F. 1965: I, S. 1967: F1, 2, 3. 1968: F1, 2. 1969: A1, 2, 3, 4, S.
456 Carlson, RA (Ray) b 02/10/1948 - WP - 1 Test (-) 1 match (-) 1972: E.
83 Carolin, HW (Paddy) b 10/04/1881 d 15/03/1967 - WP - 3 Tests (-) 18 matches (73 - 6T, 15C, 3P, 4D) 1903: BI3. 1906: S*, I.
734 Carstens, PD (Deon) b 03/06/1979 - Natal - 9 Tests (-) 10 matches (-) 2002: S, E. 2006: E1(t+R), 2(R). 2007: E1, 2(t+R), Sm1(R). 2009: BI1(R), 3(t).
9 Castens, HH (Herbert) b 23/11/1864 d 18/10/1929 - WP - 1 Test (-) 1 match (-) 1891: BI1*.
768 Chavhanga, T (Tonderai) b 24/12/1983 - WP - 4 Tests (30 - 6T) 4

matches (30 - 6T) 2005: U. 2007: NZ2(R). 2008: W1, 2.
28 Chignell, TW (Charlie) b 28/04/1866 d 17/10/1952 - WP - 1 Test (-) 1 match (-) 1891: BI3.
384 Cilliers, GD (Gert) b 28/07/1940 d 26/01/1986 - OFS - 3 Tests (3 - 1T) 6 matches (3 - 1T) 1963: A1, 3, 4.
637 Cilliers, NV (Vlok) b 26/03/1968 - WP - 1 Test (-) 1 match (-) 1996: NZ3(t).
835 Cilliers, PM (Pat) b 03/03/1987 - GL - 6 Tests (-) 6 matches (-) 2012: Arg1(t+R), 2(R), A1(R), 2(R), I(R), E4(R).
319 Claassen, JT (Johan) b 23/09/1929 - WTvl - 28 Tests (10 - 2T, 2C) 56 matches (16 - 4T, 2C) 1955: BI1, 2, 3, 4. 1956: A1, 2, NZ1, 2, 3, 4. 1958: F1*, 2*. 1960: S, NZ1, 2, 3, W, I. 1961: E, S, F, I*, A1*, 2*. 1962: BI1*, 2*, 3*, 4*.
519 Claassen, W (Wynand) b 16/01/1951 - Natal - 7 Tests (-) 13 matches (8 - 2T) 1981: I1*, 2*, NZ2*, 3*, US*. 1982: S.Am 1*, 2*.
611 Claassens, JP (Jannie) b 30/06/1969 - NTvl - No Tests - 8 matches (15 - 3T) Toured NZ. 1994 and W, S & I. 1994.
765 Claassens, M (Michael) b 28/10/1982 - FS - 8 Tests (-) 8 matches (-) 2004: W2(R), S(R), Arg(R). 2005: Arg(R), W, F3. 2007: A2(R), NZ2(R).
240 Clark, WHG (Ginger) b 22/09/1906 d 20/09/1999 - Tvl - 1 Test (-) 1 match (-) 1933: A3.
157 Clarkson, WA (Wally) b 08/07/1896 d 03/06/1973 - Natal - 3 Tests (-) 11 matches (9 - 3T) 1921: NZ1, 2. 1924: BI1.
61 Cloete, HA (Patats) b 15/06/1873 d 29/03/1959 - WP - 1 Test (-) 1 match (-) 1896: BI4.
441 Cockrell, CH (Charlie) b 10/01/1939 - WP - 3 Tests (-) 10 matches (-) 1969: S. 1970: I, W.
486 Cockrell, RJ (Robert) b 04/04/1950 d 26/05/2000 - WP - 11 Tests (4 - 1T) 25 matches (8 - 2T) 1974: F1, 2. 1975: F1, 2. 1976: NZ1, 2. 1977: WT. 1981: NZ1, 2(R), 3, US.
513 Cocks, TMD (Tim) b 29/09/1952 - Natal - No Tests - 3 matches (8 - 2T) Toured S.Am. 1980.
730 Coetzee, D (Danie) b 02/09/1977 - BB - 15 Tests (5 - 1T) 15 matches (5 - 1T) 2002: Sm. 2003: S1, 2, Arg, A1, NZ1, A2,

NZ2, [U, E, Sm(R), NZ3(R)]. 2004: S(R), Arg(R). 2006: A1(R).
463 Coetzee, JHH (Boland) b 20/01/1945 - WP - 6 Tests (-) 6 matches (-) 1974: BI1. 1975: F2(R). 1976: NZ1,2,3,4.
831 Coetzee, MC (Marcell) b 08/05/1991 - KZN - 15 Tests (5 - 1T) 15 matches (5 - 1T) 2012: E1, 2, 3, Arg1, 2, A1, NZ1(R), A2(R), NZ2(t+R), I(R), S(R), E4(R). 2013: It(R), Sam, S2(R)
724 Conradie, JHJ (Bolla) b 24/02/1978 - WP - 18 Tests (13 - 2T, 1D) 18 matches (13 - 2T, 1D) 2002: W1, 2, Arg(R), Sm, NZ1, A1, NZ2(R), A2(R), S, E. 2004: W1(R), PI, NZ2, A2. 2005: Arg. 2008: W1, 2(R), NZ1(R).
404 Conradie, SC (Faan) b 27/06/1942 d 21/10/1992 - WP - No Tests - No matches Toured I & S. 1965.
41 Cope, DG (Davie) b 14/08/1877 d 16/08/1898 - Tvl - 1 Test (2 - 1C) 1 match (2 - 1C) 1896: BI2.
53 Cotty, WAH (Bill) b 24/02/1875 d 06/09/1928 - GW - 1 Test (-) 1 match (-) 1896: BI3.
81 Crampton, G (George) b 30/03/1875 d 27/12/1946 - GW - 1 Test (-) 1 match (-) 1903: BI2.
219 Craven, DH (Danie) b 11/10/1910 d 04/01/1993 - WP - 16 Tests (6 - 2T) 38 matches (24 - 8T) 1931: W, I. 1932: S. 1933: A1, 2, 3, 4, 5. 1937: A1, 2, NZ1*, 2, 3. 1938: BI1*, 2*, 3*.
406 Cronjé, CJC (Kerneels) b 16/04/1940 d 13/05/2009 - ETvl - No Tests - No matches Toured A & NZ. 1965.
750 Cronjé, G (Geo) b 23/07/1980 - BB - 3 Tests (-) 3 matches (-) 2003: NZ. 2004: I2(R), W1(R).
758 Cronjé, J (Jacques) b 04/08/1982 - BB - 32 Tests (20 - 4T) 33 matches (25 - 5T) 2004: I1, 2, W1, PI, NZ1, A1, NZ2(R), A2(t+R), S(t+R), Arg. 2005: U, F1, 2, A1, 3, NZ1(R), 2(t), Arg, W, F3. 2006: S2(R), F(R), A1(t+R), NZ1, A2, NZ2, A3(R), I(R), E1. 2007: A2(R), NZ2, N.
447 Cronje, PA (Peter) b 21/09/1949 - Tvl - 7 Tests (10 - 3T) 15 matches (16 - 5T) 1971: F1, 2, A1, 2, 3. 1974: BI3, 4.
144 Cronjé, SN (Fanie) b 24/04/1886 d 20/09/1972 - Tvl - No Tests - 7 matches (3 - 1T) Toured BI, I & F 1912/13.
51 Crosby, JH (Jim) b 03/07/1873 d 25/02/1960 - Tvl - 1 Test (-) 1 match (-) 1896: BI2.
116 Crosby, NJ (Nic) b 21/08/1883 d 14/07/1938 - Tvl - 2 Tests (-) 2 matches (-) 1910: BI1, 3.
78 Currie, C (Clem) b 21/10/1880 d 12/10/1937 - GW - 1 Test (-) 1 match (-) 1903: BI2.

D

235 D'Alton, G (George) b 17/08/1908 d 22/11/1975 - WP - 1 Test (-) 1 match (-) 1933: A1.
614 Dalton, J (James) b 16/08/1972 - Tvl - 43 Tests (25 - 5T) 58 matches (25 - 5T) 1994: Arg1(R). 1995: [A, C], W, It, E. 1996: NZ2(R), 3, Arg1, 2, F1, 2, W. 1997: T(R), BI3, NZ2, A2, It, F1, 2, E, S. 1998: I1, 2, W1, E1, A1, NZ1, 2, A2, W2, S, I3, E2. 2002: W1, 2, Arg, NZ1, A1, NZ2, A2, F, E.
197 Daneel, GM (George) b 29/08/1904 d 19/10/2004 - WP - 8 Tests (6 - 2T) 20 matches (9 - 3T) 1928: NZ1, 2, 3, 4. 1931: W, I. 1932: E, S.
102 Daneel, HJ (Pinkie) b 04/05/1882 d 07/01/1947 - WP - 4 Tests (-) 15 matches (3 - 1T) 1906: S, I, W, E.
823 Daniel, KR (Keegan) b 05/03/1985 - KZN - 5 Tests (-) 6 matches (-) 2010: I(R). 2012: E1(R), 2(R), Arg1, 2(R).
302 Dannhauser, G (Gert) b 16/04/1918 d 07/10/1983 - Tvl - No Tests - 12 matches (-) Toured BI, I & F. 1951/52.
706 Davids, Q (Quinton) b 17/08/1975 - WP - 9 Tests (-) 13 matches (-) 2002: W2, Arg(R), Sm(R). 2003: Arg. 2004: I1(R), 2, W1, PI(t+R), NZ1(R).
700 Davidson, CD (Craig) b 23/02/1977 - Natal - 5 Tests (10 - 2T) 8 matches (10 - 2T) 2002: W2(R), Arg. 2003: Arg, NZ1(R), A2.
119 Davison, PM (Max) b 05/06/1885 d 14/11/1931 - EP - 1 Test (-) 1 match (-) 1910: BI1.
653 De Beer, JH (Jannie) b 22/04/1971 - FS - 13 Tests (181 - 2T, 33C, 27P, 8D) 14 matches (188 - 3T, 34C, 27P, 8D) 1997: BI3, NZ1, A1, NZ2, A2, F2(R), S. 1999: A2, [S, Sp, U, E, A3].
475 De Bruyn, J (Johan) b 12/10/1948 - OFS - 1 Test (-) 4 matches (-) 1974: BI3.
205 De Jongh, HPK (Manus) b 10/10/1902 d 05/09/1974 - WP - 1 Test (3 - 1T) 1 match (3 - 1T) 1928: NZ3.
806 De Jongh, JL (Juan) b 15/04/1988 - WP - 14 Tests (15 - 3T) 16 matches (20 - 4T) 2009: tour of UK - no tests. 2010: W1, F(R), It1(R), 2, A1(R), NZ3. 2011: A1, NZ1, [Fj(R), N(R).]. 2012: A2(R), NZ2(R), S, E4. 2013: Championship Squad - no tests

440 De Klerk, IJ (Sakkie) b 28/10/1938 - Tvl - 3 Tests (-) 9 matches (-) 1969: E. 1970: I, W.
464 De Klerk, KBH (Kevin) b 06/06/1950 - Tvl - 13 Tests (-) 18 matches (4 - 1T) 1974: BI1, 2, 3(R). 1975: F1, 2. 1976: NZ2(R), 3, 4. 1980: S. Am1, 2, BI2. 1981: I1, 2.
16 De Kock, AN (Arthur) b 11/01/1866 d 06/07/1957 - GW - 1 Test (-) 1 match (-) 1891: BI2.
722 De Kock, D (Deon) b 11/05/1975 - GF - 2 Tests (-) 2 matches (-) 2001: It2(R), US.
160 De Kock, JS (Sas) b 17/08/1896 d 04/11/1972 - WP - 2 Tests (-) 7 matches (6 - 2T) 1921: NZ3. 1924: BI3.
717 De Kock, NA (Neil) b 20/11/1978 - WP - 10 Tests (10 - 2T) 10 matches (10 - 2T) 2001: It1. 2002: Sm(R), NZ1(R), 2, A2, F 2003: [U(R), G, Sm(R), NZ3(R)].
75 De Melker, SC (Syd) b 31/03/1884 d 01/11/1953 - GW - 2 Tests (-) 14 matches (9 - 3T) 1903: BI2. 1906: E.
334 De Nysschen, CJ (Chris) b 31/01/1936 - Natal - No Tests - 10 matches (3 - 1T) Toured A & NZ. 1956.
112 De Villiers, DI (Dirkie) b 20/07/1889 d 01/10/1958 - Tvl - 3 Tests (3 - 1T) 3 matches (3 - 1T) 1910: BI1, 2, 3.
382 De Villiers, DJ (Dawie) b 10/07/1940 - WP - 25 Tests (9 - 3T) 53 matches (29 - 5T, 4C, 2P) 1962: BI2, 3. 1965: I, NZ1*, 3*, 4*. 1967: F1*, 2*, 3*, 4*. 1968: BI1*, 2*, 3*, 4*, F1*, 2*. 1969: A1*, 4*, E*. 1970: I*, W*, NZ1*, 2*, 3*, 4*.
95 De Villiers, HA (Boy) b 05/01/1883 d 09/11/1944 - WP - 3 Tests (-) 18 matches (22 - 6T, 1D) 1906: S, W, E.
418 De Villiers, HO (HO) b 10/03/1945 - WP - 14 Tests (26 - 7C, 4P) 29 matches (80 - 2T, 22C, 10P) 1967: F1, 2, 3, 4. 1968: F1, 2. 1969: A1, 2, 3, 4, S, E. 1970: I, W.
151 De Villiers, IB (IB) b 10/03/1892 d 09/01/1966 - Tvl - No Tests - 10 matches (35 - 10C, 5P) Toured A & NZ. 1921.
735 De Villiers, J (Jean) b 24/02/1981 - WP - 96 Tests (125 - 25T) 96 matches (125 - 25T) 2002: F. 2004: PI, NZ1, A1, NZ2, A2, W2(R), E. 2005: U, F1, 2, A1, 2, 3, NZ1, A4, NZ2, Arg, W, F3. 2006: S1, NZ2, 3, A3, I, E1, 2. 2007: E1, 2, A1, NZ1, N, [Sm.]. 2008: W1, 2, It, NZ1, 2, A1Arg, NZ3, A2, 3, W3, S, E. 2009: BI1, 2, NZ1, 2, A1, 2, 3, NZ3, I. 2010: F(t+R), It1, 2, NZ1, 2, 3, A2, 3, I, W2, S, E. 2011: A2, NZ2, [W, Sm(R), A3.]. 2012: E1*,

SPRINGBOKS 1891-2013

2*, 3*, Arg1*, 2*, A1*, NZ1*, A2*, NZ2*, I*, S*, E4*. 2013: It*, S*, Sam*, Arg1*, Arg2*, A1*, NZ1*, A2*, NZ2*, W*, S*, F*.
195 De Villiers, P du P (Pierie) b 14/06/1905 d 14/11/1975 - WP - 8 Tests (-) 28 matches (6 - 2T) 1928: NZ1, 3, 4. 1932: E. 1933: A4. 1937: A1, 2, NZ1.
400 De Vos, DJJ (Dirkie) b 08/04/1941 d 12/02/2011 - WP - 3 Tests (-) 18 matches (9 - 3T) 1965: S. 1969: A3, S.
423 De Waal, AN (Albie) b 04/02/1942 - WP - 4 Tests (-) 4 matches (-) 1967: F1, 2, 3, 4.
60 De Waal, PJ (Paul) b 02/06/1875 d 18/05/1945 - WP - 1 Test (-) 1 match (-) 1896: BI4.
429 De Wet, AE (André) b 01/08/1946 - WP - 3 Tests (-) 11 matches (-) 1969: A3, 4, E.
261 De Wet, PJ (Piet) b 12/03/1917 d 18/10/1968 - WP - 3 Tests (-) 3 matches (-) 1938: BI1, 2, 3.
335 De Wilzem, CJ (Chris) b 14/10/1932 d 02/03/2006 - OFS - No Tests - 16 matches (3 - 1T) Toured A & NZ. 1956.
145 Delaney, ETA (Ned) b 12/06/1892 d 18/10/1918 - GW - No Tests - 13 matches (-) Toured BI, I & F. 1912/13.
662 Delport, GM (Thinus) b 02/02/1975 - GL - 18 Tests (15 - 3T) 20 matches (15 - 3T) 2000: C(R), E1(t+R), A1, NZ1, A2, NZ2, A3, Arg, I, W. 2001: F2, It1. 2003: A1, NZ2, [U, E, Sm, NZ3].
297 Delport, WH (Willa) b 05/11/1920 d 14/10/1984 - EP - 9 Tests (6 - 2T) 21 matches (12 - 4T) 1951: S, I, W. 1952: E, F. 1953: A1, 2, 3, 4.
50 Devenish, CE (Charles) b 13/01/1874 d 11/01/1922 - GW - 1 Test (-) 1 match (-) 1896: BI2.
10 Devenish, GE (Tiger) b 27/07/1870 d 23/03/1930 - Tvl - 1 Test (-) 1 match (-) 1891: BI1.
45 Devenish, G St L (Long George) b 11/05/1871 d 01/02/1943 - Tvl - 1 Test (-) 1 match (-) 1896: BI2.
189 Devine, D (Dauncie) b 20/03/1904 d 22/09/1965 - Tvl - 2 Tests (-) 2 matches (-) 1924: BI3. 1928: NZ2.
814 Deysel, JR (Jean) b 05/03/1985 - KZN - 4 Tests (-) 6 matches (-) 2009: It(R). 2011: A1(R), NZ1, A2(R).
300 Dinkelmann, EE (Ernst) b 14/05/1927 d 22/10/2010 - NTvl - 6 Tests (6 - 2T) 21 matches (9 - 3T) 1951: S, I.

1952: E, F 1953: A1, 2.
597 Dirks, CA (Chris) b 23/05/1967 - Tvl - No Tests - 2 matches (10 - 2T) Toured Arg. 1993.
393 Dirksen, CW (Corra) b 22/01/1938 - NTvl - 10 Tests (9 - 3T) 11 matches (9 - 3T) 1963: A4. 1964: W. 1965: I, S. 1967: F1, 2, 3, 4. 1968: BI1, 2.
713 Dixon, PJ (Pieter) b 17/10/1977 - WP - No Tests - 1 match (-) Toured E. 2000.
762 Dlulane, VT (Tim) b 05/06/1981 - Mpu - 1 Test (-) 1 match (-) 2004: W2(R).
67 Dobbin, FJ (Uncle) b 10/10/1879 d 05/02/1950 - GW - 9 Tests (3 - 1T) 36 matches (21 - 7T) 1903: BI1, 2. 1906: S, W, E. 1910: BI1. 1912: S*, I, W.
202 Dobie, JAR (John) b 12/08/1989 - Tvl - 1 Test (-) 1 match (-) 1928: NZ2.
230 Dold, JB (Jack) b 03/01/1902 d 17/09/1968 - EP - No Tests - 10 matches (3 - 1T) Toured BI & I. 1931/32.
54 Dormehl, PJ (Pieter) b 04/11/1872 d 01/09/1958 - WP - 2 Tests (-) 2 matches (-) 1896: BI3, 4.
40 Douglass, FW (Frank) b 15/07/1875 d Post 1920 - EP - 1 Test (-) 1 match (-) 1896: BI1.
601 Drotské, AE (Naka) b 15/03/1971 - OFS - 26 Tests (15 - 3T) 34 matches (20 - 4T) 1993: Arg(2). 1995: [WS2(R)]. 1996: A1(R). 1997: T, BI1, 2, 3(R), NZ1, A1, NZ2(R). 1998: I2(R), W1(R), I3(R). 1999: It1, 2, W, NZ1, A1, NZ2, A2, [S, Sp(R), U, E, A3, NZ3].
321 Dryburgh, RG (Roy) b 01/11/1929 d 10/05/2000 - WP - 8 Tests (28 - 3T, 5C, 3P) 20 matches (116 - 15T, 13C, 15P) 1955: BI2, 3, 4. 1956: A2, NZ1, 4. 1960: NZ1*, 2*.
787 Du Plessis, BW (Bismarck) b 22/05/1984 - KZN - 57 Tests (45 - 9T) 59 matches (45 - 9T) 2007: A2(t+R), NZ2, N(R), S(R), [Sm(R), E3(R), US(R), Arg(R), E4(t).], W(R). 2008: W1(R), 2(R), It, NZ1(R), 2, Arg, NZ3, A2, 3, W3, S. 2009: BI1, 2, 3(R), NZ1, 2, A1, 2, 3, NZ3, F, I(R). 2010: I, W2, S, E. 2011: A2(R), NZ2, [W(R), Fj(R), Sm, A3(R).]. 2012: E1, 2, 3, Arg1. 2013: S(R), Sam(R), Arg1(R), Arg2(R), A1, NZ1, A2(R), NZ2, W, S(R), F
523 Du Plessis, CJ (Carel) b 24/06/1960 - WP - 12 Tests (16 - 4T) 22 matches (40 - 10T) 1982: S.Am1, 2. 1984:

E1, 2, S. Am&Sp1, 2. 1986: NZC1, 2, 3, 4. 1989: WT1, 2.
496 Du Plessis, DC (Daan) b 09/08/1948 - NTvl - 2 Tests (-) 2 matches (-) 1977: WT. 1980: S.Am2.
275 Du Plessis, F (Felix) b 24/11/1919 d 01/05/1978 - Tvl - 3 Tests (-) 3 matches (-) 1949: NZ1*, 2*, 3*.
788 Du Plessis, JN (Jannie) b 16/11/1982 - FS - 51 Tests (5 - 1T) 53 matches (5 - 1T) 2007: A2, NZ2, [Fiji, Arg(t+R).], W. 2008: A3(R), E. 2009: NZ1(t), 2(R), A1(R), 2(R), NZ3(R). 2009: tour of UK - no tests 2010: W1(R), F(R), It1, 2, NZ1, 3, A2, 3, I, W2, S, E. 2011: A2, NZ2, [W, Fj, Sm, A3.]. 2012: E1, 2, 3, Arg1, 2, A1, NZ1, A2, NZ2, I, S, E4. 2013: It, S, Sam, Arg1, Arg2, A1, NZ1, A2, NZ2.
455 Du Plessis, M (Morné) b 21/10/1949 - WP - 22 Tests (12 - 3T) 32 matches (18 - 5T) 1971: A1, 2, 3. 1974: BI1, 2, F1, 2. 1975: F1*, 2*. 1976: NZ1*, 2*, 3*, 4*. 1977: WT*. 1980: S.Am1*, 2*, BI1*, 2*, 3*, 4*, S.Am4*, F*.
537 Du Plessis, MJ (Michael) b 04/11/1958 - WP - 8 Tests (7 - 1T, 1D) 8 matches (7 - 1T, 1D) 1984: S.Am&Sp1, 2. 1986: NZC1, 2, 3, 4. 1989: WT1, 2.
166 Du Plessis, NJ (Nic) b 04/12/1894 d 10/08/1949 - WTvl - 5 Tests (-) 20 matches (-) 1921: NZ2, 3. 1924: BI1, 2, 3.
458 Du Plessis, PG (Piet) b 23/07/1947 - NTvl - 1 Test (-) 1 match (-) 1972: E.
503 Du Plessis, TD (Tommy) b 29/06/1953 - NTvl - 2 Tests (4 - 1T) 5 matches (12 - 3T) 1980: S.Am1, 2.
500 Du Plessis, W (Willie) b 04/09/1955 - WP - 14 Tests (12 - 3T) 20 matches (28 - 7T) 1980: S.Am1, 2, BI1, 2, 3, 4, S. Am3, 4, F. 1981: NZ1, 2, 3. 1982: S. Am1, 2.
317 Du Plooy, AJJ (Amos) b 31/05/1921 d 17/05/1980 - EP - 1 Test (-) 1 match (-) 1955: BI1.
375 Du Preez, FCH (Frik) b 28/11/1935 - NTvl - 38 Tests (11 - 1T, 1C, 2P) 87 matches (87 - 12T, 15C, 7P) 1961: E, S, A1, 2. 1962: BI1, 2, 3, 4. 1963: A1. 1964: W, F. 1965: A1, 2, NZ1, 2, 3, 4. 1967: F4. 1968: BI1, 2, 3, 4, F1, 2. 1969: A1, 2, S. 1970: I, W, NZ1, 2, 3, 4. 1971: F1, 2, A1, 2, 3.
701 Du Preez, GJD (De 12/06/1975 - GL - 2 Tests (5 - 1T) 5 matches (10 - 2T) 2002: Sm(R), A1(R).
327 Du Preez, JGH (Jan) b

SPRINGBOKS 1891-2013

06/10/1930 - WP - 1 Test (-) 6 matches (15 - 5T) 1956: NZ1.

757 Du Preez, PF (Fourie) b 24/03/1982 - BB - 67 Tests (75 - 15T) 67 matches (75 - 15T) 2004: I1, 2, W1, PI(R), NZ1, A1, NZ2(R), A2(R), W2, I3, E, S, Arg. 2005: U(R), F1, 2(R), A1(R)2(R), 3, NZ1(R), A4(R). 2006: S1, 2, F,A1(R), NZ1, A2, NZ2, 3, A3. 2007: N, S, [Sm, E3, US, Fiji, Arg, E4.]. 2008: Arg(R), NZ3, A2, 3, 3. 2009: BI1, 2, 3, NZ1, 2, A1, 2, 3, NZ3, F, It, 1. 2011: A2, NZ2, [W, Fj, N(R), Sm, A3.]. 2013: Arg1(R), A2, NZ2, W,S

562 Du Preez, RJ (Robert) b 19/07/1963 - Natal - 7 Tests (-) 15 matches (45 - 9T) 1992: NZ, A. 1993: F1, 2, A1, 2, 3.

792 Du Preez, WH (Wian) b 30/10/1982 - FS - 1 Test (-) 2 matches (-) 2009: It.

281 Du Rand, JA (Salty) b 16/01/1926 d 27/02/1979 - Rhodesia - 21 Tests (12 - 4T) 47 matches (27 - 9T) 1949: NZ2, 3. 1951: S, I, W. 1952: E, F. 1953: A1, 2, 3, 4. 1955: BI1, 2, 3, 4. 1956: A1, 2, NZ1*, 2, 3, 4.

619 Du Randt, JP (Os) b 08/09/1972 - OFS - 80 Tests (25 - 5T) 85 matches (25 - 5T) 1994: Arg1, 2, S, W. 1995: WS1, [A, WS2, F, NZ]. 1996: Fj, A1, NZ1, A2, NZ2, 3, 4. 1997: T, BI1, 2, 3, NZ1, A1, NZ2, A2, It, F1, 2, E, S. 1999: NZ1, A1, NZ2, A2, [S, Sp(R), U, E, A3, NZ3]. 2004: I1, 2, W1, PI, NZ1, A1, NZ2, A2, W2, I3, E, S(R), Arg(R). 2005: U(R), F1, A1, NZ1, A4, NZ2, Arg, W(R), F3. 2006: S1, 2, F, A1, NZ1, A2, NZ2, 3, A3. 2007: Sm1, NZ1, N, S, [Sm, E3, US, Fj, Arg, E4.].

208 Du Toit, AF (AF) b 12/05/1899 d 09/09/1988 - WP - 2 Tests (-) 2 matches (-) 1928: NZ3, 4.

253 Du Toit, BA (Ben) b 10/11/1912 d 25/01/1989 - Tvl - 3 Tests (3 - 1T) 10 matches (9 - 3T) 1938: BI1, 2, 3.

667 Du Toit, GS (Gaffie) b 24/03/1976 - GW - 14 Tests (108 - 5T, 25C, 11P) 23 matches (153 - 10T, 29C, 15P) 1998: I1. 1999: It1, 2, W(R), NZ1, 2. 2004: I1, W1(R), A1(R), S(R), Arg. 2006: S1(R), 2(R), F(R).

279 Du Toit, PA (Fonnie) b 13/03/1920 d 21/07/2001 - NTvl - 8 Tests (6 - 2T) 25 matches (9 - 3T) 1949: NZ2, 3, 4. 1951: S, I, W. 1952: E, F.

516 Du Toit, PG (Hempies) b 23/08/1953 - WP - 5 Tests (-) 16 matches (8 - 2T) 1981: NZ1. 1982: S. Am1, 2. 1984: E1, 2.

332 Du Toit, PS (Piet) b 09/05/1935 d 26/02/1997 - WP - 14 Tests (-) 49 matches (9 - 3T) 1958: F1, 2. 1960: NZ1, 2, 3, 4, W, I. 1961: E, S, F,I, A1, 2.

854 Du Toit, PS (Pieter-Steph) b 20/08/1992 - KZN - 2 Tests (-) 2 matches (-) 2013: W(R), F(R).

220 Du Toit, SR (Schalk) b 08/08/1902 d 18/11/1965 - WP - No Tests - 12 matches (3 - 1T) Toured BI & I. 1931/32.

1 Duff, BR (Ben) b 16/01/1867 d 25/06/1943 - WP - 3 Tests (-) 3 matches (-) 1891: BI1, 2, 3.

194 Duffy, BAA (Bernie) b 17/11/1905 d 16/03/1958 - Border - 1 Test (-) 1 match (-) 1928: NZ1.

430 Durand, PJ (Paul) b 21/01/1946 d ??/09/1988 - W Tvl - No Tests - 2 matches (-) Toured BI & I. 1969/70.

265 Duvenage, FP (Floors) b 06/11/1917 d 16/09/1999 - GW - 2 Tests (-) 2 matches (-) 1949: NZ1, 3.

E

499 Edwards, P (Pierre) b 23/05/1953 - NTvl - 2 Tests (-) 2 matches (-) 1980: S. Am1, 2.

415 Ellis, JH (Jan) b 05/01/1942 d 08/02/2013 - SWA - 38 Tests (21 - 7T) 74 matches (97 - 32T) 1965: NZ1, 2, 3, 4. 1967: F1, 2, 3, 4. 1968: BI1, 2, 3, 4, F1, 2. 1969: A1, 2, 3, 4, S. 1970: I, W, NZ1, 2, 3, 4. 1971: F1, 2, A1, 2, 3. 1972: E. 1974: BI1, 2, 3, 4, F1, 2. 1976: NZ1.

165 Ellis, MC (Mervyn) b 16/09/1892 d 24/03/1959 - Tvl - 6 Tests (-) 20 matches (3 - 1T) 1921: NZ2, 3. 1924: BI1, 2, 3, 4.

656 Els, WW (Braam) b 01/11/1971 - FS - 1 Test (-) 3 matches (-) 1997: A2(R).

836 Engelbrecht, JJ (JJ) b 22/02/1989 - BB - 12 Tests (20 - 4T) 12 matches (20 - 4T) 2012: Arg1(R). 2013: It, S, Sam, Arg1, Arg2, A1, NZ1, A2, NZ2, W(R), S(R).

347 Engelbrecht, JP (Jannie) b 10/11/1938 - WP - 33 Tests (24 - 8T) 67 matches (132 - 44T) 1960: S, W, I. 1961: E, S, F,A1, 2. 1962: BI2, 3, 4. 1963: A2, 3. 1964: W, F.1965: I, S, A1, 2, NZ1, 2, 3, 4. 1967: F1, 2, 3, 4. 1968: BI1, 2, F1, 2. 1969: A1, 2.

549 Erasmus, FS (Frans) b 19/06/1959 d 07/03/1998 - NTvl - 3 Tests (-) 3 matches (-) 1986: NZC3, 4. 1989: WT2.

649 Erasmus, J (Rassie) b 05/11/1972 - FS - 36 Tests (35 - 7T) 39 matches (35 - 7T) 1997: BI3, A2, It, F1, 2, S. 1998: I1, 2, W1, E1, A1, NZ2, A2, W2, S, I3, E2. 1999: It1, 2, W, A1*, NZ2, A2, [S, U, E, A3, NZ3]. 2000: C, E1, A1, NZ1, 2, A3. 2001: F1, 2.

692 Esterhuizen, G (Grant) b 28/04/1976 - GL - 7 Tests (-) 7 matches (-) 2000: NZ1(R), 2, A3, Arg, I, W(R), E3(t).

58 Etlinger, TE (Tommy) b 07/09/1872 d 23/02/1953 - WP - 1 Test (-) 1 match (-) 1896: BI4.

833 Etzebeth, E (Eben) b 29/10/1991 - WP - 23 Tests (-) 23 matches (-) 2012: E1, 2, 3, Arg1, 2, A1, 2, NZ2, I, S, E4. 2013: It, S, Sam, Arg1, Arg2, A1, NZ1, A2, NZ2, W, S(R), F.

F

543 Ferreira, C (Christo) b 28/08/1960 - OFS - 2 Tests (-) 2 matches (-) 1986: NZC1, 2.

540 Ferreira, PS (Kulu) b 17/03/1959 - WP - 2 Tests (4 - 1T) 2 matches (4 - 1T) 1984: S. Am & Sp1, 2.

84 Ferris, HH (Hugh) b 06/12/1877 d 17/07/1929 - Tvl - 1 Test (-) 1 match (-) 1903: BI3.

674 Fleck, RF (Robbie) b 17/07/1975 - WP - 31 Tests (50 - 10T) 36 matches (65 - 13T) 1999: It1, 2, NZ1(R), A1, NZ2(R), A2, [S, U, E, A3, NZ3]. 2000: C, E1, 2, A1, NZ1, A2, NZ2, A3, Arg, I, W, E3. 2001: F1(R), 2, It1, NZ1, A1, 2. 2002: S, E.

784 Floors, L (Kabamba) b 15/11/1980 - FS - 1 Test (-) 1 match (-) 2006: E2.

42 Forbes, HH (Spanner) b 02/01/1873 d 17/09/1955 - Tvl - 1 Test (-) 1 match (-) 1896: BI2.

229 Forrest, HM (Skaap) b 17/11/1907 d 26/01/1989 - Tvl - No Tests - 7 matches (-) Toured BI & I. 1931/32.

780 Fortuin, BA (Bevin) b 06/02/1979 - FS - 2 Tests (-) 3 matches (-) 2006: I. 2007: A2.

481 Fourie, C (Tossie) b 01/08/1950 - d 05/05/1997 - EP - 4 Tests (10 - 1T, 2P) 9 matches (14 - 2T, 2P) 1974: F1, 2. 1975: F1, 2.

752 Fourie, J (Jaque) b 04/03/1983 - GL - 72 Tests (160 - 32T) 72 matches (160 - 32T) 2003: [U, G, Sm(R), NZ3(R)]. 2004: I2, E(R), S, Arg. 2005: U(R), F2(R), A1(R), 2, 3, NZ1, A4, NZ2, Arg, W, F3. 2006: S1, A1, NZ1, A2, NZ2, 3, A3. 2007: Sm1(R), A1, NZ1, N, S, [Sm, E3, US, Fiji, Arg, E4.], W. 2008: Arg(R), W3(R), S(R), E(R). 2009: BI1(R), 2(R), 3, NZ1, 2, A1, 2, 3, NZ3, F,It, I. 2010: W1, F,It2, NZ1, 2, A1, 2, 3. 2011: A2, NZ2, [W, Fj, N, Sm, A3.]. 2013: W, S, F.

476 Fourie, TT (Polla) b 10/07/1945 - SETvl - 1 Test (-) 5 matches (12 - 3T) 1974: BI3.

SPRINGBOKS 1891-2013

339 **Fourie, WL** (Loftie) b 23/07/1936 d 23/07/2001 - SWA - 2 Tests (3 - 1T) 2 matches (3 - 1T) 1958: F1,2.

148 **Francis, JAJ** (Joe) b 24/01/1889 d 20/12/1924 - Tvl - 5 Tests (6 - 2T) 19 matches (9 - 3T) 1912: S,I,W. 1913: E,F.

218 **Francis, MG** (Tiny) b 26/08/1907 d 02/08/1961 - OFS - No Tests - 8 matches (18 - 1T,4C,1P,1D) Toured BI & I. 1931/32.

469 **Frederickson, CA** (Dave) b 17/08/1950 - Tvl - 3 Tests (-) 3 matches (-) 1974: BI2. 1980: S. Am1,2.

68 **Frew, A** (Alex) b 24/10/1877 d 29/04/1947 - Tvl - 1 Test (3 - 1T) 1 match (3 - 1T) 1903: BI1*.

492 **Froneman, DC** (Dirk) b 14/04/1954 - OFS - 1 Test (-) 1 match (-) 1977: WT.

234 **Froneman, IL** (Fronie) b 18/12/1907 d 11/08/1984 - Border - 1 Test (-) 1 match (-) 1933: A1.

294 **Fry, DJ** (Dennis) b 25/02/1926 d 25/02/2003 - WP - No Tests - 17 matches (12 - 4T) Toured BI,I & F. 1951/52.

303 **Fry, SP** (Stephen) b 14/07/1924 d 29/06/2002 - WP - 13 Tests (-) 28 matches (9 - 3T) 1951: S,I,W. 1952: E,F. 1953: A1, 2,3,4. 1955: BI1*,2*,3*,4*.

567 **Fuls, HT** (Heinrich) b 08/03/1971 - Tvl - 8 Tests (-) 21 matches (5 - 1T) 1992: NZ(R). 1993: F1,2,A1,2,3,Arg1,2.

710 **Fynn, EE** (Etienne) b 14/12/1972 - Natal - 2 Tests (-) 4 matches (-) 2001: F1, It1(R).

638 **Fyvie, WS** (Wayne) b 28/03/1972 - Natal - 3 Tests (-) 8 matches (10 - 2T) 1996: NZ4(t),5(R),Arg2(R).

G

233 **Gage, JH** (Jack) b 02/04/1907 d 30/06/1989 - OFS - 1 Test (-) 1 match (-) 1933: A1.

348 **Gainsford, JL** (John) b 04/08/1938 - WP - 33 Tests (24 - 8T) 71 matches (93 - 31T) 1960: S, NZ1,2,3,4,W, I. 1961: E,S,F,A1,2. 1962: BI1,2,3,4. 1963: A1,2,3,4. 1964: W,F 1965: I,S,A1,2, NZ1,2, 3,4. 1967: F1,2,3.

645 **Garvey, AC** (Adrian) b 25/06/1968 - Natal - 28 Tests (20 - 4T) 28 matches (20 - 4T) 1996: Arg1,2, F1,2, W. 1997: T, BI1,2,3(R), A1(t), It, F1,2, E, S. 1998: I1,2,W1,E1,A1,NZ1,2,A2,W2,S,I3, E2. 1999: [Sp].

282 **Geel, PJ** (Flip) b 07/02/1914 d 12/06/1971 - OFS - 1 Test (-) 1 match (-) 1949: NZ3.

227 **Geere, V** (Manie) b 09/09/1905 d 25/10/1989 - Tvl - 5 Tests (-) 17 matches (-) 1933: A1,2,3,4,5.

270 **Geffin, AO** (Okey) b 28/05/1921 d 16/10/2004 - Tvl - 7 Tests (48 - 9C, 10P) 17 matches (121 - 1T,26C,22P) 1949: NZ1,2, 3,4. 1951: S,I,W.

564 **Geldenhuys, A** (Adri) b 11/07/1964 - EP - 4 Tests (-) 11 matches (-) 1992: NZ,A,F1,2.

528 **Geldenhuys, SB** (Burger) b 18/05/1956 - NTvl - 7 Tests (4 - 1T) 15 matches (20 - 5T) 1981: NZ2,3,US. 1982: S.Am1,2. 1989: WT1,2.

316 **Gentles, TA** (Tommy) b 31/05/1934 d 29/06/2011 - WP - 6 Tests (-) 18 matches (9 - 3T) 1955: BI1, 2, 4. 1956: NZ2,3. 1958: F2.

283 **Geraghty, EM** (Carrots) b 20/04/1927 - Border - 1 Test (-) 1 match (-) 1949: NZ4.

514 **Gerber, DM** (Danie) b 14/04/1958 - EP - 24 Tests (82 - 19T, 1C) 35 matches (120 - 28T, 1C) 1980: S.Am3,4, F. 1981: I1, 2, NZ1, 2, 3, US. 1982: S.Am1, 2. 1984: E1, 2, S.Am&Sp1,2. 1986: NZC1,2,3,4. 1992: NZ,A,F1,2,E.

709 **Gerber, HJ** (Hendrik) b 12/04/1976 - WP - 2 Tests (-) 6 matches (-) 2003: S1,2.

337 **Gerber, MC** (Mickey) b 12/10/1935 d 07/10/2005 - EP - 3 Tests (8 - 4C) 3 matches (8 - 4C) 1958: F1, 2. 1960: S.

351 **Gericke, FW** (Mannetjies) b 08/06/1933 d 21/10/2010 - Tvl - 1 Test (3 - 1T) 1 match (3 - 1T) 1960: S.

465 **Germishuys, JS** (Gerrie) b 29/10/1949 - OFS - 20 Tests (48 - 12T) 29 matches (76 - 19T) 1974: BI2. 1976: NZ1, 2,3,4. 1977: WT. 1980: S.Am1,2,BI1,2,3,4, S.Am3,4,F.1981:I1,2,NZ2,3,US.

77 **Gibbs, EAH** (Bertie) b 25/08/1878 d 29/12/1952 - GW - 1 Test (-) 1 match (-) 1903: BI2.

641 **Gillingham, JW** (Joe) b 27/02/1974 - GL - No Tests - 7 matches (5 - 1T) Toured Arg, F & W. 1996 and It, F,E & S. 1997.

413 **Goosen, CP** (Piet) b 03/02/1937 - d 06/06/1991 - OFS - 1 Test (-) 13 matches (3 - 1T) 1965: NZ2.

839 **Goosen, JL** (Johan) b 27/07/1992 - FS - 4 Tests (8 - 1C,2P) 4 matches (8 - 1C, 2P) 2012: A1(R), NZ1(R), A2, NZ2. 2013: Tour of W,S & F - no tests.

37 **Gorton, HC** (Hubert) b 28/10/1871 d 11/01/1900 - Tvl - 1 Test (-) 1 match (-) 1896: BI1.

424 **Gould, RL** (Rodney) b 10/08/1942 - Natal - 4 Tests (3 - 1D) 7 matches (3 - 1D) 1968: BI1,2,3,4.

789 **Grant, PJ** (Peter) b 15/08/1984 - WP - 5 Tests (-) 5 matches (-) 2007: A2(R), NZ2(R). 2008: W1(t+R), It(R), A1(R).

215 **Gray, BG** (Geoff) b 28/07/1909 d 04/08/1989 - WP - 4 Tests (-) 13 matches (12 - 4T) 1931: W. 1932: E,S. 1933: A5.

729 **Greeff, WW** (Werner) b 14/07/1977 - WP - 11 Tests (31 - 4T, 4C, 1D) 11 matches (31 - 4T, 4C, 1D) 2002: Arg(R), Sm, NZ1, A1, NZ2, A2, F,S, E. 2003: [U,G].

379 **Greenwood, CM** (Colin) b 25/01/1936 d 03/10/1998 - WP - 1 Test (6 - 2T) 1 match (6 - 2T) 1961: I.

829 **Greyling, MD** (Dean) b 01/01/1986 - BB - 3 Tests (-) 3 matches (-) 2011: A1, NZ1. 2012: NZ1(R).

422 **Greyling, PJF** (Piet) b 16/05/1942 - OFS - 25 Tests (15 - 5T) 43 matches (18 - 6T) 1967: F1,2,3,4. 1968: BI1, F1,2. 1969: A1,2,3,4,S,E. 1970: I,W,NZ1,2,3,4. 1971: F1,2,A1,2,3. 1972: E*.

478 **Grobler, CJ** (Kleintjie) b 24/08/1944 d 29/09/1999 - OFS - 3 Tests (4 - 1T) 7 matches (12 - 3T) 1974: BI4. 1975: F1,2.

431 **Grobler, RN** (Rysmier) b 14/11/1946 d 26/05/1971 - NTvl - No Tests - 10 matches (9 - 3T) Toured BI & I. 1969/70.

5 **Guthrie, FEH** (Frank) b 03/11/1869 d 19/06/1954 - WP - 3 Tests (-) 3 matches (-) 1891: BI1,3. 1896: BI1.

H

766 **Habana, BG** (Bryan) b 12/06/1983 - GL - 95 Tests (265 - 53T) 97 matches (265 - 53T) 2004: E(R),S,Arg. 2005: U, F1, 2, A1, 2, 3, NZ1, A4, NZ2, Arg, W, F3. 2006: S2,F,A1,NZ1,A2,NZ2,3,I,E1,2. 2007: E1,2, S, [Sm,E3,T(R), US, Fiji,Arg,E4.],W. 2008: W1,2, It, NZ1, 2, A1, NZ3, W3, S, E. 2009: BI1, 2, NZ1,2,A1, 2,3, NZ3, F,It, I. 2010: F,It1,2, NZ1,2,A1,NZ3,A2,3,I,W. 2011: A2,NZ2, [W, N, Sm, A3.]. 2012: E1, 2, 3, Arg1, 2, A1, NZ1.A2, NZ2. 2013: It, S, Sam, Arg1, Arg2, A1, NZ1, A2, NZ2, W, S, F.

113 **Hahn, CHL** (Cocky) b 07/01/1886 - d 27/09/1948 - Tvl - 3 Tests (3 - 1T) 3 matches (3 - 1T) 1910: BI1,2,3.

SPRINGBOKS 1891-2013

714 Hall, DB (Dean) b 02/09/1977 - GL - 13 Tests (20 - 4T) 13 matches (20 - 4T) 2001: F1,2, NZ1, A1, 2, NZ2, It2, E, US. 2002: Sm, NZ1, 2, A2.
720 Halstead, TM (Trevor) b 17/06/1976 - Natal - 6 Tests (15 - 3T) 6 matches (15 - 3T) 2001: F3, It2, E, US(R). 2003: S1, 2.
15 Hamilton, GH (George) b 30/04/1863 d 07/08/1901 - EP - 1 Test (-) 1 match (-) 1891: BI1.
333 Hanekom, M v d S (Melt) b 27/07/1931 d 1997/1998 - Boland - No Tests - 9 matches (9 - 3T) Toured A & NZ. 1956.
809 Hargreaves, AJ (Alistair) b 29/04/1986 - KZN - 4 Tests (-) 7 matches (-) 2010: W1(R), It1(R). 2011: A1, NZ1.
251 Harris, TA (Tony) b 27/08/1916 d 07/03/1993 - Tvl - 5 Tests (3 - 1T) 13 matches (16 - 4T, 1D) 1937: NZ2, 3. 1938: BI1, 2, 3.
24 Hartley, AJ (Jack) b 18/08/1873 d 15/05/1923 - WP - 1 Test (-) 1 match (-) 1891: BI3.
568 Hattingh, H (Drikus) b 21/02/1968 - NTvl - 5 Tests (-) 17 matches (20 - 4T) 1992: A(R), F2(R), E. 1994: Arg1, 2.
239 Hattingh, LB (Lappies) b 01/09/1903 d 16/10/1974 - OFS - 1 Test (-) 1 match (-) 1933: A2.
623 Hattingh, SJ (Ian) b 31/10/1964 - Tvl - No Tests - 7 matches (10 - 2T) Toured W, S & I. 1994.
22 Heatlie, BH (Fairy) b 25/04/1872 d 19/08/1951 - WP - 6 Tests (6 - 3C) 6 matches (6 - 3C) 1891: BI2, 3. 1896: BI1, 4*. 1903: BI1, 3*.
657 Hendricks, M (McNeil) b 10/07/1973 - Boland - 2 Tests (5 - 1T) 4 matches (5 - 1T) 1998: I2(R), W1(R).
559 Hendriks, P (Pieter) b 13/04/1970 - Tvl - 14 Tests (10 - 2T) 23 matches (30 - 6T) 1992: NZ, A. 1994: S, W. 1995: [A, R, C]. 1996: A1, NZ1, A2, NZ2, 3, 4, 5.
57 Hepburn, TB (Tommy) b 14/02/1872 d 13/09/1933 - WP - 1 Test (2 - 1C) 1 match (2 - 1C) 1896: BI4.
521 Heunis, JW (Johan) b 26/01/1958 - NTvl - 14 Tests (41 - 2T, 6C, 7P) 24 matches (72 - 3T, 9C, 14P) 1981: NZ3(R), US. 1982: S. Am1, 2. 1984: E1, 2, S. Am&Sp1, 2. 1986: NZC1, 2, 3, 4. 1989: WT1, 2.
372 Hill, RA (Ronnie) b 20/12/1934 d 06/01/2011 - Rhodesia - 7 Tests (-) 21 matches (18 - 6T) 1960: W, I. 1961: I, A1, 2.

1962: BI4. 1963: A3.
575 Hills, WG (Willie) b 26/01/1962 - NTvl - 6 Tests (-) 13 matches (-) 1992: F1, 2, E. 1993: F1, 2, A1.
96 Hirsch, JG (Jack) b 20/02/1883 d 26/02/1958 - EP - 2 Tests (-) 18 matches (37 - 11T, 1D) 1906: I. 1910: BI1.
86 Hobson, TEC (Tommy) b 26/03/1881 d 02/09/1937 - WP - 1 Test (-) 1 match (-) 1903: BI3.
307 Hoffman, RS (Steve) b 02/12/1931 d 15/05/1986 - Boland - 1 Test (-) 1 match (-) 1953: A3.
248 Hofmeyr, SR (Koffie) b 23/08/1912 d 06/01/1975 - WP - No Tests - 11 matches (17 - 3T, 2D) Toured A & NZ. 1937.
352 Holton, DN (Dougie) b 28/09/1932 d 12/04/1994 - EP - 1 Test (-) 4 matches (-) 1960: S.
590 Honiball, HW (Henry) b 01/12/1965 - Natal - 35 Tests (156 - 1T, 38C, 25P) 45 matches (191 - 1T, 45C, 32P) 1993: A3(R), Arg2. 1995: WS1(R). 1996: Fj, A1, NZ5, Arg1, 2, F1, 2, W. 1997: T, BI1, 2, 3(R), NZ1(R), A1(R), NZ2, A2, It, F1, 2, E. 1998: W1(R), E1, A1, NZ1, 2, A2, W2, S, I3, E2. 1999: [A3(R), NZ3].
356 Hopwood, DJ (Doug) b 03/06/1934 d 10/01/2002 - WP - 22 Tests (15 - 5T) 53 matches (45 - 15T) 1960: S, NZ3, 4, W. 1961: E, S, F, I, A1, 2. 1962: BI1, 2, 3, 4. 1963: A1, 2, 4. 1964: W, F. 1965: S, NZ3, 4.
753 Hougaard, DJ (Derick) b 04/01/1983 - BB - 8 Tests (69 - 2T, 13C, 10P, 1D) 8 matches (69 - 2T, 13C, 10P, 1D) 2003: [U(R), E(R), G, Sm, NZ3]. 2007: Sm1, A2, NZ2.
807 Hougaard, F (Francois) b 06/04/1988 - BB - 27 Tests (20 - 4T) 30 matches (20 - 4T) 2009: It(R). 2010: A1(R), NZ3, A2, 3, W2(R), S, E(t). 2011: A2(t), NZ2(R), [W(R), Fj(R), N, Sm(R), A3(R).]. 2012: E1, 2, 3, Arg1, 2, A1, NZ1, A2, NZ2, I, S, E4.
330 **Howe, BF** (Pee-Wee) b 30/08/1932 d 22/04/2010 - Border - 2 Tests (3 - 1T) 18 matches (9 - 3T) 1956: NZ1, 4.
118 Howe-Browne, NRFG (Noel) b 24/12/1884 d 03/04/1943 - WP - 3 Tests (-) 3 matches (-) 1910: BI1, 2, 3.
555 Hugo, DP (Niel) b 11/11/1958 - WP - 2 Tests (-) 2 matches (-) 1989: WT1, 2.
726 Human, DCF (Daan) b 03/04/1976 - WP - 4 Tests (-) 4 matches

(-) 2002: W1, 2, Arg(R), Sm(R).
627 Hurter, MH (Marius) b 08/10/1970 - NTvl - 13 Tests (-) 18 matches (5 - 1T) 1995: [R, C], W. 1996: Fj, A1, NZ1, 2, 3, 4, 5. 1997: NZ1, 2, A2.

I

139 Immelman, JH (Jack) b 02/08/1888 d 21/07/1960 - WP - 1 Test (-) 13 matches (3 - 1T) 1913: F.

J

97 Jackson, DC (Mary) b 21/04/1885 d 17/09/1976 - WP - 3 Tests (-) 17 matches (29 - 7T, 4C) 1906: I, W, E.
80 Jackson, JS (Jack) b 01/10/1878 d 30/06/1954 - WP - 1 Test (-) 1 match (-) 1903: BI2.
721 Jacobs, AA (Adrian) b 14/08/1980 - GF - 34 Tests (35 - 7T) 35 matches (35 - 7T) 2001: It2(R), US. 2002: W1(R), Arg, Sm(R), NZ1(t+R), A1(R), F, S, E(R). 2008: W1, 2, NZ1, 2, Arg, NZ3, A2, 3, W3, S, E. 2009: BI1, 2, NZ2(R), A1(R), 2(R), 3(R), NZ3(R), F, It. 2010: I(R), E(R). 2011: A1(R), NZ1.
715 James, AD (Butch) b 08/01/1979 - Natal - 42 Tests (154 - 3T, 26C, 28P, 1D) 43 matches (159 - 3T, 27C, 29P, 1D) 2001: F1, 2, NZ1, A1, 2, NZ2. 2002: F(R), S, E. 2006: NZ1, A2, NZ2, 3(R), E1. 2007: E1, 2, A1, NZ1, N, S, [Sm, E3, US, Fiji, Arg, E4.]. 2008: W1, 2, NZ1, 2, A1, Arg, NZ3, A2, 3. 2010: It1, 2(R), NZ1(R), A1(R), 2(R). 2011: A2, [W(R).].
847 Janse van Rensburg, JC (JC) b 09/01/1986 - GL - No Tests - No matches Toured I, S & E. 2012.
436 Janse van Rensburg, MC (Martin) b 29/12/1944 - Natal - No Tests - 6 matches (10 - 2C, 2P) Toured BI & I. 1969/70.
518 Jansen, E (Eben) b 05/06/1954 - OFS - 1 Test (-) 11 matches (16 - 4T, E. 1981: NZ1.
444 Jansen, JS (Joggie) b 05/02/1948 - OFS - 10 Tests (3 - 1T) 15 matches (18 - 6T) 1970: NZ1, 2, 3, 4. 1971: F1, 2, A1, 2, 3. 1972: E.
414 Janson, A (Andrew) b 29/05/1935 d 2007 - WP - No Tests - 11 matches (24 - 8T) Toured A & NZ. 1965.
716 Jantjes, CA (Conrad) b 24/03/1980 - GL - 24 Tests (22 - 4T, C) 25 matches (22 - 4T, C) 2001: It1, A1, 2, NZ2, F3, It2, E, US. 2005: Arg, W. 2007: W(R). 2008: W1, 2, It, NZ1, 2(R), A1, Arg, NZ3(R), A2, 3, W3, S, E.

SPRINGBOKS 1891-2013

819 Jantjies, ET (Elton) b 01/08/1990 - GL - 2 Tests (6 - 2P) 3 matches (11 - 1C, 3P) 2012: A2(R), NZ2(R).
769 Januarie, ER (Ricky) b 01/02/1982 - GL - 47 Tests (25 - 5T) 50 matches (25 - 5T) 2005: U, F2, A1, 2, 3(R), NZ2, A4, NZ2. 2006: S1(R), 2(R), F(R), A1, I, E1, 2. 2007: E1, 2, Sm1, N(R), [Sm(R), T.], W. 2008: W2, It, NZ1, 2, A1, Arg, NZ3(R), A2(R), 3(R), W3(R), S, E. 2009: BI1(R), NZ1(R), 2(R), A1(R), 2(R), NZ3(R). 2010: W1, F, It1, 2, NZ1, 2, 3(R).
254 Jennings, CB (CB) b 16/08/1914 d 02/10/1989 - Border - 1 Test (-) 11 matches (9 - 3T) 1937: NZ1.
439 Jennings, MW (Mike) b 21/12/1946 - Boland - No Tests - 10 matches (6 - 2T) Toured BI & I. 1969/70.
377 Johns, RG (Bobby) b 21/02/1934 d 01/07/1990 - WP - No Tests - 1 match (-) Toured BI, I & F. 1960/61.
810 Johnson, AF (Ashley) b 16/05/1986 - FS - 3 Tests (-) 5 matches (-) 2011: A1, NZ1(R), 2(t+R).
604 Johnson, GK (Gavin) b 17/10/1966 - Tvl - 7 Tests (86 - 5T, 14C, 11P) 17 matches (173 - 9T, 25C, 26P) 1993: Arg2. 1994: NZ3, Arg1. 1995: WS1, [R, C, WS2].
291 Johnstone, PGA (Paul) b 30/06/1930 d 22/04/1996 - WP - 9 Tests (11 - 2T, 1C, 1P) 35 matches (68 - 14T, 7C, 4P) 1951: S, I, W. 1952: E, F 1956: A1, NZ1, 2, 4.
62 Jones, CH (Charlie) b 24/03/1880 d 06/03/1908 - Tvl - 2 Tests (-) 2 matches (-) 1903: BI1, 2.
30 Jones, PST (Percy) b 13/09/1876 d 08/03/1954 - WP - 3 Tests (3 - 1T) 3 matches (3 - 1T) 1896: BI1, 3, 4.
742 Jordaan, N (Norman) b 03/04/1975 - BB - 1 Test (-) 1 match (-) 2002: E(R).
271 Jordaan, RP (Jorrie) b 13/07/1920 d 22/09/1998 - NTvl - 4 Tests (-) 4 matches (-) 1949: NZ1, 2, 3, 4.
557 Joubert, AJ (André) b 15/04/1964 - OFS - 34 Tests (115 - 10T, 3C, 17P) 49 matches (258 - 18T, 39C, 30P) 1989: WT1(R). 1993: A3, Arg1. 1994: E1, 2, NZ1, 2(R), 3, Arg2, S, W. 1995: [A, C, WS2, F, NZ], W, It, E. 1996: Fj, A1, NZ1, 3, 4, 5, Arg1, 2, F1, 2, W. 1997: T, BI1, 2, A2.
711 Joubert, MC (Marius) b 10/07/1979 - Boland - 30 Tests (45 - 9T) 31 matches (45 - 9T) 2001: NZ1. 2002: W1, 2, Arg(R), Sm, NZ1, A1, NZ2, A2, F(R). 2003: S2, Arg, A1. 2004: I1, 2, W1, PI, NZ1, A1, NZ2, A2, W2, I3, E, S, Arg. 2005: U, F1, 2, A1.
110 Joubert, SJ (Steve) b 08/04/1887 - d 27/03/1939 - WP - 3 Tests (8 - 1T, 1C, 1P) 6 matches (20 - 1T, 4C, 2P, 1D) 1906: I, W, E.
689 Julies, W (Wayne) b 23/10/1978 - Boland - 11 Tests (10 - 2T) 12 matches (10 - 2T) 1999: [Sp]. 2004: I1, 2, W1, S, Arg. 2005: A2(R), 3(t). 2006: F(R). 2007: Sm1, [T.].

K
509 Kahts, WJH (Willie) b 20/02/1947 - NTvl - 11 Tests (4 - 1T) 15 matches (12 - 3T) 1980: BI1, 2, 3, S. Am3, 4, F 1981: I1, 2, NZ2. 1982: S. Am1, 2.
344 Kaminer, J (Joe) b 25/01/1934 - Tvl - 1 Test (-) 1 match (-) 1958: F2.
791 Kankowski, R (Ryan) b 14/10/1985 - KZN - 20 Tests (5 - 1T) 22 matches (5 - 1T) 2007: W. 2008: W2(R), It, A1(R), W3(R), S(R), E(R). 2009: BI3, NZ3(R), F, It. 2010: W1(R), It1(R), NZ2(R), A1, 3(R), S. 2011: A1(R), NZ1(R). 2012: E3(R).
675 Kayser, DJ (Deon) b 03/07/1970 - EP - 13 Tests (25 - 5T) 21 matches (30 - 6T) 1999: It2(R), A1(R), NZ2, A2, [S, Sp(R), U, E, A3]. 2001: It1(R), NZ1(R), A2(R), NZ2(R).
599 Kebble, GR (Guy) b 02/05/1966 - Natal - 4 Tests (-) 12 matches (5 - 1T) 1993: Arg1, 2. 1994: NZ1(R), 2.
288 Keevy, AC (Jakkals) b 12/11/1917 d 09/02/1990 - ETvl - No Tests - 13 matches (10 - 2C, 2P) Toured BI, I & F. 1951/52.
55 Kelly, EW (Ted) b 23/10/1869 d 11/03/1949 - GW - 1 Test (-) 1 match (-) 1896: BI3.
669 Kempson, RB (Robbie) b 23/02/1974 - Natal - 37 Tests (5 - 1T) 38 matches (5 - 1T) 1998: I2(R), W1, E1, A1, NZ1, 2, A2, W2, S, I3, E2. 1999: It1, 2, W. 2000: C, E1, 2, A1, NZ1, A2, 3, Arg, I, W, E3. 2001: F1, 2(R), NZ1, A1, 2, NZ2. 2003: S1(R), 2(R), Arg, A1(R), NZ1(R), A2.
286 Kenyon, BJ (Basil) b 19/05/1918 d 09/05/1996 - Border - 1 Test (-) 6 matches (13 - 2T , 2C, 1P) 1949: NZ4*.
226 Kipling, HG (Bert) b 24/12/1903 d 13/09/1981 - GW - 9 Tests (-) 24 matches (-) 1931: W, I. 1932: E, S. 1933: A1, 2, 3, 4, 5.
804 Kirchner, Z (Zane) b 16/06/1984 - BB - 24 Tests (15 - 3T) 24 matches (15 - 3T) 2009: BI3, F, It, I. 2010: W1(R), F, It1, NZ1, 2, A1, I, W2(R), S, E. 2012: E1, Arg1, 2, A1, NZ1, A2, NZ2, I, S, E4.
306 Kirkpatrick, AI (Ian) b 25/07/1930 d 18/11/2012 - GW - 13 Tests (-) 43 matches (18 - 6T) 1953: A2. 1956: NZ2. 1958: F1. 1960: S, NZ1, 2, 3, 4, W, I. 1961: E, S, F.
Kirsten, FBC (Frik) b 18/08/1988 - Blue Bulls - 2013: Springbok Tour squad member only. Not a Springbok.
143 Knight, AS (Saturday) b 16/12/1885 d 01/07/1946 - Tvl - 5 Tests (-) 18 matches (3 - 1T) 1912: S, I, W. 1913: E, F.
553 Knoetze, F (Faffa) b 18/01/1963 - WP - 2 Tests (4 - 1T) 8 matches (14 - 3T) 1989: WT1, 2.
280 Koch, AC (Chris) b 21/09/1927 d 21/03/1986 - Boland - 22 Tests (15 - 5T) 46 matches (33 - 11T) 1949: NZ2, 3, 4. 1951: S, I, W. 1952: E, F. 1953: A1, 2, 4. 1955: BI1, 2, 3, 4. 1956: A1, NZ2, 3. 1958: F1, 2. 1960: NZ1, 2.
274 Koch, HV (Bubbles) b 13/06/1921 d 02/11/2003 - WP - 4 Tests (-) 4 matches (-) 1949: NZ1, 2, 3, 4.
693 Koen, LJ (Louis) b 07/07/1975 - GL - 15 Tests (145 - 23C, 31P, 2D) 15 matches (145 - 23C, 31P, 2D) 2000: A1. 2001: It2, E, US. 2003: S1, 2, Arg, A1, NZ1, A2, NZ2, [U, E, Sm(R), NZ3(R)].
851 Kolisi, S (Siya) b 16/06/1991 - WP - 10 Tests (-) 10 matches (-) 2013: S(R), Sam(R), Arg1(R), Arg2(R), A1(R), NZ1(R), A2(R), NZ2(R), W(R), F(R).
420 Kotzé, GJM (Gert) b 12/08/1940 - WP - 4 Tests (-) 4 matches (-) 1967: F1, 2, 3, 4.
487 Krantz, EFW (Edrich) b 10/08/1954 - OFS - 2 Tests (4 - 1T) 11 matches (48 - 12T) 1976: NZ1. 1981: I1.
676 Krige, CPJ (Corné) b 21/03/1975 - WP - 39 Tests (10 - 2T) 43 matches (15 - 3T) 1999: It2*, W, NZ1. 2000: C(R), E1(R), 2, A1(R), NZ1, A2, NZ2, A3, Arg, I, W, E3. 2001: F1, 2, It1(R), A1(t+R), It2(R), E(R). 2002: W2, Arg*, Sm*, NZ1*, A1*, NZ2*, A2*, F*, S*, E*. 2003: Arg*, A1*, NZ1*, A2*, NZ2*. [E*, Sm*, NZ3*].
64 Krige, JD (Japie) b 05/07/1879 d 14/01/1961 - WP - 5 Tests (3 - 1T) 13 matches (12 - 4T) 1903: BI1, 3. 1906: S, I, W.
136 Krige, WA (Willie) b 02/12/1887 d 20/08/1961 - WP - No Tests - 9 matches (10 - 2T, 1D) Toured BI, I & F. 1912/13.
477 Kritzinger, JL (Klippies) b

01/03/1948 - Tvl - 7 Tests (4 - 1T) 12 matches (4 - 1T) 1974: BI3, 4, F1, 2. 1975: F1, 2. 1976: NZ4.
318 Kroon, CM (Colin) b 22/02/1931 d 13/11/1981 - EP - 1 Test (-) 1 match (-) 1955: BI1.
550 Kruger, PE (Piet) b 11/04/1958 - Tvl - 2 Tests (-) 2 matches (-) 1986: NZC3, 4.
832 Kruger, PJJ (Juandré) b 06/09/1985 - BB - 17 Tests (-) 17 matches (-) 2012: E1, 2, 3, A1, NZ1, I, S, E4. 2013: It, S, Sam(R), Arg1, Arg2, A1(R), NZ1(R), A2(R), NZ2 (R).
596 Kruger, RJ (Ruben) b 30/03/1970 d 27/01/2010 - OFS - 36 Tests (35 - 7T) 56 matches (105 - 21T) 1993: Arg1, 2. 1994: S, W. 1995: WS1, [A, R, WS2, F, NZ], W, It, E. 1996: Fj, A1, NZ1, A2, NZ2, 3, 4, 5, Arg1, 2, F1, 2, W. 1997: T, BI1, 2, NZ1, A1, NZ2. 1999: NZ2, A2(R), [Sp, NZ3(R)].
169 Krüger, TL (Theuns) b 17/06/1896 d 06/07/1957 - Tvl - 8 Tests (-) 21 matches (6 - 2T) 1921: NZ1, 2. 1924: BI1, 2, 3, 4. 1928: NZ1, 2.
828 Kruger, W (Werner) b 23/01/1985 - BB - 4 Tests (-) 5 matches (-) 2011: A1, NZ1. 2012: E2(R), 3(R).
364 Kuhn, SP (Fanie) b 12/06/1935 - Tvl - 19 Tests (-) 37 matches (-) 1960: NZ3, 4, W, I. 1961: E, S, F, I, A1, 2. 1962: BI1, 2, 3, 4. 1963: A1, 2, 3. 1965: I, S.
191 La Grange, JB (Paul) b 25/05/1897 d 23/05/1971 - WP - 2 Tests (-) 2 matches (-) 1924: BI3, 4.

L

694 Labuschagne, JJ (Jannes) b 16/04/1976 - GL - 11 Tests (-) 11 matches (-) 2000: NZ1(R). 2002: W1, 2, Arg, NZ1, A1, NZ2, A2, F, S, E.
820 Lambie, PJ (Patrick) b 17/10/1990 -KZN - 32 Tests (68 - 1T, 15C, 11P) 33 matches (68 - 15C, 11P) 2010: I(R), W2(R), S(R), E(R). 2011: A1(R), NZ1, 2, [Fj, N, Sm, A3.]. 2012: E1(R), 2, A1, NZ1(R), A2(R), NZ2(R), I, S, E4. 2013: It(R), S(R), Sam, Arg1(R), Arg2(R), A1(R), NZ1(R), A2(R), NZ2(R), W, S, F(R).
46 Larard, A (Alf) b 30/12/1870 d 15/08/1936 - Tvl - 2 Tests (3 - 1T) 2 matches (3 - 1T) 1896: BI2, 4.
266 Lategan, MT (Tjol) b 29/09/1925 - WP - 11 Tests (9 - 3T) 26 matches (15 - 5T) 1949: NZ1, 2, 3, 4. 1951: S, I, W. 1952: E, F. 1953: A1, 2.
620 Laubscher, TG (Tommie) b 08/10/1963 d 26/05/2007 - WP - 6 Tests (-) 12 matches (-) 1994: Arg1, 2, S, W. 1995: It, E.
396 Lawless, MJ (Mike) b 17/09/1941 - WP - 4 Tests (-) 15 matches (12 - 1T, 1P, 2D) 1964: F. 1969: E(R). 1970: I, W.
245 Lawton, AD (Dandy) b 21/08/1911 d 06/05/1967 - WP - No Tests - 5 matches (24 - 8T) Toured A & NZ. 1937.
600 Le Roux, A-H (Ollie) b 10/05/1973 - OFS - 54 Tests (5 - 1T) 68 matches (25 - 5T) 1994: E1. 1998: I1, 2, W1(R), E1(R), A1(R), NZ1(R), 2(R), A2(R), W2(R), S(R), I3(R), E2(t+R). 1999: It1(R), 2(R), W(R), NZ1(R), A1(R), NZ2(R), A2(R), [S(R), Sp, U(t+R), E(R), A3(R), NZ3(R)]. 2000: E1(t+R), 2(R), A1(R), 2(R), NZ2, A3(R), Arg(R), I(t), W(R), E3(R). 2001: F1(R), 2, It1, NZ1(R), A1(R), 2(R), NZ2(R), F3, It2, E, US(R). 2002: W1(R), 2(R), Arg, NZ1(R), A1(R), NZ2(R), A2(R).
572 Le Roux, HP (Hennie) b 10/07/1967 - Tvl - 27 Tests (34 - 4T, 1C, 4P) 51 matches (90 - 12T, 6C, 6P) 1993: F1, 2. 1994: E1, 2, NZ1, 2, 3, Arg2, S, W. 1995: WS1, [A, R, C(R), WS2, F, NZ], W, It, E. 1996: Fj, NZ2, Arg1, 2, F1, 2, W.
608 Le Roux, JHS (Johan) b 15/11/1961 - Tvl - 3 Tests (-) 7 matches (-) 1994: E2, NZ1, 2.
94 Le Roux, JSR (Japie) b 21/08/1882 d 04/03/1949 - WP - No Tests - 9 matches (30 - 10T) Toured BI, I & F. 1906/07.
510 Le Roux, M (Martiens) b 30/03/1951 d 14/10/2006 - OFS - 8 Tests (-) 12 matches (4 - 1T) 1980: BI1, 2, 3, 4, S. Am3, 4, F. 1981: I1.
103 Le Roux, PA (Pietie) b 22/01/1885 d 11/07/1954 - WP - 3 Tests (-) 16 matches (11 - 3T, 1C) 1906: I, W, E.
848 Le Roux, WJ (Willie) b 18/08/1989 - GW - 12 Tests (20 - 4T) 12 matches (20 - 4T) 2013: It, S, Sam, Arg1, Arg2, A1, NZ1, A2, NZ2, W(R), S, F.
146 Ledger, SH (Sep) b 29/04/1889 d 30/01/1918 - GW - 4 Tests (3 - 1T) 15 matches (3 - 1T) 1912: S, I. 1913: E, F.
688 Leonard, A (Anton) b 31/05/1974 - SWD - 2 Tests (5 - 1T) 2 matches (5 - 1T) 1999: A1, [Sp].
794 Liebenberg, CR (Tiaan) b 18/12/1981 - WP - 5 Tests (-) 6 matches (-) 2012: Arg2(R), A1(R), NZ1(R), A2(R), NZ2(R).
591 Linee, M (Tinus) b 23/08/1969 - WP - No Tests - 9 matches (10 - 2T) Toured A. 1993 and W, S & I. 1994.
12 Little, EM (Edward) b 01/11/1864 d ??/05/1945 - GW - 2 Tests (-) 2 matches (-) 1891: BI1, 3.
781 Lobberts, H (Hilton) b 11/06/1986 - BB - 2 Tests (-) 4 matches (-) 2006: E1(R). 2007: NZ2(R).
326 Lochner, GP (Butch) b 01/02/1931 d 27/08/2010 - WP - 9 Tests (6 - 2T) 22 matches (15 - 5T) 1955: BI3. 1956: A1, 2, NZ1, 2, 3, 4. 1958: F1, 2.
249 Lochner, GP (Flappie) b 11/01/1914 d 30/01/1996 - EP - 3 Tests (3 - 1T) 12 matches (27 - 9T) 1937: NZ3. 1938: BI1, 2.
360 Lockyear, RJ (Dick) b 26/06/1931 d 03/03/1988 - GW - 6 Tests (20 - 4C, 4P) 20 matches (97 - 32C, 11P) 1960: NZ1, 2, 3, 4, I. 1961: F.
127 Lombard, AC (Antonie) b 06/12/1885 d 22/02/1960 - EP - 1 Test (-) 1 match (-) 1910: BI2.
736 Lombard, F (Friedrich) b 04/03/1979 - FS - 2 Tests (-) 2 matches (-) 2002: S, E.
588 Lötter, D (Deon) b 10/11/1957 - Tvl - 3 Tests (-) 7 matches (5 - 1T) 1993: F2, A1, 2.
255 Lotz, JW (Jan) b 26/08/1910 d 13/08/1986 - Tvl - 8 Tests (3 - 1T) 26 matches (6 - 2T) 1937: A1, 2, NZ1, 2, 3. 1938: BI1, 2, 3.
697 Loubscher, RIP (Ricardo) b 11/06/1974 - EP - 4 Tests (-) 7 matches (-) 2002: W1. 2003: S1, [U(R), G].
85 Loubser, JA (Bob) b 06/08/1884 d 07/12/1962 - WP - 7 Tests (9 - 3T) 23 matches (66 - 22T) 1903: BI3. 1906: S, I, W, E. 1910: BI1, 3.
425 Lourens, MJ (Thys) b 15/05/1943 - NTvl - 3 Tests (3 - 1T) 11 matches (12 - 4T) 1968: BI2, 3, 4.
704 Louw, FH (Hottie) b 02/03/1976 - WP - 3 Tests (-) 7 matches (-) 2002: W2(R), Arg, Sm.
11 Louw, JS (Japie) b 30/08/1867 d 17/08/1936 - Tvl - 3 Tests (-) 3 matches (-) 1891: BI1, 2, 3.
147 Louw, LH (Louis) b 23/06/1884 d 13/09/1968 - WP - No Tests - 12 matches (3 - 1T) Toured BI, I & F. 1912/13.
815 Louw, L-FP (Francois) b 15/06/1985 - WP - 28 Tests (25 - 5T) 28 matches (25 - 5T) 2010: W1, F, It1, 2, NZ1, 2, 3(R). 2011: [Fj(t), N(t+R), A3(R).]. 2012: A1(R), NZ1, A2, NZ2, I, S, E4. 2013:

SPRINGBOKS 1891-2013

It, Sam, Arg1, Arg2, A1, NZ1, A2, NZ2, W, S, F.
454 Louw, MJ (Martiens) b 20/04/1938 d 12/10/2013 - Tvl - 2 Tests (-) 9 matches (-) 1971: A2, 3.
207 Louw, MM (Boy) b 21/02/1906 d 03/05/1988 - WP - 18 Tests (3 - 1T) 49 matches (18 - 6T) 1928: NZ3, 4. 1931: W, I. 1932: E, S. 1933: A1, 2, 3, 4, 5. 1937: A1, 2, NZ2, 3. 1938: BI1, 2, 3.
505 Louw, RJ (Rob) b 26/03/1955 - WP - 19 Tests (20 - 5T) 28 matches (44 - 11T) 1980: S. Am1, 2, BI1, 2, 3, 4, S. Am3, 4, F. 1981: I1, 2, NZ1, 3. 1982: S. Am1, 2. 1984: E1, 2, S. Am&Sp1, 2.
222 Louw, SC (Fanie) b 16/09/1909 d 13/07/1940 - WP - 12 Tests (6 - 2T) 30 matches (24 - 8T) 1933: A1, 2, 3, 4, 5. 1937: A1, NZ1, 2, 3. 1938: BI1, 2, 3.
650 Lubbe, JMF (Edrich) b 29/07/1969 - GW - 2 Tests (17 - 7C, 1P) 2 matches (17 - 7C, 1P) 1997: T, BI1.
114 Luyt, FP (Freddie) b 26/02/1888 d 06/06/1965 - WP - 7 Tests (8 - 2T, 1C) 21 matches (27 - 5T, 6C) 1910: BI1, 2, 3. 1912: S, I, W. 1913: E.
150 Luyt, JD (John) b 06/12/1884 d 03/10/1964 - EP - 4 Tests (-) 19 matches (3 - 1T) 1912: S, W. 1913: E, F.
122 Luyt, RR (Dick) b 16/04/1886 d 14/01/1967 - WP - 7 Tests (3 - 1T) 21 matches (28 - 8T, 1D) 1910: BI2, 3. 1912: S, I, W. 1913: E, F.
29 Lyons, DJ (Dykie) b 03/08/1873 d 01/05/1921 - EP - 1 Test (-) 1 match (-) 1896: BI1.
236 Lyster, PJ (Pat) b 31/05/1913 d 25/07/2002 - Natal - 3 Tests (-) 11 matches (39 - 13T) 1933: A2, 5. 1937: NZ1.

M

409 MacDonald, AW (Andy) b 27/08/1934 d 18/08/1987 - Rhodesia - 5 Tests (-) 17 matches (3 - 1T) 1965: A1, NZ1, 2, 3, 4.
470 MacDonald, DA (Dugald) b 20/01/1950 - WP - 1 Test (-) 1 match (-) 1974: BI2.
811 Maku, BG (Bandise) b 24/06/1986 - BB - 1 Test (-) 4 matches (5 - 1T) 2010: It1(R).
361 Malan, AS (Avril) b 09/04/1937 - Tvl - 16 Tests (-) 36 matches (3 - 1T) 1960: NZ1, 2, 3*, 4*, W*, I*. 1961: E*, S*, F*. 1962: BI1. 1963: A1, 2, 3*. 1964: W*. 1965: I*, S*.
556 Malan, AW (Adolf) b 06/09/1961 - NTvl - 7 Tests (-) 11 matches (-) 1989:

WT1, 2. 1992: NZ, A, F1, 2, E.
512 Malan, E (Ewoud) b 04/07/1953 - NTvl - 2 Tests (-) 2 matches (-) 1980: BI3(R), 4.
345 Malan, GF (Abie) b 18/11/1935 - WP - 18 Tests (3 - 1T) 44 matches (9 - 3T) 1958: F2. 1960: NZ1, 3, 4. 1961: E, S, F. 1962: BI1, 2, 3. 1963: A1*, 2*, 4*. 1964: W*. 1965: A1, 2, NZ1, 2.
284 Malan, P (Piet) b 13/02/1919 - Tvl - 1 Test (-) 1 match (-) 1949: NZ4.
841 Malherbe, JF (Frans) b 14/03/1991 - WP - 2 Tests (-) 2 matches (-) 2012: Rugby Championship Squad - no tests. 2013: W, S.
541 Mallett, NVH (Nick) b 30/10/1956 - WP - 2 Tests (4 - 1T) 2 matches (4 - 1T) 1984: S. Am&Sp1, 2.
687 Malotana, K (Kaya) b 30/01/1976 - Border - 1 Test (-) 1 match (-) 1999: [Sp].
708 Manana, TD (Thando) b 16/10/1977 - GW - No Tests - 3 matches (-) Toured Arg, I, W & E. 2000.
398 Mans, WJ (Wynand) b 21/02/1942 - WP - 2 Tests (5 - 1T, 1C) 19 matches (123 - 14T, 30C, 6P, 1D) 1965: I, S.
844 Mapoe, LG (Lionel) b 13/07/1988 - GL - No Tests - No matches Toured I, S & E. 2012.
685 Marais, CF (Charl) b 02/09/1970 - WP - 12 Tests (5 - 1T) 15 matches (5 - 1T) 1999: It1(R), 2(R). 2000: C, E1, 2, A1, NZ1, A2, NZ2, A3, Arg(R), W(R).
264 Marais, FP (Buks) b 13/12/1927 d 12/12/1996 - Boland - 5 Tests (10 - 1T, 2C, 1P) 18 matches (40 - 11T, 2C, 1P) 1949: NZ1, 2. 1951: S. 1953: A1, 2.
390 Marais, JFK (Hannes) b 21/09/1941 - WP - 35 Tests (3 - 1T) 75 matches (38 - 12T) 1963: A3. 1964: W, F. 1965: I, S, A2. 1968: BI1, 2, 3, 4, F1, 2. 1969: S, E, A1, 2, 3, 4. 1970: I, W, NZ1, 2, 3, 4. 1971: F1*, 2*, A1*, 2*, 3*. 1974: BI1*, 2*, 3*, 4*, F1*, 2*.
529 Marais, JH (Johan) b 28/05/1959 - NTvl - No Tests - 5 matches (4 - 1T) Toured NZ & USA. 1981.
98 Maré, DS (Dietlof) b 02/07/1885 d 14/10/1913 - Tvl - 1 Test (-) 11 matches (31 - 2T, 11C, 1P) 1906: S.
677 Markram, RL (Robert) b 15/09/1975 d 06/07/2001 - GW - No Tests - 4 matches (-) Toured BI & I. 1998.
92 Marsberg, AFW (Artie) b 24/09/1883 d 15/01/1942 - GW - 3 Tests

(-) 18 matches (15 - 5T) 1906: S, W, E.
111 Marsberg, PA (Archie) b 01/10/1885 d 23/10/1962 - GW - 1 Test (-) 1 match (-) 1910: BI1.
598 Martens, HJ (Hentie) b 29/10/1971 - OFS - No Tests - 3 matches (5 - 1T) Toured Arg. 1993.
82 Martheze, WC (Rajah) b 29/11/1877 d 16/02/1912 - GW - 3 Tests (-) 16 matches (18 - 6T) 1903: BI2. 1906: I, W.
256 Martin, HJ (Kalfie) b 10/06/1910 d 20/10/2000 - Tvl - 1 Test (-) 16 matches (9 - 3T) 1937: A2.
705 Matfield, V (Victor) b 11/05/1977 - GW - 110 Tests (35 - 7T) 114 matches (35 - 7T) 2001: It1(R), NZ1, A2, NZ2, F3, It2, E, US. 2002: W1, Sm, NZ1, A1, NZ2(R). 2003: S1, 2, Arg, A1, NZ1, A2, NZ2, [U, E, Sm, NZ3]. 2004: I1, 2, W1, NZ2, A2, W2, I3, E, S, Arg. 2005: F1, 2, A1, 2, 3, NZ1, A4, NZ2, Arg, W, F3. 2006: S1, 2, F, A1, NZ1, A2, NZ2, 3, A3. 2007: E1, 2, A1, NZ1*, N*, S*, [Sm, E3, T(R), US, Fiji, Arg, E4.]. 2008: W1(R), 2, It*, NZ1, 2*, A1*, Arg*, NZ3*, A2*, 3*, W3, S, E. 2009: BI1, 2, 3, NZ1, 2, A1, 2, 3, NZ3, F, It(R), I. 2010: W1, F, It1*, NZ1, 2, A1, NZ3, A2, 3, I*, W2*, S*, E*. 2011: A2, NZ2*, [W, Sm*, A3.].
443 McCallum, ID (Ian) b 30/07/1944 - WP - 11 Tests (62 - 10C, 14P) 17 matches (134 - 2T, 28C, 24P) 1970: NZ1, 2, 3, 4. 1971: F1, 2, A1, 2, 3. 1974: BI1, 2.
462 McCallum, RJ (Roy) b 12/04/1946 - WP - 1 Test (-) 5 matches (4 - 1T) 1974: BI1.
138 McCulloch, JD (John) b 11/04/1885 d 23/04/1953 - GW - 2 Tests (-) 11 matches (3 - 1T) 1913: E, F.
565 McDonald, I (Ian) b 22/02/1968 - Tvl - 6 Tests (-) 18 matches (25 - 5T) 1992: NZ, A. 1993: F1, A3. 1994: E2. 1995: WS1(R).
223 McDonald, JAJ (André) b 17/02/1909 - d 13/07/1991 - WP - 4 Tests (-) 15 matches (5 - 5T) 1931: W, I. 1932: E, S.
69 McEwan, WMC (Willie) b 24/10/1875 d 04/04/1934 - Tvl - 2 Tests (-) 2 matches (-) 1903: BI1, 3.
134 McHardy, EE (Boetie) b 11/06/1890 d 13/12/1959 - OFS - 5 Tests (18 - 6T) 17 matches (60 - 20T) 1912: S, I, W. 1913: E, F.
27 McKendrick, JA (Jim) b 27/07/1870 d 01/01/1895 - WP - 1 Test (

-) 1 match (-) 1891: BI3.
826 McLeod, C (Charl) b 05/08/1983 - KZN - 1 Test (-) 2 matches (-) 2011: NZ1(R).
131 Meintjes, JJ (Cooper) b 05/05/1887 d 30/01/1970 - GW - No Tests - 4 matches (-) Toured BI, I & F 1912/13.
612 Meiring, FA (FA) b 24/08/1967 - NTvl - No Tests - 7 matches (10 - 2T) Toured NZ. 1994.
48 Mellet, TB (Tom) b 29/08/1871 d 29/07/1943 - GW - 1 Test (-) 1 match (-) 1896: BI2.
172 Mellish, FW (Frank) b 26/03/1897 d 21/08/1965 - WP - 6 Tests (-) 15 matches (-) 1921: NZ1,3. 1924: BI1,2,3,4.
427 Menter, MA (Alan) b 03/10/1941 - NTvl - No Tests - 2 matches (-) Toured F. 1968.
756 Mentz, H (Henno) b 25/09/1979 - Natal - 2 Tests (-) 2 matches (-) 2004: I1,W1(R).
14 Merry, GA (George) b 03/03/1869 d 02/05/1917 - EP - 1 Test (-) 1 match (-) 1891: BI1.
79 Metcalf, HD (Henry) b 20/04/1878 d 03/03/1966 - Border - 1 Test (-) 1 match (-) 1903: BI2.
159 Meyer, C du P (Charlie) b 14/01/1897 d 31/05/1980 - WP - 3 Tests (-) 15 matches (27 - 9T) 1921: NZ1,2,3.
38 Meyer, PJ (PJ) b ??/05/1873 d 27/07/1919 - GW - 1 Test (-) 1 match (-) 1896: BI1.
663 Meyer, W (Willie) b 06/11/1967 - FS - 26 Tests (5 - 1T) 31 matches (10 - 2T) 1997: S(R). 1999: It2, NZ1(R), A1(R). 2000: C(R), E1, NZ1(R), 2(R), Arg, I, W, E3. 2001: F1(R), 2, It1, F3(R), It2, E, US(t+R). 2002: W1,2, Arg, NZ1,2, A2, F.
168 Michau, JM (Baby) b 14/08/1890 d 20/06/1945 - Tvl - 1 Test (-) 10 matches (-) 1921: NZ1.
162 Michau, JP (Mannetjies) b 06/10/1900 d 22/05/1960 - WP - 3 Tests (-) 16 matches (6 - 2T) 1921: NZ1,2,3.
109 Millar, WA (Billy) b 06/11/1883 d 18/03/1949 - WP - 6 Tests (6 - 2T) 37 matches (15 - 5T) 1906: E. 1910: BI2*,3*. 1912: I*,W*. 1913: F*.
123 Mills, WJ (Wally) b 16/06/1891 d 23/02/1975 - WP - 1 Test (3 - 1T) 13 matches (30 - 10T) 1910: BI2.
125 Moll, TM (Toby) b 20/07/1890 d 07/11/1916 - Tvl - 1 Test (-) 1 match (-) 1910: BI2.

651 Montgomery, PC (Percy) b 15/03/1974 - WP - 102 Tests (893 - 25T, 153C, 148P,6D) 104 matches (906 - 26T, 157C, 148P,6D) 1997: BI2,3, NZ1, A1, NZ2, A2, F1, 2, E, S. 1998: I1, 2, W1, E1, A1, NZ1, 2, A2, W2, S, I3, E2. 1999: It1, 2, W, NZ1, A1, NZ2, A2, [S, U, E, A3, NZ3]. 2000: C, E1, 2, A1, NZ1, A2(R), Arg, I, W, E3. 2001: F1, 2(t), It1, NZ1, F3(R), It2(R). 2004: I2, W1, PI, NZ1, A1, NZ2, A2, W2, I3, E, S. 2005: U, F1, 2, A1, 2, 3, NZ1, A4, NZ2, Arg, W, F3. 2006: S1, 2, F,A1, NZ1, A2, NZ2. 2007: E1, 2, Sm1(R), A1, NZ1, N, S, [Sm, E3, T(R), US, Fiji, Arg, E4.]. 2008: W1(R), 2(R), NZ1(R), 2, Arg(R), NZ3, A2(R), 3(R).
328 Montini, PE (Pat) b 15/06/1929 d 26/08/2008 - WP - 2 Tests (-) 11 matches (6 - 1T, 1D) 1956: A1, 2.
498 Moolman, LC (Louis) b 21/01/1951 d 10/02/2006 - NTvl - 24 Tests (-) 31 matches (12 - 3T) 1977: WT. 1980: S.Am1, 2, BI1, 2, 3, 4, S.Am3, 4, F 1981: I1, 2, NZ1, 2, 3, US. 1982: S. Am1, 2. 1984: S. Am&Sp1, 2. 1986: NZC1,2,3,4.
501 Mordt, RH (Ray) b 15/02/1957 - Zimbabwe - 18 Tests (48 - 12T) 25 matches (88 - 22T) 1980: S.Am1,2, BI1,2, 3,4, S.Am3,4, F 1981: I2, NZ1,2,3, US. 1982: S.Am1,2. 1984: S.Am&Sp1,2.
106 Morkel, DFT (Dougie) b 26/10/1885 d 20/02/1950 - Tvl - 9 Tests (38 - 3T, 7C, 5P) 40 matches (137 - 8T, 37C, 13P) 1906: I, E. 1910: BI1*, 3. 1912: S, I, W. 1913: E*, F.
66 Morkel, DJA (Andrew) b 04/08/1882 d 14/06/1965 - Tvl - 1 Test (-) 2 matches (-) 1903: BI1.
173 Morkel, HJL (Harry) b 08/12/1888 d 16/07/1956 - WP - 1 Test (-) 13 matches (6 - 2T) 1921: NZ1.
155 Morkel, HW (Henry) b 14/07/1894 d 25/12/1969 - WP - 2 Tests (-) 9 matches (18 - 6T) 1921: NZ1, 2.
171 Morkel, JA (Royal) b 30/04/1894 d 22/10/1926 - WP - 2 Tests (-) 13 matches (9 - 2T, 1D) 1921: NZ2,3.
137 Morkel, JWH (Jacky) b 13/11/1890 d 15/05/1916 - WP - 5 Tests (16 - 4T, 2C) 18 matches (34 - 6T, 4C, 2D) 1912: S, I, W. 1913: E, F.
130 Morkel, PG (Gerhard) b 15/10/1888 d 05/09/1963 - WP - 8 Tests (16 - 6C, 1D) 33 matches (79 - 33C, 3P, 1D) 1912: S, I, W. 1913: E, F 1921: NZ1, 2, 3.
211 Morkel, PK (PK) b 01/07/1905 d 24/07/1993 - WP - 1 Test (-) 1 match (-)

1928: NZ4.
128 Morkel, WH (Boy) b 02/01/1885 d 06/02/1955 - WP - 9 Tests (6 - 2T) 31 matches (21 - 7T) 1910: BI3. 1912: S, I, W. 1913: E, F 1921: NZ1*, 2*, 3*.
105 Morkel, WS (Sommie) b 26/09/1879 d 11/07/1921 - Tvl - 4 Tests (-) 16 matches (3 - 1T) 1906: S, I, W, E.
267 Moss, C (Cecil) b 12/02/1925 - Natal - 4 Tests (-) 4 matches (-) 1949: NZ1,2,3,4.
830 Mostert, G (Gerhard) b 04/10/1984 - KZN - 2 Tests (-) 2 matches (-) 2011: NZ1, A2(R).
176 Mostert, PJ (Phil) b 30/10/1898 d 03/10/1972 - WP - 14 Tests (6 - 1T, 1D) 40 matches (18 - 5T, 1D) 1921: NZ1,2,3. 1924: BI1,2,4. 1928: NZ1*,2*,3*,4*. 1931: W, I. 1932: E, S.
682 Moyle, BS (Brent) b 31/03/1974 - GF - No Tests - 1 match (-) Toured BI & I. 1998.
797 Mtawarira, T (Tendai) b 01/08/1985 - KZN - 53 Tests (10 - 2T) 54 matches (10 - 2T) 2008: W2, It, A1(R), Arg, NZ3, A2, 3, W3, S, E. 2009: BI1, 2, 3, NZ1,2, A1,2,3, NZ3, F,It(R), I. 2010: I, W2, S, E. 2011: A2, NZ2(R), [W, Fj(R), N(R), Sm.]. 2012: E1, 2, 3, Arg1, 2, A1, NZ1, A2, NZ2. 2012: tour of UK - no tests. 2013: It, S, Sam, Arg1, Arg2, A1, NZ1, A2, NZ2, W, S(R), F.
642 Muir, DJ (Dick) b 20/03/1965 - Natal - 5 Tests (10 - 2T) 10 matches (20 - 4T) 1997: It, F1, 2, E, S.
796 Mujati, BV (Brian) b 28/09/1984 - WP - 12 Tests (-) 12 matches (-) 2008: W1, It(R), NZ1(R), 2(t), A1(R), Arg(R), NZ3(R), A2(R), 3, W3(t), S(R), E(R).
405 Mulder, CG (Boet) b 21/05/1939 - ETvl - No Tests - 13 matches (20 - 7C, 2P) Toured A & NZ. 1965.
617 Mulder, JC (Japie) b 18/10/1969 - Tvl - 34 Tests (30 - 6T) 43 matches (45 - 9T) 1994: NZ2,3, S, W. 1995: WS1, [A, WS2, F, NZ], W, It, E. 1996: Fj, A1, NZ1, A2, NZ2, 5, Arg1, 2, F1, 2, W. 1997: T, BI1. 1999: It1(R), 2, W, NZ1. 2000: C(R), A1, E3. 2001: F1, It1.
428 Müller, GH (Gert) b 10/05/1948 - WP - 14 Tests (12 - 4T) 20 matches (45 - 15T) 1969: A3, 4, S. 1970: W, NZ1, 2, 3, 4. 1971: F1, 2. 1972: E. 1974: BI1,3,4.
773 Muller, GJ (Johan) b 01/06/1980 - KZN - 24 Tests (-) 26 matches (-) 2006: S1(R), NZ1(R), A2, NZ2, 3, A3, I(R), E1, 2. 2007: E1(R), 2(R), Sm1(R), A1(R), NZ1(R), A2, NZ2*, N(R), [Sm(R), E3(R),

Fiji(t+R), Arg(t+R).], W. 2009: BI3. 2011: [W(R).].
748 Müller, GP (Jorrie) b 03/01/1981 - GL - 6 Tests (5 - 1T) 6 matches (5 - 1T) 2003: A2, NZ2, [E, G(R), Sam, NZ3].
551 Müller, HL (Helgard) b 01/06/1963 - OFS - 2 Tests (-) 5 matches (-) 1986: NZC4(R). 1989: WT1(R).
277 Muller, HSV (Hennie) b 26/03/1922 d 26/04/1977 - Tvl - 13 Tests (16 - 3T, 2C, 1P) 28 matches (28 - 4T, 5C, 2P) 1949: NZ1, 2, 3, 4. 1951: S*, I*, W*. 1952: E*, F*. 1953: A1*, 2*, 3*, 4*.
563 Müller, LJJ (Lood) b 05/07/1959 - Natal - 2 Tests (-) 2 matches (-) 1992: NZ, A.
560 Müller, PG (Pieter) b 05/05/1969 - Natal - 33 Tests (15 - 3T) 52 matches (50 - 10T) 1992: NZ, A, F1, 2, E. 1993: F1, 2, A1, 2, 3, Arg1, 2. 1994: E1, 2, NZ1, S, W. 1998: I1, 2, W1, E1, A1, NZ1, 2, A2. 1999: It1, W, NZ1, A1, [Sp, E, A3, NZ3].
785 Murray, WM (Waylon) b 27/04/1986 - KZN - 3 Tests (-) 4 matches (-) 2007: Sm1, A2, NZ2.
821 Mvovo, LN (Lwazi) b 03/06/1986 - KZN - 7 Tests (5 - 1T) 8 matches (5 - 1T) 2010: S, E. 2011: A1, NZ1. 2012: Arg1, 2, A1(R).
305 Myburgh, B (Ben) b 17/06/1919 d 30/10/1984 - ETvl - No Tests - 17 matches (12 - 4T) Toured BI, I & F 1951/52.
34 Myburgh, FR (Francis) b 20/07/1871 d 30/11/1929 - EP - 1 Test (-) 1 match (-) 1896: BI1.
371 Myburgh, JL (Mof) b 24/08/1936 d 15/06/2012 - NTvl - 18 Tests (-) 57 matches (9 - 3T) 1962: BI1. 1963: A4. 1964: W, F 1968: BI1, 2, 3, F1, 2. 1969: A1, 2, 3, 4, E. 1970: I, W, NZ3, 4.
182 Myburgh, WH (Champion) b 10/10/1897 d ??/??/1978 - WTvl - 1 Test (-) 1 match (-) 1924: BI1.
N
394 Naudé, JP (Tiny) b 02/11/1936 d 28/12/2006 - WP - 14 Tests (47 - 2T, 4C, 11P) 28 matches (90 - 6T, 9C, 18P) 1963: A4. 1965: A1, 2, NZ1, 3, 4. 1967: F1, 2, 3, 4. 1968: BI1, 2, 3, 4.
774 Ndungane, AZ (Akona) b 20/02/1981 - BB - 11 Tests (5 - 1T) 13 matches (5 - 1T) 2006: A1, 2, NZ2, 3, A3, E1, 2. 2007: E2, N(R), [US.], W(R).
798 Ndungane, OM (Odwa) b 20/02/1981 - KZN - 9 Tests (10 - 2T) 12 matches (15 - 3T) 2008: It, NZ1, A3. 2009:

BI3, A3, NZ3. 2010: W1. 2011: NZ1(R), [Fj.].
401 Neethling, JB (Tiny) b 06/07/1939 d 03/04/2009 - WP - 8 Tests (-) 23 matches (3 - 1T) 1967: F1, 2, 3, 4. 1968: BI4. 1969: S. 1970: NZ1, 2.
101 Neill, WA (William) b 30/12/1882 d 03/02/1947 - Border - No Tests - 4 matches (-) Toured BI, I & F. 1906/07.
362 Nel, JA (Lofty) b 11/08/1935 - Tvl - 11 Tests (-) 24 matches (18 - 6T) 1960: NZ1, 2. 1963: A1, 2. 1965: A2, NZ1, 2, 3, 4. 1970: NZ3, 4.
329 Nel, JJ (Jeremy) b 21/09/1934 - WP - 8 Tests (3 - 1T) 23 matches (32 - 9T, 1C, 1P) 1956: A1, 2, NZ1, 2, 3, 4. 1958: F1, 2.
72 Nel, PARO (PO) b 17/04/1877 d 23/07/1928 - Tvl - 3 Tests (-) 3 matches (-) 1903: BI1, 2, 3.
199 Nel, PJ (Flip) b 17/06/1902 d 12/02/1984 - Natal - 16 Tests (3 - 1T) 46 matches (6 - 2T) 1928: NZ1, 2, 3, 4. 1931: W, I. 1932: E, S. 1933: A1*, 3*, 4*, 5*. 1937: A1*, 2*, NZ2*, 3*.
238 Nijkamp, JL (Joe) b 16/10/1904 d 03/04/1969 - Tvl - 1 Test (-) 1 match (-) 1933: A2.
369 Nimb, CF (Charlie) b 06/09/1938 d 15/06/2004 - WP - 1 Test (9 - 3C, 1P) 6 matches (20 - 2T, 4C, 2P) 1961: I.
679 Nkumane, SO (Owen) b 10/08/1975 - GL - No Tests - 4 matches (-) Toured BI & I. 1998.
767 Nokwe, JL (Jongi) b 30/12/1981 - Boland - 4 Tests (25 - 5T) 7 matches (40 - 8T) 2008: Arg, A2, 3. 2009: BI3.
408 Nomis, SH (Syd) b 15/11/1941 - Tvl - 25 Tests (18 - 6T) 54 matches (45 - 15T) 1967: F4. 1968: BI1, 2, 3, 4, F1, 2. 1969: A1, 2, 3, 4, S, E. 1970: I, W, NZ1, 2, 3, 4. 1971: F1, 2, A1, 2, 3. 1972: E.
Ntubeni, S (Scarra) b 18/02/1991 - WP - 2013: Springbok Tour squad member only. Not a Springbok.
O
289 Ochse, JK (Chum) b 09/02/1925 d 13/07/1996 - WP - 7 Tests (9 - 3T) 22 matches (48 - 16T) 1951: I, W. 1952: E, F 1953: A1, 2, 4.
295 Oelofse, JSA (Hansie) b 16/12/1926 d 31/05/1978 - Tvl - 4 Tests (6 - 2T) 13 matches (12 - 4T) 1953: A1, 2, 3, 4.
209 Oliver, JF (John) b 17/05/1897 d ??/??/1980 - Tvl - 2 Tests (-) 2 matches (-) 1928: NZ3, 4.
417 Olivier, E (Eben) b 10/04/1944 -

WP - 16 Tests (15 - 5T) 34 matches (30 - 10T) 1967: F1, 2, 3, 4. 1968: BI1, 2, 3, 4, F1, 2. 1969: A1, 2, 3, 4, S, E.
570 Olivier, J (Jacques) b 13/11/1968 - NTvl - 17 Tests (15 - 3T) 34 matches (65 - 13T) 1992: F1, 2, E. 1993: F1, 2, A1, 2, 3, Arg1. 1995: W, It(R), E. 1996: Arg1, 2, F1, 2, W.
174 Olivier, JS (Fien) b 27/05/1897 d 08/06/1980 - WP - No Tests - 13 matches (2 - 1C) Toured A & NZ. 1921.
772 Olivier, W (Wynand) b 11/06/1983 - BB - 37 Tests (5 - 1T) 41 matches (5 - 1T) 2006: S1(R), 2, F, A1, NZ1, A2, NZ2(R), 3, A3, I(R), E1, 2. 2007: E1, E2, NZ1(R), A2, NZ2, [E3(R), T, Arg(R).], W(R). 2009: BI3, NZ1(R), 2(R), F(R), It(R), I. 2010: F, It2(R), NZ1, 2, A1. 2011: A1, NZ1(R). 2012: E1(t), 2(R), 3.
33 Olver, E (Ernest) b 27/07/1874 d 12/06/1943 - EP - 1 Test (-) 1 match (-) 1896: BI1.
824 Oosthuizen, CV (Coenie) b 22/03/1989 - FS - 14 Tests (10 - 2T) 15 matches (10 - 2T) 2010: tour of UK - no tests. 2012: E1(R), NZ2(R). 2013: It(R), S(R), Sam(R), Arg1(R), Arg2(R), A1(R), NZ1(R), A2(R), NZ2(R), W(R), S(R), F.
460 Oosthuizen, JJ (Johan) b 04/07/1951 - WP - 9 Tests (8 - 2T) 14 matches (23 - 5T, 1D) 1974: BI1, F1, 2. 1975: F1, 2. 1976: NZ1, 2, 3, 4.
646 Oosthuizen, LT (Theo) b 24/02/1964 - GW - No Tests - 4 matches (15 - 3T) Toured Arg, F & W. 1996.
520 Oosthuizen, OW (Okkie) b 01/04/1955 - NTvl - 9 Tests (4 - 1T) 14 matches (12 - 3T) 1981: I1(R), 2, NZ2, 3, US. 1982: S. Am1, 2. 1984: E1, 2.
571 Oosthuysen, DE (Deon) b 04/12/1963 - NTvl - No Tests - 12 matches (20 - 4T) Toured F & E. 1992 and A. 1993.
181 Osler, BL (Bennie) b 23/11/1901 d 24/04/1962 - WP - 17 Tests (46 - 2T, 6C, 4P, 4D) 30 matches (108 - 7T, 17C, 7P, 8D) 1924: BI1, 2, 3, 4. 1928: NZ1, 2, 3, 4. 1931: W*, I*. 1932: E*, S*. 1933: A1, 2*, 3, 4, 5.
193 Osler, SG (Sharkey) b 31/01/1907 d 16/04/1980 - WP - 1 Test (-) 1 match (-) 1928: NZ1.
615 Otto, K (Krynauw) b 08/10/1971 - NTvl - 38 Tests (5 - 1T) 51 matches (30 - 6T) 1995: [R, C(R), WS2(R)]. 1997: BI3, NZ1, A1, NZ2, It, F1, 2, E, S. 1998: I1, 2, W1, E1, A1, NZ1, 2, A2, W2, S, I3, E2. 1999: It1, W, NZ1, A1, [S(R), Sp, U, E, A3, NZ3]. 2000:

C, E1, 2, A1.
359 Oxlee, K (Keith) b 17/12/1934 d 31/08/1998 - Natal - 19 Tests (88 - 5T, 14C, 14P, 1D) 48 matches (201 - 11T, 45C, 23P, 3D) 1960: NZ1, 2, 3, 4, W, I. 1961: S, A1, 2. 1962: BI1, 2, 3, 4. 1963: A1, 2, 4. 1964: W. 1965: NZ1, 2.

P

628 Pagel, GL (Garry) b 17/09/1966 - WP - 5 Tests (-) 8 matches (-) 1995: [A(R), R, C, NZ(R)]. 1996: NZ5(R).
411 Parker, WH (Hambly) b 13/04/1934 - EP - 2 Tests (-) 14 matches (-) 1965: A1, 2.
73 Partridge, JEC (Birdie) b 13/06/1879 d 01/07/1965 - Tvl - 1 Test (-) 1 match (-) 1903: BI1.
698 Passens, GA (Gavin) b 18/05/1976 - Mpu - No Tests - 3 matches (10 - 2T) Toured Arg, I, W & E. 2000.
647 Paulse, BJ (Breyton) b 25/04/1976 - WP - 64 Tests (130 - 26T) 74 matches (195 - 39T) 1999: It1, 2, NZ1, A1, 2(R), [S(R), Sp, NZ3]. 2000: C, E1, 2, A1, NZ1, A2, NZ2, A3, Arg, W, E3. 2001: F1, 2, It1, NZ1, A1, 2, NZ2, F3, It2, E. 2002: W1, 2, Arg, Sm(R), A1, NZ2, A2, F, S, E. 2003: [G]. 2004: I1, 2, W1, PI, NZ1, A1, NZ2, A2, W2, I3, E. 2005: A2, 3, NZ1, A4, F3. 2006: S1, 2, A1(R), NZ1, 3(R), A3(R). 2007: A2, NZ2.
183 Payn, C (Bill) b 09/08/1893 d 31/10/1959 - Natal - 2 Tests (-) 2 matches (-) 1924: BI1, 2.
341 Pelser, HJM (Martin) b 23/03/1934 - Tvl - 11 Tests (6 - 2T) 26 matches (18 - 6T) 1958: F1. 1960: NZ1, 2, 3, 4, W, I. 1961: F, I, A1, 2.
331 Pfaff, BD (Brian) b 02/03/1930 d 08/05/1998 - WP - 1 Test (-) 5 matches (6 - 2T) 1956: A1.
301 Pickard, JAJ (Jan) b 25/12/1927 d 30/05/1998 - WP - 4 Tests (-) 34 matches (19 - 5T, 2C) 1953: A3, 4. 1956: NZ2. 1958: F2.
584 Pienaar, JF (Francois) b 02/01/1967 - Tvl - 29 Tests (15 - 3T) 40 matches (20 - 4T) 1993: F1*, 2*, A1*, 2*, 3*, Arg1*, 2*. 1994: E1*, 2*, NZ2*, 3*, Arg1*, 2*, S*, W*. 1995: WS1*, [A*, C*, WS2*, F*, NZ*], W*, It*, E*. 1996: Fj*, A1*, NZ1*, A2*, NZ2*.
779 Pienaar, R (Ruan) b 10/03/1984 - KZN - 74 Tests (130 - 7T, 22C, 17P) 78 matches (153 - 7T, 23C, 24P) 2006: NZ2(R), 3(R), A3(R), I(t), E1(R). 2007: E1(R), 2(R), Sm1(R), A1, NZ1, A2, NZ2,
N(R), S(R), [E3(t+R), T, US(R), Arg(R).], W. 2008: W1(R), It(R), NZ2(R), A1(R), 3(R), W3, S, E. 2009: BI1, 2, 3(R), NZ1, A1(R), 2, 3, It(R), I(R). 2010: W1, F(R), It1(R), 2(R), NZ1(R), 2(R), A1, I, W2, S(R), E. 2011: A1, NZ1, [Fj(R), N(R).]. 2012: E1(R), 2(R), 3(R), Arg1(R), 2(R), A1, NZ1, A2, NZ2, I, S, E4. 2013: It(R), S, Sam, Arg1, Arg2, A1, NZ1, NZ2(R), W(R), S(R), F.
164 Pienaar, TB (Theo) b 23/11/1888 d 14/11/1960 - WP - No Tests - 10 matches (-) Toured A & NZ. 1921.
506 Pienaar, ZMJ (Gysie) b 21/12/1954 - OFS - 13 Tests (14 - 2T, 2P) 21 matches (59 - 6T, 10C, 4P, 1D) 1980: S. Am2(R), BI1, 2, 3, 4, S. Am3, 4, F. 1981: I1, 2, NZ1, 2, 3.
793 Pieterse, BH (Barend) b 23/01/1979 - FS - No Tests (-) 1 match (5 - 1T) Toured I & E. 2007.
775 Pietersen, J-PR (JP) b 12/07/1986 - KZN - 51 Tests (80 - 16T) 53 matches (80 - 16T) 2006: A3 2006: tour of UK - no tests. 2007: Sm1, A1, NZ1, A2, NZ2, N, S, [Sm, E3, T, US(R), Fiji, Arg, E4.], W. 2008: NZ2, A1, Arg, NZ3, A2, W3, S, E. 2009: BI1, 2, NZ1, 2, A1, 2, F, It, I. 2010: NZ3, A2, 3. 2011: A2, NZ2, [W, Fj, Sm, A3.]. 2012: E1, 2, 3, I, S, E4. 2013: W, S, F.
421 Pitzer, G (Gys) b 08/07/1939 - NTvl - 12 Tests (-) 16 matches (-) 1967: F1, 2, 3, 4. 1968: BI1, 2, 3, 4, F1, 2. 1969: A3, 4.
461 Pope, CF (Chris) b 30/09/1952 - WP - 9 Tests (4 - 1T) 13 matches (4 - 1T) 1974: BI1, 2, 3, 4. 1975: F1, 2. 1976: NZ2, 3, 4.
812 Potgieter, DJ (Dewald) b 22/02/1987 - BB - 6 Tests (5 - 1T) 8 matches (5 - 1T) 2009: I(t). 2010: W1, F(R), It1, 2(R), A1(R).
200 Potgieter, HJ (Hennie) b 24/10/1903 d 11/11/1957 - OFS - 2 Tests (-) 2 matches (-) 1928: NZ1, 2.
493 Potgieter, HL (Hermanus) b 11/01/1953 - OFS - 1 Test (4 - 1T) 1 match (4 - 1T) 1977: WT.
435 Potgieter, R (Ronnie) b 18/11/1943 - NTvl - No Tests - 6 matches (-) Toured BI & I. 1969/70.
834 Potgieter, UJ (Jacques) b 24/04/1986 - BB - 3 Tests (-) 3 matches (-) 2012: E3, Arg1(R), 2.
531 Povey, SA (Shaun) b 09/08/1954 - WP - No Tests - 2 matches (-) Toured NZ & USA. 1981.
52 Powell, AW (Bertie) b 18/07/1873 d 11/09/1948 - GW - 1 Test (-) 1 match
(-) 1896: BI3.
17 Powell, JM (Jackie) b 12/12/1871 d 19/12/1955 - GW - 4 Tests (-) 4 matches (-) 1891: BI2. 1896: BI3. 1903: BI1, 2*.
504 Prentis, RB (Richard) b 27/02/1947 - Tvl - 11 Tests (-) 14 matches (-) 1980: S. Am1, 2, BI1, 2, 3, 4, S. Am3, 4, F. 1981: I1, 2.
723 Pretorius, AS (André) b 29/12/1978 - GL - 31 Tests (171 - 2T, 31C, 25P, 8D) 33 matches (174 - 2T, 31C, 26P, 8D) 2002: W1, 2, Arg, Sm, NZ1, A1, NZ2, F, S(R), E. 2003: NZ1(R), A2. 2005: A2, 3, NZ1, A4, NZ2, Arg. 2006: NZ2(R), 3, A3, I, E1(t+R), 2. 2007: S(R), [Sm(R), E3(R), T, US(R), Arg(R).], W.
782 Pretorius, JC (Jaco) b 10/12/1979 - GL - 2 Tests (-) 3 matches (-) 2006: I. 2007: NZ2.
198 Pretorius, NF (Nick) b 10/12/1904 d 19/02/1990 - Tvl - 4 Tests (-) 4 matches (-) 1928: NZ1, 2, 3, 4.
577 Pretorius, PIL (Piet) b 17/08/1964 - NTvl - No Tests - 6 matches (-) Toured F & E. 1992.
392 Prinsloo, J (Poens) b 11/10/1935 - NTvl - 1 Test (-) 1 match (-) 1963: A3.
338 Prinsloo, JC (Jan) b 28/01/1935 d 28/07/1966 - Tvl - 2 Tests (-) 2 matches (-) 1958: F1, 2.
192 Prinsloo, JP (Boet) b 14/10/1905 d 04/10/1968 - Tvl - 1 Test (-) 1 match (-) 1928: NZ1.
622 Putt, KB (Kevin) b 28/07/1965 - Natal - No Tests - 11 matches (15 - 3T) Toured W, S & I. 1994 and Arg, F & W. 1996.
386 Putter, DJ (Dick) b 13/02/1937 d 31/10/2002 - WTvl - 3 Tests (-) 3 matches (-) 1963: A1, 2, 4.

R

71 Raaff, JWE (Klondyke) b 10/03/1879 d 13/07/1949 - GW - 6 Tests (3 - 1T) 20 matches (12 - 4T) 1903: BI1, 2. 1906: S, W, E. 1910: BI1.
776 Ralepelle, MC (Chiliboy) b 11/09/1986 - BB - 22 Tests (5 - 1T) 24 matches (5 - 1T) 2006: NZ2(R), E2(R). 2008: E(t+R). 2009: BI3, NZ1(R), 2(R), A2(R), NZ3(R). 2009: tour of UK - no tests. 2010: W1(R), F(R), It1, 2(R), NZ1(R), 2(R), A1(R), 2(R), 3(R), W2(R). 2011: A1(R), NZ1(R), [N(R).]. 2012: tour of UK - no tests. 2013: It(R).
488 Ras, WJ de W (De Wet) b 28/01/1954 - OFS - 2 Tests (-) 5 matches

(69 - 4T, 25C, 1P) 1976: NZ1(R). 1980: S. Am2(R).
813 **Raubenheimer, D** (Davon) b 16/07/1984 - GW - No Tests - 2 matches (-) Toured F,It,I & E. 2009.
728 **Rautenbach, SJ** (Faan) b 22/02/1976 - WP - 14 Tests (5 - 1T) 14 matches (5 - 1T) 2002: W1(R), 2(t+R), Arg(R), Sm, NZ1(R), A1, NZ2(R), A2(R). 2003: [U(R), G, Sm, NZ3]. 2004: W1, NZ1(R).
569 **Reece-Edwards, HM** (Hugh) b 05/01/1961 - Natal - 3 Tests (-) 12 matches (103 - 3T, 23C, 14P) 1992: F1, 2. 1993: A2.
87 **Reid, A** (Oupa) b 23/11/1878 d 18/05/1952 - WP - 1 Test (3 - 1T) 1 match (3 - 1T) 1903: BI3.
242 **Reid, BC** (Bunny) b 12/07/1910 d 11/09/1976 - Border - 1 Test (-) 1 match (-) 1933: A4.
107 **Reid, HG** (Bert) b 19/12/1881 - d 30/05/1944 - Tvl - No Tests - 14 matches (6 - 2T) Toured BI, I & F. 1906/07.
542 **Reinach, J** (Jaco) b 01/01/1962 d 21/01/1997 - OFS - 4 Tests (8 - 2T) 4 matches (8 - 2T) 1986: NZC1,2,3,4.
310 **Rens, IJ** (Natie) b 19/07/1929 d 19/12/1989 - Tvl - 2 Tests (19 - 5C, 2P, 1D) 2 matches (19 - 5C, 2P, 1D) 1953: A3,4.
320 **Retief, DF** (Daan) b 28/06/1925 d 22/09/2010 - NTvl - 9 Tests (12 - 4T) 21 matches (36 - 12T) 1955: BI1, 2, 4. 1956: A1, 2, NZ1, 2, 3, 4.
129 **Reyneke, HJ** (Koot) b 19/01/1882 d 22/03/1970 - WP - 1 Test (3 - 1T) 1 match (3 - 1T) 1910: BI3.
845 **Rhule, RK** (Raymond) b 06/11/1992 - FS - No Tests - No matches Toured I, S & E. 2012.
6 **Richards, AR** (Alf) b 14/12/1867 d 09/01/1904 - WP - 3 Tests (-) 3 matches (-) 1891: BI1,2,3*.
580 **Richter, AJ** (Adriaan) b 10/05/1966 - NTvl - 10 Tests (20 - 4T) 29 matches (55 - 11T) 1992: F1,2,E. 1994: E2, NZ1,2,3. 1995: [R*,C,WS2(R)].
388 **Riley, NM** (Norman) b 25/02/1939 - ETvl - 1 Test (-) 1 match (-) 1963: A3.
117 **Riordan, CA** (Cliff) b 24/12/1885 d 07/02/1958 - Tvl - 2 Tests (-) 2 matches (-) 1910: BI1,2.
573 **Roberts, H** (Harry) b 03/12/1960 - Tvl - No Tests - 6 matches (5 - 1T) Toured F & E. 1992.
480 **Robertson, IW** (Ian) b 28/04/1950 - Rhodesia - 5 Tests (3 - 1D) 10 matches (21 - 3T, 1P, 2D) 1974: F1, 2. 1976: NZ1, 2, 4.
554 **Rodgers, PH** (Heinrich) b 23/06/1962 - NTvl - 5 Tests (-) 12 matches (-) 1989: WT1, 2. 1992: NZ, F1, 2.
534 **Rogers, CD** (Chris) b 10/10/1956 - Tvl - 4 Tests (-) 4 matches (-) 1984: E1,2, S. Am&Sp1,2.
126 **Roos, GD** (Gideon) b 20/07/1890 d 08/03/1920 - WP - 2 Tests (3 - 1T) 2 matches (3 - 1T) 1910: BI2,3.
88 **Roos, PJ** (Paul) b 30/10/1880 d 22/09/1948 - WP - 4 Tests (-) 22 matches (5 - 1T, 1C) 1903: BI3. 1906: I*,W*,E*.
802 **Rose, EE** (Earl) b 12/01/1984 - GL - No Tests - 2 matches (-) Toured BI, 2008 and E, F, It & I, 2009.
322 **Rosenberg, W** (Wilf) b 18/06/1934 - Tvl - 5 Tests (6 - 2T) 9 matches (6 - 2T) 1955: BI2,3,4. 1956: NZ3. 1958: F1.
699 **Rossouw, C** (Chris) b 14/11/1976 - WP - No Tests - 4 matches (-) Toured Arg, I, W & E. 2000.
624 **Rossouw, C le C** (Chris) b 14/09/1969 - Tvl - 9 Tests (10 - 2T) 10 matches (10 - 2T) 1995: WS1, [R, WS2, F, NZ]. 1999: NZ2(R), A2(R), [Sp, NZ3(R)].
309 **Rossouw, DH** (Daantjie) b 05/09/1930 d 28/01/2010 - WP - 2 Tests (3 - 1T) 2 matches (3 - 1T) 1953: A3,4.
755 **Rossouw, DJ** (Danie) b 05/06/1978 - BB - 63 Tests (50 - 10T) 67 matches (55 - 11T) 2003: [U, G, Sm(R), NZ3]. 2004: E(R), S, Arg. 2005: U, F1, 2, A1, W(R), F3(R). 2006: S1, 2, FA1, I, E1, 2. 2007: E1, Sm1, A1(R), NZ1, S, [Sm, E3, T, Fiji, Arg, E4.]. 2008: W1(t+R), NZ3(R), A3(R), S(R), E. 2009: BI1(R), 2(R), NZ1(R), 2(R), A1(R), 3(R), NZ3(R), F(R), It, I. 2010: W1, F, NZ1(R), 2, A1, NZ3(t+R), A2(R), 3. 2011: A1, NZ1, A2, NZ2(t+R), [W, Fj, N, Sm, A3.].
578 **Rossouw, PB** (Botha) b 03/11/1969 - WTvl - No Tests - 2 matches (5 - 1T) Toured F & E. 1992.
652 **Rossouw, PWG** (Pieter) b 03/12/1971 - WP - 43 Tests (105 - 21T) 43 matches (105 - 21T) 1997: BI2,3, NZ1, A1, NZ2(R), A2(R), It, F1, 2, E, S. 1998: I1, 2, W1, E1, A1, NZ1, 2, A2, W2, S, I3, E2. 1999: It1, W, NZ1, A1(R), NZ2, A2, [S, U, E, A3]. 2000: C, E1, 2, A2, Arg(R), I, W. 2001: F3, US. 2003: Arg.
206 **Rousseau, WP** (Willie) b 11/08/1906 d 28/12/1996 - WP - 2 Tests (-) 2 matches (-) 1928: NZ3,4.
367 **Roux, F du T** (Mannetjies) b 12/04/1939 - WP - 27 Tests (18 - 6T) 56 matches (39 - 13T) 1960: W. 1961: A1, 2. 1962: BI1, 2, 3, 4. 1963: A2. 1965: A1, 2, NZ1, 2, 3, 4. 1968: BI3, 4, F1, 2. 1969: A1, 2, 3, 4. 1970: I, NZ1, 2, 3, 4.
607 **Roux, JP** (Johan) b 25/02/1969 - Tvl - 12 Tests (10 - 2T) 17 matches (20 - 4T) 1994: E2, NZ1, 2, 3, Arg1. 1995: [R, C, F(R)]. 1996: A1(R), NZ1, A2, NZ3.
426 **Roux, OA** (Tonie) b 22/02/1947 - NTvl - 7 Tests (-) 31 matches (15 - 4T, 1D) 1969: S, E. 1970: I, W. 1972: E. 1974: BI3, 4.
737 **Roux, WG** (Wessel) b 01/10/1976 - Blue Bulls - 3 Tests (-) 3 matches (-) 2002: F(R), S, E.
727 **Russell, RB** (Brent) b 05/03/1980 - Mpu - 23 Tests (40 - 8T) 23 matches (40 - 8T) 2002: W1(R), 2, Arg, A1(R), NZ2(R), A2, F, E(R). 2003: Arg(R), A1(R), NZ1, A2(R). 2004: I2(t+R), W1, NZ1(R), W2(R), Arg(R). 2005: U(R), F2(R), A1(t), Arg(R), W(R). 2006: F.
44 **Samuels, TA** (Theo) b 21/07/1873 d 16/11/1896 - GW - 3 Tests (6 - 2T) 3 matches (6 - 2T) 1896: BI2,3,4.
S
666 **Santon, D** (Dale) b 18/08/1969 - Boland - 4 Tests (-) 5 matches (-) 2003: A1(R), NZ1(R), A2(t), [G(R)].
449 **Sauermann, JT** (Theo) b 16/11/1944 - Tvl - 5 Tests (-) 11 matches (-) 1971: F1,2, A1. 1972: E. 1974: BI1.
290 **Saunders, MJ** (Cowboy) b 26/11/1927 d 17/05/2006 - Border - No Tests - 14 matches (33 - 11T) Toured BI, I & F. 1951/52.
472 **Schlebusch, JJJ** (Jan) b 05/05/1949 - OFS - 3 Tests (-) 3 matches (-) 1974: BI3, 4. 1975: F2.
346 **Schmidt, LU** (Louis) b 06/02/1936 d 23/01/1999 - NTvl - 2 Tests (-) 2 matches (-) 1958: F2. 1962: BI2.
544 **Schmidt, UL** (Uli) b 10/07/1961 - NTvl - 17 Tests (9 - 2T) 25 matches (29 - 6T) 1986: NZC1,2,3,4. 1989: WT1,2. 1992: NZ, A. 1993: F1,2, A1,2,3. 1994: Arg1,2, S, W.
391 **Schoeman, J** (Haas) b 15/03/1940 d 01/01/2006 - WP - 7 Tests (-) 23 matches (15 - 5T) 1963: A3, 4. 1965: I, S, A1, NZ1, 2.
618 **Scholtz, CP** (Christiaan) b 22/10/1970 - Tvl - 4 Tests (-) 4 matches (-) 1994: Arg1. 1995: [R, C, WS2].
732 **Scholtz, H** (Hendro) b 22/03/1979 - FS - 5 Tests (5 - 1T) 5 matches (5 - 1T)

SPRINGBOKS 1891-2013

2002: A1(R), NZ2(R), A2(R). 2003: [U(R), G].

177 Scholtz, H (Tokkie) b 29/08/1892 d 08/04/1959 - WP - 2 Tests (-) 15 matches (-) 1921: NZ1,2.

Schreuder, L (Louis) b 25/04/1990 - WP - 2013: Springbok Tour squad member only. Not a Springbok.

582 Schutte, PJW (Phillip) b 07/10/1969 - NTvl - 2 Tests (-) 8 matches (-) 1994: S,W.

36 Scott, PA (Paul) b 26/10/1872 d (unknown) - Tvl - 4 Tests (-) 4 matches (-) 1896: BI1,2,3,4.

156 Sendin, WD (Billy) b 04/10/1895 d 16/07/1977 - GW - 1 Test (3 - 1T) 9 matches (18 - 6T) 1921: NZ2.

702 Sephaka, LD (Lawrence) b 08/08/1978 - GF - 24 Tests (-) 29 matches (-) 2001: US. 2002: Sm, NZ1, A1, NZ2, A2, F 2003: S1, 2, A1, NZ1, A2(t+R), NZ2, [U,E(t+R), G]. 2005: F2, A1, 2(R), W. 2006: S1(R), NZ3(t+R), A3(R), I.

508 Serfontein, DJ (Divan) b 03/08/1954 - WP - 19 Tests (12 - 3T) 26 matches (16 - 4T) 1980: BI1,2,3,4,S.Am3,4,F 1981: I1,2, NZ1,2,3,US. 1982: S.Am1,2. 1984: E1,2, S.Am&Sp1*,2*.

849 Serfontein, JL (Jan) b 15/04/1992 - Blue Bulls - 9 Tests (5 - 1T) 9 matches (5 - 1T) 2013: It(R), S(R), Sam(R), Arg1(R), Arg2(R), A1(R), NZ1(R), A2(R), NZ2(R).

19 Shand, R (Bob) b 27/08/1866 d 01/03/1934 - GW - 2 Tests (-) 2 matches (-) 1891: BI2,3.

613 Sherrell, LR (Lance) b 09/02/1966 - NTvl - No Tests - 6 matches (31 - 3T,5C,2P) Toured NZ. 1994.

257 Sherriff, AR (Roger) b 17/03/1913 d 04/12/1951 - Tvl - 3 Tests (-) 6 matches (3 - 1T) 1938: BI1,2,3.

761 Shimange, MH (Hanyani) b 17/04/1978 - FS - 9 Tests (-) 9 matches (-) 2004: W1(R), NZ2(R), A2(R), W2(R). 2005: U(R), A1(R), 2(R), Arg(R). 2006: S1(R).

140 Shum, EH (Baby) b 17/08/1886 d 27/06/1952 - Tvl - 1 Test (-) 15 matches (6 - 2T) 1913: E.

175 Siedle, LB (Jack) b 01/07/1891 d 07/11/1962 - Natal - No Tests - 1 match (-) Toured A & NZ. 1921.

292 Sinclair, DJ (Des) b 14/07/1927 d 29/04/1996 - Tvl - 4 Tests (-) 17 matches (15 - 5T) 1955: BI1,2,3,4.

70 Sinclair, JH (Jimmy) b 16/10/1876 d 23/02/1913 - Tvl - 1 Test (-) 1 match (-) 1903: BI1.

343 Skene, AL (Alan) b 02/10/1932 d 13/08/2001 - WP - 1 Test (-) 1 match (-) 1958: F2.

659 Skinstad, RB (Bob) b 03/07/1976 - WP - 42 Tests (55 - 11T) 47 matches (70 - 14T) 1997: E(t). 1998: W1(R), E1(t), NZ1(R), 2(R), A2(R), W2(R), S, I3, E2. 1999: [S, Sp(R), U, E, A3]. 2001: F1(R), 2(R), It1*, NZ1*, A1*, 2*, NZ2*, F3*, It2*, E*. 2002: W1*, 2*, Arg, Sm, NZ1, A1, NZ2, A2. 2003: Arg(R). 2007: E2(t+R), Sm1, NZ1, A2* [E3(R), T*, US(R), Arg(R).].

416 Slabber, LJ (Louis) b 05/03/1935 d 11/05/2003 - OFS - No Tests - 7 matches (9 - 3T) Toured A & NZ. 1965.

188 Slater, JT (Jack) b 16/04/1901 d 16/02/1986 - EP - 3 Tests (6 - 2T) 3 matches (6 - 2T) 1924: BI3,4. 1928: NZ1.

546 Smal, GP (Gert) b 27/12/1961 - WP - 6 Tests (4 - 1T) 6 matches (4 - 1T) 1986: NZC1,2,3,4. 1989: WT1,2.

561 Small, JT (James) b 10/02/1969 - Tvl - 47 Tests (100 - 20T) 60 matches (135 - 27T) 1992: NZ, A, F1, 2, E. 1993: F1, 2, A1, 2, 3, Arg1, 2. 1994: E1, 2, NZ1, 2, 3(t), Arg1. 1995: WS1, [A, R, F, NZ], W, It, E(R). 1996: Fj, A1, NZ1, A2, NZ2, Arg1, 2, F1, 2, W. 1997: T, BI1, NZ1(R), A1(R), NZ2, A2, It, F1, 2, E, S.

583 Smit, FC (FC) b 13/08/1966 - WP - 1 Test (-) 4 matches (-) 1992: E.

691 Smit, JW (John) b 03/04/1978 - Natal - 111 Tests (40 - 8T) 112 matches (40 - 8T) 2000: C(t), A1(R), NZ1(t+R), A2(R), NZ2(R), A3(R), Arg, I, W, E3. 2001: F1, 2, It1, NZ1(R), A1(R), 2(R), NZ2(R), F3(R), It2, E, US(R). 2003: [U(R), E(t+R), G*, Sm, NZ3]. 2004: I1*, 2*, W1*, PI*, NZ1*, A1*, NZ2*, A2*, W2*, I3*, E*, S*, Arg*. 2005: U*, F1*, 2*, A1*, 2*, 3*, NZ1*, A4*, NZ2*, Arg*, W*, F3*. 2006: S1*, 2*, F*, A1*, NZ1*, A2*, NZ2*, 3*, A3*, I*, E1*, 2*. 2007: E1*, 2*, Sm1*, A1*, [Sm*, E3*, T(R), US*, Fiji*, Arg*, E4*.], W*. 2008: W1*, 2*, NZ1*, W3*, S*, E*. 2009: BI1*, 2*, 3*, NZ1*, 2*, A1*, A2*, A3*, NZ3*, F*, It*, I*. 2010: W1*, F*, It2*, NZ1*, 2*, A1*, NZ3*, A2*, 3*. 2011: A1*, NZ1*, A2*, NZ2(R), [W*, F]*, N*, Sm(R), A3*.].

660 Smit, PL (Philip) b 27/08/1973 - GW - No Tests - 5 matches (-) Toured It, F,E & S. 1997 and BI & I. 1998.

389 Smith, CM (Nelie) b 08/05/1934 - OFS - 7 Tests (12 - 1T, 3P) 19 matches (21 - 4T, 3P) 1963: A3,4. 1964: W, F*. 1965: A1*, 2*, NZ2*.

23 Smith, CW (Toski) b 09/04/1871 d 28/02/1934 - GW - 3 Tests (-) 3 matches (-) 1891: BI2. 1896: BI2,3.

507 Smith, DJ (David) b 09/11/1957 - Zimbabwe - 4 Tests (-) 4 matches (-) 1980: BI1,2,3,4.

21 Smith, DW (Dan) b 08/04/1869 d 27/02/1926 - GW - 1 Test (-) 1 match (-) 1891: BI2.

262 Smith, GAC (George) b 31/08/1916 d 23/03/1978 - EP - 1 Test (-) 1 match (-) 1938: BI3.

746 Smith, JH (Juan) b 30/07/1981 - FS - 69 Tests (60 - 12T) 71 matches (60 - 12T) 2003: S1(R), 2(R), A1, NZ1, A2, NZ2, [U, E, Sm, NZ3]. 2004: W2. 2005: U(R), F2(R), A2, 3, NZ1, A4, NZ2, Arg, W, F3. 2006: S1, 2, F,A1, NZ1, A2, I, E2. 2007: E1, 2, A1, N, S, [Sm, E3, T(R), US, Fiji, Arg, E4.], W. 2008: W1, 2, It, NZ1, 2, A1, Arg, NZ3, A2, 3, W3, S. 2009: BI1, 2, 3, NZ1, 2, A1, 2, 3. 2010: NZ3, A2, 3, I, W2, S, E.

643 Smith, PF (Franco) b 29/07/1972 - GW - 9 Tests (23 - 2T, 2C, 3P) 18 matches (85 - 5T, 21C, 6P) 1997: S(R). 1998: I1(t), 2, W1, NZ1(R), 2(R), A2(R), W2. 1999: NZ2.

241 Smollan, FC (Fred) b 20/08/1908 d 02/08/1998 - Tvl - 3 Tests (-) 3 matches (-) 1933: A3,4,5.

18 Snedden, RCD (Bob) b 20/03/1867 d 03/04/1931 - GW - 1 Test (-) 1 match (-) 1891: BI2*.

636 Snyman, AH (André) b 02/02/1974 - NTvl - 38 Tests (50 - 10T) 42 matches (60 - 12T) 1996: NZ3,4, Arg2(R), W(R). 1997: T, BI1,2,3, NZ1, A1, NZ2, A2, It, F1, 2, E, S. 1998: I1,2, W1, E1, A1, NZ1,2, A2, W2, S, I3, E2. 1999: NZ2. 2001: NZ2, F3, US. 2002: W1. 2003: S1, NZ1. 2006: S1,2.

453 Snyman, DSL (Dawie) b 05/07/1949 - WP - 10 Tests (24 - 1T, 1C, 4P, 2D) 22 matches (86 - 7T, 13C, 8P, 4D) 1972: E. 1974: BI1, 2(R), F1, 2. 1975: F1, 2. 1976: NZ2, 3. 1977: WT.

466 Snyman, JCP (Jackie) b 14/04/1948 - OFS - 3 Tests (18 - 6P) 7 matches (29 - 4C, 6P,1D) 1974: BI2,3,4.

473 Sonnekus, GHH (Gerrie) b 01/02/1953 - OFS - 3 Tests (4 - 1T) 3 matches (4 - 1T) 1974: BI3. 1984: E1,2.

731 Sowerby, RS (Shaun) b 01/07/1978 - Natal - 1 Test (-) 1 match (-) 2002: Sm(R).

446 Spies, JJ (Johan) b 08/05/1945 -

SPRINGBOKS 1891-2013

NTvl - 4 Tests (-) 11 matches (-) 1970: NZ1, 2, 3, 4.
777 Spies, PJ (Pierre) b 08/06/1985 - BB - 53 Tests (35 - 7T) 53 matches (35 - 7T) 2006: A1, NZ2, 3, A3, I, E1. 2007: E1(R), 2, A1. 2008: W1, 2, A1, Arg, NZ3, A2, 3, W3, S, E. 2009: BI1, 2, 3(R), NZ1, 2, A1, 2, 3, NZ3. 2010: F, It1, 2, NZ1, 2, A1, NZ3, A2, 3, I, W2, E. 2011: A2, NZ2, [W, Fj, N, Sm, A3.]. 2012: E1, 2, 3. 2013: It, S, Sam.
479 Stander, JCJ (Rampie) b 25/12/1944 d 28/08/1980 - OFS - 5 Tests (-) 8 matches (4 - 1T) 1974: BI4(R). 1976: NZ1, 2, 3, 4.
482 Stapelberg, WP (Willem) b 29/01/1947 - NTvl - 2 Tests (8 - 2T) 6 matches (12 - 3T) 1974: F1, 2.
336 Starke, JJ (James) b 16/05/1931 - WP - 1 Test (-) 8 matches (3 - 1T) 1956: NZ4.
180 Starke, KT (Kenny) b 18/06/1900 d 03/01/1982 - WP - 4 Tests (13 - 3T, 1D) 4 matches (13 - 3T, 1D) 1924: BI1, 2, 3, 4.
342 Steenekamp, J (Johan) b 02/09/1935 d 16/08/2007 - Tvl - 1 Test (-) 1 match (-) 1958: F1.
764 Steenkamp, GG (Gurthro) b 12/06/1981 - FS - 49 Tests (30 - 6T) 51 matches (30 - 6T) 2004: S, Arg. 2005: U, F2(R), A2, 3, NZ1(R), A4(R). 2007: E1(R), 2, A1, [T, Fiji(R).]. 2008: W1, 2(R), NZ1, 2, A1, W3(R), S(R). 2009: BI1(R), 3(R). 2009: tour of UK - no tests. 2010: F, It1, 2, NZ1, 2, A1, NZ3, A2, 3. 2011: A2(R), NZ2, [W(R), Fj, N, Sm(R), A3.]. 2012: S, E4. 2013: Arg1(R), Arg2(R), A1(R), NZ1(R), A2(R), NZ2(R), W(R), S, F(R).
93 Stegmann, AC (Anton) b 25/08/1883 d 23/01/1972 - WP - 2 Tests (3 - 1T) 16 matches (54 - 18T) 1906: S, I.
825 Stegmann, GJ (Deon) b 22/03/1986 - BB - 6 Tests (-) 6 matches (-) 2010: I, W2, S, E. 2011: A1, NZ1.
132 Stegmann, JA (Jan) b 21/06/1887 d 07/12/1984 - Tvl - 5 Tests (15 - 5T) 16 matches (39 - 13T) 1912: S, I, W. 1913: E, F.
350 Stewart, DA (Dave) b 14/07/1935 - WP - 11 Tests (9 - 1T, 2P) 30 matches (25 - 5T, 2C, 2P) 1960: S. 1961: E, S, F, I. 1963: A1, 3, 4. 1964: W, F. 1965: I.
678 Stewart, JC (Christian) b 17/10/1966 - WP - 3 Tests (-) 5 matches (-) 1998: S, I3, E2.
783 Steyn, FPL (Francois) b 14/05/1987 - KZN - 53 Tests (132 - 10T, 5C, 21P, 3D) 55 matches (141 - 10T, 8C, 22P,

3D) 2006: I, E1, 2. 2007: E1(R), 2(R), Sm1, A1(R), NZ1(R), S, [Sm(R), E3, T(R), US, Fiji, Arg, E4.]. W. 2008: W2(R), It, NZ1(R), 2(R), A1, NZ3(R), A2(R), W3(R), S(R), E(R). 2009: BI1, 2, 3(R), NZ1, 2, A1, 2(R), 3(R), NZ3. 2010: W1, A2, 3, W2, S, E. 2011: A2, [W, Fj, N, Sm.]. 2012: E1, 2, Arg1, 2, A1, NZ1.
803 Steyn, M (Morné) b 11/07/1984 - BB - 54 Tests (636 - 8T, 88C, 132P, 8D) 54 matches (625 - 8T, 87C, 129P, 8D) 2009: BI1(t+R), 2(R), 3, NZ1(R), 2, A1, 2, 3, NZ3, F, It, I. 2010: F, It1, 2, NZ1, 2, A1, NZ3, A2, 3, I, W2, S, E. 2011: A1, NZ1, A2(R), NZ2, [W, Fj, N, Sm, A3.]. 2012: E1, 2, 3, Arg1, A1, NZ1, S(R). 2013: It, S, Sam, Arg1, Arg2, A1, NZ1, A2, NZ2, W, S(R), F.
489 Stofberg, MTS (Theuns) b 06/06/1955 - OFS - 21 Tests (24 - 6T) 29 matches (36 - 9T) 1976: NZ2, 3. 1977: WT. 1980: S. Am1, 2, BI1, 2, 3, 4, S. Am3*, 4, F. 1981: I1, 2, NZ1*, 2, US. 1982: S. Am1, 2. 1984: E1*, 2*.
224 Strachan, LC (Louis) b 12/09/1907 d 04/03/1985 - Tvl - 10 Tests (-) 38 matches (18 - 6T) 1932: E, S. 1937: A1, 2, NZ1, 2, 3. 1938: BI1, 2, 3.
616 Straeuli, RAW (Rudolf) b 20/08/1963 - Tvl - 10 Tests (20 - 4T) 23 matches (45 - 9T) 1994: NZ1, Arg1, 2, S, W. 1995: WS1, [A, WS2, NZ(R)], E(R).
592 Stransky, JT (Joel) b 16/07/1967 - Natal - 22 Tests (240 - 6T, 30C, 47P, 3D) 36 matches (329 - 9T, 55C, 55P, 3D) 1993: A1, 2, 3, Arg1. 1994: Arg1, 2. 1995: WS1, [A, R(t), C, F, NZ], W, It, E. 1996: Fj(R), NZ1, A2, NZ2, 3, 4, 5(R).
827 Strauss, AJ (Andries) b 05/03/1984 - FS - No Tests - 1 match (-) Toured BI & I. 2010.
579 Strauss, CP (Tiaan) b 28/06/1965 - WP - 15 Tests (20 - 4T) 37 matches (55 - 11T) 1992: F1, 2, E. 1993: F1, 2, A1, 2, 3, Arg1, 2. 1994: E1, NZ1*, 2, Arg1, 2.
539 Strauss, JA (Attie) b 02/09/1959 - WP - 2 Tests (-) 2 matches (-) 1984: S. Am&Sp1, 2.
800 Strauss, JA (Adriaan) b 18/11/1985 - FS - 33 Tests (25 - 5T) 35 matches (25 - 5T) 2008: A1(R), Arg(R), NZ3(R), A2(R), 3(R). 2009: F(R), It. 2010: S(R), E(R). 2012: E1(R), 2(R), 3(R), Arg1(R), 2, A1, NZ1, A2, NZ2, 1, S, E4. 2013: It, S, Sam, Arg1, Arg2, A1(R), NZ1(R), A2, NZ2(R), W(R), S, F(R).
490 Strauss, JHP (Johan) b

27/09/1951 - Tvl - 3 Tests (-) 3 matches (-) 1976: NZ3, 4. 1980: S. Am1.
158 Strauss, SSF (Sarel) b 24/11/1891 d 06/02/1946 - GW - 1 Test (-) 12 matches (23 - 5T, 2D) 1921: NZ3.
325 Strydom, CF (Popeye) b 20/01/1932 d 31/03/2001 - OFS - 6 Tests (-) 17 matches (3 - 1T) 1955: BI3. 1956: A1, 2, NZ1, 4. 1958: F1.
586 Strydom, JJ (Hannes) b 13/07/1965 - Tvl - 21 Tests (5 - 1T) 30 matches (10 - 2T) 1993: F2, A1, 2, 3, Arg1, 2. 1994: E. 1995: [A, C, F, NZ]. 1996: A2(R), NZ2(R), 3, 4, W(R). 1997: T, BI1, 2, 3, A2.
276 Strydom, LJ (Ou-Boet) b 27/10/1921 d 11/05/2003 - NTvl - 2 Tests (-) 2 matches (-) 1949: NZ1, 2.
566 Styger, JJ (Johan) b 31/01/1962 - OFS - 7 Tests (-) 18 matches (-) 1992: NZ(R), A, F1, 2, E. 1993: F2(R), A3(R).
403 Suter, MR (Snowy) b 14/12/1939 - Natal - 2 Tests (-) 4 matches (3 - 1T) 1965: I, S.
654 Swanepoel, W (Werner) b 15/04/1973 - FS - 20 Tests (25 - 5T) 25 matches (30 - 6T) 1997: BI3(R), A2(R), F1(R), 2, E, S. 1998: I2(R), W1(R), E2(R). 1999: It1, 2(R), W, A1, [Sp, NZ3(t)]. 2000: A1, NZ1, A2, NZ2, A3.
452 Swanson, PS (Peter) b 26/12/1946 d 26/10/2003 - Tvl - No Tests - 4 matches (5 - 1T, 1C) Toured A. 1971.
595 Swart, IS de V (Balie) b 18/05/1964 - Tvl - 16 Tests (-) 31 matches (-) 1993: A1, 2, 3, Arg1. 1994: E1, 2, NZ1, 3, Arg2(R). 1995: WS1, [A, WS2, F, NZ], W. 1996: A2.
630 Swart, J (Justin) b 23/07/1972 - WP - 10 Tests (5 - 1T) 13 matches (15 - 3T) 1996: Fj, NZ1(R), A2, NZ2, 3, 4, 5. 1997: BI3(R), It, S(R).
312 Swart, JJN (Sias) b 29/07/1934 d 18/01/1993 - SWA - 1 Test (3 - 1T) 1 match (3 - 1T) 1955: BI1.

T
43 Taberer, WS (Bill) b 11/04/1872 d 10/02/1938 - GW - 1 Test (-) 1 match (-) 1896: BI2.
842 Taute, JJ (Jaco) b 21/03/1991 - GL - 3 Tests (-) 3 matches (-) 2012: A2, NZ2, I.
380 Taylor, OB (Ormy) b 05/06/1937 - Natal - 1 Test (-) 1 match (-) 1962: BI1.
603 Teichmann, GH (Gary) b 09/01/1967 - Natal - 42 Tests (30 - 6T) 52 matches (35 - 7T) 1995: W. 1996: Fj, A1,

SPRINGBOKS 1891-2013

NZ1, A2, NZ2, 3*, 4*, 5*, Arg1*, 2*, F1*, 2*, W*. 1997: T*, BI1*, 2*, 3*, NZ1*, A1*, NZ2*, A2*, It*, F1*, 2*, E*, S*. 1998: I1*, 2*, W1*, E1*, A1*, NZ1*, 2*, A2*, W2*, S*, I3*, E2*. 1999: It1*, W*, NZ1*.
668 Terblanche, CS (Stefan) b 02/07/1975 - Boland - 37 Tests (95 - 19T) 41 matches (115 - 23T) 1998: I1,2, W1, E1, A1, NZ1, 2, A2, W2, S, I3, E2. 1999: It1(R), 2, W, A1, NZ2(R), [Sp, E(t), A3(R), NZ3]. 2000: E3. 2002: W1, 2, Arg, Sm, NZ1, A1, 2(R). 2003: S1, 2, Arg, A1, NZ1, A2, NZ2, [G].
633 Theron, DF (Dawie) b 15/09/1966 - GW - 13 Tests (-) 15 matches (-) 1996: A2(R), NZ2(R), 5, Arg1, 2, F1, 2, W. 1997: BI2(R), 3, NZ1(R), A1, NZ2(R).
749 Theron, JT (Gus) b 10/01/1975 - WP - No Tests - No matches Toured Aus & NZ. 2003.
56 Theunissen, DJ (Danie) b 12/07/1869 d 19/03/1964 - GW - 1 Test (-) 1 match (-) 1896: BI3.
142 Thompson, G (Tommy) b 04/10/1886 d 20/06/1916 - WP - 3 Tests (-) 15 matches (-) 1912: S, I, W.
648 Thomson, JRD (Jeremy) b 24/06/1967 - Natal - No Tests - 4 matches (5 - 1T) Toured Arg, F & W. 1996.
161 Tindall, JC (Jackie) b 26/03/1900 d 03/05/1946 - WP - 5 Tests (-) 27 matches (3 - 1T) 1924: BI1. 1928: NZ1, 2, 3, 4.
515 Tobias, EG (Errol) b 18/03/1950 - Boland - 6 Tests (22 - 1T, 3C, 4P) 15 matches (65 - 5T, 15C, 5P) 1981: I1, 2. 1984: E1, 2, S. Am&Sp1, 2.
201 Tod, NS (Jacko) b 11/03/1904 d 01/05/1965 - Natal - 1 Test (-) 1 match (-) 1928: NZ2.
163 Townsend, WH (Taffy) b 12/03/1896 d 27/01/1943 - Natal - 1 Test (-) 11 matches (3 - 1T) 1921: NZ1.
20 Trenery, WE (Wilfred) b 21/09/1867 d 23/08/1905 - GW - 1 Test (-) 1 match (-) 1891: BI2.
635 Tromp, H (Henry) b 29/12/1966 - NTvl - 4 Tests (-) 8 matches (5 - 1T) 1996: NZ3, 4, Arg2(R), F1(R).
581 Truscott, JA (Andries) b 22/07/1968 - NTvl - No Tests - 4 matches (-) Toured F & E. 1992.
187 Truter, DR (Pally) b 19/04/1897 d 21/11/1962 - WP - 2 Tests (-) 2 matches (-) 1924: BI2, 4.
385 Truter, JT (Trix) b 05/06/1939 - Natal - 3 Tests (3 - 1T) 16 matches (33 - 11T) 1963: A1. 1964: F. 1965: A2.
680 Trytsman, JW (Johnny) b 29/07/1971 - WP - No Tests - 4 matches (-) Toured BI & I. 1998.
232 Turner, FG (Freddy) b 18/03/1914 d 12/09/2003 - EP - 11 Tests (29 - 4T, 4C, 3P) 24 matches (131 - 18T, 26C, 7P, 1D) 1933: A1, 2, 3. 1937: A1, 2, NZ1, 2, 3. 1938: BI1, 2, 3.
349 Twigge, RJ (Robert) b 24/07/1936 - NTvl - 1 Test (-) 1 match (-) 1960: S.
763 Tyibilika, S (Solly) b 23/06/1979 d 13/11/2011 - KZN - 8 Tests (15 - 3T) 8 matches (15 - 3T) 2004: S, Arg. 2005: U, A2, Arg. 2006: NZ1, A2, NZ2.

U

315 Ulyate, CA (Clive) b 11/12/1933 - Tvl - 7 Tests (6 - 1T, 1D) 16 matches (12 - 2T, 2D) 1955: BI1, 2, 3, 4. 1956: NZ1, 2, 3.
370 Uys, P de W (Piet) b 10/12/1937 d 12/12/2009 - NTvl - 12 Tests (-) 29 matches (12 - 4T) 1960: W. 1961: E, S, I, A1, 2. 1962: BI1, 4. 1963: A1, 2. 1969: A1(R), 2.
738 Uys, PJ (Pierre) b 05/02/1976 - Mpu - 1 Test (-) 1 match (-) 2002: S.

V

525 Van Aswegen, HJ (Henning) b 11/02/1955 - WP - 2 Tests (-) 10 matches (-) 1981: NZ1. 1982: S. Am2(R).
718 Van Biljon, L (Lukas) b 16/03/1976 - Natal - 13 Tests (5 - 1T) 13 matches (5 - 1T) 2001: It1(R), NZ1, A1, 2, NZ2, F3, It2(R), E(R), US. 2002: F(R), S, E(R). 2003: NZ2(R).
59 Van Broekhuizen, HD (Broekie) b 17/06/1872 d 04/08/1953 - WP - 1 Test (-) 1 match (-) 1896: BI4.
2 Van Buuren, MCWE (Mosey) b 12/08/1865 d 03/10/1951 - Tvl - 1 Test (-) 1 match (-) 1891: BI1.
250 Van de Vyver, DF (Vandie) b 14/12/1909 d 18/03/1977 - WP - 1 Test (-) 14 matches (12 - 4T) 1937: A2.
484 Van den Berg, DS (Derek) b 02/01/1946 - Natal - 4 Tests (-) 7 matches (-) 1975: F1, 2. 1976: NZ1, 2.
258 Van den Berg, MA (Mauritz) b 09/05/1909 d 09/04/1948 - WP - 4 Tests (-) 18 matches (15 - 5T) 1937: A1, NZ1, 2, 3.
684 Van den Berg, PA (Albert) b 26/01/1974 - GW - 51 Tests (20 - 4T) 55 matches (30 - 6T) 1999: It1(R), 2, NZ2, A2, [S, U(R), E(R), A3(R), NZ3(R)]. 2000: E1(t+R), A1, NZ1, A2, NZ2(R), A3(+R), Arg, I, W, E3. 2001: F1(R), 2, A2(R), NZ2(R), US. 2004: NZ1. 2005: U, F1, 2, A1(R), 2(R), 3(R), 4(R), Arg(R), F3(R). 2006: S2(R), A1(R), NZ1, A2(R), NZ2(R), A3(R), I, E1(R), 2(R). 2007: Sm1, A2(R), NZ2, N(t+R), S(R), [T, US.], W(R).
621 Van den Bergh, E (Elandré) b 09/12/1966 - EP - 1 Test (-) 8 matches (5 - 1T) 1994: Arg2(t+R).
133 Van der Hoff, AD (Apie) b 24/09/1888 d 09/03/1970 - Tvl - No Tests - 9 matches (30 - 10T) Toured BI, I & F. 1912/13.
629 Van der Linde, A (Toks) b 30/12/1969 - WP - 7 Tests (-) 18 matches (10 - 2T) 1995: It, E. 1996: Arg1(R), 2(R), F1(R), W(R). 2001: F3(R).
741 Van der Linde, CJ (CJ) b 27/08/1980 - FS - 75 Tests (20 - 4T) 80 matches (20 - 4T) 2002: S(R), E(R). 2004: I1(R), 2(R), PI(R), A1(R), NZ2(t+R), A2(R), W2(R), I3(R), E(t+R), S, Arg. 2005: U, F1(R), 2, A1(R), 3, NZ1, A4, NZ2, Arg, W, F3. 2006: S2(R), F(R), A1, NZ1, A2, NZ2, I, E1, 2. 2007: E1(R), 2, A1(R), NZ1(R), A2, NZ2, N, S, [Sm, E3(R), T, US(R), Arg, E4.], W. 2008: W1(t+R), It, NZ1, 2, A1, Arg, NZ3, A2. 2009: F(R), I(t). 2010: W1, It1(R), NZ2, A1(t+R), NZ3(R), A2(R), 3(R), I(R), W2(R), S(R), E(R). 2011: A1(t+R), NZ1(R), 2(R), [N.]. 2012: I, S(R).
323 Van der Merwe, AJ (Bertus) b 14/07/1929 d 23/11/1971 - Boland - 12 Tests (-) 26 matches (3 - 1T) 1955: BI2, 3, 4. 1956: A1, 2, NZ1, 2, 3, 4. 1958: F1. 1960: S, NZ2.
221 Van der Merwe, AV (Alvi) b 14/09/1908 d 18/09/1986 - WP - 1 Test (-) 13 matches (6 - 2T) 1931: W.
273 Van der Merwe, BS (Fiks) b 02/01/1917 d 11/07/2005 - NTvl - 1 Test (-) 1 match (-) 1949: NZ1.
703 Van der Merwe, CP (Carel) b 05/10/1971 - Boland - No Tests - 4 matches (-) Toured Arg, I, W & E. 2000.
846 Van der Merwe, F (Franco) b 15/03/1983 - GL - 1 Test (-) 1 Match (-) Toured I, S & E 2012. 2013: NZ2(R).
365 Van der Merwe, HS (Stompie) b 24/08/1936 d 04/06/1988 - NTvl - 5 Tests (-) 17 matches (6 - 2T) 1960: NZ4. 1963: A2, 3, 4. 1964: F.
790 Van der Merwe, HS (Heinke) b 03/05/1985 - GL - 4 Tests (-) 7 matches (-) 2007: W(t+R). 2012: I(R), S(R), E4(R).
433 Van der Merwe, JP (JP) b 07/12/1947 - WP - 1 Test (-) 12 matches (9 - 3T) 1970: W.

SPRINGBOKS 1891-2013

526 Van der Merwe, PR (Flippie) b 08/07/1957 - SWD - 6 Tests (-) 12 matches (-) 1981: NZ2, 3, US. 1986: NZC1, 2. 1989: WT1.

818 Van der Merwe, PR (Flip) b 03/06/1985 - BB - 34 Tests (5 - 1T) 35 matches (5 - 1T) 2010: F(R), It2(R), A1(R), NZ3, A2, 3(R), I(R), W2(R), S(R), E(R). 2011: A1. 2012: E1(R), 2(R), 3(R), Arg1(R), 2(R), A1(R), NZ1, A2(R), NZ2(R), I(R), S(R), E4(R). 2013: It(R), S(R), Sam, Arg1(R), Arg2(R), A1, NZ1, A2, W, S, F.

299 Van der Ryst, FE (Franz) b 17/10/1920 d 21/02/1981 - Tvl - No Tests - 14 matches (-) Toured BI, I & F 1951/52.

263 Van der Schyff, JH (Jack) b 11/06/1928 d 02/12/2001 - GW - 5 Tests (10 - 2C, 2P) 5 matches (10 - 2C, 2P) 1949: NZ1, 2, 3, 4. 1955: BI1.

434 Van der Schyff, PJ (Johan) b 19/01/1942 - WTvl - No Tests - 2 matches (-) Toured BI & I. 1969/70.

432 Van der Watt, AE (Andy) b 10/10/1946 - WP - 3 Tests (-) 22 matches (42 - 14T) 1969: S(R), E. 1970: I.

203 Van der Westhuizen, JC (JC) b 22/11/1905 d 08/07/2003 - WP - 4 Tests (3 - 1T) 19 matches (25 - 7T, 1D) 1928: NZ2, 3, 4. 1931: I.

609 Van der Westhuizen, JF (Cabous) b 11/01/1965 - Natal - No Tests - 11 matches (10 - 2T) Toured NZ 1994 and W, S & I. 1994.

593 Van der Westhuizen, JH (Joost) b 20/02/1971 - NTvl - 89 Tests (190 - 38T) 111 matches (280 - 56T) 1993: Arg1, 2. 1994: E1, 2(R), Arg2, S, W. 1995: WS1, [A, C(R), WS2, F, NZ], W, It, E. 1996: Fj, A1, 2(R), NZ2, 3, (R), 4, 5, Arg1, 2, F1, 2, W. 1997: T, BI1, 2, 3, NZ1, A1, NZ2, A2, It, F1. 1998: I1, 2, W1, E1, A1, NZ1, 2, A2, W2, S, I3, E2. 1999: NZ2*, A2*, [S*, Sp(R), U*, E*, A3*, NZ3*]. 2000: C, E1, 2, A1(R), NZ1(R), A2(R), Arg, I, W, E3. 2001: F1, 2, It1(R), NZ1, A1, 2, NZ2, F3, It2, E, US(R). 2003: S1*, S2*, A1, NZ1, A2(R), NZ2, [U*, E, Sm, NZ3].

213 Van der Westhuizen, JH (Ponie) b 04/11/1909 d 05/03/1995 - WP - 3 Tests (-) 16 matches (45 - 12T, 1C, 2D) 1931: I. 1932: E, S.

696 Van der Westhuyzen, JNB (Jaco) b 06/04/1978 - Mpu - 32 Tests (51 - 5T, 7C, 1P, 3D) 32 matches (51 - 5T, 7C, 1P, 3D) 2000: NZ2(R). 2001: It1(R). 2003: S1(R), 2, Arg, A1, [E, Sm, NZ3]. 2004: I1, 2, W1, PI, NZ1, A1, NZ2, A2, W2, I3, E, S, Arg. 2005: U, F1, 2, A1, 4(R), NZ2(R). 2006: S1, 2, F, A1.

437 Van Deventer, PI (Piet) b 06/06/1946 d 13/04/2013 - GW - No Tests - 12 matches (12 - 4T) Toured BI & I. 1969/70.

184 Van Druten, NJV (Jack) b 12/06/1898 d 16/01/1989 - Tvl - 8 Tests (6 - 2T) 8 matches (6 - 2T) 1924: BI1, 2, 3, 4. 1928: NZ1, 2, 3, 4.

152 Van Heerden, AJ (Attie) b 10/03/1898 d 14/10/1965 - Tvl - 2 Tests (3 - 1T) 17 matches (42 - 14T) 1921: NZ1, 3.

606 Van Heerden, FJ (Fritz) b 29/06/1970 - WP - 14 Tests (5 - 1T) 26 matches (5 - 1T) 1994: E1, 2(R), NZ3. 1995: It, E. 1996: NZ5(R), Arg1(R), 2(R). 1997: T, BI2(t+R), 3(R), NZ1(R), 2(R). 1999: [Sp].

474 Van Heerden, JL (Moaner) b 18/07/1951 - NTvl - 17 Tests (4 - 1T) 23 matches (4 - 1T) 1974: BI3, 4, F1, 2. 1975: F1, 2. 1976: NZ1, 2, 3, 4. 1977: WT. 1980: BI1, 3, 4, S. Am3, 4, F.

744 Van Heerden, JL (Wikus) b 25/02/1979 - GL - 14 Tests (5 - 1T) 16 matches (10 - 2T) 2003: S1, 2, A1, NZ1, A2(t). 2007: A2, NZ2, S(R), [Sm(R), E3, T, US, Fiji(R), E4(R).].

272 Van Jaarsveld, CJ (Hoppy) b 21/02/1917 d 08/12/1980 - Tvl - 1 Test (-) 1 match (-) 1949: NZ1.

354 Van Jaarsveldt, DC (Des) b 31/03/1929 - Rhodesia - 1 Test (3 - 1T) 1 match (3 - 1T) 1960: S*.

368 Van Niekerk, BB (Bennie) b 01/12/1937 d 21/08/2000 - OFS - No Tests - 5 matches (3 - 1T) Toured BI, I & F. 1960/61.

210 Van Niekerk, JA (Jock) b 01/06/1907 d 19/04/1983 - WP - 1 Test (-) 2 matches (-) 1928: NZ4.

719 Van Niekerk, JC (Joe) b 14/05/1980 - GL - 52 Tests (50 - 10T) 52 matches (50 - 10T) 2001: NZ1(R), A1(R), NZ2(t+R), F3(R), It2, US. 2002: W1(R), 2(R), Arg(R), Sm, NZ1, A1, NZ2, A2, F, S, E. 2003: A2, NZ2, [U, E, G, Sm]. 2004: NZ1(R), A1(t), NZ2, A2, W2, I3, E, S, Arg(R). 2005: U(R), F2(R), A1(R), 2, 3, NZ1, A4, NZ2. 2006: S1, 2, F, A1, NZ1(R), A2(R). 2008: It(R), NZ1, 2, Arg(R), A2(R). 2010: W1.

259 Van Reenen, GL (George) b 29/03/1914 d 12/11/1967 - WP - 2 Tests (6 - 2T) 11 matches (24 - 8T) 1937: A2, NZ1.

26 Van Renen, CG (Charlie) b 23/08/1868 d 20/07/1942 - WP - 3 Tests (-) 3 matches (-) 1891: BI3. 1896: BI1, 4.

65 Van Renen, WA (Willie) b 29/08/1880 d 17/02/1942 - WP - 2 Tests (-) 2 matches (-) 1903: BI1, 3.

558 Van Rensburg, JTJ (Theo) b 26/05/1967 - Tvl - 7 Tests (40 - 2C, 12P) 22 matches (182 - 7T, 21C, 34P, 1D) 1992: NZ, A, E. 1993: F1, 2, A1. 1994: NZ2.

167 Van Rooyen, GW (Tank) b 09/12/1892 d 21/09/1942 - Tvl - 2 Tests (-) 13 matches (3 - 1T) 1921: NZ2, 3.

124 Van Ryneveld, RCB (Clive) b 07/07/1891 d 25/08/1969 - WP - 2 Tests (-) 2 matches (-) 1910: BI2, 3.

631 Van Schalkwyk, D (Danie) b 01/02/1975 - NTvl - 8 Tests (10 - 2T) 8 matches (10 - 2T) 1996: Fj(R), NZ1, 2, 3. 1997: BI2, 3, NZ1, A1.

278 Van Schoor, RAM (Ryk) b 03/12/1921 d 22/03/2009 - Rhodesia - 12 Tests (6 - 2T) 23 matches (21 - 7T) 1949: NZ2, 3, 4. 1951: S, I, W. 1952: E, F. 1953: A1, 2, 3, 4.

483 Van Staden, JA (André) b 15/12/1945 - NTvl - No Tests - 3 matches (-) Toured F. 1974.

671 Van Straaten, AJJ (Braam) b 28/09/1971 - GF - 21 Tests (221 - 23C, 55P) 27 matches (294 - 5T, 46C, 59P) 1999: It2(R), W, NZ1(R), A1. 2000: C, E1, 2, NZ1, A2, NZ2, A3, Arg(R), I(R), W, E3. 2001: A1, 2, NZ2, F3, It2, E.

314 Van Vollenhoven, KT (Tom) b 29/04/1935 - NTvl - 7 Tests (15 - 4T, 1D) 23 matches (63 - 20T, 1D) 1955: BI1, 2, 3, 4. 1956: A1, 2, NZ3.

141 Van Vuuren, TFJ (Tom) b 09/07/1889 d 07/07/1947 - EP - 5 Tests (-) 17 matches (6 - 2T) 1912: S, I, W. 1913: E, F.

304 Van Wyk, CJ (Basie) b 05/11/1923 d 29/08/2002 - Tvl - 10 Tests (18 - 6T) 23 matches (24 - 8T) 1951: S, I, W. 1952: E, F. 1953: A1, 2, 3, 4. 1955: BI1.

445 Van Wyk, JFB (Piston) b 21/12/1943 - NTvl - 15 Tests (-) 19 matches (-) 1970: NZ1, 2, 3, 4. 1971: F1, 2, A1, 2, 3. 1972: E. 1974: BI1, 3, 4. 1976: NZ3, 4.

196 Van Wyk, SP (SP) b 12/01/1901 d 22/01/1978 - WP - 2 Tests (-) 2 matches (-) 1928: NZ1, 2.

378 Van Zyl, BP (Ben-Piet) b 01/08/1935 d 10/03/1973 - WP - 1 Test (6 - 2T) 5 matches (12 - 4T) 1961: I.

SPRINGBOKS 1891-2013

410 Van Zyl, CGP (Sakkie) b 01/07/1932 - OFS - 4 Tests (-) 16 matches (6 - 2T) 1965: NZ1,2,3,4.

665 Van Zyl, DJ (Dan) b 08/01/1971 - Mpu - 1 Test (-) 7 matches (10 - 2C, 2P) 2000: E(R).

340 Van Zyl, GH (Hugo) b 20/08/1932 d 08/05/2007 - WP - 17 Tests (12 - 4T) 35 matches (27 - 9T) 1958: F1. 1960: S, NZ1, 2,3,4,W,I. 1961: E,S,F,I,A1,2. 1962: BI1,3,4.

357 Van Zyl, HJ (Hennie) b 31/01/1936 - Tvl - 10 Tests (18 - 6T) 24 matches (54 - 18T) 1960: NZ1, 2, 3, 4, I. 1961: E, S, I, A1, 2.

852 Van Zyl, PE (Piet) b 14/09/1989 - FS - 2 Tests (-) 2 matches (-) 2013: S(R), Sam(R).

373 Van Zyl, PJ (Piet) b 23/07/1933 d 28/05/1988 - Boland - 1 Test (-) 17 matches (3 - 1T) 1961: I.

190 Vanderplank, BE (BV) b 29/04/1894 d 22/12/1990 - Natal - 2 Tests (-) 2 matches (-) 1924: BI3,4.

497 Veldsman, PE (Piet) b 11/03/1952 - WP - 1 Test (-) 1 match (-) 1977: WT.

634 Venter, AG (André) b 14/11/1970 - FS - 66 Tests (45 - 9T) 70 matches (50 - 10T) 1996: NZ3, 4, 5, Arg1, 2, F1, 2, W. 1997: T, BI1, 2, 3, NZ1, A1, NZ2, It, F1, 2, E, S. 1998: I1, 2, W1, E1, A1, NZ1, 2, A2, W2, S(R), I3(R), E2(R). 1999: It1, 2(R), W(R), NZ1, A1, NZ2, A2, [S, U, E, A3, NZ3]. 2000: C, E1, 2, A1, NZ1, A2, NZ2, A3, Arg, I, W, E3. 2001: F1, It1, NZ1, A1, 2, NZ2, F3(R), It2(R), E(t+R), US(R).

695 Venter, AJ (AJ) b 29/07/1973 - Natal - 25 Tests (-) 28 matches (-) 2000: W(R), E3(R). 2001: F3, It2, E, US. 2002: W1, 2, Arg, NZ1(R), 2, A2, F,S(R), E. 2003: Arg. 2004: PI, NZ1, A1, NZ2(R), A2, I3, E. 2006: NZ3, A3.

605 Venter, B (Brendan) b 29/12/1969 - OFS - 17 Tests (10 - 2T) 26 matches (30 - 6T) 1994: E1, 2, NZ1, 2, 3, Arg1, 2. 1995: [R,C,WS2(R),NZ(R)]. 1996: A1, NZ1, A2. 1999: A2, [S, U].

214 Venter, FD (Floors) b 13/04/1909 d ??/??/1992 - Tvl - 3 Tests (-) 14 matches (24 - 8T) 1931: W. 1932: S. 1933: A3.

672 Venter, SL (Lourens) b 25/06/1976 - GW - No Tests - 4 matches (15 - 3T) Toured BI & I. 1998.

838 Vermaak, J (Jano) b 01/01/1985 - BB - 3 Tests (0 - 0) 3 matches (0 - 0) 2012: Rugby Championship Squad - no tests. 2013: It, A1(R), NZ1(R), tour of W, S & F - no tests.

840 Vermeulen, DJ (Duane) b 03/07/1986 - WP - 16 Tests (5 - 1T) 16 matches (5 - 1T) 2012: A1, NZ1, A2, NZ2, I, S, E4. 2013: Arg1, Arg2, A1, NZ1, A2, NZ2, W, S, F

25 Versfeld, C (Hasie) b 24/09/1866 d 06/01/1942 - WP - 1 Test (-) 1 match (-) 1891: BI3.

7 Versfeld, M (Oupa) b 15/05/1860 d 01/09/1931 - WP - 3 Tests (-) 3 matches (-) 1891: BI1,2,3.

3 Vigne, JT (Chubb) b 23/12/1868 d 09/04/1955 - Tvl - 3 Tests (-) 3 matches (-) 1891: BI1,2,3.

448 Viljoen, JF (Joggie) b 14/05/1945 - GW - 6 Tests (6 - 2T) 10 matches (12 - 4T) 1971: F1, 2, A1, 2, 3. 1972: E.

644 Viljoen, R (Joggie) b 22/07/1976 - WP - No Tests - 3 matches (-) Toured Arg, F & W. 1996.

808 Viljoen, R (Riaan) b 04/01/1983 - GW - No Tests - 2 matches (-) Toured F, It, I & E. 2009.

451 Viljoen. JT (Hannes) b 21/04/1943 - Natal - 3 Tests (6 - 2T) 10 matches (48 - 16T) 1971: A1, 2, 3.

532 Villet, JV (John) b 03/11/1954 - WP - 2 Tests (-) 2 matches (-) 1984: E1, 2.

530 Visagie, GP (Gawie) b 31/03/1955 - Natal - No Tests - 3 matches (8 - 2T) Toured NZ & USA. 1981.

683 Visagie, IJ (Cobus) b 31/10/1973 - WP - 29 Tests (-) 29 matches (-) 1999: It1, W, NZ1, A1, NZ2, A2, [S, U, E, A3, NZ3]. 2000: C, E2, A1, NZ1, A2, NZ2, A3. 2001: NZ1, A1, 2, NZ2, F3, It2(R), E(t+R), US. 2003: S1(R), 2(R), Arg.

419 Visagie, PJ (Piet) b 16/04/1943 - GW - 25 Tests (130 - 6T, 20C, 19P, 5D) 44 matches (240 - 8T, 36C, 40P, 8D) 1967: F1, 2, 3, 4. 1968: BI1, 2, 3, 4, F1, 2. 1969: A1, 2, 3, 4, S, E. 1970: NZ1, 2, 3, 4. 1971: F1, 2, A1, 2, 3.

536 Visagie, RG (Rudi) b 27/06/1959 - OFS - 5 Tests (-) 9 matches (5 - 1T) 1984: E1, 2, S. Am&Sp1, 2. 1993: F1.

517 Visser, J de V (De Villiers) b 26/11/1958 - WP - 2 Tests (-) 12 matches (16 - 4T) 1981: NZ2, US.

625 Visser, M (Mornay) b 30/03/1969 - WP - 1 Test (-) 1 match (-) 1995: WS1(R).

237 Visser, PJ (Paul) b 25/12/1903 d 25/04/1963 - Tvl - 1 Test (-) 1 match (-) 1933: A2.

293 Vivier, SS (Basie) b 01/03/1927 d 18/10/2009 - OFS - 5 Tests (11 - 4C, 1P) 31 matches (165 - 5T, 45C, 17P, 3D) 1956: A1*, 2*, NZ2*, 3*, 4*.

471 Vogel, ML (Leon) b 22/10/1949 - OFS - 1 Test (-) 1 match (-) 1974: BI2(R).

686 Von Hoesslin, DJB (Dave) b 10/05/1975 - GW - 5 Tests (10 - 2T) 5 matches (10 - 2T) 1999: It1(R), 2, W(R), NZ1, A1(R).

681 Vos, AN (André) b 09/01/1975 - GL - 33 Tests (25 - 5T) 38 matches (30 - 6T) 1999: It1(t+R), 2, NZ1(R), 2(R), A2, [S(R), Sp*, E(R), A3(R), NZ3]. 2000: C*, E1*, 2*, A1*, NZ1*, A2*, NZ2*, A3*, Arg*, I*, W*, E3*. 2001: F1*, 2*, It1, NZ1, A1, 2, NZ2, F3, It2, E, US*.

W

491 Wagenaar, C (Christo) b 11/03/1952 - NTvl - 1 Test (-) 1 match (-) 1977: WT.

269 Wahl, JJ (Ballie) b 10/07/1920 d 25/06/1978 - WP - 1 Test (-) 1 match (-) 1949: NZ1.

170 Walker, AP (Alf) b 08/05/1893 d 17/07/1971 - Natal - 6 Tests (-) 14 matches (-) 1921: NZ1, 3. 1924: BI1, 2, 3, 4.

311 Walker, HN (Harry) b 01/07/1928 d 05/08/2008 - OFS - 4 Tests (-) 19 matches (-) 1953: A3. 1956: A2, NZ1, 4.

115 Walker, HW (Henry) b 22/02/1884 d 21/08/1951 - Tvl - 3 Tests (-) 3 matches (-) 1910: BI1, 2, 3.

397 Walton, DC (Don) b 05/04/1939 - Natal - 8 Tests (-) 31 matches (12 - 4T) 1964: F. 1965: I, S, NZ3, 4. 1969: A1, 2, E.

739 Wannenburg, PJ (Pedrie) b 02/01/1981 - BB - 20 Tests (15 - 3T) 20 matches (15 - 3T) 2002: F(R), E. 2003: S1, 2, Arg, A1(t+R), NZ1(R). 2004: I1, 2, W1, PI(R). 2006: S1(R), F, NZ2(R), 3, A3. 2007: Sm1(R), NZ1(R), A2, NZ2.

216 Waring, FW (Franky) b 07/11/1908 d 24/01/2000 - WP - 7 Tests (6 - 2T) 19 matches (12 - 4T) 1931: I. 1932: E. 1933: A1, 2, 3, 4, 5.

707 Wasserman, JG (Johan) b 29/07/1977 - SWD - No Tests - 4 matches (5 - 1T) Toured Arg, I, W & E. 2000

786 Watson, LA (Luke) b 26/10/1983 - WP - 10 Tests (-) 10 matches (-) 2007: Sm1. 2008: W1, 2, It, NZ1(R), 2(R), Arg, NZ3(R), A2(R), 3(t+R).

260 Watt, HH (Howard) b 01/03/1911 d 18/08/2005 - WP - No Tests - 7 matches

(9 - 3T) Toured A & NZ. 1937.
154 Weepner, JS (Jackie) b 16/01/1896 d 14/12/1965 - WP - No Tests - 9 matches (6 - 2T) Toured A & NZ. 1921.
587 Wegner, GN (Nico) b 03/12/1968 - WP - 4 Tests (-) 12 matches (-) 1993: F2, A1, 2, 3.
366 Wentzel, GJ (Giepie) b 28/02/1938 d 01/07/1996 - EP - No Tests - 12 matches (37 - 2T, 14C, 1P) Toured BI, I & F. 1960/61.
740 Wentzel, M v Z (Marco) b 05/05/1979 - Mpu - 2 Tests (-) 2 matches (-) 2002: F(R), S.
664 Wessels, JC (Boeta) b 30/06/1973 - GW - No Tests - 1 match (-) Toured It, F,E & S. 1997.
35 Wessels, JJ (Scraps) b 13/09/1874 d 06/04/1929 - WP - 3 Tests (-) 3 matches (-) 1896: BI1, 2, 3.
402 Wessels, JW (John) b 14/05/1935 d 22/01/2006 - OFS - No Tests - 2 matches (-) Toured I & S. 1965.
296 Wessels, PW (Piet) b 11/02/1926 d 24/08/1997 - OFS - No Tests - 14 matches (-) Toured BI, I & F. 1951/52.
459 Whipp, PJM (Peter) b 22/09/1950 - WP - 8 Tests (4 - 1T) 10 matches (4 - 1T) 1974: BI1, 2. 1975: F1. 1976: NZ1, 3, 4. 1980: S. Am1, 2.
217 White, J (Jimmy) b 20/05/1911 d 03/07/1997 - Border - 10 Tests (10 - 2T, 1D) 26 matches (23 - 5T, 2D) 1931: W. 1933: A1, 2, 3, 4, 5. 1937: A1, 2, NZ1, 2.
585 Wiese, JJ (Kobus) b 16/05/1964 - Tvl - 18 Tests (5 - 1T) 32 matches (15 - 3T) 1993: F1. 1995: WS1, [R, C, WS2, F, NZ], W, It, E. 1996: NZ3(R), 4(R), 5, Arg1, 2, F1, 2, W.
743 Willemse, AK (Ashwin) b 08/09/1981 - GL - 19 Tests (20 - 4T) 20 matches (25 - 5T) 2003: S1, 2, NZ1, A2, NZ2, [U, E, Sm, NZ3]. 2004: W2, I3. 2007: E1, 2(R), Sm1, A1, NZ1, N, S(R), [T.].
120 Williams, AE (Arthur) b 01/07/1879 d 21/07/1930 - GW - 1 Test (-) 1 match (-) 1910: BI1.
533 Williams, AP (Avril) b 10/02/1961 - WP - 2 Tests (-) 2 matches (-) 1984: E1, 2.
589 Williams, CM (Chester) b 08/08/1970 - WP - 27 Tests (70 - 14T) 47 matches (135 - 27T) 1993: Arg2. 1994: E1, 2, NZ1, 2, 3, Arg1, 2, S, W. 1995: WS1, [WS2, F, NZ], It, E. 1998: A1(t), NZ1(t). 2000: C(R), E1(t), 2(R), A1(R), NZ2, A3, Arg, I, W(R).
231 Williams, DO (Dai) b 16/06/1913 d 24/12/1975 - WP - 8 Tests (15 - 5T) 18 matches (51 - 17T) 1937: A1, 2, NZ1, 2, 3. 1938: BI1, 2, 3.
450 Williams, JG (John) b 29/10/1946 - NTvl - 13 Tests (-) 24 matches (3 - 1T) 1971: F1, 2, A1, 2, 3. 1972: E. 1974: BI1, 2, 4, F1, 2. 1976: NZ1, 2.
363 Wilson, LG (Lionel) b 25/05/1933 - WP - 27 Tests (6 - 2D) 58 matches (19 - 3T, 2C, 2D) 1960: NZ3, 4, W, I. 1961: E, F, I, A1, 2. 1962: BI1, 2, 3, 4. 1963: A1, 2, 3, 4. 1964: W, F. 1965: I, S, A1, 2, NZ1, 2, 3, 4.
495 Wolmarans, BJ (Barry) b 22/02/1953 - OFS - 1 Test (4 - 1T) 7 matches (4 - 1T) 1977: WT.
135 Wrentmore, GM (Bai) b 20/02/1893 d 16/08/1953 - WP - No Tests - 9 matches (27 - 3T, 5C, 2D) Toured BI, I & F. 1912/13.
548 Wright, GD (Garth) b 09/09/1963 - EP - 7 Tests (4 - 1T) 12 matches (4 - 1T) 1986: NZC3, 4. 1989: WT1, 2. 1992: F1, 2, E.
381 Wyness, MRK (Wang) b 23/01/1937 d 06/11/2011 - WP - 5 Tests (3 - 1T) 5 matches (3 - 1T) 1962: BI1, 2, 3, 4. 1963: A2.

Z

153 Zeller, WC (Bill) b 18/07/1894 d 27/07/1969 - Natal - 2 Tests (-) 14 matches (39 - 13T) 1921: NZ2, 3.
212 Zimerman, M (Morris) b 08/06/1911 - d 09/01/1992 - WP - 4 Tests (3 - 1T) 18 matches (42 - 14T) 1931: W, I. 1932: E, S.

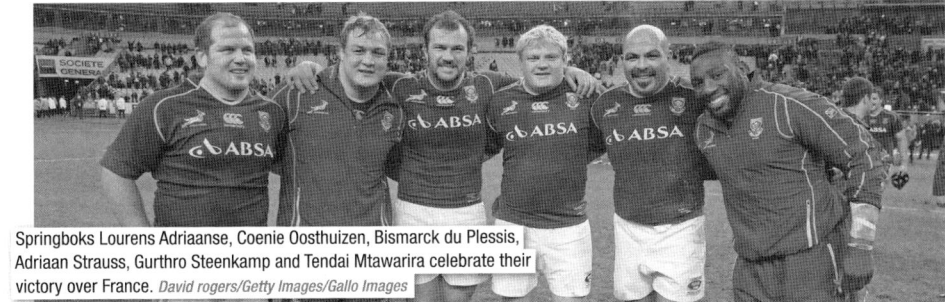

Springboks Lourens Adriaanse, Coenie Oosthuizen, Bismarck du Plessis, Adriaan Strauss, Gurthro Steenkamp and Tendai Mtawarira celebrate their victory over France. *David rogers/Getty Images/Gallo Images*

PROVINCIAL REPRESENTATION

South Africa's 854 International Players (latest PS du Toit) have come from 15 provincial unions as follows:

Western Province	257	Boland	15
Golden Lions (formerly Transvaal)	161	Falcons (Eastern Transvaal)	10
Blue Bulls (Northern Transvaal)	107	Mpumalanga (South Eastern Transvaal)	9
Free State (Orange Free State)	80	North West (Western Transvaal)	9
KwaZulu-Natal (Natal)	77	Zimbabwe (Rhodesia)	8
Griqualand West	63	South Western Districts	5
Eastern Province	34	Namibia (South West Africa)	3
Border	16	**TOTAL**	**854**

SA SEVENS INTERNATIONALS 1993-2013

† indicates 15-a-side Springbok

A
Adams, BI (Bennie) (WP) – 04 HK, Sing, Bor, Lon, Dub, SA.
Afrika, CS (Cecil) (Griffons) 09 WG, 09 Dub, SA, 10 NZ, USA, Aus, HK, Lon, Sco, CG; 10 Dub, SA; 11 USA; HK; Aus: Lon; Sco, 11 Aus, SA, 12 NZ, USA, HK; Aus; SA; , 13 Jap; Lon; RWC.
Alberts, N (Nico) (WP) - 01 Wel.
†**Aplon, GG** (Gio) (WP) 06 Wel, LA, Par, Lon 07 Lon, Sco 08 Lon, Sco, 08 Dub, SA, 09 NZ, USA, Lon, Sco, RWC.
April, C (Chelton) (WP) - 96 HK.
Arnold, P (Peet) (N Tvl) - 96 Dub; 98 Arg, Ur, Viña.

B
†**Badenhorst, C** (Chris) (FS)* - 93 HK, RWC; 96 Ur.
Basson, S (Stefan) (WP) – 04 HK, Sing, Bor, Lon. 05 Sing, Lon, Par, RWC, WG, Dub, SA, 06 Wel, LA, Par, Lon, CG, Dub, SA, 07 HK, Aus, 08 lon, Sco.
Benjamin, RS (Ryno) (Boland) 05 Sing, Lon, Par, WG, 06 Par, Lon, Dub, SA, 07 HK, Aus, 08 Dub, SA, 09 NZ, USA, HK, Aus, Lon, Sco, RWC, WG,) (Dub, 10 NZ, USA, Aus, HK, Lon, Sco, CG; 13 RWC.
Blom, J (Jandré) (FS) 05 Dub, SA, 06 HK, Sing 07 Wel, USA.
Blommetjies, C (Clayton) (SARU) 12 Sco, Lon.
†**Bobo, G** (Gcobani) (Lions) - 99 SA; 01 Lon, Car, Jap, 07 Wel, USA, HK, Aus, Lon (c), Sco (c).
Bock, AG (Alshaun) (Bol) - 03 HK.
†**Boome, CS** (Selborne) (WP) - 98 Arg, Ur, Viña .
Botha, B. (Bernardo) (Golden Lions) 10 CG; 10 Dub; SA; 11 NZ; USA; HK, 11 Aus, Dub, SA, 12 NZ, USA, HK, Jap; SA; , 13 Lon; WG.
Bouwer, G (Graeme) (NTvl) - 96 Dub; 97 RWC; 98 HK; 99 Fiji*, HK.
Bowles, J (Jovan) (Sharks) 06 Dub, SA, 07 Lon, Sco.
Brand, J (Janneman) (WP) - 96 Ur, HK.
Breytenbach, C (Conrad) (NTvl) - 96 HK.
Brink, HM (Helgard) (FS) - 99 Par, Dub, SA; 00 NZ, Fiji, Aus, HK, Jap, Fr, Dur, Dub; 01 RWC, HK, Sha, KL, Tok, Lon, Car, Jap, Dub, Dur; 02 San, Arg, Bris, Wel, Sing, KL, Bris.
Brink, S (Stephen) (FS) - 96 Ur, HK, Dub (c); 97 RWC; 98 Arg (c), Ur (c), Viña (c).
†**Britz, GJJ** (Gerrie) (FS) - 01 Dub, Dur, San, Arg.
†**Britz, WK** (Warren) (Sharks) - 99 Par, Dub, SA; 00 Ur, Arg, NZ, Fiji, Aus, HK, Jap, Fr, Dur, Dub; 01 RWC.
Brown, K (Kyle) (WP) 08 Dub, SA, 09 NZ, USA, HK, Aus, Lon, Sco, RWC, WG, 09 Dub, SA, 10 NZ, USA, Aus (c), HK (c); 10 Dub (c); SA (c) ; 11 NZ (c); USA (c); HK (c); Aus (c); Lon (c); Sco (c), 11 Aus (c), Dub (c), SA (c), 12 NZ (c), USA (c), HK (c), Jap (c), Sco (c), Lon (c); Aus (c); SA (c); , 13 RWC (c); WG (c)
†**Brüssow, HW** (Heinrich) (FS) 06 HK, Sing.
Burger, PB (Phillip) (FS) 06 Wel, LA, Par, Lon, CG, Dub, SA, 12 Sco, Lon.

C
Calitz, JP (Johan) (Leopards) - 99 Arg, San, Fiji, HK, Tok, Par; 00 HK, Tok*, Dur, Dub; 01 Wel, HK, Sha, KL, Tok, Lon, Car, Jap.
†**Chavhanga, T** (Tonderai) (Free State) – 03 Dub, SA
†**Cilliers, NV** (Vlok) (WP) - 93 HK; 94 HK; 96 Dub; 98 HK.
†**Claassens, JP** (Jannie) (NTvl)* - 93 HK, RWC; 96 HK, Dub.
Coeries, DB (Darryl) (SWD Eagles) - 02 Dub, SA; 03 Bris, NZ, HK.
Coetzee, F (Fielies) (Falcons) - 99 Arg, San.
Coetzee, R (Rudi) (Lions) - 02 Dub, SA; 03 Car, Lon.
†**Conradie, JHJ** (Bolla) (WP) - 99 Dub, SA; 00 NZ, Fiji, Aus.

D
Dames, A (Archer) (Pumas) - 99 Par.
Damons, O (Ossie) (Griffons) 05 Lon, Par.
Dazel, RL (Renfred) (Boland) 05 WG, Dub, SA, 06 Wel, LA, HK, Sing, CG, SA, 07 Wel, USA , 07 Dub, SA, 08 Wel, USA, HK, Aus 08 Dub, SA, 09 Nz, USA, HK, Aus, Lon, Sco, RWC, WG, 10 Lon, Sco, CG, 10 Dub; 11 NZ; USA, 11 Aus, Dub, 12 USA, Jap.
†**De Jongh, JL** (Juan) (WP) 08 Wel.
Delport, PS (Paul) (WP) – 03 Dub, 04 Wel, LA 06 Par, Lon, 08 Dub, Sa, 09 Nz, USA, Sco, RWC, WG, 09 Dub (c), SA (c), CG (c); 10 SA; 11 NZ; HK; Aus; Lon; Sco, 11 Aus, Dub, SA, 12 NZ, HK, Aus; Dub; SA; '13 Nz; USA; HK; Sco.
De Marigny, MRD (Marc) (Sharks) - 03 Bris, NZ, HK, Car, Lon, Dub (c), SA (c), 04 Wel, LA, HK (c), Sing (c), Bor (c), Lon (c) Dub.
Demas, D (Danwel) (WP) – 03 Dub, SA, 04 Wel, LA, HK, Sing, Bor , Lon, 05 Sing, Lon, Par, RWC, WG, Dub, SA, 06 Par, CG, Dub, SA, 07 Dub, SA, 08 Lon, Sco.
†**De Villiers, J** (Jean) (WP) - 02 San, Arg, Bris, Wel, Bei, HK, Sing, KL, Lon, Car, CG.
Dippenaar, D. (Dirk) (SARU) 12 Jap
Dippenaar, S. (Stephan) (SARU) 12 NZ, USA, HK, Jap, Sco; Aus; Dub; SA; , 13 NZ; USA; HK; Jap; Sco; Lon; RWC; WG.
†**Dirks, CA** (Chris) (Tvl)* - 94 HK.
Dry, C. (Chris) (SARU contracted) 10 Aus, HK, Lon, Sco; 11 NZ; USA; HK; Aus; Lon; Sco; 11 Aus, Dub, SA, 12 NZ, USA, HK, Jap, Sco, Lon Aus; Dub ; SA ; '13 NZ ; USA ; HK ; Jap ; Sco ; RWC
Du Plessis, M (Malan) (Bol) - 03 HK.

Key: Arg > Argentina (Mar del Plata). Aus > Australia. Bei > Beijing. Bol > Boland. Bor > Bordeaux. Bris > Brisbane. Car > Cardiff, Wales. CG > Commonwealth Games. Dub > Dubai. Dur > Durban. Fr > France. Fs > Free State. GL > Golden Lions. HK > Hong Kong. Jap > Japan. KL > Kuala Lumpur. Lon > London. NZ > New Zealand. Par > Paris. Punte > Punte del Este, Uruguay. RWC > Rugby World Cup. SA > South Africa. San > Santiago, Chile. Sha > Shangai. Sing > Singapore. Ur > Uruguay. Tok > Tokyo. Viña > Viña del Mar, Chile. Wel > Wellington, NZ. WG > World Games (Duisburg, Germany). A player's province is at his first selection for a tournament. Captains are indicated by (c).

SA SEVENS INTERNATIONALS 1993-2013

Du Plooy, JP (JP) (Lions) - 98 Arg, Ur,Viña .
Du Preez, B (Branco) (Blue Bulls) 10 NZ, USA, Aus, HK; 10 dub; SA; 11 Nz; USA; HK; Aus: Lon; Sco, 11 Dub, SA, 12 NZ, USA, HK, Jap, Sco, Lon ; Aus ; '13 USA ; HK ; Jap ; RWC.
†**Du Toit, GS** (Gaffie) (GW) - 98 CG; 02 CG.

E
Ebersohn, RT (Robert) (Free State) 08 HK, Aus, 08 Dub, SA, 09 NZ, USA, HK, Aus, Lon, RWC, 11 Aus, Dub.
Engelbrecht, G (Gerrie) (Griffons) - 00 Ur, Arg, NZ, Fiji, Aus, HK, Jap; 01 Wel.
Engelbrecht, J (Jacques) (SARU). 10 SA.
Engelbrecht, P (Pieter) (SARU) 10 Dub; SA; 11 NZ; USA; Aus; 13 NZ; USA; Sco; Lon.
Engelbrecht, P (Petrus) (SARU) 12 HK, Jap, Sco, Lon
†**Esterhuizen, G** (Grant) (Lions) - 03 NZ.
Eyre, NJ (Nicolas) (Lions) - 03 NZ, 04 bor, Lon.

F
Fihlani, IZ (Ian) (Bulldogs) - 01 Wel; 02 Bei, HK, Sing, KL, Lon, Car, Dub, SA; 03 HK, Car, Lon.
†**Floors, L** (Lucas) (SWD Eagles) – 03 Dub, SA, 04 HK, Sing, Bor 05 Dub 06 Dub (c), SA 07 SA, 08 Lon, Sco.
Foote, KW (Kevin) (Natal) - 02 Dub; 03 Bris, NZ, HK, Car, Lon, 04 Wel (c), LA(c).
Fourie, AJ (Andries) (EP) - 99 Arg, San, Fiji, HK, Par (c), Dub, SA; 00 Ur, Arg, NZ (c), Fiji (c), Aus (c), HK (c), Jap (c), Fr (c), Dur, Dub; 01 Wel, HK, Sha, KL, Tok, Lon, Car.
Fourie, DA (Deon) (Western Province) 07 Lon, Sco.
Fowles, JJ (Josh) (Bulldogs) - 02 Sing, KL.
Francis, E (Eugene) (WP) - 02 Bris, Wel, Bei, HK, Sing, KL, Lon, Car; 03 Bris, NZ, HK, Car, Lon 03 Dub, SA, 04 Wel, LA,
Fredericks, ER (Eddie) (NW) - 99 Par; 00 NZ, Fiji, Aus.04 Dub, SA, 05 Wel, LA, Lon, Par, RWC.
Frolick, S (Shandre) (WP) 05 Wel, LA 06 Dub.

G
Geduld, J (Justin) (SARU) 13 NZ; HK; Jap; Sco.
†**Gerber, HJ** (Hendrik) (WP) - 98 Arg, Ur, Viña .
†**Gillingham, JW** (Joe) (Lions) - 98 Arg, Ur, Viña , CG.
Grobler, D (??) - 99 Fiji, HK.*

H
†**Habana, BG** (Bryan) (Lions) – 04 Wel, LA.
Haupt, PJ (Hannru) (FS) - 03 Bris, NZ.
Heidtmann, DM (Dale) (Bulldogs) - 01 Wel, Dub, Dur; 02 San, Arg, Bris, Wel, Bei, HK, Sing, KL, Lon, Car, CG, 03 Dub, SA, 04 Wel, LA, HK, Sing, Bor, Lon, SA Helberg, D. (Deon) (Blue Bulls) 09 Dub, SA.
Hendriks, C. (Cornal) (SARU) 11 SA, 12 NZ, USA, HK, Jap, Sco, Lon; Aus; Dub; SA; , 13 NZ; USA; HK; Jap; Sco; Lon; RWC;
†**Honiball, HW** (Henry) (Natal) 94 HK.
Horne, FH (Frankie) (SARU contract) 07 Dub, SA, 08 Wel, USA, HK, Aus, Lon, Sco, 08 Dub, SA, 09 NZ, USA, HK, Aus, Lon, Sco, RWC, WG, 09 Dub, SA, 10 NZ, USA, Aus, HK, Lon, Sco; 10 Dub; SA; 11 NZ; USA; HK; Aus;Lon; Sco, 11 Aus, Dub, SA, 12 NZ, USA, HK, Jap, Sco, Lon; Aus; Dub; SA (c); ,13 NZ (c); USA (c); HK (c); Jap (c); Sco (c); Lon (c);
Houtshamer, J (Juan) (Falcons) - 00 HK, Jap.
Hulme, A (Alten) (BB) - 03 HK.
Human, WA (Wylie) (FS) - 00 HK, Jap, Fr.
Hunt, S. (Steven) (WP) 10 NZ, USA, Aus; 10 SA; 11 NZ; USA; Lon; Sco, 11 Aus, SA, 12 NZ, USA, Sco, Lon; Aus; Dub; '13 HK; Jap; Sco; WG.

I
Isbell, R (Ruwellyn) (SARU) '12 Aus; Dub; SA; '13 WG

J
Jackson, KL (Lesley) (Boland) 04 Dub, SA 04 RWC 05 SA, 06 HK, Sing.
†**Jacobs, AA** (Adi) (Falcons) - 00 HK, Tok.*
Jacobsz, SPE (Barry) (SWD Eagles) - 01 Jap.
†**Jantjes, CA** (Conrad) (Lions) - 99 Dub, SA; 00 Ur, Arg, NZ, Fiji, Aus, HK, Jap, Fr; 01 HK, Sha; 02 CG, Dub; 03 Car, Lon.
Johannes, R (Reuben) (SARU) '12 Aus; '13 WG
Joka, W (Wonga) (Elephants) - 00 NZ, Fiji, Aus.
Jonker, J (Jacques) (FS) - 95 HK.
Jonker, JW ("JW") (SARU contracted) 09 Dub, SA, 10 Aus, HK. Jordaan, P.(Paul) (SARU). 11 NZ; USA; HK.
†**Joubert, AJ** (André) (Natal) - 93 HK (c), RWC (c); 94 HK (c).
Juries, FM (Fabian) (EP) - 00 Dur, Dub; 01 Wel, HK, Sha, KL, Tok, Lon, Car, Jap, Dub, Dur; 02 San, Arg, Bris, Wel, CG; 03 Car, Lon, 03 Dub, Sa, 04 Wel, LA, HK, Sing, Bor, Lon, 05 Wel, LA, Sing, Lon, Par, RWC, WG, SA, 06 Wel (c), LA (c), HK, Sing, CG, 07 Dub, SA, 08 Wel, USA, HK, Aus, Lon, Sco, 10 Lon, Sco.
†**Kankowski, R** (Ryan) (KZNl) 06 Wel, LA, HK, Sing, CG.

K
†**Kayser, DJ** (Deon) (EP) - 98 HK, CG.
Kok, W (Werner) (SARU) 13 Lon; WG.
Kolbe, C (Cheslin) (SARU) 12 Lon; SA; ,13 NZ; USA.
Krause, GE (Gareth) (GW) 04 Dub, SA, 05 Wel, LA, RWC.
Kriese, D (Dieter) (Natal) - 93 HK, RWC; 95 HK.
Kruger, CR (Chris) (FS) - 98 Arg; 99 San.
†**Kruger, RJ** (Ruben) (FS) - 93 HK, RWC; 94 HK.
Kruger, HJ (Jorrie) (FS) - 96 Dub; 98 Arg, Ur, Viña .
Kruger, O. (Okkie) (Blue Bulls) 10 CG
Kuün, GWF (Derick) (Blue Bulls) 05 Wel, LA,

L
†**Loubscher, RIP** (Ricardo) (EP) - 99 Arg, San; 00 Fr; 01 RWC.
Luiters, K (Kevin) (Free State Cheetahs) '12 Dub

M
Mapoe, L G (Lionel) (Cheetahs) 09 USA, HK, Aus, RWC.
Maritz, H (Hoffman) (Cheetahs) 10 Nz, USA, Aus, HK, Lon, Sco.
Markow, A (Tony) (EP) - 95 HK.

SA SEVENS INTERNATIONALS 1993-2013

Masina, M (Mac) (Lions) - 99 Dub; 00 Ur, Arg, Dur, Dub; 02 Bris, Wel.
Mastriet, S. (Sampie) (Blue Bulls) 10 Aus, HK; 13 RWC.
Mbiyozo, MM (Mpho) (Western Province) 06 Dub, 07 Wel, USA, HK, Aus, Lon, Sco, 07 Dub, 07 SA, 08 Wel, USA, HK, Aus, Lon, Sco 08 Dub, SA, 09 NZ, USA (c); HK, Aus, lon, Sco, RWC (c), WG;09 Dub; Sa; 10 NZ; USA; Aus; HK; Lon; Sco;
Mbovane, T. (Tshotsho) (SARU). 11 HK; Aus; '12 Aus; Dub; SA; '13 NZ; USA; HK; Jap; Lon.
McBean, BJH (Baldwin) (Griquas) 07 Wel, USA, 07 Dub, SA.
Mdaka, TLP (Thobela) (Border) - 00 NZ, Fiji, Aus, HK, Jap, Fr, Dur, Dub; 01 Wel, Dub 05 Wel, LA, Sing, Lon, Par, RWC, WG, Dub,06 Wel, LA, HK, Sing, Par, Lon, CG, Dub, SA 07 HK, Aus 08 Wel, USA.
Mentz, M J ("MJ") (Griquas) 07 Lon, Sco 07 Dub, SA, 08 Wel, USA, HK, Aus, Lon, Sco, 09 Dub, SA, 10 HK, Lon, Sco, CG; 10 Dub; 11 Aus.
Minnaar, C (Chase (SARU contract) 09 HK, Aus, Lon, WG; 09 Dub; SA; 10 NZ, USA, Aus, HK, Lon, Sc, CG, 11 Aus, Dub, SA.
Mofu, Z (Zolani) 05 WG, Dub, SA, 06 Wel, LA, CG.
Mokuena, J (Jonathan) (Leopards) 05 Lon, Par, WG, Dub, SA, 06 Wel, LA, HK, Sing, Par, Lon, CG, Dub(c), SA (c) 07 Wel (c), USA (c), H K (c), Aus (c) 07 Dub, 08 Wel, USA, HK, Aus, Sco.
Mostert, H (Herman) (WP) - 99 Fiji, HK, Par; 00 NZ, Fiji, Aus, HK, Jap, Fr, Dur, Dub; 01 Wel, HK, Sha, KL, Tok, Lon, Car.
Mtembu, L. (Lubabalo) (Sharks) 10 CG; 10 Dub; 11 NZ; USA.
†**Müller, GP** (Jorrie) (Lions) - 01 HK, Sha, KL, Tok, Dub, Dur; 02 San, Arg, Bris, Wel, Lon, Car, CG, SA.
Munn, W (Wayne) (SWD Eagles) - 99 Fiji*, 99 HK.
†**Muir, DJ** (Dick) (Natal) - 93 RWC; 95 HK.

N
†**Ndungane, AZ** (Akona) (Bulldogs) – 04 Hk, Sing, Bor, Lon
Nell, R (Ryan) (SARU) 12 Sco.
Nelson, NT (Norman) (SARU contract) 08 Lon, Sco.
Noble, DC (Dusty) (Sharks) 06 Dub, SA, 07 HK, Aus, Lon, Sco.
Noble, HG (Howard) (Sharks) 07 Wel, USA, HK, Aus, 09 NZ, USA, Aus.
†**Nokwe, JL** (Jongi) (Boland) 04 SA, 05 Sing.
Nqoro, M (Milo) (Sharks) 08 SA.

O
O'Cuinneagan, D (Dion) (WP) - 93 HK, 93 RWC; 95 HK (c); 96 Ur (c), 96HK (c).
† **Olivier, J** (Jacques) (NTvl) - 93 HK, RWC; 97 RWC; 99 Arg (c), San (c), Dub (c); 00 Ur (c), Arg (c), Dur, Dub; 01 HK, Sha, KL, Tok, Lon, Car, Jap.
†**Oosthuysen, DE** (Deon) (Lions) - 99 San.

P
†**Paulse, BJ** (Breyton) (WP)* - 96 Ur, HK; 98 Arg, Ur, Viña; 01 RWC.
Payne, L (Shaun) (Natal) - 95 HK; 97 RWC; 98 Ur, Viña .
Penrose, N (Neil) (WP) - 98 HK.
Petersen, PB (Patrick) (WP) - 00 Fr.
Philander, D (Daniel) (WP) - 01 Jap.
Pietersen, JC (Johan) (WP) 04 Dub, SA.
Pietersen, WJ (Wilton) (WP) 08 HK, Aus.
Pitout, AC (Anton) (FS) - 01 Dub, Dur; 02 San, Arg, Bris, Wel, Bei, HK, Sing, KL, Lon, Car, CG, 04 Dub.
Plumtree, J (John) (Natal) - 94 HK; 95 HK.
Potgieter, R (Riaan) (EP) - 95 HK.
Potgieter, SP (Sarel) (WP) 06 HK, Sing, Par, Lon.
Powell, JD (Neil) (FS) - 01 Dur; 02 San, Arg, Bei, HK, Lon, Car, CG, Dub, SA, 07 Dub (c), SA (c), 08 Wel (c), USA (c), HK (c), Aus (c), Lon (c), Sco (c), 09 HK, Aus, Lon, Sco, RWC, WG, 09 Dub, 10 Lon, Sco, CG; 11 USA; HK; Aus; Lon; Sco, 12 Lon.
Pretorius, A (Abrie) (GW) - 96 Ur.
†**Pretorius, AS** (André) (Lions) - 00 Dur, Dub; 01 RWC, Wel, KL, Tok, Lon, Car.
†**Pretorius, JC** (Jaco) (Lions) - 02 Dub, 02 SA; 03 Bris (c), NZ (c), HK(c), Car , Lon 04 Dub, SA (c), 05 Wel (c), LA (c), Sing (c), Lon (c), Par (c), RWC (c), Dub (c), SA (c) 06 HK (c), Sing (c), Par (c), Lon (c), CG (c).
Prinsloo, B (Boom) (FS) 10 CG; 10 Dub; SA; 11 NZ; HK; Aus; Lon; Sco, 11 Aus, Dub, SA, 12 NZ, USA, HK, Jap.

†**Putt, KB** (Kevin) (Natal) - 95 HK
R
Raats, W (Werner) (WP) - 98 HK, CG.
Rafferty, AC (Ashwell) (FS) - 99 Par.
Rees, G (Grant) (Sharks) 07 Wel, USA.
Richards, M. (Mark) (SARU) 10 Dub; SA; 11 Lon; Sco, 11 Aus, Dub, SA, 12 NZ, USA ; 13 WG.
†**Richter, AJ** (Adriaan) (NTvl) - 94 HK.
†**Rose, EE** (Earl) (WP) - 03 Bris, NZ, Car, Lon, Dub, SA, 04 Wel, LA.
†**Rossouw, PWG** (Pieter) (WP) - 96 Dub; 97 RWC; 98 CG.
†**Russell, RB** (Brent) (Pumas) - 01 Dur; 02 San, Arg, Bris, Wel, Bei, HK, Sing, KL, SA. 03 SA.

S
Saayman, JIA (Izak) (Eagles) 05 SA.
Schoeman, MW (Marius) (Pumas) - 01 HK, Sha, KL, Tok, Lon, Car, Jap; 02 Bei, HK, Sing, KL, Lon, Car, CG, Dub, SA; 03 Bris, NZ, HK, Car, Lon, Dub, SA, 04 Wel, LA, Lon, 05 Sing, Lon, Par, RWC, WG (c) 06 SA, 07 Wel, USA, HK, Aus, Lon, Sco. 07 SA, 08 Wel, USA, 08 Dub, 09 Sco, WG, 09 SA, 10 NZ, USA.
Seconds, ER (Egon) (WP) - 01 Dub, Dur; 02 Bei, HK, Sing, KL, Lon, Car, CG 05 Dub.
Senatla, S (Seabelo) (SARU) 13 NZ; USA; HK; Jap; Sco; RWC; WG.
Sithole, S (Sibusiso) (Sharks) 10 CG; 10 Dub; SA; 11 HK; Aus; Lon: Sco; 13 RWC.
Siwundla, O. (Oginga) (Golden Lions) 04 Dub, SA
†**Skinstad, RB** (Bob) (WP) - 96 Dub, 97 RWC, 98 CG, 01 RWC.
Small-Smith, W. (William) (SARU). 11 Lon; Sco, 11 Dub, 12 USA, Jap.
Smith, LA (Luke) (Natal) - 95 HK.
†**Smit, PL** (Philip) (GW) - 98 Ur, Viña .
Smith, RF (Rodger) (GW) - 98 HK; 99 Mar, San, Fiji (c), HK (c), Dub, SA; 00 Ur, Arg, Par; 01 RWC; 02 Dub, SA; 03 Bris.
†**Snyman, AH** (André) (NTvl) - 97 RWC.
Snyman, PAB (Phillip) (Cheetahs) 08 Dub, SA, 09 NZ, USA, HK, Lon, Sco, RWC, WG; '12 Dub; SA; '13 NZ; USA; HK; Jap; Sco; Lon; RWC.
Stevens, J (Jeffrey) (Boland) - 96

SA SEVENS INTERNATIONALS 1993-2013 & SA UNDER-20 2008-2013

Dub; 97 RWC; 98 CG; 99 Arg, San, Fiji, HK, Tok, Par, Dub, SA; 00 Ur, Arg, NZ, Fiji, Aus, HK, Jap, Fr.
Stick, M (Mzwandile) (Elephants) – 04 HK, Sing, Bor, Lon.Dub, 05 Wel, LA, Sing, RWC, WG, Dub, SA, 06 Wel, LA, HK, Sing, CG, 07 Wel, USA, HK, Aus, Lon, Sco 07 Dub, 08 USA, HK, Aus, 08 Dub (c), SA (c), 09 NZ (c), HK (c), Aus (c), lon (c), Sco (c), WG (c), 09 Dub, SA, 10 NZ (c), USA (c), Lon (c), Sco (c)
†**Strauss, AJ** (Andries) (Sharks) 07 Lon, Sco.
Strydom, DH (Dirkie) (NTvl) - 96 Dub; 98 HK; 99 Arg, San, Fiji, Tok, Dub, SA; 00 Ur, Arg, NZ, Fiji, Aus, Fr, Dur, Dub
Strydom, W J (Willem-Johannes) (SARU) 13 Sco; Lon; WG.
T
Treu, PM (Paul) (SWD Eagles) - 99 Fiji*, HK, Dub, SA; 00 Ur, Arg, Dur, Dub; 01 RWC, Wel, HK, Sha, KL, Tok, Lon, Car, Jap, Dub, Dur; 02 San, Arg, Bris, Wel, Bei, HK, Sing, KL, Lon, Car, CG, Dub (c), SA (c).
Truter, HJ (Hendrik) (FS) - 94 HK.
U
Ulengo, J (Jamba) (SARU) 12 Sco, Lon; 13 HK; Jap; Sco; Lon; WG
V
Van den Heever, LM (Leon) (Bol) - 02 Dub, SA, 03 Bris, NZ
Van der Merwe, SM (Schalk) (Golden Lions) 05 Wel, LA, Sing, Lon, Par, RWC, WG, Dub, SA, 06 Wel, LA, Par, Lon, CG, Dub, SA, 07 Wel, USA, HK, Aus, Lon, Sco , 07 Dub, SA, 08 Wel, USA, HK, Aus, Lon, Sco.
Van der Walt, P (Phillip) (Cheetahs) 10 NZ, USA.
†**Van der Westhuizen, JH** (Joost) (NTvl) - 93 HK, RWC; 94 HK; 97 RWC (c).
Van Heerden, W (Wayne) (EP) - 01 RWC, Wel, HK, Sha, KL, Tok, Lon, Car, Dub, Dur; 02 Lon, Car, CG, 03 Dub, SA, 04 Wel, LA, HK, Sing, Bor, Lon Dub, SA, 05 Wel, LA.
†**Van Niekerk, JC** (Joe) (Lions) - 01 HK, Sha, KL, Tok, Lon, Car.
Van Rensburg, JM (José) (GW) - 02 Dub, SA; 03 Bris, NZ, HK, Car, Lon, Dub, SA, 04 Wel, LA, HK, Sing, Bor, Lon. Dub, SA, 05 Wel, LA, Sing, Lon, Par.
Van Schalkwyk, J (Jaco) (FS) - 03 HK, Car, Lon, SA, 04 HK, Sing, 04 Dub, SA.
Van Wyk, JH (Jan-Harm) (FS) - 98 Arg, Ur, Viña; 01 Dub; 02 San, Arg, Bris, Wel, Beij, HK.
Van Zyl, R (Riaan) (WP) - 96 Ur, HK.
†**Venter AG** (André) (FS) - 96 Ur, HK; 97 RWC; 98 CG.
†**Venter, AJ** (AJ) (FS) - 98 Arg, Ur, Viña .
Venter, J (Hannes) (Blue Bulls) - 99 Arg, San, Dub, SA; 00 Ur, Arg.
Venter, N (Nico) (Bor) - 98 HK.
Venter, S. (Shaun) (SARU contracted) 09 SA.
Verhoeven, AG (Antonius) (Bol) - 02 San, Arg, Bris, Wel, 06 Wel, LA, HK, Sing, Par, Lon, CG, 07 Wel, USA.
†**Vermaak, J** (Jano) (Golden Lions) 05 Wel, LA, RWC.
Verster, E (Eben) (WP) - 99 Par.
W
†**Watson, LA** (Luke) (Elephants) - 02 CG.
Whitely, W (Warren) (Golden Lions) '12 Dub; SA; '13 NZ USA
†**Willemse, AK** (Ashwin) (Bol) - 01 Dub, Dur.
†**Williams, CM** (Chester) (WP) - 93 RWC; 94 HK; 98 Arg, Ur, Viña , HK (c), CG (c); 99 SA; 00 Ur, Arg; 01 RWC.
Winter, RG (Russell) (Lions) - 98 HK, CG.
Witbooi, N (Nigel) (WP) - 96 Ur, HK.
Z
Zangqa, V (Vuyo) (Border) 07 HK, Aus, Lon, Sco, 07 Dub, SA, 08 Wel, USA, HK, Aus, Lon, Sco, 08 Dub, SA, 09 Nz, USA, HK, Aus, Lon, Sco, RWC.
* unconfirmed

SA UNDER-20 2008-2013

For a complete list of all SA U21 players from 1974-2006, please refer to previous Annuals.
† indicates 15-a-side Springbok

A
Adendorff, S (Shaun) - BB - 2012
Afrika, CS (Cecil) - Grif - 2008
B
Badenhorst, WHB (Brummer) - WP - 2010
Bali, M (Mlungisi) - BB - 2010
Bantjes, HJ (Henri) - BB - 2008
Barry, C (Craig) - WP - 2011
Beerwinkel, A (Andrew) - BB - 2013
Beyers, U (Ulrich) - BB - 2011
Blommetjies, C (Clayton) - BB - 2009
Booysen, FCF (Fabian) - GL - 2012

†**Botha, AF** (Arno) - BB - 2011
Botha, R (Ruan) - GL - 2012
Botha, ZW (Zane) - BB - 2009
Brummer, F (Francois) - BB - 2008, 2009
Bullbring, DJ (David) - GL - 2009
C
Carr, N (Nizaam) - WP - 2011
Chikukwa, TA (Tendayi) - BB - 2009
Coetzee, M (Marne) - BB - 2013
Cook, JG (Jean) - FS - 2011
Cooper, KL (Kyle) - KZN - 2009
Cronjé, L (Lionel) - FS - 2009
Cronjé, R (Ross) - KZN - 2009

D
Davis, A (Aidon) - EP - 2013
De Bruin, L (Luan) - FS - 2013
De Chaves, SJ (Sebastian) - GL - 2010
Dell, AME (Allan) - KZN - 2012
Dippenaar, SC (Stephan) - BB - 2008
Dreyer, RM (Ruan) - GL - 2010
Du Rand, CW (Wessel) - GL - 2010
Du Toit, F (Francois) - GL - 2010
Du Toit, OJJ (Jacques) - FS - 2013
†**Du Toit, PS** (Pieter-Steph) - KZN - 2012
Duvenage, DO (Dewaldt) - Bol - 2008

SA UNDER-20 2008-2013

Du Plessis, WHJ (Jacques) - BB - 2013
Du Preez, BBN, (Branco) - BB - 2010
Du Preez, CG (Cornell) - Leop - 2011
Du Preez, RJ (Rob) - KZN - 2013
E
Ebersohn, JM (Sias) - FS -2008,2009
Ebersohn, RT (Robert) - FS - 2008, 2009
Elstadt, R (Rynhardt) - WP - 2009
† **Etzebeth, E** (Eben) - WP - 2011
F
Fourie, C (Corné) - BB - 2008
G
Geduld, JG (Justin) - WP - 2013
† **Goosen, JL** (Johan) - FS - 2011
Griesel, AJ (Abrie) - BB - 2012
H
Hadebe, MS (Monde) - KZN - 2010
Hammond, D (Dean) - WP - 2012
Hanekom, NJ (Nicolaas) - WP - 2009
Hartzenberg, Y (Yaasir) - WP - 2009
Howard, PB (Patrick) - WP - 2012
Herbst, IP (Irne) - BB - 2013
Herbst, WJ (Wiehan) - Leop - 2008
Hess, CN (Cornell) - BB - 2008
† **Hougaard, F** (Francois) - BB - 2008
I
Ismaiel, TK (Travis) - BB - 2012
J
Jacobs, AJ (Adri) - BB - 2010
Jacobs, WJ (Lohan) - BB - 2010, 2011
Janse van Rensburg, Rohan - BB - 2013
Jantjies, A (Tony) - BB - 2012
† **Jantjies, ET** (Elton) - GL - 2010
Jenkinson, JR (John-Roy) - Leop - 2011
Jordaan, PA (Paul) - KZN - 2011,2012
K
Kebble, O (Oliver) - WP - 2012
Kirsten, FBC (Frik) - BB - 2008
Kirsten, JC (Jannes) - BB - 2013
Kitshoff, S (Steven) - WP - 2012
Kleinhans, F (Francois) - KZN - 2011
Kolbe, C (Cheslin) - WP - 2013
† **Kolisi, S** (Siya) - WP - 2010,2011
Koster, RN (Nick) - WP - 2008
Kotze, SC (Stephan) - FS - 2011
Kriel, JA (Jesse) - BB - 2013
L
† **Lambie, PJ** (Patrick) - KZN - 2010
Leyds, DY (Dillyn) - WP - 2012

Liebenberg, WA (Wian) - BB - 2012
Lusaseni, L (Luyvuyiso) - KZN - 2008
M
Majola, K (Khaya) - KZN - 2012
† **Mapoe, LG** (Lionel) - FS - 2008
Marais, FS (Franco) - KZN - 2012
Marais, JA (Jandré) - KZN - 2009
Marais, PC (Peet) - KZN - 2010
Marole, T (Thiliphatu) - KZN - 2008
Martinus, DR (Devon) - GL - 2013
Mastriet, S (Sampie) - BB - 2009, 2010
Mbonambi, M (Mbongeni) - BB - 2011
Mbovane, T (Tshotso) - WP - 2011, 2012
Mellett, MM (Morné) BB - 2009
Mjekevu, WG (Wandile) - GL - 2010, 2011
Moolman, BJ (Bradley) - BB - 2011
Mtembu, LS (Lubabalo) - KZN - 2010
Muller, FJ (Freddie) - WP - 2010
Muller, MD (Martin) - WP - 2008
N
Nhlapo, S (Sabelo) - KZN - 2008
O
Obi, LBS (Luther) - Leopards - 2013
Okafor, K (Kene) - KZN - 2009,2010
Oosthuizen, CR (Caylib) - GL - 2009
† **Oosthuizen, CV** (Coenie) - FS - 2009
Orie, M (Marvin) - BB - 2012
P
Paige, R (Rudy) - GL - 2009
Pietersen, WJ (Wilton) - FS 2008
Pollard, H (Handre) - WP,BB - 2012, 2013
Pretorius, M (Mark) - GL - 2012
R
Rademan, PJ (Pieter) - FS - 2011
Redelinghuys, J (Julian) - KZN - 2009
Rossouw, JJ (Jean-Jacques) - WP - 2008
† **Ruhle, RK** (Raymond) - FS - 2012
S
Sadie, J (Johann) - WP - 2009
Scheepers, JN (Nico) - FS - 2010
Schmidt, D (Marais) - GL - 2012
Schoeman, JL (Juan) - BB - 2011
Schoeman, M (Marnus) - BB - 2009
Schonert. NP (Nic) - KZN - 2011
Schreuder, L (Louis) - WP - 2010
Seabela OT (Omphile) - BB - 2008, 2009

Senatla, Seabelo - FS - 2013
† **Serfontein, JL** (Jan) - BB - 2012
Sithole, SMS (Sithembiso) - KZN - 2013
Sithole, ST (Sibusiso) - KZN - 2010
Skosan, CD (Courtnal) - BB - 2011
Small-Smith, WT (William) - BB - 2012
Smit, RA (Roelof) - BB - 2013
Smith, AS (Kwagga) - GL - 2013
Stander, CJ (CJ) - BB - 2009,2010
Stander, JH (Jannie) - GL - 2013
Steenkamp, R (Ruan) - BB - 2013
Steyn, AJ (Braam) - KZN - 2012
Swanepoel, AE (Dries) - BB - 2013
T
† **Taute, JJ** (Jaco) - GL - 2010,2011
Thomas, JN (Jason) - BB - 2012
U
Ungerer, S (Stefan) - KZN - 2013
V
Van den Heever, GJ (Gerhard) - BB - 2009
Van der Merwe, M (Marcel) - FS - 2010
Van der Walt, HS (Fanie) - FS - 2010
Van der Watt, V (Vian) - GL - 2012
Van Deventer, JC (Johan) - GL - 2008
Van Dyk, NJJ (Nico) - KZN - 2012
Van Velze, G-J (Gerrit-Jan) - BB - 2008
Van Vuuren, MT (Michael) - FS - 2011
Van Vuuren, P-W (PW) - FS - 2008
Van Wyk, JP (Kobus) - WP - 2012
Venter, HC (Hanco) - KZN - 2013
Venter, JF (Francois) - BB - 2010, 2011
Venter, RC (Ruan) - GL - 2011
Visser, D (Dennis) - BB - 2013
W
Watermeyer, S (Stefan) - BB - 2008
Wegner, C (Carl) - FS - 2011
Welthagen. JJ (Johnny) - Leop - 2011
Willemse, ME (Michael) - BB - 2013
Wiillemse, P (Paul) - GL - 2012
Williams, K (Percy) - GL - 2013
Willis, VS (Vainon) Willis - BB - 2008

SOUTH AFRICANS CAPPED OVERSEAS 1896-2013

Compiled by Stuart Farmer. † Indicates also played for South Africa.

A
Abbott, SRD (Stuart) - England - 9 Tests - 2003-2006
Abendanon, NJ (Nick) - England - 2 tests - 2007
†**Allan, J** (John) - Scotland - 9 Tests - 1990-1991
Alexander, M (Matt) - USA - 25 Tests - 1995-1998
Anderson HJ (Henry) - Ireland - 4 Tests - 1903-1906
Appleford, GN (Geoff) - England - 1 Test - 2002

B
Badenhorst, RS (Skipper) - Namibia - 2 Tests - 2007
Barnard, J (Barries) - Namibia - 22 Tests - 1990-1993
Barritt, BM (Brad) - England - 16 Tests - 2013
Bell, PJD (Patrick) - USA - 7 Tests - 2006
Binikos, A (Andrew) - Cyprus -
Black, BH (Brian) - England - 10 Tests - 1930-1933
Blom, A (André) - USA - 13 Tests - 1998-2000
Blom, ML (Morne) - Namibia - 9 Tests - 2011-2013
Botes, L-W (Lu-Wayne) - Namibia - 9 Tests 2006-2007
Botes, WT (Tobias) - Italy - 19 Tests 2012-2013
Botha, MJ (Mouritz) - England - 9 Tests - 2011-2012
Bouwer, AC (Arthur) - Namibia - 7 Tests 2012-2013
Breytenbach, CL (Conrad) - Russia - 2 Tests - 2002
Brooks, FG (Freddie) - England - 1 Test - 1906
Buchanan, JCR (John) - Scotland - 16 Tests - 1921-1925
Buitendag, A (Basie) - Namibia - 22 Tests - 1990-1993

C
Catterall, BW (Brenton) - Zimbabwe - 7 Tests - 1991-1998
Catt, MJ (Mike) - England (75 Tests), Lions (1 Test) - 1994-2007
Claassen, AD (Antonie) - France - 5 Tests - 2013
Constable R (Ryan) - Australia - 1 Test - 1994
Cuttitta, M (Marcello) - Italy - 54 Tests - 1987-1999
Cuttitta, M (Massimo) - Italy - 69 Tests - 1990-2000

D
Dalzell, K (Kevin) - USA - 42 Tests - 1996-2003
Dames, HDP (Danie) - Namibia - 8 Tests - 2011-2013
Davey, J (Jas) - England - 2 Tests - 1908-1909
Davies, MJ (Mickey) - Wales - 2 Tests - 1939
Davies, S (Shaun) - USA - 1 Test - 2013
De Jager, B (Benjamin) - Italy - 1 Test - 2006
De Jong, MG (Mike) - USA - 9 Tests - 1990-1991
De Marigny, JR (Roland).- Italy - 19 Tests - 2004-2007
De Villiers, P (Pieter) - France - 69 Tests - 1999-2007
Del Fava, CA (Carlo) - Italy - 54 Tests - 2004-2011
Dickson, WM (Walter) - Scotland - 7 Tests - 1912-1913
Dingley, J (Jon) - Hong Kong - 21 Tests - 1994-1998
Downes, GT (Graham) - USA - 1 Test - 1992
Duncan, DD (Denoon) - Scotland - 4 Tests - 1920

E
Elgie, MK (Kim) - Scotland - 8 Tests - 1954-1955
Eloff, PT (Phillip) - USA - 35 Tests - 2000-2007
Engels, JB (Jaco) - Namibia - 4 Tests - 2013
Erasmus, DJ (Danie) - Australia - 2 Tests - 1923
Erasmus, J (Jaco) - Italy - 3 Tests - 2008
Erskine, CE (Chad) - USA - 10 tests - 2007-2008
Evans, IR (Ian) - Wales - 31 Tests - 2006-2013

F
Francis, TES (Tim) - England - 4 Tests - 1926
Fourie, CH (Hendre) - England - 8 Tests - 2010-2011
Franken, HH (Henk) - Namibia - 3 Tests - 2011-2012
Freakes, HD (Hubert) - England - 3 Tests - 1938-1939

G
†**Gage, JH** (Jack) - Ireland - 4 Tests - 1926-1927
Gagiano, JR (JJ) - USA - 14 Tests - 2008-2011
Geldenhuys, Q (Quintin) - Italy - 41 Tests - 2009-2013
Gouws, J (Jurie) - USA - 8 caps - 2003-2004
Grobler, J (Juan) - USA - 33 caps - 1996-2002

H
Hauck, A (Alexander) - Germany - 6 Tests - 2009-2010
Hawkins, M (Matt) - USA - 1 cap - 2010
Goedeke, F (Frank) - Germany
Grobler, J (Juan) - USA - 33 Tests - 1996-2002
Hall, S (Steven) - France - 2 Tests - 2002
Hands, RHM (Reg) - England - 2 Tests - 1910
Harris, SW (Stan) - England (2 Tests) Lions (2 Tests) - 1920-1924
Hauck, A (Alexander) - Germany - 6 Tests - 2009-2010
Hawkins, M (Matt) - USA - 1 Test - 2010
Heatlie, BH (Fairy) - Argentina - 1 Test - 1910
Henderson, JH (Chick) - Scotland - 9 Tests - 1953-1954
Hendriks, JHF (Tenk) - Russia - 7 Tests - 2002
Hindson, RE (Ro) - Canada - 31 Tests - 1973-1990
Hofmeyr, MB (Murray) - England - 3 Tests - 1950
Hopley, FJV (John) - England - 3 Tests - 1907-1908
Horak, MJ (Michael) - England - 1 Test - 2002
Human, P (Petrus) - Namibia - 2 Tests - 2012

J
Jantjies, R (Riaan) - Namibia - 15 Tests - 1994-2000
Jeffery, D (Doug) - Namibia - 1 Test - 1990
Jones IC (Ian) - Wales - 1 Test - 1968

K
Keyter, JC (Jason) - USA - 17 Tests - 2000-2003
Klerck, GS (Gerhard) - USA - 8 Tests - 2003-2004
Kotze, DM (Dan) - France - 1 Test - 2013
Krige, JA (Jannie) - England - 1 Test - 1920

L
Labuschagne, NA (Nick) - England - 5 Tests - 1953-1955
Lentz, O (Owen) - USA - 8 Tests - 2006-2007
Le Roux, B (Bernard) - France - 3 Tests - 2013
Le Roux, JE (Jacques) - Portugal - 11 Tests - 2011-2013
Le Roux, RP (Ryan) - Spain - 4 Tests 2011-2012
Liebenberg, B (Brian) - France - 12 Tests - 2003-2005
Lipman, S (Sean) - USA - 9 Tests - 1988-1991

SOUTH AFRICANS CAPPED OVERSEAS 1896-2013

Losper, SJ (Sarel) - Namibia - 18 Tests - 1990-1991
Lupini, E (Tito) - Italy - 11 Tests - 1987-1989
Luscombe, HN (Hal) - Wales - 16 Tests - 2003-2007

M
Macdonald, DSM (Donald) - Scotland - 7 Tests - 1977-1978
MacDonald, JS (Jimmy) - Scotland - 5 Tests - 1903-1905
Marinos, AWN (Andy) - Wales - 8 Tests - 2002-2003
Maritz, WM (Willem) - Namibia - 8 Tests - 1990-1991
Marshall, KW (Kenneth) - Scotland - 8 Tests - 1934-1937
McCowat, RH (Harold) - Scotland - 1 Test - 1905
McMillan, KHD (Keith) - Scotland - 4 Tests - 1953
Mehrtens, AP (Andrew) - New Zealand - 70 Tests - 1995-2004
†**Mellish, FW** (Frank) - England - 6 Tests - 1920-1921
Melville, E (Eric) - France - 6 Tests - 1990-1991
Meyer, EA (Eden) - Namibia - 21 Tests - 1991-1996
Meyer, JM (Johannes) - Namibia - 16 Tests - 2003-2007
Milton, HC (Cecil) - England - 1 Test - 1906
Milton, JG (Jumbo) - England - 5 Tests - 1904-1907
Mulligan, PJ (Patrick) - Australia - 1 Test - 1925
Mullins, RC (Cuthbert) - British Isles - 2 Tests - 1896

N
Newman, SC (Syd) - England - 3 Tests - 1947-1948
Newton-Thompson, JO (Ossie) - England - 2 Tests - 1947
Nieuwenhuis, J (Jacques) - Namibia - 23 Tests 2006-2011

O
O'Cuinneagain, D (Dion) - Ireland - 19 Tests - 1998-2000
†**Oosthuizen, LT** (Theo) - Namibia - 7 Tests - 1990
Osler, FL (Frank) - Scotland - 2 Tests - 1911
Owen-Smith, HG (Tuppy) - England - 10 Tests - 1934-1937

P
Peens, G (Gert) - Italy - 23 Tests - 2002-2006
Pieters, W (Werner) - Russia - 2 Tests - 2002
Pieterse, W (Werner) - Russia - 7 Tests - 2002
Pocock, DW (David) - Australia - 45 Tests - 2008-2012
Poppmeier, M (Michael) - Germany - 6 Tests - 2009-2010
Pretorius, A (Andries) - Wales - 2 Tests - 2013
Proudfoot, MC (Matthew) - Scotland - 4 Tests - 1998-2003

R
Rathbone, C (Clyde) - Australia - 26 Tests - 2004-2006
Rawlinson, GP (Greg) - New Zealand - 4 Tests 2006-2007
Reid, RE (Roland) - Scotland - 2 Tests - 2001
Robertsen, JR (John) - Canada - 9 Tests - 1985-1991
Rosenblum, ME (Myer) - Australia - 4 Tests - 1928
Roxburgh, JR (James) - Australia - 9 Tests - 1968-1970

S
Small, HD (Harry) - England - 4 Tests - 1950
Smith, C (Collen) - Namibia - 2 Tests - 2012
Stevens, MJH (Matt) - England - 39 Tests - 2004-2011
†**Stewart, JC** (Christian) - Canada - 14 Tests - 1991-1995
Steyn, SSL (Stephen) - Scotland - 2 Tests - 1911-1912
Stickling, C (Conrad) - Portugal - 5 Tests - 2010
†**Strauss, CP** (Tiaan) - Australia - 11 Tests - 1999
Strauss, CR (Richardt) - Ireland - 4 Tests - 2013

T
Theron, JP (Diumpie) - Namibia - 8 Tests - 1997-1999
Thomas, RM (Rhys) - Wales - 7 Tests - 2006-2009
Tonks, GA (Greig) - Scotland - 1 Test - 2013
Trenkel, N (Nick) - Canada - 1 Test - 2007

V
Van der Merwe, AP (Arra) - Namibia - 19 Tests - 1990-1992
Van der Merwe, D (Danie) - Namibia - 1 Test - 1990
Van der Merwe, DTH - Canada - 26 Tests - 2006-2013
Van Heerden, A (Andries) - France - 2 Tests - 1992
Van Ryneveld, CB (Clive) - England - 4 Tests - 1949
Van Zyl, CC (Cornelius) - Italy - 8 Tests - 2011-2012
Van Zyl, WP (Piet) - Namibia - 18 Tests - 2007-2011
Van Zyl, R (Riaan) - USA - 13 Tests - 2003-2004
Vickerman, DJ (Dan) - Australia - 63 Tests - 2002-2011
Viljoen, F (Francois) - USA - 16 Tests - 2004-2006
Visser, W (Wim) - Italy - 22 Tests - 1999-2002
Volschenk, R (Bloues) - Russia - 9 Tests - 2002

W
Waters, FHH (Fraser) - England - 3 Tests - 2001-2004
White-Cooper, WRS (Steve) - England - 2 Tests - 2001
Williamson, RH (Rupert) - England - 5 Tests - 1908-1909
Wilson, AW (Andrew) - Scotland - 1 Test - 2005
Wilson, DS (Tug) - England - 8 Tests - 1952-1955

Z
Zaayman, C (Christian) - Namibia - 12 Tests - 1997-1999

SA SCHOOLS PLAYERS 1974-2013

† Became senior Springbok (15-man code).   * SA Schools captain (in second year if played for two years)

A
Adams, Tythan – (Paul Roos Gym) – WP - 2008
Afrika, Cecil - (Harmony Sport) - Griffons - 2006
Alberts, Nicolaas - (AHS, Pretoria) - BB - 1996
†**Alcock, Chad** - (Alexander Road) - EP - 1991
Alexander, Enwill - (Stellenberg) - WP - 2002
Anderson, Severin - (Westering) - EP – 1978
April, Garth – (Bergrivier) – Boland - 2008
April, Randall - (Bergrivier) - Boland - 2004
Arends, Neil - (McCarthy Uitenhage) - EP – 1999
Arendse, Riaan - (Brandwag Uitenhage) - (EP) - 2007
Arlow, Wium - (Nelspruit) - Mpu - 2002

B
Bakkes, Luther - (Diamantveld) - GW – 1989
Bali, Mlungisi – (St Albans) – BB – 2008
Bannink, Wimpie (Hans Strijdom) - Far North - 1992
Barker, Michael (DHS) - Natal - 1978
Barnard, Jan-Hendrik - (Menlopark) - BB - 1988
Barnard, Kierie - (Volkskool Potch.) - Leopards - 1981
Barnard, Lee - (King Edward VII) - GL - 1974-75
Barnies, Francois - (Parow HS) - WP - 2000
Baronet, Dennis - (Glenwood) - Natal - 1985
Barrett, Brett - (Kingswood Coll) - EP - 1991
¹**Barritt, Bradley** - (Kearsney Coll) - Natal – 2004
Bartle, Grant - (Middelburg THS) - Mpu - 1995
†**Bartmann, Wahl** - (Florida) - GL - 1981
Bartmann, Leon - (Florida) - GL - 1978
Basson, JP - (Boland Agric) - WP - 1994-95
Basson, Stefan - (Boland Agric) - WP – 2000
Beerwinkel, Andrew – (Porterville) - Boland - 2011
Bennett, Richard - (Dale Coll) - Border - 1992
Beukes, Chris - (DHS) - Natal - 1990
Bezuidenhout, Riaan - (Framesby) - EP – 1984
Bitterhout, Leroy – (Klein Nederb) – Boland – 2010
Bitzi, Anrich – (Grey Coll) – FS - 2010
Blignaut, Robert - (Muir Coll) - EP - 1978
†**Bobo, Gcobani** - (Dale Coll) - Border - 1996
Böhmer, Manfred - (Ermelo) - Mpu – 1998
Bolofo, Moeka - (Louis Botha) - Free State - 2007
Bolus, Robert - (Bishops) - WP - 1974-75
Bonthuys, John - (Abbots Coll) - WP - 1974-75
Bosch, Jan - (Helpmekaar) - GL – 1991
Boshoff, Marnitz – (Nelspruit) – Mpu – 2007
†**Botha, Bakkies** - (Vereeniging THS) - Valke – 1998
Bothma,* **Rikus** – (Paarl Gym) – WP – 2013
Botes, Bennie - (AHS, Pretoria) - BB - 1991
Botha, Calla - (DF Malan) - GL - 1979
Botha, Ettienne - (John Vorster, Nigel) - Valke - 1997
†**Botha, Gary** - (Overkruin) - BB - 1998-99
Botha, Justin - (Monument) - GL - 2006
Botha, Leon - (Grey Coll) - FS – 1981
Botha, Ruan – (Jeugland) – Valke - 2010
Botha, Wimpie - (Queens Coll) - Border - 1998
Breedt, Johan - (Wonderboom) - BB - 1993
Breedt, Nico - (Kearsney Coll) - Natal - 1998
Brink, Stephen - (Sentraal) - FS - 1991-92
†**Brits, Schalk** - (Paul Roos Gym.) - WP – 1999
Britz, Conraad - (Oakdale Agric) - SWD – 2005
Britz, Riaan – (Grey Coll) – FS - 2009
Bronkhorst, Stephan - (Randburg) - GL - 1992
Brown, Dick - (Pearson) - EP - 1986
Brown, John - (Hentie Cilliers) - NFS - 1999
†**Brussouw, Heinrich** - (Grey Coll) - FS – 2004
Buckle, Albertus - (Boland Agric) - Boland - 2001
†**Burger, Kobus** - (Paarl Gym.) - WP - 1980-81
Burger, Altus - (Ermelo) - Mpu - 1982-83
Burton-Moore, Mark - (Bishops) - WP - 1978
Bushney, Marais - (Roodepoort) - GL - 1989

C
Caldo, Kobus - (Oakdale Agric) - SWD - 1998-99
Campbell-McGeachy, Walter - (Pietersburg) - Far North - 1994-95
Campher, Connie - (Potchefstroom THS) - Leopards - 1985
Campher, Fanie - (Wolmaransstad THS) - Stellaland - 1974-75
Carr, Nizaam – (Bishops) – WP – 2009
†**Carstens, Deon** - (Boland Agric) - WP - 1997
Carswell, Michael - (Grey) - EP - 1984
Carty, Shane - (King Edward VII) - GL - 1974-75
Cattrell,* **Brenton** - (Maritzburg Coll) - Natal - 1987
Cawood, Mark - (Wynberg BH) - WP - 1974-75
Celliers,* **Norman** - (Ermelo) - Mpu – 1991
Chadwick, Dale – (Westville) – KwaZulu Natal - 2007
Claassen, Andrew - (Andrew Rabie) - EP - 1988
Clancy, Sean - (Selborne Coll) - Border – 1995
Cloete, Chris – (Selbourne Coll) – Border - 2009
Cloete, Hannes - (Jim Fouché) - FS - 1995
Cloete, Jan - (Waterkloof) - BB - 1996
Coetzee, Deon - (Helpmekaar) - GL – 1979
Coetzee, Eduard - (AHS, Pretoria) - BB - 1997
Coetzee, Jaco - (Ellisras) - Far North - 1988
Coetzee, Jannie - (Bloemfontein THS) - FS – 1982
Coetzee, Marne - (Waterkloof) - BB - 2011
Coetzer, Jacques - (Middelburg THS) - Mpu – 1996
†**Conradie, Bolla** - (Kasselsvlei) - WP - 1996-97
Cook, Jean – (Grey Coll) – FS - 2009
Cooper, Barney - (Paarl Gym) - WP - 1986
Cooper, John - (Soa Bras Mosselbaai) - SWD - 1998
Coyle-Meybery,* **Craig** - (Dale Coll) - Border - 1983-84
Craven, Jean - (Grey Coll) - FS - 1990
Cronjé, Frans - (Grey Coll) - FS - 1985
†**Cronjé, Jacques** - (John Vorster THS) - BB - 2000
Croy, Ricardo - (Paarl Gym.) - WP - 2004

D
Daffue, Hendrik - (Grey Coll) - FS - 1980

SA SCHOOLS PLAYERS 1974-2013

Daffue, Willem - (Grey Coll) - FS – 1977
Damens, Leneve – (Grey Coll) - FS - 2011
Dames, Arno - (Framesby) - EP - 1990
Dames, Rudi - (Vereeniging THS) - Valke - 1999
Daniller, Hennie - (Paarl Gym) - WP - 2002
Davel, Chris - (Ermelo) - Mpu – 1985
Davis, Aidon – (Daniël Pienaar) – EP - 2012
De Beer,* Conrad - (Grey Coll) - FS - 1981
De Bruin, Michael - (Nelspruit) - Mpu - 2001
De Bruyn, Corné - (Worcester) - Boland - 1994
De Coning,* Basil - (Kingswood Coll) - EP - 1990
De Haas, Pieter - (Grey Coll) - FS - 1986
De Jager, Bruce - (Bishops) - WP - 1994
De Jager, Wilhelm - (Ermelo) - Mpu - 2002
De Kock, Jason - (Hugenote HS) - Valke - 1996
De Kock, Zander - (Vereeniging THS) - Valke - 2005
De Nobrega, Paul - (Worcester) - Boland - 1984
De Ru, Ian - (Marais Viljoen THS) - GL - 1989
†**De Villiers, Jean** - (Paarl Gym) - WP Acad. - 1999
De Waal, Adriaan - (Paarl BH) - WP Acad. – 1995
Dell, Allan – (Queens Coll) – Border - 2010
Delport,* Paul - (SACS) - WP - 2001-02
Delport, Marius - (Zwartkop) - BB - 2003
Derksen, Chris - (Grey Coll) - FS - 1993
Diedericks, Ernest - (Scottsville) - WP - 1994
†**Dixon,* Pieter** - (Maritzburg Coll) - Natal - 1995
Dreyer, Hano - (Winterberg Agric) - NEC - 1995
†**Drotské, Naka** - (Grey Coll) - FS - 1989

†**Du Plessis, Carel** - (Paarl BH) - WP - 1978
†**Du Plessis, Bismarck** - (Grey Coll) - FS - 2001-02
Du Plessis, Charl - (Kroonstad Agric) - NFS – 1978
Du Plessis, Daniel - (Paul Roos Gym) - WP – 2013
Du Plessis, Jacques – (Ermelo) - Mpu - 2011
Du Plessis, Johan - (Sand du Plessis) - FS – 1985
Du Plessis, JP – (Paul Roos Gym) – WP – 2009
Du Plessis, Morne – (Waterkloof) - BB - 2011
Du Plessis, Neil - (Selborne Coll) - Border - 1984
Du Plessis, Pierre - (Port Natal) - Natal - 1987
†**Du Preez, Delarey** - (Hangklip) - Border - 1994
Du Preez, André - (Oudtshoorn THS) - SWD – 1974
Du Preez, Daniel – (Kearsney) – KZN – 2012-13
Du Preez, Fransie - (EG Jansen) - GL – 1985
Du Preez, Jean-Luc – (Kearsney) – KZN – 2012-13
Du Preez, Philip – (Monument) - GL - 2011
†**Du Preez, Wian** - (Grey Coll) - FS - 1999-00
†**Du Randt, Os** - (Piet Retief) - NEC - 1990
Du Toit, Dawie - (Vereeniging THS) - GL - 1974-75
Du Toit, Dawie - (Monument) - GL - 1992-93
Du Toit, Franna – (Grey Coll) – FS - 2008
Du Toit, Jaco - (Paarl Gym) - WP – 1999
Du Toit, Thomas - (Paarl BH) - WP – 2013
Duvenhage, Braam - (HSS Hugenote) - Valke - 1982
Duvenhage, Stoffel - (Middelburg THS) - Mpu – 2004
Dwebe, Joseph – (Florida) – GL - 2013

E
Ebersöhn, Robert – (Grey Coll) - Free State - 2007
Edgar, David - (Michaelhouse) - Natal - 2001
Ehrentraut,* Michael - (Bishops) - WP – 1989
Eksteen, Ryno – (AHS, Pretoria) – BB - 2012
Ellerd, Rialoo - (Jacobsdal) - Griquas - 2005
†**Els, Braam** - (AHS, Kroonstad) - NFS - 1990
Els,* Anton - (DHS du Plessis) - EP - 1975
Engelbrecht, Andries - (Volkskool) - Leopards - 1981
Engelbrecht,* Fanus - (R Ferreira Witrivier) - Mpu - 1983
Engelbrecht,* Frankel - (Paarl Gym) - WP - 1986
Engelbrecht, Johan - (Paul Roos Gym) - WP - 1986
Engelbrecht, Morné - (Rustenburg) - Leopards - 1994
Erasmus, Greyling - (Ermelo) - Mpu - 2000
Erasmus, Kerneels - (Frikkie Meyer) - Far North - 1982
Erlank, Karel - (Klerksdorp) - Leopards - 1979
Erwee,* Jurie - (Grey Coll) - FS - 1980
Espag,* Jaco - (Witbank THS) - Mpu - 1984-85
Esterhuizen, Francois – (Overberg) – Boland - 2012
F
Faas, Chuma – (Grey HS) – EP – 2008
Faku, Zolani – (Grey HS) – SA Acad (EP) - 2009
Farmer, Steven - (Kasselsvlei) - WP - 2001
Fenwick, Alex - (Grey Coll) - FS - 1990-91
Fenwick, Kobie - (Grey Coll) - FS – 1975
Ferreira, Andries – (AHS, Pretoria) – BB - 2008

†**Ferreira, Christo** - (Welkom Gym) - NFS - 1978
Ferreira, Freddie - (Brandwag) - EP - 1980
Ferreira, Marthinus - (Florida) - GL - 2000
Ferreira, Schalk - (Paul Roos Gym) - WP - 2002
Feurer, Lee - (Bishops) - WP - 1988
Fisher, Tyler – (Westville) – KZN - 2011
Fitchet, Christo - (Kirkwood) - EP - 1975
Flanagan, Sean - (Westville) - Natal - 1999
Forslara, Vuyani - (Grens HS) - Border - 1999
Fortuin, Sean - (Bellville South HS) - WP – 1999
Fouche, Neethling – Grey Coll) – FS - 2010
Fourie, Andries - (Framesby) - EP - 1990
Fourie, Dawie - (Kroonstad Agric) - NFS - 1978-79
Fourie, Kenneth - (Port Shepstone) - Natal - 1994
Fourie, Nel - (Ermelo) - Mpu - 2000
Fourie, Stompie - (Grey Coll) - FS - 1984
Frolick, Shandré - (Worcester Gym.) - Boland - 2004
Froneman, Stephan - (Montana) - BB - 1995
Fullard, Neil - (Paarl BH) - WP - 2000
†**Fynn, Etienne** - (St Charles) - Natal - 1990
G
Gage, Shaun - (DHS) - Natal – 1985
Galant, Warrick – (Outeniqua) – SWD – 2012-13
Geldenhuys, Jan - (Grey Coll) - FS - 1974-75
Genis, James - (DF Malan) - WP - 1977
†**Gerber,* Danie** - (Despatch) - EP - 1975-77
†**Gerber, Hendrik** - (Nico Malan) - EP - 1993-94
Gericke, Jaco - (Port Elizabeth THS) - EP – 1988

SA SCHOOLS PLAYERS 1974-2013

Gericke, Neethling – (Oakdale Agric) – SWD - 2008
Gibbs, Herchelle - (Bishops) - WP - 1992
Giezing, Kalf - (Grey Coll) - FS - 1983
†**Gillingham, Joe** - (Alberton) - GL - 1992
Glover, Shaun - (Maritzburg Coll) - Natal - 1985
Goedeke, Frank - (Carter) - Natal - 1990
Goedeke, Udo - (Maritzburg Coll) - Natal – 1987
†**Goosen, Johan** – (Grey Coll) – FS - 2010
Goosen, Niel - (Waterkloof) - BB - 1997
Goosen, Gregory - (Kearsney Coll) - Natal - 2001
Gouws, Scheepers - (Grey Coll) - FS - 1981
Gqoba, Andisa - (Hudson Park) - Border - 2003
†**Grant, Peter** - (Maritzburg Coll) - Natal - 2002
Greyling, Gert - (Sand du Plessis) - FS - 2003
Griesel, Jannie - (Verwoerdburg) - BB - 1987
Gronum, Antonie - (Oakdale Agric) - SWD - 2003
Grobler, Gerbrand - (Grey Coll) - FS - 1981
Grobler, Jacques - (FH Odendaal) - BB - 1990
Grobler, Lukas - (Hugenote HS) - Valke - 1981
Gwavu, Vincent - (Daniël Pienaar - Uitenhage) - EP - 2005
H
⁴**Hall, Stephen** - (Dale Coll) - Border - 1991
Hammer, Ernst - (Fakkel) - GL - 1993
Hancke, Wim - (Linden) - GL - 1974-75
Hankinson, Rob - (Michaelhouse) - Natal - 1974-75
†**Hargreaves,* Alistair** - (Durban HS) - Natal – 2004
Hartzenberg, Vaasir - (Paarl BHS) - WP - 2006

Hearne, Ashlyn - (Hottentots Holland) - WP - 2000
†**Hendriks, Pieter** - (Standerton) - Mpu - 1988
Hendriks, Braam - (Sandveld) - NFS – 1993
Herbst, Irne – (Waterkloof) - BB – 2011
Hermanus, Grant - (Paarl Gym) - WP – 2013
Hess, Cornel - (AHS Pretoria) - BB – 2006-07
Heuer, Merrick - (Queens Coll) - Border - 1988
Heunis, Nico - (Dirkie Uys) - Boland - 1994
Heydenrich,* Johan - (Standerton) - Mpu - 1982
Hickson, André - (Bosmansdam) - WP - 1985
Hill, Jaydon - (Glenwood) - Natal – 2002
Hlongwane, Nhlanhla – (Louis Botha) – FS (2011)
Hollenbach, Alwyn - (Grey Coll) - FS - 2003
Hopkins, Clifford - (Kearsney Coll) - Natal - 1979
Hopp, Dean - (Kairos SS) - SWD - 2000
†**Hougaard, Derick** - (Boland Agric) - Boland - 2001
Hough, André - (Framesby) - EP - 1988
Hugo, Jan-Harm - (Ermelo) - Mpu - 1997
Hugo, Werner - (Paarl BH) - WP - 1993
Hulme,* Altenstädt - (Voortrekker, CT) - WP – 1999
Human, Dewald – (Outeniqua) – SWD - 2013
Human, Gerhard - (Despatch) - EP - 1977
I
Ingles, Warren - (Alexander Road) - EP - 1987
J
†**Jacobs, Adrian** - (Scottsville) - WP - 1998
Jacobs, Divan - (Ermelo) - Mpu - 2001
Jacobs, Jaco - (Grey Coll)

- FS – 1987
Jaer, Malcolm – (Brandwag) – EP - 2013
Jamieson, Craig - (Maritzburg Coll) - Natal - 1979
Jankowitz, Anton - (Hilton Coll) - Natal – 1989
Janse van Rensburg, Nicholaas – (AHS, Pretoria) – BB – 2012
Janse van Rensburg, Rohan – (AHS, Pretoria) – BB – 2012
Janse van Vuuren, Marco – (Transvalia) – Valke - 2013
†**Jantjes, Conrad** - (CBS Boksburg) - Valke – 1997
†**Jantjies, Elton** – (Florida HS) – GL – 2008
Jantjies, Tony – (Menlo Park) – BB - 2009
†**Januarie, Enrico** - (Weston HS) - Boland – 2000
Jho, Andile (Dale Coll) – Border – 2009-10
Job, Izak - (Pres. Steyn Bloemfontein) - FS - 1998
†**Johnson, Ashley** - (Paarl Gym.) - WP - 2004
Johnson, Nicolas - (Selborne Coll) - Border - 1998
Johnston, Gordon - (Paarl BH) - WP – 1999
Jooste, Morné - (The Settlers) - WP - 2005
Jordaan, Hennie - (Menlopark) - BB – 1980
Jordaan, Paul – (Grey Coll) – FS - 2010
Joubert, Jan-Hendrik - (Oakdale Agric) - SWD - 2001
Joubert, Riaan - (Grey Coll) - FS - 1978
Joubert, Wilhelm - (Overkruin) - BB – 1982
Juries, Christopher – (Kingswood Coll) - EP - 2005
K
Kalonji, Kadima - (Pretoria THS) - BB - 1998
Kankowski, Tino - (PJ Olivier) - EP - 1977

Kaplan, Kevin - (Kimberley THS) - GW – 1980
Kapp, Divan - (Middelburg THS) - Mpu – 2005
Kapp, Neil – (Outeniqua) – SWD - 2008
Karemaker, Leon - (Bellville) - WP - 2003
Kasselman, Chris - (Sandveld) - NFS - 1979-80
Kelly, Richard - (Maritzburg Coll) - Natal - 1996
Kemp,* Scott - (Hudson Park) - Border - 1991-92
†**Kempson, Robert** - (Queens Coll) - Border – 1992
Khubeka, Sandile – (Kearsney) – KZN - 2012
King, Kelvano – (Alexandria) - Eastern Province - 2007
Kirsten, Frik - (AHS Pretoria) - BB – 2006
Kitshoff, Steven – (Paul Roos) – WP - 2010
Kleinenberg, Mark - (Selborne Coll) - Border - 1974-75
Klopper, Chris - (Die Burger) - GL – 1978
Knoetze, Frederick - (Framesby) - EP – 1982
Kobese, Bangihlonbe – (Dale Coll) – Border – 2009
Koch, Agie - (Paul Roos Gym) - WP - 1974-75
Koch, Hendrik - (Rustenburg) - Leopards – 1978
Koegelenberg, Gideon – (Hugenote) – Boland - 2012
†**Koen, Louis** - (Paarl Gym) - WP - 1993-94
Koen, Barabas - (Ermelo) - Mpu – 1991
†**Kolisi, Siyamthanda** – (Grey HS) – EP – 2008-09
Köster, Nick - (Bishops) - WP – 2006-07
Kotze, Christo - (Dirkie Uys) - Boland - 1977-78
Kotze, Divan – (Waterkloof) - BB – 2006
Kotze, Stephanus – (Grey Coll) – FS - 2009

SA SCHOOLS PLAYERS 1974-2013

Koyana, Ncedo - (Selbourne Coll) - Border – 2003
Kramer, Ruan – (Grey Coll) – FS - 2013
Krause, Piet - (Sasolburg THS) - Vaal Triangle – 1991
Kriel, Jesse – (Maritzburg Coll) – KZN - 2012
†**Krige,* Corné** - (Paarl BH) - WP - 1993
†**Kruger,* Ruben** - (Grey Coll) - FS - 1987-88
Kruger, Bertus - (Die Burger) - GL - 1989
Kruger, Ernst - (Jeugland) - GL - 1974-75
Kruger, Kobus - (Middelburg THS) - Mpu - 1996
Kruger, Morné - (Monument) - GL - 2001
Kruger, Warren - (SACS) - WP - 1974-75
Kuttel, Peter - (Bishops) - WP - 1983
Kuün, Derick - (AHS, Pretoria) - BB – 2002

L

†**Lambie, Patrick** (Michaelhouse) – Natal – 2007-08
Lanning, Andrew - (Bishops) - WP - 1989
Laubscher, Michael - (Tygerberg) - WP - 1974-75
Laufs, Gerhard - (Alberton) - GL - 1992
Le Grange, Anton - (Despatch) - EP – 1975
Le Maitre, Eugene – (Marais Viljoen) – GL – 2011
Le Marque,* Derek – (Glenwood) – Natal - 1979
†**Le Roux, Ollie** - (Grey Coll) - FS - 1991
Le Roux,* Chris - (Waterkloof) - BB - 1996-97
Le Roux, Kobus - (Boland Agric) - WP - 1995
Le Roux, Stephan - (Brits/ Waterkloof) - BB - 1993-94
Lehmann, Helmut – (Paarl Gym) – WP – 2008
Lewis, Marlon - (Bertram) - EP - 2004-05
Lewis, Jean-Paul – (Paul Roos) – WP – 2010-11
Liebenberg, Christo - (Roodepoort) - GL – 1986
Liebenberg, Wiaan – (Drostdy THS) – Boland - 2010
Lightfoot, Wessel - (Diamantveld) - GW – 1981
Linde, Jurie – (AHS, Pretoria) – BB – 2012-13
Linde, Nico - (Grey Coll) - FS - 1990
Linde, Rob - (Maritzburg Coll) - Natal – 1997
Lindeque, Piet – (Grey Coll) - FS - 2009
Lindsay, Paul - (Maritzburg Coll) - Natal - 1975-77
†**Lobberts, Hilton** - (N. Orleans Paarl) - Boland - 2004
Loest, Gary - (Queens Coll) - Border - 1985-86
†**Lombard, Friedrich** - (Frankfort) - NFS – 1997
Loubser, Pieter - (Paarl BH/Bishops) - WP - 1975-76
Louw, Coenie - (Dirkie Uys) - Boland - 1995
†**Louw, Hottie** - (Boland Agric) - WP - 1994
Louw,* Pieter - (Paarl BH) - WP - 2003
Louw, Wilco – (Drostdy) – Boland - 2012
Luiters, Kevin – (Grey Coll) – FS - 2010
Lusaseni, Luvuyo - (Selbourne Coll) - Border – 2006

M

Mabuza, Thabo – (Centurion) - Blue Bulls – 2011-12
Maherry, Chet - (Grey Coll) - FS - 1985-86
Mahlangu, Daniel - (Oosterland Secunda) - Mpu – 1999
Majola, Khaya – (Westville) – KZN - 2010
Malan, Remu – (Outeniqua) – SWD - 2013
Malgas, Warren - (PW Botha) - SWD – 2003
†**Malherbe, Frans** – (Paarl BH) – WP - 2009
†**Mallett, Nick** - (St Andrews) - EP - 1974-75
Malton, Shaun – (Glenwood) – KZN - 2008
Manuel, David - (Waterkloof) - BB - 1997-98
Manuel, Rodrique - (Ben. Heigths) - WP - 1996
Marais, Abrie - (Grey Coll) - FS - 1977
Marais, Gert - (Grey Coll) - FS – 1983
Marothodi, Ompile - Pretoria BHS - BB -2007
Martyn, Angus - (Michaelhouse) - Natal – 1998
Marutlulle, Edgar - (Potch, BHS) - Leopards - 2004-05
Marx, Malcolm – (King Edward VII) – GL - 2012
Maseko, Sizo – (Ermelo) – Mpu - 2009
Mashele, Ntokozo - (Nelspruit) - Mpu – 2006
Masina, Sibi – (Standerton) – Mpu - 2007
Masuga, Tshepo - (Monument) - GL - 2006
Matthysen, John - (Sand du Plessis) - FS - 1974-75
Mbonambi, Bongi – (St Alban's) – BB – 2009
Mbovane, Tshotso – (Paul Roos) – WP - 2010
McAlister, Daniel - (Selborne Coll) - Border - 1991
McCann, Warren - (Jeppe BH) - GL – 1985
⁵**McDonald, Aubrey** - (Winterberg HS - Fort Beaufort) - EP – 2005
⁵**McDonald, Aubrey** – (Waterkloof HS) – BB - 2006
⁶**McDonald, Barry** - (Adelaide Gym) - NEC - 1996
⁶**McDonald, Barry** - (Waterkloof) - BB - 1997
McIntyre, Mark - (Grey Coll) - FS - 1989
†**Meiring, FA** - (Gill Coll) - NEC - 1986
Mentz, Kosie - (Paarl Gym) - WP - 1988
Mentz, MJ - (Ermelo) - Mpu - 2000
Meyer, Altus - (Vredenburg HS) - Boland - 1997
Meyer, Clinton - (Maritzburg Coll) - Natal - 1989
Meyer, Pieter - (Waterkloof) - BB - 2005
Meyer, Renier - (Wessel Maree) - NFS - 1998
Mhlobiso, Luvuyo - (Daniel Pienaar) - EP - 2004
Michaels, Devan - (Kasselsvlei) - WP – 2001
Micklewood, Christopher (Westville) - Natal - 2005
Miller, Greg - (Grey Coll) - EP - 1991
Mills, David - (Maritzburg Coll) - Natal - 1978
Milton, Cliff - (AHS, Pretoria) - BB - 2001-02
Mjekevu, Wandile – (King Edward VII) – GL – 2008
Mkize, Njabula – (Westville) – KZN - 2008
Mkokeli, Tembani - (Msobomvu) - Border - 2001-02
Molapo, Matjikinyane – (Ben Vorster) – Limpopo BB - 2012
Moller, JD - (Paarl BH) - WP - 2000
†**Montgomery, Percy** - (SACS) - WP - 1992-93
Moolman, Hansie - (Ermelo) - Mpu – 2005
Morotothe, Omphile – (Pretoria BHS) – BB - 2007
Mostert, Juan-Pierre - (Brits) - Leopards - 2006
Mthula, Petros - (Glenwood) - Natal – 2001
Mtimka, Lonwaba – (Dale Coll) – Border – 1999
Mtsi, Thabani – (Selbourne Coll) – Border - 2013
†**Müller, Helgard** - (Grey Coll) - FS - 1981-82
†**Müller, Pieter** - (Grey Coll) - FS - 1987-88
†**Müller, Jorrie** - (Monument) - GL - 1999
Muller, Lourens - (Hart-

SA SCHOOLS PLAYERS 1974-2013

beespoort) - BB - 1993
Muller, Rudi - (Potch. Gym) - Leopards - 1993
Munn, Wayne - (Maritzburg Coll) - Natal - 1994
Mxoli, Sangoni - (Durban OB) - Natal - 2003
Myburgh, Jaco - (Paarl BH) - WP - 1996
Myburgh, Pieter - (Paul Roos Gym.) - WP - 2004
Myburgh, Stefaan - (Paul Roos Gym) - WP - 1996
N
Naudé, Dawie - (David Ross) - NEC – 1986
Nche, Ox – (Louis Botha THS) – FS – 2012-13
Neethling, Sydwhill - (Worcester Gym) - Boland - 2000
Nel, Boeta - (Bloemfontein THS) - FS - 1979-80
Nel, Johan - (Wolmaranstad) - Stellaland - 1987
Nel, Leon - (Nelspruit) - Mpu - 1982
Nel, Pieter - (Patriot, Witbank) - Mpu - 1983
Nell, Jacques - (Grey Coll) - FS - 1977
Ngoro, Mlindazwe - (St Johns) - Border CD - 2006
Nieuwenhuys, Jacques - (Monument) - GL - 1984
Ngonyoza, Mtobeli - (Oscar Mpetha) - WP – 2003
Nkosi, Malungisa (Giant) - (St Stithians) - GL – 2005
Nonkontwana, Abongile – (St Albans) – BB- 2012-13
North, Andrew - (Bishops) - WP - 1989
Nortjé, Danie - (Jan Viljoen) - GL – 1976
Notshe, Sikhumbuzo (Wynberg BH) – WP – 2010-11
Ntubeni, Siyabonga – (King Edward VII) – GL - 2009
Ntunja,* Kaunda - (Dale Coll) - Border - 1999-2000
Nyoka, Sinovuyo – (Dale Coll) – Border - 2008
O

²**O'Cuinneagain, Dion** - (Rondebosch BH) - WP - 1989-90
O'Neill, Pieter - (Despatch) - EP - 1988-89
Oberholster, Johan - (Vereeniging THS) - Valke – 1998
Oberholzer, Johan – (Jan Viljoen) – Golden Lions - 2007
Oberholzer, Lourens - (Linden) - GL - 1982
Ockafor, Kene – (Kearsney Coll) – Natal - 2007
Oelschig, Noël - (Grey Coll) - FS - 1997
Olckers, Riaan - (AHS, Pretoria) - BB - 1995
Olivier, HJ - (Kroonstad) - NFS – 1995
†**Oosthuizen, Coenie** – (Grey Coll) – FS - 2007
Oosthuizen. Josephus - (Grey Coll) – FS - 2005
Oosthuizen, JR - (Grey Coll) - FS - 1992
Oosthuizen,* Willie - (Helpmekaar) - GL – 1976
P
Paige, Rudy,* - (Bastion) - Golden Lions - 2007
Palmer, Shaun - (Middelburg THS) - Mpu - 1986
Penzhorn, Adrian - (Maritzburg Coll) - Natal - 2002
Petersen, Patrick - (Florida) - WP – 1995
Petersen, Sergeal – (Grey HS) – EP – 2012
Phillips, Justin – (Waterkloof) – BB – 2012-13
†**Pienaar, Francois** - (Patriot Witbank) - Mpu - 1985
Pienaar, Andries - (Paarl BH) - WP - 1975
Pienaar,* Bernard - (Paarl Gym) - WP - 1974-75
Pienaar, Pieter - (Paarl BH) - Boland – 2001
Pienaar, Roelof – (Grey Coll) - Free State - 2007
†**Pienaar, Ruan** - (Grey Coll) - FS - 2002
Pieterse, Koen - (Grey Coll) - FS - 1980

Pietersen, Ricardo - (Groot Brak) - SWD - 1999
Plaatjies, Jeremy - (Outeniqua) - SWD - 2001
Plaatjies,* Sean - (Brandwag Uitenhage) - EP – 1996
Pollard, Handré – (Paarl Gym) – WP – 2012
Poni, Onke - (Selbourne) - Border – 2002
†**Potgieter,* Dewald** (Daniël Pienaar – Uitenhage) – EP - 2005
Pretorius, Christo - (Paarl Gym) - WP - 1996
Pretorius, Herman - (Grey Coll) - FS - 2004
Pretorius, Flippie - (De Wet Nel THS) - NFS - 1979
Pretorius, Johannes - (Hentie Cilliers) - NFS - 1984
Pretorius, Riaan - (Ben Viljoen, Groblersdal) - Mpu - 1994
Pretorius, Wynand - (Sand du Plessis) - FS - 1975-76
Prinsloo, Carlo - (Paarl Gym.) - WP - 2004
Prinsloo, Jamie - (John Vorster THS) - BB - 1975
Prinsloo, Michael - (Ficksburg THS) - EFS - 1977
R
Radebe, Colin - (Secunda HS) - Mpu – 2000
Rademan, Pieter* – (Grey Coll) – FS - 2009
†**Ralepelle, Chiliboy** - (Pretoria BHS) - BB - 2002-03
Rampeta, Refuoe (Louis Botha THS) – FS - 2013
³**Rathbone, Clyde** - (Kingsway High) - Natal - 1999
†**Rautenbach, Faan** - (Kroonstad Agric) - NFS - 1993-94
Rautenbach, George - (Paul Roos Gym) - WP - 1974-75
Redelinghuys, Julian - (Monument) - GL – 2006-07
Reid, Grant - (Maritzburg Coll) - Natal - 1987

†**Reinach, Jaco** - (Grey Coll) - FS - 1979-80
Reingold, Jeremy – (Constantia) – WP - 1985
Rich, Rockey - (Kearsney Coll) - Natal - 1975
Richardson, Craig - (Despatch) - EP - 1986
Richardson, Michael - (Despatch) - EP - 1989
Richter, Jan - (Grey Coll) - FS - 1977
Richter, Toppie - (Grey Coll) - FS - 1977
Ries, Alfred - (Monument) - GL - 2006
Robberts, Steph - (Grey Coll) - FS – 2003
Robinson, Sean – (Waterkloof) – BB - 2011
Roodt, Hendrik - (Lichtenburg HS) - Leopards - 2005
†**Rose, Earl** - (Strand) - WP - 2002
Rose, Jody - (Paul Roos Gym) - WP - 2003
†**Rossouw, Chris** - (Hugenote HS) - Valke - 1987
Rossouw, Francois - (Middelburg) - Mpu – 1986
Rossouw,* Jean-Jacques - (Paarl Gym) - BB - 2006
Rossouw, Johan - (Durbanville) - WP - 1977
Roux, Daan - (Lichtenburg) - Stellaland - 1974-75
Roux, Paul - (Paul Roos Gym) - WP - 2000
Ruiters, Marlin - (Greyn Coll) - EP - 2006
S
Saaiman, Willem - (Menlopark) - BB - 1991
Saayman, Daniel - (Daniel Pienaar THS) - EP – 1992
Sadie, Ian - (Grey Coll) - FS - 1979
Scheepers, Eben - (Grey Coll) - FS – 1983
Schnetler, Fredrick – (Glenwood) – KZN - 2009
Schickerling, Adriaan - (Boland Agric) - Boland – 1984
Schickerling, JD – (Paarl

SA SCHOOLS PLAYERS 1974-2013

Gym) – WP - 2012
Schoeman, Barry - (Verwoerdburg) - BB – 1975
Schoeman, Marnus - (Waterkloof) - BB – 2006-07
Schoeman,* Pierre – (AHS, Pretoria) - BB – 2011-12
†**Scholtz, Hendro** - (Voortrekker, Bethlehem) - NFS – 1997
Schurmann, Deon - (Eldoraigne) - BB – 1984
Schwartz, Lean - (Waterkloof) – BB - 2009
Scott, Ashwin - (Parkdene) - SWD - 2003
Scriba, Hans - (Outeniqua) - SWD - 1983
Searson, Paul - (Bishops) - WP - 1989
Senekal, Dawie - (Abbots Coll) - WP - 1988
§**Serfontein,* Jan** - (Otto du Plessis) - EP - 1976-78
§†**Serfontein, Jan** – (Grey Coll) – FS - 2011
Siegelaar, Alastair - (Paul Roos Gym.) - WP – 2004
Sihunu, Akhona – (Dale Coll) – Border - 2012
Sitole, Martin - (Embalenthele) - Mpu - 2001-02
Sithole, Sibusiso – (Queens Coll) - Border - 2008
Skeate, Ross - (SACS) - WP - 2000
†**Skinstad, Bob** - (Hilton Coll) - Natal – 1994
Skosana, Brian – (St Andrews) – EP CD – 2009
Slabbert, Henk - (Potch. Gym) - Leopards - 1980
†**Small, James** - (Greenside) - GL – 1987
Small-Smith,* William – (Grey Coll) – FS - 2010
†**Smit, John** - (Pretoria BHS) - BB - 1996
Smit, Chris - (Grey Coll) - FS - 1979
Smith, André - (Paarl Gym.) - WP - 2005
†**Smith, David** - (Hamilton, Rhodesia) - Rhodesia - 1975-76
Smith, Headley – (Gey Coll) - FS
Smith, Philip - (Hangklip) - Border – 1975
Smith, Ruan – (Paarl Gym) – WP - 2008
Snyman, Earl – (Outeniqua) – SWD - 2007
Snyman, Johan - (Outeniqua) - SWD – 2004
Snyman, RG – (AHS, Pretoria) – BB - 2013
Snyman, Tiaan – (AHS, Pretoria) - BB - 1997-98
Sofoko, Jerry - (Pretoria THS) - BB - 2002
Sogidashe, Luvo - (Kama) - Border – 2002
Solomon, Chad – (Paul Roos Gym) – WP - 2012
Sonnekus, Pieter - (Bloemfontein THS) - FS - 1980
†**Sowerby, Shaun** - (Sasolburg) - Vaal Triangle - 1996
Spamer, Pieter - (Pietersburg) - Limpopo BB - 2003
Sparks, Bradley - (Selborne Coll) - Border - 1998
Squires, Brandon - (Maritzburg Coll) - Natal – 2002
Stampu, Yondela – (St Albans) - BB – 2007
Stander,* Chris – (Oakdale Agric) – SWD - 2008
Steenkamp, Buks - (Grey Coll) - FS - 1985-86
Steenkamp, Corrie - (Vereeniging THS) - Valke - 1997
Steenkamp, Wilhelm - (Paarl BH) - WP - 2003
Steenkamp, Pieta - (Grey Coll) - FS – 1990
Steenkamp,* Ruan – (Monument) - GL - 2011
Steenkamp, Virgulle - (Excelsior Belhar) - WP - 1997
Steenkamp, Willie - (Grey Coll) - FS - 2000
†**Stegmann, Deon** - (Grey Coll) - FS - 2004
Stevens, Jeffrey - (Breërivier) - Boland - 1995-96
Stevens, Kees - (Grey Coll) - FS - 1983
Stevenson, Jacques - (Ermelo) - Mpu -1989
Stewart, Clayton - (Strand HS) - WP - 2006
Stewart, Errol - (Westville) - Natal - 1987
Steyn, Christo - (Bloemfontein THS) - FS – 1976
Steyn, Francois - (AHS, Pretoria) – BB - 2013
Steyn, Jacques - (Andrew Rabie) - EP - 1995
Stoop, Ockert - (John Vorster, Nigel) - Valke - 1974-75
†**Stransky, Joel** - (Maritzburg Coll) - Natal - 1984
†**Strauss, Adriaan** - (Grey Coll) - FS - 2003
Strauss, Johan - (Kearsney Coll) - Natal - 2004
§**Strauss, Richardt** - (Grey Coll) - FS - 2003
Strydom, Emil-Jan - (Grey Coll) - FS – 1986
Swanepoel, Dries – (Grey Coll) – FS - 2011
†**Swanepoel, Werner** - (Grey Coll) - FS - 1991
†**Swart, Justin** - (Paul Roos Gym) - WP - 1991
Swart, Hakkies - (Drostdy THS) - Boland - 1988
Swart, Johan - (Paarl Gym) - WP - 1982
†**Swart, Balie** - (Paarl Gym) - WP - 1983
Swartbooi, Dewey - (Worcester Gym) - Boland – 2000
Swiel, Timothy (Bishops) – WP - 2011
Swiegers, Gielie - (Monument) - GL - 1984

T
Taute, Jaco - (Klerksdorp) - Leopards - 1989
Temple, Stephan - (Pretoria Boys High) - BB - 1993
Theron, Danie - (Kimberley THS) - GW – 1980
Theron, Gerrie - (Rustenburg) - Leopards - 1994-95
Theron, Jannie - (Sand du Plessis) - FS - 1987
Theron, Pieter - (Grey Coll) - FS - 1975
Thomas, Gray - (Volkskool) - Leopards – 1984
Thomas, Jason – (Muir Coll) – EP – 2010
Thomson, Brandon – (Ermelo) – Mpu - 2013
†**Thompson, Jeremy** - (Maritzburg Coll) - Natal - 1986
Thompson, Malcolm - (Maritzburg Coll) - Natal - 1974-75
Tile, Mandilakhe - (Dale Coll) - Border – 2005
Toerien, PJ - (Garsfontein) – BB - 2013
Tom, Siyabonga – (Glenwood) – KZN - 2011
Topkin, Gareth – (Rondebosch) – WP - 2008
†**Truscott, Andries** - (Grey Coll) - FS – 1986

U
Uys, Petrus – (Monument) – GL - 2008

V
Van Buuren, Albertus - (Hoopstad) - NFS - 1992
Van Coller, Stephan - (Volkskool) - Leopards - 1981
†**Van der Linde, CJ** - (Grey Coll) - FS - 1998
Van der Linden, Lallie - (Pretoria-Noord) - BB - 1974-75
Van der Merwe, Bennie - (Paarl BH) - WP - 1979-80
Van der Merwe, Danie - (Mariental) - SWA – 1980
Van der Merwe, Duhan – (Outeniqua) – SWD – 2012-13
Van der Merwe, Gert - (DF Malan) - WP - 1976
Van der Merwe, Jaco - (Bishops) - WP - 1983
Van der Merwe, Joepie - (Grey Coll) - FS - 1979-80
Van der Merwe, Marinus – (Standerton) – Pumas - 2010
†**Van der Merwe, Flip** -

460 SA RUGBY ANNUAL 2014   www.sarugby.co.za

SA SCHOOLS PLAYERS 1974-2013

(Grey Coll) - FS - 2003
Van der Merwe, Pikkie - (Helpmekaar) - GL - 1978
Van der Mescht, JP - (Daniel Pienaar) - EP - 1993
Van der Schyff, Jonathan - (Monument) - GL - 2001
Van der Walt, CP - (Piet Potgieter) - Far North - 1981
Van der Walt, Danie - (Ermelo) - Mpu - 1989
Van der Walt, James - (Ermelo) - Mpu - 1997
Van der Walt, Jaco – (Monument) – GL - 2011
Van der Walt, Kobus - (AHS, Pretoria) - BB – 1999
Van der Walt, Nardus – (AHS, Pretoria) – BB – 2010
Van der Walt, Nicky - (Ermelo) - Mpu - 1993
Vd Westhuizen, Chrisjan - (Menlopark) - BB – 1995
Vd Westhuizen, Dayan – (Centurion) – BB - 2012
Vd Westhuizen, Richard - (Vryburger) - GL - 1976
Vd Westhuizen, Roedolf - (AHS, Pretoria) - BB - 2000
†**Vd Westhuyzen, Jaco** - (Ben Viljoen) - Mpu - 1996
Van Genderen, Jan - (Monument) - GL - 1978
Van Genderen, Kolie - (Monument) - GL - 1980
Van Heerden, Frans - (Langenhoven) - BB – 1975
Van Heerden, Schalk – (AHS, Pretoria) – BB – 2010
Van Heerden, Wayne - (Brandwag, Uit.) - EP - 1997-98
Van Heerden, Wickus - (Voortrekkerhoogte) - BB - 1982
†**Van Niekerk, Joe** - (King Edward VII) - GL - 1997-98
Van Niekerk, Ernst - (Paarl Gym) - WP – 1986
Van Niekerk, Niekie – (De Wet Nel THS) – NFS - 1985
Van Rensburg, Charl - (Queens Coll) - Border - 1992

Van Rensburg, Robbie - (AHS, Pretoria) - BB - 1998
Van Rooyen, Leon - (Estcourt) - Natal - 1987
Van Rooyen, Nico - (Rustenburg) - Leopards – 1981
Van Rooyen, Rudi – (AHS, Pretoria) – BB – 2010
Van Vuuren, Coenraad – (Nelspruit) – Mpu - 2013
Van Vuuren, Kosie - (AHS, Kroonstad) - NFS – 1994
Van Rooyen, Marchand – (Jan Viljoen) - Golden Lions - 2007
Van Vuuren, Pieter-Willem - (Grey Coll) - FS - 2006
Van Vuuren, Rodney - (AHS, Kroonstad) - NFS - 1983
Van Westing, Carl - (Marais Viljoen THS) - GL - 1992
Van Wyk, Cobus - (Schoonspruit) - Leopards – 1976
Van Wyk, William – (Paarl Gym) – WP - 2009
Van Zyl, Jaco - (JG Meiring) - WP - 1994
Van Zyl, Willem-Petrus - (Paarl BH) - WP - 1997
Venske, Herman - (Vanderbijlpark) - GL - 1979
†**Venter, Brendan** - (Monument) - GL - 1987
[7]**Venter, André** - (Grey Coll) - FS - 1990-91
[7]**Venter, André** - (Monument) - GL - 1989
Venter, Deon - (AHS, Pretoria) - BB – 2001
Venter, Francois – (Grey Coll) – FS - 2008
Venter, Hugo - (Grey Coll) - FS – 1991
Venter, Jano – (Middelburg THS) – Mpu - 2012
Venter, Ruan – (Monument) – GL - 2010
Verhoeven, Antonius - (Charlie Hofmeyer) - Boland - 1995
†**Vermaak, Jano** - (Vereeniging THS) - Valke - 2003

Vermeulen, Gielie - (Paul Roos Gym) - WP – 1983
Vermeulen, Jacques – (Paarl Gym) – WP - 2013
Vermeulen, PJ – (Noordkaap HS) - Griquas - 2005
Vermeulen, Riaan - (Grey Coll) - FS – 2002
Viljoen, EW – (Grey Coll) – FS - 2013
Viljoen, Gert - (De Wet Nel THS) - NFS - 1980
Viljoen, Harry - (Florida) - GL - 1976-77
†**Viljoen, Roelof** - (Joggie) - (Framesby) - EP - 1993-94
Visagie, Johan - (Potchefstroom THS) - Leopards - 1974
Visagie, Ronnie - (Rob Ferreira, Witrivier) - Mpu - 1983-84
†**Visser, De Villiers** - (Voortrekker, CT) - WP - 1976
†**Visser, Mornay** - (Paarl Gym) - WP - 1988
Visser, Jacques - (Paarl Gym) - WP - 1982
Volschenk, Johan - (Oakdale Agric.) - SWD - 2004
†**Von Hoesslin, David** - (Bishops) - WP - 1993
Vundla, Tshipiso - (St Albans) - BB - 2000

W

Wagenstroom, Frank - (Tygerberg) - WP - 2003
Wait, Clayton - (Pearson) - EP - 1989
Walker, Robert - (St Johns) - GL - 1981
Walters, Clint - (Woodridge) - EP – 1993
Walters, Rowan – (Upington HS) – Griquas - 2005
Wannenburg, Callie - (Oakdale Agric.) - SWD - 2001
†**Wannenburg, Pedrie** - (Oakdale Agric.) - SWD – 1999
Watermeyer, Stefan – (Waterkloof) – BB – 2005-06
†**Watson,* Luke** - (Grey

Coll) - EP - 2001
Weideman, Greyling - (Drostdy THS) - Boland - 1996
Weitz, Gerhard - (Grey Coll) - FS - 1974-75
Wenger, Charl – (Grey Coll) – FS - 2009
White, Bruce - (Maritzburg Coll) - Natal - 1974-75
Whitfield, Brendon - (Selborne Coll) - Border - 1994
Wiese, Cornel - (Paarl Gym) - WP League - 1988
Wiggins, Deon - (Hugenote) - Boland - 1988
Willemse, Coenie - (Hendrik Verwoerd) - BB - 1982
Willemse, Martin - (Sandveld) - NFS - 1993
Williams, Jerome - (Middelande Sec.) - EP – 2004
Williams, Percey – (Oudtshoorn) – SWD - 2011
Willis, Vainon – (Waterkloof) - BB - 2006
Wilson, Warren - (Maritzburg Coll) - Natal - 1987
Wolmarans, Jan - (Wonderboom) - BB - 1982

Z

Zaltsman, Neil - (Northlands) - Natal – 1985
Zass, Leolin - (Hermanus) – Boland - 2013

[1] Appeared for England at full international level [2] Appeared for Ireland at full international level. [3] Appeared for Australia at full international level. [4] Appeared for France at full international level. [5, 6 & 7] Earned SA Schools caps from two different provinces. [8] Jan (snr) and Jan (jnr) Serfontein are the first father-son combination to have represented the SA Schools team. [9] Appeared for Ireland at full international level

Five SA Schools players gained senior national colours in other sports than rugby: Warren McCann, Jaco Reinach, Herrman Venske (athletics); and Errol Stewart and Herschelle Gibbs (cricket).

Two SA School players later coached the Springbok team: Harry Viljoen and Nick Mallett

REFEREES

Kaplan, Henning bid farewell

IN 2013 WE BID FAREWELL TO TWO MEN who have made a lasting contribution to refereeing in South Africa and in the rest of the world, men whom it is so hard to emulate, let alone replace – Tappe Henning and Jonathan Kaplan.

Henning has moved to Scotland to take over Scottish refereeing, which certainly needs a boost. Kaplan has retired from top rugby but will go on refereeing at clubs and schools in the Western Province.

His record speaks for itself: 70 Tests (more than anybody else), more Six Nations Tests (17) than anybody else, refereed one country (All Blacks, 18 times) more than anybody else, more Bledisloe Cup matches (8), more Super Rugby matches (107) and more Currie Cup matches (161) than anybody else.

Kaplan has refereed 13 matches at the four World Cups that he attended – in 1999, 2003, 2007 and 2011, including the semi-final between England and France in 2007. He was the first official in the world to referee 50 Tests. Kaplan refereed three Super Rugby Finals, including that one in the fog in Christchurch, and six Currie Cup finals, including the 2013 final at Newlands, his last match as a professional referee in South Africa. He has refereed 425 first-class matches and 1,040 matches altogether.

Henning is five years older than Kaplan but in many ways their careers ran together. After playing for Northern Transvaal Under-20, he started refereeing in 1987 and first got on the National Panel in 1994. The year 1995 was great one for him. At 34, he became the youngest referee to referee a Currie Cup final – a record broken by Craig Joubert in 2010. In 1995 he also refereed his first Test match – Scotland vs Western Samoa at Murrayfield, where he is now based. In 1997 Henning refereed the Super Rugby final between the Auckland Blues and the Brumbies at Eden Park. In all he refereed 14 Tests. He was at the 1999 World Cup in Wales but not, bizarre as it seemed at the time, at the 2003 World Cup. His contribution since then has been immense. He has an outstanding knowledge of the laws and how they should work and he is an outstanding presenter with a good sense of humour. His work as a coach, selector, appraiser of referees and wise man has been of inestimable value, and he has served the IRB well, especially as a selector. He worked with the Springboks in improving their knowledge of the laws. Born in Nigel, Tappe, who inherited his nickname from his grandfather, is known throughout the refereeing world.

The 2013 season will also be remembered for the new referees that came onto the top panel – Quin-

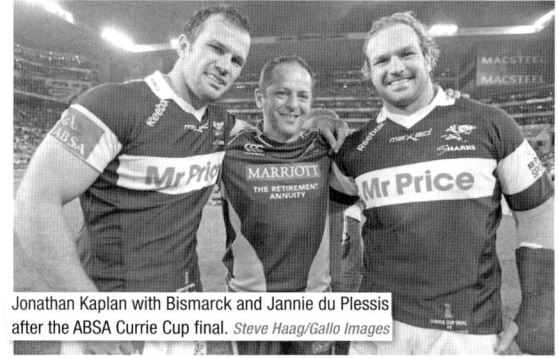

Jonathan Kaplan with Bismarck and Jannie du Plessis after the ABSA Currie Cup final. *Steve Haag/Gallo Images*

ton Immelman, Jason Jaftha and Rasta Rasivhenge. Later Marius van der Westhuizen also came onto the panel.

The Elite Panel were a young group. Craig Joubert and Lourens van der Merwe were the oldest and they were only 35. Immelman and Peyper were 32, Berry was 31, Mayende 30, Van der Westhuizen 29, Jaftha 28 and Rasivhenge 27. The new man joining them in 2014, Jaco van Heerden, is 30. Nine of the ten Elite referees are 35 or younger. The present is bright and the future looks bright as well. That SA referees are able to bring through young referees of great class is a feather in the cap of management.

It was a golden year for Marius van der Westhuizen. He became a Currie Cup referee in 2013, refereed, brilliantly, a semi-final of the Currie Cup, was named a Super Rugby referee for 2014 and has been named on SA Referees' Elite Panel – all of that apart from the honours he achieved on the IRB Sevens circuit. Also on the Elite Panel is Rasta Rasivhenge, who has been brilliant on the Sevens circuit, and Jaco van Heerden who has not yet refereed a Currie Cup match in the Premier Division. Back on this panel are Christie du Preez, who concentrated nationally on being an assistant referee for a while, and Pro Legoete.

It is obvious that the management of South African referees is in good hands as there are constantly really good referees coming through the system. That system relies heavily on hard work by both management and referees. There are several courses during the year, nationally and regionally, there are peer groups and TMO discussions each week, there are fitness tests and law exams, there is the Athletic Management System which is a closed comms system to panel referees and to the provincial societies, there are the reports of coaches and assessors, there is the expert help of Balie Swart on scrumming and there is communication to the 14 societies. Despite the effort, referees are regularly criticised by commentators and spectators, mostly when the commentators and spectators are wrong. André Watson and Mark Lawrence have regularly been a part of Boots 'n All in an effort to improve communication with commentators and journalists. In addition the society has a website (www.sareferees.co.za) and a quarterly newsletter, In Touch.

Sevens has been fertile ground for SA referees. There were five South Africans at the World Cup Sevens in Moscow – Banks Yantolo (assessor), Tappe Henning (IRB Selector), and referees Rasta Rasivhenge, Marius van der Westhuizen and Marlize Jordaan. Yantolo was appointed the IRB selector of women's Sevens for the Southern Hemisphere. In 2013, the South African duo of Rasivenghe and Van der Westhuizen had an outstanding series. Rasivenghe refereed three finals, Van der Westhuizen two. Marlize Jordaan was appoointed to four tournaments – Dubai, USA, Brazil and China. The Bloemfontein mother of a 12-year-old has refereed rugby in England, Italy, China, Brazil, the USA, Hong Kong, the United Arab Emirates, Kenya and Russia. She has travelled more widely as a referee than she did playing for South Africa.

The following referees refereed Test matches during the season: Jonathan Kaplan, Craig Joubert, Jaco Peyper, Stuart Berry (whose very first Test was between Japan and the world champion All Blacks), Lourens van der Merwe, Lesego Legoete and Marlize Jordaan.

Tappe Henning was an IRB selector; Shaun Veldsman, Johann Meuwesen, Deon van Blommestein and Gerrie Coetzee were TMOs at Tests. Test assessors were Tappe Henning and Dennis Immelman. Test assistant referees were Craig Joubert, Jaco Peyper, Lourens van der Merwe, Stuart Berry, Christie du Preez, Cobus Wessels, Loyiso Bosman, Denis Mpiti, Marius Jonker and Cobus Wessels. Timekeepers at Tests were Gabriel Pappas, Albert Mocke and Paul Ackerman. Stuart Berry refereed at the Junior World Cup in France and the following refereed age-group internationals: Quinton Immelman, Lihan Pretorius and Jaco Kotze.

Executive: Stephen Meintjes (chairman), Douglas Holwill, Mnininzi Plaaitjie, Banks Yantolo
Staff: Andre Watson (manager), Neville Heilbron, Mark Lawrence, Tappe Henning, Aletta Coetzee, Eugene de Villiers.

REFEREE PANELS FOR 2013 (ALPHABETICAL):

ELITE GROUP:
Stuart Berry (Sharks), Quinton Immelman (Western Province), Jason Jaftha (South Western Districts), Marius Jonker (Sharks), Craig Joubert (Sharks), Jonathan Kaplan (Western Province), Sindile Mayende (Border), Jaco Peyper (Free State), Rasta Rasivhenge (Golden Lions), Marius van der Westhuizen (Western Province), Lourens van der Merwe (Free State).
Reserves: Ben Crouse (Blue Bulls), Lusanda Jam (Border), Tiaan Jonker (Golden Lions), Jaco Kotze (Free State), Jaco van Heerden (Blue Bulls)

NATIONAL GROUP:
Rodney Bonaparte (Eastern Province), Gerrie de Bruin (Blue Bulls), Daniel Fortuin (Western Province), Stephan Geldenhuys (Blue Bulls), Francois Groenewald (Western Province), Cwengile Jadezweni (Western Province), Pieter Janse van Vuuren (Free State), Matt Kemp (Western Province), Lesego Legoete (Golden Lions), Eduan Nel (Golden Lions), Francois Pretorius (Western Province), Lihan Pretorius (Valke), Oregopotse Rametsi (Leopards), Archie Sehlako (KwaZulu Natal)
Reserves: Christie du Preez (Eastern Province), Marlize Jordaan (Free State), Tahla Ntshakaza (Golden Lions), Jaco Pretorius Valke), Ricus van der Hoven (Pumas), Renier Vermeulen (Golden Lions).

CONTENDERS' SQUAD:
Blake Beattie (Sharks), Loyiso Bosman (Border), Tony Correia (Blue Bulls), Eugene de Wet (Valke), Wilko Esterhuizen (Blue Bulls), Andre Goliath (South Western Districts), AJ Jacobs (Griffons), Pieter Maritz (Blue Bulls), Ruan Meiring (South Western Districts), Sakkie Meyer (Free State), Denis Mpiti (Border), Vusumuzi Msibi (Sharks), Norris Mark (Eastern Province), Henchalla Oerson (South Western Districts), Nico Schmahl (Griquas), Nathan Swartz (Western Province), Fernando Uithaler (Eastern Province), James van Oudtshoorn (Leopards), Henrico van Rooyen (Griffons), Jan Venter (Blue Bulls), Terence Westcott (Blue Bulls).
Reserves: Jan Ruaan du Preez (Golden Lions), Quinten Pretorius (Golden Lions), Morebe Godwill (Leopards), Naka Bulelani (Border), Watson Zane (Sharks).

SPECIALISED ASSISTANT REFEREES PANEL:
Stefan Breytenbach (Pumas), Attie Buitendag (Blue Bulls), Francois de Bruin (Griquas), Christie du Preez (Eastern Province), Linston Manuels (Boland), Reuben Rossouw (Sharks), Sieg van Staden (Valke), Marc van Zyl (Western Province), Cobus Wessels (Blue Bulls)

SARU TMO PANEL:
Gerrie Coetzee (Free State), Johan Greeff (Blue Bulls), Johann Meuwesen (Eastern Province), Deon van Blommestein (Western Province), Shaun Veldsman (Boland), Reuben Rossouw (Sharks)

SARU TIMEKEEPERS:
Paul Ackerman (Sharks), Albert Mocke (Free State), Gabriel Pappas (SARU), Kat Swanepoel (Griquas), Pieter van der Merwe (Golden Lions).

SARU REFEREE SELECTORS:
Banks Yantolo (convener), Tappe Henning (Manager: Performance Measurement), Mark Lawrence, Neville Heilbron, Eugene de Villiers (Women), Pierre Oelofse.

SARU REFEREE PERFORMANCE REVIEWERS:
Tappe Henning (Manager: Performance Measurement), Eska Claasen, Gerrit Coetzer, Keith Hendricks, Jacques Hugo, Dennis Immelman, Theuns Janse van Vuuren, Marius Jonker, Allan O'Connell, Pierre Oelofse, Willie Roos, Arrie Schoonwinkel, Balie Swart (Scrum Consultant), Mngqibisa Thuso, Pieter White, Banks Yantolo.

COACHES:
International Coaches and Mentors: Mark Lawrence (Manager Performance Enhancement), Andre Watson, Tappe Henning, Neville Heilbron, Balie Swart (Scrum Consultant).
National Coaches: Dries Breytenbach, Deon van Blommestein, Banks Yantolo, Johan Zurich.
Regional Coaches: Philip du Toit, Johann Meuwesen, Kim Smit.
Academy Coaches: Eugene Daniels (Manager Academy Squad), Marius Franken, Hendrik Greyvenstein, Jamiel Panday.
Peer Coaches: Craig Joubert, Jonathan Kaplan, Jaco Peyper.
Scouting: Eugene Daniels, Theuns Naudé.

FINAL REFEREES

Vodacom Super Rugby: Craig Joubert
Absa Currie Cup: Jonathan Kaplan
Absa 1st Division Final: Craig Joubert
Promotion Relegation (two matches):
Jonathan Kaplan and Craig Joubert
Vodacom Cup: Marius van der Westhuizen
Cell C Community Cup: Jaco Kotze
Absa Under-21A: Rasta Rasivhenge
Absa Under-21B: Francois Pretorius
Absa Under-19A: Rodney Bonaparte
Absa Under-19B: Christie du Preez

Amateur Provincial Final: Pieter Maritz
Varsity Cup: Marius van der Westhuizen
Koshuis Final: Cwengile Jadezweni
Young Guns: Daniel Fortuin
Final Match at Coca-Cola Craven Week:
Lihan Pretorius
Women's Provincial A Section Final:
Christie du Preez
Women's Provincial A Section Final:
Mark Norris

SOUTH AFRICAN REFEREES IN FIRST-CLASS RUGBY - 2013

Name	Vodacom Cup	Currie Cup	Super Rugby	Tests	TOTAL
Stuart Berry	1	4	7	1	13
Ben Crouse	4	5	-	-	9
Gerrie de Bruin	2	-	-	-	2
Stephan Geldenhuys	1	-	-	-	1
Francois Groenewald	1	-	-	-	1
Quinton Immelman	2	5	-	-	7
Cwengile Jadezweni	1	-	-	-	1
Jason Jaftha	2	9	6	-	17
Lusanda Jam	2	1	-	-	3
Pieter Janse van Vuuren	1	-	-	-	1
Marius Jonker	4	11	-	-	15
Tiaan Jonker	4	3	-	-	7
Craig Joubert	1	6 (FINAL 1ST)	10 (FINAL)	7	24
Jonathan Kaplan	1	10 (FINAL PREM)	8	2	21
Matt Kemp	2	-	-	-	2
Jaco Kotze	1	2	-	-	3
Pro Legoete	2	4	-	2	8
Sindile Mayende	5	4	-	-	9
Eduan Nel	1	-	-	-	1
Jaco Peyper	-	5	12	5	22
Francois Pretorius	2	-	-	-	2
Linan Pretorius	1	-	-	-	1
Rasta Rasivhenge	4	6	-	-	10
Nic Rocono	2	-	-	-	2
Archie Sehlako	2	-	-	-	2
Juan Sylvestre (Argentina)	3	-	-	-	3
Lourens van der Merwe	2	7	8	4	21
Marius van der Westhuizen	4 (FINAL)	9	-	-	13
Jaco van Heerden	5	3	-	-	8
29 Referees	**63**	**94**	**51**	**21**	**-**

OBITUARIES

BEN ALBERTS

BEN ALBERTS was many things: University of Pretoria graduate and a member of the convocation, chairman of the university's council, philanthropist, naturalist, environmentalist and wise man. Barend Christiaan Alberts was born in Pretoria on 16 September 1939. He inherited his father's names and also his noemnaam – Ben. He graduated with a BSc in 1963 and then an MSc, in mining engineering, in 1965. He achieved great things in the mining industry and in 2011 was honoured with its top award – the SA Institute of Mining & Metallurgy Brigadier Stokes Memorial Award. Alberts had a farm in the Piet Retief district when he started the Alberts Bursary for needy students. He took special delight in Skuta Ndlangomandle, a farm boy whom he helped to a BEd, after which the young man went back to Piet Retief to teach. From 1960-1967, he played prop for Northern Transvaal 23 times, at a time when they had the likes of Mof Myburgh and Jaap Bekker. He suffered a stroke and died in Pretoria on 8 April 2013, aged 73, survived by wife Ansie (nee Van der Wath of Ermelo) and three sons, three daughters, two adopted children and many grandchildren.

GERT AUGUSTYN

GERT AUGUSTYN was chairman of Randfontein for many years, then its president for 16 years and then an honorary life president for the next 10 years until his death. He became a vice-president of the Transvaal Rugby Union in 1984 and then deputy president to Louis Luyt during the glorious 1990s. Augustyn played for his club and had one match for a Transvaal XV, against Rhodesia in 1956. He was also a useful heavyweight boxer.

Gert Matthys Augustyn was born in Calvinia on 4 October 1927 and went to Calvinia High School. His wife Rika died in January 2011 after 65 years of marriage and he died of general organ failure on 2 September 2013, aged 85. He was survived by daughter Sarita, wife of Mpumalanga Pumas coach Jimmy Stonehouse, seven grandchildren and four great-grandchildren. Grandson Gert van Schalkwyk played for the Pumas in the Currie Cup.

ROBBIE BARNARD

ROBBIE BARNARD was wholeheartedly a Transvaler. An earnest hooker, he played for Diggers and from 1964 to 1972 was capped 69 times for Transvaal. He and younger brother Jannie made their debuts in the same year. Jannie, the l'enfant terrible of SA rugby with the dazzling feet, played for South Africa before Robbie did. He also died before Robbie did. Jannie was 20 when he played five Tests for South Africa in 1965 but he was killed in a car crash outside Potchefstroom in 1985. Barnard played 12 times for the Springboks but his only Test appearance was as a replacement for injured Piston van Wyk against New Zealand at Newlands in 1970.

Robert William Barnard was born in Pretoria on 26 November 1941 and educated at Hoërskool Fakkel. He died of cancer, aged 71. Barnard's wife Dawn died in 2007. He is survived by their two sons Robert and Johannes.

KOOS BASSON

KOOS BASSON, a man of Stellenbosch by birth, education and choice, gave enormous service to rugby over many years. He died watching the Springboks playing the All Blacks in Auckland with his wife Stella in Paradyskloof, Stellenbosch. He suffered a heart attack. His health had not been good after suffering a slight stroke on a visit to Nelspruit and he had gone home from hospital on the Monday before his death. Basson, who attended Paul Roos Gymnasium and read law at Stellenbosch, was a partner in the law firm Cluver Markötter, for whom he still consulted. He was chairman of the Van der Stel rugby club. Western Province soon roped him in on the disciplinary committee in 1966. He served under four presidents, including Ronnie Masson, from whom he took over in 2002. One of his great contributions to the Union was the part he played in the unification of rugby in the province. He was also vice-president of SARU from 2006-2008.

Jacobus Adriaan Albertus Basson was born on 11 October 1938. He died on 14 September 2013, aged 74, survived by Stella, his wife of 49 years, son Jacques, daughter Jianni and three grandchildren.

ATTIE BOTHA

IN 1946 Northern Transvaal won the Currie Cup for the first time when they beat WP in a thrilling final that was celebrated long and noisily afterwards. Attie Botha played centre in that match. In all he played 34 times for Northern Transvaal from 1945-48. He attended the Springbok trials in 1949 when the All Blacks came but by then he was past his best. Andreas de Wet Botha was born in Oudtshoorn on 15 January 1924. He died in July 2013, aged 89.

KOPPEL BROWN

KOPPEL BROWN came to the University of Cape Town in 1948 from Wynberg Boys' High where he was a legendary all-round sportsman. At UCT his coach Louis Barrow described him as being "as slippery as an eel at flyhalf, steady as a rock at fullback". In 1951 he played for Western Province. Brown graduated BArch in 1953 and he headed to Northern Rhodesia, now Zambia. Just married he and Maureen went up Luanshya near Ndola in the Copperbelt. He eventually started his own practice in Kitwe, doing work for the mines. He was elected deputy mayor of Kitwe. Despite travelling difficulties Brown played twice in Currie Cup matches for Rhodesia in 1954. In retirement he found a way to eradicate moles in Maureen's garden and then became known as Mr Mole, servicing troubled homes around the suburbs.

Koppel Brown was born on 17 February 1930 and died in Claremont on 19 September 2013, aged 83, survived by Maureen, his wife of 60 years, their children Martine and Gareth, and a grandchild.

RAY CONNELLAN

RAY CONNELLAN was a man of the Eastern Cape, educated at Selborne College in East London and Rhodes University in Grahamstown. He taught science at Queen's College in Queenstown before heading to Wynberg Boys' High in 1973 as a vice-principal. He stayed for 25 years, retiring in 1997 as deputy headmaster to Keith Richardson. An intensely loyal man, he gave his greatest effort to whatever body he was involved with. Rugby was his greatest passion. He coached at Queen's, including a stint as the 1st XV coach, and then at Wynberg where he was the 1st XV coach for 11 years. Connellan and his wife went to the UK to visit their three children and their grandchildren. Three days after they returned he died, six weeks after he had been diagnosed with terminal cancer.

Raymond Peter Connellan was born on 11 February 1938. He died on 9 June 2013, aged 75, survived by wife Daphne, children Bev, Tim and Howard, their spouses Mark, Sally and Caroline, and nine grandchildren.

MORGAN CUSHE

MORGAN CUSHE died of renal failure in the Cuyler Clinic in Uitenhage on 6 October 2013, aged 65. He had suffered kidney problems for some time and had been in and out of hospital. Cushe had a great career, following in the footsteps of older brother Meshak, whose nickname was Stampo, from a powerful figure in comic books at the time. Like Stampo, who died some years ago, Morgan was a hero for the Swallows club in Uitenhage. He first played for EP in 1968 and in 1971 was chosen for the African Springboks to play the SA Rugby Football Federation team, the Proteas, at Athlone Stadium. Stampo was also in the side and kicked two conversions as the Africans won 10-3. In the return match they won 13-6 at Wolfson Stadium, Morgan creating a try for Jack Dolomba. In his career of 19 'Tests', Cushe also played against England in 1972 and 1984, Italy in 1973 and 1974 when he scored a try in each match, the Lions in 1974 and 1980, France in 1975 and the All Blacks in 1976. In 1980 Cushe captained his side, then called the Leopards, against the Lions, captained by Derek Quinnell. In addition, in 1975 he played in South Africa's first mixed-race team, the President's XV, against France at Newlands and went on tour in 1979 with the highly successful SA Barbarians with Chick Henderson as the manager and Dougie Dyers as the coach. One of his trademarks was running with the ball in one hand, like Jan Ellis. After his playing days Cushe and his brother coached Swallows.

Morgan William Cushe, nicknamed Koktjana, was born in Kirkwood on 17 May 1948. He is survived by his ex-wife, six children and 10 grandchildren.

ERIC DE WET

ERIC DE Wet, a prominent man of Upington, had a long provincial career, signing off when he was 39. He was an important farmer on Kanoneiland, the biggest island on the Orange River, and a director of Oranjerivier-Wynkelders (OWK). De Wet was born in Kakamas but went to school in Upington and represented North West Cape at Craven Week in 1972. From school he went to Stellenbosch University and played for the Maties. Back in Upington in 1977 he played for the town club, which he captained from 1977-89, and was chosen for North West Cape who were then in the Sport Pienaar competition, a tier below Currie Cup. He captained the team from 1981-90, playing flank or No 8. In all he played provincial rugby from 1977-93.

Frederick Petrus de Wet was born on 2 April 1954. On 21 August 2013 he was at a function with daughter Marize and husband Dawid. He left to go home. Marize then got a phone call from De Wet to say that he had been in a car accident. They found him injured in his bakkie and took him to the Upington MediClinic, where he died on 24 August, aged 59, survived by wife Debbie, children Corné, Marize, Erika, Debbie and Albert, and grandchildren.

GRAHAM DOWNES

GRAHAM DOWNES, a South African who played rugby for the USA, had a tragic end. At the time he was a celebrated architect living in San Diego, California. He and some colleagues were drinking at his house. After the others had gone, he and Higinion Salgado, his property manager, were in a heated, job-related argument that became a fight. Police found them outside the house, Downes severely injured. He was taken to hospital; his brother Simon flew over and was at his bedside when the machines keeping him alive were switched off two days later. Downes had died of strangulation and severe head, neck and chest trauma. Salgado was charged with murder, his bail was set at $3 million and he opted to stay in custody to stand trial in January 2014. Downes was born in Durban and attended DHS after which he read architecture at Natal University. While doing his army training in Kroonstad he played for Northern Free State from 1981. Back in Durban he played for Natal from 1983-85, including the surprise Currie Cup final at Newlands in 1984. In 1986 he went to San Diego and played for the USA at the inaugural Rugby World Cup in 1987.

Graham Trouncer Downes was born on 17 July 1956 and died on 21 April 2013, aged 56. The club for which he had played and coached, OMBAC (Old Mission Beach Athletic Club), established the Graham Downes Scholarship Fund.

JAN ELLIS

JAN ELLIS'S death on 8 February 2013, aged 71, came as a shock because of all Springboks he seemed indestructible: those strong legs striding, ball in one hand, face impassive, red hair flying. When he retired he had worn a Springbok jersey 74 times, 38 times in Tests, then a record. And he did it all on his own and in his own way. More than any other, he was a self-made Springbok and one of the greatest players of his era. Ellis might just have been the fittest Springbok of all time and his training was legendary, running in punishing heat up sand dunes carrying bricks. He played his first Test against the All Blacks in New Zealand in 1965 and his last against the All Blacks in Durban in 1976. In that time the Springboks played 39 Tests and Ellis played in all but the 1969 match against England, when he was injured. Ellis played a team game and yet was a loner. He avoided after-match functions, content to sit in the bus and wait for the others. On tour he was in bed early with a book. He was not a popular man, not even amongst those who admired him most. Jan Hendrik Ellis was born in Brakpan on 5 January 1942. He was young when he moved to Gobabis in South West Africa (now Namibia) and went to school there. From that remote town he captained South West African schools and then moved to Windhoek determined to make his way as a rugby player. In 1962, aged 20, he was chosen as a lock against the British & Irish Lions. From that remote part he became a Springbok at the age of 22. His career coincided with a topsy-turvy period in South African rugby, as it teetered on the brink of isolation and mixed ignominious defeats with outstanding victories – two series wins over New Zealand, a 3-0 series win over the Lions, a whitewash of the Wallabies and almost total domination of the French. Ellis played for most of his career in South West Africa but ended it at Transvaal from 1975-6. He played his club rugby for Otjiwarongo, United (Windhoek), Windhoek Wanderers and Kempton Park. He was an auctioneer and then a garage proprietor. In December 2000 he was shot in an armed robbery at his garage and his health suffered as a result. He is survived by wife Heila, a son, a daughter and five grandchildren, one of whose weddings he attended on the Saturday before he died.

PROFESSOR FRITZ ELOFF

FRITZ ELOFF, who died on 5 September 2013, was a great achiever and a gentleman, a professor with a cauliflower ear and a flattened boxer's nose. He was a man of great endurance. Eloff did everything at great length. He lived till he was 93, he was head of zoology at Pretoria University for 31 years, on the executive of the SA Rugby Board for 30 years, president of Northern Transvaal for 26 years, chairman of the National Parks Board for 16 years, chaired the Council of Curators, Transvaal Museum, for 28 years and served on the International Rugby Board for 27 years. He was 16 when he left Pietersburg Hoërskool and entered the University of Pretoria, 90 when he published a book on desert elephants and 93 when, in 2013, he published his last book. Of course he wrote many papers beside that for he was world-famous as a scientist, especially for his work in the Kalahari and with lions, most sensationally the white lions of Timbevati. In rugby Eloff was a player and an administrator. A wing at school, he eventually found that his speed was no good and played tighthead. He captained Tukkies for three years and played for Northern Transvaal from 1944-50 as a lock, eighthman and prop. He was a Springbok triallist in 1949. Studying in England in 1951 on a British Council bursary, he played for London Harlequins. His playing days over, Eloff coached Tukkies for four years, starting in 1954 when he also became head of the Department of Zoology. He retired in 1985 after 42 years of service. In 1960 Eloff was elected vice-president of the Northern Transvaal rugby Union and in 1965 he succeeded Dr Gert Potgieter as president and in his time Northern Transvaal were great. The combination of Eloff and Buurman van Zyl seemed unbeatable. Eloff became Craven's vice-president and actually took over as co-executive president when Craven died in 1993. He was part of the whole process of unity and chaired the first annual general meeting of SARFU in 1994. Eloff was the chairman of the International Rugby Board from 1989-90, when the office was for two years only. When Eloff retired he and wife Valerie (née Schraader) lived at Larmenier Village in Pretoria. Valerie died in August 2012 at the age of 84. They had been married for 65 years.

Frederick Christoffel Eloff was born on a farm between Pietersburg and Louis Trichardt on 18 May 1920. He is survived by daughters Elize and Marita, and two grandchildren.

GIBSON GAWULAYO

GIBSON GAWULAYO died in May 2012, aged 61, but his family did not hear about it till July 2013. He was born in Cape Town but moved to the Eastern Cape where he became a famous player. Back in Cape Town he was living on his own in a squatter camp and doing casual work when he became ill and went to Tygerberg Hospital, where he died. The hospital had nobody to contact and his body was donated to scientific research but the medical faculty of Stellenbosch University, which uses Tygerberg as its teaching hospital, returned his remains to his family in the Eastern Cape. The family then arranged a funeral service on 20 July 2013 and Gawulayo was laid to rest in the Matanzima cemetery in Uitenhage. Gawulayo rose to prominence as a schoolboy in East London at a time when Wallace Xotyeni and Norman Mbiko were the incumbent scrumhalves. He was chosen against the Proteas of the Federation in 1973 when the African Springboks/Leopards won 16-13 in East London and Gawulayo harassed the experienced Attie Lategan and scored a try. He, Xotyeni and Mbiko then swapped places regularly and in 1974 all three went on a tour to Italy. Xotyeni was at scrumhalf in the 'Test' with Mbiko on the flank.

Gawulayo was the Leopards' scrumhalf against France in 1975 when the French won at Mdantsane in East London and in 1976 when the Proteas beat them 13-6 at Newlands.

STEVE HILLOCK

YOU COULD not live in the Kenilworth-Rondebosch area of Cape Town and not know Steve Hillock, a lively and gregarious man whose dog was his constant companion. The thought of his dying seemed absurd. As a boy, Hillock was at Rondebosch Boys' High, captaining the 1st XV in 1965. In 2012 his son, Tim, a flyhalf, captained Rondebosch. Both father and son attended UCT. He was a wiry eighthman who played for WP from 1969-72. After UCT, he studied at Palmer College in Davenport, Iowa, and returned to South Africa to open a chiropractic practice.

Stephen Louis Hillock was born on 3 December 1947 and died in Vincent Pallotti Hospital on 26 April 2013, aged 65. He had developed severe circulatory problems, which required the amputation of his legs. He was survived by his two sons. He was an enormously popular man.

GEOFF HOLMES

GEOFF HOLMES came to the University of Cape Town from St Andrew's College in Grahamstown. Holmes was an outstanding wing who played for WP from 1959-60 as a centre. In 1959, WP won the Currie Cup and in the two crucial matches against Transvaal Holmes was a centre with Colin Greenwood, later a Springbok. In 1960, Holmes was at centre with Daantjie Bornman of Stellenbosch for Southern Universities against the All Blacks, who won 14-3 at Newlands. Holmes graduated from UCT with BSc Engineering (1960) and BCom (1963) degrees.

Geoffrey Noel Carleton Holmes was born on 20 October 1937 and died on 28 January 2013, aged 75.

DAANTJIE IMMELMAN

DAANTJIE IMMELMAN not only played and coached but was also the first of three generations of prominent referees. Flying and rugby were great loves of his. Born in Prieska in the Northern Cape, he joined the South African Air Force and fought in World War II and the Korean War. In all he was in the air force for 44 years, long based at Langebaanweg. There was a remarkable incident in the last days of the Korean war which made a tiny bit of history. The war ended in August 1953 but in April, Immelman's 2nd Squadron, the Flying Cheetahs, played a rugby match in Tokyo against Waseda University, still a prominent side in Japan. Playing days over he became a first-league referee in Boland for many years. His son Dennis became a provincial referee and now flies to many parts of the world to assess referees working for the IRB. Dennis's son Quinton is currently on SA's elite panel of 10 referees.

Daniel Gerhardus Immelman was born on 27 January 1923 and grew up near Marydale, a son of the Karoo. He died on 18 August 2012, aged 89, survived by Daphne, his wife of 62 years, daughter Cheryll-Anne and son Dennis, grandchildren and great grandchildren.

LAURIE KAY

NOBODY WHO was at Ellis Park for that thrilling, glorious World Cup final in 1995 will forget the SAA Boeing 747 that flew over Ellis Park. It made a massive statement that all South Africans associated with. It was a moment that will live on in rugby's recorded history for ever, a story to tell the world, yet strangely enough pilot Laurie Kay's widow, Adrienne, says that he did not think it special – just another day's work. But the impact was astonishing. His main concern was being able to get back to watch the match! When the Hollywood film Invictus was made, Kay was required to give Clint Eastwood advice and he struck up a friendship with Morgan Freeman, who played Nelson Mandela. Through the flypast, which was a first of its kind and took the world by storm, Kay got to know people all over the world and through it he became involved in guide dogs. He had a DVD made of the flyover and sold many of them. All the money from every DVD went to the South African Guide Dog Association. Adrienne says that Laurie claimed he had never done a day's work in his life, such was his love of flying and everything associated with it. He was six when he joined the South African Air Boys Club in Malvern, Johannesburg. He would get a lift on an older boy's bicycle to Rand Airport. He would later get flips on SAA aircraft. When he finished school at Jeppe, he applied to join the Air Force, but was turned down. Not daunted, he wrote to air forces around the world and the RAF accepted him in 1967. Trained, he came back to South Africa and joined SAA. After retiring from commercial flying at 60, he was a member of the Harvard Club of South Africa and at the time of his death Kay, who loved the Bushveld, was in the Kruger Park flying helicopters in an effort to thwart rhino poachers.

Laurence Arnold Kay was born in Johannesburg on 5 May 1945. He died of a heart attack at Skukuza in the Kruger National Park, survived by Adrienne, his wife of 36 years, children Roy, Helen and Laurienne & grandchildren.

JOHAN KEMP

JOHAN KEMP'S death was horrible. Three burglars broke into his Randburg home while he and his wife were sleeping in the early hours of the morning. They shot and killed him as he lay in bed. Fortunately their two young sons were left alone. Not long afterwards a Zimbabwean suspect was arrested. He went to school at Westcliff in Bellville and made his provincial debut for the Golden Lions in the Vodacom Cup, playing six times for them. Then he went to Port Elizabeth and played for EP.

Johan Kemp was born in February 1979 and was killed on 28 March 2013, aged 34, survived by wife Elaine and children Christopher (4) and Christiaan (2).

MARTIENS LOUW

MARTIENS LOUW and Robbie Barnard [see separate entry], hooker and prop, who played together for Transvaal and South Africa, died just over a week apart. Louw died in Pretoria on 12 October 2013 and Barnard on 20 October. Louw was 75, Barnard 71. Louw played for Transvaal from 1969-74. He and Barnard both played in the front row for Piet Greyling's Transvaal team when they drew the 1971 Currie Cup final but neither was in the winning team that beat Eastern Transvaal the following year. That year Louw broke an ankle early in the season. Louw and Barnard were both were chosen for the 1971 Springbok tour of Australia. After his playing days, Louw was a Transvaal selector, coached Vereeniging and when Vaal Triangle was formed in 1984 he was the new province's vice-president and their coach. He played for Vereeniging at a time when it was one of the strongest clubs in Transvaal.

Marthinus Johannes Louw was born in Germiston on 20 April 1938 and educated at Hoërskool Vereeniging. He suffered heart problems for several years and died in a Pretoria Hospital on 12 October 2013, aged 75, three months after a heart attack. He is survived by wife Suzette, their three daughters Riana Barkhuizen, Suzette Miller and Erika Delport, and five grandchildren.

DR LOUIS LUYT

LOUIS LUYT, one of the outstanding personalities in South African rugby, died on 1 February 2013, aged 80. Luyt, who became a vastly wealthy man and a generous one, was certainly not born with a silver spoon in his mouth. His biological father, Poley, turned out to be a bigamist, which left the family desperately poor when he was found out and fled to his first family in Cape Town. His mother married Charles Luyt, a labourer, and Luyt took his stepfather's surname. Louis Luyt was born in Britstown on 18 June 1932, when the Great Depression was at its worst, and spent his youth in dire poverty, rescued by hard work at school and by rugby. By the time he was 11, he was the second of nine children, and was required to be up at 4.30am on icy Karoo mornings to work in a bakery or even at 1.30am to irrigate a vegetable garden. He delivered meat from the butcher in return for some to take home to a family that often had no food to eat. Home was sometimes a corrugated iron shack as the family shifted about. But he showed an aptitude for rugby and played – as a fullback – for the Hanover senior team where he was spotted by the coach at the Colesberg school, who offered him two years with free books and free boarding though even that was not enough and Luyt worked his holidays for meagre pay. Matriculated at 16, he went to Bloemfontein and a job as a labourer on the railways. Luyt joined the Railway club in Bloemfontein and graduated from fullback to flyhalf to eighthman to lock, and at 19 he first played for Free State, against Eastern Transvaal on 27 May 1952, the first of 52 caps. His last game was on 6 July 1960 when Free State beat the All Blacks 9-8. It was not the end of his playing career for in 1965 he played a match for Northern Transvaal. From the railways in Bloemfontein he worked underground on a gold mine in Welkom, then was a salesman for Caltex and then a rep for Fisons, the fertiliser company. When his commission earned him twice the managing director's pay, Fisons dropped his commission from 7.5% to 2%. Luyt moved to Pretoria and started Louis Luyt Enterprises. He was to start Triomf and become the fertiliser king of South Africa at the age of 38. In all the work and play, Luyt managed to study after hours and ended with an earned doctorate as well as an honorary one. With his brusque manner, he was not a popular man except to those who knew him and knew of his kindness. His achievements for rugby were enormous – he helped Dr Craven in brokering the deals with the ANC that led to the unification of rugby; he saved Ellis Park, turning around a substantial debt into a healthy profit, and an offshore investment of R67 million when he resigned; he ran what was till then the best run, most lucrative Rugby World Cup and then he saved rugby when he fought off the attempt by Kerry Packer and his men to take over the sport. Luyt was at the birth of SANZAR, which negotiated a massive deal with Rupert Murdoch and got Super Rugby and Tri-Nations going. In the negotiations with Murdoch he managed to get a better deal for South Africa than the other two got. He was an excellent chairman of meetings with his crisp efficiency, and he became the president of SARFU – the unified South African rugby Football Union. As the leader he took the blame.

The founding of the Citizen newspaper and the subsequent Infogate scandal that toppled Prime Minister John Vorster was a bad idea. The 1986 New Zealand Cavaliers rebel tour was a questionable idea. When SARFU took Nelson Mandela to court, Luyt was blamed though it was a SARFU decision. He resigned from rugby after the case, though Mandela remained warm and friendly. When he had been inaugurated as South Africa's president in 1994, he mentioned two rugby names in his speech – Doc Craven and Louis Luyt, for they of all establishment sports administrators met the ANC. Luyt thereafter became a member of parliament and it was at his home that the Democratic Alliance was formed.

Born Oswald Louis Petrus Poleÿ he was adopted by his mother's husband Charles Luyt. Luyt met Adri in 1957 and married her in 1958. They had four children – two daughters and two sons. He is survived by Adri, their children Corlia, Lucien, Louis and Nossie, and grandchildren.

MADODA MAVALELISO

MADODANDILE MAVALELISO came to DHS from Port Elizabeth on a rugby scholarship and showed great promise, a popular boy whose nickname was Madoda. He played for DHS's Under-14 side against Hoerskool Transvalia in the Bizsport rugby tournament hosted by Glenwood. After the match he felt ill and was taken to Entabeni Hospital, not far from Glenwood. When Madoda arrived at the hospital he was in a coma and despite medical efforts to save him, he died of bacterial meningitis on 28 March 2013. The illness was not related to rugby. Out of respect, Glenwood then withdrew its teams from the tournament and its 1st XV from Maritzburg College's 150th birthday festivities.

VUYO MBULI

VUYO MBULI was a particularly popular SABC television and radio announcer, known in particular for his Morning Live television programme, which he hosted for 13 years. He was in Bloemfontein for the Super Rugby match between the Cheetahs and the Reds at the Free State Stadium. On the morning before the evening match he had been to see his 75-year-old father before driving to Bloemfontein with his son Sithenkosi. During the match Mbuli collapsed. He was treated at the ground and then rushed to the nearby Medi-Clinic, where he died, aged 46, on 18 May 2013, survived by wife Savita and their children.

FRANCIS MELLISH

YOU DO not easily find men of greater integrity, loyalty and dependability than Francis Mellish. When his conviction told him that he had to do something, he did it. The Mellishes came to South Africa as 1820 Settlers but Francis's family came from the Eastern Cape to Cape Town where he was born. The family farm was called Vredehoek. Now there is a suburb of that name where the farm was. Francis went to SACS which was then in town and close to the farm, and he stayed loyal to SACS till he died. He was a vice-president of the SACS Old Boys' Union. When the school moved to Newlands, Francis was close by and for years, a heavy man, he refereed the Under-15 side with intense concentration. After school Francis joined Old Mutual, where he stayed all his life. The head office was then in town and Francis naturally played for Hamiltons, whom he captained. He first played prop for WP in 1939. When World War II broke out, Francis joined up. He did his basics in Potchefstroom prior to going up north. While there he played for the Garrison side and Western Transvaal. Back from the War, Francis went back to Hamiltons, one of 17 Mellishes to play for SA's oldest club! After his playing days he coached the 1st XV. When the Old Mutual sent Francis to Bloemfontein, he coached Old Greys and famously dropped Basie Viviers, the Springbok captain, from his team, saying that Ben Kloppers of Old Greys and Free State was "100%" better than Viviers. In Jan Pickard's time, when Newlands was virtually rebuilt, Francis served as his senior vice-president, and had a great deal to do with the negotiations that led to clubs of the Federation and the SA Coloured Rugby Board's joining of the union and then the more demanding 1990s when politically acceptable unification was set in motion.

Francis Carr Bayly Mellish was born in Cape Town in 1917. He was thus 96 when he died at his home in Somerset West in 2013. He had enjoyed good health but suffered a stroke the week before he died. He is survived by wife Moraig (nee Stewart), children Eddie, Liz and Charles, grandchildren and great grandchildren.

FRIKKIE MEYER

FRIKKIE MEYER was a man of Despatch near Port Elizabeth. He was born there, educated there, played rugby there, did business there, died and is buried there. Meyer, a centre or wing, first played for EP in 1967 and was a Springbok triallist eight times. He was the first Despatch player ever invited to Springbok trials. He could play on either wing but was mostly a right wing with a remarkable sidestep. He ended his provincial career in 1975, after playing 75 times for EP, sometimes as captain. In Despatch there is a furniture business – Frikkie Meyer Meubels – which Frikkie started. Father and son were close – both in the furniture business and both rugby players. Frikkie Jnr played for EP age-group teams in the 1990s and then from 1995 for Eastern Province B in the President's Cup for seven years.

Frederick Benjamin Meyer was born in Graaff-Reinet on 4 December 1945 and he died on 28 July 2013, aged 67, survived by wife Florence, sons Frikkie Jnr and Charl, daughter Marie and four grandchildren.

SIMON MJO

SIMO MJO'S talents went beyond rugby but on the field he is regarded as the best-ever scrumhalf for the African Springboks. In addition he became the first black actor to feature in East London's Guild Theatre, in a drama adapted from John Steinbeck's classic 1937 novel, Of Mice and Men, staged in 1975. He later moved to PE where he worked in the insurance industry and established the Port Elizabeth Classics. Mjo was a dedicated member of the ANC and so was arrested and imprisoned at Viljoen's Drift Prison in Kroonstad. In prison he started a vocal group called The Lords. Out of jail, he found getting employment difficult and so spent time organising sporting events and started a choir, The East London Harmony Set, which performed African music as well as European classics. But it was at rugby that Mjo made his name in a great career cut short by his arrest. He and flyhalf Eric Majola, called the Black Brewis, formed a great combination. When Mjo was arrested Majola gave up, believing that no other scrumhalf could look after him the way Mjo did. In 1956, when Mjo was playing for Swallows in East London, he made his debut for Border and in 1959 for the African Springboks in a drawn match against the SA Coloured Board team in Johannesburg. He was in the team again for the next 'Test' when the African Springboks won 12-6. The next match was in September 1963, which was after Mjo had been arrested and jailed, causing Majola to pull out.

Simon Mzwandile Cyril Mjo was born at KwaTsolo Township in East London on 2 July 1935. He was educated at the Presbyterian Church's Upper Mission Primary School, Welsh High School and Fort Hare, where his captain was the tough flank Dumile Kondile, now a retired judge. He died on 18 June 2013, aged 77, survived by his wife, seven children, seven grandchildren and two great-grandchildren.

KWENA MOREMI

KWENA MOREMI was playing prop for Leopards Under-19 when they and their Under-21 team went down to East London to play Border, whom they beat 19-16. Moremi started the match at loosehead. After the match, the two teams from the dry interior went down to the beach. He and a dozen others were caught in a rip tide. Despite help Moremi drowned. Moremi was born in Kempton Park and attended Rhodesfield Technical High School in Kempton Park and played for the Valke Under-16 at the Grant Khomo Week in 2009 and 2010. He then moved to HTS Louis Botha in Bloemfontein and played for Free State in the 2011 Craven Week. From school he went up to Rustenburg to the Impala-Leopards Sports Academy where he played rugby and studied engineering.

Kwena Collins Moremi was born on 24 March 1994 and died on 13 September 2013, aged 19, survived by his parents living in Thembisa.

BOBBY MURTAGH

BOBBY MURTAGH, an energetic lock, was most popular with all who knew him, but not one who settled easily. His death was a miserable one, killed in a train accident at Vasco Station in Cape Town. Murtagh played for Villagers and Goodwood and for San Dona in Italy for three seasons. In 1978, when he was just 21, he played twice for Western Province.

Robert George Murtagh was born in Cape Town on 30 April 1957. He went to school at Pinelands Junior and then at De Villiers Graaff High in Villiersdorp. At the time of his death he was working for a fresh produce company in Montagu Gardens. He died on 7 July 2012, aged 55, survived by ex-wife Anna-Marie and children Monique and Robert.

WALLY NEWING

WALLY NEWING was a career soldier who rose to a great rank and lived to a great age. He was Brigadier General WJ Newing of the South African Defence Force, whom he joined from school. He played on the flank for Northern Transvaal from 1941-52. Not originally invited to the 1949 Springbok trials in Pretoria when the All Blacks came to South Africa, he nonetheless played in them. His club was Garrison in Pretoria. After his playing days Newing was a Northern Transvaal selector and the coach of the Defence team.

Wallace Jefferson Newing was born in Kokstad on 16 May 1919. He attended Kokstad High where he captained the rugby team before going on to the Army College where he played for Northern Natal. He and his wife Madeleine Susan had two children, Maliene-Sue and Jeffery William, who died before his father. Newing died in Pretoria on 12 June 2013, aged 94. He is survived by five grandchildren and eight great-grandchildren.

IVAN NURICK

IVAN NURICK did not play rugby but he had the most astonishing knowledge of the game's history and especially that of the University of Cape Town RFC, which was for over 60 years his passion and to which he was utterly loyal. Ask him about the 1952 Intervarsity and he could give a commentary of the game, tell you who scored tries, kicked conversions and penalties and the names of the teams and the referee. But he was not dry but rather a lively and entertaining man, this anaesthetist and raconteur. He read history at UCT and clearly he had a freakish memory. Sadly, much information died with him. Ivan James Nurick was born in Indwe, an Eastern Cape town between Dordrecht and Elliot, once an important coal-mining centre. Nurick's father had a hotel there and Nurick went to school there and then at Queen's College in Queenstown, from where he went to UCT to read medicine.

Nurick was born on 25 August 1934 and died after a long battle with cancer in Cape Town in November 2013, aged 79, survived by wife Shirley, sons Matthew, Philip and Gideon and their wives, and nine grandchildren.

PIET OLIVIER

IT'S HARD to establish ranking in Pretoria where so many people have titles but being Mayor of Pretoria and President of the Blue Bulls Rugby Union must rank high, and Piet Olivier was both of those.

Olivier studied on a bursary at Pretoria University, graduating with a science degree in iron and steel studies and an MBA. The Bursary came from Iscor for whom he worked from 1953-93, ending as the managing director of Steelforged, an Iscor subsidiary. He began a career in rugby administration in 1977 as the chairman of the Iscor RFC, a position he held till 1992 when the club amalgamated with Pretoria Technikon RFC and he was then the chairman of the new club till 1998. He served on the committee of the Northern Transvaal Rugby Union from 1979-84. He became the deputy president to Hentie Serfontein in 1996. From 1998-2001 he was president of the Union. From 1990-2001 he served on the Pretoria city council and the executive of the Pretoria metro council. In 1996 he became the mayor of the Greater Pretoria, succeeded by Joyce Ngele of the ANC, who defeated Olivier, of the National Party, in an election.

Petrus Johannes Olivier was born in Springs on 2 March 1935. He died of cancer in the Little Company of Mary Hospital in Pretoria on 14 January 2013, aged 77, survived by wife Colleen and their children.

PA PELSER

PA PELSER was a great rugby man and a great teacher, much revered as a player and then as a coach, a man who combined dedication with a great sense of humour.

He went to school at Monument in Krugersdorp, a tall boy, his height enhanced by piled up hair on the top of his head, who first played in the 1st XV in 1941. He matriculated in 1944 and went off to Potchefstroom Normal College. Then he went back to Monument to teach. There he played for West Rand RFC which won the Pirates Grand Challenge in 1947 and 1952 and shared it with Diggers in 1956. Between his debut in 1947 and his retirement in 1955, he played 60 times for Transvaal, a vast number for those days. In 1947 he was in the Transvaal team beaten by Western Province in the Currie Cup final at Newlands. In 1949 Pelser played in the Springbok trials to pick the team to play the touring All Blacks. He was in the Transvaal side, captained by his great friend Piet Malan, that lost 6-3 to the All Blacks. In 1953 Basie Wyk captained Transvaal when Pelser scored a try and Transvaal beat the Wallabies 20-14. He played twice against the great 1955 Lions, for Transvaal and then for the Junior Springboks, whom he captained. He was the sort of player who would have played many Tests in the modern era. He coached Transvaal from 1972, when they won the Currie Cup, to 1974 and again from 1985 to 1988 when Transvaal were twice losing finalists.

Pieter Andries Pelser was born in Rustenburg in 1924, his names inherited from his grandfather and it was his initials, not any aged appearance, that gave him his nickname, Pa. After his retirement he and his wife Rina settled in St Francis Bay. His health deteriorated in his last years and he died in Port Elizabeth on 29 October 2013, survived by Rina and their three daughters, and six grandchildren.

ALAN READ

ALAN READ was so full of life that it's hard to think of him dying – handsome, confident and laughing.

After school at Cradock Boys' High, Read went to Cape Town to learn about being a building contractor and played for Hamiltons. Later he played for Stellenbosch. In 1970, Read made his debut for Western Province at centre against Griquas in Kimberley, the same match in which Morné du Plessis made his debut. The big, blond, fearless three-quarter was more effective on the wing, using his speed and strength to good effect. He played for WP from 1970-74. In 1974, he was a Springbok triallist. In 1974, playing left wing, Read scored a try against the Lions. Read was also a lifesaver at famous, glamorous Clifton with it beaches. A building contractor, Read lived by himself at Keurbooms River, near Plettenberg Bay. Two weeks before he died, Springboks Peter Whipp and Dugald Macdonald went up to see him and Read proclaimed himself well.

Alan Oliver Read was born in Cradock on 3 September 1948 and died suddenly at his home in Keurbooms River on 29 January 2013, aged 64, survived by two daughters.

BASJAN REINHARDT

BASJAN REINHARDT, the principal of Paarl Gim from 1992-2008, died suddenly of a heart attack in the early hours of Saturday morning, 19 October 2013, in Dwarskersbos on the West Coast where he and his wife were on holiday. He had turned 65 the day before. Reinhardt started his teaching career at Hoërskool Warrenton where he had matriculated. He then moved to Kathu, Hugenote in Wellington and then on to Cradock, where he was the principal, after which he came to Paarl Gim. On his retirement, Reinhardt returned to the Northern Cape and for three years was attached to Hoërskool Diamantveld as its operations manager. He was then able to start his Super Schools programme with sponsorship from Wildeklawer. The first tournament was held at Paarl Gim with 12 of South Africa's top schools present by invitation. The next year it moved to Affies with 16 schools. In 2010, 2011 and 2012 it was held at Diamantveld before moving in 2013 to Maritzburg College as a part of that great school's 150th birthday celebrations.

Born in Boshof on 18 October 1948, Sebastiaan Reinhardt is survived by wife Harriet, whom he first met in Kuruman, their two children Basie and Riëtte and three grandchildren.

HENDRIK ROODT

HENDRIK ROODT, whose unfortunate nickname was Verwoerd, was a tough hooker who did the basics so well that he played for Northern Transvaal, making his debut in 1989 when the number-one hooker was Uli Schmidt. He was a policeman and when transferred to Port Elizabeth in 1992 he hooked for Eastern Province and for Despatch for two seasons till suddenly transferred back to Pretoria. In 1989, Roodt was a member of the South African Police team that toured Chile. Hendrik Lambertus Roodt was born in Lichtenburg on 4 July 1965. He went to Hoërskool Lichtenburg and represented Stellaland at Craven Week. He died of heart complications on 11 September 2013, aged 48, survived by wife Dedrei and their children Marlize, Vean and Dewalt.

Like his father, son Vean is a hooker, excellent at his basics and as a fourth loose forward. He is at Hoërskool Centurion and represented the Blue Bulls at the 2012 and 2013 Craven Weeks.

RODERICK ROSSOUW

RODERICK ROSSOUW was a dedicated schoolmaster. He was 25 and on the staff when Bertram Secondary School opened in January 1985 in the north of Port Elizabeth. He started rugby at the school. Later he was the force behind the Night Series for Port Elizabeth schools rugby. When the school celebrated its 25th birthday in 2010 Rossouw was happily there, proud that his school was the best rugby school in the area. Rossouw was an assistant coach of the EP senior team.

In January 2013 he was diagnosed with cancer cancer and on 23 March 2013 he died at the age of 53, survived by wife Cheryl and daughters Tarryn, Ronia and Chelsey.

GENèVE SCHOLTZ

GENÈVE SCHOLTZ, a young, promising women's rugby player died after being injured in a match in her home town of Middelburg in the Karoo. She was playing flank for the Middelburg Stormers against the Kwaru Girls. Medics at the match attended to her and she was rushed by ambulance to Humansdorp Hospital. He condition was clearly critical and she was being taken by helicopter to hospital in Port Elizabeth when she died. She was 23. In 2008, she was chosen for South Africa Under-20 to play the USA and in 2011 she was called up to the SA Women's training squad.

Genève Scholtz was born in Middelburg in 1990 and died on 9 March 2013, survived by mother Lena Meyer and her sisters.

NIC SLABBERT

NIC SLABBERT, whose nickname was Butch, was once described by Danie Craven as "that great leader of forwards". Slabbert was born in Lichtenburg before moving to Pretoria Technical College where he captained the 1st XV for three years. He then captained Northern Transvaal Under-19 before moving to Wits University whom he captained from 1940-45, described as one of Wits' greatest captains. He had played for Transvaal from 1942-45 when he moved to Kimberley and played for Griquas from 1946-48. Slabbert graduated from Wits with a degree in mining engineering. Kimberley was a good place to start and when the goldfields were opened in the Free State he moved there and ended his working life as manager of the Hartebeesfontein gold mine, then the second largest in the world. After he retired he lived on there, managing a dairy farm. Then in 2006, incredibly at the age of 88, he and his wife emigrated to Fort Smith in Arkansas to be with their family there.

Nicolaas Johannes Slabbert was born in Lichtenburg on 28 September 1918. He died in Fort Smith in the USA on 17 August 2013, aged 94, survived by his wife of 66 years Sannie-Marie, whom he had met at Wits, daughters Zephnè Ferreira, Nicolette Atkins, son Christiaan and their spouses, and five grandchildren.

TOMMY SYMONS

TOMMY SYMONS enjoyed a twelve-season career for Transvaal, one of the union's most charismatic players. He played for Transvaal 85 times between 1966 and 1977 – a centre, wing or (twice) a fullback, scoring 45 tries. In 1971 he played against France and in the Currie Cup final. In fact he played in three finals – one drawn, one won and one lost. In 1973, he scored five tries in a match against Newport. In 1974, he played against the great Lions and in 1976 against the All Blacks, who beat Transvaal 12-10. He was also a Junior Springbok – in the days when it was virtually a Springbok second team – and a Springbok triallist in 1974.

Thomas Alfred Williams Symons was born in Germiston on 8 April 1945. He went to school at Dr EG Jansen in Boksburg and played for Germiston Simmer. He died on 30 January 2013, aged 67, in Pretoria after a long period of kidney problems, survived by wife Estelle, their children and grandchildren. He was a draughtsman.

MORNé VAN DER MERWE

MORNÉ VAN der Merwe was a powerful loosehead prop forward but he was only 39 when he died. In rugby he was a wanderer, taking his strength and skill to many places. Born in Port Elizabeth, he played first for Eastern Province in 1995 and then for the Lions, Sharks, Wellington in New Zealand and for Western Province and the Stormers. He was in the Wellington side in 2000 when it won New Zealand's NPC. He had gone to New Zealand as part of his honeymoon. The next year he was back playing for WP and the Stormers. He ended his playing career in 2004, when he was 32. He played 11 times for the Stormers and 29 times for WP. In all he played over 100 first-class matches. Van der Merwe, a genial, highly religious man, fought a two-year battle against brain cancer before he died.

Morné van der Merwe was born 28 March 1973. He attended school at Westering in Port Elizabeth. He died in Cape Town on 18 January 2013, survived by wife Cindy and their young sons Joshua and Matthew.

PIET VAN DEVENTER

PIETER IGNATIUS van Deventer was born in Krugersdorp on 6 June 1946. He went to school at Barkly East. He was first in the police force and played for Pretoria Police. He then moved to the manganese mines and played for Ammosal and Griqualand West. He was just 19 when he first played for Griquas and played 55 times for them between 1966 and 1974. He was on the flank for Griquas in 1970 when they did the impossible, beating Northern Transvaal to win the Currie Cup final. He became a Springbok in 1969 when he went on the demo tour to the UK and Ireland, playing in 12 of the matches, but not in any Tests.

A remarkably fit man in his playing days, Piet van Deventer suffered a heart attack on Thursday 14 March 2013, went to the doctor during the early hours of Friday morning and died in Krugersdorp Hospital early on Saturday morning, 16 March 2013, aged 66. He was survived by wife Marietjie.

FRANS VAN JAARSVELD

FRANS VAN Jaarsveld first played prop for Western Province in 1980 and then played five more times in 1981, the year before WP started their triumphant run of five successive Currie Cup victories. Van Jaarsveld was a policeman for 35 years, first in the railway police and then with the SAP after amalgamation, ending in 2000 as a detective inspector. After leaving the police force he worked for Auction Alliance for 10 years. He was setting up for an auction in Maitland when he felt a pain in his chest. He thought it was heartburn but he was rushed to Vincent Pallotti Hospital where he, a healthy, fit and strong man, died of a heart attack.

Frans Johan Niklaas van Jaarsveld was born in Cape Town on 21 August 1949. He died on 18 November 2013, aged 64, survived by Lynette, his wife of 42 years, daughters Zelda and Francette and two grandsons.

SAILOR VAN SCHALKWYK

SAILOR VAN Schalkwyk was playing for Police when he was chosen to play prop in one match for Northern Transvaal in 1953. After his playing days were over, he became a referee, a heavy man who was very much one of the characters of his day. When he left school at Paul Roos in Stellenbosch, Van Schalkwyk joined the navy and was in the armoury where he learnt the armourer's trade. In the police force, he was a brilliant armourer and travelled to many parts. When he retired he had the rank of warrant officer, but when asked his rank he would answer, "Oom Sailor". When he was doing his police training in Pretoria he shared a room with another trainee, Tom van Vollenhoven, the great Springbok three-quarter. When Sailor married hairdresser Yvonne, Van Vollenhoven was his best man. Pieter Jacobus van Schalkwyk was born in Stellenbosch on 14 May 1930 and died in the Wilgers Hospital in Pretoria on 2 June 2013, aged 83, survived by Yvonne, his wife of 58 years, their son and daughter, two grandchildren and a great-granddaughter who was born just before he died and whose picture he was shown.

GERDA VON SOLMS

RUGBY IS a man's game, they say, but mostly the efficient organisation is in the hands of women. Gerda van Solms was very much one of those women, ending her long career as the CEO of the Free State Rugby Union. If you wanted anything of the union, you phoned Gerd'. After all she was there for 37 years – not just was there, but very much in control. When Gerda van der Westhuizen, then aged 21, and Gerdri Fourie went to work at the Union in 1976, they were the first full-time secretaries the organisation had had. She advanced to manager in 1998 and CEO in 2003, the first woman in South African rugby to hold such a position. Gerda von Solms was born in Bloemfontein on 1 February 1955 and caught rugby fever from her father, making scrapbooks when a schoolgirl.

Gerda von Solms died on 5 April 2013, aged 58, after leaving work the day before with a stomach pain. She was admitted to hospital and died the next day, survived by husband Piet, whom she married in 1986, and three stepchildren.

BRETT WILLIAMS

BRETT WILLIAMS' death is unique in the history of South African rugby and probably its blackest. Williams was born in South Africa but moved with his family to Liverpool when a child. He joined the Royal Marines in 2001 and saw action in Afghanistan and Iraq. After he left the Marines in 2012, he was employed by a maritime security company to protect cargo against pirates off East Africa. His ship docked in Durban and he went to watch rugby at Kings Park prior to heading to an uncle in Johannesburg, intending to re-enlist with the Marines when he got back to England. After the match he got into an argument with five Sharks supporters. This led to a fight and in it he was killed. Five men were arrested and brought to court.

Brett Williams was 29 when he was killed on 23 March 2013, survived by fiancée Louise Scott, their four-year-old daughter, Lailah, his parents and other relatives.

A-Z OF FIRST-CLASS PLAYERS IN 2013

A complete list of all 851 players who appeared in a first-class match in South Africa in 2013.

A

Abrahams, Keenan Marc (Klein Nederburg HS) b 07/08/1991, Paarl. 1.89m. 140kg. Prop. FC DEBUT: 2013. PROV CAREER: Boland 2013 1-0-0-0-0-0. FC RECORD: 1-0-0-0-0-0. RECORD IN 2013: (Boland) 1-0-0-0-0-0.

Abrahams, Yuseph Williams (Boela) (Hentie Cilliers HS) b 23/07/1988, Port Elizabeth. 1.63m. 65kg. Scrumhalf. FC DEBUT: 2007. PROV CAREER: Griffons 2007-09 4-0-0-0-0-0. EP Kings 2011-13 20-0-0-0-0. REP HONOURS: SA Kings 2011 2-0-0-0-0-0. SA Barbarians 2012 1-0-0-0-0-0. FC RECORD: 27-0-0-0-0-0. RECORD IN 2013: (EP Kings) 7-0-0-0-0-0.

Acker, Daniel Enrico (Outeniqua HS, George & UFS) b 23/09/1990, Bloemfontein. 1.74m. 80kg. Scrumhalf. FC DEBUT: 2011. PROV CAREER: Cheetahs 2011 8-3-0-0-0-15. Griffons 2013 1-0-0-0-0-0. Griquas 2013 6-2-0-0-0-10. FC RECORD: 15-5-0-0-0-25. RECORD IN 2013: (Griquas, Griffons) 7-2-0-0-0-10.

Adams, Duane Hershelle Nicholas (Despatch HS) b 02/03/1992, De Aar. 1.87m. 91kg. Fullback. FC DEBUT: 2013. PROV CAREER: Bulldogs 2013 4-1-0-0-0-5. FC RECORD: 4-1-0-0-0-5. RECORD IN 2013: (Bulldogs) 4-1-0-0-0-5.

Adams, Tythan Franco (Paul Roos Gymnasium. & US) b 31/08/1990, Vredenburg. 1.75m. 82kg. Wing. FC DEBUT: 2012. PROV CAREER: Eagles 2012 1-0-0-0-0-0. Boland 2013 8-2-0-0-0-10. FC RECORD: 9-2-0-0-0-10. RECORD IN 2013: (Boland) 8-2-0-0-0-10.

Adendorff, Jonathan Wallis (Napier HS & US) b 23/08/1985, Napier. 1.91m. 102kg. Flank. FC DEBUT: 2011. PROV CAREER: Pumas 2011 5-0-0-0-0-0. Griquas 2012-13 19-2-0-0-0-10. FC RECORD: 24-2-0-0-0-10. RECORD IN 2013: (Griquas) 9-1-0-0-0-5.

Adendorff, Shaun (Glenwood HS & UP) b 28/05/1992, Durban. 1.85m. 100kg. Flank. FC DEBUT: 2012. PROV CAREER: Blue Bulls 2013 3-0-0-0-0-0. REP HONOURS: SA U20 2012 3-2-0-0-0-10. FC RECORD: 6-2-0-0-0-10. RECORD IN 2013: (Blue Bulls) 3-0-0-0-0-0.

Adongo, Daniel Ojambo (Strathmore HS & Varsity College) b 12/10/1989, Nairobi. 1.97m. 112kg. Lock. FC DEBUT: 2011. PROV CAREER: Sharks XV 2011 10-3-0-0-0-0. Blue Bulls 2012 8-1-0-0-0-5. EP Kings 2013 4-0-0-0-0-0. SUPERRUGBY: Southern Kings 2013 5-0-0-0-0-0. FC RECORD: 27-4-0-0-0-20. RECORD IN 2013: (Southern Kings, EP Kings) 9-0-0-0-0-0.

Adriaanse, Lourens Cornelius (Paarl Gymnasium & Stellenbosch Univ.) b 05/02/1988, Cape Town. 1.81m. 115kg. Prop. FC DEBUT: 2009. PROV CAREER: Griquas 2011-13 37-3-0-0-0-15. SUPERRUGBY: Cheetahs 2011-13 30-0-0-0-0-0. REP HONOURS: SA 2013 1-0-0-0-0-0. SA Students 2009 2-0-0-0-0-0. MISC INFO: Brother of Jacobie Adriaanse. FC RECORD: 70-3-0-0-0-15. RECORD IN 2013: (SA, Cheetahs S15, Griquas) 23-0-0-0-0-0.

Afrika, Cecil Sebastian (Hentie Cilliers HS) b 03/03/88, Port Elizabeth. 1.77m. 65kg. Fullback. FC DEBUT: 2006. PROV CAREER: Griffons 2006-09 48-36-2-0-1-187. REP HONOURS: SA U20 2008 4-1-0-0-0-5. SA Sevens 2009-13. SA Schools 2006. MISC INFO: IRB Sevens PoY 2010 -11. SARU Sevens PoY 2012. FC RECORD: 52-37-2-0-1-192. RECORD IN 2013: (SA Sevens).

Afrika, Leroy Danny (St. Albans HS) b 17/08/1992, Kimberley. 1.80m. 82kg. Centre. FC DEBUT: 2013. PROV CAREER: Young Lions 2013 1-0-0-0-0-0. FC RECORD: 1-0-0-0-0-0. RECORD IN 2013: (Young Lions) 1-0-0-0-0-0.

Agaba, Timothy Ernest Victor Kwizera (Stirling HS & NMMU) b 23/07/1989, Kampala. 1.93m. 106kg. Eightman. FC DEBUT: 2013. PROV CAREER: EP Kings 2013 12-2-0-0-0-10. REP HONOURS: SA Univ 2013 1-0-0-0-0-0. FC RECORD: 13-2-0-0-0-10. RECORD IN 2013: (EP Kings, SA Univ) 13-2-0-0-0-10.

Alberts, Gert Dirk Jacobus (Jacques) (Helpmekaar HS, Jhbg) b 17/01/1991, Johannesburg. 2.02m. 98kg. Lock. FC DEBUT: 2011. PROV CAREER: Valke 2011-13 32-1-0-0-0-5. FC RECORD: 32-1-0-0-0-5. RECORD IN 2013: (Valke) 17-0-0-0-0-0.

Alberts, Willem Schalk (Monument HS, Krugersdorp) b 11/05/1984, Pretoria. 1.92m. 1209kg. Lock. FC DEBUT: 2005. PROV CAREER: Lions 2005 & 07-09 35-7-0-0-0-35. Lions XV 2007-08 2-1-0-0-0-5. Young Lions 2005 3-0-0-0-0-0. KZN 2010-13 19-4-0-0-0-20. Sharks XV 2013 2-2-0-0-0-10. SUPERRUGBY: Lions 2007-09 37-4-0-0-0-20. Sharks 2010-13 48-5-0-0-0-25. REP HONOURS: SA 2010-13 Tests: 30-7-0-0-0-35. Tour: 1-0-0-0-0-0. Total: 31-7-0-0-0-35. FC RECORD: 177-30-0-0-0-150. RECORD IN 2013 (SA, Sharks, KZN, Sharks XV) 19-4-0-0-0-20.

Albertse, Louis Erasmus (Michaelhouse & UJ) b 02/04/1990, Ermelo. 1.81m. 100kg. Prop. FC DEBUT: 2013. PROV CAREER: Blue Bulls 2013 6-0-0-0-0-0. FC RECORD: 6-0-0-0-0-0. RECORD IN 2013: (Blue Bulls) 6-0-0-0-0-0.

Alexander, Guy Walter Clive (Hilton College) b 19/04/1992, Durban. 1.92m. 94kg. Flank. FC DEBUT: 2013. PROV CAREER: Sharks XV 2013 2-1-0-0-0-5. FC RECORD: 2-1-0-0-0-5. RECORD IN 2013: (Sharks XV) 2-1-0-0-0-5.

Am, Lukhanyo (De Vos Malan HS) b 28/11/1993, Kingwilliamstown. 1.86m. 93kg. Centre. FC DEBUT: 2013. PROV CAREER: Bulldogs 2013 2-0-0-0-0-0. FC RECORD: 2-0-0-0-0-0. RECORD IN 2013: (Bulldogs) 2-0-0-0-0-0.

Annandale, Gavin Barnard (Brandwag HS) b 27/04/1989, Welkom. 1.94m. 112kg. Lock. FC DEBUT: 2009. PROV CAREER: Valke 2009 5-0-0-0-0-0. Griffons 2010-12 27-2-0-0-0-10. Young Lions 2013 2-0-0-0-0-0. Leopards 2013 1-0-0-0-0-0. FC RECORD: 35-2-0-0-0-10. RECORD IN 2013: (Young Lions, Leopards) 3-0-0-0-0-0.

Aplon, Gio Giaan (Hawston HS) b 06/10/1982, Hermanus. 1.75m. 78kg. Fullback. FC DEBUT: 2005. PROV CAREER: WP 2005-13 95-32-2-0-0-164. SUPERRUGBY: Stormers 2007-08 & 10-13 76-16-0-1-1-86. REP HONOURS: SA 2010-12 Tests: 17-5-0-0-0-25. Tour: 1-0-0-0-0-0. Total: 18-5-0-0-0-25. SA Sevens 2006-07. WP XV 2006 1-2-0-0-0-10. MISC INFO: Try of the Year 2006 (WP vs. Bulls). Super PoY 2011 nominee. FC RECORD: 190-55-2-1-1-285. RECORD IN 2013: (Stormers, WP) 28-8-0-0-0-40.

Apollis, Kerwin Riedewaan (PW Botha College) b 06/02/1993, George. 1.63m. 73kg. Scrumhalf. FC DEBUT: 2013. PROV CAREER: Eagles 2013 1-1-0-0-0-5. FC RECORD: 1-1-0-0-0-5. RECORD IN 2013: (Eagles) 1-1-0-0-0-5.

April, Brendon Terence (Bergrivier HS) b 20/12/1983, Paarl. 1.80m. 75kgs. Wing. FC DEBUT: 2005. PROV CAREER: Valke 2005-06 32-12-0-0-0-60. Griffons 2007 2-0-0-0-0-0. Boland 2010-13 66-34-0-0-0-170. FC RECORD: 100-46-0-0-0-230. RECORD IN 2013: (Boland) 18-8-0-0-0-40.

April, Garth Graham (Bergrivier HS) b 16/07/1991, Cape Town. 1.7m. 74kg. Fullback/Flyhalf. FC DEBUT: 2012. PROV CAREER: Young Lions 2012 5-2-0-0-0-10. Boland 2013 4-0-2-0-0-4. FC RECORD: 9-2-2-0-0-14. RECORD IN 2013: (Boland) 4-0-2-0-0-4.

Arendse, Ederies (Aloe HS) b 25/11/1987, Cape Town. 1.84m. 78kg. Wing. FC DEBUT: 2009. PROV CAREER: Valke 2009 6-3-0-0-0-15. WP 2011-13 15-5-0-0-0-25. FC RECORD: 21-8-0-0-0-40. RECORD IN

A-Z OF FIRST-CLASS PLAYERS IN 2013

2013: (WP) 1-0-0-0-0-0.
Armand, Donovan Wade (Maritzburg College & UCT) b 23/09/1988, Harare, Zimbabwe. 1.91m. 112kg. Flanker. FC DEBUT: 2012. PROV CAREER: WP 2012-13 19-1-0-0-0-5. SUPERRUGBY: Stormers 2012-13 15-0-0-0-0-0. FC RECORD: 34-1-0-0-0-5. RECORD IN 2013: (Stormers,WP) 11-0-0-0-0-0.
Arnold, Rory Wiremu (Murwillumbath HS) b 01/07/1990, Wagga Wagga. 2.08m. 127kg. Lock. SA FC debut: 2013. PROV CAREER: Griquas 2013 6-2-0-0-0-10. SA FC RECORD: 6-2-0-0-0-10. RECORD IN 2013: (Griquas) 6-2-0-0-0-10.
Aspeling, Karlo Gericke (Outeniqua HS, George & TUT) b 13/12/1987, George. 1.79m. 88kg. Flyhalf. FC DEBUT: 2012. PROV CAREER: Valke 2012 14-4-25-10-2-106. Bulldogs 2013 20-1-11-23-1-99. FC RECORD: 34-5-36-33-3-205. RECORD IN 2013: (Bulldogs) 20-1-11-23-1-99.
Astle, John-Charles (Pionier HS & UOFS) b 30/08/1990, Queenstown. 1.98m. 92kg. Lock. FC DEBUT: 2010. PROV CAREER: Cheetahs 2010-11 12-0-0-0-0-0. Free State XV 2012 4-0-0-0-0-0. Boland 2013 13-1-0-0-0-5. FC RECORD: 29-1-0-0-0-5. RECORD IN 2013: (Boland) 13-1-0-0-0-5.

B
Badenhorst, Willem Hermanus Brummer (Brummer) (Outeniqua HS, George & US) b 06/09/1990, Durban. 1.89m. 122kg. Prop. FC DEBUT: 2012. PROV CAREER: Cheetahs 2012 2-0-0-0-0-0. Griquas 2013 13-1-0-0-0-5. REP HONOURS: SAU20 2010 4-1-0-0-0-5. FC RECORD: 19-2-0-0-0-10. RECORD IN 2013: (Griquas) 13-1-0-0-0-5.
Bali, Mlungisi (St Albans HS) b 01/06/1990, East London. 1.96m. 105kg. Lock. FC DEBUT: 2010. PROV CAREER: Griffons 2013 13-0-0-0-0-0. REP HONOURS: SA U20 2010 4-0-0-0-0-0. FC RECORD: 17-0-0-0-0-0. RECORD IN 2013: (Griffons) 13-0-0-0-0-0.
Barends, Alfredo Hilton (Diazville HS & CPUT) b 23/09/1987, Vredenburg. 1.78m. 85kg. FC DEBUT: 2009. PROV CAREER: Boland 2009 4-1-0-0-0-5. Griffons 2013 2-0-0-0-0-0. FC RECORD: 6-1-0-0-0-5. RECORD IN 2013: (Griffons) 2-0-0-0-0-0.
Barnard, Eben Philip (Brandwag HS) b 29/01/1992, Paarl. Wing. FC DEBUT: 2013. PROV CAREER: EP Kings 2013 4-0-0-0-0-0. FC RECORD: 4-0-0-0-0-0. RECORD IN 2013: (EP Kings) 4-0-0-0-0-0.
Barnes, Ryno Joseph (Paarl Gymnasium) b 05/11/81, Cape Town. 1.86m. 110kg. Hooker. FC DEBUT: 2006. PROV CAREER: WP 2006 13-0-0-0-0-0. Valke 2007-08 41-5-0-0-0-25. Griquas 2009-13 82-9-0-0-0-45. Cheetahs XV 2010 1-0-0-0-0-0. SUPERRUGBY: Cheetahs 2010-13 30-0-0-0-0-0. REP HONOURS: Royal XV 2009 1-1-0-0-0-5. FC RECORD: 168-15-0-0-0-75. RECORD IN 2013: (Cheetahs S15, Griquas) 19-0-0-0-0-0.
Basson, Bjorn Alberic (Dale College) b 11/02/87, King Williams Town. 1.85m. 84kg. Wing/Fullback. FC DEBUT: 2008. PROV CAREER: Griquas 2008-10 56-47-0-0-0-235. Blue Bulls 2011-13 15-13-0-0-0-65. SUPERRUGBY: Cheetahs 2009-10 9-6-0-0-0-30. Bulls 2011-13 46-20-0-0-0-100. REP HONOURS: SA 2010-13 Tests: 11-3-0-0-0-15. Emerging Springboks 2008-09 4-1-0-0-0-5. Royal XV 2009 1-0-0-0-0-0. MISC INFO: Holds SA record for most tries in a Currie Cup season (21 in 2010 for Griquas). Brother of Logan Basson. Holds Bulls record for most tries in a season (10 in 2012). FC RECORD: 143-90-0-0-0-400. RECORD IN 2013: (SA, Bulls, Blue Bulls) 21-6-0-0-0-30.
Basson, Logan Andrew (Dale College) b 09/03/1989, King Williamstown. 1.91m. 77kg. Flyhalf. FC DEBUT: 2010. PROV CAREER: Bulldogs 2010 & 12 19-9-13-13-0-110. Griquas 2010-11 & 13 12-2-8-1-0-29. Eagles 2011 2-0-0-0-0-0. MISC INFO: Brother of Bjorn Basson. FC RECORD: 33-11-21-14-0-139. RECORD IN 2013: (Griquas) 1-0-0-0-0-0.

Beerwinkel, Andrew (Porterville HS) b 05/03/1993, Saron. 1.86m. 115kg. Prop. FC DEBUT: 2013. REP HONOURS: SA U20 2013 4-1-0-0-0-5. FC RECORD: 4-1-0-0-0-5. RECORD IN 2013: (SA U20) 4-1-0-0-0-5.
Bekker, Andries (Paul Roos Gymnasium) b 05/12/83, Cape Town. 2.08m. 120kg. Lock. FC DEBUT: 2003. PROV CAREER: WP 2004-09 & 12 38-12-0-0-0-60. SUPERRUGBY: Stormers 2005-13 105-15-0-0-0-75. REP HONOURS: SA 2008-10 & 12 Tests 29-1-0-0-0-5 Tour: 2009 2-0-0-0-0-0. Totals 31-1-0-0-0-5. SA U21 2003-04 7-1-0-0-0-5. FC RECORD: 181-29-0-0-0-145. MISC INFO: Son of HJ (Hennie) Bekker, SA (1981). Tallest Springbok ever at 2.08m. Holds Stormers record for most matches in a career (94). RECORD IN 2013: (Stormers) 11-4-0-0-0-20.
Bell, John-Wessel (JW) (Eldoraigne HS & UP) b 18/01/1990, Cape Town. 1.75m. 73kg. Fullback. FC DEBUT: 2011. PROV CAREER: Valke 2011-12 29-12-0-0-0-60. Pumas 2013 25-15-0-0-0-75. FC RECORD: 54-27-0-0-0-135. RECORD IN 2013: (Pumas) 25-15-0-0-0-75.
Benjamin, Rayno Shannon (Weston HS) b 03/08/83, St Helena Bay. 1.84m. 83kg. Wing. FC DEBUT: 2004. PROV CAREER: Boland 2004-06 42-35-0-0-0-175. Lions 2007-08 23-13-0-0-0-65. Lions XV 2008 1-1-0-0-0-5. Cheetahs 2011-13 19-2-0-0-0-10. Emerging Cheetahs 2011 1-1-0-0-0-5. SUPERRUGBY: Stormers 2006 11-2-0-0-0-10. Lions 2008 12-2-0-0-0-10. Cheetahs 2011-13 28-7-0-0-0-35. REP HONOURS: SA Sevens 2005-07 & 13. FC RECORD: 137-63-0-0-0-315. RECORD IN 2013: (Cheetahs S15, Cheetahs, SA Sevens) 19-2-0-0-0-10.
Bernardo, Rynier Mark (Framesby HS) b 27/08/1991, Pretoria. 1.99m. 102kg. Lock. FC DEBUT: 2012. PROV CAREER: EP Kings 2012-13 17-0-0-0-0-0. SUPERRUGBY: Southern Kings 2013 10-0-0-0-0-0. FC RECORD: 27-0-0-0-0-0. RECORD IN 2013: (Southern Kings, EP Kings) 15-0-0-0-0-0.
Bester, Alwyn (Boland Agric HS) b 15/04/87, Vredendal. 1.93m. 105kg. Eightman. FC DEBUT: 2009. PROV CAREER: Boland 2009 & 2011-13 64-10-0-0-0-50. Pumas 2010 7-1-0-0-0-5. FC RECORD: 71-11-0-0-0-55. RECORD IN 2013: (Boland) 10-1-0-0-0-5.
Bester, Juan b 04/12/1992, Kempton Park. Flanker. FC DEBUT: 2012. PROV CAREER: Bulldogs 2012-13 3-1-0-0-0-5. FC RECORD: 3-1-0-0-0-5. RECORD IN 2013: (Bulldogs) 2-1-0-0-0-5.
Beyers, Ulrich (Ermelo HS) b 22/01/1991, Pretoria. 1.89m. 87kg. Fullback. FC DEBUT: 2011. PROV CAREER: Blue Bulls 2011-13 27-3-1-0-1-20. SUPERRUGBY: Bulls 2013 2-0-0-0-0-0. REP HONOURS: SAU20 2011 4-0-0-0-0-0. FC RECORD: 33-3-1-0-1-20. RECORD IN 2013: (Bulls, Blue Bulls) 15-0-1-0-0-2.
Bezuidenhout, Carl (Union HS, Graaff-Reinet) b 10/02/86, Grahamstown. 1.90m. 90kg. Fullback. FC DEBUT: 2006. PROV CAREER: KZN 2006 1-1-0-0-0-5. Sharks XV 2006 & 08-09 10-1-0-0-0-5. Elephants 2009 8-2-8-7-0-47. Pumas 2010-13 67-12-101-65-2-463. REP HONOURS: SA Pres XV 2013 3-0-2-7-0-25. FC RECORD: 89-16-111-79-2-545. RECORD IN 2013: (SA Pres XV, Pumas) 28-6-81-60-0-378.
Bezuidenhout, Martin Johannes (Klerksdorp HS & UJ) b 21/08/1989, Orkney. 1.82m. 102kg. Hooker. FC DEBUT: 2010. PROV CAREER: Golden Lions 2010-13 33-1-0-0-0-5. Young Lions 2010-11 10-1-0-0-0-5. SUPERRUGBY: Lions 2011-12 24-3-0-0-0-15. Lions P/R 2013 2-0-0-0-0-0. Stormers 2013 8-0-0-0-0-0. FC RECORD: 77-5-0-0-0-25. RECORD IN 2013: (Lions S15, Stormers, Lions) 12-0-0-0-0-0.
Bezuidenhout, Stephanus Marthinus (Stephan) (HTS Potchefstroom) b 10/05/1986, Vereeniging. 1.85m. 128kg. Prop. FC DEBUT: 2011. PROV CAREER: Leopards 2011-13 38-1-0-0-0-5. Leopard XV 2013 2-0-0-0-0-0. FC RECORD: 40-1-0-0-0-5. RECORD IN 2013: (Leop-

A-Z OF FIRST-CLASS PLAYERS IN 2013

ards, Leopard XV) 8-1-0-0-0-5.
Bholi, Thembelani (Jamangile HS) b 18/01/1990, East London. 1.95m. 92kg. Eighthman. FC DEBUT: 2013. PROV CAREER: EP Kings 2013 4-0-0-0-0-0. FC RECORD: 4-0-0-0-0-0. RECORD IN 2013: (EP Kings) 4-0-0-0-0-0.
Bitterhout, Leroy Hurzell (Klein Nederburg HS) b 16/11/1992, Paarl. 1.7m. 68kg. Wing. FC DEBUT: 2012. PROV CAREER: Free State XV 2012-13 6-2-0-0-0-10. FC RECORD: 6-2-0-0-0-10. RECORD IN 2013: (Free State XV) 2-0-0-0-0-0.
Blom, Jandré (Riebeeckstad HS) b 24/12/84, Vredendal. 1.74m. 75kg. Scrumhalf. FC DEBUT: 2005. PROV CAREER: Cheetahs 2005-09 46-9-37-39-1-239. Griffons 2008 8-1-3-1-2-20. Eagles 2009-10 & 13 45-5-26-23-0-146. Griquas 2011 5-2-0-0-0-10. REP HONOURS: SA Sevens 2005-07. FC RECORD: 104-17-66-63-3-415. RECORD IN 2013: (Eagles) 12-1-0-0-0-5.
Blommetjies, Clayton (New Orleans SSS & UP) b 30/08/1990, Paarl. 1.85m. 75kg. Wing. FC DEBUT: 2009. PROV CAREER: Blue Bulls 2011-13 32-8-0-0-0-40. REP HONOURS: SA Students 2009 1-2-0-0-0-10. SAU20 2009 2-0-0-0-0-0. SA Sevens 2012. FC RECORD: 35-10-0-0-0-50. RECORD IN 2013: (Blue Bulls) 13-3-0-0-0-15.
Bock, Alshaun Gerswon (Weltevrede HS, Wellington) b 16/05/1982, Wellington. 1.79m. 78kg. Wing. FC DEBUT: 2002. PROV CAREER: Boland 2002-04 & 07-08 38-19-0-0-0-95. Griquas 2005-06 22-13-0-0-0-65. WP 2009 1-1-0-0-0-5. Eagles 2012-13 35-29-0-0-0-145. REP HONOURS: SA Pres XV 2013 3-2-0-0-0-10. SA Sevens 2003; SA U21 2003 5-9-0-0-0-45. MISC INFO: CC First Division PoY nominee 2013. FC RECORD: 104-73-0-0-0-365. RECORD IN 2013: (SA Pres XV, Eagles) 23-22-0-0-0-110.
Boesak, Marshell (Parkdene HS) b 14/09/1989, George. 1.80m. 90kg. Flank. FC DEBUT: 2013. PROV CAREER: Eagles 2013 2-1-0-0-0-5. FC RECORD: 2-1-0-0-0-5. RECORD IN 2013: (Eagles) 2-1-0-0-0-5.
Bondesio, Michael (Lichtenburg HS) b 10/03/85, Middelburg. 1.76m. 84kg. Scrumhalf. FC DEBUT: 2008. PROV CAREER: Leopards 2008-10 52-13-0-0-0-65. Lions 2011-13 25-0-0-0-0-0. Young Lions 2011 & 13 14-4-0-0-0-20. SUPERRUGBY: Lions 2012 7-1-0-0-0-5. FC RECORD: 98-18-0-0-0-90. RECORD IN 2013: (Lions, Young Lions) 8-1-0-0-0-5.
Bondesio, Murray (Grey College, Bloemfontein & UP) b 04/12/1992, Pretoria. 1.78m. 88kg. Flank. FC DEBUT: 2013. PROV CAREER: Sharks XV 2013 2-1-0-0-0-5. FC RECORD: 2-1-0-0-0-5. RECORD IN 2013: (Sharks XV) 2-1-0-0-0-5.
Booi, Chumani Nande (Union HS, Graaff-Reinet) b 15/02/80, Sada, Whittlesea. 1.75m. 75kgs. Fullback. FC DEBUT: 2001. PROV CAREER: Border 2001-03 & 09-13 105-28-14-7-0-189. Pumas 2003 14-6-0-0-0-30. Griquas 2004-06 23-8-2-0-0-44. WP 2006 5-0-0-0-0-0. SUPERRUGBY: Sharks 2004 5-0-0-0-0-0. Cats 2005 10-1-0-0-0-5. Stormers 2006 5-0-0-0-0-0. REP HONOURS: SA 'A' 2004 2-1-0-0-0-5. WP XV 2006 1-0-0-0-0-0. SA U21s 2001 4-3-0-0-0-15; CW Elephants 1997-98. FC RECORD: 174-47-16-7-0-288. RECORD IN 2013: (Bulldogs) 4-2-0-0-0-10.
Booyse, Pieter Johannes Frederik b 23/03/1991. Wing. FC DEBUT: 2013. PROV CAREER: Limpopo 2013 3-0-0-0-0-0. FC RECORD: 3-0-0-0-0-0. RECORD IN 2013: (Limpopo) 3-0-0-0-0-0.
Booysen, Fabian Connal Frazer (Florida HS & UJ) b 21/03/1992, Caledon. 1.9m. 103kg. Eighthman. FC DEBUT: 2012. PROV CAREER: Young Lions 2012-13 3-0-0-0-0-0. REP HONOURS: SA Univ 2013 1-0-0-0-0-0. SAU20 2012 5-0-0-0-0-0. FC RECORD: 9-0-0-0-0-0. RECORD IN 2013: (SA Univ, Young Lions) 3-0-0-0-0-0.
Booysen, Franco (Brakpan HS) b 26/03/87, Welkom. 1.83m. 90kg. Centre. FC DEBUT: 2008. PROV CAREER: Valke 2008-11 & 13 39-6-0-0-

0-30. FC RECORD: 39-6-0-0-0-30. RECORD IN 2013: (Valke) 1-0-0-0-0-0.
Booysen, Stefanus Johannes (Fanie) (Hoogenhout HS) b 14/09/1990, Nigel. 1.83m. 92kg. Flyhalf. FC DEBUT: 2011. PROV CAREER: Blue Bulls 2011 1-0-0-0-0-0. Young Lions 2013 1-0-0-0-0-0. FC RECORD: 2-0-0-0-0-0. RECORD IN 2013: (Young Lions) 1-0-0-0-0-0.
Bosch, Christopher (Paarl Gymnasium) b 27/03/1992, Pretoria. 1.83m. 90kg. Centre. FC DEBUT: 2013. PROV CAREER: Blue Bulls 2013 1-0-0-0-0-0. FC RECORD: 1-0-0-0-0-0. RECORD IN 2013: (Blue Bulls) 1-0-0-0-0-0.
Boshoff, Henri Bossau (Nelspruit HS & UJ) b 08/02/1992, Nelspruit. 1.86m. 110kg. Hooker. FC DEBUT: 2013. PROV CAREER: Young Lions 2013 2-1-0-0-0-5. FC RECORD: 2-1-0-0-0-5. RECORD IN 2013: (Young Lions) 2-1-0-0-0-5.
Boshoff, Jan Hendrik (Jannie) (Maritzburg College) b 13/01/86, Newcastle. 1.78m. 87kg. Centre. FC DEBUT: 2006. PROV CAREER: Golden Lions 2006-11 34-9-0-0-0-45. Lions XV 2007 1-1-0-0-0-5. Young Lions 2006-11 13-3-0-0-0-15. Griquas 2012-13 13-7-0-0-0-35. SUPERRUGBY: Lions 2007-09 & 11 24-3-0-0-0-15. FC RECORD: 85-23-0-0-0-115. RECORD IN 2013: (Griquas) 4-1-0-0-0-5.
Boshoff, Marnitz Louis (Nelspruit HS & TUKS) b 11/01/89, Nelspruit. 1.76m. 78kg. Flyhalf. FC DEBUT: 2009. PROV CAREER: Blue Bulls 2009-11 24-3-23-21-2-130. Griquas 2012 13-0-11-5-0-37. Lions 2013 11-2-20-14-0-92. Young Lions 2013 6-0-18-16-4-96. SUPERRUGBY: Lions P/R 2013 1-0-0-0-0-0. Misc onfo: VC PoY nominee 2013. FC RECORD: 55-5-72-56-6-355. RECORD IN 2013: (Lions S15, Lions, Young Lions) 18-2-38-30-4-188.
Bosman, Hendrik Meyer (Oakdale Agric. HS & Free State Univ.) b 19/04/85, Bethlehem. 1.91m. 94kg. Utility back. FC DEBUT: 2005. PROV CAREER: Cheetahs 2005-10 59-10-21-9-0-119. KZN 2011-12 23-2-19-28-0-132. SUPERRUGBY: Cheetahs 2006-10 61-4-27-38-0-188. Sharks 2011-13 47-7-11-0-0-57. REP HONOURS: SA Tests: 2005-06 3-0-2-1-0-7. Tour: 2006,09 3-0-0-0-0-0. Total: 6-0-2-1-0-7. Emerging Springboks 2007 2-0-0-0-0-0. FC RECORD: 198-23-80-76-0-503. RECORD IN 2013: (Sharks) 13-3-9-0-0-33.
Botes, Louis Jacques (Jacques) (Potchefstroom Gymnasium) b 12/04/80, Nelspruit. 1.81m. 97kg. Eighthman. FC DEBUT: 2002. PROV CAREER: Pumas 2002-04 42-6-0-0-0-30. KZN 2005-13 120-42-0-0-0-210. Sharks XV 1-0-0-0-0-0. Sharks Inv XV 2009-10 2-5-1-0-0-27. SUPERRUGBY: Sharks 2005-13 114-27-0-0-0-135. REP HONOURS: Emerging Springboks 2009 1-0-0-0-0-0. FC RECORD: 280-80-1-0-0-402. RECORD IN 2013: (Sharks, KZN) 19-5-0-0-0-25.
Botha, Andries Hendrik (Nylstroom HS & NWU) b 08/05/1990, Nylstroom. 1.80m. 80kg. Scrumhalf. FC DEBUT: 2010. PROV CAREER: Leopards 2010 1-0-0-0-0-0. Limpopo 2013 2-0-0-0-0-0. FC RECORD: 3-0-0-0-0-0. RECORD IN 2013: (Limpopo) 2-0-0-0-0-0.
Botha, Arnoldus Francois (Arno) (Nylstroom HS) b 26/10/1991, Modimolle. 1.90m. 102kg. Flank. FC DEBUT: 2011. PROV CAREER: Blue Bulls 2011-12 17-4-0-0-0-20. SUPERRUGBY: Bulls 2012-13 22-1-0-0-0-5. REP HONOURS: SA Tests: 2013 2-0-0-0-0-0. SAU20 2011 5-7-0-0-0-35. Misc: SA U20 PoY 2011. FC RECORD: 46-12-0-0-0-60. RECORD IN 2013: (SA, Bulls) 14-1-0-0-0-5.
Botha, Bernardo Carl (Florida HS) b 04/07/88, Oudtshoorn. 1.81m. 86kg. Wing. FC DEBUT: 2009. PROV CAREER: Young Lions 2009-10 8-4-0-0-0-20. Griffons 2013 5-0-0-0-0-0. SUPERRUGBY: Lions 2010 2-0-0-0-0-0. Rep. honours: SA Sevens 2010-13. FC RECORD: 15-4-0-0-0-20. RECORD IN 2013: (Griffons, SA Sevens) 5-0-0-0-0-0.
Botha, John Philip (Bakkies) (Vereeniging THS/Middelburg THS) b 22/09/79, Newcastle. 2.02m. 118kg. Lock. FC DEBUT: 1999. PROV CAREER: Valke 1999-2000 22-2-1-0-0-12. Blue Bulls 2001-02 &

A-Z OF FIRST-CLASS PLAYERS IN 2013

04-05 & 09-10 53-10-0-0-0-50. SUPERRUGBY: Bulls 2002-11 100-11-0-0-0-55. REP HONOURS: SA 2002-05 & 07-11 & 13 Tests: 78-7-0-0-0-35. 2010 Tour: 1-1-0-0-0-5. Total: 79-8-0-0-0-40. SA 'A' 2001-03 6-1-0-0-0-5; SA U23s 2001 3-1-0-0-0-5; SA Schools 1998 (captain); CW Pumas 1997. British Barbarians 2008 1-0-0-0-0-0. MISC INFO: PoY nominee 2003, 2004, 2005. Locked together with Victor Matfield in 64 tests (world record). FC RECORD: 264-33-1-0-0-167. RECORD IN 2013: (SA) 2-0-0-0-0-0.

Botha, Chrysander Antonio (Walvis Bay HS) b 13/07/1988, Walvis Bay. 1.88m. 72kg. Fullback. SA FC DEBUT: 2010. PROV CAREER: Valke 2010 11-3-0-3-0-24. Lions 2013 6-0-0-0-0-0. Young Lions 2013 5-5-1-0-0-27. SUPERRUGBY: Lions P/R 2013 2-0-0-0-0-0. SA FC RECORD: 24-8-1-3-0-51. REP HONOURS: Welwitschias 2010. RECORD IN 2013: (Lions S15, Lions, Young Lions) 13-5-1-0-0-27.

Botha, Ruan (Jeugland HS) b 10/01/1992, Brakpan. 2.03m. 113kg. Lock. FC DEBUT: 2012. PROV CAREER: Young Lions 2012 1-0-0-0-0-0. WP 2013 1-1-0-0-0-5. SUPERRUGBY: Lions 2012 5-0-0-0-0-0. REP HONOURS: SAU20 2012 5-0-0-0-0-0. FC RECORD: 12-1-0-0-0-5. RECORD IN 2013: (WP) 1-1-0-0-0-5.

Botha, Van Zyl (Grey College, Bloemfontein & UJ) b 25/01/1991, Middelburg, EC. 1.86m. 120kg. Prop. FC DEBUT: 2012. PROV CAREER: Young Lions 2012-13 7-1-0-0-0-5. FC RECORD: 7-1-0-0-0-5. RECORD IN 2013: (Young Lions) 4-1-0-0-0-5.

Bothma, Renaldo (Volkskool Heidelberg) b 18/09/1989, Alberton. 1.87m. 100kg. Flanker. FC DEBUT: 2010. PROV CAREER: Golden Lions 2010 7-2-0-0-0-10. Young Lions 2011 6-1-0-0-0-5. Leopards 2011 1-0-0-0-0-0. Pumas 2012-13 37-15-0-0-0-75. REP HONOURS: SA Pres XV 2013 2-1-0-0-0-5. FC RECORD: 53-19-0-0-0-95. RECORD IN 2013: (SA Pres XV, Pumas) 20-9-0-0-0-45.

Bothma, Rinus Luan (Noordheuwel HS) b 03/08/1989, Roodepoort. 2.0m. 109kg. Lock. FC DEBUT: 2013. PROV CAREER: Valke 2013 9-1-0-0-0-5. FC RECORD: 9-1-0-0-0-5. RECORD IN 2013: (Valke) 9-1-0-0-0-5.

Bouwer, Willem Sterrenberg Jacobus Marais (Jaco) (Waterkloof HS, Pretoria) b 04/09/85, Kempton Park, 1.84m. 97kg. Flank. FC DEBUT: 2007. PROV CAREER: Leopards 2007-08 34-8-0-0-0-40. Pumas 2009-13 97-44-0-0-0-220. REP HONOURS: SA Pres XV 2013 4-0-0-0-0-0. SA Barbarians 2012 1-0-0-0-0-0. FC RECORD: 136-52-0-0-0-260. RECORD IN 2013: (SA Pres XV, Pumas) 25-8-0-0-0-40.

Brache, Marcel Girard (Rondebosch Boys HS & UCT) b 15/10/1987, Los Angeles. 1.90m. 88kg. Centre. FC DEBUT: 2010. PROV CAREER: WP 2010-13 44-6-0-0-0-30. SUPERRUGBY: Stormers 2012 1-0-0-0-0-0. MISC INFO: VC PoY 2012 nominee. FC RECORD: 45-6-0-0-0-30. RECORD IN 2013: (WP) 5-0-0-0-0-0.

Breet, Jan-Jacobus (Ben Vorster HS, Tzaneen & TUT) b 14/06/1991, Pretoria. 1.98m. 105kg. Lock. FC DEBUT: 2013. PROV CAREER: Lions 2013 2-0-0-0-0-0. Young Lions 2013 5-2-0-0-0-10. FC RECORD: 7-2-0-0-0-10. RECORD IN 2013: (Lions, Young Lions) 7-2-0-0-0-10.

Bresler, Anton (Durban HS) b 16/02/1988, Windhoek. 1.97m. 106kg. Lock. FC DEBUT: 2010. PROV CAREER: KZN 2010-12 28-1-0-0-0-5. Sharks XV 2010-11 15-0-0-0-0-0. Sharks Inv XV 2010 1-0-0-0-0-0. SUPERRUGBY: Sharks 2011-13 34-1-0-0-0-5. FC RECORD: 78-2-0-0-0-10. RECORD IN 2013: (Sharks) 10-0-0-0-0-0.

Briedenhann, Jannie Gysbert (Gys) (Jim Fouche HS) b 14/05/85, Kempton Park. 1.97m. 111kg. Lock. FC DEBUT: 2007. PROV CAREER: Griffons 2007-09 28-3-0-0-0-15. Leopards 2010 8-0-0-0-0-0. Free State XV 2013 1-0-0-0-0-0. MISC INFO: Brother of Marnus Briedenhann. FC RECORD: 37-3-0-0-0-15. RECORD IN 2013: (Free State XV) 1-0-0-0-0-0.

Briedenhann, Marnus (Jim Fouche HS) b 24/08/87, Kempton Park. 1.92m. 106kg. Lock. FC DEBUT: 2008. PROV CAREER: Cheetahs 2008-09 15-1-0-0-0-5. Griffons 2009-11 & 13 40-3-0-0-0-15. Free State XV 2013 6-0-0-0-0-0. MISC INFO: Brother of Gys Briedenhann. FC RECORD: 61-4-0-0-0-20. RECORD IN 2013: (Griffons, Free State XV) 11-1-0-0-0-5.

Brits, Schalk Burger (Paul Roos Gymnasium & Stellenbosch Univ.) b 16/05/81, Empangeni. 1.82m. 98kg. Hooker. FC DEBUT: 2002. PROV CAREER: WP 2002-03 & 06-08 39-6-0-0-0-30. Lions 2004-05 35-11-0-0-0-55. SUPERRUGBY: Cats 2005 11-0-0-0-0-0. Stormers 2006-09 & 2011 52-4-0-0-0-20. REP HONOURS: SA 2008 & 12 Tests: 5-0-0-0-0-0. Emerging Springboks 2007 3-2-0-0-0-10. SA 'A' 2004 3-2-0-0-0-10. WP XV 2006. British Barbarians 2007,09,10,13 5-1-0-0-0-5. SA Schools 1999. MISC INFO: YPoY nominee 2004. FC RECORD: 154-26-0-0-0-130. RECORD IN 2013: (British Barbarians) 2-1-0-0-0-5.

Brits, Coenraad Johannes (Oakdale HS) b 28/07/87, Mossel Bay. 1.85m. 99kg. Flank. FC DEBUT: 2008. PROV CAREER: WP 2008-09 13-2-0-0-0-10. EP Kings 2011-13 31-4-0-0-0-20. FC RECORD: 44-6-0-0-0-30. RECORD IN 2013: (EP Kings) 13-1-0-0-0-5.

Britz, Rudolph Martinus (Rudi) (Hentie Cilliers HS) b 03/03/1989, Virginia. 1.89m. 126kg. Prop. FC DEBUT: 2012. PROV CAREER: Griffons 2012-13 30-2-0-0-0-10. FC RECORD: 30-2-0-0-0-10. RECORD IN 2013: (Griffons) 15-0-0-0-0-0.

Britz, Willem Stephanus (Willie) (Diamantveld HS, Kimberley & UFS) b 31/08/88, Cape Town. 1.91m. 98kg. FC DEBUT: 2009. PROV CAREER: Cheetahs 2009 & 2011 5-2-0-0-0-10. Griffons 2010-12 28-8-0-0-0-40. Lions 2012-13 20-3-0-0-0-15. Young Lions 2013 7-1-0-0-0-5. Emerging Cheetahs 2011 1-0-0-0-0-0. SUPERRUGBY: Lions P/R 2013 2-0-0-0-0-0. FC RECORD: 63-14-0-0-0-70. RECORD IN 2013: (Lions S15, Lions, Young Lions) 19-4-0-0-0-20.

Brown, Kyle Gie (SACS & UCT) b 06/02/1987, Cape Town. 1.82m. 96kg. Rep. Honours: SA Sevens 2008-13. RECORD IN 2013: (SA Sevens).

Brüssow, Heinrich Wilhelm (Grey College, Bloemfontein) b 21/07/86, Bloemfontein. 1.81m. 103kg. Flank. FC DEBUT: 2006. PROV CAREER: Cheetahs 2006-09 & 2011-12 59-25-0-0-0-125. Cheetahs XV 2010 1-0-0-0-0-0. SUPERRUGBY: Cheetahs 2007-13 70-6-0-0-0-30. REP HONOURS: SA 2008-09 & 2011 Tests: 20-1-0-0-0-5. SA Sevens 2006, SA Schools 2004. MISC INFO: YPoY nominee 2008, PoY Nominee 2009. FC RECORD: 150-32-0-0-0-160. RECORD IN 2013: (Cheetahs S15) 15-0-0-0-0-0.

Brummer, Francois (Waterkloof HS, Pretoria) b 17/05/1989, Pretoria. 1.82m. 90kg. Flyhalf. FC DEBUT: 2008. PROV CAREER: Blue Bulls 2008-11 49-6-66-91-15-480. Griquas 2012-13 33-3-38-33-2-196. SUPERRUGBY: Bulls 2010 1-0-1-0-0-2. Cheetahs 2013 1-0-0-1-0-3. REP HONOURS: SAU20 2008-09 9-3-24-13-1-105. FC RECORD: 93-12-129-138-18-786. RECORD IN 2013: (Cheetahs S15, Griquas) 17-1-20-12-0-81.

Brummer, Johannes Gerhardus (JP) (Kempton Park HS) b 25/03/1992, Pretoria. 1.84m. 96kg. Flanker. FC DEBUT: 2012. PROV CAREER: Valke 2012-13 4-0-0-0-0-0. FC RECORD: 4-0-0-0-0-0. RECORD IN 2013: (Valke) 3-0-0-0-0-0.

Buckle, Christiaan Johannes (Boland Agric. HS & US) b 15/07/1985, Paarl. 1.76m. 103kg. Hooker. FC DEBUT: 2011. PROV CAREER: Boland 2011 & 13 12-2-0-0-0-10. FC RECORD: 12-2-0-0-0-10. RECORD IN 2013: (Boland) 3-1-0-0-0-5.

Bullbring, David James (Alexander Road HS & UJ) b 12/09//89,

A-Z OF FIRST-CLASS PLAYERS IN 2013

Port Elizabeth. 1.98m. 104kg. Lock. FC DEBUT: 2009. PROV CAREER: Golden Lions 2010 7-0-0-0-0-0. Young Lions 2009-11 19-4-0-0-0-20. EP Kings 2012 24-1-0-0-0-5. Blue Bulls 2013 6-1-0-0-0-5. SUPERRUGBY: Lions 2010-11 3-0-0-0-0-0. SUPERRUGBY: Southern Kings 2013 16-0-0-0-0-0. P/R 2013 2-0-0-0-0-0. REP HONOURS: SA Barbarians 2012 1-0-0-0-0-0. SAU20 2009 5-0-0-0-0-0. FC RECORD: 83-6-0-0-0-30. RECORD IN 2013: (Southern Kings, Blue Bulls) 24-1-0-0-0-5.
Burden, Craig Bruce (Maritzburg College) b 13/05/85, Durban. 1,84m, 98kg. Hooker. FC DEBUT: 2005. PROV CAREER: KZN 2005-13 71-23-0-0-0-115. Sharks XV 2005-11 27-9-0-0-0-45. Sharks Inv XV 2007 & 09-10 3-1-0-0-0-5. SUPERRUGBY: Sharks 2006 & 08 & 10-13 47-4-0-0-0-20. REP HONOURS: SA 2012 - no tests. FC RECORD: 148-37-0-0-0-185. RECORD IN 2013: (Sharks, KZN) 14-0-0-0-0-0.
Burger, Schalk Willem Petrus (Paarl Gymnasium) b 13/04/83, Port Elizabeth. 1.93m. 110kg. Flank. FC DEBUT: 2002. PROV CAREER: WP 2003-05 & 08-11 & 13 37-7-0-0-0-35. SUPERRUGBY: Stormers 2004-12 88-7-0-0-0-35. REP HONOURS: SA 2003-11 Tests: 68-13-0-0-0-65; SA U21 2002-03 8-4-0-0-0-20; British Barbarians 2004 & 08,09,13 4-0-0-0-0-0. S Hemisphere XV 2005 1-1-0-0-0-5. MISC INFO: SA PoY 2004. IRB PoY 2004. IRPA PoY & YPoY 2004. Super PoY nominee 2011. SARU PoY 2011. SA YPoY nominee 2003, 2004; Holds SA record for most Tests as a Flank - 66 (also two at No.8). Son of 1984-86 Springbok SWP (Schalk) Burger. FC RECORD: 206-32-0-0-0-160. RECORD IN 2013: (WP, British Barbarians): 6-0-0-0-0-0.
Butterworth, Eugene Francois (Monument Park HS) b 19/09/1984, Belville. Prop. FC DEBUT: 2011. PROV CAREER: Boland 2011 15-0-0-0-0-0. Griquas 2012-13 6-0-0-0-0-0. FC RECORD: 21-0-0-0-0-0. RECORD IN 2013: (Griquas) 2-0-0-0-0-0.
Buys, Jarryd Andrew (Selborne College & US) b 02/02/1990, Elliot. 1.89m. 91kg. Fullback. FC DEBUT: 2013. PROV CAREER: Leopards 2013 8-4-1-0-0-22. FC RECORD: 8-4-1-0-0-22. RECORD IN 2013: (Leopards) 8-4-1-0-0-22.
Buys, Kevin (Dr E G Jansen HS) b 26/04/86, Benoni. 1.91m. 120kgs. Eightman. FC DEBUT: 2007. PROV CAREER: Blue Bulls 2007 6-0-0-0-0-0. Blue Bulls XV 2007 1-0-0-0-0-0. Golden Lions 2009-10 19-0-0-0-0-0. Young Lions 2010-11 5-0-0-0-0-0. EP Kings 2012 2-0-0-0-0-0. SUPERRUGBY: Lions 2010-11 13-0-0-0-0-0. Southern Kings 2013 15-0-0-0-0-0. P/R 2013 2-0-0-0-0-0. FC RECORD: 63-0-0-0-0-0. RECORD IN 2013 (Southern Kings) 17-0-0-0-0-0.
Byleveldt, Zander (Tom Naude HS) b 27/10/1987, Newcastle. 1.74m. 74kg. Fullback. FC DEBUT: 2013. PROV CAREER: Limpopo 2013 1-0-0-0-0-0. FC RECORD: 1-0-0-0-0-0. RECORD IN 2013: (Limpopo) 1-0-0-0-0-0.

C

Carney, Deon (Northern Cape HS) b 30/08/1991, Brits. 1.80m. 84kg. Eightman. FC DEBUT: 2013. PROV CAREER: Griquas 2013 8-2-0-0-0-10. FC RECORD: 8-2-0-0-0-10. RECORD IN 2013: (Griquas) 8-2-0-0-0-10.
Carr, Nizaam (Bishops HS) b 04/04/1991, Cape Town. 1.84m. 93kg. Flank. FC DEBUT: 2011. PROV CAREER: WP 2011-13 17-1-0-0-0-5. SUPERRUGBY: Stormers 2012-13 21-0-0-0-0-0. REP HONOURS: SAU20 2011 4-2-0-0-0-10. FC RECORD: 42-3-0-0-0-15. RECORD IN 2013: (Stormers) 24-1-0-0-0-5.
Cassiem, Uzair (Strand HS & Boland College) b 17/03/1990, Strand. 1.89m. 98kg. Flank. FC DEBUT: 2011. PROV CAREER: Young Lions 2012 4-0-0-0-0-0. Golden Lions XV 2011 1-1-0-0-0-5. Valke 2012 3-2-0-0-0-10. Pumas 2012-13 33-11-0-0-0-55. REP HONOURS: SA Pres XV 2013 4-2-0-0-0-10. FC RECORD: 45-16-0-0-0-80. RECORD IN 2013: (SA Pres XV, Pumas) 27-9-0-0-0-45.

Catrakilis, Demetri (St Johns College UJ & UCT) b 06/09/1989, Johannesburg. 1.76m 82kg. Flyhalf. FC DEBUT: 2011. PROV CAREER: WP 2011-13 40-1-66-111-8-494. SUPERRUGBY: Southern Kings 2013 14-0-14-37-1-142. P/R 2013 1-0-0-3-0-9. MISC INFO: VC PoY 2012. FC RECORD: 55-1-80-151-9-645. Record in 2013: (Southern Kings, WP) 21-1-19-56-3-220.
Chadwick, Dale Michael (Westville Boys HS) b 20/06/89, Westville. 1.83m. 105kg. Prop. FC DEBUT: 2009. PROV CAREER: KZN 2009 & 2011-13 34-2-0-0-0-10. Sharks XV 2010-12 13-2-0-0-0-10. Sharks Inv XV 2009 1-0-0-0-0-0. SUPERRUGBY: Sharks 2012 10-0-0-0-0-0. FC RECORD: 58-4-0-0-0-20. RECORD IN 2013: (KZN) 9-0-0-0-0-0.
Cilliers, Patric Michael (Michaelhouse HS) b 03/03/87, Pietermaritzburg. 1.85m. 101kg. Prop. FC DEBUT: 2007. PROV CAREER: KZN 2007-10 34-5-0-0-0-25. Sharks XV 2007-10 18-3-0-0-0-15. Sharks Inv XV 2009-10 2-0-0-0-0-0. Lions 2011-12 17-4-0-0-0-20. WP 2013 12-0-0-0-0-0. SUPERRUGBY: Sharks 2007 & 09-10 3-0-0-0-0-0. Lions 2011-12 28-1-0-0-0-5. Stormers 2013 13-0-0-0-0-0. REP HONOURS: SA 2012 Tests: 6-0-0-0-0-0. Emerging Springboks 2009 1-0-0-0-0-0. FC RECORD: 134-13-0-0-0-65. RECORD IN 2013: (Stormers, WP) 25-0-0-0-0-0.
Classen, Neil (Daniel Pienaar HS) b 26/09/1992, Pretoria. 1.94m. 85kg. Prop. FC DEBUT: 2012. PROV CAREER: Free State XV 2012-13 9-1-0-0-0-5. FC RECORD: 9-1-0-0-0-5. RECORD IN 2013: (Free State XV) 7-1-0-0-0-5.
Clark, Nolan. Lock. FC DEBUT: 2007. PROV CAREER: Sharks XV 2008-09 10-0-0-0-0-0. Sharks Inv XV 2007 1-1-0-0-0-5. Griquas 2009 6-0-0-0-0-0. EP Kings 2009-10 16-0-0-0-0-0. EP Inv XV 2010 1-0-0-0-0-0. Boland 2012-13 28-3-0-0-0-15. REP HONOURS: SA Barbarians 2012 1-0-0-0-0-0. FC RECORD: 63-4-0-0-0-20. RECORD IN 2013: (Boland) 9-0-0-0-0-0.
Cloete, Christopher Anthony (Selborne College) b 15/02/1991, East London. 1.76m. 91kg. Flanker. FC DEBUT: 2012. PROV CAREER: Sharks XV 2012 7-1-0-0-0-5. WP 2013 4-5-0-0-0-25. FC RECORD: 11-6-0-0-0-30. RECORD IN 2013: (WP) 4-5-0-0-0-25.
Cloete, Wesley Wyndham (Selborne College) b 08/02/1990, East London. 1.77m. 100kg. Prop. FC DEBUT: 2012. PROV CAREER: Bulldogs 2012-13 34-0-0-0-0-0. FC RECORD: 34-0-0-0-0-0. RECORD IN 2013: (Bulldogs) 21-0-0-0-0-0.
Coetzee, Andries (Middelburg Tech. HS) b 01/03/1990, Bethal. 1.81m. 86kg. Fullback. FC DEBUT: 2011. PROV CAREER: Lions 2012-13 18-3-1-0-0-17. Young Lions 2012-13 2-2-5-0-0-20. Golden Lions XV 2011 1-0-0-0-0-0. SUPERRUGBY: Lions 2012 12-0-0-0-1-3. Sharks 2013 1-0-0-0-0-0. FC RECORD: 34-5-6-0-1-40. RECORD IN 2013: (Sharks, Lions, Young Lions) 10-3-0-0-0-15.
Coetzee, Armand Dirk (Port Natal HS) b 12/11/1988, Potchefstroom. 1.92m. 120kg. Lock. FC DEBUT: 2013. PROV CAREER: Eagles 2013 1-0-0-0-0-0. FC RECORD: 1-0-0-0-0-0. RECORD IN 2013: (Eagles) 1-0-0-0-0-0.
Coetzee, Jacques (Volkskool HS) b 22/10/83, Bethal. 1.77m. 78kg. Scrumhalf. FC DEBUT: 2007. PROV CAREER: Pumas 2007-10 71-16-14-5-0-123. EP Kings 2011 10-1-0-0-0-5. Griquas 2012-13 39-6-0-0-0-30. SUPERRUGBY: Lions 2010 10-0-0-0-0-0. Cheetahs 2012 1-0-0-0-0-0. REP HONOURS: Royal XV 2009 1-0-0-0-0-0. FC RECORD: 132-23-14-5-0-158. RECORD IN 2013: (Griquas) 20-3-0-0-0-15.
Coetzee, Marcell Cornelius (Port Natal HS) b 08/05/1991, Potchefstroom. 1.91m. 106kg. Loose Forward. FC DEBUT: 2011. PROV CAREER: KZN 2011-13 24-1-0-0-0-5. Sharks XV 2011 8-3-0-0-0-15. SUPERRUGBY: Sharks 2011-13 39-5-0-0-0-25. REP HONOURS: SA 2012-13 Tests: 15-1-0-0-0-5. MISC INFO: YPoY 2012 nominee. Super PoY 2012 nominee. FC RECORD: 86-10-0-0-0-50. RECORD IN 2013: (SA, Sharks,

A-Z OF FIRST-CLASS PLAYERS IN 2013

KZN) 24-4-0-0-0-20.
Coetzee, Marne (Waterkloof HS, Pretoria, Pretoria & Glenwood HS, Durban) b 17/09/1993, Pretoria. 1.8m. 114kg. Hooker. FC DEBUT: 2013. REP HONOURS: SA U20 2013 4-0-0-0-0-0. FC RECORD: 4-0-0-0-0-0. RECORD IN 2013: (SA U20) 4-0-0-0-0.
Coctzee, Robin Leendert (Robbie) (Eldoraigne HS, Centurion) b 02/05/1989, Pretoria. 1.85m. 105kg. Hooker. FC DEBUT: 2012. PROV CAREER: Blue Bulls 2012 11-1-0-0-0-5. Lions 2013 10-1-0-0-0-5. Young Lions 2013 6-1-0-0-0-5. SUPERRUGBY: Lions P/R 2013 2-0-0-0-0-0. FC RECORD: 29-3-0-0-0-15. RECORD IN 2013: (Lions S15, Lions, Young Lions) 18-2-0-0-0-10.
Coetzee, Stephanus Hendrik (Paarl Boys HS) b 09/01/1982, Worcester. 1.85m. 105kg. Hooker. FC DEBUT: 2013. PROV CAREER: WP 2013 8-0-0-0-0-0. FC RECORD: 8-0-0-0-0-0. RECORD IN 2013: (WP) 8-0-0-0-0-0.
Coetzer, Johannes Micheil b 24/11/1985. Prop. FC DEBUT: 2013. PROV CAREER: Limpopo 2013 7-0-0-0-0-0. FC RECORD: 7-0-0-0-0-0. RECORD IN 2013: (Limpopo) 7-0-0-0-0-0.
Coetzer, Marius (Waterkloof HS, Pretoria) b 04/04/84, Pretoria. 2.00m. 104kg. Lock. FC DEBUT: 2005. PROV CAREER: Blue Bulls 2005 1-0-0-0-0-0. WP 2006 5-0-0-0-0-0. Valke 2007-08 26-0-0-0-0-0. Pumas 2009-11 & 13 67-9-0-0-0-45. SUPERRUGBY: Lions 2012 5-0-0-0-0-0. Stormers 2013 1-0-0-0-0-0. FC RECORD: 105-9-0-0-0-45. RECORD IN 2013: (Stormers, Pumas) 14-1-0-0-0-5.
Coleman, Kurt Kendall (Grey HS & Stellenbosch Univ.) b 29/01/1990, Knysna. 1.77m. 82kg. Flyhalf. FC DEBUT: 2011. PROV CAREER: WP 2011-13 39-6-31-39-0-209. Eagles 2012 4-0-7-7-0-35. SUPERRUGBY: Stormers 2011 & 13 6-1-4-6-0-31. FC RECORD: 49-7-42-52-0-275. RECORD IN 2013: (Stormers, WP) 18-0-21-34-0-144.
Colyn, Frederick Hendrik (Erick) (Outeniqua HS, George & UFS) b 07/08/1990, Oudtshoorn. 1.78m. 77kg. Flyhalf. FC DEBUT: 2011. PROV CAREER: Cheetahs 2011 2-0-0-0-0-0. Free State XV 2013 1-0-0-0-0-0. FC RECORD: 3-0-0-0-0-0. RECORD IN 2013: (Free State XV) 1-0-0-0-0-0.
Combrink, Ruan Jacobus (Michaelhouse HS) b 10/05/1990, Vryheid. 1.83m. 96kg. Wing. FC DEBUT: 2010. PROV CAREER: WP 2010 1-0-0-0-0-0. Lions 2012 9-4-0-2-0-26. Young Lions 2012 5-3-0-0-0-15. SUPERRUGBY: Lions 2012 7-4-0-1-0-3. P/R 2013 2-0-0-0-0-0. FC RECORD: 24-7-0-3-0-44. RECORD IN 2013: (Lions S15) 2-0-0-0-0-0.
Conradie, Johannes Haindly Joseph (Bolla) (Kasselsvlei SS) b 24/02/78, Cape Town. 1.69m. 75kg. Scrumhalf. FC DEBUT: 1998. PROV CAREER: WP 2001-09 & 13 86-16-0-0-0-80. Boland 2010-12 50-13-0-0-0-65. SUPERRUGBY: Stormers 2002-09 77-10-0-0-1-53. REP HONOURS: SA 2002 & 04-05 & 08 Tests 18-2-0-0-1-13. SA 'A' 2001 & 03 6-0-0-0-0-0. SA U23s 2001 5-0-0-0-0-0. SA U21s 1998 3-0-0-0-0-0. SA Sevens 1999-00. SA Schools 1996-97. CW WP 1996-97. FC RECORD: 245-41-0-0-2-211. RECORD IN 2013: (WP) 7-0-0-0-0-0.
Constant, Ashton (Voortrekker HS, Cape Town, UWC) b 28/09/83, Cape Town. 1.82m. 110kg. Hooker. FC DEBUT: 2004. PROV CAREER: WP 2004-05 5-0-0-0-0-0. Pumas 2006-08 47-6-0-0-0-30. Eagles 2009 11-1-0-0-0-5. Boland 2010-13 48-6-0-0-0-30. REP HONOURS: Emerging Springboks 2007 3-1-0-0-0-5. SA Pres XV 2013 3-0-0-0-0-0. SA U21 2004 5-1-0-0-0-5. FC RECORD: 122-15-0-0-0-75. RECORD IN 2013: (SA Pres XV, Boland) 9-2-0-0-0-10.
Cook, Jean George (Grey College, Bloemfontein & UCT) b 14/08/1991, Pietermaritzburg. 1.93m. 102kg. Flank. FC DEBUT: 2011. PROV CAREER: Cheetahs 2011 1-0-0-0-0-0. Blue Bulls 2012-13 17-3-0-0-0-15. SUPERRUGBY: Bulls 2013 1-0-0-0-0-5. REP HONOURS: SAU20 2011 5-0-0-0-0-0. FC RECORD: 24-4-0-0-0-20. RECORD IN 2013: (Bulls,

Blue Bulls) 10-3-0-0-0-15.
Cooke, Ronald John (Ronnie) (Noord-Kaap HS) b 05/01/85, Pretoria. 1.83m. 79kgs. Centre. FC DEBUT: 2004. PROV CAREER: Leopards 2004-05 26-14-0-0-0-70. Griquas 2006-07 14-3-0-0-0-15. EP Kings 2013 4-0-0-0-0-0. SUPERRUGBY: Cheetahs 2006-07 24-5-0-0-0-25. Southern Kings 2013 15-2-0-0-0-10. P/R 2013 2-0-0-0-0-0. REP HONOURS: SA U21 2005 3-0-0-0-0-0. FC RECORD: 88-24-0-0-0-120. RECORD IN 2013: (Southern Kings, EP Kings) 21-2-0-0-0-10.
Cooper, Kyle Lorran (Glenwood HS) b 10/02/1989, Johannesburg. 1.77m. 107kg. Hooker. FC DEBUT: 2010. PROV CAREER: KZN 2010-13 38-2-0-0-0-10. Sharks XV 2010-12 27-2-0-0-0-10. Sharks Inv XV 2010 1-1-0-0-0-5. SUPERRUGBY: Sharks 2012-13 17-1-0-0-0-5. REP HONOURS: SAU20 2009 5-0-0-0-0-0. FC RECORD: 88-6-0-0-0-30. RECORD IN 2013: (Sharks, KZN) 28-2-0-0-0-10.
Cornelius, Lionel Curtis (Hermanus HS) b 29/10/86, Hermanus. 1.75m. 91kg. Fullback. FC DEBUT: 2007. PROV CAREER: Boland 2007-10 56-9-15-18-0-129. Eagles 2013 2-0-0-0-0-0. FC RECORD: 58-9-15-18-0-129. RECORD IN 2013: (Eagles) 2-0-0-0-0-0.
Craill, Bronwyn b 07/03/1988. Fullback. FC DEBUT: 2013. PROV CAREER: Limpopo 2013 6-0-1-5-0-17. FC RECORD: 6-0-1-5-0-17. RECORD IN 2013: (Limpopo) 6-0-1-5-0-17.
Cresswell, Rory Charles b 25/03/1988. Lock. FC DEBUT: 2013. PROV CAREER: Limpopo 2013 1-0-0-0-0-0. FC RECORD: 1-0-0-0-0-0. RECORD IN 2013: (Limpopo) 1-0-0-0-0-0.
Crocker, Quinton (Port Natal HS) b 26/06/1987, Kempton Park. 1.87m. 96kg. Flyhalf/Fullback. FC DEBUT: 2012. PROV CAREER: Bulldogs 2012-13 32-4-5-2-0-36. FC RECORD: 32-4-5-2-0-36. RECORD IN 2013: (Bulldogs) 21-3-2-0-0-19.
Cronje, Coert Frederick (Jeugland HS & UJ) b 11/05/1988, Vereeniging. 1.82m. 86kg. Centre. FC DEBUT: 2010. PROV CAREER: Valke 2010-13 57-26-0-0-0-130. FC RECORD: 57-26-0-0-0-130. RECORD IN 2013: (Valke) 20-6-0-0-0-30.
Cronje, Guy (Michaelhouse) B 26/07/89, Johannesburg. 1.76m. 75kg. Flyhalf. FC DEBUT: 2009. PROV CAREER: KZN 2009 7-0-3-0-0-6. Sharks XV 2009 & 2011 12-2-16-4-0-54. Sharks Inv XV 2009 1-0-0-0-0-0. Lions 2012-13 8-0-1-0-0-2. Young Lions 2012-13 6-2-24-9-0-85. SUPERRUGBY: Lions P/R 2013 2-0-0-0-0-0. MISC INFO: Twin brother of Ross Cronje. FC RECORD: 36-4-44-13-0-147. RECORD IN 2013: (Lions S15, Lions, Young Lions) 10-2-12-0-0-34.
Cronje, Lionel (Queens College & UOFS) b 25/05/1989, Bloemfontein. 1.84m. 90kg. Flyhalf. FC DEBUT: 2010. PROV CAREER: WP 2010-11 21-6-33-13-0-135. Blue Bulls 2012 5-0-0-0-0-0. Lions 2013 5-0-0-0-0-0. Young Lions 2013 5-3-2-0-0-19. SUPERRUGBY: Stormers 2010-11 7-0-4-8-0-32. REP HONOURS: SAU20 2009 4-5-2-0-0-29. Misc: Vodacom Cup POY 2011. FC RECORD: 47-14-41-21-0-215. RECORD IN 2013: (Lions, Young Lions) 10-3-2-0-0-19.
Cronje, Ross (Michaelhouse) b 26/7/89, Johannesburg. 1.81m. 79kg. Scrumhalf. FC DEBUT: 2009. PROV CAREER: KZN 2009 & 2011 14-0-0-0-0-0. Sharks XV 2009-11 22-3-11-4-0-49. Lions 2012-13 16-1-0-0-0-5. Young Lions 2013 7-0-3-0-0-6. SUPERRUGBY: Sharks 2009 1-0-0-0-0-0. Lions 2012 6-0-0-0-0-0. Lions P/R 2013 1-0-0-0-0-0. REP HONOURS: SAU20 2009 5-1-0-0-0-5. MISC INFO: Twin brother of Guy Cronje. FC RECORD: 72-5-14-4-0-65. RECORD IN 2013: (Lions S15, Lions, Young Lions) 13-0-3-0-0-6.
Crous, Christiaan Petro (Overkruin HS & UP) b 21/07/1988, Pretoria. 1.94m. 109kg. Hooker. FC DEBUT: 2013. PROV CAREER: Limpopo 2013 2-0-0-0-0-0. FC RECORD: 2-0-0-0-0-0. RECORD IN 2013: (Limpopo) 2-0-0-0-0-0.
Croy, Ricardo (Paarl Gymnasium) b 07/12/86, Belville. 1.72m.

A-Z OF FIRST-CLASS PLAYERS IN 2013

77kg. Flyhalf. FC DEBUT: 2006. PROV CAREER: WP 2006 & 08 14-2-14-6-0-56. Eagles 2008-09 22-4-37-31-2-193. Pumas 2010-11 27-4-32-33-4-195. Boland 2012-13 25-0-14-15-0-73. REP HONOURS: SA Barbarians 2012 1-0-0-0-0. SA Pres XV 2013 2-0-3-4-0-18. SA U19 2005. MISC INFO: Son of former WP scrumhalf Richard Croy. FC RECORD: 91-10-100-89-6-535. RECORD IN 2013: (SA Pres XV, Boland) 15-0-11-10-0-52.

D

Dames, Hendrik Daniel Petrus (Danie) (Duineveld HS) b 07/02/86, Pretoria. 1.90m. 84kg. Utility back. FC DEBUT: 2008. PROV CAREER: Sharks XV 2008-09 12-0-0-0-0-0. Leopards 2009-13 58-22-0-0-0-110. Leopard XV 2013 7-5-0-0-0-25. MISC INFO: Represented Namibia at RWC 2011. FC RECORD: 77-27-0-0-0-135. RECORD IN 2013: (Leopards, Leopard XV) 21-11-0-0-0-55.

Daniel, Keegan Rhys (Dale College) b 05/03/85, Humansdorp. 1.85m. 100kg. Flank. FC DEBUT: 2006. PROV CAREER: KZN 2006-13 104-33-0-0-0-165. Sharks XV 2006-09 9-4-0-0-0-20. Sharks Inv XV 2009-10 2-2-1-0-0-12. SUPERRUGBY: Sharks 2006-13 96-15-0-0-0-75. REP HONOURS: SA 2010 & 12 Tests: 5-0-0-0-0-0. Tour: 1-0-0-0-0-0. Total: 6-0-0-0-0-0. SA U21 2006 5-3-0-0-0-15. MISC INFO: U21 PoY 2006, VC PoY 2006, YPoY nominee 2006, IRB PoY nominee 2006. SARU Poy 2012 nominee. Super PoY 2012. FC RECORD: 222-57-1-0-0-287. RECORD IN 2013: (Sharks, KZN) 23-6-0-0-0-30.

Daniller, Hendrik Joseph (Hennie) (Paarl Gymnasium) b 05/04/84, Cape Town. 1.95m. 95kg. Fullback. FC DEBUT: 2003. PROV CAREER: Blue Bulls 2003 & 05-06 19-1-0-0-0-5. Boland 2006-07 19-1-0-0-0-5. Cheetahs 2008-13 71-11-0-0-0-55. Griffons 2008 5-0-0-0-0-0. Cheetahs XV 2010 1-0-0-0-0-0. SUPERRUGBY: Bulls 2004 7-0-0-0-0-0. Cheetahs 2008-13 76-7-0-0-0-35. REP HONOURS: SA U21 2004-05 9-3-0-0-0-15. SA U19 2003. SA Schools 2002. FC RECORD: 207-23-0-0-0-115. RECORD IN 2013: (Cheetahs S15, Cheetahs) 27-3-0-0-0-15. MISC INFO: Brother of Tertius Daniller.

Daniller, Tertius (Paarl Gymnasium) b 04/08/1989, Paarl. 1.94m. 88kg. Eightman. FC DEBUT: 2010. PROV CAREER: WP 2010-11 17-1-0-0-0-5. Griffons 2013 11-2-0-0-0-10. Free State XV 2013 7-2-0-0-0-10. FC RECORD: 35-5-0-0-0-25. RECORD IN 2013: (Griffons, Free State XV) 18-4-0-0-0-20. MISC INFO: Brother of Hennie Daniller.

Davel, Cornelius Andries (Nollie) (DF Malan HS & UP) b 09/11/1988, Vereeniging. 1.70m. 75kg. Scrumhalf. FC DEBUT: 2013. PROV CAREER: Limpopo 2013 5-0-0-0-0-0. FC RECORD: 5-0-0-0-0-0. RECORD IN 2013: (Limpopo) 5-0-0-0-0-0.

Davel, Louw Lodewickus b 24/08/1985. Centre. FC DEBUT: 2013. PROV CAREER: Limpopo 2013 6-0-0-0-0-0. FC RECORD: 6-0-0-0-0-0. RECORD IN 2013: (Limpopo) 6-0-0-0-0-0.

Davids, Ashlon (Schoonspruit HS) b 24/06/1993, Malmesbury. 1.70m. 75kg. Flyhalf. FC DEBUT: 2013. PROV CAREER: Young Lions 2013 2-3-3-0-0-21. FC RECORD: 2-3-3-0-0-21. RECORD IN 2013: (Young Lions) 2-3-3-0-0-21.

Davis, Aidon (Daniel Pienaar HS) b 29/04/1994, Uitenhage. 1.91m. 100kg. Flank. FC DEBUT: 2013. PROV CAREER: EP Kings 2013 7-2-0-0-0-10. SUPERRUGBY: Southern Kings 2013 1-0-0-0-0-0. REP HONOURS: SA U20 2013 3-0-0-0-0-0. FC RECORD: 11-2-0-0-0-10. RECORD IN 2013: (Southern Kings, EP Kings, SA U20) 11-2-0-0-0-10. MISC INFO: Brother of Dalton Davis.

Davis, Dalton (Daniel Pienaar THS) b 19/11/1990, Uitenhage. 1.91m. 103kg. Lock. FC DEBUT: 2013. PROV CAREER: EP Kings 2013 10-2-0-0-0-10. Griquas 2013 3-1-0-0-0-5. FC RECORD: 13-3-0-0-0-15. RECORD IN 2013: (Griquas, EP Kings) 13-3-0-0-0-15. MISC INFO: Brother of Aidon Davis.

De Allende, Damian (Milnerton HS) b 25/11/1991, Cape Town. 1.89m. 96kg. Centre. FC DEBUT: 2012. PROV CAREER: WP 2012-13 24-6-0-0-0-30. SUPERRUGBY: Stormers 2013 14-0-0-0-0-0. FC RECORD: 38-6-0-0-0-30. RECORD IN 2013: (Stormers, WP) 26-4-0-0-0-20.

De Bruin, Johann (Kempton Park HS) b 23/07/86, Kempton Park. 1.98m. 95kg. Lock. FC DEBUT: 2008. PROV CAREER: Valke 2008-13 63-7-0-0-0-35. FC RECORD: 63-7-0-0-0-35. RECORD IN 2013: (Valke) 5-1-0-0-0-5.

De Bruin, Luan (Affies, Pretoria) b 13/02/1993, Pretoria. 1.83m. 124kg. Prop. FC DEBUT: 2013. REP HONOURS: SA U20 2013 4-1-0-0-0-5. FC RECORD: 4-1-0-0-0-5. RECORD IN 2013: (SA U20) 4-1-0-0-0-5.

De Bruyn, Matthewus Johannes (Tewis) (Grey College, Bloemfontein) b 05/08/82, Hoopstad. 1.73m. 81kg. Scrumhalf. FC DEBUT: 2002. PROV CAREER: Leopards 2002-03 23-2-16-3-1-54. Eagles 2004-06 51-6-10-7-1-74. Boland 2006-07 14-0-12-4-0-36. Cheetahs 2007-12 74-13-38-3-0-150. Griffons 2013 1-0-0-0-0-0. Free State XV 2013 5-2-5-10-0-50. Cheetahs XV 2010 1-0-1-2-0-8. Emerging Cheetahs 2011 1-0-0-0-0-0. SUPERRUGBY: Cheetahs 2008-13 57-3-2-2-0-25. FC RECORD: 227-26-84-31-2-397. RECORD IN 2013: (Cheetahs S15, Griffons, Free State XV) 7-2-5-10-0-50.

De Bruyn, Robert James (Michaelhouse HS & UJ) b 26/02/1991, Johannesburg. 1.79m. 90kg. Centre. FC DEBUT: 2011. PROV CAREER: Lions 2013 7-0-0-0-0-0. Young Lions 2012 7-3-0-0-0-15. Golden Lions XV 2011 1-1-0-0-0-5. FC RECORD: 15-4-0-0-0-20. RECORD IN 2013: (Lions) 7-0-0-0-0-0.

De Jager, Lodewyk (Hugenote HS & NWU) b 17/12/1992, Alberton. 2.05m. 118kg. Lock. FC DEBUT: 2013. PROV CAREER: Cheetahs 2013 10-0-0-0-0-0. SUPERRUGBY: Cheetahs 2013 17-0-0-0-0-0. FC RECORD: 27-0-0-0-0-0. RECORD IN 2013: (Cheetahs S15, Cheetahs) 27-0-0-0-0-0.

De Jongh, Juan Leon (Hugenot HS) b 15/04/88, Paarl. 1.77m. 84kg. Centre. FC DEBUT: 2009. PROV CAREER: WP 2009-13 39-14-0-0-0-70. SUPERRUGBY: Stormers 2010-13 57-9-0-0-0-45. REP HONOURS: SA 2009-12 Tests: 14-3-0-0-0-15. Tour 2009 2-1-0-0-0-5. Total: 16-4-0-0-0-20. MISC INFO: YPOY Nominee 2009. FC RECORD: 112-27-0-0-0-135. RECORD IN 2013: (Stormers, WP) 18-5-0-0-0-25.

De Klerk, Francois (Waterkloof HS, Pretoria) b 19/10/1991, Nelspruit. 1.69m. 66kg. Scrumhalf. FC DEBUT: 2012. PROV CAREER: Pumas 2012-13 46-3-0-0-0-15. FC RECORD: 46-3-0-0-0-15. RECORD IN 2013: (Pumas) 28-1-0-0-0-5.

De Klerk, Jan Jonathan Stephanus (JJ) (Grey College, Bloemfontein) b 24/02/1992, Lichtenburg. 1.77m. 80kg. Centre. FC DEBUT: 2013. PROV CAREER: Griquas 2013 1-0-0-0-0-0. FC RECORD: 1-0-0-0-0-0. RECORD IN 2013: (Griquas) 1-0-0-0-0-0.

De Klerk, Pieter Rossouw (Paarl Gymnasium) b 21/08/89. Vredenburg. 1.86m. 110kg. Prop. FC DEBUT: 2009. PROV CAREER: Blue Bulls 2009-12 33-0-0-0-0-0. Cheetahs 2013 7-0-0-0-0-0. Griffons 2013 1-0-0-0-0-0. Free State XV 2013 7-1-0-0-0-5. SUPERRUGBY: Bulls 2010-11 14-0-0-0-0-0. FC RECORD: 62-1-0-0-0-5. RECORD IN 2013: (Cheetahs, Griffons, Free State XV) 15-1-0-0-0-5.

De Kock, Jacobus Johannes (Kobus) (Paarl Boys HS) b 29/03/1988, Paarl. 1.89m. 98kg. Fullback. FC DEBUT: 2011. PROV CAREER: Sharks XV 2011 8-7-7-0-0-49. Lions 2013 2-0-0-0-0-0. Young Lions 2013 3-0-1-0-0-2. FC RECORD: 13-7-8-0-0-51. RECORD IN 2013: (Lions, Young Lions) 5-0-1-0-0-2.

De Lange, Jean-Jacques (JJ) b 20/04/1992. Lock. FC DEBUT: 2013. PROV CAREER: Limpopo 2013 6-0-0-0-0-0. FC RECORD: 6-0-0-

A-Z OF FIRST-CLASS PLAYERS IN 2013

0-0-0. RECORD IN 2013: (Limpopo) 6-0-0-0-0.

De Swardt, Albertus Jacobus (Albie) (Outeniqua HS, George) b 10/08/1990, George. 1.86m. 98kg. Hooker. FC DEBUT: 2011. PROV CAREER: WP 2011 1-0-0-0-0-0. EP Kings 2013 11-0-0-0-0-0. FC RECORD: 12-0-0-0-0-0. RECORD IN 2013: (EP Kings) 11-0-0-0-0-0.

De Villiers, Jean (Paarl Gymnasium) b 24/02/81, Paarl. 1.90m. 100kg. Centre. FC DEBUT: 2001. PROV CAREER: WP 2001-05 & 08 & 10-13 50-30-0-0-0-150. SUPERRUGBY: Stormers 2005-09 & 11-13 96-27-0-0-0-135. REP HONOURS: SA 2002 & 2004-13 Tests: 96-25-0-0-0-125. Total: 96-25-0-0-0-125. SA XV 2006 1-0-0-0-0-0. SA Sevens 2002. SA U21s 2001-02 9-7-0-0-0-35; SA U19 2000. SA Schools 1999; CW WP Academy 1999. British Barbarians 2008 & 13 2-2-0-0-0-10. MISC INFO: SA Rugby PoY 2008. PoY nominee 2005. SA Rugby PoY 2013. Holds SA Record for most tests as a centre - 81. Son of former WP lock André de Villiers. FC RECORD: 254-91-0-0-0-455. RECORD IN 2013: (SA, Stormers, WP, British Barbarians) 30-12-0-0-0-60.

De Wet, Philip Albert (Grey College, Bloemfontein & NWU) b 14/02/1989, Kuruman. 1.87m. 98kg. Flank. FC DEBUT: 2011. PROV CAREER: Leopards 2011-13 29-13-0-0-0-65. FC RECORD: 29-13-0-0-0-65. RECORD IN 2013: (Leopards) 8-2-0-0-0-0.

De Wet, Pieter-Steyn (Paarl Gymnasium) b 08/01/1991, Caledon. 1.75m. 83kg. Flyhalf. FC DEBUT: 2012. PROV CAREER: Free State XV 2012 4-0-0-0-0-0. Griquas 2013 5-0-13-6-1-47. FC RECORD: 9-0-13-6-1-47. RECORD IN 2013: (Griquas) 5-0-13-6-1-47.

Deale, Johannes Jacobus (Hanco) (Affies, Pretoria) b 12/08/1993, Pretoria. 1.77m. 80kg. Fullback. FC DEBUT: 2013. PROV CAREER: Young Lions 2013 2-0-1-0-0-2. FC RECORD: 2-0-1-0-0-2. RECORD IN 2013: (Young Lions) 2-0-1-0-0-2.

Dell, Allan Michael Elgin (Queens College) b 16/03/1992, Humansdorp. 1.85m. 112kg. Prop. FC DEBUT: 2012. PROV CAREER: KZN 2012 1-0-0-0-0-0. Sharks XV 2012-13 10-0-0-0-0-0. REP HONOURS: SAU20 2012 4-0-0-0-0-0. FC RECORD: 15-0-0-0-0-0. RECORD IN 2013: (Sharks XV) 6-0-0-0-0-0.

Delo, Layle Antonio (Outeniqua HS) b 28/10/1989, George. 1.86m. 115kg. Hooker. FC DEBUT: 2011. PROV CAREER: Eagles 2011-13 27-2-0-0-0-10. FC RECORD: 27-2-0-0-0-10. RECORD IN 2013: (Eagles) 14-1-0-0-0-5.

Delport, Paul Stephen (SACS) b 13/10/84, Cape Town. 1.72m. 79kg. Scrumhalf. FC DEBUT: 2004. PROV CAREER: WP 2004-08 52-6-0-0-0-30. SUPERRUGBY: Cats 2004-05 11-0-0-0-0-0. REP HONOURS: WP XV 2006 1-1-0-0-0-5. SA Sevens 2003-13. SA U21 2004-05 9-3-0-0-0-15. SA U19 (captain) 2003. SA Schools 2001-2002 (captain). CW WP 2001-2002. FC RECORD: 73-10-0-0-0-50. RECORD IN 2013: (SA Sevens).

Demas, Danwel (New Orleans HS) b 15/10/81, Paarl. 1.86m. 79kg. Wing. FC DEBUT: 2004. PROV CAREER: Pumas 2004 & 12-13 19-8-0-0-0-40. Blue Bulls 2005-08 27-8-0-0-0-40. Boland 2008 & 2011 19-21-0-0-0-105. Cheetahs 2009 12-3-0-0-0-15. Cheetahs XV 2010 1-0-0-0-0-0. Griffons 2013 2-1-0-0-0-5. SUPERRUGBY: Bulls 2006 & 08 4-0-0-0-0-0. Cheetahs 2009-10 21-2-0-0-0-10. REP HONOURS: Emerging Springboks 2009 1-1-0-0-0-5. SA Barbarians 2012 1-0-0-0-0-0. SA Sevens 2003-06. FC RECORD: 107-44-0-0-0-220. RECORD IN 2013: (Pumas, Griffons) 4-7-0-0-0-35.

Des Fountain, Dylan (Paarl Gymnasium) b 07/06/85. 1.87m. 84kg. Centre. FC DEBUT: 2004. PROV CAREER: Blue Bulls 2004 1-0-0-0-0-0. WP 2007-10 24-4-0-0-0-20. Lions 2011-13 17-1-0-0-0-5. Young Lions 2011 & 13 8-2-0-0-0-10. SUPERRUGBY: Stormers 2007-09 18-3-0-0-0-15. Lions 2011 6-1-0-0-0-5. Lions P/R 2013 2-0-0-0-0-0. FC RECORD: 76-11-0-0-0-55. RECORD IN 2013 (Lions S15, Lions, Young Lions).

16-1-0-0-0-5.

Deysel, Jean Roy (Hentie Cilliers HS) b 05/03/85, Virginia. 1.92m. 103kg. Flank. FC DEBUT: 2005. PROV CAREER: Lions 2005-07 21-1-0-0-0-5. KZN 2007-13 61-7-0-0-0-35. Sharks XV 2007-08 & 2011-12 8-1-0-0-0-5. Sharks Inv XV 2007,09 2-3-0-0-0-15. SUPERRUGBY: Sharks 2008-13 54-0-0-0-0-0. REP HONOURS: SA 2009,2011 Tests 4-0-0-0-0-0. Tour: 2009 2-0-0-0-0-0. Total: 6-0-0-0-0-0. Emerging Springboks 2009 1-0-0-0-0-0. SA Students 2007 1-0-0-0-0-0. MISC INFO: Absa CC PoY 2008. FC RECORD: 154-12-0-0-0-60. RECORD IN 2013: (Sharks, KZN) 20-1-0-0-0-5.

Dippenaar, Stephanus Christiaan (Stephan) (Paul Roos Gymnasium) b 03/01/88, Moorreesburg. 1.88m. 88kg. Centre. FC DEBUT: 2008. PROV CAREER: Blue Bulls 2008-11 32-6-0-0-0-30. SUPERRUGBY: Bulls 2008 & 10-11 21-1-0-0-0-5. REP HONOURS: SAU20 2008 2-1-0-0-0-5. SA Sevens 2012-13. FC RECORD: 55-8-0-0-0-40. RECORD IN 2013: (SA Sevens).

Dobson, Matthew Grayson (St Charles College & US) b 16/12/1986, Pietermaritzburg. 1.83m. 110kg. Hooker. FC DEBUT: 2011. PROV CAREER: Griquas 2011-13 41-2-0-0-0-10. FC RECORD: 41-2-0-0-0-10. RECORD IN 2013: (Griquas) 18-0-0-0-0-0.

Dolo, Maputhla Stephen (Ben Vorster HS & UFS) b 13/03/1992, Polokwane. 1.78m. 82kg. Fullback. FC DEBUT: 2013. PROV CAREER: Free State XV 2013 5-0-0-0-0-0. FC RECORD: 5-0-0-0-0-0. RECORD IN 2013: (Free State XV) 5-0-0-0-0-0.

Dorfling, Tiaan Arno (Framesby HS & North West Univ.) b 26/07/1990, Port Elizabeth. 1.75m. 80kg. Scrumhalf. FC DEBUT: 2010. PROV CAREER: Leopards 2010 & 12-13 12-1-0-0-0-5. Leopard XV 2013 4-0-0-0-0-0. FC RECORD: 16-1-0-0-0-5. RECORD IN 2013: (Leopards, Leopard XV) 13-1-0-0-0-5.

Downey, Justin (Northwood HS) b 11/11/86, Johannesburg. 1.93m. 102kg. Flank. FC DEBUT: 2008. PROV CAREER: KZN 2009 & 13 7-0-0-0-0-0. Sharks XV 2008-10 18-3-0-0-0-15. Sharks Inv XV 2009-10 2-0-0-0-0-0. Griquas 2010-13 48-4-0-0-0-20. SUPERRUGBY: Cheetahs 2012 12-0-0-0-0-0. FC RECORD: 87-7-0-0-0-35. RECORD IN 2013: (KZN, Griquas) 12-2-0-0-0-10.

Dreyer, Marthinus Chrisstoffel (Martin) (Wonderboom HS & NWU) b 25/08/1988, Rustenburg. 1.85m. 112kg. Prop. FC DEBUT: 2011. PROV CAREER: Leopards 2011 & 13 13-1-0-0-0-5. Leopard XV 2013 4-0-0-0-0-0. REP HONOURS: SA Univ 2013 1-0-0-0-0-0. SA Pres XV 2013 4-0-0-0-0-0. FC RECORD: 22-1-0-0-0-5. RECORD IN 2013: (SA Univ, SA Pres XV, Leopards, Leopard XV) 20-1-0-0-0-5.

Dreyer, Ruan Martin (Monument HS, Krugersdorp) b 16/09/1990, Carletonville. 1.86m. 113kg. Prop. FC DEBUT: 2010. PROV CAREER: Lions 2012-13 13-2-0-0-0-10. Young Lions 2010-13 17-1-0-0-0-5. Golden Lions XV 2011 1-0-0-0-0-0. SUPERRUGBY: Lions 2012 4-1-0-0-0-5. Lions P/R 2013 2-0-0-0-0-0. REP HONOURS: SAU20 2010 5-0-0-0-0-0. FC RECORD: 42-4-0-0-0-20. RECORD IN 2013: (Lions S15, Lions, Young Lions) 18-2-0-0-0-10.

Dry, Christopher Adriaan (Grey College, Bloemfontein & CUT.) b 13/02/88, Cape Town. 1.91m. 95kg. FC DEBUT: 2009. PROV CAREER: Cheetahs 2009-10 5-0-0-0-0-0. Rep. Honours: SA Sevens 2010-13. FC RECORD: 5-0-0-0-0-0. RECORD IN 2013: (SA Sevens).

Du Plessis, Bismarck Wilhelm (Grey College, Bloemfontein & UFS) b 22/05/1984, Bethlehem. 1.89m. 112kg. Hooker. FC DEBUT: 2003. PROV CAREER: Cheetahs 2003 2-0-0-0-0-0. KZN 2005-11 & 13 39-10-0-0-0-50. Sharks XV 2005-08 3-2-0-0-0-10. SUPERRUGBY: Sharks 2005-13 103-14-0-0-0-70. REP HONOURS: SA 2007-13 Tests: 57-9-0-0-0-45. Tour: 2007 2-0-0-0-0-0. Total: 59-9-0-0-0-45. SA U21 2005 1-1-0-0-0-5.

A-Z OF FIRST-CLASS PLAYERS IN 2013

British Barbs. 2009 & 13 2-2-0-0-0-10. MISC INFO: PoY nominee 2008, 2011, 2013. Super PoY 2011 and 2012 nominee. Brother of Sharks prop Jannie du Plessis. Son of former EOFS prop Francois du Plessis. FC RECORD: 209-38-0-0-0-190. RECORD IN 2013: (SA, Sharks, KZN, British Barbarians) 18-6-0-0-0-30.

Du Plessis, Charl Francois (Monument HS, Krugersdorp) b 08/04/87, Cape Town. 1.87m. 113kg. Prop. FC DEBUT: 2008. PROV CAREER: Young Lions 2008-10 7-0-0-0-0-0. Valke 2009 9-0-0-0-0-0. Boland 2010-12 31-0-0-0-0-0. EP Kings 2012-13 27-0-0-0-0-0. SUPERRUGBY: Southern Kings 2013 2-0-0-0-0-0. P/R 2013 1-0-0-0-0-0. FC RECORD: 77-0-0-0-0-0. RECORD IN 2013: (Southern Kings, EP Kings) 19-0-0-0-0-0.

Du Plessis, Christo John (George HS) b 02/06/1989, George. 1.86m. 92kg. Flanker. FC DEBUT: 2010. PROV CAREER: Eagles 2010 & 12-13 33-5-0-0-0-25. FC RECORD: 33-5-0-0-0-25. RECORD IN 2013: (Eagles) 18-4-0-0-0-20.

Du Plessis, Jan Nathaniël (Jannie) (Grey College, Bloemfontein) b 16/11/82, Bethlehem. 1.88m. 120kg. Prop. FC DEBUT: 2003. PROV CAREER: Cheetahs 2003-07 69-3-0-0-0-15. KZN 2008-13 35-3-0-0-0-15. SUPERRUGBY: Cheetahs 2006-07 26-0-0-0-0-0. Sharks 2008-13 88-0-0-0-0-0. REP HONOURS: SA 2007-13 Tests: 51-1-0-0-0-5. Tour: 2007, 09 2-0-0-0-0-0. Total: 53-1-0-0-0-5. SA U21 2003 4-0-0-0-0-0. MISC INFO: Brother of Natal Sharks hooker Bismarck du Plessis. Son of former EOFS prop Francois du Plessis. Medical doctor. FC RECORD: 275-7-0-0-0-35. REP HONOURS: CW Free State 2000. RECORD IN 2013: (SA, Sharks, KZN) 27-0-0-0-0-0.

Du Plessis, Jean-Pierre (JP) (HTS Middelburg) B 06/05/1992, Volksrust. 1.85m. 105kg. Centre. FC DEBUT: 2012. PROV CAREER: Young Lions 2012-13 3-1-0-0-0-5. FC RECORD: 3-1-0-0-0-5. RECORD IN 2013: (Young Lions) 2-1-0-0-0-5.

Du Plessis, Willem Hendrik Jacques (Jacques) (Ermelo HS & UP) b 12/08/1993, Pongola. 2.01m. 119kg. Flank. FC DEBUT: 2013. PROV CAREER: Blue Bulls 2013 12-2-0-0-0-10. SUPERRUGBY: Bulls 2013 1-0-0-0-0-0. REP HONOURS: SA U20 2013 5-1-0-0-0-5. MISC INFO: SA U20 PoY nominee 2013. FC RECORD: 18-3-0-0-0-15. RECORD IN 2013: (Bulls, Blue Bulls, SA U20) 18-3-0-0-0-15.

Du Plessis, Willem Nicolaas Frederik (Willie) (Affies, Pretoria & UP) b 05/06/1990, Pretoria. 1.86m. 90kg. Flyhalf. FC DEBUT: 2012. PROV CAREER: Blue Bulls 2012-13 7-4-33-0-0-86. Cheetahs 2013 9-0-3-0-0-6. FC RECORD: 16-4-36-0-0-92. RECORD IN 2013: (Blue Bulls, Cheetahs) 16-2-33-0-0-76.

Du Preez, Branco Bewinn Nazeem (PW Botha College) b 08/05/1990, George. 1.66m. 72kg. Flyhalf. REP HONOURS: SAU20 2010 4-1-0-0-0-5. SA Sevens 2010-13. FC RECORD: 4-1-0-0-0-5. RECORD IN 2013: (SA Sevens).

Du Preez, Cornell Gerard (Framesby HS & NWU) b 23/03/1991, Port Elizabeth. 1.92m. 106kg. Loose Forward. FC DEBUT: 2012. PROV CAREER: EP Kings 2012-13 23-11-0-0-0-55. SUPERRUGBY: Southern Kings 2013 14-3-0-0-0-15. P/R 2013 2-0-0-0-0-0. REP HONOURS: SAU20 2011 5-1-0-0-0-5. FC RECORD: 44-15-0-0-0-75. RECORD IN 2013: (Southern Kings, EP Kings) 20-5-0-0-0-25.

Du Preez, Hermanus Carel (Noordkaapland Agric.) b 30/04/1983, Hartswater. 1.98m. 100kg. Eightman. FC DEBUT: 2013. PROV CAREER: WP 2013 3-0-0-0-0-0. FC RECORD: 3-0-0-0-0-0. RECORD IN 2013: (WP) 3-0-0-0-0-0.

Du Preez, Petrus Fourie (Affies, Pretoria) b 24/03/82, Pretoria. 1.82m. 91kg. Scrumhalf. FC DEBUT: 2001. PROV CAREER: Blue Bulls 2001-05 & 08-09 52-19-0-0-0-95. SUPERRUGBY: Bulls 2003-11 112-22-0-0-0-110. REP HONOURS: SA 2004-09 & 2011 & 13 67-15-0-0-0-75.

SA U21 2002-03 9-1-0-0-0-5. SA U19 2001. British Barbarians 2008, 09 2-0-0-0-0-0. MISC INFO: YPoY nominee 2003, 2004, PoY 2006 PoY nominee 2007. S14 PoY 2007. SA Rugby POY 2009. IRB Rugby POY Nominee 2009. Son of former Northern Transvaal No. 8 Fourie du Preez (Snr) FC RECORD: 242-57-0-0-0-285. RECORD IN 2013: (SA) 5-2-0-0-0-10.

Du Preez, Robert James (Kearsney College) b 30/07/1993, Durban. 1.92m. 95kg. Scrumhalf. FC DEBUT: 2013. REP HONOURS: SA U20 2013 4-0-8-4-0-28. FC RECORD: 4-0-8-4-0-28. RECORD IN 2013: (SA U20) 4-0-8-4-0-28. MISC INFO: Son of former Springbok scrumhalf Robert du Preez.

Du Preez, Vernon (Stoffberg HS) b 23/04/1986, Springs. 1.75m. 108kg. Hooker. FC DEBUT: 2010. PROV CAREER: Valke 2010-13 15-1-0-0-0-5. FC RECORD: 15-1-0-0-0-5. RECORD IN 2013: (Valke) 3-0-0-0-0-0.

Du Preez, Wian Hunter (Grey College, Bloemfontein) b 30/10/82, Bloemfontein. 1.85m. 113kg. Prop. FC DEBUT: 2003. PROV CAREER: Cheetahs 2003-09 & 13 110-7-0-0-0-35. SUPERRUGBY: Sharks 2005 2-0-0-0-0-0. Cheetahs 2006-10 59-0-0-0-0-0. REP HONOURS: Tests SA Tests: 2009 1-0-0-0-0-0. Tour 2009 1-0-0-0-0-0. Total: 2-0-0-0-0-0. Emerging Springboks 2009 1-0-0-0-0-0. FC RECORD: 174-7-0-0-0-35. RECORD IN 2013: (Cheetahs) 5-0-0-0-0-0.

Du Rand, Christiaan Wessel (Dr EG Jansen HS & UJ) b 23/05/1990, Boksburg. 1.81m. 118kg. Prop. FC DEBUT: 2012. PROV CAREER: Valke 2013 12-1-0-0-0-5. Young Lions 2012 5-0-0-0-0-0. REP HONOURS: SAU20: 2010 3-0-0-0-0-0. FC RECORD: 20-1-0-0-0-5. RECORD IN 2013: (Valke) 12-1-0-0-0-5.

Du Toit, Francois (Florida HS & UJ) b 17/08/1990, Johannesburg. 1.78m. 103kg. Hooker. FC DEBUT: 2011. PROV CAREER: Lions 2012-13 3-0-0-0-0-0. Young Lions 2011-13 14-3-0-0-0-15. Pumas 2013 10-1-0-0-0-5. REP HONOURS: SA Students 2012 2-0-0-0-0-0. SAU20 2010 4-0-0-0-0-0. FC RECORD: 33-4-0-0-0-20. RECORD IN 2013: (Lions, Young Lions, Pumas) 18-2-0-0-0-10.

Du Toit, Francois Cornelius (Franna) (Grey College, Bloemfontein & UFS) b 16/03/1990, Vryburg. 1.83m. 84kg. Flyhalf. FC DEBUT: 2011. PROV CAREER: Cheetahs 2011 1-1-0-0-0-5. Griffons 2013 4-0-10-0-0-20. REP HONOURS: SA Students 2012 2-0-2-1-0-7. FC RECORD: 7-1-12-1-0-32. RECORD IN 2013: (Griffons) 4-0-10-0-0-20.

Du Toit, Lourens Marthinus (Framesby & Oueteniqua HS) b 29/08/1992, Port Elizabeth. 1.94m. 105kg. Lock. FC DEBUT: 2013. PROV CAREER: Eagles 2013 4-0-0-0-0-0. FC RECORD: 4-0-0-0-0-0. RECORD IN 2013: (Eagles) 4-0-0-0-0-0.

Du Toit, Ockert Jacobus Jacques (Grey College, Bloemfontein & UFS) b 19/11/1993, Bloemfontein. 1.86m. 102kg. Hooker. FC debut: 2013. REP HONOURS: SA U20 2013 5-1-0-0-0-5. FC RECORD: 5-1-0-0-0-5. RECORD IN 2013: (SA U20) 5-1-0-0-0-5.

Du Toit, Ozard Martin (Hottentots Holland HS) b 27/06/1989, Welkom. 1.82m. 80kg. Fullback. FC DEBUT: 2012. PROV CAREER: Eagles 2012-13 22-4-0-0-0-20. FC RECORD: 22-4-0-0-0-20. RECORD IN 2013: (Eagles) 18-4-0-0-0-20.

Du Toit, Pieter Stephanus (Pieter-Steph) (Swartland HS) b 20/08/1992, Cape Town. 2m. 116kg. Lock. FC DEBUT: 2012. PROV CAREER: Sharks XV 2012 5-1-0-0-0-5. KZN 2013 5-0-0-0-0-0. SUPERRUGBY: Sharks 2012-13 19-0-0-0-0-0. REP HONOURS: SA 2013 Tests: 2-0-0-0-0-0. SAU20 2012 5-1-0-0-0-5. FC RECORD: 36-2-0-0-0-10. RECORD IN 2013: (SA, Sharks, KZN) 20-0-0-0-0-0. MISC INFO: Grandson of PS du Toit (SA 1956-1961). YPoY nominee 2013.

A-Z OF FIRST-CLASS PLAYERS IN 2013

Dukisa, Ntabeni (Loyolo HS) b 25/07/1988. Wing. FC DEBUT: 2010. PROV CAREER: Bulldogs 2010-12 26-5-19-34-0-165. Griffons 2012 5-0-0-0-0-0. EP Kings 2013 18-3-6-8-1-54. REP HONOURS: SA Barbarians 2012 1-1-0-0-0-5. FC RECORD: 50-9-25-42-1-224. RECORD IN 2013: (EP Kings) 18-3-6-8-1-54.

Dumond, Cecil (Orkney HS) b 08/04/87, Klerksdorp. 1.82m. 84kgs. Flyhalf. FC DEBUT: 2007. PROV CAREER: Leopards 2007 & 09-11 26-2-18-29-2-139. Eagles 2011-12 13-1-1-4-0-19. Bulldogs 2013 7-0-2-1-0-7. MISC INFO: Brother of Monty Dumond. FC RECORD: 46-3-21-34-1-165. RECORD IN 2013: (Bulldogs) 7-0-2-1-0-7.

Dunlop, Wesley Roy (Grey HS, PE) b 12/05/87, Durban. 1.85m. 92kg. Flyhalf. FC DEBUT: 2009. PROV CAREER: EP Kings 2009 & 12-13 35-5-42-40-1-232. Blue Bulls 2011-12 8-0-14-6-0-46. Leopards 2011 12-2-18-11-1-82. FC RECORD: 55-7-74-57-2-360. RECORD IN 2013: (EP Kings) 10-1-11-16-0-75.

Duvenage, Dewaldt Otto (Paarl Gymnasium) b 22/05/88, Bellville. 1.76m. 75kg. Scrumhalf. FC DEBUT: 2007. PROV CAREER: Boland 2007-08 24-3-0-0-0-15. WP 2008-12 51-5-2-1-0-32. SUPERRUGBY: Stormers 2009-13 67-2-4-4-0-30. REP HONOURS: SA U20 2008 4-0-0-0-0-0. FC RECORD: 146-10-6-5-0-77. RECORD IN 2013: (Stormers) 11-0-0-0-0-0.

Dyanti, Mzoxolo (Willie) (Kwezi Lomso) b 10/10/85, Port Elizabeth. 1.65m. 75kg. Scrumhalf. FC DEBUT: 2006. PROV CAREER: Griffons 2006 11-0-0-0-0-0. Eagles 2007-09 & 2011-13 55-7-0-0-0-35. FC RECORD: 66-7-0-0-0-35. RECORD IN 2013: (Eagles) 14-2-0-0-0-10.

Dyer, Robert James (Otto du Plessis HS) b 04/12/86, Port Elizabeth. 1.82m. 103kg. FC DEBUT: 2008. PROV CAREER: EP Kings 2008-13 37-5-0-0-0-25. EP Inv XV 2010 1-0-0-0-0-0. FC RECORD: 38-5-0-0-0-25. RECORD IN 2013: (EP Kings) 2-0-0-0-0-0.

E

Ebersohn, Robert Thompson (Grey College, Bloemfontein) b 23/02/89, Bloemfontein. 1.80m. 82kg. Centre. FC DEBUT: 2008. PROV CAREER: Cheetahs 2008-13 72-11-0-0-0-55. SUPERRUGBY: Cheetahs 2010-13 59-11-0-0-0-55. REP HONOURS: SAU20 10-4-0-0-0-20. MISC INFO: YPoY 2008. Sasol u 20 PoY 2008. Twin brother of Sias Ebersohn. REP HONOURS: SA Sevens 2008 & 2012. FC RECORD: 141-26-0-0-0-130. RECORD IN 2013: (Cheetahs S15, Cheetahs) 28-6-0-0-0-30.

Ehlers, Chris Erich (Wesvalia HS) b 22/05/1988, Kroonstad. 1.99m. 95kg. Lock. FC DEBUT: 2010. PROV CAREER: Valke 2010-11 30-1-0-0-0-5. Griffons 2012-13 32-3-0-0-0-15. FC RECORD: 62-4-0-0-0-20. RECORD IN 2013: (Griffons) 14-1-0-0-0-5.

Elstadt, Rynhardt (Montagu HS) b 02/12/1989, Johannesburg. 1.98m. 112kg. Lock. FC DEBUT: 2010. PROV CAREER: WP 2010 & 12-13 24-0-0-0-0-0. SUPERRUGBY: Stormers 2011-13 37-0-0-0-0-0. REP HONOURS: SAU20 2009 3-0-0-0-0-0. FC RECORD: 64-0-0-0-0-0. RECORD IN 2013: (Stormers, WP) 17-0-0-0-0-0.

Engelbrecht, Adriaan Erasmus (Volkskool, Potchefstroom) b 14/09/1990, Pretoria. 1.85m. 98kg. Centre. FC DEBUT: 2011. PROV CAREER: Leopards 2011-13 36-9-48-23-0-210. Leopard XV 2013 7-2-2-0-0-14. REP HONOURS: SA Pres XV 2013 4-1-0-0-0-5. FC RECORD: 47-12-50-23-0-229. RECORD IN 2013: (SA Pres XV, Leopards, Leopard XV) 26-5-45-19-0-172.

Engelbrecht, Gabriel Joubert (Upington HS & NWU) b 27/06/1989, Kimberley. 1.89m. 90kg. Centre. FC DEBUT: 2010. PROV CAREER: Leopards 2010-12 36-14-0-0-0-70. Griffons 2013 9-1-5-1-0-18. Cheetahs 2013 1-0-0-0-0-0. Free State XV 2013 7-4-0-0-0-20. REP HONOURS: SA Students 2012 1-0-0-0-0-0. SA Barbarians 2012 1-1-0-0-0-5. FC RECORD: 55-20-5-1-0-113. RECORD IN 2013: (Cheetahs, Griffons, Free State XV) 17-5-5-1-0-38.

Engelbrecht, Jacques Jacobus (Monument HS, Krugersdorp) b 10/06/85, Cape Town. 1.94m. 105kg. Flank. FC DEBUT: 2007. PROV CAREER: WP 2007-08 2-0-0-0-0-0. Eagles 2008-10 48-3-0-0-0-15. EP Kings 2011-12 24-5-0-0-0-25. Blue Bulls 2013 8-0-0-0-0-0. SUPERRUGBY: Southern Kings 2013 15-1-0-0-0-5. P/R 2013 2-0-0-0-0-0. REP HONOURS: SA Kings 2011 2-0-0-0-0-0. SA Barbarians 2012 1-1-0-0-0-5. SA Sevens 2010-11. FC RECORD: 102-10-0-0-0-50. RECORD IN 2013: (Southern Kings, Blue Bulls) 25-1-0-0-0-5.

Engelbrecht, Johannes Jacobus (JJ) (Grey HS, PE) b 22/02/1989, Port Elizabeth. 1.90m. 94kg. Wing/Centre. FC DEBUT: 2009. PROV CAREER: WP 2009-11 38-24-0-0-0-120. Blue Bulls 2012-13 9-0-0-0-0-0. SUPERRUGBY: Bulls 2012-13 33-7-0-0-0-35. REP HONOURS: SA 2012-13 Tests: 12-4-0-0-0-20. FC RECORD: 92-35-0-0-0-175. RECORD IN 2013: (SA, Bulls, Blue Bulls) 28-8-0-0-0-40.

Engelbrecht, Nicolaas Johannes Els (Oos Moot HS) b 02/11/1989, Klerksdorp. 1.91m. 108kg. Prop. FC DEBUT: 2010. PROV CAREER: Valke 2010-13 46-6-0-0-0-30. FC RECORD: 46-6-0-0-0-30. RECORD IN 2013: (Valke) 12-0-0-0-10.

Engelbrecht, Petrus Johannes Jacobus (Pieter) (Paul Roos Gymnasium) b 14/03/87, Bloemfontein. 1.83m. 100kg. Centre. FC DEBUT: 2009. PROV CAREER: Golden Lions 2009-10 11-1-0-0-0-5. Young Lions 2010 7-2-0-0-0-10. Pumas 2011 2-1-0-0-0-5. Griquas 2013 1-0-0-0-0-0. REP HONOURS: SA Sevens 2010-13. FC RECORD: 21-4-0-0-0-20. RECORD IN 2013: (Griquas, SA Sevens) 1-0-0-0-0-0.

Engels, Jaco (Volkskool, Potchefstroom) b 17/12/80, Oranjemund. 1.85m. 118kg. Prop. FC DEBUT: 2003. PROV CAREER: Leopards 2003-04 40-6-0-0-0-30. Boland 2005 22-4-0-0-0-20. Blue Bulls 2006-10 67-6-0-0-0-30. EP Kings 2011-13 34-4-0-0-0-20. SUPERRUGBY: Bulls 2006-10 40-2-0-0-0-10. Southern Kings 2013 4-0-0-0-0-0. REP HONOURS: SA Kings 2011 3-1-0-0-0-5. S/Kings 2009 1-0-0-0-0-0. FC RECORD: 211-23-0-0-0-115. RECORD IN 2013: (Southern Kings, EP Kings) 9-0-0-0-0-0. MISC INFO: Namibia international.

Engledoe, Damien Courtney (New Orleans HS) b 07/03/1993, Paarl. 1.72m. 63kg. Wing. FC DEBUT: 2013. PROV CAREER: Young Lions 2013 1-0-0-0-0-0. FC RECORD: 1-0-0-0-0-0. RECORD IN 2013: (Young Lions) 1-0-0-0-0-0.

Erasmus, Dual Lance (Wesbank HS & US) b 14/01/1990, Malmesbury. 1.69m. 77kg. Scrumhalf. FC DEBUT: 2013. PROV CAREER: Boland 2013 2-0-0-0-0-0. FC RECORD: 2-0-0-0-0-0. RECORD IN 2013: (Boland) 2-0-0-0-0-0.

Erasmus, Ernst Lodewyk (AHS, Kroonstad & NWU, UFS) b 09/08/1990, Kroonstad. 1.85m. 95kg. Fullback. FC DEBUT: 2012. PROV CAREER: Leopards 2012 1-0-0-0-0-0. Free State XV 2013 7-3-0-0-0-15. FC RECORD: 8-3-0-0-0-15. RECORD IN 2013: (Free State XV) 7-3-0-0-0-15.

Erasmus, Renier Devon (Grey HS, PE) b 07/12/1991, Port Elizabeth. 1.80m. 94kg. Flank. FC DEBUT: 2013. PROV CAREER: EP Kings 2013 1-0-0-0-0-0. FC RECORD: 1-0-0-0-0-0. RECORD IN 2013: (EP Kings) 1-0-0-0-0-0.

Erwee, Reinhardt (Jim Fouche HS & UFS) b 10/01/1988, Bloemfontein. 1.81m. 85kg. Flyhalf. FC DEBUT: 2011. PROV CAREER: Griffons 2011-13 24-4-20-12-0-96. Boland 2013 3-0-0-0-0-0. FC RECORD: 27-4-20-12-0-96. RECORD IN 2013: (Griffons, Boland) 5-0-0-0-0-0.

Esau, Ashley Anthony (Durbanville & CPUT) b 02/04/1992, Cape Town. 1.81m. 77kg. Flyhalf. FC DEBUT: 2013. PROV CAREER: Boland 2013 1-0-0-0-0-0. FC RECORD: 1-0-0-0-0-0. RECORD IN 2013: (Boland) 1-0-0-0-0-0.

Espag, Ivann (Monument HS, Krugersdorp) b 08/09/87. Prop. FC DEBUT: 2008. PROV CAREER: Blue Bulls 2008 & 10 8-0-0-0-0-0.

A-Z OF FIRST-CLASS PLAYERS IN 2013

Boland 2009 6-0-0-0-0-0. Griquas 2010-12 35-0-0-0-0-0. Pumas 2013 10-1-0-0-0-5. REP HONOURS: SA Pres XV 2013 4-0-0-0-0-0. MISC INFO: Son of former Pumas, Transvaal & SWD prop Jaco Espag. FC RECORD: 63-1-0-0-0-5. RECORD IN 2013: (SA Pres XV, Pumas) 14-1-0-0-0-5.

Esterhuizen, Adriaan Pieter (Andre) (Klerksdorp HS) b 30/03/1994, Potchefstroom. 1.92m. 102kg. Wing. FC DEBUT: 2013. PROV CAREER: Sharks XV 2013 3-0-0-0-0-0. FC RECORD: 3-0-0-0-0-0. RECORD IN 2013: (Sharks XV) 3-0-0-0-0-0.

Esterhuizen, John-Ronald Andrew (Paarl Gymnasium & UJ) b 24/02/1991, Worcester. 1.80m. 90kg. Wing. FC DEBUT: 2011. PROV CAREER: Lions 2012 4-0-0-0-0-0. Young Lions 2012-13 4-3-0-0-0-15. Golden Lions XV 2011 1-0-0-0-0-0. REP HONOURS: SA Univ 2013 1-1-0-0-0-5. FC RECORD: 10-4-0-0-0-20. RECORD IN 2013: (SA Univ, Young Lions) 2-1-0-0-0-5.

Etzebeth, Eben (Tygerberg HS) b 29/10/1991, Cape Town. 2.03m. 117kg. Lock. FC DEBUT: 2012. PROV CAREER: WP 2012-13 6-0-0-0-0-0. SUPERRUGBY: Stormers 2012-13 21-2-0-0-0-10. REP HONOURS: SA 2012-13 Tests: 23-0-0-0-0-0. SAU20 2011 5-1-0-0-0-5. MISC INFO: SARU PoY 2012 & 2013 nominee. YPoY 2012 & 2013. Super PoY 2012 nominee. FC RECORD: 55-3-0-0-0-15. RECORD IN 2013: (SA, Stormers, WP) 23-1-0-0-0-5.

Ewerts, Charlton Dean (Brighton HS) b 18/11/1989, Oudtshoorn. 1.61m. 64kg. Wing. FC DEBUT: 2010. PROV CAREER: Eagles 2010 & 12-13 6-1-0-0-0-5. FC RECORD: 6-1-0-0-0-5. RECORD IN 2013: (Eagles) 2-0-0-0-0-0.

F

Ferreira, Andries Stephanus (Affies, Pretoria & TUT) b 29/03/1990, Despatch. 1.97m. 117kg. Lock. FC DEBUT: 2012. PROV CAREER: Cheetahs 2012 3-1-0-0-0-5. Griffons 2013 1-0-0-0-0-0. Free State XV 2013 3-0-0-0-0-0. SUPERRUGBY: Cheetahs 2012 14-1-0-0-0-5. FC RECORD: 21-2-0-0-0-10. RECORD IN 2013: (Griffons, Free State XV) 4-0-0-0-0-0.

Ferreira, Hendrik Matthys Stefanus (Affies, Pretoria & US) b 13/09/1980, Pretoria. 1.89m. 125kg. Prop. FC DEBUT: 2013. PROV CAREER: WP 2013 6-0-0-0-0-0. FC RECORD: 6-0-0-0-0-0. RECORD IN 2013: (WP) 6-0-0-0-0-0.

Ferreira, Jean Pierre b 25/06/1983. Hooker. FC DEBUT: 2013. PROV CAREER: Limpopo 2013 4-0-0-0-0-0. FC RECORD: 4-0-0-0-0-0. RECORD IN 2013: (Limpopo) 4-0-0-0-0-0.

Ferreira, Martin (Grey HS, PE & NMMU & UFS) b 24/01/1989, Port Elizabeth. 1.88m. 115kg. Hooker. FC DEBUT: 2011. PROV CAREER: Eagles 2011 & 13 22-6-0-0-0-30. REP HONOURS: SA Univ 2013 1-2-0-0-0-10. FC RECORD: 23-8-0-0-0-40. RECORD IN 2013: (Eagles, SA Univ) 13-5-0-0-0-25

Ferreira, Schalk Jakobus Petrus (Paul Roos Gymnasium) b 09/02/84, Pretoria. 1.88m. 107kg. Prop. FC DEBUT: 2004. PROV CAREER: WP 2005-09 & 12 58-2-0-0-0-10. Boland 2009 1-0-0-0-0-0. EP Kings 2012 12-1-0-0-0-5. SUPERRUGBY: Stormers 2007-09 16-0-0-0-0-0. Southern Kings 2013 15-1-0-0-0-5. P/R 2013 2-1-0-0-0-5. REP HONOURS: SA U21 2004 3-0-0-0-0-0. SA U19 2003. SA Schools 2002. CW WP 2002. FC RECORD: 107-5-0-0-0-25. RECORD IN 2013: (Southern Kings) 17-2-0-0-0-10.

Fihlani, Lwazi Samora (Lumnko HS) b 14/05/85, East London. 1.98m. 104kg. Lock. FC DEBUT: 2008. PROV CAREER: Bulldogs 2008-12 61-5-0-0-0-25. Griffons 2012 7-0-0-0-0-0. EP Kings 2013 17-3-0-0-0-15. REP HONOURS: SA Barbarians 2012 1-0-0-0-0-0. FC RECORD: 86-8-0-0-0-40. RECORD IN 2013: (EP Kings) 17-3-0-0-0-15.

Fisher, Tyler Luke (Westville Boys HS) b 19/11/1993, Westville. 1.89m. 93kg. Centre. FC DEBUT: 2013. PROV CAREER: Sharks XV 2013 5-2-0-0-0-10. FC RECORD: 5-2-0-0-0-10. RECORD IN 2013: (Sharks XV) 5-2-0-0-0-10.

Flink, Damien Juan b 01/09/1989. Wing. FC DEBUT: 2013. PROV CAREER: Limpopo 2013 6-0-0-0-0-0. FC RECORD: 6-0-0-0-0-0. RECORD IN 2013: (Limpopo) 6-0-0-0-0-0.

Floors, Lucas (Kabamba) (Morestēr SS) b 15/11/80, Oudtshoorn. 1.75m. 84kg. Flank. FC DEBUT: 2003. PROV CAREER: Eagles 2003-04 & 2013 50-21-0-0-0-105. Cheetahs 2005-10 & 12 95-25-0-0-0-125. SUPERRUGBY: Cheetahs 2006-11 57-10-0-0-0-50. REP HONOURS: SA 2006 Tests: 1-0-0-0-0-0. SA 'A' 2004. Emerging Springboks 2007 3-2-0-0-0-10. SA Sevens 2003-06. MISC INFO: Holds Eagles record for most tries in a CC season (14) and shares record for most in all matches in a season (18). PPoY 2006. CC PoY 2006. FC RECORD: 207-58-0-0-0-290. RECORD IN 2013: (Eagles) 17-3-0-0-0-15.

Fortuin, Bradley b 03/12/82. 1.90m. 101kg. Flanker. FC DEBUT: 2009. PROV CAREER: Valke 2009-12 45-4-0-0-0-20. WP 2010 3-1-0-0-0-5. Boland 2013 20-0-0-0-0-0. FC RECORD: 68-5-0-0-0-25. RECORD IN 2013: (Boland) 20-0-0-0-0-0.

Fouche, Louis Daniel van Zyl (Rustenburg HS) b 04/01/1990, Pretoria. 1.86m. 92kg. Flyhalf. FC DEBUT: 2011. PROV CAREER: Blue Bulls 2011-12 24-2-43-55-5-276. SUPERRUGBY: Bulls 2012-13 21-2-5-5-0-35. FC RECORD: 45-4-48-60-5-311. RECORD IN 2013: (Bulls) 11-2-4-5-0-33.

Fourie, Armon (George Randall HS) b 07/01/80, East London. 1.89m. 132kg. Prop. FC DEBUT: 2003. PROV CAREER: Bulldogs 2003,07-08 & 10-2012 35-1-0-0-0-5. Boland 2013 1-0-0-0-0-0. FC RECORD: 36-1-0-0-0-5. RECORD IN 2013: (Boland) 1-0-0-0-0-0.

Fourie, Corne (Waterkloof HS, Pretoria) b 02/09/1988, Roodepoort. 1.87m. 116kg. Prop. FC DEBUT: 2010. PROV CAREER: Blue Bulls 2010-11 16-3-0-0-0-15. Pumas 2012-13 52-6-0-0-0-30. REP HONOURS: SA Barbarians 2012 1-0-0-0-0-0. SAU20 2008 4-0-0-0-0-0. FC RECORD: 73-9-0-0-0-45. RECORD IN 2013: (Pumas) 29-3-0-0-0-15.

Fourie, Deon André (Pietersburg HS) b 25/09/86, Pretoria. 1.76m. 97kg. Hooker. FC DEBUT: 2006. PROV CAREER: WP 2006-13 90-22-0-0-0-110. SUPERRUGBY: Stormers 2008-13 69-10-0-0-0-50. REP HONOURS: SA Sevens 2007. MISC INFO: CC PoY 2012. FC RECORD: 159-32-0-0-0-160. RECORD IN 2013: (Stormers, WP) 25-8-0-0-0-40.

Fourie, Francois Petrus (Middelburg HS) b 14/02/1991, East London. 1.94m. 100kg. Flanker. FC DEBUT: 2012. PROV CAREER: Pumas 2012 1-0-0-0-0-0. Valke 2013 13-0-0-0-0-0. FC RECORD: 14-0-0-0-0-0. RECORD IN 2013: (Valke) 13-0-0-0-0-0.

Fourie, Jaque (Monument HS, Krugersdorp, RAU) b 04/03/83, Carletonville. 1.90m. 105kg. Fullback. FC DEBUT: 2002. PROV CAREER: Lions 2002-05 & 08 43-25-0-0-0-125. WP 2010-11 3-0-0-0-0-0. SUPERRUGBY: Cats 2003-06 44-15-0-0-0-75. Lions 2007-09 24-9-0-0-0-45. Stormers 2010-11 30-13-0-0-0-65. REP HONOURS: SA 2003-11 & 13 Tests: 72-32-0-0-0-160. Tour: 2007 2-0-0-0-0-0. Total: 73-32-0-0-0-160. S Hemisphere XV 2005 1-1-0-0-0-5. SA XV 2006 1-0-0-0-0-0. British Barbs. 2009 1-0-0-0-0-0. MISC INFO: YPoY nominee 2002, 2003. FC RECORD: 221-95-0-0-0-475. RECORD IN 2013: (SA) 3-0-0-0-0-0.

Francis, Burton Kenvin (Klein Nederburg HS) b 02/01/87, Paarl. 1.84m. 85kg. Flyhalf. FC DEBUT: 2008. PROV CAREER: Blue Bulls 2008-09 28-3-42-30-7-210. Golden Lions 2010-11 12-3-14-123-0-79. Young Lions 2011 3-0-8-8-0-40. Eagles 2012 4-0-2-1-2-13. WP 2012 1-0-0-0-0-0. SUPERRUGBY: Bulls 2008-09 9-1-3-1-0-14. Lions 2010-11 12-0-10-11-1-56. Stormers 2012 6-0-0-0-0-0. Cheetahs 2013 6-0-7-15-1-62. FC RECORD: 81-7-86-78-11-474. RECORD IN 2013: (Cheetahs S15) 6-0-7-15-1-62.

A-Z OF FIRST-CLASS PLAYERS IN 2013

Francke, Jonathan Charles (Strand HS & Boland College) b 17/05/1986, Strand. 1.80m. 92kg. Fullback. FC DEBUT: 2011. PROV CAREER: Boland 2011-13 55-16-0-0-0-80. Griquas 2013 1-0-0-0-0-0. FC RECORD: 56-16-0-0-0-80. RECORD IN 2013: (Boland, Griquas) 21-3-0-0-0-15.

Franklin, Johannes (Hannes) (Bekker HS) b 06/10/81, Randfontein. 1.82m. 99kg. Hooker. FC DEBUT: 2003. PROV CAREER: Valke 2003-04 22-1-0-0-0-5. Pumas 2005, 09-10 53-12-0-0-0-60. Eagles 2006-08 58-18-0-0-0-90. EP Kings 2011-13 53-3-0-0-0-15. SUPERRUGBY: Lions 2010 12-2-0-0-0-10. Southern Kings 2013 8-1-0-0-0-5. P/R 2013 2-0-0-0-0-0. REP HONOURS: SA Kings 2011 3-0-0-0-0-0. SA Barbarians 2012 1-1-0-0-0-5. FC RECORD: 212-38-0-0-0-190. RECORD IN 2013: (Southern Kings, EP Kings) 18-2-0-0-0-10.

Fredericks, Edrick Reginald (Eddie) (Cloetesville HS) b 31/12/77, Stellenbosch. 1.80m. 80kg. Wing. FC DEBUT: 1997. PROV CAREER: WP 1998 4-1-0-0-0-5 ; Leopards 1999 17-0-0-0-0-0; Griffons 2000, 09-11 38-20-0-0-0-100; Cheetahs 2001-09 & 2011 114-53-0-0-0-265. Free State XV 2013 4-1-0-0-0-5. SUPERRUGBY: Bulls 2003-04 20-6-0-0-0-30. Cats 2005 3-0-0-0-0-0. Cheetahs 2006-08 33-7-0-0-0-35. REP HONOURS: SA Sevens 1999-00. SA 'A' 2003-04 2-1-0-0-0-5. SA U21s 1997 1-0-0-0-0-0. FC RECORD: 236-89-0-0-0-445. RECORD IN 2013: (Free State XV) 4-1-0-0-0-5.

Fritz, George b 08/03/1991. Hooker. FC DEBUT: 2012. PROV CAREER: Bulldogs 2012-13 2-0-0-0-0-0. FC RECORD: 2-0-0-0-0-0. RECORD IN 2013: (Bulldogs) 1-0-0-0-0-0.

Fuzani, Mthetheleli Godfrey (Bellville HS) b 18/01/1991, Uitenhage. 1.97m. 118kg. Lock. FC DEBUT: 2013. PROV CAREER: WP 2013 9-0-0-0-0-0. FC RECORD: 9-0-0-0-0-0. RECORD IN 2013: (WP) 9-0-0-0-0.

G

Gates, Shane Edward (Muir College Boys HS) b 27/09/1993, Port Elizabeth. 1.82m. 91kg. Flyhalf. FC DEBUT: 2011. PROV CAREER: EP Kings 2012-13 10-2-0-0-0-10. SUPERRUGBY: Southern Kings 2013 5-0-0-0-0-0. P/R 2013 2-0-0-0-0-0. REP HONOURS: SA Kings 2011 1-0-0-0-0-0. FC RECORD: 18-2-0-0-0-10. RECORD IN 2013: (Southern Kings, EP Kings) 11-0-0-0-0-0.

Geduld, Justin Gilberto (Tygerberg HS) b 01/10/1993, Cape Town. 1.75m. 70kg. Centre. FC DEBUT: 2013. REP HONOURS: SA U20 2013 3-2-0-0-0-10. SA Sevens 2013. FC RECORD: 3-2-0-0-0-10. RECORD IN 2013: (SA U20, SA Sevens) 3-2-0-0-0-10.

Geel, Albertus Daniel (Barry) (FH Odendaal HS) b 30/04/82, Springs. 1.83m. 87kg. Centre. FC DEBUT: 2002. PROV CAREER: Leopards 2002-06 91-21-0-0-0-105. Griquas 2007-11 80-26-0-0-0-130. Cheetahs 2012 4-0-0-0-0-0. Free State XV 2012-13 6-3-0-0-0-15. Cheetahs XV 2010 1-0-0-0-0-0. SUPERRUGBY: Cheetahs 2010-13 8-0-0-0-0-0. FC RECORD: 190-50-0-0-0-250. RECORD IN 2013: (Cheetahs S15, Free State XV) 2-0-0-0-0-0.

Geldenhuys, Ross (St. Andrews College) b 19/04/83, Cape Town. 1.89m. 122kg. Prop. FC DEBUT: 2005. PROV CAREER: Bulldogs 2005 3-0-0-0-0-0. Pumas 2007 17-2-0-0-0-10. Lions 2008-10 22-1-0-0-0-5. Young Lions 2009 & 2011 11-0-0-0-0-0. Boland 2012 5-0-0-0-0-0. Griffons 2012 2-0-0-0-0-0. Cheetahs 2012 8-2-0-0-0-10. EP Kings 2013 14-1-0-0-0-5. SUPERRUGBY: Lions 2008 & 10 19-0-0-0-0-0. REP HONOURS: SA Barbarians 2012 1-0-0-0-0-0. MISC INFO: Son of former WP flank Piet Geldenhuys. FC RECORD: 102-6-0-0-0-30. RECORD IN 2013 (EP Kings) 14-1-0-0-0-5.

Gerber, Du Randt (Outeniqua HS) b 28/02/1992, George. 1.86m. 94kg. Flyhalf. FC DEBUT: 2013. PROV CAREER: Griquas 2013 6-0-1-0-0-2. FC RECORD: 6-0-1-0-0-2. RECORD IN 2013: (Griquas) 6-0-1-0-0-2.

Gerber, Johann Abraham (Braam) (Affies, Pretoria) b 13/07/87, Oudtshoorn. 1.88m. 87kg. Centre. FC DEBUT: 2007. PROV CAREER: Blue Bulls 2007-08 10-6-0-0-0-30. Blue Bulls XV 2007 1-0-0-0-0-0. Boland 2011-13 46-7-0-0-0-35. FC RECORD: 57-13-0-0-0-65. RECORD IN 2013: (Boland) 19-5-0-0-0-25.

Gerber, Rayno (Framesby HS) b 28/01/81, Port Elizabeth. 1.89m. 123kg. Prop. FC DEBUT: 2002. PROV CAREER: Cheetahs 2003-04 41-4-0-0-0-20. Blue Bulls 2006-08 & 12 49-0-0-0-0-0. KZN 2013 5-0-0-0-0-0. SUPERRUGBY: Bulls 2007-09 & 12 38-0-0-0-0-0. REP HONOURS: SA U21 2002 4-0-0-0-0-0. MISC INFO: Son of former EP centre Orlando. Leeds (Eng) 2005-06. FC RECORD: 137-4-0-0-0-20. RECORD IN 2013: (KZN) 5-0-0-0-0-0.

Gerber, Stephan Ehlers (Carolina HS) b 27/08/1980, Durban. 1.95m. 110kg. Lock. FC DEBUT: 2005. PROV CAREER: Leopards 2005 3-0-0-0-0-0. Pumas 2006-07 32-2-0-0-0-10. Griquas 2008 22-5-0-0-0-25. Bulldogs 2013 12-1-0-0-0-5. FC RECORD: 69-8-0-0-0-40. RECORD IN 2013: (Bulldogs) 12-1-0-0-0-5.

Geswindt, Merlin Zane (PW Botha College) b 15/01/1991, George. 1.81m. 83kg. Centre. FC DEBUT: 2013. PROV CAREER: Eagles 2013 1-0-0-0-0-0. FC RECORD: 1-0-0-0-0-0. RECORD IN 2013: (Eagles) 1-0-0-0-0-0.

Gilbert, Warren James (Affies, Pretoria b 19/03/1992, Nelspruit. 1.80m. 90kg. Flyhalf. FC DEBUT: 2013. PROV CAREER: Leopards 2013 6-0-1-0-0-2. Leopard XV 2013 4-0-0-4-0-12. FC RECORD: 10-0-1-4-0-14. RECORD IN 2013: (Leopsards, Leopard XV) 10-0-1-4-0-14.

Godfrey, Roy Andrew Michael (Selborne College & NMMU) b 11/09/1989, East London. 1.88m. 118kg. Prop. FC DEBUT: 2013. PROV CAREER: Eagles 2013 14-5-0-0-0-25. REP HONOURS: SA Univ 2013 1-1-0-0-0-5. FC RECORD: 15-6-0-0-0-30. RECORD IN 2013: (Eagles, SA Univ) 15-6-0-0-0-30.

Goliath, Robin Vernon (Middelburg HTS) b 24/10/1990, Cape Town. 1.75m. 67kg. Fullback. FC DEBUT: 2013. PROV CAREER: Limpopo 2013 5-0-0-0-0-0. FC RECORD: 5-0-0-0-0-0. RECORD IN 2013: (Limpopo) 5-0-0-0-0-0.

Goosen, Gerhardus (Paarl Gymnasium) b 28/03/1990, Alexander. 1.94m. 87kg. Lock. FC DEBUT: 2013. PROV CAREER: Boland 2013 1-0-0-0-0-0. FC RECORD: 1-0-0-0-0-0. RECORD IN 2013: (Boland) 1-0-0-0-0-0.

Goosen, Johannes Lodewikus (Johan) (Grey College, Bloemfontein) b 27/07/1992, Burgersdorp. 1.85m. 85kg. Flyhalf. FC DEBUT: 2011. PROV CAREER: Cheetahs 2011-13 17-2-23-26-3-143. Emerging Cheetahs 2011 1-0-0-0-0-0. SUPERRUGBY: Cheetahs 2012-13 13-3-25-40-1-188. REP HONOURS: SA 2012 Tests: 4-0-1-2-0-8. SAU20 2011 5-0-23-10-1-79. MISC INFO: YPoY 2011 and 2012 nominee. FC RECORD: 40-5-72-78-5-419. RECORD IN 2013: (Cheetahs S15, Cheetahs) 6-0-9-10-0-48.

Gossmann, Ludwig Adolf. Flyhalf. FC DEBUT: 2013. PROV CAREER: Limpopo 2013 7-0-0-0-0-0. FC RECORD: 7-0-0-0-0-0. RECORD IN 2013: (Limpopo) 7-0-0-0-0-0.

Gouws, Gideon Petrus (Grey College, Bloemfontein & CUT) b 24/09/1990, Bloemfontein. 1.79m. 99kg. Hooker. FC DEBUT: 2013. PROV CAREER: Griffons 2013 1-0-0-0-0-0. FC RECORD: 1-0-0-0-0-0. RECORD IN 2013: (Griffons) 1-0-0-0-0-0.

Gqoboka, Lizo Pumzile (Ntabankuku HS) b 24/03/1990, Mount Free. 1.83m. 115kg. Prop. FC DEBUT: 2012. PROV CAREER: EP Kings 2012-13 30-2-0-0-0-10. FC RECORD: 30-2-0-0-0-10. RECORD IN 2013: (EP Kings) 21-1-0-0-0-5.

Graaff, Johannes Petrus Jacobus (Hansie) (Wonderboom HS & TUT) b 10/09/1989, Pretoria. 1.9m. 94kg. Wing/Fullback. FC DE-

A-Z OF FIRST-CLASS PLAYERS IN 2013

BUT: 2012. PROV CAREER: Griffons 2012-13 27-7-46-15-2-178. MISC INFO: CC First Div PoY 2012. FC RECORD: 27-7-46-15-2-178. RECORD IN 2013: (Griffons) 9-0-8-4-1-31.

Grant, Peter John (Maritzburg College) b 15/08/84, Durban. 1.88m. 90kg. Flyhalf. FC DEBUT: 2004. PROV CAREER: WP 2004-09 55-9-52-43-1-281. SUPERRUGBY: Stormers 2006-13 90-10-116-179-0-819. REP HONOURS: SA 2007-08 Tests: 5-0-0-0-0-0. Emerging Springboks 2007 3-0-10-8-0-44. WP XV 2006 1-0-2-0-0-4. British Barbarians 2007 1-0-0-0-0-0. SA U19 2003. SA Schools 2002. CW KZN 2002. FC RECORD: 155-19-180-232-1-1148. RECORD IN 2013: (Stormers) 2-0-0-0-0-0.

Greeff, Carel Fredrick Kirsten (Schoonspruit HS) b 20/05/1990, Klerksdorp. 1.83m. 99kg. Flank. FC DEBUT: 2011. PROV CAREER: Golden Lions XV 2011 1-0-0-0-0-0. Griquas 2013 8-3-0-0-0-15. FC RECORD: 9-3-0-0-0-15. RECORD IN 2013: (Griquas) 8-3-0-0-0-15.

Greeff, Stephan (Gill College) b 24/12/1989, Cape Town. 1.98m. 103kg. Lock. FC DEBUT: 2010. PROV CAREER: WP 2010-11 6-0-0-0-0-0. Lions 2013 2-0-0-0-0-0. Young Lions 2012-13 2-0-0-0-0-0. Leopards 2013 2-0-0-0-0-0. SUPERRUGBY: Lions 2012 5-0-0-0-0-0. FC RECORD: 17-0-0-0-0-0. RECORD IN 2013: (Lions, Young Lions, Leopards) 5-0-0-0-0-0.

Grey, Siyanda (Hlumani HS) b 16/08/1989, Komga. 1.79m. 79kg. Centre. FC DEBUT: 2010. PROV CAREER: EP Kings 2010-13 30-14-0-0-0-70. SUPERRUGBY: Southern Kings 2013 4-0-0-0-0-0. REP HONOURS: SA Kings 2011 3-6-0-0-0-30. FC RECORD: 37-20-0-0-0-100. RECORD IN 2013: (Southern Kings, EP Kings) 13-4-0-0-0-20.

Greyling, MacGuyver Dean (Affies, Pretoria) b 01/01/86, Potgietersrus. 1.92m, 122kg. Prop. FC DEBUT: 2005. PROV CAREER: Blue Bulls 2005,07-13 69-7-0-0-0-35. SUPERRUGBY: Bulls 2008 & 10-13 38-4-0-0-0-20. REP HONOURS: SA 2011-12 Tests: 3-0-0-0-0-0. S/Kings 2009 1-0-0-0-0-0. FC RECORD: 111-11-0-0-0-55. RECORD IN 2013 (Bulls, Blue Bulls) 14-3-0-0-0-15.

Greyvenstein, Willem b 27/08/1992. Prop. FC DEBUT: 2013. PROV CAREER: Valke 2013 1-0-0-0-0-0. FC RECORD: 1-0-0-0-0-0. RECORD IN 2013: (Valke) 1-0-0-0-0-0.

Griesel, Werner (Welkom Gymnasium) b 01/07/86, Welkom. 1.80m. 90kg. Centre. FC DEBUT: 2008. PROV CAREER: Griffons 2008-13 114-26-0-0-0-130. Cheetahs 2011 1-1-0-0-0-5. FC RECORD: 115-27-0-0-0-135. RECORD IN 2013: (Griffons) 19-5-0-0-0-25.

Grobbelaar, Hendrik (Dirk) (Hans Strijdom HS) b 08/02/1992, Benoni. 1.89m. 106kg. Flank. FC DEBUT: 2013. PROV CAREER: Griffons 2013 2-0-0-0-0-0. FC RECORD: 2-0-0-0-0-0. RECORD IN 2013: (Griffons) 2-0-0-0-0-0.

Grobler, Francois Jacobus (Jaco) (Framesby HS & NWU) b 11/06/1992, Newton Park. 1.72m. 84kg. Scrumhalf. FC DEBUT: 2012. PROV CAREER: Leopards 2012-13 18-2-0-0-0-10. Leopard XV 2013 2-0-0-0-0-0. FC RECORD: 20-2-0-0-0-10. RECORD IN 2013: (Leopards, Leopard XV) 6-0-0-0-0-0.

Grobler, Douw Gerbrandt (Affies, Pretoria) b Nelspruit. 1.99m. 95kg. Lock. FC DEBUT: 2012. PROV CAREER: WP 2012-13 15-0-0-0-0-0. SUPERRUGBY: Stormers 2013 5-0-0-0-0-0. FC RECORD: 20-0-0-0-0-0. RECORD IN 2013: (Stormers, WP) 19-0-0-0-0-0.

Grobler, Roedolf Jacobus (Ben Vorster HS, Tzaneen) b 28/02/1986, Pietersburg. 1.91m. 110kg. Lock. FC DEBUT: 2013. PROV CAREER: Limpopo 2013 5-1-0-0-0-5. FC RECORD: 5-1-0-0-0-5. RECORD IN 2013: (Limpopo) 5-1-0-0-0-5.

Groenewald, Bernardus Jacobus b 26/06/1990. Prop. FC DEBUT: 2013. PROV CAREER: Limpopo 2013 6-1-0-0-0-5. FC RECORD: 6-1-0-0-0-5. RECORD IN 2013: (Limpopo) 6-1-0-0-0-5.

Groenewald, Lambert Smith (Paul Roos Gymnasium) b 01/02/1989, Worcester. 1.89m. 106kg. Flanker. FC DEBUT: 2010. PROV CAREER: Sharks XV 2010-11 14-1-0-0-0-5. Lions 2013 6-0-0-0-0-0. SUPERRUGBY: Sharks 2011 1-0-0-0-0-0. FC RECORD: 21-1-0-0-0-5. RECORD IN 2013: (Lions) 6-0-0-0-0-0.

Groenewald, Marcel Breytenbach (Oudtshoorn HS) b 10/03/1990, Pretoria. 1.89m. 88kg. Eightman. FC DEBUT: 2012. PROV CAREER: Leopards 2012 2-0-0-0-0-0. Leopard XV 2013 1-0-0-0-0-0. FC RECORD: 3-0-0-0-0-0. RECORD IN 2013: (Leopard XV) 1-0-0-0-0-0.

Groenewald, Wilmar Romano (Hentie Cilliers HS) b 30/04/1990, George. 1.84m. 81kg. Flanker. FC DEBUT: 2010. PROV CAREER: Griffons 2010-13 15-2-0-0-0-10. FC RECORD: 15-2-0-0-0-10. RECORD IN 2013: (Griffons) 8-2-0-0-0-10.

Gronum, Anthonie Johannes (Oakdale Agricultural HS) b 15/06/85, Knysna. 2.02m. 112kg. Lock. FC DEBUT: 2006. PROV CAREER: Blue Bulls 2006 2-0-0-0-0-0. Leopards 2007-10 55-2-0-0-0-10. Bulldogs 2011-13 34-0-0-0-0-0. FC RECORD: 91-2-0-0-0-10. RECORD IN 2013: (Bulldogs) 3-0-0-0-0-0.

Groom, Nicholas James (Rondebosch Boys HS & UCT) b 21/02/1990, King Williams Town. 1.71m. 81kg. Scrumhalf. FC DEBUT: 2011. PROV CAREER: WP 2011-13 49-7-0-0-0-35. SUPERRUGBY: Stormers 2011 & 13 11-1-0-0-0-5. FC RECORD: 60-8-0-0-0-40. RECORD IN 2013: (Stormers, WP) 21-2-0-0-0-10.

Gwavu, Lubabalo Vincent (Daniel Pienaar HTS) b 04/09/87, Port Elizabeth. 1.84m. 99kg. Flank. FC DEBUT: 2008. PROV CAREER: Blue Bulls 2008-11 23-2-0-0-0-10. Eagles 2009 2-1-0-0-0-5. Valke 2013 14-1-0-0-0-5. REP HONOURS: SA Pres XV 2013 1-0-0-0-0-0. FC RECORD: 40-4-0-0-0-20. RECORD IN 2013: (SA Pres XV, Valke) 15-1-0-0-0-5.

H

Habana, Bryan Gary (KES & RAU) b 12/06/83, Johannesburg. 1.80m. 94kg. Wing. FC DEBUT: 2003. PROV CAREER: Lions 2003-04 21-17-0-0-0-85. Blue Bulls 2005 & 08-09 14-9-0-0-0-45. WP 2010-12 8-2-0-0-0-10. SUPERRUGBY: Bulls 2005-09 61-37-0-0-0-185. Stormers 2010-13 57-19-0-0-0-95. REP HONOURS: SA Tests: 2004-13 95-53-0-0-0-265. Tour: 2007 2-0-0-0-0-0. Total: 97-53-0-0-0-265. SA Sevens 2004. SA U21 2004 3-3-0-0-0-15. British Barbarians 2008,09,11 3-3-0-0-0-15. MISC INFO: SARU PoY 2005, 2007, 2012 . YPoY 2004, S12 PoY 2005. IRB PoY 2007. IRB PoY nominee 2005. IRPA YPoY 2005. Try of the year 2012 (SA vs All Blacks). Leading FC try-scorer 2004,2005,2007. Holds SA record for most tries in a season (13 in 2007) Holds SA record for most tries in Tests - 53. Holds SA record for most Tests as a wing - 94 (also one at centre). Holds SA record for most tries in Superrugby (56 - Bulls 37 & Stormers 19) FC RECORD: 263-143-0-0-0-715. RECORD IN 2013: (SA, Stormers) 24-9-0-0-0-45.

Hadebe, Monde Sakhile (Westville HS) b 09/12/1990, Durban. 1.77m. 102kg. Hooker. FC DEBUT: 2011. PROV CAREER: KZN 2011-13 13-0-0-0-0-0. Sharks XV 2011-13 19-0-0-0-0-0. REP HONOURS: SAU20 2010 5-0-0-0-0-0. FC RECORD: 37-0-0-0-0-0. RECORD IN 2013: (Sharks XV, KZN) 12-0-0-0-0-0.

Halvorsen, Thorleif (Boland Agric. HS) b 09/05/1988, Cape Town. 1.93m. 107kg. Eightman. FC DEBUT: 2010. PROV CAREER: Boland 2010-13 39-3-0-0-0-15. FC RECORD: 39-3-0-0-0-15. RECORD IN 2013: (Boland) 10-2-0-0-0-10.

Hamman, Stephan (Os) (Paul Roos Gymnasium. & US) b 14/10/1988, Cape Town. 1.84m. 130kg. Prop. FC DEBUT: 2012. REP HONOURS: SA Students 2012 2-0-0-0-0-0. SA Univ 2013 1-1-0-0-0-5. FC RECORD: 3-1-0-0-0-5. RECORD IN 2013: (SA Univ) 1-1-0-0-0-5.

A-Z OF FIRST-CLASS PLAYERS IN 2013

Hancke, Shane (THS Welkom) b 20/02/83, Welkom. 1.75m. 85kg. Utility Back. FC DEBUT: 2005. PROV CAREER: Griffons 2005,08-13 79-23-0-0-0-115. FC RECORD: 79-23-0-0-0-115. Record in 2013 (Griffons) 13-3-0-0-0-15.
Hanekom, Morne (Boland Agric. & Stellenbosch Univ.) b 15/02/88, Malmesbury. 1.94m. 112kg. FC DEBUT: 2009. PROV CAREER: WP 2009 1-0-0-0-0-0. EP Kings 2010-11 7-2-0-0-0-10. Leopards 2011-13 29-5-0-0-0-25. Leopard XV 2013 7-4-0-0-0-20. FC RECORD: 44-11-0-0-0-55. RECORD IN 2013: (Leopards, Leopard XV) 18-7-0-0-0-35.
Hanekom, Nicolaas Johannes (Stokkies) (Paarl Gymnasium) b 17/05/1989, Citrusdal. 1.93m. 101kg. Centre. FC DEBUT: 2012. PROV CAREER: Eagles 2012 14-5-0-0-0-25. Lions 2013 1-1-0-0-0-5. Young Lions 2013 1-0-0-0-0-0. SUPERRUGBY: Lions P/R 2013 2-2-0-0-0-10. REP HONOURS: SAU20 2009 5-2-0-0-0-10. FC RECORD: 23-10-0-0-0-50. RECORD IN 2013: (Lions S15, Lions, Young Lions) 4-3-0-0-0-15.
Hanekom, Pierre Francois (Marlow Agric. & UFS) b 06/02/1989, Port Elizabeth. 1.86m. 120kg. Prop. FC DEBUT: 2012. PROV CAREER: Boland 2012-13 32-0-0-0-0-0. Sharks XV 2012 1-0-0-0-0-0. FC RECORD: 33-0-0-0-0-0. RECORD IN 2013 (Boland) 18-0-0-0-0-0.
Harris, Juan (Brok) (Bastion HS) b 22/02/85, Roodepoort. 1.83m. 113kg. Prop. FC DEBUT: 2006. PROV CAREER: WP 2006-13 109-14-0-0-0-70. SUPERRUGBY: Stormers 2007-13 84-2-0-0-0-10. FC RECORD: 193-16-0-0-0-80. RECORD IN 2013: (Stormers,WP) 21-0-0-0-0-0.
Harris, Robert Lee (Glenwood BHS) b 30/03/82, Durban. 1.80m. 114kg. Prop. FC DEBUT: 2005. PROV CAREER: Pumas 2005 2-0-0-0-0-0. KZN 2006-08 21-0-0-0-0-0. Sharks XV 2006-08 & 2011 & 13 20-2-0-0-0-10. Sharks Inv XV 2007 1-0-0-0-0-0. FC RECORD: 44-2-0-0-0-10. RECORD IN 2013: (Sharks XV) 2-1-0-0-0-5.
Hartnick, Lyndon Lee (Kairos HS) b 08/07/86, Heidelberg. 1.90m. 97kgs. Flanker. FC DEBUT: 2008. PROV CAREER: Bulldogs 2008 6-0-0-0-0-0. Eagles 2010-13 56-9-0-0-0-45. FC RECORD: 62-9-0-0-0-45. RECORD IN 2013: (Eagles) 14-4-0-0-0-20.
Hattingh, Grant Neil (Kingswood College) b 03/10/1990, Johannesburg. 2.01m. 105kg. Lock. FC DEBUT: 2011. PROV CAREER: WP 2011-12 2-0-0-0-0-0. Blue Bulls 2012-13 18-0-0-0-0-0. SUPERRUGBY: Lions 2012 9-1-0-0-0-5. Bulls 2013 12-0-0-0-0-0. FC RECORD: 41-1-0-0-0-5. RECORD IN 2013: (Bulls, Blue Bulls) 22-0-0-0-0-0.
Haupt, Kurt Stanley (St Albans & UP) b 17/01/1989, Johannesburg. 1.90m. 112kg. Hooker. FC DEBUT: 2013. PROV CAREER: Blue Bulls 2013 2-0-0-0-0-0. FC RECORD: 2-0-0-0-0-0. RECORD IN 2013: (Blue Bulls) 2-0-0-0-0-0.
Havenga, Wayne Raymond (Weston College) b 29/11/1985, Johannesburg. 1.98m. 89kg. Flanker. FC DEBUT: 2010. PROV CAREER: Valke 2010 & 13 4-0-0-0-0-0. FC RECORD: 4-0-0-0-0-0. RECORD IN 2013: (Valke) 1-0-0-0-0-0.
Hay, Wiehan (Jeugland HS) b 02/02/1992, Kempton Park. 1.96m. 122kg. Lock. FC DEBUT: 2013. PROV CAREER: Sharks XV 2013 1-0-0-0-0-0. FC RECORD: 1-0-0-0-0-0. RECORD IN 2013: (Sharks XV) 1-0-0-0-0-0.
Heiberg, Chris (Wynberg Boys HS) b 01/06/1985, Cape Town. 1.83m. 115kg. Prop. FC DEBUT: 2013. PROV CAREER: WP 2013 7-0-0-0-0-0. FC RECORD: 7-0-0-0-0-0. RECORD IN 2013: (WP) 7-0-0-0-0-0.
Helberg, Gideon Gerhardus (Middelburg THS) b 27/09/1989, Lichtenburg. 1.87m. 91kg. Wing. FC DEBUT: 2010. PROV CAREER: Blue Bulls 2010 10-4-0-0-0-20. Lions 2012-13 18-5-0-0-0-25. Young Lions 2013 7-2-0-0-0-10. SUPERRUGBY: Bulls 2010 1-0-0-0-0-0. Lions P/R 2013 1-0-0-0-0-0. FC RECORD: 37-11-0-0-0-55. RECORD IN 2013: (Lions S15, Lions, Young Lions) 18-4-0-0-0-20.
Hendricks, Carlyle (Kyle) (Excelsior HS) b 12/12/86, Cape Town. 1.74m. 70kg. Wing. FC DEBUT: 2009. PROV CAREER: Valke 2009-13 61-28-16-10-0-202. FC RECORD: 61-28-16-10-0-202. RECORD IN 2013: (Valke) 20-4-4-3-0-37.
Hendricks, Cornal (Berg River HS) b 18/04/88, Paarl. 1.88m. 85kg. Wing. FC DEBUT: 2008. PROV CAREER: Boland 2008-12 68-27-0-0-0-135. REP HONOURS: SA Barbarians 2012 1-0-0-0-0-0. SA Sevens 2012-13. FC RECORD: 69-27-0-0-0-135. RECORD IN 2013 (SA Sevens).
Herbert, Colin (Goudveld HS) b 19/03/1992, Welkom. 1.9m. 85kg. Flyhalf. FC DEBUT: 2012. PROV CAREER: Griffons 2012-13 9-1-1-0-0-70. MISC INFO: Son of former Free State and Griffons flyhalf Eric Herbert. FC RECORD: 9-1-1-0-0-7. RECORD IN 2013: (Griffons) 7-1-1-0-0-7.
Herbst, Irne Philip (Waterkloof HS, Pretoria) b 04/05/1993, Witbank. 1.97m. 117kg. Lock. FC DEBUT: 2013. REP HONOURS: SA U20 2013 5-1-0-0-0-5. FC RECORD: 5-1-0-0-0-5. RECORD IN 2013: (SA U20) 5-1-0-0-0-5.
Herbst, Johan David (Boland Agric. & US) b 18/05/1987, Stellenbosch. 1.77m. 93kg. Scrumhalf. FC DEBUT: 2011. PROV CAREER: Griquas 2011 4-3-0-0-0-15. Eagles 2012-13 23-10-0-0-0-50. SUPERRUGBY: Southern Kings 2013 1-0-0-0-0-0. FC RECORD: 28-13-0-0-0-65. RECORD IN 2013: (Southern Kings, Eagles) 4-1-0-0-0-5.
Herbst, Wiehahn Jovan (Klerksdorp HS & Unisa) b 05/07/88, Klerksdorp. 1.80m. 110kg. Prop. FC DEBUT: 2009. PROV CAREER: KZN 2009-13 52-1-0-0-0-5. Sharks XV 2009-11 21-0-0-0-0-0. Sharks Inv XV 2009-10 2-0-0-0-0-0. SUPERRUGBY: Sharks 2010-13 39-0-0-0-0-0. REP HONOURS: SAU20 2008 4-0-0-0-0-0. FC RECORD: 118-1-0-0-0-5. RECORD IN 2013: (Sharks, KZN) 28-1-0-0-0-5.
Herne, Frank (Grey College, Bloemfontein & UOFS) b 31/10/1989, Ficksburg. 1.78m. 101kg. Hooker. FC DEBUT: 2011. PROV CAREER: EP Kings 2011-12 39-4-0-0-0-20. Pumas 2013 21-8-0-0-0-40. REP HONOURS: SA Kings 2011 3-0-0-0-0-0. SA Pres XV 2013 4-0-0-0-0-0. FC RECORD: 67-12-0-0-0-60. RECORD IN 2013: (SA Pres XV, Pumas) 25-8-0-0-0-40.
Hess, Cornell Norman (Affies, Pretoria) b 01/03/1989, Wynberg. 2.0m. 106kg. Lock. FC DEBUT: 2010. PROV CAREER: Blue Bulls 2010-13 39-0-0-0-0-0. REP HONOURS: SAU20 2008 5-0-0-0-0-0. FC RECORD: 44-0-0-0-0-0. RECORD IN 2013: (Blue Bulls) 4-0-0-0-0-0.
Hewitt, Edwin Westley (Affies, Pretoria) b 28/03/1988, Pretoria. 1.94m. 115kg. Lock. FC DEBUT: 2010. PROV CAREER: Griquas 2010-13 32-1-0-0-0-5. Eagles 2011 1-0-0-0-0-0. KZN 2013 9-0-0-0-0-0. SUPERRUGBY: Sharks 2013 3-0-0-0-0-0. FC RECORD: 45-1-0-0-0-5. RECORD IN 2013: (Sharks, KZN, Griquas) 20-1-0-0-0-5.
Heyns, Ian b 08/08/1991, Brackenfell. 1.84m. 86kg. Wing. FC DEBUT: 2013. PROV CAREER: Leopard XV 2013 1-4-0-0-0-20. FC RECORD: 1-4-0-0-0-20. RECORD IN 2013: (Leopard XV) 1-4-0-0-0-20.
Heyns, Kirsten Ralph (Hentie Cilliers HS) b 31/07/1993, George. 1.82m. 87kg. Centre. FC DEBUT: 2013. PROV CAREER: Eagles 2013 2-0-0-0-0-0. FC RECORD: 2-0-0-0-0-0. RECORD IN 2013: (Eagles) 2-0-0-0-0-0.
Hollenbach, Alwyn Wilhelm Cornelius Johannes (Grey College, Bloemfontein) b 14/06/85, Johannesburg. 1.90m. 95kg. Wing. FC DEBUT: 2005. PROV CAREER: Cheetahs 2005-07,09 41-11-0-0-0-55. Griquas 2008 2-0-0-0-0-0. Lions 2009 & 2011-12 33-8-0-0-0-40. Young Lions 2010-11 & 13 13-2-0-0-0-10. SUPERRUGBY: Cheetahs 2007 2-0-0-0-0-0. Lions 2011-12 14-1-0-0-0-5. FC RECORD: 105-22-0-0-0-110. RECORD IN 2013: (Young Lions) 5-0-0-0-0-0.
Hope, Devlin (Bryanston HS & UJ, UP) b 27/04/1990, Johannesburg. 1.80m. 94kg. Hooker. FC DEBUT: 2013. PROV CAREER: Valke

A-Z OF FIRST-CLASS PLAYERS IN 2013

2013 1-0-0-0-0-0. FC RECORD: 1-0-0-0-0-0. RECORD IN 2013: (Valke) 1-0-0-0-0-0.
Hopp, Dean Lionel John (Kairos SS) b 07/09/82, Heidelberg. 1.76m. 142kg. Hooker. FC DEBUT: 2002. PROV CAREER: Eagles 2002-03 & 2011-13 41-4-0-0-0-20. Elephants 2005 19-1-0-0-0-5. Griquas 2006-08 21-3-0-0-0-15. REP HONOURS: SA U21 2002 2-0-0-0-0-0. SA Barbarians 2012 1-0-0-0-0-0. FC RECORD: 84-8-0-0-0-40. RECORD IN 2013: (Eagles) 9-0-0-0-0-0
Horn, Joubert Prinsloo (Burgersdorp HS & Grey College & UOFS) b 08/10/1988, Welkom. 1.95m. 100kg. Lock. FC DEBUT: 2010. PROV CAREER: Griffons 2010-12 30-2-0-0-0-10. Griquas 2013 5-0-0-0-0-0. FC RECORD: 35-2-0-0-0-10. RECORD IN 2013: (Griquas) 5-0-0-0-0-0.
Horne, Francis Henry (Frankie) (Huguenot HS) b 24/02/83, Port Elizabeth. 1.87m. 100kg. Flanker. FC DEBUT: 2005. PROV CAREER: Boland 2005-08 22-0-0-0-0-0. Rep. Honours: SA Sevens 2007-13. FC RECORD: 22-0-0-0-0-0. RECORD IN 2013: (SA Sevens).
Hougaard, Francois (Paul Roos Gymnasium.) b 06/04/88, Paarl. 1.79m. 92kg. Scrumhalf. FC DEBUT: 2007. PROV CAREER: WP 2007 3-0-0-0-0-0. Blue Bulls 2008-10 & 12 38-11-0-0-0-55. SUPERRUGBY: Bulls 2008-13 56-18-0-0-0-90. REP HONOURS: SA 2009-12 Tests: 27-4-0-0-0-20. Tour: 2009-10 3-0-0-0-0-20. Total: 30-4-0-0-0-20. SAU20 2008 3-0-0-0-0-0. S/Kings 2009 1-0-0-0-0-0. MISC INFO: PoY nominee 2011. YPoY nominee 2009, 2011. FC RECORD: 131-33-0-0-0-165. RECORD IN 2013: (Bulls) 11-2-0-0-0-10.
Horn, Gido (Kempton Park HS) b 15/01/88, Kempton Park. 1.79m. 90kg. Flyhalf. FC DEBUT: 2009. PROV CAREER: Valke 2009-10 & 13 18-2-11-5-0-47. FC RECORD: 18-2-11-5-0-47. RECORD IN 2013: (Valke) 1-0-0-0-0-0.
Howard, Patrick Benjamin (Michaelhouse HS) b 27/03/1992, Pietermaritzburg. 1.87m. 101kg. Centre. FC DEBUT: 2012. PROV CAREER: WP 2012-13 14-3-0-0-0-15. REP HONOURS: SAU20 2012 3-1-0-0-0-5. FC RECORD: 17-4-0-0-0-20. RECORD IN 2013: (WP) 11-3-0-0-0-15.
Huggett, Elandre (Premier HS) b 05/10/1991, Cape Town. 1.76m. 93kg. Hooker. FC DEBUT: 2011. PROV CAREER: Cheetahs 2011-12 4-0-0-0-0-0. Free State XV 2012-13 12-2-0-0-0-10. Griffons 2013 3-1-0-0-0-5. FC RECORD: 19-3-0-0-0-15. RECORD IN 2013: (Griffons, Free State XV) 8-2-0-0-0-10.
Hugo, Abraham Pieter Marnus (Paarl Gymnasium) b 24/09/86, Paarl. 1.70m. 84kg. Scrumhalf. FC DEBUT: 2006. PROV CAREER: Boland 2006 & 08-09 & 2011 32-4-0-0-0-20. Griquas 2010-13 57-1-0-0-0-5. SUPERRUGBY: Cheetahs 2010 2-0-0-0-0-0. FC RECORD: 91-5-0-0-0-25. RECORD IN 2013: (Griquas) 17-0-0-0-0-0.
Hugo, Daniel Pieter (Reniel) (Paul Roos Gymnasium & US) b 19/07/1990, Belville. 1.97m. 112kg. Lock. FC DEBUT: 2011. PROV CAREER: WP 2011 2-0-0-0-0-0. REP HONOURS: SA Univ 2013 1-0-0-0-0-0. FC RECORD: 3-0-0-0-0-0. RECORD IN 2013: (SA Univ) 1-0-0-0-0-0. MISC INFO: Son of former Springbok lock Niel Hugo.
Human, Petrus Gerhardus (Pote) (Grey HS, Port Elizabeth) b 12/01/86, Port Elizabeth. 1.91m. 101kg. Flank. FC DEBUT: 2006. PROV CAREER: Blue Bulls 2006-07 23-1-0-0-0-5. Lions 2008 3-0-0-0-0-0. Cheetahs 2010 5-0-0-0-0-0. Griquas 2010 & 13 9-0-0-0-0-0. FC RECORD: 40-1-0-0-0-5. RECORD IN 2013: (Griquas) 1-0-0-0-0-0. MISC INFO: Son of Pote Human (EP & FS)
Hunt, Steven Mark (Grey HS, PE & Stellenbosch Univ.) b 14/10/88, Port Elizabeth. 1.79m. 81kg. FC DEBUT: 2009. PROV CAREER: WP 2009 & 2011 4-0-0-0-0-0. Rep. Honours: SA Sevens 2010-13. FC RECORD: 4-0-0-0-0-0. RECORD IN 2013: (SA Sevens).

I
Ismaiel, Travis Keenan (Tygerberg HS & UP) b 02/06/1992, Cape Town. 1.83m. 92kg. Wing. FC DEBUT: 2012. PROV CAREER: Blue Bulls 2013 10-7-0-0-0-35. REP HONOURS: SA U20 2012 1-0-0-0-0-0. FC RECORD: 11-7-0-0-0-35. RECORD IN 2013: (Blue Bulls) 10-7-0-0-0-35.

J
Jacobs, Adri Justin (Schoonspruit HS) b 08/07/1990, Stellenbosch. 1.80m. 93kg. Centre. FC DEBUT: 2010. PROV CAREER: Boland 2013 2-0-0-0-0-0. REP HONOURS: SA U20 2010 1-0-0-0-0-0. FC RECORD: 3-0-0-0-0-0. RECORD IN 2013: (Boland) 2-0-0-0-0-0.
Jacobs, Neill (Affies, Pretoria) b 30/06/88, Pretoria. 1.83m. 91kg. Flyhalf. FC DEBUT: 2009. PROV CAREER: Leopards 2009-11 14-0-6-5-1-30. Bulldogs 2012-13 31-3-1-1-0-20. MISC INFO: Twin brother of Ruan Jacobs. FC RECORD: 45-3-7-6-1-50. RECORD IN 2013: (Bulldogs) 21-1-1-1-0-10.
Jacobs, Ruan (Affies, Pretoria & NWU) b 30/06/88, Pretoria. 1.82m. 92kg. Centre. FC DEBUT: 2008. PROV CAREER: Cheetahs 2008-09 7-1-0-0-0-5. Leopards 2011 1-0-0-0-0-0. Bulldogs 2012-13 23-4-0-0-0-20. MISC INFO: Twin brother of Neill Jacobs. FC RECORD: 31-5-0-0-0-25. RECORD IN 2013: (Bulldogs) 17-0-0-0-0-0.
Jacobs, Willem Johannes (Lohan) (Affies, Pretoria) b 23/04/1991, Krugersdorp. 1.76m. 88kg. Scrumhalf. FC DEBUT: 2011. PROV CAREER: Blue Bulls 2011-13 15-0-0-0-0-0. REP HONOURS: SAU20 2010-11 6-0-0-0-0-0. FC RECORD: 21-0-0-0-0-0. RECORD IN 2013: (Blue Bulls) 9-0-0-0-0-0.
James, Andrew David (Butch) (Maritzburg College) b 08/01/79, Johannesburg. 1.84m. 98kg. Flyhalf. FC DEBUT: 1999. PROV CAREER: KZN 1999-03 & 06 & 13 73-11-96-81-1-493. Lions 2011-12 14-0-10-17-0-71. SUPERRUGBY: Sharks 2001 & 03-07 & 13 59-6-63-74-4-390. Lions 2011-12 16-1-8-10-0-51. REP HONOURS: SA 2001-02 & 06-08 & 10-11 Tests 42-3-26-28-1-154. Tour: 2007 1-0-1-1-0-5. Total: 43-3-27-29-1-159; SA U21s 1999-2000 7-3-1-0-0-17; SA U23s 2000 5-1-7-1-0-22. SA 'A' 2002-03 2-0-4-2-0-14. MISC INFO: Holds Sharks Super record for most points (390), pens (74) and drop goals (4) in a career. FC RECORD: 219-25-216-214-6-1217. RECORD IN 2013: (Sharks, KZN) 10-0-5-11-0-43.
James, Eldred Garth (Parkdene HS) b 22/04/1993, Swellendam. 1.82m. 77kg. Centre. FC DEBUT: 2013. PROV CAREER: Eagles 2013 1-0-0-0-0-0. FC RECORD: 1-0-0-0-0-0. RECORD IN 2013: (Eagles) 1-0-0-0-0-0.
Janke, Grant Donovan (Welkom HS) b 02/11/1990, Cape Town. 1.78m. 87kg. Wing. FC DEBUT: 2011. PROV CAREER: Griffons 2011-12 9-0-0-0-0-0. Leopards 2012 3-0-0-0-0-0. Lions 2013 1-0-0-0-0-0. Young Lions 2013 1-0-0-0-0-0. FC RECORD: 14-0-0-0-0-0. RECORD IN 2013: (Lions, Young Lions) 2-0-0-0-0-0.
Janse van Rensburg, Jakobus Christo (JC) (Oakdale HS) b 09/01/86, Prins Albert. 1.85m. 109kg. Prop. FC DEBUT: 2006. PROV CAREER: Lions 2006-12 67-0-0-0-0-0. Lions XV 2007-08 2-0-0-0-0-0. Young Lions 2006-09 & 13 10-1-0-0-0-5. SUPERRUGBY: Lions 2008-12 50-1-0-0-0-5. Lions P/R 2013 2-0-0-0-0-0. Sharks 2013 3-0-0-0-0-0. REP HONOURS: SA 2012 - no tests. SA U19 2005. MISC INFO: CC PoY 2012 nominee. FC RECORD: 134-2-0-0-0-10. RECORD IN 2013: (Sharks, Lions S15, Young Lions) 7-0-0-0-0-0.
Janse van Rensburg, Marko Louis (Vredenburg HS & US) b 01/11/1991, Vanderbijlpark. 1.81m. 104kg. Hooker. FC DEBUT: 2013. PROV CAREER: Boland 2013 4-0-0-0-0-0. FC RECORD: 4-0-0-0-0-0. RECORD IN 2013: (Boland) 4-0-0-0-0-0.
Janse van Rensburg, Rohan (Waterkloof HS, Pretoria) b 11/09/1994, Welkom. 1.86m. 100kg. Centre. FC DEBUT: 2013. PROV

A-Z OF FIRST-CLASS PLAYERS IN 2013

CAREER: Blue Bulls 2013 6-4-0-0-0-20. REP HONOURS: SA U20 2013 2-0-0-0-0-0. FC RECORD: 8-4-0-0-0-20. RECORD IN 2013: (Blue Bulls, SA U20) 8-4-0-0-0-20.

Jansen, Jaquin (Bergrivier HS) b 27/05/86, Paarl. 1.75m. 83kg. Flyhalf. FC DEBUT: 2008. PROV CAREER: Boland 2008-13 66-21-60-39-0-342. REP HONOURS: SA Barbarians 2012 1-0-0-0-0-0. SA Pres XV 2013 2-0-0-0-0-0. FC RECORD: 69-21-60-39-0-342. RECORD IN 2013: (SA Pres XV, Boland) 19-5-6-4-0-49.

Jansen, Rocco Reginald (Queens College) b 21/07/86, Queenstown. 1.79m. 88kg. Wing. FC DEBUT: 2007. PROV CAREER: Blue Bulls 2007-09 28-22-0-0-0-110. Blue Bulls XV 2007 1-1-0-0-5. Elephants 2009 5-6-0-0-0-30. Sharks Inv XV 2009 1-0-0-0-0-0. Griquas 2010-13 65-28-0-0-0-140. SUPERRUGBY: Cheetahs 2012 4-0-0-0-0-0. REP HONOURS: Emerging Springboks 2008 3-1-0-0-0-5. FC RECORD: 107-58-0-0-0-290. RECORD IN 2013: (Griquas) 18-7-0-0-0-35.

Jantjies, Altonio (Tony) (Menlopark HS) b 19/04/1992, Cape Town. 1.78m. 90kg. Flyhalf. FC DEBUT: 2012. PROV CAREER: Blue Bulls 2012-13 14-3-32-24-0-151. REP HONOURS: SA U20 2012 3-0-2-5-0-19. MISC INFO: Brother of Elton Jantjies. FC RECORD: 17-3-34-29-0-170. RECORD IN 2013: (Blue Bulls) 9-2-22-18-0-108.

Jantjies, Elton Thomas (Florida HS & UJ) b 01/08/1990, Graaff Reinet. 1.76m. 84kg. Flyhalf. FC DEBUT: 2010. PROV CAREER: Golden Lions 2010-13 42-4-75-101-2-479. Young Lions 2010-11 2-0-1-0-0-2. SUPERRUGBY: Lions 2011-12 27-0-33-53-1-228. Lions P/R 2013 2-0-3-6-0-24. Stormers 2013 13-0-1-3-0-11. REP HONOURS: SA 2012 Tests: 2-0-0-2-0-6. 2010 Tour: 1-0-1-1-0-5. Total: 3-0-1-3-0-11. SAU20 2010 5-2-1-0-0-12. MISC INFO:YPoY 2011 and 2012 nominee. CC PoY 2012 nominee. MISC INFO: Brother of Tony Jantjies. FC RECORD: 94-6-115-166-3-762. RECORD IN 2013: (Stormers, Lions S15, Lions) 24-2-15-20-0-100.

Jenkinson, John-Roy (Glenwood HS & NWU) b 26/03/1991, Worcester. 1.77m. 127kg. Prop. FC DEBUT: 2011. PROV CAREER: Leopards 2011-13 16-0-0-0-0-0. Cheetahs 2013 2-0-0-0-0-0. REP HONOURS: SA Students 2012 2-1-0-0-0-5. SA U2O 2011 5-0-0-0-0-0. FC RECORD: 25-1-0-0-0-5. RECORD IN 2013: (Leopards, Cheetahs) 8-0-0-0-0-0.

Jenner, Dwayne (Dr. EG Jansen HS) b 17/11/1990, Benoni. 1.83m. 99kg. Wing. FC DEBUT: 2010. PROV CAREER: Bulldogs 2011-13 26-3-0-0-0-15. Sharks Inv XV 2010 1-1-0-0-5. FC RECORD: 27-4-0-0-0-20. RECORD IN 2013: (Bulldogs) 8-2-0-0-0-10.

Jho, Andile (Dale College & NMMU) b 21/04/1992, Kingwilliamstown. 1.73m. 83kg. Centre. FC DEBUT: 2013. PROV CAREER: EP Kings 2013 6-0-0-0-0-0. FC RECORD: 6-0-0-0-0-0. RECORD IN 2013: (EP Kings) 6-0-0-0-0-0.

Jobo, Vincent Thabiso (KES, UJ & UCT) b 01/02/1991, Krugersdorp. 1.86m. 104kg. Eightman. FC DEBUT: 2013. PROV CAREER: WP 2013 1-0-0-0-0-0. FC RECORD: 1-0-0-0-0-0. RECORD IN 2013: (WP) 1-0-0-0-0-0.

Johannes, Reuben Benjamin (Paul Roos Gymnasium & US) b 05/10/1990, Belville. 1.83m, 96kg, Flank. FC DEBUT: 2011. PROV CAREER: WP 2011-12 7-3-0-0-0-15. REP HONOURS: SA Sevens 2012-13. FC RECORD: 7-3-0-0-0-15. RECORD IN 2013: (SA Sevens).

Jongbloed, Theyman b 16/12/1983. Scrumhalf. FC DEBUT: 2013. PROV CAREER: Limpopo 2013 2-0-0-0-0-0. FC RECORD: 2-0-0-0-0-0. RECORD IN 2013: (Limpopo) 2-0-0-0-0-0.

Jordaan, Daniel Barend (Fochville HS & NWU) b 25/01/1991, Johannesburg. 1.96m. 104kg. Lock. FC DEBUT: 2012. PROV CAREER: Leopards 2012-13 2-0-0-0-0-0. FC RECORD: 2-0-0-0-0-0. RECORD IN 2013: (Leopards) 1-0-0-0-0-0.

Jordaan, Daniel Niell (Grey College, Bloemfontein) b 13/01/1992, Newcastle. 1.90m. 103kg. Eightman. FC DEBUT: 2013. PROV CAREER: Free State XV 2013 4-0-0-0-0-0. FC RECORD: 4-0-0-0-0-0. RECORD IN 2013: (Free State XV) 4-0-0-0-0-0.

Jordaan, Jeremy (Fichardtpark HS, Bloemfontein) b 06/01/1991, Bloemfontein. 1.96m. 121kg. Lock. FC DEBUT: 2013. PROV CAREER: Griffons 2013 14-2-0-0-0-10. FC RECORD: 14-2-0-0-0-10. RECORD IN 2013: (Griffons) 14-2-0-0-0-10.

Jordaan, Paul Abraham (Grey College, Bloemfontein) b 04/01/1992, Somerset East. 1.80m. 88kg. Centre. FC DEBUT: 2011. PROV CAREER: KZN 2012 11-3-0-0-0-15. Sharks XV 2011-12 3-1-0-0-0-5. SUPERRUGBY: Sharks 2012-13 18-2-0-0-0-10. Rep. Honours: SAU20 2011-12 8-1-0-0-0-5. SA Sevens 2010-11. FC RECORD: 40-7-0-0-0-35. RECORD IN 2013: (Sharks) 8-0-0-0-0-0.

Jordaan, Zandre (Paarl Boys HS) b 24/09/87, Empangeni. 1.91m. 93kg. FC DEBUT: 2009. PROV CAREER: Boland 2009-13 66-21-0-0-0-105. WP 2009 4-2-0-0-0-10. REP HONOURS: SA Barbarians 2012 1-0-0-0-0-0. SA Pres XV 2013 2-1-0-0-0-5. FC RECORD: 73-24-0-0-0-120. RECORD IN 2013: (SA Pres XV, Boland) 12-4-0-0-0-20.

Josephs, Creswin (PW Botha College & NMMU) b 01/04/1993, George. 1.80m. 80kg. Centre. FC DEBUT: 2013. PROV CAREER: Eagles 2013 3-0-0-0-0-0. FC RECORD: 3-0-0-0-0-0. RECORD IN 2013: (Eagles) 3-0-0-0-0-0.

Joubert, Christo (Kempton Park HS) b 25/04/1987, Johannesburg. 1.82m. 104kg. Centre. FC DEBUT: 2013. PROV CAREER: Valke 2013 3-0-0-0-0-0. FC RECORD: 3-0-0-0-0-0. RECORD IN 2013: (Valke) 3-0-0-0-0-0.

Joubert, Marius Charl (Paarl Gymnasium) b 10/07/79, Paarl. 1.88m. 94kgs. Centre. FC DEBUT: 1999. PROV CAREER: Boland 1999-01 37-18-0-0-0-90. WP 2002-04 15-7-0-0-0-35. Cheetahs 2007 15-2-0-0-10. KZN 2011-12 18-1-0-0-0-5. Sharks XV 2012=13 11-1-0-0-0-5. SUPERRUGBY: Stormers 2002-06 46-11-0-0-0-55. Cheetahs 2007 12-0-0-0-0-0. Sharks 2012 3-0-0-0-0-0. REP HONOURS: SA 2000-05 Tests 30-9-0-0-0-45, Tour 1-0-0-0-0-0, Total 31-9-0-0-0-45; SA 'A' 2001 4-2-0-0-0-10; SA U23s 2000-01 8-9-0-0-0-45; SA U21s 2000 5-1-0-0-0-5. MISC INFO: YPoY nominee 2000. IRB & SA PoY nominee 2004. FC RECORD: 205-61-0-0-0-305. RECORD IN 2013: (Sharks XV) 7-1-0-0-0-5.

K

Kamanga, Fhumulani Wiseman (M Viljoen HS & UJ) b 14/11/1991, Johannesburg. 1.88m. 114kg. Prop. FC DEBUT: 2012. PROV CAREER: Young Lions 2012-13 4-0-0-0-0-0. FC RECORD: 4-0-0-0-0-0. RECORD IN 2013: (Young Lions) 1-0-0-0-0-0.

Kankowski, Ryan (St Andrew's College) b 14/10/85, Port Elizabeth. 1.93m. 103kg. Eighthman. FC DEBUT: 2006. PROV CAREER: KZN 2006-11 59-16-0-0-0-80. Sharks XV 2009 & 12-13 3-0-0-0-0-0. SUPERRUGBY: Sharks 2007-13 82-18-0-0-0-90. REP HONOURS: SA 2007-12 Tests: 20-1-0-0-0-5. Tour: 2-0-0-0-0-0. Total: 22-1-0-0-0-5. SA Sevens 2004. MISC INFO: PoY nominee 2008. YPoY nominee 2008. Son of former EP, Border & Griquas wing Tino Kankowski. FC RECORD: 166-35-0-0-0-175. RECORD IN 2013: (Sharks, Sharks XV) 8-2-0-0-0-10.

Karemaker, Leon (Bellville HS) b 18/05/85, Cape Town. 1.92m. 98kgs. FC DEBUT: 2004. PROV CAREER: WP 2005-06 14-5-0-0-0-25. Griquas 2010-13 59-23-0-0-0-115. SUPERRUGBY: Cheetahs 2011 2-0-0-0-0-0. REP HONOURS: SA U21 2004 2-0-0-0-0-0. SA U19s 2003-2004. SA Schools 2002-03. CW WP 2003. FC RECORD: 77-28-0-0-0-140. RECORD IN 2013: (Griquas) 15-6-0-0-0-30.

Katzen, Joshua Mathew (Wynberg Boys HS & UCT) b 07/06/1992, Cape Town. 1.81m. 95kg. Flank. FC DEBUT: 2013. PROV CAREER: WP 2013 2-0-0-0-0-0. FC RECORD: 2-0-0-0-0-0. RECORD IN

A-Z OF FIRST-CLASS PLAYERS IN 2013

2013: (WP) 2-0-0-0-0-0.
Kebe, Ntando Lucky (Thubalethu HS & Univ. Fort Hare) b 19/08/1988, East London. 1.79m. 80kg. Scrumhalf. FC DEBUT: 2010. PROV CAREER: Bulldogs 2010-12 42-4-0-0-0-20. Boland 2013 21-1-0-0-0-5. REP HONOURS: SA Barbarians 2012 1-0-0-0-0-0. SA Pres XV 2013 4-0-0-0-0-0. FC RECORD: 68-5-0-0-0-25. RECORD IN 2013: (SA Pres XV, Boland) 25-1-0-0-0-5.
Keet, Alister Edward (Grantleigh College) b 24/12/1991, Cape Town. 1.98m. 100kg. Lock. FC DEBUT: 2013. PROV CAREER: Bulldogs 2013 7-0-0-0-0-0. FC RECORD: 7-0-0-0-0-0. RECORD IN 2013: (Bulldogs) 7-0-0-0-0-0.
Kelly, Dwayne (Westville Boys HS & NMMU) b 19/10/1991, Bloemfontein. 1.80m. 88kg. Scrumhalf. FC DEBUT: 2013. PROV CAREER: EP Kings 2013 12-0-0-0-0-0. REP HONOURS: SA Univ 2013 1-0-0-0-0-0. FC RECORD: 13-0-0-0-0-0. RECORD IN 2013: (EP Kings, SA Univ) 13-0-0-0-0-0.
Kember, Reginald (RW) (Daniel Pienaar THS) b 15/04/83, Adelaide. 1.87m. 105kg. Eighthman. FC DEBUT: 2006. PROV CAREER: Elephants 2006-07 30-5-0-0-0-25. Leopards 2008-11 51-7-0-0-0-35. Lions 2008 6-0-0-0-0-0. Pumas 2011-13 58-16-0-0-0-80. SUPERRUGBY: Lions 2008 1-0-0-0-0-0. REP HONOURS: Royal XV 2009 1-0-0-0-0-0. FC RECORD: 147-28-0-0-0-140. RECORD IN 2013: (Pumas) 24-9-0-0-0-45.
Kemp, Grant Dale (Wynberg Boys HS, UCT & UP) b 31/10/1988, Cape Town. 1.87m. 119kg. Prop. FC DEBUT: 2012. PROV CAREER: Eagles 2012-13 24-4-0-0-0-20. SUPERRUGBY: Southern Kings 2013 12-0-0-0-0-0. P/R 2013 1-0-0-0-0-0. FC RECORD: 37-4-0-0-0-20. RECORD IN 2013: (Southern Kings, Eagles) 23-2-0-0-0-10.
Kerrod, Simon. b 25/08/1992. Prop. FC DEBUT: 2013. PROV CAREER: Sharks XV 2013 2-0-0-0-0-0. FC RECORD: 2-0-0-0-0-0. RECORD IN 2013: (Sharks XV) 2-0-0-0-0-0.
Khan, Wayne (PW Botha HS) b 21/01/1991, Cape Town. 1.84m. 79kg. Hooker. FC DEBUT: 2011. PROV CAREER: Griffons 2011 3-0-0-0-0-0. Eagles 2012-13 15-2-0-0-0-10. FC RECORD: 18-2-0-0-0-10. RECORD IN 2013: (Eagles) 5-0-0-0-0-0.
Killian, Michael (Muir College, Uitenhage) b 22/11/83, Uitenhage. 1.82m. 84kg. Wing. FC DEBUT: 2004. Prov career; EP Kings 2004-07 & 12-13 83-27-0-0-0-135. Lions 2008-11 45-21-0-0-0-105. Young Lions 2008-09 & 12 12-4-0-0-1-23. Lions XV 2008. SUPERRUGBY: Lions 2009-12 37-10-0-0-0-50. Southern Kings 2013 4-0-0-0-0-0. REP HONOURS: SA Students 2005,07 2-0-0-0-0-0. FC RECORD: 184-62-0-0-1-313. RECORD IN 2013: (Southern Kings, EP Kings) 19-4-0-0-0-20.
Kilroe, James Alexander Gibson (Bishops College & UCT) b 29/11/1991, Cape Town. 1.95m. 100kg. Lock. FC DEBUT: 2013. PROV CAREER: WP 2013 1-0-0-0-0-0. FC RECORD: 1-0-0-0-0-0. RECORD IN 2013: (WP) 1-0-0-0-0-0.
Kirchner, Zane (PW Botha College) b 16/06/84, George. 1.84m. 92kg. Fullback. FC DEBUT: 2003. PROV CAREER: Griquas 2003-04 & 06-07 58-9-32-22-0-175. Blue Bulls 2008-12 43-6-2-0-0-34. SUPERRUGBY: Bulls 2008-13 82-21-0-0-0-105. REP HONOURS: SA 2009-10 & 12-13 Tests: 28-5-0-0-0-25. Emerging Springboks 2009 1-0-0-0-0-0. CW SWD 2002. MISC INFO: VC PoY 2007. FC RECORD: 212-41-34-22-0-339. RECORD IN 2013: (SA, Bulls) 15-3-0-0-0-15.
Kirkwood, Shane Monro (Marais Viljoen HS) b 06/09/89, Alberton. 1.94m. 113kg. Forward. FC DEBUT: 2009. PROV CAREER: Valke 2013 9-1-0-0-0-5. Young Lions 2009 3-1-0-0-0-5. FC RECORD: 12-2-0-0-0-10. RECORD IN 2013: (Valke) 9-1-0-0-0-5.
Kirsten, Frederick Barend Christoffel (Frik) (Affies, Pretoria) b 18/08/1985, Sandton. 1.93m. 118kg. Prop. FC DEBUT: 2008. PROV CAREER: Blue Bulls 2008-13 47-0-0-0-0-0. SUPERRUGBY: Bulls 2009 & 2012-13 31-0-0-0-0-0. REP HONOURS: 2013: Springbok tour squad member. SAU20 2008 5-1-0-0-0-5. MISC INFO: Son of former Eastern Transvaal Flank Barend Kirsten and brother of Blue Bulls lock Jannes Kirsten. FC RECORD: 83-1-0-0-0-5. RECORD IN 2013: (Bulls, Blue Bulls) 23-0-0-0-0-0.
Kirsten, Johannes Casper (Affies, Pretoria & UP) b 01/12/1993, Johannesburg. 1.96m. 107kg. Lock. FC DEBUT: 2013. PROV CAREER: Blue Bulls 2013 1-0-0-0-0-0. REP HONOURS: SA U20 2013 1-0-0-0-0-0. FC RECORD: 2-0-0-0-0-0. RECORD IN 2013: (Blue Bulls, SA U20) 2-0-0-0-0-0. MISC INFO: Brother of Frik Kirsten.
Kitshoff, Johannes Jakobus (Hanno) (Worcester Gymnasium) b 25/01/1984, George. 1.91m. 92kg. Flanker. FC DEBUT: 2012. PROV CAREER: Boland 2012-13 15-0-0-0-0-0. FC RECORD: 15-0-0-0-0-0. RECORD IN 2013: (Boland) 8-0-0-0-0-0.
Kitshoff, Rohan (Drostdy THS) b 13/09/85, Windhoek. 1.81m. 95kg. Flank. FC DEBUT: 2007. PROV CAREER: Griquas 2007-10 59-12-0-0-0-60. WP 2011-13 22-7-0-0-0-35. SUPERRUGBY: Stormers 2013 1-0-0-0-0-0. MISC INFO: Represented Namibia at RWC 2011. FC RECORD: 82-19-0-0-0-95. RECORD IN 2013: (Stormers, WP) 8-0-0-0-0-0.
Kitshoff, Steven (Paul Roos Gymnasium) b 10/02/1992, Somerset West. 1.83m. 114kg. Prop. FC DEBUT: 2011. PROV CAREER: WP 2011-13 32-1-0-0-0-5. SUPERRUGBY: Stormers 2011-13 35-0-0-0-0-0. REP HONOURS: SA U20 2012 5-1-0-0-0-5. FC RECORD: 72-2-0-0-0-10. RECORD IN 2013: (Stormers, WP) 27-0-0-0-0-0.
Klaasen, Berton Wesley (Somerset West HS) b 24/01/1990, Somerset West. 1.87m. 92kg. Centre. FC DEBUT: 2011. PROV CAREER: WP 2011-13 24-2-0-0-0-10. FC RECORD: 24-2-0-0-0-10. RECORD IN 2013: (WP) 10-2-0-0-0-10.
Kleinhans, Francois (Glenwood HS) b 07/01/1991, Parklands. 1.84m. 96kg. Flank. FC DEBUT: 2011. PROV CAREER: KZN 2011-12 7-0-0-0-0-0. Sharks XV 2011-13 20-3-0-0-0-15. REP HONOURS: SAU20 2011 3-1-0-0-0-5. FC RECORD: 30-4-0-0-0-20. RECORD IN 2013: (Sharks XV) 7-1-0-0-0-5.
Kleinhans, Johannes Frederik (Brackenfell HS & US) b 13/06/1991, Riversdal. 1.89m. 125kg. Prop. FC DEBUT: 2013. PROV CAREER: Boland 2013 1-0-0-0-0-0. FC RECORD: 1-0-0-0-0-0. RECORD IN 2013: (Boland) 1-0-0-0-0-0.
Kloppers, Pieter Hugo (Worcester Gymnasium & US) b 14/10/1988, Worcester. 1.97m. 99kg. Lock. FC DEBUT: 2010. PROV CAREER: WP 2010 4-0-0-0-0-0. Lions 2013 4-0-0-0-0-0. Young Lions 2013 4-0-0-0-0-0. REP HONOURS: SA Students 2012 2-1-0-0-0-5. FC RECORD: 14-1-0-0-0-5. RECORD IN 2013: (Lions, Young Lions) 8-0-0-0-0-0.
Knoop, Graham Peter (Bishops College) b 17/09/1987, Cape Town. 1.92m. 105kg. Flank. FC DEBUT: 2013. PROV CAREER: WP 2013 3-0-0-0-0-0. FC RECORD: 3-0-0-0-0-0. RECORD IN 2013: (WP) 3-0-0-0-0-0.
Koch, Vincent Philip (Hugenote HS) b 13/03/1990, Empangeni. 1.85m. 118kg. Prop. FC DEBUT: 2012. PROV CAREER: Blue Bulls 2012 3-1-0-0-0-5. Pumas 2012-13 30-6-0-0-0-30. REP HONOURS: SA Pres XV 2013 2-0-0-0-0-0. FC RECORD: 35-7-0-0-0-35. RECORD IN 2013: (SA Pres XV, Pumas) 28-6-0-0-0-30.
Kock, Fredericque Arafaat (Menlo Park & Florida HS & Wits) b 24/07/1991, Krugersdorp. 1.76m. 83kg. Scrumhalf. FC DEBUT: 2011. PROV CAREER: Valke 2011 & 13 8-0-0-0-0-0. FC RECORD: 8-0-0-0-0-0. RECORD IN 2013: (Valke) 7-0-0-0-0-0.
Koegelenberg, Gideon (Hugenote HS) b 25/11/1994, Wellington. 1.99m. 108kg. Lock. FC DEBUT: 2013. PROV CAREER: Sharks XV

A-Z OF FIRST-CLASS PLAYERS IN 2013

2013 1-0-0-0-0-0. FC RECORD: 1-0-0-0-0-0. RECORD IN 2013: (Sharks XV) 1-0-0-0-0-0.

Koekemoer, Hendrik Lambert (Luhan) (Middelburg THS & UJ) b 13/11/87, Middelburg. 1.99m. 102kg. Lock. FC DEBUT: 2009. PROV CAREER: Eagles 2011-12 14-0-0-0-0-0. Young Lions 2009 3-0-0-0-0-0. Boland 2011 9-0-0-0-0-0. Griffons 2013 14-1-0-0-0-5. FC RECORD: 40-1-0-0-0-5. RECORD IN 2013: (Griffons) 14-1-0-0-0-5.

Kok, Werner (Nelspruit HS) b 17/01/1993, Nelspruit. 1.79m. 88kg. Wing. REP HONOURS: SA Sevens 2013. RECORD IN 2013: (SA Sevens).

Kolbe, Cheslin (Brackenfell HS) b 28/10/1993, Kraaifontein. 1.7m. 69kg. Utility back. FC DEBUT: 2013. PROV CAREER: WP 2013 19-7-0-0-0-35. REP HONOURS: SA U20 2013 5-2-0-0-0-10. SA Sevens 2012-13. MISC INFO: YPoY nominee 2013. SA U20 PoY 2013. CC Premier Division PoY nominee 2013. FC RECORD: 24-9-0-0-0-45. RECORD IN 2013: (WP,SA U20, SA Sevens) 24-9-0-0-0-45.

Kolisi, Siya (Grey HS, PE) b 16/06/1991, Port Elizabeth. 1.86m. 99kg. Eightman. FC DEBUT: 2011. PROV CAREER: WP 2011-13 23-5-0-0-0-25. SUPERRUGBY: Stormers 2012-13 29-3-0-0-0-15. REP HONOURS: SA 2013 Tests: 10-0-0-0-0-0. SAU20 2010-11 8-2-0-0-0-10. MISC INFO: YPoY nominee 2013. FC RECORD: 70-10-0-0-0-50. RECORD IN 2013: (SA, Stormers, WP) 26-2-0-0-0-10.

Koster, Armandt (Pionier HS & UFS) b 20/01/1990, Vryheid. 1.92m. 105kg. Flanker. FC DEBUT: 2012. PROV CAREER: Griffons 2012-13 11-0-0-0-0-0. Free State XV 2012 2-0-0-0-0-0. FC RECORD: 13-0-0-0-0-0. RECORD IN 2013: (Griffons) 5-0-0-0-0-0.

Kotze, Andre Jacques (Nelspruit HS) b 17/06/1991, Vredendal. 1.83m. 124kg. Prop. FC DEBUT: 2013. PROV CAREER: Boland 2013 13-0-0-0-0-0. Young Lions 2013 1-0-0-0-0-0. FC RECORD: 14-0-0-0-0-0. RECORD IN 2013: (Boland, Young Lions) 14-0-0-0-0-0.

Kotze, Jaun (Ben Vorster HS, Tzaneen) b 18/05/1992. 1.75m. 70kg. Flyhalf. FC DEBUT: 2011. PROV CAREER: Valke 2011-13 42-8-66-27-6-271. FC RECORD: 42-8-66-27-6-271. RECORD IN 2013: (Valke) 21-4-31-11-5-130.

Kotze, Stephan Clyde (Grey College, Bloemfontein) b 21/01/1991, Kimberley. 1.88m. 119kg. Prop. FC DEBUT: 2011. PROV CAREER: Cheetahs 2011 3-0-0-0-0-0. Free State XV 2012 2-0-0-0-0-0. Pumas 2013 5-0-0-0-0-0. REP HONOURS: SAU20 2011 2-0-0-0-0-0. FC RECORD: 12-0-0-0-0-0. RECORD IN 2013: (Pumas) 5-0-0-0-0-0.

Krause, Gareth Edward (Dale College & UNISA) b 30/12/81, East London. 1.90m. 100kg. Flank. FC DEBUT: 2002. PROV CAREER: Bulldogs 2002-03,09,12-13 78-13-0-0-0-65. Griquas 2004-08 97-19-0-0-0-95. SUPERRUGBY: Cheetahs 2004-05. REP HONOURS: SA Sevens 2004-05. FC RECORD: 182-32-0-0-0-160. RECORD IN 2013: (Bulldogs) 19-1-0-0-0-5.

Kriel, Jacobus Albertus (Jaco) (Standerton HS & UJ) b 21/08/1989, Standerton. 1.83m. 86kg. Flanker. FC DEBUT: 2010. PROV CAREER: Golden Lions 2010-13 23-7-0-0-0-35. Young Lions 2010-13 26-7-0-0-0-35. SUPERRUGBY: Lions 2011-12 7-2-0-0-0-10. P/R 2013 2-1-0-0-0-0. MISC INFO: VC PoY 2012 nominee. FC RECORD: 58-17-0-0-0-85. RECORD IN 2013: (Lions S15, Lions, Young Lions) 18-9-0-0-0-45.

Kriel, Jason (Dirkie Uys HS & UP) b 30/01/1990, Moorreesburg. 1.90m. 102kg. Wing. FC DEBUT: 2013. PROV CAREER: Boland 2013 1-2-0-0-0-10. FC RECORD: 1-2-0-0-0-10. RECORD IN 2013: (Boland) 1-2-0-0-0-10.

Kriel, Jesse Andre (Maritzburg College & UP) b 15/02/1994, Cape Town. 1.86m. 95kg. Fullback. FC DEBUT: 2013. REP HONOURS: SA U20 2013 4-2-0-0-0-10. FC RECORD: 4-2-0-0-0-10. RECORD IN 2013: (SA U20) 4-2-0-0-0-10.

Kritzinger, Inus Michael (Wilgeriver HS, Frankfort & UFS) b 13/05/1989, Welkom. 1.76m. 83kg. Scrumhalf. FC DEBUT: 2011. PROV CAREER: Griffons 2011-13 19-6-5-0-0-40. Free State XV 2012 4-1-0-0-0-5. REP HONOURS: SA Pres XV 2013 1-0-0-0-0-0. FC RECORD: 24-7-5-0-0-45. RECORD IN 2013: (SA Pres XV, Griffons) 11-4-5-0-0-30.

Kruger, Petrus Johannes Juandre (Juandre) (Paul Roos Gymnasium.) b 06/09/85, Cape Town. 1.99m. 112kg. Lock. FC DEBUT: 2007. PROV CAREER: WP 2007 6-2-0-0-0-10. Blue Bulls 2008 & 10-12 55-9-0-0-0-45. SUPERRUGBY: Bulls 2012-13 31-1-0-0-0-5. REP HONOURS: SA 2012-13 Tests: 17-0-0-0-0-0. FC RECORD: 109-12-0-0-0-60. RECORD IN 2013: (SA, Bulls) 23-0-0-0-0-0.

Kruger, Pieter Gerhardus (Grenswag HS) b 28/03/1991, Rustenburg. 1.93m. 121kg. Prop. FC DEBUT: 2013. PROV CAREER: Bulldogs 2013 1-0-0-0-0-0. FC RECORD: 1-0-0-0-0-0. RECORD IN 2013: (Bulldogs) 1-0-0-0-0-0.

Kruger, Robert Albertus (Standerton HS & Potch Univ.) b 28/04/1988, Johannesburg. 1.94m. 106kg. FC DEBUT: 2009. PROV CAREER: Lions 2009-10 4-0-0-0-0-0. Young Lions 2009-11 5-1-0-0-0-5. Leopards 2011-13 33-2-0-0-0-10. Leopard XV 2013 7-2-0-0-0-10. SUPERRUGBY: Lions 2009-10 9-0-0-0-0-0. FC RECORD: 58-5-0-0-0-25. RECORD IN 2013: (Leopards, Leopard XV) 17-3-0-0-0-15.

Kruger, Rossouw (Boland Agric. HS) b 03/05/1989, Cape Town. 121kg. Prop. FC DEBUT: 2010. PROV CAREER: Boland 2010-13 41-3-0-0-0-15. FC RECORD: 41-3-0-0-0-15. RECORD IN 2013: (Boland) 11-1-0-0-0-5.

Kruger, Stephanus Johannes Paulus (Paul) b 16/06/1992. Lock. FC DEBUT: 2013. PROV CAREER: Valke 2013 5-0-0-0-0-0. FC RECORD: 5-0-0-0-0-0. RECORD IN 2013: (Valke) 5-0-0-0-0-0.

Kruger, Victor Eric (Strand HS & NWU) b 19/01/1989, Welkom. 1.99m. 112kg. Lock. FC DEBUT: 2011. PROV CAREER: Leopards 2011-13 14-1-0-0-0-5. Griquas 2013 2-0-0-0-0-0. FC RECORD: 16-1-0-0-0-5. RECORD IN 2013: (Leopards, Griquas) 4-0-0-0-0-0.

Kruger, Werner (Kempton Park HS) b 23/01/85, Kempton Park. 1.90m. 107kg. Prop. FC DEBUT: 2003. PROV CAREER: Blue Bulls 2003 & 05-07-13 112-7-0-0-0-35. Blue Bulls XV 2007 1-0-0-0-0-0. SUPERRUGBY: Bulls 2008-13 92-8-0-0-0-40. REP HONOURS: SA 2011-12 Tests: 4-0-0-0-0-0. Tour: 2010 1-0-0-0-0-0. Total: 5-0-0-0-0-0. Emerging Springboks 2009 1-0-0-0-0-0. SA U21 2005-06 6-0-0-0-0-0. FC RECORD: 217-15-0-0-0-75. RECORD IN 2013: (Bulls, Blue Bulls) 24-2-0-0-0-10.

Kyd, Blake Jonathan (Maritzburg College) b 10/06/1988, Pietermaritzburg. 1.78m. 94kg. Prop. FC DEBUT: 2012. PROV CAREER: Bulldogs 2012-13 33-2-0-0-0-10. FC RECORD: 33-2-0-0-0-10. RECORD IN 2013: (Bulldogs) 14-1-0-0-0-5.

L

Labuschagne, Pieter Hermias Cornelius (Grey College, Bloemfontein & UFS) b 11/01/1989, Pretoria. 1.89m. 103kg. Flank. FC DEBUT: 2011. PROV CAREER: Cheetahs 2011-13 39-10-0-0-0-50. Free State XV 2012 2-0-0-0-0-0. Emerging Cheetahs 2011 1-0-0-0-0-0. SUPERRUGBY: Cheetahs 2012-13 19-2-0-0-0-10. FC RECORD: 61-12-0-0-0-60. RECORD IN 2013: (Cheetahs S15, Cheetahs) 27-4-0-0-0-20.

Lacombe, Virgile. b 07/07/1984. Hooker. SA FC DEBUT: 2013. PROV CAREER: EP Kings 2013 3-1-0-0-0-5. SUPERRUGBY: Southern Kings 2013 4-0-0-0-0-0. REP HONOURS: Argentinia. SA FC RECORD: 7-1-0-0-0-5. RECORD IN 2013: (Southern Kings, EP Kings) 7-1-0-0-0-5.

Ladendorf Ernst (Marais Viljoen HS) b 05/02/1992, Alberton. 2.0m. 103kg. Flank. FC DEBUT: 2013. PROV CAREER: Bulldogs 2013 3-0-0-0-0-0. FC RECORD: 3-0-0-0-0-0. RECORD IN 2013: (Bulldogs) 3-0-0-0-0-0.

A-Z OF FIRST-CLASS PLAYERS IN 2013

Laker, Johannes Jacobus Barend (Johann) (Paul Roos Gymnasium. & US & NWU) b 24/03/1988, Gordons Bay. 1.77m. 83kg. Scrumhalf. FC DEBUT: 2011. PROV CAREER: Leopards 2011-13 40-8-0-0-0-40. FC RECORD: 40-8-0-0-0-40. RECORD IN 2013: (Leopards) 14-4-0-0-0-20.

Lambie, Patrick Jonathan (Michaelhouse) b 17/10/90, Durban. 1.78m. 87kg. Flyhalf. FC DEBUT: 2009. PROV CAREER: KZN 2009-13 28-6-47-63-2-319. Sharks Inv XV 2009 1-0-1-1-0-5. SUPERRUGBY: Sharks 2010-13 50-8-65-114-1-515. REP HONOURS: SA 2010-13 Tests: 32-1-15-11-0-68. Tour: 1-0-0-0-0-0. Total: 33-1-15-11-0-68. SAU20 2010 5-4-17-9-0-75. British Barbarians 2013 1-0-4-0-0-8. MISC INFO: SARU PoY 2011 and 2012 nominee. SA Rugby YPoY 2011. MISC INFO: Son of former Natal utility back Ian Lambie. Grandson of Nic Labuschagne (England and Natal) and former President of the KZNRU. FC RECORD: 118-19-149-198-3-990. RECORD IN 2013: (SA, Sharks, KZN, British Barbarians) 31-3-35-54-3-256.

Landman, Rynard Jaco (Despatch HS) b 24/07/86, East London. 1.97m. 114kg. Lock. FC DEBUT: 2008. PROV CAREER: Leopards 2008-11 41-2-0-0-0-10. Boland 2011 13-4-0-0-0-20. Griquas 2012-13 23-7-0-0-0-35. SUPERRUGBY: Lions 2009 2-0-0-0-0-0. Cheetahs 2013 14-0-0-0-0-0. REP HONOURS: Royal XV 2009 1-0-0-0-0-0. FC RECORD: 94-13-0-0-0-65. RECORD IN 2013: (Cheetahs S15, Griquas) 18-0-0-0-0-0.

Larson, Raoul Jonathan (Grey College, Bloemfontein) b 14/05/84, Katima Mulilo. 1.85m. 120kgs. Prop. FC DEBUT: 2006. PROV CAREER: Cheetahs 2006-07 16-0-0-0-0-0. Griffons 2007 9-0-0-0-0-0. Elephants 2009 9-0-0-0-0-0. Boland 2010 7-0-0-0-0-0. Eagles 2012-13 14-0-0-0-0-0. FC RECORD: 55-0-0-0-0-0. RECORD IN 2013: (Eagles) 12-0-0-0-0-0.

Lawson, Richard James (Wynberg Boys HS) b 20/10/86, Johannesburg. 1.83m. 87kg. Fullback. FC DEBUT: 2006. PROV CAREER: WP 2006-08 16-3-0-0-0-15. Griquas 2009-13 47-14-0-0-0-70. REP HONOURS: Emerging Springboks 2008 3-0-0-0-0-0. FC RECORD: 66-17-0-0-0-85. RECORD IN 2013: (Griquas) 10-2-0-0-0-10.

Le Maitre, Eugene (Marais Viljoen HS) b 13/02/1993, Alberton. 1.79m. 96kg. Hooker. FC debut: 2013. PROV CAREER: Young Lions 2013 1-0-0-0-0-0. FC RECORD: 1-0-0-0-0-0. RECORD IN 2013: (Young Lions) 1-0-0-0-0-0.

Le Roux, Abraham Jacobus (AJ) (Overkruin HS, Pretoria) b 12/12/1990, Pretoria. 1.80m. 108kg. Hooker. FC DEBUT: 2010. PROV CAREER: Blue Bulls 2010 2-0-0-0-0-0. Cheetahs 2012-13 7-1-0-0-0-5. Young Lions 2011-12 9-0-0-0-0-0. Golden Lions XV 2011 1-0-0-0-0-0. Griffons 2013 5-2-0-0-0-10. FC RECORD: 24-3-0-0-0-15. RECORD IN 2013: (Cheetahs, Griffons) 9-3-0-0-0-15.

Le Roux, Christo (Oakdale Agri. HS) b 28/03/85, Bloemfontein. 1.91m. 108kg. Eighthman. FC DEBUT: 2008. PROV CAREER: Eagles 2008 15-3-0-0-0-15. Pumas 2009-13 97-14-0-0-0-70. SUPERRUGBY: Lions 2012 1-0-0-0-0-0. FC RECORD: 113-17-0-0-0-85. RECORD IN 2013: (Pumas) 17-4-0-0-0-20.

Le Roux, Grant (Flippie) (Vereeniging THS & Potch Univ.) b 13/01/86, Sasolburg. 1.97m. 110kg. Lock. FC DEBUT: 2009. PROV CAREER: Boland 2009-11 44-1-0-0-0-5. Eagles 2012-13 32-3-0-0-0-15. FC RECORD: 76-4-0-0-0-20. RECORD IN 2013: (Eagles) 14-1-0-0-0-5.

Le Roux, Hendrik Frederik (Erik) (Grey College, Bloemfontein & UFS) b 24/02/1988, Bloemfontein. 1.90m. 96kg. Eighthman. FC DEBUT: 2011. PROV CAREER: Griffons 2011-13 29-2-0-0-0-10. Cheetahs 2011 1-0-0-0-0-0. FC RECORD: 30-2-0-0-0-10. RECORD IN 2013: (Griffons) 10-1-0-0-0-5.

Le Roux, Willem Jacobus (Willie) (Paul Roos Gymnasium) b 18/08/1989, Cape Town. 1.86m. 88kg. Flyhalf. FC DEBUT: 2010. PROV CAREER: Boland 2010-11 39-27-31-6-2-221. Griquas 2012-13 11-1-0-0-0-5. SUPERRUGBY: Cheetahs 2012-13 33-13-0-0-0-65. REP HONOURS: SA 2013 Tests: 12-4-0-0-0-20. British Barbarians 2013 1-0-0-0-0-0. MISC INFO: SA PoY nominee 2013. SR PoY nominee 2013. FC RECORD: 96-45-31-6-2-311. RECORD IN 2013: (SA, Cheetahs S15, Griquas, British Barbarians) 32-10-0-0-0-50.

Lehmann, Helmut Werner (Paarl Gymnasium. & US) b 28/09/1990, Paarl. 1.84m. 104kg. Flank. FC DEBUT: 2011. PROV CAREER: WP 2011-13 8-0-0-0-0-0. REP HONOURS: SA Students 2012 2-0-0-0-0-0. SA Univ 2013 1-0-0-0-0-0. FC RECORD: 11-0-0-0-0-0. RECORD IN 2013: (WP, SA Univ) 2-0-0-0-0-0.

Lemley, Wayne (Daniel Pienaar HS) b 15/05/1991, Uitenhage. 1.93m. 113kg. Prop. FC DEBUT: 2013. PROV CAREER: Bulldogs 2013 7-0-0-0-0-0. FC RECORD: 7-0-0-0-0-0. RECORD IN 2013: (Bulldogs) 7-0-0-0-0-0.

Leonardi, Tomas. Lock. SA FC DEBUT: 2013. PROV CAREER: EP Kings 2013 4-0-0-0-0-0. SUPERRUGBY: Southern Kings 2013 1-0-0-0-0-0. REP HONOURS: Argentinia. SA FC RECORD: 5-0-0-0-0-0. RECORD IN 2013: (Southern Kings, EP Kings) 5-0-0-0-0-0.

Lerm, Ruan Stephan (Dr. EG Jansen) b 25/03/1992, Kempton Park. 1.92m. 93kg. Eightman. FC DEBUT: 2012. PROV CAREER: Young Lions 2012-13 8-1-0-0-0-5. FC RECORD: 8-1-0-0-0-5. RECORD IN 2013: (Young Lions) 1-1-0-0-0-5.

Lewies, Joseph Stephanus Theuns b 27/01/1992. Lock. FC DEBUT: 2012. PROV CAREER: Sharks XV 2012-13 2-0-0-0-0-0. KZN 20213 5-0-0-0-0-0. FC RECORD: 7-0-0-0-0-0. RECORD IN 2013: (KZN, Sharks XV) 6-0-0-0-0-0.

Lewis, Clemen (Boland Agricultural HS) b 10/10/83. 1.75m. 90kg. Flank. FC DEBUT: 2006. PROV CAREER: Boland 2006-13 102-7-0-0-0-35. REP HONOURS: SA Barbarians 2012 1-0-0-0-0-0. FC RECORD: 103-7-0-0-0-35. RECORD IN 2013: (Boland) 17-1-0-0-0-5.

Lewis, Jean-Paul (Paul Roos Gymnasium & US) b 20/10/1983, Stellenbosch. 1.76m. 72kg. Centre. FC DEBUT: 2013. REP HONOURS: SA Univ 2013 1-3-0-0-0-15. FC RECORD: 1-3-0-0-0-15. RECORD IN 2013: (SA Univ) 1-3-0-0-0-15.

Leyds, Dillyn Yullrich (Bishops College & UCT) b 12/09/1982, Somerset West. 1.85m. 78kg. Flyhalf. FC DEBUT: 2012. PROV CAREER: WP 2013 2-0-1-1-0-5. REP HONOURS: SA U20 2012 4-0-0-0-0-0. FC RECORD: 6-0-1-1-0-5. RECORD IN 2013: (WP) 2-0-1-1-0-5.

Liebenberg, Christiaan Rudolph (Tiaan) (Grey College, Bloemfontein) b 18/12/81, Kimberley. 1.85m. 107kg. Hooker. FC DEBUT: 2002. PROV CAREER: KZN 2002 2-0-0-0-0-0. Griquas 2003-06 64-4-1-0-0-22. WP 2006-07,09-13 61-6-0-0-0-30. SUPERRUGBY: Cheetahs 13-1-0-0-0-5. Stormers 2007-13 67-5-0-0-0-25. REP HONOURS: SA 2012 Tests: 5-0-0-0-0-0. SA 2007 Tour: 1-0-0-0-0-0. Total: 6-0-0-0-0-0. Emerging Springboks 2009 1-0-0-0-0-0. MISC INFO: Brother of FS hooker Hercu. Son of former GW & FS flyhalf & fullback Henning Liebenberg. FC RECORD: 214-16-1-0-0-82. RECORD IN 2013: (Stormers, WP) 7-1-0-0-0-5.

Liebenberg, Herculaas Johannes (Hercu) (Grey College, Bloemfontein) b 16/05/86, Bloemfontein. 1.78m. 104kg. Hooker. FC DEBUT: 2006. PROV CAREER: Cheetahs 2006-08 & 10-13 57-0-0-0-0-0. Elephants 2009 11-1-0-0-0-5. Griffons 2011 2-0-0-0-0-0. Emerging Cheetahs 2011 1-0-0-0-0-0. Free State XV 2013 7-0-0-0-0-0. SUPERRUGBY: Cheetahs 2012 6-0-0-0-0-0. MISC INFO: Brother of GW & WP hooker Tiaan. Son of former GW & FS flyhalf & fullback Henning Liebenberg. FC RECORD: 84-1-0-0-0-5. RECORD IN 2013: (Cheetahs, Free State XV) 16-0-0-0-0-0.

Liebenberg, RJ (Voortrekker HS, Bethlehem) b 11/12/1990,

A-Z OF FIRST-CLASS PLAYERS IN 2013

Bethlehem. 1.84m. 101kg. Flank. FC DEBUT: 2011. PROV CAREER: Golden Lions XV 2011 1-0-0-0-0-0. Griquas 2013 9-0-0-0-0-0. REP HONOURS: SA Univ 2013 1-0-0-0-0-0. FC RECORD: 11-0-0-0-0-0. RECORD IN 2013: (Griquas, SA Univ) 10-0-0-0-0-0.

Liebenberg, Willem Andries (Wiaan) (Drostdy HS) b 31/08/1992, Bellville. 1.89m. 100kg. Flanker. FC DEBUT: 2012. PROV CAREER: Blue Bulls 2012-13 18-10-0-0-0-50. REP HONOURS: SA U20 2012 (captain) 4-0-0-0-0-0. FC RECORD: 22-10-0-0-0-50. RECORD IN 2013: (Blue Bulls) 16-10-0-0-0-5.

Lindeque, Petrus Johannes (Piet) (Grey College, Bloemfontein) b 31/01/1991, Winburg. 1.82m. 88kg. Centre. FC DEBUT: 2010. PROV CAREER: Sharks XV 2011-12 9-4-0-0-0-20. Sharks Inv XV 2010 1-0-0-0-0-0. Blue Bulls 2013 1-1-0-0-0-5. Cheetahs 2013 6-0-0-0-0-0. SUPERRUGBY: Sharks 2013 5-1-0-0-0-5. FC RECORD: 22-6-0-0-0-30. RECORD IN 2013: (Sharks, Blue Bulls, Cheetahs) 12-2-0-0-0-10.

Lobberts, Hilton (New Orleans SS) b 11/06/86, Paarl. 1.90m. 102kg. Flank. FC DEBUT: 2005. PROV CAREER: Blue Bulls 2006-08 37-5-0-0-0-25. Boland 2009-10 17-0-0-0-0-0. WP 2009 & 2011-12 34-3-0-0-0-15. Griquas 2013 4-0-0-0-0-0. SUPERRUGBY: Bulls 2007-08 7-0-0-0-0-0. Stormers 2009 5-0-0-0-0-0. REP HONOURS: SA 2006-07 Tests: 2-0-0-0-0-0. Tour: 2006,07 2-0-0-0-0-0. Total: 4-0-0-0-0-0. Emerging Springboks 2007 1-0-0-0-0-0. SA U21 2005-06 10-1-0-0-0-5. SA U19s 2004-05. FC RECORD: 119-9-0-0-0-45. RECORD IN 2013: (Griquas) 4-0-0-0-0-0.

Loock, Wilhelm Hendrik (Oakdale HS & US) b 14/01/1987, George. 1.80m. 90kg. Wing. FC DEBUT: 2011. PROV CAREER: Pumas 2011-13 33-13-0-0-0-65. FC RECORD: 33-13-0-0-0-65. RECORD IN 2013: (Pumas) 11-4-0-0-0-20.

Louw, Jacobus Johannes Petrus (Jaco) b 26/07/1983. Flank. FC DEBUT: 2013. PROV CAREER: Limpopo 2013 5-0-0-0-0-0. FC RECORD: 5-0-0-0-0-0. RECORD IN 2013: (Limpopo) 5-0-0-0-0-0.

Louw, Johann Barnard (Pakuranga College) b 08/03/1991, Bellville. 1.83m. 91kg. Scrumhalf. FC DEBUT: 2013. PROV CAREER: Valke 2013 2-0-0-0-0-0. FC RECORD: 2-0-0-0-0-0. RECORD IN 2013: (Valke) 2-0-0-0-0-0.

Louw, Louis-Francois Pickard (Francois) (Bishops) b 15/06/85, Cape Town. 1.90m. 114kg. Flank. FC DEBUT: 2006. PROV CAREER: WP 2006-10 65-13-0-0-0-65. SUPERRUGBY: Stormers 2008-11 52-4-0-0-0-20. REP HONOURS: SA 2010-13 Tests: 28-5-0-0-0-25. British Barbarians 2013 1-0-0-0-0-0. MISC INFO: Grandson of former Springbok Jan Pickard. FC RECORD: 146-22-0-0-0-110. RECORD IN 2013: (SA, British Barbarians) 12-2-0-0-0-10.

Louw, Sarel Jacobus (Goudveld HS, Welkom) b 27/04/78, Odendaalsrus. 1.87m. 108kg. Prop. FC DEBUT: 2001. PROV CAREER: Griffons 2001-04,07-13 140-13-0-0-0-65. MISC INFO: Son of former Norhern Free State prop Sarel Louw. FC RECORD: 140-13-0-0-0-65. RECORD IN 2013: (Griffons) 7-0-0-0-0-0.

Louw, Willem Johannes (Hans Strijdom HS) b 03/02/1988, Pietersburg. 1.93m. 119kg. Lock. FC DEBUT: 2013. PROV CAREER: Limpopo 2013 1-0-0-0-0-0. FC RECORD: 1-0-0-0-0-0. RECORD IN 2013: (Limpopo) 1-0-0-0-0-0.

Louw, Wilmaure Derrick (Carlton van Heerden HS) b 02/02/87, Upington. 1.83m. 86kg. Centre. >> FC debut 2009. PROV CAREER: Griquas 2009-12 63-11-0-0-0-55. Pumas 2013 24-1-0-0-0-5. SUPERRUGBY: Cheetahs 2010-11 6-0-0-0-0-0. REP HONOURS: SA Pres XV 2013 3-1-0-0-0-5. FC RECORD: 96-13-0-0-0-65. RECORD IN 2013: (SA Pres XV, Pumas) 27-2-0-0-0-10.

Louwrens, Lodewikus (Oakdale Agric. & NMMU) b 30/08/1991, Riversdal. 1.80m. 115kg. Prop. FC debut: 2013. PROV CAREER: Eagles 2013 2-0-0-0-0-0. FC RECORD: 2-0-0-0-0-0. RECORD IN 2013: (Eagles) 2-0-0-0-0-0.

Luckan, Ghafoer (Rylands HS) b 18/12/85, Cape Town. 1.78m. 85kg. Wing. FC DEBUT: 2009. PROV CAREER: Bulldogs 2009 11-3-0-0-0-15. Leopards 2010 2-0-0-0-0-0. Eagles 2012-13 15-7-0-0-0-35. WP 2012 2-1-0-0-0-5. FC RECORD: 30-11-0-0-0-55. RECORD IN 2013: (Eagles) 10-1-0-0-0-5.

Ludik, Louis (Dr EG Jansen) b 08/10/86, Kempton Park. 1.82m. 92kg. Wing. FC DEBUT: 2006. PROV CAREER: Lions 2006-09 45-12-0-0-0-60. Lions XV 2008 1-1-0-0-0-5. Young Lions 2006-08 12-4-0-0-0-20. KZN 2010-13 44-7-0-0-0-35. Sharks XV 2010 3-1-0-0-0-5. Sharks Inv XV 2010 1-0-0-0-0-0. SUPERRUGBY: Lions 2007-09 36-4-0-0-0-20. Sharks 2011-13 40-7-0-0-0-35. REP HONOURS: Emerging Springboks 2007 1-0-0-0-0-0. MISC INFO: CC PoY 2012 nominee. FC RECORD: 183-36-0-0-0-180. RECORD IN 2013: (Sharks, KZN) 17-4-0-0-0-20.

Luiters, Kevin (Grey College, Bloemfontein & UFS) b 02/07/1992, Port Elizabeth. 1.72m. 75kg. Scrumhalf. FC DEBUT: 2011. PROV CAREER: Cheetahs 2011 & 13 6-1-0-0-0-5. Free State XV 2012-13 6-0-0-0-0. REP HONOURS: SA Sevens 2012-13. FC RECORD: 12-1-0-0-0-5. RECORD IN 2013: (Cheetahs, Free State XV, SA Sevens) 8-1-0-0-0-5.

Lusaseni, Luvuyiso (Selborne College & Ethekwini College) b 16/12/88, East London. 1.96m. 102kg. FC DEBUT: 2009. PROV CAREER: Sharks XV 2009-10 11-1-0-0-0-5. Griquas 2010 3-0-0-0-0-0. Leopards 2011-13 43-2-0-0-0-10. Leopard XV 2013 4-0-0-0-0-0. REP HONOURS: SA Barbarians 2012 1-0-0-0-0-0. SAU20 2008 1-0-0-0-0-0. SA Univ 2013 1-0-0-0-0-0. FC RECORD: 64-2-0-0-0-15. RECORD IN 2013: (SA Univ, Leopards, Leopard XV) 19-1-0-0-0-5.

M

Maarman, Marzuq (Muir College) b 23/09/1992, Port Elizabeth. 1.81m. 112kg. Prop. FC DEBUT: 2013. PROV CAREER: EP Kings 2013 1-0-0-0-0-0. FC RECORD: 1-0-0-0-0-0. RECORD IN 2013: (EP Kings) 1-0-0-0-0-0.

Maarman, Tertius (Hentie Cilliers HS, Virginia) b 14/04/87, Port Elizabeth. 1.69m. 79kg. Utility back. FC DEBUT: 2008. PROV CAREER: Griffons 2008-13 70-20-4-0-0-108. FC RECORD: 70-20-4-0-0-108. RECORD IN 2013: (Griffons) 14-4-3-0-0-24.

Mahoney, Andries Stefanus (Klerksdorp HS) b 29/01/85, Klerksdorp. 1.70m. 76kgs. Scrumhalf. FC DEBUT: 2006. PROV CAREER: Leopards 2006-07 17-2-0-0-0-10. Griffons 2011-13 47-3-0-0-0-15. REP HONOURS: SA Barbarians 2012 1-0-0-0-0-0. FC RECORD: 65-5-0-0-0-25. RECORD IN 2013: (Griffons) 9-1-0-0-0-5.

Mahuza, Sylvian (Outeniqua HS, George & NWU) b 29/07/1993, George. 1.78m. 80kg. Wing. FC DEBUT: 2013. PROV CAREER: Leopards 2013 3-1-0-0-0-5. REP HONOURS: SA U20 2013 no appearances. FC RECORD: 3-1-0-0-0-5. RECORD IN 2013: (Leopards, SA U20) 3-1-0-0-0-5.

Majola, Khaya (Westville Boys HS) b 13/03/1992, Kokstad. 1.85m. 98kg. Flanker. FC DEBUT: 2012. PROV CAREER: Sharks XV 2012-13 8-0-0-0-0-0. REP HONOURS: SAU20 2012 1-0-0-0-0-0. FC RECORD: 9-0-0-0-0-0. RECORD IN 2013: (Sharks XV) 7-0-0-0-0-0.

Maku, Bandise Grey (Dale College) b 24/06/86, King William's Town. 1.87m. 111kg. Hooker. FC DEBUT: 2006. PROV CAREER: Blue Bulls 2006-10 & 13 69-3-0-0-0-15. Lions 2011-12 23-1-0-0-0-5. SUPERRUGBY: Bulls 2008 & 10 19-0-0-0-0-0. Lions 2011 14-0-0-0-0-0. Southern Kings 2013 16-0-0-0-0-0. P/R 2013 2-0-0-0-0-0. REP HONOURS: SA 2010 Tests: 1-0-0-0-0-0. Tour: 2009-10 3-1-0-0-0-5. Total: 4-1-0-0-0-5. Emerging Springboks 2007,09 2-0-0-0-0-0. SA U21 2006 3-0-0-0-0-0. FC RECORD: 152-5-0-0-0-25. RECORD IN 2013: (Southern Kings, Blue Bulls) 26-0-0-0-0-0.

A-Z OF FIRST-CLASS PLAYERS IN 2013

Malherbe, Jozua Francois (Paarl Boys HS) b 14/03/1991, Paarl. 1.90m. 120kg. Prop. FC DEBUT: 2011. PROV CAREER: WP 2011-13 33-0-0-0-0. SUPERRUGBY: Stormers 2011-13 32-0-0-0-0. REP HONOURS: SA 2012-13 2-0-0-0-0-0. FC RECORD: 67-0-0-0-0. RECORD IN 2013: (SA, Stormers, WP) 17-0-0-0-0.
Mamojele, Thabo (Patriot HS) b 29/07/86, Witbank. 1.95m. 104kg. Flank. FC DEBUT: 2007. PROV CAREER: KZN 2007 2-2-0-0-0-10. Valke 2008 5-0-0-0-0. Leopards 2009 & 2011 16-0-0-0-0. EP Kings 2012-13 16-2-0-0-0-10. SUPERRUGBY: Southern Kings 2013 1-0-0-0-0. FC RECORD: 40-4-0-0-0-20. RECORD IN 2013: (Southern Kings, EP Kings) 12-1-0-0-0-5.
Mangweni, Siyabonga (Tiger) (Ntsonkotha SS) b 20/06/80, Nxaruni. 1.87m. 80kg. Fullback. FC DEBUT: 2001. PROV CAREER: Bulldogs 2001-05 63-17-29-20-0-203. Griquas 2005-07 22-3-2-3-0-28. Blue Bulls 2008-10 46-15-0-0-1-78. EP Kings 2010-13 64-11-0-0-0-55. SUPERRUGBY: Stormers 2005 2-0-0-0-0. Cheetahs 2007 7-1-0-0-0-5. Bulls 2010 1-0-0-0-0-0. REP HONOURS: SA 'A' 2004 2-0-0-0-0-0. S/Kings 2009 1-0-0-0-0-0. MISC INFO: CC First Division PoY nominee 2013. FC RECORD: 208-47-31-23-1-369. RECORD IN 2013: (EP Kings) 23-4-0-0-0-20.
Mapoe, Lionel Granton (Fichardtpark HS, Bloemfontein) b 13/07/88, Port Elizabeth. 1.82m. 84kg. Wing. FC DEBUT: 2008. PROV CAREER: Cheetahs 2008 12-6-0-0-0-30. Cheetahs XV 2010 1-0-0-0-0. Lions 2011-13 20-5-0-0-0-25. SUPERRUGBY: Cheetahs 2010 5-1-0-0-0-5. Lions 2011-12 23-2-0-0-0-10. Bulls 2013 12-2-0-0-0-10. REP HONOURS: SA 2012 - no tests. SAU20 2008 4-5-0-0-0-25. MISC INFO: YPOY Nominee 2009. FC RECORD: 77-21-0-0-0-105. RECORD IN 2013: (Bulls, Lions) 15-2-0-0-0-10.
Marais, Brenvin Bradley (Weston HS) b 15/01/1993, Vredenburg. 1.82m. 86kg. Centre. FC DEBUT: 2013. PROV CAREER: Griffons 2013 1-0-0-0-0. FC RECORD: 1-0-0-0-0. RECORD IN 2013: (Griffons) 1-0-0-0-0.
Marais, Charles Maclean (Paarl Boys HS & UOFS) b 29/08/1988, Paarl. 1.91m. 114kg. Prop. FC DEBUT: 2010. PROV CAREER: Cheetahs 2010-11 7-0-0-0-0. Free State XV 2012-13 8-0-0-0-0. Griffons 2012-13 6-1-0-0-0-5. FC RECORD: 21-1-0-0-0-5. RECORD IN 2013: (Griffons, Free State XV) 5-0-0-0-0-0.
Marais, Daniel Rudolf (Niel) (Grey College, Bloemfontein & UFS) b 21/01/1992, Bloemfontein. 1.81m. 97kg. Fullback. FC DEBUT: 2013. PROV CAREER: Free State XV 2013 6-0-0-0-0. FC RECORD: 6-0-0-0-0. RECORD IN 2013: (Free State XV) 6-0-0-0-0.
Marais, Edmar b 24/10/1991. Wing. FC DEBUT: 2013. PROV CAREER: Leopards 2013 15-11-0-0-0-55. Leopard XV 2013 7-3-0-0-0-15. FC RECORD: 22-14-0-0-0-70. RECORD IN 2013: (Leopards, Leopard XV) 22-14-0-0-0-70.
Marais, Franco Stephan (Transvalia HS) b 23/09/1992, Vereeniging. 1.86m. 94kg. Hooker. FC DEBUT: 2012. PROV CAREER: KZN 2012 1-0-0-0-0. Sharks XV 2013 8-1-0-0-0-5. SAU20 2012 1-0-0-0-0-0. FC RECORD: 10-1-0-0-0-5. RECORD IN 2013: (Sharks XV) 8-1-0-0-0-5.
Marais, Jacobus Johannes (Kobus) (Waterkloof HS, Pretoria) b 05/07/1994, Richards Bay. 1.83m. 92kg. Flyhalf. FC DEBUT: 2013. PROV CAREER: Blue Bulls 2013 2-0-0-0-0. FC RECORD: 2-0-0-0-0. RECORD IN 2013: (Blue Bulls) 2-0-0-0-0.
Marais, Jan Andre (Jandre) (Welkom Gymnasium) b 14/06/89. 1.97m. 115kg. Lock. FC DEBUT: 2009. PROV CAREER: KZN 2011-12 22-0-0-0-0. Sharks XV 2009-13 36-2-0-0-0-10. Sharks Inv XV 2009 1-0-0-0-0. SUPERRUGBY: Sharks 2012-13 12-1-0-0-0-5. REP HONOURS: SAU20 2009 4-1-0-0-0-5. MISC INFO: Brother of Peet Marais. FC RECORD: 75-4-0-0-0-20. RECORD IN 2013: (Sharks, Sharks XV) 11-0-0-0-0-0.
Marais, Peet Celliers (Welkom Gymnasium) b 31/10/1990, Welkom. 1.98m. 115kg. Lock. FC DEBUT: 2011. PROV CAREER: KZN 2011-13 18-0-0-0-0. Sharks XV 2011-13 23-0-0-0-0. REP HONOURS: SAU20 2010 2-0-0-0-0-0. MISC INFO: Brother of Jandre Marais. FC RECORD: 43-0-0-0-0. RECORD IN 2013: (KZN, Sharks XV) 20-0-0-0-0-0.
Marais, Sarel Petrus (Paarl Boys HS) b 16/03/1989. 1.84m. 80kg. Wing. PROV CAREER: Leopards 2010 2-3-1-0-0-17. EP Kings 2011-12 36-18-4-0-0-98. KZN 2013 11-4-0-0-0-20. SUPERRUGBY: Southern Kings 2013 8-0-0-0-0. P/R 2013 2-0-0-0-0. REP HONOURS: SA Kings 2011 3-0-0-0-0. FC RECORD: 62-25-5-0-0-135. RECORD IN 2013: (Southern Kings, KZN) 21-4-0-0-0-20.
Maritz, Gert Coenraad Frederik (Franco) (Waterkloof HS, Pretoria & TUT) b 20/02/1991, Kempton Park. 1.77m. 92kg. Centre. FC DEBUT: 2013. PROV CAREER: Valke 2013 4-1-0-0-0-5. FC RECORD: 4-1-0-0-0-5. RECORD IN 2013: (Valke) 4-1-0-0-0-5.
Maritz, Hoffman Van Heerden (Voortrekker HS, Bethlehem) b 29/03/1989, Bethlehem. 1.85m. 93kg. Wing. FC DEBUT: 2011. PROV CAREER: Young Lions 2011 5-0-0-0-0. Leopards 2011-12 29-9-0-0-0-45. Leopard XV 2013 4-1-0-0-0-5. REP HONOURS: SA Barbarians 2012 1-0-0-0-0. SA Pres XV 2013 1-1-0-0-0-5. SA Univ 2013 1-0-0-0-0. FC RECORD: 41-11-0-0-0-55. RECORD IN 2013: (SA Pres XV, SA Univ, Leopard XV) 6-2-0-0-0-10.
Martinus, Devon Roy (Bredasdorp HS & UWC) b 28/01/1993, Bredasdorp. 1.86m. 122kg. Prop. FC DEBUT: 2013. PROV CAREER: Young Lions 2013 3-0-0-0-0. REP HONOURS: SA U20 2013 1-0-0-0-0. FC RECORD: 4-0-0-0-0. RECORD IN 2013: (SA U20, Young Lions) 4-0-0-0-0-0.
Marutlulle, Edgar (Potchefstroom HS) b 20/12/87, Boksburg. 1.77m. 91kg. Hooker. FC DEBUT: 2007. PROV CAREER: Golden Lions 2010 13-1-0-0-0-5. Young Lions 2011-12 11-3-0-0-0-15. Leopards 2012-13 26-1-0-0-0-50. Leopard XV 2013 1-0-0-0-0. SUPERRUGBY: Lions 2011 8-0-0-0-0. Southern Kings: 2013 4-0-0-0-0. REP HONOURS: SA Students 2007-09 4-0-0-0-0-0. FC RECORD: 67-14-0-0-0-70. RECORD IN 2013: (Southern Kings, Leopards, Leopard XV) 18-6-0-0-0-30.
Marx, Noel Petrus Johannes (Diamantveld HS, Kimberley & CUT) b 30/10/1992, Bloemfontein. 1.79m. 78kg. Centre. FC DEBUT: 2013. PROV CAREER: Free State XV 2013 3-1-0-0-0-5. FC RECORD: 3-1-0-0-0-5. RECORD IN 2013: (Free State XV) 3-1-0-0-0-5.
Marx, Tiaan (Nelspruit HS) b 17/03/86, Nelspruit. 1.86m. 82kg. Flyhalf. FC DEBUT: 2007. PROV CAREER: Leopards 2007 8-1-2-2-0-15. KZN 2008 6-2-6-2-1-31. Pumas 2008-13 82-15-31-17-1-191. MISC INFO: Son of former Lowveld flank Gawie Marx. FC RECORD: 96-18-39-21-2-237. RECORD IN 2013: (Pumas) 14-2-17-2-0-50.
Maseko, Sizophilo Sabelo (Ermelo HS & US) b 03/03/1991, Ermelo. 1.84m. 88kg. Wing. FC DEBUT: 2013. PROV CAREER: KZN 2013 4-1-0-0-0-5. Sharks XV 2013 8-5-0-0-0-25. FC RECORD: 12-6-0-0-0-30. RECORD IN 2013: (KZN, Sharks XV) 12-6-0-0-0-30.
Masimla, Godlen Herschelle Derrick (Hugenote HS & UWC) b 11/08/1992, Wellington. 1.77m. 80kg. Scrumhalf. FC DEBUT: 2013. PROV CAREER: WP 2013 9-0-0-0-0. FC RECORD: 9-0-0-0-0. RECORD IN 2013: (WP) 9-0-0-0-0.
Mastriet, Sampie (Drostdy HS) b 03/08/1990, Mairsdas. 1.80m. 84kg. Wing. FC DEBUT: 2011. PROV CAREER: Blue Bulls 2011-13 34-20-0-0-0-100. SUPERRUGBY: Bulls 2013 1-1-0-0-0-5. REP HONOURS: SAU20 2009-10 6-4-0-0-0-20. SA Sevens 2013. FC RECORD: 41-25-0-0-

A-Z OF FIRST-CLASS PLAYERS IN 2013

0-12 5. RECORD IN 2013: (Bulls, Blue Bulls, SA Sevens) 14-10-0-0-0-50.
Mateus, Franco da Silva (Welkom Gymnasium & CUT) b 04/09/1989, Welkom. 1.76m. 102 kg. Hooker. FC DEBUT: 2013. PROV CAREER: Griffons 2013 3-0-0-0-0-0. FC RECORD: 3-0-0-0-0-0. RECORD IN 2013: (Griffons) 3-0-0-0-0-0.
Mathee, Rudi (Otto du Plessis HS) b 25/02/86, Port Elizabeth. 1.95m. 108kg. Lock. FC DEBUT: 2006. PROV CAREER: Lions 2006-07 6-1-0-0-0-5. Leopards 2008-09 26-6-0-0-0-30. Cheetahs 2010 6-2-0-0-0-10. Griffons 2010 6-2-0-0-0-10. Pumas 2011-13 50-4-0-0-0-20. REP HONOURS: SA Students 2007 1-1-0-0-0-5. Royal XV 2009 1-0-0-0-0-0. SA Barbarians 2012 1-0-0-0-0-0. MISC INFO: CC First Div PoY 2012 nominee. FC RECORD: 97-16-0-0-0-80. RECORD IN 2013: (Pumas) 10-1-0-0-0-5.
Mathie, Scott (Durban HS) b 01/02/83. 1.80m. 82kg. Scrumhalf. FC DEBUT: 2004. PROV CAREER: Blue Bulls 2004 16-3-0-0-0-15. KZN 2006-08 41-4-0-0-0-20. KZN XV 2007 1-0-0-0-0-0. EP Kings 2012-13 23-0-0-0-0-0. SUPERRUGBY: Sharks 2006 5-0-0-0-0-0. FC RECORD: 86-7-0-0-0-35. RECORD IN 2013: (EP Kings) 13-0-0-0-0-0.
Mathonsi, Thulani Densel b 10/10/1983. Prop. FC DEBUT: 2013. PROV CAREER: Limpopo 2013 7-0-0-0-0-0. FC RECORD: 7-0-0-0-0-0. RECORD IN 2013: (Limpopo) 7-0-0-0-0-0.
Matthee, Pieter (Dr EG Jansen HS & UFS) b 18/02/1992, Benoni. 1.90m. 102kg. Lock. FC DEBUT: 2013. PROV CAREER: Free State XV 2013 3-0-0-0-0-0. FC RECORD: 3-0-0-0-0-0. RECORD IN 2013: (Free State XV) 3-0-0-0-0-0.
Matyeshana, Dumisani (Selborne College) b 11/02/81, Mdansane. 1.85m. 92kg. Centre. FC DEBUT: 2004. PROV CAREER: Bulldogs 2004-06,09 44-13-0-0-0-65. Leopards 2007 & 10-11 & 13 36-15-0-0-0-75. KZN 2007-08 4-0-0-0-0-0. KZN XV 2007 1-0-0-0-0-0. FC RECORD: 85-28-0-0-0-140. RECORD IN 2013: (Leopards) 2-0-0-0-0-0.
Matsushima, Kotaro (Toin Gukuen HS) b 26/02/1993, Pretoria. 1.76m. 86kg. Fullback. FC DEBUT: 2013. PROV CAREER: Sharks XV 2013 2-1-0-0-0-5. FC RECORD: 2-1-0-0-0-5. RECORD IN 2013: (Sharks XV) 2-1-0-0-0-5.
Mbiyozo, Mpho Mzukisi (Grey HS, PE & UCT) b 07/02/83, Lusikisiki. 1.82m. 94kg. Flank. FC DEBUT: 2005. PROV CAREER: WP 2005-06 18-2-0-0-0-10. Boland 2008 1-0-0-0-0-0. EP Kings 2010-13 54-10-0-0-0-50. SUPERRUGBY: Southern Kings 2013 1-1-0-0-0-5. REP HONOURS: SA Kings 2011 1-0-0-0-0-0. S/Kings 2009 1-1-0-0-0-5. SA Barbarians 2012 1-0-0-0-0-0. SA Sevens 2008. FC RECORD: 77-14-0-0-0-70. RECORD IN 2013: (Southern Kings, EP Kings) 17-10-0-0-0-50.
Mbonambi, Mbongeni Theo (Bongi) (Voortrekker HS, Bethlehem, St Albans HS & TUT) b 07/01/1991, Bethlehem. 1.80m. 97kg. Hooker. FC DEBUT: 2012. PROV CAREER: Blue Bulls 2012-13 19-0-0-0-0-0. SUPERRUGBY: Bulls 2012 2-0-0-0-0-0. REP HONOURS: SAU20 2011 5-0-0-0-0-0. FC RECORD: 26-0-0-0-0-0. RECORD IN 2013: (Blue Bulls) 13-0-0-0-0-0.
Mboto, Vuyo (Lukhozi HS). b 28/09/1988. Wing. FC DEBUT: 2010. PROV CAREER: Bulldogs 2010-12 26-7-0-0-0-35. Griffons 2013 16-2-0-0-0-10. FC RECORD: 42-9-0-0-0-45. RECORD IN 2013: (Griffons) 16-2-0-0-0-10.
Mbovane, Tshotsho (Paul Roos Gymnasium) b 01/08/1992, Cape Town. 1.75m. 82kg. Wing. FC DEBUT: 2011. REP HONOURS: SAU20 2011-12 7-5-0-0-0-25. FC RECORD: 7-5-0-0-0-25. SA Sevens 2011-13. RECORD IN 2013: (SA Sevens).
McDonald, Aubrey Neville (Winterberg Agric. & UJ) b 03/02/1988, Port Elizabeth. 1.83m. 87kg. Fullback. FC DEBUT: 2008. PROV CAREER: Blue Bulls 2008 1-0-0-0-0-0. Griffons 2013 15-3-0-0-15. FC RECORD: 16-3-0-0-0-15. RECORD IN 2013: (Griffons) 15-3-0-0-0-15.
McGeer, Shaun Steven (Dr Johan Jurgens HS & CUT) b 29/03/1990, Roodepoort. 1.95m. 107kg. Lock. FC DEBUT: 2013. PROV CAREER: Valke 2013 9-0-0-0-0-0. FC RECORD: 9-0-0-0-0-0. RECORD IN 2013: (Valke) 9-0-0-0-0-0.
McLeod, Charl (Wonderboom HS, Pretoria) b 05/08/83, Johannesburg. 1.79m. 82kg. Scrumhalf. FC DEBUT: 2005. PROV CAREER: WP 2005-06 12-1-0-0-0-5. Lions 2007 6-3-0-0-0-15. Valke 2007 11-2-0-0-0-10. KZN 2008-13 59-12-0-0-0-60. Sharks XV 2008-10 19-7-0-0-0-35. Sharks Inv XV 2009-10 2-2-0-0-0-10. Lions XV 2007 1-0-0-0-0-0. SUPERRUGBY: Sharks 2009-13 55-5-0-0-0-25. REP HONOURS: SA 2011 Tests: 1-0-0-0-0-0. Tour 2010: 1-0-0-0-0-0. Total: 2-0-0-0-0-0. FC RECORD: 167-32-0-0-0-160. RECORD IN 2013: (Sharks, KZN) 25-5-0-0-0-25.
Mdaka, Siyabulela (George Campbell HS & NWU) b 14/02/1988, Umtata. 1.88m. 102kg. Flank. FC DEBUT: 2011. PROV CAREER: Leopards 2011 4-0-0-0-0-0. Bulldogs 2012-13 20-1-0-0-0-5. FC RECORD: 24-1-0-0-0-5. RECORD IN 2013: (Bulldogs) 17-1-0-0-0-5.
Mellet, Morne Melvin (Dr. EG Jansen HS) b 02/10/1988, Boksburg. 1.87m. 115kg. Prop. FC DEBUT: 2010. PROV CAREER: Blue Bulls 2010-13 23-2-0-0-0-10. SUPERRUGBY: Bulls 2013 12-0-0-0-0-0. REP HONOURS: SAU20 2009 5-0-0-0-0-0. FC RECORD: 40-2-0-0-0-10. RECORD IN 2013: (Bulls, Blue Bulls) 17-0-0-0-0-0.
Memese, Sinthamdile Amos b 22/02/1982. Flank. FC DEBUT: 2013. PROV CAREER: Limpopo 2013 1-0-0-0-0-0. FC RECORD: 1-0-0-0-0-0. RECORD IN 2013: (Limpopo) 1-0-0-0-0-0.
Meslane, Dumisane Kelvin (Ithembelhle HS) b 11/05/85, Port Elizabeth. 1.86m. 92kg. Flanker. FC DEBUT: 2008. PROV CAREER: Bulldogs 2008-10 42-7-0-0-0-35. Eagles 2011-13 26-8-0-0-0-40. FC RECORD: 68-15-0-0-0-75. RECORD IN 2013: (Eagles) 10-1-0-0-0-5.
Meyer, Johan Gert (Queens College) b 26/02/1993, Port Elizabeth. 1.93m. 104kg. Eightman. FC DEBUT: 2013. PROV CAREER: Sharks XV 2013 5-0-0-0-0-0. FC RECORD: 5-0-0-0-0-0. RECORD IN 2013: (Sharks XV) 5-0-0-0-0-0.
Meyer, Tian Carel (Westville HS) b 20/09/1988, Pietermaritzburg. 1.76m. 71kg. Scrumhalf/Centre. FC DEBUT: 2010. PROV CAREER: Pumas 2010-11 36-10-0-0-0-50. Sharks XV 2013 4-0-0-0-0-0. Lions 2013 6-0-0-0-0-0. SUPERRUGBY: Lions 2012 11-2-0-0-0-10. FC RECORD: 57-12-0-0-0-60. RECORD IN 2013: (Lions, Sharks XV) 10-0-0-0-0-0.
Mhlongo, Shembiso Santo (Siyahomula HS & UP) b 13/05/1987, Pietermaritzburg. 2.01m. 112kg. Lock. FC DEBUT: 2013. PROV CAREER: Bulldogs 2013 9-1-0-0-0-5. FC RECORD: 9-1-0-0-0-5. RECORD IN 2013: (Bulldogs) 9-1-0-0-0-5.
Mienie, Daniel Jacobus (Danie) (Merensky HS) b 01/03/1991, Polokwane. 1.78m. 104kg. Prop. FC DEBUT: 2012. PROV CAREER: KZN 2013 6-0-0-0-0-0. Sharks XV 2012-13 13-0-0-0-0-0. SUPERRUGBY: Sharks 2013 1-0-0-0-0-0. FC RECORD: 20-0-0-0-0-0. RECORD IN 2013: (Sharks, KZN, Sharks XV) 13-0-0-0-0-0.
Mienie, Shane b 25/02/1992. Prop. FC DEBUT: 2013. PROV CAREER: Limpopo 2013 3-0-0-0-0-0. FC RECORD: 3-0-0-0-0-0. RECORD IN 2013: (Limpopo) 3-0-0-0-0-0.
Minnie, Derick Johannes (Marais Viljoen HS) b 29/10/86, Alberton. 1.86m. 95kg. Flank. FC DEBUT: 2006. PROV CAREER: Golden Lions 2006-13 60-19-0-0-0-95. Young Lions 2006-09 & 13 22-5-0-0-0-25. Lions XV 2007 1-0-0-0-0-0. SUPERRUGBY: Lions 2010-12 42-6-0-0-0-30. Lions P/R 2013 2-1-0-0-0-5. Sharks 2013 3-3-0-0-0-15. FC RECORD: 130-34-0-0-0-170. RECORD IN 2013: (Sharks, Lions S15, Lions, Young Lions) 18-11-0-0-0-55.
Mkhafu, Khwezilokusa (Kwezi) (Lebogang HS) b 17/06/1988, Engcobo. 1.77m. 97kg. Hooker. FC DEBUT: 2010. PROV CAREER:

A-Z OF FIRST-CLASS PLAYERS IN 2013

Bulldogs 2010-13 70-6-0-0-0-30. REP HONOURS: SA Pres XV 2013 2-1-0-0-0-5. FC RECORD: 72-7-0-0-0-35. RECORD IN 2013: (SA Pres XV, Bulldogs) 23-6-0-0-0-30.

Mnisi, Xolane Howard (Standerton HS & NMMU) b 13/07/1989, Elukwatini. 1.86m. 96kg. Centre. FC DEBUT: 2011. PROV CAREER: Sharks XV 2011 3-1-0-0-0-5. Griquas 2013 11-1-0-0-0-5. SUPERRUGBY: Cheetahs 2013 1-0-0-0-0-0. REP HONOURS: SA Students 2012 1-0-0-0-0. SA Univ 2013 1-0-0-0-0-0. FC RECORD: 17-2-0-0-0-10. RECORD IN 2013: (SA Univ, Cheetahs S15, Griquas) 13-1-0-0-0-5.

Mnyaka, Abongile Enoch. b 18/10/1993. Prop. FC DEBUT: 2013. PROV CAREER: EP Kings 2013 1-0-0-0-0-0. FC RECORD: 1-0-0-0-0-0. RECORD IN 2013: (EP Kings) 1-0-0-0-0-0.

Mohoje, Teboho Stephen (Louis Botha THS & UFS) b 03/08/1990, Qwa Qwa. 1.92m. 103kg. Lock. FC DEBUT: 2012. PROV CAREER: Griffons 2012-13 6-0-0-0-0-0. Cheetahs 2013 11-0-0-0-0-0. Free State XV 2013 5-2-0-0-0-10. FC RECORD: 22-2-0-0-0-10. RECORD IN 2013: (Cheetahs, Free State XV, Griffons) 21-2-0-0-0-10.

Mokgoto, Photole Walter (Tom Naude HS, Polokwane) b 13/10/1988, Tzaneen. 1.75m. 70kg. Flank. FC DEBUT: 2013. PROV CAREER: Limpopo 2013 4-0-0-0-0-0. FC RECORD: 4-0-0-0-0-0. RECORD IN 2013: (Limpopo) 4-0-0-0-0-0.

Momberg, Christiaan Jacobus (Jacques) (Waterkloof HS, Pretoria & UP) b 18/02/1991, Pretoria. 1.8m. 105kg. Hooker. FC DEBUT: 2012. PROV CAREER: Blue Bulls 2012 2-0-0-0-0-0. Pumas 2013 17-2-0-0-0-10. FC RECORD: 19-2-0-0-0-10. RECORD IN 2013: (Pumas) 17-2-0-0-0-10.

Moolman, Bradley Johannes (Monument HS, Krugersdorp) b 18/01/1991, Welkom. 1.80m. 90kg. Centre. FC DEBUT: 2011. PROV CAREER: Blue Bulls 2011 4-0-0-0-0-0. Young Lions 2012-13 8-4-0-0-0-20. REP HONOURS: SAU20 2011 2-0-0-0-0-0. FC RECORD: 14-4-0-0-0-20. RECORD IN 2013: (Young Lions) 1-0-0-0-0-0.

Moolman, Whestley (Monument HS, Krugersdorp) b 04/02/90, Welkom. 1.7m. 80kg. FC DEBUT: 2009. PROV CAREER: Leopards 2011 15-4-0-0-0-20. Lions 2012 1-0-0-0-0-0. Young Lions 2009 & 13 4-0-0-0-0-0. FC RECORD: 20-4-0-0-0-20. RECORD IN 2013: (Young Lions) 1-0-0-0-0-0.

Mostert, Francois John (Franco) (Brits HS & UP) b 27/11/1990, Bloemfontein. 1.98m. 103kg. Lock. FC DEBUT: 2012. PROV CAREER: Blue Bulls 2012 12-2-0-0-0-10. Young Lions 2013 3-0-0-0-0-0. FC RECORD: 15-2-0-0-0-10. RECORD IN 2013: (Young Lions) 3-0-0-0-0-0.

Mostert, Juan-Pierre Francois (JP) (Brits HS & US) b 22/01/1988, Brits. 1.93m. 106kg. Flank. FC DEBUT: 2011. PROV CAREER: Pumas 2011-12 21-1-0-0-0-5. Valke 2012-13 20-8-0-0-0-40. FC RECORD: 41-9-0-0-0-45. RECORD IN 2013: (Valke) 18-8-0-0-0-40.

Moyake, Kuselo (CH Boklein HS & UCT) b 07/08/1986, Ntlaza. 1.84m. 93kg. Flank. FC DEBUT: 2013. PROV CAREER: EP Kings 2013 8-0-0-0-0-0. FC RECORD: 8-0-0-0-0-0. RECORD IN 2013: (EP Kings) 8-0-0-0-0-0.

Mtawarira, Tendai (Beast) (Peterhouse) b 01/07/85, Harare. 1.83m. 115kg. Prop. FC DEBUT: 2006. PROV CAREER: KZN 2006-13 37-3-0-0-0-15. Sharks XV 2006-08 & 12 9-0-0-0-0-0. Sharks Inv XV 2010 1-1-0-0-0-5. SUPERRUGBY: Sharks 2007-13 88-2-0-0-0-10-. REP HONOURS: SA 2008-13 Tests 53-2-0-0-0-10. 2010 Tour: 1-0-0-0-0-0. Total: 54-2-0-0-0-10. British Barbs. 2009 & 13 2-0-0-0-0-0. MISC INFO: PoY nominee 2008. YPoY nominee 2008. FC RECORD: 191-8-0-0-0-40. RECORD IN 2013: (SA, Sharks, KZN, British Barbarians) 27-2-0-0-0-10.

Mtembu, Lubabalo Siphosethu (Dale College) b 09/12/1990, East London. 1.87m. Eightman. FC DEBUT: 2011. PROV CAREER: Sharks XV 2011-13 16-4-0-0-0-20. KZN 2012-13 11-1-0-0-0-5. SUPER-RUGBY: Sharks 2012-13 7-1-0-0-0-5. Rep. honours: SAU20 2010 4-0-0-0-0-0. SA Sevens 2010-11. FC RECORD: 38-6-0-0-0-30. RECORD IN 2013: (Sharks, KZN, Sharks XV) 15-1-0-0-0-5.

Mtyanda, Lubabalo (Cowan HS) b 19/03/86, Port Elizabeth. 1.99m. 116kgs. Lock. FC DEBUT: 2006. PROV CAREER: Elephants 2006 13-0-0-0-0-0. Lions 2007 4-0-0-0-0-0. Eagles 2010-13 70-8-0-0-0-40. Pumas 2013 18-2-0-0-0-10. REP HONOURS: SA Pres XV 2013 4-0-0-0-0-0. FC RECORD: 109-10-0-0-0-50. RECORD IN 2013: (SA Pres XV, Eagles, Pumas) 29-2-0-0-0-10.

Muir, Dean (Glenwood HS) b 06/02/1989, Durban. 1.81m. 102kg. Hooker. FC DEBUT: 2012. PROV CAREER: Bulldogs 2012-13 31-4-0-0-0-20. FC RECORD: 31-4-0-0-0-20. RECORD IN 2013: (Bulldogs) 18-3-0-0-0-15.

Muller, Bruce (Klerksdorp HS) b 24/02/1989, Klerksdorp. 1.76m. 116kg. Prop. FC DEBUT: 2012. PROV CAREER: Valke 2012-13 18-4-0-0-0-20. FC RECORD: 18-4-0-0-0-20. RECORD IN 2013: (Valke) 12-3-0-0-0-15.

Muller, Frederick Jacobus (Hugenote HS & UWC) b 03/02/1990, Belville. 1.68m. 78kg. Scrumhalf. FC DEBUT: 2013. REP HONOURS: SA U20 2010 no appearances. SA Univ 2013 1-0-0-0-0-0. FC RECORD: 1-0-0-0-0-0. RECORD IN 2013: (SA Univ) 1-0-0-0-0-0.

Muller, Reg-Hack (Marais Viljoen HS) b 06/03/86, Johannesburg. 1.89m. 104kg. Eighthman. FC DEBUT: 2007. PROV CAREER: KZN 2007 3-0-0-0-0-0. Valke 2008-13 72-26-0-0-0-130. FC RECORD: 75-26-0-0-0-130. RECORD IN 2013: (Valke) 1-0-0-0-0-0.

Muller, Ruan b 10/10/1985. Centre. FC DEBUT: 2013. PROV CAREER: Limpopo 2013 6-1-0-0-0-5. FC RECORD: 6-1-0-0-0-5. RECORD IN 2013: (Limpopo) 6-1-0-0-0-5.

Murray, Keith Michael (Falcon College) b 25/02/1987, Harare. 1.73m. 82kg. Hooker. FC DEBUT: 2013. PROV CAREER: Young Lions 2013 1-0-0-0-0-0. FC RECORD: 1-0-0-0-0-0. RECORD IN 2013: (Young Lions) 1-0-0-0-0-0.

Murray, Waylon Michael (Westville Boys' High) b 27/04/86, Durban. 1.90m. 105kg. Centre. FC DEBUT: 2005. PROV CAREER: KZN 2005-09 52-18-0-0-0-90. Sharks XV 2005-10 8-0-0-0-0-0. Golden Lions 2010-12 19-5-0-0-0-25. Blue Bulls 2013 6-0-0-0-0-0. EP Kings 2013 1-0-0-0-0-0. SUPERRUGBY: Sharks 2006-10 41-5-0-0-0-25. Lions 2011-12 14-3-0-0-0-15. Southern Kings 2013 7-0-0-0-0-0. P/R 2013 1-0-0-0-0-0. REP HONOURS: SA Tests: 2007 3-0-0-0-0-0. Tour: 1-0-0-0-0-0. Total: 4-0-0-0-0-0. SA U21 2006 5-3-0-0-0-15. FC RECORD: 158-34-0-0-0-170. RECORD IN 2013: (Southern Kings, EP Kings, Blue Bulls) 15-0-0-0-0-0.

Mvovo, Lwazi Ncedo (Maria Louw HS) b 03/06/86, Unthatha. 1.85m. 94kg. Wing. FC DEBUT: 2007. PROV CAREER: KZN 2007-13 57-25-0-0-0-125. Sharks XV 2007-10 20-9-0-0-0-45. Sharks Inv XV 2009 1-0-0-0-0-0. SUPERRUGBY: Sharks 2010-13 52-17-0-0-0-85. REP HONOURS: SA 2010-12 Tests: 7-1-0-0-0-5. Tour: 1-0-0-0-0-0. Total: 8-1-0-0-0-5. FC RECORD: 138-52-0-0-0-260. RECORD IN 2013: (Sharks, KZN) 24-6-0-0-0-30.

Mxunyelwa, Buhle (Stirling HS) b 25/06/86, East London. 1.87m. 129kg. Prop. FC DEBUT: 2008. PROV CAREER: Bulldogs 2008-09 19-2-0-0-0-10. E/Cape XV 2008 1-0-0-0-0-0. WP 2010 8-0-0-0-0-0. Leopards 2011-12 6-0-0-0-0-0. Leopard XV 2013 3-0-0-0-0-0. MISC INFO: Brother of Siya Mxunyelwa. FC RECORD: 37-2-0-0-0-10. RECORD IN 2013: (Leopard XV) 3-0-0-0-0-0.

N

Nagel, Ignis Joseph (Paarl Boys HS & UFS) b 30/04/1993, Middelburg. 1.90m. 130kg. Prop. FC DEBUT: 2013. PROV CAREER: Free State XV 2013 3-0-0-0-0-0. FC RECORD: 3-0-0-0-0-0. RECORD IN 2013: (Free State XV) 3-0-0-0-0-0.

A-Z OF FIRST-CLASS PLAYERS IN 2013

Ndungane, Akona Zilindlovu (Hudson Park HS, East London) b 20/02/81, Umtata. 1.83m. 86kg. Wing. FC DEBUT: 2003. PROV CAREER: Elephants 2003 13-6-0-0-0-30. Bulldogs 2004-05 17-14-0-0-0-70. Blue Bulls 2005-06 & 08-13 62-27-0-0-0-135. SUPERRUGBY: Bulls 2005-09 & 11-13 96-32-0-0-0-160. REP HONOURS: SA 2006-07 Tests: 11-1-0-0-0-5. Tour: 2007 2-0-0-0-0-0. Total: 13-1-0-0-0-5. SA 'A' 2004 1-3-0-0-0-15. SA Sevens 2004. MISC INFO: Holds Border record for most CC tries in a season (10). Twin Brother of Natal Sharks wing Odwa Ndungane. FC RECORD: 202-83-0-0-0-415. RECORD IN 2013: (Bulls, Blue Bulls) 19-6-0-0-0-30.

Ndungane, Odwa Mzuzo (Hudson Park HS & Eastern Cape Tech.) b 20/02/81, Umtata. 1.83m. 93kg. Wing. FC DEBUT: 2000. PROV CAREER: Bulldogs 2000-03 49-25-0-0-0-125. Blue Bulls 2004 2-0-0-0-0-0. KZN 2005-13 78-29-1-0-0-147. Sharks XV 2005-08 & 12 4-0-0-0-0-0. SUPERRUGBY: Bulls 2004 10-3-0-0-0-15. Sharks 2005-13 95-24-0-0-0-120. REP HONOURS: SA 2008-11 Tests: 9-2-0-0-0-10. Tour: 2009-10 3-1-0-0-0-5. Total: 12-3-0-0-0-15. SA 'A' 2004 2-2-0-0-0-10. Emerging Springboks 2007 2-0-0-0-0-0. SA U21 2002 1-0-0-0-0-0. MISC INFO: Twin brother of Springbok and Blue Bulls wing Akona Ndungane. FC RECORD: 255-86-1-0-0-432. RECORD IN 2013: (Sharks, KZN) 22-2-0-0-0-10.

Ndiweni, Mbekezeli (Dickson) b 17/12/1983. Hooker. FC DEBUT: 2013. PROV CAREER: Limpopo 2013 5-0-0-0-0-0. FC RECORD: 5-0-0-0-0-0. RECORD IN 2013: (Limpopo) 5-0-0-0-0-0.

Nel, Adriaan Ruhan (Brandwag HS) b 17/05/1991. 1.92m. 88kg. Wing. FC DEBUT: 2012. PROV CAREER: Lions 2013 3-1-0-0-0-5. Young Lions 2012-13 4-1-0-0-0-5. FC RECORD: 7-2-0-0-0-10. RECORD IN 2013: (Lions, Young Lions) 6-2-0-0-0-0.

Nel, Arno (Klerksdorp HS) b 23/01/1991, Welkom. 1.89m. 94kg. Flank. FC DEBUT: 2013. PROV CAREER: Leopard XV 2013 1-0-0-0-0-0. FC RECORD: 1-0-0-0-0-0. RECORD IN 2013: (Leopard XV) 1-0-0-0-0-0.

Nel, Jacobus Andreas (Cobus) (Grey College, Bloemfontein) b 05/05/1992, Johannesburg. 1.91m. 90kg. Lock. FC DEBUT: 2013. PROV CAREER: WP 2013 4-0-0-0-0-0. FC RECORD: 4-0-0-0-0-0. RECORD IN 2013: (WP) 4-0-0-0-0-0.

Nel, Jacobus Paulus (JP) (Worcester Gymnasium & Tygerberg College) b 09/01/81, Worcester. 1.83m. 91kg. Centre. FC DEBUT: 2000. PROV CAREER: WP 2000 1-0-0-0-0-0; Blue Bulls 2001-07 78-39-1-0-0-197. Griquas 2012-13 12-0-0-0-0-0. SUPERRUGBY: Bulls 2001-02 & 04-09 78-15-0-0-0-75. REP HONOURS: SA U21 2002 5-2-0-0-0-10. FC RECORD: 172-56-1-0-0-282. RECORD IN 2013: (Griquas) 9-0-0-0-0-0.

Nel, Jacques Jehan (Brandwag HS) b 17/03/1993, Port Elizabeth. 1.66m. 88kg. Centre. FC DEBUT: 2013. PROV CAREER: Young Lions 2013 3-0-0-0-0-0. FC RECORD: 3-0-0-0-0-0. RECORD IN 2013: (Young Lions) 3-0-0-0-0-0.

Nel, Japie (Goudveld HS, Welkom) b 20/11/82, Welkom. 1.90m. 105kg. Wing. FC DEBUT: 2005. PROV CAREER: Griffons 2005-07 & 2011-13 79-30-0-0-0-150. Leopards 2008-10 35-4-0-0-0-20. FC RECORD: 114-34-0-0-0-170. RECORD IN 2013: (Griffons) 18-9-0-0-0-45.

Nell, Darron Paul (Muir College) b 08/03/80, Uitenhage. 1.94m. 108kg. Eighthman. FC DEBUT: 2002. PROV CAREER: Cheetahs 2002-08 66-11-0-0-0-55. EP Kings 2010-13 50-9-0-0-0-45. SUPERRUGBY: Cheetahs 2007-08 10-2-0-0-0-10. Southern Kings 2013 5-0-0-0-0-0. P/R 2013 2-0-0-0-0-0. REP HONOURS: SA Kings 2011 2-0-0-0-0-0. S/Kings 2009 1-0-0-0-0-0. FC RECORD: 136-22-0-0-0-110. RECORD IN 2013: (Southern Kings, EP Kings) 15-1-0-0-0-5.

Nell, Ryan Desmond (Paarl Gymnasium. & US) b 04/09/1990, Port Elizabeth. 1.91m. 95kg. Utility back. >> PROV CAREER: WP 2013 2-0-0-0-0-0. REP HONOURS: SA Univ 2013 1-0-0-0-0-0. SA Sevens 2012.

FC RECORD: 3-0-0-0-0-0. RECORD IN 2013: (WP, SA Univ) 3-0-0-0-0-0.

Nelson, Norman Tsimba (Patensie HS) b 10/08/83, Patensie. 1.75m. 81kg. Wing. FC DEBUT: 2006. PROV CAREER: EP Kings 2006-08 & 10-13 92-56-0-0-0-280. E/Cape XV 2008 1-0-0-0-0-0. Eagles 2009 20-15-1-0-0-77. Griffons 2013 5-3-0-0-0-15. REP HONOURS: SA Barbarians 2012 1-1-0-0-0-5. FC RECORD: 119-75-1-0-0-377. RECORD IN 2013: (EP Kings, Griffons) 6-3-0-0-0-15.

Nepgen, Jaco (Hangklip) b 03/01/86. 1.98m. 103kg. Lock. FC DEBUT: 2008. PROV CAREER: Griquas 2010-13 48-4-0-0-0-20. Eagles 2011 1-0-0-0-0-0. REP HONOURS: SA Students 2008-09 3-1-0-0-0-5. FC RECORD: 52-5-0-0-0-25. RECORD IN 2013: (Griquas) 12-1-0-0-0-5.

Newman, Christopher William (Willie) (Monument HS, Krugersdorp) b 26/07/1993, Pretoria. 1.84m. 94kg. Flank. FC DEBUT: 2013. PROV CAREER: Young Lions 2013 3-1-0-0-0-5. FC RECORD: 3-1-0-0-0-5. RECORD IN 2013: (Young Lions) 3-1-0-0-0-5.

Ngam, Yamkela (Dale College & NMMU) b 06/09/1991, Butterworth. 1.76m. 81kg. Wing. FC DEBUT: 2013. PROV CAREER: EP Kings 2013 3-2-0-0-0-10. FC RECORD: 3-2-0-0-0-10. RECORD IN 2013: (EP Kings) 3-2-0-0-0-10.

Ngcobo, Sandile Caleb (Stix) (Highlands North HS & UJ) b 01/08/1989, Thembisa. Wing. FC DEBUT: 2012. PROV CAREER: Valke 2012-13 30-6-0-0-0-30. FC RECORD: 30-6-0-0-0-30. RECORD IN 2013: (Valke) 17-2-0-0-0-10.

Ngoza, Thato Frederick Ntandyenkosi (Volksrust HS & UFS) b 20/10/1991, Piet Retief. 1.90m. 105kg. Lock. FC DEBUT: 2011. PROV CAREER: Griffons 2011 & 13 7-1-0-0-0-5. Cheetahs 2013 4-0-0-0-0-0. Free State XV 2013 2-1-0-0-0-5. FC RECORD: 13-2-0-0-0-10. RECORD IN 2013: (Cheetahs, Griffons, Free State XV) 11-2-0-0-0-10.

Nhlapo, Sabelo (Highlands North Boys HS) b 17/12/88, Johannesburg. 1.90m. 116kg. Prop. FC DEBUT: 2009. PROV CAREER: Sharks XV 2009-11 20-0-0-0-0-0. Boland 2013 8-0-0-0-0-0. REP HONOURS: SA U20 2008 3-1-0-0-0-5. FC RECORD: 31-1-0-0-0-5. RECORD IN 2013: (Boland) 8-0-0-0-0-0.

Niemand, Samuel Jacobus (SJ) (Klerksdorp HS & NWU) b 06/03/1991, Pretoria. 1.87m. 103kg. Eighthman. FC DEBUT: 2012. PROV CAREER: Leopards 2012-13 7-2-0-0-0-10. FC RECORD: 7-2-0-0-0-10. RECORD IN 2013: (Leopards) 6-1-0-0-0-5.

Nieuwenhuyzen, Shaun David (Welkom HTS) b 01/06/1992, Welkom. 1.96m. 106kg. Fullback. FC DEBUT: 2013. PROV CAREER: Bulldogs 2013 2-0-0-0-0-0. FC RECORD: 2-0-0-0-0-0. RECORD IN 2013: (Bulldogs) 2-0-0-0-0-0.

Nkuna, Musa Phanuel (Ben Vorster HS, Tzaneen & TUT) b 08/03/1985, Tzaneen. 1.89m. 96kg. Lock. FC DEBUT: 2013. PROV CAREER: Limpopo 2013 4-0-0-0-0-0. FC RECORD: 4-0-0-0-0-0. RECORD IN 2013: (Limpopo) 4-0-0-0-0-0.

Nokwe, Jongikhaya Lutric (Jongi) (Kwamfundo SS) b 30/12/81, Ngxalawe, Ciskei. 1.82m. 80kg. Wing. FC DEBUT: 2003. PROV CAREER: Boland 2003-07 55-33-0-0-0-165. Cheetahs 2008-10 35-26-0-0-0-130. Cheetahs XV 2010 1-0-0-0-0-0. Griffons 2011 1-0-0-0-0-0. EP Kings 2012 6-3-0-0-0-15. Valke 2013 14-6-0-0-0-30. SUPERRUGBY: Stormers 2006 6-2-0-0-0-10. Cheetahs 2008-10 30-15-0-0-0-75. REP HONOURS: SA 2008-09 Tests: 4-5-0-0-0-25. Tour: 2006,09 3-3-0-0-0-15. Total: 7-8-0-0-0-40. SA Sevens 2004-05. MISC INFO: YPoY 2005. FC RECORD: 155-93-0-0-0-465. RECORD IN 2013: (Valke) 14-6-0-0-0-30.

Norris, Quinton (Helpmekaar HS, Jhbg) b 16/03/1982, Alberton. 1.8m. 80kg. Wing. FC DEBUT: 2012. PROV CAREER: Bulldogs 2012 2-0-0-0-0-0. Free State XV 2013 1-0-0-0-0-0. FC RECORD: 3-0-0-0-0-0. RECORD IN 2013: (Free State XV) 1-0-0-0-0-0.

Nortier, Gerhard Johan (Oudtshoorn HS & NWU) b 04/03/1989,

A-Z OF FIRST-CLASS PLAYERS IN 2013

George. 1.8m. 88kg. Flyhalf. FC DEBUT: 2012. PROV CAREER: Leopards 2012-13 15-2-2-1-0-17. FC RECORD: 15-2-2-1-0-17. RECORD IN 2013: (Leopards) 1-0-0-0-0-0.
Nortje, Oshwill (Hentie Cilliers HS, Virginia) b 03/12/1990, George. 1.65m. 67kg. Scrumhalf. FC DEBUT: 2011. PROV CAREER: Griffons 2011-13 26-6-0-0-0-30. FC RECORD: 26-6-0-0-0-30. RECORD IN 2013: (Griffons) 19-4-0-0-0-20.
Notshe, Sikhumbuzo (Wynberg Boys HS) b 28/05/1993, Kingwilliamstown. 1.90m. 100kg. Eightman. FC DEBUT: 2013. PROV CAREER: WP 2013 9-2-0-0-0-10. FC RECORD: 9-2-0-0-0-10. RECORD IN 2013: (WP) 9-2-0-0-0-10.
Ntleki, Lonwabo Iicholus (King Edward HS) b 07/08/1992, Alice. 1.78m. 87kg. Centre. FC DEBUT: 2012. PROV CAREER: EP Kings 2012-13 4-0-0-0-0-0. FC RECORD: 4-0-0-0-0-0. RECORD IN 2013: (EP Kings) 2-0-0-0-0-0.
Ntubeni, Siyabonga (Scarra) (King Edward HS) b 18/02/1991, East London. 1.77m. 92kg. Hooker. FC DEBUT: 2011. PROV CAREER: WP 2011-13 32-1-0-0-0-5. SUPERRUGBY: Stormers 2011-13 11-0-0-0-0-0. REP HONOURS: 2013 Springbok team squad member. CC Premier Division PoY 2013. FC RECORD: 43-1-0-0-0-5. RECORD IN 2013: (Stormers, WP) 18-0-0-0-0-0.
Nyakane, Trevor Ntando (Ben Vorster HS, Tzaneen) b 04/05/1989, Bushbuck Ridge. 1.78m. 109kg. Prop. FC DEBUT: 2010. PROV CAREER: Cheetahs 2010-13 37-2-0-0-0-10. Griffons 2011 1-0-0-0-0. Emerging Cheetahs 2011 1-0-0-0-0-0. SUPERRUGBY: Cheetahs 2012-13 27-2-0-0-0-10. REP HONOURS: SA Tests: 2013 3-1-0-0-0-5. FC RECORD: 69-5-0-0-0-25. RECORD IN 2013: (SA, Cheetahs S15, Cheetahs) 28-3-0-0-0-15.
Nyoka, Sinovuyo (Dale College) b 07/08/1990, King Williams Town. 1.68m. 67kg. Scrumhalf. FC DEBUT: 2010. PROV CAREER: Bulldogs 2010-13 49-2-0-0-0-10. REP HONOURS: SA Pres XV 2013 3-0-0-0-0-0. FC RECORD: 52-2-0-0-0-10. RECORD IN 2013: (SA Pres XV, Bulldogs) 19-1-0-0-0-5.

O

Oberholzer, Johan Christiaan (Jan Viljoen HS) b 14/11/1989, Krugersdorp. 1.78m. 92kg. Hooker. FC DEBUT: 2010. PROV CAREER: Leopards 2010-13 8-0-0-0-0-0. Leopard XV 2013 1-0-0-0-0-0. REP HONOURS: SA Univ 2013 1-0-0-0-0-0. FC RECORD: 10-0-0-0-0-0. RECORD IN 2013: (SA Univ, Leopards, Leopard XV) 5-0-0-0-0-0.
Obi, Luther Banks St Charles (St Benedicts College) b 29/04/1993, Aba. 1.75m. 86kg. Wing. FC DEBUT: 2013. PROV CAREER: Leopards 2013 14-8-0-0-0-40. REP HONOURS: SA U 20 2013 5-4-0-0-0-20. FC RECORD: 19-12-0-0-0-60. RECORD IN 2013: (Leopards, SA U20) 19-12-0-0-0-60.
O' Brien, Patrick Lloyd (Paul Roos Gymnasium & US) b 25/12/1989, Durban. 1.89m. 109kg. Lock. FC DEBUT: 2013. PROV CAREER: Griquas 2013 9-0-0-0-0-0. FC RECORD: 9-0-0-0-0-0. RECORD IN 2013: (Griquas) 9-0-0-0-0-0.
Odendaal, Miegiel Burger (Monument HS, Krugersdorp & UP) b 15/04/1993, Bloemfontein. 1.87m. 95kg. Utility Back. FC DEBUT: 2013. PROV CAREER: Blue Bulls 2013 1-0-0-0-0-0. FC RECORD: 1-0-0-0-0-0. RECORD IN 2013: (Blue Bulls) 1-0-0-0-0-0.
Odendaal, Willem Adriaan (Eldoraigne HS, Centurion) b 11/07/1990, Pretoria. 1.83m. 92kg. Scrumhalf. FC DEBUT: 2010. PROV CAREER: Valke 2010-13 63-14-0-0-0-70. FC RECORD: 63-14-0-0-0-70. RECORD IN 2013: (Valke) 18-6-0-0-0-30.
Oelofse, Schalk Wentzel (Daniel Pienaar THS & NMMU) b 02/11/1988, Port Elizabeth. 1.97m. 111kg. Lock. FC DEBUT: 2013. PROV CAREER: EP Kings 2013 1-0-0-0-0-0. Eagles 2013 11-1-0-0-0-5.

REP HONOURS: SA Univ 2013 1-0-0-0-0-0. FC RECORD: 13-1-0-0-0-5. RECORD IN 2013: (EP Kings, Eagles, SA Univ) 13-1-0-0-0-5.
Okafor, Kenechukwu (Kenny) (Kearsney HS & Varsity College) b 08/12/1990, Lagos. 1.95m. 103kg. Lock. FC DEBUT: 2011. PROV CAREER: Golden Lions XV 2011 1-0-0-0-0-0. Leopard XV 2013 6-1-0-0-0-5. REP HONOURS: SAU20 2009-10 10-1-0-0-0-5. FC RECORD: 17-2-0-0-0-10. RECORD IN 2013: (Leopard XV) 6-1-0-0-0-5.
Olivier, Brenden Hercules (Nico Malan HS) b 19/03/1992, Kareedouw. 1.89m. 110kg. Prop. FC DEBUT: 2012. PROV CAREER: EP Kings 2012-13 17-0-0-0-0-0. FC RECORD: 17-0-0-0-0-0. RECORD IN 2013: (EP Kings) 15-0-0-0-0-0.
Olivier, Friedle (Dr Johan Jurgens HS) b 27/05/1992, Pretoria. 1.98m. 94kg. Flank. FC DEBUT: 2013. PROV CAREER: Valke 2013 9-1-0-0-0-5. FC RECORD: 9-1-0-0-0-5. RECORD IN 2013: (Valke) 9-1-0-0-0-5.
Olivier, Jacques (Centurion HS) b 07/08/1992, Pretoria. 1.84m. 92kg. Scrumhalf. FC DEBUT: 2012. PROV CAREER: Leopards 2012 1-0-0-0-0-0. Leopard XV 2013 5-1-0-0-0-5. FC RECORD: 6-1-0-0-0-5. RECORD IN 2013: (Leopard XV) 5-1-0-0-0-5.
Olivier, Leonard (Affies, Pretoria) b 19/01/86, Pretoria. 1.80m. 86kg. Flyhalf. FC DEBUT: 2006. PROV CAREER: Blue Bulls 2006 12-1-16-12-1-76. Valke 2007-08 33-3-29-13-0-112. Sharks XV 2009 7-0-4-3-0-17. Boland 2013 6-0-10-6-0-38. FC RECORD: 58-4-59-34-1-243. RECORD IN 2013: (Boland) 6-0-10-6-0-38
Olivier, Ryan (Belville HS) b 17/08/1988, Cape Town. 1.94m. 121kg. Lock. FC DEBUT: 2013. PROV CAREER: WP 2013 2-0-0-0-0-0. FC RECORD: 2-0-0-0-0-0. RECORD IN 2013: (WP) 2-0-0-0-0-0.
Olivier, Wynand (Affies, Pretoria) b 11/06/83, Welkom. 1.84m. 87kg. Centre. FC DEBUT: 2003. PROV CAREER: Blue Bulls 2003-06 & 08-11 72-26-0-0-0-130. SUPERRUGBY: Bulls 2005-13 110-29-0-0-0-145. REP HONOURS: SA 2006-07 & 09-12 Tests: 37-1-0-0-0-5. Tour: 4-0-0-0-0-0. Total: 41-1-0-0-0-5. SA XV 2006 1-0-0-0-0-0. SA U21 2004 5-2-0-0-0-10. MISC INFO: YPoY nominee 2005. FC RECORD: 229-58-0-0-0-290. RECORD IN 2013: (Bulls) 7-0-0-0-0-0.
Oosthuizen, Caylib Rees (Oudtshoorn HS & UJ) b 01/09/1989, Cape Town. 1.86m. 114kg. Prop. FC DEBUT: 2011. PROV CAREER: Lions 2012 2-0-0-0-0-0. Young Lions 2011 2-0-0-0-0-0. Cheetahs 2013 3-0-0-0-0-0. Free State XV 2013 3-0-0-0-0-0. SUPERRUGBY: Lions 2012 6-1-0-0-0-5. REP HONOURS: SA U20 2009 5-0-0-0-0-0. FC RECORD: 21-1-0-0-0-5. RECORD IN 2013: (Cheetahs, Free State XV) 6-0-0-0-0-0.
Oosthuizen, Coenraad Victor (Grey College, Bloemfontein) b 22/03/89, Potchefstroom. 1.81m. 127kg. Prop. FC DEBUT: 2008. PROV CAREER: Cheetahs 2008-13 53-11-0-0-0-55. Cheetahs XV 2010 1-0-0-0-0-0. SUPERRUGBY: Cheetahs 2010-13 57-8-0-0-0-40. REP HONOURS: SA Tests: 2012-13 14-2-0-0-0-10. 2010 Tour: 1-0-0-0-0-0. Total: 15-2-0-0-0-10. British Barbarians 2013 1-0-0-0-0-0. SAU20 2009 5-0-0-0-0-0. FC RECORD: 132-21-0-0-0-105. RECORD IN 2013: (SA, Cheetahs S15, Cheetahs, British Barbarians) 32-4-0-0-0-20.
Oosthuizen, Devin Andre (John Vorster THS, Pretoria) b 28/05/1988. 1.94m. 104kg. Flanker. FC DEBUT: 2010. PROV CAREER: Blue Bulls 2010 10-1-0-0-0-5. EP Kings 2010-13 52-10-0-0-0-50. SUPERRUGBY: Southern Kings 2013 9-0-0-0-0-0. P/R 2013 2-0-0-0-0-0. REP HONOURS: SA Kings 2011 3-0-0-0-0-0. FC RECORD: 76-11-0-0-0-55. RECORD IN 2013: (Southern Kings, EP Kings) 25-3-0-0-0-15.
Oosthuizen, Jaco (Waterkloof HS, Pretoria) b 08/03/1990, Johannesburg. 1.85m. 97kg. Wing. FC DEBUT: 2012. PROV CAREER: Valke 2012-13 16-4-0-0-0-20. FC RECORD: 16-4-0-0-0-20. RECORD IN 2013: (Valke) 5-1-0-0-0-5.
Oosthuizen, Schalk Willem (Wolmaransstad HS & NWU) b

A-Z OF FIRST-CLASS PLAYERS IN 2013

07/03/1990, Wolmaransstad. 1.88m. 91kg. Fullback. FC DEBUT: 2011. PROV CAREER: Leopards 2011 & 13 4-0-2-0-0-4. FC RECORD: 4-0-2-0-0-4. RECORD IN 2013: (Leopards) 2-0-0-0-0-0.

P

Paige, Rudy (Bastion HS & UJ) b 02/08/1989, Riversdal. 1.67m. 70kg. Scrumhalf. FC DEBUT: 2010. PROV CAREER: Lions 2011 2-0-0-0-0-0. Young Lions 2010-12 10-0-0-0-0-0. Blue Bulls 2012-13 18-2-0-0-0-10. SUPERRUGBY: Bulls 2013 4-0-0-0-0-0. REP HONOURS: SA Students 2012 2-0-0-0-0-0. SAU20 2009 4-0-0-0-0-0. FC RECORD: 40-2-0-0-0-10. RECORD IN 2013: (Bulls, Blue Bulls) 18-1-0-0-0-5.

Parkes, Hadleigh. Wing. SA FC DEBUT: 2013. PROV CAREER: EP Kings 2013 2-1-0-0-0-5. SUPERRUGBY: Southern Kings 2013 5-0-0-0-0-0. P/R 2013 2-0-0-0-0-0. Auckland Blues. SA FC RECORD: 9-1-0-0-0-5. RECORD IN 2013: (Southern Kings, EP Kings) 9-1-0-0-0-5.

Parks, Buran Joshua (Harmony Sports Academy) b 27/06/1992, George. 1.80m. 85kg. Eighthman. FC DEBUT: 2011. PROV CAREER: Eagles 2011-13 25-1-0-0-0-5. FC RECORD: 25-1-0-0-0-5. RECORD IN 2013: (Eagles) 16-1-0-0-0-5.

Payi, Mbembe Xolela (Durban HS) b 18/09/1993, Port Elizabeth. 1.72m. 74kg. Fullback. FC DEBUT: 2013. PROV CAREER: Eagles 2013 5-0-0-0-0-0. FC RECORD: 5-0-0-0-0-0. RECORD IN 2013: (Eagles) 5-0-0-0-0-0.

Pedro, Hentzwill Nowellen (George HS) b 21/07/1987, George. 1.86m. 80kg. Wing. FC DEBUT: 2013. PROV CAREER: Eagles 2013 3-1-0-0-0-5. FC RECORD: 3-1-0-0-0-5. RECORD IN 2013: (Eagles) 3-1-0-0-0-5.

Pelser, Justen Christopher (Merensky HS) b 12/12/1990, Johannesburg. 1.84m. 98kg. Wing. FC DEBUT: 2013. PROV CAREER: Limpopo 2013 7-0-0-0-0-0. FC RECORD: 7-0-0-0-0-0. RECORD IN 2013: (Limpopo) 7-0-0-0-0-0.

Petersen, Sergeal (Grey HS, PE) b 01/08/1994, Port Elizabeth. 1.71m. 82kg. Wing. FC DEBUT: 2013. PROV CAREER: EP Kings 3-0-0-0-0-0. SUPERRUGBY: Southern Kings 2013 8-4-0-0-0-20. FC RECORD: 11-4-0-0-0-20. RECORD IN 2013: (Southern Kings, EP Kings) 11-4-0-0-0-20.

Peterson, Dylan (KES & UJ) b 10/02/1990, Alberton. 1.90m. 102kg. Lock. FC DEBUT: 2011. PROV CAREER: Golden Lions XV 2011 1-0-0-0-0-0. Young Lions 2013 3-0-0-0-0-0. FC RECORD: 4-0-0-0-0-0. RECORD IN 2013: (Young Lions) 3-0-0-0-0-0.

Pienaar, Ruan (Grey College, Bloemfontein) b 10/03/84, Bloemfontein. 1.87m. 92kg. Scrumhalf. FC DEBUT: 2004. PROV CAREER: Cheetahs 2004 9-2-1-0-0-12. KZN 2005-06 & 08-10 33-7-5-9-36-0-261. SUPERRUGBY: Sharks 2005-10 67-10-35-42-2-252. REP HONOURS: SA 2006-13 Tests: 74-7-22-17-0-130. Tour 2006,07, 09 4-0-1-7-0-23. Total: 78-7-23-24-1-153. SA XV 2006 1-0-0-0-0-0. British Barbarians 2011 1-0-1-0-0-2. SA U21 2004-05 10-1-3-0-0-11. SA U19 2003. SA Schools 2002. CW Free State 2002. MISC INFO: YPoY nominee 2005, Son of 1980-81 Springbok Gysie Pienaar. FC RECORD: 199-27-122-102-3-694. RECORD IN 2013: (SA) 11-0-0-0-0-0.

Pienaar, Wynand Christo (Welkom Gymnasium) b 05/08/1989, Welkom. 1.86m. 95kg. Fullback. FC DEBUT: 2013. PROV CAREER: Boland 2013 6-1-0-0-0-5. FC RECORD: 6-1-0-0-0-5. RECORD IN 2013: (Boland) 6-1-0-0-0-5.

Pieters, Jean Jacques (Ben Viljoen HS, Grolersdal) b 06/08/1992, Middelburg. 1.98m. 93kg. Wing. FC DEBUT: 2013. PROV CAREER: Limpopo 2013 1-0-0-0-0-0. FC RECORD: 1-0-0-0-0-0. RECORD IN 2013: (Limpopo) 1-0-0-0-0-0.

Pietersen, Johan Christiaan (Joe) (Grey College, Bloemfontein) b 18/05/84, Vryheid. 1.78m. 78kg. Wing. FC DEBUT: 2004. PROV CAREER: WP 2004-09 & 12 65-23-48-57-5-397. SUPERRUGBY: Stormers 2006 & 08-10 & 12-13 50-9-35-86-0-373. REP HONOURS: WP XV 2006. SA Sevens 2006. CW Free State 2002. FC RECORD: 116-32-83-143-5-770. RECORD IN 2013: (Stormers) 15-0-19-44-0-170.

Pietersen, Jon-Paul Roger (JP) (General Hertzog HS, Witbank) b 12/07/86, Stellenbosch. 1.90m. 106kg. Wing/Fullback. FC DEBUT: 2005. PROV CAREER: KZN 2005-06 & 08-12 42-17-0-0-0-85. SUPERRUGBY: Sharks 2006-13 98-33-0-0-0-165. REP HONOURS: SA 2006-13 Tests: 51-16-0-0-0-80. Tour: 2-0-0-0-0-0. Total: 53-16-0-0-0-80. SA U21 2006 5-2-0-0-0-10. Misc. info: YPoY nominee 2005, 2006. SARU PoY 2012 nominee. Super PoY 2012 nominee. SARPA PPoY 2012. FC RECORD: 198-68-0-0-0-340. RECORD IN 2013: (SA, Sharks) 14-2-0-0-0-10.

Pitzer, Brendan (Eden Glen HS & US) b 10/10/1991, Welkom. 1.81m. 120kg. Prop. FC DEBUT: 2013. PROV CAREER: Griquas 2013 1-0-0-0-0-0. FC RECORD: 1-0-0-0-0-0. RECORD IN 2013: (Griquas) 1-0-0-0-0-0.

Poley, Arno Pieter (Dr Malan HS) b 14/03/1991, Barberton. 1.94m. 95kg. Fullback. FC DEBUT: 2011. PROV CAREER: Valke 2011-13 43-3-1-0-1-20. FC RECORD: 43-3-1-0-1-20. RECORD IN 2013: (Valke) 12-1-0-0-0-5.

Pollard, Handre (Paarl Gymnasium) b 11/03/1994, Somerset West. 1.88m. 97kg. Flyhalf. FC DEBUT: 2012. PROV CAREER: Blue Bulls 2013 8-0-16-14-1-77. REP HONOURS: SA U20 2012-13 9-0-20-11-1-76. FC RECORD: 17-0-36-25-2-153. RECORD IN 2013: (Blue Bulls, SA U20) 13-0-24-20-1-111.

Poppmeier, Michael (Graham College) b 24/07/82, Durban. 1.97m. 112kg. Lock. FC DEBUT: 2009. PROV CAREER: Elephants 2009 1-0-0-0-0-0. WP 2013 2-0-0-0-0-0. FC RECORD: 3-0-0-0-0-0. RECORD IN 2013: (WP) 2-0-0-0-0-0.

Potgieter, Dewald Johan (Daniel Pienaar THS, Uitenhage) b 22/02/87, Port Elizabeth. 1.90m. 98kg. Eighthman. FC DEBUT: 2007. PROV CAREER: Blue Bulls 2007-12 63-10-0-0-0-50. SUPERRUGBY: Bulls 2008-13 67-4-0-0-0-20. REP HONOURS: SA Tests: 2009-10 6-1-0-0-0-5. Tour: 2009 2-0-0-0-0-0. Total: 8-1-0-0-0-5. Emerging Springboks 2009 1-0-0-0-0-0. FC RECORD: 139-15-0-0-0-75. RECORD IN 2013: (Bulls) 13-0-0-0-0-0.

Potgieter, Ulrich Jacques (Daniel Pienaar HTS) b 24/04/86, Port Elizabeth. 1.94m. 115kg. Lock. FC DEBUT: 2008. PROV CAREER: KZN 2008 2-0-0-0-0-0. EP Kings 2009-11 36-4-0-0-0-20. Blue Bulls 2011-13 9-2-0-0-0-10. SUPERRUGBY: Bulls 2012-13 23-4-0-0-0-20. REP HONOURS: SA 2012 Tests: 3-0-0-0-0-0. SA Kings 2011 2-1-0-0-0-5. FC RECORD: 75-11-0-0-0-55. RECORD IN 2013: (Bulls, Blue Bulls) 11-2-0-0-0-10.

Powell, Albertus Hendrik (Birtie) (John Vorster THS, Pretoria) b 18/04/81, Pretoria. 1.75m. 100kgs. Hooker. FC DEBUT: 2004. PROV CAREER: Pumas 2004 4-0-0-0-0-0. Griffons 2005 19-1-0-0-0-5. Leopards 2006 13-1-0-0-0-5. Valke 2012-13 22-2-0-0-0-10. FC RECORD: 55-4-0-0-0-20. RECORD IN 2013: (Valke) 17-2-0-0-0-10.

Pretorius, André Stefan (Dinamika HS) b 29/12/78, Johannesburg. 1.76m. 90kgs. Flyhalf. FC DEBUT: 1998. PROV CAREER: Lions 1999-06,09 45-7-120-72-15-536. Young Lions 2009 & 2011 6-0-9-13-1-60. KZN 2010 8-0-6-0-0-12. Leopards 2012 21-0-59-30-4-220. Leopard XV 2013 6-2-28-9-0-93. SUPERRUGBY: Cats 2002-06 47-10-74-95-5-498. Lions 2007 & 09 & 11 25-1-28-26-8-163. REP HONOURS: SA 2002-03 & 05-07 Tests: 31-2-31-25-8-171. Tour: 2007 2-0-0-1-0-3. Total: 33-2-31-26-8-174. SA 'A' 2004 3-1-11-0-0-27. SA U23s 2001 2-2-2-0-0-14; SA Sevens 2000-01 (inc RWC 7s); SA U21s 1998 6-3-7-9-1-59; SA Barbarians

A-Z OF FIRST-CLASS PLAYERS IN 2013

2001 1-0-0-0-0-0. MISC INFO: Holds Cats/Lions record for most career points (661), cons (102), pens (121), drop goals (13). SA 7s PoY 2001; Leading scorer U21s champs. 1999 (129 points) & 1998 (80 points). FC RECORD: 203-28-375-280-42-1856. RECORD IN 2013: (Leopard XV) 6-2-28-9-0-93.

Pretorius, Dewald Petrus (Stilfontein HS) b 29/11/86, Welkom. 1.86m. 96kg. Centre. FC DEBUT: 2007. PROV CAREER: Blue Bulls 2007 3-2-0-0-0-10. Valke 2008 14-4-0-0-0-20. Griquas 2009-10 20-10-0-0-0-50. Pumas 2011-13 37-7-0-0-0-35. FC RECORD: 74-23-0-0-0-115. RECORD IN 2013: (Pumas) 16-1-0-0-0-5.

Pretorius, Jerome (Voortrekker HS, Boksburg) b 22/03/1988, Boksburg. 1.81m. 85kg. Centre. FC DEBUT: 2010. PROV CAREER: Sharks XV 2010-11 18-7-0-0-0-35. Blue Bulls 2012 4-1-0-0-0-5. Pumas 2012-13 25-7-0-0-0-35. REP HONOURS: SA Pres XV 2013 3-0-0-0-0-0. FC RECORD: 50-15-0-0-0-75. RECORD IN 2013: (SA Pres XV, Pumas) 20-5-0-0-0-25.

Pretorius, Johannes Hendrik (Juan) (Klerksdorp HS) b 22/10/1987, Klerksdorp. 1.90m. 101kg. Flank. FC DEBUT: 2011. PROV CAREER: Leopards 2011-12 28-4-0-0-0-20. Bulldogs 2013 20-2-0-0-0-10. FC RECORD: 48-6-0-0-0-30. RECORD IN 2013: (Bulldogs) 20-2-0-0-0-10.

Pretorius, Mark (Nelspruit HS) b 09/06/1992, Nelspruit. 1.76m. 102kg. Hooker. FC DEBUT: 2013. PROV CAREER: Young Lions 2013 1-0-0-0-0-0. REP HONOURS: SAU20 2012 4-1-0-0-0-5. FC RECORD: 5-1-0-0-0-5. RECORD IN 2013: (Young Lions) 2013 1-0-0-0-0-0.

Pretorius, Nicolaas (John Vorster THS, Pretoria & UP) b 29/02/84, Pretoria. 1.84m. 119kg. Prop/Hooker. FC DEBUT: 2006. PROV CAREER: Griffons 2006 10-0-0-0-0-0. Valke 2007-08 & 12-13 53-1-0-0-0-5. Griquas 2013 1-0-0-0-0-0. FC RECORD: 64-1-0-0-0-5. RECORD IN 2013: (Valke, Griquas) 18-0-0-0-0-0.

Pretorius, Sarel Johannes (Reitz HS) b 18/04/84, Reitz. 1.75m. 75kg. Scrumhalf. FC DEBUT: 2006. PROV CAREER: Valke 2006-07 37-16-0-0-0-80. Griquas 2007-11 65-25-0-0-0-125. Cheetahs 2012-13 22-7-0-0-0-35. Cheetahs XV 2010 1-0-0-0-0-0. SUPERRUGBY: Cheetahs 2009-11 & 13 53-19-0-0-0-95. REP HONOURS: Emerging Springboks 2008 3-0-0-0-0-0. Royal XV 2009 1-0-0-0-0-0. MISC INFO: Super PoY 2011. Brother of former Cheetahs fullback Herman Pretorius. FC RECORD: 182-67-0-0-0-335. RECORD IN 2013: (Cheetahs S15, Cheetahs) 25-7-0-0-0-35.

Pretorius, Stephanus Johannes Petrus (Steph) (Grey College, Bloemfontein & UP) b 29/06/1991. Nelspruit. 1.82m. 115kg. Prop. FC DEBUT: 2011. PROV CAREER: Blue Bulls 2011 & 13 10-0-0-0-0-0. FC RECORD: 10-0-0-0-0-0. RECORD IN 2013: (Blue Bulls) 4-0-0-0-0-0.

Pretorius, Ulrich De Beer (Marlow Agric, Cradock & NMMU) b 21/11/1988, Eliott. 1.85m. 110kg. Hooker. FC DEBUT: 2013. PROV CAREER: Boland 2013 16-6-0-0-0-30. FC RECORD: 16-6-0-0-0-30. RECORD IN 2013: (Boland) 16-6-0-0-0-30.

Pretorius, Walter b 23/04/1982. Lock. FC DEBUT: 2013. PROV CAREER: Limpopo 2013 2-0-0-0-0-0. FC RECORD: 2-0-0-0-0-0. RECORD IN 2013: (Limpopo) 2-0-0-0-0-0.

Prins, Shaun b 22/05/1989. Wing. FC DEBUT: 2013. PROV CAREER: Griffons 2013 5-0-0-0-0-0. FC RECORD: 5-0-0-0-0-0. RECORD IN 2013: (Griffons) 5-0-0-0-0-0.

Prinsloo, Johannes Gerhardus (Boom) (Grey College, Bloemfontein) b 12/03/1989, Bloemfontein. 1.87m. 95kg. Flanker. FC DEBUT: 2010. PROV CAREER: Cheetahs 2010-12 31-9-0-0-0-45. Emerging Cheetahs 2011 1-0-0-0-0-0. Free State XV 2013 3-5-0-0-0-25. SUPERRUGBY: Cheetahs 2012-13 13-1-0-0-0-5. Rep. honours: SA Sevens 2010-12. FC RECORD: 48-15-0-0-0-75. RECORD IN 2013: (Chee-

tahs S15, Cheetahs, Free State XV) 26-9-0-0-0-45.

Prinsloo, Johannes Gouws (Gouws) (Marlow Agric, Cradock) b 19/07/1990, East London. 1.79m. 80kg. Fullback. FC DEBUT: 2011. PROV CAREER: KZN 2011-12 4-0-0-0-0-0. Sharks XV 2011-13 21-7-28-30-0-181. Griquas 2013 9-0-8-14-0-58. MISC INFO: VC PoY 2012 nominee. FC RECORD: 34-7-36-44-0-239. RECORD IN 2013: (Sharks XV, Griquas) 17-1-8-14-0-63

R

Ralepelle, Mahlatse Chilliboy (Pretoria BHS) b 11/09/1986, Tzaneen. 1.80m. 104kg. Hooker. FC DEBUT: 2005. PROV CAREER: Blue Bulls 2006 & 08-12 35-3-0-0-0-15. SUPERRUGBY: Bulls 2006-07 & 09-13 69-4-0-0-0-20. Rep. honours: Tests: SA 2006 & 08-11 & 13 22-1-0-0-0-5. Tour: 2006,09 2-0-0-0-0-0. Total: 24-1-0-0-0-5. SA U21 2005-06 9-0-0-0-0-0. SA U19 2004-05, SA Schools 2002-03. CW Blue Bulls. MISC INFO: IRB U19 PoY nominee 2005. FC RECORD: 137-8-0-0-0-40. RECORD IN 2013 (SA, Bulls) 18-2-0-0-0-10.

Rams-Tshoshane, Brendan Thato (St Albans College) b 10/04/1989, Johannesburg. 1.84m. 113kg. Hooker. FC DEBUT: 2013. PROV CAREER: Valke 2013 5-0-0-0-0-0. FC RECORD: 5-0-0-0-0-0. RECORD IN 2013: (Valke) 5-0-0-0-0-0.

Ras, Egbert Olivier (Grey College, Bloemfontein) b 09/07/1991, Bloemfontein. 1.85m. 88kg. Flank. FC DEBUT: 2011. PROV CAREER: Cheetahs 2011 5-0-0-0-0-0. Free State XV 2012 2-0-0-0-0-0. Griffons 2013 4-0-0-0-0-0. MISC INFO: Son of former Springbok De Wet Ras. FC RECORD: 11-0-0-0-0-0. RECORD IN 2013: (Griffons) 4-0-0-0-0-0.

Raubenheimer, Davon (Pacaltsdorp SS) b 16/07/1984, Knysna. 1.94m. 92kg. Flank. FC DEBUT: 2005. PROV CAREER: Eagles 2005-08 60-5-0-0-0-25. Griquas 2009-11 56-4-0-0-0-20. Cheetahs 2012-13 16-0-0-0-0-0. Free State XV 2012-13 6-0-0-0-0-0. Griffons 2013 5-0-0-0-0-0. SUPERRUGBY: Cheetahs 2010-12 20-2-0-0-0-10. REP HONOURS: SA Tour: 2009 2-0-0-0-0-0. Emerging Springboks 2008 2-0-0-0-0-0. Royal XV 2009 1-0-0-0-0-0. SA U21 2005 3-0-0-0-0-0. FC RECORD: 171-11-0-0-0-55. RECORD IN 2013: (Cheetahs, Griffons, Free State XV) 14-0-0-0-0-0.

Raubenheimer, Shaun (George Hill HS) b 10/11/83, George. 1.80m. 94kg. Flanker. FC DEBUT: 2008. PROV CAREER: Bulldogs 2008 15-2-0-0-0-10. Eagles 2009-10 & 12-13 59-20-0-0-0-100. Griffons 2011 13-2-0-0-0-10. REP HONOURS: SA Barbarians 2012 1-0-0-0-0-0. FC RECORD: 88-24-0-0-0-120. RECORD IN 2013: (Eagles) 12-5-0-0-0-25.

Redelinghuys, Julian (Monument HS, Krugersdorp) b 11/09/89, Pretoria. 1.76m. 100kg. Prop. FC DEBUT: 2009. PROV CAREER: KZN 2009 & 2011-12 9-0-0-0-0-0. Sharks XV 2010-11 8-0-0-0-0-0. Lions 2013 3-0-0-0-0-0. Young Lions 2013 4-1-0-0-0-5. SUPERRUGBY: Lions P/R 2013 2-0-0-0-0-0. REP HONOURS: SAU20 2009 4-0-0-0-0-0. FC RECORD: 30-1-0-0-0-5. RECORD IN 2013: (Lions S15, Lions, Young Lions) 9-1-0-0-0-5.

Reinach, Jacobus Meyer (Cobus) (Grey College, Bloemfontein) b 07/02/1990, Bloemfontein. 1.75m. 83kg. Scrumhalf. FC DEBUT: 2011. PROV CAREER: KZN 2011-13 26-4-0-0-0-20. Sharks XV 2011-12 19-4-0-0-0-20. SUPERRUGBY: Sharks 2012-13 13-1-0-0-0-5. MISC INFO: Son of former Springbok Jaco Reinach. FC RECORD: 58-9-0-0-0-45. RECORD IN 2013: (Sharks, KZN) 24-3-0-0-0-15.

Reynecke, Ethienne (Huguenot HS) b 20/03/82, Kempton Park. 1.75m. 98kg. Hooker. FC DEBUT: 2004. PROV CAREER: Lions 2004 & 06-09 32-3-0-0-0-15. Young Lions 2004,06-09 11-0-0-0-0-0. Griffons 2005 17-2-0-0-0-10. Lions XV 2008 1-0-0-0-0-0. WP 2011 2-0-0-0-0-0. Cheetahs 2013 4-0-0-0-0-0. SUPERRUGBY: Lions 2007-08 20-2-0-0-0-

A-Z OF FIRST-CLASS PLAYERS IN 2013

10.Stormers 2011 2-0-0-0-0-0. FC RECORD: 89-7-0-0-0-35. RECORD IN 2013: (Cheetahs) 4-0-0-0-0-0

Reynecke, Jody Tylon (Tygerberg HS) b 02/08/1991, Somerset West. 1.82m. 95kg. Flank. FC DEBUT: 2013. PROV CAREER: WP 2013 6-2-0-0-0-10. FC RECORD: 6-2-0-0-0-10. RECORD IN 2013: (WP) 6-2-0-0-0-10.

Rhodes, Michael Kenworthy (Michaelhouse) b 19/12/87, Durban. 1.97m. 110kg. Lock. FC DEBUT: 2007. PROV CAREER: KZN 2009-10 19-1-0-0-0-5. Sharks XV 2008-10 18-5-0-0-0-25. Sharks Inv XV 2007 & 10 2-1-0-0-0-5. Lions 2011-12 21-5-0-0-0-25. Young Lions 2011 1-0-0-0-0-0. WP 2013 11-3-0-0-0-15. SUPERRUGBY: Lions 2011 11-2-0-0-0-10. Stormers 2013 3-1-0-0-0-5. FC RECORD: 86-18-0-0-0-90. RECORD IN 2013: (Stormers,WP) 14-4-0-0-0-20.

Rhoode, Deroy Elizandro (Groot Brak HS) b 28/10/88. 1.6m. 64kg. FC DEBUT: 2009. PROV CAREER: Eagles 2009-13 53-4-12-3-0-53. FC RECORD: 53-4-12-3-0-53. RECORD IN 2013: (Eagles) 14-1-0-0-0-5.

Rhule, Raymond Kofi (Louis Botha THS, Bloemfontein & UFS) b 06/11/1992, Accra (Ghana). 1.78m. 78kg. Wing. FC DEBUT: 2012. PROV CAREER: Cheetahs 2012=13 22-15-0-0-0-75. Free State XV 2012 1-0-0-0-0-0. SUPERRUGBY: Cheetahs 2013 17-5-0-0-0-25. MISC INFO: YPoY 2012 nominee. CC PoY 2012 nominee. REP HONOURS: SA 2012 - no tests. SAU20 2012 3-2-0-0-0-10. FC RECORD: 43-22-0-0-0-110. RECORD IN 2013: (Cheetahs S15, Cheetahs) 27-12-0-0-0-60.

Richards, Mark (Michaelhouse HS) b 09/09/1989, Springs. 1.75m. 81kg. Wing. FC DEBUT: 2010. PROV CAREER: KZN 2011 4-1-0-0-0-5. Sharks XV 2010-11 16-6-0-0-0-30. Sharks Inv XV 2010 1-1-0-0-0-5. Rep. honours: SA Sevens 2010-13. FC RECORD: 21-8-0-0-0-40. RECORD IN 2013: (SA Sevens).

Richter, Anrich (Dr EG Jansen HS) b 30/05/1991, Kempton Park. 78kg. Scrumhalf. FC DEBUT: 2011. PROV CAREER: Valke 2011-13 43-15-0-0-0-75. FC RECORD: 43-15-0-0-0-75. RECORD IN 2013: (Valke) 21-7-0-0-0-35.

Rick, Shannon Michael Kendrick (Dale College) b 21/10/1988, East London. 1.78m. 86kg. Scrumhalf. FC DEBUT: 2011. PROV CAREER: Eagles 2011 1-0-0-0-0-0. Griquas 2011 3-0-0-0-0-0. Sharks XV 2012 1-0-0-0-0-0. Bulldogs 2013 18-2-0-0-0-10. FC RECORD: 23-2-0-0-0-10. RECORD IN 2013: (Bulldogs) 18-2-0-0-0-10.

Roberts, Cheslyn Dean (John Ramsey HS) b 10/04/1990, Cape Town. 1.76m. 91kg. Wing. FC DEBUT: 2013. PROV CAREER: Boland 2013 11-1-0-0-0-5. FC RECORD: 11-1-0-0-0-5. RECORD IN 2013: (Boland) 11-1-0-0-0-5.

Roberts, Daniel Cornelius (PW Botha College) b 20/01/1992, Riversdal. 1.85m. 73kg. Fullback. FC DEBUT: 2013. PROV CAREER: Eagles 2013 10-0-0-0-0-0. FC RECORD: 10-0-0-0-0-0. RECORD IN 2013: (Eagles) 10-0-0-0-0-0.

Roberts, Wesley Aidan (Northcliff HS & UJ) b 15/02/1987, Cape Town. 1.82m. 90kg. Flyhalf. FC DEBUT: 2013. PROV CAREER: Valke 2013 15-1-10-7-0-46. FC RECORD: 15-1-10-7-0-46. RECORD IN 2013: (Valke) 15-1-10-7-0-46.

Roberts, Willem Andries Stephanus (Steph) (Grey College, Bloemfontein) b 20/03/85, Bloemfontein. 1.80m. 108kg. Prop. FC DEBUT: 2005. PROV CAREER: Cheetahs 2005-07 15-0-0-0-0-0. Griquas 2008-13 111-4-0-0-0-20. REP HONOURS: Royal XV 2009 1-0-0-0-0-0. SA Students 2007 1-0-0-0-0-0. FC RECORD: 128-4-0-0-0-20. RECORD IN 2013: (Griquas) 17-0-0-0-0-0.

Robinson, Sean Jack (Waterkloof HS, Pretoria) b 02/11/1993, Pretoria. 1.81m. 85kg. Wing. FC DEBUT: 2013. PROV CAREER: Sharks XV 2013 1-1-0-0-0-5. SUPERRUGBY: Sharks 2013 3-0-0-0-0-0. FC RECORD: 4-1-0-0-0-5. RECORD IN 2013: (Sharks, Sharks XV) 4-1-0-0-0-5.

Roelfse, Heinrich Rashid (George HS) b 25/01/1990, Mossel Bay. 1.86m. 110kg. Prop. FC DEBUT: 2012. PROV CAREER: Griffons 2012-13 14-0-0-0-0-0. FC RECORD: 14-0-0-0-0-0. RECORD IN 2013: (Griffons) 8-0-0-0-0-0.

Rogers, Dylan (Selborne College & UCT) b 05/07/1984, East London. 1.87m. 110kg. Prop. FC DEBUT: 2013. PROV CAREER: WP 2013 3-0-0-0-0-0. FC RECORD: 3-0-0-0-0-0. RECORD IN 2013: (WP) 3-0-0-0-0-0.

Roodt, Hendrik Lambertus (Lichtenburg HS) b 06/11/1987, Lichtenburg. 1.98m. 121kg. Lock. FC DEBUT: 2007. PROV CAREER: Blue Bulls 2007-08 19-1-0-0-0-5. Blue Bulls XV 2007 1-0-0-0-0-0. Griquas 2010-11 25-3-0-0-0-15. Lions 2012 6-1-0-0-0-5. Young Lions 2012-13 12-1-0-0-0-5. SUPERRUGBY: Lions 2012 7-0-0-0-0-0. P/R 2013 2-0-0-0-0-0. REP HONOURS: Emerging Springboks 2008 3-0-0-0-0-0. FC RECORD: 75-6-0-0-0-30. RECORD IN 2013: (Lions S15, Young Lions) 8-0-0-0-0-0.

Roos, Juan-Claude (Waterkloof HS, Pretoria) b 12/09/1990, Witbank. 1.83m. 94kg. Flyhalf. FC DEBUT: 2011. PROV CAREER: Blue Bulls 2011 1-0-0-0-1-3. Pumas 2011-13 30-2-78-63-1-358. Valke 2013 1-0-1-1-0-5. REP HONOURS: SA Barbarians 2012 1-0-4-1-0-11. FC RECORD: 33-2-83-65-2-377. RECORD IN 2013: (Valke, Pumas) 8-0-19-15-1-86.

Ross, Jonathan Montague (Jono) (St Stithians HS) b 27/10/1990, Sandton. 1.88m. 107kg. Flank. FC DEBUT: 2011. PROV CAREER: Blue Bulls 2011-13 22-2-0-0-0-10. SUPERRUGBY: Bulls 2013 4-0-0-0-0-0. FC RECORD: 26-2-0-0-0-10. RECORD IN 2013: (Bulls, Blue Bulls) 14-1-0-0-0-5.

Rossouw, Jacques Nelius (Piketberg HS & UP) b 29/04/1993, Piketberg. 1.84m. 85kg. Fullback. FC DEBUT: 2013. REP HONOURS: SA Univ 2013 1-0-0-0-0-0. FC RECORD: 1-0-0-0-0-0. RECORD IN 2013: (SA Univ) 1-0-0-0-0-0.

Rossouw, Jean Jacques (Paarl Gymnasium) b 06/04/1988, George. 1.84m. 120kg. Prop. FC DEBUT: 2010. PROV CAREER: Boland 2010 3-0-0-0-0-0. Leopards 2011 4-0-0-0-0-0. Eagles 2012-13 21-1-0-0-0-5. REP HONOURS: SAU20 2008 2-0-0-0-0-0. FC RECORD: 30-1-0-0-0-5. RECORD IN 2013: (Eagles) 7-0-0-0-0-0.

Roux, Jacobus Stephanus (Bees) (Marlow Agric, Cradock) b 09/12/81, Upington. 1.86m. 115kg. Forward. FC DEBUT: 2005. PROV CAREER: Leopards 2005-06 41-1-0-0-0-5. Griquas 2007-09 31-1-0-0-0-5. Blue Bulls 2010 7-0-0-0-0-0. Lions 2013 2-0-0-0-0-0. SUPERRUGBY: Cheetahs 2008-09 17-0-0-0-0-0. Bulls 2010 14-0-0-0-0-0. REP HONOURS: Royal XV 2009 1-0-0-0-0-0. FC RECORD: 113-2-0-0-0-10. RECORD IN 2013: (Lions) 2-0-0-0-0-0.

S

Sabbagh, Dale Gavin (Selborne College) b 02/02/1991, East London. 1.85m. 85kg. Flyhalf. FC DEBUT: 2011. PROV CAREER: Bulldogs 2011-13 22-0-23-26-1-127. FC RECORD: 22-0-23-26-1-127. RECORD IN 2013: (Bulldogs) 11-0-12-17-0-75.

Sadie, Johann (Paarl Gymnasium & Univ. Stellenbosch) b 23/01/1989, Malmesbury. 1.88m. 88kg. Wing. FC DEBUT: 2010. PROV CAREER: WP 2010-11 24-12-0-0-0-60. Blue Bulls 2012 3-0-0-0-0-0. Cheetahs 2013 11-3-0-0-0-15. SUPERRUGBY: Stormers 2011 7-2-0-0-0-10. Bulls 2012 10-0-0-0-0-0. Cheetahs 2013 17-5-0-0-0-25. REP HONOURS: SAU20 2009 4-1-0-0-0-5. FC RECORD: 76-23-0-0-0-115. RECORD IN 2013: (Cheetahs S15, Cheetahs) 28-8-0-0-0-40.

Sampson, Marcello Edward Dennis (Wynberg Boys HS & UWC) b 27/03/1987, Cape Town. 1.83m. 85kg. Wing. FC DEBUT: 2011. PROV CAREER: EP Kings 2011-13 37-19-0-0-0-95. SUPERRUGBY: Southern Kings 2013 13-0-0-0-0-0. P/R 2013 1-1-0-0-0-5. REP

A-Z OF FIRST-CLASS PLAYERS IN 2013

HONOURS: SA Kings 2011 1-0-0-0-0-0. FC RECORD: 52-20-0-0-0-100. RECORD IN 2013: (Southern Kings, EP Kings) 19-1-0-0-0-5.
Scheepers, Jacobus Nicolaas (Nico) (Nico Malan HS & UFS) b 27/02/1990, Port Elizabeth. 1.86m. 90kg. Wing. FC DEBUT: 2011. PROV CAREER: Cheetahs 2011-12 16-3-17-27-0-130. Free State XV 2012-13 8-3-12-5-0-54. Emerging Cheetahs 2011 1-0-0-0-0-0. Griquas 2013 7-1-5-12-0-51. SUPERRUGBY: Cheetahs 2012 3-0-0-0-0-0. REP HONOURS: SAU20 2010 4-1-0-0-0-5. FC RECORD: 39-8-34-44-0-240. RECORD IN 2013: (Griquas, Free State XV) 11-1-8-14-0-63.
Schmidt, David (Marais) (Krugersdorp HS) b 23/04/1992, Sandton. 1.83m. 83kg. Flyhalf. FC DEBUT: 2011. PROV CAREER: Young Lions 2012-13 6-1-10-7-0-46. Golden Lions XV 2011 1-0-2-2-0-10. REP HONOURS: SAU20 2012 1-0-0-0-0-0. FC RECORD: 8-1-12-9-0-56. RECORD IN 2013: (Young Lions) 1-0-0-3-0-9.
Schoeman, Danie Burger (Boland Agric HS) b 26/09/1988, Paarl. 1.90m. 105kg. Eightman. FC DEBUT: 2010. PROV CAREER: Griquas 2010-13 37-5-0-0-0-25. Griffons 2011-12 3-2-0-0-0-10. FC RECORD: 40-7-0-0-0-35. RECORD IN 2013: (Griquas) 10-1-0-0-0-5.
Schoeman, Marnus (Waterkloof HS, Pretoria) b 09/02/89, Edenvale. 1.78m. 95kg. Flank. FC DEBUT: 2009. PROV CAREER: Blue Bulls 2009 & 2011 12-3-0-0-0-15. Griquas 2011-13 41-25-0-0-0-125. REP HONOURS: SAU20 2009 5-0-0-0-0-0. FC RECORD: 58-28-0-0-0-140. RECORD IN 2013: (Griquas) 17-12-0-0-0-60.
Schoeman, Paul (Marlow Agric, Cradock) b 19/12/1992, Cradock. 1.90m. 97kg. Eightman. FC DEBUT: 2013. PROV CAREER: EP Kings 2013 8-2-0-0-0-10. FC RECORD: 8-2-0-0-0-10. RECORD IN 2013: (EP Kings) 8-2-0-0-0-10.
Schoeman, Renier (Walla) (Ben Viljoen HS, Tzaneen) b 27/05/83, Potgieterus. 1.90m. 128kg. Prop. FC DEBUT: 2005. PROV CAREER: Pumas 2005 3-0-0-0-0-0. Leopards 2007-08 7-0-0-0-0-0. Griquas 2007 2-0-0-0-0-0. Eagles 2009 6-0-0-0-0-0. Bulldogs 2011-13 40-0-0-0-0-0. FC RECORD: 42-0-0-0-0-0. RECORD IN 2013 (Bulldogs) 16-0-0-0-0-0.
Schoeman, Stephanus (Paarl Gymnasium & UP) b 12/05/1991, Somerset West. 1.95m. 120kg. Prop. FC DEBUT: 2013. PROV CAREER: Valke 2013 7-0-0-0-0-0. FC RECORD: 7-0-0-0-0-0. RECORD IN 2013: (Valke) 7-0-0-0-0-0.
Scholtz, Deon (Skurweberg HS) b 12/09/85, Ceres. 1.69m. 75kg. Wing/Centre. FC DEBUT: 2008. PROV CAREER: Boland 2008-09 27-8-0-0-0-40. Leopards 2010 21-10-0-0-0-50. Pumas 2011-13 34-9-0-0-0-45. REP HONOURS: SA Barbarians 2012 1-1-0-0-0-5. FC RECORD: 83-28-0-0-0-140. RECORD IN 2013: (Pumas) 1-0-0-0-0-0.
Scholtz, Xavier Grant (PW Botha HS) b 22/04/85, George. 1.68m. 83kgs. Hooker. FC DEBUT: 2006. PROV CAREER: Griquas 2006-07 5-0-0-0-0-0. Eagles 2011-13 15-0-0-0-0-0. FC RECORD: 20-0-0-0-0-0. RECORD IN 2013: (Eagles) 1-0-0-0-0-0.
Schonert, Nicholas Peter (Nic) (Maritzburg College) b 20/09/1991, Durban. 1.89m. 118kg. Prop. FC DEBUT: 2012. PROV CAREER: Sharks XV 2012 1-0-0-0-0-0. Griquas 2013 14-0-0-0-0-0. REP HONOURS: SAU20 2011 5-0-0-0-0-0. FC RECORD: 20-0-0-0-0-0. RECORD IN 2013: (Griquas) 14-0-0-0-0-0.
Schreuder, Louis (Paarl Gymnasium) b 25/04/1990, Paarl. 1.84m. 82kg. Wing. FC DEBUT: 2010. PROV CAREER: WP 2010-13 44-3-0-0-0-15. SUPERRUGBY: Stormers 2011-13 27-1-0-0-0-5. REP HONOURS: 2013 Springbok team squad member. SAU20 2010 5-0-0-0-0-0. FC RECORD: 76-4-0-0-0-20. RECORD IN 2013: (Stormers, WP) 22-1-0-0-0-5.
Schroeder, Ricky Darryl (Paul Roos Gymnasium & UCT) b 05/01/1991, Worcester. 1.68m. 77kg. Scrumhalf. FC DEBUT: 2012. PROV CAREER: WP 2012-13 7-0-0-0-0-0. Boland 2013 10-0-0-0-0-0. FC RECORD: 17-0-0-0-0-0. RECORD IN 2013: (WP, Boland) 11-0-0-0-0-0.
Scott, Ashwin Robert (Parkdene HS) b 02/06/85. 1.74m. 80kg. Wing. FC DEBUT: 2004. PROV CAREER: Eagles 2004-08 39-11-0-0-1-58. Pumas 2009-13 50-11-0-0-0-55. Griffons 2013 2-0-0-0-0-0. REP HONOURS: SA Schools 2003. CW SWD 2003. FC RECORD: 91-22-0-0-1-113. RECORD IN 2013: (Pumas, Griffons) 5-4-0-0-0-20.
Scott, Wenstley Shane (Florida HS) b 09/04/1988, George. 1.74m. 83kg. Centre. FC DEBUT: 2010. PROV CAREER: Eagles 2010-13 33-5-0-0-0-25. FC RECORD: 33-5-0-0-0-25. RECORD IN 2013: (Eagles) 7-0-0-0-0-0.
Seegers, Albertus (Phalaborwa HS) b 30/08/1984, Limpopo. 1.83m. 103kg. Hooker. FC DEBUT: 2013. PROV CAREER: Limpopo 2013 1-0-0-0-0-0. FC RECORD: 1-0-0-0-0-0. RECORD IN 2013: (Limpopo) 1-0-0-0-0-0.
Seerane, Johannes (Joe) (Merensky HS & NWU) b 30/03/1987, Ackonhoek. 1.72m. 85kg. FC DEBUT: 2011. PROV CAREER: Leopards 2011 1-1-0-0-0-5. Bulldogs 2012-13 10-6-0-0-0-30. REP HONOURS: SA Students 2012 2-1-0-0-0-5. SA Pres XV 2013 1-0-0-0-0-0. FC record 14-8-0-0-0-40. RECORD IN 2013: (SA Pres XV, Bulldogs) 8-4-0-0-0-20.
Senatla, Seabelo Mohanoe (Riebeeckstad HS & CUT) b 10/02/1993, Welkom. 1.86m. 76kg. Wing. FC DEBUT: 2013. REP HONOURS: SA U20 2013 5-7-0-0-0-35. SA Sevens 2013. MISC INFO: SA U20 PoY nominee. FC RECORD: 5-7-0-0-0-35. RECORD IN 2013: (SA U20, SA Sevens) 5-7-0-0-0-35.
September, Franzel Julio (Bergrivier HS) b 06/06/86, Paarl. 1.80m. 100kg. FC DEBUT: 2009. PROV CAREER: Eagles 2009 1-0-0-0-0-0. Boland 2010-13 65-24-0-0-0-120. FC RECORD: 65-24-0-0-0-120. RECORD IN 2013: (Boland) 18-4-0-0-0-20.
Serfontein, Jan Lodewyk (Grey HS, PE) b 15/04/1993, Port Elizabeth. 1.87m. 97kg. Centre. FC DEBUT: 2012. PROV CAREER: Blue Bulls 2012-13 11-4-0-0-0-20. SUPERRUGBY: Bulls 2013 12-2-0-0-0-10. MISC INFO: VC PoY 2012 nominee. SA U20 PoY 2012. IRB U/20 PoY 2012. YPoY nominee 2013. Brother of Willem Serfontein (Pumas). Son of former EP No. 8 Jan Serfontein. REP HONOURS: SA Tests: 2013 9-1-0-0-0-5. SAU20 2012 5-4-0-0-0-20. FC RECORD: 37-11-0-0-0-55. RECORD IN 2013: (SA, Bulls, Blue Bulls) 22-3-0-0-0-15.
Serfontein, Willem Jacob (Framesby HS & Unisa) b 16/09/88, Port Elizabeth. 1.95m. 112kg. Lock. FC DEBUT: 2009. PROV CAREER: Blue Bulls 2009 8-1-0-0-0-5. Pumas 2010-13 62-1-0-0-0-5. REP HONOURS: SA Barbarians 2012 1-0-0-0-0-0. MISC INFO: Brother of Jan Serfontein. Son of former EP No. 8 Jan Serfontein. FC RECORD: 71-2-0-0-0-10. RECORD IN 2013: (Pumas) 10-0-0-0-0-0.
Shabangu, Simphiwe Brian (Glenwood HS) b 11/04/1988, Durban. 1.73m. 96kg. Flanker. FC DEBUT: 2012. PROV CAREER: Bulldogs 2012-13 26-4-0-0-0-20. REP HONOURS: SA Pres XV 2013 3-0-0-0-0-0. FC RECORD: 29-4-0-0-0-20. RECORD IN 2013: (SA Pres XV, Bulldogs) 15-2-0-0-0-10.
Short, Basil Gordon (Standerton HS & UP) b 19/05/1991, Vryheid. 1.89m. 116kg. Prop. FC DEBUT: 2012. PROV CAREER: Blue Bulls 2012-13 9-2-0-0-0-10. FC RECORD: 9-2-0-0-0-10. RECORD IN 2013: (Blue Bulls) 2-1-0-0-0-5.
Sisita, Frans Leonardo (Sand du Plessis HS, Bloemfontein & CUT) b 06/08/1990, Vryburg. 1.86m. 103kg. Wing. FC DEBUT: 2013. PROV CAREER: Griffons 2013 1-0-0-0-0-0. FC RECORD: 1-0-0-0-0-0. RECORD IN 2013: (Griffons) 1-0-0-0-0-0.
Sithole, Sibusiso Camagu Thokazani (Varsity College) b 14/06/1990, Queenstown. 1.78m. 90kg. Wing. FC DEBUT: 2010. PROV CAREER: KZN 2011-12 19-4-0-0-0-20. Sharks XV 2010-13 20-12-0-0-0-60. SUPERRUGBY: Sharks 2013 2-0-0-0-0-0. Rep. honours: SAU20

A-Z OF FIRST-CLASS PLAYERS IN 2013

2010 3-4-0-0-0-20. SA Sevens 2010-11 & 13. FC RECORD: 44-20-0-0-0-100. RECORD IN 2013: (Sharks, Sharks XV, SA Sevens) 7-4-0-0-0-20.
Sithole, Simphiwe Martin (Kusaselethu SS) b 03/02/1984, Pietermaritzburg. 1.81m. 95kg. Flanker. FC DEBUT: 2005. Prov. career: Pumas 2008-11 37-6-0-0-0-30. Griffons 2011-13 38-14-0-0-0-70. Rep. honours: SA U21 2005 1-0-0-0-0-0. SA Barbarians 2012 1-0-0-0-0-0. CW Pumas 2001-02. FC RECORD: 77-20-0-0-0-100. Record in 2013 (Griffons) 16-5-0-0-0-25.
Sithole, Sithembiso Mfundo Siphesihle (Westville Boys HS & UCT) b 31/03/1993, Durban. 1.79m. 104kg. Prop. FC DEBUT: 2013. REP HONOURS: SA U20 2013 4-0-0-0-0-0. FC RECORD: 4-0-0-0-0-0. RECORD IN 2013: (SA U20) 4-0-0-0-0-0.
Skorbinski, Alfred Henry (Framesby HS & NWU) b 25/09/1990, Port Elizabeth. 1.84m. 93kg. Centre. FC DEBUT: 2011. PROV CAREER: Leopards 2011-13 18-3-0-0-0-15. Leopard XV 2013 2-1-0-0-0-5. FC RECORD: 20-4-0-0-0-20. RECORD IN 2013: (Leopards, Leopards XV) 10-3-0-0-0-15.
Skosan, Courtnall Douglas (Brackenfell HS) b 24/07/1991, Cape Town. 1.83m. 90kg. Utility back. FC DEBUT: 2011. PROV CAREER: Blue Bulls 2011-13 12-7-0-0-0-35. REP HONOURS: SAU20 2011 3-1-0-0-0-5. FC RECORD: 15-8-0-0-0-40. RECORD IN 2013: (Blue Bulls) 4-5-0-0-0-25.
Skosana, Mthangala Brian JR (St Andrews College) b 05/12/1991, Johannesburg. 1.80m. 89kg. Wing. FC DEBUT: 2013. PROV CAREER: EP Kings 2013 12-1-0-0-0-5. FC RECORD: 12-1-0-0-0-5. RECORD IN 2013: (EP Kings) 12-1-0-0-0-5.
Small-Smith, William Thomas (Grey College, Bloemfontein) b 31/03/1982, Johannesburg. 1.84m. 91kg. Centre. FC DEBUT: 2011. PROV CAREER: Blue Bulls 2011 & 13 6-3-0-0-0-15. Rep. Honours: SAU20 2012 3-2-0-0-0-10. SA Sevens 2011-12. FC RECORD: 9-5-0-0-0-25. RECORD IN 2013: (Blue Bulls) 4-2-0-0-0-10.
Smid, Rayn (Rondebosch HS) b 26/03/1992, Cape Town. 1.93m. 107kg. Eightman. FC DEBUT: 2013. PROV CAREER: WP 2013 10-2-0-0-0-10. FC RECORD: 10-2-0-0-0-10. RECORD IN 2013: (WP) 10-2-0-0-0-10.
Smit, Adriaan Jacobus (Riaan) (THS Springs) b 28/04/84, Springs. 1.78m. 85kg. Fullback. FC DEBUT: 2006. PROV CAREER: Leopards 2006,09 7-2-7-6-0-42. Pumas 2007 15-5-14-12-0-89. Valke 2008 11-3-9-3-0-42. Griffons 2010 2-0-4-2-0-14. Cheetahs 2010-13 35-10-20-19-0-147. Free State XV 2012-13 6-1-11-3-1-39. Emerging Cheetahs 2011 1-1-2-3-0-18. SUPERRUGBY: Cheetahs 2011-13 24-3-11-23-0-106. FC RECORD: 101-25-78-71-1-497. RECORD IN 2013: (Cheetahs S15, Cheetahs, Free State XV) 18-3-20-26-0-133.
Smit, Dillon (Middelburg HS) b 11/12/1992, Bethal. 1.75m. 83kg. Scrumhalf. FC DEBUT: 2013. PROV CAREER: Bulldogs 2013 5-0-0-0-0-0. FC RECORD: 5-0-0-0-0-0. RECORD IN 2013: (Bulldogs) 5-0-0-0-0-0.
Smit, Roelof Andries (Hangklip HS) b 11/01/1993, Queenstown. 1.90m. 90kg. Flank. FC DEBUT: 2013. PROV CAREER: Blue Bulls 2013 3-2-0-0-0-10. REP HONOURS: SA U20 2013 4-0-0-0-0-0. FC RECORD: 7-2-0-0-0-10. RECORD IN 2013: (Blue Bulls, SA U20) 7-2-0-0-0-10.
Smith, Albertus Stephanus (Kwagga).(Middelburg THS) b 11/06/1993, Lydenburg. 1.80m. 80kg. Flank. FC DEBUT: 2013. REP HONOURS: SA U20 2013 3-2-0-0-0-10. FC RECORD: 3-2-0-0-0-10. RECORD IN 2013: (SA U20) 3-2-0-0-0-10.
Smith, Gerhardus Phillipus Johannes (Gerrit) (FH Odendaal HS, Pretoria & UP & NMMU) b 12/02/88, Pretoria. 1.79m. 91kg. Centre. FC DEBUT: 2009. PROV CAREER: Valke 2009 1-0-0-0-0-0. Eagles 2013 12-3-11-2-0-43. FC RECORD: 13-3-11-2-0-43. RECORD IN 2013: (Eagles) 12-3-11-2-0-43.

Smith, Johan (Joe) (Volkskool Potchefstroom) b 02/12/1991, Fochville. 1.83m. 99kg. Hooker. FC DEBUT: 2012. PROV CAREER: Leopards 2012-13 9-0-0-0-0-0. Leopard XV 2013 3-1-0-0-0-5. FC RECORD: 12-1-0-0-0-5. RECORD IN 2013: (Leopards, Leopard XV) 11-1-0-0-0-5.
Smith, Mynhardt b 25/02/1989. Wing. FC DEBUT: 2013. PROV CAREER: Limpopo 2013 3-0-0-0-0-0. FC RECORD: 3-0-0-0-0-0. RECORD IN 2013: (Limpopo) 3-0-0-0-0-0.
Snyman, Brendon Michael (Pietersburg HS) b 21/08/84, Pietersburg. 122kg. Forward. FC DEBUT: 2005. PROV CAREER: Eagles 2005 16-1-0-0-0-5. Griquas 2006-09 67-9-0-0-0-45. EP Kings 2009-10 10-0-0-0-0-0. EP Inv XV 2010 1-0-0-0-0-0. Leopards 2011-13 46-5-0-0-0-25. Leopard XV 2013 7-0-0-0-0-0. REP HONOURS: SA Pres XV 2013 4-0-0-0-0-0. FC RECORD: 151-15-0-0-0-75. RECORD IN 2013: (SA Pres XV, Leopards, Leopard XV) 23-3-0-0-0-15.
Snyman, Jacobus Phillipus (Jaco) (Schweizer Reneke HS) b 09/06/86, Schweizer Reneke. 1.75m. 78kg. Scrumhalf. FC DEBUT: 2007. PROV CAREER: Lions 2007-08 4-0-0-0-0-0. Valke 2009-13 46-8-0-0-0-40. FC RECORD: 50-8-0-0-0-40. RECORD IN 2013: (Valke) 6-0-0-0-0-0.
Snyman, Phillipus Albertus Borman (Phillip) (Grey College, Bloemfontein) b 26/03/87, Bloemfontein. 1.88m. 95kg. Centre. FC DEBUT: 2008. PROV CAREER: Griffons 2008-09 6-0-0-0-0-0. Cheetahs 2008-12 59-19-0-0-0-95. Emerging Cheetahs 2011 1-0-0-0-0-0. SUPERRUGBY: Cheetahs 2011-12 20-1-0-0-0-5. REP HONOURS: SA Sevens 2008 & 12-13. FC RECORD: 86-20-0-0-0-100. RECORD IN 2013: (SA Sevens).
Snyman, Ruan (Affies, Pretoria) b 09/03/87, Pretoria. 1.85m. 80kg. Scrumhalf. FC DEBUT: 2008. PROV CAREER: Blue Bulls 2008-13 69-12-0-0-0-60. SUPERRUGBY: Bulls 2010 1-1-0-0-0-5. FC RECORD: 70-13-0-0-0-65. RECORD IN 2013: (Blue Bulls) 11-4-0-0-0-20.
Snyman, Willem Adolph b 24/01/1985. Flank. FC DEBUT: 2013. PROV CAREER: Limpopo 2013 1-0-0-0-0-0. RECORD IN 2013: (Limpopo) 1-0-0-0-0-0.
Soyizwapi, Siviwe Sonwabile (Dale College) b 07/12/1992, Mthatha. 1.72m. 75kg. Wing. FC DEBUT: 2012. PROV CAREER: EP Kings 2012-13 9-4-0-0-0-20. SUPERRUGBY: Southern Kings 2013 6-0-0-0-0-0. FC RECORD: 15-4-0-0-0-20. RECORD IN 2013: (Southern Kings, EP Kings) 14-4-0-0-0-20.
Speckman, Rosko Shane (Mary Waters HS) b 28/04/1989, Grahamstown. 1.66m. 70kg. Wing. FC DEBUT: 2010. PROV CAREER: KZN 2012 1-0-0-0-0-0. Sharks XV 2010-12 13-5-0-0-0-25. Pumas 2013 25-23-0-0-0-115. REP HONOURS: SA Pres XV 2013 3-1-0-0-0-5. MISC INFO: VC PoY nominee 2013. CC First Division PoY 2013. FC RECORD: 42-29-0-0-0-145. RECORD IN 2013: (SA Pres XV, Pumas) 28-24-0-0-0-120.
Spies, Pierre Johan (Affies, Pretoria) b 08/06/1985, Pretoria. 1.94m. 108kg. Loose Forward. FC DEBUT: 2005. PROV CAREER: Blue Bulls 2005-06 & 08-10 17-4-0-0-0-20. SUPERRUGBY: Bulls 2005-13 102-25-0-0-0-125. REP HONOURS: SA 2006-13 Tests: 53-7-0-0-0-35. SA U21 2006 4-3-0-0-0-15. SA Students 2005 1-1-0-0-0-5. MISC INFO: SA record of 48 Tests as a No.8. YPoY 2006. Son of former N-Tvl and Transvaal wing and Springbok Athlete Pierre Spies. FC RECORD: 177-40-0-0-0-200. RECORD IN 2013: (SA, Bulls) 16-1-0-0-0-5.
Spring, Shane Michael (Dale College) b 25/03/1988, King Williams Town. 1.86m. 94kg. Flank. FC DEBUT: 2011. PROV CAREER: Bulldogs 2011-13 42-7-0-0-0-35. FC RECORD: 42-7-0-0-0-35. RECORD IN 2013: (Bulldogs) 11-1-0-0-0-5.
Stander, Brynard (Westville Boys HS) b 27/04/1990, Durban. 1.9m. 97kg. Flanker. FC DEBUT: 2012. PROV CAREER: KZN 2012-13

A-Z OF FIRST-CLASS PLAYERS IN 2013

8-1-0-0-0-5. Sharks XV 2012-13 16-5-0-0-0-25. FC RECORD: 24-6-0-0-0-30. RECORD IN 2013: (KZN, Sharks XV) 12-3-0-0-0-15.
Stander, Jan Hendrik (Jannie) (Monument HS, Krugersdorp) b 21/04/1993, Phalaborwa. 1.96m. 107kg. Lock. FC DEBUT: 2013. PROV CAREER: Young Lions 2013 3-0-0-0-0-0. REP HONOURS: SA U20 2013 no appearances. FC RECORD: 3-0-0-0-0-0. RECORD IN 2013: (SA U20, Young Lions) 3-0-0-0-0-0.
Stander, Johannes Hendrik (Janneman) (Oakdale Agric. HS) b 08/09/1993, George. 1.88m. 94kg. Flank. FC DEBUT: 2013. PROV CAREER: Young Lions 2013 1-0-0-0-0-0. FC RECORD: 1-0-0-0-0-0. RECORD IN 2013: (Young Lions) 1-0-0-0-0-0.
Steenkamp, Carel Gert (Callie) (Boland Agric HS) b 09/06/1982, Somerset West. 1.82m. 137kg. Prop. FC DEBUT: 2011. PROV CAREER: Boland 2011 & 13 6-0-0-0-0-0. FC RECORD: 6-0-0-0-0-0. RECORD IN 2013: (Boland) 1-0-0-0-0-0.
Steenkamp, Cornelius Jacobus (Corné) (Ermelo HS) b 20/02/82, Ermelo. 1.80m. 94kg. Flank. FC DEBUT: 2005. PROV CAREER: Pumas 2005-11 & 13 141-28-0-0-0-140. FC RECORD: 141-28-0-0-0-140. RECORD IN 2013: (Pumas) 22-5-0-0-0-25.
Steenkamp, Gurthrö Garth (Paarl Boys HS & UFS) b 12/06/81, Paarl. 1.89m. 122kg. Prop. FC DEBUT: 2001. PROV CAREER: Cheetahs 2002-04 42-2-0-0-0-10. Blue Bulls 2005 & 08-10 24-5-0-0-0-25. SUPERRUGBY: Cats 2004 10-1-0-0-0-5. Bulls 2005, 07-11 60-1-0-0-0-5. REP HONOURS: SA Tests: 2004-05, 07-13 49-6-0-0-0-30. Tour: 2007, 09 2-0-0-0-0-0. Total: 51-6-0-0-0-30. SA U21s 2001-02 8-1-0-0-0-5; CW WP 1998-99. FC RECORD: 195-16-0-0-0-80. RECORD IN 2013: (SA) 9-0-0-0-0-0.
Steenkamp, Jabez Wilhelmus Arnoldus (Wilhelm) (Paarl Boys HS) b 07/02/85, Calvinia. 2.00m. 104kg. Lock. FC DEBUT: 2006. PROV CAREER: Blue Bulls 2006-10 & 12-13 87-5-0-0-0-25. Cheetahs 2011 8-1-0-0-0-5. SUPERRUGBY: Bulls 2008-09 & 12-13 36-0-0-0-0-0. Sharks 2010 5-0-0-0-0-0. Cheetahs 2011 13-1-0-0-0-5. REP HONOURS: Emerging Springboks 2007, 09 4-0-0-0-0-0. SA U21 2006 5-2-0-0-0-10. Misc. info: Brother of De Kock Steenkamp. FC RECORD: 158-9-0-0-0-45. RECORD IN 2013: (Bulls, Blue Bulls) 13-0-0-0-0-0.
Steenkamp, Michiel de Kock (Paarl Boys HS & Stellenbosch Univ.) b 16/02/87, Calvinia. 1.97m. 106kg. Lock. FC DEBUT: 2009. PROV CAREER: WP 2009-13 62-1-0-0-0-5. SUPERRUGBY: Stormers 2010-13 47-0-0-0-0-0. Misc. info: Brother of Wilhelm Steenkamp. FC RECORD: 109-1-0-0-0-5. RECORD IN 2013: (Stormers, WP) 25-0-0-0-0-0.
Steenkamp, Ruan (Monument HS, Krugersdorp) b 02/02/1993, Krugersdorp. 1.82m. 92kg. Eighthman. FC DEBUT: 2013. REP HONOURS: SA U20 2013 5-2-0-0-0-10. FC RECORD: 5-2-0-0-0-10. RECORD IN 2013: (SA U20) 5-2-0-0-0-10.
Stegmann, Gideon Johannes (Deon) (Grey College, Bloemfontein) b 22/03/86, Cradock. 1.81m. 99kg. Flank. FC DEBUT: 2007. PROV CAREER: Blue Bulls 2007-12 57-8-0-0-0-40. SUPERRUGBY: Bulls 2008-13 75-5-0-0-0-25. REP HONOURS: SA 2010-11 Tests: 6-0-0-0-0-0. FC RECORD: 138-13-0-0-0-65. RECORD IN 2013: (Bulls) 15-4-0-0-0-20.
Stemmet, Jean (Stellenbosch Univ.) b 06/06/86. 1.85m. 92kg. FC DEBUT: 2009. PROV CAREER: Sharks XV 2010 9-3-0-0-0-15. Griquas 2010-13 45-15-0-0-0-75. REP HONOURS: SA Students 2009 1-0-0-0-0-0. FC RECORD: 55-18-0-0-0-90. RECORD IN 2013: (Griquas) 15-3-0-0-0-15.
Stemmet, Pieter Franz (Paul Roos Gymnasium) b 18/02/1992, Paarl. 1.84m. 115kg. Prop. FC DEBUT: 2012. PROV CAREER: WP 2012 1-1-0-0-0-5. EP Kings 2013 1-0-0-0-0-0. FC RECORD: 2-1-0-0-0-5. RECORD IN 2013: (EP Kings) 1-0-0-0-0-0.

Stevens, Kevin Bruce (Grey College, Bloemfontein) b 30/01/87, Virginia. 1.86m. 112kg. FC DEBUT: 2009. PROV CAREER: Cheetahs 2007 & 2009 6-0-0-0-0-0. Griffons 2009-13 72-3-0-0-0-15. Griquas 2011 1-0-0-0-0-0. FC RECORD: 79-3-0-0-0-15. RECORD IN 2013: (Griffons) 15-0-0-0-0-0.
Stevens, Wayne (Grey College, Bloemfontein) b 17/05/88. 1.85m. 86kg. Centre. FC DEBUT: 2008. PROV CAREER: Cheetahs 2009-10 10-1-0-0-0-5. EP Kings 2010-13 56-13-0-0-0-65. REP HONOURS: SA Students 2008 1-0-0-0-0-0. SA Kings 2011 3-0-0-0-0-0. SA Barbarians 2012 1-0-0-0-0-0. FC RECORD: 71-14-0-0-0-70. RECORD IN 2013: (EP Kings) 21-4-0-0-0-20.
Steyl, Heinrich Diederick (Boland Agric & US) b 06/07/1990, Belville. 1.80m. 82kg. Fullback. FC DEBUT: 2011. PROV CAREER: WP 2011 2-0-0-0-0-0. Blue Bulls 2013 2-0-0-0-0-0. FC RECORD: 4-0-0-0-0-0. RECORD IN 2013: (Blue Bulls) 2-0-0-0-0-0.
Steyn, Dauw Petrus Jacobus (Elspark HS & UJ) b 26/05/1988, Johannesburg. 1.78m. 98kg. Flyhalf. FC DEBUT: 2011. PROV CAREER: Leopards 2011 5-1-3-6-0-29. Valke 2013 3-0-0-0-0-0. FC RECORD: 8-1-3-6-0-29. RECORD IN 2013: (Valke) 3-0-0-0-0-0.
Steyn, Dawie (Affies, Pretoria) b 05/01/84, Pretoria. 1.89m. 124kg. Prop. FC DEBUT: 2008. PROV CAREER: Pumas 2008-11 78-3-0-0-0-15. Blue Bulls 2012-13 15-0-0-0-0-0. SUPERRUGBY: Bulls 2012 2-0-0-0-0-0. FC RECORD: 95-3-0-0-0-15. RECORD IN 2013: (Bulls, Blue Bulls) 6-0-0-0-0-0.
Steyn, Francois Philippus Lodewyk (Frans) (Grey College, Bloemfontein) b 14/05/87, Aliwal North. 1.91m. 110kg. Utility back. FC DEBUT: 2006. PROV CAREER: KZN 2006 & 08 & 13 20-4-12-6-1-65. SUPERRUGBY: Sharks 2007-09 & 12-13 50-4-7-10-7-85. REP HONOURS: SA 2006-12 Tests: 53-10-5-21-3-132. Tour: 2-0-3-1-0-9. Total: 55-10-8-22-3-141. SA U19 2005-06. British Barbarians 2008 1-0-0-0-0-0. MISC INFO: YPoY 2007. U19 PoY 2006. YPOY Nominee 2009. IRB POY Nominee 2009. FC RECORD: 126-18-27-38-11-291. RECORD IN 2013: (Sharks, KZN) 12-0-0-0-0-0.
Steyn, Morné (Sand du Plessis HS, Bloemfontein) b 11/07/84, Bellville. 1.84m. 91kg. Flyhalf. FC DEBUT: 2003. PROV CAREER: Blue Bulls 2003-10 & 12 95-26-180-106-11-841. SUPERRUGBY: Bulls 2005-13 123-13-242-275-25-1449. REP HONOURS: SA 2009-13 Tests: 54-8-88-132-8-636. SA 'A' 2004 1-0-1-0-0-2. SA U21 2005 5-3-17-7-1-73. British Barbs. 2009 1-0-1-0-3. CW Free State 2001-2002. MISC INFO: YPoY nominee 2005. Holds SA record for most penalty goals by a player in a test (8 vs. New Zealand in 2009). Holds SA record for most penalty goals in a season (40 in 2010). Holds SA record for most test matches as a flyhalf (52, also one at fullback and one at centre). Holds Bulls Super record for most cons in a season (38) and a career (242). Holds Bulls record for most penalties in a season (57) and a career (275). Holds Bulls record for most drop goals in a match (4), in a season (11) and a career (25). Holds Bulls and SA record for most points in a Super career (1449). SA S14 POY 2009. POY Nominee 2009. FC RECORD: 279-50-528-521-45-3004. RECORD IN 2013: (SA, Bulls) 29-3-61-86-1-398.
Steyn, Nicolaas Phillipus Jacobus (Nicky) (Welkom Gymnasium) b 02/08/85, Kroonstad. 1.90m. 101kg. Loose Forward. FC DEBUT: 2006. PROV CAREER: Cheetahs 2006-08 19-12-0-0-0-60. Griffons 2008-13 88-38-0-0-0-190. REP HONOURS: SA Barbarians 2012 1-0-0-0-0-0. FC RECORD: 108-50-0-0-0-250. RECORD IN 2013: (Griffons) 13-5-0-0-0-25.
Stighling, Jade Kyle (Hans Moore HS) b 27/05/1993, Johannesburg. 1.83m. 85kg. Centre. FC DEBUT: 2013. PROV CAREER: Blue Bulls 2013 1-0-0-0-0-0. FC RECORD: 1-0-0-0-0-0. RECORD IN 2013:

A-Z OF FIRST-CLASS PLAYERS IN 2013

(Blue Bulls) 1-0-0-0-0-0.

Strauss, Andries Jacobus (Grey College, Bloemfontein) b 05/03/84, Pretoria. 1.87m. 90kg. Centre. FC DEBUT: 2004. PROV CAREER: Cheetahs 2004-05 & 2011-12 26-6-0-0-0-30. KZN 2006-10 55-6-3-0-0-36. Sharks XV 2006-10 22-4-4-2-0-34. Sharks Inv XV 2007,09-10 3-2-0-0-0-10. SUPERRUGBY: Sharks 2006 & 08-10 22-1-0-0-0-5. Cheetahs 2011-12 18-3-0-0-0-15. Southern Kings 2013 14-0-0-0-0-0. REP HONOURS: SA 2010 Tour: 1-0-0-0-0-0. SA Sevens 2007. SA U21 2004 2-0-0-0-0-0. MISC INFO: Brother of Cheetahs hooker Richardt Strauss and cousin of Cheetahs hooker Adriaan. FC RECORD: 163-22-7-2-0-130. RECORD IN 2013: (Southern Kings) 14-0-0-0-0-0.

Strauss, Jan Adriaan (Grey College, Bloemfontein) b 18/11/85, Bloemfontein. 1.84m. 114kg. Hooker. FC DEBUT: 2005. PROV CAREER: Blue Bulls 2005-06 22-3-0-0-0-15. Cheetahs 2007-13 56-9-0-0-0-45. SUPERRUGBY: Bulls 2006 8-0-0-0-0-0. Cheetahs 2007-13 81-8-0-0-0-40. REP HONOURS: SA 2008-10 & 12-13 Tests: 33-5-0-0-0-25. Tour: 2-0-0-0-0-0. Total: 35-5-0-0-0-25. British Barbarians 2011 1-0-0-0-0. SA U21 2005-06 8-2-0-0-0-10. SA U19 2004. SA Schools 2003. CW Free State 2003. MISC INFO: Holds Cheetahs Super rugby record for most matches in a career (81). Cousin of Andries (SA 2010) and Richardt Strauss (Ireland 2012). SR PoY 2013. FC RECORD: 211-27-0-0-0-135. RECORD IN 2013: (SA, Cheetahs S15, Cheetahs) 31-4-0-0-0-20.

Strydom, Louis Isias (Welkom THS) b 21/10/80, Welkom. 1.78m. 72kg. Flyhalf. FC DEBUT: 2001. PROV CAREER: Griffons 2001-03 & 13 33-5-45-59-1-295. Blue Bulls 2003-04 23-3-59-23-0-202. Valke 2005-06 42-3-70-83-6-422. Lions 2007-08 24-1-20-23-2-120. Lions XV 2007-08 2-1-5-0-0-15. Cheetahs 2009-11 44-1-81-68-1-374. EP Kings 2011 12-1-23-18-1-108. SUPERRUGBY: Lions 2007-08 12-0-4-18-0-62. Cheetahs 2010 1-0-1-0-0-2. REP HONOURS: SA Kings 2011 3-1-5-10-0-45. FC RECORD: 196-16-313-302-11-1645. RECORD IN 2013: (Griffons) 7-0-20-14-1-85.

Strydom, Willem Johannes (WJ). (Affies, Pretoria) b 26/11/1993, Vereeniging. 1.73m. 70kg. Fullback. REP HONOURS: SA Sevens 2013. RECORD IN 2013: (SA Sevens).

Swanepoel, Andries Ebenaezer (Dries) (Grey College, Bloemfontein) b 19/02/1993, Delareyville. 1.84m. 92kg. Centre. FC DEBUT: 2013. PROV CAREER: Blue Bulls 2013 6-6-0-0-0-30. REP HONOURS: SA U20 2013 4-1-0-0-0-5. FC RECORD: 10-7-0-0-0-3. RECPORD IN 2013: (Blue Bulls, SA U20) 10-7-0-0-0-35.

Swart, Henro-Pierre (HP) (Framesby HS & NWU) b 17/03/1989, Port Elizabeth. 1.89m. 108kg. Eightman. FC DEBUT: 2012. PROV CAREER: Leopards 2012-13 13-2-0-0-0-10. Leopard XV 2013 4-1-0-0-5. FC RECORD: 17-3-0-0-0-15. RECORD IN 2013: (Leopards, Leopard XV) 13-2-0-0-0-10.

Swart, Jacobus Ockert (Jaco) b 11/07/1979. Eightman. FC DEBUT: 2013. PROV CAREER: Limpopo 2013 6-0-0-0-0-0. FC RECORD: 6-0-0-0-0-0. RECORD IN 2013: (Limpopo) 6-0-0-0-0-0.

Swart, Malherbe (Volkskool) b 27/03/1991, Klerksdorp. 1.79m. 68kg. Scrumhalf. FC DEBUT: 2013. PROV CAREER: Leopard XV 2013 3-1-0-0-0-5. FC RECORD: 3-1-0-0-0-5. RECORD IN 2013: (Leopard XV) 3-1-0-0-0-5.

Swiel, Timothy Gregory (Bishops College) b 04/06/1993, Taunton. 1.80m. 85kg. Fullback. FC DEBUT: 2013. PROV CAREER: WP 2013 9-2-3-0-1-19. FC RECORD: 9-2-3-0-1-19. RECORD IN 2013: (WP) 9-2-3-0-1-19.

Sykes, Steven Robert (Marlow HS) b 05/08/84, Middelburg, Cape. 1.97m. 106kg. Lock. FC DEBUT: 2005. PROV CAREER: KZN 2005-10 & 12 88-5-0-0-0-25. Sharks XV 2005-08 21-0-0-0-0-0. EP Kings 2013 6-3-0-0-0-15. SUPERRUGBY: Sharks 2007-12 69-9-0-0-0-45. Southern Kings 2013 13-1-0-0-0-5. P/R 2013 2-1-0-0-0-5. REP HONOURS: Emerging Springboks 2009 1-0-0-0-0-0. FC RECORD: 200-19-0-0-0-95. RECORD IN 2013: (Southern Kings, EP Kings) 21-5-0-0-0-25.

T

Tack, Bouke Marnus (Volkskool, Potchefstroom) b 25/05/1993, Magaliesburg. 1.94m. 100kg. Centre. FC DEBUT: 2013. PROV CAREER: Leopards 2013 1-0-0-0-0-0. FC RECORD: 1-0-0-0-0-0. RECORD IN 2013: (Leopards) 1-0-0-0-0-0.

Taljaard, Matthew (Hudson Park HS, East London) b 08/09/1985. Hooker. FC DEBUT: 2008. PROV CAREER: Bulldogs 2008-13 67-8-0-0-0-40. FC RECORD: 67-8-0-0-0-40. RECORD IN 2013: (Bulldogs) 5-1-0-0-0-5.

Taljard, Jeffrey John (Hudson Park HS, East London) b 22/04/87, East London. 1.81m. 90kg. Utility back. FC DEBUT: 2008. PROV CAREER: Bulldogs 2008-10 33-6-23-28-0-160. E/Cape XV 2008 2-0-0-0-0-0. Eagles 2011-13 51-10-19-11-0-121. FC RECORD: 86-16-42-39-0-281. RECORD IN 2013: (Eagles) 18-2-19-11-0-81.

Taute, Jacob Johannes (Jaco) (Monument HS, Krugersdorp) b 21/03/91, Springs. 1.87m. 95kg. Fullback. FC DEBUT: 2009. PROV CAREER: Lions 2009-12 31-13-0-1-0-68. Young Lions 2010 3-0-2-0-0-4. SUPERRUGBY: Lions 2010-12 31-9-0-2-0-51. Stormers 2013 4-0-0-0-0-0. REP HONOURS: SA 2012 Tests: 3-0-0-0-0-0. SAU20 2010-11 7-4-0-0-0-20. MISC INFO: YPoY nominee 2011. FC RECORD: 79-26-2-3-0-143. RECORD IN 2013 (Stormers) 4-0-0-0-0-0.

Tecklenburg, Warwick John (Uplands College) b 22/01/1987, Nelspruit. 1.88m. 102kg. Flank. FC DEBUT: 2011. PROV CAREER: Blue Bulls 2011-12 22-4-0-0-0-20. Lions 2013 11-1-0-0-0-5. Young Lions 2013 7-1-0-0-0-5. SUPERRUGBY: Lions P/R 2013 2-0-0-0-0-0. FC RECORD: 42-6-0-0-0-30. RECORD IN 2013: (Lions S15, Lions, Young Lions) 20-2-0-0-0-10.

Temperman, Emile Nicolaas George (Nelspruit HS & UP) b 05/12/1991, Nylstroom. 1.73m. 81kg. Scrumhalf. FC DEBUT: 2013. PROV CAREER: Blue Bulls 2013 1-0-0-0-0-0. FC RECORD: 1-0-0-0-0-0. RECORD IN 2013: (Blue Bulls) 1-0-0-0-0-0.

Terblanche, De-Jay (Knysna HS) b 25/06/85, Knysna. 1.89m. 124kg. Prop. FC DEBUT: 2008. PROV CAREER: Pumas 2008-13 103-6-0-0-0-30. FC RECORD: 103-6-0-0-0-30. RECORD IN 2013: (Pumas) 27-3-0-0-0-15.

Thomas, Jason Neil (Muir College) b 03/08/1992, Uitenhage. 1.84m. 103kg. Hooker. FC DEBUT: 2012. PROV CAREER: Blue Bulls 2013 1-0-0-0-0-0. REP HONOURS: SA U20 2012 3-0-0-0-0-0. FC RECORD: 4-0-0-0-0-0. RECORD IN 2013: (Blue Bulls) 1-0-0-0-0-0.

Tobias, Sidney (Paul Roos Gymnasium) b 20/03/1989, Caledon. 1.75m. 93kg. Hooker. FC DEBUT: 2010. PROV CAREER: WP 2010-12 22-2-0-0-0-10. Eagles 2012 13-0-0-0-0-0. Blue Bulls 2013 1-0-0-0-0-0. MISC INFO: Son of former Springbok Errol Tobias. FC RECORD: 36-2-0-0-0-10. RECORD IN 2013: (Blue Bulls) 1-0-0-0-0-0.

Tom, Siphosethu (Grey College, Bloemfontein) b 12/02/1992, Port Elizabeth. 1.74m. 85kg. Wing. FC DEBUT: 2012. PROV CAREER: Free State XV 2012-13 6-2-0-0-0-10. FC RECORD: 6-2-0-0-0-10. RECORD IN 2013: (Free State XV) 5-1-0-0-0-5.

Tonga, Nomani (Tonga HS) b 16/05/83, Vava'u. 108kg. Lock. SA FC DEBUT: 2008. PROV CAREER: Bulldogs 2008-13 67-5-0-0-0-25. E/Cape XV 2008 2-0-0-0-0-0. SA FC RECORD: 69-5-0-0-0-25. RECORD IN 2013: (Bulldogs) 11-0-0-0-0-0.

Tossel, George de la Rey (Middelburg THS & NWU) b 05/03/1988, Pretoria. 1.93m. 105kg. Fullback. FC DEBUT: 2011. PROV CAREER: Leopards 2011-13 31-9-2-2-0-55. Leopard XV 2013 7-0-0-0-0-

A-Z OF FIRST-CLASS PLAYERS IN 2013

0. FC RECORD: 38-9-2-2-0-55. RECORD IN 2013: (Leopards, Leopard XV) 21-4-0-0-0-20.
Tredoux, Francois Jakobus (Waterkloof HS, Pretoria) b 12/02/1993, Pretoria. 1.80m. 81kg. Flyhalf. FC DEBUT: 2013. PROV CAREER: Blue Bulls 2013 1-0-0-0-0-0. FC RECORD: 1-0-0-0-0-0. RECORD IN 2013: (Blue Bulls) 1-0-0-0-0-0.
Truter, Jan Andries (Vredendal HS) b 29/05/1991, Vredendal. 1.83m. 87kg. Scrumhalf. FC DEBUT: 2013. PROV CAREER: Boland 2013 2-0-0-0-0-0. FC RECORD: 2-0-0-0-0-0. RECORD IN 2013: (Boland) 2-0-0-0-0-0.
Trytsman, Albert Meyer (Brandwag HS) b 05/11/1987, Knysna. 1.86m. 95kg. Centre. FC DEBUT: 2013. PROV CAREER: Boland 2013 3-1-0-0-0-5. FC RECORD: 3-1-0-0-0-5. RECORD IN 2013: (Boland) 3-1-0-0-0-5.
Tshibidi, Claude Kalombo (Potchefstroom Boys HS) b 31/03/1993, Tembisa. 1.90m. 92kg. Flank. FC debut: 2013. PROV CAREER: Young Lions 2013 2-0-0-0-0-0. FC RECORD: 2-0-0-0-0-0. RECORD IN 2013: (Young Lions) 2-0-0-0-0-0.

U

Ulengo, Jamba Isaac (Jim Fouche HS, Bloemfontein & UFS) b 07/01/1990, Vryburg. 1.85m. 88kg. Wing. FC DEBUT: 2012. PROV CAREER: Free State XV 2012 1-0-0-0-0-0. SA Sevens 2012-13. FC RECORD: 1-0-0-0-0-0. RECORD IN 2013: (SA Sevens).
Ungerer, Stefan (Maritzburg College) b 23/11/1993, Pietermaritzburg. 1.85m. 88kg. Scrumhalf. FC DEBUT: 2013. PROV CAREER: Sharks XV 2013 4-0-0-0-0-0. REP HONOURS: SA U20 2013 4-1-0-0-0-5. FC RECORD: 8-1-0-0-0-5. RECORD IN 2013: (SA U20, Sharks XV) 8-1-0-0-0-5.
Uys, BG (Paarl Gymnasium) b 20/06/88. 1.90m. 113kg. Prop. FC DEBUT: 2008. PROV CAREER: Leopards 2010-13 61-8-0-0-0-40. Leopard XV 2013 5-1-0-0-0-5. REP HONOURS: SA Students 2008-09 3-1-0-0-0-5. SA Barbarians 2012 1-0-0-0-0-0. FC RECORD: 70-10-0-0-0-50. RECORD IN 2013: (Leopards, Leopard XV) 19-4-0-0-0-20.
Uys, Francois Jacobus (Dr EG Jansen) b 12/03/86, Springs. 1.91m. 103kg. Flank. FC DEBUT: 2006. PROV CAREER: Lions 2006-08 24-5-0-0-0-25. Cheetahs 2009-13 58-7-0-0-0-35. Griffons 2008 & 10 & 12 14-1-0-0-0-5. Lions XV 2008 1-0-0-0-0-0. Emerging Cheetahs 2011 1-0-0-0-0-0. Free State XV 2012 5-1-0-0-0-5. SUPERRUGBY: Cheetahs 2009 & 2011-13 33-0-0-0-0-0. REP HONOURS: SA U19 2005. FC RECORD: 136-14-0-0-0-70. RECORD IN 2013: (Cheetahs S15, Cheetahs) 18-0-0-0-0-0.
Uys, Johannes Lodewicus (Linden HS & NWU) b 11/01/1991. Johannesburg. 1.95m. 95kg. Lock. FC DEBUT: 2012. PROV CAREER: Leopards 2012 2-0-0-0-0-0. Boland 2013 7-0-0-0-0-0. FC RECORD: 9-0-0-0-0-0. RECORD IN 2013: (Boland) 7-0-0-0-0-0.
Uys, Wiehan. Lock. FC DEBUT: 2013. PROV CAREER: Limpopo 2013 4-0-0-0-0-0. FC RECORD: 4-0-0-0-0-0. RECORD IN 2013: (Limpopo) 4-0-0-0-0-0.

V

Van Aswegen, Gary Jacques (Standerton HS & Univ. Stellenbosch) b 18/02/1990, Pretoria. 1.76m. 83kg. Flyhalf. FC DEBUT: 2010. PROV CAREER: WP 2010-13 13-0-16-16-2-86. SUPERRUGBY: Stormers 2011-13 15-0-3-7-1-30. FC RECORD: 28-0-19-23-3-116. RECORD IN 2013: (Stormers, WP) 16-0-11-12-2-64.
Van den Heever, Gerhard Jacobus (Affies, Pretoria) b 13/04/89, Bloemfontein. 1.90m. 93kg. Wing. FC DEBUT: 2009. PROV CAREER: Blue Bulls 2009-11 41-19-0-0-0-95. WP 2012-13 24-3-0-0-0-15. SUPERRUGBY: Bulls 2009-11 31-12-0-0-0-60. Stormers 2012-13 26-2-0-0-0-10. REP HONOURS: SAU20 2009 4-3-0-0-0-15. FC RECORD: 126-39-0-0-0-195. RECORD IN 2013 (Stormers, WP) 23-2-0-0-0-10.
Van der Berg, Arrie (Ben Viljoen HS, Tzaneen & UP) b 10/02/1993, Polokwane. 1.92m. 94kg. Flank. FC DEBUT: 2013. PROV CAREER: Limpopo 2013 7-0-0-0-0-0. FC RECORD: 7-0-0-0-0-0. RECORD IN 2013: (Limpopo) 7-0-0-0-0-0.
Van der Heever, Martin Jacobus (Jim Fouche HS, Bloemfontein & UFS) b 20/11/1990, Bloemfontein. 1.86m. 115kg. FC DEBUT: 2013. PROV CAREER: Griffons 2013 1-0-0-0-0-0. FC RECORD: 1-0-0-0-0-0. RECORD IN 2013: (Griffons) 1-0-0-0-0-0.
Van der Linde, Christoffel Johannes (CJ) (Grey College, Bloemfontein) b 27/08/80, Welkom. 1.90m. 123kg. Prop. FC DEBUT: 2000. PROV CAREER: Cheetahs 2002-05 & 10 49-6-0-0-0-30. Lions 2011-13 18-0-0-0-0-0. SUPERRUGBY: Cats 2004-05 19-1-0-0-0-5. Cheetahs 2006-08 19-2-0-0-0-10. Stormers 2011 11-0-0-0-0-0. Lions 2012 7-0-0-0-0-0. REP HONOURS: SA 2002 & 2004-12 Tests: 75-4-0-0-0-20. Tour: 2006,07,09,10 5-0-0-0-0-0. Total: 78-4-0-0-0-20. SA U21s 2000-01 8-0-0-0-0-0; SA U19s 1999; SA Schools 1998; CW Cheetahs 1998. FC RECORD: 211-13-0-0-0-65. RECORD IN 2013: (Lions) 9-0-0-0-0-0.
Van der Merwe, Armand (Outeniqua HS, George & NWU) b 17/06/1991, Vanderbijlpark. 1.78m 106kg. Hooker. FC DEBUT: 2013. PROV CAREER: Leopards 2013 9-0-0-0-0-0. Leopard XV 2013 6-2-0-0-0-10. FC RECORD: 15-2-0-0-0-10. RECORD IN 2013: (Leopards, Leopard XV) 15-2-0-0-0-10.
Van der Merwe, Daniel Joubert (Wilgerivier HS, Frankfort) b 24/01/1989, Frankfort. 1.83m. 119kg. Prop. FC DEBUT: 2010. PROV CAREER:Young Lions 2010 1-0-0-0-0-0. Griffons 2012-13 18-2-0-0-0-10. FC RECORD: 19-2-0-0-0-10. RECORD IN 2013: (Griffons) 15-0-0-0-0-0.
Van der Merwe, Franco (Hartswater HS) b 15/03/83, Paarl. 1.98m. 116kg. Lock/Flank. FC DEBUT: 2004. PROV CAREER: Leopards 2004-06 58-8-0-0-0-40. Lions 2006-13 100-10-0-0-0-50. Lions XV 2007-08 2-0-0-0-0-0. Young Lions 2009 2-0-0-0-0-0. SUPERRUGBY: Lions 2007-12 75-7-0-0-0-35. Lions P/R 2013 2-0-0-0-0-0. Sharks 2013 16-0-0-0-0-0. REP HONOURS: SA 2013 Tests: 1-0-0-0-0-0. Emerging Springboks 2009 1-0-0-0-0-0. SA U21 2004 3-0-0-0-0-0. FC RECORD: 260-25-0-0-0-125. RECORD IN 2013: (SA, Sharks, Lions S15, Lions) 27-1-0-0-0-5.
Van der Merwe, Frans Jacobus (Franco) (Grey College, Bloemfontein & UFS) b 16/12/1989, Bloemfontein. 1.94m. 118kg. Prop. FC DEBUT: 2013. PROV CAREER: Free State XV 2013 2-0-0-0-0-0. FC RECORD: 2-0-0-0-0-0. RECORD IN 2013: (Free State XV) 2-0-0-0-0-0.
Van der Merwe, Marcel (Paarl Boys HS) b 24/10/1990, Welkom. 1.89m. 121kg. Prop. FC DEBUT: 2011. PROV CAREER: Cheetahs 2011-12 32-13-0-0-0-65. Emerging Cheetahs 2011 1-0-0-0-0-0. Free State XV 2012 6-4-0-0-0-20. Blue Bulls 2013 8-1-0-0-0-5. SUPERRUGBY: Cheetahs 2012 3-0-0-0-0-0. REP HONOURS: SAU20 2010 5-2-0-0-0-10. FC RECORD: 55-20-0-0-0-100. RECORD IN 2013: (Blue Bulls) 8-1-0-0-0-5.
Van der Merwe, Phillip Rudolph (Flip) (Grey College, Bloemfontein) b 03/06/85, Potchefstroom. 1.96m. 120kg. Lock. FC DEBUT: 2006. PROV CAREER: Cheetahs 2006-09 37-2-0-0-0-10. Griffons 2007 1-0-0-0-0-0. Blue Bulls 2009-12 36-5-0-0-0-25. SUPERRUGBY: Cheetahs 2007-09 6-1-0-0-0-5. Bulls 2010-13 57-2-0-0-0-10. REP HONOURS: SA 2010-13 Tests: 34-1-0-0-0-5. Tour: 1-0-0-0-0-0. Total: 35-1-0-0-0-5. SA Students 2007 1-0-0-0-0-0. MISC INFO: Son of Springbok Flippie van der Merwe. FC RECORD: 173-11-0-0-0-55. RECORD IN 2013: (SA, Bulls) 26-0-0-0-0-0.
Van der Merwe, Schalk Willem (Duineveld HS, Upington & Grey College) b 04/12/1990, Tzaneen. 1.84m. 104kg. Prop. FC DEBUT: 2011. PROV CAREER: Cheetahs 2011-13 15-2-0-0-0-10. Emerging Cheetahs 2011 1-0-0-0-0-0. Griffons 2013 5-1-0-0-0-5. FC RECORD:

A-Z OF FIRST-CLASS PLAYERS IN 2013

21-3-0-0-0-15. RECORD IN 2013: (Cheetahs, Griffons) 10-3-0-0-0-15.
Van der Merwe, Senan Delin Clint (Pionier HS) b 02/02/1986, Robertson. 1.87m. 82kg. Wing. FC DEBUT: 2012. PROV CAREER: Boland 2012-13 26-6-0-0-0-30. FC RECORD: 26-6-0-0-0-30. RECORD IN 2013: (Boland) 11-3-0-0-0-15.
Van der Merwe, Stephan Gerhardus (Paul Roos Gymnasium & UFS) b 25/02/1992, Cape Town. 1.83m. 88kg. Centre. FC DEBUT: 2011. PROV CAREER: Cheetahs 2011 3-0-0-0-0. Free State XV 2012 3-1-0-0-0-5. Griquas 2013 9-1-0-0-0-5. FC RECORD: 9-1-0-0-0-5. RECORD IN 2013: (Griquas) 3-0-0-0-0-0.
Van der Sluys, Wilhelm (Paarl Boys HS & US) b 14/08/1991, Paarl. 1.98m. 103kg. Lock. FC DEBUT: 2012. PROV CAREER: WP 2012-13 19-0-0-0-0-0. FC RECORD: 19-0-0-0-0-0. RECORD IN 2013: (WP) 5-0-0-0-0-0.
Van der Spuy, Michael George (Grey College, Bloemfontein & US) b 20/02/1991, Bethlehem. 1.80m. 86kg. Flyhalf. FC DEBUT: 2011. PROV CAREER: WP 2011-13 24-5-0-0-0-25. FC RECORD: 24-5-0-0-0-25. RECORD IN 2013: (WP) 13-3-0-0-0-15.
Van der Walt, Andre Jacobus (Marlow Agric HS, Cradock) b 10/07/1989, Middelburg. 1.79m. 82kg. Scrumhalf. FC DEBUT: 2012. PROV CAREER: Free State XV 2012-13 13-0-0-0-0-0. FC RECORD: 13-0-0-0-0-0. RECORD IN 2013: (Free State XV) 6-0-0-0-0-0.
Van der Walt, Andries Petrus (Peet) (Outeniqua HS, George) b 19/09/1991, Kimberley. 1.94m. 103kg. Flank. FC DEBUT: 2013. PROV CAREER: Leopards 2013 12-0-0-0-0-0. Leopard XV 2013 5-0-0-0-0-0. FC RECORD: 17-0-0-0-0-0. RECORD IN 2013: (Leopards, Leopard XV) 17-0-0-0-0-0.
Van der Walt, Christoffel Philippus (Philip) (Adelaide Gymnasium & UOFS) b 14/07/1989, Adelaide. 1.94m. 105kgs. Eightman. FC DEBUT: 2010. PROV CAREER: Cheetahs 2010-13 31-4-0-0-0-20. Griffons 2011 1-1-0-0-0-5. SUPERRUGBY: Cheetahs 2010-13 41-3-0-0-0-15. FC RECORD: 73-8-0-0-0-40. RECORD IN 2013: (Cheetahs S15, Cheetahs) 25-2-0-0-0-10.
Van der Walt, Eduan Raymond (Zwartkop HS, Centurion) b 20/03/87, Pretoria. 1.97m. 103kg. Lock. FC DEBUT: 2008. PROV CAREER: Blue Bulls 2008 2-0-0-0-0-0. Pumas 2008-13 94-10-0-0-0-50. REP HONOURS: SA Barbarians 2012 1-0-0-0-0-0. SA Pres XV 2013 3-1-0-0-0-5. FC RECORD: 100-11-0-0-0-55. RECORD IN 2013: (SA Pres XV, Pumas) 25-4-0-0-0-20.
Van der Walt, Hendrik Bernardus (Nardus) (Affies, Pretoria) b 22/02/1992, Rustenburg. 1.89m. 100kg. Lock. FC DEBUT: 2013. PROV CAREER: Blue Bulls 2013 8-3-0-0-0-15. FC RECORD: 8-3-0-0-0-15. RECORD IN 2013: (Blue Bulls) 8-3-0-0-0-15.
Van der Walt, Petrus Willem (Wimpie) (Nelspruit HS) b 06/01/1989, Brits. 1.87m. 102kg. Flanker. FC DEBUT: 2010. PROV CAREER: WP 2010-11 17-5-0-0-0-25. EP Kings 2012 17-3-0-0-0-15. SUPERRUGBY: Southern Kings 2013 15-6-0-0-0-30. P/R 2013 2-0-0-0-0-0. FC RECORD: 51-14-0-0-0-70. RECORD IN 2013: (Southern Kings) 17-6-0-0-0-30.
Van der Walt, Vian (Florida HS) b 18/11/1992, Springs. 1.68m. 77kg. Scrumhalf. FC DEBUT: 2011. PROV CAREER: Golden Lions XV 2011 1-0-0-0-0-0. Young Lions 2012-13 3-2-0-0-0-10. SUPERRUGBY: Lions P/R 2013 1-0-0-0-0-0. REP HONOURS: SAU20 2012 5-2-0-0-0-10. FC RECORD: 10-4-0-0-0-20. RECORD IN 2013: (Lions S15, Young Lions) 3-2-0-0-0-10.
Van der Westhuizen, Dandre (Affies, Pretoria) b 06/11/1991, Pretoria. 1.86m. 114kg. Prop. FC DEBUT: 2011. PROV CAREER: Blue Bulls 2011 2-0-0-0-0-0. Valke 2012-13 14-0-0-0-0-0. FC RECORD: 16-0-0-0-0-0. RECORD IN 2013: (Valke) 10-0-0-0-0-0.

Van der Westhuizen, Ewald (Voortrekker HS & UJ) b 03/04/1990, Ladysmith. 1.82m. 114kg. Prop. FC DEBUT: 2013. PROV CAREER: Griquas 2013 1-0-0-0-0-0. FC RECORD: 1-0-0-0-0-0. RECORD IN 2013: (Griquas) 1-0-0-0-0-0.
Van der Westhuizen, Zander b 26/02/1987. Centre. FC DEBUT: 2013. PROV CAREER: Young Lions 2013 1-0-0-0-0-0. FC RECORD: 1-0-0-0-0-0. RECORD IN 2013: (Young lions) 1-0-0-0-0-0.
Van der Westhuyzen, Dane Robert (St Andrews College) b 16/08/1992, Queenstown. 1.80m. 95kg. Hooker. FC DEBUT: 2013. PROV CAREER: EP Kings 2013 10-0-0-0-0-0. FC RECORD: 10-0-0-0-0-0. RECORD IN 2013: (EP Kings) 10-0-0-0-0-0.
Van Breda, Scott (Rondebosch Boys HS) b 12/12/1991. Fullback/Wing. FC DEBUT: 2012. PROV CAREER: EP Kings 2012-13 39-8-34-45-0-243. SUPERRUGBY: Southern Kings 2013 1-0-0-0-0-0. P/R 2013 1-1-2-3-0-18. FC RECORD: 41-9-36-48-0-261. RECORD IN 2013: (Southern Kings, EP Kings) 21-4-36-42-0-218.
Van Coller, Drew (Waterkloof HS, Pretoria) b 09/02/87, Johannesburg. 1.87m. 116kg. Prop. FC DEBUT: 2008. PROV CAREER: Cheetahs 2008 8-0-0-0-0-0. Griquas 2009 2-0-0-0-0-0. Pumas 2012-13 22-2-0-0-0-10. FC RECORD: 32-2-0-0-0-10. RECORD IN 2013: (Pumas) 10-1-0-0-0-5.
Van Dyk, Hans Jacob (Middelburg THS) b 29/04/82, Bethal. 1.75m. 102kg. Hooker. FC DEBUT: 2005. PROV CAREER: Leopards 2005-06 43-3-0-0-0-15. Griquas 2007-08 37-6-0-0-0-30. Lions 2009 15-1-0-0-0-5. Young Lions 2010 5-1-0-0-0-5. Pumas 2010-11 13-1-0-0-0-5. Eagles 2012-13 22-0-0-0-0-0. Boland 2012 6-0-0-0-0-0. SUPERRUGBY: Cheetahs 2007 6-0-0-0-0-0. Lions 2009-10 15-0-0-0-0-0. MISC INFO: Brother of BW van Dyk. FC RECORD: 162-12-0-0-0-60. RECORD IN 2013: (Eagles) 12-0-0-0-0-0.
Van Dyk, Nicolaas Johannes (Paarl Boys HS) b 21/01/1992, Johannesburg. 1.86m. 113kg. Prop. FC DEBUT: 2012. PROV CAREER: Sharks XV 2012-13 10-0-0-0-0-0. REP HONOURS: SAU20 2012 4-0-0-0-0-0. FC RECORD: 14-0-0-0-0-0. RECORD IN 2013: (Sharks XV) 8-0-0-0-0-0.
Van Eeden, Marco-Pieter (Ermelo HS) b 11/04/1989, Ermelo. 1.91m. 104kg. Eightman. FC DEBUT: 2012. PROV CAREER: Pumas 2012 1-0-0-0-0-0. Valke 2013 17-1-0-0-0-5. FC RECORD: 18-1-0-0-0-5. RECORD IN 2013: (Valke) 17-1-0-0-0-5.
Van Greyn, Cornelius Hendrik b 08/11/1985. Flank. FC DEBUT: 2013. PROV CAREER: Limpopo 2013 1-0-0-0-0-0. FC RECORD: 1-0-0-0-0-0. RECORD IN 2013: (Limpopo) 1-0-0-0-0-0.
Van Heerden, Derrick (Strand HS) b 15/02/1988. 1.78m. 103kg. Hooker. FC DEBUT: 2010. PROV CAREER: Griffons 2010-13 61-4-0-0-0-20. FC RECORD: 61-4-0-0-0-20. RECORD IN 2013: (Griffons) 17-1-0-0-0-5.
Van Heerden, Johan Cornelius Bernardus (Grey College, Bloemfontein) b 22/04/1991, Barkly East. 1.8m. 108kg. Hooker. FC DEBUT: 2012. PROV CAREER: Valke 2012-13 9-1-0-0-0-5. FC RECORD: 9-1-0-0-0-5. RECORD IN 2013: (Valke) 5-0-0-0-0-0.
Van Heerden, Pieter Schalk (Waterkloof HS, Pretoria) b 31/01/1992, Thabazimbi. 1.98m. 100kg. Lock. FC DEBUT: 2012. PROV CAREER: Blue Bulls 2012-13 4-0-0-0-0-0. MISC INFO: Son of former Springbok Moaner van Heerden and brother of former Springbok Wikus van Heerden. FC RECORD: 4-0-0-0-0-0. RECORD IN 2013: (Blue Bulls) 3-0-0-0-0-0.
Van Heerden, Wayne (Brandwag HS, Uitenhage) b 29/03/79, Graaff-Reinet. 1.97m. 95kg. Flank. FC DEBUT: 2000. PROV CAREER: EP Kings 2000-05 & 2011-13 121-22-0-0-0-110. Griquas 2006-08 70-10-0-0-0-50. SUPERRUGBY: Sharks 2002-03 15-1-0-0-0-5. Cheetahs 2009

13-2-0-0-0-10. REP HONOURS: SA 'A' 2001-02 4-0-0-0-0-0; SA Kings 2011 3-0-0-0-0-0. SA Sevens 2001-05 (inc RWC 7s); SA U23s 2001 3-2-0-0-0-10; SA U21s 2000 3-1-0-0-0-5; SA U19s 1998; SA Schools 1997-98; CW Elephants 1997. FC RECORD: 232-38-0-0-0-190. RECORD IN 2013: (EP Kings) 13-0-0-0-0-0.

Van Heese, Werner b 23/02/1992. Centre. FC DEBUT: 2013. PROV CAREER: Limpopo 2013 2-0-0-0-0-0. FC RECORD: 2-0-0-0-0-0. RECORD IN 2013: (Limpopo) 2-0-0-0-0-0.

Van Jaarsveld, Torsten George (Hendrik Verwoerd HS, Pretoria) b 30/06/87. 1.75m. 89kg. Hooker. FC DEBUT: 2008. PROV CAREER: Pumas 2008-12 73-8-0-0-0-40. Free State XV 2013 2-0-0-0-0-0. REP HONOURS: SA Barbarians 2012 1-0-0-0-0-0. FC RECORD: 76-8-0-0-0-40. RECORD IN 2013: (Free State XV) 2-0-0-0-0-0.

Van Niekerk, Johannes Lambrechts (Janru) (Paarl Boys HS) b 05/11/82, Worcester. 1.82m. 110kg. Prop. FC DEBUT: 2006. PROV CAREER: Boland 2006-11 106-5-0-0-0-25. Griquas 2012-13 22-4-0-0-0-20. REP HONOURS: Emerging Springboks 2008 3-0-0-0-0-0. FC RECORD: 131-9-0-0-0-45. RECORD IN 2013: (Griquas) 10-2-0-0-0-10.

Van Niekerk, Marlou Du Plessis (Marlow Agric, Cradock) b 19/05/1993, Douglas. 1.86m. 92kg. Flyhalf. FC DEBUT: 2013. PROV CAREER: EP Kings 2013 6-1-1-0-0-7. FC RECORD: 6-1-1-0-0-7. RECORD IN 2013: (EP Kings) 6-1-1-0-0-7.

Van Niekerk, Rikus (Monument HS, Krugersdorp) b 19/03/1992, Alberton. 1.86m. 95kg. Hooker. FC DEBUT: 2013. PROV CAREER: Young Lions 2013 3-0-0-0-0-0. FC RECORD: 3-0-0-0-0-0. RECORD IN 2013: (Young Lions) 3-0-0-0-0-0.

Van Rensburg, Andries Gideon (Deon) (Potch THS) b 24/01/82, Potchefstroom. 1.78m. 92kg. Centre. FC DEBUT: 2004. PROV CAREER: Leopards 2004-09 92-44-0-0-0-220. Golden Lions 2010-12 27-10-0-0-0-50. Young Lions 2013 6-4-0-0-0-20. SUPERRUGBY: Lions 2009-12 41-3-0-0-0-15. P/R 2013 1-0-0-0-0-0. REP HONOURS: Emerging Springboks 2009 1-0-0-0-0-0. Royal XV 2009 1-0-0-0-0-0. FC RECORD: 169-61-0-0-0-305. RECORD IN 2013: (Lions S15, Young Lions) 7-4-0-0-0-20.

Van Rooyen, Bernard Daniel (Bernie) (Potchefstroom HS) b 28/11/1988, Potchefstroom. 1.75m. 85kg. Flanker. FC DEBUT: 2012. PROV CAREER: Leopards 2012-13 19-0-0-0-0-0. Leopard XV 2013 1-0-0-0-0-0. FC RECORD: 20-0-0-0-0-0. RECORD IN 2013: (Leopards, Leopard XV) 14-0-0-0-0-0.

Van Rooyen, Jacques (Pretoria North HS & UP, TUT) b 24/10/1986, Pretoria. 1.86m. 122kg. Prop. FC DEBUT: 2013. PROV CAREER: Lions 2013 11-2-0-0-0-10. Young Lions 2013 6-0-0-0-0-0. FC RECORD: 17-2-0-0-0-10. RECORD IN 2013: (Lions, Young Lions) 17-2-0-0-0-10.

Van Rooyen, James-Lenn b 29/04/1985. FC DEBUT: 2013. PROV CAREER: Eagles 2013 6-0-0-0-0-0. FC RECORD: 6-0-0-0-0-0. RECORD IN 2013: (Eagles) 6-0-0-0-0-0.

Van Rooyen, Reynier (Rob Ferreira HS) b 25/04/1990, Nelspruit. 1.72m. 74kg. Scrumhalf. FC DEBUT: 2012. PROV CAREER: EP Kings 2012 5-0-0-0-0-0. Pumas 2013 13-1-0-0-0-5. FC RECORD: 18-1-0-0-0-5. RECORD IN 2013: (Pumas) 13-1-0-0-0-5.

Van Schalkwyk, Chrislyn John (Schoonspruit HS) b 12/10/1990, Porterville. 1.8m. 75kg. Wing. FC DEBUT: 2012. PROV CAREER: Bulldogs 2012-13 25-6-0-0-0-30. FC RECORD: 25-6-0-0-0-30. RECORD IN 2013: (Bulldogs) 15-2-0-0-0-10.

Van Schalkwyk, Robert (Voortrekker HS & UOFS) b 25/05/1990, Pietermaritzburg. 1.91m. 98kg. Wing. FC DEBUT: 2010. PROV CAREER: Cheetahs 2010-11 12-4-0-0-0-20. Emerging Cheetahs 2011 1-0-0-1-0-3. Free State XV 2012-13 3-1-0-0-0-5. Griffons 2012 2-0-0-0-0-0. FC RECORD: 18-5-0-1-0-28. RECORD IN 2013: (Free State XV) 1-0-0-0-0-0.

Van Staden, Justin (Merensky HS) b 03/06/1990, Tzaneen. 1.79m. 86kg. Centre. FC DEBUT: 2010. PROV CAREER: Blue Bulls 2010 1-0-0-0-0-0. EP Kings 2012 7-0-6-18-1-66. Eagles 2013 12-1-25-26-2-139. REP HONOURS: SA Univ 2013 1-0-5-0-0-10. FC RECORD: 21-1-36-44-3-215. RECORD IN 2013: (Eagles, SA Univ) 13-1-30-26-2-149.

Van Tonder, Jaco (Outeniqua HS, George) b 07/04/1991, Cape Town. 1.86m. 95kg. Centre. FC DEBUT: 2012. PROV CAREER: Sharks XV 2012-13 8-2-0-0-0-10. KZN 2013 6-0-0-0-0-0. SUPERRUGBY: Sharks 2013 1-0-0-0-0-0. FC RECORD: 15-2-0-0-0-10. RECORD IN 2013: (Sharks, KZN, Sharks XV) 13-2-0-0-0-10.

Van Vuuren, Elric (Despatch HS) b 08/04/85, Port Elizabeth. 1.83m. 95kg. Fullback. FC DEBUT: 2006. PROV CAREER: Elephants 2006 & 08 24-7-0-0-0-35. Bulldogs 2007 10-1-4-3-0-22. Eagles 2011-13 31-14-66-37-0-313. SUPERRUGBY: Southern Kings 2013 2-0-0-0-0-0. FC RECORD: 67-22-70-40-0-370. RECORD IN 2013: (Southern Kings, Eagles) 5-0-3-2-0-12.

Van Wyk, Andrew Justerine Deometrie (Diamantveld HS, Kimberley & NWU) b 04/08/1989, Prieska. 1.77m. 85kg. Wing. FC DEBUT: 2011. PROV CAREER: Leopards 2011-12 8-0-0-0-0-0. Leopard XV 2013 4-0-0-0-0-0. Bulldogs 2013 12-5-0-0-0-25. FC RECORD: 24-5-0-0-0-25. RECORD IN 2013: (Bulldogs, Leopard XV) 16-5-0-0-0-25.

Van Wyk, Coenraad George (Coenie) (Paul Roos Gymnasium) b 08/01/88, Bellville. 1.83m. 80kg. FC DEBUT: 2009. PROV CAREER: WP 2009 5-0-1-0-0-2. Griquas 2010 3-2-7-1-0-27. Pumas 2011-13 64-32-35-20-0-290. REP HONOURS: SA Barbarians 2012 1-0-0-0-0-0. SA Pres XV 2013 3-0-0-0-0-0. FC RECORD: 76-34-43-21-0-319. RECORD IN 2013: (SA Pres XV, Pumas) 27-11-12-0-0-79.

Van Wyk, Damian (Kempton Park HS & UP) b 24/04/1992, Kempton Park. 1.79m. 85kg. Wing. FC DEBUT: 2013. PROV CAREER: Blue Bulls 2013 3-0-0-0-0-0. FC RECORD: 3-0-0-0-0-0. RECORD IN 2013: (Blue Bulls) 3-0-0-0-0-0.

Van Wyk, Francois Daniel (Boland Agric HS & UCT) b 30/07/1991, Belville. 1.89m. 114kg. Prop. FC DEBUT: 2013. PROV CAREER: WP 2013 2-0-0-0-0-0. FC RECORD: 2-0-0-0-0-0. RECORD IN 2013: (WP) 2-0-0-0-0-0.

Van Wyk, Hendrik Jacobus (Hencus) (Nylstroom HS) b 02/03/1992, Nigel. 1.83m. 116kg. Prop. FC DEBUT: 2011. PROV CAREER: Blue Bulls 2011 & 13 5-1-0-0-0-5. SUPERRUGBY: Bulls 2013 1-0-0-0-0-0. FC RECORD: 6-1-0-0-0-5. RECORD IN 2013: (Bulls, Blue Bulls) 5-1-0-0-0-5.

Van Wyk, Jacobus Petrus (Kobus) (Paarl Gymnasium) b 22/01/1992, Nababeep. 1.90m. 94kg. Centre. FC DEBUT: 2012. PROV CAREER: WP 2013 5-3-0-0-0-15. REP HONOURS: SA U20 2012 1-0-0-0-0-0. FC RECORD: 6-3-0-0-0-15. RECORD IN 2013: (WP) 5-3-0-0-0-15.

Van Wyk, Jan Christoffel (JC) (Monument HS, Krugersdorp & UFS) b 29/03/1988, Randfontein. 1.82m. 101kg. Hooker. FC DEBUT: 2012. PROV CAREER: Griffons 2012-13 14-0-0-0-0-0. FC RECORD: 14-0-0-0-0-0. RECORD IN 2013: (Griffons) 9-0-0-0-0-0.

Van Wyk, Russell Steven (Jan Mohr HS & CUT) b 12/08/1990, Tsumeb. 1.80m 83kg. Wing. SA FC DEBUT: 2013. PROV CAREER: Valke 2013 11-1-0-0-0-5. SA FC RECORD: 11-1-0-0-0-5. REP HONOURS: Welwitchias 2010-11. RECORD IN 2013: (Valke) 11-1-0-0-0-5.

Van Wyk, Rynardt Ian (Merensky HS) b 06/03/1991, Rustenburg. 1.88m. 97kg. Prop. FC DEBUT: 2012. PROV CAREER: Bulldogs 2012-13 27-4-0-0-0-20. FC RECORD: 27-4-0-0-0-20. RECORD IN 2013: (Bulldogs) 21-3-0-0-0-15.

Van Wyk, Stephanus Jacobus b 31/01/1987. Scrumhalf. FC DEBUT: 2013. PROV CAREER: Limpopo 2013 6-0-0-0-0-0. FC RECORD: 6-0-0-0-0-0. RECORD IN 2013: (Limpopo) 6-0-0-0-0-0.

A-Z OF FIRST-CLASS PLAYERS IN 2013

Van Zyl, Christopher Machiel (Chris) (Rondebosch HS & US) b 12/07/1986, Cape Town. 1.97m. 112kg. Lock. FC DEBUT: 2013. PROV CAREER: Lions 2013 7-0-0-0-0-0. Young Lions 2013 3-0-0-0-0-0. FC RECORD: 10-0-0-0-0-0. RECORD IN 2013: (Lions, Young Lions) 10-0-0-0-0-0. MISC INFO: Brother of Anton van Zyl.

Van Zyl, Divan (Noord-Kaap HS & UJ) b 14/10/88, Kuruman. 1.81m. 80kg. Flyhalf/Centre. FC DEBUT: 2008. PROV CAREER: Cheetahs 2008-09 11-1-0-0-0-5. Bulldogs 2010 9-0-0-0-0-0. Griquas 2010 6-0-1-0-0-2. REP HONOURS: SA Students 2012 2-1-0-0-0-5. SA Univ 2013 1-0-0-0-0-0. FC RECORD: 29-2-1-0-0-12. RECORD IN 2013: (SA Univ) 1-0-0-0-0-0.

Van Zyl, Kayle Deon (Nico Malan HS & NMMU) b 10/12/1991, Johannesburg. 1.85m. 88kg. Scrumhalf. FC DEBUT: 2013. PROV CAREER: EP Kings 2013 15-3-6-1-0-30. FC RECORD: 15-3-6-1-0-30. RECORD IN 2013: (EP Kings) 15-3-6-1-0-30.

Van Zyl, Ockert Petrus (Ockie) (Fichardt Park HS, Bloemfontein) b 17/08/82, Bloemfontein. 1.97m. 110kg. Flank. FC DEBUT: 2004. PROV CAREER: Griffons 2004-06 & 08-09 51-11-0-0-0-55. Griquas 2007 11-0-0-0-0-0. Cheetahs 2011 1-0-0-0-0-0. Free State XV 2012-13 9-2-0-0-0-10. SUPERRUGBY: Cheetahs 2006 8-0-0-0-0-0. FC RECORD: 80-13-0-0-0-65. RECORD IN 2013: (Free State XV) 2-0-0-0-0-0.

Van Zyl, Petrus Erasmus (Pieter) (Grey College, Bloemfontein & UOFS) b 14/09/1989, Pretoria. 1.74m. 81kg. Scrumhalf. FC DEBUT: 2010. PROV CAREER: Cheetahs 2010-13 31-6-0-0-0-30. Emerging Cheetahs 2011 1-0-0-0-0-0. SUPERRUGBY: Cheetahs 2012-13 32-5-0-0-0-25. REP HONOURS: SA 2013 Tests: 2-0-0-0-0-0. FC RECORD: 66-11-0-0-0-55. RECORD IN 2013: (SA, Cheetahs S15, Cheetahs) 26-4-0-0-0-20.

Van Zyl, Philippus Jacobus (PJ) (Bergsig HS) b 23/04/1988, Rustenburg. 1.93m. 91kg. Flank. FC DEBUT: 2011. PROV CAREER: Boland 2011-13 58-10-0-0-0-50. FC RECORD: 58-10-0-0-0-50. RECORD IN 2013: (Boland) 21-5-0-0-0-25.

Venter, Anver (Oudtshoorn HS) b 01/02/1990, Aliwal North. 1.86m. 80kg. Wing. FC DEBUT: 2013. PROV CAREER: Eagles 2013 1-1-0-0-0-5. FC RECORD: 1-1-0-0-0-5. RECORD IN 2013: (Eagles) 1-1-0-0-0-5.

Venter, Benjamin Christoffel Gerhardus (Ben) (Hennenman HS) b 15/05/1987, Johannesburg. 1.97m. 116kg. Lock. FC DEBUT: 2010. PROV CAREER: Bulldogs 2010-13 32-3-0-0-0-15. Griquas 2010 1-0-0-0-0-0. Boland 2013 18-0-0-0-0-0. FC RECORD: 51-3-0-0-0-15. RECORD IN 2013: (Boland) 18-0-0-0-0-0.

Venter, Elardus Desederus (Merensky HS & NWU) b 26/03/1990, Nelspruit. 1.85m. 123kg. Prop. FC DEBUT: 2013. PROV CAREER: Leopards 2013 10-0-0-0-0-0. Leopard XV 2013 5-0-0-0-0-0. FC RECORD: 15-0-0-0-0-0. RECORD IN 2013: (Leopards, Leopard XV) 15-0-0-0-0-0.

Venter, Hanco Charles (Monument HS, Krugersdorp) b 07/01/1991, Witbank. 1.76m. 82kg. Scrumhalf. FC DEBUT: 2012. PROV CAREER: Sharks XV 2012-13 7-1-0-0-0-5. REP HONOURS: SA U20 2013 3-0-0-0-0-0. FC RECORD: 10-1-0-0-0-5. RECORD IN 2013: (SA U20, Sharks XV) 9-1-0-0-0-5.

Venter, Jacobus Francois (Grey College, Bloemfontein & UP) b 19/04/1991, Bloemfontein. 1.85m. 91kg. Centre. FC DEBUT: 2011. PROV CAREER: Blue Bulls 2011-13 43-12-0-0-0-60. SUPERRUGBY: Bulls 2012-13 11-0-0-0-0-0. REP HONOURS: SAU20 2010-11 9-7-0-0-0-35. FC RECORD: 63-19-0-0-0-95. RECORD IN 2013: (Bulls, Blue Bulls) 13-5-0-0-0-25.

Venter, Ruan Christov (Monument HS, Krugersdorp) b 11/05/1992, Rustenburg. 1.98m. 108kg. Lock. FC DEBUT: 2011. PROV CAREER: Lions 2013 2-0-0-0-0-0. REP HONOURS: SA U20 2011 2-0-0-0-0-0. FC RECORD: 4-0-0-0-0-0. RECORD IN 2013: (Lions) 2-0-0-0-0-0.

Venter, Shaun Harold (Affies, Pretoria) b 16/03/87, Witbank. 1.80m. 80kg. Scrumhalf. FC DEBUT: 2007. PROV CAREER: Pumas 2007-13 105-28-0-0-0-140. SUPERRUGBY: Southern Kings 2013 16-2-0-0-0-10. P/R 2013 2-0-0-0-0-0. REP HONOURS: SA Barbarians 2012 1-2-0-0-0-10. SA Sevens 2009. FC RECORD: 124-32-0-0-0-160. RECORD IN 2013: (Southern Kings, Pumas) 21-2-0-0-0-10.

Venter, Walter (Monument HS, Krugersdorp) b 07/08/84, Virginia. 1.80m. 86kg. Centre. FC DEBUT: 2005. PROV CAREER: Lions 2005,07-09 18-7-0-0-0-35. Lions XV 2007-08 2-0-0-0-0-0. Young Lions 2005-09 13-5-0-0-0-25. Leopards 2006 & 10-11 25-5-0-0-0-25. Valke 2007 4-0-0-0-0-0. Griquas 2012-13 14-1-0-0-0-5. SUPERRUGBY: Lions 2008-10 18-1-0-0-0-5. FC RECORD: 94-19-0-0-0-95. RECORD IN 2013: (Griquas) 4-0-0-0-0-0.

Venter, Wynand Johannes (Jeugland HS) b 08/05/1993, Brakpan. 1.74m. 78kg. Scrumhalf. FC DEBUT: 2013. PROV CAREER: Young Lions 2013 1-0-0-0-0-0. FC RECORD: 1-0-0-0-0-0. RECORD IN 2013: (Young Lions) 1-0-0-0-0-0.

Vergallo, Nicolas. b 20/04/1983. Scrumhalf. SA FC DEBUT: 2013. PROV CAREER: EP Kings 2013 5-1-0-0-0-5. SUPERRUGBY: Southern Kings 2013 14-1-0-0-0-5. REP HONOURS: Argentina. SA FC RECORD: 19-2-0-0-0-10. RECORD IN 2013: (Southern Kings, EP Kings) 19-2-0-0-0-10.

Vermaak, Alistair Fernando (Hillside HS & Hentie Cilliers HS, Virginia) b 28/04/1989, Port Elizabeth. 1.79m. 108kg. Prop. FC DEBUT: 2011. PROV CAREER: WP 2011-12 7-1-0-0-0-5. Boland 2013 3-0-0-0-0-0. REP HONOURS: SA Univ 2013 1-0-0-0-0-0. FC RECORD: 11-1-0-0-0-5. RECORD IN 2013: (SA Univ, Boland) 4-0-0-0-0-0.

Vermaak, Jacobus Cornelius (Jacques) (Volkskool Potch) b 17/09/1991, Potchefstroom. 1.78m. 95kg. Hooker. FC DEBUT: 2013. PROV CAREER: Leopards 2013 6-0-0-0-0-0. Leopard XV 2013 5-2-0-0-0-10. FC RECORD: 11-2-0-0-0-10. RECORD IN 2013: (Leopards, Leopard XV) 11-2-0-0-0-10.

Vermaak, Jano (Vereeniging THS) b 01/01/85, Graaff-Reinet. 1.70m. 82kg. Scrumhalf. FC DEBUT: 2005. PROV CAREER: Lions 2005-11 74-20-3-4-0-118. Young Lions 2005-08 & 10 6-1-0-0-0-5. Lions XV 2008 1-0-0-0-0-0. Blue Bulls 2011-12 15-5-0-0-0-25. SUPERRUGBY: Cats 2006 11-1-0-0-0-5. Lions 2007-11 62-10-3-4-0-68. Bulls 2012-13 31-6-0-0-0-30. REP HONOURS: SA 2012-13 Tests: 3-0-0-0-0-0. Emerging Springboks 2007,09 4-2-0-0-0-10. SA U21 2006 5-2-0-0-0-10. SA Sevens 2005. MISC INFO: Son of former EP & NEC hooker Deon Vermaak. FC RECORD: 212-47-6-8-0-271. RECORD IN 2013: (SA, Bulls) 19-5-0-0-0-25.

Vermaak, Michael (Brandwag HS, Uitenhage) b 10/10/79, Uitenhage. 1.89m. 102kg. Flanker. FC DEBUT: 2001. PROV CAREER: Elephants 2001 & 05-06 & 08-09 45-5-0-0-0-25. Cheetahs 2003-04 6-1-0-0-0-5. Valke 2006-07 28-3-0-0-0-15. E/Cape XV 2008 2-0-0-0-0-0. Eagles 2012-13 26-2-0-0-0-10. FC RECORD: 107-11-0-0-0-55. RECORD IN 2013: (Eagles) 26-2-0-0-0-10.

Vermeulen, Daniel Johannes (Duane) (Nelspruit HS) b 03/07/86, Nelspruit. 1.93m. 108kg. Flank/No. 8. FC DEBUT: 2005. PROV CAREER: Pumas 2005-06 26-4-0-0-0-20. Cheetahs 2007-08 28-2-0-0-0-10. WP 2009-10 & 12-13 38-7-0-0-0-35. SUPERRUGBY: Cheetahs 2007-08 20-3-0-0-0-15. Stormers 2009-13 62-2-0-0-0-10. REP HONOURS: SA 2012-13 Tests: 16-1-0-0-0-5. Emerging Springboks 2009 1-0-0-0-0-0. British Barbarians 2013 1-1-0-0-0-5. MISC INFO: Super PoY nominee 2011. SA PoY nominee 2013. SR PoY nominee 2013. FC RECORD: 192-20-0-0-0-100. RECORD IN 2013: (SA, Stormers, WP, British Barbarians) 23-2-0-0-0-10.

Vermeulen, Petrus Jacobus (PJ) (Northern Cape HS) b

A-Z OF FIRST-CLASS PLAYERS IN 2013

03/03/87, De Aar. 1.82m. 86kg. Centre. FC DEBUT: 2007. PROV CAREER: WP 2007-09 26-6-0-0-0-30. Boland 2009-11 39-6-0-0-0-30. Griquas 2012-13 21-5-1-0-0-27. FC RECORD: 86-17-1-0-0-87. RECORD IN 2013: (Griquas) 13-3-1-0-0-17.

Vermeulen, Petrus Van der Walt (Waltie) (Grey College, Bloemfontein) (UOVS) b 11/11/88. 1.99m. 108kg. Lock. FC DEBUT: 2008. PROV CAREER: Cheetahs 2009-13 44-0-0-0-0. Free State XV 2012-13 4-0-0-0-0-0. Cheetahs XV 2010 1-0-0-0-0-0. SUPERRUGBY: Cheetahs 2010-13 23-1-0-0-0-5. REP HONOURS: SA Students 2008 1-0-0-0-0-0. FC RECORD: 73-1-0-0-0-5. RECORD IN 2013: (Cheetahs S15, Cheetahs, Free State XV) 10-0-0-0-0-0.

Verwey, Tobie Jacques (Middelburg HS) b 09/12/89, Middelburg. 1.94m. 91kg. Flank. FC DEBUT: 2009. PROV CAREER: Pumas 2009 4-0-0-0-0-0. Blue Bulls 2012-13 2-0-0-0-0-0. Valke 2013 12-0-0-0-0-0. FC RECORD: 18-0-0-0-0-0. RECORD IN 2013: (Blue Bulls, Valke) 13-0-0-0-0-0.

Viljoen, Francis Jacobus Nicolas (Frans) (Grey College, Bloemfontein) b 22/10/82, Ficksburg. 1.89m. 104kg. Flank. FC DEBUT: 2002. PROV CAREER: Leopards 2002-04 40-16-0-0-0-80. Griquas 2005-08 60-14-0-0-0-70. Cheetahs 2009 & 12 23-9-0-0-0-45. Cheetahs XV 2010 1-0-0-0-0-0. Griffons 2012 1-0-0-0-0-0. SUPERRUGBY: Cheetahs 2006 & 09-11 & 13 34-1-0-0-0-5. FC RECORD: 159-40-0-0-0-200. RECORD IN 2013: (Cheetahs S15) 8-0-0-0-0-0.

Viljoen, Riaan (Klerksdorp HS) b 04/01/83, Carletonville. 1.81m. 86kg. Utility back. FC DEBUT: 2005. PROV CAREER: Valke 2005-07 57-17-32-18-5-218. Griquas 2008-11 74-16-42-42-6-308. Cheetahs XV 2010 1-0-0-0-0-0. KZN 2012 9-1-4-1-1-19. Sharks XV 2013 2-1-0-0-0-5. SUPERRUGBY: Cheetahs 2010-11 26-5-1-4-2-45. Sharks 2012-13 23-8-0-0-0-40. REP HONOURS: SA Tour: 2009 2-0-0-0-0-0. Royal XV 2009 1-0-1-0-0-2. FC RECORD: 195-48-80-65-14-637. RECORD IN 2013: (Sharks, Sharks XV) 13-5-0-0-0-25.

Visagie, Callie-Theron (Paarl Boys HS & US) b 09/07/1988, Paarl. 1.89m. 103kg. Hooker. FC DEBUT: 2010. PROV CAREER: WP 2010 9-0-0-0-0-0. Lions 2012 10-0-0-0-0-0. Young Lions 2013 1-0-0-0-0-0. Blue Bulls 2013 4-0-0-0-0-0. SUPERRUGBY: Lions 2012 16-0-0-0-0-0. Bulls 2013 7-1-0-0-0-5. FC RECORD: 47-1-0-0-0-5. RECORD IN 2013: (Bulls, Blue Bulls, Young Lions) 12-1-0-0-0-5.

Visagie, Gerrit Jacobus (Jaco) (Augsburg HS & UP) b 08/07/1992, Cape Town. 1.88m. 98kg. Hooker. FC DEBUT: 2013. PROV CAREER: Blue Bulls 2013 4-0-0-0-0-0. FC RECORD: 4-0-0-0-0-0. RECORD IN 2013: (Blue Bulls) 4-0-0-0-0-0.

Visser, Dennis (Kempton Park & Affies Pretoria) b 20/01/1993, Benoni. 2m. 120kg. Lock. FC DEBUT: 2013. REP HONOURS: SA U20 2013 5-0-0-0-0-0. FC RECORD: 5-0-0-0-0-0. RECORD IN 2013: (SA U20) 5-0-0-0-0-0.

Visser, Petrus Jurgen (Paarl Gymnasium) b 13/09/89, Paarl. 1.91m. 88kg. Flyhalf. FC DEBUT: 2009. PROV CAREER: WP 2009-10 8-1-9-4-1-38. Blue Bulls 2011-13 37-7-2-5-0-54. SUPERRUGBY: Bulls 2013 11-1-0-0-0-5. FC RECORD: 56-9-11-9-1-97. RECORD IN 2013: (Bulls, Blue Bulls) 21-3-1-4-0-29.

Volmink, Anthonie Alfred (Bredasdorp THS) b 10/02/90, Bredasdorp. 1.80m. 85kg. Wing. FC DEBUT: 2009. PROV CAREER: Boland 2009 2-1-0-0-0-5. Lions 2012-13 16-9-0-0-0-45. Young Lions 2012-13 14-19-1-0-0-97. SUPERRUGBY: Lions 2012 4-0-0-0-0-0. P/R 2013 2-0-0-0-0-0. FC RECORD: 38-29-1-0-0-147. RECORD IN 2013: (Lions S15, Lions, Young Lions) 20-19-1-0-0-97.

Vorster, Harold William (Frans du Toit HS, Phalaborwa) b 11/10/1993, Phalaborwa. 1.86m. 92kg. Centre. FC DEBUT: 2012. PROV CAREER: Young Lions 2012-13 6-1-0-0-0-5. FC RECORD: 6-1-0-

0-0-5. RECORD IN 2013: (Young Lions) 3-1-0-0-0-5.

Vulindlu, Luzuko (Durban HS) b 14/11/87, Grahamstown. 1.83m. 98kg. Centre. FC DEBUT: 2008. PROV CAREER: KZN 2009-10 6-1-0-0-0-5. Sharks XV 2008-11 13-2-0-0-0-10. Sharks Inv XV 2009 1-0-0-0-0-0. Griquas 2012-13 11-2-0-0-0-10. Eagles 2013 3-0-0-0-0-0. SUPERRUGBY: Sharks 2009 9-1-0-0-0-5. REP HONOURS: Emerging Springboks 2009 1-0-0-0-0-0. FC RECORD: 44-6-0-0-0-30. RECORD IN 2013: (Griquas, Eagles) 11-2-0-0-0-10.

W

Wagman, Clinton Andrew (Florida HS) b 05/10/1990, George. 1.79m. 78kg. Wing. FC DEBUT: 2011. PROV CAREER: Eagles 2011-13 43-12-0-0-0-60. FC RECORD: 43-12-0-0-0-60. RECORD IN 2013: (Eagles) 17-6-0-0-0-30.

Waka, Lolo Yanga (Forbes Grant SS, NWU & UJ) b 23/12/1986, King Williams Town. 1.8m. 86kg. Wing. FC DEBUT: 2007. PROV CAREER: Bulldogs 2007,09 & 13 22-8-0-0-0-40. Griquas 2012 3-1-0-0-0-5. REP HONOURS: Emerging Springboks 2008 1-1-0-0-0-5. FC RECORD: 26-10-0-0-0-50. RECORD IN 2013: (Bulldogs) 6-0-0-0-0-0.

Walters, Peter-John (Upington HS & UJ) b 23/04/1993, Keetmanshoop. 1.87m. 97kg. Wing. FC DEBUT: 2013. PROV CAREER: Young Lions 2013 2-0-0-0-0-0. FC RECORD: 2-0-0-0-0-0. RECORD IN 2013: (Young Lions) 2-0-0-0-0-0.

Watermeyer, Stefan (Waterkloof HS, Pretoria) b 03/06/88, Nelspruit. 1.85m. 95kg. FC DEBUT: 2007. PROV CAREER: Blue Bulls 2008-11 55-20-9-2-0-124. Blue Bulls XV 2007 1-0-0-0-0-0. Griquas 2012 3-0-0-0-0-0. Pumas 2013 24-9-0-0-0-45. SUPERRUGBY: Bulls 2010 1-0-0-0-0-0. REP HONOURS: SA Pres XV 2013 3-0-0-0-0-0. SAU20 2008 4-4-0-0-0-20. FC RECORD: 91-33-9-2-0-189. RECORD IN 2013: (SA Pres XV, Pumas) 27-9-0-0-0-45.

Watson, Luke Asher (Grey HS, PE) b 26/10/83, Port Elizabeth. 1.84m. 97kg. Flank. FC DEBUT: 2002. PROV CAREER: EP Kings 2002 & 2011-13 27-24-0-0-0-120. KZN 2003-04 19-2-0-0-0-10. WP 2005-09 48-26-0-0-0-130. SUPERRUGBY: Sharks 2003-04 20-1-0-0-0-5. Stormers 2005-09 62-10-0-0-0-50. Southern Kings 2013 6-2-0-0-0-10. REP HONOURS: SA 2007-08 Tests: 10-0-0-0-0-0. SA U21 2004 (captain) 2-1-1-0-0-7. SA Kings 2011 2-0-0-0-0-0. WP XV 2006. SA Sevens 2002. SA U19 2002 (captain). SA Schools 2001 (captain). CW EP 2001. MISC INFO: YPoY nominee 2004. S14 PoY 2006. CC First Div PoY 2012 nominee. Son of former Eastern Free State & EP winger and current President of the EP Rugby Union Cheeky Watson. FC RECORD: 197-66-1-0-0-332. RECORD IN 2013: (Southern Kings, EP Kings) 7-3-0-0-0-15.

Watts, Elgar Graeme (Klein Nederberg HS) b 24/09/85, Paarl. 1.81m. 84kg. Flyhalf. FC DEBUT: 2008. PROV CAREER: Boland 2008-09 & 2011-12 75-21-101-45-1-445. Pumas 2010 22-10-17-9-0-111. Cheetahs 2013 11-4-8-9-0-63. Free State XV 2013 2-0-3-1-0-9. SUPERRUGBY: Cheetahs 2013 6-0-7-8-0-38. REP HONOURS: SA Barbarians 2012 1-0-3-0-0-6. Misc: First Division POY 2011. FC RECORD: 117-35-139-72-1-672. RECORD IN 2013: (Cheetahs S15, Cheetahs, Free State XV) 19-4-18-18-0-110.

Weideman, Charl Francois Marais (Paul Roos Gymnasium) b 07/04/88, Bloemfontein. 1.89m. 87kgs. Centre. FC DEBUT: 2008. PROV CAREER: WP 2008 1-0-1-0-0-2. Griffons 2010 11-1-0-0-0-5. Cheetahs 2011 3-0-0-0-0-0. Leopards 2011-13 16-0-0-0-0-0. Leopard XV 2013 3-0-0-0-0-0. FC RECORD: 34-1-1-0-0-7. RECORD IN 2013: (Leopards, Leopard XV) 8-0-0-0-0-0.

Welgemoed, Rhyk (Framesby HS) b 21/12/1990, Port Elizabeth. 1.91m. 90kg. Eightman. FC DEBUT: 2013. PROV CAREER: Leopards 2013 2-0-0-0-0-0. Leopard XV 2013 7-4-0-0-0-20. FC RECORD: 9-4-0-0-0-